ऋग्वेद-संहिता

RGVEDA SAMHITĀ

SANSKRIT TEXT, ENGLISH TRANSLATION

Parimal Sanskrit Series No. 45

ऋग्वेद-संहिता

ṚGVEDA SAṀHITĀ

VOL. III
[MAṆḌALAS – 6,7,8]

SANSKRIT TEXT, ENGLISH TRANSLATION AND NOTES
According to the translation of

H. H. WILSON
and
BHĀṢYA OF SĀYAṆĀCĀRYA

Edited & Revised *with an exhaustive introduction and notes*

by

RAVI PRAKASH ARYA
K. L. JOSHI

PARIMAL PUBLICATIONS
DELHI

Published by

PARIMAL PUBLICATIONS

Office : 27/28, Shakti Nagar, Delhi-110007 (INDIA)
Retail Outlet : 22/3, Shakti Nagar, Delhi-110007 (INDIA)
ph. : +91-11-23845456, 47015168
e-mail : order@parimalpublication.com
url : http://www.parimalpublication.com

Forth Reprint Edition : Year 2016

ISBN : 978-81-7110-141-2 (Vol. 3)
        978-81-7110-138-2 (Set)

Price : ₹ 2000.00 (Set of 4 Vols.)

Printed at

Chawla Offset Printers
Ashok Vihar, Delhi-52

CONTENTS

॥अथ षष्ठं मण्डलम्॥

SIXTH MANDALA

ANUVĀKA 1

[सूक्त- १]

[ऋषि– भरद्वाज बार्हस्पत्य। देवता– अग्नि। छन्द– अनुष्टुप्; ११ शक्वरी।]

४३६९. त्वं ह्यग्ने प्रथमो मनोतास्या धियो अभवो दस्म होता।
त्वं सीं वृषन्नकृणोर्दुष्टरीतु सहो विश्वस्मै सहसे सहध्यै॥१॥

1. You *Agni*, are the first of the gods; a deity to whom their minds are devoted; pleasing of aspect, you are the invoker of the deities at this rite: showerer (of benefits), bestow upon us unsurpassable strength, where with to sustain all (hostile) prowess.

Tvam hi Agne prathamo manotā: the last lord is interpreted *devānām mano yatrotam, sambaddham,* where, on whom, the mind of the gods is attached; or, as more fully explained in the scholia on the *Aitareya Brāhmaṇa,* on this and other texts which occur, ii.10.1; *devānām manāmsi etani dṛḍhapraviṣṭāni yasyām devatāyām sa manotā,* the divinity on whom the minds of the gods are fastened, that is, firmly concentrated, he is called *Manotā.*[1]

४३७०. अधा होता न्यसीदो यजीयानिळस्पद इषयन्नीड्यः सन्।
तं त्वा नरः प्रथमं देवयन्तो महो राये चितयन्तो अनु गमन्॥२॥

2. Offerer of the oblation, frequent celebrator of sacrifice, now sit down on the foot-mark of *Iḷā*, accepting the (sacrificial) food, and being glorified: devout men, expectant of great riches, have recourse to you as to the first (of the gods).

४३७१. वृतेव यन्तं बहुभिर्वसव्यै३ स्वे रयिं जागृवांसो अनु गमन्।
रुशन्तमग्निं दर्शतं बृहन्तं वपावन्तं विश्वहा दीदिवांसम्॥३॥

3. Those who are assiduous in (worshipping) you for riches follow you, going with many *Vasus* by the path (of the firmament); you, the radiant *Agni*, of goodly aspect, mighty, fed with burnt-offerings, and blazing every day.

---

१. अग्निः सर्वा मनोताग्नौ मनोताः संगच्छन्ते (ऐ० ब्रा० २.१०)।

४३७२. __पदं__ देवस्य __नर्मसा__ व्यन्त___: श्रवस्यव___: श्रवं आपन्नमृक्तम्।
नामानि चिद्दधिरे यज्ञियानि भद्रायां ते रणयन्त __सन्दृष्टौ__।।४।।

4. Men desirous of food obtain abundance unopposed when
repairing to the station of the divinity with oblations; and when
delighting, *Agni*, in yours auspicious presence, they repeat those
your names which are to be uttered at sacrifices.

They Repeat those your names which, Etc.— *Nāmāni cid dadhire
yajñīyāni,* that is, such appellations as *Jātavedas, Vaiśvānara,* and atevials
or means of adoration, *stotrāṇi namanasādhanāni.*

४३७३. त्वां वर्धन्ति क्षितयः पृथिव्यां त्वां रायं __उभयासो__ जनानाम्।
त्वं __त्राता__ __तरणे__ चेत्यौ भूः पिता माता सदमिन्मानुषाणाम्।।५।।

5. Men exalt you upon earth: they exalt you for both kinds of
affluence, (cattle and treasure, which you bestow upon) men: you
who extricate (us from evil) are to be known as our preserver, as
the unfailing father and mother of mankind.

Which You Bestow upon, Men— *Janānām* may also mean, for the
gift of men, that is, of male posterity.

४३७४. सपर्येण्यः स प्रियो विश्वइ__ग्निर्होता__ __मन्द्रो__ नि षसादा यज्ञीयान्।
तं त्वां वयं दम आ दीदिवांसमुप __जुबाधो__ नर्मसा सदेम।।६।।

6. *Agni*, who is adorable, affectionate, the offerer of oblations
amongst men, the giver of delight, the celebrator of worship, has
sat down (upon the altar): let us approach you, kindled in our
dwellings, on bended knees, with praise.

४३७५. तं त्वां वयं सुध्योइ३ नव्यमग्ने सुम्नायव ईमहे देवयन्तः।
त्वं विशो अनयो दीद्यानो दिवो अग्ने बृहता रोचनेन।।७।।

7. Intelligent, hoping for happiness, and devout, we glorify
you, adorable *Agni*; do you, shining with exceeding lustre, lead
men to heaven.

४३७६. विशां कविं विश्पतिं शश्वतीनां नितोशनं वृषभं चर्षणीनाम्।
प्रेतीषणिमिषयर्यन्तं पावकं राजन्तमग्निं यजतं रयीणाम्।।८।।

8. (We glorify) the lord of men of ever-existing men; the wise,
the destroyer (of foes) the showerer (of benefits) on mankind, the
moving, the bestower of food, the purifier, the resplendent, *Agni*,
who is worshipped for (the sake of) riches.

The Lord of Men— *Viṣpatim viśām śaśvatīnām*; the epithet is explained *nityānām ṛtvigyajamānalakṣaṇānām*, perhaps, their regular and perpetual observance of religions institutes.

४३७७. सो अग्ने ईजे शशमे च मर्तो यस्त आनट् समिधा हव्यदातिम्।
य आहुतिं परि वेदा नमोभिर्विश्वेत्स वामा दधते त्वोतः॥९॥

9. The man, *Agni*, who worships you, who praises you, who offers oblations to you with kindled fuel, who presents burnt-offerings to you with prostrations, he verily, protected by you, obtains all desired wealth.

४३७८. अस्मा उ ते महि महे विधेम नमोभिरग्ने सामिधोत हव्यैः।
वेदी सूनो सहसो गीर्भिरुक्थैरा ते भद्रायां सुमतौ यंतेम॥१०॥

10. To you, mighty *Agni*, we offer exceeding adoration with prostrations, with fuel, with oblations: (we glorify you) on the altar, son of strength, with hymns and with prayers: may we be successful in our efforts (to gain) you auspicious favour.

४३७९. आ यस्ततन्थ रोदसी वि भासा श्रवोभिश्च श्रवस्यं स्तरुत्रः।
बृहद्भिर्वाजैः स्थविरेभिरस्मे रेवद्भिरग्ने वितरं वि भाहि॥११॥

11. Do you, *Agni*, who have spread heaven and earth with light, who are the preserver (of man), and (who are) to be glorified with praises, shine brightly upon us with abundant food, and with substantial riches.

४३८०. नृवद्वसो सदमिद्धेह्यस्मे भूरि तोकाय तनयाय पश्यः।
पूर्वीरिषो बृहतीरारेअघा अस्मे भद्रा सौश्रवसानि सन्तु॥१२॥

12. Possessor of wealth, bestow upon us at all times opulence conjoined with dependants, and (grant) abundance of cattle to our sons and grandsons: may there be to us abundant food, satisfying our wishes, and free from blame; and may there be auspicious and reputable (means of subsistence).

४३८१. पुरूण्यग्ने पुरुधा त्वाया वसूनि राजन्वसुता ते अश्याम्।
पुरूणि हि त्वे पुरुवार सन्त्यग्ने वसु विधते राजनि त्वे॥१३॥

13. Royal *Agni*, may I obtain from you your many and various treasures whereby to be enriched; for, *Agni*, who are the desired of multitudes, infinite are the riches (aggregated) in you, fit, monarch, for your worshipper.

[सूक्त- २]

[ऋषि- भरद्वाज बार्हस्पत्य। देवता- अग्नि। छन्द- अनुष्टुप्; ११ शक्वरी]

४३८२. त्वं हि क्षैतवद्यशोऽग्ने मित्रो न पत्यसे।

त्वं विचर्षणे श्रवो वसो पुष्टिं न पुष्यसि॥१॥

1. You alight, *Agni*, like *Mitra*, upon the oblation offered with the dry fuel: therefore, beholder of all, possessor of riches, you cherish us with food and nourishment.

४३८३. त्वां हि ष्मा चर्षणयो यज्ञेभिर्गीर्भिरीळते।

त्वां वाजी यात्यवृको रजस्तूर्विश्वचर्षणिः॥२॥

2. Men verily worship you with sacrifice and with praises: the inoffensive sun, the sender of rain, the beholder of the universe, proceeds to you.

The Sun . . . . . Proceeds to you— The sun, it is said, at the evening enters into fire, whence it is that the latter is visible throughout the night: the term for sun, in the text, is, *vājin*, he who goes swiftly, and it is an appellative also of fire and wind, as by another text, *agnirvāyuḥ sūryas te vai vājinaḥ*,[1] fire, wind, the sun, they verily are *vājins*.

४३८४. सजोषस्त्वा दिवो नरो यज्ञस्य केतुमिन्धते।

यद्ध स्य मानुषे जनः सुम्नायुर्जुह्वे अध्वरे॥३॥

3. The offerers of praise, sympathizing in satisfaction, kindle you the banner of the sacrifice, when man, the descendant of *Manu*, desiring happiness; invokes you to the rite.

४३८५. ऋध्वद्यस्ते सुदानवे धिया मर्तः शशमते।

ऊती ष बृहतो दिवो द्विषो अंहो न तरति॥४॥

4. May the mortal prosper who propitiates you (his) benefactor, by holy rites: through the protection of you who are resplendent, he overcomes those who hate him, as if they were mortal sins.

Sāmaveda, 365, but the reading of the first line is a little different.

४३८६. समिधा यस्त आहुतिं निशितिं मर्त्यो नशत्।

वयावन्तं स पुष्यति क्षयमग्ने शतायुषम्॥५॥

---

१. अग्निर्वायुः सूर्यस्ते वै वाजिनः (तै॰ ब्रा॰ १.६.३.९)।

5. The mortal who feeds your consecrated burnt offering with fuel enjoys, *Agni*, a dwelling peopled with descendants, and a life of a hundred years.

४३८७. त्वेषस्तें धूम ऋण्वति दिवि षञ्छुक्र आततंः।
सूरो न हि द्युता त्वं कृपा पांवक् रोचंसे।।६।।

6. The pure smoke of you the resplendent spreads through the firmament, matures (in clouds), and you, the purifier, shine with radiance like the sun, when propitiated by praise.

Shine with Radiance, etc.— *Dyutā tvaṁ kṛpā rocase*, you shine with light by praise; *kṛpā* is of rather doubtful import: it occurs subsequently in the unmistakeable sense of *dīptyā*, with lustre, as if the word was properly in the nominative *kṛp;* Sāyaṇa here explains it by *stutyā*, by praise, metaphorically, or literally, by that which is able to compel the presence of a deity, *abhimukhīkaraṇa-sāmarthya*; occurs in a passage quoted, in the *Nirukta*, 6.8, where it apparently the sense of praise; but there is no explanation beyond its derivation from *kṛp*, to be able or capable; Mahīdhara; *Yajuṣ,* 17.10, explains *kṛp, sāmarthyena, diptyā vā*, by ability, power, or by lustre.

४३८८. अधा हि विश्ववीङ्ग्योऽसिं प्रियो नो अतिंथिः।
रण्वः पुरींव जूर्यः सूनुर्न त्रंययाय्यं: ।।७।।

7. You are now to be praised among the people, for you are our well beloved guest, venerated like an elder in the city, and to be cherished like a son.

Venerated like an elder in a City— *Raṇvaḥ purīva jūryaḥ, sūnur na, trayayāyyaḥ*; the first part is interpreted *nagaryām vṛddho hitopadeṣṭā rājā iva ramaṇīyaḥ*, to be had recourse to as to an old *Rājā* giving good council in a city: the second half, *putra iva pālanīyaḥ*, to be cherished like a son; or *trayayāyya*[1] may be explained, endowed with three merits, learning, penance, devotion; or one having had three births, the natural, investiture with the sacred string, and initiation or preparation for sacred rites, *dīkṣā*.

४३८९. क्रत्वा हि द्रोणें अज्यसेऽग्नें वाजी न कृत्यंः।
परिज्मेव स्वधा गयोऽत्यो न ह्वार्यं: शिशुं:।।८।।

8. You are manifested in the timber, *Agni*, by the act of attrition: you are the bearer (of the oblation) as a horse (is of his

---

१. मातुरग्रेऽधिजननं द्वितीयं मौञ्जिबन्धनात्। तृतीयं यज्ञदीक्षाया इति जन्मत्रयं स्मृतम् (मनु॰
२.१६९)।

rider): you are like the circumambient wind: you are food and dwelling; you are like a (newborn) babe, and variable (in movement) as a horse.

You are Food and Dwelling— *Svadhā gayaḥ* are rendered *annam gṛham ca*; there is no verb, but the Scholiast supplies *bhavasi*, you are.

४३९०. त्वं त्या चिदच्युताग्ने पशुर्न यवसे।

धामा ह यत्ते अजर वना वृश्चन्ति शिक्वस:॥९॥

9. You consume *Agni*, the unfallen (trees) as an animals (feeds) upon pasture, when, undecaying deity, the flames of you who are resplendent shear the forests.

४३९१. वेषि ह्यध्वरीयतामग्ने होता दमे विशाम्।

समृधो विश्पते कृणु जुषस्व हव्यमङ्गिर:॥१०॥

10. You enter as the ministrant priest into the habitations of men who wish to perform sacrifice: render them prosperous, benefactor of mankind: be propitiated, *Aṅgiras*, by the oblation.

४३९२. अच्छा नो मित्रमहो देव देवानग्ने वोच: सुमतिं रोदस्यो: वीहि स्वस्ति। सुक्षितिं दिवो नृन्द्विषो अंहांसि दुरिता तरेम ता तरेम तवावसा तरेम॥११॥

11. Divine *Agni*, reverenced as a friend, who are abiding in heaven and earth, communicate our praise to the gods: conduct the offerer of adoration to domestic felicity; and may we overcome our adversaries, our iniquities, our difficulties; may we overcome those (sins of a prior existence); may we overcome them by your protection.

My we overcome those (Sins)— The text has *tā tarema*, may we cross over those, which Sāyaṇa interprets *janmāntarakṛtāni pāpāni*.

[सूक्त- ३]

[ऋषि– भरद्वाज बार्हस्पत्य। **देवता–** अग्नि। **छन्द–** त्रिष्टुप्।]

४३९३. अग्ने स क्षेषदृतपा ऋतेजा उरु ज्योतिर्नशते देवयुष्टे।

यं त्वं मित्रेण वरुण: सजोषा देव पासि त्यजसा मर्तमंह:॥१॥

1. The offerer of sacrifice, born for religious rites, who lives devoted, *Agni*, to you, obtains abundant light, and is a man whom you, sympathizing in satisfaction with *Mitra* and *Varuṇa*, protect by your shield from iniquity.

By your shield, *Tyajasā*, which is explained, *tyājanasādhanena āyudhena*, by a weapon which is the instrument of causing abandonment or escape.

४३९४. ईजे यज्ञेभिः शशमे शमीभिॠधद्वारायाग्नयें ददाश।
एवा चन तं यशसामजुष्टिर्नाहो मर्तं नशते न प्रदृप्तिः॥२॥

2. He who has presented (oblations) to *Agni*, the possessor of desired (wealth), sacrifices with (all) sacrifices, and is sanctified by (all) holy acts: him, the wand of excellent (posterity) does not afflict, nor does sin or pride affect a mortal.

४३९५. सूरो न यस्य दृशतिररेपा भीमा यदेति शुचतस्त आ धीः।
हेषस्वतः शुरुधो नायमक्तोः कुत्रा चिद्रण्वो वसतिर्वनेजाः॥३॥

3. When the fearful flames of you, whose appearance is (as) faultless as (that of) the sun, spread on every side as (if they were) the lowing heifers of the night, then this *Agni*, the asylum of all, generated in the woods, is everywhere beautiful.

Spread on Every side as if they were, Etc.— *Heṣasvataḥ śurudho na ayam aktoḥ kutrā cid raṇvaḥ,* is not very intelligible: according to Sāyaṇa, *śurudhaḥ* means obstructors, or removers of sorrow, *i.e.,* cows, *śokasya rodhayitṛ gāḥ*; *aktu*, night, he considers *pur* for night-walkers, *Rākṣasas rākṣasādeḥ svabhūtā dadāti*, she, night, gives them their properties, is understood; *raṇvaḥ* is an epithet of *ayam*, this, *Agni*, *ramaṇīya*, agreeable, beautiful.

४३९६. तिग्मं चिदेम महि वर्पो अस्य भसदश्वो न यमसान आसा।
विजेहमानः परशुन जिह्वां द्रविनं द्रावयति दारु धक्षत्॥४॥

4. Sharp is his path, and his vast body shines like a horse champing fodder with his mouth, darting forth his tongue like a hatchet, and burning timber to ashes, like a goldsmith who fuses (metal).

Like a Goldsmith who fuses (Metal)— *Dravir na drāvayati dāru dhakṣat*, is, literally, as a melter causes to melt, he burns the timber; or, as Sāyaṇa explains it, *yathā svarṇakāraḥ svarṇādikam drāvayati tathāgnir vanam bhasmasāt karoti*, as a goldsmith fuses gold and the rest, so *Agni* reduces the wood to ashes: perhaps something more than simple fusion of metals is implied: the alchemical calcining or permutation of them would be more analogous to the burning of timber, or its reduction to ashes.

४३९७. स इदस्तेव प्रति धादसिष्यञ्छिशीत तेजोऽयसो न धाराम्।
चित्रध्रजतिररतियों अक्रोर्वेनं दुष्द्वां रघुपत्मजंहाः॥५॥

5. He casts (afar his flames) as an archer (his arrows), and sharpens when about to dart his radiance, as (a warrior whets) the edge of his iron (weapons), he who, variously moving, passes through the night, like the light-falling foot of a bird perched upon a tree.

The Edge of His Iron (Weapons)— *Ayaso na dhārām, ·ayas* has here the force of the Latin *ferrum*.

४३९८. स ई रेभो न प्रति वस्त उस्राः शोचिषा रारपीति मित्रमंहाः।
नक्तं य ईमरुषो यो दिवा नृनमंर्त्यो अरुषो यो दिवा नृन्।।६।।

6. Like the adorable sun, he clothes himself with brilliant (rays): diffusing friendly light, he crackles with (his fame): (he it is) who is luminous by night, and who lights men (to their work) by day; who is immortal and radiant; who lights men by day.

४३९९. दिवो न यस्य विधतो नवीनोद्वृषा रुक्ष ओषधीषु नूनोत्।
घृणा न यो ध्रजंसा पत्मंना यन्ना रोदंसी वसुंना दं सुपत्नीं।।७।।

7. Of whom a sound is heard when scattering his rays like (that) of the sun: the brilliant showerer (of benefits) clamours among the (burning) plants; he who, moving not with a shifting, variable motion, but, humbling (our foes), fills the well-wedded earth and heaven with wealth.

Fills your well-wedded earth and Heaven with Wealth— *ā rodasī vasunā supātnī, śobhanapatikā dyāvā pṛthivyau dhanena pūrayati* is the amplification of the comment, he fills with wealth heaven and earth, both having a brilliant husband or lord: who that is, is not specified, unless it be *Agni* or *Indra*.

४४००. धायोभिर्वा यो युज्येभिरर्कैर्विद्युन्न दविद्योत्स्वेभिः शुष्मैः।
शर्धो वा यो मरुतां ततक्ष ऋभुर्न त्वेषो रभसानो अद्यौत्।।८।।

8. He who (goes) with sacred (rays), as if with self-harnessed, well-governed (steeds), who shines like lightning with his own scorching (flames), who impairs the vigour of the *Maruts*, he glows radiant and rapid as the-wide-shining sun.

As the Wide-shining Sun— *Ṛbhur-na* is explained *uru bhāsamāna sūrya iva*.

[सूक्त-४]

[**ऋषि**– भरद्वाज बार्हस्पत्य। **देवता**– अग्नि। **छन्द**– त्रिष्टुप्।]

४४०१. यथा होतर्मनुषो देवताता यज्ञेभिः सूनो सहसो यजासि।
एवा नों अद्य समना समानानुशर्त्रग्न उशतो यक्षि देवान्।।१।।

1. Son of strength, invoker (of the gods), in like manner as at the worship of the gods by *Manu*, your did offer worship with sacrifice so now, *Agni*, with willing mind, worship for us the assenting deities, regarding them as your equals.

४४०२. स नो विभावा चक्षणिर्न वस्तोरग्निर्वन्दारु वेद्यश्रनो धात्।
विश्वायुर्यो अमृतो मर्त्येषूषर्भुद्भूदतिथिर्जातवेदा:॥२॥

2. May that *Agni*, who, like the illuminator of the day, is resplendent and cognizable (by all), grant us commendable food; he who is the life of all, immortal, who knows all that exists, who is our guest, waking among men at dawn.

४४०३. द्यावो न यस्य पनयन्त्यभ्वं भासांसि वस्ते सूर्यो न शुक्र:।
वि य इनोत्यजर: पावको श्रस्य चिच्छिश्रथत्पूर्व्याणि॥३॥

3. Whose great deeds his worshippers now celebrate, who is clothed with light, radiant as the sun, exempt from decay, the purifier, he illumes (all things), and destroys the ancient cities of the dispersed (evil beings).

Of the Dispersed (Evil Beings)— *Aśnasya cid*: from *aś* to pervade, *vyāpanaśīlasya*, of the pervader, that is, according to Sāyaṇa, *rākṣasādeḥ*, of the *Rākṣasas*, and the like, it may possibly be intended for a proper name.

४४०४. वद्मा हि सूनो अस्यद्मसद्वा चक्रे अग्निर्जनुषाज्मात्रम्।
स त्वं न ऊर्जसन ऊर्जं धा राजेव जेरवृके क्षेष्यन्त:॥४॥

4. Son of strength, you are to be praised: *Agni*, sitting upon the (sacrificial) viands, has given (to his worshippers), from their birth, habitation and food: giver of strength, bestow strength upon us: triumph like a price, so that you may abide in our unassailed (dwelling).

४४०५. नितिक्ति यो वारणमन्नमत्ति वायुर्न राष्ट्र्यत्येत्यक्तून्।
तुर्याम यस्त आदिशामरातीरत्यो न हुत: पततः परिहुत्॥५॥

5. He who whets his (gloom) dispersing (radiance), who eats the (offered) oblation, a sovereign like *Vāyu*, overcomes the nights: may we prevail (over him) who is not a donor of the oblations that are due, (*Agni*), to you, and do you, (swift) as a horse be the destroyer of the foes assailing (us).

४४०६. आ सूर्यो न भानुमद्भिरर्कैरग्ने ततन्थ रोदसी वि भासा।
चित्रो नयत्परि तमांस्यक्त: शोचिषा पत्मन्नौशिजो न दीयन्॥६॥

6. You over spread, *Agni*, heaven and earth with radiance, like the sun with his lustrous rays: the wonderful *Agni* disperses the glooms like the adored (sun) moving on his path, imbued with light.

४४०७. त्वां हि मन्द्रतममर्कशोकैर्ववृमहे महि न: श्रोष्यग्ने।
इन्द्रं न त्वा शर्वसा देवता वायुं पृणन्ति राधसा नृतमा:॥७॥

7. We celebrate you, who are most adorable, with sacred praises: hear, *Agni*, our laudation: the leaders (of rites) earnestly honour you with offerings, you who are divine like *Indra,* and like *Vāyu* in strength.

With Sacred Praises— *Arkaśokaiḥ, praśasyair dīptikaraṇaiḥ stotraiḥ* with excellent illustrating praises, or it may be an epithet of *Agni* with *yukta* understood, endowed with, or possessed of, excellent radiance; *praśasyair dīptibhir yuktam agnim:* Mahīdhara, *Yajurveda,* 33.13, explains it *Iarkavat śucante,* which shine like the sun; and hence *Iarkaśokaiḥ* means, he says, *mantraiḥ,* with prayers.

४४०८. नू नो अग्नेऽवृकेभि: स्वस्ति वेषि राय: पथिभि: पर्षंह:।
ता सूरिभ्यो गृणते रासि सुम्नं मदेम शतहिमा: सुवीरो:॥८॥

8. Quickly conduct us, *Agni*, by unmolested paths, to riches and prosperity: (convey us) beyond sin: those delights which you give to your adorers (extend) to him who (now) glorifies you, and may we, living for a hundred winters, and blessed with excellent posterity, be happy.

[सूक्त-५]

[ऋषि– भरद्वाज बार्हस्पत्य। देवता– अग्नि। छन्द– त्रिष्टुप्।]

४४०९. हुवे व: सूनुं सहसो युवानमद्रोघवाचं मतिभिर्यविष्ठम्।
य इन्वति द्रविणानि प्रचेता विश्ववाराणि पुरुवारो अध्रुक्॥१॥

1. I invoke you, *Agni*, the son of strength, the youthful, the irreproachable, the very young; you who are wise, the sought of many, the merciful, who bestow treasures acceptable to all.

४४१०. त्वे वसूनि पुवर्णीक होतर्दोषा वस्तोररिरे यज्ञियास:।
क्षामेव विश्वा भुर्वनानि यस्मिन्त्सं सौभगानि दधिरे पावके॥२॥

2. Bright blazing *Agni*, invoker of the gods, to you the adorable deities have appropriated, by night and day, the riches (on the

oblation): they have deposited in the purifier (*Agni*) all good things,[1] as they have placed all beings upon earth.

The Adorable Deities— *Yajñiyāsaḥ, yajñārhaḥ*, entitled to sacrifices, an appellative ordinarily applied to the *devas*; but here the Scholiast would render it *yajamānaḥ*, the sacrificers, a sense obviously incompatible with what follows.

४४११. त्वं विक्षु प्रदिवः सीद आसु क्रत्वा रथीरभवो वार्याणाम्।
अतं इनोषि विधते चिकित्वो व्यानुषग्जातवेदो वसूनि॥३॥

3. You, abide from of old in these people, and by your deeds have been (to them) the conveyer of good things: thence, sage *Jātavedas*, you bestow continually wealth upon the sacrificer.

४४१२. यो नः सनुत्यो अभिदासदग्ने यो अन्तरो मित्रमहो वनुष्यात्।
तमजरैभिर्वृषभिस्तव स्वैस्तपां तपिष्ठ तपसा तपस्वान्॥४॥

4. Do you, protector of (your) friends, who are most resplendent, blazing with radiance, consume with your own imperishable flames him who injures us abiding in secret, or when near to us design us harm.

४४१३. यस्ते यज्ञेन समिधा य उक्थैरर्केभिः सूनो सहसो ददाशत्।
स मर्त्येष्वमृत प्रचेता राया द्युम्नेन श्रवसा वि भाति॥५॥

5. He who propitiates you, son of strength, with sacrifice, with fuel, with prayers, with praises, shines immortal amongst men, eminent in wisdom and possessed of splendid opulence and (abundant) food.

४४१४. स तत्कृधीषितस्तूर्यमग्ने स्पृधो बाधस्व सहसा सहस्वान्।
यच्छस्यसे द्युभिरक्तो वचोभिस्तज्जुषस्व जरितुर्घोषि मन्म॥६॥

6. Accomplish quickly, *Agni*, that for which you are solicited: endowed with strength, oppose by strength our adversaries: be pleased, you who are anointed with radiance, by loud vociferation of you worshipper, by whom you are adored with hymns.

४४१५. अश्याम तं काममग्ने तवोती अश्याम रयिं रयिवः सुवीरम्।
अश्याम वाजमभि वाजयन्तोऽश्याम द्युम्नमजराजरं ते॥७॥

7. May we obtain through your protection, *Agni*, that which we desire: giver of riches, may we obtain of your riches and

---

१. अग्नौ वामं वसु सं न्यदधत (तै० सं० १.५.१.१)।

— —

descendants: desiring food, may we obtain food: may we obtain, imperishable *Agni*, imperishable fame (through you).
Yajurveda, 18.74.

[सूक्त-६]

[ऋषि– भरद्वाज बार्हस्पत्य। देवता– अग्नि। छन्द– त्रिष्टुप्।]

४४१६. प्र नव्यसा सहस: सूनुमच्छा यज्ञेन गातुमव इच्छमान:।
वृश्चद्वनं कृष्णयामं रुशन्तं वीती होतारं दिव्यं जिगाति॥१॥

1. He who is desirous of food has recourse with a new sacrifice, approachable son of strength (*Agni*), to you the consumer of forests, the dark-pathed, the bright shining, the ministrant (to the gods) of (sacrificial) food, the divine;

४४१७. स श्वितानस्तन्यतू रोचनस्था अजरेभिर्नानदद्भिर्यविष्ठ:।
य: पावक: पुरुतम: पुरूणि पृथून्यग्निरनुयाति भर्वन्॥२॥

2. (You who are) white-hued, vociferous, abiding in the firmament, (associated) with the imperishable, resounding (winds), the youngest (of the gods), *Agni*, who, purifying and most vast, proceeds, feeding upon numerous and substantial (forests).

४४१८. वि ते विष्वग्वातजूतासो अग्ने भामास: शुचे शुचयश्चरन्ति।
तुविम्रक्षासो दिव्या नवग्वा वना वनन्ति धृषता रुजन्त:॥३॥

3. Pure *Agni*, your bright flames, fanned by the wind, spread wide in every direction, consuming abundant (fuel); divine, fresh-rising, they play upon the woods, enveloping them in lustre.

४४१९. ये ते शुक्रास: शुचय: शुचिष्म: क्षां वपन्ति विषितासो अश्वा:।
अध भ्रमस्त उर्विया वि भाति यातयमानो अधि सानु पृश्ने:॥४॥

4. Resplendent *Agni*, your bright rays, horses let loose (from the rein), shear the earth; yours (band of flame), mounting above the high-lands of the many-tinted (earth), blazes fiercely.

Shear the Earth— *Kṣām vapanti, muṇḍayanti*, lit, shave the earth, the plants of which constitute the hair: see vol. I. verse 752-53.

Mounting above the highlands, Etc.— *Yātayamāno adhi sānu pṛśneḥ, bhumer-upari parvatāgrādikam prati svakīyam agram vyāpārayan*, displaying its own point or flame upon the summit, and the like, of the mountains upon the earth: volcanic eruptions may be possibly alluded to.

४४२०. अर्ध जिह्वा पांपतीति प्र वृष्णो गोषुयुधो नाशनिं: सृजाना।
शूरस्येव प्रसिति: क्षातिरग्नेर्दुर्वर्तुर्भीमो दंयते वनानि॥५॥

5. The flame of the showerer, (*Agni*), repeatedly descends like the hurled thunderbolt of the rescuer of the cattle: like the prowess of a hero is the destroying (energy) of *Agni*: irresistible and fearful, he consumes the forests.

४४२१. आ भानुना पार्थिवानि ज्रयांसि महस्तोदस्यं धृषता ततन्थ।
स बाधस्वाप भया सहोभि: स्पृधो वनुष्यन्वनुषो नि जूर्व॥६॥

6. You overspread the accessible places of the earth with light by the energy of you powerful, exciting (influence): do you disperse all perils, and, baffling (our) adversaries by your mighty (powers), destroy (our) foes.

४४२२. स चित्र चित्रं चितयन्तमस्मे चित्रंक्षत्र चित्रततमं वयोधाम्।
चन्द्रं रयिं पुरुवीरं बृहन्तं चन्द्र चन्द्राभिर्गृणते युवस्व॥७॥

7. Wonderful *Agni*, of wonderful strength, bestower of delight, grant to us, and to him who praises you with gratifying (praises), wonderful, most wonderful riches, conferring fame, supplying food, comprehending male descendants, delectable and infinite.

In the first half to the stanza the word *citra*, wonderful, in the second, *candra*, delightful, are illiteratively repeated, *sa citra citram citayantam asme citrakṣatra citratamam*, and *candram rayim candra candrābhiḥ*, etc.

[सूक्त-७]

[ऋषि– भरद्वाज बार्हस्पत्य। देवता– वैश्वानर अग्नि।
छन्द– त्रिष्टुप्; ६-७ जगती।]

४४२३. मूर्धानं दिवो अरतिं पृथिव्या वैश्वानरमृत आ जातमग्निम्।
कविं सम्राजमतिथिं जनानामासन्ना पात्रं जनयन्त देवा:॥१॥

1. The gods have generated *Vaiśvānara*, *Agni*, as the brow of heaven, the unceasing pervader of earth, born for (the celebration of) sacrifice, wise, imperial, the guest of men, in whose mouth (is) the vessel (that conveys the oblation to the gods).

Sāmaveda, 67, 1140; *Yajurveda*, 7.24: Mahīdhara's explanation is to the same effect as Sāyaṇa's, only more fall.

The Gods— *Deva* may also be applied to the priests who generate *Agni* by attrition: *Vaiśvānara* is variously explained, but it most usually implies, what or who belongs to or is beneficial to, all (*viśva*) men (*naraḥ*).

४४२४. नाभिं यज्ञानां सद॑नं रयीणां महामाॅहावमभि सं न॑वन्त।
वैश्वान॑रं र॒थ्यमध्वराणां य॒ज्ञस्य॑ के॒तुं ज॒नयन्त देवाः॥२॥

2. (The worshippers) glorify together, (*Agni*), the bond of sacrifices, the abode of riches, the great receptacle of burnt-offerings: the gods generate *Vaiśvānara*, the conveyer of oblations, the emblem of sacrifice.

Sāmaveda, 1142.

The Bond of Sacrifices— *Nābhiṁ yajñānām; nābhi* is here explained *vahanam, bandhakam,* the connecting link or binding of different religious rites.

४४२५. त्वद्विप्रो॑ जायते वाज्य॑ग्ने त्वद्वीरासो॑ अभिमातिषाह॑ः।
वैश्वा॑नर॒ त्वम॒स्मासु॑ धेहि॒ वसू॑नि राज॒न्त्स्पृह॒याय्या॑णि॥३॥

3. The offerer of (sacrificial) food becomes wise, *Agni*, from you from you heroes become the vanquishers of foes: therefore do you, royal *Vaiśvānara*, bestow upon us enviable riches.

४४२६. त्वां विश्वे॑ अमृत जाय॑मानं शिशुं न॒ देवा॒ अभि सं न॑वन्ते।
तव॒ क्रतु॑भिरमृतत्वमाय॑न्वैश्वान॑र॒ यत्पित्रोरदीद॑ेः॥४॥

4. All the worshippers together praise you, immortal, *Agni*, when born like an infant: when you shine *Vaiśvānara*, between the parental (heaven and earth) they obtain immortality through your (sacred) rites.

४४२७. वैश्वा॑नर॒ तव॒ तानि॑ व्रतानि॑ महान्य॑ग्ने॒ नकि॑रा द॑धर्ष।
यज्जाय॑मानः॒ पित्रोरुपस्थे॑ऽविन्दः॑ के॒तुं व॒युनेष्वह्ना॑म्॥५॥

5. *Agni, Vaiśvānara*, these your mighty deeds no one can resist: when born on the lap of your parents, your have stationed the banner of the days on the paths of the firmament.

When Born on the Lap of your Parents— That is, according to the Scholiast, in the *Antarikṣa,* or firmament.

४४२८. वैश्वान॒रस्य॒ विमि॑तानि॒ चक्ष॑सा॒ सानू॑नि दि॒वो अ॒मृत॑स्य के॒तुना॑।
तस्ये॒दु विश्वा॒ भुव॒नाधि॑ मू॒र्धनि॒ वया॑ इव रुरुहुः स॒प्त वि॒स्रुह॑ः॥६॥

6. The summits of the firmament are measured by the light of *Vaiśvānara*, the manifester of ambrosial (rain): all the regions are overspread (by the vapour) on his brow, and the seven gliding (streams) spring from thence like branches.

All the Regions are Overspread, Etc.— This idea has occured before: the smoke that rises from sacrificial fires becomes clouds in the atmosphere, whence rain falls and rivers are filled.

४४२९. वि यो रजांस्यमिमीत सुक्रतुर्वैश्वानरो वि दिवो रोचना कवि:।
परि यो विश्वा भुवनानि पप्रथेऽदब्धो गोपा अमृतस्य रक्षिता॥७॥

7. Vaiśvānara, the performer of sacred acts, is he who made the regions; foreseeing (he has made) the luminaries of heaven, and has spread throughout all worlds: the irresistible guardian (of all), the protector of ambrosial (rain).

[सूक्त-८]

[ऋषि— भरद्वाज बार्हस्पत्य। देवता— वैश्वानर अग्नि।
छन्द— जगती; ७ त्रिष्टुप्।]

४४३०. पृक्षस्य वृष्णो अरुषस्य नू सह: प्र नु वोचं विदथा जातवेदस:।
वैश्वानराय मतिर्नव्यसी शुचि: सोम इव पवते चारुरग्नये॥१॥

1. I commemorate promptly at the holy ceremony the might of the all-pervading Jātavedas, the showerer, the radiant: new, pure, and graceful praise issues (from me) like the Soma juice (from the filter), to Agni Vaiśvānara.

४४३१. स जायमान: परमे व्योमनि व्रतान्यग्निर्व्रतपा अरक्षत।
व्यं१न्तरिक्षममिमीत सुक्रतुर्वैश्वानरो महिना नाकमस्पृशत्॥२॥

2. That Agni who, as soon as born in the highest heaven, the protector of sacred rites, protects the pious acts (of men), he has made the manifold firmament: Vaiśvānara, the performer of good deeds, has attained heaven by his greatness.

४४३२. व्यस्तभ्नाद्रोदसी मित्रो अद्भुतोऽन्तर्वावदकृणोज्ज्योतिषा तम:।
वि चर्मणीव धिषणे अवर्तयद्वैश्वानरो विश्वमधत्त वृष्ण्यम्॥३॥

3. The friend (of all), the wonderful (Agni), has upheld heaven and earth; he has hidden darkness within light; he has spread out the two sustaining (worlds heaven and earth), like two skin; Vaiśvānara comprehends all (creative) energy.

४४३३. अपामुपस्थे महिषा अगृभ्णत विशो राजानमुप तस्थुर्ऋग्मियम्।
आ दूतो अग्निमभरद्विवस्वतो वैश्वानरं मातरिश्वा परावत:॥४॥

4. The mighty *Maruts* have seized upon him on the lap of the
waters (in firmament), and men have acknowledged him as their
adorable sovereign: *Mātariśvan*, the messenger of the gods, has
brought *Agni Vaiśvānara*, (hither) from the distant (sphere of the)
sun.

४४३४. युगेयुगे विदथ्यं गृणद्भ्योऽग्ने रयिं यशसं धेहि नव्यसीम्।
पव्येव राजन्नघशंसमजर नीचा नि वृश्च वनिनं न तेजसा॥५॥

5. To those, *Agni*, who repeat new (praises) to you, the object
of their worship from age to age, grant riches and famous
(posterity): strike down, undecaying sovereign, the sinner with
your blaze like the thunderbolt, as if he were a tree.

४४३५. अस्माकमग्ने मघवत्सु धारयानामि क्षत्रमजरं सुवीर्यम्।
वयं जयेम शतिनं सहस्रिणं वैश्वानर वाजमग्ने तवोतिभिः॥६॥

6. Grant, *Agni*, to us who are affluent in (offerings), wealth
that cannot be taken away, that is exempt from decay, and that
comprehends excellent male descendants: may we obtain, *Agni
Vaiśvānara,* hundreds and thousands of viands through your
protection.

४४३६. अदब्धेभिस्तव गोपाभिरिष्टेऽस्माकं पाहि त्रिषधस्थ सूरीन्।
रक्षा च नो ददुषां शर्धो अग्ने वैश्वानर प्र च तारीः स्तवानः॥७॥

7. Adored *Agni*, present in the three worlds, protect your
worshippers with your irresistible protections, preserve the
strength of us who offer (oblations): glorified (by us), *Agni
Vaiśvānara*, transport us (beyond evil).

[सूक्त-९]

[**ऋषि**- भरद्वाज बार्हस्पत्य। **देवता**- वैश्वानर अग्नि। **छन्द**- त्रिष्टुप्।]

४४३७. अहश्च कृष्णमहरर्जुनं च वि वर्तेते रजसी वेद्याभिः।
वैश्वानरो जायमानो न राजावातिरज्ज्योतिषाग्निस्तमांसि॥१॥

1. The dark day and the light day revolve alternate, affecting
(the world) by their recognizable (properties): *Agni Vaiśvānara*,
manifested like a prince, dispels darkness by his lustre.

४४३८. नाहं तन्तुं न वि जानाम्योतुं न यं वयन्ति समरेऽतमानाः।
कस्य स्वित्पुत्र इह वक्त्वानि परो वदात्यवरेण पित्रा॥२॥

2. I understand not the threads (of the warp), nor the threads of the woof, nor that (cloth) which those who are assiduous in united exertion weave: of what (man) may the son declare the words that are to be spoken in the next world, (instructed) by a father abiding below.

The first half of the stanza reads *nāham tantum na vijānāmy-otum, na yaṁ vayanti samare atamānāḥ*, and implies, according to those who know tradition, *sampradāyavidaḥ*, says Sāyaṇa, a figurative allusion to the mysteries of sacrifice: the threads of the warp, *tantu*, are the metres of the Vedas, those of the woof, *otu*, the liturgic prayers and ceremonial, the combination of which two is the cloth, or sacrifice: the *ātamavidaḥ*, or, *Vedantis*, understand it, as alluding to the mysteries of creation, the threads of the warp being the subtile elements, those of the woof the gross, and their combination the universe: either interpretation is sufficiently intelligible, but the former harmonizes best with the character of the Veda: it is less easy to give intelligibility to the second half, *kasya svit putra iha vaktvāni, paro vadati avareṇa pitrā* and the Scholiast does not materially help us: of whom (may) the son (say) in this world the words that are to be said, (which) the subsequent (may say) by the father being after of below, is, with a little assistance, the literal translation: Sāyaṇa explains *putra* by *manuṣya*, a man, *vaktvāni* by *vaktavyāni, para* by *parastāt*, or *amuṣmin* like *vartamāno yaḥ sūryaḥ*, the sun who is abiding in the other or future world, he being instructed, *anuśiṣṭaḥ san,* by the father abiding below, or in this world, *pitrā avastāt asmin loke vartamānena*, that is, by *Agni Vaiśvānara, vaiśvānara agninā*, as it is elsewhere said, *vaiśvānarasya putro cāsau parastād-divi yaḥ sthitaḥ* he is the son of *vaiśvānara*, who is stationed above, or in heaven; all that may be intended is, that no human being can explain the mysteries of sacrifice, although the sun may be able to do so, having been intended is, that no human being can explain the mysteries of sacrifice, although the sun may be able to do so, having been instructed in them by *Agni*, his parent or source, the sun being no more than the *Agni* of heaven; as regards the mysteries of creation, Sāyaṇa explains the passage, no man, however taught by a father born after creation, can rightly know any thing previous to his birth, either in this world or the next.

४४३९. स इत्तन्तुं स वि जानात्योतुं स वक्त्वान्यृतुथा वंदाति।
य ई चिकेतदमृतस्य गोपा अवश्चरन्परो अन्येन पश्यन्॥३॥

3. He verily knows the threads of the warp and or the woof, he speaks in due season what is to be said, who comprehends all this (universe); who is the protector of ambrosial water, sojourning both above and below, and contemplating (the world) under a different (manifestation).

Contemplating the worlds under a different manifestation— Or as the sun, whilst upon earth *Agni* or *Vaiśvānara* is manifest as fire.

४४४०. अयं होता प्रथमः पश्यतेममिदं ज्योतिरमृतं मर्त्येषु।

अयं स जज्ञे ध्रुव आ निषत्तोऽमर्त्यस्तन्वा३ वर्धमानः ॥४॥

4. This *Vaiśvānara* is the first offerer of burnt offerings: behold him: this is the light immortal amongst mortals: he has been born in a bodily shape, immoveable, all-pervading, immortal, ever increasing.

४४४१. ध्रुवं ज्योतिर्निहितं दृशये कं मनो जविष्ठं पतयत्स्वन्तः।

विश्वे देवाः समनसः सकैता एकं क्रतुमभि वि यन्ति साधु ॥५॥

5. A steady light, swifter than thought, stationed among moving beings to show (the way) to happiness all the gods being of one mind, and of like wisdom, proceed respectfully to the presence of the one (chief) agent, (*Vaiśvānara*)

A Steady light, Etc.— According to the *Vedāntin* view of the text, the light is *Brahma*, seated spontaneously in the heart as the means of true knowledge, to which all the senses, together with the mind and consciousness, refer, as to the one cause of creation, or *Paramātmā* supreme spirit.

४४४२. वि मे कर्णा पतयतो वि चक्षुर्वी३दं ज्योतिर्हृदय आहितं यत्।

वि मे मनश्चरति दूरआधीः किं स्विद्वक्ष्यामि किमु नू मनिष्ये ॥६॥

6. Mine ears are turned (to hear him), mine eyes (to behold him); this light that is placed in the heart (seeks to know him); my mind, the receptacle of distant (objects) hastens (towards him): what shall I declare him)? How shall I comprehend him?

४४४३. विश्वे देवा अनमस्यन्भियानास्त्वामग्ने तमसि तस्थिवांसम्।

वैश्वानरोऽवतूतये नोऽमर्त्योऽवतूतये नः ॥७॥

7. All the gods, alarmed, venerate you, *Agni*, abiding in darkness: may *vaiśvānara* preserve us with his protection: may the immortal *Agni* preserve us with his protection.

[सूक्त-१०]

[ऋषि– भरद्वाज बार्हस्पत्य। देवता– अग्नि।

छन्द– त्रिष्टुप्, ७ द्विपदा विराट्।]

४४४४. पुरो वो मन्द्रं दिव्यं सुवृक्तिं प्रयति यज्ञे अग्निमध्वरे दधिध्वम्।

पुर उक्थेभिः स हि नो विभावा स्वध्वरा करति जातवेदाः ॥१॥

1. Place before you at the progressive, uninterrupted sacrifice, the divine, adorable, perfect *Agni*, with prayers; for he, the resplendent *Jātavedas*, makes us prosperous in sacred rites.

४४४५. तमुं द्युमः पुर्वणीक होतरग्ने अग्निभिर्मनुष इधानः।
स्तोमं यर्मस्मै ममतेव शूषं घृतं न शुचिं मतर्यः पवन्ते॥२॥

2. Brilliant, many-rayed *Agni*, invoker of the gods, kindled with many fires, (hear) this (praise) of men; which delightful praise, pure as the clarified butter (that has been filtered), his worshippers offer unto him as *Mamatā* (formerly offered it).

४४४६. पीपाय स श्रवसा मर्त्येषु यो अग्नयें ददाश विप्र उक्थैः।
चित्राभिस्तमूतिभिश्चित्रशोचिर्व्रजस्य साता गोमंतो दधाति॥३॥

3. He thrives in abundance amongst men, who, pious, presents to *Agni* (oblations) with prayers: the wonderfully radiant *Agni* places him with marvellous protection in the enjoyment of pasturage full of herds of cattle.

४४४७. आ यः पप्रौ जार्यमान उर्वी दूरेदृशा भासा कृष्णाध्वां।
अध बहु चित्तम् ऊर्म्यायास्तिरः शोचिषां ददृशे पावकः॥४॥

4. The dark-pathed, as soon as generated, filled with his afar-seen light the two spacious (worlds): he, the purifier, is now beheld dispersing with his radiance the thick glooms of night.

४४४८. नू नश्चित्रं पुरुवाजाभिरूती अग्ने रयिं मघवद्भ्यश्च धेहि।
ये राधसा श्रवसा चात्यन्यान्त्सुवीर्यैरभिष्चाभि सन्ति जनान्॥५॥

5. Bestow quickly, *Agni*, upon us who are affluent (in oblations), wondrous wealth, with abundant viands and protections, such as enrich other men with wealth with food, and with male descendants.

४४४९. इमं यज्ञं चनो धा अग्न उशन्यं तं आसानो जुहुते हविष्मान्।
भरद्वाजेषु दधिषे सुवृक्तिमवीर्वाजस्य गर्ध्यस्य सातौ॥६॥

6. *Agni* desirous (of the offering), accept this sacrifice, this food which the presenter (of the oblation), sitting down (before you), offers unto you: accept the blameless (praises) of the *Bhāradvāja* (race), and favour them that they may obtain many sorts of food.

४४५०. वि द्वेषांसीनुहि वर्धयेळां मदेम शतहिमाः सुवीराः॥७॥

7. Scatter (our) enemies; augment our abundance; and may we, blessed with virtuous male descendants, enjoy happiness for a hundred winters.

[सूक्त-११]

[ऋषि– भरद्वाज बार्हस्पत्य। देवता– अग्नि। छन्द– त्रिष्टुप्।]

४४५१. यजस्व होतरिषितो यजीयानग्ने बाधो मरुतां न प्रयुक्ति।
आ नौ मित्रावरुणा नासत्या द्यावा होत्रायं पृथिवी ववृत्याः॥१॥

1. *Agni*, invoker of the gods, do you who are adorable, being instigated by us, worship at our present rite the foe-repelling (troop) of the *Maruts*, and bring to our sacrifice *Mitra* and *Varuṇa*, the *Nāsatyās*, and Heaven and Earth.

४४५२. त्वं होता मन्द्रतमो ना अध्वगन्तर्देवो विदथा मर्त्येषु।
पावकया जुह्वा३ वह्निरासाग्ने यजस्व तन्वं३ तव स्वाम्॥२॥

2. You are amidst mortals at the celebration (of sacrifice), the invoker of the gods, you who are) most deserving of praise, a divinity doing us no harm: the bearer (of the oblations) offers (the gods), *Agni*, your own body with purifying flame as if with their mouth.

४४५३. धन्या चिद्धि त्वे धिषणा वष्टि प्र देवाञ्जन्मं गृणते यजध्यै।
वेपिष्ठो अङ्गिरसां यद्ध विप्रो मधुच्छन्दो भनति रेभ इष्टौ॥३॥

3. Praise solicitous of wealth, is ever addressed, *Agni*, to you, inasmuch as your manifestation (enables) the worshipper to sacrifice to the gods, when the pious sage, the most earnest adorer amongst the *Aṅgirasas*, the reciter (of the hymns), repeats at the ceremony the gratifying measure.

४४५४. अदिद्युतत्स्वपाको विभावाग्ने यजस्व रोदसी उरूची।
आयुं न यं नमसा रातहव्या अञ्जन्ति सुप्रयसं पञ्च जनाः॥४॥

4. The brilliant *Agni*, mature in wisdom, has shone resplendently: offer worship to the wide-spread heaven and earth, you whom, well-fed, the five races of men, bearing oblations, propitiate, with (sacrificial) food, as if you were a mortal guest.

४४५५. वृञ्जे ह यन्नमसा बर्हिरग्नावयामि सुघृतवन्ती सुवृक्तिः।
अम्यक्षि सद्म सदने पृथिव्या अश्रायि यज्ञः सूर्ये न चक्षुः॥५॥

5. When the holy grass has been cut, (to be presented) to *Agni*, with the oblation; when the well-trimmed ladle, filled with butter, has been lifted up; then your receptacle, (the altar), has been prepared on the surface of the earth, and the sacred rite is had recourse to, as light (concentrates) in the sun.

४४५६. दशस्या नः पुर्वणीक होतर्देवेभिरग्ने अग्निभिरिधानः।
राय: सूनो सहसो वावसाना अतिं स्नसेम वृजनं नांहः॥६॥

6. *Agni*, many-rayed, invoker of the gods, blazing with brilliant fires, bestow upon us riches; and may we, Son of strength, clothing you with oblations, overcome iniquity (like) a foe.

[सूक्त-१२]

[**ऋषि**– भरद्वाज बार्हस्पत्य। **देवता**– अग्नि। **छन्द**– त्रिष्टुप्।]

४४५७. मध्ये होता दुरोणे बर्हिषो राळग्निस्तोदस्य रोदसी यजध्यै।
अयं स सूनुः सहस ऋतावा दूरात्सूर्यो न शोचिषा ततान॥१॥

1. *Agni*, the invoker of the gods, the lord of sacrifice, abides in the dwelling of the institutor of the rite, to offer sacrifice to heaven and earth: he, the Son of strength, the observer of truth, has overspread (the world) from afar, like the sun, with light.

Of the institutor of the Rite— *Todasya*, from *tud*, to torment or distress, he who is distressed by ascetic devotion, *tapasā pidyate*, that is, the *yajamāna*.

४४५८. आ यस्मिन्त्वे स्वपाके यजत्र यक्षद्राजन्त्सर्वतातेव नु द्यौः।
त्रिषधस्थस्ततरुषो न जंहो हव्या मघानि मानुषा यजध्यै॥२॥

2. Adorable and resplendent *Agni*, to whom, mature in wisdom, the worshipper offers oblations at every sacred rite, do you, who are present in the three (worlds), move with the speed of the traverser (of the sky, the sun), to convey the valuable oblations of men (to the gods).

४४५९. तेजिष्ठा यस्यारतिर्वनेराट् तोदो अध्वन्न वृधसानो अद्यौत्।
अद्रोघो न द्रविता चेतति त्मन्नमर्त्योऽवत्र ओषधीषु॥३॥

3. He, whose pure and spreading flame blazes in the forest, shines with increasing intensity, like the sun on his (celestial) path: rushing like the innoxious (wind) amongst the plants, immortal, unimpeded, he lights up (all things) by his own (lustre).

Like the Sun— *todo adhvan na*: here *toda* is said to signify the sun as the *sarvasya preraka*, the urger, impeller, or animator of all.

Like the innoxious Winds— *Adrogha na* may also mean, according to Sāyaṇa, as of one not liable to be oppressed or harmed, *adrogdhavya*, or it may imply the vital air, the non-injurer, the sustainer of all, *prāṇarūpeṇa sarveṣām adrogdha*, that is, the wind, *vāyuḥ*.

४४६०. सास्माकेंभिरेतरी न शूषैरग्निः ष्वे दम आ जातवेदाः।
द्वन्नो वन्वन् क्रत्वा नार्वोस्रः पितेवं जारयायिं यज्ञैः॥४॥

4. *Agni*, who knows all that exists, is propitiated in our dwelling by our praises, like those gratifying (commendations which proceed) from one soliciting (a favour): feeder upon trees, consumer of forests, impetuous in act as the bull, the (progenitor of calves), he is glorified by the celebration of sacrifices.

From one soliciting a Favour— *Etari na etari* is explained *gantari*, a goer; *yācamāne puruṣe vidyamānāni stotrāṇi yathā atyantaṁ sukhakarāṇi*, like praises which being present in a man soliciting, going, or applying to another, are the yielders of very great pleasure.

४४६१. अर्धं स्मास्य पनयन्ति भासो वृथा यत्क्षदनुयातिं पृथ्वीम्।
सयो यः स्पन्द्रो विषितो धर्वीयानृणो न तायुरति धन्वां राट्॥५॥

5. They glorify his flames in this world: when, easily thinning the woods, they spread over the earth; he, who glides along unarrested, and rapid in movement as a fast flying thief, shines over the desert.

४४६२. स त्वं नों अर्वन्निदांया विश्वेभिरग्ने अग्निभिरिधानः।
वेषिं रायो वि यासि दुच्छुना मदेम शतहिमाः सुवीराः॥६॥

6. Quick-moving *Agni*, kindled with all (your) fires, (guard) us from reproach: you bestow riches, you scattered adversaries: may we, blessed with excellent male descendants, enjoy happiness for a hundred winters.

[सूक्त-१३]

[ऋषि– भरद्वाज बार्हस्पत्य। देवता– अग्नि। छन्द– त्रिष्टुप्।]

४४६३. त्वद्विश्वा सुभग सौभगान्यग्ने वि यन्ति वनिनो न वयाः।
श्रुष्टी रयिर्वाजो वृत्रतूर्यें दिवो वृष्टिरीड्यों रीतिरपाम्॥१॥

1. Auspicious *Agni*, all good things proceed from you like branches (from the trunk) of a tree, renowned riches, vigour for the

destruction of foes, the rain of heaven: you are to be glorified the sender of the waters.

४४६४. त्वं भगो न आ हि रत्नमिषे परिज्मेव क्षयसि दस्मवर्चाः।

अग्ने मित्रो न बृहत ऋतस्यासि क्षत्ता वामस्य देव भूरेः॥२॥

2. Do you, who are adorable, bestow upon us precious wealth; beautiful with radiance, you pass (around) like the circumambient (wind): you, divine *Agni*, are like *Mitra*, the giver of abundant water and ample wealth.

Who are Adorable— *Tvaṁ Bhago na* might be rendered, you like *Bhaga*; but the Scholiast makes the first an adjective, *bhajanīya*, to be worshipped or propitiated, and considers *na* as *naḥ*, us.

४४६५. स सत्यपतिः शर्वसा हन्ति वृत्रमग्ने विप्रो वि पणेर्भर्ति वाजम्।

यं त्वं प्रचेत ऋतजात राया सजोषा नप्त्रापां हिनोषि॥३॥

3. That man, the protector of the virtuous, destroys, *Agni*, his enemy by his strength, and baffles, intelligent, the might of (the *Asura*) *Paṇi*, whom you, the wise, the parent of sacrifice, consentient with the grandson of the waters, encourage (in the hope) of riches.

Consentient with the Grandson of the Waters— *Sajoṣā naptrāpām*, the grandson of the waters is said here to mean the lightning, *vidyutagninā saṅgatās-tvam* you associated with the lightning-fire.

४४६६. यस्ते सूनो सहसो गीर्भिरुक्थैर्यज्ञैर्मर्तो निशितिं वेद्यानट्।

विश्वं स देव प्रति वारमग्ने धत्ते धान्यं पत्यते वसव्यैः॥४॥

4. The mortal who by praise, by prayers, by sacrifices, attracts, Son of strength, your heightened (radiance) to the altar, enjoys all-sufficiency and corn, and abounds in wealth.

४४६७. ता नृभ्य आ सौश्रवसा सुवीराग्ने सूनो सहसः पुष्यसे धाः।

कृणोषि यच्छर्वसा भूरि पश्वो वयो वृकायारये जसुरये॥५॥

5. Grant, Son of strength, to men (who praise you), those abundant viands and excellent descendants, (that may contribute) to their prosperity: grant also that copious sustenance from cattle, which by your strength you take away from a churlish and malignant adversary.

४४६८. वद्मा सूनो सहसो नो विहाया अग्ने तोकं तनयं वाजि नो दाः।

विश्वाभिर्गीर्भिरभि पूर्तिमश्यां मदेम शतहिमाः सुवीराः॥६॥

6. *Agni*, Son of strength, do you who are mighty be our councillor; give us sons and grandsons, together with food; may I, by all my praises, obtain the fulfilment of my desires; may we, blessed with excellent male descendants, enjoy happiness for a hundred winters.

This is the same passage as occurs in *Sūkta* III.V.11.

[सूक्त-१४]

[**ऋषि**– भरद्वाज बार्हस्पत्य। **देवता**– अग्नि। **छन्द**– अनुष्टुप्; ६ शक्वरी।]

४४६९. अग्ना यो मर्त्यो दुवो धियं जुजोष धीतिभिः।

भसन्नु ष प्र पूर्व्य इषं वुरीतावसे॥१॥

1. May the mortal who propitiates *Agni* by devotion and worship, together with praises, quickly become distinguished as first (amongst men), and acquire ample food for the support (of his children).

४४७०. अग्निरिद्धि प्रचेता अग्निर्वेधस्तम ऋषिः।

अग्निं होतारमीळते यज्ञेषु मनुषो विशः॥२॥

2. *Agni* verily is most wise; he is the chief performer of religious rites, a holy sage: the progeny of men glorify *Agni* as the invoker of the gods at sacrifices.

४४७१. नाना ह्य१ग्नेऽवसे स्पर्धन्ते रायो अर्यः।

तूर्वन्तो दस्युमायवो व्रतैः सीक्षन्तो अव्रतम्॥३॥

3. The manifold treasures of the enemy (detached from them) are emulous, *Agni*, for the preservation (of your worshippers): men who worship you, triumphing over the spoiler, seek to shame him who celebrates no sacred rite by (their) observances.

४४७२. अग्निरप्सामृतीषहं वीरं ददाति सत्पतिम्।

यस्य त्रसन्ति शवसः सङ्क्षि शत्रवो भिया॥४॥

4. *Agni* bestows (upon his worshippers) a male descendant, (the performer of good) works, the subduer of foes, the protector of the virtuous, at whose appearance his enemies tremble through fear of his prowess.

४४७३. अग्निर्हि विद्मना निदो देवो मर्तमुरुष्यति।

सहावा यस्यावृतो रयिर्वाजेष्ववृतः॥५

5. The mighty and divine *Agni*, endowed with knowledge, protects the mortal from reproach whose rich (offerings) are unobstructed (by evil spirits), and unshared by other (offerers) at sacrifices.

४४७४. अच्छा नो मित्रमहो देव देवानग्ने वोच: सुमतिं रोदस्यो:। वीहि
स्वस्तिसुक्षितिं दिवो नन्द्रिषो अंहांसि दुरिता तरेम ता तरेम तवावंसा
तरेम।।६।।

6. Divine *Agni*, revered as a friend, who, abiding in heaven and earth, communicates our praise to the gods, conduct the offerer of adoration to domestic felicity, and may we overcome our adversaries, our iniquities, our difficulties: may we overcome them by your protection.

[सूक्त-१५]

[**ऋषि**– भरद्वाज बार्हस्पत्य अथवा वीतहव्य आङ्गिरस। **देवता**– अग्नि।
छन्द– जगती, ३, १५; ६ अतिशक्वरी; १०, १४, १६, १९
त्रिष्टुप्; १६ अनुष्टुप् ; १८ बृहती।]

४४७५. इममू षु वो अतिथिमुषर्बुधं विश्वासां विशां पतिमृञ्जसे गिरा।
वेतीद्दिवो जनुषा कच्चिदा शुचिर्ज्योर्किंचदत्ति गर्भो यदच्युतम्।।१।।

1. Propitiate by praises this guest who wakes at dawn, the cherisher of all people, who on every occasion descends, pure of origin, from heaven, and, present as the embryo (in the wood of attrition), consumes immediately the offered (oblation).

४४७६. मित्रं न यं सुधितं भृगवो दधुर्वनस्पतावीड्यमूर्ध्वशोचिषम्।
स त्वं सुप्रीतो वीतहव्ये अद्भुत प्रशस्तिभिर्महयसे दिवेदिवे।।२।।

2. Wonderful *Agni*, whom, adorable and upward flaming, the *Bhṛgus* regard as a friend, deposited in the wood of (attrition), be pleased with *Vītahavya*, since you are glorified by (his) praise every day.

Vītahavya— If applied to *Bharadvāja* this will be an appellative, he by whom oblations are offered.

४४७७. स त्वं दक्षस्यावृको वृधो भूर्यः परस्यान्तरस्य तरुषः। राय: सूनो
सहसो मर्त्येष्वा छर्दिर्यच्छ वीतहव्याय सप्रथो भरद्वाजाय
सप्रथ:।।३।।

3. Do you, who are unresisted, become the benefactor of him who is skilled (in sacred rites), his defender against a near of distant enemy; Son of strength, who are ever renowned, grant wealth and a dwelling to *Vītahavya*, the offerer of the oblation.

To *Vītahavya*, **the offerer of the Oblation**—*vītahavyāya bharadvājāya*, either of these may be taken as the name or the epither; to *Vītahavya*, the bearer, *bharat*, of the oblation, *vāja*, or to *Bharadvāja*, by whom is offered, *vīta*, the oblation, *havya*.

४४७८. द्युतानं वो अतिथिं स्वर्णरमग्निं होतारं मनुष: स्वध्वरम्।
विप्रं न द्युक्षवचसं सुवृक्तिभिर्हव्यवाहंमरतिं देवमृञ्जसे॥४॥

4. Propitiate with pious praises the radiant *Agni*, your guest, the guide to heaven, the invoker of the gods (at the sacrifice) of *Manu*, the celebrator of holy rites, the speaker of brilliant words like a learned sage, the bearer of oblations (to the gods), the lord, the divine.

४४७९. पावकया यश्चितयन्त्या कृपा क्षामन्नुरुच उषसो न भानुना।
तूर्वन्न यामन्नेतशस्य नू रण आ यो घृणे न तृतृषाणो अजर:॥५॥

5. (Propitiate him) who shines upon the earth with purifying and enlightening lustre, as the dawns with light; him, who like (a warrior) discomfiting (his foes) quickly blazed forth in the contest in defence of *Etaśa*; him, who is satiated (with food), exempt from decay.

In Defence of *Etaśa*— See vol. I. verse 707: Mahīdhara, *Yajuṣ.* 10.10, explains *etaśa* by its other meaning, a horse, but his interpretation of the passage is not very distinct.

४४८०. अग्निमग्निं व: समिधा दुवस्यत प्रियंप्रियं वो अतिथिं गृणीषणि। उप
वो गीर्भिरमृतं विवासत देवो देवेषु वनते हि वार्यं देवो देवेषु वनते
हि नो दुव:॥६॥

6. Worship repeatedly the adorable *Agni* with fuel (him) who is ever your dear friend, your guest; approach the immortal *Agni* with praises, for he, a god among gods, accepts our homage.

४४८१. समिद्धमग्निं समिधा गिरा गृणे शुचिं पावकं पुरो अध्वरे ध्रुवम्।
विप्रं होतारं पुरुवारमद्भुहं कविं सुम्नैरीमहे जातवेदसम्॥७॥

7. I glorify with praise the kindled *Agni*, pure purifying, permanent, (placed) before (us) at the sacrifice; let us celebrate with pleasant (hymns) the wise *Agni*, the invoker of the gods, the

adored of many, the benevolent, the far-seeing, him who knows all
that exists.

४४८२. त्वां दूतमग्ने अमृतं युगेयुगे हव्यवाहं दधिरे पायुमीड्यम्।
देवासश्च मर्तासश्च जागृवि विभुं विश्पतिं नर्मसा नि षेदिरे॥८॥

8. You, *Agni*, have gods and men in every age retained as thier
messenger, immortal bearer of oblations, beneficent, adorable;
they have placed him with reverence (upon the altar), vigilant,
pervading, the protector of mankind.

४४८३. विभूषन्नग्न उभयाँ अनु व्रता दूतो देवानां रजसी समीयसे।
यत्ते धीतिं सुमतिमावृणीमहेऽध स्मा नस्त्रिवरूथ: शिवो भव॥९॥

9. Showing grace, *Agni*, to both (gods and men), and at each
sacred rite the messenger of the gods, you traverse earth and
heaven: inasmuch as we offer you worship and praise, therefore do
you, who are the guardian of the three (regions), be auspicious to
us.

This and the two preceding stanzas occur in the *Sāmaveda*, 1569.

४४८४. तं सुप्रतीकं सुदृशं स्वञ्चमविद्वांसो विदुष्टरं सपेम।
स यक्षद्विश्वा वयुनानि विद्वान्त्र हव्यमग्निरमृतेषु वोचत्॥१०॥

10. We of little wisdom adore the most wise *Agni*, the well-
formed, the well-looking the graceful-moving; may *Agni*, who
knows all things that are to be known offer the sacrifice; may he
announce the oblation to the immortals.

४४८५. तमग्ने पास्युत तं पिपर्षि यस्त आनट् कवये शूर धीतिम्।
यज्ञस्य वा निशितिं वोदितिं वा तमित्पृणक्षि शवसोत राया॥११॥

11. You cherish, you protect, *Agni*, that may who offers
worship, hero, to you, the far-seeing; you reward with strength and
with riches him (who undertakes) the institution, (who effects) the
accomplishment, of the sacrifice.

Who Effects the Accomplishments of the Acrifice— *Yajñasya vā*
niśitim vā uditim vā: the first is explained by Sāyaṇa, *saṁskāra*,
perfection, accomplishment the second, *udgamanam*, going up or over,
perhaps, finishing; the relation of either to *yajña* is questionable, as they
are both separated from it by the disjunctive, *vā*, or.

४४८६. त्वमग्ने वनुष्यतो नि पाहि त्वमु न: सहसावन्नवद्यात्।
सं त्वा ध्वस्मन्वदभ्येतु पाथ: सं रयि: स्पृहयाय्य: सहस्री॥१२॥

12. Protect us, *Agni*, from the malignant, preserve us, mighty one, from wickedness; may the offering come to you free from defects; may desirable riches, by you sands, (reach us).

४४८७. अग्निहोता गृहपति: स राजा विश्वा वेद जनिमा जातवेदा:।
देवानामुत यो मर्त्यानां यजिष्ठ: स प्र यंजतामृतावां।।१३।।

13. *Agni*, is the invoker of the gods, the lord of the house, the ruler, who knows all that is, knows all existing beings; he is the most assiduous worshipper amongst gods or men; let him who is observant of truth offer worship.

४४८८. अग्ने यद्य विशो अध्वरस्य होत: पार्वकशोचे वेष्वं हि यज्वा।
ऋता यजासि महिना वि यद्भूर्हव्या वह यविष्ठ या ते अद्य।।१४।।

14. *Agni*, minister of the sacrifice, bright with purifying lustre, approve of that (worship) which is this day celebrated by the institutor of the rite: you verily are the sacrificer, therefore address the worship (to the gods); and since by your greatness you are all-pervading, therefore, youngest (of the gods), accept the oblations which are today (presented) to you.

४४८९. अभि प्रयांसि सुधितानि हि ख्यो नि त्वा दधीत रोदसी यजध्यै।
अवां नो मघवन्वाजसातावग्ने विश्वानि दुरिता तरेम ता तरेम
तवावंसा तरेम।।१५।।

15. Look, *Agni*, upon the (sacrificial) viands duly deposited (upon the alter): Heaven and earth detain you to sacrifice (to the gods): opulent *Agni*, protect us in battle, whereby we may pass safe over all evils: may we pass over those of a prior existence; may we pass over them by your protection.

See the last verse of the of preceding *Sūkta*.

४४९०. अग्ने विश्वेभि: स्वनीक देवैरूर्णावन्तं प्रथम: सीद योनिम्।
कुलायिनं घृतवन्तं सवित्रे यज्ञं नय यजमानाय साधु।।१६।।

16. Bright-rayed *Agni*, sit down first with all the gods, upon the altar lined with wool, a nest (of perfumes) and suffused with *ghee*, and rightly convey (to the deities) the sacrifice of the institutor of the rite, of the presenter of the oblation.

Lined with Wool, Etc.— *urṇāvantam, kulāyinam ghṛtavantam*; the stanza is quoted in the *Aitareya Brāhmaṇa*, with a partial explanation, which is amplified by Sāyaṇa; the altar is built up like the nest of a bird, *kulaya*, with circles, *pardhayaḥ*, of the wood of the *khayar* or *devadāru*, in which, *aviṣambandaḥ romaviśeṣaḥ*, sheep's wool; and fragrant resins, the materials of incense (*guggulu dhupāt dhanam*) are placed, *ete uttaravedyām sthāpitaḥ*, these appurtenances are placed in the northern altar.

Of the presenter of the Oblation— *Savitre yajamānāya*, according to Sāyaṇa should be in the genitive case, *ṣaṣṭyarthe caturthyeṣa;* but in his comment on the *Brāhmaṇa* he explains the terms *anuṣṭātre yajamānāya tadupakārārtham*, for the sake of the benefit of the sacrificing institutor of the ceremony.

Wandering Deviously, but not Bewildered— *Aṅkuyantam amuram*: the first refers, according to the Scholiast, to the legend of *Agni*'s attempting at first to run way from the gods, *devebhyaḥ pālayamānam*.

४४९१. इममु त्यमथर्ववदग्निं मन्थन्ति वेधसः।
      यमङ् कूयन्तमानयन्नमूरं श्याव्याभ्यः॥१७॥

17. The priests churn you, *Agni*, as was done by *Atharvan*, and bring him from the glooms of might wandering deviously, but not bewildered.

४४९२. जनिष्वा देववीतये सर्वताता स्वस्तयें।
      आ देवान् वक्ष्यमृताँ ऋतावृधौ यज्ञं देवेषु पिस्पृशः॥१८॥

18. Be born, *Agni*, at the sacrifice, for the welfare of the offerer (of the oblation) to the gods: bring hither the immortal deities, the augmenters of the (sacred) rite preser⬤ our sacrifice to the gods.

४४९३. वयमु त्वा गृहपते जनानामग्ने अर्कं समिधा बृहन्तम्।
      अस्थूरि नो गार्हपत्यानि सन्तु तिग्मेन नस्तेजसा सं शिशाधि॥१९॥

19. Lord of the house, *Agni*, we, amongst men, promote your increase by fuel: may our domestic fires be supplied with all that is essential: eliven us with brilliant radiance.

With all that is Essential— *Asthūri* for *asthūriṇa gārhapatyāni santu isthūri* is properly a one-horse car or waggon which bring either the *Soma* plant or fuel; with the negative prefix *asthūri* it implies a non-one-horse cart, that is a earth with a full team, and, metonymically, its contents, or a full supply of what is wanted for a perfect sacrifice, such as children, cattle, riches, *asthūriṇi putra-paśu-dhanādibhiḥ sampūrṇāni*.

ANUVAKA II

[सूक्त- १६]

[**ऋषि**– भरद्वाज बार्हस्पत्य। **देवता**– अग्नि। **छन्द**– गायत्री; १, ६ वर्धमाना;
२७, ४७-४८ अनुष्टुप्; ४६ त्रिष्टुप्।]

४४९४. त्वमग्ने यज्ञानां होता विश्वेषां हित:। देवोभिर्मानुषे जनें।।१।।

1. You, *Agni*, have been appointed by the gods, the ministrant
for men, the descendants of *Manu*, at all sacrifices.
Sāmaveda, 2, 1474.

४४९५. स नौ मन्द्राभिरध्वरे जिह्वाभिर्यजा मह:।

आ देवान्वक्षि यक्षि च।।२।।

2. Therefore do you at our sacrifice offer oblations to the great
deities with exhilarating flames; bring hither the gods; offer them
worship.
Sāmaveda, 1475.

४४९६. वेत्था हि वेधो अध्वन: पथश्च देवाञ्जसा। अग्ने यज्ञेषु सुक्रतो।।३।।

3. *Agni*, doer of great deeds, creator, you know (how to travel
over) with speed (great) roads and (little) paths at sacrifices.
Road and Paths— *Adhvanaḥ pathaśca* are explained severally
mahāmārgān, great roads, *kṣudra mārgāṁśca*, little roads or paths; that is,
according to Sāyaṇa put the sacrificer into the right way when he is going
wrong in the ceremonial or sacrifice.

४४९७. त्वामीळे अध द्विता भरतो वाजिभि: शुनम्। ईजे यज्ञेषु यज्ञियम्।।४।

4. *Bharata*, with the presenters of the oblation, has joyfully
praised you in your (two-fold capacity), and has worshipped you,
the adorable, with sacrifices.
Bharata— Sāyaṇa considers *Bharata* here to be the *Rājā*, the son of
Duṣyanta.
In your two-fold capacity— In the character of bestowing what is
wished for and removing what is undesired, is twofold; *iṣṭa prāptyaniṣṭa-*
parihārarūpeṇāgnir dvidhā.

४४९८. त्वमिमा वार्या पुरु दिवोदासाय सुन्वते। भरद्वाजाय दाशुषे।।५।।

5. As you have conferred these many blessings upon *Divodāsa*
when presenting libations, (so now grant them) to the (actual)
offerer, *Bharadvāja*.

४४९९. त्वं दूतो अमर्त्य आ वहा दैव्यं जनम्। शृण्वन्विप्रस्य सुष्टुतिम्।।६।।

6. Hearing the adoration of the sage, do you, who are the immortal messenger, bring hither the celestial people.

४५००. त्वामग्ने स्वाध्योऽइ मर्तासो देववीतये। यज्ञेषु देवमीळते।।७।।

7. Pious mortals invoke you, divine *Agni*, at sacrifices, to convey their (sacrificial) food to the gods.

४५०१. तव प्र यक्षि सन्दृशमुत क्रतुं सुदानवः। विश्वे जुषन्त कामिनः।।८।।

8. I glorify your splendour, and the acts of you the liberal giver all who, (through your favour) enjoy their desires, glorify you.

४५०२. त्वं होता मनुर्हितो वह्निरासा विदुष्टरः। अग्ने यक्षि दिवो विशः।।९।।

9. You have been appointed by *Manu*, the invoker of the gods, the most wise bearer of oblations (to them) by your mouth; worship, *Agni*, the people of heaven.

४५०३. अग्न आ याहि वीतये गृणानो हव्यदातये।

नि होता सत्सि बर्हिषि।।१०।।

10. Come, *Agni*, to the (sacrificial) food: being lauded, (come) to convey the oblation (to the gods): sit down as the ministrant priest upon the sacred grass.

Sāmaveda, 1 & 660 the stanza is twice translated by Mr. Colebrooke in his "Essays on the Religious Ceremonies of the *Brahmans*'. Asiatic Researches, vol. v., p.364; vol., p.272.

४५०४. तं त्वा समिद्भिरङ्गिरो घृतेन वर्धयामसि। बृहच्छोचा यविष्ठ्य।।११।।

11. We augment you, *Aṅgiras*, with fuel and with cutter; blaze fiercely, youngest (of the gods).

Sāmaveda, 661, *Yajurveda*, 3.3

४५०५. स नः पृथु श्रवाय्यमच्छा देव विवाससि। बृहदग्ने सुवीर्यम्।।१२।।

12. Divine *Agni*, bestow upon us (wealth), excellent, great, and (comprehending) worthy male descendants.

Sāmaveda, 662; *suvīra* or *suvīrya* always implies having male descendants, *bonos viros habens,* or *bonorum virorum possessio.*

४५०६. त्वामग्ने पुष्कराद्ध्यथर्वा निरमन्थत। मूर्ध्नो विश्वस्य वाघतः।।१३।।

13. The sage, *Atharvan*, extracted you from upon the lotus-leaf, the head, the support of the universe.

Tvaṁ puṣkarād adhi atharvo niramanthata, murdhno viṣvasya vāghataḥ: the verse occurs in the *Sāmaveda*, 9, and the *Yajurveda*, 2.32:

according to Sāyaṇa, *puṣkarādadhi* means *puṣkaraparṇe*, or the lotus-leaf, as by the text *puṣkara-parṇe, Prajāpatir bhūmim aprathayat*, upon the lotus-leaf *Prajāpati* made manifest the earth, which probably suggested one of the accounts of the creation in *Manu* 1: hence, as it supported the earth it may be termed the head, *mūrdhan*, or the bearer, *vāghata* for *vāhaka*, of all things; Mahīdhara cites a text to show that *atharvan* means *prāṇa*, vital air extracted fire or animal heat from the water, *prāṇa udakasakāśād-agniṁ niśeṣeṇa mathitavān*; to *vāghata* he assigns the usual import of *ṛtvij*, ministrant priest, and explains the last sentence, all the priests churned you out of the head or top of the wood of attrition; he gives also another explanation, which agrees with that of Sāyaṇa.

४५०७. तमु॒ त्वा द॒ध्य॒ङ्ङृषि॑: पुत्र॒ ईधे॒ अथ॑र्वण॑:। वृ॒त्रह॑णं॒ पुर॑न्दर॒म्॥१४॥

14. The *Ṛṣi*, Dadhyañc, the son of *Atharvan*, kindled the slayer of *Vṛtra*, the destroyer of the cities of the *Asuras*.

४५०८. तमु॒ त्वा पा॒थ्यो॒ वृ॒षा स॒मीधे॑ दस्यु॒हन्त॑मम्। ध॒नञ्ज॑यं र॒णेर॑णे॥१५॥

15. (The *Ṛṣi*) *Pāthya*, the showerer, kindled you the destroyer of the *Dasyu*, the winner of spoil in battle.

४५०९. एह्यु॒षु ब्रवा॑णि ते॒ऽग्न इ॒त्थेत॑रा गिर॑:। ए॒भिर्व॑र्धास॒ इन्दु॑भि:॥१६॥

16. Come, *Agni*, that I may address to you other praises in this manner: augment with these libations.

Other Praises in this Manner— *Itthetarā giraḥ ittha, anena prakāreṇa*, thus, in this manner; *tiara*, other may mean also, according to Sāyaṇa, offered by others, or by the *Asuras, asuraiḥ kṛtā*: in his commentary on the *Aitareya Brāhmaṇa*, where the verse is cited, 3.49, he understands it differently, or, other than those offered to the gods, or adverse to the gods, propitiatory of the *Asuras, asurebhiyaḥ hitaḥ devavākyāditara devavirodhinya ityarthaḥ*.

४५१०. यत्र॒ क्व च ते॒ मनो॒ दक्षं॑ दध॒स उत्त॑रम्। तत्रा॒ सद॑: कृणवसे॥१७॥

17. Wheresoever, and upon whatsoever your mind is directed, you bestow uncommon vigour, and there you make your abode.

४५११. न॒हि ते॑ पू॒र्तम॑क्षिपद्धुवद्वने॑मानां वसो। अथा॒ दुवो॒ वनवसे॥१८॥

18. Let not your full (blaze) be distressing to the eye, giver of dwellings to your humble votaries, and, therefore accept our worship.

Distressing to the Eye— The text has *nahi pūrtam akṣipadbhuvat; akṣi-pat, akṣṇo patākaṁ vināśakam*, the offender or destroyer of the eye; the verse occurs *Sāmaveda*, 707, and *Yajurveda*, 26, 13 the preceding verse also occurs in the former 11.56.

४५१२. आग्निर॑र्गामि भार॑तो वृत्र॒हा पु॑रुचेत॑नः। दि॒वौदा॑सस्य॒ सत्प॑तिः॥१९॥

19. *Agni*, the bearer, (of oblations), the destroyer of the enemies of *Divopāsa*, the cognizant of many, the protector of the good, has been brought hither (by our praises).

४५१३. स हि विश्वाति पार्थि॑वा र॒यिं दाश॑न्महि॒त्व॑ना।

वन्व॒न्न॒वा॒तो अस्तृ॑तः॥२०॥

20. Surpassing all earthly things, may he bestow upon us riches, destroying his enemies by his greatness, unresisted, unassailed.

४५१४. स प्र॒त्न॒व॒न्नवी॑यसा॒ग्ने द्यु॒म्नेन॑ सं॒यता॑। बृ॒ह॒त्तन्थ॒ भानु॑ना॥२१॥

21. You, have overspread, *Agni*, this vast (firmament) with radiant concentrated lustre, recent like that of old.

४५१५. प्र वः॑ सखायो अग्नये॒ स्तोम॑ य॒ज्ञं च॑ धृष्णु॒या।

अर्च॑ गा॒य च॑ वे॒धसे॑॥२२॥

22. Sing praise and offer sacrifice, my friends, to the foe-discomfiting, the creator, *Agni*.

४५१६. स हि यो मानु॑षा यु॒गा सीद॒द्धोता॑ क॒विक्र॑तुः।

दू॒तश्च॑ हव्य॒वाह॑नः॥२३॥

23. May that *Agni* indeed sit down (at our sacrifice), who in every age of man has been the invoker of the gods, doer of wise deeds, the messenger of the gods, the bearer of oblations.

४५१७. ता राजा॑ना॒ शुचि॑व्रता॒दित्या॒न्मारु॑तं ग॒णम्। वसो॒ यक्षी॒ह रोद॑सी॥२४॥

24. Giver of dwellings, worship on this occasion the two regal divinities, *Mitra* and *Varuṇa*, whose acts are holy, the *Ādityas*, the company of the *Maruts*, and heaven.

४५१८. वस्वीं॑ ते अग्ने सं॒दृष्टि॑रिष॒यते॒ मर्त्या॑य। ऊर्जो॑ नपाद॒मृत॑स्य॥२५॥

25. Son of strength, *Agni*, the glorious radiance of you who are immortal, bestows food upon (your) mortal worshipper.

४५१९. क्रत्वा॒ दा अ॑स्तु॒ श्रेष्ठो॒ऽद्य त्वा॒ वन्व॒न्त्सुरे॑कणः।

मर्त॑ आनाश सुवृ॒क्तिम्॥२६॥

26. May the donor (of the oblation), propitiating you by his acts toady, be exalted, and (rendered) very opulent: may (such) mortal be diligent in (your) praise.

४५२०. ते तें अग्ने त्वोता इषयन्तो विश्वमायुः।
तरन्तो अर्यो अरातीर्वन्वन्तों अर्यो अराती:॥२७॥

27. Those, *Agni*, who are protected by you, wishing for the whole (term of) life (obtain it), overcoming hostile assailants, destroying hostile assailants.

४५२१. अग्निस्तिग्मेन शोचिषा यासद्विश्वं न्यऽत्रिणम्।
अग्निनों वनते रयिम्॥२८॥

28. May *Agni*, with his sharp flame, demolish the devourer (of the oblation); may *Agni* grant us riches.

४५२२. सुवीरं रयिमा भर जातवेदो विचर्षणे। जहि रक्षांसि सुक्रतो॥२९॥

29. *Jātavedas*, all-beholder, bring us wealth with good posterity; doer of good deeds, destroy the *Rākṣasas*.

४५२३. त्वं नः पाह्यंहसो जातवेदो अघायतः। रक्षा णो ब्रह्मणस्कवे॥३०॥

30. Preserve us, *Jātavedas*, from sin; enunciator of prayer, protect us from the malevolent.

Enunciator of Prayer— *Brahmaṇaskave* is explained *mantrasya śabdayitā*, or sounder or articulator of prayer; for *Agni*, it is said, generates articulate sound, and the *Smṛti* is cited as authority; *manaḥ kāyāgnim ahanti, sa prerayati manutam, marutas-tu urasi caran, mandiam janayati svaram,* mind excites the fire of the body, that excites the collective vital airs, and they, passing into the breast, engender agreeable, articulate sound.

४५२४. यो नौ अग्ने दुरेव आ मर्तों वधाय दाशति।
तस्मान्नः पाह्यंहसः॥३१॥

31. The malevolent mortal who threatens us with murderous weapon from defend us, and also from sin.

४५२५. त्वं तं देव जिह्वया परि बाधस्व दुष्कृतम्।
मर्तो यो नो जिघांसति॥३२॥

32. Scatter, divine *Agni*, by your flame, that evil-doer, the man who seeks to kill us.

४५२६. भरद्वाजाय सप्रथः शर्म यच्छ सहन्त्य। अग्ने वरेण्यं वसु॥३३॥

33. Subduer of foes, grant to *Bharadvāja* infinite happiness and desirable wealth.

४५२७. अग्निर्वृत्राणि जङ्घनद्द्रविणस्युर्विपन्यया।
समिद्धः शुक्र आहुतः॥३४॥

34. May *Agni*, propitiated by praise, desirous of (sacrificial) affluence, kindled, bright, and fed with burnt-offerings, destroy all adversaries.

Sāmaveda, 4, 1396; *Yajurveda*, 33.9: Mahīdhara interprets the first part somewhat differently, *Agni* entirely destroys all by manifold worship.

४५२८. गर्भे मातुः पितुष्पिता विदिद्युतानो अक्षरे। सीदन्नृतस्य योनिमा॥३५॥

35. Radiant in the embryo of the maternal (earth), on the imperishable (altar); the cherisher of the paternal (heaven), sitting on the seat of sacrifice.

The Cherisher of the Paternal Heaven— *he mātuḥ, pituṣpitā*: here, as before, the mother of *Agni* is the earth, the father is heaven: *Agni* is said to be the father or fosterer of his parent heaven, by transmitting to it the flame and smoke of burnt-offerings: also *Sāmaveda*, 1397.

४५२९. ब्रह्म प्रजावदा भर जातवेदो विचर्षणे। अग्ने यद्दीदयद्दिवि॥३६॥

36. Bring to us, *Jātavedas*, all-beholder, food with progeny; such (food) as is brilliant in heaven.

Sāmaveda, 1398.

४५३०. उप त्वा रण्वसन्दृशं प्रयस्वन्तः सहस्कृत। अग्ने ससृज्महे गिरः॥३७।

37. Strength-begotten *Agni*, we, offering (sacrificial) food, address praises to you who are of pleasing aspect,

Sāmaveda, 1705.

४५३१. उपच्छायामिव घृणेरगन्म शर्म ते वयम्। अग्ने हिरण्यऽसन्दृशः॥३८॥

38. We have recourse, *Agni*, to the shelter of you, the lustrous, the golden-feathered, as to the shade (of a tree).

४५३२. य उग्रइव शर्यहा तिग्मशृङ्गो न वंसगः। अग्ने पुरो रुरोजिथ॥३९॥

39. You, *Agni*, who are like a fierce archer, or like a sharp-horned bull, have destroyed the cities (of the *Asuras*).

The Scholiast here identifies *Agni* with *Rudra* as the destroyer of the cities of *Tripura*; the identification is authorized by the Vedic text, *Rudro vā eṣo yad Agniḥ*, also *Sāmaveda*, 1707.

४५३३. आ यं हस्ते न खादिनं शिशुं जातं न बिभ्रति। विशामग्निं स्वध्वरम्॥४०॥

40. (Worship) that *Agni* whom (the priests) bear in their hands like a new-born babe; the devourer (of the oblation), the (conveyer of the) holy sacrifices of men.

४५३४. प्र देवं देववीतये भरंता वसुवित्तंमम्।
आ स्वे योनौ नि षींदतु ॥४१॥

41. Conduct the divine (*Agni*), the bestower of infinite wealth, to (receive charge of) the food of the gods; let him sit down on his appropriate seat.

४५३५. आ जातं जातवेदसि प्रियं शिशीतातिथिम्।
स्योन आ गृहपंतिम् ॥४२॥

42. (Welcome him) as soon as born, like a beloved guest, and place the lord of the mansion upon the sacred (altar) whence wisdom is derived.

This and the preceding verse are to be recited, it is said, when the fire that has been produced by attrition is applied to kindle the *āhavanīya*, or fire of burnt-offerings they are both quoted in the *Aitareya Brāhmaṇa*, i.16, and with Sāyaṇa's gloss to this effect, but some of the terms are differently explained and applied; thus, *Agni* is to be considered as the guest, not of the sacrificer, but of the *āhavanīya* fire, and *jātavedasi* is also applies to the latter, as knowing the birth of the churned fire, to whom it is a giver of delight, *śyona, sukhakara,* by giving him a welcome reception.

४५३६. अग्ने युक्ष्वा हि ये तवाश्वांसो देव साधवः। अरं वहन्ति मन्यवे ॥४३॥

43. Harness, divine *Agni*, your well-trained horses, who bear you quickly to the sacrifice.

To the Sacrifice— *Manyave,* synonymous with *yajñāya,* as *manyur, yāhaḥ*; Mahīdhara, *Yajus,* 13,36, gives the same interpretation; it occurs also *Sāmaveda,* 25.

४५३७. अच्छा नो याह्या वहाभि प्रयांसि वीतयें। आ देवान्त्सोमंपीतये ॥४४॥

44. Come, *Agni*, to our presence; bring hither the gods to partake of the (sacrificial) viands, to drink the *Soma* juice.

४५३८. उदंग्ने भारत द्युमदजस्रेण दविद्युतत्। शोचा वि भाह्यजर ॥४५॥

45. Blaze up, *Agni*, bearer of oblations; shine, undecaying *Agni*, radiant with undecaying lustre.

४५३९. वीती यो देवं मर्तो दुवस्येदग्निमीळीताध्वरे हविष्मान्।
होतारं सत्ययजं रोदस्योरुत्तानहस्तो नमसा विवासेत् ॥४६॥

46. Whatever mortal, offering oblations, worships a deity with (sacrificial) food, let him at the ceremony also worship *Agni*, the invoker of heaven and earth, the sacrificer with truth; let him adore (*Agni*) with uplifted hands.

४५४०. आ तें अग्न ऋचा हविर्हृदा तष्टं भंरामसि।
ते तें भवन्तूक्षण ऋष्णभासों वशा उत।।४७।।

47. We offer to you, *Agni*, the oblation sanctified by the heart, and (identified) with the sacred verse may the vigorous bulls and the cows be (as such an oblation) to you.

May the Vigorous Bulls and the Cows, Etc.— *Te te bhavantu ūkṣaṇa ṛṣabhāso vaśā uta*, may these vigorous bulls or the cows be for you; the Scholiast intimates their being offered to *Agni* as victims *ṛṣabhavaśārūpeṇa pariṇatam san tvabhakṣa ṇāya (havir) bhavatu*, let the oblation, matured in the from of bulls or cows, be for your food.

४५४१. अग्निं देवासों अग्रियमिन्धते वृत्रहन्तंमम्।
येनां वसून्याभृता तृह्ळहा रक्षांसि वाजिनां।।४८।।

48. The gods kindle *Agni* as the chief (of them); as the especial destroyer of *Vṛtra*; by whom the treasures (of the *Asuras*) are carried off; by whom the *Rākṣasas* are destroyed.

[सूक्त- १७]

[ऋषि– भरद्वाज बार्हस्पत्य। देवता– इन्द्र।
छन्द– त्रिष्टुप्; १५ द्विपदा त्रिष्टुप्।]

४५४२. पिबा सोमंमभि यमुग्रे तर्दं ऊर्वं गव्यं महिं गृणान इन्द्र।
वि यो धृष्णो वधिषों वज्रहस्त विश्वां वृत्रमंमित्रिया शवोंभिः।।१।।

1. Fierce *Indra*, glorified by us, drink the *Soma*, (animated) by which you have discovered the vast herd of cattle (stolen by *Paṇis*), and, overcomer of enemies, wielder of the thunderbolt, you have slain, by your strength all opposing foes.

४५४३. स ईं पाहि य ऋजीषी तरुंत्रो यः शिप्रंवान् वृष्भो यो मंतीनाम्।
यो गौत्रभिद्वज्रभृद्यो हरिष्ठाः स इन्द्र चित्रां अभि तृन्धि वाजान्।।२।।

2. Drink it, *Indra,* you who enjoy the flavourless *Soma*; you who are the preserver, the handsome-chinned, the showerer (of benefits) on those who praise you; who are the breaker of mountains, the wielder of the thunderbolt, the curber of steeds, do you bestow upon us various food.

४५४४. एवा पाहि प्रत्नथा मन्दतु त्वा श्रुधि ब्रह्म वावृधस्वोत गीर्भिः।
आविः सूर्यं कृणुहि पीपिहीषो जहि शत्रूँरभि गा इन्द्र तृन्धि ।।३।।

3. Drink it as of old, and may it exhilarate you; hear our prayer, and be exalted by our praises; make the sun visible, nourish us with food, destroy our enemies, rescue the cattle.

४५४५. ते त्वा मदा बृहदिन्द्र स्वधाव इमे पीता उक्षयन्त द्युमन्तम्।
महामनूनं तवसं विभूतिं मत्सरासो जर्हृषन्त प्रसाहम् ।।४।।

4. Abounding in food, *Indra*, let these exhilarating draughts copiously bedew you, the resplendent; let the inebriating juices delight you who are mighty, deficient in no (excellence), powerful, manifold, the overcomer of foes.

४५४६. येभिः सूर्यमुषसं मन्दसानोऽवासयोऽपँ दुळ्हानि दर्दृत्।
महामद्रिं परि गा इन्द्र सन्तं नुत्था अच्युतं सदसः परि स्वात् ।।५।।

5. By which (juices) being exhilarated you have appointed the sun and the dawn (to their offices), driving away the solid (glooms); you have penetrated, *Indra*, the mountain, unmoved from its own seat, concealing the cattle.

४५४७. तव क्रत्वा तव तद्दंसनाभिरामासु पक्वं शच्या नि दीधः।
और्णोर्दुरँ उस्रियाभ्यो वि दुळ्होदूर्वादगा असृजो अङ्गिरस्वान् ।।६।।

6. By your wisdom, by your deeds, through your power, you have developed the mature (milk) in the immature (udders), you have opened the strong doors for the cattle (to come forth); associated with the *Angirasas*, you have liberated the cows from their fold.

४५४८. पप्राथ क्षां महि दंसो व्युर्वीमुप द्यामृष्वो बृहदिन्द्र स्तभायः।
अधारयो रोदसी देवपुत्रे प्रत्ने मातरा यह्वी ऋतस्य ।।७।।

7. You have filled the wide earth, *Indra*. With (the of) your deeds; you, the mighty one, have propped up the vast heaven; you have sustained the heaven and earth, whose children are the gods, (and who are) the old and mighty parents of sacrifice.

The old and mighty parents of sacrifice— *Pratne mātarā yahvir ṛtasya*, which may be also rendered, according to Sāyaṇa, the ancient parents, the offspring of *Brahmā*; *ṛtasya, brahmaṇa, yahvi putryau, yahu* being a synonym of *Āpatya, Nighaṇṭu*, 2.2.

४५४९. अध त्वा विश्वे पुर इन्द्र देवा एकं तवसं दधिरे भराय।
अदेवो यदभ्यौहिष्ट देवान्त्स्वर्षाता वृणत इन्द्रमत्रे ॥८॥

8. All the gods then placed you, *Indra*, as their mighty chief in front for battle; when the impious (*Asuras*) assailed the deities; the *Maruts* supported *Indra* in the conflict.

The *Maruts* supported *Indra* in the conflict— According to the legend the gods ran away, the *Maruts* alone stood by *Indra*.

४५५०. अध द्यौश्चित्ते अप सा नु वज्राद्द्वितानंमद्रियसा स्वस्य मन्यो:।
अहिं यदिन्द्रो अभ्योहंसानं नि चिद्द्विधायुः शयथे जघानं ॥९॥

9. The heaven bowed down in the two-fold dread of your thunderbolt, and your individual wrath, when *Indra*, the giver of food, struck to the sleep (of death) the assailing *Ahi*.

४५५१. अध त्वष्टा ते मह उग्र वज्रं सहस्रभृष्टिं ववृतच्छताश्रिम्।
निकांममरमणसं येन नवन्तमहिं सं पिणगृजीषिन् ॥१०॥

10. Fierce *Indra*, *Tvaṣṭā* constructed for you, the mighty one, the thousand-edged, the hundred-angles thunderbolt, wherewith you have crushed the ambitious audacious, loud-shouting *Ahi*.

४५५२. वर्धान्यं विश्वे मरुतः सजोषाः पर्चच्छतं महिषाँ इन्द्र तुभ्यम्।
पूषा विष्णुस्त्रीणि सरांसि धावन्वृत्रहणं मदिरमंशुमस्मै ॥११॥

11. For you, *Indra*, whom all the *Maruts*, alike pleased, exalt, may *Pūṣan* and *Viṣṇu* dress for you a hundred buffaloes, and to him may the three streams flow with the inebriating, foe-destroying *Soma*.

Dress for you a hundred Buffaloes— *Pacat śatam mahiṣān tubhyam,* may he cook for you a hundred male animals; *pum-paśūn pacet* is the explanation; there is no nominative except *Pūṣan,* which is in the following hemstitch, and which is followed by *Viṣṇu* without a copulative.

Three Streams— *Trīṇi sarāṁsi* mean, according to the Scholiast, three cups or vessels called *Āhavanis,* holding the *Soma* which has been purified or filtered into the pitcher, the *droṇakalaśa.*

४५५३. आ क्षोदो महि वृतं नदीनां परिष्ठितमसृज ऊर्मिमपाम्।
तासामनु प्रवतं इन्द्र पन्थां प्रार्दयो नीचीरपसः समुद्रम् ॥१२॥

12. You have set free the greatly obstructed and arrested water of the rivers, the flux of the waters; you have directed them, *Indra*,

upon their downward paths; you have sent them rapidly down to the ocean.

४५५४. एवा ता विश्वा चकृवांसमिन्द्रं महामुग्रमजुर्यं संहोदाम्।
सुवीरं त्वा स्वायुधं सुवज्रमा ब्रह्म नव्यमवसे ववृत्यात्॥१३॥

13. May our new prayer bring to our protection you, *Indra*, who are the maker of all these (things that exist); who are mighty, fierce, undecaying, the giver of strength, having excellent descendants, the *Maruts*, well-armed, the bearer of the thunderbolt.

४५५५. स नो वाजाय श्रवस इषे च राये धेहि द्युमत इन्द्र विप्रान्।
भरद्वाजे नृवतं इन्द्र सूरीन्दिवि च स्मैधि पार्ये न इन्द्र॥१४॥

14. Do you, resplendent *Indra*, uphold us who are devout, for (the obtaining of) food, of sustenance, of nourishment, of wealth; bestow upon *Bhardvāja* pious posterity, with numerous attendants; be with us, *Indra*, every future day.

For Food, Sustenance, Nourishment, Wealth— *Vājāya, śaravase, iṣe ca rāye;* the three first are synonyms, meaning food.

४५५६. अया वाजं देवहितं सनेम मदेम शतहिमाः सुवीराः॥१५॥

15. May we, by this (praise), obtain food granted by the deity; may we, blessed with excellent male descendants, be happy for a hundred winters.

[सूक्त-१८]

[**ऋषि**- भरद्वाज बार्हस्पत्य। **देवता**- इन्द्र।
छन्द- त्रिष्टुप्; १५ द्विपदा त्रिष्टुप्।]

४५५७. तमु ष्टुहि यो अभिभूत्योजा वन्वन्नवातः पुरुहूत इन्द्रः।
अषाल्हमुग्रं सहमानमाभिर्गीर्भिर्वर्ध वृषभं चर्षणीनाम्॥१॥

1. Praise him who is *Indra*, the invoker of many, endowed with overpowering vigour, the destroyer (of foes), unharmed by them; exalt with these praises the irresistible, fierce, victorious *Indra*, the showerer (of benefits) upon mankind.

४५५८. स युध्मः सत्वा खजकृत्समद्वा तुविमाक्षो नदनुमाँ ऋजीषी।
बृहद्रेणुश्च्यवनो मानुषीणामेकः कृष्टीनामभवत्सहावा॥२॥

2. He is ever the combatant, the donor, the engaged in battle, the sympathizer (with the sacrificer), the benefactor of many, the

loud-sounding, the partaker of the stale libation, the stirrer up of
dust (in strife), the chief protector of men the descendants of
Manu, the endowed with strength.

४५५९. त्वं ह॒ नु त्यद॑दमायो॒ दस्यूँ॒रेक॑: कृ॒ष्टीर॑वनोरार्या॑य।

अस्ति॒ स्विन्नु वी॒र्यं१॑ तत्त॑ इन्द्र॒ न स्विद॑स्ति॒ तदृ॑तु॒था वि वो॑च:॥३॥

3. You are he who has quickly humbled the *Dasyus*: you are
the chief one who has given posterity to the *Arya*: but, *Indra*, is not
verily your power such? If it be not, then in due season confess.

Not beholding *Indra*, the Scholiast says, the *Ṛṣi* begins to question
his attributes and power; in the succeeding verse he expresses his belief in
their existence.

४५६०. सदि॒द्धि ते॑ तुविजा॒तस्य॑ मन्ये॒ सह॑: सहिष्ठ तु॒रत॑स्तु॒रस्य॑।

उ॒ग्रमु॒ग्रस्य॑ तव॒सस्तवी॒योऽर॑ध्रस्य र॒ध्रतु॑रो बभूव॥४॥

4. Yet, most mighty one, I believe that power is verily always
in you, who are manifest at many rites, and are the enemy of (our)
enemies; (the power) that is fierce in the fierce one, most mighty
in the mighty one, most unassailable in the subduer (of foes).

४५६१. तन्न॑: प्र॒त्नं स॒ख्यम॑स्तु युष्मे॒ इ॒त्था वद॑द्भि॒र्वल॑मङ्गि॒रोभि॑:।

हन्न॑च्युत॒च्युद्द॒स्मेष॑यन्त॒मृणो॑: पु॒रो वि दुरो॑ अस्य॒ विश्वा॑:॥५॥

5. May that our ancient friendship with you ever endure; as
when, along with the *Aṅgirasas*, celebrating your praises, you,
beautiful *Indra*, caster down of the immoveable (rocks), did verily
slay *Bala*, hurling (his darts against you), and force open his cities,
and all his gates.

४५६२. स हि धी॒भिर्ह॒व्यो अस्त्यु॒ग्र ई॒शान॑कृ॒न्मह॑ति वृ॒त्रतू॑र्ये।

स तो॒कसा॑ता॒ तन॑ये॒ स व॒ज्री वि॑त॒न्तसा॒य्यो॑ अभव॒त्समत्सु॑॥६॥

6. Fierce *Indra*, maker of rulers you are he who is to be
invoked with praise in a great conflict; you are he (who is to be
invoked) for sons and grandsons, he, the wielder of the
thunderbolt, who is to be especially glorified in battles.

४५६३. स म॒ज्मना॒ जनि॑म॒ मानु॑षाणाम॒मर्त्ये॑न॒ नाम्ना॒ति प्र स॑र्स्रे।

स द्यु॒म्नेन॒ स शव॑सो॒त रा॒या स वी॒र्ये॑ण॒ नृत॑म॒: समो॑का:॥७॥

7. With immortal, foe-humiliating might he has promoted the
(multiplied) birth of mankind; he, the chief of leaders, dwells in

the same dwelling with fame, with strength, with riches, with heroism.

४५६४. स यो न मुहे न मिथू जनो भूत्सुमन्तुनामा चुमुरिं धुनिं च।
वृणक्पिपुं शम्बरं शुष्णमिन्द्रः पुरां च्यौत्नाय शयथाय नू चित्॥८॥

8. He who is never perplexed, who is no engenderer of that which is in vain, whose name is renowned, who promptly (exerts himself) for the overturning of the cities (of the *Asuras*), and for the destruction (of his foes); you, (*Indra*), have indeed slain *Cumuri, Dhuni, Pipru, Śambara,* and *Śuṣṇa.*

All these have been mentioned before, see vols., I. and II.

४५६५. उदावता त्वक्षसा पन्यसा च वृत्रहत्याय रथमिन्द्र तिष्ठ।
धिष्व वज्रं हस्त आ दक्षिणत्राभि प्र मन्द पुरुदत्र मायाः॥९॥

9. (Endowed) with upward-rising, foe-thinning, and glorified (vigour), ascend your car for the destruction of *Vṛtra*; take the thunderbolt in your right hand, an baffle, giver of wealth, the devices (of the *Asuras*).

४५६६. अग्निर्न शुष्कं वनमिन्द्र हेती रक्षो नि धक्ष्यशनिर्न भीमा।
गम्भीरय ऋष्वया यो रुरोजाध्वानयद्दुरिता दम्भयच्च॥१०॥

10. In like manner as *Agni* consumes the dry forest, so, *Indra*, your weapon (destroys your enemies); as (formidable as you) fearful shaft, consume the *Rākṣasas;* you who have shouted aloud (in the combat) and demolished all evil things.

४५६७. आ सहस्रं पथिभिरिन्द्र राया तुविद्युम्न तुविवाजेभिर्वर्वाक्।
याहि सूनो सहसो यस्य नू चिददेव ईशे पुरुहूत योतोः॥११॥

11. Opulent, *Indra*, Son of strength, the invoker of many, whose union (with energy) the impious is unable to disjoint, come down to us with thousands of riches by very powerful conveyances.

Very Powerful Conveyances— *Pathibhistuvi vājebhiḥ:* Sāyaṇa renders the first by *vāhaiḥ*, vehicles, or sometimes horses, so considered: the epithet he translates *bāhubalaiḥ*, very strong or powerful.

४५६८. प्र तुविद्युम्नस्य स्थविरस्य घृष्वेर्दिवो ररप्शे महिमा पृथिव्याः।
नास्य शत्रुर्न प्रतिमानमस्ति न प्रतिष्ठिः पुरुमायस्य सह्योः॥१२॥

12. The vastness of the affluent, ancient (*Indra*), the demolisher (of foes), exceeds that of the heaven and the earth;

there is no antagonist, no counterpart, no recipient of him abounding in wisdom, victorious (in war).

४५६९. प्र तत्ते अद्या करणं कृतं भूत्कुत्सं यदायुमतिथिग्वमस्मै।
पुरू सहस्रा नि शिशा अभि क्षामुत्तूर्वयाणं धृषता निनेथ॥१३॥

13. That exploit is celebrated in the present day (which you have) achieved for *Kutsa*, for *Āyu*, for *Atithigvave*: to him you have given many thousands (of riches), and you have quickly elevated *Turvayāṇa* over the earth by your power.

Turvayāṇa— The same as *Divodās*, to whom *Indra* gave the spoils of *Śambara*.

४५७०. अनु त्वाहिघ्ने अर्ध देव देवा मदन्विश्वे कवितमं कवीनाम्।
करो यत्र वरिवो बाधिताय दिवे जनाय तन्वे गृणानः॥१४॥

14. Divine *Indra*, all the gods have glorified you, the wisest of the wise, for the destruction of *Ahi*; when propitiated, you have given wealth to the distressed worshipper, and to his posterity.

When Propitiated, you have given Wealth, Etc.— *Yatra varīvo bādhitāya dive janāya tanve gṛṇānaḥ karaḥ* is explained *yasmin kāle piditya stotre janāya, tat-tanayāya ca dhanam stūyamāṇo adadaḥ,* as translated in the text; but Sāyaṇa admits another rendering, which he makes, when being praised, you have given ease to the celestial people through the relief, *tanve, śobhāyai,* caused by the demolition of *Ahi*.

४५७१. अनु द्यावापृथिवी तत्त ओजोऽमर्त्या जिहत इन्द्र देवाः।
कृष्वा कृत्नो अकृतं यत्ते अस्त्युक्थं नवीयो जनयस्व यज्ञैः॥१५॥

15. The heaven and earth, and the immortal gods, acknowledge your might; doer of many deeds, do that which is yet undone by you, give birth to a new hymn at (your) sacrifice.

[सूक्त-१९]

[ऋषि– भरद्वाज बार्हस्पत्य। देवता– इन्द्र। छन्द– त्रिष्टुप्।]

४५७२. महाँ इन्द्रो नृवदा चर्षणिप्रा उत द्विबर्हा अमिनः सहोभिः।
अस्मद्र्यग्वावृधे वीर्यायोरुः पृथुः सुकृतः कर्तृभिर्भूत्॥१॥

1. May the great *Indra*, who is as a monarch the fulfiller (of the desires) of men, come hither; may he who is mighty over the two (realms of space), uninjurable by (hostile) offers, increase (in capacity) for heroism in our presence; may he who is great (in

body), eminent (in qualities), be honoured by the performers (of pious acts).

Yajurveda, 7.39; Mahīdhara's explanation is to the same purport, although he renders some of the epithets rather differently.

४५७३. इन्द्रमेव धिषणा सातये धाद्बृहन्तमृष्वमजरं युवानम्।
अषाळ्हेन शवसा शूशुवांसं सद्यश्चिद्यो ववृधे असामि॥२॥

2. Our praise encourages *Indra* to munificence, the vast, quick-moving, undecaying, ever-youthful *Indra,* mighty with unsurpassable strength, who rapidly grows to greatness.

४५७४. पृथू करस्ना बहुला गर्भस्ती अस्मद्र्यऽक्सं मिमीहि श्रवांसि।
यूथेव पश्वः पशुपा दमूना अस्माँ इन्द्राभ्या ववृत्स्वाजौ॥३॥

3. Extend towards us your long, active, and bountiful hands, (to bring us) food; be about us, lowly-minded *Indra,* in battle, as a herdsman (tends) the herds of cattle.

४५७५. तं व इन्द्रं चतिनमस्य शाकैरिह नूनं वाजयन्तो हुवेम।
यथा चित्पूर्वे जरितारं आसुरनेद्या अनवद्या अरिष्टाः॥४॥

4. Desiring sustenance, we invoke you, the renowned *Indra,* on this occasion, the destroyer (of enemies), together with his powerful allies (the *Maruts*); as his ancient adorers have been, (may we be), exempt from blame, irreproachable, unharmed.

४५७६. धृतव्रतो धनदाः सोमवृद्धः स हि वामस्य वसुनः पुरुक्षुः।
सं जग्मिरे पथ्याऽ३ रायो अस्मिन्त्समुद्रे न सिन्धवो यादमानाः॥५॥

5. In him who is observant of pious rites, who is a giver of wealth, who is exalted by the *Soma* beverage, the (lord) of desirable riches, the distributer of food, (in him) the treasures fit (for his worshippers) congregate like rivers flowing into ocean.

४५७७. शविष्ठं न आ भर शूर शव ओजिष्ठमोजो अभिभूत उग्रम्।
विश्वा द्युम्ना वृष्ण्या मानुषाणामस्मभ्यं दा हरिवो मादयध्यै॥६॥

6. Bestow upon us, hero *Indra,* most vigorous vigour; subduer (of enemies, bestow upon us) most energetic and fierce energy; grant, lord of steeds, all the bright and invigorating (treasures) fit for men, to make us happy.

४५७८. यस्ते मदः पृतनाषाळमृध्र इन्द्र तं न आ भर शूशुवांसम्।
येन तोकस्य तनयस्य सातौ मंसीमहि जिगीवांसस्त्वोताः॥७॥

7. Impart to us, *Indra*, that your invigorating exultation which overcomes enemies, and is irresistible, where by, protected by you, triumphant we may glorify you for the sake of (obtaining) sons and grandsons.

४५७९. आ नो॒ भर॒ वृष॑णं शु॒ष्ममि॑न्द्र धन॒स्पृतं॑ शूशु॒वांसं॑ सु॒दक्ष॑म्।
येन॒ वंसा॑म॒ पृत॑नासु॒ शत्रू॒न्तवोति॑भिरु॒त जामी॒ँरजा॑मीन्॥८॥

8. Bestow upon us, *Indra*, vigorous strength, the realizer of wealth, great and propitious, wherewith, through your protection, we may destroy our enemies in battles, whether they be kinsmen or strangers.

४५८०. आ ते॒ शुष्मो॑ वृष॒भ ए॑तु प॒श्चादोत्त॒रादध॑रादा पु॒रस्ता॑त्।
आ वि॒श्वतो॑ अ॒भि स॒मेत्व॑र्वाङिन्द्र॑ द्यु॒म्नं स्व॑र्व॒द्धेह्य॒स्मे॥९॥

9. May your invigorating strength come from the west, from the north, from the south, from the east; may it come to us from every quarter; grant use riches combined with felicity.

४५८१. नृ॒वत्त॒ इन्द्र॒ नृत॑माभिरू॒ती वं॒सी॑महि॒ वाम॒ श्रोम॑तेभिः।
ईक्षे॒ हि वस्व॑ उ॒भय॑स्य रा॒जन्धा रत्नं॒ महि॑ स्थू॒रं बृ॒हन्त॑म्॥१०॥

10. We enjoy, *Indra*, through your guiding protection, desirable affluence along with descendants and reputation: grant us, sovereign, who rule over (earthly and heavenly) riches, vast, desirable, and infinite treasures.

४५८२. म॒रुत्वं॑तं वृष॒भं वा॑वृधा॒नमक॑वारिं दि॒व्यं शास॒मिन्द्र॑म्।
वि॒श्वासाह॒मव॑से॒ नूत॑नायो॒ग्रं स॒होदा॒मिह तं हु॑वेम॥११॥

11. We invoke on this occasion for his present protection, that *Indra* who is attended by the *Maruts*; who is the showerer (of benefits); augmenting (in prowess); the unreviled of foes, radiant, ruling, all-subduing, fierce, the giver of strength.

४५८३. जनं॑ वज्रिन्महि॒ चिन्म॒न्य॑मानमे॒भ्यो नृभ्यो॑ र॒न्धया॒ येष्व॑स्मि॑।
अधा॒ हि त्वा॑ पृथि॒व्यां शूर॑सा॒तौ हवा॑महे॒ तन॑ये॒ गोष्व॒प्सु॥१२॥

12. Wielder of the thunderbolt, humble that man who looks upon himself as the greatest amongst those men of whom I am; we invoke you now to (descend) upon the earth at the time of battle, and for (the sake of obtaining) sons and grandsons.

४५८४. वयं तं एभि: पुरुहूत सख्यै: शत्रों: शत्रोरुत्तर इत्स्याम।

घ्नन्तौ वृत्राण्युभयानि शूर राया मंदेम बृहता त्वोता:॥१३॥

13. Invoked of many, may we, through these your friendly
(praises), ever be superior to successive foes, destroying, oh. hero,
both (classes of) enemies, (kindred or unallied); and may we,
protected by you, be happy with abundant riches.

[सूक्त-२०]

[ऋषि– भरद्वाज बार्हस्पत्य। देवता– इन्द्र। छन्द– त्रिष्टुप्; ७ विराट्।]

४५८५. द्यौर्न य इन्द्राभि भूमार्यस्तस्थौ रयि: शर्वसा पृत्सु जनान्।

तं न: सहस्रभरमुर्वरासां दद्धि सूनो सहसो वृत्रतुर्म्॥१॥

1. *Indra*, Son of strength, grant us (a son), the possessor of
thousands, the owner of cultivated lands, the subduer of foes, the
riches that may overcome men in battles by strength, as the radiant
(sun) overspreads the earth by his rays.

Grant us a Son— The text has no substantive, but the epithets
evidently allude to some one individual, or, as Sāyaṇa understands them,
to a son, *putram*, who is metaphorically the riches of a family, and its
defence against enemies, *putrarūpaṁ dhanam, rayir yo śavasā śavasā
śatrūn ākramet*.

४५८६. दिवो न तुभ्यमन्विन्द्र संत्रासुर्यं देवेभिर्धायि विश्वम्।

अहिं यद्वृत्रमपो वव्रिवांसं हन्नृजीषिन्विष्णुना सचान:॥२॥

2. To you, *Indra*, as to the sun, all strength has verily been
given by the gods; so that, drinker of the stale *Soma*, associated
with *Viṣṇu*, your mightest slay the hostile *Ahi* obstructing the
waters.

Given by the Gods— *Devebhiḥ*, Sāyaṇa renders by *stotṛbhiḥ*
observing, *stotraiḥ stuyamānā devatā balavatī*, a deity becomes strong,
being praised with praises.

The Hostile *Ahi*— *Ahim vṛtram* may be also rendered the destroyer,
hantāram, Vṛtra.

४५८७. तूर्वन्नोजीयान्तवसस्तवीयान्कृतब्रह्मेन्द्रो वृद्धमंह:।

राजाभवन्मधुन: सोम्यस्य विश्वासां यत्पुरां दर्तुमावत्॥३॥

3. When *Indra*, the destroyer, the most mighty, the strongest of
the strong, the giver of food, the possessor of vast splendour,
received (the thunderbolt), the shatterer of all the cities (of the
Asuras), he became the lord of the sweet *Soma* beverage.

४५८८. शतैरपद्रन्पणयं इन्द्रात्र दशोणये कवये३र्कसातौ।
वधै: शुष्णस्याशुष्वष्य माया: पित्वो नारिरिचीत्किं चन प्र।।४।।

4. The *Paṇis, Indra*, fled, with hundreds (of *Asuras*), from the
sage, your worshipper (and ally) in battle; neither did he, (*Indra*),
suffer the deceptions of the powerful *Śuṣṇa* to prevail over his
weapons, nor did he (leave him) any of his sustenance.

From the Sage, your Worshipper— *Daśoṇaye kavaye;* the
Scholiast asserts that the dative is put for the ablative, and that the terms
are equivalent to *bahu kaviṣkāt medhāvinaḥ,* from the wise man offering
many oblations, that is *tvatsahāyakutsāt,* from *kutsa,* your ally; in verse 8
of this *Sūkta, Daśoṇi* occurs, as elsewhere, as the name of an *Asura*.

४५८९. महो दुहो अप विश्वायुं धायि वज्रस्य यत्पतने पादि शुष्ण:।
उरु ष सरथं सारथये करिन्द्र: कुत्साय सूर्यस्य सातौ।।५।।

5. When *Śuṣṇa* passed away upon the falling of the
thunderbolt, then the universal strength of the great oppressor was
annihilated; and *Indra* enlarged their common car for (the use of)
his charioteer *Kutsa*, for (the sake of) the worship of the sun.

For the sake of the worship of the Sun— *sūryasya sātau, bhāhane
nimittabhūte* is the explanation of *Sāyaṇa,* and *samānuratham, vistīrṇam
akarot* is his interpretation of the *uru ṣa saratham kar* of the text; *Kutsa* is
the reputed author of the hymns to *Sūrya* and *Uṣas* see vol. I. *Sūkta* 113
and 115.

४५९०. प्र श्येनो न मंदिरमंशुमंस्मै शिरो दासस्य नमुचेर्मथायन्।
प्रावन्नमीं साप्यं ससन्तं पृणग्राया समिषा सं स्वस्ति।।६।।

6. And the hawk bore to *Indra* the exhilarating *Soma*, when,
bruising the head of the oppressor Namuci, and protecting the
slumbering *Nami*, the son of *Sapya*, he provided, for the well-
being (of the sage), riches and food.

४५९१. वि पिप्रोरहिंमायस्य दृूल्हा: पुरो वज्रिञ्छर्वसा न दर्द:।
सुदामन्तद्रेकणों अप्रमृष्यमृजिश्वने दात्रं दाशुषे दा:।।७।।

7. You have scattered by force, wielder of the thunderbolt, the
strong cities of the deadly-deluding *Pipru*; you have given,
bountiful *Indra*, uninjurable wealth to *rijiṣvat*, the donor of
sacrificial gifts.

Pipru— See vol. I. verse 604.

४५९२. स वैतसुं दशमायं दशोणिं तूतुजिमिन्द्र: स्वभिष्टिसुम्न:।
आ तुग्रं शश्वदिभं द्योतनाय मातुर्न सीमुप सृजा इयध्यै।।८।।

8. *Indra*, the granter of wished-for felicity, compelled the many-fraudulent *Etaśa* and *Dasoṇi*, *Tūtuji*, *Tugra*, and *Ibha*, always to come submissively to (the *Rājā*) *Dyotana*, as a son (comes before a mother).

४५९३. स इं स्पृधो वनते अप्रतीतो बिभ्रद्वज्रं वृत्रहणं गभस्तौ।
तिष्ठद्धरी अध्यस्तेव गर्तें वचोयुजा वहत इन्द्रमृष्वम्॥९॥

9. Bearing in his hand the foe-destroying thunderbolt, *Indra*, unresisted, demolishing those his adversaries; he mounts his two-horse (car), as a warrior (ascends) his chariot; harnessed at a word, his steeds, convey the mighty *Indra*.

४५९४. सनेम तेऽवसा नव्य इन्द्र प्र पूर्वः स्तवन्त एना यज्ञैः।
सप्त यत्पुरः शर्म शारदीर्दर्द्धन्दासीः पुरुकुत्साय शिक्षन्॥१०॥

10. (Favoured) by your protection, *Indra*, we solicit new (wealth); by this adoration men glorify you at sacrifices, for that you have shattered with your bolt the seven cities of *Śarat*, killing the opponents (of sacred rites), and giving (their spoils) to *Purukutsa*.

Men— *Puravaḥ* is the term of the text rendered *manuṣyaḥ* in the comment.

Śarat— *śarat* is said to be the name of an *Asura*.

४५९५. त्वं वृध इन्द्र पूर्व्यो भूर्वरिवस्यन्नुशने काव्याय।
परा नववास्त्वमनुदेयं महे पित्रे ददाथ स्वं नपातम्॥११॥

11. Desirous of opulence, you, *Indra*, have been an ancient benefactor of *Uśanas*, the son of *Kavi*; having slain *Navavāstva*, you have given back his own grandson, who was (fit) to be restored to the grandfather.

४५९६. त्वं धुनिरिन्द्र धुनिमतीर्ऋणोरपः सीरा न स्रवन्तीः।
प्र यत्समुद्रमति शूर पर्षि पारया तुर्वशं यदुं स्वस्ति॥१२॥

12. You, *Indra*, who make (your enemies) tremble, have caused the waters, detained by *Dhuni*, to flow like rushing rivers; so, hero, when, having crossed the ocean, you have reached the shore, you have brought over in safety *Turvaśa* and *Yadu*.

Samudram atipraparṣi, samudram atikramya pratirṇo, bhavasi, when you are crossed, having traversed the ocean, you have brought across *Turvaśa* and *Yadu*, both standing on the further shore, *samudrapāre tiṣṭhantau apārayaḥ*.

४५९७. तवं ह त्यदिन्द्र विश्वमाजौ सस्तो धुनीचुमुरी या ह सिष्वप् ।
दीदयदित्तुभ्यं सोमेभि: सुन्वन्दभीतिरिधमभृति: पक्थ्यइ कैं: ॥१३॥

13. All this, *Indra*, has been your work in war; you have put to sleep, (in death), the slumbering *Dhuni* and *Cumuri*; and thereupon *Dabhīti*, pouring the libation, preparing the oblation, and supplying the fuel, has glorified you with *Soma* offerings.

[सूक्त-२१]

[**ऋषि**– भरद्वाज बार्हस्पत्य। **देवता**– इन्द्र; ९, ११ विश्वेदेवा।
छन्द– त्रिष्टुप्।]

४५९८. इमा उ त्वा पुरुतमस्य कारोर्हव्वं वीर हव्या हवन्ते ।
धियो रथेष्ठामजरं नवीयो रयिर्विभूतिरीयते वचस्या ॥१॥

1. These earnest adorations of the much-desiring worshipper glorify you, hero, *Indra*, who are adorable; mounted on you car, undecaying, ever new, and to whom the wealth (of sacrifice), the most excellent opulence, proceeds.

४५९९. तमु स्तुष इन्द्रं यो विदानो गिर्वाहसं गीर्भिर्यज्ञवृद्धम् ।
यस्म दिवमति महा पृथिव्या: पुरुमायस्य रिरिचे महित्वम् ॥२॥

2. I glorify that *Indra* who is propitiated by praises, exalted by sacrifices, who knows all things; the magnitude of whom, the possessor of various wisdom, exceeds in vastness (that of) heaven and earth.

४६००. स इत्तमोऽवयुनं ततन्वत्सूर्येण वयुनवच्चकार ।
कदा ते मर्ता अमृतस्य धामेर्यक्षन्तो न मिनन्ति स्वधाव: ॥३॥

3. He who made the indistinct, wide-spreading darkness distinct with the sun; whenever, possessor of strength, mortals are seeking to adore the dwelling of you who are immortal, they harm not (any living being).

They Harm not (any living being)— The text has only *na minanti, na hiṁsanti*; the Scholiast supplies the object, *kim api praṇijātam*.

४६०१. यस्ता चकार स कुहं स्विदिन्द्र: कमा जनं चरति कासु विक्षु ।
कस्तै यज्ञो मनसे शं वराय को अर्क इन्द्र कतम: स होता ॥४॥

4. What is he, the *Indra* who has done these deeds? What region does he frequent? Among what people (does he abide)? What worship, *Indra*, gives satisfaction to your mind? What praise

is able to gratify you? which of your invokers (is most acceptable to you)?

४६०२. इदा हि ते वेविषतः पुराजा: प्रत्ना आसुः पुरुकृत्सखायः।
ये मध्यमास उत नूतनास उतावमस्य पुरुहूत बोधि ॥५॥

5. Doer of many deeds, these adders, born in former times, engaged in sacred rites, have been, as they are now, your friends; so have those of mediaeval and those of recent (date); therefore, invoked of many, take notice of your (present) humble (adorer).

४६०३. तं पृच्छन्तोऽवरासः पराणि प्रत्ना त इन्द्र श्रुत्यानु येमुः।
अर्चामसि वीर ब्रह्मवाहो यादेव विद्म तात्वां महान्तम् ॥६॥

6. Humble (worshippers), adoring him, commemorate, *Indra*, your excellent, ancient, and glorious (deeds); so, hero, who are attracted by prayer, we praise you who are mighty, for those great actions with which we are acquainted.

Who are Attracted by Prayer— *Brahmavāaḥ* is explained *mantrairvahanīyaḥ,* to *ve* borne or conveyed by prayers.

४६०४. अभि त्वा पाजो रक्षसो वि तस्थे महि जज्ञानमभि तत्सु तिष्ठ।
तव प्रत्नेन युज्येन सख्या वज्रेण धृष्णो अप ता नुदस्व ॥७॥

7. The strength of the *Rākṣasas* is concentrated against you; bear up well against that mighty manifested (effort); scatter them, valiant (*Indra*), with your old associate, your friend, the thunderbolt.

४६०५. स तु श्रुधीन्द्र नूतनस्य ब्रह्मण्यतो वीर कारुधायः।
त्वं ह्या३ पिः प्रदिवि पितृणां शश्वद्बभूथ सुहव एष्टौ ॥८॥

8. Supporter of (your) worshippers, hero, *Indra*, listen (to the praises) of your present adorer, for you have always attended to invocations at sacrifices in ancient times, as the kinsman of our forefather.

As the Kinsman of our Forefathers— *Pitṛṇām āpiḥ, bandhuḥ*; according to Sāyaṇa the *Aṅgirasas* are intended.

४६०६. प्रोतये वरुणं मित्रमिन्द्रं मरुतः कृष्वावसे नो अद्य।
प्र पूषणं विष्णुमग्निं पुरन्धिं सवितारमोषधी: पर्वतांश्च ॥९॥

9. Propitiate today, for our protection and preservation, *Varuṇa, Mitra, Indra,* and the *Maruts, Pūṣan, Viṣṇu, Agni,* of many rites, *Savitā,* the herbs, the mountains.

४६०७. इम॒ उ त्वा॑ पुरुशाक॒ प्रय॒ज्यो᳚ जरि॒तारो॑ अ॒भ्य॑र्चन्त्य॒र्कैः॑ ।
श्रु॒धी हव॒मा हु॒वतो॒ हुवा॑नो॒ न त्वावाँ॒ अ॒न्यो अ॑मृत॒ त्वद॑स्ति ॥१०॥

10. *Indra*, of great power, and to be devoutly worshipped, these your adorers glorify you with hymns; do you, who are invoked, hear the invocation of (him) invoking you, for there is no other divinity than you, immortal (*Indra*), such as you are.

४६०८. नू म॒ आ वाच॒मुप॑ याहि वि॒द्वान् विश्वे॑भिः सूनो सह॑सो य॒जत्रैः॑ ।
ये अ॑ग्निजि॒ह्वा ऋ॑तसा॒प॒ आसु॒र्ये मनुं॑ च॒क्रुरुप॑रं॒ दसा॑य ॥११॥

11. Come quickly, Son of strength, you who know (all things), upon my prayer; together with all the adorable (divinities); they who, with the tongue of *Agni*, are partakers of the sacrifice, who rendered *Manu* (victorious) over his adversaries.

Who rendered *Manu* Victorious, etc.— *Ye Manum cakrur uparam dasāya śatrūṇām,* or *dasyūnām uparibhavam,* who made *Manu* the *Rājarṣi, manum rājarṣim,* over, or the overcomer of enemies, or the *Dasyus.*

४६०९. स नो॑ बोधि पुर॒ऐता॑ सु॒गेषू॒त दु॒र्गेषु॑ प॒थिकृ॒द्विदा॑नः । ये अश्र॑मा॒   स
उ॒रवो॒ वहि॑ष्ठास्ते॒भिर्न॑ इन्द्रा॒भि व॑क्षि॒ वाज॑म् ॥१२॥

12. Constructor of paths, who are cognizant (of all things), be our preceder, whether in easy or difficult (ways); bring to us food, *Indra*, with those your (steeds), who are unwearied, large, and bearers of great burthens.

[सूक्त-२२]

[ऋषि- भरद्वाज बार्हस्पत्य। देवता- इन्द्र। छन्द- त्रिष्टुप्।]

४६१०. य ए॒क इद्धव्य॑श्च॒र्षणी॑नामि॒न्द्रं तं गी॒र्भिर॒भ्य॑र्च आ॒भिः । यः पत्य॑ते वृष॒भो वृष्ण्या॑वान्त्स॒त्यः सत्वा॑ पुरु॒मा॒यः सह॑स्वान् ॥१॥

1. I glorify with these praises, *Indra*, who alone is to be invoked by man; who comes (to his worshippers) the showerer (of benefits), the vigorous, the observer of truth, the subduer of foes, the possessor of manifold knowledge, the mighty.

४६११. तमु॑ नः॒ पूर्वे॑ पि॒तरो॒ नव॑ग्वाः स॒प्त विप्रा॑सो अ॒भि वा॑जय॒न्तः ।
न॒क्ष॒द्दा॒भं ततु॑रिं प॒र्वते॑ष्ठामद्रो॑घवाचं म॒तिभिः॒ शवि॑ष्ठम् ॥२॥

2. To him the seven sages, our ancient progenitors, performing the nine days' rite, were offerers of (sacrificial) food, celebrating

with hymns the very strong (*Indra*), the humiliator of foes, the traverser of the heavens, the dweller in the clouds, whose commands are not to be disobeyed.

४६१२. तमीमहे इन्द्रमस्य रायः पुरुवीरस्य नृवतः पुरुक्षोः।
यो अस्कृधोयुरजरः स्वर्वान्तमा भर हरिवो मादयध्यै॥३॥

3. We solicit that *Indra* for wealth, comprehending numerous descendants, followers, and much cattle, and which is undisturbed, imperishable, and the source of felicity; such riches, lord of steeds, bestow upon us to make us happy.

४६१३. तन्नो वि वोचो यदि ते पुरा चिज्जरितार आनशुः सुम्नमिन्द्र।
कस्ते भागः किं वयो दुध्र खिद्वः पुरुहूत पुरूवसोऽसुरघ्नः॥४॥

4. If, *Indra*, your worshippers have formerly obtained felicity, confer that also upon us; irresistible *Indra*, subduer of foes, invoked of many, abounding in wealth, what is the portion, what the offering (due) to you who are the slayer of the *Asuras*?

४६१४. तं पृच्छन्ती वज्रहस्तं रथेष्ठामिन्द्रं वेपी वक्वरी यस्य नू गीः।
तुविग्राभं तुविकूर्मिं रभोदां गातुमिषे नक्षते तुम्रमच्छ॥५॥

5. He whose ceremonial and eulogistic hymn is commemorating *Indra*, the holder of the thunderbolt, seated in his car, the accepter of many, the doer of many great deeds, the bestower of strength, proceeds promptly to acquire happiness, and encounters (with confidence) the malevolent.

४६१५. अया ह त्वं माययौ वावृधानं मनोजुवा स्वतवः पर्वतेन।
अच्युता चिद्वीळिता स्वोजो रुजो वि दृळ्हा धृषता विरप्शिन्॥६॥

6. Self-invigorated *Indra*, you have crushed by your knotted (thunderbolt), quick a thought, that *Vṛtra*, growing in strength by this cunning; very radiant and mighty (*Indra*), you have demolished by (your) irresistible (shaft) the unyielding, compact, and strong (cities of the *Asuras*).

Growing in strength by this Cunning— *Ayā māyayā vāvṛdhānam*, by this guile or deception, but what that was is not specified.

४६१६. तं वो धिया नव्यस्या शविष्ठं प्रत्नं प्रत्नवत्परितंसयध्यै।
स नो वक्षदनिमानः सुवह्वेन्द्रो विश्वान्यति दुर्गहाणि॥७॥

7. (I have undertaken) to spread around with a new hymn, as it was done of old, (the glory of) you, the ancient and most mighty

(Indra); may that *Indra*, who is illimitable, and is a sure conveyance, bear us over all difficulties.

४६१७. आ जनाय दुर्हृणे पार्थिवानि दिव्यानि दीपयोऽन्तरिक्षा।

तपा वृषन्विश्वतः शोचिषा तान्ब्रह्मद्विषे शोचय क्षामपश्च ॥८॥

8. Make hot the regions of earth, of heaven, of mid air, for the oppressive race (of the *Rākṣasas*); showerer (of benefits), consume them everywhere with your radiance, make the heaven and the firmament (too) hot for the impious.

The Impious— *Brahmadviṣe*; the Scholiast explains *brāhmaṇa-dveṣṭre*, the hater of *Brāhmaṇs*, but it may also import the enemy or hater of the Veda, or of prayer.

४६१८. भुवो जनस्य दिव्यस्य राजा पार्थिवस्य जगतस्त्वेषसन्दृक्।

धिष्व वज्रं दक्षिण इन्द्र हस्ते विश्वा अजुर्य दयसे वि मायाः ॥९॥

9. Bright-flaming *Indra*, you are the king of the people of heaven, and of the moving races of earth; grasp in your right hand the thunderbolt, wherewith, *Indra*, who are beyond all praise, you baffles all the devices (of the *Asuras*).

४६१९. आ संयतमिन्द्र णः स्वस्ति शत्रुतूर्याय बृहतीममृध्राम्।

यया दासान्यार्याणि वृत्रा करो वज्रिन्त्सुतुका नाहुषाणि ॥१०॥

10. Bring to us, *Indra*, concentrated, vast, and unassailable prosperity beyond the reach of enemies, and by which, wielder of the thunderbolt, you have rendered human enemies, whether *Dāsas* or *Āryas*, easy to be overcome.

४६२०. स नो नियुद्भिः पुरुहूत वेधो विश्ववाराभिरा गहि प्रयज्यो।

न या अदेवो वरते न देव आभिर्याहि तूयमा मंद्रयद्रिक् ॥११॥

11. Invoked of many, creator, object of sacrifices, come to us with your all-admired steeds, whom neither *Asura* nor deity arrests; come with them quickly to our presence.

[सूक्त-२३]

[ऋषि- भरद्वाज बार्हस्पत्य। देवता- इन्द्र। छन्द- त्रिष्टुप्।]

४६२१. सुत इत्त्वं निमिश्ल इन्द्र सोमे स्तोमे ब्रह्माणि शस्यमान उक्थे।

यद्वा युक्ताभ्यां मघवन्हरिभ्यां बिभ्रद्वज्रं बाह्वोरिन्द्र यासि ॥१॥

1. When the *Soma* juice, *Indra*, is being effused, the sacred hymn chaunted, the prayer recited, be you prepared (to harness your horses), or, *Maghavan*, with your horses ready harnessed, come (hither), bearing the thunderbolt in your hand.

४६२२. यद्वा॒ दिवि॒ पार्ये॒ सुष्वि॑मिन्द्र वृ॒त्रह॒त्येऽव॑सि शूर॒सातौ॑।

यद्वा॒ दक्ष॑स्य॒ बिभ्युषो॒ अबि॑भ्यद॒रंध्यः॒ शर्ध॑त॒ इन्द्र॒ दस्यू॑न्॥२॥

2. Or as, although engaged in heaven in the hero-animating conflict with foes, you protect the offerer of the libation, and humblest, undaunted *Indra*, the *Dasyus*, the disturbers of the pious and terrified worshipper, (so do you come when the *Soma* is effused).

(So do you come when the *Soma* is Effused)— There is no verb in the text, but the commentator considers that 'come' is brought on from the preceding stanza, and adds, when the *Soma* is poured forth.

४६२३. पाता॑ सु॒तमिन्द्रो॒ अस्तु॒ सोमं॒ प्रणे॑नीरु॒ग्रो ज॑रि॒तारं॑मू॒ती।

कर्ता॑ वी॒राय॒ सुष्व॑य उ लो॒कं दा॒ता वसु॒ स्तुव॑ते की॒रये॑ चि॒त्॥३॥

3. May *Indra* be the drinker of the effused *Soma*, he who is the fierce conductor of the worshipper to security; may he be the donor of the world to the presenter of the libation, the giver of wealth to the man who adores him.

४६२४. गन्ते॑या॒न्ति सव॑ना॒ हरि॑भ्यां ब॒भ्रिर्व॒ज्रं प॑पि॒ः सोमं॑ द॒दिर्गाः॑।

कर्ता॑ वी॒रं नर्यं॒ सर्व॑वीरं॒ श्रोता॒ हवं॑ गृ॒णतः॒ स्तोम॑वाहाः॑॥४॥

4. May *Indra*, with his steeds, come to as many (daily) rites (as may be celebrated), bearing the thunderbolt, drinking the *Soma*, bestowing cattle, granting manly and multiplied posterity, hearing the invocation of his adorer, and being the accenter of (our) praises.

४६२५. अस्मै॑ व॒यं यद्वा॒वान॒ तद्वि॑विष्म॒ इन्द्रा॑य॒ यो नः॑ प्र॒दिवो॒ अपस्कः॑।

सु॒ते सोमे॑ स्तुमसि॒ शंस॒दुक्थे॒न्द्रा॑य॒ ब्रह्म॒ वर्ध॑नं यथास॑त्॥५॥

5. To that *Indra*, who of old has rendered us good offices, we address (the praise) that he is pleased by; we celebrate him when the *Soma* is effused, repeating the prayer that the (sacrificial) food (offered) to *Indra* may be for his augmentation.

४६२६. ब्रह्मा॑णि॒ हि च॒क्रुषे॒ वर्ध॑नानि॒ ताव॑त्त इन्द्र म॒तिभि॑र्विविष्मः॑।

सु॒ते सोमे॑ सुतपाः॒ शन्त॑मानि॒ रान्ध्यां॑ क्रियास्म व॒र्क्षणा॑नि य॒ज्ञैः॑॥६॥

6. Since, *Indra*, you have made the (sacred) prayers (the means of) your augmentation, we address such to you, along with our praises; may we, drinker of the effused libation, offer gratifying and acceptable eulogies with (our) sacrifices.

४६२७. स नो॑ बोधि पुरोळाशं॒ रराण॒: पिबा॒ तु सोमं॑ गो॒र्ऋजी॒कमिन्द्र॑।
एदं ब॒र्हिर्यज॑मानस्य सीदो॒रुं कृ॑धि त्वा॒यत॒ उ लोक॑म्॥७॥

7. Accept, *Indra*, who are condescending, our cakes and butter; drink the *Soma* mixed with curds; sit down upon this sacred grass (strewn by) the worshipper; grant ample possessions to him who depends upon you.

४६२८. स म॑न्दस्वा॒ ह्यनु॒ जोष॑मुग्र॒ प्र त्वा॑ य॒ज्ञास॑ इ॒मे अ॑श्नुवन्तु।
प्रेमे हवा॑स: पुरुहू॒तम॒स्मे आ त्वे॒यं धीर्व॑स इन्द्र य॒म्या:॥८॥

8. Rejoice, fierce *Indra*, according to your pleasure; let these libations reach you; invoked of many, may these our invocations ascend to you; may this praise influence you for our protection.

४६२९. तं वः॒ सखा॑य॒: सं य॒था सु॒तेषु॑ सोमे॑भिरीं पृ॒णता॑ भो॒जमिन्द्र॑म्।
कु॒वित्त॒स्मा असति॒ नो॒ भरा॑य॒ न सु॒ष्विमिन्द्रो॒ऽव॑से मृ॒धाति॑॥९॥

9. Friends, when the libations are effused, do you satisfy that liberal *Indra* with the *Soma* juices; let there be plenty for him, that (he may provide) for our nourishment; *Indra* never neglects the care of him who presents copious libations.

४६३०. ए॒वेदिन्द्र॑: सु॒ते अ॑स्तावि॒ सोमे॑ भर॒द्वाजे॑षु क्षय॒दिन्म॒घोन॑:।
अस॒द्यथा॑ ज॒रित्र॑ उ॒त सू॒रिरिन्द्रो॑ रा॒यो वि॒श्ववा॑रस्य॒ दाता॑॥१०॥

·10. Thus has *Indra*, the lord of the opulent, been glorified by the *Bhāradvājas*, upon the libation being effused, that he may be the director of his eulogist (to virtue), that *Indra* may be the giver of all desirable riches.

ANUVAKA III

[सूक्त-२४]

[ऋषि- भरद्वाज बार्हस्पत्य। **देवता**- इन्द्र। **छन्द**- त्रिष्टुप्।]

४६३१. वृषा॒ मद॒ इन्द्रे॒ श्लोक॑ उ॒क्था सचा॒ सोमे॑षु सुत॒पा ऋ॑जीषी।
अर्च॒त्र्यो॒ मघ॑वा नृभ्य॑ उ॒क्थैर्द्यु॒क्षो राजा॑ गि॒रामक्षि॑तोति:॥१॥

1. At the rites at which the *Soma* (is offered) the exhilaration (produced) in *Indra* is a shower (of benefits to the offerer); so is the chaunted hymn with the (recited) prayer; therefore the drinker of the *Soma*, the partaker of the stale *Soma*, *Maghavan*, is to be propitiated by men with praises; dweller in heaven, he is the lord of sacred songs, unwearied in the protection (of his votaries).

४६३२. ततुरिर्वीरो नर्यो विचेताः श्रोता हवं गृणत उव्यूतिः।

वसुः शंसो नरां कारुधाया वाजी स्तुतो विदथे दाति वाजम्॥२॥

2. The surpasser (of foes), a hero, the friend of man, the discriminator, the hearer of the invocation, the great protector of his adorers, the giver of dwellings, the ruler of men, the cherisher of his worshippers, the bestower of food, grants us, when glorified at the sacrifice, (abundant) sustenance.

४६३३. अक्षो न चक्र्योः शूर बृहन्न ते महा रिरिचे रोदस्योः।

वृक्षस्य नु ते पुरुहूत वया व्यूे तयो रुरुहुरिन्द्र पूर्वीः॥३॥

3. Mighty hero, by your magnitude, (the extent) of heaven and earth is exceeded, as the axle by the (circumference of the) wheels; invoked of many, your numerous benefits, *Indra*, spread our like the branches of a tree.

४६३४. शचीवतस्ते पुरुशाक शाका गवामिव स्रुतयः सञ्चरणीः।

वत्सानां न तन्तयस्त इन्द्र दामन्वन्तो अदामानः सुदामन्॥४॥

4. Accomplisher of many acts, the energies of you who are (ever) active (congregate from all directions), like the converging tracks of cattle; they are the bonds (of foes), themselves unfettered, munificent *Indra*, like the tethers of (many) calves.

The Energies— *Śākāḥ śaktayaḥ*, abilities, energies; the following text has no verb; the Scholiast supplies *sarvataḥ saṁcarantī*, come together from all sides, and he explains the simile *gavām iva srutayaḥ sañcaraṇīḥ* by *dhenūnām mārgāḥ yathā sarvatra sañcāriṇo bhavanti*, as the paths of milch kine are everywhere going together.

Like the Tethers of Many Calves— *Vatsānām na tantayaḥ*, like long ropes used to tie a number of calves together, is Sāyaṇa's translation.

४६३५. अन्यदद्य कर्वरमन्यदु श्वोऽसच्च सन्मुहुराचक्रिरिन्द्रः।

मित्रो नो अत्र वरुणश्च पूषार्यो वशस्य पर्येतास्ति॥५॥

5. *Indra* achieves one act toady, another tomorrow, evil and good repeatedly; may he, and *Mitra*, *Varuṇa*, *Pūṣan*, *Arya*, be on this occasion promoters of the desired result.

४६३६. वि त्वदापो न पर्वतस्य पृष्ठादुकथेभिरिन्द्रानयन्त यज्ञै:।
तं त्वाभि: सुष्टुतिभिर्वाजयन्त आजिं न जग्मुर्गिर्वाहो अश्वा:॥६॥

6. By praises and by sacrifices, *Indra*, (men) bring down (what they desire) from you, as the waters (descend) from the top of the mountain; desirous of food, they approach you, who are accessible by praise, with these their eulogies, as (eagerly as) coursers rush to battle.

The verse occurs in the *Sāmaveda*, 68, but with some variety of reading, and is there addressed to *Agni*.

४६३७. न यं जरन्ति शरदो न मासा न द्याव इन्द्रमवकर्शयन्ति।
वृद्धस्य चिद्वर्धतामस्य तनू: स्तोमेभिरुक्थैश्च शस्यमाना॥७॥

7. May the person of that vast *Indra*, celebrated by praises and prayers, ever increase; *Indra*, whom neither years nor months make old, nor days enfeeble.

४६३८. न वीळवे नमते न स्थिराय न शर्धते दस्युजूताय स्तवान्।
अज्ञा इन्द्रस्य गिरयश्चिदृष्वा गम्भीरे चिद्भवति गाधमस्मै॥८॥

8. Glorified by us, he bows not down to the robust, nor to the resolute, nor to the persevering (worshipper) who is instigated by the (irreligious) *Dasyus*; the lofty mountains are easy of access to *Indra*; to him there is a bottom in the (lowest) deep.

४६३९. गम्भीरेण न उरुणामत्रिन्प्रेषो यन्धि सुतपावन्वाजान्।
स्था ऊ षु ऊर्ध्व ऊती अरिषण्यन्नक्तोर्व्युष्टौ परितक्म्यायाम्॥९॥

9. Powerful *Indra*, drinker of the *Soma* juice, (actuated) by a profound and comprehensive (purpose), grant us food and strength: be ever diligent, benevolent *Indra*, for our protection by day and by night.

४६४०. सचस्व नायमवसे अभीके इतो वा तमिन्द्र पाहि रिष:।
अमा चैनमरण्ये पाहि रिषो मदेम शतहिमा: सुवीरा:॥१०॥

10. Accompany, *Indra*, the leader in battle for his protection; defend him against a near (or distant) foe; protect him from an enemy, whether in (his) house or in a forest, and may we, blessed with excellent male descendants, be happy for a hundred winters.

[सूक्त-२५]

[ऋषि– भरद्वाज बार्हस्पत्य। **देवता**– इन्द्र। **छन्द**– त्रिष्टुप्।]

४६४१. या त॑ ऊति॒रव॑मा या प॒रमा या म॒ध्यमेन्द्र॑ शुष्मिन्नस्ति॑।

ताभिरू॒ षु वृ॑त्रह॒त्येऽव॑वीर॒न् एभि॑श्च॒ वाजै॒र्महा॒न्त उ॑ग्र॥१॥

1. Powerful *Indra*, with these (your protections), whether the
protection be little, great, or middling, defend us for the
destruction of our foes: supply us, fierce *Indra*, who are mighty,
with those viands (that are needed).

४६४२. आभि॑: स्पृधो॑ मिथ॒तीरर्षि॑षण्य॒न्नमि॑त्रस्य॒ व्यथ॑या॒ मन्युमि॑न्द्र।

आभि॑र्विश्वा॑ अभि॒युजो॒ विषू॑ची॒रार्या॑य॒ विशो॑ऽव तारी॒र्दास॑ी:॥२॥

2. (Induced) by these (praises), protecting our assailing host,
baffle, *Indra*, the wrath of the enemy: (induced) by them,
overthrow, on the part of the *Ārya*, all the servile races everywhere
abiding.

४६४३. इन्द्रे॑ जा॒मय॑ उ॒त येऽजा॑मयो॒ऽर्वा॑चीनासो॒ वनु॑षो युयुज्रे।

त्वमे॑षां॒ विथु॑रा॒ शवां॑सि ज॒हि वृष्ण्या॑नि कृणु॒ही प॒राच॑:॥३॥

3. Annihilate, *Indra*, the strength of those who, whether
kinsmen or unrelated, present themselves before us, exerting
themselves as adversaries: enfeeble their prowess, put them to
flight.

४६४४. शूरो॑ वा॒ शूरं॑ वन॒ते शरी॑रैस्त॒नूरुचा॒ तरु॑षि॒ यत्कृ॒ण्वैते॑।

तोके॑ वा॒ गोषु॒ तन॑ये॒ यद॒प्सु वि क्र॒न्दसी॑ उ॒र्वरा॑सु॒ ब्रवै॑ते॥४॥

4. The hero, (favoured by you), assuredly slays the (hostile)
hero by his bodily prowess, when, both excelling in personal
strength, they strive together in conflict, or when, clamorous, they
dispute for (the sake of) sons, of grandson, of cattle, of water, of
land.

४६४५. नहि त्वा॑ शूरो॒ न तु॒रो न धृष्णु॒र्न त्वा॑ यो॒धो म॒न्यमा॑नो युयोध।

इन्द्र॒ नकि॑ष्ट्वा॒ प्रत्य॑स्त्येषां॒ विश्वा॑ जा॒तान्य॒भ्यसि॒ तानि॑॥५॥

5. But you (no one) resists, neither the hero, nor the fleet
runner, nor the resolute, nor the combatant confiding (in his
valour); neither of these, *Indra*, is a match for you: you are
superior to all these persons.

४६४६. स पंत्यत उभयोंर्नृम्ण्ममयोर्यदीं वेधसः समिथे हवन्ते।

वृत्रे वां महो नृवति क्षयें वा व्यचंस्वन्ता यदिं वितन्तसैतैं।।६।।

6. Of both these (disputants), that one acquires wealth whose priests invoke (*Indra*) at the sacrifice, whether the content emulous for (the overthrow of) a powerful enemy, or for a dwelling peopled with dependants.

४६४७. अर्धं स्मा ते चर्षणयो यदेजानिन्द्रं त्रातोत भंवा वरूता।

अस्माकांसो ये नृतंमासो अर्यं इन्द्र सूर्यों दधिरे पुरो नंः।।७।।

7. Therefore, *Indra*, when your people tremble (with fear), protect them; be to them a defender: may those who are our chief leaders be enjoyers (of your favour), as well as those (your) worshippers who have placed us foremost (to perform the sacrifice).

४६४८. अनुं ते दायि मह इंन्द्रियाय सत्रा ते विश्वमनुं वृत्रहत्यें।

अनुं क्षत्रमनु सहों यज्त्रेन्द्रं देवेभिरनुं ते नृष्ह्यें।।८।।

8. All (power) has been successively conceded verily to you, *Indra*, who are mighty, for the destruction of the foe: suitable vigour, suitable strength in battle (has been given) to you, adorable *Indra*, by the gods.

४६४९. एवा नः स्पृधः समंजा समत्स्विन्द्रं रारन्धि मिथंतीरदेंवीः।

विद्यांम वस्तोरर्वंसा गृणन्तों भरद्वाजा उत तं इन्द्र नूनम्।।९।।

9. So (glorified by us), *Indra*, animate us (to overcome) our enemies in battle: overthrow our impious, malevolent (foes), and may we, *Bhāradvājas*, praising you, assuredly possess habitations, with (abundant) food.

[सूक्त-२६]

[ऋषि- भरद्वाज बार्हस्पत्य। देवता- इन्द्र। छन्द- त्रिष्टुप्।]

४६५०. श्रुधी नं इन्द्र ह्वयूमसि त्वा महो वार्जस्य सातौ वांवृषाणः।

सं यद्विशोऽर्यन्त शूरंसाता उग्रं नोऽव: पार्यें अहन्दाः।।१।।

1. Hear us, *Indra*, when, offering libations, we call upon you for obtaining abundant food: grant us decided protection when on a future day men are assembling for battle.

४६५१. त्वां वाजी हवते वाजिनेयो महो वाजस्य गध्यस्य सातौ।

त्वां वृत्रेष्विन्द्र सत्पतिं तरुत्रं त्वां चष्टे मुष्टिहा गोषु युध्यन्।।२।।

2. The son of *Vājini*, (*Bharadvāja*), offering (sacrificial) viands, invokes you for (the sake of) acquiring obtainable and abundant food: (he invokes) you, *Indra*, the preserver of the good, the defender (from the wicked), when enemies (assail him): he depends upon you when, lifting up his fist, he is fighting for (his) cattle.

४६५२. त्वं कविं चौदयोऽर्कसातौ त्वं कुत्साय शुष्णं दाशुषे वर्क्।

त्वं शिरो अमर्मणः पराहन्नतिथिग्वाय शंस्यं करिष्यन्।।३।।

3. You have animated the sage with (the hope of) obtaining food: you have cut to pieces *Śuṣṇa* for *Kutsa*, the donor of the oblation: you have struck off the head (of *Śambara*), imagining himself invulnerable, intending to give pleasure to *Atithigvan*.

Imagining Himself Invulnerable— The text has only *amarmaṇaḥ*, which the commentator explains *marmahīnam ātmānam manyamānasya*, of him thinking himself devoid of any fatally vulnerable part: he applies it also to *Śambara*.

४६५३. त्वं रथं प्र भरो योधमृष्वमावो युध्यन्तं वृषभं दशद्युम्।

त्वं तुग्रं वेतसवे सचाहन्त्वं तुजिं गृणन्तमिन्द्र तूतोः।।४।।

4. You have brought to *Vṛṣabha* a great war-chariot; you have protected him warring for ten days: you have slain *Tugra* along with *Vetasu*: you have exalted *Tuji* glorifying you.

Vetasave sacā: Vetasu[1] is in other places the name of an *Asura*, and it may be so here, the fifth case being used for the third, or *Vetasunā saha*; but Sāyaṇa suggests that it may be the name of a *Rājā*, of whom *Indra* is the ally against *Tugra*, whom he has slain for the sake of *Vetasu*; *Vṛṣabha* is also said to be the name of a prince.

४६५४. त्वं तदुक्थमिन्द्र बर्हणा कः प्र यच्छता सहस्रा शूर दर्षि।

अव गिरेर्दासं शम्बरं हन्प्रावो दिवोदासं चित्राभिरूती।।५।।

5. *Indra*, who are the subduer (of foes), you have achieved a glorious (deed), inasmuch as you have scattered, hero, the hundreds and thousands (of the host of *Śambara*), have slain the slave *Śambara* (when issuing) from the mountain, and have protected *Divodāsa* with marvellous protections.

---

१. (ऋ॰ सं॰ १०.४.४)।

४६५५. त्वं श्रद्धाभिर्मन्दसानः सोमैर्दभीतये चुमुरिमिन्द्र सिष्वप्।
त्वं रजिं पिठीनसे दशस्यन्षष्टिं सहस्रा शच्या सचाहन्॥६॥

6. Delighted by libations offered with faith, you have consigned *Cumuri* to the sleep (of death) on behalf of *Dabhīti*, and, bestowing (the maiden) *Raji* upon *Piṭhīnas*, you have, by your contrivance, destroyed sixty thousand (warriors) at once.

Piṭhīnas–– *Rajim Piṭhīinase daśasyan:* Raji explained by the Scholiast *etadākhyām kanyām* a made called; or it may be a synonym of *rājyam*, kingdom, dominion.

By your Contrivance— *Śacyā*, which the Scholiast renders *prajñāyā*; but it may also import *karmaṇā*, by act or exploit: as to the number of slain, although probably *Asuras* are intended, yet the specification intimates familiarity with numerous armies and sanguinary conflicts.

४६५६. अहं चन तत्सूरिभिरानश्यां तव ज्यायं इन्द्र सुम्नमोजः।
त्वया यत्स्तवन्ते सधवीर वीरास्त्रिवरूथेन नहुषा शविष्ठ॥७॥

7. May I, with my fellow-worshippers, obtain that your most excellent felicity and vigour, which, most mighty *Indra*, associate of heroes, the pious celebrate (as bestowed) by you, who are the humiliator (of foes), the protector of the three (worlds).

४६५७. वयं ते अस्यामिन्द्र द्युम्नहूतौ सखायः स्याम महिन प्रेष्ठाः।
प्रातर्दनिः क्षत्रश्रीरस्तु श्रेष्ठो घने वृत्राणां सनये धनानाम्॥८॥

8. May we, adorable *Indra*, your friends, at this your worship, offered for (the acquirement of) wealth, be held most dear to you: may *Kṣatraśrī*, the son of *Pratardana*, (my patron), by most illustrious through the destruction of foes, and the attainment of riches.

[सूक्त- २७]

[ऋषि- भरद्वाज बार्हस्पत्य। देवता- इन्द्र, ८ अभ्यावर्ती चायमान
(दान स्तुति)। छन्द- त्रिष्टुप्।]

४६५८. किमस्य मदे किम्वस्य पीताविन्द्रः किमस्य सख्ये चकार।
रणा वा ये निषदि किं ते अस्य पुरा विविद्रे किमु नूतनासः॥१॥

1. What has *Indra* done in the exhilaration of this (*Soma*)? What has he done on quaffing this (libation)? what has he done in

friendship for this (*Soma*)? What have former, What have recent adorers obtained from you in the chamber of this (libation)?

According to Sāyaṇa the *Ṛṣi* here expresses his impatience at the dealing of the reward of his praises: in the next verse he sings his recatation.

४६५९. सदस्य मदे सद्वस्य पीताविन्द्रः सदस्य सख्ये चकार।
रणा वा ये निषदि सत्ते अस्य पुरा विविद्रे सदु नूतनासः ।।२।।

2. Verily, in the exhilaration of this (*Soma*) *Indra* has done a good deed; on quaffing the libation (he has done) a good deed; (he has done) a good deed in friendship for this *Soma*: former as well as recent adorers have obtained good of you in the chamber (of the libation).

४६६०. नहि नु ते महिमनः समस्य न मघवन् मघवत्त्वस्य विद्म।
न राधसोराधसो नूतनस्येन्द्र नकिर्ददृश इन्द्रियं ते ।।३।।

3. We acknowledge no one, *Maghavan*, of greatness equal to yours, nor one of like affluence, nor one of equally glorifiable riches, none has (such as) your power been ever seen (in any other).

४६६१. एतत्त्यत्त इन्द्रियमचेति येनावधीर्वरशिखस्य शेषः।
वज्रस्य यत्ते निहतस्य शुष्मात्स्वनाच्चिदिन्द्र परमो ददार ।।४।।

4. Such as your power (is) it has been comprehended (by us) as that wherewith you have slain the race of *Varaśikha*, when the boldest (of them) was demolished by the noise of your thunderbolt hurled with (all your) force.

Varaśikha— The name of an *Asura*, but the context would rather imply the name of a tribe or people.

४६६२. वधीदिन्द्रो वरशिखस्य शेषोऽभ्यावर्तिने चायमानाय शिक्षन्।
वृचीवता यद्धरियूपीयायां हन्पूर्वे अर्धे भियसापरो दर्त् ।।५।।

5. Favefling *Abhyāvartin*, the son of *Cāyamāna*, *Indra* destroyed the race of *Varaśikha*, killing the descendants of *Vṛcīvat*, (who were stationed) on the *Hariyupīya*, on the eastern part, whilst the western (troop) was scattered through fear.

Abhyāvartin, Cāyamāna— The names of *Rājās*. *Vṛcīvat* is the first-born of the sons of *Varaśikha*, whence the rest are named: *Hariyūpīya* is the name either of a river or a city according to the comment.

४६६३. त्रिंशच्छतं वर्मिणं इन्द्र साकं यव्यावर्त्यां पुरुहूत श्रवस्या। -

वृचीवन्त: शर्वे पर्त्यमाना: पात्रा भिन्दाना न्यर्थान्यायन्।।६।।

6. *Indra*, the invoked of many, thirty hundred mailed warriors (were collected) together on the *Yavyāvatī*, to acquire glory, but the *Vṛcīvats* advancing hostilely, and breaking the sacrificial vessels, went to (their own) annihilation.

Thirty Hundred— *Triṁśac-chataṁ varmiṇaḥ*: Sāyaṇa makes the number one hundred and thirty, *triṁśada-dhikaśatam*, of *kavacabhṛtas*, wearers of breastplates or armour.

Yavyāvatī— The same as the *Hariyūpīya*, according to Sāyaṇa.

४६६४. यस्य गावांवरुषा सूर्यवस्यू अन्तरू षु चर्रतो रेरिहाणा।

स सृञ्जयाय तुर्वशं परांदाद्वृचीवंतो देववाताय शिक्षन्।।७।।

7. He those bright prancing horses, delighted with choice fodder, proceed between (heaven and earth), gave up *Turvaśa* to *Sṛñjaya*, subjecting the *Vṛcīvats* to the descendant of *Devavāta*, (*Abhyāvartin*).

Sṛñjaya— There are several princes of this name in the *Purāṇas*: one of them, the son of *Haryaśva*, was one of the five *Pāñcāla* princes: the name is also that of a people, probably in the same direction, the north-west of India, or towards the Punjab: *Viṣṇu Purāṇa*, pp.193, 454: what is meant by the phrase, he gave up, *parādāt, Turvaśa* to *Sṛñjaya*, may be conjectured but is not explained.

४६६५. द्वयाँ अग्ने रथिनों विंशतिं गा वधूमंतो मघवा महाँ सम्राट्।

अभ्यावर्ती चांयमानो दंदाति दूणाशेयं दक्षिणा पार्थवानाम्।।८।।

8. The opulent supreme sovereign *Abhyāvartin*, the son of *Cāyamāna*, presents, *Agni*, to me two damsels riding in cars, and twenty cows: this donation of the descendant of *Pṛthu* cannot be destroyed.

Two Damsels riding in Cars and twenty Cows— *Dvayān rathino vimśati gā vadhūmantaḥ* is explained by the Scholiast, *rathasahitān vadhūmataḥ strīyuktān, dvayān mithunabhūtān,* being in pairs, having women together with cars: twenty animals, *paśūn*: the passage is obscure and might be understood to mean that the gift consisted of twenty pair of oxen yoked two and two in chariots: the gift of females to saintly persons, however, is nothing unusual: see Maṇḍala 1. Sūkta 125.

This Donation . . . . . Cannot be Destroyed— *Dūṇāśeyam dakṣiṇā pārthavānām: nāśayitum aśakyā* is the translation of the first: the last implies *Abhyāvartin*, as descended from *Pṛthu*, the plural being used honorifically: the name of this member of the race of *Pṛthu* does not occur apparently in the *Purāṇas*.

[सूक्त-२८]

[ऋषि– भरद्वाज बार्हस्पत्य। देवता– गौएँ; २, ८ इन्द्र अथवा गौएँ।
छन्द– त्रिष्टुप्; २-४ जगती; ८ अनुष्टुप्।]

४६६६. आ गावो अग्मन्नुत भद्रमक्रन्त्सीदन्तु गोष्ठे रणयन्त्वस्मे।
प्रजावती: पुरुरूपा इह स्युरिन्द्राय पूर्वीरुषसो दुहाना:॥१॥

1. May the cows come and bring good fortune; let them lie down in (our) stalls and be pleased with us: may the many-coloured kine here be parboiled milk for *Indra* on many dawns.

४६६७. इन्द्रो यज्वने पृणते च शिक्षत्युपेद्ददाति न स्वं मुषायति।
भूयोभूयो रयिमिदस्य वर्धयन्नभिन्ने खिल्ये नि दधाति देवयुम्॥२॥

2. *Indra* grants the desires of the man who offers to him sacrifice and praise; he ever bestows upon him wealth, and deprives him not of that which is his own: again and again increasing his riches, he places the devout man in an inaccessible fortress.

In An Inaccessible Fortress— *Abhinna khilye:* The first is explained *śatrubhirabhetavye*, not to be breached by enemies: and the second is considered the same as *khila*, commonly, waste land, but here said to mean *apratihatasthānam*, an unassailed or unassailable place, one, rich is unapproachable by others, *gantumaśakye sthale.*

४६६८. न ता नशन्ति न दभाति तस्करो नासामामित्रो व्यथिरा दधर्षति।
देवाँश्च याभिर्यजते ददाति च ज्योगित्ताभि: सचते गोपति: सह॥३॥

3. Let not the Cows be lost: let no thief carry them away: let no hostile weapon fall upon them: may the master of the cattle be long possessed of those with which he sacrifices, and which he presents to the gods.

Let not the Cows be lost— *Na tā naśanti:* in this we have the third person plural of the present tense indicative mood, but Sāyaṇa assigns it the force of the imperative, *na naśyantu:* in the following, *na dabhāti taskaraḥ, na vyathir ādadharṣati,* we have the Vedic imperative, *Let.*

४६६९. न ता अर्वा रेणुककाटो अश्नुते न संस्कृतत्रमुप यन्ति ता अभि।
उरुगायमभयं तस्य ता अनु गावो मर्तस्य वि चरन्ति यज्वन:॥४॥

4. Let not the dust-spurning (war) horse reach them nor let them fall in the way of sacrificial consecration let the cattle of the man who offers sacrifice wander about at large and without fear.

Nor let them Fall, Etc.— *Na saṁskṛtatram abhyupayanti*: Sāyaṇa interprets *viśasanādisaṁskādisaṁskāram nābhyupagacchantu,* let them not go night to the consecration of immolation and the rest, as if he understood the Veda to authorize the sacrifice of cattle as victims: but the use of metonymy is so common, that perhaps by cows, in this place, we are to understand their produce, milk and butter, which are constantly offered.

४६७०. गावो भगो गाव इन्द्रो मे अच्छान् गाव: सोमस्य प्रथमस्य भक्ष:।
इमा या गाव: स जनास इन्द्र इच्छामीद्धृदा मनसा चिदिन्द्रम्॥५॥

5. May the Cows be (for our) affluence: may *Indra* grant me cattle: may the Cows yield the food of the first libation: these Cows, oh men, are the *Indra*, the *Indra* whom I desire with heart and mind.

These Cows are the *Indra*— I rather strong personation, and which the Scholiast weakens by understanding it to mean that the cows may be considered as *Indra*, as they nourish him by their milk and butter presented in sacrifices: so, perhaps, the first phrase, *gāvo bhayaḥ*, which he renders *mahyaṁ dhanaṁ bhavantu*, may they be to me affluence, may mean the cows are *Bhaga*, the impersonations of the deity of good fortune and riches.

४६७१. यूयं गावो मेदयथा कृशं चिदश्रीरं चित्कृणुथा सुप्रतीकम्।
भद्रं गृहं कृणुथ भद्रवाचो बृहद्वो वय उच्यते सभासु॥६॥

6. Do you, Cows, give us nourishment: render the emaciated, the unlovely body the reverse: do you, whose lowing is auspicious, make my dwelling prosperous: great is the abundance that is attributed to you in religious assemblies.

Great is the Abundance that is, Etc.— *Bṛhad vo vaya ucyate sabhāsu*: great of you the food is said in assemblies: Sāyaṇa understands it rather differently, great is the food given to you in assemblies, it is given by all, *sarvair dīyate ityarthaḥ.*

४६७२. प्रजावती: सूयवसं रिशन्तीं: शुद्धा अप: सुप्रपाणे पिबन्ती:।
मा व: स्तेन ईशत माघशंस: परि वो हेती रुद्रस्य वृज्या:॥७॥

7. May you, Cows, have many calves grazing upon good pasture, and drinking pure water at accessible ponds: may no thief be your master; no beast of prey (assail you), and may the (fatal) weapon of *Rudra* avoid you.

Rudra is here said to be the Supreme Being identical with time, *kālātmakasya parameśvarasya.*

४६७३. उपेदमुपपर्चनमासु गोषूपं पृच्यताम्।

उपं ऋषभस्य रेतस्युपेन्द्र तवं वीर्यैं।।८।।

8. Let the nourishment of the *Cows* be solicited, let the vigour
of the bull (be requested), *Indra*, for your invigoration.

Let the Vigour of the Bull, Etc.— That is, the milk and butter which
are required for *Indra's* nutriment are dependent upon the cows bearing
calves.

[सूक्त-२९]

[ऋषि– भरद्वाज बार्हस्पत्य। देवता– इन्द्र। छन्द– त्रिष्टुप्।]

४६७४. इन्द्रं वो नरः सख्यायं सेपुर्महो यन्तः सुमतयें चकानाः।

महो हि दाता वज्रहस्तो अस्तिं महामुं रण्वमवंसे यजध्वम्।।१।।

1. Your priests, (oh worshippers), propitiate *Indra* for his
friendship, offering great (praise), and desirous of his favour; for
the wielder of the thunderbolt is the giver of vast (wealth): worship
him, therefore, who is mighty and benevolent, (to obtain) his
protection.

Offering Great Praise and Desirous of his Favour— *Maho yantaḥ
sumataye cakānāḥ,* may also, according to Sāyaṇa, be rendered *mahat
karmma anutiṣṭhantaḥ,* performing great worship, and *stutiṁ
śabdāyantaḥ,* soupling or uttering praise.

४६७५. आ यस्मिन्हस्ते नर्या मिमिक्षुरा रथे हिरण्ययें रथेष्ठाः।

आ रश्मयो गर्भस्त्यो: स्थूरयोराध्वन्नश्वांसो वृषणो युजानाः।।२।।

2. In whose hand (riches) good for man are accumulated, the
chariot-mounted in a golden car; in whose arms the rays of light
(are collected); whose vigorous horses, yoked (to his car, convey
him) on the road (of the firmament).

In whose Hand— *Yasmin havee* may also be interpreted, according
to a note cited from Yāska, *Nirukta,* 1.7, "in whom, the slayer of foes,"
yasmin hantari.

४६७६. श्रिये ते पादा दुव आ मिमिक्षुर्धृष्णुर्वज्री शर्वसा दक्षिणावान्।

वसानो अत्कं सुरभिं दृशे कं स्वर्ण नृतविषिरो बभूथ।।३।।

3. They offer adoration at your feet to acquire prosperity, for
you are the overthrower of enemies by (your) strength, the wielder
of the thunderbolt, the bestower of donations: leader (of rites), you
are like the rolling sun, wearing in the sight (of all) a graceful and
ever moving form.

Wearing . . . . a graceful and ever moving from— *Vasāno atkaṁ surabhim*: the commentator explains *satatagamanaśīlam praśastam rūpam, sarveṣāṁ darśanārtham ācchādayan*, putting on, for the sake of the seeing of all, an excellent form endowed with perpetual movement.

४६७७. स सोम आमिश्लतमः सुतो भूद्यस्मिन्पक्तिः पच्यते सन्तिं धानाः।

इन्द्रं नरः स्तुवन्तों ब्रह्मकारा उक्था शंसन्तो देववाततमाः ॥४॥

4. That libation is most perfectly mixed when, upon its being effused, the cakes are baked, and the barley is friend, and the priests, glorifying *Indra*, offering the (sacrificial) food, and reciting holy prayers, are approaching most nigh to the gods.

४६७८. न ते अन्तः शर्वसो धाय्यस्य वि तु बाबधे रोदसी महित्वा।

आ ता सूरिः पृणति तूतुजानो यूथेवाप्सु समीजमान ऊती ॥५॥

5. No limit of your strength has been assigned; heaven and earth are intimidated by its greatness: the pious worshipper, hastening (to sacrifice), and earnestly performing worship, gratifies you with the offering, as (the cow-keeper satisfies) the herds with water.

With the Offering— *Ūtī* for *ūtya*, is here explained *tarpakena haviṣā*, with the satisfying oblation.

४६७९. एवेदिन्द्रः सुहवं ऋष्वो अस्तूती अनूती हिरिशिप्रः सत्वा।

एवा हि जातो असमात्योजाः पुरू च वृत्रा हनति नि दस्यून् ॥६॥

6. Thus may the mighty *Indra* be successfully invoked; he, the azure-chinned, the giver of wealth, whether by coming or not coming (to the sacrifice); and may he who is of unequalled strength destroy, as soon as manifested, many opposing (evil spirits) and (hostile) *Dasyus*.

The Azure-Chinned— *Hiriśipra, haritavarṇaḥ śipro yasya*: he whose chin or nose is of a green colour, alluding possibly to the sky, considered as a feature of *Indra*.

Whether by coming or not coming— *Ūti anūti* are explained *āgamanena, anāgamanena*, by coming or not coming: *svayam āgato anāgato api stotṛbhyo dhanaṁ prayacchati*, whether he may have come himself or not, he gives wealth to the praisers.

[सूक्त-३०]

[ऋषि– भरद्वाज बार्हस्पत्य। देवता– इन्द्र । छन्द– त्रिष्टुप्।]

४६८०. भूय इद्वावृधे वीर्यायैं एको अजुर्यों दयते वसूनि।

प्र रिरिचे दिव इन्द्रः पृथिव्या अर्धमिदस्य प्रति रोदसी उभे।।१।।

1. Again has *Indra* increased (in strength) for (the display of) heroism: he, the chief (of all), the undecayable, bestows riches (on his votaries): *Indra* surpasses heaven and earth: a mere portion of him is equal to both earth and heaven.

४६८१. अधा मन्ये बृहदसुर्यमस्य यानि दाधार नकिरा मिनाति।
दिवेदिवे सूर्यो दर्शतो भूद्धि सद्यान्युर्विया सुक्रतुर्धात्।।२।।

2. I now glorify his vast and *Asura*-destroying (vigour): those exploits that he has determined (to achieve) no one can resist: (by him) the sun was made daily visible; and he, the doer of great deeds, spread out the spacious regions (of the universe).

The Sun was made daily Visible— That is, by *Indra's* breaking asunder the clouds.

४६८२. अद्या चिन्नू चित्तदपो नदीनां यदाभ्यो अरदो गातुमिन्द्र।
नि पर्वता अद्मसदो न सेदुस्त्वया दृळ्हानि सुक्रतो रजांसि।।३।।

3. At present, verily as of old, that act, (the liberation) of the rivers, is effective; whereby you have directed them on their course: the mountains have settled (at your command) like (men) seated at their meals: doer of great deeds, by you have the worlds been rendered stationary.

४६८३. सत्यमित्तन्न त्वावाँ अन्यो अस्तीन्द्र देवो न मर्त्यो ज्यायान्।
अहन्नहिं परिशयानमर्णोऽवासृजो अपो अच्छा समुद्रम्।।४।।

4. Verily it is the truth, *Indra*, that there is no other such as you, no god nor mortal is (your) superior: you have slain *Ahi* obstructing the waters, you have set them free (to flow) to the ocean.

४६८४. त्वमपो वि दुरो विषूचीरिन्द्र दृळ्हमरुजः पर्वतस्य।
राजाभवो जगतश्चर्षणीनां साकं सूर्यं जनयन् द्यामुषासम्।।५।।

5. You have set the obstructed waters free to flow in all directions: you have fractured the solid (barrier) of the cloud: you are lord over the people of the world, making manifest together the sun, the sky, and the dawn.

[सूक्त-३१]

[ऋषि- सुहोत्र भारद्वाज। देवता- इन्द्र। छन्द- त्रिष्टुप्; ४ शक्वरी।]

४६८५. अभूरेको रयिपते रयीणामा हस्तयोरधिथा इन्द्र कृष्टी:।
वि तोके अप्सु तनये च सूरेऽवोचन्त चर्षणयो विवाच:॥१॥

1. You, lord of riches, are the chief (sovereign) over riches:
you hold men in your two hands, and men glorify you with various
praises for (the sake of obtaining) sons, and valiant grandsons, and
rain.

४६८६. त्वद्द्वियेन्द्र पार्थिवानि विश्वाच्युता चिच्च्यावयन्ते रजांसि।
द्यावाक्षामा पर्वतासो वनानि विश्वं दृळ्हं भयते अज्मन्ना ते॥२॥

2. Through fear of you, Indra, all the regions of the firmament
cause the unfallen (rain) to descend: the heavens, the earth, the
mountains, the forests, all the solid (universe) is alarmed at your
approach.

४६८७. त्वं कुत्सेनाभि शुष्णमिन्द्राशुषं युध्य कुयवं गविष्टौ।
दश प्रपित्वे अध सूर्यस्य मुषायश्चक्रमविवे रपांसि॥३॥

3. You, Indra, with Kutsa, have warred against the
inexhaustible Śuṣṇa: you have overthrown Kuyava in battle: in
conflict you have carried off the wheel (of the chariot) of the sun;
you have driven away the malignant (spirits).

You have carried off the wheel, Etc.— See vol. I. verse 1368.

४६८८. त्वं शतान्यव शम्बरस्य पुरो जघन्थाप्रतीनि दस्यो:। अशिंक्षो यत्र
शच्या शचीवो दिवोदासाय सुन्वते सुतक्रे भरद्वाजाय गृणते
वसूनि॥४॥

4. You have destroyed the hundred impregnable cities of the
Dasyu, Śambara, when sagacious Indra, you, who are brought by
the libation, have bestowed in your liberality riches upon Divodāsa
presenting to you libations, and upon Bharadvāja hymning your
praise.

The Dasyu, Śambara— Śambara is more usually styled an Asura,
and hence it would appear that Dasyu and Asura are synonymous, so that
the latter is equally applied to the unbelieving or anti-Hindu mortal
inhabitant of India.

४६८९. स संत्यसत्वन्महते रणाय रथमा तिष्ठ तुविनृम्ण भीमम्।
याहि प्रपथिन्रवसोप मद्रिकप्र चं श्रुत श्रावय चर्षणिभ्यः॥५॥

5. Leader of true heroes, possessor of infinite wealth, mount your formidable car for the arduous conflict: come to me, pursuer of a forward path, for my protection: do you who are renowned, proclaim (our renown) amongst men.

[सूक्त-३२]

[**ऋषि–** सुहोत्र भारद्वाज। **देवता–** इन्द्र। **छन्द–** त्रिष्टुप्।]

४६९०. अपूर्व्या पुरुतमान्यस्मै महे वीराय तवसे तुराय।
विरप्शिने वज्रिणे शन्तमानि वचांस्यासा स्थविराय तक्षम्॥१॥

1. I have fabricated with my mouth unprecedented, comprehensive, and gratifying praises to that mighty, heroic, powerful, rapid, adorable, and ancient wielder of the thunderbolt.

This verse occurs *Sāmaveda*, 322, but the reading of the last portion somewhat varies in the printed edition: instead of *vacāṁsi asa sthavirāya takṣam*, we have *vacāṁsi asmai sthavīrya takṣuḥ*, they have fabricated praises to that ancient, etc.

४६९१. स मातरा सूर्येणा कवीनामवासयदुजदद्रिं गृणानः।
स्वाधीभिर्ऋक्वभिर्वावशान उदुस्त्रियाण्मसृजन्निदानम्॥२॥

2. He has obtained the parent (worlds, heaven and earth), with the sun, for the sake of the sages, (the *Aṅgirasas*), and, glorified (by them), he has shattered the mountain: repeatedly wished for by his adorers intently meditating (upon him), he has cast off the fetters of the kine.

४६९२. स वह्निभिर्ऋक्वभिर्गोषु शश्वन्मितज्ञुभिः पुरुकृत्वा जिगाय। पुरः पुरोहा
सखिभिः सखीयन्दृळ्हा रुरोज कविभिः कविः सन्॥३॥

3. He, the achiever of many deeds, together with his worshippers ever offering oblations upon bended knees, has overcome (the *Asuras*) for (the rescue of) the cows: friendly with his friends (the *Aṅgirasas*), far-seeing with the far-seeing, the destroyer of cities has demolished the strong cities (of the *Asuras*).

४६९३. स नीव्याभिर्जरितारमच्छा महो वाजेभिर्महद्भिश्च शुष्मैः।
पुरुवीराभिर्वृषभ क्षितीनामा गिर्वणः सुविताय प्र याहि॥४॥

4. Showerer (of benefits), propitiated by praise, come to him who glorifies you to make him happy amongst men with abundant food, with exceeding strength, and with young (mares) with numerous colts.

With Young Mares with Numerous Colts— *Nīvyābhiḥ puruvīrābhiḥ* are translated by Sāyaṇa, *navatarābhiḥ bahūnām vīrayitrībhir-vaḍavābhiḥ,* with very new or young mares bearing male progeny of many.

४६९४. स सर्गेण शर्वसा तक्तो अत्यैरप इन्द्रो दक्षिणतस्तुराषाट्।
इत्था सृजाना अनपावृदर्थं दिवेदिवे विविषुरप्रमृष्यम्।।५।।

5. Endowed with natural force possessed of (swift) horses, *Indra,* the overcomer of adversaries, (sets free) the waters at the southern (declination): thus liberated the waters expand daily to the insatiable goal whence there is no returning.

The Waters at the Southern Declination— The text has only *āpo dakṣiṇataḥ,* the waters from or at the south: there is no verb: Sāyaṇa considers the *dakṣiṇāyana* to be intended the sun's course south from the northern limit of the tropics, which, in India, is in fact the commencement of the rainy season.

[सूक्त-३३]

[ऋषि- शुनहोत्र भारद्वाज। देवता- इन्द्र। छन्द- त्रिष्टुप्।]

४६९५. य ओजिष्ठ इन्द्र तं सु नो दा मदो वृषन्त्स्वभिष्टिर्दास्वान्।
सौवश्व्यं यो वनवत्स्वश्वो वृत्रा समत्सु सासहदमित्रान्।।१।।

1. Showerer (of benefits), *Indra,* grant us a son who shall be most vigorous, a delighter (of you by praise), a pious sacrificer, a liberal giver, who, mounted on a good steed, shall overthrow numerous good steeds, and conquer opposing enemies in combats.

४६९६. त्वां हीन्द्रावसे विवाचो हवन्ते चर्षणयः शूरसातौ।
त्वं विप्रेभिर्वि पणीँरशायस्त्वोत इत्सनिता वाजमर्वा।।२।।

2. Men of various speech invoke you, *Indra,* for their defence in war: you, with the sages, (the *Aṅgirasas*), have slain the *Paṇis*: protected by you, the liberal (worshipper) obtains food.

Men of Various Speech— *Vivācaḥ,* the commentator renders *vividhastutirūpā vāco yeṣām,* they of whom the speech has the form of many kinds of praise, which meaning he assigned to the same word in the first verse of *Sūkta* XXXI; he is probably right, although the more simple explanation would be, "of various speech."

४६९७. त्वं ताँ इं॒द्रोभ॒याँ अमि॒त्रान्दा॒सा॑ वृ॒त्राण्यार्या॑ च शूर।

वधी॑र्वनेव सु॒धि॒तेभि॒रत्कै॑रा पृ॒त्सु द॒र्षि नृ॒णां नृ॑तम।।३।।

3. You, hero, *Indra*, destroyed both (classes of) enemies, (both) *Dāsa* and *Ārya*, adversaries: chief leader of leaders, you cut your foes in pieces in battles with well-plied weapons, as (wood-cutters fell) the forests.

४६९८. स त्वं न॑ इ॒न्द्राक॑वाभिरू॒ती स॒खा वि॒श्वायु॒रवि॑ता वृ॒धे भूः॑।

स्व॒र्षाता॒ यद्ध्व॒यामसि॑ त्वा॒ यु॒ध्यन्तो॒ नेम॑धिता पृ॒त्सु शूर॑।।४।।

4. Do you, *Indra*, who are all-pervading, be a friend, and a protector with irreproachable protections for our prosperity; when warring in number-thinning conflicts, we invoke you for the acquirement of wealth.

When Warring in number-thinning Conflicts— *Yudhyanto nemadhitā pṛtsu, nema* is synonymous with *ardha*, a half, or here, some, *katipayāḥ puruṣā dhīyanta eṣu*, in those battles, *pṛtsu*, in which some men are engaged or killed; the first case plural, *nemadhitā*, or, properly, *nemadhitaya*, being used for the seventh case plural.

For the Acquirement of Wealth— *Svaraṣātā* is explained *suṣṭhu araṇīyam dhanam tasya sambhajanārtham*, very precious wealth for the sake of enjoying it, that is, by the spoils of the enemy.

४६९९. नू॒नं न॑ इ॒न्द्रापरा॑यं च स्या॒ भवा॑ मृ॒ळीक॑ उ॒त नो॑ अभि॒ष्टौ।

इ॒त्था गृ॒णन्तो॒ महि॑न॒स्य शर्म॑न्दि॒वि ष्या॑म पा॒र्ये॑ गो॒षत॑माः।।५।।

5. Do you, *Indra*, now and at (all) other times be verily ours; be the bestower of happiness according to our condition: and in this manner, worshipping at dawn, and glorifying you, may we abide in the brilliant and unbounded felicity of you who are mighty.

Worshipping at Dawn— *Goṣatamā* is left unexplained by Sāyaṇa, unless he intends-to explain it by *vartamānā bhavema*, may we be present, but this may merely express the *syāma* of the text, may we be, or may we abide: the word is unusual, and the rendering is conjectural only, one sense of *goṣa* being the dawn.

[सूक्त-३४]

[ऋषि– शुनहोत्र भारद्वाज। देवता– इन्द्र। छन्द– त्रिष्टुप्।]

४७००. सं च॒ त्वे ज॒ग्मुर्गिर॒ इन्द्र॑ पू॒र्वीर्वि च॒ त्वद्यन्ति॑ वि॒भ्वो॑ म॒नीषाः॑।

पुरा नूनं च॑ स्तुतय ऋषीणां पस्पृध्र इन्द्रे अध्युक्थार्का ॥१॥

1. Many praises, *Indra*, are concentrated in you; from you
abundant commendations diversely proceed; to you, formerly and
at present, the praises of the sages, their prayers and hymns, vie (in
glorifying) *Indra*.

From you Abundan commendations diversely proceed— *Vica
tvad yanti manīṣāḥ, tvattaḥ stotṛṇām* approbations of the praisers
variously go forth, is the explanation of Sāyaṇa.

४७०१. पुरुहूतो य॒: पुरुगूर्त॑ ऋभ्वाँ॑ एक॑: पुरुप्रशस्तो अस्ति॑ यज्ञै॑:।
रथो न म॒हे श॒र्वसे युजा॒नो३े॒ स्माभिरिन्द्रो॑ अनुमाद्यो॑ भूत् ॥२॥

2. May that *Indra* ever be propitiated, by us who is the invoked
of many, mighty and chief, especially honoured by sacrifices, and
to whom, as to a conveyance, we are attached for (the attainment
of) great strength.

४७०२. न यं हिंसं॑न्ति धीतयो न वाणीरिन्द्रं॑ नक्ष॒न्तीद॒भि व॒र्धयन्ती॑:।
यदि स्तोतारं॑: शतं यत्स॒हस्रं॑ गृणन्ति गिर्वणसं॑ शं तद॑स्मै ॥३॥

3. All praises contributing to his exaltation proceed to *Indra*,
whom no acts, no words can harm, since hundreds and thousands
of adorers glorify him who is entitled to praise, and so afford him
gratification.

४७०३. अस्मा॑ एतद्दिव्यं॒ चेव॑ मासा मिमिक्ष इन्द्रे न्य॑यामि सोमं॑:।
जनं॑ न धन्व॒न्नभि सं यदाप॑: सत्रा वा॑वृधुर्हवनानि यज्ञै॑: ॥४॥

4. The mixed *Soma* juice has been prepared for *Indra*, (to be
offered) on the day (of sacrifice), with reverence-like adoration,
when praises, together with offerings, yield him increase, as when
water (revives) a man in a desert waste.

With Reverence-like Adoration— *Divyarceva māsā* is explained
divase sautye ahani arcana-sādhanena stotṛṇeva mānena, with respect,
like praise, the instrument of worship on the day for the libation; the
Scholiast cites in illustration a *mantra* beginning *Vṛtraghna*, slayer of
Vṛtra, etc., but he also proposes another explanation, *divi dyotake, arceva
arkaḥ, sūrya iva, māsā-māsas candramāḥ sa iva*, which, with the
following word, *mimikṣa,* explained *vṛṣṭyudakānām sektā*, the sprinkler of
rain-waters, is applied to *Indra, ya Indro vartate*, that *Indra* who is the
shedder of rain, like the sun and the moon in heaven: this is scarcely more
satisfactory than the interpretation first given, although that is not very
explicitly.

४७०४. अस्मा एतन्महाङ्घूषमस्मा इन्द्राय स्तोत्रं मतिभिरवाचि।
असद्यथा महति वृत्रतूर्य इन्द्रो विश्वायुरविता वृधश्च।।५।।

5. To this *Indra* has this earnest eulogy been addressed by the devout, in order that the all-pervading *Indra* may be our defender and exalter in the great conflict with (our) foes.

[सूक्त-३५]

[ऋषि– नर भारद्वाज। देवता– इन्द्र । छन्द– त्रिष्टुप्।]

४७०५. कदा भुवन्नरथक्षयाणि ब्रह्म कदा स्तोत्रे सहस्रपोष्यं दाः।
कदा स्तोमं वासयोऽस्य राया कदा धियः करसि वाजरत्नाः।।१।।

1. When may our prayers (be with you) in your chariot? When will you grant to your adorer the (means of) maintaining thousands? When will you recompense my adoration with riches? When will you render sacred rites productive of food?

४७०६. कर्हि स्वित्तदिन्द्र यत्नृभिर्नृन्वीरैर्वीरान्नीळयासे जयाजीन्।
त्रिधातु गा अधि जयासि गोष्विन्द्र द्युम्नं स्वर्वद्धेह्यस्मे।।२।।

2. When, *Indra*, will you bring together leaders with leaders, heroes with heroes, and give us victory in battles? When will you conquer from the enemy the threefold-food-supplying cattle? (When will you grant) us, *Indra*, diffusive wealth?

Threefold-food-supplying Cattle— *Tridhātu gāḥ:* cows having three elements of nutriment, as a milk, curds and butter.

४७०७. कर्हि स्वित्तदिन्द्र यज्जरित्रे विश्वप्सु ब्रह्म कृणवः शविष्ठ।
कदा धियो न नियुतो युवासे कदा गोमघा हवनानि गच्छाः।।३।।

3. When, most vigorous *Indra*, will you grant your worshipper that food which is all-sufficing? When will you combine (in yourself) worship and praises? When will you render oblations productive of cattle?

४७०८. स गोमघा जरित्रे अश्वश्चन्द्रा वाजश्रवसो अधि धेहि पृक्षः।
पीपिहीषः सुदुघामिन्द्र धेनुं भरद्वाजेषु सुरुचो रुरुच्याः।।४।।

4. Grant, *Indra*, to your adorer (abundant) food, productive of cattle, pleasant with horses, and renowned for vigour: multiply nourishment, and (cherish) the kine easily milked, and render them so that they may be resplendent.

४७०९. तमा नूनं वृजनमन्यथा चिच्छूरो यच्छक्र वि दुरो गृणीषे।
मा निरंरं शुक्रदुघस्य धेनोराङ्गिरसान्ब्रह्मणा विप्र जिन्व।।५।।

5. Direct him who is actually our adversary into a different (course): mighty *Indra*, who are a hero, the destroyer (of enemies), therefore are you glorified: never may I desist from the praise of the giver of pure (gifts): satisfy, sage *Indra*, the *Aṅgirasas* with food.

Into a different Course— That is, consign him to death, a course different from that of living beings.

Never may I desist from the Praise— *Mā niraram śukradughasya dhenoḥ* is, literally, may I not cease from the cow the yielder of pure milk; but *dhenoḥ* is interpreted by the Scholiast in this place *vacas*, *stotrat*, from praise; or he wishes as an alternative, may I never depart from the milch cows given, *Indra*, by you.

[सूक्त-३६]

[ऋषि– नर भारद्वाज। देवता– इन्द्र। छन्द–त्रिष्टुप्।]

४७१०. सत्रा मदासस्तव विश्वजन्याः सत्रा रायोऽध ये पार्थिवासः।
सत्रा वाजानामभवो विभक्ता यद्देवेषु धारयथा असुर्यम्।।१।।

1. Truly are your exhilarations beneficial to all men: truly are the riches which exist on earth (beneficial to all men): truly are you the distributor of food; wherefore you maintain vigour amongst the gods.

४७११. अनु प्र येजे जन ओजो अस्य सत्रा दधिरे अनु वीर्याय।
स्यूमगृभे दुधयेऽर्वते च क्रतुं वृञ्जन्त्यपि वृत्रहत्ये।।२।।

2. The worshipper praises especially the strength of that *Indra*, verily they rely upon him for heroic deeds: they offer sacrifices to him as the seizer of an uninterrupted series of foes, their assailant, their subduer, and also for the destruction of *Vṛtra*.

Seizer of an Uninterrupted Series of Foes— *Syūmagṛbhe, syūtān avicchedena vartamānān śatrūn gṛhṇate,* to him who seizes enemies being lines or threads without interruption.

४७१२. तं सध्रीचीरूतयो वृष्ण्यानि पौंस्यानि नियुतः सश्चुरिन्द्रम्।
समुद्रं न सिन्धव उक्थशुष्मा उरुव्यचसं गिर आ विशन्ति।।३।।

3. The associated *Maruts*, heroic energies, virile strength, and the *Niyut* steeds, attend upon *Indra* and, praises powerful in sacred song centre in him as river flow into the ocean.

४७१३. स रायस्खामुरपं सृजा गृणानः पुरुश्चन्द्रस्य त्वमिन्द्र वस्वः।
पतिर्बभूथासमो जनानामेको विश्वस्य भुवनस्य राजा॥४॥

4. Glorified by us, *Indra*, let flow the stream of much
delighting, home-conferring affluence, for you are the unequalled
lord of men, the sole sovereign of all the world.

४७१४. स तु श्रुधि श्रुत्या यो दुवोयुर्द्यौर्न भूमाभि रायो अर्यः।
असो यथा नः शर्वसा चकानो युगेयुगे वयसा चेकितानः॥५॥

5. Hear, *Indra*, (the praises) that may be heard (by you), you,
who are gratified by our adoration, and, like the sun, (prevail) over
the ample riches of the enemy: endowed with strength, being
glorified in every age, rendered comprehensible by (sacrificial)
food, be to us no other (than such as you have been).

Like the Sun, Prevail, etc.— *Dyaur-na bhūmābhi rāyo aryaḥ; arer
dhanāni bahutarāṇi sūrya iva abhibhavasi*: the prefix *abhi*, as is frequent
in the Veda, being put for the compound verb *abhibhu*.

By to us no other— *Aso yathā naḥ* is, literally, not he as to us:
Sāyaṇa, to make this intelligible, says, *yena prakāreṇa asmākam
asādhāraṇo asi sa tathā saḥ syāḥ,* in what manner you are especially of
exclusively ours, so may you be that, our property or friend.

[सूक्त- ३७]

[**ऋषि**– भरद्वाज बार्हस्पत्य। **देवता**– इन्द्र। **छन्द**– त्रिष्टुप्।]

४७१५. अर्वाग्रथं विश्ववारं त उग्रेन्द्र युक्तासो हरयो वहन्तु।
कीरिश्चिद्धि त्वा हवंते स्वर्वानृधीमहि सधमादस्ते अद्य॥१॥

1. Fierce *Indra*, let your harnessed steeds bring down your all-
desired chariot: your devoted adorer verily invokes you: may we
today, partaking of your exhilaration, increase toady (in
prosperity).

४७१६. प्रो द्रोणे हरयः कर्माग्मन्मनुनानास ऋज्यन्तो अभूवन्।
इन्द्रो नो अस्य पूर्व्यः पपीयादद्युक्षो मदस्य सोम्यस्य राजा॥२॥

2. The green *Soma* juices flow at our sacrifice, and purified,
proceed direct into the pitcher: may the ancient illustrious *Indra*,
the sovereign of the exhilarating *Soma* libation, drink of this our
offering.

४७१७. आसस्राणास: शवसानमच्छेन्द्रं सुचक्रे रथ्यासो अश्वा:।

अभि श्रव ऋज्यन्तो वहेयुर्नू चिन्नु वायोरमृतं वि दस्येत्।।३।।

3. May the everywhere-going, straight-proceeding, chariot-bearing steeds, bring the mighty *Indra* in his strong-wheeled car to our rite: let not the ambrosial *Soma* waste in the wind.

Let not the Ambrosial *Soma* waste in the Wind— The *Soma* Juice, it is said, if allowed to remain some time in the vessel containing it, may be dried up by the air: *Indra* is therefore urged to drink it before it evaporates.

४७१८. वरिष्ठो अस्य दक्षिणामियर्तीन्द्रो मघोनां तुविकूर्मितम:।

यया वज्रिव: परियास्यंहो मघा च धृष्णो दयसे वि सूरीन्।।४।।

4. The very strong *Indra*, the performer of many great deeds, instigates the donation of this (institutor of the ceremony) amongst the opulent, whereby, wielder of the thunderbolt, you remove sin, and, firm of purpose, bestow riches upon the worshippers.

४७१९. इन्द्रो वाजस्य स्थविरस्य दातेन्द्रो गीर्भिर्वर्धतां वृद्धमंहा:।

इन्द्रो वृत्रं हनिष्ठो अस्तु सत्वा ता सूरि: पृणति तूतुजान:।।५।।

5. *Indra* is the donor of substantial food; may the very illustrious *Indra* increase (in glory) through our praises: may *Indra*, the destroyer (of menies), be the especial slayer of *Vṛtra*: may he, the animator the quick-mover, grant us those (riches which we desire).

[सूक्त-३८]

[**ऋषि**– भरद्वाज बार्हस्पत्य। **देवता**– इन्द्र। **छन्द**– त्रिष्टुप्।]

४७२०. अपादित उदु नश्चित्रतमो महीं भर्षद्द्युमतीमिन्द्रहूतिम्।

पन्यसीं धीतिं दैव्यस्य यामञ्जनस्य रातिं वनते सुदानु:।।१।।

1. May the most marvellous *Indra* drink from this (our cup): may he acknowledge our earnest and brilliant invocation: may the munificent (*Indra*) accept the offering and the praiseworthy adoration at the sacrifice of the devout worshipper.

४७२१. दूराच्चिदा वसतो अस्य कर्णा घोषादिन्द्रस्य तन्यति ब्रुवाण:।

एयमेनं देवहूतिर्ववृत्यान्मद्र्यगिन्द्रमियमृच्यमाना।।२।।

2. Reciting (his praise, the worshipper) calls aloud, that by the sound he may reach the ears of *Indra*, although abiding afar off: may this invocation of the deity, inducing, him (to come), bring *Indra* to may presence.

४७२२. तं वो॑ धिया॒ प॑रम॒या॑ पुरा॒जाम॒जर॑मिन्द्र॑म॒भ्य॑नूष्य॒कैः॑।
ब्रह्मा॑ च गि॒रो॑ दधिरे॒ स॒म॑स्मिन्मह॑श्च॒ स्तोमो॒ अधि॑ वर्धदिन्द्रे॑ ।।३।।

3. I glorify you with hymns and with pious worship, the ancient undecaying *Indra*, for in him are oblations and praises concentrated, and great adoration is enhanced (when addressed to him).

४७२३. वर्धा॒द्यं य॒ज्ञ उ॒त सोम॑ इन्द्रं॑ वर्धा॒द्ब्रह्म॑ गि॒र॑ उ॒क्था च॒ मन्म॑।
वर्धाहै॑नमु॒षसो॒ याम॑न्न॒क्तोर्व॑र्धा॒न्मासाः॑ श॒रदो॒ द्याव॑ इन्द्र॑म् ।।४।।

4. *Indra*, whom the sacrifice, whom the libation exalts, whom the oblation, the praises, the prayers, the adoration exalt, whom the course of day and night exalts, whom months, and years, and days exalt.

४७२४. ए॒वा ज॒ज्ञा॒नं सह॑से॒ अ॒सा॑मि वावृ॒धा॒नं राध॑से च श्रु॒ताय॑।
महामु॒ग्रम॑व॒से वि॒प्र नू॒नमा॑ वि॑वासेम वृत्र॒तूर्ये॑षु ।।५।।

5. So, wise *Indra*, may we today propitiate you who are manifested, to overcome (our foes), you who are greatly augmenting, mighty and free, for (the sake of) wealth, fame, and protection, and for the destruction of (our) enemies.

[सूक्त-३९]

[ऋषि– भरद्वाज बार्हस्पत्य। **देवता–** इन्द्र। **छन्द–** त्रिष्टुप्।]

४७२५. मन्द्रस्य॑ क॒वेर्दि॒व्यस्य॒ वह्ने॑र्वि॒प्रम॑न्मनो व॒चन॑स्य॒ मध्वः॑।
अपा॑ न॒स्तस्य॒ सच॑नस्य दे॒वेषो॒ युव॑स्व गृ॒णते॑ गो॒अग्राः॑ ।।१।।

1. Drink, *Indra*, of that our sweet, exhilarating, inspiring, celestial, fruit-yielding *Soma*, commended by the wise, and entitled to praise and preparation; bestow upon him who glorifies you, divine (*Indra*), food, the chiefest of which is cattle.

Sweet, exhilarating, etc.— Several of the epithets in the text are unusual, and, agreeably to European notions, very inapplicable to a beverage; they are, severally, *mandra*, exhilarating, *kavi*, explained *vikrānta,* heroic; *divya*, divine; *vahni* rendered *voḍhā*, bearing fruit;

vipramanman, of which sages are the praisers, *stotāraḥ; vacana* laudable, *stutya; sacana* to be served or honoured, *sevya*.

The Chiefest of which is Cattle— *Iṣo yuvasva gṛṇate go agrāḥ* is explained *annam sanyojaya*, combine or supply food to the praiser: *yāsām iṣam gāvo agre*, of which viands, cows are in the first place; is this to be understood literally? And were cows, in the time of the Vedas, a principal article of food? Of course, a *Brahman* would interpret it metonymically, cows being put for their produce, milk and butter; Sāyaṇa is silent, but there does not seem to be any thing in the Veda that militates against the literal interpretation.

४७२६. अयमुंशानः पर्यद्रिंमुस्ता ऋतधीतिभिर्ऋतयुर्युजानः।
रुजदरुग्णं वि वलस्य सानुं पर्णींर्वचोभिरभि यौधदिन्द्रः॥२॥

2. Determined (to recover) the cattle hidden in the mountain, associated with the animated by (their) veracious (praise), this (*Indra*) fractured the infrangible rock of *Bala*, and overwhelmed the *Paṇis* with reproaches.

४७२७. अयं द्योतयदद्द्युतो व्यइकूनदोषा वस्तोः शरद इन्दुरिन्द्र।
इमं केतुमंदधुर्नू चिदह्नां शुचिंजन्मन उषसंश्चकार॥३॥

3. This *Soma*, *Indra*, (quaffed by you), has lighted up the unlustrous nights, and days and nights, and years: (the gods) of old have established it as the ensign of days, and it he made the dawns generated in light.

This Soma— The text has *ayam Induḥ*, which, as a synonym of *Soma*, implies both the moon and the *Soma* juice: it is the former that is here held in veiw at the expense of consistency: according to Sāyaṇa, *Soma* is here *candrātmā nabhasi vartamānaḥ*, the same as the moon present in the sky, and as, *candragatyādhīnatvāt tithivibhāgaḥ*, the divisions of lunar days are dependent upon the motions of the moon, it may be said to be the cause of days, weeks, months and years, the first term, *aktun*, is said by the Scholiast to imply fortnights, months and years, or the longest periods of time: the phrase in the parenthesis is not in the text, but is supplied by the Scholiast, *tvayā pīyamānaḥ*, to be drunk by you, but it is justified by the pronoun *ayam*, this which could not apply as something present to the moon.

४७२८. अयं रोचयदरुचो रुचानोऽयं वासयद्व्यृ‍इ तेनं पूर्वीः।
अयमीयत ऋतयुग्भिरश्वैः स्वार्वदा नाभिना चर्षणिप्राः॥४॥

4. This radiant (*Indra*) has illumed the non-radiant (worlds): he has pervaded many dawns with true lustre the benefactor of men moves in (a chariot) drawn by horses, harnessed by praise, laden with riches.

४७२९. नू गृणानो गृणते प्रत्न राजन्निषः पिन्व वसुदेयाय पूर्वीः।
अप ओषधीरविषा वनानि गा अर्वतो नॄनृचसे रिरीहि ॥५॥

5. Sovereign of old, do you, when glorified, bestow upon him who praises you, and to whom affluence is due abundant food: grant to the worshipper water, plants, innoxious woods, cattle horses, and men.

[सूक्त-४०]

[**ऋषि–** भरद्वाज बार्हस्पत्य। **देवता–** इन्द्र। **छन्द–** त्रिष्टुप्।]

४७३०. इन्द्र पिब तुभ्यं सुतो मदायाव स्य हरी वि मुञ्चा सखाया।
उत प्र गाय गण आ निषद्याथा यज्ञाय गृणते वयो धाः ॥१॥

1. Drink, *Indra*, (the *Soma*) that is effused for your exhilaration: stop your friendly steeds: let them loose; sitting in our society, respond to our hymns; give food to him who lauds and worships you.

Sitting in our Society, respond to our Hymns— *Uta pra gāya gaṇe ā niṣadya: pragāya* is explained *asmābhiḥ kṛtam stotram upaślokaya,* return verses to the praise made by us.

४७३१. अस्य पिब यस्य जज्ञान इन्द्र मदाय क्रत्वे अपिबो विरप्शिन्।
तमु ते गावो नर आपो अद्रिरिन्दुं सम्हन्नपीतये समस्मै ॥२॥

2. Drink, *Indra*, of this (libation), of which you, mighty one, have drunk as soon as born, for excitement to (great) deeds: that *Soma* juice which the kine, the priests, the waters, the stones, combine to prepare for your drinking.

४७३२. समिद्धे अग्नौ सुत इन्द्र सोम आ त्वां वहन्तु हरयो वहिष्ठाः।
त्वायता मनसा जोहवीमीन्द्रा याहि सुविताय महे नः ॥३॥

3. The fire is kindled; the *Soma, Indra,* is effused let your vigorous horses bring you hither: I invoke you, *Indra,* with a mind wholly devoted to you; come for our great prosperity.

४७३३. आ याहि शश्वदुशता ययाथेन्द्र महा मनसा सोमपेयम्।
उप ब्रह्माणि शृणव इमा नोऽथा ते यज्ञस्तन्वे वयो धात् ॥४॥

4. You have ever gone (to similar rites): come now with a great mind disposed to drink the *Soma:* hear these our praises: may the worshipper present to you (sacrificial) food for (the nourishment of) your person.

४७३४. यदिन्द्र दिवि पार्ये यदृधग्यद्वा स्वे सदने यत्र वासि।
अतो नो यज्ञमवसे नियुत्वान्त्सजोषाः पाहि गिर्वणो मरुद्भिः॥५॥

5. Whether, *Indra*, you abide in the distant heaven, in any other place, or in your own abode, or wheresoever (you may by), from thence do you, who are propitiated by praise, putting to your steeds, protect, together with the *Maruts*, well pleased, our sacrifice, for our preservation.

[सूक्त-४१]

[ऋषि– भरद्वाज बार्हस्पत्य। देवता– इन्द्र। छन्द– त्रिष्टुप्।]

४७३५. अहेळमान उप याहि यज्ञं तुभ्यं पवन्त इन्दवः सुतासः।
गावो न वज्रिन्त्स्वमोको अच्छेन्द्रा गहि प्रथमो यज्ञियानाम्॥१॥

1. Unirascible (*Indra*), come to the sacrifice; the effused juices are purified for you: they flow, thunderer, (into the pitchers), as cows go to their stalls; come, *Indra*, the first of those who are to be worshipped.

४७३६. या ते काकुत्सुकृता या वरिष्ठा यया शश्वत्पिबसि मध्व ऊर्मिम्।
तया पाहि प्र ते अध्वर्युरस्थात्सं ते वज्रो वर्ततामिन्द्र गव्युः॥२॥

2. Drink, *Indra*, with that well-formed and expanded tongue wherewith you ever quaffest the juice of the sweet (*Soma*); before you stands the ministrant priest; let your bolt, *Indra*, designed (to recover) the cattle, be hurled (against your foes).

४७३७. एष द्रप्सो वृषभो विश्वरूप इन्द्राय वृष्णे समकारि सोमः।
एतं पिब हरिवः स्थातरुग्र यस्येशिषे प्रदिवि यस्ते अन्नम्॥३॥

3. This dropping, omniform *Soma*, the showerer (of benefits), has been duly prepared for *Indra*, the showerer (of rain): lord of steeds, ruler over all, mighty (*Indra*), drink this over which you have of old presided, which is your food.

४७३८. सुतः सोमो असुतादिन्द्र वस्यानयं श्रेयाञ्चिकितुषे रणाय।
एतं तितिर्व उप याहि यज्ञं तेन विश्वास्तविषीरा पृणस्व॥४॥

4. The enused *Soma*, *Indra*, is more excellent than that which is not effused: it is better (qualified) to give pleasure to you, who are capable of judging: overcomer (of enemies), approach this sacrifice, and thereby perfect all your powers.

४७३९. ह्वयामसि त्वेन्द्र याह्ववाङरं ते सोमस्तन्वे भवाति।

शतक्रतो मादयस्वा सुतेषु प्रास्माँ अव पृतनासु प्र विक्षु॥५॥

5. We invoke you, *Indra*, come down: may the *Soma* be sufficient for (the satisfaction of) your person: exult *Śatakratu* with the libations, defend us in combats, and against the people.

Defend us in combats and against the people— *Pra asmān avapṛtanāsu pra vikṣu: pra* is put for *prasakṣ*, especially protect us, *na kevalam saṅgrāmeṣu kintu sarvāsu prajāsu*, not only in wars, but in or against all people this looks as if the religious party had opponents amongst the people in general.

[सूक्त-४२]

[**ऋषि**– भरद्वाज बार्हस्पत्य। **देवता**– इन्द्र। **छन्द**– अनुष्टुप्; ४ - बृहती।]

४७४०. प्रत्यस्मै पिपीषते विश्वानि विदुषे भर।

अरङ्गमाय जग्मयेऽपश्चाद्दघ्वने नरं॥१॥

1. Offer, (priests), the libation to him who is desirous to drink; who knows all things; whose movements are all-sufficient; who goes readily (to sacrifices); the leader (of holy rites), following no one.

Sāmaveda, 352 1440.

४७४१. एमेनं प्रत्येतन सोमेभिः सोमपातमम्।

अमत्रेभिर्ऋजीषिणमिन्द्रं सुतेभिरिन्दुभिः॥२॥

2. Proceed to the presence of that deep quaffer of the *Soma*, with the *Soma* juices; to the vigorous *Indra* with vessels (filled) with the effused libations.

This and the two following verses also occur in the *Sāma*, 1441-43.

४७४२. यदीं सुतेभिरिन्दुभिः सोमेभिः प्रतिभूषथ।

वेदा विश्वस्य मेधिरो धृषत्तन्तमिदेषते॥३॥

3. When, with the effused and flowing *Soma* juices, you come into his presence, the sagacious (*Indra*) knows your wish, and the suppresser (of enemies) assuredly grants it, whatever it may be.

Tam tam id eṣate: the repetition of the relative with reference to the antecedent *kāmam* may perhaps be so rendered.

४७४३. अस्माअस्मा इदन्धसोऽध्वर्यो प्र भरा सुतम्।

कुवित्समस्य जेन्यस्य शर्धतोऽभिशस्तेरवस्परत्॥४॥

4. Offer, priest, to him, and him (only) this libation of (sacrificial) food, and may he ever defend us against the malignity of every superable adversary.

[सूक्त-४३]

[ऋषि– भरद्वाज बार्हस्पत्य। देवता– इन्द्र । छन्द– उष्णिक्।]

४७४४. यस्य त्यच्छम्बरं मदे दिवोदासाय रन्धयः।
अयं स सोम इन्द्र ते सुतः पिब।।१।।

1. This *Soma*, in the exhilaration of which it is known that you have subdued *Śambara* for (the sake of) *Divodāsa*, is poured our, *Indra*, for you: drink.

It is Known— *Yasya tyacchambaram made: tyat* is explained by Sāyaṇa as equivalent to *tat prasiddham yatha bhavati tatha*, such as that which is notorious.

Sāmaveda, 392.

४७४५. यस्य तीव्रसुतं मदं मध्यमन्तं च रक्षसे।
अयं स सोम इन्द्र ते सुतः पिब।।२।।

2. This *Soma*, the exhilarating draught of which, when fresh effused (at dawn), or at noon, or at the last (or evening worship), you cherish, is poured out, *Indra*, for you: drink.

४७४६. यस्य गा अन्तरश्मनो मदे दृळ्हा अवासृजः।
अयं स सोम इन्द्र ते सुतः पिब।।३।।

3. This *Soma*, in the exhilaration of which you have liberated the cattle, firm (fastened) within the rock, is poured out, *Indra*, for you: drink.

४७४७. यस्य मन्दानो अन्धसो माघोनं दधिषे शवः।
अयं स सोम इन्द्र ते सुतः पिब।।४।।

4. This *Soma*, exhilarated (by drinking) of which (sacrificial) food you possessed the might of *Maghavan*, is poured out, *Indra*, for you: drink.

The Might of Maghavan— *Māghonam śavas*, the rank of office of *Indra*, is engendered by the *Soma*, *Somam Indratvam jātam*.

ANUVAKA IV

[सूक्त-४४]

[ऋषि– शंयु बार्हस्पत्य। देवता– इन्द्र। छन्द– त्रिष्टुप्, १-६ अनुष्टुप्; ७-९
विराट्; ८ त्रिष्टुप् अथवा विराट्।]

४७४८. यो रयिवो रयिन्तमो यो द्युम्नैर्द्युम्नवत्तम:।
सोम: सुत: स इन्द्र तेऽस्ति स्वधापते मद:॥१॥

1. Opulent *Indra*, the *Soma* that abounds with riches, and is
most resplendent with glories, is poured out: it is your exhilaration,
Indra, lord of the offering.

Lord of the Offering— *Svadhāpati* may also mean the cherisher or
protector of the *Soma* libation, *svadhāyā annasya somalakṣaṇasya
pālanāt;* also *Sāmaveda,* 351.

४७४९. य: शग्मस्तुविशग्म ते रायो दामा मतीनाम्।
सोम: सुत: स इन्द्र तेऽस्ति स्वधापते मद:॥२॥

2. The *Soma*, possessor of felicity, which gives you delight,
and which is the bestower of riches on your votaries, is poured out:
it is your exhilaration, *Indra*, lord of the offering.

४७५०. येन वृद्धो न शवसा तुरो न स्वाभिरूतिभि:।
सोम: सुत: स इन्द्र तेऽस्ति स्वधापते मद:॥३॥

3. The *Soma*, whereby you are augmented in strength, and,
together with your defenders, (the *Maruts*), are victorious (over
your foes), is poured out: it is your exhilaration, *Indra*, lord of the
offering.

४७५१. त्यमु वो अप्रहणं गृणीषे शवसस्पतिम्।
इन्द्रं विश्वासाहं नरं मंहिष्ठं विश्वचर्षणिम्॥४॥

4. (Worshippers), for you I glorify that *Indra* who disappointed
not (his adorers); the lord of strength, the all-subduing, the leader
(of rites), the most beautiful, the beholder of the universe.

४७५२. यं वर्धयन्तीदि्गिर: पतिं तुरस्य राधस:।
तमिन्वस्य रोदसी देवी शुष्मं सपर्यत:॥५॥

5. The divine heaven and earth adore that vigour of his, which
our hymns augment, the appropriator of the riches of the foe.

४७५३. तद्वां उक्थस्य॑ बर्हणेन्द्रा॒योप॑स्तृणीषणि ।

विपो॒ न यस्यो॒तयो॒ वि यद्रो॒हन्ति॑ स॒क्षित॑:॥६॥

6. (Worshippers), the efficacy of your eulogy is to be
manifested to that *Indra*, whose protections, like (those) of a
sensible man, are displayed as abiding along with him.

Like those of a sensible Man— *Vipo na, medhāvirat iva;* that is, the
protective measures or expedients of a sensible or wise man are capable
for all affairs, *sarva kāryakuśalaḥ.*

४७५४. अवि॑न्दद्द॒क्षं मि॒त्रो न॒वीयान्प॒पानो दे॒वेभ्यो॒ वस्यो॒ अचैत् ।

ससवान्स्तौ॒लाभि॒र्धौत॑री॒भिरुरुष्या॑ पा॒युर॑भवत्स॒खिभ्य॑:॥७॥

7. *Indra*, appreciates him who is skilled (in holy rites): a recent
friend, quaffing (the libation), he heaps excellent (wealth) upon the
devout: partaking of (the sacrificial) food, (and brought) by his
robust agitators (of the earth, his steeds), he, through his
benevolence, is a protector to his friends.

By his Robust Agitators— *Sthaulābhir dhautarībhiḥ* explained
sthūlābhiḥ kampanakāriṇībhiḥ, with the stout causers of trembling: the
Scholiast supplies *vaḍavābhiḥ yuktaḥ,* joined with such mares; or the
epithets, although feminine, the Scholiast says may be applied to the
Maruts.

४७५५. ऋ॒तस्य॒ पथि॑ वे॒धा अ॑पायि श्रि॒ये म॒नांसि॑ दे॒वासो॑ अक्रन् ।

दधा॑नो॒ नाम॑ म॒हो वचो॑भि॒र्वपु॒र्दृशये॒ वेन्यो॒ व्याव॑:॥८॥

8. The *Soma*, creator (of all), on the path of sacrifice, has been
drunk: the worshippers have presented it to gratify the mind (of
Indra): may he, the humiliator (of his foes), possessing a vast
body, propitiated by our praises, become manifest to our view.

४७५६. द्यु॒मत्त॑मं॒ दक्षं॑ धे॒ह्यस्मे॒ सेधा॒ जना॑नां पू॒र्वीररा॒ती॑: ।

वर्षी॑यो॒ वयः॑ कृणुहि॒ शची॑भि॒र्धन॑स्य सा॒ताव॒स्माँ अ॑विड्ढि॥९॥

9. Bestow upon us most brilliant vigour: oppose the numerous
enemies of your worshippers: grant us, for our pious acts, abundant
food: secure us in the enjoyment of wealth.

४७५७. इन्द्र॒ तुभ्य॒मिन्म॑घवन्न॒भूम॑ व॒यं दा॒त्रे हरि॑वो॒ मा वि वे॑न: ।

नकि॑रा॒पिर्द॒दृशे॑ मर्त्य॒त्रा किम॒ङ्ग र॑ध्र॒चोद॑नं त्वाहु:॥१०॥

10. *Indra*, possessor of affluence, we have recourse to you, the
bountiful, lord of steeds, be not unfavourable to us: no other

kinsman is beheld (by us) amongst men: who else have they called you the bestower of wealth?

४७५८. मा जस्वने वृषभ नो ररीथा मा ते रेवतः सख्ये रिषाम।
पूर्वीष्ट इन्द्र निष्षिधो जनेषु जह्यसुष्वीन्प्र वृहापृणतः॥११॥

11. Give us not up, showerer (of benefits), to the obstructor (of our rites): relying upon the friendship of you, lord of riches, may we be unharmed: many are the hindrances (opposed) to you amongst men: slay those who make no libations, root out those present no offerings.

४७५९. उद्भ्राणीव स्तनयन्नियर्तीन्द्रो राधांस्यश्व्यानि गव्या।
त्वमसि प्रदिवः कारुधाया मा त्वादामान आ दभन्मघोनः॥१२॥

12. As *Indra*, when thundering raises the clouds, so he (heaps upon his worshippers) riches of horses and cattle: you, *Indra*, are the ancient upholder of the sacrificer: let not the opulent wrong you, not presenting (oblations).

४७६०. अध्वर्यो वीर प्र महे सुतानामिन्द्राय भर स ह्यस्य राजा।
यः पूर्व्याभिरुत नूतनाभिर्गीर्भिर्ववृधे गृणतामृषीणाम्॥१३॥

13. Ministrant priests offer libations to the mighty *Indra*, for he is their king, he who has been exalted by the ancient and recent hymns of adoring sages.

४७६१. अस्य मदे पुरु वर्पांसि विद्वानिन्द्रो वृत्राण्यप्रती जघान।
तमु प्र होषि मधुमन्तमस्मै सोमं वीराय शिप्रिणे पिबध्यै॥१४॥

14. In the exhilaration of this *Soma*, the wise *Indra*, irresistible, has destroyed numerous opposing enemies: offer the sweet-flavoured beverage to that hero, the handsome-chinned, to drink.

४७६२. पाता सुतमिन्द्रो अस्तु सोमं हन्ता वृत्रं वज्रेण मन्दसानः।
गन्ता यज्ञं परावतश्चिदच्छा वसुर्धीनामविता कारुधायाः॥१५॥

15. May *Indra* be the drinker of this effused *Soma* juice, and, exhilarated by it, become the destroyer of *Vṛtra* by the thunderbolt: may he come, although from afar, to our sacrifice, (he who is) the giver of dwellings, the upholder of the celebrator (of religious).

४७६३. इदं त्यत्पात्रमिन्द्रपानमिन्द्रस्य प्रियममृतमपायि।
मत्सद्यथा सौमनसाय देवं व्यर्ंस्मद्द्वेषो युयवद्वधं हः॥१६॥

16. May this ambrosia, the appropriate beverage of *Indra*, of which he is fond, be quaffed (by him), so that it may inspire the divinity with favourable feelings (towards us), and that he may remove from us our adversaries, and (all) iniquity.

४७६४. एना मंन्दानो जहि शूर शत्रूञ्जामिमजामिं मघवन्नमित्रान्।
अभिषेणाँ अभ्याइंदेदिशानान्परांच इन्द्र प्र मृणा जंही चं।।१७।।

17. Exhilarated by it, valiant *Maghavan*, slay our unfriendly adversaries, whether kinsman or unrelated (to us): put to flight, *Indra*, hostile armies menacing us (with their weapons), and slay them.

४७६५. आसु ष्मां णो मघवन्निन्द्र पृत्स्वइं समभ्यं महिं वरिंवः सुगं कं:।
अपां तोकस्य तनयस्य जेष इन्द्रं सूरीन्कंणुहि स्मां नो अर्धम्।।१८।।

18. Affluent *Indra*, facilitate to us (the acquirement of) vast riches in these our battles: (enable us) to gain the victory: make us prosperous with rain, and with sons and grandsons.

४७६६. आ त्वा हर्यो वृषणो युजाना वृषरथासो वृषरश्मयोऽत्यां:।
अस्मत्राञ्ज्ञो वृषणो वज्रवाहो वृष्णे मर्दाय सुयुजों वहन्तु।।१९।।

19. Let your vigorous steeds, harnessed of their own will, drawing your wish-bestowing chariot, guided by shower-yielding reins, quick-moving, hastening towards us, youthful, thunder-bearing, well-yoked, bring you to the bountiful, exhilarating (libation).

४७६७. आ ते वृष्न्वृषणो द्रोणमस्थुर्घृतप्रुषो नोर्मयो मर्दन्तः।
इन्द्र प्र तुभ्यं वृषभिं: सुतानां वृष्णे भरन्ति वृषभाय सोमंम्।।२०।।

20. Showerer (of benefits), your vigorous water-shedding steeds, like the waves (of the sea), exulting, are harnessed to your car; for they, (the priests), offer to you, the showerer (of benefits), ever youthful, the libation of the *Soma* juices expressed by the stones.

४७६८. वृषांसि दिवो वृषभ: पृथिव्या वृषा सिन्धूनां वृषभः स्तियांनाम्।
वृष्णे त इन्दुर्वृषभ पीपाय स्वादू रसों मधुपेयो वरांय।।२१।।

21. You, *Indra*, are the showerer of heaven, the berewer of earth, the feeder of the rivers, the supplier of the aggregated (waters): for you, showerer (of desires), who are the most excellent

shedder of rain, the sweet *Soma*, the honey-flavoured juice, is
ready to be quaffed.

In this and the two preceding stanzas we have the usual abuse of the
derivatives of *Vṛṣa,* to sprinkle, to rain; *Indra's* horses are *vṛṣaṇa*; they
draw a *vṛṣa ratha,* and are guided by *vṛṣarasmayaḥ*: again, the steeds are
vṛṣaṇa, explained, *nityatāruṇṇu,* always young, and *Indra* is *vṛṣan, vṛṣ,*
and *vṛṣabha,* the showerer of rain or of benefits: in most of the instances a
grosser sense is probably implied.

४७६९. अयं देव: सहसा जायमान इन्द्रेण युजा पणिमस्तभायत्।
अयं स्वस्य पितुरायुधानीन्दुरमुष्णादशिवस्य माया:॥२२॥

22. This divine *Soma*, with *Indra* for its ally, crushed, as soon
as generated, *Paṇi* by force: this *Soma* baffled the devices and the
weapons of the malignant secreter of (the stolen) wealth, (the
cattle).

४७७०. अयमकृणोदुषस: सुपत्नीरयं सूर्ये अदधाज्ज्योतिरन्त:।
अयं त्रिधातु दिवि रोचनेषु त्रितेषु विन्ददमृतं निगूळहम्॥२३॥

23. This *Soma* made the dawns happily wedded to the sun: this
Soma placed the light within the solar orb: this (*Soma*) has found
the threefold ambrosia hidden in heaven in the three bright regions.

Ayaṁ tridhātu divi rocaneṣu, triteṣu, triteṣu vindat amṛtam nigūḷham;
according to the Scholiast, this may merely mean that the *Soma* becomes
as it were ambrosia when received or concealed in the vessels at the three
diurnal ceremonies, which ambrosia is properly deposited with the gods
abiding in the third bright sphere, or in heaven.

४७७१. अयं द्यावापृथिवी वि ष्कभायदयं रथमयुनक्सप्तरश्मिम्।
अयं गोषु शच्या पक्वमन्त: सोमो दाधार दर्शयन्त्रमुत्सम्॥२४॥

24. This (*Soma*) has fixed heaven and earth: this has harnessed
the seven-rayed chariot (of the sun): this *soma* has developed of
its own will the mature deeply-organized secretion in the kine.

This has Fixed Heaven, Etc.— These functions are ascribed to the
Soma as being the source of the energies of *Indra*. Who is the real agent,
both in this and the preceding verse, this *Indra* has made the dawns, etc.

Deeply-Organized Secretion— *Daśayantram utsam* is literally a
well with ten machines: here *utsa* is explained by Sāyaṇa, *utsaraṇaśīlam,*
having the property of flowing forth, *payas,* milk: the epithet
daśayantram is of a less precise purport, and is somewhat mystified: in
one sense it implies aggregated bodily existence, or organs and functions
of the body, which are the result of the nutriment furnished to the child by
the matured milk agreeably to a *khila,* or supplementary verse quoted by

the Scholiast: *cakṣuśca śrotram-ca, manaśca, vāk-ca, prāṇāpanau, deha, idam śarīram, dvau prat yañcāvanulomau visargāv-etam tam manye diśayantram utsam*, I consider the eye, the ear, the mind, the speech, the two vital airs, the form, the body, the two creations inverted and direct, as the tenfold *utsa*, or state of being: another explanation makes the phrase imply the *Soma's* being offered with nine texts to *Indra* and other deities at the morning sacrifice: (*Aitareya Brāhmaṇa*, 3,1.

[सूक्त-४५]

[ऋषि– शंयु बार्हस्पत्य। देवता– इन्द्र; ३१- ३३ बृबुतक्षा। छन्द– गायत्री, २९ अतिनिचृत्, ३१ पाद निचृत् (गायत्री), ३३ अनुष्टुप्।]

४७७२. य आनयत्परावतः सुनीती तुर्वशं यदुम्।

इन्द्रः स नो युवा सखा।।१।।

1. May that youthful *Indra*, who, by good guidance, brought *Turvaśa* and *Yadu* from afar, (be) our friend.

४७७३. अविप्रे चिद्वयो दधदनाशुना चिदर्वता। इन्द्रो जेता हितं धनम्।।२।।

2. *Indra* gives sustenance, even to the undevout he is the conqueror of wealth accumulated (by enemies) though (going against) them with a slow-paced steed.

४७७४. महीरस्य प्रणीतयः पूर्वीरुत प्रशस्तयः। नास्य क्षीयन्त ऊतयः।।३।।

3. Vast are his designs, manifold are his praises, his protections are never withdrawn.

४७७५. सखायो ब्रह्मवाहसेऽर्चत प्र च गायत। स हि नः प्रमतिर्मही।।४।।

4. Offer worship and praises, friends, to him who is to be attracted by prayers; for he verily is our great intelligence.

४७७६. त्वमेकस्य वृत्रहन्नविता द्वयोरसि। उतेदृशे यथा वयम्।।५।।

5. Slayer of *Vṛtra*, you are the protector of one (adorer), or of two, and of such as we are.

४७७७. नयसीद्वति द्विषः कृणोष्युक्थशंसिनः। नृभिः सुवीर उच्यसे।।६।।

6. You remove (far from us) those who hate us: you prosper those who repeat your praise: bestower of excellent male descendants, you are glorified by man.

Bestower of Excellent male Descendants— *Suvīra* is here explained *śobhanair vīraiḥ putrapautrādibhir dātavyair-upetaḥ*, endowed with or possessed of sons, grandsons, and the like to be given.

४७७८. ब्रह्माणं ब्रह्मवाहसं गीर्भिः सखायमृग्मियम्। गां न दोहसे हुवे ॥७॥

7. I invoke with hymns *Indra,* our friends, who is *Brahma,*
who is attracted by prayer and entitled to adoration, to milk him as
a cow.

Brahma— *Brahmāṇam,* the Scholiast interprets *Parivṛḍham,* great,
mighty.

४७७९. यस्य विश्वानि हस्तयोरूचुर्वसूनि नि द्विता। वीरस्य पृतनाषहः ॥८॥

8. In the hands of whom, the heroic subduer of hostile armies,
(the sages) have declared, are all the treasures in both (heaven and
earth).

४७८०. वि दृळ्हानि चिद्द्रिवो जनानां शचीपते। वृह माया अनानत ॥९॥

9. Wielder of the thunderbolt, lord of *Śacī,* demolish the strong
(cities) of men: (baffle), unbending (*Indra*) their devices.

४७८१. तमु त्वा सत्य सोमपा इन्द्र वाजानां पते। अहूमहि श्रवस्यवः ॥१०॥

10. Veracious *Indra,* drinker of the *Soma,* provider of
sustenance, we, desirous of food, invoke such as you are.

Such as your Are— *Tam tvā ahūmahi,* we invoke you (who are)
that, or such as has been described in the preceding verses.

४७८२. तमु त्वा यः पुरासिथ यो वा नूनं हिते धने।

हव्यः स श्रुधी हवम् ॥११॥

11. (We invoke) you, such as you are, you who have been
invocable of old, and who are now to be invoked for the wealth
held (by the foe): hear our invocation.

४७८३. धीभिर्वद्द्रिवर्वतो वाजाँ इन्द्र श्रवाय्यान्।

त्वया जेष्म हितं धनम् ॥१२॥

12. (Favoured) by you, *Indra,* (who are propitiated, by our
hymns, (we overcome) with our steeds the steeds (of the enemy),
and we conquer abundant food, and the wealth held (by the foes).

The stanza is literally, with praises, by horses, horses food, excellent
Indra by you, we conquer deposited wealth.

४७८४. अभूरु वीर गिर्वणो महाँ इन्द्र धने हिते। भरे वितन्तसाय्यः ॥१३॥

13. Heroic and adorable *Indra,* verily you are mighty in battle,
and victor of the wealth held (by the enemy).

४७८५. या त ऊतिरमित्रहन्मक्षूज्वस्तमासति। तया नो हिनुही रथम् ॥१४॥

14. Destroyer of enemies with that your velocity, which is of exceeding swiftness, impel our chariots (against the foe).

४७८६. स रथेन रथीतमोऽस्माकेनाभियुग्वना।

जेषि जिष्णो हितं धनम्॥१५॥

15. Victorious *Indra*, who are the chief of charioteers, conquer the wealth that is held (by the enemy) with our assailing car.

४७८७. य एक इत्तमं ष्टुहि कृष्टीनां विचर्षणिः। पतिर्जज्ञे वृषक्रतुः॥१६॥

16. Praise that *Indra* who alone has been born the supervisor (of all), the lord of men, the giver of rain.

४७८८. यो गृणतामिदासिथापिरूती शिवः सखा।

स त्वं न इन्द्र मृळय॥१७॥

17. *Indra*, who has ever been the friend of those who praise you, and the insurer of their happiness by your protection, grant us felicity.

४७८९. धिष्व वज्रं गभस्त्यो रक्षोहत्याय वज्रिवः।

सासहीष्ठा अभि स्पृधः॥१८॥

18. Wielder of the thunderbolt, take the bolt in your hands for the destruction of the *Rākṣasas*, and utterly overthrow those who defy you.

४७९०. प्रतं रयीणां युजं सखायं कीरिचोदनम्। ब्रह्मवाहस्तमं हुवे॥१९॥

19. I invoke the ancient *Indra*, the giver of riches, (our) friend, the encourager of his adorers, who is to be propitiated by prayer.

४७९१. स हि विश्वानि पार्थिवाँ एको वसूनि पत्यते।

गिर्वणस्तमो अध्रिगुः॥२०॥

20. He alone rules over all terrestrial riches, he who is entitled to especial praise, he who is irresistible.

४७९२. स नो नियुद्भिरा पृण कामं वाजेभिरश्विभिः।

गोमद्भिर्गोपते धृषत्॥२१॥

21. Lord of cattle, (coming) with your mares, satisfy our desires completely with (abundant) food, with horses, and with kine.

४७९३. तद्वो गाय सुते सचा पुरुहूताय सत्वने। शं यद्गवे न शाकिने॥२२॥

22. Sing praises, when your libation is poured out, to him who is the invoked of many, the subduer (of foes), giving him gratification, like (fresh pasture) to cattle.

Sāmaveda, 115.

४७९४. न घा॒ वसूनि॒ यंमते॒ दानं॒ वाजस्य गोमंतः। यत्सीमुप॒ श्रवद्गिरः।।२३।।

23. The giver of dwellings verily withholds not the gift of food conjoined with cattle, when he hears our praises.

४७९५. कुवित्संस्य॒ प्र हि॒ व्रजं॒ गोमंतं॒ दस्युहा गमत्।

शची॒भिरप॑ नो वरत्।।२४।।

24. Then the destroyer of the *Dasyus*, proceeds to the cattle-crowded folds of *Kuvitsa*, and by his acts opens them for us.

Sāmaveda,1668: *kuvitsa* is termed merely a certain person who does much (*kuvit*) harm, (*syati*).

४७९६. इमा उ॑ त्वा शतक्रतोऽभि॒ प्र नोनुवुर्गिरः।

इन्द्रं॒ वत्सं॒ न मातरः।।२५।।

25. *Indra*, performer of many exploits, these our praises repeatedly recur to you as parent (cows) to their young.

४७९७. दूणाशं॒ सख्यं॒ तव॒ गौरसि वीर गव्यते। अश्वो॑ अश्वायते भव॑।।२६।।

26. Your friendship, *Indra*, is not easily lost: you, hero are (the giver of) cattle to him who desires cattle (of) horses him who desires horses.

४७९८. स मंदस्वा॒ ह्यन्धसो॒ राधसे तन्वा॑ महे। न स्तो॒तारं॒ निदे॒ करः।।२७।।

27. Delight your person with the (beverage of the) libation (offered) for the sake of great treasure: subject not your worshipper to his reviler.

४७९९. इमा उ॑ त्वा सुते॒सुते॒ नक्षंते गिर्वणो गिरः।

वत्सं॒ गावो॒ न धेनवः।।२८।।

28. These our praises tend, as the libations are repeatedly poured out, eagerly to you who are gratified by praise, as the milch kine (hasten) to their calves.

४८००. पुरूतमं॑ पुरूणां॒ स्तोतॄणां विवाचि। वाजेभिर्वाजयताम्।।२९।।

29. May the praises of many worshippers offered at the sacrifice, (accompanied) by (sacrificial) viands, invigorate you, destroyer of multitudes.

At the Sacrifice— *Vivāci,* at the sacrifice called *Vivac,* because various praises and prayers are then repeated.

४८०१. अस्माकमिन्द्र भूतु ते स्तोमो वाहिष्ठो अन्तमः।
अस्मान्नाये महे हिनु॥३०॥

30. May our most elevating praise be near, *Indra,* to you, and urge us to (the acquirement of) great riches.

Most Elevating Praise— *Stomo vāhiṣṭhaḥ, voḍhṛtama,* most bearing, uplifting, elevating.

४८०२. अधि बृबुः पणीनां वर्षिष्ठे मूर्धन्नस्थात्। उरुः कक्षो न गाङ्ग्यः॥३१॥

31. *Bṛbu* presided over the high places of the *Paṇis,* like the elevated bank of the Ganges.

Bṛbu paṇinām varṣiṣṭhe mūrdhan adhyasthāt, he stood over upon the high place, as if it were on the forehead of the *Paṇis, mūrdhavat ucchrite sthale:* the *Paṇis* May be either merchants or traders, or *Asuras,* so termed: for *Bṛbu* see note on verse 33.

Like the Elevated Bank of the Ganges— *Uruḥ kakṣo na gāṅgyaḥ* is explained by the Scholiast *gaṅgāyāḥ kule vistīrṇe ivā,* as on the broad bank of the Ganges, that is, as the bank is high above the bed of the river.

४८०३. यस्य वायोरिव द्रवद्भद्रा रातिः सहस्रिणी। सद्यो दानाय मंहते॥३२॥

32. Of whom, prompt as the wind, the liberal donation of thousands (of cattle) has been quickly given to (me) soliciting a gift.

४८०४. तत्सु नो विश्वे अर्य आ सदा गृणन्ति कारवः।
बृबुं सहस्रदातमं सूरिं सहस्रसातमम्॥३३॥

33. Whom, therefore, we all, who are the profferers and bestower of praise ever commend, as the pious *Bṛbu,* the donor of thousands (of cattle), the receiver of thousands (of laudations).

This and the two preceding stanzas from a *Trica* in praise of the liberality of a person named *Bṛbu* to *Bharadvāja,* the *Ṛṣi* of the hymn: Sāyaṇa calls him the *Takṣā* the carpenter or artificer of the *Paṇis:* the legend is preserved by *Many,* 10.107, the illustrious *Bharadvāja,* with his son, distressed by hunger in a lonely forest, accepted many cows from the carpenter *Bṛbu:* the *Niti Mañjarī* tells the same story, and attributes the *Tṛca* to *Sayu,* the son of *Bharadvāja:* the moral of the illustration in *Manu* and the *Niti Mañjarī* is, that *Brāhmaṇs,* in times of distress, may accept assistance from persons, of low castes: the object of the *Sūkta,* although it might be so understood, is rather that persons of inferior condition become eminent by liberality: in which sense Sāyaṇa interprets it *jātito hino api dātṛtvāt sarvatra śreṣṭho bhavati,* a person inferior by caste becomes everywhere distinguished by generosity.

[सूक्त-४६]

[**ऋषि**– शंयु बार्हस्पत्य । **देवता**– इन्द्र।

छन्द– बार्हत प्रगाथ- (विषमा बृहती, समासतो बृहती)।]

४८०५. त्वामिद्धि हवामहे साता वाजस्य कारवः।
त्वां वृत्रेष्विन्द्र सत्पतिं नरस्त्वां काष्ठास्वर्वतः ॥१॥

1. We worshippers invoke you for the acquirement of food: you, *Indra*, the protector of the good, (do) men (invoke for aid) against enemies, and in places where horses (encounter).

Where Horses Encounter— *Kāṣṭhāsu arvataḥ*, in the quarters or regions of the horse, where horses are engaged, or, according to Sāyaṇa, the field of battle: Mahīdhara, *Yajurveda*, 27, 37, separates the two words, and explains them, as men invoke you for victory.

४८०६. स त्वं नश्चित्र वज्रहस्त धृष्णुया महः स्तवानो अद्रिवः।
गामश्वं रथ्यमिन्द्र सं किर सत्रा वाजं न जिग्युषे ॥२॥

2. Wonderful wielder of the thunderbolt, *Indra*, the lord of clouds, mighty in resolution, being glorified by us, grant us cattle, and horses fit for chariots, as (you grant) abundant food to him who is victorious (in battle).

The Lord of Clouds— *Adrivas* is, more properly, wielder of the thunderbolt, but we have just had that epithet in *vajrahasta*.

Abundant Food to him who is Victorious—*Satrā vājam na jigyuṣe*: the Scholiast has *satrā, prabhūtam*, abundant: Mahīdhara, *Yajus*, 27, 38, makes it an pleases him also to understand *jigyuṣe*, valorous, not as applicable to a man, *puruṣāya*, but to a horse or elephant, *aśvāya hastine vā*, which is quite gratuitous: see also *Sāmaveda*, 810.

४८०७. यः सत्राहा विचर्षणिरिन्द्रं तं हूमहे वयम्।
सहस्रमुष्क तुविनृम्ण सत्पते भवा समत्सु नो वृधे ॥३॥

3. We invoke that *Indra* who is the destroyer of mighty foes, the supervisor (of all things): do you, the many organed, the protector of the good, the distributor of wealth, be unto us (the insurer of) success in combats.

Sāmaveda, 286: this is said to be the first verse of *Prayātha*.

४८०८. बाधसे जनान् वृषभेव मन्युना घृषौ मीळह ऋचीषम।
अस्माकं बोध्यविता महाधने तनूष्वप्सु सूर्ये ॥४॥

4. Such, *Indra*, as you are represented in holy texts, assail (our) adversaries with fierceness like (that of) a bull in close conflict:

regard yourself as our defender in war, (that we may long enjoy) posterity, water, and the sight of the) sun.

Represented in Holy Texts— *Ṛcīṣama* is explained by Sāyaṇa *rgyādṛśam rūpaṁ pratipādayati tādṛg-rūpendraḥ*: such form as the *Ṛc* exhibits, such in form is *Indra*.

Posterity water and Sun— The text only *tanuṣu apsu, sūrye,* in descendants, in waters, in the sun, but they may be connected with what precedes, *asmākaṁ bodhi avitā mahādhane,* know yourself to be our protector in battle, in descendants, etc., that is in securing to us these good things and long life.

४८०९. इन्द्र ज्येष्ठं न आ भरँ ओजिष्ठं पपुरि श्रवः।

येनेमे चित्र वज्रहस्त रोदसी ओभे सुशिप्र प्राः ॥५॥

5. *Indra*, bring to us most excellent, most invigorating and nutritious food, wherewith, wonderful wielder of the thunderbolt, the handsome-chinned, you sustain both heaven and earth.

४८१०. त्वामुग्रमवसे चर्षणीसहं राजन्देवेषु हूमहे।

विश्वा सु नो विथुरा पिंब्दना वसोऽमित्रान्त्सुषहान्कृधि ॥६॥

6. We invoke for protection you, royal *Indra*, who are mighty among the gods, the subduer of men; granter of dwellings, repel all evil spirits, and render our enemies easy of discomfiture.

४८११. यदिन्द्र नाहुषीष्वाँ ओजो नृम्णं च कृष्टिषु।

यद्वा पञ्च क्षितीनां द्युम्नमा भर सत्रा विश्वानि पौस्या ॥७॥

7. Whatever strength and opulence (exist) amongst human beings, whatever be the sustenance of the five classes of men, bring *Indra* to us, as well (as) all great manly energies.

४८१२. यद्वा तृक्षौ मघवन् द्रुह्यावा जने यत्पूरौ कच्च वृष्ण्यम्।

अस्मभ्यं तद्रिरीहि सं नृषाह्येऽमित्रान्पृत्सु तुर्वणे ॥८॥

8. Whatever vigour, *Maghavan*, (existed) in *Tṛkṣu*, in *Druhyu*, in *Puru*, bestow fully upon us in conflicts with foes, so that we may destroy our enemies in war.

४८१३. इन्द्र त्रिधातु शरणं त्रिवरूथं स्वस्तिमत्।

छर्दिर्यच्छ मघवंद्वयश्च महां च यावयां दिद्युमेभ्यः ॥९॥

9. Give, *Indra*, to the affluent, and to me also, a sheltering and prosperous dwelling combining three elements, and defending in three ways and keep from them the blazing (weapon of our foes).

४८१४. ये गॅव्यॅता मॅनसा॒ शॅत्रुमॅदाभुरॅभिप्रॅघ्नन्तिॅ धृष्णुॅया।
अधॅ स्मा नो मघवन्निन्द्र गिर्वणस्तॅनूपा अॅन्तॅमो भव॥१०॥

10. Affluent *Indra*, propitiated by praise, be nigh to us, as the
defender of our persons (against those) who assail (us as) enemies,
with a mind bent upon carrying off (our) cattle, or who assault us
with arrogance.

४८१५. अधॅ स्मा नो वॅधे भॅवेन्द्र॒ नायॅमॅवा युधि।
यॅदॅन्तॅरिॅक्षे पॅतयॅन्ति पॅर्णिनो॒ दिॅद्यॅवॅस्तिॅग्ममूॅर्धानॅ:॥११॥

11. *Indra*, be (favourable) at present to our success: protect our
leader in battle when the feathered, sharp-pointed, shining shafts
fall from the sky.

४८१६. यॅत्रॅ शूॅरासॅस्तॅन्वो॒ वितॅन्वॅते प्रियाॅ शॅर्मॅ पितृॅणाम्।
अधॅ स्मा यॅच्छ तॅन्वे॒इॅ तॅने॒ च छॅदिॅरॅचिॅत्तॅ यावॅय द्वेॅषॅ:॥१२॥

12. When heroes rest their persons (until abandoning) the
pleasant abodes of their progenitors: grant us, for ourselves and
our posterity, an unsuspected defence, and scatter our enemies.

The Pleasant Abode of their Progenitors— *Priyā śarma pitṛṇām* is
explained *priyāṇi sthānāni janakānām sambandhinī*, the beloved places in
relation with progenitors, but the want of a verb makes the sense doubtful:
the Scholiast extends to it the government of *vitanvate, tanvo vitanvate*,
they spread out or rest their persons; or they spread out, he says, before
the enemy the sites won by their forefathers until they abandon them,
parityajanti yāvat: perhaps it should be, until they, the enemy, desist from
the attack.

An Unsuspected Defence— *Chardiracittam* the commentator
renders *kavacaṁ śatrubhir ajñātam* armour unknown by the enemies; the
connexion of the sense runs through the two following verses: the
unknown armours is solicited when a charge of horse takes place: it may
possibly allude to the superiority of the arms of the *Āryas*, the mail worn
by them being unknown to the *Dasyus*, or barbarians, like the steel
helmets or caresses of the Spaniards to the Mexicans and Peruvians.

४८१७. यॅदिॅन्द्र सॅर्गे अॅर्वॅतॅश्चोॅदयाॅसे महाधॅने।
असॅमने अॅध्वॅनि वृॅजिॅने पॅथि श्येॅना॒ इॅव श्रॅवस्यॅतॅ:॥१३॥

13. (At the time) when, in the effort (made) in an arduous
conflict, you urge our horses over an uneven road, like falcons
darting upon their food through the difficult path (of the
firmament).

४८१८. सिन्धूँरिव प्रवण आ॑शुया य॒तो यदि॑ क्लोशमनु॒ ष्वणिं॑।

आ ये वयो॑ न व॑र्वृ॒तत्यामि॑षि गृभी॒ता बा॒ह्वोर्गविं॑॥६४॥

14. Rushing rapidly like rivers in their downward course and although reiging loudly through terror, they yet, tight-girthed, return repeatedly (to the conflict) for cattle, like birds darting on their prey.

[सूक्त-४७]

[**ऋषि**– गर्ग भारद्वाज, **देवता**– इन्द्र, १-५, सोम, २० देवभूमि, बृहस्पति-इन्द्र, २२-२५ सांर्ज्य प्रस्तोक (दान स्तुति) २६-२८ रथ, २९-३० दुंदुभि, ३१ दुंदुभि तथा इन्द्र। **छन्द**– त्रिष्टुप् १४ - बृहती, २३ अनुष्टुप्,२४ गायत्री, २५ द्विपदा त्रिष्टुप्, २७ जगती।]

४८१९. स्वादुष्किला॒यं मधु॑माँ उता॒यं ती॒व्रः किला॒यं रस॑वाँ उता॒यम्।

उ॒तो न्व॑स्य प॑पिवांसमिन्द्रं॒ न कश्च॒न स॒हत आह॑वेषु॥१॥

1. Savoury indeed is this (*Soma*); sweet is it, sharp, and full of flavour: no one is able to encounter *Indra* in battles after he has been quaffing this (beverage).

४८२०. अ॒यं स्वादुरि॒ह मदि॑ष्ठ आस॒ यस्येन्द्रो॑ वृ॒त्रह॒त्ये म॒माद॑।

पु॒रूणि॒ यश्च्यौ॒त्ना शम्ब॑रस्य॒ वि न॑व॒तिं नव॑ च दे॒ह्यो३॒ हन्॑॥२॥

2. This savoury *Soma*, drunk on this occasion, has been most exhilarating: by drinking of it *Indra* has been elevated to the slaying of *Vṛtra*, and it has destroyed the numerous hosts of *Śambara* and the ninetynine cities.

Ninety-nine Cities— *Dehyaḥ* is the term in the text for *dehiḥ*, explained by Sāyaṇa, *digdhaḥ,* the smeared or plastered, implying *puriḥ,* cities; as if they consisted of stuccoed or plastered houses: the ninety-nine cities of *Śambara* have frequently occured: see Vol. II. verses 2199 etc.

४८२१. अ॒यं मे॑ पी॒त उदि॑यर्ति॒ वाच॒मयं म॑नी॒षामु॒शती॑मजीग॒ः।

अ॒यं ष॒ळु॒र्वीर॑मिमीत॒ धीरो॒ न याभ्यो॒ भुव॑नं॒ कच्च॒नारे॑॥३॥

3. This beverage inspires my speech; this develops the desired intelligence: this sagacious (*Soma*) has created the six vast conditions, from which no creature is distinct.

Six Vast Conditions— They are said to be heaven earth, day, night, water, and plants.

४८२२. अयं॒ स यो व॒रिमाणं॑ पृथिव्या॒ वर्ष्माणं॑ दि॒वो अकृ॑णोद॒यं सः॑।
अ॒यं पी॒यूषं॑ ति॒सृषु॒ प्रव॑त्सु सो॒मो दा॑धारो॒र्वन्तरि॑क्षम्।।४।।

4. This it is which formed the expanse of the earth, the
compactness of the heaven: this *Soma* has deposited the ambrosia
in its three principal (receptacles), and has upheld the spacious
firmament.

Three Principal Receptacles— In plant, water, and cows.

Has Upheld the Spacious firmament— See *Ṛg*: i, 91. 22[1] here, as in
that *Sūkta*, there is an obviously designed confusion between the *Soma*
plant, and *Soma* the moon.

४८२३. अ॒यं विं॑द॒च्चित्र॒दृशी॑क॒मर्णः॒ शुक्रसद्म॑नामु॒षसा॑मनी॒के।
अ॒यं म॒हान्म॑ह॒ता स्क॒म्भने॒नोद् द्यामस्त॑भ्नाद् वृष॒भो म॒रुत्वा॑न्।।५।।

5. This makes known the wonderfully beautiful and inspiring
(solar radiance) at the appearance of the dawns, whose dwelling is
the firmament: this mighty (*Soma*) has sustained the heaven with a
powerful support, the sender of rain, the leader of the winds.

४८२४. धृ॒षत्पि॑ब॒ कल॑शे॒ सोम॑मिन्द्र वृत्र॒हा शूर॑ स॒मरे॒ वसू॑नाम्।
मा॒ध्यन्दि॑ने॒ सव॑न॒ आ वृ॑षस्व रयि॒स्थानो॑ र॒यिम॒स्मासु॑ धेहि।।६।।

6. Hero, *Indra*, who are the slayer of foes in contests for (the
acquirement of) treasures, drink boldly from the pitcher: drink
copiously at the noonday rite: receptacle of riches, bestow riches
upon us.

४८२५. इन्द्र॒ प्र णः॑ पुरए॒तेव॑ पश्य॒ प्र नो॑ नय प्रत॒रं वस्यो॒ अच्छ॑।
भवा॑ सु॒पारो॑ अति॒पार॑यो नो॒ भवा॑ सुनी॒तिरु॒त वा॑मनी॒तिः।।७।।

7. Like one who goes before us, *Indra*, (on the road), look out,
bring before us infinite wealth; be our conductor beyond the
bounds (of want), convey us safely over (peril); be our careful
guide, our guide to desirable (affluence).

Look Out— *Pra ṇaḥ pura eteva paśya*, like one who is preceding us,
look: the Scholiast says, look after the travellers under the charge of the
mārgarakṣaka, the protector of the road, an escort, or, possibly, the leader
of a *kāfilā*, may be intended.

---

1. त्वमिमा ओषधी: सोम विश्वास्त्वामपो अजनयस्त्वं गाः। त्वमा ततन्थोर्वन्तरिक्षम् (ऋ० सं०
1.91.22)।

४८२६. उरुं नों लोकमनुं नेषि विद्वान्त्स्वर्वज्ज्योतिरभयं स्वस्ति।

ऋष्वा तं इन्द्र स्थविरस्य बाहू उपं स्थेयाम शरणा बृहन्ता।।८।।

8. Do you, *Indra*, who are wise, conduct us to the spacious world (of heaven), to a blessed state of happiness, light, and safety: may we recline in the graceful, protecting, and mighty arms of you the ancient one.

४८२७. वरिष्ठे न इन्द्र वन्धुरें धा वहिष्ठयो: शतावन्नश्वयोरा।

इषमा वक्षीषां वर्षिष्ठां मा नंस्तारीन्मघवन्रायों अर्य:।।९।।

9. Place us, possessor of riches, in your ample chariot, (behind) your powerful horses: bring to us from among all viands the most excellent food: let not, *Maghavan*, any opulent man surpass us in wealth.

४८२८. इन्द्र मृळ महां जीवातुमिच्छ चोदयं धियमयसो न धारां।

यत्किञ्चाहं त्वायुरिदं वदांमि तज्जुषस्व कृधि मां देववन्तम्।।१०।।

10. Make me happy, *Indra*; be pleased to prolong my life: sharpen my intellect like the edge of an iron sword: whatsoever, desirous (of propitiating) you, I may utter, be pleased by it: render me the object of divine protection.

४८२९. त्रातारमिन्द्रमवितारमिन्द्रं हवेहवे सुहवं शूरमिन्द्रम्।

ह्वयामि शक्रं पुरुहूतमिन्द्रं स्वस्ति नों मघवां धात्विन्द्र:।।११।।

11. I invoke, at repeated sacrifice, *Indra*, the preserver, the protector, the hero, who is easily propitiated, *Indra*, the powerful, the invoked of many: may *Indra*, the lord of affluence, bestow upon us prosperity.

Sāmaveda, 333; *Yajurveda*, 20.50.

४८३०. इन्द्र: सुत्रामा स्ववाँ अवोंभि: सुमृळीको भंवतु विश्ववेदा:।

बाधतां द्वेषो अभयं कृणोतु सुवीर्यस्य पतंय: स्याम।।१२।।

12. May the protecting, opulent *Indra* be the bestower of felicity by his protections: may he, who is all-knower of felicity by his protections: may he, who is all-knowing, foil our adversaries: may he keep us out of danger, and may we be the possessors of excellent posterity.

४८३१. तस्यं वयं सुमतौ यज्ञियस्यापि भद्रे सौमनसे स्यांम।

स सुत्रामा स्ववाँ इन्द्रो अस्मे आराच्चिद् द्वेष: सनुतर्युयोतु।।१३।।

13. May we continue in the favour of that adorable (deity) even in his auspicious good-will: may that protecting and opulent *Indra* drive far from us, into extinction, all those who hate us. See *Yajurveda*, 20. 52.

४८३२. अव॒ त्वे इन्द्र॒ प्रव॒तो नोर्मिर्गिरो॑ ब्रह्मा॑णि नियु॒तो॑ धवन्ते।
उ॒रू न रा॒धः सर्व॑ना पुरू॒ण्यपो॑ गा॒ वज्रि॒न्युव॑से समि॒न्दून्॑।।१४।।

14. To you the praises and prayers of the worshipper hasten like a torrent down a declivity; and you thunderer, aggregate the immense wealth (of sacrificial offerings), copious libations, and milk, and the juices of the *Soma*.

Apo gāḥ yuvase samindūn: the first is explained *vasatīvarī* which is said by Kātyāyana, *Sūtra*, 8,9,7-10, to be portions of water taken from a running stream on the evening previous to the ceremony, and kept in jars in different parts of the sacrificial chamber, to be mixed with the *Soma*: see *Yajurveda*, 6.23, and the *Taittirīya Yajuṣ, Prapāṭhaka* III. *Anuvāka* XII.

४८३३. क ई॒ स्तव॒त्कः पृ॒णात्को॒ यजा॑ते॒ यदु॒ग्रमिन्म॒घवा॑ विश्वहा॒वेत्।
पादा॑विव॒ प्रह॒रन्न॒न्य॒मन्यं॑ कृ॒णोति॑ पूर्व॒मप॑रं॒ शची॑भिः।।१५।।

15. Who may (adequately) praise him? Who may satisfy him? Who offer worthy adoration? Since *Maghavan* is daily conscious of his own terrible (power): by his acts he makes first one and then the other precede and follow, as (a man) throws out his feet (alternately in walking).

Makes first one and then, Etc.— That is, *Indra*, at his pleasure, makes the first of his worshippers the last, and the last the first.

४८३४. शृ॒ण्वे वी॒र उ॒ग्रमु॑ग्रं॒ दमा॑यन्न॒न्य॒मन्य॑मतिने॒नीय॑मानः।
ए॒धमा॑नद् वि॒ळुभ॑यस्य रा॒जा चो॒ष्कू॒यते॒ विश॒ इन्द्रो॑ मनु॒ष्यान्॑।।१६।।

16. The hero *Indra* is renowned; humiliating every formidable (foe), and repeatedly changing the place of one (worshipper) with that of another; *Indra*, the enemy of the arrogant, the sovereign of both (heaven and earth), calls again and again (to encourage) the men who are his worshippers.

४८३५. परा॒ पूर्वे॑षां स॒ख्या वृ॑णक्ति वित॒र्तुराणो॒ अप॑रेभि॒रेति।
अना॑नुभू॒तिर॑वधून्वा॒नः पू॒र्वीरिन्द्रः॒ शर॒दस्त॑र्तरीति।।१७।।

17. *Indra* rejects the friendship of those who are foremost (in pious acts), and, despoiling them, associates with (their) inferiors:

or (again) shaking off those who neglect his worship, *Indra* abides many years with those who serve him.

४८३६. रूपंरूपं प्रतिरूपो बभूव तदस्य रूपं प्रतिचक्षणाय।

इन्द्रो मायाभिः पुरुरूपं ईयते युक्ता ह्यस्य हरयः शता दशा।।१८।।

18. *Indra*, the prototype, has assumed various forms, and such is his form as that which (he adopts) for his manifestation: *Indra*, multiform by his illusions, proceeds (to his many worshippers), for the horses, yoked to his car are a thousand.

Indra has Assumed Various Forms— *Indra* presents himself as *Agni, Viṣṇu,* or *Rudra,* or any other deity who is the actual object of worship, and is really the deity to be adored: he is identifiable with each.

Horses Yoked to his Car are a thousand— His chariots and horses are multiplied according to the forms in which he manifests himself: agreeably to the *Vaidāntika* interpretation of the stanza, *Indra* is here identified with *Parameśvara,* the supreme first cause, identical with creation.

४८३७. युज्जानो हरिता रथे भूरि त्वष्टेह राजति।

को विश्वाहा द्विषतः पक्षं आसत उतासीनेषु सूरिषु।।१९।।

19. Yoking his horses to his car, *Tvaṣṭā* shines in many places here in the three worlds: who (else), so-journing daily amongst his present worshippers, is their protector against adversaries?

Sāyaṇa regards this name as, in this place, an appellative of *Indra.*

४८३८. अगव्यूति क्षेत्रमार्गन्म देवा उर्वी सती भूमिरंहूरणाभूत्।

बृहस्पते प्र चिकित्सा गविष्टावित्था सते जरित्र इन्द्र पन्थाम्।।२०।।

20. We have wandered, gods, into a desert where there is no track of cattle: the vast extant earth has become the protectress of murderers: direct us, *Bṛhaspati,* in our search for cattle: shew the path, *Indra,* to your votary being they astray.

Garga, the author of the *Sūkta,* having, it is said, lost his way in a desert, repeated this stanza to *Bṛhaspati* and *Indra,* who thereupon enabled him to regain his road.

No Track of Cattle— *Agavyūti kṣetram, gosañcararahitaṁ deśam,* a place devoid of the grazing of cattle.

४८३९. दिवेदिवे सदृशीरन्यमर्धं कृष्णा असेधदप सध्नो जाः।

अहन्दासा वृषभो वस्नयन्तोदव्रजे वर्चिनं शम्बरं च।।२१।।

21. *Indra,* becoming manifest from his abode (in the firmament), dissipates, day by day, the resembling glooms, (so that

he may distinguish) the other portion, (or the day); and the showerer has slain the two wealth-seeking slaves, *Varcin* and *Śambara*, in (the country of) *Udavraja*.

The Country of Udavraja— So Sāyaṇa explains *Udavraja, deśa-viśeṣaḥ*, a sort of country, one into which the waters flow, *udakāni vrajantyasmin*.

४८४०. प्रस्तोक इन्नु राधसस्त इन्द्र दश कोश्यीर्दिर्शं वाजिनोऽदात्।
दिवोदासादतिथिग्वस्य राधः शाम्बरं वसु प्रत्यग्रभीष्म॥२२॥

22. *Prastoka* has given to your worshipper, *Indra*, ten purses of gold, and ten horses, and we have accepted this treasure from *Divodās*, the spoil won by *Atithigva* from *Śambara*.

Ten Purses of Gold— *Daśa kośaiḥ, suvarṇa-pūrṇan daśakośān*, the ten bags or chests full of gold.

Atithigva— *Prastoka, Divodāsa,* and *Atithigva*, are different names of the same person, a *Rājā*, the son of *Sṛñjaya*.

४८४१. दशाश्वान्दश कोशान्दश वस्त्राधिभोजना।
दशो हिरण्यपिण्डान्दिवोदासादसानिषम्॥२३॥

23. I have received ten horses, ten purses, clothes, and ample food, and ten lumps of gold from *Divodāsa*.

४८४२. दश रथान्प्रष्टिमतः शतं गा अथर्वभ्यः। अश्वथः पायवेऽदात्॥२४॥

24. *Aśvattha* has given to *Pāyu* ten chariots with their horses, and a hundred cows to the priests.

To the Priests— *Atharvabhyaḥ* is the term in the text which Sāyaṇa explains, to the *Ṛṣis* of the *Atharvagotra: Pāyu* is the brother of *Garga; Aśvattha* is the same as *Prastoka*.

४८४३. महि राधो विश्वजन्यं दधानान् भरद्वाजान्त्साञ्जयो अभ्ययष्ट॥२५॥

25. The son of *Sṛñjaya* has reverenced the *Bharadvājas* who have accepted such great wealth for the good of all men.

४८४४. वनस्पते वीड्वङ्गो हि भूया अस्मत्संखा प्रतरणः सुवीरः।
गोभिः सन्नद्धो असि वीळयस्वास्थाता ते जयतु जेत्वानि॥२६॥

26. (Chariot made of the) forest lord, be strong of fabric; be our friend; be our protector, and be manned by warriors; you are girt with cow-hides: keep us steady; and may he who rides in you be victorious over conquered (foes).

Be Manned by Warriors— *Suvīro bhava*, Sāyaṇa explain *śūrabhaṭṭ aiḥ putrādibhir vā yuktaḥ*, joined with warriors, or with sons and the rest:

the latter could scarcely be predicated of a car, except as the source, figuratively speaking, of prosperity, and so far of descendants.

You are Girt with Cow-Hides— *Gobhiḥ sannaddhosi*; literally, you are bound together by cow: but both Sāyaṇa and Mahīdhara, *Yajurveda*, 29, 52, explain this *govikāraiḥ*, by what are formed from cattle: so, in the next verse, *gobhirāvṛtam* is interpreted *carmabhiḥ parita aveṣṭitam*, encompassed round with hides, as if the exterior of the war-chariot especially were so strengthened: Mahīdhara gives us an alternative, encompassed with rays of light, or with splendours, *gobhiḥ, tejobhiḥ*.

४८४५. दिवस्पृथिव्याः पर्योज उद्धृतं वनस्पतिभ्यः पर्याभृतं सहः।
अपामोज्मानं परि गोभिरावृतमिन्द्रस्य वज्रं हविषा रथं यज ॥२७॥

27. Worship with oblations the chariot constructed of the substance of heaven and earth, the extracted essence of the forest lords; the velocity of the waters; the encompassed with the cow-hide; the thunderbolt (of *Indra*).

४८४६. इन्द्रस्य वज्रो मरुतामनीकं मित्रस्य गर्भो वरुणस्य नाभिः।
सेमां नो हव्यदातिं जुषाणो देव रथ प्रति हव्या गृभाय ॥२८॥

28. Do you, divine chariot, who are the thunderbolt of *Indra*, the precursor of the *Maruts*, the embryo of *Mitra*, the navel of *Varuṇa*, propitiated by this our sacrifice, accept the oblation.

The Precursor of Maruts, Etc.— *Marutām anikam, Mitrasya garbho, Varuṇasya nābhiḥ: anīkam* the Scholiast interprets *agrabhūtam*, being before, out-stripping in speed; Mahīdhara explains it *mukhyam*, principal or leader; the *garbha* of *Mitra*-Sāyaṇa endeavours to make sense of, by saying, the car is to be considered as contained by *Mitra,* the ruler of the day, as moving by day, whilst by the *nābhi* of *Varuṇa* it is intimated to be a fixed point or centre for the deity ruling over the night, when the car of *Indra* or *Sūrya* stands still: Mahīdhara derives *garbha* from *gṛ*, to praise, and considers *mitrasya garbha* equivalent to *sūryeṇa stūyamāna*, to be praised by the sun: *nābhi* he derives from *nābh*, to injure, and translates it, the weapon of *Varuṇa*: both Scholiasts labour superfluously to attach meaning to what was never intended to have any.

४८४७. उप श्रासय पृथिवीमुत द्यां पुरुत्रा ते मनुतां विष्ठितं जगत्।
स दुन्दुभे सजूरिन्द्रेण देवैर्दूराद्दवीयो अप सेध शत्रून् ॥२९॥

29. War-drum, fill with your sound both heaven and earth; and let all things, fixed or moveable, be aware of it: do you, who are associated with *Indra* and the gods, drive away our foes to the remotest distance.

४८४८. आ क्रन्दय बलमोजो न आ धा निः ष्टनिहि दुरिता बाधमानः।
अप प्रोथ दुन्दुभे दुच्छुना इत इन्द्रस्य मुष्टिरसि वीळयस्व॥३०॥

30. Sound loud against the (hostile) host: animate our prowess: thunder aloud, terrifying the evil-minded: rapid, drum, those whose delight it is to harm us: you are the fist of *Indra*: inspire us with fierceness.

४८४९. आमूरज प्रत्यावर्तयेमाः केतुमद् दुन्दुभिर्वावदीति।
समश्वपर्णाश्चरन्ति नो नरोऽस्माकमिन्द्र रथिनो जयन्तु॥३१॥

31. Recover these our cattle, *Indra*: bring them back: the drum sounds repeatedly as a signal: our leaders, mounted on their steeds, assemble: may our warriors, riding in their cars, *Indra*, be victorious.

This and the two preceding verses occur in the *Yajus*, 29, 55-57.

[सूक्त-४८]

[**ऋषि**– शंयु बार्हस्पत्य, **देवता**– १-१० अग्नि, ११-१५, मरुद्गण अथवा (१३-१५ लिङ्गोक्त देवता, १६-१९ पूषा देवता) २२ पृश्नि, द्यावाभूमि अथवा मरुद्गण। **छन्द**– प्रगाथ १, ३, ५, ९, १४, १९, २० बृहती; २, ४, १०, १२, १७ सतोबृहती; ६, ८, महासतो बृहती; ७, २१ महाबृहती ११, १६, ककुप्, १३,१८ पुरउष्णिक १५ अतिजगती, २२ अनुष्टुप्।]

४८५०. यज्ञायज्ञा वो अग्नये गिरागिरा च दक्षसे।
प्र प्र वयममृतं जातवेदसं प्रियं मित्रं न शंसिषम्॥१॥

1. At every sacrifice (honour) the mighty *Agni* with your reiterated praise, whilst we glorify him, the immortal, who knows all things, our dear friend.

Sāmaveda, 35, 703.

४८५१. ऊर्जो नपातं स हिनायमस्मयुदर्शिम हव्यदातये।
भुवद् वाजेष्वविता भुवद्वृध उत त्राता तनूनाम्॥२॥

2. The son of strength, for he verily is propitious to us, to whom let us offer oblations as to the conveyer of them (to the gods): may he be our defender in battles: may he be our benefactor and the grandsire of our offspring.

४८५२. वृषा ह्यग्ने अजरो महान्विभास्यर्चिषा।
अजस्रेण शोचिषा शोशुचच्छुचे सुदीतिभिः सु दीदिहि॥३॥

3 *Agni*, who are the showerer (of benefits), mighty, and exempt from decay, you shine with (great) splendour; you are resplendent, brilliant (*Agni*), with unfading lustre: shine forth with glorious rays.

४८५३. महो देवान्यजसि यक्ष्यानुषक्त्व क्रत्वोत दंसना।
अर्वाचं: सीं कृणुह्यग्नेऽवसे रास्व वाजोत वंस्व॥४॥

4. You sacrifice to the mighty gods: sacrifice (for us) continually, for (sacrifice is perfected) by your wisdom and your acts: bring them down, *Agni*, for our salvation: present (to them) the sacrificial food, partake of it yourself.

४८५४. यमापो अद्रयो वना गर्भमृतस्य पिप्रति।
सहसा यो मथितो जायते नृभि: पृथिव्या अधि सानवि॥५॥

5. (You are he) whom the waters, the mountains, the woods, nourish as the embryo of sacrifice; who, churned with strength by the performers (of the rite), are generated in the highest place of the earth.

Whom the waters, the Mountains, Etc.— *Yam āpo, adrayo vanā piprati*, may bear the more humble meanings of the water prepared to mix with the *Soma*, the *vasatīvarī*, the stones for grinding the *Soma*, and the wood for attrition.

४८५५. आ य: पप्रौ भानुना रोदसी उभे धूमेन धावते दिवि। तिरस्तमों
ददृश ऊर्म्यास्वा श्यावास्वरुषो वृषा श्यावा अरुषो वृषा॥६॥

6. He who fills both heaven and earth with light, who mounts with smoke into the sky, this radiant showerer (of benefits) is beheld in the dark nights dispersing the gloom: this radiant showerer (of benefits) presides over the dark nights.

४८५६. बृहद्भिरग्ने अर्चिभि: शुक्रेण देव शोचिषा। भरद्वाजे समिधानो
यरिछ्य रेवत्र: शुक्र दीदिहि द्युमत्पावक दीदिहि॥७॥

7. Divine, resplendent *Agni*, youngest (of the gods), when kindled by *Bharadvāja*, shines with many flames, with pure lustre, (conferring) riches upon us; shine, resplendent purifier.

४८५७. विश्वासां गृहपतिर्विशामसि त्वमग्ने मानुषीणाम्। शतं पूर्भिर्यविष्ठ
पाह्यंहस: समेद्धारं शतं हिमा: स्तोतृभ्यो ये च ददति॥८॥

8. You, *Agni*, are the lord of the dwelling, and of all men the descendants of *Manu*: protect me, youngest (of the gods), when

kindling you, with a hundred defences against iniquity: (grant me) a hundred winters, (as well as to those) who bestow gifts upon your worshippers.

The Lord of the Dwelling— *Gṛhapati*, master or protector of the house.

४८५८. त्वं नश्चित्र ऊत्या वसो राधांसि चोदय।

अस्य रायस्त्वमग्ने रथीरसि विदा गाधं तुचे तु नः॥९॥

9. Wonderful (*Agni*), giver of dwellings, encourage us by (your) protection, and (the gift of) riches, for you are the conveyer, *Agni*, of this wealth: quickly bestow permanence upon our progeny.

Sāmaveda, 41, 1623.

४८५९. पर्षि तोकं तनयं पर्तृभिष्ट्वमदब्धैरप्रयुत्वभिः।

अग्ने हेळांसि दैव्या युयोधि नोऽदेवानि ह्वरांसि च॥१०॥

10. You protect with uninjurable, irremovable defences (our) sons and grandsons: remove far from us celestial wrath and human malevolence.

Sāmaveda, 1624.

४८६०. आ संखायः सबर्दुघां धेनुमजध्वमुप नव्यसा वचः।

सृजध्वमनपस्फुराम्॥११॥

11. Approach, friends the milk-yielding cow with a new song, and let her loose unharmed.

The Milk-Yielding Cow— The milch cow, *dhenu*, is here introduced because this is the first of a series of stanzas of which the *Maruts* are the deities, either with reference to the milk which is their appropriate offering at sacrifices, or to *Pṛśni*, the mythological mother of the *Maruts*, in the form of a cow.

४८६१. या शर्धाय मारुताय स्वभानवे श्रवोऽमृत्यु धुक्षत।

या मृळीके मरुतां तुराणां या सुमैरेवयावरी॥१२॥

12. She who yields immortal food to the powerful, self-irradiating band of the *Maruts*, who (is anxious) for the gratification of the self-moving *Maruts*, who traverses the sky with (the passing waters), shedding delight.

Who Traverses the Sky . . . . Shedding Delight— The text has only *sumnair-evayāvarī*: the first is explained by the Scholiast, being with the means of the happiness, *sukhahetubhūaiḥ*, the substantive being implied in the compound attributive of *dhenu*, or *evayāvarī*, from *eva*, who or what goes, as a horse, or the water of mad-air, the rain, and *yāvarī*, she who goes with, *saha yāti ya,* that is, who proceeds with rains, giving pleasure to others, *anyeṣām sukhārtham vṛṣṭijālaiḥ saha gacchanti.*

४८६२. भरद्वाजायाव॒र्वं धु॒क्षत द्वि॒ता।

धे॒नुं च॑ वि॒श्वदो॑ह॒समि॒षं च॑ वि॒श्वभो॑जसम्॥१३॥

13. Milk for *Bharadvāja* the twofold (blessing), the cow that gives milk to the universe, food that is sufficient for all.

४८६३. तं व॑ इन्द्रं॒ न सु॒क्रतुं॒ वरुणमिव मा॒यिन॑म्।

अ॒र्य॒मणं॒ न म॒न्द्रं सु॒प्रभो॑ज॒सं विष्णुं॒ न स्तुष॒ आदि॒शे॥१४॥

14. I praise you, the (company of *Maruts*), for the distribution of wealth: (the company that), like *Indra*, is the achiever of great deeds; sagacious like *Varuṇa*; adorable as *Aryaman*, and munificent as *Viṣṇu*.

४८६४. त्वे॒षं शर्धो॒ न मारुतं॑ तु॒विष्व॒ण्यन॑र्वाणं॒ पू॒षणं॒ सं यथा॒ शता॑। सं स॒हस्रा॑ का॒रिष॑च्चर्ष॒णिभ्य॒ आँ आ॑विर्गू॒ळ्हा वसू॑ करत्सु॒वेद॒ नो॒ वसू॑ करत्॥१५॥

15. I now (glorify) the brilliant vigour of the company of the *Maruts*, loud-sounding, irresistible, cherishing, whereby hundreds and thousands (of treasures) are bestowed collectively upon men; may that (company) make hidden wealth manifest; may it render the wealth easily accessible to us.

४८६५. आ मा॑ पूष॒न्नुप॑ द्रव॒ शंसि॑षं॒ नु ते॑ अपिक॒र्ण आ॑घृणे।

अ॒घा अ॒र्यो अरा॑तयः॥१६॥

16. Hasten, *Pūṣan*, to me: (repel), bright deity, (all) deadly assailing foes: close at your side I repeat your praise.

Close at your-side I repeat your Praise— *Saṁśiṣam nu te karṇa,* literally, I celebrate your praise quickly at your ear.

४८६६. मा कां॒क॒म्बीरमुद्वृ॑हो॒ वनस्पति॒मशस्ती॒र्वि हि नी॑नश॑ः।

मोत सूरो॒ अ॒ह॒ एवा॒ च॒न ग्री॒वा आद॑ध॒ते वे॑ः॥१७॥

17. Uproot not, *Pūṣan*, the forest lord with its propeny of crows: utterly destroy those who are my revilers: let not the adversary ensnare me, as (fowlers) set snares for birds.

Progeny of Crows— *Kākambīram vanaspatim*: the first is said by the Scholiast to amply metaphorically the author of the *Sūkta*, with his children and dependants.

As Fowlers set Snares for Birds— *Evā cana grīvā ādadhate veḥ* even as sometimes they place snares for a bird: *grīvā* is said to have here the unusual signification of *damam, jālarūpam,* a snare of the nature of a net.

४८६७. दूतेरिव तेऽवृकमंस्तु सख्यम्।

अच्छिद्रस्य दधन्वतः सुपूर्णस्य दधन्वतः॥१८॥

18. May your friendship be unbroken, like (the surface) of a skin without a flaw, containing curds.

Skin containing Curds— Such a skin of curds, Sāyaṇa says, is always carried in *Pūṣan's* chariot.

४८६८. परो हि मर्त्यैरसिं समो देवैरुत श्रिया।

अभि ख्यः पूषन् पृतनासु नस्त्वमवा नूनं यथा पुरा॥१९॥

19. Supreme are you above mortals: equal in glory are you to the gods: therefore. *Pūṣan,* regard us (favourably) in battles: defend us at present as (you have defended) those of old.

४८६९. वामी वामस्य धूतयः प्रणीतिरस्तु सूनृता।

देवस्य वा मरुतो मर्त्यस्य वेजानस्य प्रयज्यवः॥२०॥

20. *Maruts,* agitators, especially to be adored, may your kind and true speech be our conductress; that pleasant (speech which is the guide) to desirable (wealth) for both gods and sacrificing mortals.

४८७०. सद्यश्चिद्यस्य चर्कृतिः परि द्यां देवो नैति सूर्यः। त्वेषं शवो दधिरे नामं यज्ञियं मरुतो वृत्रहं शवो ज्येष्ठं वृत्रहं शवः॥२१॥

21. Whose functions spread quickly round the heavens, like (the light of) the divine sun, since the *maruts* possess brilliant, foe-humiliating, and adorable foe-destroying strength, most excellent foe-destroying strength.

४८७१. सकृद्ध द्यौरजायत सकृद्भूमिरजायत।

पृश्न्यां दुग्धं सकृत्पयस्तदन्यो नानु जायते॥२२॥

22. Once, indeed, was the heaven generated; once was the earth born; once was the milk of *Prśni*[1] drawn other than that was not similarly generated.

---

१. पृश्निये वै पयसो मरुतो जाताः (तै॰ सं॰ २.२.११.४)।

Once Indeed was the heaven Generated, Etc.— This is rather at variance with the doctrine of the succession of worldly existences, but the Scholiast so understands it: *sakṛd ha dyaur ajāyata, utpadyate,* and once born it is permanent, *sakṛd-utpannaiva sthitā bhavati,* or, being destroyed, no other similar heaven is born, *na punas-tasyām naṣṭāyām anya tat-sadṛśī dyaur jāyate.*

Other than that was not Similarly Generated— *Tadanyo nānujāyate* is explained; *tataḥ param anyaḥ padārthastatsadṛśo notpadyate,* after that another object or thing like that (object or thing) is not produced.

[सूक्त-४९]

[**ऋषि**– ऋजिश्वा भारद्वाज। **देवता**– विश्वेदेवा। **छन्द**– त्रिष्टुप्,१५ शक्वरी]

४८७२. स्तुषे जनं सुव्रतं नव्यसीभिर्गीर्भिर्मित्रावरुणा सुम्नयन्ता।

त आ गमन्तु त इह श्रुवन्तु सुक्षत्रासो वरुणो मित्रो अग्निः॥१॥

1. I commend with new hymns the man observant of his duty, and the beneficent *Mitra* and *Varuṇa*: may they, the mighty ones, *Varuṇa, Mitra, Agni,* come to our rite, and listen (to our praises).

The Man Observant of his Duty— *Stuṣe janam suvratam* the Scholiast interprets *daivyam janam,* the divine people, *devasaṅgham,* the company of the gods, which is not incompatible with the purport of the hymn.

४८७३. विशोविश इड्यमध्वरेष्वदृप्तक्रतुमरतिं युवत्योः।

दिवः शिशुं सहसः सूनुमाग्ने यज्ञस्य केतुमरुषं यजध्यै॥२॥

2. (I incite the worshipper) to offer worship to *Agni,* who is to be adored at the sacrifices of every man; whose acts are free from arrogance; the lord of two youthful (brides, heaven and earth); the child of heaven, the son of strength, the brilliant symbol of sacrifice.

४८७४. अरुषस्य दुहितरा विरूपे स्तृभिरन्या पिपिशे सूरो अन्या।

मिथस्तुरा विचरन्ती पावके मन्म श्रुतं नक्षत ऋच्यमाने॥३॥

3. May the two daughters of the radiant (sun) of various form, of whom one glitters with stars, the other (is bright) with the sun, mutually opposed, proceeding diversely, purifying (all things), and entitled to our laudation, be pleased by the praise they hear (from us).

The two Daughters— Day and night, who may be called the daughters of the sun, as, directly or indirectly, their cause.

४८७५. प्र वायुमच्छा बृहती मनीषा बृहद्रयिं विश्ववारं रथप्राम्।

द्युतद्यामा नियुतः पत्यमानः कविः कविमियक्षसि प्रयज्यो ।।४।।

4. May our earnest praise proceed to the presence of *Vāyu*, the possessor of vast riches, the desired of all, the filler of his chariot (with wealth for his worshippers): most adorable (*Vāyu*), who are riding in a radiant car, and driving your *Niyut* (steeds), do you, who are far-seeing, show favour to the sage, (your adorer).

Show Favour to the Sage— *Kavim iyakṣasi prayajyo:* Mahīdhara, *Yajurveda*, 33, 55 applies *prayajyo* to the priest, the *Adhvaryu*; worship, venerable priest, the wise *Vāyu*, etc.

४८७६. स मे वपुश्छदयदश्विनोर्यो रथो विरुक्मान्मनसा युजानः।

येन नरा नासत्येषयध्यै वर्तिर्याथस्तनयाय त्मने च।।५।।

5. May that splendid car of the *Aśvins*, which is harnessed at a thought, clothe my form (with radiance): that (car) with which, *Nāsatyās*, leaders of (rites), you go to the dwelling (of the worshipper) to fulfil his desires for his posterity and himself.

४८७७. पर्जन्यवाता वृषभा पृथिव्याः पुरीषाणि जिन्वतमप्यानि।

सत्यश्रुतः कवयो यस्य गीर्भिर्जगतः स्थातर्जगदा कृणुध्वम्।।६।।

6. *Parjanya* and *Vāta*, showerers of rain, and from the firmament available waters: sage *Maruts*, hearers of truth, establishers of the world, multiply the moveable (wealth of him) by whose praises (you are propitiated).

Multiply the moveable Wealth— *Jagad ākṛṇudhvam:* according to Sāyaṇa, *jagat* here comprehends fixed as well as moveable, all living things, *jagat sthāvara-jaṅgamātmakaṁ sarvaṁ prāṇijātam.*

४८७८. पावीरवी कन्या चित्रायुः सरस्वती वीरपत्नी धियं धात्।

ग्नाभिरच्छिद्रं शरणं सजोषा दुराधर्षं गृणते शर्म यंसत्।।७।।

7. May the purifying, amiable, graceful *Sarasvatī*, the bride of the hero, favour our pious rite: may she, together with the wives of the gods, well pleased, bestow upon him who praises her a habitation free from defects and impenetrable (to wind and rain), and (grant him), felicity.

Amiable— *Kanyā*, literally a maiden, is here explained[1] *kamanīyā*, to be desired or loved; the usual sense being incompatible with the following

---

१. ग्ना: गायज्ज्यादीनि छन्दांसि। छन्दांसि वै ग्ना: (तै॰ सं॰ ५.१.७.२)।

epithet, *vīrapatni*, the wife of the hero, meaning, according to the Scholiast, *Prajāpati* or *Brahmā*; or it might mean the protectress of heroes or of men.

४८७९. पथस्पथः परिपतिं वचस्या कामेन कृतो अभ्यानळर्कम् ।
स नौ रासच्छुरुध॑श्चन्द्राग्रा॒ धियंधियं॑ सीषधाति॒ प्र पूषा ॥८॥

8. May (the worshipper), influenced by the hope (of reward), approach with praise the adorable (*Pūṣan*), protector of all paths: may he bestow upon us cows with golden horns: may *Pūṣan* bring to perfection our every rite.

Yajurveda, 34.42: Mahīdhara's explanation differs in some respects from Sāyaṇa's.

Protector of all Paths— *Pathaspathaḥ paripatim*: *Pūṣan* is especially customs *viarum*, see vol. I. *Sūkta* 42.

४८८०. प्रथमभाजं॒ यश॑सं वयो॒धां सु॒पाणि॑ दे॒वं सु॒गभ॑स्तिमृभ्व॑म् ।
होता॑ य॒क्षद्यज॑तं प॒स्त्याना॒मग्निस्त्वष्टा॑रं॒ सुह॑वं॒ विभावा॑ ॥९॥

9. May the illustrious *Agni*, the invoker of the gods, worship (with this oblation), *Tvaṣṭā*, the first divider (of forms), the renowned, the giver of food, the well-handed, the vast, the adored of householders, the readily invoked.

The Adored of Householders— *Yajatam pastyānām: pastyam* is a house, here used by metonymy for householder, according to Sāyaṇa, *gṛhasthair yajanīyam*.

४८८१. भुव॑नस्य पि॒तरं॑ गी॒र्भिरा॒भी रु॒द्रं दि॒वा व॑र्धया॒ रु॒द्रम॒क्तौ ।
बृह॒न्तमृष्व॒मज॑रं॒ सुषु॒म्नमृध॒ग्घुवेम॒ क॒विने॑षि॒तास॑: ॥१०॥

10. Exalt *Rudra*, the parent of the world, with these hymns by day; (exalt) *Rudra* (with them) by night; animated by the far-seeing, we invoke him, mighty, of pleasing aspect, undecaying, endowed with felicity, (the source of) prosperity.

४८८२. आ यु॒वान॑: क॒वयो॑ य॒ज्ञिया॑सो॒ मरु॑तो॒ गन्त॑ गृ॒णतो॒ वर॒स्याम् ।
अ॒चित्रं॑ चि॒द्धि जि॒न्व॑था वृ॒धन्त॑ इ॒त्था नक्ष॑न्तो नरो अङ्गि॒रस्वत् ॥११॥

11. Ever youthful wise, and adorable *Maruts*, come to the praise of your adorer: thus augmenting, leaders (of rites), and spreading (through the firmament), like rays)of light), refresh the scanty woods (with rain).

Like Rays of Light— *Nakṣanto aṅgirasvat* the Scholiast renders *aṅgirasaḥ, gamanaśīlaraśmayaḥ*, rays endowed with motions: *te yathā* *śīghram nabhastalam vyāpnuvanti tad vat,* as they spread quickly through the sky, so) do the winds): or if *aṅgiras* retain its more usual signification of *Ṛṣi* or *Ṛṣis,* so named, then the property of rapid movement is assigned to them, *yad vā Ṛṣayastad-vacchīghragāminaḥ.*

Refresh the Scanty Woods with Rain— *Acitraṁ cid hi jinvatha: citram* is said to mean a place thick with shrubs and trees: with the negative prefix it implies the contrary, a place with little timber: the *Maruts* are solicited to satisfy such a place, with rain understood.

४८८३. प्र वीराय प्र तवसे तुरायाजा यूथेव पशुरक्षिरस्तम् ।
स पिस्पृशति तन्विं श्रुतस्य स्तृभिर्न नाकं वचनस्य विपः ॥१२॥

12. Offer adoration to the valiant, powerful, swift-moving (company of the *Maruts*), as the herdsman (drives his) herd to their stall: may that (company) appropriate to its own body the praises of the pious worshipper, as the firmament (is studded) with stars.

४८८४. यो रजांसि विममे पार्थिवानि त्रिश्चिद्विष्णुर्मनवे बाधिताय ।
तस्य ते शर्मन्नुपदद्यमाने राया मंदेम तन्वा३ तना च ॥१३॥

13. May we be happy in a home, in riches, in person, in children, bestowed upon us by you, *Viṣṇu*, who with three (steps) made the terrestrial regions for *Manu* when harassed (by the *Asuras*).

४८८५. तन्नोऽहिर्बुध्न्यो अद्रिरर्कंस्तत्पर्वंतस्तत्सविता चनो धात् ।
तदोषधीभिरभि रातिषाचो भगः पुरन्धिर्जिन्वतु प्र राये ॥१४॥

14. May *Ahirbudhnya* (propitiated) by (our) hymns, and *Parvata* and *Savitā* give us food with water: may the bountiful (gods supply us), addition, with vegetable (grains); and may the all-wise *Bhaga* be propitious (to us) for (the acquirement of) riches.

Ahirbudhnya— *Budhna* is explained *Iantarikṣa,* firmament, and *budhnya* is, what or who is there born: *ahi* is interpreted he who goes, that is, in the sky, but the etymology is not satisfactory.

Parvata— The commentator is rather at a loss to explain *Parvata:* it may mean, he says, the filler, *pūrayitrī,* or the wielder of the thunderbolt, *parvavad-vajram, tadvān;* or enemy of the mountain, *gireḥ śatru:* in either sense it is obviously *Indra.*

With Vegetable Grains— *Tad oṣadhibhir-abhi; oṣadhayas tila-māṣādayaḥ,* the vegetables are sesamum, pulse, and the like.

४८८६. नू नों रयिं रथ्यं चर्षणिप्रां पुरुवीरं महे ऋतस्यं गोपाम्। क्षयं दाताजरं
येन॒ जना॒न्त्स्पृधो॒ अदे॑वीर॒भि च॑ क्रमा॒म विश॒ आदे॑वीर॒भ्य१॑
श्नवा॑म॥१५॥

15. Grant us, (universal gods), riches, comprehending chariots, numerous dependants, many male offspring, (wealth) the giver of efficiency to the solemn rite, and a dwelling free from decay, wherewith we may overcome malevolent men and unrightious (spirits), and afford support to those people who are devoted to the gods.

ANUVAKA V

[सूक्त-५०]

[ऋषि– ऋजिश्वा भारद्वाज। देवता– विश्वेदेवा। छन्द– त्रिष्टुप्]

४८८७. हुवे वो॑ दे॒वीमदि॑तिं॒ नमो॑भिर्मृ॒ळी॒का॑य॒ वरु॑णं मि॒त्रम॒ग्निम्।
अ॒भि॒क्ष॒दाम॑र्य॒मणं॑ सु॒शेवं॑ त्रा॒तॄन्दे॒वान्त्स॑वि॒तारं॒ भगं॑ च॥१॥

1. I invoke with adorations, for the sake of felicity, the divine *Aditi* and *Varuṇa*, *Mitra* and *Agni*, *Aryaman*, the overthrower of foes, worthy of devotion, *Savitā* and *Bhaga*, and (all) protecting divinities.

४८८८. सु॒ज्योति॑ष॒: सूर्य॒ दक्ष॑पितॄन॒नागा॑स्त्वे सु॒महो॑ वीहि दे॒वान्।
द्वि॒ज॒न्मानो॒ य ऋ॑त॒सापः॑ स॒त्याः स्वर्व॑न्तो यज॒ता अ॑ग्निजि॒ह्वाः॥२॥

2. Radiant *Sūrya*, render the luminous deities, who have *Dakṣa* for their progenitor, void of offence towards us; they who are twice born, desirous of sacrifice, observant of truth, possessors of wealth, deserving of worship, whose tongue is *Agni*.

Who have *Dakṣa* for their Progenitor— *Dakṣapitṛn, dakṣaḥ pitāmaho yeṣām,* they of whom *Dakṣa* is the grandfather: the grandchildren of *Dakṣa,* however, were sundry sentiments and passions: see *Viṣṇu Purāṇa,* 55, and *pitara,* therefore, must here be understood, according to Sāyaṇa, only in the general sense of priority or seniority.

They who are Twice Born— *Dvijanmānaḥ,* they who are have two births, means agreeably to Sāyaṇa, they who are manifest or present in two spheres, heaven and earth.

४८८९. उ॒त द्यावा॑पृथि॒वी क्ष॒त्रमु॒रु बृ॒ह॒द्रोद॑सी॒ शर॑णं सु॒षुम्ने॑।
महस्क॒रथो॒ वरि॑वो॒ यथा॑ नो॒ऽस्मे क्ष॒याय॑ धि॒षणे॑ अ॒नेहः॑॥३॥

3. Or bestow, Heaven and Earth, vast strength: give us, Earth and Heaven, a spacious habitation for our comfort: so arrange, that infinite wealth may be ours, remove, beneficent deities, iniquity from our abode.

४८९०. आ नो रुद्रस्य सूनवो नमन्तामद्या हूतासो वसवोऽधृष्टाः।
यदीमर्भे महति वा हितासो बाधे मरुतो अह्वाम देवान्॥४॥

4. May the sons of *Rudra*, givers of dwellings, the unsubdued, invoked on this occasion, stoop down to us, inasmuch as we call upon the divine *Maruts* that they may be our helpers in difficulty, great or small.

४८९१. मिम्यक्ष येषु रोदसी नु देवी सिषक्ति पूषा अभ्यर्धयज्वा।
श्रुत्वा हवं मरुतो यद्ध याथ भूमा रेजन्ते अध्वनि प्रविक्ते॥५॥

5. With whom the divine Heaven and Earth are associated; whom *Pūṣan*, the rewarder (of his worshippers) with prosperity, honours: when, *Maruts*, having heard our invocation, you come hither, then on your several paths all beings tremble.

४८९२. अभि त्यं वीरं गिर्वणसमर्चेन्द्रं ब्रह्मणा जरितर्नवेन।
श्रवदिद्धवमुप च स्तवानो रासद्वाजाँ उप महो गृणानः॥६॥

6. Praise, worshipper, with a new hymn, that hero, *Indra*, who is deserving of praise: may he, so glorified hear our invocation: may he, so lauded, bestow upon us abundant food.

४८९३. ओमानमापो मानुषीरमृक्तं धात तोकाय तनयाय शं योः।
यूयं हि ष्ठा भिषजो मातृतमा विश्वस्य स्थातुर्जगतो जनित्रीः॥७॥

7. Waters, friendly to mankind, grant uninterrupted (life) preserving (food) for (the perpetuation of our) sons and grandsons; grant us security and the removal (of all evil), for you are more than maternal physicians; you are the parents of the stationary and moveable universe.

Security and the Removal of all Evil— *Śaṁyoḥ*: the first is explained *śamanam upadravāṇām*, the appeasing of oppressions or violences; and the second, *yāvanam, pṛthak-karaṇaṁ pṛthakkartvyānām*, the making separate of those things which are to be kept off.

४८९४. आ नो देवः सविता त्रायमाणो हिरण्यपाणिर्यजतो जगम्यात्।
यो दत्रवाँ उषसो न प्रतीकं व्यूर्णुते दाशुषे वार्याणि॥८॥

8. May the adorable, golden-handed *Savitā*, the preserver, come to us; he, the munificent, who, like the opening of the dawn, displays desirable (riches) to the offerer of the oblation.

४८९५. उत त्वं सूनो सहसो नो अद्या देवाँ अस्मिन्नध्वरे ववृत्याः।
स्यामहं ते सदमिद्रातौ तव स्यामग्नेऽवसा सुवीरः॥९॥

9. And do you, son of strength, bring back toady the deities to this our sacrifice; may I be ever in (the enjoyment of) your bounty: may I, through your protection, *Agni*, be blessed with excellent male descendants.

४८९६. उत त्या मे हवमा जग्म्यातं नासत्या धीभिर्युवमङ्ग विप्रा।
अत्रिं न महस्तमसोऽमुमुक्तं तूर्वतं नरा दुरितादभीके॥१०॥

10. Wise *Nāsatyās* come quickly to my invocation (united) with holy acts: (extricate us) from thick darkness, as you did extricate *Atri*; protect us, leaders (of rites) from danger in battle.

४८९७. ते नौ रायो द्युमतो वाजवतो दातारो भूत नृवतः पुरुक्षोः।
दशस्यन्तो दिव्याः पार्थिवासो गोजाता अप्या मृळता च देवाः॥११॥

11. Be unto us, gods, donors of splendid, invigorating riches, comprising male descendants, and celebrated by many: celestial *Ādityas*, terrestrial *Vasus*, offspring of *Pṛśni*, children of the waters, granting our desires, make us happy.

Celestial *Ādityas*, terrestrial *Vasus*, Etc.— The text has epithets only, the Scholiast supplies the nomencalture: thus *divyā*, the celestial, that is, the *Ādityas*; *pārthivāsāh*, terrestrials, that is, the *Vasus;* *go-jātāh*, cow-born, born of *Pṛśni*, the *Maruts;* *apyāh*, the aquatic, born in the firmament, the *Rudras*.

४८९८. ते नौ रुद्रः सरस्वती सजोषा मीळ्हुष्मन्तो विष्णुर्मृळन्तु वायुः।
ऋभुक्षा वाजो दैव्यो विधाता पर्जन्यावाता पिप्यतामिषं नः॥१२॥

12. May *Rudra* and *Sarasvatī*, alike well pleased and *Viṣṇu* and *Vāyu*, make us happy, sending rain; and *Ribhukṣin*, and *Vāja*, and the divine *Vidhātā*: and may *Parjanya* and *Vāta* grant us abundant food.

४८९९. उत स्य देवः सविता भगो नोऽपां नपादवतु दानु पत्रिः।
त्वष्टा देवेभिर्जनिभिः सजोषा द्यौर्देवेभिः पृथिवी समुद्रैः॥१३॥

13. And may the divine *Savitā* and *Bhaga*, and the grandson of the waters, (*Agni*), the prodigal of gifts, preserve us; and may *Tvaṣṭā* with the gods, and Earth with the seas, (preserve us).

४९००. उत नोऽहिर्बुध्न्यः शृणोत्वज एकपात्पृथिवी समुद्रः। विश्वे देवा
ऋतावृधौ हुवानाः स्तुता मन्त्राः कविशस्ता अवन्तु॥१४॥

14. May *Ahirbudhnya*, *Aja-Ekapād*, and Earth and Ocean, hear
us; may the universal gods, who are exalted by sacrifice, they who
are invoked and praised (by us), to whom mystical prayers are
addressed, and who have been glorified by (ancient) sages,
preserve us.

Yajurveda, 34,53.

४९०१. एवा नपातो मम तस्य धीभिर्भरद्वाजा अभ्यर्चन्त्यकैः।
ग्ना हुतासो वसवोऽधृष्टा विश्वे स्तुतासौ भूता यजत्राः॥१५॥

15. Thus do my sons, of the race of *Bharadvāja*, worship the
gods with sacred rites and holy hymns; and so, adorable (deities),
may you, who are worshipped and glorified, the givers of
dwellings, the invincible, universal gods, ever be adored, (together
with your) wives.

[सूक्त-५१]

[ऋषि– ऋजिश्वा भारद्वाज। देवता– विश्वेदेवा।
छन्द– त्रिष्टुप्, १३-१५ उष्णिक्, १६ अनुष्टुप्]

४९०२. उदु त्यच्चक्षुर्महि मित्रयोराँ एति प्रियं वरुणयोरदब्धम्।
ऋतस्य शुचि दर्शतमनीकं रुक्मो न दिव उदिता व्यद्यौत्॥१॥

1. The expansive, illuminating, unobstructive, pure, and
beautiful radiance of the sun, grateful to *Mitra* and *Varuṇa*, having
risen, shines like the ornament of the sky.

४९०३. वेद यस्त्रीणि विदथान्येषां देवानां जन्म सनुतरा च विप्रः।
ऋजु मर्तेषु वृजिना च पश्यन्नभि चष्टे सूरो अर्य एवान्॥२॥

2. He who knows the three congziable (worlds); the sage (who
knows) the mysterious birth of the divinities (abiding in them); he
who is beholding the good and evil acts of mortals, he, the sun, the
lord, makes manifest their intentions.

The Divinities Abiding in them— Of the *Vasus* on earth, the *Rudras*
in the firmament, the *Ādityas* in heaven.

४९०४. स्तुष उ वो मह ऋतस्य गोपानदिति मित्रं वरुणं सुजातान्।
अर्यमणं भगमदब्धधीतीनच्छां वोचे सधन्यः पावकान्॥३॥

3. I praise you, protectors of the solemn sacrifice, the well-born *Aditi, Mitra* and *Varuṇa*, and *Aryaman* and *Bhaga*; I celebrate the gods whose acts are unimpeded, the bestowers of wealth, the dispensers of purity;

४९०५. रिशादसः सत्पतीँरदब्धान्महो राज्ञः सुवसनस्य दातॄन्।
यूनः सुक्षत्रान्क्षयतो दिवो नॄनादित्यान्याम्यदितिं दुवोयु॥४॥

4. The scatterers of the malevolent, the defenders of the virtuous, the irresistible, the mighty lords, the donors of good dwellings, ever young, very powerful, omnipresent, leader of heaven, the sons of *Āditya*: I have recourse to *Aditi*, who is gratified by mine adoration.

४९०६. द्यौष्पितः पृथिवि मातरधुगग्ने भ्रातर्वसवो मृळतां नः।
विश्व आदित्या अदिते सजोषा अस्मभ्यं शर्म बहुलं वि यन्त॥५॥

5. Father Heaven, innocent mother Earth, brother *Agni*, and you, *Vasus*, grant us happiness; all you sons of *Aditi*, and you *Aditi*, alike well-pleased, bestow upon us ample felicity.

४९०७. मा नो वृकाय वृक्यै समस्मा अघायते रीरधता यजत्राः।
यूयं हि ष्ठा रथ्यो नस्तनूनां यूयं दक्षस्य वर्चसो बभूव॥६॥

6. Subject us not, adorable (deities), to the robber or his wife; not to any one designing us harm; for you are the regulators of our persons, of our strength, of our speech.

To the Robber of his Wife— *Mā no vṛkāya vṛkye rīradhatā,* the substantives are explained *hiṁsakāya, stenāya,*to the injurer, the thief, and *tasya striyai,* to his woman, or wife; or *vṛka* may retain its ordinary sense of wild-dog, or wolf, *araṇya śvān,* and *vṛki* import its female.

४९०८. मा व एनो अन्यकृतं भुजेम मा तत्कर्म वसवो यच्चयध्वे।
विश्वस्य हि क्षयथ विश्वदेवाः स्वयं रिपुस्तन्वं रीरिषीष्ट॥७॥

7. Let us not suffer for the sin committed by another: let us not do that which, *Vasus*, you prohibit: you rule universal gods, over the universe: (so provide that) mine enemy may inflict injury on his own person.

४९०९. नम इदुग्रं नम आ विवासे नमो दाधार पृथिवीमुत द्याम्।
नमो देवेभ्यो नम ईश एषां कृतं चिदेनो नमसा विवासे॥८॥

8. Reverence be to the potent (company of universal gods): I offer (them) reverence: reverence sustains both earth and heaven:

reverence be to the gods: reverence is sovereign over them: I expiate by reverence whatever sin may have been committed.

Reverence sustains both Earth and Heaven— The Scholiast says that earth and heaven, by receiving the *namas* or *namaskāra*, the reverential salutation or homage of mortals, continue throughout a long period for their enjoyment.

४९१०. ऋतस्य वो रथ्यः पूतदक्षानृतस्य पस्त्यसदो अदब्धान्।
ताँ आ नमोभिरुरुचक्षसो नृन्विश्वान्व आ नमे महो यंजत्राः॥९॥

9. Adorable (deities), I venerate with reverential salutations all you who are mighty, the mighty, the regulators of your sacrifice, of pure vigour, dwellers in the chamber of worship, unsubdued, far-seeing, leaders (of rites).

The Regulators of your Sacrifice— *Ritasya rathyaī, yajñasya ranhitṛn, netṛn,* the leaders or conveyers of the sacrifice offered to them.

४९११. ते हि श्रेष्ठवर्चसस्त उ नस्तिरो विश्वानि दुरिता नयन्ति।
सुक्षत्रासो वरुणो मित्रो अग्निर्ऋतधीतयो वक्मराजसत्याः॥१०॥

10. May they, exceeding in splendour, so guide us, that all iniquities may disappear; they, the very powerful *Varuṇa, Mitra, Agni*, practisers of truth, and faithful to those who are prominent in (their) praise.

४९१२. ते न इन्द्रः पृथिवी क्षाम वर्धन्पूषा भगो अदितिः पञ्च जनाः।
सुशर्माणः स्ववसः सुनीथा भवन्तु नः सुत्रात्रासः सुगोपाः॥११॥

11. May they, *Indra*, Earth, *Pūṣan, Bhaga, Aditi*, and the five orders of beings, give increase to our habitations; may they be to us granters of happiness, bestowers of food, guides to good, our gracious defenders and preservers.

४९१३. नू सद्मानं दिव्यं नंशि देवा भारद्वाजः सुमतिं यांति होता।
आसानेभिर्यजमानो मियेधैर्देवानां जन्म वसूयुर्ववन्द॥१२॥

12. May the presenter of the oblation, *Bharadvāja*, quickly obtain, gods, a celestial abode, as he solicits your good-will: the institutor of the ceremony, together with pious associates, desirous of riches, glorifies the assembly of the gods.

४९१४. अप त्यं वृजिनं रिपुं स्तेनमग्ने दुराध्यम्।
दविष्ठमस्य सत्पते कृधी सुगम्॥१३॥

13. Drive away, *Agni,* to a distance the wicked, felonious, malignant enemy: grant us felicity, protector of the virtuous.
*Sāvaveda,*105.

४९१५. ग्रावाण: सोम नो हि कं सखित्वनाय वावशु:।

जही न्य१त्रिणं पणिं वृको हि ष:॥१४॥

14. These our grinding stones are anxious, *Soma,* for your friendship: destroy the voracious *Paṇi,* for verily he is a wolf.

Destroy the Voracious Paṇi, Etc.— *Jahī ninatriṇam paṇim vṛko hi saḥ: Paṇi* may here mean a trader, a greedy trafficker, who gives no offerings to the gods, no presents to the priests: hence he comes to be identified with an *asura,* or enemy of the gods: *vṛka* may be also rendered a robber, an extortioner, from the root *vṛk,* to seize or take away, *adane.*

४९१६. यूयं हि ष्ठा सुदानव इन्द्रज्येष्ठा अभिद्यव:।

कर्ता नो अध्वत्रा सुगं गोपा अमा॥१५॥

15. You are munificent and illustrious, gods, with *Indra,* for your chief, be with us, protectors, on the road, and grant us happiness.

४९१७. अपि पन्थामगन्महि स्वस्तिगामनेहसम्।

येन विश्वा: परि द्विषो वृणक्ति विन्दते वसु॥१६॥

16. We have travelled along the road prosperously traversed and free from evil, and by which (a man) avoids adversaries and acquires wealth.

[सूक्त-५२]

[ऋषि- ऋजिश्वा भारद्वाज। देवता- विश्वेदेवा।

छन्द- त्रिष्टुप्, ७-१२ गायत्री, १४ जगती]

४९१८. न तद्दिवा न पृथिव्यानु मन्ये न यज्ञेन नोत शमीभिरिभाभि:।

उब्जन्तु तं सुभ्व१: पर्वतासो नि हीयतामतियाजस्य यष्टा॥१॥

1. I do not regard it as worthy (of the gods) of heaven, or (those) of earth, as (fit to be compared) with the sacrifice (I offer), or with these (our) sacred rites: let, then, the mighty mountains overwhelm him; let the employer of *Atiyāja* be ever degraded.

Let the Employer of Atiyāja be ever Degraded— According to Sāyaṇa, *Ṛjiśvan* here pronounces an imprecation upon *Ātiyāja,* a rival priest.

४९१९. अति॑ वा॒ यो म॒रुतो॑ म॒न्य॑ते नो॒ ब्रह्म॑ वा॒ यः क्रि॒यमा॑णं॒ निनि॑त्सात्।

तपूं॑षि॒ तस्मै॑ वृ॒जिना॑नि सन्तु ब्रह्म॒द्विष॒मभि॒ तं शो॑चतु॒ द्यौः॥२॥

2. *Maruts*, may the energies of that man be enfeebled: may heaven consume that impious adversary who thinks himself superior to us, and who pretends to depreciate the worship that we offer.

That impious Adversary— *Brahmadviṣam*, and again, in the next verse, *brahmadviṣe*: the first is explained by Sāyaṇa simply *taṁ śatrum* that enemy, with reference to the word *brahma*, which has gone before, religious act or praise, the enemy or obstructer of prayer or praise: in the second place he interprets it *brāhmaṇa-dveṣṭā*, the hater or enemy of the *Brāhmaṇas*.

४९२०. किम॒ङ्ग त्वा॒ ब्रह्म॑णः सोम गो॒पां किम॒ङ्ग त्वा॑हुरभिशस्ति॒पां नः॑।

किम॒ङ्ग नः॑ पश्यसि निद्य॒मा॑नान् ब्रह्म॒द्विषे॒ तपु॑षिं हे॒तिम॑स्य॥३॥

3. Why have they called you, *Soma*, the protector of pious prayer? Why (have they called you) our defender against calumny? Why do you behold us subjected to reproach? Why do you behold us subjected to reproach? Cast your destroying weapon upon the adversary of the *Brahman*.

४९२१. अव॑न्तु मा॒मुष॑सो॒ जाय॑माना॒ अव॑न्तु मा॒ सिन्ध॑वः॒ पिन्व॑मानाः।

अव॑न्तु मा॒ पर्व॑तासो ध्रु॒वासो॒ऽव॑न्तु मा॒ पि॒तरो॑ देव॒हूतौ॑॥४॥

4. May the opening dawns preserve me: may the swelling rivers preserve me: may the firm-set mountains preserve me: may the progenitors (present) at the invocation of the gods preserve me.

४९२२. विश्व॑दानीं सु॒मन॑सः स्याम॒ पश्ये॒म॒ नु सूर्य॑मु॒च्चर॑न्तम्।

तथा॒ कर॑द्सु॒पति॑र्व॒सू॑नां दे॒वाँ ओहा॑नोऽव॒साग॑मिष्ठः॥५॥

5. May we at all seasons be possessed of sound minds: may we ever behold the rising sun: such may the affluent lord of riches, (*Agni*), render us, ever most ready to come (at our invocation), charged with our oblation to the gods.

४९२३. इन्द्रो॑ ने॒दिष्ठ॑म॒वसाग॑मिष्ठः॒ सर॑स्वती॒ सिन्धु॑भिः॒ पिन्व॑माना।

पर्ज॒न्यो न॒ ओष॑धीभि॒र्मयो॑भुर॒ग्निः सु॒शंसः॑ सु॒हवः॑ पि॒तेव॑॥६॥

6. May *Indra* be most prompt to come nigh for our protection, and *Sarasvatī* dwelling with (tributary) rivers: may *Parjanya*, with

the plants, be a giver of happiness; and may *Agni*, worthily praised and earnestly invoked, (be to us) like a father.

४९२४. विश्वे॒ देवास॒ आ गॅत शृणुता॑ मॅ इ॒मं हव॑म्। एदं ब॒र्हिर्नि षी॑दत।७॥

7. Come, universal gods, hear this my invocation: sit down upon this sacred grass.

४९२५. यो वो॑ देवा घृ॒तस्नु॑ना ह॒व्येन॑ प्रति॒भूष॑ति। तं विश्व॒ उप॑ गच्छथ॥८॥

8. Come, gods, to him who honours you with the butter dripping oblation.

४९२६. उप॑ नः सू॒नवो॒ गिरः॑ शृ॒ण्वन्त्व॒मृत॑स्य॒ ये। सु॒मृ॒ळी॒का भ॑वन्तु नः॥९॥

9. May the sons of the immortal hear our praises, and be to us the givers of felicity.

Son of the Immortal— *Amṛtasya sūnavaḥ* the Scholiast calls the sons of *Prajāpati*, the *Viśvadevas*: see *Sāmaveda*, 1595, *Yajurveda*, 33, 77.

४९२७. विश्वे॒ देवा ऋ॒तावृ॑ध ऋ॒तुभि॑र्हवन॒श्रुत॑:। जु॒षन्तां॒ युज्यं॒ पयः॑॥१०॥

10. Universal gods, augmenters of sacrifice, listening to praises (uttered) at due seasons, accept your appropriate milk-offering.

Appropriate Milk-Offering— *Yujyaṁ payas,* a mixture of milk and curds termed *āmikṣā*, as the text, *tapte payasi dadhyānayati sā vaiśvadevyāmikṣā* when the milk is boiled he brings the curds, that is, the *āmikṣā*, proper for the *Viśvadevas*.

४९२८. स्तोत्रमि॒न्द्रो म॒रुद्ग॑णस्त्वष्टृ॑मान् मि॒त्रो अ॒र्यमा।

इ॒मा ह॒व्या जु॑षन्त नः॥११॥

11. *Indra*, with the company of the *Maruts*, *Mitra*, with *Tvaṣṭā* and *Aryaman*, accept our praise and these our oblations.

४९२९. इ॒मं नो॑ अग्ने अ॒ध्वरं॒ होत॑र्वयु॒नशो॑ यज। चि॒कि॒त्वान्दैव्यं॒ जन॑म्॥१२॥

12. *Agni*, invoker of the gods, cognizant (which of) the divine assembly (is be honoured), offer this our sacrifice according to the proper order.

४९३०. विश्वे॑ देवाः॒ शृणु॒तेमं हवं॑ मे॒ ये अ॒न्तरि॑क्षे॒ य उप॒ द्यवि॒ ष्ठ।

ये अ॒ग्निजि॑ह्वा उ॒त वा॒ यज॑त्रा आ॒सद्या॒स्मिन्ब॒र्हिषि॑ मादयध्वम्॥१३॥

13. Universal gods, hear this my invocation, whether you be in the firmament or in the heaven: you who (receive oblations) by the

tongue of *Agni*, or are to be (otherwise) worshipped: seated on this sacred grass, be exhilarated (by the *Soma*).

४९३१. विश्वे॒ दे॒वा मम॑ शृण्वन्तु य॒ज्ञिया॑ उ॒भे रोद॑सी अ॒पां नपा॑च्च॒ मन्म॑।
मा वो॒ वचां॑सि परि॒चक्ष्या॑णि वोचं सु॒म्नेष्वि॒द्वो अ॒न्त॑मा मदेम॥१४॥

14. May the adorable, universal deities, and both heaven and earth, and the grandson of the waters, hear my praise: let me not utter words to be disregarded, but let us, (brought) most nigh unto you, rejoice in the happiness (you bestow).

४९३२. ये के च॒ ज्मा महि॑नो अ॒हिमा॑या दि॒वो ज॒ज्ञिरे॒ अ॒पां स॒धस्थे॑।
ते अ॒स्मभ्य॒मिष॑ये वि॒श्वमा॒गुः क्ष॒रं उ॒ष्णा व॒रिव॒स्यन्तु॑ दे॒वाः॥१५॥

15. May those mighty deities, having power to destroy, whether they have been manifested upon earth or in heaven, or in the abode of the waters, bestow upon us and our posterity abundant sustenance both by night and day.

Having Power to Destroy— *Ahimāyāḥ*, is explained *āhantṛprajñāḥ*, having the wisdom or knowledge that kills.

Our Posterity— *Asmabhyam iṣaye*; the latter, *iṣi*, is derived from *iṣ*, to wish, and is explained *putrādi*, sons and the rest, *asmabhyām tasmai ca*, to us and to it, that is, posterity, as the object of desire.

४९३३. अग्नीप॑र्जन्यावव॒तं धियं॑ मे॒ऽस्मिन्ह॒वे सु॑ह॒वा सु॒ष्टुतिं॑ नः।
इळा॒मन्यो॑ जन॒यद् गर्भ॑मन्यः प्र॒जाव॑ती॒रिष॒ आ ध॑त्तमस्मे॥१६॥

16. *Agni* and *Parjanya*, prosper my pious acts: (accept), you who are reverently invoked, our praise at this sacrifice: one of you generates food, the other posterity: grant us, therefore, food productive of descendants.

One of you Generates food, the other Posterity— *Iḷām anyo janayat garbham anyaḥ: Parjanya*, by sending rain, causes the growth of corn, and *Agni*, as the main agent in digestion, produces the vigour necessary for procreation.

४९३४. स्ती॒र्णे ब॒र्हिषि॑ समि॒धाने॑ अ॒ग्नौ सू॒क्तेन॑ म॒हा नम॑सा वि॒वासे॑।
अ॒स्मिन्नो॑ अ॒द्य वि॒दथे॑ यजत्रा॒ विश्वे॑ देवा ह॒विषि॑ मादयध्वम्॥१७॥

17. When the sacred grass is strewn; when the fire is kindled, and when I worship (you) with a hymn, and with profound veneration, then, adorable universal gods, rejoice in the oblation (offered) today at this our sacrifice.

[सूक्त-५३]

[**ऋषि–** भरद्वाज बार्हस्पत्य। **देवता–** पूषा। **छन्द–** गायत्री, ८ अनुष्टुप्]

४९३५. वयमु त्वा पथस्पते रथं न वाजसातये। धिये पूषन्नयुज्महि।।१।।

1. *Pūṣan*, lord of paths, we attach you to us like a chariot, for (the sake of) bringing food, and of (accomplishing our) solemnity.

४९३६. अभि नो नर्यं वसु वीरं प्रयतदक्षिणम्। वामं गृहपतिं नय।।२।।

2. Conduct us to a gracious householder, friendly to men, liberal in (bestowing) wealth, the giver of pious donations.

Liberal in Bestowing Wealth— *Vasuvīram*, literally, a hero of riches, that is, according to the Scholiast, one who is especially the instigator of poverty to acquire wealth, *dhanam abhiprāptum vīram dāridrasya viśeṣeṇa erayitāram*.

४९३७. अदित्सन्तं चिदाघृणे पूषन्दानाय चोदय। पणेश्चिद्वि म्रदा मनः।।३।।

3. Resplendent *Pūṣan*, instigate the niggard to liberality, soften the heart of the miser.

४९३८. वि पथो वाजसातये चिनुहि वि मृधो जहि।

साधन्तामुग्र नो धियः।।४।।

4. Pierce *Pūṣan*, select (fit) roads for the passage of provisions: drive away all obstructors, (thieves, or the like), so that our holy rites may be accomplished.

४९३९. परि तृन्धि पणीनामारया हृदया कवे। अथेमस्मभ्यं रन्धय।।५।।

5. Pierce with a goad the hearts of the avaricious, wise *Pūṣan*, and so render them complacent towards us.

Pierce with a Goad— *Paritṛndhi ārayā: ārā* is described as a stick with a slender point of iron; *pratoda*, a goad; the common vernacular derivative, *ārāḥ*, is a saw.

४९४०. वि पूषन्नारया तुद पणेरिच्छ हृदि प्रियम्। अथेमस्मभ्यं रन्धय।।६।।

6. Pierce with a goad, *Pūṣan*, the heart of the avaricious; generate generosity in his heart, and so render him complacent towards as.

४९४१. आ रिख किकिरा कृणु पणीनां हृदया कवे।

अथेमस्मभ्यं रन्धय।।७।।

7. Abrade, wise *Pūṣan*, the hearts of the avaricious; relax (their hardness), and so render them complacent towards us.

४९४२. यां पूषन्ब्रह्मचोद॑नीमारां बिभर्ष्या॒घृणे।

तया॑ सम॒स्य॒ हृद॑यमा रि॑ख किकि॑रा कृ॒णु।।८।।

8. Resplendent *Pūṣan*, with that food-propelling goad which you bearest, abrade the heart of every miser, and render it relaxed.

४९४३. या ते॑ अ॒ष्ट्रा गोऔपशा॑घृणे पशु॒साध॑नी। तस्या॑स्ते सु॒म्नमी॑महे।।९।।

9. Resplendent *Pūṣan*, we ask of you the service of that your weapon, which is the guide of cows, the director of cattle.

४९४४. उ॒त नो॑ गो॒षणि॑ धि॒यमश्व॑सां वा॒जसा॑मुत। नृ॒वत् कृ॒णुहि॑ वी॒तये॑।।१०।।

10. Make our pious worship productive of cows, of horses, of food, of dependants, for our enjoyment.

[सूक्त-५४]

[ऋषि– भरद्वाज बार्हस्पत्य। **देवता–** पूषा। **छन्द–** गायत्री**]**

४९४५. सं पूषन् विदुषा॑ नय॒ यो अ॒ङ्जसानुशा॑स॒ति। य ए॒वेदमिति॒ ब्रव॑त्।।१।।

1. Bring us, *Pūṣan*, into communication with a wise man who may rightly direct us, who may even say, this is so.

Who may Even say, this is So— *Ya evedam iti bravat*: Sāyaṇa's explanation of this is curious, and is justified by what follows: by *Viduṣā*, a wise man, he understands a cunning man, a conjurer: the last phrase, he therefore interprets to mean, one who says, this, your property, has been lost, and the passage that precedes he explains as directing the way to the recovery of the lost or stolen goods: this is a new attribute of *Pūṣan* as the patron of fortune-tellers and recoverers of stolen property.

४९४६. सम॑ पू॒ष्णा ग॑मेम॒हि॒ यो गृ॒हाँ अ॑भि॒शास॑ति।

इ॒म ए॒वेति॑ च॒ ब्रव॑त्।।२।।

2. May we, by the favour of *Pūṣan*, come in communication with (the man) who may direct us to the houses (where our goods are secreted), and may say, verily these are they.

४९४७. पू॒ष॒णश्च॒क्रं न रि॑ष्यति॒ न कोशो॒ऽव॑ पद्यते।

नो अ॑स्य व्यथते प॒विः।।३।।

3. The discus of *Pūṣan* does not destroy; its sheathe is not discarded, its edge harms not us.

४९४८. यो अस्मै हविषाविधन्नं तं पूषापि मृष्यते। प्रथमो विन्दते वसुं।।४।।

4. *Pūṣan* inflicts not the least injury on the man who propitiates him by oblations: he is the first who acquires wealth.

४९४९. पूषा गा अन्वेतु न: पूषा रंक्षत्वर्वर्वत:। पूषा वाजं सनोतु न:।।५।।

5. May *Pūṣan* come to (guard) our cattle, may *Pūṣan* protect our horses; may *Pūṣan* give us food.

४९५०. पूषन्नु प्र गा इहि यर्जमानस्य सुन्वन्त:। अस्माकं स्तुवतामुत।।६।।

6. Come, *Pūṣan*, to (guard) the cattle of the institutor of the rite presenting libations, and also of us repeating (your) praises.

४९५१. माकिर्नेशन्माकीं रिषन्माकीं सं शारि केवंटे। अथारिष्टाभिरा गंहि।।७।

7. Let not, *Pūṣan*, our cattle perish; let them not be injured; let them not be hurt by falling into a well; come, therefore, along with them unharmed.

४९५२. शुण्वन्तं पूषणं वयमिर्यमनष्टवेदसम्। ईशानं राय ईमहे।।८।।

8. We solicit of *Pūṣan*, who hears (our eulogies); who is the averter (of poverty); the preserver of that which is not lost, the ruler (over all).

४९५३. पूषन्तवं व्रते वयं न रिष्येम कदां चन। स्तोतारस्त इह स्मसि।।९।।

9. May we never suffer detriment when engaged, *Pūṣan*, in your worship: we are at this time your adorers.

Yajurveda, 33.41.

४९५४. परि पूषा परस्ताद्धस्तं दधातु दक्षिणम्। पुनर्नो नष्टमाजतु।।१०।।

10. May *Pūṣan* put forth his right hand (to restrain our cattle) from going astray: may he bring again to us that which has been lost.

[सूक्त-५५]

[ऋषि- भरद्वाज बार्हस्पत्य। देवता- पूषा। छन्द- गायत्री]

४९५५. एहि वां विमुचों नपादाघृणे सं संचावहै। रथीर्ऋतस्यं नो भव।।१।।

1. Come illustrious grandson of *Prajāpati* to (me your) worshipper: let us two be associated: become the conveyer of our sacrifice.

Grandson of *Prajāpati*— *Vimuco napāt*: the first is rendered by *Prajāpati* as he who, at the period of creation, lets loose, *vimuñcati*, *visṛjati*, all creatures from himself, *svasakāśāt sarvāḥ prajāḥ*.

Come to me, your worshipper— *Ehi vām: Vā,* according to Sāyaṇa, here means praiser, from the root *va,* to go, to have odour, *vāṁ gantāram stotāraṁ mām, ehi, āgaccha.*

४९५६. रथीतमं कपर्दिनमीशानं राधसो महः। रायः सखायमीमहे ॥२॥

2. We solicit riches of our friend, (*Pūṣan*), the chief of charioteers, the wearer of a braid (of hair), the lord of infinite wealth.

The Wearer of a Braid of Hair— *Kapardinam, kapardaścūḍā tadvantam;* but it is more usually an epithet of *Śiva,* importing a braid of hair, not the *cūḍā,* or lock left on the crown of the head at tonsure.

४९५७. रायो धारास्याघृणे वसो राशिरंजाश्च। धीवतोधीवतः सखा ॥३॥

3. Illustrious *Pūṣan,* you are a torrent of riches: you, who have a goat for your steed, are a heap of wealth; the friend of every worshipper.

४९५८. पूषणं न्वंश्वजाश्वमुरुं स्तोषाम वाजिनम्। स्वसुर्यो जार उच्यते ॥४॥

4. We glorify *Pūṣan,* the rider of the goat, the giver of food, him who is called the gallant of his sister.

Who is called the Gallant of his sister— *Svasur yo jāra ucyate,* the sister of *Pūṣan* is the dawn, with whom he, as the sun, may be said to associate amorously.

४९५९. मातुर्दिधिषुमब्रवं स्वसुर्जारः शृणोतु नः। भ्रातेन्द्रस्य सखा मम ॥५॥

5. I glorify *Pūṣan,* the husband of his mother: may the gallant of his sister hear us; may the brother of *Indra* be our friend. .

The Husband of his Mother— *Mātur didhiṣum, rāreḥ patim,* the lord or husband of the night.

The Brother of Indra— As one of the *Ādityas,* or sons of *Aditi,* he may be called the brother of *Indra,* who is also one of the number.

४९६०. आजासः पूषणं रथे निशृम्भास्ते जनश्रियम्।
देवं वहन्तु बिभ्रतः ॥६॥

6. May the harnessed goats, drawing the deity in his car, bring hither *Pūṣan,* the benefactor of man.

[सूक्त-५६]

[ऋषि– भरद्वाज बार्हस्पत्य। देवता– पूषा। छन्द– गायत्री, ६ अनुष्टुप्]

४९६१. य एनमादिदेशति करम्भादिति पूषणम्। न तेन देव आदिशे ॥१॥

1. No (other) deity is indicated by him who declares the offering of mixed meal and butter to be intended for *Pūṣan.*

Mixed Meal and Butter— *Karambhāt iti: karambha* is said to be a mixture of parched barley-meal land butter.

४९६२. उत घा स रथीतंमः सख्या_ सर्त्पतिर्युजा। इन्द्रौ वृत्राणि जिघ्नते॥२॥

2. He, the chief of charioteers, the protector of the virtuous, *Indra*, destroys his foes, with his friend *Pūṣan* for his ally.

४९६३. उतादः प॑रुषे गविं सूरँश्चक्रं हिरण्ययंम्। न्यैरयद्रथीतंमः॥३॥

3. He, the impeller, the chief of charioteers, (*Pūṣan*) ever urges on that golden wheel (of his car) for the radiant sun

For the Radiant Sun— *Paruṣe gavi:* the first is explained *parvavati, bhāsvati vā,* the period-having or the shining: the second is rendered *Āditya,* he who moves or revolves, *gacchatīti gaur-ādityaḥ.*

४९६४. यद्ध त्वा॑ पुरुष्टुत ब्रवांम दस्र मन्तुमः। तत्सु नो॑ मन्मं साधय॥४॥

4. Since, intelligent *Pūṣan*, of godly aspect, the praised of many, we celebrate you today, therefore grant us the desired wealth.

४९६५. इमं चं नो गवेषणं॑ सातयें सीषधो गणम्। आरात् पूषन्नसि श्रुतः॥५॥

5. Gratify this our assembly, desirous of cattle, by their acquisition: you, *Pūṣan*, are renowned afar.

४९६६. आ ते॑ स्वस्तिमीमहे आरे अंघामुप॑वसुम्।

अद्या चं सर्वतांतये श्वश्च॑ सर्वतांतये॥६॥

6. We deserve of your well-being, remote from evil, approximate to wealth, both for the sake of general sacrifice toady, for the sake of general sacrifice to-marrow.

General Sacrifice today, Etc.— *Adya ca sarvatātaye, śvaś-ca sarvatātaye:* the substantive is explained *yajña,* that which is conducted by all the priest, *sarvair-ṛtvigbhis-tāyate;* or it may mean for the dissemination of all enjoyment, *sarveṣām bhogānām vistārāya.*

[सूक्त-५७]

[**ऋषि**- भरद्वाज बार्हस्पत्य। **देवता**- इन्द्र पूषा। **छन्द**- त्रिष्टुप्, २ जगती]

४९६७. इन्द्रा नु पूषणा॑ वयं सख्यायं॑ स्वस्तयें। हुवेम वाजसातये॥१॥

1. We invoke you, *Indra* and *Pūṣan*, for your friendship, for our well-being, and for the obtaining of food.

Sāmaveda, 202.

४९६८. सोमंमन्य उपासदत्पातवे चम्वौः सुतम्। करम्भमन्य इच्छति॥२॥

2. One (of you) approaches to drink the *Soma* poured out into ladles, the other desires the buttered meal.

The Buttered Meal–*Karambham*: see the preceding *Sūkta*, note on I.

४९६९. अजा अन्यस्य वह्नयो हरी अन्यस्य सम्भृता।
ताभ्यां वृत्राणि जिघ्नते॥३॥

3. Goats are the bearers of the one, two well-fed horses of the other, and with them he destroys his foes.

४९७०. यदिन्द्रो अनयद्रितो महीरपो वृषन्तमः। तत्र पूषाभवत्सचा॥४॥

4. When the showerer *Indra* sends down the falling and mighty waters, there is *Pūṣan* along with him.

Sāmaveda, 148.

४९७१. तां पूष्णः सुमतिं वयं वृक्षस्य प्र वयामिव। इन्द्रस्य चा रभामहे॥५॥

5. We depend upon the good-will of *Pūṣan*, and of *Indra*, as (we cling) to the branches of a tree.

४९७२. उत्पूषणं युवामहेऽभीशूँरिव सारथिः। मह्या इन्द्रं स्वस्तये॥६॥

6. We draw to us, for our great welfare, *Pūṣan* and *Indra*, as a charioteer (pulls tight) his reins.

[सूक्त-५८]

[ऋषि– भरद्वाज बार्हस्पत्य। देवता– पूषा। छन्द– त्रिष्टुप्, २ जगती]

४९७३. शुक्रं ते अन्यद्यजतं ते अन्यद्विषुरूपे अहनी द्यौरिवासि।
विश्वा हि माया अवसि स्वधावो भद्रा ते पूषन्निह रातिरस्तु॥१॥

1. One of your forms, (*Pūṣan*), is luminous, one is venerable: so that the day is variously complexioned: for you are like the sun: verily, bestower of food, you protect all intelligences: may your auspicious liberality be manifested on this occasion.

Sāmaveda, 75, also *Nirukta*, 12.17, Sāyaṇa follows Yāska.

You are like the Sun— *Pūṣan* is here identified with both day and night, or is considered as their regulator.

४९७४. अजाश्वः पशुपा वाजपस्त्यो धियञ्जिन्वो भुवने विश्वे अर्पितः।
अष्ट्रां पूषा शिथिरामुद्वरीवृजत् सञ्चक्षाणो भुवना देव ईयते॥२॥

2. The rider of the goat, the protector or animals, in whose dwelling good is abundant, the propitiated by sacred rites, who has been placed over the whole (world), the divine *Pūṣan*, brandishing his loosened goad, proceeds (in the sky), contemplating all beings.

Placed over the whole World— Placed so by *Prajāpati*, according to the Scholiast, in his capacity of nourishing all things, *poṣakatvena*.

Proceeds in the Sky, Etc.— As identval with the sun.

४९७५. यास्ते॑ पूष॒न्नावो॒ अन्तः॑ स॒मुद्रे॒ हिर॑ण्ययी॒रन्तरि॑क्षे॒ चर॑न्ति ।
ताभि॑र्यासि दू॒त्यां॑ सूर्य॑स्य॒ कामे॑न कृ॒त॒ श्रव॑ इ॒च्छमा॑नः ॥३॥

3. With those your golden vessels, which navigate within the ocean-firmament, you discharge the office of messenger of the sun: desirous of the sacrificial food, you are propitiated by (that which is) willingly offered.

Messenger of the Sun— *Yāsi dūtyām sūryasya*: Sāyaṇa relates a legend which says, that on one occasion, when *Sūrya*, with the gods, had set out to fight the *Asuras*, he sent *Puṣan* to his abode to console his wife, who was greatly afflicted by his going to the wars; for which office *Puṣan* is here commended.

४९७६. पू॒षा सु॒बन्धु॒र्दिव॒ आ पृ॑थि॒व्या इ॒ळस्पति॒र्मघ॑वा॒ दस्म॑वर्चाः ।
यं दे॒वासो॒ अद॑दुः॒ सूर्या॑यै॒ कामे॑न कृ॒तं तव॑सं स्व॒ञ्चम् ॥४॥

4. *Pūṣan* is the kind kinsman of heaven and earth, the lord of food, the possessor of opulence, of goodly form; whom the gods gave to *Sūrya*, vigorous, well-moving, propitiated by (that which is) willingly offered.

Propitiated by that which is Willingly Offered— *Kāmena kṛtaḥ* is the whole text; the Scholiast fills it up with *paśvādiviṣayena stotṛbhir vaśīkṛtaḥ asi,* you are subjected or propitiated by worshippers by means of the *Paśu* and other offerings.

[सूक्त-५९]

[ऋषि- भरद्वाज बार्हस्पत्य। देवता- इन्द्राग्नी।

छन्द- बृहती, (७-१० अनुष्टुप्]

४९७७. प्र नु वो॑चा सु॒तेषु॑ वां वी॒र्या॑ यानि॑ चक्र॒थुः ।
ह॒तासो॑ वां पि॒तरो॑ दे॒वश॑त्रव॒ इन्द्रा॑ग्नी जी॒वथो॑ युव॒म् ॥१॥

1. When the libation is effused I celebrate, *Indra* and *Agni*, your heroic exploits: the *Pitras*, the enemies of the gods, have been slain by you, and you survive.

The *Pitras*— By *Pitras*, in this place, the Scholiast says *Asuras* are intended, as derived from the root *pi* to injure, *piyatir-hiṁsākarme.*

४९७८. ब॒ळि॒त्था म॑हि॒मा वा॑मिन्द्रा॒ग्नी प॑नि॒ष्ठ आ ।
स॒मानो॑ वां ज॒नि॒ता भ्रात॑रा यु॒वं य॒माविहे॒हमा॑तरा ॥२॥

2. Your greatness, *Indra* and *Agni*, is after this fashion, and is most deserving of praise: the same is your progenitor: twin brethren are you, having a mother everywhere present.

Having a mother everywhere Present— *Ihehamātarau*, of whom the mother is here and there: *Aditi* is their mother, in common with all the gods, and she is here identified with the wide extended earth, *vistīrṇa bhūmiḥ,* according to Sāyaṇa.

४९७९. ओकिवांसा सुते सचाँ अश्वा सप्ती इवादने ।

इन्द्रान्व१र्ग्नी अवसेह वज्रिणा वयं देवा हवामहे ॥३॥

3. You approach together, when the libation is effused, like two fleet coursers to their forage: we invoke today *Indra* and *Agni*, deities armed with the thunderbolt, to this ceremony for our preservation.

४९८०. य इन्द्राग्नी सुतेषु वां स्तवत्तेष्वृतावृधा ।

जोषवाकं वदतः पज्रहोषिणा न देवा भसर्थश्चन ॥४॥

4. Divine *Indra* and *Agni*, augmenters of sacrifice by whom the acclamation (of praise) is received, you partake not of the (*Soma*) of him who, when the libation is effused, praises you (improperly), uttering unacceptable eulogies.

Praises you Improperly— *Yo vaṁ stavat* is explained by the commentator, he who may praise you badly, *kutsitaṁ stūyāt*.

Uttering Unacceptable Eulogies— *Joṣavākam vadataḥ* : the first is explained, *prītihetutvena kartavyaṁ svay aprītikaraṁ vacam*, speech to be uttered with the design of gaining affection, but of itself producing disaffection or dislike; so in the *Nirukta*, 5.22, as quoted by Sāyaṇa, *ya Indragnī suteṣu vām someṣu stauti teṣu na tasya aśnīthaḥ*, of him who praises you two, *Agni* and *Indra*, when the *Soma* juices are effused you do not eat (the offering): the printed *Nirukta* has, you eat, omitting the negative: of *joṣavākam*, it is first said, *avijñātanāmadheyam joṣayitavyaṁ bhavati*, that being of unknown name is to be propitiated; and again, *yo ayaṁ joṣavākaṁ vadati vijañjapaḥ na tasya aśnīthaḥ*, this person who utters, *joṣavākam*, repeating incessantly, or silently, propitiatory prayer of various object, of that man, you two do not eat the offering.

४९८१. इन्द्राग्नी को अस्य वां देवौ मर्तश्चिकेतति ।

विषूचो अश्वान्युयुजान ईयत एकः समान आ रथै ॥५॥

5. What mortal, divine *Indra* and *Agni*, is a judge of that (your act), when one of you, harnessing his diversely-going horses, proceeds in the common car.

One of you. . . . . Proceeds in the Common Car— *Viṣūco aśvān yuyujāna īyate ekaḥ samāne rathe*: the one is *Indra*, who, as identical with the sun, goes over the world in a car which is common to him and *Agni*, as being also identified with the sun: the same identity being kept in view, *Indra* yokes the multiform horses, months, weeks, days, to a monoform car, or the year.

४९८२. इन्द्राग्नी अपादियं पूर्वागात्पद्वतीभ्यः।

हित्वी शिरो जिह्वया वावदच्चरत्रिंशत्पदा न्यक्रमीत्॥६॥

6. This footless (dawn), *Indra* and *Agni*, comes before the footed sleepers, animating the head (of living beings with consciousness), causing them to utter loud sounds with their tongues, and passing onwards she traverses thirty steps.

Animating the Head— *Hitvī śiras*, literally, exciting the head, which is the whole of the text, is explained *prāṇinām śiro prerayitrī*, urging or animating the head of living beings: or it may apply to the dawn, as being headless, *śiras tyaktvā svayam aśiraskā satī*, she having abandoned the head, being of herself headless, though what they may mean is doubtful: so *Sāmaveda*, 281, and *Yajuṣ*, 33.93: Mahīdhara, after proposing the same interpretation as Sāyaṇa, suggests another, in which he refers the epithets to *vāc*, speech, *apād*, footless, meaning prose, *gadyātmikā*, and so on, but this is obviously fanciful.

Thirty Steps— The thirty *muhūrtas*, the divisions of the day and might.

४९८३. इन्द्राग्नी आ हि तन्वते नरो धन्वानि बाह्वोः।

मा नो अस्मिन्महाधने परा वर्क्तं गविष्टिषु॥७॥

7. *Indra* and *Agni*, men verily stretch their bows with their arms, but do not you desert us contending for cattle in the great combat.

४९८४. इन्द्राग्नी तपन्ति माघा अर्यो अरातयः।

अप द्वेषांस्या कृतं युयुतं सूयादधि॥८॥

8. *Indra* and *Agni*, murderous, aggressive enemies harass us: drive away mine adversaries: separate them from (sight of) the sun.

४९८५. इन्द्राग्नी युवोरपि वसु दिव्यानि पार्थिवा।

आ न इह प्र यच्छतं रयिं विश्वायुपोषसम्॥९॥

9. *Indra* and *Agni*, yours are both celestial and terrestrial treasures: bestow upon us, on this occasion, life sustaining riches.

४९८६. इन्द्राग्नी उक्थवाहसा स्तोमैर्भिर्हवनश्रुता।

विश्वाभिर्गीर्भिरा गंतमस्य सोमस्य पीतयेे॥१०॥

10. *Indra* and *Agni*, who are to be attracted by hymns; you, who hear our invocation (accompanied) by praise and by all adorations, come hither to drink of this *Soma* libation.

[सूक्त-६०]

[**ऋषि**– भरद्वाज बार्हस्पत्य। **देवता**– इन्द्राग्नी।

छन्द– गायत्री, १-३, १३ त्रिष्टुप्, १४ बृहती, १५ अनुष्टुप्]

४९८७. श्रथद्वृत्रमुत संनोति वाजमिन्द्रा यो अग्नी सहुरी सपर्यात्।

इर्ज्यन्तां वसव्यस्य भूरे: सहस्तमा सहसा वाजयन्तां॥१॥

1. He overcomes his enemy, and acquires food, who worships the victorious *Indra* and *Agni*, the lords of infinite opulence, most powerful in strength, desirous of (sacrificial) food.

४९८८. ता यौधिष्टमभि गा इंन्द्र नूनमप: स्वर्रुषसों अग्न ऊळ्हा:।

दिश: स्वर्रुषस इन्द्र चित्रा अपो गा अग्ने युवसे नियुत्वान्॥२॥

2. *Indra* and *Agni*, verily you have combated for (the recovery of) the cows, the waters, the sun, the dawns that had been carried away (by the *Asuras*): you reunitest, *Indra*, (with the world), the quarters of the horizon, the sun, the wonderful waters, the dawns, the cattle, and so do you, *Agni*, who have the *Niyut* steeds.

४९८९. आ वृत्रहणा वृत्रहभि: शुष्मैरिन्द्रे यातं नमोभिरग्ने अर्वाक्।

युवं राधोभिरकंवेभिरिन्द्राग्नेे अस्मे भवतमुत्तमेभि:॥३॥

3. Slayers of *Vṛtra*, *Indra* and *Agni*, come down with foe-subduing energies, (to be invigorated) by (our) offerings: be manifest to us, *Indra* and *Agni*, with unblameable and most excellent riches.

४९९०. ता हुवे ययौरिदं पप्ने विश्वं पुरा कृतम्। इन्द्राग्नी न मर्धत:॥४॥

4. I invoke those two, the whole of whose deeds of old have been celebrated: *Indra* and *Agni* harm us not.

Sāmaveda, 853.

४९९१. उग्रा विघनिंता मृध इन्द्राग्नी हवामहे। ता नौ मृळात ईदृशे॥५॥

5. We invoke the fierce *Indra* and *Agni*, the slayers of enemies: may they give us success in similar warfare.

Maṇḍala 6, Sūkta 60   **133**

Sāmaveda, 854. Yajurveda, 33.61.

४९९२. हतो वृत्राण्यार्या हतो दासानि सर्पती। हतो विश्वा अप द्विषः॥६॥

6. Counteract all oppressions (committed) by the pious:
counteract all oppressions (committed) by the impious; protectors
of the virtuous, destroy all those who hate us.

Oppressions Committed by the Pious, Etc.— Hato vṛtrāny-āryā
hato dāsāni, vṛtrāṇi and dāsāni, being neuter, can scarcely signify aryas
and dāsas themselves: therefore the Scholiast interprets them āryaiḥ and
dāsaiḥ kṛtāni, things done by them severally, that is, upadravajātāni,
things generated by violence or oppression and the like; also Sāmaveda,
855.

४९९३. इन्द्राग्नी युवामिमेऽभि स्तोमा अनूषत। पिबतं शम्भुवा सुतम्॥७॥

7. Indra and Agni, these hymns glorify you both: drink,
bestowers of happiness, the libation.

४९९४. या वां सन्ति पुरुस्पृहौ नियुतो दाशुषे नरा।

इन्द्राग्नी ताभिरा गंतम्॥८॥

8. Indra and Agni, leaders (of rites), whose Niyut steeds are
desired by many, come with them to the donor (of the libation).

४९९५. ताभिरा गच्छतं नरोपेदं सर्वनं सुतम्। इन्द्राग्नी सोमपीतये॥९॥

9. Come with them, leaders (of rites), to the effused libation, to
drink, Indra and Agni, of the Soma.

This and the two preceding occur Sāmaveda, 991-93.

४९९६. तमीळिष्व यो अर्चिषा वना विश्वा परिष्वजत्।

कृष्णा कृणोति जिह्वया॥१०॥

10. Glorify that Agni who envelopes all the forest with flame,
who blackens them with (his) tongue.

४९९७. य इद्ध आविवासति सुम्नमिन्द्रस्य मर्त्यः।

द्युम्नाय सुतरा अपः॥११॥

11. The mortal who presents the gratifying (oblation) to Indra
in the kindled (fire), to him (Indra grants) acceptable waters for his
sustenance.

४९९८. ता नो वाजवतीरिष आशून्पिपृतमर्वतः। इन्द्रमग्निं च वोळ्हवे॥१२॥

12. May those two grant us strengthening food, and swift
horses to convey (our offerings).

Sāmaveda, 1151.

४९९९. उभा वामिन्द्राग्नी आहुवध्यां उभा राधंसः सह मांदयध्यै।

उभा दातारांविषां रंयीणामुभा वार्जस्य सांतयें हुवे वाम्॥१३॥

13. I invoke you both, *Indra* and *Agni*, to be present at the sacrifice; and both together to be exhilarated by the (sacrificial) food; for you are both donors of food and riches, and therefore I invoke you both for the obtaining of sustenance.

५०००. आ नो गव्यैभिरश्व्यैर्वसव्यैइरुपं गच्छतम्।

सखांयौ देवौ संख्यार्यं शम्भुवेन्द्राग्नी ता हंवामहे॥१४॥

14. Come to us with herds of cattle, with troops of horses, with ample treasures, divine friends, *Indra* and *Agni*: givers of happiness, we invoke you as such for your friendship.

५००१. इन्द्राग्नी शृणुतं हवं यर्जमानस्य सुवन्तः।

वीतं हव्यान्या गंतं पिबतं सोम्यं मधुं॥१५॥

15. Hear, *Indra* and *Agni*, the institutor of the rite as he offers the libation: partake of the offering: come, quaff the sweet *Soma* beverage.

[सूक्त-६१]

[**ऋषि**– भरद्वाज बार्हस्पत्य। **देवता**– सरस्वती।

छन्द– गायत्री, १-3, १3 जगती, १४ त्रिष्टुप्]

५००२. इयमंददाद्रभसमृणच्युतं दिवौदासं वध्र्यश्वांय दाशुषें।

या शश्वन्तमाचखादांवसं पणिं ता तें दात्रांणि तविषा सरस्वति॥१॥

1. She gave to the donor of the oblations, *Vadhryaśva*, a son *Divodāsa* endowed with speed, and acquitting the debt (due to gods and progenitors); she who destroyed the churlist niggard, (thinking) only of himself: such are your great bounties, *Sarasvatī*.

Divodāsa— The *Viṣṇu Purāṇa* makes the father of *Divodāsa*, *Bahvasva* but this is a various or erroneous reading: it is another representation of the name *Bandhyasva*: a MSS. of the *Vāyu Purāṇa* is cited in the note for the reading of our text, *Badhryaśva*; *Viṣṇu Purāṇa*, p.454, note 51.

The Churlish Niggard thinking only of himself— *Pani* as usual.

५००3. इयं शुष्मेभिर्बिसखाइवारुजत्सानु गिरीणां तविषेभिरूर्मिभिः।

पारावतघ्नीमर्वसे सुवृक्तिभिः सरस्वतीमा विवासेम धीतिभिः॥२॥

2. With impetuous and mighty waves she breaks down the precipices of the mountains, like a digger for the lotus fibres: we adore for our protection, the praises and with sacred rites, *Sarasvatī* the underminer of both her banks.

With Impetuous and mighty Waves— In the first stanza *Sarasvatī* has been addressed as a goddess: here she is praised as a river: the confusion pervades the entire *Sūkta*.

Like a Digger for the Lotus-Fibres— *Bisa-khā iva, bisam khanati,* who digs the *bisa*, the long fibres of the stem of the lotus, in delving for which he breaks down the banks of the pond.

Like a Digger for the Lotus-Fibres—

५००४. सरस्वति देवनिदो नि बर्हय प्रजां विश्वस्य बृसयस्य मायिनः।
उत क्षितिभ्योऽवनीरविन्दो विषमेभ्यो अस्रवो वाजिनीवति ॥३॥

3. Destroy, *Sarasvatī*, the revilers of the gods, the offspring of the universal deluder, *Bṛsaya*: giver of sustenance, you have acquired for men the lands (seized by the *Asuras*), and have showered water upon them.

Bṛsaya— *Bṛsaya* is a name of *Tvaṣṭā*, whose son was *Vṛtra*: in Sāyaṇa's introduction to the *Black, Taittirīya Yajuṣ*, a curious legend is related, intended to illustrate the importance of correctly accentuating the words of the Veda: *Indra,* it is said, had killed a son of *Tvaṣṭā*, named *Viśvarūpa*, in consequence of which there was enmity between them, and, upon the occasion of a *Soma*-sacrifice celebrated by *Tvaṣṭā*, he omitted to include *Indra* in his invitations to the gods: *Indra*, however, came an uninvited guest, and by force took a part of the *Soma* libation; with the remainder *Tvaṣṭā* performed a sacrifice for the birth of an individual who should avenge his quarrel and destroy his adversary, directing the priest to pray, now let a man be born and prosper, the killer of *Indra*: in uttering the *Mantra,* however, the officiating priest made a mistake in the accentuation of the term *Indraghātaka,* slayer of *Indra*, in which sense, as a *Tat-puruṣa* compound, the acute accent should have been placed upon the last syllable; instead of which the reciter of the *Mantra* placed the accent on the first syllable, whereby the compound became a *Bahuvrīhi* epithet, signifying one of whom *Indra* is the slayer: consequently, when, by virtue of the rite, *Vṛtra* was produced, he was foredoomed by the wrong accentuation to be put to death by *Indra* instead of becoming his destroyer: *Taittirīya Yajuṣ*, p.43.

You have Acquired for men the Lands, Etc.— *Kṣitibhyo avanīravindo viṣam abhyo asravaḥ* may also admit of a different interpretation, according to Sāyaṇa, or, you have shed poison upon them, or destroyed them.

५००५. प्र णो देवी सरस्वती वाजेभिर्वाजिनीवती। धीनामवित्र्यवतु ॥४॥

4. May the divine *Sarasvatī*, the acceptress of (sacrificial) food, the protectress of her worshippers, sustain us with (abundant) viands.

५००६. यस्त्वा देवि सरस्वत्युपब्रूते धनें हिते। इन्द्रं न वृत्रतूर्यें ।।५।।

5. Divine *Sarasvatī*, protect him engaged in conflict for the sake of wealth, who glorifies you like *Indra*.

५००७. त्वं देवि सरस्वत्यवा वाजेषु वाजिनि। रदा पूषेव नः सनिम् ।।६।।

6. Divine *Sarasvatī*, abounding in food, protect us in combat, and, like *Pūṣan*, give us gifts.

५००८. उत स्या नः सरस्वती घोरा हिरण्यवर्तनिः। वृत्रघ्नी वष्टि सुष्टुतिम् ।।७।

7. May the fierce *Sarasvatī*, riding in a golden chariot, the destructress of enemies, be pleased by our earnest laudation.

५००९. यस्या अनन्तो अह्रुतस्त्वेषश्चरिष्णुरर्णवः। अमश्चरति रोरुवत् ।।८।।

8. May she whose might, infinite, undeviating, splendid, progressive, water-shedding, proceeds loud-sounding.

५०१०. सा नो विश्वा अति द्विषः स्वसृॄरन्या ऋतावरी। अतन्नहेव सूर्यः ।।९।।

9. Overcome all our adversaries, and bring to us her other water-laden sisters, as the ever-rolling sun (leads on) the days.

Bring to us her other water-laden sisters— *Ati svasṝranyā ṛtāvarī: ati* is put, it is said, for *atini*, to lead over or beyond, or in the order of the text, *ati dviṣaḥ*, may the other sisters overcome those who hate us.

५०११. उत नः प्रिया प्रियासु सप्तस्वसा सुजुष्टा। सरस्वती स्तोम्या भूत् ।।१०।

10. May *Sarasvatī*, who has seven sister, who is dearest amongst those dear to us, and is fully propitiated, be ever adorable.

Seven Sisters— *Saptasvasā*: either the seven metres of the Vedas, or the seven rivers.

५०१२. आपप्रुषी पार्थिवान्युरु रजो अन्तरिक्षम्। सरस्वती निदस्पातु ।।११।।

11. May *Sarasvatī*, filling (with radiance) the expanse of earth and heaven, defend us from the reviled.

५०१३. त्रिषधस्था सप्तधातुः पञ्च जाता वर्धयन्ती।
वाजेवाजे हव्या भूत् ।।१२।।

12. Abiding in the three worlds, comprising seven elements, cherishing the five races (of beings), she is ever to be invoked in battle.

Seven Elements— *Saptadhātu,* as before, either the metres or the rivers.

५०१४. प्र या महिम्ना महिनासु चेकिते द्युम्नेभिरन्या अपसामपस्तमा।
रथं इव बृहती विभ्वने कृतोपस्तुत्या चिकितुषा सरस्वती।।१३।।

13. She who is distinguished amongst them as eminent in greatness and in her glories; she who is the most impetuous of all other streams; she who has been created vast in capacity as a chariot, she, *Sarasvatī,* is to be glorified by the discreet (worshipper).

Amongst them— *Āsu,* amongst them, divinties, or rivers, *devatānām nadīnām madhye.*

Vast in Capacity as a Chariot— *Ratha iva bṛhatī vibhvane kṛta:* made great in vastness, like a chariot created by *Prajāpati,* so created, *vibhvane, vibhutvāya,* for greatness or vastness.

५०१५. सरस्वत्यभि नो नेषि वस्यो मापं स्फरीः पर्यसा मा न आ धक्।
जुषस्व नः सख्या वेश्या च मा त्वत्क्षेत्राण्यरणानि गन्म।।१४।।

14. Guide us, *Sarasvatī,* to precious wealth: reduce us not to insignificance; overwhelm us not with (excess of) water; be pleased by our friendly (services) and access to our habitations, and let us not repair to places unacceptable to you.

Reduce us not to Insignificance— *Mā apa spharīḥ: sphara,* it is said, means increase, greatness, prosperity; with the prefix, it implies the reverse, *apravṛddhān mā kārṣīḥ,* do not make us unimportant or adject.

ANUVAKA VI

[सूक्त-६२]

[**ऋषि**- भरद्वाज बार्हस्पत्य। **देवता**- अश्विनीकुमार। **छन्द**- त्रिष्टुप्]

५०१६. स्तुषे नरा दिवो अस्य प्रसन्ताश्विना हुवे जरमाणो अर्कैः।
या सद्य उस्रा व्युषि ज्मो अन्तान्युयूषतः पर्युरू वरांसि।।१।।

1. I praise the two leaders of heaven, the presiders over this world: I invoke the *Aśvins,* glorifying them with sacred hymns, them, who are ever the discomfiture (of foes), who at dawn scatter the investing glooms to the ends of the earth.

५०१७. ता यज्ञमा शुचिभिश्चक्रमाणा रथस्य भानुं रुरुचू रजोभिः।
पुरू वरांस्यमिता मिमानापो धन्वान्यति याथो अज्रान्।।२।।

2. Coming to the sacrifice with their bright splendours, they light up the lustre of (their) car; emitting vast and infinite radiance; they drive their horses over deserts (refreshing them) with water.

५०१८. ता ह त्यद्वर्तिर्यदरध्रमुग्रेत्था धियं ऊहथुः शश्वदश्वैः।
मनोजवेभिरिषिरैः शयध्यै परि व्यथिर्दाशुषो मर्त्यस्य॥३॥

3. Fierce *Asvins*, from that humble mansion to which (you have repaired), you have ever borne with your desirable horses, as swift as thought, the pious worshippers in some manner (to heaven): Let the injurer of the liberal man (be consigned by you) to (final) repose.

५०१९. ता नव्यसो जरमाणस्य मन्मोप भूषतो युयुजानसप्ती।
शुभं पृक्षमिषमूर्जं वहन्ता होता यक्षत्प्रत्नो अध्रगुयुवाना॥४॥

4. Harnessing their horses, bringing excellent food, nourishment, and strength, they approach (to receive) the adoration of their recent worshipper; and may the benevolent ancient invoker of the gods (*Agni*) sacrifice to the ever youthful (deities).

५०२०. ता वल्गू दस्रा पुरुशाकतमा प्रत्ना नव्यसा वचसा विवासे।
या शंसते स्तुवते शम्भविष्ठा बभूवतुर्गृणते चित्रराती॥५॥

5. I worship with a new hymn those two quick-moving good-looking ancient (*Asvins*), the achievers of many exploits, who are the givers of great felicity to him who prays to (them), or praises (them); the bestowers of wondrous gifts on him who adores (them).

५०२१. ता भुज्युं विभिरद्भ्य समुद्रातुग्रस्य सूनुमूहथु रजोभिः।
अरेणुभिर्योजनेभिर्भुजन्ता पतत्रिभिरर्णसो निरुपस्थात्॥६॥

6. They bore up from the waters, from the ocean, by the winged horses attached to their car, (passing) by roads unsoiled by dust, *Bhujyu*, the son of *Tugra*; they (bore them) from out of the lap of the water.

From out of the lap of the Water— *Arṇaso nirupasthāt*, from the womb of the water, *jalasya yoneh, samudrād, adbhyo nir agamayatam*:

५०२२. वि जयुषा रथ्या यातमद्रिं श्रुतं हवं वृषणा वध्रिमत्याः।
दशस्यन्ता शयवे पिप्यथुर्गामिति च्यवाना सुमतिं भुरण्यू॥७॥

7. Riders in you car, you have penetrated the mountain by your triumphant chariot: showerers (of benefits) you heard the invocation of *Vadhrimatī*: you have nourished, bountiful givers, the cow for *Śayu*—and in this manner displaying benevolence are you everywhere present.

Vadhrimatī- Śayu- Rathyā- See *Ṛg.* i, 116. 20 & 22

५०२३. यद्रोदसी प्रदिवो अस्ति भूमा हेळो देवानामुत मर्त्यात्रा।
तदादित्या वसवो रुद्रियासो रक्षोयुजे तपुरघं दधात॥८॥

8. Heaven and Earth, *Ādityas, Vasus, Maruts,* render that dread anger of the gods which (has) of old (been directed) against mortals, destructive and fatal to him who is associated with the *Rākṣasas*.

Who is Associated with the *Rākṣasas*— *Rakṣoyuje* is explained *Rākṣasam svāmine, prerakāya vā;* for, *Rakṣobhir yuktāya yajvane,* one who sacrifices, assisted for joined by the *Rākṣasas*.

५०२४. य ई राजानावृतुथा विदधद्रजसो मित्रो वरुणश्चिकेतत्।
गम्भीराय रक्षसे हेतिमस्य द्रोघाय चिद्वचस आनवाय॥९॥

9. *Mitra* and *Varuṇa* recognize him who of all the world worships the royal (*Aśvins*) in due season; he hurls his weapon against the strong *Rākṣasa*, against the malignant menaces of man.

Against the Malignant Menaces of Man— *Droghāya cid vacase ānavāya* is explained, *abhidrohātmakāya manuṣyasaṁbhandine vacanāya eva.*

५०२५. अन्तरैश्चक्रैस्तनयाय वर्तिर्द्युमता यातं नृवता रथेन।
सनुत्येन त्यजसा मर्त्यस्य वनुष्यतामपि शीर्षा ववृक्तम्॥१०॥

10. Come with your shining and well-guided chariot, (fitted) with excellent wheels, to our dwelling, (to bestow upon us) male offspring: cut off with secret indignation the heads of those obstructing (the adoration) of the mortal (who worships you).

Well-Guided Chariot— *Nṛvata rathena,* having a leader, a driver; or *nṛ* may mean a horse.

With Excellent Wheels— *Antaraiścakraiḥ,* The commentator explains the adjective *anikṛṣṭaiḥ,* with not inferior wheels.

With Secret Indignation— *Sanutyena tyajasā* are explained *tirohitena krodhena.*

५०२६. आ परमाभिरुत मध्यमाभिर्नियुद्भिर्यातमवमाभिर्वाक्।
दृळ्हस्य चिद् गोमतो वि व्रजस्य दुरो वर्त गृणते चित्रराती॥११॥

11. Come down, whether with the most excellent, or middling, or inferior *Niyut* steeds; set upon the doors of the fast-shut stall of the cattle: be bountiful to him who praises you.

[सूक्त-६३]

[**ऋषि**– भरद्वाज बार्हस्पत्य। **देवता**– अश्विनीकुमार।

छन्द– त्रिष्टुप्, ११ एकपदा त्रिष्टुप्]

५०२७. क्रष्टत्या वल्गू पुरुहूताद्य दूतो न स्तोमोऽविदन्नमस्वान्।

आ यो अर्वाङ्नासत्या ववर्त प्रेष्ठा ह्यासथो अस्य मन्मन्।।१।।

1. Where may our praise and oblations find today for a messenger, those two splendid (*Aśvins*), the invoked of many, and bring the *Nāsatyās* to our presence? Be propitiated (*Aśvins*) by the adoration of this (your worshipper).

५०२८. अरं मे गन्तं हवनायास्मै गृणाना यथा पिबाथो अन्धः।

परि ह त्यद्वर्तिर्याथो रिषो न यत्परो नान्तरस्तुर्यात्।।२।।

2. Praised, that you may drink the (sacrificial) beverage, you come promptly upon this may invocation: keep guard around the dwelling against (all) adversaries, so that neither one that abides at a distance nor a neighbour may do us harm.

५०२९. अकारि वामन्धसो वरीमन्नस्तारि बर्हिः सुप्रायणतमम्।

उत्तानहस्तो युवयुर्ववन्दा वां नक्षन्तो अद्रय आञ्जन्।।३।।

3. (What is essential) for the copious effusion of (the sacrificial) food has been done for you: the very delicate sacred grass has been strewn: the (priest with) uplifted hands desirous of your presence praises you; the stones express (the *Soma* juice), designing it for you.

५०३०. ऊर्ध्वो वामग्निरध्वरेष्वस्थात्प्र रातिरेति जूर्णिनी घृताची।

प्र होता गूर्तमना उराणोऽयुक्त यो नासत्या हवीमन्।।४।।

4. *Agni* is above for you: he is present at (your) sacrifices: the oblation flows diffusive and redolent of *ghī*: deligent and zealous is the ministrant priest who is engaged, *Nāsatyās*, in your invocation.

५०३१. अधि श्रिये दुहिता सूर्यस्य रथं तस्थौ पुरुभुजा शतोतिम्।

प्र मायाभिर्मायिना भूतमत्र नरा नृतू जनिमन्यज्ञियानाम्।।५।।

5. Protectors of many, the daughter of *Sūrya* ascended your chariot the defence of hundreds, for refuge: sagacious leaders and guides, you have excelled by your devices (all others) at this appearance of the adorable (deities).

Leaders and Guides— *Nārā-nṛtyu* would be, literally, guides and dancers.

You have Excelled by your Devices, etc.— It is not very clear what is intended: the Scholiast refers to the legend of the *Aśvins* carrying off in their car the daughter of *Sūrya* from the other gods, as narrated in the *Aitareya Brāhmaṇa* iv.7.

५०३२. युवं श्रीभिर्दर्शताभिराभिः शुभे पुष्टिमूहथुः सूर्यायाः।
प्र वां वयो वपुषेऽनु पप्तन्नक्षद्राणी सुष्टुता धिष्ण्या वाम्॥६॥

6. You have provided with these beautiful splendours, gratification for the enjoyment of *Sūrya*, your horses have descended for felicity, deserving of praise, the laudation (of the sages) has reached you glorified.

५०३३. आ वां वयोऽश्वासो वहिष्ठा अभि प्रयो नासत्या वहन्तु।
प्र वां रथो मनोजवा असर्जीषः पृक्ष इषिधो अनु पूर्वीः॥७॥

7. May your rapid burthen-bearing steeds bring you *Nāsatyās* to the (sacrificial) food: your chariot swift as thought has dispensed substantial, desirable, abundant food.

५०३४. पुरु हि वां पुरुभुजा देष्णं धेनुं न इषं पिन्वतमस्क्राम्।
स्तुतश्च वां माध्वी सुष्टुतिश्च रसाश्च ये वामनु रातिमग्मन्॥८॥

8. Protectors of many, vast (wealth) is to be distributed by you: give us then nutritious and invariable food. Givers of delight, there are to you, adorers, and fit praise, and libations, which are prepared to acknowledge your liberality.

Nutritious and Invariable Food— The expression is singular, *dhenum na iṣam pinvatam askrām,* literally, give us a cow, food, that does not stray, Sāyaṇa explains *dhenu* by *prīṇayitrī*, gratifying: or *iṣam* may be the adjective for *eṣaṇīyam,* give us a desirable cow.

५०३५. उत मं ऋज्रे पुरयस्य रघ्वी सुमीळ्हे शतं पेरुके च पक्वा।
शाण्डो दाद्धिरणिनः समद्दिष्टीन् दश वशासो अभिषाचं ऋष्वान्॥९॥

9. May the two straight-going, light-moving, (mares) of *Puraya* be mine: may the hundred cows belonging to *Sumiḷha,* may the dressed viands prepared by *Peruka* be for me: may *Śaṇḍa*

bestow upon me ten handsome golden chariots, and obedient, valiant, and well-favoured (dependants).

We have nothing in this verse but epithets; in the first half, *ṛjre raghvī*, two straight-right-going, require some such noun as *vadave*, mares: to *śatam*, a hundred, the Scholiast supplies *gavām*, of cows: and to *pakva*, for *pakvāni*, he adds, *annāni*, viands: in the second half we have *hiraṇinaḥ vasmād, diṣṭin daśa*, ten golden to us handsome, *i.e.*, *rathān*, cars, understood; and again, *vaśāsaḥ abiśāca ṛṣvān*, obedient, valorous, handsome—what? We must ask the Scholiast. The answer is, *puruṣān*, men. If we render the stanza literally, it is utterly unintelligible: the greater part of the *Sūkta* is very obscure.

५०३६. सं वां शता नासत्या सहस्राश्वानां पुरुपन्था गिरे दात्।

भरद्वाजाय वीर नू गिरे दाद्धता रक्षांसि पुरुदंससा स्युः॥२०॥

10. May *Purupanthā, Nāsatyās*, grant to him who praises you, hundreds and thousands of horses: may he give them, heroes, to *Bharadvāja*: achievers of great deeds, may the *Rākṣasas* be slain.

५०३७. आ वां सुम्ने वरिमन्तस्सूरिभिः ष्याम्॥२१॥

11. May I be associated with the pious in the abundant felicity bestowed by you.

[सूक्त- ६४]

[ऋषि- भरद्वाज बार्हस्पत्य। देवता- उषा। छन्द- त्रिष्टुप्]

५०३८. उदु श्रिय उषसो रोचमाना अस्थुरपां नोर्मयो रुशन्तः।

कृणोति विश्वं सुपथा सुगान्यभूदु वस्वी दक्षिणा मघोनी॥१॥

1. The white and shining tints of the dawn have spread like the waves of the waters, for the beautifying (of the world); she renders all good roads easy to be traversed; she who is replete with delight, excellence, and health.

५०३९. भद्रा ददृक्ष उर्विया वि भास्युतै शोचिर्भानवो द्यामपप्तन्।

आविर्वक्षः कृणुषे शुभमानोषो देवि रोचमाना महोभिः॥२॥

2. Divine *Uṣas*, you are seen auspicious: you shine afar: your bright rays spread over the sky, lovely and radiant with great (splendours), you display your person.

५०४०. वहन्ति सीमरुणासो रुशन्तो गावः सुभगामुर्विया प्रथानाम्।

अपेजते शूरो अस्तेव शत्रून् बाधते तमो अजिरो न वोल्हा॥३॥

3. Ruddy and resplendent kine bear the auspicious, expanding, illustrious dawn: like a warrior, who, casting his darts, or a swift charger scattering enemies, she drives away the glooms.

Kine— *Gāvaḥ* is rendered by Sāyaṇa, *raśmayaḥ*, rays: one of its meanings it is true, but rather incompatible here with the verb *vahanti*, *vehunt*.

५०४१. सुगोत ते सुपथा पर्वतेष्ववाते अपस्तरसि स्वभानो।
सा न आ वह पृथुयामतृष्वे रयिं दिवो दुहितरिषयध्यै ॥४॥

4. Yours are good roads and easy to be traversed in mountains and inaccessible places: you pass self-irradiating over the waters: bring to us, daughter of heaven, in your spacious and beautiful chariot, desirable riches.

५०४२. सा वह योक्षभिरवातोषो वरं वहसि जोषमनु।
त्वं दिवो दुहितर्यां हं देवी पूर्वहूतौ मंहना दर्शता भूः ॥५॥

5. Do you *Uṣas* bring me opulence, for unopposed you bear with your oxen (wealth to your worshippers), according to your satisfaction: daughter of heaven, you who are divine, who are lovely, are to be worshipped at the first (daily) rite.

५०४३. उत्ते वयश्चिद्वसतेरपप्तन्नरश्च ये पितुभाजो व्युष्टौ।
अमा सते वहसि भूरि वाममुषो देवि दाशुषे मर्त्याय ॥६॥

6. At your dawning, divine *Uṣas*, the birds spring up from their nests, and men who have to gain their sustenance (arise): you, divine *Uṣas*, bring ample wealth to the mortal who is nigh you, the offerer of the oblation.

[सूक्त-६५]

[ऋषि- भरद्वाज बार्हस्पत्य। देवता- उषा। छन्द- त्रिष्टुप्]

५०४४. एषा स्या नौ दुहिता दिवोजाः क्षितीरुच्छन्ती मानुषीरजीगः।
या भानुना रुशता राम्यास्वज्ञायि तिरस्तमंसश्चिदक्तून् ॥१॥

1. This heaven-born daughter (of the sky), driving away the darkness for us, makes visible human beings; she who with bright lustre is perceived dissipating the glooms, and (extinguishing) the planets (shining) in the nights.

Makes Visible Human Beings— *Udgirati mānuṣīḥ prajāḥ*, is, literally, vomits them, *i.e.*, brings them up out of darkness into light.

In the Nights— *Rāmyāsu,* for *yāmyāsu, rātriṣu,* or being substituted for *y*: see the similar change in Burman articulation.

५०४५. वि तद्ययुररुणयुग्भिरश्वैश्चित्रं भान्त्युषसश्चन्द्ररथाः।

अग्रं यज्ञस्य बृहतो नयन्तीर्विं ता बाधन्ते तम ऊर्म्यायाः॥२॥

2. The Dawns in beautiful chariots drawn by purple steeds in pairs, shine gloriously as they proceed (along the heaven): bringing on the commencement of the great (morning) sacrifice, they disperse the darkness of the night.

५०४६. श्रवो वाजमिषमूर्जं वहन्तीर्नि दाशुषं उषसो मर्त्याय।

मघोनीर्वीरवत्पत्यमाना अवों धात विदुषते रत्नमद्य॥३॥

3. Dawns, bringing fame, and food, and sustenance, and strength to the mortal, the donor (of the oblation), abounding in wealth, and proceeding (through the sky), bestow upon the worshipper today food, with male descendants and riches.

५०४७. इदा हि वों विदुषते रत्नमस्तीदा वीराय दाशुषं उषासः।

इदा विप्राय जरते यदुक्था नि ष्म मावते वहथा पुरा चित्॥४॥

4. Verily, Dawns, there is at present wealth to give to your worshipper, to the man offering (oblations) to the sage repeating your praise; if the praises (are accepted), then bring to him who is like me such wealth as has been formerly bestowed (upon myself).

५०४८. इदा हि तं उषो अद्रिसानो गोत्रा गवामङ्गिरसो गृणन्ति।

व्यर्केण बिभिदुर्ब्रह्मणा च सत्या नृणामभवद्देवहूतिः॥५॥

5. Verily, *Uṣas,* the *Aṅgirasas* through your (favour) recover the herd of cattle from the summit of the mountain: by adoration and by prayer they have divided (the rock): unfailing was the praise of the gods uttered by the leaders (of rites).

५०४९. उच्छा दिवो दुहितः प्रत्नवन्नों भरद्वाजवद्विधते मघोनि।

सुवीरं रयिं गृणते ररीह्युरुगायमधि धेहि श्रवों नः॥६॥

6. Daughter of heaven, dawn upon us upon those of old: possessor of riches (down) upon the worshipper, as (you have done upon) *Bharadvāja:* grant to him who glorifies you, wealth with male descendants: give to us food that may be distributed to many.

[सूक्त-६६]

[ऋषि- भरद्वाज बार्हस्पत्य। देवता- मरुद्गण। छन्द- त्रिष्टुप्]

५०५०. वपुर्नु तच्चिकितुषे चिदस्तु समानं नाम धेनु पत्यमानम्।
मर्तेष्वन्यद्दोहसे पीपाय सकृच्छुक्रं दुदुहे पृश्निरूध:॥१॥

1. May the like-formed, benevolent, all-pervading, all humiliating troop (of the *Maruts*) be promptly with the prudent man: the troop that ever cherishes all that amongst mortals is designed to yield (them) advantage; and (at whose will) *Pṛśni* gives milk from (her) bright udder once (in the year).

That ever Cherishes all that, Etc.— The phraseology is obscure, *marttesu anyad dohase pīpāya*. It is amplified by Sāyaṇa, *tad rūpam* (*marutām*), *martyaloke anyad osadhi-vanaspatyādikam kāmān dogdhum āpyāyagoti*, that from of the *Maruts* causes one or other thing in the world, as herbaceous plants, forest trees, and the like, of flourish, so as to milk or yield what is desired.

Pṛśni— *Pṛśni* is said here to imply the firmament, which, by the influence of the winds, sends down its milk, *ie.*, rain, once, *i.e.*, at the rainy season.

५०५१. ये अग्नयो न शोशुचन्त्रिधाना द्वियर्तिर्मरुतो वावृधन्त।
अरेणवो हिरण्ययास एषां साकं नृम्णै: पौंस्येभिश्च भूवन्॥२॥

2. Unsoiled by dust the golden chariots of those *Maruts*, who are shining like kindled fires, enlarging themselves (at will) twofold and threefold, and (charged) with riches and virile energies, are manifest.

५०५२. रुद्रस्य ये मीळ्हुष: सन्ति पुत्रा यांश्रो नु दाधृविभिरध्यै।
विदे हि माता महो मही षा सेतृपृश्नि: सुभ्वे३ गर्भमाधात्॥३॥

3. They (who are) the sons of the showerer *Rudra*, whom the nursing (firmament is able) to sustain, and of whom, the mighty ones, it is known that the great *Pṛśni* has received the germ for the benefit (of man).

५०५३. न य ईषन्ते जनुषोऽया न्वइन्त: सन्तोऽवद्यानि पुनाना:।
निर्यद् दुहे शुचयोऽनु जोषमनु श्रिया तन्वमुक्षमाणा:॥४॥

4. They who approach not to men by any conveyance, being already in their hearts, purifying their defects: when brilliant they supply their milk (the rain) for the gratification (of their

worshippers): they are watering the earth (manifesting their collective): from with splendour.

Being Already in their Hearts— The *Maruts* are here regarded as identical with the *Prāṇaḥ*, vital airs.

५०५४. मधू न येषु दोहसें चिदया आ नार्म धृष्णु मारुतं दधाना:।

न ये स्तौना अयासों मह्ना नू चित्सुदानुर्वं यासदुग्रान्॥५॥

5. Approaching nigh to whom, and repeating the mighty name of the *Maruts*, (the worshipper is able) quickly to obtain (his wished): the liberal donor pacifies the angry *Maruts*, who are otherwise in their might the resistless plunderers (of their wealth).

Plunderers of their Wealth— The words are unusual, and the construction elliptical and involved: he pacifies those *na ye staunā ayāso mahnā nu cid*, who now are thieves going with greatness verily ever.

५०५५. त इदुग्रा: शर्वसा धृष्णुषेणा उभे युजन्त रोदसी सुमेके।

अध स्मैषु रोदसी स्वशोंचिरार्मवत्सु तस्थौ न रोक:॥६॥

6. Those fierce and powerfully arrayed (*Maruts*) unite by their strength the two beautiful (regions) heaven and earth; in them, the self-radiant, heaven and earth abide: the obstruction (of light) dwells not in those mighty ones.

Unite by their Strength— By the rain, which may be said to form a bond of union between heaven and earth.

५०५६. अनेनो वों मरुतो यामों अस्त्वनश्विश्विद्यमजत्यरथी:।

अनवसो अनभीशू रंजस्तूर्वि रोदसी पथ्यां याति साधर्न्॥७॥

7. May your chariot, *Maruts*, be devoid of wickedness; that which (the worshipper) impels, and which without driver, without horses, without provender, without traces, scattering water and accomplishing (desires), traverses heaven and earth and the paths (of the firmament).

५०५७. नास्यं वर्ता न तरुता न्वस्ति मरुतो यमवंथ वार्जसातौ।

तोके वा गोषु तनंये यमप्सु स व्रजं दर्ता पार्ये अध द्यो:॥८॥

8. There is no propeller, no obstructer, of him, whom, *Maruts*, you protect in battle: he whom (you prosper) with sons, grandsons, cattle, and water, is in war the despoiler of the herds of his ardent (foes).

Despoiler of the Herds of his Ardent Foe— *Sa vrajam dartā pārye adha dyoḥ,* is explained, *sa gavām saṅgham dārayitā saṅgrāme—dyoḥ,* is rendered by *vijigiṣor vā śatroḥ*, of one desirous to overcome, or an enemy.

५०५८. प्र चित्रमर्कं गृणते तुराय मारुताय स्वतवसे भरध्वम्।

ये सहांसि सहसा सहन्ते रेजते अग्ने पृथिवी मखेभ्यः॥९॥

9. Offer to the loud-sounding, quick-moving, self-invigorating company of the *Maruts*, excellent (sacrificial) food: (to them) who overcome strength by strength: the earth trembles, *Agni*, at the adorable (*Maruts*).

५०५९. त्विषीमन्तो अध्वरस्येव दिद्युत्तृषुच्यवसो जुह्वो३ नाग्नेः।

अर्चत्रयो धुनयो न वीरा भ्राजज्जन्मानो मरुतो अधृष्टाः॥१०॥

10. The *Maruts* are resplendent as if illuminators of the sacrifice, (bright) as the flames of *Agni*: entitled are they to donation, and like heroes making (adversaries) tremble: brilliant are they from birth, and invincible.

५०६०. तं वृधन्तं मारुतं भ्राजदृष्टिं रुद्रस्य सूनुं हवसा विवासे।

दिवः शर्धाय शुचयो मनीषा गिरयो नाप उग्रा अस्पृध्रन्॥११॥

11. I worship with oblations that exalted company of the *Maruts*, the progeny of *Rudra*, armed with shining lances: the pure and earnest praises of the devout (adorer) are emulous in the invigoration (of the *Maruts*), as the clouds (vie in the emission of the rain).

The Pure and Earnest Praises, Etc.— *Divaḥ śardhāya śucayo maniṣā girayo nāpa ugrā aspṛdhran*, is, literally, of heaven of the strength pure praises mountains like waters fierce have vied: Sāyaṇa renders *divaḥ* by *stotuḥ*, of the praiser or worshipper; *śardhāya, mārutāya*, for the strength of the *Maruts*: and *giri* by *megha*, a cloud: the line is a fair specimen of the whole *Sūkta*, which is very elliptical and obscure.

[सूक्त-६७]

[**ऋषि**– भरद्वाज बार्हस्पत्य। **देवता**– मित्रावरुण। **छन्द**– त्रिष्टुप्]

५०६१. विश्वेषां वः सतां ज्येष्ठतमा गीर्भिर्मित्रावरुणा वावृधध्यै।

सं या रश्मेव यमतुर्यमिष्ठा द्वा जनाँ अस्मा बाहुभिः स्वैः॥१॥

1. (I proceed) by my praises to exalt you, *Mitra* and *Varuṇa*, the eldest of all existing things: you two, though not the same, are

the firmest restrainers with your arms, and hold men back (from evil) as they check (horses) with reins.

५०६२. इयं मद्रां प्र स्तृणीते मनीषोपं प्रिया नर्मसा बहिरच्छे।

यन्तं नौं मित्रावरुणावधृष्टं धर्दियंद्वां वरूथ्यं सुदानू।।२।।

2. This my praise is addressed to you both, and proceeds to you beloved (deities) together with the oblation: the sacred grass is spread before you: grant us, *Mitra* and *Varuṇa*, an unassailable dwelling, that through your favour, munificent divinties, may be a (secure) shelter.

५०६३. आ यांतं मित्रावरुणा सुशस्त्युपं प्रिया नर्मसा हूयमांना।

सं यार्वंपः स्थो अपसेंव जनाँछुधीयतश्चिद्यतथो महित्वा।।३।।

3. Come, *Mitra* and *Varuṇa*, beloved by all, and invoked with reverence to the propitious rite, you who by your bounty support men labouring for sustenance as a work man (maintains himself) by work.

५०६४. अश्वा न या वाजिनां पूतर्बन्धू ऋता यद् गर्भमदितिर्भरध्यै।

प्र या महि महान्ता जार्यमाना घोरा मर्ताय रिपवे नि दीधः।।४।।

4. Who (are) strong as horses, accepters of pious praise, observers of truth, whom *Aditi* conceived: whom, mighty of the mighty at your birth and formidable to mortal foes, she bore.

५०६५. विश्वे यद्रां मंहना मन्दमांनाः क्षत्रं देवासो अदधुः सजोषाः।

परि यद्भूथो रोदसी चिदुर्वी सन्ति स्पशो अदब्धासो अमूराः।।५।।

5. Inasmuch as all the gods equally pleased and rejoicing in your greatness conferred strength upon you, and since you are preeminent over the wide heaven and earth, your courses are unobstructed, unimpeded.

Your Courses are Unobstructed— *Spaśo adabdhāso amūrā*—the Scholiast explains, *spaśaḥ* by *raśmayas, cāra vā*, rays, or perhaps reins, or goings, which are *ahinsita*, uninjured, *amūḍhā*, not bewildered.

५०६६. ता हि क्षत्रं धारयेथे अनु द्यून् दुंहेथे सानुंमुपमादिंव द्योः।

दुळ्हो नक्षत्र उत विश्वदेवो भूमिमातान्द्वां धासिनायोः।।६।।

6. You manifest vigour daily, you strengthen the summit of the sky as if with a pillar; the solid firmament and the universal deity (the sun) replenish earth and heaven with the food of man.

As if with a Pillar— *Upamād iva—upamāt* is explained, *sthūṇa*, a post or pillar—the post to which a calf is tied, according to the commentator.

५०६७. ता विग्रं धैथे जठरं पृणध्या आ यत्सद्म सभृतय: पृणन्ति।

न मृष्यन्ते युवतयोऽवाता वि यत्पयौं विश्वजिन्वा भरन्ते॥७॥

7. You two support the sage (worshipper), filling his belly when he and his dependants fill the sacrificial chamber; when, sustainers of all, the rain (is sent down by you), and the young (rivers) are not obstructed, but, undried, diffuse (fertility) around.

५०६८. ता जिह्वया सदमेदं सुमेधा आ यद्वां सत्यो अरतिर्ऋते भूत्।

तद्वां महित्वं घृतान्नावस्तु युवं दाशुषे वि चयिष्टमंहः॥८॥

8. The wise man always (solicits) you his prayers for this (supply of water), when approaching you sincere in sacrifice: may your magnanimity be such that you, the feeders upon *ghi*, may exterminate sin in the donor (of the oblation).

With his Prayers— Literally, with his tongue, *jihvayā*.

५०६९. प्र यद्वां मित्रावरुणा स्पूर्धन्प्रिया धाम युवधिता मिनन्ति।

न ये देवास ओहसा न मर्ता अयज्ञसाचो अप्यो न पुत्राः॥९॥

9. (Exterminate also), *Mitra* and *Varuṇa*, those who, emulously contending, disturb the rites that are agreeable and beneficial to you both: those divinities, those mortals, who are not diligent in adoration, those who performing works perform not sacrifices, those who do not propitiate you.

Exterminate Also— There is no verb to govern the objects specified, and the Scholiast brings on, from the preceding verse, *vicayiṣṭam, vināśayatam*, destroy: the expressions in the second half of the stanza are somewhat equivocal, *na ye devāsa ohasā na martā ayajñasāco apyo na putrāḥ: ohasā* is explained, *vahanasādhanena,* by the means of conveying—wishes it may be supposed, *ie., stotreṇa*, by praise: *apyaḥ* is rendered *karmavantaḥ*, doing acts, from *apas, opus*, but not sacrificing or sacrificing in vain; *vṛthā karmāṇi kurvantaḥ: na putrāḥ*, not sons, is rendered *apṛṇantaḥ*, not pleasing, or satisfying.

५०७०. वि यद्वाचं कीस्तासो भरन्ते शंसन्ति के चित्रिविदो मनाना:।

आद्वां ब्रवाम सत्यान्युक्था नर्किर्देवेभिर्यतथो महित्वा॥१०॥

10. When the intelligent (priests) offer praise, then some of them, glorifying (*Agni* and other deities), recite the *Nivid* hymns: such being the case, we address to you sincere adoration, for in

consequence of your greatness you do not associate with (other) divinities.

You do not Associate with other Divinities— *Na kir devebhir yatathaḥ*, you do not go, *gacchathaḥ*, with other gods, *anyair devaiḥ saha*; you are not associated with them at sacrifice.

५०७१. अवोरित्था वां छर्दिषो अभिष्टौ युवोर्मित्रावरुणावस्कृधोयु।
अनु यद् गाव: स्फुरानृजिप्यं धृष्णुं यद्रणे वृषणं युनजन्।।११।।

11. Upon your approach, *Mitra* and *Varuṇa*, protectors of the dwelling, your (bounty) is unlimited; when (your) praises are uttered, and the sacrificers add in the ceremony the *Soma* that inspires straightforwardness and resolution, and is the showerer (of benefits).

Your Bounty is Unlimited— *Yuvor askṛdhoyu;* there is no substantive: the Scholiast supplies *yuvābhyāṁ deyaṁ gṛhādikam avicchinnaṁ bhavati*, that which is to be given by you, as houses and the like, is unchecked; *askṛdhoyu* is explained by Yāska, long-lived, *akṛdhvāyuḥ kṛdhu* meaning short, or *nikṛttam*, cut off; and he cities a text in which it is associated with *ajara*, as *yo askṛdhoyur ajaraḥ svarvān*, who is long-lived, free from decay, an occupant of heaven[1].

[सूक्त-६८]

[ऋषि- भरद्वाज बार्हस्पत्य। देवता- इन्द्रावरुण।
छन्द- त्रिष्टुप्, ९-१० जगती]

५०७२. श्रुष्टी वां यज्ञ उद्यत: सजोषा मनुष्वद् वृक्तबर्हिषो यजध्यै।
आ य इन्द्रावरुणाविषे अद्य महे सम्मायं मह आववर्तत्।।१।।

1. Mighty *Indra* and *Varuṇa*, promptly has the *Soma* returned, engaged conscientiously (with the priests) to offer sacrifice to you to obtain food for him by whom, like *Manu*, the sacred grass has been clipped: he who (invited you hither) today for exceeding happiness.

५०७३. ता हि श्रेष्ठा देवताता तुजा शूराणां शविष्ठा ता हि भूतम्।
मघोनां मंहिष्ठा तुविशुष्म ऋतेन वृत्रतुरा सर्वसेना।।२।।

2. You two are the principal (divinities) at the worship of the gods; the distributors of wealth; the most vigorous of heroes; the

---

१. अस्कृधोयुरकृध्वायु:। कृध्विति ह्रस्वनाम निकृत्तं भवति (निरु० ६.३)।

most liberal among the opulent; possessed of vast strength; destroyers of foes by truth; entire hosts (of yourselves).

५०७४. ता गृणीहि नमस्यैभि: शूषै: सुम्नेभिरिन्द्रावरुणा चकाना।
वज्रेणान्य: शर्वसा हन्ति वृत्रं सिषक्त्यन्यो वृजनेषु विप्र:॥३॥

3. Praise *Mitra* and *Varuṇa*, renowned for all glorious energies and enjoyment: one of whom slays *Vṛtra* with the thunderbolt, the other, intelligent by his might, comes to the aid (of the pious when) in difficulties.

५०७५. ग्नाश्च यन्नरश्च वावृधन्त विश्वे देवासो नरां स्वगूर्ता:।
प्रैभ्यं इन्द्रावरुणा महित्वा द्यौश्च पृथिवि भूतमुर्वी॥४॥

4. When amongst mankind, both males and females, and when all the gods spontaneously striving glorify you, *Indra* and *Varuṇa*, you become pre-eminent in greatness over them, as do you, wide heaven and earth (surpass them also).

५०७६. स इत्सुदानु: स्ववाँ ऋतावेन्द्रा यो वां वरुण दाशति त्मन्।
इषा स द्विषस्तरेद्दास्वान्वंसद्रयिं रयिवतश्च जनान्॥५॥

5. He who spontaneously presents you, *Indra* and *Varuṇa* (oblations), is liberal, wealthy and upright: he has prosper with the food of his adversary, and possess riches, and opulent descendants.

५०७७. यं युवं दाश्वध्वराय देवा रयिं धत्थो वसुमन्तं पुरुक्षुम्।
अस्मे स इन्द्रावरुणावपि ष्यात्प्र यो भनक्ति वनुषामशस्ती:॥६॥

6. May that opulence comprising treasure and abundant food, which you bestow, deities, upon the donor (of the oblation), that, *Indra* and *Varuṇa*, which baffles the calumnies of the malevolent, be ours.

५०७८. उत न: सुत्रात्रो देवगोपा: सूरिभ्य इन्द्रावरुणा रयि: ष्यात्।
येषां शुष्म: पृतनासु साह्वान्प्र सद्यो द्युम्ना तिरते तर्तुरि:॥७॥

7. May that opulence, *Indra* and *Varuṇa*, which is a sure defence, and of which the gods are the guardians, be ours, celebrating our praise, whose destroying prowess in battles victorious (over foes) speedily obscures (their) fame.

५०७९. नू नं इन्द्रावरुणा गृणाना पृङ्क्तं रयिं सौश्रवसाय देवा।
इत्था गृणन्तो महिनस्य शर्धोऽपो न नावा दुरिता तरेम॥८॥

8. Divine and glorified *Indra* and *Varuṇa*, quickly bestow upon us wealth for our felicity; and thus eulogising the strength of you two, mighty (deities), may we pass over all difficulties as (we cross) the waters with a boat.

५०८०. प्र सम्राजे॑ बृह॒ते मन्म॒ नु प्रि॒यमर्च॑ दे॒वाय॒ वरु॑णाय स॒प्रथः॑।
अ॒यं य उ॒र्वी म॑हि॒ना महि॑व्रतः॒ क्रत्वा॑ वि॒भात्य॒जरो॒ न शोचि॑षा॥९॥

9. Repeat acceptable and all-comprehensive praise to the imperial mighty divine *Varuṇa*, he who, endowed with greatness, with wisdom, and with splendour, illumes the spacious (heaven and earth).

५०८१. इन्द्रा॑वरुणा सुतपाविमं सु॒तं सोमं॑ पिब॒तं म॒द्यं॑ धृ॒तव्रता।
यु॒वो रथो॑ अध्व॒रं दे॒ववी॑तये॒ प्रति॒ स्वस॑रमुप॒ याति॑ पी॒तये॑॥१०॥

10. *Indra* and *Varuṇa*, observant of holy duties, drinkers of the *Soma* juice, drink this exhilarating effused libation: your chariot approaches along the road to the sacrifice, (that you may partake) of the food of the gods and drink (the *Soma*).

५०८२. इन्द्रा॑वरुणा॒ मधु॑मत्तमस्य॒ वृष्णः॒ सोम॑स्य वृषणा वृषेथाम्।
इ॒दं वा॒मन्धः॒ परि॑षिक्तम॒स्मे आ॒सद्या॒स्मिन्ब॒र्हिषि॑ मादयेथाम्॥११॥

11. Drink, *Indra* and *Varuṇa*, showerers (of benefits), of the most sweet *Soma*, the shedder (of blessings): this your beverage, is poured forth by us: sitting on the sacred grass, be exhilarated (by the draught).

[सूक्त-६९]

[**ऋषि**– भरद्वाज बार्हस्पत्य। **देवता**– इन्द्र-विष्णु। **छन्द**– त्रिष्टुप्]

५०८३. सं वां॒ कर्म॑णा॒ समि॒षा हि॑नोमीन्द्राविष्णू अ॒पस॒स्पारे॑ अ॒स्य।
जु॒षेथां॑ य॒ज्ञं द्रवि॑णं च धत्तमरि॒ष्टैर्नः॑ प॒थिभिः॑ पार॒यन्ता॑॥१॥

1. I earnestly propitiate you, *Indra* and *Viṣṇu*, by worship and (sacrificial) food: upon the completion of the rite, accept the sacrifice, and grant us wealth, conducting us by safe path.

५०८४. या विश्वा॑सां ज॒नित॑ारा म॒तीना॒मिन्द्रा॒विष्णू॑ क॒लशा॑ सोम॒धाना॑।
प्र वां॒ गिरः॑ श॒स्यमा॑ना अवन्तु॒ प्र स्तोमा॑सो गी॒यमा॑नासो अ॒र्कैः॑॥२॥

2. May the prayers that are repeated to you reach you, *Indra* and *Viṣṇu*: may the praises that are chaunted reach you: you are the generators of all praises, pitchers recipient of the *Soma* libation.

५०८५. इन्द्राविष्णू मदपती मदानामा सोमं यातं द्रविणो दधाना।

सं वामञ्जन्त्वक्तुभिर्मतीनां सं स्तोमासः शस्यमानास उक्थैः ।।३।।

3. *Indra* and *Viṣṇu*, lords of the exhilaration, of the exhilarating juices, come to (drink) the *Soma*, bringing (with you) wealth: may the encomiums of the praises repeated along with the prayers anoint you completely with radiance.

५०८६. आ वामश्वासो अभिमातिषाह इन्द्राविष्णू सधमादो वहन्तु।

जुषेथां विश्वा हवना मतीनामुप ब्रह्माणि शृणुतं गिरो मे ।।४।।

4. May your equally-spirited steeds, *Indra* and *Viṣṇu*, the triumphant over enemies, bear you hither: be pleased with all the invocations of your worshippers: hear my prayers and praises.

५०८७. इन्द्राविष्णू तत्पनयाय्यं वां सोमस्य मद उरु चक्रमाथे।

अकृणुतमन्तरिक्षं वरीयोऽप्रथतं जीवसे नो रजांसि ।।५।।

5. *Indra* and *Viṣṇu*, that (exploit) is to be glorified, by which, in the exhilaration of the *Soma*, you have strode over the wide (space): you have traversed the wide firmament: you have declared the worlds (fit) for our existence.

५०८८. इन्द्राविष्णू हविषा वावृधानाग्राद्वाना नमसा रातहव्या।

घृतासुती द्रविणं धत्तमस्मे समुद्रः स्थः कलशः सोमधानः ।।६।।

6. *Indra* and *Viṣṇu*, teeders upon clarified butter, drinkers of the fermented *Soma*, thriving upon oblations, accepting them offered with reverence, bestow upon us wealth; for you are an ocean, a pitcher, the receptacle of the libation.

५०८९. इन्द्राविष्णू पिबतं मध्वो अस्य सोमस्य दस्रा जठरं पृणेथाम्।

आ वामन्धांसि मदिराण्यग्मन्नुप ब्रह्माणि शृणुतं हवं मे ।।७।।

7. *Indra* and *Viṣṇu*, agreeable of aspect, drink of this sweet *Soma*; fill with it your bellies: may the inebriating beverage reach you: hear my prayers, my invocation.

५०९०. उभा जिग्यथुर्न परा जयेथे न परा जिग्ये कतरश्चनैनोः।

इन्द्रश्च विष्णो यदपस्पृधेथां त्रेधा सहस्रं वि तदैरयेथाम् ।।८।।

8. You have both (ever) been victorious: never have been conquered; neither of you two has been vanquished: with whomsoever you have contended you have thrice conquered thousands.

You have thrice Conquered Thousands— *Tredhā sahasram vi tad airayethām, vyakramethām:* the passage is somewhat doubtful: the treble manner of kinds, it is said, mean the world, the Vedas, and speech; *lokavedavāgātmanā tridhā sthitam,* being in three ways, consisting of speech, the Vedas, the world; *sahasram, amitam,* unmeasured, infinite. Sāyaṇa cites the *Aitareya Brāhmaṇa* for an explanation, which, with his own scholia, imports, that after *Indra* and *Viṣṇu* had overcome the *Asuras, Indra* said to them, we will divide the universe with you: whatever *Viṣṇu* traverses with three steps shall be ours the rest shall be for you: to which the *Asuras* consented. With his first step *Viṣṇu* traversed the three worlds: with his second he traversed, *vicakrame,* what that means must be left to the *Brāhmaṇas,* the Vedas; and with the third he crossed over all speech: *sarvasya vāco upari tṛtīyam pādam prakṛptavān,* so that, in fact, nothing was left for the *Asuras:* so far *tredhā* is somewhat made out; but what is the meaning of *sahasram?* To this it is answered, that it implies infinite, or the whole, which is necessarily implied by combining all worlds, all Vedas, all modes of speech. Sāyaṇa also quotes the *Taittirīya,* seventh *Kāṇḍa,* for the meaning of *sahasra,* being here, *sarvam jagat,* the whole world. *Ait. Brāhm.* vi.15

[सूक्त-७०]

[**ऋषि**– भरद्वाज बार्हस्पत्य। **देवता**– द्यावा-पृथ्वी। **छन्द**– जगती]

५०९१. घृतवंती भुवनानामभिश्रियोर्वी पृथ्वी मंधुदुघे सुपेर्शसा।
द्यावांपृथिवी वरुणस्य धर्मणा विष्कंभिते अजरे भूरिरेतसा।।१।।

1. Radiant Heaven and Earth, the asylum of created beings, you are spacious, manifold, water-yielding, lovely, separately fixed by the functions of *Varuṇa,* undecaying, many-germed.
Sāmaveda, 378; *Yajurveda,* 34, 35.

५०९२. असंश्चन्ती भूरिधारे पर्यस्वती घृतं दुंहाते सुकृते शुचिव्रते।
राजन्ती अस्य भुवनस्य रोदसी अस्मे रेतः सिञ्चतं यन्मनुर्हितम्।।२।।

2. Uncollapsing, many-showering, water retaining, yielding moisture, beneficent, pure in act: do you two, Heaven and Earth, rulers over created beings, grant us vigour, that may be favourable to (the increase of) mankind.

५०९३. यो वांमृजवे क्रमणाय रोदसी मर्तों ददाश धिषणे स सांधति।
प्र प्रजाभिर्जायते धर्मणस्परि युवोः सिक्ता विषुरूपाणि सव्रता।।३।।

3. Firm-set Heaven and Earth, the mortal who has offered (oblations) for your straight-forward course, accomplishes (his objects), he prospers with progeny, and invigorated by your operation, many beings of various forms, but similar functions, are engendered.

५०९४. घृतेन द्यावापृथिवी अभीवृते घृतश्रिया घृतपृचा घृतावृधा।
उर्वी पृथ्वी होतृवूर्यें पुरोहिते ते इद्विप्रा ईळते सुम्नमिष्टये॥४॥

4. You are surrounded, Heaven and Earth, by water: you are the asylum of water: imbued with water: the augmenters of water: vast and manifold; you are first propitiated in the sacrifice: the pious pray to you for happiness, that the sacrifice (may be celebrated).

Pray to you for Happiness, Etc.— *Iḷate sumnam iṣṭaye*, ask happiness for the sacrifice: for, Sāyaṇa observes, when there is happiness, sacrifices proceed, *sukhe sati yāgaḥ pravartante*.

५०९५. मधु नो द्यावापृथिवी मिमिक्षतां मधुश्रुतां मधुदुघे मधुव्रते।
दधाने यज्ञं द्रविणं च देवता महि श्रवो वाजमस्मे सुवीर्यम्॥५॥

5. May Heaven and Earth, the effusers of water, the milkers of water, dischargers of the functions of water, divinities, the promoters of sacrifice, the bestowers of wealth, of renown, of food, of male posterity, combine together.

५०९६. ऊर्जं नो द्यौश्च पृथिवी च पिन्वतां पिता माता विश्वविदा सुदंससा।
संरराणे रोदसी विश्वशंभुवा सनिं वाजं रयिमस्मे समिन्वताम्॥६॥

6. May father Heaven, may mother Earth, who are all knowing, and doers of good deeds, grant us sustenance: may Heaven and Earth, mutually co-operating and promoting the happiness of all, bestow upon us posterity, food, and riches.

[सूक्त-७१]

[**ऋषि**– भरद्वाज बार्हस्पत्य। **देवता**– सविता। **छन्द**– जगती, ४-६ त्रिष्टुप्]

५०९७. उदु ष्य देव: सविता हिरण्यया बाहू अयंस्त सवनाय सुक्रतु:।
घृतेन पाणी अभि प्रुष्णुते मखो युवा सुदक्षो रजसो विधर्मणि॥१॥

1. The divine and benevolent *Savitā* puts forth his golden arms for (making) donations: the adorable, youthful, sagacious (deity), stretches out his hands, filled with water, in the various service of the world.

५०९८. देवस्य वयं सवितुः सवीमनि श्रेष्ठे स्याम वसुनश्च दावने।

यो विश्वस्य द्विपदो यश्चतुष्पदो निवेशने प्रसवे चासि भूमन:॥२॥

2. May we be amongst the progeny of the divine *Savitā*, and (have power) to offer him most excellent donations: for you are he who (are absolute) in the procreation and perpetuation of many (living beings), bipeds or quadrupeds.

५०९९. अदब्धेभिः सवितः पायुभिष्ट्वं शिवेभिरद्य परि पाहि नो गयम्।

हिरण्यजिह्वः सुविताय नव्यसे रक्षा माकिर्नो अघशंस ईशत॥३॥

3. Do you, *Savitā*, prosper today our dwelling with uninjurable protections, confirming happiness: do you, who are golden-tongued, (be vigilant) for our present prosperity: protect us; let not any calumniator have power (to harm) us.

Golden-Tongued— *Hiraṇyajihva* may also mean one whose speech is pleasant and beneficial, *hita ramaṇīya*[1] *vāk*. Mahīdhara says that *jihvā* may imply *jvalā*, flame, when the epithet will signify, he whose light or heat is beneficial.—*Yajur,*. 33.69.

५१००. उदु ष्य देवः सविता दमूना हिरण्यपाणिः प्रतिदोषमस्थात्।

अयोहनुर्यजतो मन्द्रजिह्व आ दाशुषे सुवति भूरि वामम्॥४॥

4. May the divine, munificent, golden-handed, golden-jawed, adorable, sweet-spoken *Savitā*, rise regularly at the close of night: when he bestows abundant and desirable (food) upon the donor of the oblation.

५१०१. उदू अयाँ उपवक्तेव बाहू हिरण्यया सविता सुप्रतीका।

दिवो रोहांस्यरुहत्पृथिव्या अरीरमत्पतयत्कच्चिदभ्वम्॥५॥

5. May *Savitā* put forth like an orator his golden well-formed arms: (he who), from the ends of the earth, ascends to the summit of the sky, and, moving along, delights every thing that is.

Like an Orator— *Upavaktā-iva* like one who addresses or advises.

५१०२. वाममद्य सवितर्वाममु श्वो दिवेदिवे वाममस्मभ्यं सावीः।

वामस्य हि क्षयस्य देव भूरेरया धिया वामभाजः स्याम॥६॥

6. Beget for us, *Savitā*, wealth today, wealth tomorrow, wealth day by day: you are the giver of ample wealth, of a (spacious) mansion: may we, by this praise, become partakers of wealth.

---

१. हितरमणं भवतीति वा (निरु॰ २.१०)।

Yajurveda, 8,6; Mahīdhara interprets *Vāma*, which Sāyaṇa renders **dhanam**, by **karmaphalam**, the reward of holy acts or sacrifice, both interpreting it as usual, *vananīyam*, that which it is desirable to obtain, and which will apply equally to wealth or reward: *kṣaya* he renders residence, and *bhūreḥ*, *bahukālinasya*, long protracted, that is, residence in heaven, *Svargaṇivāsaḥ*.

[सूक्त-७२]

[ऋषि– भरद्वाज बार्हस्पत्य। देवता– इन्द्र-सोम। छन्द– त्रिष्टुप्]

५१०३. इन्द्रासोमा महि तद्वां महित्वं युवं महानि प्रथमानि चक्रथुः।
युवं सूर्यं विविदथुर्युवं स्वर्विश्वा तमांस्यहतं निदश्च ॥१॥

1. Great, *Indra* and *Soma*, is that your greatness, for you have made great and principal (beings): you have made known (to men) *Sūrya* and the waters: you have dissipated the glooms and (destroyed) the revilers.

५१०४. इन्द्रासोमा वासयथ उषासमुत्सूर्यं नयथो ज्योतिषा सह।
उप द्यां स्कम्भथुः स्कम्भनेनाप्रथतं पृथिवीं मातरं वि ॥२॥

2. *Indra* and *Soma*, you have led on the dawns; you have upraised the sun with his splendour, you have propped up the sky with he supporting pillar (of the firmament): you have spread out the earth, the mother (of all).

५१०५. इन्द्रासोमावहिमपः परिष्ठां हथो वृत्रमनु वां द्यौरमन्यत।
प्राणांस्यैरयतं नदीनामा समुद्राणि पप्रथुः पुरूणि ॥३॥

3. *Indra* and *Soma*, you slew *Ahi* and *Vṛtra*, the obstructer of the water; for which the heaven venerates you both: you have urged on the waters of the rivers until they have replenished numerous oceans.

५१०६. इन्द्रासोमा पक्वमामास्वन्तर्नि गवामिद्धथुर्वक्षणासु।
जगृभथुरनपिनद्धमासु रुशच्चित्रासु जगतीष्वन्तः ॥४॥

4. *Indra* and *Soma*, you have deposited the mature (milk) in the immature udders of the kine: you have retained the white (secretion), although not shut up within those many-coloured cattle.

५१०७. इन्द्रासोमा युवमङ्ग तरुत्रमपत्यसाचं श्रुत्यं रराथे।
युवं शुष्मं नर्यं चर्षणिभ्यः सं विव्यथुः पृतनाषाहमुग्रा ॥५॥

5. *Indra* and *Soma*, do you promptly bestow upon us preservative, renowned (riches), accompanied by offspring; for you, fierce (divinities), have disseminated amongst men, strength, useful to man, victorious over hostile hosts.

[सूक्त-७३]

[ऋषि– भरद्वाज बार्हस्पत्य। देवता– बृहस्पति। छन्द– त्रिष्टुप्]

५१०८. यो अद्रिभित्प्रथमजा ऋतावा बृहस्पतिराङ्गिरसो हविष्मान्।
द्विबर्हज्मा प्राघर्मसत्पिता न आ रोदसी वृषभो रौरवीति॥१॥

1. *Bṛhaspati*, who is the breaker of the mountain, the first-born (of *Prajāpati*), the observer of truth, the descendant of *Aṅgiras*, the partaker of the oblation, the traverser of two worlds, abiding in the region of light, is to us as a father: he, the showerer, thunders loud in heaven and earth.

In the first instance it is said *Bṛhaspati* was born of the seed of *Prajāpati*, afterwards from the *Aṅgirasas*, upon the authority of the *Aitareya Brāhmaṇa*, where a strange and filthy legend is told of the origin of various deities from the seed of *Prajāpati* converted into burning coals: from some of these proceeded, it is said, the *Aṅgirasas; and* afterwards, from other cinders, not yet cool, *Bṛhaspati*: this, however, does not agree exactly with the text, in which *Aṅgirasa*, as a patronymic, implies the descent of *Bṛhaspati* from *Aṅgiras. Aitareya Brāhmaṇa*, iii.34.

५१०९. जनाय चिद्य ईवत उ लोकं बृहस्पतिर्देवहूतौ चकार।
घ्नन्वृत्राणि वि पुरो दर्दरीति जयञ्छत्रूँरमित्रान्पृत्सु साहन्॥२॥

2. *Bṛhaspati*, who has appointed a region for the man who attends deligently at divine worship, destroying impediments, conquering foes, overcoming enemies, demolished various cities (of the *Asuras*).

५११०. बृहस्पतिः समजयद्वसूनि महो व्रजान् गोमतो देव एषः।
अपः सिषासन्त्स्वरप्रतीतो बृहस्पतिर्हन्त्यमित्रमर्कैः॥३॥

3. This divine *Bṛhaspati* has conquered the treasures (of the enemy), and the spacious pastures with the cattle: purposing to appropriate the waters (of the firmament), he destroys with sacred prayers the adversary of heaven.

[सूक्त-७४]

[ऋषि– भरद्वाज बार्हस्पत्य। देवता– सोम-रुद्र। छन्द– त्रिष्टुप्]

५१११. सोमारुद्रा धारयेथामसुर्यं प्र वामिष्टयोऽरमश्नुवन्तु।

दमेदमे सप्त रत्ना दधाना शं नौ भूतं द्विपदे शं चतुष्पदे।।१।।

1. *Soma* and *Rudra*, confirm (in us the strength) of *Asuras* may sacrifices in every dwelling adequately reach you: do you, possessors of the seven precious things, bestow happiness upon us: happiness upon our bipeds and quadrupeds.

Possessors of the Seven Precious Things— *Sapta ratnā dadhānā*; no explanation is given by the Scholiast as to what they are.

५११२. सोमारुद्रा वि वृहतं विषूचीममीवा या नो गयमाविवेश।

आरे बाधेथां निर्ऋतिं पराचैरस्मे भद्रा सौश्रवसानि सन्तु।।२।।

2. *Soma* and *Rudra*, expel the widespread sickness that has entered into our dwellings; keep off *Nirṛti*, so that she may be far away, and may prosperous means of sustenance be ours.

Keep off *Nirṛti*— *Nirṛti* is here interpreted *alakṣmī* misfortune and poverty.

५११३. सोमारुद्रा युवमेतान्यस्मे विश्वा तनूषु भेषजानि धत्तम्।

अव स्यतं मुञ्चतं यन्नो अस्ति तनूषु बद्धं कृतमेनो अस्मत्।।३।।

3. *Soma* and *Rudra*, grant all these medicaments for (the ailments of) our bodies: detach, set free, the perpetrated iniquity that has been bound up in our persons.

Set Free, the Perpetrated Iniquity, Etc.— That is, disease is regarded as the consequence and evidence of some committed sin; and the removal of the malady is proof of its expiation.

५११४. तिग्मायुधौ तिग्महेती सुशेवौ सोमारुद्राविह सु मृळतं नः।

प्र नो मुञ्चतं वरुणस्य पाशाद् गोपायतं नः सुमनस्यमाना।।४।।

4. Sharp-weaponed, sharp-arrowed, profoundly-honoured *Soma* and *Rudra*, grant us happiness in this world: propitiated by our praise, preserve us: liberate us from the bonds of *Varuṇa*.

[सूक्त-७५]

[**ऋषि**– पायु भारद्वाज। **देवता**– (संग्राम के अंग) १ वर्म, २ धनु, ३ ज्या, ४ आर्त्नी, ५ इषुधि, ६ पूर्वा. सारथी, उत्त. रश्मियां, ७ अनेक अश्व, ८ रथ ९ रथ गोप, १० ब्राह्मण, पितृ, सोम, द्यावा-पृथिवी, पूषा, ११-१२, १५-१६ इषु समूह, १३ प्रतोद, १४ हस्तघ्न, १७ युद्धभूमि, ब्रह्मणस्पति तथा अदिति, १८ वर्म-सोम-वरुण, १९ देवब्रह्म. **छन्द**– त्रिष्टुप्, ६-१० जगती, १२, १३, १५, १६, १९ अनुष्टुप्, १७ पंक्ति]

५११५. जीमूतस्येव भवति प्रतीकं यद्वर्मी याति समदामुपस्थे।

अनाविद्धया तन्वा जय त्वं स त्वा वर्मणो महिमा पिपर्तु॥१॥

1. When the mailed warrior advances in the front of battles, his form is like that of a cloud: with his body unwounded to you conquer; may the strength of the armour defend you.

In the front of Battles— *Pratīkaṁ rūpam:* Mahīdhara, *Yajurveda,* 29,58, explains it, front of the army, *senāmukham:* the whole *Sūkta* occurs in the *Yajus,* with the exception of two stanzas, the ninth and fifteenth; the first four stanzas occur in the same order, as do 38 to 51; the 11th, 17th, 18th are in the seventeenth *Adhyāya,* verses 45, 48, 49.

५११६. धन्वना गा धन्वनाजिं जयेम धन्वना तीव्राः समदो जयेम।

धनुः शत्रोरपकामं कृणोति धन्वना सर्वाः प्रदिशो जयेम॥२॥

2. May we conquer the cattle (of the enemies) with the bow: with the bow may we be victorious in battle may we overcome our fierce-exulting (enemies) with the bow: may the bow disappoint the hope of the foe: may we subdue with the bow all (hostile) countries.

Exulting— *Samadaḥ* is explained either, *sa,* with, *mada,* exhilaration, or *sam,* entirely, and *ad,* who devours[1].

५११७. वक्ष्यन्तीवेदा गनीगन्ति कर्णं प्रियं सखायं परिषस्वजाना।

योषेव शिङ्क्ते वितताधि धन्वज्या इयं समने पारयन्ती॥३॥

3. This bowstring; drawn tight upon the bow, and making way in battle, repeatedly approaches the ear (of the warrior), as if embracing its friend (the arrow), and proposing to say something agreeable, as a woman whispers (to her husband).

---

1. *Nir.* IX.17 & IX 18 For *mantra* 5117

५११८. ते आ॒चर॒न्ती॒ स॒म॒ने॒व॒ योषा॒ मा॒तेव॑ पु॒त्रं बि॑भृता॒मुप॒स्थे।
अप॒ शत्रू॑न् विध्यतां सं॒विदा॑ने आ॒र्ती इ॒मे वि॒ष्फु॒रन्ती॒ अमि॑त्रान्॥४॥

4. May the two extremities of the bow, acting consentaneously, like a wife sympathizing (with her husband), uphold
(the warrior), as a mother nurses her child upon her lap; and may
they, moving concurrently, and harassing the foe, scatter his
enemies.

Like a Wife . . . the Warrior— *Bibhṛtām*, Sāyaṇa explains *rājānam
dhārayetām;* Mahīdhara, *dhārayatām samam*, support the arrow.
Samaneva yoṣā he considers as the singular put for the dual, the two
extremities drawing close to the archer, like two women to their lover,
Striyau yathā kāntam āgacchataḥ.

५११९. ब॒ह्वीनां॑ पि॒ता ब॒हुर॑स्य पु॒त्रश्चि॒श्चा कृ॑णोति सम॒नाव॑ग॒त्य।
इ॒षु॒धिः सं॒काः पृत॑ना॒श्च सर्वाः॑ पृ॒ष्ठे नि॒नद्धो॑ जयति प्र॒सूतः॑॥५॥

5. The quiver, the parent of many, of whom many are the sons,
clangs as it enters into the battle: slung at the back (of the warrior),
prolific (of its shafts), it overcomes all shouting hosts.

Shouting Hosts— *Saṅkāḥ pṛtanāḥ*—Sāyaṇa explains *saṅkā*,
sounding together, *saṁ kāyanti*; Mahīdhara, following Yāska, *Nir,*
IX.14, derives it from *sac*, to be assembled, or *saṁ*, with, *kṛ*, to be renowned,
armies in which there are assembled, or celebrated warriors.

५१२०. रथे॒ तिष्ठ॒न्नय॑ति वा॒जिनः॑ पु॒रो यत्र॒यत्र॒ काम॑यते सुषार॒थिः।
अ॒भीशू॑नां महि॒मानं॑ पनायत॒ मनः॑ प॒श्चाद॒नु य॑च्छन्ति र॒श्मयः॑॥६॥

6. The skilful charioteer, standing in the car, drives his horses
before him whatsoever he will; praise the efficacy of the reins, for
the reins from the back (of the car compel the steeds) to follow the
intention (of the driver).

Nir. IX.16.

५१२१. ती॒व्रान् घोषा॑न् कृ॒ण्वते॒ वृष॑पाण॒योऽश्वा॒ रथे॑भिः स॒ह वा॒जय॑न्तः।
अ॒व॒क्राम॑न्तः प्र॒पदै॒रमि॑त्रान् क्षि॒णन्ति॒ शत्रूँ॒रन॑प॒व्यय॑न्तः॥७॥

7. The horses raising the dust with their hoofs, rushing on with
the chariots, utter loud neighings, retreating not (from the charge),
but trampling with their fore feet upon the enemies, they destroy
them.

The Horses Raising, Etc.— *Vṛṣapāṇayo aśvaḥ, pāṁsunām varṣaka-
khura,* with hoofs the showerers of dust: Mahīdhara explains the epithet,
aśvavāra. riders: *vṛṣab aśvāḥ haste yeṣām te aśvavāraḥ,* and makes it the

nominative to *kṛṇvate-ghoṣān*, calling out, *jaya, jaya*; but he again refers the verb to *āśeva*, the horses make a noise: *heṣādi Śabdān*, neighing, and the like.

५१२२. रथवाहनं हविरस्य नाम यत्रायुधं निहितमस्य वर्म।
तत्रा रथमुप शग्मं सदेम विश्वाहा वयं सुमनस्यमाना:॥८॥

8. The spoil borne off in his car, in which his weapons and armour are deposited, is the appropriate oblation of the warrior; therefore let us, exulting, daily do honour to the joy-bestowing car.

The Joy-Bestowing Car— *Rathavāhanam,* Mahīdhara explains *anas*, a car, or truck on which the car is placed.

५१२३. स्वादुष्ंसद: पितरौ वयोधा: कृच्छ्रेश्रित: शक्तीवन्तो गभीरा:।
चित्रसेना इषुबला अमृध्रा: सतोवीरा उरवो व्रातसाहा:॥९॥

9. The guards (of chariot), revelling in the savoury (spoil), distributors of food, protectors in calamity, armed with spears, resolute, beautifully arranged, strong in arrows, invincible, of heroic valour, robust, and conquerors of numerous hosts.

The Guards of the Chariot— *Pitaraḥ* is the only substaintive in the text, which both Scholiasts render *pālayitāraḥ*, guards, defenders, a body of spearmen, *Śaktivantaḥ,* apparently, attendants on the war chariot of the chief: Mahīdhara's explanation of this verse is much the same as Sāyaṇa's with some trifling variations.

५१२४. ब्राह्मणास: पितर: सोम्यास: शिवे नो द्यावापृथिवी अनेहसा।
पूषा न: पातु दुरितादृतावृधो रक्षा माकिर्नो अघशंस ईशत॥१०॥

10. May the *Brāhmaṇas*, the progenitors presenters of the *Soma* the observers of truth, protect us: may the faultless heaven and earth be propitious to us: may *Pūṣan* preserve us from misfortune, let no caluminator prevail over us.

The Observers of Truth— *Ṛtāvṛdhaḥ rakṣā*, which occur in the second half of the verse, are retained in their places by Mahīdhara; of deities, *deva, rakṣatasmān*, protect us: both commentators affirm that *rakṣa* in the singular is put for *rakṣata* in the plural: the verse, however seems out of place.

५१२५. सुपर्णं वस्ते मृगो अस्या दन्तो गोभि: सन्नद्धा पतति प्रसूता।
यत्रा नर: सं च वि च द्रवन्ति तत्रास्मभ्यमिषव: शर्म यंसन्॥११॥

11. The arrow puts on a (feathery) wing: the (horn of the) deer is its point: it is bound with the sinews of the cow: it alights where

directed: whenever men assemble or disperse, there may the shafts
fall for an advantage.

Deer is its Point— *Mṛgo asyā danta*, the deer is its tooth: that is,
according to Sāyaṇa, the horn of the deer: Mahīdhara and Yāska make
mṛga an adjective, that which seeks or reaches the enemy. *Nir.* IX.19.

With the Sinews of the Cow— *Gobhiḥ sannaddha*: all the
commentators agree that this means *govikāraiḥ snāyubhiḥ*, with tendons
derived from the cow.

५१२६. ऋजीते परि वृङ्ग्धि नोऽश्मा भवतु नस्तनूः।
सोमो अधि ब्रवीतु नोऽदितिः शर्म यच्छतु॥१२॥

12. Straight-flying (arrow), defend us: may our bodies be
stone: may *Soma* speak to us encouragement: may *Aditi* grant us
success.

५१२७. आ जङ्घन्ति सान्वेषां जघनाँ उप जिघ्नते।
अश्वाजनि प्रचेतसोऽश्वान्त्समत्सु चोदय॥१३॥

13. Whip, with which the skilful (charioteers) lash their thighs
and scourge their flanks, urge the horses in battles.

Skilful Charioteers.— *Pracetasaḥ* is applied by Yāska IX.20, and
Mahīdhara, to *aśvān*, the intelligent horses but Sāyaṇa is better advised, as
there is no other nominative to the verbs *jaṅghanti* and *jighnate*.

५१२८. अहिरिव भोगैः पर्येति बाहुं ज्यायाः हेतुं परिबाधमानः।
हस्तघ्नो विश्वा वयुनानि विद्वान् पुमान्पुमांसं परि पातु विश्वतः॥१४॥

14. The ward of the fore-arm protecting it from the abrasion of
the bow-string, surrounds the arm like a snake with its
convolutions: may the brave man, experienced in the arts of war,
defend a combatant on every side.

So Yāska, IX.15. Mahīdhara, suggests another interpretation, and
explains *hastaghna*, a shield, as well as the guard of the fore-arm.

With its Convolutions— *Ahiriva bhogaiḥ*: the latter is rendered
śarīreṇa, with the body, by all the interpreters.

५१२९. आलाक्ता या रुरुशीर्ष्ण्यथो यस्या अयो मुखम्।
इदं पर्जन्यरेतस इष्वै देव्यै बृहन्नमः॥१५॥

15. This praise (be offered) to the large celestial arrow, the
growth of *Parjanya,* whose point is anointed with venom, whose
blade is iron.

The Growth of *Parjanya*— The stem of the arrow formed of the
śara reed or grass growing in the rainy season.

५१३०. अवसृष्टा परा पत शरव्ये ब्रह्मसंशिते।
गच्छामित्रान्प्र पद्यस्व मामीषां कं चनोच्छिषः।।१६।।

16. Arrow, whetted by charms, fly when discharged go: light amongst the adversaries: spare not one of the enemy.

Sāmaveda, 1863; *Yajurveda*, 17, 45.

५१३१. यत्र बाणाः सम्पतन्ति कुमारा विशिखाइव।
तत्रा नो ब्रह्मणस्पतिरदितिः शर्म यच्छतु विश्वाहा शर्म यच्छतु।।१७।।

17. Where arrows alight like shaven-headed boys may *Brahmaṇaspati*, may *Aditi*, grant us happiness grant us happiness every day.

Like Shaven-Headed Boys— *Kumārā viśikhā iva*, like boys without the lock of hair left at shaving: *muṇḍitā muṇḍaḥ*, shorn-headed; the point of comparison is not very obvious, but it may mean, that the arrows fall where they list, as boys before they are left with the lock of hair, before the religious tonsure, play about wherever they like, *Sāmaveda*, 1866; *Yajurveda*, 17, 48.

५१३२. मर्माणि ते वर्मणा छादयामि सोमस्त्वा राजामृतेनानु वस्ताम्।
उरोर्वरीयो वरुणस्ते कृणोतु जयन्तं त्वानु देवा मंदन्तु।।१८।।

18. I cover your vital parts with armour; may the royal *Soma* invest you with ambrosia; may *Varuṇa* amplify your ample felicity: may the gods rejoice (at beholding you) triumphant.

May *Varuṇa* Amplify your Ample Felicity— *Uror-varīyo varuṇas te kṛṇotu*, may *Varuṇa* make the increase of the large: that is, according to Sāyaṇa, *sukham,* happiness: Mahīdhara applies the phrase to the *varma,* or mail, may he make it ample of ample. *Sāmaveda*, 1870; *Yajurveda*, 17, 49.

५१३३. यो नः स्वो अरणो यश्च निष्ट्यो जिघांसति।
देवास्तं सर्वे धूर्वन्तु ब्रह्म वर्म ममान्तरम्।।१९।।

19. Whoever, whether an unfriendly relative or a stranger, desires to kill us, may all the gods destroy him: prayer is my best armour.

Sāmaveda, 1872: it adds to brahma varma mamantaram, śarma varma mamantarm, my best happiness my armour.

॥इति षष्ठं मण्डलम्॥

End of the Sixth Maṇḍala

||अथ सप्तमं मण्डलम्||

SEVENTH MANDALA

ANUVĀKA 1

[सूक्त- १]

[ऋषि–वसिष्ठ मैत्रावरुणि, देवता– अग्नि। छन्द– विराट्, १९-२५ त्रिष्टुप्।]

५१३४. अग्निं नरो दीधितिभिररण्योर्हस्तच्युती जनयन्त प्रशस्तम्।
दूरेदृशं गृहपतिमथर्युम्॥१॥

1. Men generate the excellent, far-gleaming master of the mansion, the accessible *Agni*, present in the two sticks by attrition with their fingers.

Sāmaveda, 72; the printed copy reads, *atharya*: Sāyana explains it, *āgamya-atanavat*, not spreading or dispersing.

५१३५. तमग्निमस्ते वसवो न्यृण्वन्त्सुप्रतिचक्षमवसे कुतश्चित्।
दक्षाय्यो यो दम आस नित्य:॥२॥

2. The dwellers have placed in the mansion, for its constant protection, that visible *Agni*, who has been from ever, who is to be honoured in every house.

५१३६. प्रेद्धो अग्ने दीदिहि पुरो नोऽजस्रया सूर्म्या यविष्ठ।
त्वां शश्वन्त उप यन्ति वाजा:॥३॥

3. Well-kindled, youthful *Agni*, shine before us with undecaying radiance: to you abundant sacrificial viands proceed.

With Undecaying Radiance— *Ajasrayā sūrmyā*-Mahīdhara gives to *surmi*, for one meaning, *samitkāṣṭham*, kindled wood; or it may mean an iron stake or post, red hot: it is therefore, figuratively, flame,[1]

५१३७. प्र ते अग्नयोऽग्निभ्यो वरं नि: सुवीरासः शोशुचन्त द्युमन्त:।
यत्रा नर: समासते सुजाता:॥४॥

4. Those radiant fires, at which the well-born sacrificers assemble, shine more brightly, and are more bountiful bestower of progeny (and other blessings), than the fires (of common life).

---

१. See *Yajurveda*, 17.76: also *Sāmaveda*, 1375

५१३८. दा नो अग्ने धिया रयिं सुवीरं स्वपत्यं सहस्य प्रशस्तम्।
न यं यावा तरति यातुमावान्।।५।।

5. Vigorous *Agni*, grant to us, (in requital) of our praises, excellent riches, worthy male offspring, and descendants: (wealth), which an enemy attempting to assail, may not despoil.

५१३९. उप यमेति युवतिः सुदक्षं दोषा वस्तोर्हविष्मती घृताचीं।
उप स्वैनमरमतिर्वसूयुः।।६।।

6. Whom vigorous, the young damsel (the ladle) charged with the oblation, presenting the melted butter, day and night approaches; him, his own lustre approaches, favourable to (the bestowal of) wealth.

५१४०. विश्वा अग्नेऽप दहारातीर्येभिस्तपोभिरदहो जरूथम्।
प्र निस्वरं चातयस्वामीवाम्।।७।।

7. Consume, *Agni*, all enemies; with the same flames with which you have consumed *Jarūtha*, drive away febrile disease.

Jarūtha— *Jarūtha* is explained the harsh-voiced, or the threatening, *Rākṣasam paruṣaśabdakāriṇam.*

५१४१. आ यस्ते अग्न इधते अनीकं वसिष्ठ शुक्र दीदिवः पावक।
उतो न एभिः स्तवथैरिह स्याः।।८।।

8. Eminent, pure, radiating purifier, *Agni*, be present (at the sacrifice) of him who lights up your blaze, and at ours, (who address you) with these praises.

५१४२. वि ये ते अग्ने भेजिरे अनीकं मर्ता नरः पित्र्यासः पुरुत्रा।
उतो न एभिः सुमना इह स्याः।।९।।

9. Patriarchal mortals, leaders or rites have shared, *Agni*, you radiance in many places: (propitiated) by these our (praises, as by theirs), be present at this sacrifice.

५१४३. इमे नरो वृत्रहत्येषु शूरा विश्वा अदेवीरभि सन्तु मायाः।
ये मे धियं पनयन्त प्रशस्ताम्।।१०।।

10. May those men who commend this my sacred rite, heroes, in battles with foes, overcome all impious devices.

५१४४. मा शूनै अग्ने नि षंदाम नृणां माशेषंसोऽवीरंता परि त्वा।
प्रजावंतीषु दुर्यांसु दुर्य॥११॥

11. Let us not sit down, *Agni*, in an empty dwelling, (nor in those) of (other) men: let us not be without successors; or, being without male posterity, let us, friend of dwellings, (by) worshipping you, (come to abide) in houses filled with progeny.

५१४५. यमश्वी नित्यंमुपयाति यज्ञं प्रजावंतं स्वपत्यं क्षयं नः।
स्वजंन्मना शेषंसा वावृधानम्॥१२॥

12. To whatsoever sacrifice the lord of horses regularly repairs, render, (*Agni*), our dwelling blessed with progeny, with excellent posterity, prospering with lineal successors.

५१४६. पाहि नो अग्ने रक्षसो अजुष्टात् पाहि धूर्तेररुषो अघायोः।
त्वा युजा पृतनायूँरभि ष्याम्॥१३॥

13. Protect us, *Agni*, from the odious *Rākṣasas*; protect us from the malignant, the illiberal, the iniquitous; may I, with you for my ally, triumph over the hostile.

५१४७. सेदग्निरग्गींरत्यस्त्वन्यान्यत्र वाजी तनयो वील्वुपाणिः।
सहस्रंपाथा अक्षरां समेति॥१४॥

14. May that fire (kindled by me) surpass all other fires, at which a vigorous son, firm-handed, possessing a thousand means (of living), co-operates in imperishable (praise).

५१४८. सेदग्निर्यो वंनुष्यतो निपाति समेद्धारमंहंस उरुष्यात्।
सुजातासः परि चरन्ति वीराः॥१५॥

15. Verily he is *Agni*, who defends from the malevolent and from heinous sin (the worshipper) kindling (the fire): he (it is) whom the well-born worshippers adore.

५१४९. अयं सो अग्निराहुतः पुरुत्रा यमीशानः समिदिन्धे हविष्मांन्।
परि यमेत्यध्वरेषु होता॥१६॥

16. This is the *Agni* invoked in many places: whom the prince, presenting oblations to, kindles, whom the ministrant priest circumambulates at sacrifices.

५१५०. त्वे अग्न आहवंनानि भूरीशानास आ जुहुयाम नित्या।
उभा कृण्वन्तो वहतू मियेधे॥१७॥

17. To you, *Agni*, may we, who are of exalted rank, offer many perpetual oblations, (employing) means, prayer and praise), attracting you to the sacrifice.

५१५१. इमो अग्ने वीततमानि हव्याजस्तो वक्षि देवतातिमच्छ।
प्रति न ईं सुरभीणि व्यन्तु॥१८॥

18. Do you, who are imperishable, bear these most acceptable oblations to the presence of the assembly of the gods; and may our fragrant (offering) gratify them severally.

५१५२. मा नो अग्नेऽवीरते परा दा दुर्वाससेऽमतये मा नो अस्यै। मा नः
क्षुधे मा रक्षसं ऋतावो मा नो दमे मा वन आ जुहूर्थाः॥१९॥

19. Relinquish us not, *Agni*, to the want of male offspring: nor to deficient clothing: nor to such destruction: leave us not to hunger, not to the *Rākṣasas:* expose us not, observer of truth, to evil, whether in the house or in the forest.

५१५३. नू मे ब्रह्माण्यग्न उच्छशाधि त्वं देव मघवद्भ्य: सुषूद:।
रातौ स्यामोभयासः आ ते यूयं पात स्वस्तिभि: सदा नः॥२०॥

20. Bestow upon me, *Agni*, quickly, abundant whole some food: send sustenance, divine *Agni*, to those who are opulent in oblations: may we, both (priests and employer), be comprehended in you munificence: do you ever cherish us with blessings.

Do you Ever Cherish us with Blessings— *Yūyam pāta svastibhiḥ sadā naḥ,* the burthen of numerous *Sūktas*, both prior and subsequent: *yūyam* is considered equivalent to *tvam*, the plural being put honorifically for the singular; but in a subsequent recurrence of the passage, verse 25, the Scholiast interprets it, you and your attendants, *yūyam tvat parivārāśca sarve.*

५१५४. त्वमग्ने सुहवो रण्वसन्दृक् सुदीती सूनो सहसो दिदीहि। मा त्वे
सचा तनये नित्य आ धङ्मा वीरो अस्मन्नर्यो वि दासीत्॥२१॥

21. Shine with bright lustre, *Agni*, son of strength, you who are earnestly invoked, and of pleasant aspect: consume not the begotten son with whom you are associated: let not our male offspring, beneficial to man, perish.

५१५५. मा नो अग्ने दुर्भृतये सचैषु देवेद्धेष्वग्निषु प्र वोच:।
मा ते अस्मान्दुर्मतयो भृमाच्चिद्देवस्य सूनो सहसो नशन्॥२२॥

22. Command not the fires kindled by the priests with which you are united to work us evil: let not the displeasure, even in error, of you, the son of strength, who are divine, fall upon us.

५१५६. स मर्तो अग्ने स्वनीक रेवानमर्त्ये य आजुहोति हव्यम्।

स देवता वसुवनिं दधाति यं सूरिरर्थी पृच्छमान एति।।२३।।

23. Radiant *Agni*, the mortal who offers oblations to the immortal becomes affluent: that deity (*Agni*) favours the presenter of (sacrificial) wealth, to whom the devout solicitant inquiring applies.

To whom the Devout Solicitant Inquiring Applies— *Yam sūrir arthī prcchamāna, etc.*, the inquirer is supposed to ask, either where is the liberal giver of the wealth for which he prays, or who is that *Agni* to whom the petition is to be addressed.

५१५७. महो नौ अग्ने सुवितस्य विद्वान् रयिं सूरिभ्य आ वहा बृहन्तम्।

येन वयं सहसावन्मदेमाविक्षितास आयुषा सुवीराः।।२४।।

24. *Agni*, who are cognizant of our solemn and auspicious (worship), bring to the worshippers abundant riches, whereby, mighty *Agni*, we, blessed with uncontracted life, and excellent male descendants, may be happy.

५१५८. नू मे ब्रह्माण्यग्न उच्छशाधि त्वं देव मघवद्भ्यः सुषूदः।

रातौ स्यामोभयास आ ते यूयं पात स्वस्तिभिः सदा नः।।२५।।

25. Bestow upon me, *Agni*, quickly, abundant whole some food: send sustenance, divine *Agni*, to those who are opulent in oblations: may we, both (priests and employer), be comprehended in your munificence: do you ever cherish us with blessings.

This is a repetition of verse 20.

[सूक्त- २]

[**ऋषि**– वसिष्ठ मैत्रावरुणि, **देवता**– आप्री सूक्त (१ ईध्म , समिद्ध अग्नि, २ नराशंस, ३ इळ; ४ बर्हि, ५ देवीद्वार ६, उषासानक्ता, ७ दिव्यहोता- प्रचेतस्, ८ सरस्वती, भारती, इळा-तिस्रो देव्य:, ९ त्वष्टा, १० वनस्पति, ११ स्वाहाकृति)। **छन्द**– त्रिष्टुप्।]

५१५९. जुषस्व नः समिधमग्ने अद्य शोचा बृहद्यजतं धूममृण्वन्।

उप स्पृश दिव्यं सानु स्तूपैः सं रश्मिभिस्ततनः सूर्यस्य।।१।।

1. Be gratified, *Agni*, by the (sacred fire) kindled by us today, emitting abundant adorable smoke: touch with your scorching flames the celestial summit; combine with the rays of the sun.

Kindled— *Samiddham*: here, as usual, it implies one of the *Ápris*, or forms of fire, although used as an epithet.

५१६०. नराशंसस्य महिमानमेषामुपं स्तोषाम यजतस्यं यज्ञैः।
ये सुक्रतंवः शुचयो धियंधाः स्वदन्ति देवा उभयांनि हव्या॥२॥

2. We celebrate with sacrifices the greatness of the adorable *Narāśaṁsa* amongst those who are divinities, the performers of good works, the bright-shining, the upholders of rites, who partake of both kinds of oblations.

Both kinds of Oblations— Oblations of *ghī* and libations of *Soma*, or other offerings. *Nir.* viii.6.

५१६१. ईळेन्यं वो असुरं सुदक्षमन्तर्दूतं रोदसी सत्यवाचम्।
मनुष्वदग्निं मनुना समिद्धं समध्वराय सदमिन्महेम॥३॥

3. Let us ever worship the *Agni* who is to be adored by us; the mighty, the destrous, the messenger passing between heaven and earth, the speaker of truth, kindled (of old) by Manu, as now by men, that (he may come) to the solemnity.

Tanūnapāt, who usually comes next, is omitted, because, according to Sāyaṇa, the *Sūkta* is called an *Āprī Sūkta, Apra śabdoktatvān-idam Tanūnapād rahitam.*

Agni who is to be Adored by Us— *Īḷenyam Agnim* is the *Īḷita* of the other *āprī Sūktas*: the verb is *mahema* in the first person plural, the Scholiast says, substituted for the second, to you (priests) worship.

५१६२. सपर्यवो भरमाणा अभिज्ञु प्र वृञ्जते नमसा बर्हिरग्नौ।
आजुह्वांना घृतपृष्ठं पृषद्वदध्वर्यवो हविषा मर्जयध्वम्॥४॥

4. The worshippers bearing the sacred grass offer it with reverence, upon their knees, to *Agni*: worship him, priests, with oblations, invoking him to (sit down) on the spotted (grass), smeared with clarified butter.

५१६३. स्वाध्यो३ वि दुरो देवयन्तोऽशिश्रयू रथयुर्देवतांता।
पूर्वी शिशुं न मातरां रिहाणे समग्रुवो न समनेष्वञ्जन्॥५॥

5. The devout performers of holy rites, desirous of chariots, have had recourse to the doors (of the sacrificial chamber): (the

ladles), placed to the east, are plying the fire with *ghee* at
sacrifices, as the mother cows lick the calf, or as rivers (water the
fields).

The Doors of the Sacrificial Chamber— The doors are always
named amongst the *Āpris*: the second half of the stanza is obscurely
constructed, although the sense may be made out, *Pūrvī śiśum na mātarā
rihāṇe samagruvo na samaneṣu-añjan*: literally, the prior (or eastern) calf-
like two mothers licking rivers, like in sacrifices they anoint: the Scholiast
explains *pūrvī-prāgagre juhūpabhṛtau*, the two ladles—the *juhu* and
upabhṛt—placed at sacrifices with their ends to the east.

५१६४. उत योषणे दिव्ये मही न॑ उषासान॒क्ता॑ सुदु॒घेव धेनुः।
बर्हिष॒दा॑ पुरुहू॒ते म॒घोनी॑ आ य॒ज्ञिये॑ सुवि॒ताय॑ श्रयेताम्॥६॥

6. May the two youthful females, the divine and mighty day
and night, the invoked of many, the possessed of wealth, seated on
the sacred grass, entitled to adoration, be with us like an easily-
milked cow for our welfare.

५१६५. विप्रा॑ य॒ज्ञेषु॒ मानु॑षेषु का॒रू म॒न्ये वां॑ जात॒वेद॑सा य॒जध्यै॑।
ऊ॒र्ध्वं नो॑ अध्व॒रं कृ॑तं ह॒वेषु॒ ता दे॒वेषु॒ वनथो॒ वार्या॑णि॥७॥

7. I am minded to adore you two sages, the ministrants at
sacrifices of men, from celebrated, convey our offspring aloft, and
acquire (for our use) the precious (treasures preserved) amongst
the gods.

५१६६. आ भार॑ती॒ भार॑तीभिः स॒जोषा॒ इळा॑ दे॒वैर्म॑नु॒ष्ये॑भिर॒ग्निः।
सर॑स्वती सारस्व॒तेभि॒र॑र्वाक् ति॒स्रो दे॒वीर्ब॒र्हिरेदं स॑दन्तु॥८॥

8. May Bharati, associated with the Bharatis; Iḷa with gods and
men; and *Agni* and *Sarasvatī* with the *Sarasvatas*; may the three
goddesses sit down before us upon this sacred grass.

Iḷā with Gods and Man— *Iḷā devabhir-manuṣyebhir agniḥ*: the
Scholiast here changes the order, and associates *Iḷā* with men, and *Agni*
has to do here amongst the goddesses, unless the name were in apposition
with *Iḷā*, the *Agni Iḷā*. This and three following verses are repeated from
the second *Aṣṭaka*, see verse 2487 etc.: in such cases Sāyaṇa does not
usually repeat his comments, but here he says, as some interval has
occurred he does so summarily: he does so, also, with one or two
variations of explanation of no great importance.

५१६७. तन्न॑स्तु॒रीप॑मध॒ पोष॑यि॒त्नु देवं॑ त्वष्ट॒र्वि र॑राण॒ः स्यस्व॑।
यतो॒ वीरः॒ कर्म॑ण्यः सु॒दक्षो॑ यु॒क्तग्रा॑वा जाय॑ते दे॒वका॑मः॥९॥

9. Divine *Tvaṣṭā*, being well pleased, give issue to our procreative vigour, whence (a son) manly, devout, vigorous, wielder of the *Soma*-bruising stone, and reverencing the gods, may be born.

५१६८. वनस्पतेऽव सृजोप देवान्ग्निहविः शमिता सूदयाति।

सेदु होता सत्यतरो यजाति यथा देवानां जनिमानि वेद ॥१०॥

10. Vanaspati, bring the gods night: may *Agni*, the immolator, prepare the victim: let him who is truth officiate as the ministering priest, for verily he knows the birth of the gods.

५१६९. आ याह्ग्ने समिधानो अर्वाङ् इन्द्रेण देवैः सरथं तुरेभिः।

बर्हिर्न आस्तामदितिः सुपुत्रा स्वाहा देवा अमृता मादयन्ताम् ॥११॥

11. *Agni*, kindled (into flame), come to our presence in the same chariot with *Indra*, and with the swift moving gods: may *Aditi*, the mother of excellent sons, sit down on the sacred grass, and may the immortal gods be satisfied with the reverentially-offered oblation.

[सूक्त-३]

[ऋषि– वसिष्ठ मैत्रावरुणि। देवता– अग्नि। छन्द– त्रिष्टुप्।]

५१७०. अग्निं वो देवमग्निभिः सजोषा यजिष्ठं दूतमध्वरे कृणुध्वम्।

यो मर्त्येषु निध्रुविर्ऋतावा तपुर्मूर्धा घृतान्नः पावकः ॥१॥

1. Appoint (gods) the most adorable, divine *Agni*, consentient with (all other) fires, your messenger at the sacrifice: him who is permanently present amongst men, the observer of truth, who is crowned with flame, the purifier, whose food is butter.

Sāmaveda, 1219

५१७१. प्रोथदश्वो न यवसेऽविष्यन्यदा महः संवरणाद्व्यस्थात्।

आदस्य वातो अनु वाति शोचिरध स्म ते व्रजनं कृष्णमस्ति ॥२॥

2. When, like a neighing steed about to feed upon the forage, (*Agni*) springs up from the vast-enclosing (forest) then the wind fans his flame: and black, (*Agni*), is your course.

Sāmaveda, 1220; *Yajurveda*, 15.62.

५१७२. उद्यस्य ते नवजातस्य वृष्णोऽग्ने चरन्त्यजरा इधानाः।

अच्छा द्यामरुषो धूम एति सं दूतो अग्न ईयसे हि देवान् ॥३॥

3. The kindled undecaying flames of you, the newly born, the showerer, rise up: the luminous smoke spreads along the sky: and you, *Agni*, proceedest as their messenger to the gods.

Sāmaveda, 1221

५१७३. वि यस्य ते पृथिव्यां पाजो अश्रेत्तृषु यदन्ना समवृक्त जम्भैः।
सेनेव सृष्टा प्रसितिष्ट एति यवं न दंस्म जुह्वा विवेक्षि ॥४॥

4. The light of whom quickly spreads over the earth when with his teeth (of flame) he devours his food: your blaze rushes along like a charging host, when *Agni*, of goodly aspect, you spreadest with your flame (amongst the trees) as if (they were) barley.

You Spreadest with your Flame.—*Yavam na dasma juhvā vivekṣi* is explained, *Darśanīyāgner tvam yavam iva jvālayā kāṣṭhādīni bhakṣayasi,* when you eatest wood and other things like barley, with flame.

५१७४. तमिद्दोषा तमुषसि यविष्ठमग्निमत्यं न मर्जयन्त नरः।
निशिशाना अतिथिमस्य योनौ दीदाय शोचिराहुतस्य वृष्णः ॥५॥

5. Men cherish that youthful *Agni* at evening and at dawn, as (they tend) a horse: lighting him as a guest in his proper station: the radiance of the showerer (of benefits), to whom the oblation is offered, shines brightly.

५१७५. सुसन्दृक्ते स्वनीक प्रतीकं वि यद्रुक्मो न रोचस उपाके।
दिवो न ते तन्यतुरेति शुष्मश्चित्रो न सूरः प्रति चक्षि भानुम् ॥६॥

6. Resplendent *Agni*, when you shinest nigh at hanc like gold, your appearance is beautiful: your might issues like the thunderbolt from the firmament, and like the wonderful sun, you displayest your lustre.

५१७६. यथा वः स्वाहाग्नये दाशेम परीळाभिर्घृतवद्भिश्च हव्यैः।
तेभिर्नो अग्ने अमितैर्महोभिः शतं पूर्भिरायसीभिर्नि पाहि ॥७॥

7. When we present to you, *Agni*, the sacred offering along with oblations mixed with milk and butter, then protect us, *Agni*, with those vast unbounded, innumerable golden cities.

Protect us, Agni, with those, Etc.— *Tebhir amitair mahobhiḥ śatam pūrbhir-āyasībhir nipāhi* is literally rendered in the text according to the interpretation of Sāyaṇa; he gives no explanation of what meant.

५१७७. या वा ते सन्ति दाशुषे अधृष्टा गिरो वा याभिर्नृवतीरुरुष्याः।
ताभिर्नः सूनो सहसो नि पाहि स्मत्सूरीञ्जरितॄञ्जातवेदः ॥८॥

8. Son of strength, *Jātavedas*, with those unobstructed (splendours) which belong to you, a munificent donor, and with those praises wherewith you protectest people with their posterity, do you protect us your worshippers and praisers.

५१७८. निर्यत्पूतेव॒ स्वधि॑ति॒: शुचि॑र्गा॒त् स्व॒या॑ कृ॒पा त॒न्वा॑३े रोच॑मान:।
आ यो मा॒त्रोरु॒शेन्यो॑ ज॒निष्ट॑ दे॒वय॒ज्या॑य सु॒क्रतु॑: पाव॑क:॥९॥

9. When the bright *Agni*, radiant with his own diffusive lustre, issues (from the touchwood) like a sharpened exe; and he who is desirable, the doer of great deeds, the purifier, is born of his two parents: (he appears) for the worship of the gods.

५१७९. ए॒ता नो॑ अग्ने॒ सौभ॑गा दिदी॒ह्यपि॒ क्रतुं॑ सु॒चेत॑सं वतेम। वि॒श्वा॑ स्तो॒तृभ्यो॑ गृ॒णते॑ च॒ सन्तु यू॒यं पा॑त स्व॒स्तिभि॒: सदा॑ न:॥१०॥

10. Illume for us, *Agni*, these auspicious (riches): may we possess (a son) intelligent, the celebrator of sacred rites: may all (good things) be the your praisers, and to him who eulogizes (you): and do you ever cherish us with blessings.

[सूक्त- ४]

[ऋषि- वसिष्ठ मैत्रावरुणि। **देवता-** अग्नि। **छन्द-** त्रिष्टुप्।]

५१८०. प्र व॒: शु॒क्राय॒ भान॑वे भरध्वं ह॒व्यं म॒तिं चा॒ग्नये॑ सु॒पूत॑म्।
यो दैव्या॑नि॒ मानु॑षा ज॒नूंष्य॒न्तर्विश्वा॑नि वि॒द्मना॒ जिगा॑ति॥१॥

1. Offer your sacred oblation, and praise the bright and radiant *Agni*, who passes with wisdom between all divine and human beings.

५१८१. स गृ॒त्सो अ॑ग्निस्तरु॒णश्चि॑दस्तु॒ यतो॒ यवि॑ष्ठो अ॒जनि॑ष्ट मातु:।
सं यो वना॑ युव॒ते शुचि॑द॒न् भूरि॑ चि॒दन्ना॒ समि॑द॒त्ति स॒द्य:॥२॥

2. May the sagacious *Agni* be our conductor from the time that he is born, most youthful, of his mother: he who, bright-toothed, attacks the forest, and quickly devours his abundant food.

५१८२. अस्य॑ दे॒वस्य॒ संस॒द्यनी॑के॒ यं मर्ता॑स: श्ये॒तं ज॑गृ॒भ्रे।
नि॒यागृभं॒ पौरु॑षेयीमुवोच॑ दु॒रोक॑म॒ग्निरा॒यवे॑ शुशोच॥३॥

3. Whom mortals apprehend as white (shining) in the principal station of that divinity; he who assents to manly adoration, and blazes for the good of man, and the discomfiture (of his foes).

As white (Shining) in the Principal Stations— *Asya devasya samsadi anīke yam martāsaḥ śyetam jagṛbhre*, is rendered literally according to the obvious purport of the words, confirmed by the Scholiast: what it means is not so clear.

५१८३. अयं कविरकविषु प्रचेता मर्तेष्वग्निरमृतो नि धायि।

स मा नो अत्र जुहुर: सहस्व: सदा त्वे सुमनस: स्याम॥४॥

4. This far-seeing, sagacious, immortal *Agni*, has been stationed among short-sighted mortals: harm us not, vigorous *Agni*, in this world, that we may ever be devoted to you.

५१८४. आ यो योनिं देवकृतं ससाद क्रत्वा ह्यग्निरमृताँ अतारीत्।

तमोषधीश्च वनिनश्च गर्भं भूमिश्च विश्वधायसं बिभर्ति॥५॥

5. The herbs, and the trees, and the earth, contain as a germ that all-supporting *Agni*, who occupies a place provided by the gods, that by his functions he may convey (the offerings) to the immortals.

५१८५. ईशे ह्यग्निरमृतस्य भूरीशे राय: सुवीर्यस्य दातो:।

मा त्वा वयं सहसावन्नवीरा माप्सव: परि षदाम मादुव:॥६॥

6. *Agni* has power to grant abundant food: he has power to grant riches with male posterity: vigorous *Agni*, let us not sit down before you devoid of sons, of beauty, of devotion.

Devoid of Beauty— *Māpsavaḥ, rūpa-rahitaḥ: apsas* is a synonym of *rūpa* in the *Nighaṇṭu*.[1]

५१८६. परिषद्यं ह्यरणस्य रेक्णो नित्यस्य राय: पतय: स्याम।

न शेषो अग्ने अन्यजातमस्त्यचेतानस्य मा पथो वि दुक्ष:॥७॥

7. Wealth is competent to the acquittance of debt: may we be masters of permanent riches: that is not offspring which is begotten by another: alter not the paths (of the generation) of a blockhead.

Wealth is Competent to the Acquittance of Debt— *Pariṣadyam hi araṇasya reknas*, may also mean, *anṛṇasya dhanam parihartavyam*, the wealths of one not indebted is to be accepted.

Alter not the Paths of the Generation of a Blockhead— *Acetānasya mā patho vidukṣa*, is literally, consume not the paths of the universe; but Sāyaṇa, following *Yāska, Nir*. iii.2, explains it, *aviduṣaḥ*

---

१. अप्स इति रूप नाम (निरु० ५.१३)

putrotpādāna pramukhān mārgān mā viduduṣaḥ, change not (*duṣ,*
vaikṛtye) the principal paths of begetting a son of the unwise.

५१८७. नहि ग्रभायारेण: सुशेवोऽन्योदर्यो मनसा मन्तवा उं।

अधा चिदोक: पुनरित्स एत्या नौ वाज्यभीषाळेतु नव्य:॥८॥

8. One not acquitting debts, although worthy of regard, yet
begotten of another, is not to be contemplated even in the mind (as
fit) for acceptance: for verily he returns to his own house; therefore
let there come to us (a son) new-born, possessed of food,
victorious over foes.

One not Acuitting Debts— *Araṇa* is explained in this place
aramamāṇa, one not pleasing or delighting: in the proceeding verse it is
rendered *Anṛṇa*, one free from debt, implying not only literal debt, but the
obligations due to men, progenitors and gods.

Therefore Let there come to us a Son, Etc.— This looks like a
prohibition of adoption, confining inheritance either to direct descent
through a son, or to collateral descent through the son of a daughter: *Nir,*
iii.3: this verse is considered as an explanation of the preceding, the drift
of the two being the preference of lineal male descent.

५१८८. त्वमग्ने वनुष्यतो नि पाहि त्वमु न: सहसावन्नवद्यात्।

सं त्वा ध्वस्मन्वदभ्येतु पाथ: सं रयि: स्पृहयाय्य: सहस्री॥९॥

9. Do you, Agni, defend us against, the malignant; do you,
who are endowed with strength, (preserve us) from sin: may the
(sacrificial) food come to you free from defect: may the riches that
we desire come to us by thousands.

५१८९. एता नौ अग्ने सौभगा दिदीह्यपि क्रतुं सुचेतसं वतेम। विश्वा
स्तोतृभ्यों गृणते च सन्तु यूयं पात स्वस्तिभि: सदा न:॥१०॥

10. Illume for us, *Agni*, these auspicious (riches): may we
possess (a son) intelligent, the celebrator of sacred rites: may all
(good things) be to your praisers and to him who eulogizes (you):
and do you ever cherish us with blessings.

See last verse of preceding *Sūkta*.

[सूक्त-५]

[**ऋषि**– वसिष्ठ मैत्रावरुणि। **देवता**– वैश्वानर अग्नि। **छन्द**– त्रिष्टुप्।]

५१९०. प्रागन्यें तवसें भरध्वं गिरं दिवो अरतयें पृथिव्या:।

यो विश्वेषाममृतानामुपस्थें वैश्वानरो वावृधे जागृवद्भि:॥१॥

1. Offer praise to the strong *Agni*, traversing without hindrance heaven and earth: he who (as) *Vaiśvānara* prospers at the sacrifices of all the immortals, being associated with the awaking divinities.

५१९१. पृष्टो दिवि धाय्यग्निः पृथिव्यां नेता सिन्धूनां वृषभः स्तियानाम्।
स मानुषीरभि विशो वि भाति वैश्वानरो वावृधानो वरेण॥२॥

2. *Agni*, the leader of the rivers, the showerer of the waters, the radiant, has been stationed in the firmament and upon earth: *Vaiśvānara* augmenting with the most excellent (oblation) shines upon human beings.

५१९२. त्वद्भिया विश आयन्नसिक्नीरसमना जहतीर्भोजनानि।
वैश्वानर पूर्वे शोशुचानः पुरो यदग्ने दरयन्नदीदेः॥३॥

3. Through fear of you, *Vaiśvānara*, the dark-complexioned races, although of many minds, arrived, abandoning their possessions, when, *Agni*, shing upon *Puru*, you have blazed, consuming the cities of his foe.

Puru— In a former passage, *Rg* I.63.7, *Purave* occurs as an epithet of *Sudasa*, one who fills or satisfies with offerings: *Tridhatu* is here interpreted *Antarikṣam*.

५१९३. तव त्रिधातु पृथिवी उत द्यौर्वैश्वानर व्रतमग्ने सचन्त।
त्वं भासा रोदसी आ ततन्थाजस्रेण शोचिषा शोशुचानः॥४॥

4. *Vaiśvānara Agni*, the firmament, the earth, the heaven, combine in your worship: shining with undecaying splendour, you overspreadest heaven and earth with light.

५१९४. त्वामग्ने हरितो वावशाना गिरः सचन्ते धुनयो घृताचीः।
पतिं कृष्टीनां रथ्यं रयीणां वैश्वानरमुषसां केतुमह्णाम्॥५॥

5. The horses (of *Indra*), full of ardour, worship you, *Agni*; the praises (of men), dispersers (of iniquity), accompanied by oblations, (honour you), the lord of men, the conveyer of riches, the *Vaiśvānara* of dawns, the manifester of days.

५१९५. त्वे असुर्यं वसवो न्यृण्वन्क्रतुं हि ते मित्रमहो जुषन्त।
त्वं दस्यूँरोकसो अग्न आज उरु ज्योतिर्जनयन्नार्याय॥६॥

6. Reverencer of friends, *Agni*, the *Vasus* have concentrated vigour in you: they have been propitiated by your acts: generating vast splendour for the *Arya*, do you, *Agni*, expel the *Dasyus* from the dwelling.

५१९६. स जार्यमानः परमे व्योमन्वायुर्न पाथः परि पासि सद्यः।
त्वं भुर्वना जनयन्नभि क्रन्नपत्याय जातवेदो दशस्यन्॥७॥

7. Born in the highest heaven, you ever drinkest the (*Soma*)
beverage like *Vāyu*: generating the waters, you thunderest,
granting (his wishes) to your offspring, the worshipper.

Drinkest the Soma ....like *Vāyu*— According to Sāyaṇa, in the cups
dedicated to two deities the libation is offered first to *Vāyu* or to
Vaisvānara: or it may be explained, you drinkest or driest up water like
the wind.

५१९७. तामग्ने अस्मे इषमेरयस्व वैश्वानर द्युमतीं जातवेदः।
यया राधः पिन्वसि विश्ववार पृथु श्रवो दाशुषे मर्त्याय॥८॥

8. Send to us, *Agni*, (who are) *Vaisvānara Jātavedas*, that
brilliant sustenance whereby you conferrest wealth, and (grantest),
all-desired *Agni*, abundant food to the mortal, the donor (of the
oblation).

५१९८. तं नो अग्ने मघवद्भ्यः पुरुक्षुं रयिं नि वाजं श्रुत्यं युवस्व।
वैश्वानर महि नः शर्म यच्छ रुद्रेभिरग्ने वसुभिः सजोषाः॥९॥

9. Bestow upon us who are affluent (in offerings), *Agni*, ample
riches and renowned strength; associated with the *Rudras*, with the
Vasus, grant us, *Agni Vaisvānara*, infinite happiness.

[सूक्त- ६]

[ऋषि- वसिष्ठ मैत्रावरुणि। देवता- वैश्वानर अग्नि। छन्द- त्रिष्टुप्।]

५१९९. प्र सम्राजो असुरस्य प्रशस्तिं पुंसः कृष्टीनामनुमाद्यस्य।
इन्द्रस्येव प्र तवसस्कृतानि वन्दे दारुं वन्दमानो विवक्मि॥१॥

1. I salute the demolisher (of cities), glorifying the excellence
of the powerful male, the universal sovereign who is the
reverenced of all men: I proclaim his exploits (which are) like
those of the mighty *Indra*.

Sāmaveda, 78; the reading rather differs.

I Salute the Demolisher of Cities— *Dārum vande*: the first is
interpreted by Sāyaṇa, *puram bhettāram*.

५२००. कविं केतुं धासिं भानुमद्रेर्हिन्वन्ति शं राज्यं रोदस्योः।
पुरन्दरस्य गीर्भिरा विवासेऽग्नेर्व्रतानि पूर्व्या महानि॥२॥

2. They propitiate the wise, the manifesting, the sustaining, the enlightener of the pious, the giver of happiness, the sovereign of heaven and earth: I glorify with hymns the ancient and mighty works of *Agni*, the demolisher of cities.

५२०१. न्यॅक्रॅतून् ग्रथिनो मृध्रवाच: पॅणीॅरॅश्रॅद्धाँ अॅवृॅधाँ अॅयज्ञान्।
प्रप्र ताॅन्दॅयूँरॅग्निॅर्विवाय पूॅर्वॅश्चॅकाॅरापॅराँ अॅयॅज्यून्।।३।।

3. May *Agni* utterly confound those *Dasyus* who perform no (sacred) rites, who are babblers defective in speech, niggards, unbelievers, not honquiring (*Agni*), offering no sacrifice: *Agni* preceding, has degraded those who institute no sacred ceremonies.

५२०२. यो अॅपाचीने तॅमॅसि मॅदॅन्ती: प्राॅचीॅश्चॅकार नृॅतॅम: शॅचीॅभि:।
तॅमीशाॅनॅ वॅस्वोॅ अॅग्निॅ गृॅणीषेॅऽनॅनॅतॅ दॅमॅयॅन्तॅ पृॅतॅन्यून्।।४।।

4. The chief of leaders has, by the benefits (bestowed upon them), guided those praising (him) through the accumulated gloom (of night): I glorify that *Agni*, the unbending lord of wealth, the tamer of adversaries.

Guided those praising him, Etc.— *Pūrvaś-cakāra aparam ayayitun* is explained, *Agnir mukhyaḥ san ayajamānān aparān jaghanyān cakāra;* or it may be rendered he who enlightens by the manifestation of dawn those praising him in the night.

५२०३. यो देॅह्योॅॅ3े अॅनॅमॅयॅद्वॅधॅस्नैॅर्यो अॅर्यॅपॅतीॅरुषॅसॅश्चॅकार।
स निॅरुॅध्या नॅहुॅषो यॅह्वो अॅग्निॅर्विॅशॅश्चॅक्रे बॅलिॅहृॅत: सॅहोॅभि:।।५।।

5. The might *Agni*, who by his fatal (weapons) has baffled the devices (of the *Asuras*), who has created the lawns, the birds of the sun, having coerced the people by his strength, has made them the tributaries of *Nahuṣa*.

Baffled the Devices of the Asuras— *Dehyo anamayat*, has bowed or humbled, is the sense of the verb: that of *Dehyaḥ dehairūpacita*, connected with, or collected bodies, is not so obvious: the Scholiast interprets it, *Āsurī vidyā*, the learning or science of the *Asuras*.

५२०४. यॅस्यॅ शॅर्मॅन्नुॅप विॅश्वे जॅनाॅसु एॅवैॅस्तस्थुॅ: सुॅमॅतिॅ भिॅक्षॅमाणा:।
वैॅश्वानरो वॅरॅमा रोॅदॅस्योॅराॅग्निॅ: संॅसाद पिॅत्रोॅरुॅपॅस्थॅम्।।६।।

6. *Agni Vaiśvānara*, whom all men approach with pious offerings, soliciting his favour for the sake of (obtaining felicity), has come to the excellent station (intermediate) between his parents, heaven and earth.

५२०५. आ देवो ददे बुध्न्या३ वसूनि वैश्वानर उदिता सूर्यस्य।
आ समुद्रादवरादा परस्मादाग्निर्ददे दिव आ पृथिव्या:॥७॥

7. The divine *Agni Vaiśvānara* has removed from the
firmament the investing (glooms) at the rising of the sun: he has
removed them from the lower firmament of the earth, from the
upper firmament of heaven.

From the Firmament, Etc.— *Ā samudrād, avarād, ā parasmād,
diva ā pṛthivyāḥ,* or it might be from the lower firmament, from the
higher, from heaven, from earth.

[सूक्त-७]

[**ऋषि–** वसिष्ठ मैत्रावरुणि। **देवता–** अग्नि। **छन्द–** त्रिष्टुप्।]

५२०६. प्र वो देवं चित् सहसानमग्निमश्वं न वाजिनं हिषे नमोभि:।
भवा नो दूतो अध्वरस्य विद्वान्त्मना देवेषु विविदे मितद्रु:॥१॥

1. I propitiate with oblations the divine, vigorous *Agni*, rapid
as a horse: do you, knowing (our desires), be our messenger of the
sacrifice: he, the consumer of forests, is known spontaneously
among the gods.

५२०७. आ याह्यग्ने पथ्या३अनु स्वा मन्द्रो देवानां सख्यं जुषाण:।
आ सानु शुष्मैर्नदयन्पृथिव्या जम्भेभिर्विश्वमुशधग्वनानि॥२॥

2. Come, *Agni*, rejoicing by thine own paths, gratified by the
friendship of the gods: roaring with withering flames above the
high places of the earth: threatening to consume all the forests.

५२०८. प्राचीनो यज्ञ: सुधितं हि बर्हि: प्रीणीते अग्निरीळितो न होता।
आ मातरा विश्ववारे हुवानो यतो यविष्ठ जज्ञिषे सुशेव:॥३॥

3. The sacrifice is present; the sacred grass is strewn; *Agni*
lauded is satisfied, and is the ministrant priest invoking the all-
desired parents of whom you, honoured *Agni*, the youngest (of the
gods), are born.

५२०९. सद्यो अध्वरे रथिरं जनन्त मानुषासो विचेतसो य एषाम्।
विशामधायि विश्पतिर्दुरोणे३ऽग्निर्मन्द्रो मधुवचा ऋतावा॥४॥

4. Judicious men promptly generate at the sacred rite the
directing (*Agni*), who (may convey) their (oblations): *Agni*, the
lord of men, the giver of delight, the sweet-spoken, the celebrator
of sacrifices, has been established in the dwelling of the people.

Who may Convey their Oblations— The text has only *ya eṣām*, who their: the Scholiast supplies the rest.

५२१०. असादि वृतो वह्निराजगन्वानग्निर्ब्रह्मा नृषद्ने विधर्ता।
द्यौश्च यं पृथिवी वावृधाते आ यं होता यजति विश्ववारम्॥५॥

5. Investes (with the priestly office), the bearer (of the oblation), *Agni*, the directing priest, the sustainer (of all), is seated in the house of man, he whom heaven and earth extol, and whom, the desired of all, the ministrant priests worship.

५२११. एते द्युम्नेभिर्विश्वमातिरन्त मन्त्रं ये वारं नर्या अतक्षन्।
प्र ये विशस्तिरन्त श्रोषमाणा आ ये मे अस्य दीर्घयन्नृतस्य॥६॥

6. These men nourish the universe with viands who offer (to *Agni*) fitting commendation; those people also who eagerly listen (to his laudation) augment (the plenty of the world), as do these my (associates), who are glorifiers of this truthful (deity).

५२१२. नू त्वामग्न ईमहे वसिष्ठा ईशानं सूनो सहसो वसूनाम्।
इषं स्तोतृभ्यो मघवद्भ्य आनड्यूयं पात स्वस्तिभिः सदा नः॥७॥

7. We *Vasiṣṭhas* implore you, *Agni*, son of strength, the lord of treasures, that you wilt quickly bestow food upon thine adorers who are affluent (in oblations), and do you ever cherish us with blessings.

[सूक्त-८]

[ऋषि– वसिष्ठ मैत्रावरुणि। देवता– अग्नि। छन्द– त्रिष्टुप्।]

५२१३. इन्धे राजा समर्यो नमोभिर्यस्य प्रतीकमाहुतं घृतेन।
नरो हव्येभिरीळते सबाध आग्निरग्रे उषसामशोचि॥१॥

1. The royal (*Agni*), the master (of the sacrifice), is kindled with praises, he whose person is invoked with (offerings of) butter, whom men associated worship with oblations, *Agni*, who is lighted before the dawn.
Sāmaveda, 70.

५२१४. अयमु ष्य सुमहाँ अवेदि होता मन्द्रो मनुषो यह्वो अग्निः।
वि भा अकः ससृजानः पृथिव्यां कृष्णपविरोषधीभिर्ववक्षे॥२॥

2. This great *Agni* has been known amongst man as invoker (of the gods), the giver of delight, the mighty: he has spread light (in

the firmament), he, the darkpathed at large upon the earth, is
nourished by the plants.

५२१५. कया नो अग्ने वि वस: सुवृक्तिं कामुं स्वधामृणव: शस्यमांन:।

कदा भंवेम पतयं: सुदत्र रायो वन्तारों दुष्टरंस्य साधो:॥३॥

3. By what oblation, *Agni*, dost you clothe our praise? What
offering dost you, when glorified, accept? When, giver of good,
may we be the possessors and enjoyers of perfect and unmolested
riches?

५२१६. प्रप्रायमग्निर्भंरतस्य शृण्वे वि यत्सूर्यों न रोचंते बृहद्धा:।

अभि य: पूरुं पृतंनासु तस्थौ द्युतानों दैव्यो अतिंथि: शुशोच॥४॥

4. This *Agni* is greatly celebrated by the institutor of the rite
when he shines resplendent as the sun: he who overcame *Puru* in
battle, and shone glorious as the guest of the gods.

Is Greatly Celebrated— *Bharatasya śṛṇve, yajamānasya prathito
bhavati*, is Sāyaṇa's explanation: Mahīdhara, *Yajuṣ*, 12.34, interprets it,
yajamānasya āhvānam śṛṇoti, he hears the invocation of the worshipper.

५२१७. असन्निंत्त्वे आहवंनानि भूरि भुवो विश्वेभि: सुमनां अनीकैं:।

स्तुतश्चिंदग्ने शृण्विषे गृणान: स्वयं वर्धस्व तन्वं सुजात॥५॥

5. In you, *Agni*, are many offerings: do you with all your
flames be propitious: favourably hear (the praises) of the
worshipper; and do you of auspicious manifestation being
glorified, spontaneously magnify (your) person.

५२१८. इदं वचं: शतसां: संसहस्त्रमुदग्नयें जनिषीष्ट द्विबर्हां:।

शं यत्स्तोतृभ्यं आपयें भवाति द्युमदंमीवचातनं रक्षोहा॥६॥

6. *Vasiṣṭhā* illustrious in both heaven and earth, rich with a
hundred and a thousand (head of cattle), has addressed this hymn
to *Agni*, that such fame-conferring disease-removing, fiend-
destroying (laudation) may be (the means of) happiness to the
eulogists and their kindred.

Illustrious in Both Heaven and Earth— *Dvibarhaḥ, dvayoḥ
sthānayor, mahān*, is Yāska's interpretation, cited by Sāyaṇa, who
himself proposes *vidyākarmābhyām bṛhana* eminent in both wisdom and
devotion.

५२१९. नू त्वामग्न ईमहे वसिष्ठा ईशानं सूनो सहसो वसूनाम्।

इषं स्तोतृभ्यों मघवंद्भ्य आनड्यूयं पातं स्वस्तिभि: सदां न:॥७॥

7. We *Vasiṣṭhas* implore you, *Agni*, son of strength, the lord of treasures, that you wilt quickly bestow food upon thine adorers, who are affluent (in oblations), and do you ever cherish us with blessings.

Same as last verse of the preceding *Sūkta*.

[सूक्त-९]

[ऋषि– वसिष्ठ मैत्रावरुणि। **देवता**– अग्नि। **छन्द**– त्रिष्टुप्।]

५२२०. अबोधि जार उषसामुपस्थाद्धोता मन्द्रः कवितमः पावकः।
दधाति केतुमुभयस्य जन्तोर्हव्या देवेषु द्रविणं सुकृत्सु॥१॥

1. The waster away (of living creatures), the invoker (of the gods), the giver of delight, the wisest of the wise, the purifier, (*Agni*), has been manifested from the lap of the dawn: he gives consciousness to both classes of beings (men and animals), oblations to the gods, and wealth to the pious.

५२२१. स सुक्रतुर्यो वि दुरः पणीनां पुनानो अर्कं पुरुभोजसं नः।
होता मन्द्रो विशां दमूनास्तिरस्तमो ददृशे राम्याणाम्॥२॥

2. He, the doer of great deeds, who forced open the doors of the *Panis*, recovering for us the sacred food-bestowing (herd of kine), he who is the invoker of the gods, the giver of delight, the lowly-minded, is seen of all people dissipating the gloom of the nights.

५२२२. अमूरः कविरदितिर्विवस्वान्त्सुसंसन्मित्रो अतिथिः शिवो नः।
चित्रभानुरुषसां भात्यग्रेऽपां गर्भः प्रस्वं आ विवेश॥३॥

3. Upreplexed, far-seeing elevated, resplendent, right-directing, a friend, a guest, the bestower of prosperity upon us, the wonderfully radiant he shines before the dawns the embryo of the waters, he has entered into the nascent plants.

He has Entered into the Nascent Plants— *Prasva a viveśa*: the first is explained, *jayamana oṣadhih*.

५२२३. ईळेन्यो वो मनुषो युगेषु समनगा अंशुचज्जातवेदाः।
सुसन्दृशा भानुना यो विभाति प्रति गावः समिधानं बुधन्त॥४॥

4. You, *Agni*, are to be glorified in (all) the ages of men: you, *Jātavedas*, who are illustrious when engaged in battle: our praises wake up the kindling (*Agni*), him who shines with conspicious splendour.

५२२४. अग्ने याहि दूत्यं॑ मा रि॑षण्यो देवाँ अच्छा॑ ब्रह्म॒कृता॑ ग॒णेन॑।
सर॑स्वतीं म॒रुतो॑ अ॒श्विना॒पो य॒क्षि देवान् र॑त्न॒धेया॑य॒ विश्वा॑न्।।५।।

5. Repair, *Agni*, to the presence of the gods in your office of messenger, (sent) by the assembly engaged in prayer: neglect us not: offer worship to Sarasvati, the *Maruts*, the *Aśvins*, the waters, the universal gods, that they may bestow treasures (upon us).

५२२५. त्वाम॑ग्ने समि॒धानो॑ वसि॒ष्ठो ज॒रूथं॑ हन्य॒क्षि रा॒ये पुर॑न्धिम्।
पु॒रु॒णी॒था जा॒तवे॑दो जरस्व॒ यूयं॑ पा॑त स्व॒स्तिभि॒: सदा॑ न:।।६।।

6. *Vasiṣṭha* is kindling you, *Agni*: destroy the malignant: worship the object of many rites, (the company of the gods), on behalf of the wealthy (institutor of the sacrifice), praise (the gods), *Jātavedas*, with manifold praises, and do you ever cherish us with blessings.

[सूक्त-१०]

[ऋषि– वसिष्ठ मैत्रावरुणि। देवता– अग्नि। छन्द– त्रिष्टुप्।]

५२२६. उ॒षो न जा॒र: पृ॒थु पाजो॑ अ॒श्रेद्द॒विद्यु॒तद्दीद्य॒च्छोशु॑चान:।
वृषा॑ ह॒रि: शुचि॑रा भा॑ति भा॒सा धियो॑ हि॒न्वान उ॑श॒तीरजीग॑:।।१।।

1. *Agni*, like the lover of the dawn (the sun), radiant, bright, resplendent, displays extensive lustre, the showerer (of benefits), the receiver (of oblations), he shines with splendour, encouraging holy rites: he arouses (mankind), desiring (his presence).

५२२७. स्व१॒र्ण वस्तो॑रु॒षसा॒मरो॑चि य॒ज्ञं त॒न्वाना॑ उ॒शिजो॒ न मन्म॑।
अ॒ग्निर्ज॒न्मानि॑ दे॒व आ वि वि॒द्वान्द्र॒वद् दू॒तो दे॑व॒याव॒ा वनि॑ष्ठ:।।२।।

2. *Agni*, preceding the dawn, is radiant by day as the sun, and the priests celebrating the sacrifice repeat his praise: the divine, munificent *Agni*, the messenger (of the gods), cognizant of their birth, repairing to the deities, hastens in various directions.

५२२८. अच्छा॑ गिरो॑ म॒तयो॑ देव॒यन्ती॒रग्निं॑ यन्ति द्रवि॑णं भिक्ष॑माणा:।
सु॒सं॒दृशं॑ सु॒प्रती॑कं॒ स्वं१॒चं ह॒व्यवा॑ह॒मर॑तिं॒ मानु॑षाणाम्।।३।।

3. Devout praises and hymns, soliciting riches, proceed to *Agni*, who is of pleasing aspect, agreeable form, of graceful movement, the bearer of oblations, the ruler of men.

५२२९. इन्द्रं नो अग्ने वसुभिः सजोषा रुद्रं रुद्रेभिरा वहा बृहन्तम्।
आदित्येभिरदितिं विश्वजन्यां बृहस्पतिमृक्वभिर्विश्ववारम्।।४।।

4. Consentient with the *Vasus*, *Agni*, bring hither *Indra*, with
the *Rudras*, the benevolent *Aditi*, with the *Ādityas* and *Bṛhaspati*,
the desired of all, with the adorable (*Aṅgirasas*).

५२३०. मन्द्रं होतारमुशिजो यविष्ठमग्निं विश ईळते अध्वरेषु।
स हि क्षपावाँ अभवद्रयीणामतन्द्रो दूतो यजथाय देवान्।।५।।

5. Men desiring him celebrate at sacrifices the youthful *Agni*,
the giver of delight, the invoker of the gods: he, the ruler of the
night, has been the diligent envoy of the opulent (institutors of
sacrifices) for the worship of the gods.

[सूक्त-११]

[**ऋषि**– वसिष्ठ मैत्रावरुणि। **देवता**– अग्नि। **छन्द**– त्रिष्टुप्।]

५२३१. महाँ अस्यध्वरस्य प्रकेतो न ऋते त्वदमृता मादयन्ते।
आ विश्वेभिः सरथं याहि देवैर्न्यग्ने होता प्रथमः सदेह।।१।।

1. Great are you, *Agni*, the manifester of the solemnity without
you the immortals do not rejoice: come in the same chariot with all
the gods: sit down here the chief, the ministrant priest.

५२३२. त्वामीळते अजिरं दूत्याय हविष्मन्तः सदमिन्मानुषासः।
यस्य देवैरासदो बर्हिरग्नेऽहान्यस्मै सुदिना भवन्ति।।२।।

2. Men offering oblations, ever solicit you the quick-going (to
undertake) the office of their messenger, for to him, on whose
sacred grass you sittest with the gods, the days are prosperous.

५२३३. त्रिश्चिदक्तोः प्र चिकितुर्वसूनि त्वे अन्तर्दाशुषे मर्त्याय।
मनुष्वदग्न इह यक्षि देवान्भवा नो दूतो अभिशस्तिपावा।।३।।

3. In you, *Agni*, thrice in the day, (the priests) make manifest
the treasures (of the oblation) for the (benefit of the) mortal donor:
worship the gods on this occasion, *Agni*, as (you didst) for Manu:
be our messenger, our protector against malignity.

५२३४. अग्निरीशे बृहतो अध्वरस्याग्निर्विश्वस्य हविषः कृतस्य।
क्रतुं ह्यस्य वसवो जुषन्ताथा देवा दधिरे हव्यवाहम्।।४।।

4. *Agni* presides over the sokemn rite, over every consecrated oblation: the Vasus approved of his acts: the gods have made him the bearer of the offering.

५२३५. आग्ने॑ वह ह॒विर॑द्या॒य दे॒वानिन्द्र॒ज्ये॒ष्ठास॒ इह॒ मा॑दयन्ताम्।
इ॒मं य॒ज्ञं दि॒वि दे॒वेषु॑ धेहि यू॒यं पा॑त स्व॒स्तिभि॒: सदा॑ न:॥५॥

5. *Agni*, bring the gods to eat of the oblation: may they, of whom *Indra* is the cheif, be delighted on this occasion: convey this sacrifice to the deities in heaven, and do you ever cherish us with blessings.

[सूक्त-१२]

[ऋषि- वसिष्ठ मैत्रावरुणि। देवता- अग्नि। छन्द- त्रिष्टुप्।]

५२३६. अग॑न्म म॒हा नम॑सा॒ यवि॑ष्ठं॒ यो दी॒दाय॑ स॒मिद्धः॒ स्वे दु॑रो॒णे।
चि॒त्रभा॑नुं॒ रोद॑सी अ॒न्तरु॑र्वी॒ स्वा॑हुतं वि॒श्वत॒: प्रत्य॑ञ्चम्॥१॥

1. Let us approach with profound reverence the youngest (of the gods), who shines when kindled in his own abode; who is blazing wonderfully between heaven and earth, and, piously invoked, is coming from every quarter.

५२३७. स म॒ह्ना विश्वा॑ दुरि॒तानि॑ सा॒ह्वानग्निः॒ ष्टवे॒ दम॒ आ जा॒तवे॑दाः।
स नो॑ रक्षिषद् दुरि॒तादव॒द्यादस्मा॑न्गृ॒णत॑ उ॒त नो॑ म॒घोन॑:॥२॥

2. May that *Agni* who by his greatness is the overcomer of all evils, who is praised as *Jātavedas* in the (sacrificial) chamber, protect us, glorifying him, and affluent (in oblations), from all sin and reproach.

५२३८. त्वं वरु॑ण उ॒त मि॒त्रो अ॑ग्ने त्वां व॒र्धन्ति॑ म॒तिभि॒र्वसि॑ष्ठाः।
त्वे वसु॑ सुष॒णना॑नि सन्तु यू॒यं पा॑त स्व॒स्तिभि॒: सदा॑ न:॥३॥

3. You are *Varuṇa*, you are *Mitra*, *Agni*: the *Vasiṣṭhas* augment you with praises: may liberally distributed riches be (extant) in you, and do you ever cherish us with blessings.

Sāmaveda, 1304-1306.

[सूक्त-१३]

[ऋषि- वसिष्ठ मैत्रावरुणि, देवता- वैश्वानर अग्नि, छन्द- त्रिष्टुप्।]

५२३९. प्राग्न॑ये॒ विश्व॑शुचे॒ धिय॒न्धैऽसु॒रघ्ने॒ मन्म॑ धी॒तिं भ॑रध्वम्।
भरे॑ ह॒विर्न ब॒र्हिषि॑ प्रीणा॒नो वै॑श्वान॒राय॑ य॒तये॑ म॒तीनाम्॥१॥

1. Offer praise and worship to *Agni*, the enlightener of all, the accepter of pious rites, the destroyer of the *Asuras*: propitiating him, I now present the oblation on the sacred grass to *Vaiśvānara*, the granter of desires.

५२४०. त्वमग्ने शोचिषा शोशुचान आ रोदसी अपृणा जार्यमान:।
तं देवाँ अभिशस्तेरमुञ्चो वैश्वानर जातवेदो महित्वा ॥२॥

2. You, *Agni*, radiant with lustre, fillest the heaven and earth (with light) as soon as born: you, *Vaiśvānara*, from whom wealth proceeds, hast by your mighty liberated the gods from malevolent (foes).

५२४१. जातो यदग्ने भुर्वना व्यख्य: पशून्न गोपा इर्य: परिज्मा।
वैश्वानर ब्रह्मणे विन्द गातुं यूयं पात स्वस्तिभि: सदा न: ॥३॥

3. When you are born, *Agni*, the lord, the circumambient, you watchest over all creatures as a herdsman over his cattle: be willing, *Vaiśvānara*, to requite our praise, and do you cherish us ever with blessings.

Watchest over all Creatures, Etc.— *Vaiśvānara brahmaṇe vinda gātum*, know, or find, to go according to the prayer or praise: the sense is not very obvious.

[सूक्त-१४]

[ऋषि– वसिष्ठ मैत्रावरुणि। देवता–अग्नि। छन्द– त्रिष्टुप्, १–बृहती]

५२४२. समिधा जातवेदसे देवाय देवहूतिभि:।
हविर्भि: शुक्रशोचिषे नमस्विनो वयं दाशेमाग्नये ॥१॥

1. Let us, laden with oblations, offer worship with fuel and invocations of the gods to the divine *Jātavedas*, to the purely lustrous *Agni*.

५२४३. वयं ते अग्ने समिधा विधेम वयं दाशेम सुष्टुती यजत्र।
वयं घृतेनाध्वरस्य होतर्वयं देव हविषा भद्रशोचे ॥२॥

2. May we perform your rites, *Agni*, with fuel: may we offer you, adorable *Agni*, pious praises: may we (gratify you), ministrant of the sacrifice, with clarified butter; divine *Agni*, of auspicious lustre, may we (worship you) with oblations.

५२४४. आ नो देवेभिरुप देवहूतिमग्ने याहि वषट्कृतिं जुषाण:।
तुभ्यं देवाय दाशत: स्याम यूयं पात स्वस्तिभि: सदा न: ॥३॥

3. Come to our sacrifice, *Agni*, with the gods, propitiated by the sanctified oblations: may we be the offerers (of worship) to you who are divine, and do you ever cherish us with blessings.

[सूक्त- १५]

[**ऋषि**– वसिष्ठ मैत्रावरुणि। **देवता**–अग्नि। **छन्द**– त्रिष्टुप्, गायत्री]

५२४५. उपसद्याय मीळ्हुषं आस्यें जुहुता हविः। यो नो नेदिष्ठमाप्यम्॥१॥

1. Offer the oblation to the present *Agni*, the showerer (of benefits); pour it into the mouth of him who (bears) to us the nearest relationship.

५२४६. यः पञ्च चर्षणीरभि निषसाद दमेदमे। कविर्गृहपतिर्युवा॥२॥

2. Who, juvenile, wise, the lord of the dwelling, abides with the five classes of men in every dwelling.

५२४७. स नो वेदो अमात्यमग्नी रक्षतु विश्वतः। उतास्मान्पात्वंहसः॥३॥

3. May he defend for us the wealth that has been acquired, and preserve us from iniquity.

५२४८. नवं नु स्तोममग्नये दिवः श्येनाय जीजनम्।
वस्वः कुविद्वनाति नः॥४॥

4. May *Agni*, to whom as to a (swift) hawk in heaven, I address this new hymn, bestow upon us am;e wealth.

५२४९. स्पार्हा यस्य श्रियो दृशे रयिर्वीरवतो यथा। अग्ने यज्ञस्य शोचतः॥५।

5. Of whom, blazing in the front of the sacrifice, the enviable honours are to be seen, like the riches of a man having male offspring.

५२५०. सेमां वेतु वर्षट्कृतिमग्निर्जुषत नो गिरः। यजिष्ठो हव्यवाहनः॥६॥

6. May that most adorable *Agni*, the bearer of oblations, accept our offering, gratified by our praises.

५२५१. नि त्वां नक्ष्य विश्पते द्युमन्तं देव धीमहि। सुवीरमग्न आहुत॥७॥

7. Divine *Agni*, the approachable: the lord of men, the invoked of all, we set you down (upon the altar), the resplendent, the righteously glorified.

The Approachable— Nakṣya upagantavya; nakṣati, vyāpti karmā from nakṣ, to pervade.

The **Righteously Glorified**— *Suvīram* is here interpreted *kalyāṇastotṛkam,* the object of auspicious or pious praise.

५२५२. क्षप॑ उ॒स्रश्च॑ दी॒दिहि॒ स्व॒ग्नय॑स्त्वया॒ व॒यम्। सु॒वीर॑स्त्व॒म॑स्म॒युः॥८॥

8. Blaze, *Agni*, night and day, that by you we may be possessed of sacred fires: mayest you, friendly to us, be righteously praised.

५२५३. उप॑ त्वा॒ सा॒तये॒ न॒रो वि॒प्रासो॑ यन्ति धी॒तिभिः॑।

उपा॒क्षरा॑ स॒हस्रिणी॑॥९॥

9. Wise men approach you with sacred rites for the acquirement of riches: perpetual, infinite (praise is addressed to you).

Praise is Addressed to you— The text has only *upākṣarā sahasriṇī,* imperishable, thousand-fold, near: the Scholiast supplies the substantive *vāk,* speech or praise, and the prefix *upa* implies the compound verb *upayati,* approaches.

५२५४. अ॒ग्नी र॒क्षांसि॑ सेधति शु॒क्रशो॑चिरम॒र्त्यः। शुचिः॑ पा॒वक॒ ईड्यः॑॥१०॥

10. May the bright, radiant, immortal, pur, purifying, adorable *Agni,* keep off the *Rākṣasas.*

५२५५. स नो॒ राधां॑स्या॒ भरे॒शान॑: स॒हसो॑ यहो। भग॑श्च॒ दातु॒ वार्य॑म्॥११॥

11. Son of strength, who are the lord (of all), bestow riches upon us: and may *Bhaga* give us wealth.

५२५६. त्वम॑ग्ने वी॒रव॒द्यशो॒ दे॒वश्च॑ सवि॒ता भगः॑। दि॒तिश्च॑ दाति॒ वार्य॑म्॥१२॥

12. Do you, *Agni*, give us food along with male issue, and may the divine *Savitā, Bhaga* and *Diti,* give us wealth.

५२५७. अग्ने॑ र॒क्षा णो॒ अंह॑सः प्र॒ति ष्म॑ देव॒ रीष॑तः। त॒पिष्ठै॑रज॒रो द॑ह॥१३॥

13. Preserve us, *Agni*, from sin: divine (*Agni*), who are exempt from decay, consume (our) foes with (your) hottest flames.
Sāmaveda, 24.

५२५८. अ॒धा म॒ही न॒ आ॒य॒स्य॒नाधृ॒ष्टो नृ॒पीत॑ये। पूर्भ॑वा श॒तभु॑जिः॥१४॥

14. Do you, who are irresistible to us, for the protection of our posterity, like the vast spacious, ironwalled cities (of the *Rākṣasas*).

५२५९. त्वं नः॑ पा॒ह्यंह॑सो दो॒षाव॑स्तरघा॒यतः॑। दिवा॒ नक्तं॑मदाभ्य॑॥१५॥

15. Uninjurable *Agni,* dispeller of darkness, preserve us night and day from sin, and from the malevolent.

[सूक्त-१६]

[ऋषि– वसिष्ठ मैत्रावरुणि। देवता– अग्नि।
छन्द– प्रगाथ (विषमा बृहती, समा सतोबृहती)]

५२६०. एना वो अग्निं नमसोर्जो नपातमा हुवे।
प्रियं चेतिष्ठमरतिं स्वध्वरं विश्वस्य दूतममृर्तम्॥१॥

1. I invoke for you with this hymn, *Agni*, the son of strength,
the kind, the most knowing, the unobstructed: the fit object of
sacred rites, the messenger of all the immortals.

The Unobstructed— *Aratim gantāram*, the goer, or *Svāminam*,
lord; Mahīdhara, *Yajurveda*, XV.32, explains it, either having sufficient
understanding, *paryāpta matim*, or one never desisting from activity,
uparamarahitam sadodyamayutam: the verse recurs, also *Sāmaveda*,
45.749.

५२६१. स योजते अरुषा विश्वभोजसा स दुद्रवत्स्वाहुतः।
सुब्रह्मा यज्ञः सुशमी वसूनां देवं राधो जनानाम्॥२॥

2. May he harness his brilliant protecting (steeds to his car),
when earnestly invoked: may he hasten (to bring the gods): may
the sacrificial wealth of the worshippers (proceed to) that deity
who is the giver of abundant food, the adorable, the doer of great
deeds.

This and the preceding are curiously blended in point of arrangement
in the *Yajurveda*, 15.32-34: also *Sāmaveda*, 750. Mahīdhara's especially
as regards the last phrase, *vasūnām devam rādho janānām:* Sāyaṇa
explains it, *tam dhanānām madhye devam atyantoparakṣamāṇam dhanam
yajamānānām,* may *Agni*, who harnesses, etc., be re gardful of the
brilliant wealth of the worshippers amongst riches. Mahīdhara, connecting
it with what has preceded, renders the whole, *Agni* goes quickly where the
worship of the *Vasus, Rudras,* and *Ādityas* is celebrated, and the
sacrificial wealth of the worshippers is offered.

५२६२. उदस्य शोचिरस्थादाजुह्वानस्य मीळ्हुषः।
उद्धूमासो अरुषासो दिविस्पृशः समग्निर्मिन्धते नरः॥३॥

3. The radiance of that showerer (of benefits), repeatedly
invoked, rises up, as does the fiery sky-lambent smoke when men
kindle *Agni*.

५२६३. तं त्वा दूतं कृण्महे यशस्तमं देवाँ आ वीतये वह।
विश्वा सूनो सहसो मर्तभोजना रास्व तद्यच्त्वेमहे॥४॥

4. We constitute you our most renowned messenger: bring the gods to partake (of the oblations): bestow upon us, son of strength, all human blessings: whatsoever we solicit of you.

५२६४. त्वमग्ने गृहपतिस्त्वं होता नो अध्वरे।
त्वं पोता विश्ववार प्रचेता यक्षि वेषि च वार्यम्॥५॥

5. All-desired *Agni*, you are the lord of the mansion: you are the invoker of the gods: you are the assistant priest: do you, who are wise, present (the oblation to the gods), and partake (of it yourself).

The Assistant Priest— The *Potā*: he had just been called the *Hotā*. *Sāmaveda*. 61.

५२६५. कृधि रत्नं यजमानाय सुक्रतो त्वं हि रत्नधा असि।
आ न ऋते शिशीहि विश्वमृत्विजं सुशंसो यश्च दक्षते॥६॥

6. Doer of good deeds, bestow treasure upon the institutor of the solemnity, for you are the bestower of treasure:: inspire all the priests at our sacrifice: (prosper him) who, offering worthy praise, is prosperous.

Who Offering Worthy Praise is Prosperous— *Suśanso yaścha dakṣate,* offering good praise, may indicate either a son or the *Hotri*, according to Sāyaṇa, who completes the phrase thus, *yo vardhate tam vardhaya,* increase him who increases.

५२६६. त्वे अग्ने स्वाहुत प्रियासः सन्तु सूर्यः।
यन्तारो ये मघवानो जनानामूर्वान्दयन्त गोनाम्॥७॥

7. *Agni*, piously invoked, may those devout worshippers be dear to you, who are liberal, opulent, and the bestowers upon man of herds of cattle.

Who are Liberal, Opulent, and the Bestowers, Etc.— *Yantāro ye maghavāno janānām ūrvān dayanta gonām,* is rendered by Mahīdhara, may those who, amongst men, are self-restrained, opulent, and donors of butter and offerings; translating *ūrvān annaviśeṣam puroḍāśādīn,* and understanding by *gonām* the products of the cow, *Yajurveda,* 33.14; also *Sāmaveda,* 38.

५२६७. येषामिळा घृतहस्ता दुरोण आँ अपि प्राता निषीदति।
ताँस्त्रायस्व सहस्य दुहो निदो यच्छा नः शर्म दीर्घश्रुत्॥८॥

8. Strength-bestowing *Agni*, protect from the oppressor and the revilers those in whose dwelling Iḷa, butter-handed, sits down satisfied, and grant to us felicity long renowned.

Iḷa, Butter-Handed— *Iḷā ghṛtahastā*: the name is explained, *annarūpa havirlakṣaṇā devī*, a goddess, the impersonation of food, that is, of sacrificial food, or the oblation personified.

५२६८. स मन्द्रया च जिह्वया वह्निरासा विदुष्टरः।

अग्ने रयिं मघवद्भ्यो न आ वह हव्यदातिं च सूदय।।९।।

9. The most wise *Agni* is the bearer (of oblations), as the mouth of the gods with his graceful tongue (of flame): bring riches, *Agni*, to the affluent (in sacrifices): encourage the donor of the oblation.

५२६९. ये राधांसि ददत्यश्व्या मघा कामेन श्रवसो महः।

ताँ अंहसः पिपृहि पर्तृभिष्ट्वं शतं पूर्भिर्यविष्ठ्य।।१०।।

10. Youngest (of the gods), protect with your protections from iniquity, (and reward) with numerous cities those who, through the desire of extended fame, bestow riches, comprehending horses and treasure.

५२७०. देवो वो द्रविणोदाः पूर्णां विवष्ट्यासिचम्।

उद्वा सिञ्चध्वमुप वा पृणध्वमादिद्वो देव ओहते।।११।।

11. The divine *Agni*, the giver of wealth, desires the ladle filled full. Pour out (the contents), and replenish (the vessel), and then the deity bears (your oblations to the gods).

Pour out the Contents and Replenish the Vessel— *Udva siñcadhvam upa vā pṛṇadhvam*, and sprinkle and fill up, is the whole of the text: the Scholiast would seem to apply the first to the vessel, and the second to *Agni, Dhruvā graheṇa hotṛ, tve tvayi camasam pūrayata, śa Agnaye Somam yacchata, ityarthaḥ* : the meaning is, both fill the vessel with the *dhruvāgraha* and present the *Soma* to *Agni*. *Sāmaveda*, 55.1513

५२७१. तं होतारमध्वरस्य प्रचेतसं वह्निं देवा अकृण्वत।

दधाति रत्नं विधते सुवीर्यमग्निर्जनाय दाशुषे।।१२।।

12. The gods have made the wise (*Agni*) the ministrant priest, and bearer of the sacrifice. *Agni* gives to the man who performs the prescribed rite and presents (the offering), wealth, with virtuous male posterity.

Sāmaveda, 1514

[सूक्त-१७]

[**ऋषि**- वसिष्ठ मैत्रावरुणि। **देवता**- अग्नि। **छन्द**- द्विपदा त्रिष्टुप्।]

५२७२. अग्ने भव सुषमिधा समिद्ध उत बर्हिरुर्विया वि स्तृणीताम्।।१।।

1. Be kindled, *Agni*, with suitable fuel: let the (priest) strew the plentiful sacred grass.

५२७३. उत द्वारा उशतीर्वि श्रयन्तामुत देवाँ उशत आ वहेह।।२।।

2. Let the willing doors and the chamber of sacrifice) be thrown open; bring hither the willing gods.

५२७४. अग्ने वीहि हविषा यक्षि देवान्त्स्वध्वरा कृणुहि जातवेदः।।३।।

3. *Agni Jātavedas*, repair to the gods, worship them with the oblation, render them pleased by the sacrifice.

५२७५. स्वध्वरा करति जातवेदा यक्षद्देवाँ अमृतान्पिप्रयच्च।।४।।

4. May *Jātavedas* render the immortal gods, pleased by the sacrifice: let him sacrifice (to them), and gratify them (what praise).

५२७६. वंस्व विश्वा वार्याणि प्रचेतः सत्या भवन्त्वाशिषो नो अद्य।।५।।

5. Bestow upon us, sage *Agni*, all desirable (riches): may the blessings (vouchsafed) to us this day be sacrificed.

५२७७. त्वामु ते दधिरे हव्यवाहं देवासो अग्न ऊर्ज आ नपातम्।।६।।

6. The gods have made you, *Agni*, who are the son of strength, the bearer of the oblation.

५२७८. ते ते देवाय दाशतः स्याम महो नो रत्ना वि दध इयानः।।७।।

7. May we be the presenters (of offerings) to you who are divine: and you, the mighty one, being solicited, bestow upon us treasures.

ANUVĀKA II

[सूक्त-१८]

[ऋषि– वसिष्ठ मैत्रावरुणि। देवता– इन्द्र, २२-२५ सुदास पैजवन।
छन्द– त्रिष्टुप्।]

५२७९. त्वे ह यत्पितरश्चिन्न इन्द्र विश्वा वामा जरितारो असन्वन्।
त्वे गावः सुदुघास्त्वे ह्यश्वास्त्वं वसुं देवयते वनिष्ठः।।१।।

1. Our forefathers, *Indra*, glorifying you, have obtained all desirable (riches); in your gift are cows easy to be milked, and horses, and you are the liberal donor of wealth to the devout.

In your Gift— Literally, in you, *tve, tvayi.*

५२८०. राजेव हि जनिभिः क्षेष्येवाव द्युभिरभि विदुष्कविः सन्।
पिशा गिरो मघवन् गोभिरश्वैस्त्वायतः शिशीहि राये अस्मान्।।२।।

2. You dwellest with your glories like a *Rājā* with his wives; *Maghavan*, who are wise and experienced, (reward our) praises with the precious metals, with cows, with horses: conduct us who are dependent on you for riches.

With the Precious Metals— *Piśā*, silver or gold, and the like: *rūpeṇa hiraṇyādinā vā,* or *rūpa* may mean beauty.

५२८१. इमा उ त्वा पस्पृधानासो अत्रं मन्द्रा गिरो देवयन्तीरुप स्थुः।
अर्वाची ते पथ्या राय एतु स्याम ते सुमताविन्द्र शर्मन्।।३।।

3. These gratifying and pious hymns, emulous (in earnestness), are addressed on this occasion to you, may the path of your riches lead downwards: may we, *Indra*, (diligent) in your praise, enjoy felicity.

५२८२. धेनुं न त्वा सूयवसे दुदुक्षन्नुप ब्रह्माणि ससृजे वसिष्ठः।
त्वामिन्मे गोपतिं विश्व आहा न इन्द्रः सुमतिं गन्त्वच्छ।।४।।

4. Desirous of milking you like a milch cow at pasture, *Vasiṣṭha* has let loose his prayers to you: every one of my people proclaims you the lord of cattle: may *Indra* be present at our praises.

५२८३. अर्णांसि चित्पप्रथाना सुदास इन्द्रो गाधान्यकृणोत्सुपारा।
शर्धन्तं शिम्युमुचथस्य नव्यः शापं सिन्धूनामकृणोदशस्तीः।।५।।

5. The adorable *Indra* made the well-known deep waters (of the *Pasruṣṇi*) fordable for *Sudāsa*, and converted the vehement awakening imprecation of the sacrificer into the calumination of the rivers.

Converted the Vehement Awakening Imprecation, Etc.— *Sardhantam śimyum ucathasya śāpam sindhūnām akṛṇod aśastīḥ,* is explained, *utsahmānām bodhamānām stotuḥ śāpam abhiśasatīḥ sindhūnām akarot,* he made the exerting awakening curse of the praiser the imprecations of the rivers: some legend is perhaps alluded to, but it is not detailed: the only other explanation furnished by Sāyaṇa is *viśvarūpodbhavam ātmano abhiśāpam,* the imprecation on his (*Indra*) has its birth in *viśvarūpa.*

५२८४. पुरोळा इत्तुर्वशो यक्षुरासीद्राये मत्स्यासो निशिता अपीव।
श्रुष्टिं चक्रुर्भृगवो द्रुह्यवश्च सखा सखायमतरद्विषूचः॥६॥

6. *Turvaśa*, who was preceding (at solemn rites), diligent in sacrifice, (went to *Sudāsa*) for wealth; but like fishes restricted (to the element of water), the *Bhrigus* and *Druhyus* quickly assailed them: of these two everywhere going the friend (of *Sudāsa, Indra*) rescued his friend.

Indra Rescued his Friend— The legend, such as it is, is very obscurely told : as *Indra* saved one of the two, *Sudāsa*, Sāyaṇa infers he slew the other, *Turvaśam avadhīt,* but why does not appear: not does it follow from another proposed rendering, understanding by *Matsyaso niśitaḥ*, fishes limited to water, but the people of the country *Matsya* attacked by *Turvaśa, tena matsyajanapada bādhitaḥ*: again, the expression, *Śruṣṭim cakruḥ*, as applied to the *Bhrigus*, is rendered either *Aśuprāptim cakruḥ* or *sukham Turvaśasya cakruḥ*, making the *Bhrigus* and *Druhyus* the allies of *Turvaśa.*

५२८५. आ पक्थासो भलानसो भनन्तालिनासो विषाणिनः शिवासः।
आ योऽनयत्सधमा आर्यस्य गव्या तृत्सुभ्यो अजगन्युधा नॄन्॥७॥

7. Those who dress the oblation, those who pronounce auspicious words, those who abstain from penance, those who bear horns (in their hands), those who bestow happiness (on the world by sacrifice), glorify that *Indra*, who recovered the cattle of the *Arya* from the plunderers, who slew the enemies in battle.

Those who Dress the Oblations, Etc.— The terms so rendered are severally, according to the Scholiast, denominations of the persons assisting at religious rites, viz., *Pakthāsaḥ*, the *haviṣam pācakaḥ*, cooks of the butter offered in oblation; 2. *Bhalānasaḥ, bhadra-vācinaḥ*, speakers of that which is lucky; 3. *Alināsaḥ, tapobhir apravṛddhaḥ*, not eminent by austerities; 4. *Viṣāṇinaḥ*, having black horns in their hands for the purpose of scratching *kaṇḍuyanārtham*, the same as *dīkṣitaḥ*, having undergone the preliminary purification called *Dīkṣā*; and 5. *Śivāsaḥ, yāgādinā sarvasya lokasya śivakaraḥ*, the makers happy of all people by sacrifice and the like.

५२८६. दुराध्यो३ अदितिं स्रेवयन्तोऽचेतसो वि जगृभ्रे परुष्णीम्।
महाविव्यक् पृथिवीं पत्यमानः पशुष्कविरशयच्चायमानः॥८॥

8. The evil-disposed and stupid (enemies of *Sudāsa*), crossing the humble *Paruṣṇi* river, have broken down its banks; but he by his greatness pervades the earth, and *Kavi*, the son of *Cāyamana*, like a falling victim, sleeps (in death).

Sleeps in Death— Killed by *Sudās*: the application of these incidents to whom is entirely the work of the Scholiast.

५२८७. ईयुरर्थं न न्यर्थं परुष्णीमाशुश्चनेदभिपित्वं जगाम।

सुदास इन्द्रः सुतुकाँ अमित्रानरन्धयन्मानुषे वध्रिवाचः॥९॥

9. The waters followed their regular course to the *Paruṣṇi*, nor (wandered) beyond it: the quick courser (of the king) came to the accessible places, and *Indra* made the idly-talking enemies, with their numerous progeny, subject among men (to *Sudās*).

Indra is said to have reparied the banks of the river so that the waters—*iyur artham na nyartham*—went to their object, that is, their former bed, not below or beyond it: the enemies *Amitrān* are called *vadhrivācaḥ,* which Sāyaṇa explains *jalpakān.*

५२८८. ईयुर्गावो न यवसादगोपा यथाकृतमभि मित्रं चितासः।

पृश्निगावः पृश्निनिप्रेषितासः श्रुष्टिं चक्रुर्नियुतो रन्तयश्च॥१०॥

10. They who ride on particoloured cattle, (the *Maruts*), despatched by *Pṛṣṇi*, and recalling the engagement made by them with their friend (*Indra*), came like cattle from the pasturage, when left without a herdsman: the exulting *Niyut* steeds brought them quickly (against the foe).

५२८९. एकं च यो विंशतिं च श्रवस्या वैकर्णयोर्जनान्राजा न्यस्तः।

दस्मो न सद्मन्नि शिशाति बर्हिः शूरः सर्गमकृणोदिन्द्र एषाम्॥११॥

11. The hero *Indra* created the *Maruts* (for the assistance of the *Rājā*), who, ambitious of fame, slew one-and-twenty of the men on the two banks (of the *Paruṣṇi*), as a well-looking priest lops the sacred grass in the chamber of sacrifice.

५२९०. अध श्रुतं कवषं वृद्धमप्स्वनु दुह्वं नि वृणग्वज्रबाहुः।

वृणाना अत्र सख्याय सख्यं त्वायन्तो ये अमदन्ननु त्वा॥१२॥

12. You, the bearer of the thunderbolt, didst drown *Sruta*, *Kavaṣa*, *Vṛddha*, and afterwards *Druhyu*, in the waters: for they, *Indra*, who are devoted to you, and glorify you, preferring your friendship, enjoy it.

५२९१. वि सद्यो विश्वा दृंहितान्येषामिन्द्रः पुरः सहसा सप्त दर्दः।

व्यानवस्य तृत्सवे गयं भाग्जेष्मं पूरुं विदथे मृध्रवाचम्॥१३॥

13. *Indra*, in his might, quickly demolished all their strongholds, and their seven (kinds of) cities: he has given the

dwelling of the son of *Anu* to *Tṛtsu*: may we, (by propitiating *Indra*), conquer in battle the ill-speaking man.

Seven kinds of Cities— *Puraḥ sapta* : would be rather seven cities: but Sāyaṇa renders it *nagarīḥ sapta prakāraḥ*: perhaps the last should be *prakāraḥ*, seven-walled.

Conquer in Battle the Ill-Speaking Man—*Jeṣma pūrum manuṣyam mṛdhravācam*, which we have had before in the same sense of speaking imperfectly or barbarously: Sāyaṇa here renders it *baddhavācam*, which is rather equivocal, but may mean threatening, whose speech is obstructive or adverse.

५२९२. नि गव्यवोऽनवो दुह्रवश्च षष्टिः शता सुषुपुः षट् सहस्रा।
षष्टिर्वीरासो अधि षड् दुवोयु विश्वेदिन्द्रस्य वीर्या कृतानि॥१४॥

14. The warriors of the *Anus* and *Druhyus*, intending (to carry off the) cattle, (hostile) to the pious (*Sudās*) perished to the number of sixty-six thousand six hundred and sixty: such are all the glorious act of *Indra*.

Sixty-six Thousand six Hundred and Sixty— The enumeration is very obscurely expressed, *ṣaṣṭiḥ śata śat sahasra ṣaṣṭir adhi śat*, literally, sixty hundreds, six thousands, sixty, with six more: Sāyaṇa understand by *śatāni,* thousands, *sahasrānītyartham.*

५२९३. इन्द्रेणैते तृत्सवो वेविषाणा आपो न सृष्टा अधवन्त नीचीः।
दुर्मित्रासः प्रकलविन् मिमाना जहुर्विश्वानि भोजना सुदासे॥१५॥

15. These hostile, *Tṛtsus*, ignorantly contending with *Indra*, fled prouted as rapidly as rivers on a downward course, and being discomfited, abandoned all their possessions to *Sudāsa*.

५२९४. अर्धं वीरस्य शृतपामनिन्दं परा शर्धन्तं नुनुदे अभि क्षाम्।
इन्द्रो मन्युं मन्युम्यो मिमाय भेजे पथो वर्तनिं पत्यमानः॥१६॥

16. *Indra* has scattered over the earth the hostile rival of the hero (*Sudāsa*), the senior of *Indra*, the appropriator of the oblation: *Indra* has baffled the wrath of the wrathful enemy, and the (foe) advancing on the way (against *Sudāsa*) has taken the path of flight.

५२९५. आश्रेण चित्तद्वेकं चकार सिंहं चित्पेत्वेना जघान।
अव स्रक्तीर्वेश्यावृश्चदिन्द्रः प्रायच्छद्विश्वा भोजना सुदासे॥१७॥

17. *Indra*, has effected a valuable (donation) by a pauper: he has slain an old lion by a goat: he has cut the angles of the sacrificial post with a needle: he has given all the spoils (of the enemy) to *Sudāsa*.

Indra has Effected a Valuable Donation, Etc.— Sāyaṇa says, these three impossible acts are specified as illustrations of the wonderful power of *Indra,* to whom they are possible.

५२९६. शर्श्वन्तो हि शत्रवो रारधुष्टे भेदस्य चिच्छर्धतो विन्द रन्धिम् ।

मताँ एनः स्तुवतो यः कृणोति तिग्मं तस्मिन्नि जहि वज्रमिन्द्र ॥१८॥

18. Your numerous enemies, *Indra,* have been reduced to subjection, effect at some time or other the subjugation of the turbulent *Bheda,* who holds men praising you as guilty of wickedness; fiurl, *Indra,* your sharp thunderbolt against him.

Bheda— *Bheda,* who breaks or separates, may mean, Sāyaṇa says, an unbeliever, *nāstika;* or it may be the name of an enemy of *Sudas.*

५२९७. आवदिन्द्रं यमुना तृत्सवश्च प्रात्रं भेदं सर्वताता मुषायत् ।

अजासश्च शिग्रवो यक्षवश्च बलिं शीर्षाणि जभ्रुरश्व्यानि ॥१९॥

19. The dwellers on the *Yamuna* and the *Tṛtsus* glorified *Indra* when he killed *Bheda* in battle: the *Ajas,* the *Śigrus,* the *Yakṣas,* offered to him as a sacrifice the heads of the horses (killed in the combat).

Offered to him as a Sacrifice, Etc.— *Balim śīrṣāṇi jabhrur-aśvyāni* may mean also, according to the Scholiast, they presented the best horses, taken; but *bali* more usually imports a sacrifice.

५२९८. न तं इन्द्र सुमतयो न रायः सञ्चक्षे पूर्वा उषसो न नूत्नाः ।

देवकं चिन्मान्यमानं जघन्थाव त्मना बृहतः शम्बरं भेत् ॥२०॥

20. Your favours, *Indra,* and your bounties, whether old or new, cannot be counted like the (recurring) dawn: you hast slain Devaka, the son of Manyamany, and of thine own will hast cast down Shambara from the vast (mountain).

५२९९. प्र ये गृहादममदुस्त्वाया पराशरः शतयातुर्वसिष्ठः ।

न ते भोजस्य सख्यं मृषन्ताधा सूरिभ्यः सुदिना व्युच्छान् ॥२१॥

21. *Parāśara,* the destroyer of hundreds (of *Rākṣasas*), and *Vasiṣṭha* they who, devoted to you, have glorified you in every dwelling, neglect not the friendship of you (their) benefactor: therefore prosperous days dawn upon the pious.

The Destroyer of hundreds of *Rākṣasas*— *Śatayātu;* that is, *Śakti,* the son of *Vasiṣṭha,* the father of *Parāśara, Viṣṇu Purāṇa,* 8.4, and note.

५३००. द्वे नप्तुर्देववत: शते गोद्रा रथा वधूमन्ता सुदास:।
अर्हन्नग्ने पैजवनस्य दानं होतेव सद्म पर्येमि रेभन्।।२२।।

22. Praising the liberality of *Sudāsa*, the grandson of *Devavat*,
the son of *Paijavana*, the donor of two hundred cows, and of two
chariots with two wives, I, worthy (of the gift), circumambulate
you, *Agni*, like the ministrant priest in the chamber (of sacrifice).

५३०१. चत्वारो मा पैजवनस्य दाना: स्मद्दिष्टय: कृशनिनो निरेके।
ऋज्रासो मा पृथिविष्ठा: सुदासस्तोकं तोकाय श्रवसे वहन्ति।।२३।।

23. Four (horses), having golden trappings, going steadily on a
difficult road, celebrated on the earth, the excellent and acceptable
gifts (made) to me by *Sudāsa*, the son of *Paijavana*, bear me as a
son (to obtain) food and progeny.

The Excellent and Acceptable Gifts made to Me— *Smaddiṣṭayaḥ*,
an epithet of *Aśvaḥ*, understood, is explained, *praśastatisarjanā-
śraddhādidānāṅgayuktā*, being or having part of a donation made in the
belief of presenting what is excellent.

५३०२. यस्य श्रवो रोदसी अन्तरुर्वी शीर्ष्णेशीर्ष्णे विबभाजा विभक्ता।
सप्तेदिन्द्रं न स्त्रवतो गृणन्ति नि युध्यामधिमशिशादभीके।।२४।।

24. The seven worlds praise (*Sudāsa*) as if he were *Indra*; him
whose fame (spreads) through the spacious heaven and earth: who,
munificent, has distributed (wealth) on every eminent person, and
(for whom) the flowing (rivers) have destroyed Yudhyamadhi in
war.

५३०३. इमं नरो मरुत: सश्चतानु दिवोदासं न पितरं सुदास:।
अविष्टना पैजवनस्य केतं दूणाशं क्षत्रमजरं दुवोयु।।२५।।

25. *Maruts*, leaders (of rits), attend upon this (prince) as you
did upon Divodasa, the father of *Sudāsa*: favour the prayers of the
devout son of Pijavana, and may his strength be unimpaired,
undecaying.

[सूक्त-१९]

[ऋषि- वसिष्ठ मैत्रावरुणि। देवता- इन्द्र। छन्द- त्रिष्टुप्।]

५३०४. यस्तिग्मशृङ्गो वृषभो न भीम एक: कृष्टीश्च्यावयति प्र विश्वा:।
य: शश्वतो अदाशुषो गयस्य प्रयन्तासि सुष्विंतराय वेद:।।१।।

1. *Indra*, who is formidable as a sharp-horned bull, singly
expels all men (from their stations): you who are the despoiler of

the ample wealth of him who makes no offerings are the giver of riches to the presenter of frequent oblations.

५३०५. त्वं ह त्यदिन्द्र कुत्समाव: शुश्रूषमाणस्तन्वां समर्ये।

दासं यच्छुष्णं कुयवं न्यस्मा अरन्धय आर्जुनेयाय शिक्षन्॥२॥

2. Aiding him with your person, *Indra*, you had defended *Kutsa* in combat when you had subjugated *Dasa*, *Śuṣṇa* and *Kuyava*, giving (their spoil) to that son of *Arjuni*.

५३०६. त्वं धृष्णो धृषता वीतहव्यं प्रावो विश्वाभिरूतिभि: सुदासम्।

प्र पौरुकुत्सिं त्रसदस्युमाव: क्षेत्रसाता वृत्रहत्येषु पूरुम्॥३॥

3. Undaunted (*Indra*), you had protected with all your protections *Sudāsa*, the offerer of oblations: you hast protected in battles with enemies for the possession of the earth *Trasadasyu*, the son of *Purukutsa*, and *Puru*.

५३०७. त्वं नृभिर्नृमणो देववीतौ भूरीणि वृत्रा हर्यश्च हंसि।

त्वं नि दस्युं चुमुरिं धुनिं चास्वापयो दभीतये सुहन्तु॥४॥

4. You, the lord of horses, who are honoured by men, hast destroyed, along with the *Maruts*, numerous enemies at the sacrifice to the gods: you hast put to sleep with the thunderbolt the *Dasyus*, *Chumuri*, and *Dhuni*, on behalf of *Dabhīti*.

५३०८. तव च्यौत्नानि वज्रहस्त तानि नव यत्पुरो नवतिं च सद्य:।

निवेशने शततमाविवेषीरहंश्च वृत्रं नमुचिमुताहन्॥५॥

5. Such, wielder of the thunderbolt, are your mighty powers, that when you hadst quickly destroyed ninety and nine cities, you hast occupied the hundredth as a place of abode: you hast slain *Vṛtra*: you hast also slain *Namuci*.

५३०९. सना ता त इन्द्र भोजनानि रातहव्याय दाशुषे सुदासे।

वृष्णे ते हरी वृषणा युनज्मि व्यन्तु ब्रह्माणि पुरुशाक वाजम्॥६॥

6. Your favours, *Indra*, to *Sudāsa*, the donor (of offerings), the presenter of oblations, are infinite: showerer (of benefits), I yoke for you (your vigorous) steeds: may our prayers reach you who are mighty, to whom many rites are addressed.

५३१०. मा ते अस्यां सहसावन्परिष्टावघाय भूम हरिव: परादै।

त्रायस्व नोऽवृकेभिर्वरूथैस्तव प्रियास: सूरिषु स्याम॥७॥

7. Powerful *Indra*, lord of horses, let us not be exposed at this ceremony, addressed to you, to the murderous despoiler: protect us with impregnable defences: may we be held dear among your worshippers.

५३११. प्रियास इत्ते मघवन्नभिष्टौ नरो मदेम शरणे सखाय:।
नि तुर्वशं नि यार्द्वं शिशीह्यतिथिग्वाय शंस्यं करिष्यन्॥८॥

8. May we, *Maghavan*, leaders in your adoration, regarded as dear friends, be happy in our homes: about to bestow felicity upon *Atithigvan*, humiliate *Turvasa*; (humiliate) the son of *Yadu*.

५३१२. सद्यश्चिन्नु ते मघवन्नभिष्टौ नर: शंसन्त्युक्थशासं उक्था।
ये ते हवेभिर्वि पणींरदाशन्नस्मान्वृणीष्व युज्याय तस्मै॥९॥

9. The leader (of rites), reciters of prayers, offer, *Maghavan*, prayers devoutly for your adoration: they by their praises have appropriated the wealth of the niggards: select us (as the objects) of your friendship.

By their Praises have Appropriated the Wealth of the Niggards—
Ye te havebhir, vi pāṇin adaśan: the connection of *havebhir, stotraiḥ* with what follows is not very obvious the rest is explained, *apradānaśīlān vaṇijo api dhanāni viśeṣeṇadāpayan*, they have made to give, or have mulched, especially in their riches, those traders who are not donors of offerings.

५३१३. एते स्तोमां नरां नृतम तुभ्यमस्मद्र्यञ्चो ददतो मघानि।
तेषामिन्द्र वृत्रहत्ये शिवो भू: सखां च शूरोऽविता च नृणाम्॥१०॥

10. Chief leader (of rites), these praises of man addressed to you revert to us, who are the offerers of (sacrificial) riches: do you be propitious to such men, (*Indra*), in conflicts with enemies: be their friend, their hero, and protector.

५३१४. नू इंद्र शूर स्तवंमान ऊती ब्रह्मजूतस्तन्वां वावृधस्व।
उपं नो वाजान्निमीह्युप स्तीन्यूयं पात स्वस्तिभि: सदां न:॥११॥

11. Hero, *Indra*, glorified on the present occasion, and propitiated by praise, be amplified in your person for our protection: bestow upon us food and habitations: and do you ever cherish us with blessings.

[सूक्त-२०]

५३१५. उग्रो जज्ञे वीर्याय स्वधावाञ्चक्रिरपो नर्यो यत्कंरिष्यन्।
जग्मिर्युर्वा नृषदंनमवोभिस्त्राता न इन्द्र एनसो महश्चित्।।१॥

1. The fierce and powerful (*Indra*) has been born for heroic
(deeds): friendly to man, he is the accomplisher of whatever act he
undertakes to perform; ever youthful, he invests the (sacrificial)
hall with defences (against interruption): be our preserver, *Indra*,
from heinous sin.

५३१६. हन्ता वृत्रमिन्द्रः शूशुंवानः प्रावींनु वीरो जरितारंमूती।
कर्ता सुदासे अहं वा उ लोकं दाता वसु मुहुरा दाशुषे भूत्।।२॥

2. *Indra*, dilating in bulk, is the slayer of Vritra: the hero
defends his worshipper promptly with his protection, whether he
be the giver of dominion to *Sudāsa*, or the donor repeatedly of
wealth to the offerer (of oblations).

५३१७. युध्मो अनर्वा खजकृत्समद्वा शूरः सत्राषाङ्जनुषेमषाळ्हः।
व्यासं इन्द्रः पृतनाः स्वोजा अधा विश्वं शत्रूयन्तं जघान।।३॥

3. A warrior who turns not back in battle, a combatant, one
engaged in tumults, a hero, victorious over (his) foes from birth,
invincible, of great vigour, this *Indra* scatters (hostile) hosts and
slays all (his) adversaries.

५३१८. उभे चिदिन्द्र रोदंसी महित्वा पंप्राथ तविषीभिस्तुविष्मः।
नि वज्रमिन्द्रो हरिंवान्मिमिक्षन्त्समन्धसा मदेषु वा उवोच।।४॥

4. Opulent *Indra*, you hast filled both heaven and earth with
your magnitude, your energies: *Indra*, the lord of horses,
brandishing the thunderbolt, is gratified at sacrifices by the
(sacrificial) food.

५३१९. वृषा जजान वृषणं रणाय तमुं चित्रारीं नर्यं ससूव।
प्र यः सेनानीरध नृभ्यो अस्तीनः सत्वा गवेषणः स धृष्णुः।।५॥

5. (His) progenitor begot *Indra*, the showerer (of benefits) for
(of benefits) for (the purposes of) war: his mother brought him
forth the benefactor of man: the leader of armies who is chief over
men, he is the lord, the conqueror, the recoverer of the kine, the
subduer of foes.

५३२०. नू चित्स भ्रेषते जनो न रेषन्मनो यो अस्य घोरमाविवासत्।
यज्ञैर्य इन्द्रे दधते दुर्वांसि क्षयत्स राय ऋतपा ऋतेजा:॥६॥

6. He who devotes his mind to the terrible *Indra* never falls (from his condition), nor will he perish: the protector of sacred rites, the progeny of sacrifice, bestows riches on him who offers to *Indra* praises and prayers with sacrifices.

५३२१. यदिन्द्र पूर्वो अपराय शिक्षन्नयज्ज्यायान् कनीयसो देष्णम्।
अमृत इत्यर्यासीत दूरमा चित्र चित्र्यं भरा रयिं न:॥७॥

7. That (wealth) *Indra*, which the prior has given to the posterior: which the elder may accept from the younger: with which (the son) yet living dwells far away (separated from his father), confer, wonderful *Indra*, such precious riches upon us.

Which the Prior has given to the Posterior, Etc.— *Yad Indra purvo aparaya sikṣan*, what the father has given to the son, or the elder to the younger brother: and so in the next case, that which the father receives from the son or the elder brother from the younger.

५३२२. यस्त इन्द्र प्रियो जनो ददाशदस्त्रिरेके अद्रिव: सखा ते।
वयं ते अस्यां सुमतौ चनिष्ठा: स्याम वरूथे अघ्नतो नृपीतौ॥८॥

8. May the man who is dear to you, *Indra*, present (Oblations): may he be your friend, wielder of the thunderbolt, he (assiduous) in donations: may we be abounding in food through this favour of you who are devoid of cruelty, (may we be in the enjoyment of) a dwelling giving shelter to men.

५३२३. एष स्तोमो अचिक्रदद्वृषा त उत स्तामुर्मघवन्नक्रपिष्ट।
रायस्कामो जरितारं त आगन्त्वमङ्ग शक्र वस्व आ शंको न:॥९॥

9. For you, *Maghavan*, this showering *Soma* (libation) cries aloud: to you the worshipper has recited praises: the desire of riches has fallen upon thine adorer, do you, therefore, *Sakra*, bestow quickly upon us wealth.

५३२४. स न इन्द्र त्वयताया इषे धास्तमना च ये मघवानो जुनन्ति।
वस्वी षु ते जरित्रे अस्तु शक्तिर्यूयं पात स्वस्तिभि: सदा न:॥१०॥

10. Enable us, *Indra*, (to partake of) food granted by you, as well as those who, opulent (in sacrificial presentations), spontaneously offer (you oblations): may there be power in thine adorer (to repeat) many laudations: and do you ever cherish us with blessings.

May there be Power in thine Adorer— *Vasvī ṣu te jaritre astu śaktiḥ* is explained *atyanta praśastāsu stutiṣu tava stotre samarthyam astu*, as in the text.

[सूक्त-२१]

[ऋषि- वसिष्ठ मैत्रावरुणि। **देवता-** इन्द्र। छन्द- त्रिष्टुप्।]

५३२५. असावि देवं गोऋजीकमन्धो न्यस्मिन्निन्द्रो जनुषेमुवोच।
बोधामसि त्वा हर्यश्व यज्ञैर्बोधा नः स्तोममन्धसो मदेषु।।१।।

1. I bright sacrificial food mixed with curds and milk has been poured out: *Indra* delights in it from his birth: lord of bay horses, we wake you up with sacrifices, acknowledge our praises in the exhilaration of the *Soma* beverage.

५३२६. प्र यन्ति यज्ञं विपयन्ति बर्हिः सोममादो विदथे दुध्रवाचः।
न्यु भ्रियन्ते यशसो गृभादा दूरउपब्दो वृषणो नृषाचः।।२।।

2. They repair to the sacrifice, they strew the sacred grass: the (grinding) stones at the ceremony are of difficulty suppressed noise: famous priests, whose voices are heard far off, bring the stones from the interior of the dwelling.

५३२७. त्वमिन्द्र स्रविंतवा अपस्कः परिष्ठिता अहिना शूर पूर्वीः।
त्वद्वावक्रे रथ्योइ न धेना रेजन्ते विश्वा कृत्रिमाणि भीषा।।३।।

3. You, hero, hast enabled the many waters arrested by Ahi to flow: by you the rivers rushed forth like charioteers: all created worlds trembled through fear of you.

५३२८. भीमो विवेषायुधेभिरेषामपांसि विश्वा नर्याणि विद्वान्।
इन्दुः पुरो जर्हृषाणो वि दूधोद्वि वज्रहस्तो महिना जघान।।४।।

4. The formidable (*Indra*), knowing all actions beneficial to man, intimidated those (*Asuras*) by his weapons: *Indra*, exulting, shook their cities: armed with his thunderbolt he slew them in his might.

५३२९. न यातव इन्द्र जूजुवुर्नो न वन्दना शविष्ठ वेद्याभिः।
स शर्धदर्यो विषुणस्य जन्तोर्मा शिश्नदेवा अपि गुर्ऋतं नः।।५।।

5. Let not the *Rākṣasas*, *Indra*, do us harm: let not the evil spirits do harm to our progeny, most powerful (*Indra*): let the

sovereign lord, (*Indra*), exert himself (in the restraint) of disorderly beings, so that the unchaste may not disturb our rite.

Let not the *Rākṣasas* **do us Harm**— *Na vandana vedyabhiḥ* are rendered by Sāyaṇa *vandanani, rakṣansi,* and *prajabhyaḥ.*

The Unchaste— *Śiṣnadevaḥ, abrahmacharya ityarthaḥ,* following *Yaska,* IV.19, but it may have the sense of those who hold the *Linga* for a deity.

५३३०. अभि क्रत्वेन्द्र भूरध ज्मन्न ते विव्यङ्महिमानं रजांसि ।

स्वेना हि वृत्रं शवंसा जघन्थ न शत्रुरन्तं विविदद्युधा ते ॥६॥

6. You, *Indra*, by your function, presidest over the beings (of earth): all the regions (of the world) do not surpass your magnitude: by thine own strength you hast slain Vritra: no enemy has effected your destruction in battle.

५३३१. देवाश्चित्ते असुर्याय पूर्वे ऽनु क्षत्राय ममिरे सहांसि ।

इन्द्रो मघानि दयते विष्वहेन्द्रं वाजस्य जोहुवन्त सातौ ॥७॥

7. The older deities have confessed your vigour superior to their destructive strength, *Indra* having subdued his foes, gives the rich spoils (to his worshippers): they invoke *Indra* to obtain food.

The Older Deities— *Devas chit purve,* the *Asuras,* who, in the received mythology, are considered as older than the gods. The construction is somewhat obscure, *asūryaya kṣatraya anumamire sahansi; anu,* Sāyaṇa of *Panini: Hine,* I.4.86, they have confessed inferiority to your strength: *tava balebhyo hina mamire; asuraya,* he renders, *balaya,* to strength, and *kṣatraya* he derives from *kṣadi,* to injure, *hinsayam.*

५३३२. कीरिश्चिद्धि त्वामवसे जुहावेशानमिन्द्र सौभगस्य भूरेः ।

अवो बभूथ शतमूते अस्मे अभिक्षत्तुस्त्वावतो वरूता ॥८॥

8. The worshipper has invoked you the sovereign *Indra*, for protection: protector of many, you hast been to us the guardian of great fortune: be our defender against every overpowering (assailant) like to you.

५३३३. सखायस्त इन्द्र विश्वह स्याम नमोवृधासो महिना तरुत्र ।

वन्वन्तु स्मा तेऽवसा समीके ऽभीतिमर्यो वनुषां शवांसि ॥९॥

9. May we, daily increasing in reverence, be (regarded), *Indra*, (as) your friends: through the protection of you, surpasser in greatness, may (your worshippers) repulse the attack of the foe in battle, the strength of the malevolent.

५३३४. स नं इन्द्र त्वयंताया इषे धास्तमना च ये मघवांनो जुनन्ति।

वस्वी षु तें जरित्रे अस्तु शक्तिर्यूयं पांत स्वस्तिभिः सदां नः॥१०॥

10. Enable us, *Indra*, (to partake of) food granted by you, as well as those who, opulent (in sacrificial presentations), spontaneously offer the (oblations): may there be ability in thine adorer (to repeat) may laudations: and do you ever cherish us with blessings.

[सूक्त-२२]

[ऋषि– वसिष्ठ मैत्रावरुणि। **देवता**– इन्द्र। **छन्द**– विराट्, ९ त्रिष्टुप्।]

५३३५. पिबा सोममिन्द्र मन्दंतु त्वा यं तें सुषावं हर्यश्वाद्रिः।

सोतुर्बाहुभ्यां सुयंतो नार्वा॥१॥

1. Drink, *Indra*, the *Soma*: may it exhilarate you, that which the stone tightly held like a horse (by the reins), by the arms of the grinder, has expressed, lord of bay horses for you.

Sāmaveda, 398, 927.

५३३६. यस्तें मदो युज्यश्चारुरस्ति येनं वृत्राणि हर्यश्व हंसिं।

स त्वामिन्द्र प्रभूवसो ममत्तु॥२॥

2. May the exhilarating beverage which is fit for an suitable to you, by which, lord of bay horses, you slayest Vritras, exhilarate you, *Indra*, abounding in riches.

Sāmaveda, 278-29.

५३३७. बोधा सु मे मघवन्वाचमेमां यां ते वसिष्ठो अर्चति प्रशस्तिम्।

इमा ब्रह्मं सधमादें जुषस्व॥३॥

3. Understand thoroughly, *Maghavan*, this my speech, this praise of you, which *Vasiṣṭha* recites; be pleased by these prayers at the sacrifice.

५३३८. श्रुधी हवं विपिपानस्याद्रेर्बोधा विप्रस्यार्चतो मनीषाम्।

कृष्वा दुवांस्यन्तमा सचेमा॥४॥

4. Hear the invocation of the (grinding) stone, (of me) repeatedly drinking (the *Soma*), comprehend the hymn of the adoring sage, and, friendly (with us), take to your near consideration these adorations.

Of me Repeatedly Drinking the Soma— *Śrudhi havam vipipanasya adraḥ*, the Scholiast inserts, *mama* as *vipipana*, the frequentative of *pa*, to drink, explained *vipitavat* or *vipivat*, would be not a very appropriate epithet of *adri*.

Take to your near Consideration these Adorations— *Kṛṣva duvansi antama sachema*, is explained *mani paricharanani antikatamani buddhisthani sahayabhuta san kuru*, the explanation is not very intelligible.

५३३९. न ते गिरो अपि मृष्ये तुरस्य न सुष्टुतिमसुर्यस्य विद्वान् ।

सदा ते नाम स्वयशो विवक्मि ।।५।।

5. Knowing of your strength, I refrain not from the praise nor from the glorification of you, the destroyer (of foes), but ever proclaim your especial care.

५३४०. भूरि हि ते सर्वना मानुषेषु भूरि मनीषी हवते त्वामित् ।

मारे अस्मन्मघवज्ज्योककः ।।६।।

6. Many are the sacrifices offered, *Maghavan*, to you amongst mankind; constantly does worshipper indeed invoke you; therefore be not far nor be a long time from us.

This and the two preceding occur in *Sāmaveda*, 1798-1800.

५३४१. तुभ्येदिमा सर्वना शूर विश्वा तुभ्यं ब्रह्माणि वर्धना कृणोमि ।

त्वं नृभिर्हव्यो विश्वधासि ।।७।।

7. To you, hero, I indeed offer these sacrifices, to you I address these elevating praises: you are to be in all ways invoked by the leaders (of rites).

५३४२. नू चिन्नु ते मन्यमानस्य दस्मोदश्नुवन्ति महिमानमुग्र ।

न वीर्यमिन्द्र ते न राधः ।।८।।

8. *Indra*, of goodly aspect, none attain the greatness of you who are to be honoured, nor, fierce *Indra*, your heroism, nor your wealth.

५३४३. ये च पूर्व ऋषयो ये च नूत्ना इन्द्र ब्रह्माणि जनयन्त विप्राः ।

अस्मे ते सन्तु सख्या शिवानि यूयं पात स्वस्तिभिः सदा नः ।।९।।

9. May your auspicious regards, *Indra*, be directed towards us, as they have been to those pious sages, ancient or recent, who have originated (your) praises, and do you ever cherish us with blessings.

[सूक्त-२३]

[**ऋषि**– वसिष्ठ मैत्रावरुणि। **देवता**– इन्द्र। **छन्द**– त्रिष्टुप्।]

५३४४. उदु ब्रह्माण्यैरत श्रवस्येन्द्रं समर्ये महया वसिष्ठ।

आ यो विश्वानि शवसा ततानोपश्रोता म ईवतो वचांसि॥१॥

1. (The sages) have offered prayers to (*Indra*) for food, worship *Indra*, *Vasiṣṭha* at the sacrifice: may that *Indra* who has spread out all (the regions) by his might, be the hearer of my words when approaching him.

५३४५. अयामि घोषं इन्द्र देवजामिरिरज्यन्त यच्छुरुधो विवाचि।

नहि स्वमायुश्चिकिते जनेषु तानीदंहांस्यति पर्षस्मान्॥२॥

2. When, *Indra*, the plants grow up, the sound (of praise) acceptable to the gods, (uttered) by the worshipper, has been raised: by no one among men, is his own life understood; convey us beyond all those sins (by which life is shortened).

When the Plants Grow Up— *Yacchurudho irajyanta* is explained *oṣadhyo varddhante*: in a former passage *śurudh* was interpreted, a cow.

५३४६. युजे रथं गवेषणं हरिभ्यामुप ब्रह्माणि जुजुषाणमस्थुः।

वि बाधिष्टस्य रोदसी महित्वेन्द्रौ वृत्राण्यप्रती जघन्वान्॥३॥

3. I harness (by praises) the kine-bestowing chariot (of *Indra*) with his horses: (my) prayers have reached him who is pleased (by devotion): he has surpassed in magnitude heaven and earth, slaying the unresisting enemies.

Slaying the Unresisting Enemies— *vritranyaprati jaghanvān*: the meaning of *aprati* is not very obvious: Sāyaṇa explains it, *dvandvani*, twofold, doubled.

५३४७. आपश्चित्पिप्युः स्तर्यो३ न गावो नक्षन्नृतं जरितारस्त इन्द्र।

याहि वायुर्न नियुतो नो अच्छा त्वं हि धीभिर्दयसे वि वाजान्॥४॥

4. May the waters increase like young: may your worshippers, *Indra*, possess water (in abundance): come like the wind with the *Niyut* steeds, for you, (propitiated) by holy rites, verily bestowest upon us food.

Yajurveda, 33. 18: Mahīdhara gives a totally different meaning to the first phrase, *apaschit pipyuh staryo na gavah,* the waters augment the *Soma* juice as those *Vaidik* texts by which the *Soma* is effused.

५३४८. ते त्वा॒ मदा॑ इन्द्र॒ माद॑यन्तु शुष्मिणं॑ तुविरा॒धसं॑ जरि॒त्रे।

एको॒ देव॒त्रा द॑यसे॒ हि मर्ता॒नस्मिञ्छू॑र॒ सव॑ने मादयस्व॑।।५।।

5. May these inebriating draughts exhilarate you, *Indra*: bestow upon the praiser (a son vigorous and wealthy): for you alone amongst the gods are compassionate to mortals: be exhilarated here at this sacrifice.

५३४९. ए॒वेदिन्द्रं॑ वृ॒षणं॑ व॒ज्रबाहुं॑ वसि॒ष्ठासो॑ अ॒भ्यर्च॑न्त्य॒र्कैः।

स न॑: स्तु॒तो वी॒रव॑द्धातु॒ गोम॑द्यू॒यं पा॑त स्व॒स्तिभि॑: स॒दा न॑:।।६।।

6. In this manner the *Vasiṣṭhas* glorify with hymns *Indra*, the showerer, the bearer of the thunderbolt: may he so glorified grant us wealth, comprising male posterity and cattle: and do you ever cherish us with blessings.

Yajurveda, 20.54: the concluding phrase, which has so often occurred, Mahīdhara considers addressed to the priests, *yuyam Ritvijaḥ*.

[सूक्त-२४]

[ऋषि– वसिष्ठ मैत्रावरुणि। देवता– इन्द्र। छन्द– त्रिष्टुप्।]

५३५०. योनि॒ष्ट इन्द्र॒ सद॑ने अकारि॒ तमा नृभि॑: पुरुहूत॒ प्र या॑हि।

असो॒ यथा॑ नो॒ऽविता॑ वृ॒धे च॒ ददो॒ वसू॑नि म॒मद॑श्च सोमै॑:।।१।।

1. A place has been prepared for you in the sacrificial chamber: proceed to it, invoked of many, along with the leaders (of rites the *Maruts*), inasmuch as you are our protector, (promote our) prosperity: grant us riches: be exhilarated by the *Soma*.

५३५१. गभी॒तं ते॒ मन॑ इन्द्र द्वि॒बर्हा॑: सु॒त: सोम॑: परि॒षिक्ता॒ मधू॑नि।

विसृ॒ष्टधे॑ना भरते सुवृ॒क्तिरि॒यमिन्द्रं॒ जोहु॑वती म॒नीषा॑।।२।।

2. Your purpose, *Indra*, is apprehended, you who are mighty in the two (worlds): the *Soma* is effused: the sweet juices are poured (into the vessels): this perfect praise uttered with loosened tongue propitiates *Indra* with repeated invocations.

Mighty in the two Worlds— *Dvibhara*, according to the Scholiast, should be *dvibarhasaḥ*, agreeing with *te-dvayoḥ sthanayoḥ pari vṛdhasya tava man gṛhitam*, the mind of you who are enlarged in both is apprehended: what places is not explained; perhaps heaven and earth may be intended.

५३५२. आ नौ दिव आ पृथिव्या ऋजीषिन्निदं बर्हिः सौमपेयाय याहि।

वहन्तु त्वा हरयो मद्र्यञ्चमाङ्गूषमच्छा तवसं मदाय॥३॥

3. Come, Rijishin, from the sky, or from the firmament, to this sacred grass , to drink the *Soma*: let your horses bear you who are vigorous to my presence to (receive my) praise and for (thine) exhilaration.

५३५३. आ नो विश्वाभिरूतिभिः सजोषा ब्रह्म जुषाणो हर्यश्व याहि।

वरीवृजत् स्थविरेभिः सुशिप्रास्मे दधद्वृषणं शुष्ममिन्द्र॥४॥

4. Lord of bay steeds, propitiated by our praise, come to us with all your protections, sharing in satisfaction, handsome-chinned, with the ancient (*Maruts*), overthrowing repeatedly (your) foes, and granting us a strong and vigorous (son).

५३५४. एष स्तोमो मह उग्राय वाहे धुरीइव वात्यो न वाजयन्नधायि।

इन्द्र त्वायमर्क ईं वसूनां दिवीव द्यामधि नः श्रोमतं धाः॥५॥

5. This invigorating praise, like a horse attached to car, has been addressed to you who are mighty and fierce, the up-bearer (of the world): this thine adorer desires of you, *Indra*, riches: do you grant us sustenance notorious as the sky in heaven.

Notorious as the Sky in Heaven— *Diviva dyam adhi na śromatam dhaḥ*: the Scholiast gives no explanation of the comparison: *śromatam* he interprets *sravaniyam*, applicable either to food or fame.

५३५५. एवा न इन्द्र वार्यस्य पूर्धि प्र ते महीं सुमतिं वेविदाम।

इषं पिन्व मघवद्भ्यः सुवीरां यूयं पात स्वस्तिभिः सदा नः॥६॥

6. In this manner, *Indra*, satisfy us (with the gift) of desirable (wealth): may we repeatedly experience your great giver: bestow upon us who are opulent (in offerings) food with male descendants: do you ever cherish us with blessings.

[सूक्त-२५]

[ऋषि- वसिष्ठ मैत्रावरुणि। **देवता-** इन्द्र। छन्द- त्रिष्टुप्।]

५३५६. आ ते मह इन्द्रोत्युग्र समन्यवो यत्समरन्त सेनाः।

पताति दिद्युन्नर्यस्य बाह्वोर्मा ते मनो विष्वद्र्यइग्व चारीत्॥१॥

1. Fierce *Indra*, when animated by like fierce armies, encounter them: let the bright (weapon) wielded by the arms of

you who are mighty and the friend of man descend for our protection; let not your all-pervading mind wander (away from us).

५३५७. नि दुर्ग इन्द्र श्रथिह्यमित्रानभि ये नो मर्तासो अमन्ति।

आरे तं शंसं कृणुहि निनित्सोरा नौ भर सम्भरणं वसूनाम्।।२।।

2. Destroy, *Indra*, our adversaries in battle, those men who overpower us: remove far from us the calumny of the reviler: bring to us abundance of treasures.

५३५८. शतं ते शिप्रिन्नूतयः सुदासे सहस्रं शंसा उत रातिरस्तु।

जहि वर्धर्वनुषो मर्त्यस्यास्मे द्युम्नमधि रत्नं च धेहि।।३।।

3. May hundreds of your protections, handsome-chinned, be (secured) to the liberal donor (of oblations): may thousands of blessings be bestowed (upon me) us well as wealth: cast the fatal weapon on the mischievous mortal: grant us food and wealth.

Wealth— *Dyumnam* may mean either food or fame. *Nir.* v.5.

५३५९. त्वावतो हीन्द्र क्रत्वे अस्मि त्वावतोऽवितुः शूर रातौ।

विश्वेदहानि तविषीव उग्रं ओकः कृणुष्व हरिवो न मर्धीः।।४।।

4. I am (in dependence), *Indra*, upon the acts of such as you are, upon the liberality of a protector, hero, such as you: vigorous and fierce *Indra*, give us a dwelling for all our days: lord of bay steeds, do us no harm.

५३६०. कुत्सा एते हर्यश्वाय शूषमिन्द्रे सहो देवजूतमियानाः।

सत्रा कृधि सुहना शूर वृत्रा वयं तरुत्राः सनुयाम वाजम्।।५।।

5. These (*Vasiṣṭhas*) are offering grateful (adoration) to the lord of bay steeds, soliciting the strength assigned by the gods to *Indra*: make our enemies, *Indra*, easy to be overcome, and may we, safe from peril, enjoy abundance.

५३६१. एवा न इन्द्र वार्यस्य पूर्धि प्र ते महीं सुमतिं वेविदाम।

इषं पिन्व मघवद्भयः सुवीरां यूयं पात स्वस्तिभिः सदा नः।।६।।

6. In this manner, *Indra*, satisfy us with the gift of desirable (wealth): may we repeatedly experience your great favour: bestow upon us who are opulent in offerings food with male descendants: do you ever cherish us with blessings.

[सूक्त-२६]

[ऋषि– वसिष्ठ मैत्रावरुणि। देवता– इन्द्र। छन्द– त्रिष्टुप्।]

५३६२. न सोम इन्द्रमसुतो ममाद नाब्रह्माणो मघवानं सुतासः।
तस्मा उक्थं जनये यज्जुजोषन्नृवन्नवीयः शृणवद्यथा नः॥१॥

1. The *Soma* uneffused delights not *Indra*: the effused juices please not *Maghavan*, unaccompanied by prayer: therefore I offer to him praise that he may be pleased with: that, like a prince, he may listen to a novel (strain).

५३६३. उक्थउक्थे सोम इन्द्रं ममाद नीथेनीथे मघवानं सुतासः।
यदीं सबाधः पितरं न पुत्राः समानदक्षा अवसे हवन्ते॥२॥

2. The *Soma* effused with reiterated prayer delights *Indra*: the effused juices, (offered) with repeated praise, (exhilarate) *Maghavan*: therefore (the priests), combining together and making like exertion, invoke *Indra* for protection, as sons (apply) to a father.

५३६४. चकार ता कृणवन्नूनमन्या यानि ब्रुवन्ति वेधसः सुतेषु।
जनीरिव पतिरेकः समानो नि मामृजे पुर इन्द्रः सु सर्वाः॥३॥

3. Such exploits as his worshippers, when the *soma* is effused, proclaim that he has achieved, let him now perform: may *Indra*, equal (to the task) and unaided, spossess all the cities (of the *Asuras*) as a husband his wives.

५३६५. एवा तमाहुरुत शृण्व इन्द्र एको विभक्ता तरणिर्मघानाम्।
मिथस्तुर ऊतयो यस्य पूर्वीरस्मे भद्राणि सश्चत प्रियाणि॥४॥

4. Such have they proclaimed him: *Indra* is still celebrated as the distributor of riches, the transporter (beyond calamity), of whom many and emulous are the protections: may acceptable benefits attend us.

५३६६. एवा वसिष्ठ इन्द्रमूतये नॄन्कृष्टीनां वृषभं सुते गृणाति।
सहस्रिण उप नो माहि वाजान् यूयं पात स्वस्तिभिः सदा नः॥५॥

5. Thus does Vashishtha glorify *Indra*, the showerer (of benefits) upon the worshippers for the preservation of mankind: bestow upon us, (*Indra*), thousands of viands: do you ever cherish us with blessings.

[सूक्त- २७]

[ऋषि– वसिष्ठ मैत्रावरुणि। देवता– इन्द्र। छन्द– त्रिष्टुप्।]

५३६७. इन्द्रं नरो नेमधिता हवन्ते यत्पार्या युञ्जते धियस्ताः।
शूरो नृषाता शवसश्चकान आ गोमति व्रजे भजा त्वं नः॥१॥

1. Men invoke *Indra* in battle when those actions which lead to victory are performed: do you who are hero, the benefactor of man, the desirer of provess, place us in possession of pastures abounding with cattle.

Sāmaveda, 318.

५३६८. य इन्द्र शुष्मो मघवन्ते अस्ति शिक्षा सखिभ्यः पुरुहूत नृभ्यः।
त्वं हि दृळ्हा मघवन्विचेता अपा वृधि परिवृतं न राधः॥२॥

2. *Indra*, who are the invoked of many, give to those men who are your friends that strength which, *Maghavan*, is thine: you, *Maghavan*, (hast forced open) the firm (shur, gates of cities): discover, discriminator (of truth), the treasure now concealed.

Hast Forced open Firm shut Gates of Cities— The text has only *tvam hi dridha maghavan,* you, *Maghavan,* verily the firm (plur, acc. fem.).

५३६९. इन्द्रो राजा जगतश्चर्षणीनामधि क्षमि विषुरूपं यदस्ति।
ततो ददाति दाशुषे वसूनि चोदद्राध उपस्तुतश्चिदर्वाक्॥३॥

3. *Indra* is lord of the earth and of men: (his is) the various wealth that exists upon the earth: thence he gives riches to the donor (of oblations): may he, glorified by us, bestow upon us wealth.

५३७०. नू चित्र इन्द्रो मघवा सहूती दानो वाजं नि यमते न ऊती।
अनूना यस्य दक्षिणा पीपाय वामं नृभ्यो अभिवीता सखिभ्यः॥४॥

4. May the affluent and liberal *Indra*, upon being invoked together (with the *Maruts*), quickly bestow food for our reservation, he whose unlimited, experienced liberality yields desirable (wealth) to those men (who are his) friends.

५३७१. नू इन्द्र राये वरिवस्कृधी न आ ते मनो ववृत्याम मघाय।
गोमदश्वावद्रथवद्व्यन्तो यूयं पात स्वस्तिभिः सदा नः॥५॥

5. *Indra*, grant quickly wealth for our enrichment: may we attract your favour by our adoration: granting us (riches),

comprising cattle, and horses, and chariots: do you ever cherish us
with blessings.

[सूक्त- २८]

[ऋषि- वसिष्ठ मैत्रावरुणि। देवता- इन्द्र। छन्द- त्रिष्टुप्।]

५३७२. ब्रह्मा ण इन्द्रोप याहि विद्वानवांश्चस्ते हरय: सन्तु युक्ता:।

विश्वे चिद्धि त्वां विहवन्त मर्ता अस्माकमिच्छृणुहि विश्वमिन्व॥१॥

1. *Indra*, who are wise, come to our adoration: let your horses
harnessed by before us: gratified of all (men), all mortals severally
invoke you: hear therefore our (invocation).

५३७३. हवं त इन्द्र महिमा व्यानड् ब्रह्म यत्पासि शवसिन्तृषीणाम्।

आ यद्वज्रं दधिषे हस्त उग्र घोर: सन्क्रत्वा जनिष्ठा अषाळ्ह:॥२॥

2. Endowed with strength, since you grantest the prayers of the
Ṛsis, let your greatness, *Indra*, extend to thine invoker: and as,
fierce deity, you holdest the thunderbolt in your hand, then
formidable by your expolits you hast become invincible.

५३७४. तव प्रणीतीन्द्र जोहुवानान्त्सं यत्रत्र रोदसी निनेथ।

महे क्षत्राय शर्वसे हि जज्ञेऽतूतुजिं चित्तूतुजिरशिश्रत्॥३॥

3. Since, *Indra*, by your guidance, you hast conducted men,
you zealous worshippers, over heaven and earth, you are born to
(bestow) great wealth and strength, whence the presenter of
offerings overcomes him who offers them not.

Hast Conducted men......over heaven and Earth— *Nriti na rodasi
san ninetha*; the verb is explained *sangamayasi*, you bringest together;
divi pṛthivyam ca stotrin pratiṣṭhapayasi, you establishest the worshippers
in heaven and in earth: no notice is taken of the particle *na*: but it cannot
well be the negative.

५३७५. एभिर्न इन्द्राहभिर्दशस्य दुर्मित्रासो हि क्षितय: पवन्ते।

प्रति यच्चष्टे अनृतमनेना अवं द्विता वरुणो मायी न: सात्॥४॥

4. Grant us, *Indra*, with these days, (wealth), for unfriendly
men approach: may the untruth which the wise and sinless *Varuṇa*
observes in us, (through your favour, *Indra*), doubly disappear.

Doubly Disappear— *Dvita avasat*: the verb is explained by
vimochana, loosing, setting free; but there is no explanation of *dvita* or
dvidha, twofold: perhaps it may mean now and hereafter, or body and
mind, or word and deed.

५३७६. वोचेमेदिन्द्रं मघवानमेनं महो रायो राधंसो यद्दंत्र:।

यो अर्चतो ब्रह्मकृतिमविंक्षो यूयं पातं स्वस्तिभि: सदां न:॥५॥

5. Let us glorify that opulent *Indra*, that he may give us great and valuable riches, he who is the cheif protector of the pious rites of the worshipper: do you ever cherish us with blessings.

[सूक्त-२९]

[ऋषि– वसिष्ठ मैत्रावरुणि। देवता– इन्द्र। छन्द– त्रिष्टुप्।]

५३७७. अयं सोमं इन्द्र तुभ्यं सुन्व आ तु प्र यांहि हरिवस्तदोका:।

पिबा त्वंऽस्य सुषुंतस्य चारोर्ददों मघानिं मघवन्नियान:॥१॥

1. This *Soma* is poured out, *Indra*, for you: come, lord of bay steeds, to that dwelling (where it is prepared) drink of the plentifully-effused and grateful libation), give us, Maghavan, when solicited for them, riches.

५३७८. ब्रह्मन्वीर ब्रह्मकृतिं जुषाणोऽर्वाचीनो हरिभिर्याहि तूयम्।

अस्मिन्नू षु सवंने मादयस्वोप ब्रह्माणि शृणव इमा नं:॥२॥

2. Magnified hero, *Indra*, approving of the sacred rite, come to us speedily with your steeds: be exhilarated at this sacrifice; hear these our prayers.

In the Variously Clamorous Strife— *Vivācī* is explained *vividha vaco yasmin pradurbhavanti tasmin yuddhe,* in that war or combat in which many words are manifested: the nominative *Śūra*, heroes, gives plausibility to the interpretation.

For the ling Enjoyment of the Sun— *Sūryasya satum, cirakāla, prāptyartham,* for the sake of having long life: *Āyur atra sūrya vivakṣitaḥ, Sūrya* her expresses life.

५३७९. का ते अस्त्यरंङ्कृति: सूक्तै: कदा नूनं ते मघवन् दाशेम।

विश्वां मतीरा ततने त्वायाधां म इन्द्र शृणवो हवेमा॥३॥

3. What satisfaction is there to you from our hymns? When, *Maghavan*, may we indeed present to you (oblations)? I expatiate in all praises addressed to you: hear, *Indra*, these my invocations.

५३८०. उतो घा ते पुरुष्याऽइ इदांसन्येषां पूर्वेषामश्रृणोर्ऋषीणाम्।

अधाहं त्वां मघवञ्जोहवीमि त्वं नं इन्द्रासि प्रमति: पितेवं॥४॥

4. Friendly to man were those of the ancient *Ṛṣis* whose praises you hast listened to; therefore I repeatedly invoke you, *Maghavan*: you, *Indra*, are well affected towards us as a parent.

५३८१. वोचेमेदिन्द्रं मघवानमेनं महो रायो राधसो यद्दनः।
यो अर्चतो ब्रह्मकृतिमविष्ठो यूयं पात स्वस्तिभिः सदा नः॥५॥

5. Let us glorify that opulent *Indra*, that he may give us vast and valuable riches, he who is the cheif protector of the religious rites of the worshippers: do you ever cherish us with blessings.

[सूक्त-३०]

[ऋषि– वसिष्ठ मैत्रावरुणि। **देवता**– इन्द्र। **छन्द**– त्रिष्टुप्।]

५३८२. आ नों देव शवसा याहि शुष्मिन्भवा वृध इन्द्र रायः अस्य।
महे नृम्णाय नृपते सुवज्र महि क्षत्राय पौंस्याय शूर॥१॥

1. Divine and powerful (*Indra*), come to us with your strength: be the augmenter of our riches: be to us, king of men, wielder of the thunderbolt, for (a source of) vigour, of great prowess, hero, of manhood.

५३८३. हवन्त उ त्वा हव्यं विवाचि तनूषु शूराः सूर्यस्य सातौ।
त्वं विश्वेषु सेन्यो जनेषु त्वं वृत्राणि रन्धया सुहन्तु॥२॥

2. Warriors invoke you, worthy to be invoked, in the variously clamorous (strife), for (the safety of their) persons, and for the (long) enjoyment of the sun: you are a fit leader over all men: humble our enemies by the fatal (bolt).

५३८४. अहा यदिन्द्र सुदिना व्युच्छान्दधो यत्केतुमुपमं समत्सु।
न्यग्निः सीददसुरो न होता हुवानो अत्र सुभगाय देवान्॥३॥

3. When, *Indra*, fortunate days arise, when you advancest thine emblem in battles, the strong *Agni*, the invoker of the gods, summoning the gods hither for our benefit, sits down on the sacred grass.

५३८५. वयं ते तं इन्द्र ये च देव स्तवन्त शूर ददतो मघानि।
यच्छा सूरिभ्य उपमं वरूथं स्वाभुवो जरणामश्नवन्त॥४॥

4. We, divine *Indra*, who are thine, are they, hero, who are praising you and offering rich libations: grant to (your) pious (worshippers) an excellent abode: and may they, prosperous, attain old age.

५३८६. वोचेमेदिन्द्रं मघवानमेनं महो रायो राधसो यद्ददन्न:।
यो अर्चतो ब्रह्मकृतिमविश्वो यूयं पात स्वस्तिभि: सदा न:॥५॥

5. Let us glorify the opulent *Indra*, that he may give us vast
and valuable riches: he who is the cheif protector of the religious
rites of the worshippers: do you ever cherish us with blessings.

[सूक्त- ३१]

[ऋषि– वसिष्ठ मैत्रावरुणि। देवता– इन्द्र। छन्द– गायत्री, १०-१२ विराट्।]

५३८७. प्र व इन्द्राय मादनं हर्यश्वाय गायत। सखाय: सोमपाव्ने॥१॥

1. Sing, friends, an exhilarating hymn to *Indra*, the lord of bay
steeds, the drinker of the *Soma*.
　Sāmaveda, 156, 716.

५३८८. शंसेदुक्थं सुदानव उत द्युक्षं यथा नर:। चकृमा सत्यराधसे॥२॥

2. Repeat to the liberal *Indra* such brilliant praise as other
(men repeat): let us offer it to him who is affluent in truth.

५३८९. त्वं न इन्द्र वाजयुस्त्वं गव्यु: शतक्रतो। त्वं हिरण्ययुर्वसो॥३॥

3. Do you, *Indra*, be willing to give us food: be willing,
Shatakratu, to give us cattle: be willing, donor of dwelling, to us
gold.

५३९०. वयमिन्द्र त्वायवोऽभि प्र णोनुमो वृषन्।
विद्धी त्वस्य नो वसो॥४॥

4. Devoted to you, showerer (of benefits), we glorify you: be
cognizant, giver of dwellings, of this our praise.
　Sāmaveda, 132.

५३९१. मा नो निदे च वक्तवेऽर्यो रन्धीररावणे। त्वे अपि क्रतुर्ममं॥५॥

5. *Indra*, who are lord, subject us not to the reviler, to the
abuser, to the withholder of offerings: may my worship verily (find
favour) with you.
　May my Worship Verily find favour with you— *Tve a kratur
mama*, in you ever my act, means, says Sāyana, *asmadiyam stotran,
bhavacchitte praviśatu*, may my praise enter into your heart.

५३९२. त्वं वर्मासि सप्रथ: पुरोयोधश्च वृत्रहन्। त्वया प्रति ब्रुवे युजा॥६॥

6. Slayer of enemies, you, *Indra*, are our armour, vast and our
preceder in battle: with you for my ally I defy (the foe).

५३९३. महाँ उतासि यस्य॒ ते॒नु॒ स्व॒धाव॑री स॒ह:। म॒म्नाते॑ इन्द्र॒ रोद॑सी।।७।।

7. You verily are great; and heaven and earth abounding with food, respect, *Indra*, your strength.

५३९४. तं त्वा॑ म॒रुत्व॑ती॒ परि॑ भुव॒द्वाणी॑ स॒यावं॑री। न॒क्ष॒माणा॑ स॒ह द्यु॒भि:।।८।।

8. May the praises of thine adorers, accompanying you (wherever you goest), such as you are, and spreading around with radiance, reach you.

५३९५. ऊ॒र्ध्वास॑स्त्वान्विन्द॒वो भुव॑न्दस्ममुप॑ द्य॒वि। सं ते॑ नमन्त कृ॒ष्टय॑:।।९।।

9. The ascending libations proceed, *Indra*, to you, abiding in heaven, of goodly aspect: men bow in reverence before you.

५३९६. प्र वो॑ म॒हे महि॒वृधे॑ भरध्वं॒ प्रचे॑तसे॒ प्र सु॒मतिं॑ कृणुध्वम्।

विश॑: पू॒र्वी: प्र च॑रा चर्षणि॒प्रा:।।१०।।

10. Bring (libations) to the great (*Indra*), the giver of great (wealth): offer praise to the wise *Indra*: fulfiller (of the desires) of men, come to the people offering many (oblations).

Sāmaveda, 328, 1793.

५३९७. उ॒रुव्य॑चसे म॒हिन॑े सुवृ॒क्तिमिन्द्रा॑य॒ ब्रह्म॑ जनयन्त॒ विप्रा॑:।

तस्य॑ व्र॒तानि॑ न मि॒नन्ति॒ धीरा॑:।।११।।

11. The sages engender sacred praise and (sacrificial) food for the wide-pervading, mighty *Indra*: the prudent impede not his functions.

५३९८. इन्द्रं॑ वा॒णीरनु॑त्तमन्यु॒मेव॑ स॒त्रा राजा॑नं दधिरे॒ सह॑ध्यै।

हर्य॑श्वाय बर्हया॒ समा॑पीन्।।१२।।

12. Praises truly enable the universal monarch, *Indra*, whose wrath is irresistible, to overcome (his foes): urge your kinsmen, (worshippers, to glorify) the lord of bay steeds.

[सूक्त-३२]

[ऋषि– वसिष्ठ मैत्रावरुणि, २६ पूर्वार्द्ध ऋचा वसिष्ठ अथवा शक्ति वासिष्ठ।

देवता– इन्द्र। छन्द– प्रगाथ (विषमा बृहती, समासतो बृहती),

३ द्विपदा विराट्।]

५३९९. मो षु त्वा॑ वाघत॑श्चना॒रे अ॒स्मन्नि री॑रमन्।

आ॒रात्ता॑च्चित्स॒धमादं॒ न आ ग॑हीह॒ वा॒ सन्नुप॑ श्रुधि।।१।।

1. Let not, *Indra*, (other) worshippers detain you far from us: come from whatever distance to our assembly: present at this ceremony, hear our (prayers).

५४००. इमे हि ते ब्रह्मकृतः सुते सचा मधौ न मक्ष आसते।
इन्द्रे कामं जरितारो वसूयवो रथे न पादमा दधुः॥२॥

2. When the libation is effused for you, these offerers of sacrifice swarm like flies round honey: the pious praisers, desiring riches, fix their hope upon *Indra*, like a foot upon a chariot. (*Sāmaveda*, 1676).

५४०१. रायस्कामो वज्रहस्तं सुदक्षिणं पुत्रो न पितरं हुवे॥३॥

3. Desirous of riches, I call upon the benevolent wielder of the thunderbolt, as a son upon a father.

५४०२. इम इन्द्राय सुन्विरे सोमासो दध्याशिरः।
ताँ आ मदाय वज्रहस्त पीतये हरिभ्यां याह्योक आ॥४॥

4. These *Soma* Juices, mixed with curds, are poured out to *Indra*: come, wielder of the thunderbolt, with your horses of our dwelling, to drink there for (thine) exhilaration (*Sāmaveda*, 293.)

५४०३. श्रवच्छ्रुत्कर्ण ईयते वसूनां नू चिन्नो मर्धिषद् गिरः।
सद्यश्चिद्यः सहस्राणि शता ददन्नकिर्दित्सन्तमा मिनत्॥५॥

5. May *Indra*, whose ear is ready to hear, listen to the suppliant for riches, and never disappoint our prayers: he who is the giver of hundreds and thousands: may no one ever hinder him when willing to give.

५४०४. स वीरो अप्रतिष्कुत इन्द्रेण शूशुवे नृभिः।
यस्ते गभीरा सर्वनानि वृत्रहन्त्सुनोत्या च धावति॥६॥

6. Slayer of *Vṛtra*, the hero who offers sacrifices to you, who eagerly approaches you (with praises), he, (protected) by *Indra*, is unresisted (by any one), and is honoured by men.

५४०५. भवा वरूथं मघवन्मघोनां यत्समजासि शर्धतः।
वि त्वाहतस्य वेदनं भजेमह्या दूणाशो भरा गयम्॥७॥

7. Be a defence, *Maghavan*, to the wealthy (offerers in oblations), for you are the discomfiter of (our) adversaries: may we divide the spoil of the enemy slain by you do you, who are indestructible, bring it to our dwelling.

५४०६. सुनोता॒ सोमपा॒व्ने सोम॒मिन्द्राय॑ व॒ज्रिणे॑।

पच॑ता प॒क्तीर॑व॒से कृ॒णु॒ध्व॒मित्पृ॒ण॒न्नित्पृ॑णते म॒र्यः॑॥८॥

8. Pour out the libation to *Indra*, the thunderer, the drinker of
the *Soma*: prepare the baked (cakes) to satisfy him: do (what is
agreeable to him), for he bestows happiness on (the worshipper)
who pleases him.

Sāmaveda, 285.

५४०७. मा स्रे॑धत सोमि॒नो द॒क्षता॑ म॒हे कृ॒णु॒ध्वं राय॒ आतु॑जे।

तर॒णिरिज्ज॑यति॒ क्षेति॒ पुष्य॑ति॒ न दे॒वासः॑ क॒वत्न॒वे॑॥९॥

9. Offerers of the libation, do not hesitate: be active: sacrifice
to the mighty benefactor for the sake of riches: the assiduous
worshipper conquers (his enemies), dwells in a habitation, and
prospers: the gods favour not the imperfect rite.

The Gods Favour not the Imperfect Rite— *Na devāsaḥ karatnave*:
karatnuḥ is explained *kutsita kriya*, bad or defective act of religion: the
Scholiast seems to render it men do not become gods by such means,
devā na bhavanti.

५४०८. नकिः॑ सु॒दासो॒ रथं॒ पर्या॑स॒ न री॑रमत्।

इन्द्रो॒ यस्या॑वि॒ता यस्य॑ म॒रुतो॒ गम॒त्स गोम॑ति व्र॒जे॑॥१०॥

10. No one overturns, no one arrests the chariot of the liberal
sacrificer: he, of whom *Indra* is the protector, of whom the *Maruts*
(are the defenders), will walk in pastures filled with cattle.

५४०९. गम॒द्वाजं॒ वाज॑य॒न्निन्द्र॒ मर्त्यो॒ यस्य॒ त्वमवि॑ता भु॒वः॑।

अ॒स्माकं॑ बोध्यवि॒ता र॒थाना॑म॒स्माकं॑ शूर॒ नृ॒णाम्॑॥११॥

11. Let the man of whom you, *Indra*, are the protector,
invigorating (you with praise), enjoy (abundant) food: be the
preserver, hero, of our chariots, (the preserver) of our people.

Be the Preserver— *Bodhi avitā*: the Scholiast makes *bodhi* the
second person singular imperative of *bhu* for *bhava*, *b* being substituted
for *bh*.

५४१०. उदिव्र॑स्य रि॒च्यते॒ंऽशो धनं॒ न जि॒ग्युषः॑।

य इन्द्रो॒ हरि॑वा॒न्न दभ॑न्ति॒ तं रि॒पो दक्षं॑ दधाति सोमि॒नि॑॥१२॥

12. Verily (*Indra*'s) share (of the *Soma*) exceeds (that of other
deities) like the wealth of the victorious: enemies overcome not

him, who is the lord of bay steeds, who gives strength to the offerer of the libation.

५४११. मन्त्रमखर्वं सुधितं सुपेशसं दधात यज्ञियेष्वा।

पूर्वीश्चन प्रसितयस्तरन्ति तं य इन्द्रे कर्मणा भुवत्॥१३॥

13. Address (to *Indra*), amongst the gods, the ample, well-uttered, and graceful prayer: many bonds entangle not him who, by his devotion, abides in *Indra*.

५४१२. कस्तमिन्द्र त्वावसुमा मर्त्यो दधर्षति।

श्रद्धा इत्ते मघवन्पार्ये दिवि वाजी वाजं सिषासति॥१४॥

14. What mortal, *Indra*, injures him who has you for his support ? He who offers you (sacrificial) food, *Maghavan*, with faith, he obtains food on the day of the libation.

Obtains food on the Day of the Libation— *Pārye divi vājī vajam, siṣāsati, sautye ahani sa haviṣmān annam sevate* is the explanation of Sāyaṇa.

५४१३. मघोनः स्म वृत्रहत्येषु चोदय ये ददति प्रिया वसु।

तव प्रणीती हर्यश्व सूरिभिर्विश्वा तरेम दुरिता॥१५॥

15. Animate (those men) for the destruction of their foes, who offer treasures which are dear to you, the abounder in wealth: may we, lord of bay steeds, along with (your) worshippers, pass over all difficulties by your guidance.

५४१४. तवेदिन्द्रावमं वसु त्वं पुष्यसि मध्यमम्।

सत्रा विश्वस्य परमस्य राजसि नर्किष्ट्वा गोषु वृण्वते॥१६॥

16. Thine, *Indra*, is the vast valuable wealth: you cherish the middling: you rule over all that which is the most precious: no one opposes you in (the recovering of the) cattle.

No one opposes you in the recovering of the cattle— *Na kiś tva goṣu vrinvate*: the Scholiast explains it, *goṣu nimitteṣu ke api tvām na vārayanti,* none resist or oppose you on account of the cows.

५४१५. त्वं विश्वस्य धनदा असि श्रुतो य ईं भवन्त्याजयः।

तवायं विश्वः पुरुहूत पार्थिवोऽवस्युर्नाम भिक्षते॥१७॥

17. You are celebrated as the giver of wealth to all even where battles occur: all the people of the earth-desirous of protection, solicit of you, the invoked of many.

Art Celebrated as the giver of Wealth Etc.— *Dhanadā asi śruto ye īm bhavantyajāyaḥ:* The Scholiast explains the last, *ye ete ājayo yuddhāni bhavanti teṣu api dhanadāḥ śrutosi.*

५४१६. यदिन्द्र यावतस्त्वमेतावदहमीशीय।
स्तोतारमिद्दिधिषेय रदावसो न पापत्वाय रासीय॥१८॥

18. If I were lord of as much (affluence) as you are, *Indra*, then might I support (your) worshippers, dispenser of wealth, and not squander it upon wickedness.
Sāmaveda, 310, 1796.

५४१७. शिक्षेयमिन्महयते दिवेदिवे राय आ कुहचिद्विदे।
नहि त्वदन्यन्मघवन्न आप्यं वस्यो अस्ति पिता चन॥१९॥

19. May I daily distribute wealth to the venerable wherever abiding: no other, *Maghavan*, than you is to be sought by us: (no other is to us) a most excellent protector.
Sāmaveda, 1797.

५४१८. तरणिरित्सिषासति वाजं पुरन्ध्या युजा।
आ व इन्द्रं पुरुहूतं नमे गिरा नेमिं तष्टेव सुद्र्वम्॥२०॥

20. The prompt offers (of praise), with solemn rites combined, acquires food: I bend down with adoration to you, *Indra*, the invoked of many, as a carpenter bends the wooden circumference of the wheel.
Sāmaveda 238, 867.

५४१९. न दुष्टुती मर्त्यो विन्दते वसु न स्रेधन्तं रयिर्नशत्।
सुशक्तिरिन्मघवन्तुभ्यं मावते देष्णं यत्पार्ये दिवि॥२१॥

21. A man acquires not wealth by unbecoming praise: affluence devolves not upon one obstructing (sacrifice): in you, *Maghavan*, is the power whereby bounty (may be shown) to such as I am on the day of libation.
Sāmaveda, 868.

५४२०. अभि त्वा शूर नोनुमोऽदुग्धाइव धेनवः।
ईशानमस्य जगतः स्वर्दृशमीशानमिन्द्र तस्थुषः॥२२॥

22. We glorify you, hero, (*Indra*), the lord of all movable and stationary things, the beholder of the universe, with ladles filled with *Soma*), like (the udders of) unmilked kine.

Sāmaveda, 233, 680. *Yajurveda*, 27. 35.

Like Udders of Unmilked Kine— *Adugdha iva dhenavo* occurs in the first line, and *Mahīdhara, Yajuṣ* 27. 36, explains it, we praise you as unmilked kine praise their calves, which is not very intelligible: in order to make sense of it, Sāyaṇa inserts, the fullness of ladles, *yathā dhenavaḥ kṣirapūr-ṇodhastvena vartante tad vat somapūrṇacamastvena vartamānā vayam bhṛśam abhiṣ—umaḥ,* as the cows remain with the state of the udders being full of milk, so we, abiding with the state of the ladle full of *Soma,* glorify you.

५४२१. न त्वावाँ अन्यो दिव्यो न पार्थिवो न जातो न जनिष्यते।

अश्वायन्तों मघवन्निन्द्र वाजिनों गव्यन्तंस्त्वा हवामहे॥२३॥

23. No other such as you are, celestial or terrestrial, has been or will be born: desirous of horses, of food, of cattle affluent *Indra,* we invoke you.

५४२२. अभी षतस्तदा भरेन्द्र ज्याय: कनीयस:।

पुरूवसुर्हि मघवन्त्सनादसि भरेभरे च हव्य:॥२४॥

24. Elder *Indra,* bring that (wealth to me), being the junior, for, *Maghavan,* you hast form the beginning been possessed of infinite treasure, and are to be adored at repeated sacrifices.

Sāmaveda, 680; *Yajurveda.* 27. 36.

५४२३. परा णुदस्व मघवन्नमित्रान्त्सुवेदां नो वसू कृधि।

अस्माकं बोध्यविता महाधने भवां वृध: सखीनाम्॥२५॥

25. Drive away, *Maghavan,* our enemies: render riches easy of acquisition: be our preserver in war: be the augmenter of (the prosperity) of (your) friends..

५४२४. इन्द्र क्रतुं न आ भर पिता पुत्रेभ्यो यथा।

शिक्षा णो अस्मिन्नुरुहूत यामनि जीवा ज्योतिरशीमहि॥२६॥

26. Bring to us, *Indra,* wisdom, as a father (gives knowledge) to his sons: bestow wealth upon us on this occasion, you the invoked of many, so that we, living at the solemnity may (long) enjoy the light (of existence).

Sāmaveda, 259, 1456.

५४२५. मा नो अज्ञाता वृजना दुराध्यो३े माशिवासो अव क्रमु:।

त्वयां वयं प्रवत: शश्वतीरपोऽति शूर तरामसि॥२७॥

27. Let no unknown, wicked, malevolent, malignant (enemies) overpower us: may we, protected by you, cross over many waters.
Sāmaveda, 1457.

This, although in some places rather obscure, is upon the whole intelligible enough, and seems to be a popular *Sūkta*; thirteen of the stanzas have been adopted into the *Sāmaveda*, some of them twice over.

[सूक्त-३३]

[**ऋषि–** वसिष्ठ मैत्रावरुणि, १०-१४ वसिष्ठ पुत्रगण। **देवता–** १-९ वसिष्ठ पुत्रगण, १०-४४ वसिष्ठ गायत्री, १०-१२। **छन्द–** त्रिष्टुप्।]

५४२६.   श्वित्यञ्चों मा दक्षिणतस्कपर्दा धियंजिन्वासों अभि हि प्रमन्दुः।

उत्तिष्ठन्वोचे परि बर्हिषो नॄन्न मे दूरादवितवे वसिष्ठाः॥१॥

1. The white-complexioned accomplishers of holy ceremonies, wearing the lock of hair on the right side, have afforded me delight, when, rising up I call the leaders (of rites) to the sacred grass: the *Vasiṣṭhas,* (my sons) should never be far from me.

White-Complexioned Accomplishers of Holy Ceremonies— The text has *Śvity, ñcaḥ,* which Sāyaṇa explains *Śvetavarṇaḥ,* white-coloured: it is a curious epithet as applied to the *Vasiṣṭhas.*

Wearing the Lock of Hair on the Right Side— *Dakṣiṇatas kapardāḥ: kaparda* is the *chuḍa* or single lock of hair left on the top of the head at tonsure, which, according to the Scholiast, it is characteristic of the *Vasiṣṭhas* to wear on the right of the crown of the head, *dakṣiṇe śiraso bhāge.*

५४२७.   दूरादिन्द्रमनयत्रा सुतेन तिरो वैशन्तमति पान्तमुग्रम्।

पाशद्युम्नस्य वायतस्य सोमात्सुतादिन्द्रोऽवृणीता वसिष्ठान्॥२॥

2. Disgracing (Pāśadyumna), they brought from afar the fierce *Indra,* when drinking the ladle of *Soma* at his sacrifice, to (receive) the libation (of *Sudāsa*): *Indra* hastened from the effused *Soma* of Pāśadyumna, the son of Vāyata, to the *Vasiṣṭhas.*

They Brought ...Indra— This is explained by a legend which relates, that when the sons of *Vasiṣṭha* had undertaken a *Soma* sacrifice to *Indra* on behalf of *Sudas,* they found that he was present at a similar solemnity instituted by the *Rājā Pāśadyumna,* the son of *Vāyata,* on which they abused the *Rājā,* broke off his sacrifice, and, by their *mantras,* compelled *Indra* to come to that of their patrons.

५४२८.   एवेन्नु कं सिन्धुमेभिस्ततारेवेन्नु कं भेदमेभिर्जघान।

एवेन्नु कंदाशराज्ञे सुदासं प्रावदिन्द्रो ब्रह्मणा वो वसिष्ठाः॥३॥

3. In the same manner was he, (*Sudāsa*) enabled by them easily to cross the *Sindhu* river: in the same manner, through them he easily slow his foe: so in like manner, *Vasiṣṭhas*, through your prayers, did *Indra* defend *Sudāsa* in the war with the ten kings.

He Easily Slow his Foe— *Bhedam jaghāna*: *Bheda* may be a proper name.

In the War with the Ten Kings— *Dāśarājñe* is explained *Daśabhī rājabhiḥ saha yuddhe*: the same war is subsequently alluded to: see *Sūkta* 83 of this *Maṇḍala*.

५४२९. जुष्टी नरो ब्रह्मणा वः पितृणामक्षमव्ययं न किलां रिषाथ।
यच्छक्करीषु बृहता रवेणेन्द्रे शुष्ममदधाता वसिष्ठ:॥४॥

4. By your prayers, leaders (of rites), is effected the gratification of your progenitors: I have set in motion the axle (of the chariot): be not you inert, for by your sacred metres, *Vasiṣṭhas*, (chaunted) with a loud voice, you sustain vigour in *Indra*.

Of Your Progenitors— *Pitṛṇām*, in the gen., plur., may be used only honorifically, implying father, *i.e.*, *Vasiṣṭha*.

I have Set in Motion the Axle of the Chariot— *Akṣam avyayam*, the Scholiast interprets *rathasya akṣam avyayāmi, cālayāmi*, I cause to move the axle of the car, ascribing the words to *Vasiṣṭha*, as announcing his intention to return to his hermitage.

५४३०. उद् द्यामिवेतृष्णजो नाथितासोऽदींधयुर्दाशराज्ञे वृतासः।
वसिष्ठस्य स्तुवत इन्द्रो अश्रोदुरुं तृत्सुभ्यो अकृणोदु लोकम्॥५॥

5. Suffering from thirst, soliciting (rain), supported (by the *Tṛtsus*) in the war with the ten *Rājās*, (the *Vasiṣṭhas*) made *Indra* radiant as the sun: *Indra* heard (the praises) of *Vasiṣṭha* glorifying him, and bestowed a spacious region on the *Tṛtsus*.

५४३१. दण्डाइवेद्रोअर्जनास आसन्परिच्छिन्ना भरता अर्भकास:।
अर्भवच्च पुरएता वसिष्ठ आदित्तृत्सूनां विशो अप्रथन्त॥६॥

6. The *Bharatas*, inferior (to their foes), were shorn (of their possessions), like the staves for driving cattle, (stripped of their leaves and branches): but *Vasiṣṭha* became their family priest, and the people of the *Tṛtsus* prospered.

The People of the *Tṛtsus*— The *Tṛtsus* are the same as the *Bharatas*: according to the *Mahābhārata, Samvarana*, the son of *Ṛkṣa*, the fourth in descent from Bharata the son of Duṣyanta, was driven from his kingdom by the *Pancālas*, and obliged to take refuge with his tribe amongst the thickets on the *Sindhu* until *Vasiṣṭha* came to them, and consented to be the *Rājā's* Purohit, when they recovered their territory.

५४३२. त्रयः कृण्वन्ति भुवनेषु रेतस्तिस्रः प्रजा आर्या ज्योतिरग्राः।
त्रयो घर्मास उषसं सचन्ते सर्वाँ इत्ताँ अनु विदुर्वसिष्ठाः॥७॥

7. Three shed moisture upon the regions, three are their
glorious progeny, of which the chief is night: three communicators
of warmth accompany the dawn: verily the *Vasiṣṭhas* understand
all these.

Three Shed Moisture— Sāyaṇa quotes *Śātyāyana* for the
explanation of this verse: the three who send rain on the three regions of
earth, mid-air, and heaven, are *Agni*, *Vāyu*, and *Āditya*, and they also
diffuse warmth: their offspring are the *Vasus* the *Rudras*, the *Ādityas*, the
latter of whom are the same with *Jyotis* light.

५४३३. सूर्यस्येव वक्षथो ज्योतिरेषां समुद्रस्येव महिमा गंभीरः।
वातस्येव प्रजवो नान्येन स्तोमो वसिष्ठा अन्वेतवे वः॥८॥

8. The glory of these *Vasiṣṭhas* is like the splendour of the sun:
their greatness as profound as (the depth of) the ocean: your praise,
Vasiṣṭhas, has the velocity of the wind: by no other can it be
surpassed.

५४३४. त इन्निण्यं हृदयस्य प्रकेतैः सहस्रवल्शमभि सं चरन्ति।
यमेन ततं परिधिं वयन्तोऽप्सरस उप सेदुर्वसिष्ठाः॥९॥

9. By the wisdom seated in the heart the *Vasiṣṭhas* traverse the
hidden thousand branched world, and the *Apsarasas* sit down
wearing the vesture spread out by Yama.

The Hidden Thousand-Branched World— *Niṇyam sahasravalśam
abhisañcaranti*, they completely go over the *hidden, tirohitam*, or
durjñānam, ignorant, *sahasra valśam*, thousand-branched, that is,
saṁsāram, the revolving world of various living beings, or the succession
of many births: an allusion is intended, the Scholiast appears to intimate,
to the repeated births of *Vasiṣṭha*: the plural here being put for the
singular, he having been first one of the *Prajāpatis*, or mind-born sons of
Brahmā, and, secondly, one of the sons of *Urvaśī*; or it may perhaps
intend, by the expression *hṛdayasya praketaiḥ prajñānaiḥ*, internal
convictions or knowledge, to imply the detachment of *Vasiṣṭha* or his
sons from the world.

**The Apsarasas sit Down, Wearing the Vesture Spread out by
Yama**— *Yamena tatam paridhim vayanto apsarasa upaseduru vasiṣṭhāḥ* is
somewhat dark: *vivsiṣṭhāḥ* has no business in this part of the construction,
and must be connected with the first word in the verse, *te vasiṣṭhāḥ, those
Vasiṣṭhas* or that *Vasiṣṭha*: *yamena* is explained *sarvaniyantrā*, by the
restrainer or regulator of all: *kāraṇātmanā*, identical with cause, that is, by

acts, as the causes of vital condition: the garb *paridhim, vastram,* spread, *tatam,* by him, is the revolution of life and death: *janmādipravāhāḥ,* weaving, *vayantaḥ,* as the masc, plural, should agree with *vasiṣṭhāḥ,* but Sāyaṇa connects it with *apsarasaḥ,* the nymphs, or, more properly, the nymph *Urvaśī,* who sat down or approached in the capacity of a mother, *Jananītvena,* wearing that vesture which he was destined by former acts to wear: the general purpose is not doubtful, but it is obscurely expressed.

५४३५. विद्युतो ज्योतिः परि संजिहानं मित्रावरुणा यदपश्यतां त्वा।
तत्ते जन्मोतैकं वसिष्ठागस्त्यो यत्त्वा विश आजभार॥१०॥

10. When *Mitra* and *Varuṇa* be held you, *Vasiṣṭha,* quitting the lustre of the lightning (for a different form), then one of your births (took place), inasmuch as *Agastya* bore you from your (former) abode.

Inasmuch as *Agastya* Bore you from your Former Abode— *Agastyo yat tvā viśā ājabhāra* is interpreted *yadā purvavasthānāt tvām ājahāra,* when *Agastya* took you from the former condition, the only interpretation of which is *mitrāvaruṇau-āvām janayiṣyāva,* we two *Mitra* and *Varuṇa,* will beget; or *āvābhyām ayam jāyeta iti samakalpatām* the two divinities determined this *Vasiṣṭha* shall be begotten by us: but what *Agastya* has to do with this is left unexplained.

५४३६. उतासि मैत्रावरुणो वसिष्ठोर्वश्या ब्रह्मन्मनसोऽधि जातः।
द्रप्सं स्कन्नं ब्रह्मणा दैव्येन विश्वे देवाः पुष्करे त्वाददन्त॥११॥

11. Verily, *Vasiṣṭha* you are the son of *Mitra* and *Varuṇa,* born, *Brahmā,* of the will of *Urvaśī,* after the seminal effusion: all the gods have sustained you, (endowed) with celestial and Vedic vigour in the lake.

Born of the will of Urvaśī— The Paurāṇik version, which here appears to be of *Vaidika* origin is well known: according to the Scholiast, *Urvaśī,* on seeing the birth of the *Ṛṣi,* said to herself, let this be my son.

Endowed with Celestial and Vedic Vigour— *Brahmaṇā daivyena,* according to the Scholiast, requires the addition of *yuktam,* joined with, as the epithet of *tvam, devasambandhina vedarāśināhambhuva yuktam. Puṣkara* may meant the *kumbha,* or pitcher, used at sacrifice, or the *vasatīvara,* the pool of water prepared for the same, but Sāyaṇa proceeds with a legend which seems intended to attach its usual sense to *puṣkara,* the vessel running over, some contents fell upon the earth, and from them *Vasiṣṭha* was born: *Agastya* was born of those in the vessel: the overflowing fluid being collected together, *Vasiṣṭha* remained in the lake, *tato apsu gṛhyamāṇāsu vasiṣṭhāḥ puṣkare sthitaḥ: Puṣkara* is also the name of the lake in Ajmer; but, according to the *Padma Purāṇa,* it was the site of the hermitage of *Agastya,* not of *Vasiṣṭha: Sṛṣṭi Khaṇḍa,* c. 22.

५४३७. स प्रॅकेत उभयॅस्य प्रविद्वान्त्सहस्त्रॅदान उत वा सदाॅनः।
यमेनॅ ततं पॅरिधिं वॅयिष्यत्रॅप्सरसः पॅरि जज्ञे वसिॅष्ठः।।१२।।

12. He, the sage, cognizant of both worlds, was the donor of
thousands: he was verily donation: wearing the vesture spread by
Yama, *Vasiṣṭha* was born of the *Apsaras*.

५४३८. सत्रे हॅ जाताॅविॅषिता नमोॅभिः कुम्भे रेॅतः सिषिचतुः समानॅम्।
ततोॅ हॅ मान उदिॅयाय मध्याॅत्ततोॅ जातमृॅषिमाहुॅर्वसिॅष्ठम्।।१३।।

13. Consecrated for the sacrifice, propitiated by praises, they,
Mitra and *Varuṇa*, poured a common effusion into the water-jar,
from the midst of which *Māna* uprose, and from which also, they
say, *Vasiṣṭha* was born.

Consecrated for the Sacrifice— *Satre jātau* is explained *yage
dīkṣitau*, prepared by preliminary purifications for the ceremony.

Māna— *Māna* is said to be a name of *Agastya* with reference to his
being of the *measure* of a span at his birth: as by the text *udiyāya tato
Agastyaḥ śamyamātro mahitapaḥ, mānena sammito yasmād mānya
ihocyate,* thence arose the great ascetic *Agastya* of the measure of a span,
as measured by a measure, (*māna*): he is thence called upon earth *Mānya*:
Agastya is not reckoned amongst the *Prajāpatis*: According to one legend
he was, in a preceding birth, the son of *Pulastya*; but he is evidently the
creation of a later date than *Vasiṣṭha* and the other primary *Rṣis*, although
of great and early celebrity, as recorded in both the *Rāmāyaṇa* and
Mahābhārata.

५४३९. उक्थॅभृतं सामॅभृतं बिभर्तिॅ ग्रावाॅणं बिभ्रत्रॅ वॅदात्यग्रॅे।
उपैॅनमाध्वं सुमनस्यॅमाॅना आ वोॅ गच्छाति प्रतृॅदो वसिॅष्ठः।।१४।।

14. *Pratṛts*, Agastya comes to you; welcome him with devoted
minds, and he is the foremost station directs the reciter of the
prayer, the chaunter of the hymn, the grinder of the stone, and
repeats (what is to be repeated).

Pratṛts—The same as the *Tṛtsus*.

In the Foremost Station—*Agre*, in front, *i.e.,* as their *Purohit*.

ANUVAKA III

[सूक्त-३४]

[**ऋषि**- वसिष्ठ मैत्रावरुणि। **देवता**- विश्वेदेवा, १६ अहि, १७ अहिर्बुध्न्य।
छन्द- द्विपदा विराट् २२-२५ त्रिष्टुप्।]

५४४०. प्र शुक्रैॅतु देवी मॅनीषा अस्मत्सुतॅष्ट्ये रथो न वाजी।।१।।

1. May pure and divine praise proceed from us (to the gods) like a swift well-constructed chariot.

५४४१. विदुः पृथिव्या दिवो जनित्रं शृण्वन्त्यापो अध क्षरन्तीः ॥२॥

2. The flowing waters having known the origin of earth and heaven: may they now hear (our praises).

Waters have Known the Origin of Earth and Eaven—An allusion perhaps to the subsequently received cosmogony, as in *Manu*, that water was the first of created things.

५४४२. आपश्चिदस्मै पिन्वन्त पृथ्वीवृतेषु शूरा मंसन्त उग्राः ॥३॥

3. The vast waters offer nourishment to *Indra:* fierce warriors. (combating) with foes, glorify him.

५४४३. आ धूर्वस्मै दधाताश्वानिन्द्रो न वज्री हिरण्यबाहुः ॥४॥

4. Yoke for him the horses of his chariot, the *Indra* is the wielder of the thunderbolt, the golden-armed.

५४४४. अभि प्र स्थाताहैव यज्ञं यातेव पत्मन्त्मना हिनोत ॥५॥

5. Proceed to the sacrifice like one who goes along the road; proceed of your own accord.

५४४५. त्मना समत्सु हिनोत यज्ञं दधात केतुं जनाय वीरम् ॥६॥

6. Go of your own accord to battle: celebrate the significant and expiatory sacrifice for (the good of) mankind.

५४४६. उदस्य शुष्माद्भानुनार्तं बिभर्ति भारं पृथिवी न भूम ॥७॥

7. From the force of this (sacrifice) the sun rises: it sustains the burden (of the world) as (earth) supports many (beings).

५४४७. ह्वयामि देवाँ अयातुरग्ने साधन्नृतेन धियं दधामि ॥८॥

8. I invoke the gods, *Agni*, propitiating them by an inoffensive rite, I celebrate a pious act.

By an Inoffensive Rite Etc.— *Ayātuḥ sādhanṛtena*, the Scholiast puts *ayātuḥ* into the instrumental case, *ayātuna*, and makes it the epithet of *ṛtena, ahinsakena, yajñena*, intending perhaps one without animal victims: if taken as it stands, as the gen. of *Ayātri*, the meaning would be much the same by the rite of one not sacrificing victims.

५४४८. अभि वो देवीं धियं दधिध्वं प्र वो देवत्रा वाचं कृणुध्वम् ॥९॥

9. Offer, (worshippers) your heavenly worship: earnestly address you praises to the gods.

५४४९. आ चष्ट आसां पाथो नदीनां वरुण उग्रः सहस्रचक्षाः॥१०॥

10. The fierce *Varuṇa*, the thousand-eyes, contemplates the water of these rivers.

५४५०. राजा राष्ट्रानां पेशौ नदीनामनुत्तमस्मै क्षत्रं विश्वायु॥११॥

11. He is the king of kings: the beauty of the rivers his all-pervading strength is irresistible.

५४५१. अविष्टो अस्मान्विश्वासु विश्ववद्यं कृणोत शंसं निनित्सो:॥१२॥

12. Protect us, gods, among all people: render extinct the calumny of the malevolent.

५४५२. व्यैतु दिद्युद् द्विषामशेवा युयोत विष्वग्रपस्तनूनाम्॥१३॥

13. May the blazing (weapons) of foes pass by innocuous: separate, (gods), universally (from us) the sin of our bodies.

५४५३. अवीनो अग्निर्हव्यान्नमोभिः प्रेष्ठो अस्मा अधायि स्तोमः॥१४॥

14. May *Agni,* the feeder on oblations, propitiated by our homage, protect us: to him has our praise been addressed.

५४५४. सजूर्देवेभिरपां नपातं सखायं कृध्वं शिवो नो अस्तु॥१५॥

15. Glorify along with the gods our friend, the grand son of the waters: may he be propitious to us.

५४५५. अब्जामुक्थैरहिं गृणीषे बुध्ने नदीनां रजःसु षादन्॥१६॥

16. I glorify with hymns the disperser of the clouds in the firmament: the water-born, sitting amongst the waters of the rivers.

The Disperser of the Glouds in the Firmament— *Ahim gṛṇīṣe budhne,* dividing two words usually put together. *Ahirbudhna:* Sāyaṇa explains the former, *māghānāmāhantāram,* the latter, upon the authority of *Yāska,* the firmament, or the region in which the waters of rains are bound or detained, *baddhā asmin dhṛtā āpa viti vyutpatteḥ: Nir.* x. 44: in the next stanza the words are reunited as a name of *Agni.*

५४५६. मा नोऽहिर्बुध्न्यो रिषे धान्मा यज्ञो अस्य स्त्रिधदूतायो:॥१७॥

17. Let not *Ahirbudhnya* be disposed to work us harm: let not the sacrifice of the worshipper be disregarded.

५४५७. उत न एषु नृषु श्रवो धुः प्र राये यन्तु शर्धन्तो अर्यः॥१८॥

18. May (the gods) bestow food upon our people let foes contending for our riches perish.

५४५८. तर्पन्ति शत्रुं स्वर्ऽण भूमा महासेनासो अमेंभिरेषाम्॥१९॥

19. Leaders of great armies, by the power of these (divinities), consume their foes, as the sun (scorches) the regions.

Of These Divinities— *Eṣām,* of these: the Scholiast supplies either *Davānām* or *Marutām,* of these *Maruts*.

५४५९. आ यत्रः पत्नीर्गमन्त्यच्छा त्वष्टा सुपाणिर्दधातु वीरान्॥२०॥

20. When the wives (of the gods) come before us, may the dextrous *Tvaṣṭā* grant us male progeny.

Wives of the Gods— The addition of the comment, *devānam,* seems somewhat superfluous: human wives would have been more in keeping with the prayer.

५४६०. प्रतिं नः स्तोमं त्वष्टा जुषेत स्यादस्मे अरमतिर्वसूयुः॥२१॥

21. May *Tvaṣṭā* be propitiated by this our praise: may he who is of comprehensive understanding be inclined to give us wealth.

५४६१. ता नों रासन्रातिषाचो वसून्या रोदसी वरुणानी शृणोतु।

वरूत्रीभिः सुशरणो नों अस्तु त्वष्टा सुदत्रो वि दधातु रायः॥२२॥

22. May they who are the givers of gifts bestow upon us the treasure (we desire) : may *Rodasī* and *Varuṇam* hear (our supplications): may the generous *Tvaṣṭā* together with these (our) protectresses, he our sure refuge: may be give us riches.

५४६२. तन्नो रायः पर्वतास्तन्न आपस्तद्रातिषाच ओषधीरुत द्यौः।

वनस्पतिंभिः पृथिवी सजोषा उभे रोदसी परिं पासतो नः॥२३॥

23. May the mountains, the waters, the liberal (wives of the gods), the plants, also the heaven and the earth, consentient with the forest lords and both the heaven and earth, preserve for us those (coveted) riches.

The Liberal Wives of the Gods— The wives of the gods, according to Sāyaṇa.

५४६३. अनु तदुर्वी रोदसी जिहातामनु द्युक्षो वरुण इन्द्रसखा।

अनु विश्वे मरुतो ये सहासो रायः स्याम धरुणं धियध्यै॥२४॥

24. Let the vast heaven and earth consent let the brilliant *Varuṇa,* of whom *Indra* is the friend consent: let all the victorious *Maruts* consent that we may be a receptacle for the retention of riches.

५४६४. तन्न॒ इन्द्रो॒ वरुणो मित्रो॒ अग्निराप॒ ओष॑धीर्वनिनो॑ जुषन्त।
शर्म॑न्त्स्याम॒ मरुता॑मुप॒स्थे यू॒यं पा॑त स्व॒स्तिभि॒: सदा॑ न:॥२५॥

25. May *Indra, Varuṇa, Mitra, Agni*, the waters the herbs, the trees, be pleased by our (praise): may we, (reclining) on the lap of the *Maruts,* enjoy felicity: and do you ever cherish us with blessings.

Do you ever Cherish us with Blessings— The burden of many previous *Sūktas.*

[सूक्त-३५]

[ऋषि- वसिष्ठ मैत्रावरुणि। देवता- विश्वेदेवा। छन्द- त्रिष्टुप्।]

५४६५. शं न॑ इन्द्रा॒ग्नी भ॑वता॒मवो॑भि: शं न॑ इन्द्रा॒वरुणा॑ रा॒तह॑व्या।
शमि॑न्द्रासोमा॑ सुवि॒ताय॒ शं यो: शं न॑ इन्द्रा॒पूषणा॒ वाज॑सातौ॥१॥

1. May *Indra* and *Agni* be (with us) with their protections for our happiness: may *Indra* and *Varuṇa*, to whom oblation are offered, (be with us) for our happiness: may *Indra* and *Soma* be (with us) for our happiness, our prosperity, our good: may *Indra* and *Puṣan* be (with us) in battle for our triumph.

Yajurveda, 36. 11.

May Indra and Agni be with us with their protections for our Happiness— The construction of the leading phrase through thirteen stanzas is the same, *śama na bhavatām*, sometimes slightly varied, literally may they tow be our happiness: the commentator explains *śam* by *śantyai* for our peace or happiness; but the bolder expression is probably the more correct.

५४६६. शं नो॒ भग॒: शम्ु न॑: शंसो॑ अस्तु॒ शं न॑: पुर॑न्धि॒: शम्ु सन्तु॒ राय॒:।
शं न॒: स॒त्यस्य॑ सु॒यम॑स्य॒ शंस॒: शं नो॑ अर्य॒मा पु॑रुजा॒तो अस्तु॥२॥

2. May *Bhaga* (promote) our happiness: may Śaṅsa be our happiness: may *Purandhi* be (with us for) our happiness: may riches be (a source of) happiness: may the benediction of the true and virtuous yield us happiness: may the variously-manifested *Aryaman* be (with us) for our felicity.

Śaṅsa— For *Naraśaṅsa.*

Purandhi— The possessor of much intelligence: see vol. II. 3976.

५४६७. शं नो॑ धा॒ता शम्ु ध॒र्ता नो॑ अस्तु॒ शं न॑ उ॒रूची॑ भवतु स्व॒धाभि॑:।
शं रोद॑सी बृह॒ती शं नो॒ अद्रि॒: शं नो॑ दे॒वानां॑ सुह॒वानि॑ सन्तु॥३॥

3. May the creator be to us for happiness: may the discriminator (between virtue and vice, *Varuṇa*), be (with us) for our happiness: may the wide earth (contribute) with sustenance to our happiness: may the vast heaven and earth be (to us for) happiness: may the mountains (yield) us happiness: may our pious invocations of the gods secure us happiness.

५४६८. शं नो॒ अ॒ग्निज्यों॑ति॒रनी॑को अस्तु शं नो॑ मि॒त्रावरु॑णाव॒श्विना॑ शम्।
शं न॑: सु॒कृतां॑ सु॒कृता॑नि सन्तु शं न॑ इ॒षि॒रो अ॒भि वा॒तु वात॑:॥४॥

4. May *Agni*, whose countenance is light, be (with us) for our happiness: may *Mitra* and *Varuṇa*, may the *Aśvins* be (present) for our felicity: may the virtuous be (promotive of) our happiness: may the restless wind blow for our happiness.

५४६९. शं नो॒ द्यावा॑पृथि॒वी पू॒र्वहू॑तौ॒ शम॒न्तरि॑क्षं दृ॒शये॑ नो अस्तु।
शं न॑ ओष॑धी॒र्वनि॑नो॑ भवन्तु॒ शं नो॒ रज॑सस्प॒तिर॑स्तु जि॒ष्णु:॥५॥

5. May heaven and earth, the first invoked, (promote) our happiness: may the firmament be happiness to our view: may the herbs, the trees, (yield) us happiness: may the victorious lord of the world, (*Indra*), be (favourable to) our felicity.

५४७०. शं न॒ इन्द्रो॒ वसु॑भि॒र्देवो॑ अस्तु॒ शमा॑दि॒त्येभि॑र्वरु॑ण: सु॒शंस॑:।
शं नो॑ रु॒द्रो रु॒द्रेभि॑र्ज॒लाष॑: शं न॒स्त्वष्टा॒ ग्नाभि॒रिह शृ॒णोतु॑॥६॥

6. May the divine (*Indra*), with the *Vasus*, grant us happiness: may the justly-praised *Varuṇa*, with the *Ādityas,* be (friendly to) our happiness: may the grief-assuaging *Rudra*, with the *Rudras*, be (for) our happiness: may *Tvaṣṭā*, with the wives of the gods, be (with us) for our happiness, and hear us at this solemnity.

५४७१. शं न॒: सोमो॑ भवतु॒ ब्रह्म॒ शं न॒: शं नो॒ ग्रावा॑ण: श॒मु सन्तु य॒ज्ञ:।
शं न॒: स्व॒रूणां॑ मि॒तयो॑ भवन्तु॒ शं न॒: प्र॒स्व॑: श॒म्वस्तु वे॒दि:॥७॥

7. May the *Soma* be (offered for) our happiness: may the prayer be (uttered for) our happiness: may the stones (grind the *Soma*), the sacrifice be (solemnized for) our happiness: may the measured lengths of the sacrificial posts be (conducive to) our felicity: may the sacred grass be (strewn) for our happiness: may the altar be (raised for) our happiness.

५४७२. शं न॒: सूर्य॑ उरु॒चक्षा॒ उदे॑तु॒ शं न॒श्चत॑स्र: प्र॒दिशो॑ भवन्तु।
शं न॒: पर्व॑ता ध्रु॒वयो॑ भवन्तु॒ शं न॒: सिन्ध॑व: श॒मु सन्त्वाप॑:॥८॥

8. May the wide-seeing sun rise (for) our happiness: may the four quarters of the horizon (exist for) our felicity: may the firm-set mountains be (for) our happiness: may the rivers, may the waters, be (diffused) for our happiness.

५४७३. शं नो अदितिर्भवतु व्रतेभिः शं नो भवन्तु मरुतः स्वर्काः। शं नो विष्णुः शर्मु पूषा नो अस्तु शं नो भवित्रं शर्म्वस्तु वायुः॥९॥

9. May *Aditi*, with holy observances, be (for) our happiness: may the glorified *Maruts* be (friendly to) our felicity: may *Viṣṇu*, may *Pūṣan*, be (promoters of) our happiness: may the firmament be propitious to us: may *Vāyu* (blow for) our happiness.

५४७४. शं नो देवः सविता त्रायमाणः शं नो भवन्तूषसो विभातीः। शं नः पर्जन्यो भवतु प्रजाभ्यः शं नः क्षेत्रस्य पतिरस्तु शम्भुः॥१०॥

10. May the divine preserving *Savitā* be (radiant for) our happiness: may the opening dawns (break for) our happiness: may Parjanya be (the granter of happiness) to our posterity: may Shambhu, the lord of strength, be (the conferrer of) happiness upon us.

Śambhu— *Śambhu* is here said to imply *sukhasya bhāvayitā*, the causer of the condition of pleasure: it is ordinarily a name of *Śiva*.

५४७५. शं नो देवा विश्वदेवा भवन्तु शं सरस्वती सह धीभिरस्तु। शर्मभिषाचः शर्मु रातिषाचः शं नो दिव्याः पार्थिवाः शं नो अप्र्याः॥११॥

11. May the divine universal gods be (favourable) to our felicity; may *Sarasvatī*, with holy rites, be happiness: may those who assist at sacrifices, those who are liberal of gifts. Be (conducive to) our happiness: may celestial, terrestrial and aquatic things be (subservient to) our happiness.

५४७६. शं नः सत्यस्य पतयो भवन्तु शं नो अर्वन्तः शर्मु सन्तु गावः। शं न ऋभवः सुकृतः सुहस्ताः शं नो भवन्तु पितरो हवेषु॥१२॥

12. May the lords of truth be (propitious to) our happiness: may horses, may cattle, (contribute to) our happiness: may the virtuous, the dexterous *Ṛbhus*, be to us (for) felicity: may the progenitors be (Promoters of) our happiness at the seasons of worship.

५४७७. शं नो॒ अज॒ एक॑पा॒देवो॑ अस्तु॒ शं नो॒ऽहि॒र्बु॒ध्न्यः॑: शं स॑मु॒द्रः।
शं नो॒ अपां॒ नपा॑त्पे॒रुर॑स्तु॒ शं नः॒ पृश्नि॑र्भवतु दे॒वगो॑पा।।१३।।

13. May the divine Aja-Ekapad be (favourable to) our happiness: may Ahirbudhnya, may the firmament, be (promotive of) our happiness: may the grandson of the waters, the protector, be (the securer of) our felicity: may Prishni, of whom the gods are the guardians, be to us (a granter of) happiness.

५४७८. आ॒दि॒त्या रु॒द्रा वस॑वो जुषन्ते॒दं ब्रह्म॑ क्रि॒यमा॑णं न॒वीय॑:।
शृ॒ण्वन्तु॑ नो दि॒व्याः पार्थि॑वासो गो॒जाता॑ उ॒त ये य॒ज्ञिया॑स:।।१४।।

14. May the *Ādityas* the *Rudras*, the *Vasu*s, be gratified by this new and now repeated praise: may celestial and terrestrial (beings), the progeny of the cow, (*Pṛṣni*), and those who were entitled to worship, hear our (invocations).

५४७९. ये दे॒वानां॑ य॒ज्ञिया॑ य॒ज्ञिया॑नां॒ मनो॑र्य॒जत्रा॑ अ॒मृता॑ ऋत॒ज्ञाः॑।
ते नो॑ रासन्तामुरुगा॒यम॒द्य यू॒यं पा॑त स्व॒स्तिभि॒: सदा॑ नः।।१५।।

15. May those who are the most adorable of the adorable divinities, those who were the adored of *Manu*, those who are immortal, the observers of truth, bestow upon us this day (a son, of widely-spread renown: and do you ever cherish us with blessings.

[सूक्त-३६]

[**ऋषि**– वसिष्ठ मैत्रावरुणि। **देवता**– विश्वेदेवा। **छन्द**– त्रिष्टुप्।]

५४८०. प्र ब्रह्मै॑तु॒ सद॑ना॒दृत॑स्य॒ वि र॒श्मिभि॑: ससृजे॒ सूर्यो॒ गाः।
वि सानु॑ना॒ पृथि॑वी स॒स्र उ॒र्वी पृ॒थु प्र॒तीक॒मध्ये॑धे॒ अ॒ग्निः।।१।।

1. Let the prayer proceed from the nail of the sacrifice, for Sūrya with his rays lets loose the waters: the spacious earth spreads (studded) with mountains, and *Agni* blazes on the extensive plains.[1]

Agni Blazes on the Extensive Plans— *Pṛthā pratīkam adhyedhe agniḥ; pratīkam* is said to be *pṛthivyā avayavam* a portion or member of the earth.

---

१. याभिरादित्यस्तपति रश्मिभिस्ताभि: पर्जन्यो वर्षन्यो वर्षति (तै॰ आ॰ १०.६३)।

५४८१. इमां वां मित्रावरुणा सुवृक्तिमिषं न कृण्वे असुरा नवीय:।
इनो वामन्य: पंदवीरदंब्धो जनं च मित्रो यतति ब्रुवाण:॥२॥

2. Powerful *Mitra* and *Varuṇa*. To you I offer this new praise
as if it were (sacrificial) food: one of you, (*Varuṇa*). The invincible
lord, is the guide to the path (of virtue) *Mitra, when* praised.
Animates men to exertion.

Mitra, when Praised, Animates men to Exertion— *Janam ca mitro*
yatati bruvānaḥ: the phrase has occured before: see *Ṛg.*, 3111, 59.1.

५४८२. आ वातंस्य ध्रजंतो रन्त इत्या अपीपयन्त धेनवो न सूदां:।
महो दिवं: सदंने जायंमानोऽचिंक्रदद् वृषभं: सस्मिन्नूधंन्॥३॥

3. The movements of the restless wind sport around: the milk-
yielding kine are in good condition: the showerer generated in the
dwelling of the mighty sun has cried aloud in that his place of
abiding, (the firmament).

The Showerer Generated, Etc.— *Acikradad vṛṣabhaḥ sasmin*
ūdhan, rendered, as in the text, *parjanya* has cried in that firmament,
tasmin antarikṣe acikradat.

५४८३. गिरा य एता युनज्ध्वरीं तं इन्द्रं प्रिया सुरथां शूर धायू।
प्र यो मन्युं रिरिंक्षतो मिनात्या सुक्रतुंमर्यमणं ववृत्याम्॥४॥

4. Hero, *Indra*, (come to the sacrifice of the man) who, by his
adoration, has harnessed (to your car) these your favourite,
graceful, and vigorous horses: may I bring hither *Aryaman*, the
doer of good deeds, who baffles the wrath of the malevolent.

५४८४. यजन्ते अस्य सख्यं वयंश्च नमस्विन: स्व ऋतस्य धामंन्।
वि पृक्षो बाबधे नृभि: स्तवानं इदं नमौं रुद्राय प्रेष्ठम्॥५॥

5. Let the offerers of adoration, engaging (in pious acts),
worship (*Rudra*) in their own hall of sacrifice, (solicitous) of his
friendship: praised by the leaders (of rites), he lavishes food (upon
them): this most acceptable adoration is addressed to *Rudra*.

५४८५. आ यत्साकं यशसौं वावशाना: सरंस्वती सप्तथीं सिन्धुंमाता।
या: सुष्वयन्त सुदुघां: सुधारा अभि स्वेन पयंसा पीप्यांना:॥६॥

6. May the seventh (stream), *Sarasvatī*, the mother of the
Sindhu and those rivers that flow copious and fertilizing,
bestowing abundance of food, and nourishing (the people) by their
waters come at once together.

The Mother of the Sindhu— *Sindhu mātrā* may mean, according to the Scholiast, *apāṃ mātṛbhūtā,* being the mother of the waters.

५४८६. उत त्ये नो॒ म॒रुतो॑ मन्दसाना धि॒यं तोक॑ च॒ वा॒जिनो॑ऽवन्तु।
मा नः॒ परि॑ ख्य॒दक्ष॑रा॒ चर॒न्त्यवी॑वृध॒न्युज्यं॑ ते र॒यिं नः॑॥७॥

7. May these joyous and swift-going *Maruts* protect our sacrifice and our offspring: let not the imperishable goddess of speech, deserting us, speak (kindly) to our (adversaries): and may both (she and the *Marut* associated augment our riches.

Let not the Imperishable Goddess of Speech, Etc.— *Mā naḥ parikhyad akṣarā caranti* is explained by Sāyaṇa, *akṣarā vyāptā, caranti vāgdevatā, asmān parityaktvā asmād vyatiriktā mā drākṣīt,* let not the diffusive deity of speech, having abandoned us, look upon our opponents.

५४८७. प्र वो॑ म॒हीमर॑मतिं कृणुध्वं॒ प्र पू॒षणं॑ विद॒थ्यं३ न वी॒रम्।
भग॑ धि॒यो॑ऽवि॒तारं॑ नो अ॒स्याः सा॒तौ वाज॑ रा॒तिषाच॑ पुर॒न्धिम्॥८॥

8. Invoke, (worshippers), the unresisting earth, and the adorable hero, *Puṣan*: (invoke) *Bhaga*, the protector of this our sacrifice, and *Vāja*, the sustainer of old, the liberal of gifts to our solemnity.

५४८८. अच्छा॑य॒ वो॑ मरुतः श्लोक॑ ए॒त्वच्छ॑ विष्णुं॑ निषि॒क्तपा॑मवो॒भिः।
उ॒त प्र॒जायै॑ गृ॒णते॑ व॒यो धु॒र्यूयं॑ पात॑ स्व॒स्तिभिः॒ सदा॑ नः॥९॥

9. May this praise come, *Maruts*, before you: (may it come) before *Viṣṇu*, the guardian of the embryo, with his protecting faculties: man they both bestow upon (me), their adorer, progeny and food: and do you ever cherish us with blessings.

[सूक्त-३७]

[ऋषि– वसिष्ठ मैत्रावरुणि। देवता– विश्वेदेवा। छन्द– त्रिष्टुप्।]

५४८९. आ वो॑ वा॒हिष्ठो॑ वहतु स्तव॒ध्यै रथो॑ वाजा ऋ॒भुक्ष॒णो अमृ॑क्तः।
अ॒भि त्रि॒पृष्ठैः॑ सर्व॑नेषु॒ सोमै॒र्मदे॑ सु॒शिप्रा॑ म॒हभिः॑ पृणध्वम्॥१॥

1. Vajas, possessors of energy, let your capacious, commendable, and unobstructed chariot bring you (hither): be satiated, handsome-chinned, with the copious triply-combined libation (poured out) for your exhilaration at our sacrifices.

With the Copious Triply-Combined Libations— *Tripṛṣṭhaiḥ somaiḥ,* with *Soma* juices mixed with milk curds and meal.

५४९०. यूयं ह॒ रत्नं॑ म॒घव॑त्सु धत्थ॒ स्व॒र्दृश॑मृ॒भुक्ष॒णो अ॒मृक्त॑म्।
       सं य॒ज्ञेषु॑ स्वधावन्तः पि॒बध्वं॒ वि नो॒ राधां॑सि म॒तिभि॑र्दयध्वम्॥२॥

2. For you, *Rbhuksins*, beholders of heaven, preserve
unmolested the precious (treasure) for us who are affluent (in
sacrificial offerings): do you who are possessed of strength, drink
fully at (our) solemnities, and with (favourable) minds bestow
upon us riches.

५४९१. उ॒वोचि॑थ॒ हि म॑घवन्दे॒ष्णं म॒हो अ॒र्भस्य॒ वसु॑नो वि॒भागे॑।
       उ॒भा ते॑ पू॒र्णा वसु॑ना॒ गभ॑स्ती॒ न सू॑नृ॒ता नि य॑मते व॒सव्या॑॥३॥

3. You, *Maghavan*, have determined what is to be given in the
apportionment of much or of little wealth, for both your hands are
full of treasure, and your sincere (promises) of riches do not
restrain them.

५४९२. त्वमि॑न्द्र स्व॒यशा॑ ऋ॒भुक्षा॒ वाजो॒ न सा॒धुर॒स्तमे॒ष्यृक्वा॑।
       व॒यं नु ते॑ दा॒श्वांसः॑ स्याम॒ ब्रह्म॑ कृ॒ण्वन्तो॑ हरिवो वसिष्ठाः॥४॥

4. Do you, *Indra*, who are *Rbhuksin*, and of especial renown,
who, like food, are the fulfiller (of wants), come to the dwelling of
the worshipper: lord of bay horses, may we, *Vasisthas*, be today
the donors (of the offerings) to you, the celebrators of your praise.

५४९३. स॒नि॒तासि॑ प्र॒वतो॑ दा॒शुषे॑ चि॒द्याभि॑र्वि॒वेषो॑ हर्यश्व धी॒भिः।
       व॒वन्मा॒ नु ते॑ युज्या॒भिरू॒ती कदा॒ न इ॑न्द्र॒ राय॒ आ द॑शस्येः॥५॥

5. Lord of bay horses, you are the giver of descending (wealth)
to the donor (of the oblation), by whose sacred rites you are
magnified: when may you bestow upon us riches: when may we be
secure by your appropriate protections.

५४९४. वासय॑सी॒व वे॒धस॒स्त्वं नः॒ कदा॒ न इ॑न्द्र॒ वच॑सो बु॒बोधः॑।
       अस्तं॒ तात्या॑ धि॒या र॒यिं सु॒वीरं॑ पृ॒क्षो नो॒ अर्वा॒ न्यु॑हीत वा॒जी॥६॥

6. When, *Indra*, wilt you appreciate our praise: at present you
establish us (thine) adorers in our dwelling: let your swift horse,
(influenced) by our protracted solemnity, convey to our abode
riches, male offspring, and food,

You Establish us your Adorers in our Dwelling— *Vāsayasīva
vedhasas tvam nah* is explained *asmān stotrn idānīm svakīye sthāne
avasthāpayasi*, as translated: perhaps *svakiye*, own, may refer to *Indra* in
his own dwelling, that is, in *Svarga*.

५४९५. अभि यं देवी निर्ऋतिश्चिदीशे नक्षन्त इन्द्रं शरदः सुपृक्षः।
उप त्रिबन्धुर्जरदष्टिमेत्यस्वर्ववेशं यं कृणवन्त मर्ताः॥७॥

7. *Indra*, the upholder of the three regions, whom the divine *Nirṛti* acknowledges as ruler, whom abundant years pass over, whom mortals detain from his own abode, approaches to (recruit) his decaying strength.

The Upholder of the three Regions— *Upa tribandhur jaradaṣṭim eti: trayāṇām lokānām bandhaka* is Sāyaṇa's rendering of the epithet *tribandhu: jaradaṣṭim* he explains *jīrṇam raśanam, yasya balasya hetubhūtam tad balam upagacchati,* he approaches that strength of which or of whose strength it is the cause: the explanation is not very clear.

Nirṛti— *Nirṛti* is said here to mean the earth.

५४९६. आ नो राधांसि सवितः स्तवध्या आ रायो यन्तु पर्वतस्य रातौ।
सदा नो दिव्यः पायुः सिषक्तु यूयं पात स्वस्तिभिः सदा नः॥८॥

8. May riches worthy of laudation come, *Savitā*, to us; riches that are in the bestow of *Parvata*: may the heavenly protector (of all) ever preserve us; and, do you (Universal gods), ever cherish us with blessings.

[सूक्त-३८]

[ऋषि– वसिष्ठ मैत्रावरुणि, देवता–१-५ तथा ६ के पूर्वार्द्ध– सविता, ६ उत्तरार्द्ध– सविता अथवा भग, ७-८ वाजिन्। छन्द–त्रिष्टुप्।]

५४९७. उदु ष्य देवः सविता ययाम हिरण्ययीममतिं यामशिश्रेत्।
नूनं भगो हव्यो मानुषेभिर्वि यो रत्ना पुरूवसुर्दधाति॥१॥

1. The divine *Savitā* has diffused the golden radiance on high, of which he is the asylum: verily *Bhaga* is to be absorbed by men who, abounding in wealth, distributes treasures (amongst them).

५४९८. उदु तिष्ठ सवितः श्रुध्यस्य हिरण्यपाणे प्रभृतावृतस्य।
व्युर्वीं पृथ्वीममतिं सृजान आ नृभ्यो मर्तभोजनं सुवानः॥२॥

2. Rise up *Savitā*: hear (our solicitations) upon the celebration of this ceremony, (you who are) diffusing light over the spacious earth, and bestowing human enjoyment upon men.

५४९९. अपि ष्टुतः सविता देवो अस्तु यमा चिद्विश्वे वसवो गृणन्ति।
स नः स्तोमान्नमस्यश्च्छ्रवो धाद्विश्वेभिः पातु पायुभिर्नि सूरीन्॥३॥

3. Glorified be the divine *Savitā*, whom all the gods praise: may that adorable (divinity) requite our praises (with) food: may he always protect the devout with all his protections.

Whom all the Gods Praise— The text has *yam viśve vasavo gṛṇanti*, whom all the *Vasus* praise: Sāyaṇa makes it *Devaḥ*.

५५००. अभि यं देव्यदितिर्गृणाति सवं देवस्य सवितुर्जुषाणा।

अभि सम्राजो वरुणो गृणन्त्यभि मित्रासो अर्यमा सजोषाः॥४॥

4. Whom the divine *Aditi*, delighting at the birth of the divine *Savitri*, glorifies, whom the supreme sovereigns, *Varuṇa, Mitra, Aryaman*, (and other gods), consentaneously adore.

Mitra and other Gods— *Mitra* occurs in the plural *Mitrāsaḥ*, meaning, according to the commentator *Mitra* and others.

५५०१. अभि ये मिथो वनुषः सर्पन्ते रातिं दिवो रातिषाचः पृथिव्याः।

अहिर्बुध्न्य उत नः शृणोतु वरूत्र्येकधेनुभिर्नि पातु॥५॥

5. Whom those solicitous for wealth those enjoying (it), mutually worship, the benefactor of heaven and earth: may Ahirbudhnya hear us: may the protectress (the goddess of speech), cherish us with excellent cattle.

Ahirbudhnya— According to Sāyaṇa this is a name of *Agni*, of the middle region or firmament.

The Protectress, the Goddess of Speech— The text has only *varutra*, which Sāyaṇa renders *vāgdevatā*.

५५०२. अनु तन्नो जास्पतिर्मंसीष्ट रत्नं देवस्य सवितुरियानः।

भगमुग्रोऽवसे जोहवीति भगमनुग्रो अध याति रत्नम्॥६॥

6. May the protector of progeny, when solicited, consent to bestow upon us the precious (wealth of the divine *Savitā*: the ardent (adorer) invokes repeatedly *Bhaga* for protection; the less ardent solicits *Bhaga* for wealth.

५५०३. शं नो भवन्तु वाजिनो हवेषु देवताता मितद्रवः स्वर्काः।

जम्भयन्तोऽहिं वृकं रक्षांसि सनेम्यस्मद्युयवन्नमीवाः॥७॥

7. May the *Vājins*, with slackened speed, bringing excellent food, be (disposed) for our happiness, upon our invocations at the worship of the gods: destroying the murderer, the robber, the *Rākṣasas*, and keeping from us ancient maladies.

The Vājins— Sāyaṇa interprets the term *etadabhidhāyakādevatāḥ*, divinities so denominated: *Mahīdhara* renders it *aśvaḥ*, horse *Yajurveda*, 9. 16.

The Murderer, the Robber— *Jambhayanto ahim vṛkam Mahīdhara* renders literally, destroying the snake, the wolf: Sāyaṇa renders them *hantāram,coram: vaje-vaje saveṣu yuddheṣu:* Sāyaṇa, *sarvasmin anne upasthite* when all food is nigh *Mahīdhara, Yajuṣ,* IX. 18.

५५०४. वाजेवाजेऽवत वाजिनो नो धनेषु विप्रा अमृता ऋतज्ञाः।
अस्य मध्वः पिबत मादयध्वं तृप्ता यात पथिभिर्देवयानैः ॥८॥

8. Wise, immortal Vājins, observers of truth, defined us in very conflict, and for the sake of wealth: drink of this sweet (*Soma* beverage), be exhilarated (thereby) and satisfied; proceed by the paths traversed by the gods.

[सूक्त-३९]

[**ऋषि**– वसिष्ठ मैत्रावरुणि। **देवता**– विश्वेदेवा। **छन्द**– त्रिष्टुप्।]

५५०५. ऊर्ध्वो अग्निः सुमतिं वस्वो अश्रेत्प्रतीची जूर्णिर्देवतातिमेति।
भेजाते अद्री रथ्येव पन्थामृतं होता न इषितो यजाति ॥१॥

1. Let *Agni*, risen on high, accept the praise of the worshipper: she who makes (all creatures) old, looking to the west, goes to the sacrifice: the pious pair, like two riders in a chariot, follow the path (of the ceremony): let the *Holā*, as enjoined, celebrate the rite.

She who makes all Creatures Old— *Pratīcī devatalion eti, sarvāsām prajānām jarayitrī* the cause of the decay or age of all progeny, that is, *Uṣodevatā,* the dawn, whose successive revolutions constitute old age.

The Pious Pair— *Bhejāte adri:* The latter is explained, *ādriyantau, śraddhāvantau,* the two reverencing or believing, that is, the *Yajamāna* and his wife.

५५०६. प्र वावृजे सुप्रया बर्हिरेषामा विशपतीव बीरिट इयाते।
विशामक्षोरुषसः पूर्वहूतौ वायुः पूषा स्वस्तये नियुत्वान् ॥२॥

2. The food-bestowing sacred grass of these (the worshippers) is strewn: may the two lords of people, Vāyu, with the *Niyut* steeds, and *Pūṣan,* invoked before the dawn upon the close of the night, appear now in the firmament for the welfare of mankind.

The Two Lords of People— *Viśpatīve vīrite iyāte, antrikṣe āgacchatām:* Sāyaṇa says *iva* here means *idanīm* now; but he states it may also intimate, as usual, a comparison, comparing *Vāyu* and *Pūṣan* to two *Rājās* appearing amongst a crowd of attendants, *yathā manuṣyāṇām gaṇe rajānau:* so *Mahīdhara, Yajurveda* 33. 44 and *Yaska Nirukta,* v. 28.

Upon the Close of the Night— *Aktor uṣasaḥ pūrvahūtau* is explained by Sāyaṇa, *rātreḥ sambandhinyā uṣasaḥ sakaśāt pūrvasmin āhvāne sati*, there being the invocation preceding the proximity of the dawn in connection with the night: *Mahīdhara* seems to understand it somewhat differently: *Pūṣan*, as the sun, appears after the prior invocation of the dawn upon the lighting of the sacrificial fire: whilst by *Vāyu* is to be understood *Agni*, of whom he is the friend; and who is the divinity of the nocturnal sacrifice.

५५०७. ज्मया अत्र वसवो रन्त देवा उरावन्तरिक्षे मर्जयन्त शुभ्राः।
अर्वाक् पथ उरुव्रयः कृणुध्वं श्रोता दूतस्य जग्मुषो नो अस्य॥३॥

3. May the divine *Vasu*s sport on this occasion upon the earth: the brilliant (*Maruts*) in the expansive firmament are being worshipped: swift-moving deities, direct your paths towards us: hear (the words) of this our messenger, (*Agni*), approaching to you.

५५०८. ते हि यज्ञेषु यज्ञियास ऊमाः सधस्थं विश्वे अभि सन्ति देवाः।
ताँ अध्वर उशतो यक्ष्यग्ने श्रुष्टी भगं नासत्या पुरन्धिम्॥४॥

4. These universal adorable guardian deities occupy a common station at sacrifices: worship, *Agni*, those divinities, deservers (of oblations) at the ceremony, the swift *Bhaga*, the *Nāsatyās* and *Purandhi*.

Purandhi— *Indra*.

५५०९. आग्ने गिरो दिव आ पृथिव्या मित्रं वह वरुणमिन्द्रमग्निम्।
आर्यमणमदितिं विष्णुमेषां सरस्वती मरुतो मादयन्ताम्॥५॥

5. Bring *Agni*, whether from heaven or earth, the adorable deities, *Mitra*, *Varuṇa*, *Indra* and *Agni*. *Aryaman*, *Aditi* and *Viṣṇu*, (for the good) of these (worshippers): and may *Sarasvatī* and the Maruts be delighted (by our offerings).

५५१०. रे हव्यं मतिभिर्यज्ञियानां नक्षत्कामं मर्त्यानामसिन्वन्।
धाता रयिमविदस्यं संदासां संक्षीमहि युज्येभिनु देवैः॥६॥

6. The oblation is offered together with praises to the adorable deities: may (*Agni*), unaverse to the desire of mortals, be present: bestow (upon us gods), unwasting, all-benefiting riches; and may we today be associated with the assembled deities.

५५११. नू रोदसी अभिष्टुते वसिष्ठैर्ऋतावानो वरुणो मित्रो अग्निः।
यच्छन्तु चन्द्रा उपमं नो अर्कं यूयं पात स्वस्तिभिः सदा नः॥७॥

7. Heaven and earth are now glorified by the *Vasiṣṭhas*, as are *Varuṇa*, the object of worship, and *Mitra* and *Agni*: may they, the conferrers of joy, bestow upon us excellent food: and do you (all) ever cherish us with blessings.

[सूक्त-४०]

[ऋषि- वसिष्ठ मैत्रावरुणि। देवता–विश्वेदेवा। छन्द–त्रिष्टुप्।]

५५१२. ओ श्रुष्टिर्विदथ्या३ समेतु प्रति स्तोमं दधीमहि तुराणाम्।
यद्ध देव: सविता सुवाति स्यामास्य रत्निनों विभागे।।१।।

1. May the satisfaction derived from pious rites come to us as we contemplate the glorification of the swift moving (divinities): may we be included in the apportionment by that wealth-bestowing deity (of the riches) which the divine *Savitā* today distributes.

५५१३. मित्रस्तन्नो वरुणो रोदसी च द्युभक्तमिन्द्रो अर्यमा ददातु।
दिदेष्टु देव्यदिति रेक्णों वायुश्च यन्त्रियुवैते भगश्च।।२।।

2. May *Mitra* and *Varuṇa*, heaven and earth, *Indra* and *Aryaman*, give us that (wealth) which is merited by brilliant (laudations): may the divine *Aditi* be disposed to give us riches, which Vāyu and *Bhaga* may preserve ever in our keeping.

५५१४. सेदुग्रो अस्तु मरुत: स शुष्मी यं मर्त्यं पृषदश्वा अवाथ।
उतेमग्नि: सरस्वती जुनन्ति न तस्य रांय: पर्येतास्ति।।३।।

3. *Maruts*, whose steeds are the spotted deer, may the mortal whom you protect be resolute, be strong, for him *Agni* and *Sarasvatī* also defend, and there be no despoiler of his riches.

५५१५. अयं हि नेता वरुण ऋतस्य मित्रो राजानो अर्यमापो धु:।
सुहवों देव्यदितिरनर्वा ते नो अंहो अति पर्षन्नरिष्टान्।।४।।

4. This *Varuṇa*, the leader of the rite, and the royal *Mitra* and *Aryaman*, uphold my acts, and the divine unopposed *Aditi*, earnestly invoked: may they convey us safe beyond evil.

५५१६. अस्य देवस्य मीळ्हुषों वया विष्णोरेषस्य प्रभृथे हविर्भि:।
विदे हि रुद्रो रुद्रियं महित्वं यासिष्टं वर्तिरश्विनाविरावत्।।५।।

5. I propitiate with oblations the ramifications of that divine attainable *Viṣṇu*, the showerer of benefits: *Rudra*, bestow upon us

the magnificence of his nature: the *Aśvins* have come to our dwelling abounding with (sacrificial) food.

The Ramifications— Vayāḥ, branches: all other deities are, as it were, branches of *Viṣṇu*, anye *devāḥ śākhā iva bhavanti:* as by a text cited by the Scholiast, *Viṣṇu* is all divinities, *Viṣṇuḥ sarā devatā iti śruteḥ.*[1]

५५१७. मात्रे पूषन्नाघृण इरस्यो वरूत्री यद्रातिषाच्चश्च रासन्।

मयोभुवौ नो अर्वन्तो नि पान्तु वृष्टिं परिज्मा वातो ददातु॥६॥

6. Resplendent *Puṣan*, oppose not (hindrance) on this occasion: may the protectress, (*Sarasvatī*), and the liberal (wives of the gods), grant us wealth: may the ever-moving deities, the sources of happiness, protect us: may the circumambient *Vāta* send us rain.

५५१८. नू रोदसी अभिष्टुते वसिष्ठैर्ऋतावानो वरुणो मित्रो अग्निः।

यच्छन्तु चन्द्रा उपमं नो अर्कं यूयं पात स्वस्तिभिः सदा नः॥७॥

7. Heaven and earth are now glorified by the *Vasiṣṭhas*, as are *Varuṇa* the object of worship, and *Mitra* and *Agni*: may they, the conferrers of joy, bestow upon us excellent food: and do you (all) ever cherish us with blessings.

[सूक्त-४१]

[**ऋषि**– वसिष्ठ मैत्रावरुणि। **देवता**– लिङ्गोक्त देवता, (अग्नि, इन्द्र, मित्रावरुण, अश्विनीकुमार, भग, पूषा, ब्रह्मणस्पति, सोम, रुद्र) २-६ भग, ७ उषा। **छन्द**– त्रिष्टुप् जगती।]

५५१९. प्रातरग्निं प्रातरिन्द्रं हवामहे प्रातर्मित्रावरुणा प्रातरश्विना।

प्रातर्भगं पूषणं ब्रह्मणस्पतिं प्रातः सोममुत रुद्रं हुवेम॥१॥

VII.3.8. The whole of this *Sukta* occurs in he *Yajuṣ*, XXXIV. 34-40.

1. We invoke at dawn *Agni*: at dawn *Indra*: at dawn *Mitra* and *Varuṇa*: at dawn the *Aśvins*: at dawn *Bhaga*, *Puṣan*, *Brahmaṇaspati*: at dawn *Soma* and *Rudra*.

५५२०. प्रातर्जितं भगमुग्रं हुवेम वयं पुत्रमदितेर्यो विधर्ता।

आध्रश्चिद्यं मन्यमानस्तुरश्चिद्राजा चिद्यं भगं भक्षीत्याह॥२॥

2. We invoke at dawn to be altorious fierce *Bhaga*, the son of *Aditi*, who is the sustainer (of the world), to whom the poor man

---

१. विष्णुः सर्वा देवताः (ऐ० ब्रा० १.१)।

praising him applies, saying, give (me wealth), to whom the opulent prince (addresses the same prayer).

To whom the Poor man, Etc.— *Adhraśchid yam manyanianas, turaśchid raja cid yam bhagam bhakṣity-aha*: *Mahīdhara* explains the terms somewhat differently: the *Adhra* he renders unsatisfied, hungry, or poor: *tura* he makes the same as *atura,* sick, or it may mean *yama*: *raja* is the same.

५५२१. भग प्रणेतर्भग सत्यराधो भगेमां धियमुदवा ददन्नः।
भग प्र णो जनय गोभिरश्वैर्भग प्र नृभिर्नृवन्तः स्याम।।३।।

3. *Bhaga*, chief leader of rited, *Bhaga*, faithful promn granting (our wishes), fructify ceremony, enrich us with cattle and horses: may we *Bhaga*, be eminent with male descendants and followers.

५५२२. उतेदानीं भगवन्तः स्यामोत प्रपित्व उत मध्ये अह्नाम्।
उतोदिता मघवन्त्सूर्यस्य वयं देवानां सुमतौ स्याम।।४।।

4. May we now have *Bhaga* (for our lord), whether in the forenoon or at mid-day, or at sun-rise: may we, *Maghavan*, enjoy the favour of the gods.

May we now have Bhaga for our Lord— *Utedanim bhagavantaḥ syama*, may we be now possessors of *Bhaga*; or it may mean, may we be possessors of wealth; in which sense *Mahīdhara* understands *bhagavantah*, or, he says also, possessors of knowledge: *jnanavantah.*

At Sunrise— *Prapitve* Sāyaṇa explains purvahne: Mahīdhara, sūryasya prapatane, astomaye, sun-down, sunset.

५५२३. भग एव भगवाँ अस्तु देवास्तेन वयं भगवन्तः स्याम।
तं त्वां भग सर्व इज्जोहवीति स नो भग पुरएता भवेह।।५।।

5. May *Bhaga*, gods, be the possessor of opulence, and, through him, may we be possessed of wealth, every one verily repeatedly invokes you, *Bhaga*: do you, *Bhaga*, be our preceder at this solemnity.

May Bhaga be the Possessor of Opulence— *Bhaga eva bhagavān, astu, dhanavān,* having wealth.

Do you, Bhaga, be our Preceder— *Pura eta, puro-ganta,* one who goes before: it may mean *purohita,* or family priest.

५५२४. समध्वरायोषसो नमन्त दधिक्रावेव शुचये पदाय।
अर्वाचीनं वसुविदं भगं नो रथमिवाश्वा वाजिन आ वहन्तु।।६।।

6. May the Dawn come to our sacrifice as a horse to a suitable station: as rapid steeds convey a chariot, so may the Dawns bring to us *Bhaga*, down-descending, charged with riches.

To a Suitable Station— *Śucaaye padaya*, Sāyaṇa interprets *gamanayogyaya sthanaya: Mahīdhara* supplies *agnyadhanartham śucai padam*, a pure place for the receptacle of the fire, as if he understood by *dadhikra* of the text, not any horse, although he renders it simply *aśve*, but the one intended for sacrifice.

५५२५. अश्वावती॒र्गोमं॑तीर्न॒ उषा॑सो॒ वीर॑वती: स॒दमु॑च्छन्तु भ॒द्रा:।

घृ॒तं दुहा॑ना वि॒श्वत॑: प्र॒पीता यू॒यं पा॑त स्व॒स्तिभि॑: स॒दा न॑:॥७॥

7. May the auspicious Dawns ever break, bestowing horses and cattle and male descendants, shedding water, and endowed with all good things: and do you ever cherish us with blessings.

[सूक्त-४२]

[ऋषि– वसिष्ठ मैत्रावरुणि। देवता– विश्वेदेवा। छन्द– त्रिष्टुप्।]

५५२६. प्र ब्र॒ह्माणो॑ अ॒ङ्गि॑रसो नक्षन्त प्र क्रन्द॒नुर्न॑भ॒न्य॑स्य वेतु।

प्र धे॒नव॑ उद॒प्रुतो॑ नवन्त यु॒ज्यातामद्री॒ अ॑ध्व॒रस्य॒ पेश॑:॥१॥

1. May the *Brahmāṇas*, the *Aṅgirasas*, be everywhere present: may Krandanu be conscious of (our) adoration: may the rivers glide along, distributing water may the pious couple, (the *Yajamāna* and his wife), conjointly appreciate the beauty of the sacrifice.

Krandanu— *Krandanu* is said to be a synonym of *Parjanya*.

The Rivers— *Dhenavaḥ* is here explained *Nadyaḥ*, consistently with what is said of *udapruto navantaḥ*.

५५२७. सु॒गस्ते॑ अग्ने स॒न॑वित्तो अध्वा॑ यु॒क्ष्वा सु॒ते ह॒रितो॑ रोहित॑श्च।

ये वा॒ स॒द्म॑नरु॒षा वी॒रवा॑हो॒ हु॒वे दे॒वानां॒ जनि॑मानि स॒न्त॑:॥२॥

2. Pleasant, *Agni*, be your long-familiar path, invoke the libation the bay, the ruddy horses, who, brilliant shining, are the conveyers of (you), the hero, to the hall of sacrifice, where seated. I invoke the companies of the gods.

५५२८. समु॑ वो य॒ज्ञं म॑हयन्त्रमो॒भि: प्र होता॑ म॒न्द्रो रि॑रिच उ॒पाके॑।

यज॑स्व॒ सु पु॒र्वणी॑क दे॒वाना॑ यज्ञि॒याम॑र॒मतिं॑ ववृत्या॒:॥३॥

3. The (worshippers) offer you, (gods), this sacrifice, with prostrations: the ministrant priest, who is near us repeating pious praise, excels (all others): worship well the gods: resplendent (*Agni*), make the venerable earth revolve.

५५२९. यदा वीरस्य रेवतो दुरोणे स्योनशीरतिथिराचिकेतत्।
सुप्रीतो अग्नि: सुधितो दम आ स विशे दाति वार्यमियर्त्यै।।४।।

4. When *Agni*, reposing at his ease in the dwelling of the liberal worshipper, is welcomed as a guest, thus suitably placed in the hall of sacrifice, he gives well-pleased, desirable (wealth) to the people who approach him.

५५३०. इमं नो अग्ने अध्वरं जुषस्व मरुत्स्विन्द्रे यशसं कृधी न:।
आ नक्ता बर्हि: संदतामुषासोशन्ता मित्रावरुणा यजेह।।५।।

5. Be gratified, *Agni*, by this our sacrifice: render our (worship) renowned among *Indra* and the *Maruts*: let the days and nights sit down on the sacred grass: worship (*Agni*), at this rite, *Mitra* and *Varuṇa*, desiring (the oblation).

५५३१. एवाग्नि सहस्यं वसिष्ठो रायस्कामो विश्वप्स्न्यस्य स्तौत्।
इषं रयिं पप्रथद्वाजमस्मे यूयं पात स्वस्तिभि: सदा न:।।६।।

6. Thus has *Vasiṣṭha* wishing for riches, glorified the vigorous *Agni* for the sake of every sort of wealth: may be bestow upon us food, riches, strength: and do you, (gods), ever cherish us with blessings.

[सूक्त-४३]

[**ऋषि**– वसिष्ठ मैत्रावरुणि। **देवता**– विश्वेदेवा। **छन्द**– त्रिष्टुप्।]

५५३२. प्र वो यज्ञेषु देवयन्तो अर्चन्द्यावा नमोभि: पृथिवी इषध्यै।
येषां ब्रह्माण्यसमानि विप्रा विष्वग्वियन्ति वनिनो न शाखा:।।१।।

1. Devout worshippers seek to attain you, gods, by praises at sacrifices: they (worship) the heaven and earth, they of whom the diversified adorations spread everywhere like the branches of trees.

५५३३. प्र यज्ञ एतु हेत्वो न सप्तिरुद्यच्छध्वं समनसो घृताची:।
स्तृणीत बर्हिरध्वराय साधूर्ध्वा शोचींषि देवयून्यस्थु:।।२।।

2. Let the sacrifice proceed like a swift course (to the gods: elevate, (priests), with one occured, your ladles, charged with butter: spread for the solemnity the sacred grass: let the flames (of the burnt-offering) to the gods ascend on high.

५५३४. आ पुत्रासो न मातरं विभृत्राः सानौ देवासो बर्हिषः सदन्तु।
आ विश्वाचीं विदथ्यामनक्त्वग्ने मा नौ देवताता मृधस्कः॥३॥

3. Let the gods sit down on the summit of the sacred grass, like children nursed on the (lap of the) mother: let the full ladle, *Agni*, pour (the oblation) on the sacrificial flame: give us not up to our adversaries in battle.

५५३५. ते सीषपन्त जोषमा यजत्रा ऋतस्य धाराः सुदुघा दुहानाः।
ज्येष्ठं वो अद्य मह आ वसूनामा गन्तन समनसो यति ष॥४॥

4. May the adorable deities, who are the bestowers of water, the shedders of showers, be fully propitiated (by our praises): may the most precious and commendable of your treasure (be ours) today: and do you with one accord come hither.

And do you with one accord come Hither— *Āgantana samanasaḥ* are followed by *yatiṣṭha*, which are unexplained, apparently through a hiatus in the manuscripts: *stha* may be the second pers. plur. pres. of *as*, to be; but it is difficult to assign a meaning to *yati*, unless it be intended, or an error, for *yadi*, if, when the sentence may be rendered, if you are of one mind.

५५३६. एवा नो अग्ने विश्वा दशस्य त्वया वयं सहसावन्नास्राः।
राया युजा सधमादो अरिष्टा यूयं पात स्वस्तिभिः सदा नः॥५॥

5. Be glorified, *Agni*: grant us (wealth) among the people: may we, vigorous *Agni*, ever be undeserted by you, but always be rejoicing and unmolested in the possession of riches: and do you, (gods), ever cherish us with blessings.

[सूक्त-४४]

[**ऋषि**– वसिष्ठ मैत्रावरुणि। **देवता**– दधिक्रा; १ लिङ्गोक्त देवता (दधिक्रा, अश्विनीकुमार, उषा, अग्नि, भग, इन्द्र, विष्णु, पूषा, ब्रह्मणस्पति, आदित्य द्यावा-पृथिवी आपः)। **छन्द**– त्रिष्टुप्, १ जगती।]

५५३७. दधिक्रां वः प्रथममश्विनोषसमग्निं समिद्धं भगमूतये हुवे।
इन्द्रं विष्णुं पूषणं ब्रह्मणस्पतिमादित्यान्द्यावापृथिवी अपः स्वः॥१॥

1. For your preservation, (worshippers), I invoke, first, Dadhikra, then the *Aśvins*, the Dawn, the kindled *Agni*, *Bhaga*, *Indra*, *Viṣṇu*, *Pūṣan*, Bramhanaspati, the *Ādityas*, heaven and earth, the waters, the sun.

५५३८. दधिक्रामु नर्मसा बोधर्यन्त उदीराणा यज्ञमुपप्रयन्तः।
इळां देवीं बर्हिषि सादर्यन्तोऽश्विना विप्रा सुहवा हुवेम॥२॥

2. Arousing and animating *Dadhikrā*, proceeding diligently
with the sacrifice: seating the divine *Iḷa* on the sacred grass, let us
invoke the intelligent and worthily-invoked *Aśvins*.

५५३९. दधिक्रावाणं बुबुधानो अग्निमुपं ब्रुव उषसं सूर्यं गाम्।
ब्रध्नं मैंश्चतोर्वरुणस्य बभ्रुं ते विश्वास्मद् दुरिता यावयन्तु॥३॥

3. Propitiating Dadhikrāvan, I glorify *Agni*, *Uṣas*, the sun, the
earth, the great brown horse of *Varuṇa*, who is mindful of his
adorers: may they put far away from us iniquities.

५५४०. दधिक्रावा प्रथमो वाज्यर्वाग्रे रथानां भवति प्रजानन्।
संविदान उषसा सूर्येणादित्येभिर्वसुभिरङ्गिरोभिः॥४॥

4. Dadhikravan, the swift steed, the first (of horses), knowing
(his office), is in the front of the chariots (of the gods), consentient
with *Uṣas*, with Sūrya, with the *Ādityas*, with the *Vasus*, with the
Aṅgirasas.

५५४१. आ नो दधिक्राः पथ्यामनकत्वृतस्य पन्थामन्वेतवा उं।
शृणोतु नो दैव्यं शर्धो अग्निः शृण्वन्तु विश्वे महिषा अमूराः॥५॥

5. May Dadhikrā sprinkle our path (with water), that we may
follow the road of sacrifice: may *Agni*, the strength of the gods,
here our (invocation): may the mighty, unperplexed, universal
deities hear it.

[सूक्त-४५]

[**ऋषि**- वसिष्ठ मैत्रावरुणि। **देवता**- सविता। **छन्द**- त्रिष्टुप्।]

५५४२. आ देवो यातु सविता सुरत्नोंऽन्तरिक्षप्रा वहंमानो अश्वैः।
हस्ते दधानो नर्या पुरूणि निवेशयंश्च प्रसुवंश्च भूर्म॥१॥

1. Borne by his steeds, may the divine *Savitā*, who is possessed
of precious treasure, and filling the firmament (with radiance),
come hither, holding in his hands many things good for man, and
(both) tranquillizing and animating living beings.

Both Tranquillizing and animating Living Beings— *Niveśayan c
prasuvan ca bhūma* is explained *bhūtani ratriṣu sve sthāpayansca ahaḥsu
prerayansca,* placing beings at night in their own stations, and urging
them on by day.

५५४३. उद॑स्य बा॒हू शि॒थि॒रा बृ॒ह॒न्ता हि॑र॒ण्यया॒ दि॒वो अन्ताँ॑ अनष्टाम्॑।
नू॒नं सो अ॑स्य महि॒मा प॑निष्ट सूर॑श्चिद॒स्मा अनु॑ दादप॒स्याम्॑।।२।।

2. May the outspread, vast, and golden arms of *Savitā* extend
to the ends of the sky: verily his greatness is glorified (by us): may
the sun impart energy unto him.

May the Sun Impart Energy unto Him— *Suraścid asmā anudād
apasyām* is explained, *Sūryo asmin Savitre karmecchāṁ anudadātu*, may
Sūrgy subsequently give to that *Savitā* the desire for acts.

५५४४. स घा॑ नो दे॒वः स॑वि॒ता साह॑वा सावि॒षद्वसु॑पति॒र्वसू॑नि।
वि॒श्रय॑माणो अम॒तिमुरू॑चीं॒ मर्त॑भोज॒नमध॑ रासते नः।।३।।

3. May the divine *Savitā*, who is endowed with energy, the
lord of treasure, bestow treasures upon us concentrating infinite
lustre: may he bestow upon us wealth, the source of the enjoyment
of mortals.

Appeaser of the Wind— *Svapivāta*, which is left untranslated by the
Scholiast: it is somewhat difficult to assign it a meaning: *Svapi* may be
derived from *Svap*, to sleep, and *vata* is usually the mind; or it may mean
disorders arising from the windy humour which *Rudra*, as the deity of
medicines, may be supposed to allay: this, however, would be an early
indication of the humoral pathology.

५५४५. इ॒मा गिरः॑ सवि॒तारं॑ सु॒जि॒ह्वं॒ पू॒र्णग॑भस्तिमीळते सु॒पा॒णिम्॑।
चि॒त्रं वयो॑ बृ॒हद॒स्मे द॑धातु यू॒यं पा॑त स्व॒स्तिभिः॒ सदा॑ नः।।४।।

4. These praises glorify the eloquent-tongued, dextrous-
handed, whose hands are full (of wealth): may he bestow upon us
manifold and abundant food: and do you, (gods), ever cherish us
with blessings.

[सूक्त-४६]

[ऋषि– वसिष्ठ मैत्रावरुणि। **देवता**– रुद्र। **छन्द**– जगती ४ त्रिष्टुप्।]

५५४६. इ॒मा रु॒द्राय॑ स्थि॒रध॑न्वने॒ गिरः॒ क्षि॒प्रेष॑वे दे॒वाय॑ स्व॒धाव्ने॑।
अ॒षा॒ळ्हाय॒ सह॑मानाय वे॒धसे॑ ति॒ग्माय॑ध्याय भरता शृणोतु॑ नः।।१।।

1. Offer these praises to the divine *Rudra*, armed with the
strong bow and fast-flying arrows, the bestower of food, the
invincible, the conqueror, the creator, the, wielder of sharp
weapons: may he hear our (praises).

५५४७. स हि क्षयेण क्षम्यस्य जन्मनः साम्राज्येन दिव्यस्य चेतति ।
अवत्रवन्तीरुपं नो दुरश्चरानमीवो रुद्र जासु नो भव ॥२॥

2. He is known by his rule over those of terrestrial birth, by his sovereignty over those of celestial (origin): protecting our progeny, *Rudra*, propitiating you (by praise), come to our dwellings, and be to them a guardian against disease.

५५४८. या ते दिद्युदवसृष्टा दिवस्परि क्षमया चरति परि सा वृणक्तु नः ।
सहस्रं ते स्वपिवात भेषजा मा नस्तोकेषु तनयेषु रीरिषः ॥३॥

3. May your blazing (weapon), which, discharged from heaven, traverses the earth, avoid us: thine, appeaser of the wind, are a thousand medicaments: inflict not evil upon our sons and grandsons.

५५४९. मा नो वधी रुद्र मा परा दा मा ते भूम प्रसितौ हीळितस्य ।
आ नो भज बर्हिषि जीवशंसे यूयं पात स्वस्तिभिः सदा नः ॥४॥

4. Harm us not, *Rudra*: abandon us not: let us not fall under the bondage of you when displeased: make us partakers of the life-promotion sacrifice: and do you, (gods), ever cherish us with blessings.

[सूक्त-४७]

[**ऋषि**– वसिष्ठ मैत्रावरुणि। **देवता**– आपः। **छन्द**- त्रिष्टुप्।]

५५५०. आपो यं वः प्रथमं देवयन्त इन्द्रपानमूर्मिमकृण्वतेळः ।
तं वो वयं शुचिमरिप्रमद्य घृतप्रुषं मधुमन्तं वनेम ॥१॥

1. We solicit from you, *Waters,* today, that pure, faultless, rain-shedding, sweet essence of the earth, which devout have first consecrated as the beverage of *Indra*.

Sweet Essence of the Earth— *Prathamam ūrmimakṛṇvata iḷaḥ*: *ūrmi* is said here to imply the *Soma* juice, *bhūmyāḥ sambhūtam*, produced from the earth.

५५५१. तमूर्मिमापो मधुमत्तमं वोऽपां नपादवत्वाशुहेमा ।
यस्मिन्निन्द्रो वसुभिर्मादयाति तमश्याम देवयन्तो वो अद्य ॥२॥

2. May the swift-moving grandson of the Waters protect, *Waters,* your most sweet essence, wherewith may *Indra* and the *Vasu*s be delighted: and may we, devoted to the gods, partake (of it).

५५२. शतपवित्रा: स्वधया मदन्तीर्देवीर्देवानामपि यन्ति पाथ:।

ता इन्द्रस्य न मिनन्ति व्रतानि सिन्धुभ्यो हव्यं घृतवज्जुहोत।।३।।

3. The divine *Waters,* the purifiers of many, gratifying men with food, pursue the paths of the gods: they impede not the sacred rites of *Indra*: offer, (priests), the butter-charged oblation to the rivers.

५५३. या: सूर्यो रश्मिभिरातताना याभ्य इन्द्रो अरदद् गातुमूर्मिम्।

ते सिन्धवो वरिवो धातना नो यूयं पात स्वस्तिभि: सदा न:।।४।।

4. *Waters,* whom the sun has evaporized by his rays, for whom *Indra* has opened a path by which to issue, bestow upon us wealth: and do you (also) ever cherish us with blessings.

Indra has Opened a Path by which to Issue— The sun having converted the waters of the earth into clouds, *Indra*, by his thunderbolt, cleaves the latter, and the water condensed falls as rain.

[सूक्त-४८]

[**ऋषि–** वसिष्ठ मैत्रावरुणि। **देवता–** ऋभुगण, ४ विश्वेदेवा अथवा ऋभुगण । **छन्द–** त्रिष्टुप्।]

५५४. ऋभुक्षणो वाजा मादयध्वमस्मे नरो मघवान: सुतस्य।

आ वोऽर्वाच: क्रतवो न यातां विभ्वो रथं नर्यं वर्तयन्तु।।१।।

1. *Ṛbhu,* (*Vibhu*), and *Vāja,* leaders of rites, possessors of opulence; be exhilarated by our effused (libation): may your active and powerful (horses) bring to our presence your chariot, beneficial to mankind.

Ṛbhu, Vibhu and Vāja— The text has *Ṛbhukṣaṇo Vājaḥ,* the use of the plurals implying, according to the Scholiast, that the three brothers are intended.

५५५. ऋभुर्ऋभुभिरभि व: स्याम विभ्वो विभुभि: शवसा शवांसि।

वाजो अस्माँ अवतु वाजसाताविन्द्रेण युजा तरुषेम वृत्रम्।।२।।

2. Mighty with the *Ṛbhus,* opulent with the *Vibhus,* may we overcome by strength the strength (of our foes): may *Vāja* defend us in battle: with *Indra,* our ally, may we destroy the enemy.

Ṛbhus Opulent with the Vibhus— *Ṛbhur ṛbhubhiḥ vibhvo vibhubhiḥ* are rather unintelligible phrases: the commentator explains *Ṛbhu* and *uru,* great, and *Vibhu, vibhavaḥ,* rich or powerful: but he leaves unexplained why the first should be in the singular and the second in the plural: it is an evident play upon words, as is the following, *Vājo vājasātau.*

५५५६. ते चिद्धि पूर्वीरभि सन्ति शासा विश्वाँ अर्य उपरताति वन्वन्। इन्द्रो विभ्वाँ ऋभुक्षा वाजो अर्य: शत्रोर्मिथत्या कृणवन्वि नृम्णम्॥३॥

3. They verily, (*Indra* and the *Ṛbhus*), overcome multitudes by their prowess: they overcome all enemies in the missile conflict: may *Indra*, *Vibhvan*, *Ṛbhukśin* and *Vāja*, the subduers of foes, annihilate by their wrath the strength of the enemy.

In the Missile Conflict— *Uparatāti: upara* is explained *upala,* a stone: *upalaiḥ paṣānasadṛśair āyudhais tāyate yuddham,* war that is waged with weapons like stones, is *uparatati.*

५५५७. नू देवासो वरिव: कर्तना नो भूत नो विश्वेऽवसे सजोषा:। समस्मे इषं वसवो ददीरन् यूयं पात स्वस्तिभि: सदा न:॥४॥

4. Grant us, deities, this day opulence: may you all, well pleased alike, be (ready) for our protection: may the exalted (*Ṛbhus*) bestow upon us food: and do you (all) ever cherish us with blessings.

The Exalted Ṛbhus— The text has *uasavaḥ,* which might be *Vasus*; but Sāyaṇa explains it *praśasyaḥ,* an epithet of *Ṛbhavaḥ* understood.

[सूक्त-४९]

[ऋषि– वसिष्ठ मैत्रावरुणि। देवता– आप:। छन्द– त्रिष्टुप्।]

५५५८. समुद्रज्येष्ठा: सलिलस्य मध्यात्पुनाना यन्त्यनिविशमाना:। इन्द्रो या वज्री वृषभो रराद ता आपो देवीरिह मामवन्तु॥१॥

1. The waters, with their ocean-chief, proceed from the midst of the firmament, purifying (all things), flowing unceasingly: may the divine waters, whom the thunder-bearing *Indra*, the showerer, sent forth, protect me here (on earth).

Form the Midst of the Firmament— *Samudrajyeṣṭhā, salilasya madhyāt: salila* is said here to mean *antarikṣa.*

५५५९. या आपो दिव्या उत वा स्रवन्ति खनित्रिमा उत वा या: स्वयंजा:। समुद्रार्था या: शुचय: पावकास्ता आपो देवीरिह मामवन्तु॥२॥

2. May the waters that are in the sky, or those that flow (on the earth), those (whose channels) have being dug, or those that have

sprung up spontaneously, and those that seek the ocean. All pure and purifying, may those divine waters protect me here (on earth).

Those whose Channels have been Dug— *Khanitrimā, khananena nivṛttaḥ*, formed, or perhaps stopped by digging, canals or reservoirs; in either case a proof of the practice of irrigation.

५५६०. यासां राजा वरुणो याति मध्ये सत्यानृते अवपश्यञ्जनानाम्।
मधुश्चुतः शुचयो याः पावकास्ता आपो देवीरिह मामवन्तु॥३॥

3. Those whose sovereign, *Varuṇa*, passes in the middle sphere, discriminating the truth and falsehood of mankind; those shedding sweet showers, pure and purifying; may those divine waters protect me here (on earth).

५५६१. यासु राजा वरुणो यासु सोमो विश्वे देवा यासूर्जं मदन्ति।
वैश्वानरो यास्वग्निः प्रविष्टस्ता आपो देवीरिह मामवन्तु॥४॥

4. May they in which their king, *Varuṇa*, in which *Soma*, abides, in which the gods delight (to receive) the sacrificial food, into which *Agni Vaiśvānara* entered, may those divine waters protect me here (on earth).

[सूक्त-५०]

[ऋषि– वसिष्ठ मैत्रावरुणि। देवता– १ मित्रावरुण, २ अग्नि, ३ विश्वेदेवा, ४ गंगाद्या नद्यः। छन्द– जगती, ४ अतिजगती अथवा शक्वरी॥]

५५६२. आ मां मित्रावरुणेह रक्षतं कुलाययद् विश्वयन्मा न आ गन्।
अजकावं दुर्दृशीकं तिरो दधे मा मां पद्येन रप्सा विदत्त्सरुः॥१॥

1. *Mitra* and *Varuṇa*, protect me here (in this world) let not the insidious and spreading (poison) reach me may the equally malignant and undiscernible (venom) disappear: let not the tortuous (snake) recognize me by the sound of my footsteps.

Let not the Insidious and Spreading Poison Reach me— *Kulāyayat viśvayat mā na ā gan*: the first term is explained *sthānam kurvat*, making a place or a nest; the second, *viśeṣeṇa vardhamānam*, especially increasing: the Scholiast supplies the substantive *viṣam*.

Malignant and Undiscernible Venom— Here again we have only epithets, *ajakāvam, durdṛśīkam*: the first is explained, *ajakā nāma rogaviśeṣaḥ, tad vat*: *ajakā* is the name of a disease like that, a malignant poison, according to Sāyaṇa; the second is rendered *durdarśanam*, difficult or disagreeable to be seen: each verse of this *Sūkta* is to be repeated as an antidote.

The Tortuous Snake— *Tsarus, chadmagāmī jihmagaḥ sarpa ityarthaḥ: tsaru* means what goes stealthily or crookedly, that is to say a snake.

५५६३. यद्द्विजामन्परुषि वन्दनं भुवदष्ठीवन्तौ परि कुल्फौ च देहत्।
अग्निष्टच्छोचन्त्रपं बाधतामितो मा मां पद्येन रप्सा विदत्सरुः॥२॥

2. May the brilliant *Agni* counteract that poison which is generated in the manifold knots (of trees) and the like, or which is smeared upon the knees or ankles: let not the tortuous snake recognize me by the sound of my footsteps.

Poison Generated in the...Knots of Trees— *Yad vijāman paruṣi vandanam* is thus explained, *vandanam etat sañjñakam viṣam: vandana* is a poison so named: *yad vividha janmani vṛkṣādīnām parvaṇi udbhavet,* which may originate in the variously-born joints of trees and others.

Which is Smeared upon the Knees or Ankles— *Asthīvantau parikulphau ca dehat:* the substantive are in common use for the knee and ankle: *paridehat* is explained, *upacitam kuryat,* let him smear: but there does not seem to be any nominative.

५५६४. यच्छल्मलौ भवति यन्त्रदीषु यदोषधीभ्यः परि जायते विषम्।
विश्वे देवा निरितस्तत्सुवन्तु मा मां पद्येन रप्सा विदत्सरुः॥३॥

3. The poison that is in the *Śalmalī* tree, in the rivers, or which is generated from plants, may the universal gods remove from hence: let not the tortuous (snake) recognize me by the sound of my footsteps.

५५६५. याः प्रवतो निवत उद्वत उदन्वतीरनुदकाश्च याः। ता अस्मभ्यं पयसा
पिन्वमानाः शिवा देवीरशिपदा भवन्तु सर्वा नद्यो अशिमिदा
भवन्तु॥४॥

4. May the divine rivers, whether flowing down declivities, in hollow places, or upwards, whether filled with water or dry, nourishing all with their water, be auspicious to us communicating not disease: may all the rivers be unproductive of harm.

Communicating not Disease— *Aśipadā bhavantu: śipada* is said to be the name of a malady, may they be unproductive of the *śipada* complaint: perhaps it is the *Vedic* a form of *slipada,* the Cochin leg.

Unproductive of Harm— *Aśimidā bhavantu: śimi,* it is said, means *vadha,* killing, with the negative prefix, and *da* which gives: *ahiṃsa prada,* not doing harm or injury.

[सूक्त-५१]

[**ऋषि**– वसिष्ठ मैत्रावरुणि। **देवता**– आदित्यगण। **छन्द**– त्रिष्टुप्।]

५५६६. आ॒दि॒त्याना॒मव॑सा॒ नूत॑नेन सक्षी॒महि॒ शर्म॑णा॒ शन्त॑मेन।

अना॒गास्त्वे॒ अदि॑तित्वे तु॒रास॒ इमं॑ य॒ज्ञं द॑धतु॒ श्रोष॑माणाः॥१॥

1. May we, through the protection of the *Ādityas*, be in the enjoyment of a new and comfortable dwelling; may the swift-moving *Ādityas*, listening to our praises, preserve this their worshipper in sinlessness and independence.

५५६७. आ॒दि॒त्यासो॒ अदि॑तिर्मादयन्तां मि॒त्रो अ॑र्य॒मा वरु॑णो॒ रजि॑ष्ठाः।

अ॒स्माकं॑ सन्तु॒ भुव॑नस्य गो॒पाः पिब॑न्तु॒ सोम॑म॒वसे॑ नो अ॒द्य॥२॥

2. May the *Ādityas* and *Aditi*, and the upright *Mitra*, *Aryaman*, and *Varuṇa*, be exhilarated (by the libation): may the guardians of the world be ours also: may they drink the *Soma* today for our preservation.

५५६८. आ॒दि॒त्या विश्वे॑ म॒रुत॑श्च॒ विश्वे॑ दे॒वाश्च॒ विश्व॑ ऋ॒भव॑श्च॒ विश्वे॑।

इन्द्रो॑ अ॒ग्निर॒श्विना॑ तु॒ष्टुवा॑ना यू॒यं पा॑त स्व॒स्तिभिः॒ सदा॑ नः॥३॥

3. All the *Ādityas*, all the *Maruts*, all the gods, all the *Ṛbhus*, *Indra*, *Agni*, and the *Aśvins*, (have been) glorified (by us): do you all ever cherish us with blessings.

[सूक्त-५२]

[**ऋषि**– वसिष्ठ मैत्रा-वरुणि। **देवता**– आदित्यगण। **छन्द**– त्रिष्टुप्।]

५५६९. आ॒दि॒त्यासो॒ अदि॑तयः स्याम पू॒र्देवत्रा॒ वस॑वो॒ मर्त्य॑त्रा।

सने॑म मि॒त्रावरुणा॒ सन॑न्तो भवे॑म द्यावापृथिवी॒ भव॑न्तः॥१॥

1. *Ādityas*, may we be independent: *Vasu*s, (dwelling) among the gods, may your protection (extend) to mortals: offering (oblations to you), *Mitra* and *Varuṇa*, may we partake (of your bounty): may we, heaven and earth exist (through your favour).

५५७०. मि॒त्रस्त॒न्नो॒ वरु॑णो मामहन्त॒ शर्म॒ तोका॑य॒ तन॑याय गो॒पाः।

मा वो॑ भुजेमान्य॒जात॑मेनो॒ मा त॒त्कर्म॑ वसवो॒ यच्च॒यध्वे॑॥२॥

2. May *Mitra* and *Varuṇa* bestow upon us felicity: (may they), the guardians (of all men, bestow felicity) upon our sons and grandsons: let us not suffer (gods), for offences committed by

another: let us not, *Vasus*, do any act by which you may be offended.

५५७१. तुरण्यवोऽङ्गिरसो नक्षन्त रत्नं देवस्य सवितुरियाना:।

पिता च तन्नो महान् यजत्रो विश्वे देवा: समनसो जुषन्त।।३।।

3. The *Aṅgirasas*, prompt (in worship), soliciting him obtain precious (wealth) from *Savitā*: may the mighty adorable parent, and the universal god alike favourable minded, approve (of the donation).

The Mighty Adorable Parent— *Pita* may be *Varuṇa*, the father of *Vasiṣṭha,* or *Prajāpati*, the father of all.

[सूक्त-५३]

[ऋषि- वसिष्ठ मैत्रावरुणि। देवता- द्यावा-पृथिवी। छन्द- त्रिष्टुप्।]

५५७२. प्र द्यावा यज्ञै: पृथिवी नमोभि: सबाधं ईळे बृहती यजत्रे।

ते चिद्धि पूर्वे कवयो गृणन्त: पुरो मही दधिरे देवपुत्रे।।१।।

1. Attended by a concourse (of priests) I worship the adorable and mighty Heaven and Earth with sacrifices and praises, those two great ones of whom the gods are the sons, whom ancient sages glorifying have formerly detained.

५५७३. प्र पूर्वजे पितरा नव्यसीभिर्गीर्भि: कृणुध्वं सदने ऋतस्य।

आ नो द्यावापृथिवी दैव्येन जनेन यातं महि वां वरूथम्।।२।।

2. Place before (us) in the hall of sacrifice, with new songs, the ancient parents (of all beings): come to us, Heaven and Earth, with the celestial people, for vast is your protecting (wealth).

५५७४. उतो हि वां रत्नधेयानि सन्ति पुरूणि द्यावापृथिवी सुदासे।

अस्मे धत्तं यदसदस्कृधोयु यूयं पात स्वस्तिभि: सदा न:।।३।।

3. Many, Heaven and Earth, are the treasures fit to be given to the pious donor (of the oblation): give to us that wealth which is unlimited: and do you ever cherish us with blessings.

[सूक्त-५४]

[ऋषि- वसिष्ठ मैत्रा-वरुणि। देवता- वास्तोष्पति। छन्द- त्रिष्टुप्।]

५५७५. वास्तोष्पते प्रति जानीह्यस्मान्त्स्वावेशो अनमीवो भवा न:।

यत्त्वेमहे प्रति तन्नो जुषस्व शं नो भव द्विपदे शं चतुष्पदे।।१।।

1. Protector of the dwelling, recognize us: be to us an excellent abode the non-inflicter of disease: whatever we ask of you, be pleased to grant: be the bestower of happiness on our bipeds and quadrupeds.

Protector of the Dwelling— *Vastoṣpati*: *pati*, lord or protector of the *Vastu*, the foundation of a house, put for the house itself: this *Sukta* is translated by Mr. Colebrooke, *Asiatic Researches*, Vol. VIII. p. 390.

५५७६. वास्तोष्पते प्रतरणो न एधि गयस्फानो गोभिरश्वेभिरिन्दो।

अजरासस्ते सख्ये स्याम पितेव पुत्रान्प्रति नो जुषस्व॥२॥

2. Protector of the dwelling, be our preserver and the augmenter of our wealth: possessed of cattle and horses, *Indra*, may we, through your friendship, be exempt from decay: be favourable to us, like a father to his sons.

५५७७. वास्तोष्पते शग्मया संसदा ते सक्षीमहि रण्वया गातुमत्या।

पाहि क्षेम उत योगे वरं नो यूयं पात स्वस्तिभिः सदा नः॥३॥

3. Protector of the dwelling, may we be possessed of a comfortable, delightful, opulent abode, bestowed by you: protect our wealth, whether in possession or expectation: and do you, (gods), ever cherish us with blessings.

Opulent— *Gatumatya* is rendered by Mr. Colebrooke melodious, from *ga*, to sing: Sāyaṇa interprets it here by *dhanavatī*, having wealth.

And do You God— Or *yuyam* may be put for *tvam*, do you *Vāstoṣpati*, etc.

[सूक्त-५५]

[ऋषि– वसिष्ठ मैत्रावरुणि। **देवता**– वास्तोष्पति, २-८ इन्द्र (प्रस्वापिनी उपनिषद्)। **छन्द**– १ गायत्री, २-४ उपरिष्टाद् बृहती, ५-८ अनुष्टुप्।]

VII. The occasion of this *Sūkta* is narrated from the *Bṛhaddevatā*: *Vasiṣṭha* coming by night to the house of *Varuṇa*, intended to sleep there: the watch-dog barking, was about to lay hold of him, when he appeased the animal by this hymn: according to another story briefly told by Sāyaṇa, and found in the *Nīti Mañjarī*, *Vasiṣṭha* had passed three days without being able to get any food; on the night of the fourth he entered the house of *Varuṇa* to steal something to eat, and had made his way to the larder, the *Koṣṭagara*, when the god set upon him, but was put to sleep by these verses, wherefore they are to be recited on similar occasions by thieves and burglars.

५५७८. अमीवहा वास्तोष्पते विश्वा रूपाण्याविशन्।
सखा॑ सुशेव॑ एधि न॒:।।१।।

1. Protector of the dwelling, remover of disease, assuming all (kinds of) forms, be to us a friend, the granter of happiness.

५५७९. यद॑र्जुन सारमेय द॒त: पि॑शङ्ग॒ यच्छसे।
वीव॑ भ्राजन्त ऋष्टय॒ उप॑ स्रक्वे॑षु बप्सतो॒ नि षु स्वप।।२।।

2. White offspring of *Saramā,* with tawny limbs, although barking you display your teeth against me, bristling like lances in your gums, nevertheless, go quietly to sleep.

White Offspring of Sarama— *Sārameya,* progeny of *Saarmā,* bitch of *Indra:* he is called *arjuna,* white, as well as *piṅgala,* tawny: the latter, according to Sāyaṇa, in some members, *keṣucidaṅgeṣu.*

५५८०. स्ते॒नं राय॑ सारमेय तस्क॑रं वा पुन॒:सर।
स्तोतृनिन्द्रस्य रायसि॒ किमस्मान्दुच्छुनायसे॒ नि षु स्वप।।३।।

3. Offspring of *Saramā,* returning (to the charge), attack the pilferer or the thief: why dose you assail the worshippers of *Indra* ? Why dose you intimidate us ? Go quietly to sleep.

The Pilferer or the Thief— *Stenam taskaram ca:* the first is he who steals privily or hidden property, the latter carries it off openly.

५५८१. त्वं सूक॑रस्य दर्द्धि तव॑ दर्दर्तु॒ सूक॑र:।
स्तोतृनिन्द्रस्य रायसि॒ किमस्मान्दुच्छुनायसे॒ नि षु स्वप।।४।।

4. Do you rend the hog: let the hog rend you: why dose you assail the worshippers of *Indra* ? Why dose you intimidate us ? Go quietly to sleep.

५५८२. सस्तु॒ माता॒ सस्तु॒ पिता॒ सस्तु॒ श्वा सस्तु॒ विश्पति॑:।
ससन्तु॒ सर्वे॑ ज्ञातय॒: सस्त्वयमभितो॒ जन॑:।।५।।

5. Let the mother sleep let the father sleep, let the dog sleep, let the son-in-law sleep, let all the kindred sleep, let the people (who are stationed) around sleep.

Let the Son-in-Law Sleep— *Sastu viśpati:* the latter is explained *Jāmatṛ,* or, literally, the master of all: *gṛhi,* the householder.

५५८३. य आस्ते॒ यश्च॒ चरति॒ यश्च॒ पश्यति नो जन॑:।
तेषां सं ह॑न्मो अक्षाणि॒ यथेदं ह॒र्म्यं तथा॑।।६।।

6. The man who sits, or he who walks, or he who sees us, of
these we shut up the eyes, so that they may be as unconscious as
the mansion.

५५८४. सहस्त्रशृङ्गो वृषभो यः समुद्रादुदाचरत्।

तेना सहस्येना वयं नि जनान्त्स्वापयामसि ॥७॥

7. We put men to sleep through the irresistible might or the
bull with a thousand horns, who rises out of the ocean.

The Bull with a Thousand Horns, Etc.— *Sahasraśṛṅgo vṛṣabho
yaḥ samudrād udācarat,* the sun with a thousand rays: through the
worship of the sun, at a later date, *Kumara* was the patron of house-
breakers.

५५८५. प्रोष्ठेशया वह्येशया नारीर्यास्तल्पशीवरीः।

स्त्रियो याः पुण्यगन्धास्ता सर्वाः स्वापयामसि ॥८॥

8. We put to sleep all those women are lying in the courtyard
in litter on the bed, the women who are decorated with holiday
perfumes.

The Women who are Decorated with Holiday Perfumes— *Striyo
yāḥ puṇyagandhāḥ, maṅgalya gandhāḥ,* wearing garlands of fragrant
flowers on festival occasions, as at marriages and the like.

ANUVAKA IV

[सूक्त-५६]

[**ऋषि**– वसिष्ठ मैत्रा-वरुणि। **देवता**– मरुद्गण। **छन्द**– त्रिष्टुप्, ९-११
द्विपदा विराट्।]

५५८६. क ईं व्यक्ता नरः सनीळा रुद्रस्य मर्या अधा स्वश्वाः ॥१॥

1. Who are these resplendent chiefs, the dwellers in one abode,
the sons of *Rudra*, friends of man, at present well mounted ?
Sāmaveda 433.

५५८७. नकिर्ह्येषां जनूंषि वेद ते अङ्ग विद्रे मिथो जनित्रम् ॥२॥

2. No one indeed knows their origin, they alone respectively
know their birth.

५५८८. अभि स्वपूर्भिर्मिथो वपन्त वातत्स्वनसः श्येना अस्पृध्रन् ॥३॥

3. They go together by their own pure paths: roaring like the
wind, and fleet as falcons, they mutually rival each other.

५५८९. एतानि धीरो निण्या चिकेत पृश्निर्यदूधो मही जभार ॥४॥

4. The sage may know those white-complexioned beings (the *Maruts*), whom the vast Prishni born at her udder.

White-Complexioned beings, the Maruts— *Etāni ninya,* which Sāyaṇa explains, *śveta varṇāni bhūtāni marutātmakāni,* white-coloured beings, identical with, the *Maruts.*

Bore at her Udder— *Udho babhāra: udhas* may mean the firmament of the womb, according to Sāyaṇa.

५५९०. सा विट् सुवीरा मरुद्भिरस्तु सनात्सहन्ती पुष्यन्ती नृम्णम् ॥५॥

5. May the people, through (the favours of) the *Maruts,* always victorious, possessed of male posterity, and in the enjoyment of wealth.

५५९१. यामं येष्वा: शुभा शोभिष्ठा: श्रिया सम्मिश्ला ओजोभिरुग्रा: ॥६॥

6. The *Maruts* rapidly repair to the place (of their destination), richly decorated with ornaments, invested with beauty, terrible by their strength.

५५९२. उग्रं व ओज: स्थिरा शवांस्यधा मरुद्भिर्गणस्तुविष्मान् ॥७॥

7. Terrible be your strength, steadfast your energies, prosperous be the company of the *Maruts.*

५५९३. शुभ्रो व: शुष्म: क्रुध्मी मनांसि धुनिर्मुनिरिव शर्धस्य धृष्णो: ॥८॥

8. Glorious is your vigour, unrelenting are your minds; (the exertion) of your irresistible force, the agitator (of the trees), is like (the manifold tone of the prayers of) a *muni.*

Like the Manifold tone of the Prayers of a Muni— The text has *dhuni muniriva,* the agitation like a *muni;* the sounds produced by the shaking of the trees are like the varied intonations of a reciter of praises, is Sāyaṇa's explanation.

५५९४. सनेम्यस्मद्युयोत दिद्युं मा वो दुर्मतिरिह प्रणङ्न: ॥९॥

9. Withhold from us your ancient blazing (weapon) let not your displeasure light upon us at this sacrifice.

५५९५. प्रिया वो नाम हुवे तुराणामा यत्तृपन्मरुतो वावशाना: ॥१०॥

10. I invoke your beloved names, *Maruts,* destroyers (of foes), that they who are desirous of the offering may be satisfied.

५५९६. स्वायुधास इष्मिण: सुनिष्का उत स्वयं तन्व: शुम्भमाना: ॥११॥

11. Bearers are (the *Maruts*) of bright weapons, rapid are they in motion, wearers of brilliant ornaments, and self-radiators of their persons.

५५९७. शुचीं वो हव्या मरुतः शुचीनां शुचिं हिनोम्यध्वरं शुचिभ्यः।

ऋतेन सत्यमृतसाप आयञ्छुचिजन्मानः शुचयः पावकाः॥१२॥

12. Pure oblations be offered, *Maruts*, to you who are pure: the shedders of water proceed by truth to truth, pure, purifying, of pure birth.

५५९८. अंसेष्वा मरुतः खादयो वो वक्षःसु रुक्मा उपशिश्रियाणाः।

वि विद्युतो न वृष्टिभी रुचाना अनु स्वधामायुधैर्यच्छमानाः॥१३॥

13. Bright ornaments, *Maruts*, are on your shoulders, shining (necklaces) are pendant on your breasts, glittering with rain, like lightnings, you are distributing the waters with your weapons.

Bright Ornaments— *Khādayo alaṅkāra viśeṣaḥ*: *khādi* occurs before for a guard for the hand, I. 23. 4. 3. ; it is more usual to describe the *Maruts* as bearing lances on their shoulders.

Shining Necklaces— The text has only *rukma, rocamāna,* shining: the Scholiast supplies *hara*: elsewhere the *Maruts* are said to have golden cuirasses on their breasts, and possibly *rukma* here implies the same.

५५९९. प्र बुध्न्या व ईरते महांसि प्र नामानि प्रयज्यवस्तिरध्वम्।

सहस्रियं दम्यं भागमेतं गृहमेधीयं मरुतो जुषध्वम्॥१४॥

14. Your celestial splendours, *Maruts*, spread wide: objects of worship, you send down (the waters) that beat down (the dust): accept, *Maruts*, this your portion of the domestic worship of the household multiplied a thousand-fold.

Waters that Beat Down the Dust— *Nāmāni tiradhvam, pāṅsūn namayanti; nāmāni udakāni: namani* means waters, for they bend down the dust.

Multiplied a Thousand-Fold— How can one portion become a thousand? Asks the Scholiast; and he answers by quoting a rather obscurely expressed text, which implies that the amounts of an offering is computed, not by its actual number, but by that assigned to it by the divinity to whom it is offered, *yāvad ekā devatā kāmayate, yāvadekā tāvad āhutiḥ prathate.*

५६००. यदि स्तुतस्य मरुतो अधीथेत्था विप्रस्य वाजिनो हवीमन्।

मक्षू रायः सुवीर्यस्य दात नू चिद्यमन्य आदभदरावा॥१५॥

15. If, *Maruts*, you justly appreciate the praise of the devout offerer of (sacrificial) food, conjoined with oblations, then promptly bestow (upon us) riches, comprehending excellent male posterity, such as no unfriendly man can take away.

५६०१. अत्यासो न ये मरुतः स्वञ्चो यक्षदृशो न शुभयन्त मर्याः।

ते हर्म्येष्ठाः शिशवो न शुभ्रा वत्सासो न प्रक्रीळिनः पयोधाः॥१६॥

16. The swift-moving *Maruts* are like rapid horses, shining like men gazing at a festival innocent as children in the (paternal) mansion, frolicksome as calves, they are the dispensers of water.

५६०२. दशस्यन्तो नो मरुतो मृळन्तु वरिवस्यन्तो रोदसी सुमेके।

आरे गोहा नृहा वधो वो अस्तु सुम्नेभिरस्मे वसवो नमध्वम्॥१७॥

17. May the munificent *Maruts*, filling the beautiful heaven and earth with their glory, make us happy: your fatal weapon, the render of clouds, the destroyer of men, be far from us: bend down to us, *Vasus*, with blessings.

५६०३. आ वो होता जोहवीति सत्तः सत्राचीं रातिं मरुतो गृणानः।

य ईवतो वृषणो अस्ति गोपाः सो अद्वयावी हवते व उक्थैः॥१८॥

18. Praising your universal liberality, *Maruts*, the ministrant priest repeatedly worships you, seated (in the sacrificial chamber): he, showerers (of benefits), who is the guardian of the zealous (worshipper), he (the priest), who is void of insincerity, glorifies you with hymns.

५६०४. इमे तुरं मरुतो रामयन्तीमे सहः सहस आ नमन्ति।

इमे शंसं वनुष्यतो नि पान्ति गुरु द्वेषो अररुषे दधन्ति॥१९॥

19. These, *Maruts*, give pleasure to the zealous (worshipper): these humble the strength of the strong man: these protect their adorers from the malignant: they entertain severe displeasure towards the withholder of offerings.

५६०५. इमे रध्रं चिन्मरुतो जुनन्ति भृमिं चिद्यथा वसवो जुषन्त।

अप बाधध्वं वृषणस्तमांसि धत्त विश्वं तनयं तोकमस्मे॥२०॥

20. These *Maruts*, encourage the prosperous man: they encourage the (poor) wanderer: they, as *Vasus*, are pleased (with you): showerers (of benefits), dissipate the darkness: grant us many sons and grandsons.

५६०६. मा वो दात्रान्मरुतो निरराम मा पश्चाद्घ्म रथ्यो विभागे। आ नः

स्पार्हे भजतना वस्व्ये३ यदीं सुजातं वृषणो वो अस्ति॥२१॥

21. Never, *Maruts*, may we be excluded from your bounty: let us not, lords of chariots, be last in its apportionment: make us

sharers in that desirable opulence which, showerers (of benefits), in born of you.

५६०७. सं यद्धनन्त मन्युभिर्जनास: शूरा यह्वीष्वोषधीषु विक्षु।
अर्ध स्मा नो मरुतो रुद्रियासक्त्रातारों भूत पृतनास्वर्य:॥२२॥

22. When heroic men, filled with wrath, assemble for (the sake of conquering) many plants and people, then, *Maruts*, sons of *Rudra*, be our defenders in battles against our enemies.

Many Plants and People— *Bahviṣu, oṣadhiṣu vikṣu* is explained, *mahatīṣu oṣadhiṣu prajāsu jetavyāsu* in great plants and people to be subdued; by plants or vegetables, *oṣadhi,* we may perhaps understand cultivated lands.

५६०८. भूरि चक्र मरुत: पित्र्याण्युक्थानि या व: शस्यन्ते पुरा चित्।
मरुद्भिरुग्र: पृतनासु साळ्हा मरुद्भिरित्सनिता वाजमर्वा॥२३॥

23. You have bestowed, *Maruts*, many (benefits) on our forefathers, which praiseworthy (benefits) have been celebrated in former times: by the (favour of the) *Maruts* the fierce (warrior) is victorious in combats: by the (favour of the) *Maruts* the worshipper ever obtains food.

The Worshipper ever Obtains Food— *Marudbhir, it, sanitā vājam arvā:* the last word is explained, *stotrair abhigantā,* one who overcomes by praises; or it may have its usual sense of a house, when the sentence may be rendered, through the *Maruts* a horse is the obtainer (of success) in war.

५६०९. अस्मे वीरो मरुत: शुष्म्यस्तु जनानां यो असुरो विधर्ता।
अपो येन सुक्षितये तरेमाध स्वमोको अभि व: स्याम॥२४॥

24. May our male progeny, *Maruts*, be vigorous, one who is intelligent, the scatterer of (hostile) men, by whom we may cross the water (of enmity) to a secure dwelling: may we, your (servants), dwell in our own abode.

५६१०. तन्न इन्द्रो वरुणो मित्रो अग्निराप ओषधीर्वनिनो जुषन्त।
शर्मन्त्स्याम मरुतामुपस्थे यूयं पात स्वस्तिभि: सदा न:॥२५॥

25. May *Indra, Varuṇa, Mitra, Agni,* the waters, the plants, the trees, be pleased with us: may we recline in happiness upon the lap of the *Maruts:* and do you ever cherish us with blessings.

[सूक्त-५७]

[**ऋषि**– वसिष्ठ मैत्रा-वरुणि। **देवता**– मरुद्गण। **छन्द**– त्रिष्टुप्।]

५६११. मध्वों वो नाम मारुतं यजत्राः प्र यज्ञेषु शवसा मदन्ति।

ये रेजयन्ति रोदसी चिदुर्वी पिन्वन्त्युत्सं यदयासुरुग्राः॥१॥

1. Adorable (*Maruts*), the worshippers vigorously celebrate at sacrifices your appellation of company of the *Maruts*, they who cause the spacious heaven and earth to tremble, the clouds to rain, the move everywhere terrible.

५६१२. निचेतारो हि मरुतो गृणन्तं प्रणेतारो यजमानस्य मन्म।

अस्माकमद्य विदथेषु बर्हिरा वीतये सदत पिप्रियाणाः॥२॥

2. The *Maruts* verily are the benefactors of him who praises them, the gratifiers of the wishes of the institutor of the solemnity: do you, being pleased, sit down today upon the grass at our ceremony, to partake (of the sacrificial food).

५६१३. नैतावदन्ये मरुतो यथेमे भ्राजन्ते रुक्मैरायुधैस्तनूभिः।

आ रोदसी विश्वपिशः पिशानाः समानमञ्ज्यञ्जते शुभे कम्॥३॥

3. No other (deities give) such (good things) as the *Maruts*, as they shine with brilliant (ornaments), weapons and persons: illumining heaven and earth, wide-radiating, they heighten their common lustre for (our) good.

५६१४. ऋधक्सा वो मरुतो दिद्युदस्तु यद्व आगः पुरुषता कराम।

मा वस्तस्यामपि भूमा यजत्रा अस्मे वो अस्तु सुमतिश्चनिष्ठा॥४॥

4. May that blazing (weapon) of your, *Maruts*, be far from us, although, through human infirmities, we offer you offence: let us not, adorable *Maruts*, be exposed to your (shaft): may your favour, the source of abundance. Ever be shown unto us.

५६१५. कृते चिदत्र मरुतो रणन्तानवद्यासः शुचयः पावकाः।

प्र णोऽवत सुमतिभिर्यजत्राः प्र वाजेभिस्तिरत पुष्यसे नः॥५॥

5. May the *Maruts* who are irreproachable, pure, and purifying, delight in this our ceremony: protect us, adorable *Maruts*, with favourable thoughts: be ever anxious to sustain us with food.

५६१६. उत स्तुतासो मरुतो व्यन्तु विश्वेभिर्नामभिर्नरो हवींषि।

ददात नो अमृतस्य प्रजायै जिगृत राय: सूनृता मघानि।।६।।

6. May the glorified *Maruts* partake of the oblations, they who, accompanied by the bending waters, are the leaders of rites: bestow water, *Maruts*, upon our progeny, return suitable opulence for (the donation of sacrificial) riches.

५६१७. आ स्तुतासो मरुतो विश्व ऊती अच्छा सूरीन्त्सर्वताता जिगात।

ये नस्त्मना शतिनो वर्धयन्ति यूयं पात स्वस्तिभि: सदा न:।।७।।

7. Glorified *Maruts*, do you all come at the time of sacrifice to the presence of the worshippers along with your protections, for you are they who, of your own will, multiply our hundreds: do you ever cherish us with blessings.

Who...Multiply our Hundreds— *Ye nas tmanā śatino vardhayanti,* who increase us, that with sons, grandsons, and the like, we may become hundreds.

[सूक्त-५८]

[ऋषि– वसिष्ठ मैत्रा-वरुणि। **देवता–** मरुद्गण। **छन्द–** त्रिष्टुप्।]

५६१८. प्र साकमुक्षे अर्चता गणाय यो दैव्यस्य धाम्नस्तुविष्मान्।

उत क्षोदन्ति रोदसी महित्वा नक्षन्ते नाकं निर्ऋतेरवंशात्।।१।।

1. Offer worship to the company (of the *Maruts*), the associated dispensers of moisture, which is powerful over the celestial region: the *Maruts*, by their greatness, oppress both heaven and earth: they spread from the earth and the firmament to heaven.

They Spread, from the Earth and the Firmament to Heaven— *Nakṣante nākam nirṛti avaṁsāt: nirṛti* is here said to be a synonym of *bhūmi,* and *avaṁsa* of the *antarikṣa.*

५६१९. जनूश्छिद्रो मरुतस्त्वेष्येण भीमासस्तुविमन्यवोऽयास:।

प्र ये महोभिरोजसोत सन्ति विश्वो वो यामन्भयते स्वर्दृक्।।२।।

2. Formidable, high-spirited, quick-moving *Maruts*, your birth is from the illustrious *Rudra*: every gazer on the sun is alarmed with the course of you who are preeminent in lustre and strength.

Every Gazer on the Sun— *Viśvaḥ svardṛk,* that is, all living creatures; or it may mean also, according to Sāyaṇa, what looks up to the sky, that is, a tree, trees being naturally alarmed at the approach of the wind.

५६२०. बृहद्द्यौं मघवंद्भ्यो दधात जुजोषन्निन्मरुतः सुष्टुतिं नः।
गतो नाध्वा वि तिर्रति जन्तुं प्र णः स्पार्हाभिरूतिभिस्तिरेत ॥३॥

3. Grant, *Maruts*, to us who are affluent (in sacrificial offering) abundant food; accept complacently our earnest praise: the path you follow is not hurtful to living beings: may it increase our (prosperity) by (your) desirable protections.

५६२१. युष्मोतो विप्रो मरुतः शतस्वी युष्मोतो अर्वा सहुरिः सहस्री।
युष्मोतः सम्राळुत हंन्ति वृत्रं प्र तद्वो अस्तु धूतयो देष्णम् ॥४॥

4. The pious man protected, *Maruts*, by you, is the possessor of hundreds: the assailant, overcomer (of his foes), protected by you, is he possessor of thousands: protected by you, the Emperor slays his enemy: may the wealth that is given, agitators, by you ever by abundant.

५६२२. ताँ आ रुद्रस्य मीळ्हुषों विवासे कुविन्नंसन्ते मरुतः पुनर्नः।
यत्सस्वर्तां जिहीळिरे यदाविरव तदेन ईमहे तुराणाम् ॥५॥

5. I adore those sons of the showerer, *Rudra*: may the *Maruts*, repeatedly invoked, again come to us: may we expiate (by praise) whatever we have committed secretly or openly against the swift-moving *Maruts*, by which they are displeased.

५६२३. प्र सा वाचि सुष्टुतिर्मघोनामिदं सूक्तं मरुतो जुषन्त।
आराच्चिद्द्वेषों वृषणो युयोत यूयं पांत स्वस्तिभिः सदां नः ॥६॥

6. The pious praise of the opulent *Maruts* has been recite: may the *Maruts* be gratified by this hymn: remove far from us, showerers (of benefits), those who hate us: and do you ever cherish us with blessings.

[सूक्त-५९]

[ऋषि- वसिष्ठ मैत्रावरुणि। देवता- मरुद्गण, १२ रुद्र (मृत्यु विमोचनी)।
छन्द- प्रगाथ (विषमा बृहती, समा सतोबृहती), ७-८ त्रिष्टुप्, ९-११ गायत्री,
१२ अनुष्टुप्।]

५६२४. यं त्रायध्व इदमिदं देवासो यं च नयथ।
तस्मा अग्ने वरुण मित्रार्यमन्मरुतः शर्म यच्छत ॥१॥

1. *Agni, Varuṇa, Mitra, Maruts*, grant happiness, gods, to him whom you preserve from (the perils of) this (world), whom you guide here (to the paths of virtue).

From this World...to the Paths of Virtue— *Yam trāyadhvam idam idam, yam ca nayatha*: *idam* is explained, in the first place, by *itas,* from this, *bhayahetoḥ,* cause of peril; in the second, *idam* implies *san-mārgam,* road of virtue.

५६२५. युष्माकं देवा अवसाहनि प्रिय ईजानस्तरति द्विष:।

प्र स क्षयं तिरते वि महीरिषो यो वो वराय दाशति॥२॥

2. Through your protection, gods, the man who worships on an auspicious day overcomes his adversaries: he who offers abundant (sacrificial) food to you to detain you (at his rite) enlarges his habitation.

५६२६. नहि वश्चरमं चन वसिष्ठ: परिमंसते।

अस्माकमद्य मरुत: सुते सचा विश्वे पिबत कामिन:॥३॥

3. *Vasiṣṭha* overlooks not the very lowest among you: *Maruts,* who are desirous (of the libation), do you all drink together today of our effused *Soma* juices.

Sāmaveda, 241.

५६२७. नहि व ऊति: पृतनासु मर्धति यस्मा अराध्वं नर:।

अभि व आवर्त्सुमतिर्नवीयसी तूयं यात पिपीषव:॥४॥

4. Your protection, leaders (of rites), yields no detriment to him whom you defend in battles: may your latest favour return to us: come quickly, eager to drink the *Soma.*

५६२८. ओ षु घृष्विराधसो यातनान्धांसि पीतये।

इमा वो हव्या मरुतो ररे हि कं मो ष्व1ऽन्यत्र गन्तन॥५॥

5. Do you whose riches are connected together come to partake of the (sacrificial) viands, for, *Maruts,* I offer to you these oblations, therefore go not away to any other (sacrifice).

५६२९. आ च नो बर्हि: सदताविता च न: स्याहणि दातवे वसु।

अस्रेधन्तो मरुत: सोम्ये मधौ स्वाहेह मादयाध्वै॥६॥

6. Sit down on our sacred grass: come to bestow upon us desirable riches: doing no harm, *Maruts* delight in the sweet *Soma* libation presented at this season.

५६३०. सस्वश्चिद्धि तन्व: शुम्भमाना आ हंसासो नीलपृष्ठा अपप्तन्।

विश्वं शर्धो अभितो मा नि षेद नरो न रण्वा: सवने मदन्त:॥७॥

7. May the *Maruts* yet unrevealed, decorating their persons, descend like black-backed swans: let the entire company gather round me like happy men rejoicing together at a solemn rite.

५६३१. यो नों मरुतो अभि दुर्हणायुस्तिरश्चित्तानि वसवो जिघांसति।
     द्रुह: पाशान्प्रति स मुचीष्ट तपिष्ठेन हन्मेना हन्तना तम्॥८॥

8. The man, *Maruts*, who wounds our feelings, he who, rebuked by all, yet seeks, *Vasus*, to kill us, he would bind us in the wounds of (*Varuṇa*), the avenger (of iniquity), such a man do you destroy with a consuming fatal weapon.

५६३२. सान्तपना इदं हविर्मरुतस्तज्जुजुष्टन। युष्माकोती रिशादस:॥९॥

9. *Maruts*, destroyers of foes, this oblation is designed for you: do you, who are the devourers of enemies, (coming) with your protections, graciously accept it.

५६३३. गृहमेधास आ गेत मरुतो माप भूतन। युष्माकोती सुदानव:॥१०॥

10. Objects of domestic worship, munificent *Maruts*, come with your protections: go not away.

५६३४. इहेहं व: स्वतवस: कवेय: सूर्यत्वच:। यज्ञं मरुत आ वृणे॥११॥

11. *Maruts*, of independent strength, who are far-seeing, glorious as the sun, come hither, come hither, I invoke you to the sacrifice.

Glorious as the Sun— The text has *Sūrya tvacas,* literally, sun-skinned.

५६३५. त्र्यम्बकं यजामहे सुगन्धिं पुष्टिवर्धनम्।
     उर्वारुकमिव बन्धनान्मृत्योर्मुक्षीय मामृतात्॥१२॥

12. We worship *Tryambaka,* whose fame is fragrant, the augmenter of increase: may I be liberated from death, and, like the *Urvāruka* from its stalk, but not to immortality: let us worship *Trayambaka,* whose fame is fragrant, the augmenter of increase: may I be liberated from death like the *Urvaruka* from its stalk, but not unto immortality.

Tryambaka— According to the Scholiast the term streams the father, *ambuka,* of the three deities, *Brahma, Viṣṇu* and *Rudra*: the *Ṛg-vidhan* identifies him with *mahatva*: but the authority is of no great weight.

Whose Fame is Fragrant— *Sugandhim* is explained, *prasāritapuṇya kīrtim,* whose fame of virtue is spread; or as illustrated by another text quoted in the comment, in like manner as the fragrance of a tree full in flower sheds sweetness, so spreads the gragrance of holy actions; the memory of the just, smell sweet and blossoms in the dust.

The Augmenter of Increase— *Puṣṭi-vardhanam,* the augmenter of nutrition, is interpreted, *jagad-vījam,* the seed of the world; but the simple meaning of the multiplier of good things subservient to objects of bodily enjoyment, as wealth, *śarīradhanadiviṣayān vardhayati yaḥ,* is preferable.

May I be Liberated from Death— *Mṛtyor makṣiya* may also mean, may I be liberated from the world, or the revolutions of life and death: may I attain *mokṣa.*

Urvāruka— The *urvāruka* is called also the *karkaṭi,* a species of cucumber.

But not to Immortality— *Māmṛtāt mā ā amṛta,* not to or until the immortal or immortality, understanding thereby either the long life of the gods or *svarga* paradise. The wish expressed being for final emancipation: this notion, and the denomination *Tryambaka,* are, in my opinion, decisive of the spuriousness of this stanza: the repetition of the half stanza to make up a whole is something unusual; the verse occurs in the *Yajurveda,* 3. 60, and is, in some instances differently interpreted: *Tryambaka* is termed *nātratrayopetām Rudram,* the triocular *Rudra:* *sugandhim, divya-gandhopetām,*[1] of celestial fragrance: the *urvāruka* is said to mean the *karkandhu,* which, when ripe falls of itself from its stalk.

[सूक्त-६०]

[ऋषि- वसिष्ठ मैत्रावरुणि। **देवता**- मित्रावरुण, १ सूर्य। **छन्द**- त्रिष्टुप्।]

५६३६. यदद्य सूर्य ब्रवोऽनागा उद्यन्मित्राय वरुणाय सत्यम्।
वयं देवत्रादिते स्याम् तव प्रियासो अर्यमन् गृणन्तः॥१॥

1. Sūrya, when rising today, declare the truth to *Mitra* and *Varuṇa,* that we are void of sin: may we, *Aditi,* be (approved of) among the gods: praising you, *Aryaman,* may we be dear to you.

५६३७. एष स्य मित्रावरुणा नृचक्षा उभे उदेति सूर्यो अभि ज्मन्।
विश्वस्य स्थातुर्जगतश्च गोपा ऋजु मर्तेषु वृजिना च पश्यन्॥२॥

2. This Sūrya, the beholder of man, rises, *Mitra* and *Varuṇa,* upon both (heaven and earth), moving (in the sky): he who is the preserver of all that is stationary or moveable, witnessing the upright acts or the sins of mortals.

---

१. यथा वृक्षस्य संपुष्पितस्य दूराद्गन्धो वात्येवं पुण्यस्य कृर्मणो दूराद्गन्धो वाति (तै० आ०
१०.९)।

५६३८. अयुक्त सप्त हरितः सधस्थादा ई वहन्ति सूर्यं घृताचीः।
धामानि मित्रावरुणा युवाकुः सं यो यूथेव जनिमानि चष्टे॥३॥

3. He has harnessed his seven bay steeds, *Mitra* and *Varuṇa*, (to come) from your common dwelling-place, (the firmament): the horses that, shedding water, convey that *Sūrya* who, friendly to your both, (contemplates all) regions, and looks carefully upon living creatures as (a herdsman) upon the herd.

५६३९. उद्वां पृक्षासो मधुमन्तो अस्थुरा सूर्यो अरुहच्छुक्रमर्णः।
यस्मा आदित्या अध्वनो रदन्ति मित्रो अर्यमा वरुणः सजोषाः॥४॥

4. For you, (*Mitra* and *Varuṇa*), the sweet-flavoured viands have been prepared: the sun has ascended the shining firmament, for whom the *Ādityas* and the consentient *Mitra, Varuṇa, Aryaman* make ready the paths.

५६४०. इमे चेतारो अनृतस्य भूरेर्मित्रो अर्यमा वरुणो हि सन्ति।
इम ऋतस्य वावृधुर्दुरोणे शग्मासः पुत्रा अदितेरदब्धाः॥५॥

5. These (deities), *Mitra, Aryaman, Varuṇa*, are the detectors of much untruth: these unconquered sons of *Aditi*, dispensers of happiness, are magnified in the hall of sacrifice.

५६४१. इमे मित्रो वरुणो दूळभासोऽचेतसं चिच्चितयन्ति दक्षैः।
अपि क्रतुं सुचेतसं वर्तन्तस्तिरश्चिदंहः सुपथा नयन्ति॥६॥

6. These, the unsubdued *Mitra, Varuṇa*, and *Aryaman*, animate with energies the unconscious (sleepers): repairing to the intelligent performer (of pious acts), they lead (him), by safe paths (to heaven), removing all iniquity.

५६४२. इमे दिवो अनिमिषा पृथिव्याश्चिकित्वांसो अचेतसं नयन्ति।
प्रव्राजे चिन्नद्यो गाधमस्ति पारं नो अस्य विष्पितस्य पर्षन्॥७॥

7. (Beholding) with unclosing eyes, and cognizant (of the things) of heaven and earth, they conduct the ignorant man (to duty): in the lowest depth of the river, (through them), there is a bottom: may they lead us to the opposite shore of the vast expanse.

To the Opposite Shore of the Vast Expanse— *Viśpitasya parṣam*: the former is explained only by *vyāptitasya,* expanded: Sāyaṇa supplies the substantive *karmaṇaḥ* act duty.

५६४३. यद् गोपावददितिः शर्म भद्रं मित्रो यच्छन्ति वरुणः सुदासे।
तस्मिन्ना तोकं तनयं दधाना मा कर्म देवहेळनं तुरासः॥८॥

8. Including our sons and grandsons in that preserving and auspicious felicity which *Aditi*, *Mitra*, and *Varuṇa* confer upon the liberal donor (of the oblation), may we never, acting precipitately, incur the displeasure of the deities.

५६४४. अव वेदिं होत्राभिर्यजेत रिपः काश्चिद्विरुणधृतः सः।
परि द्वेषोभिरर्यमा वृणक्तूरुं सुदासे वृषणा उ लोकम्॥९॥

9. Let my adversary desecrate the altar by (ill-expressed) praises: repelled by *Varuṇa*, may he (undergo) various sufferings: may *Aryaman* defend us from those who hate us: confer, showerers (of benefits), a vast region upon the liberal donor (of oblations).

५६४५. सस्वश्चिद्धि समृतिस्त्वेष्येषामपीच्येन सहसा सहन्ते।
युष्मद्भिया वृषणो रेजमाना दक्षस्य चिन्महिना मृळता नः॥१०॥

10. The association of these (three deities) is of mysterious lustre: by their secret strength they overcome (all enemies): showerers (of benefits), through fear (of you our opponents) are trembling: have mercy upon us in the mightiness of your strength.

५६४६. यो ब्रह्मणे सुमतिमायजाते वाजस्य सातौ परमस्य रायः।
सीक्षन्त मन्युं मघवानो अर्य उरु क्षयाय चक्रिरे सुधातु॥११॥

11. These munificent (deities) conjointly accept the praise of the worshipper, and bestow a spacious mansion for a dwelling upon him who, for the sake of food and excellent riches, devotes his mind to your glorification.

Who Devotes his Mind to your Glorification— *Yo brahmane sumatim āyajāte* is explained, *yo yajamāno dadāti śobhanām buddhim yuṣmat stoktrūpāya*, the institutor of the rite, who gives pure or pious understanding to the nature or form of your praise.

५६४७. इयं देव पुरोहितिर्युवभ्यां यज्ञेषु मित्रावरुणावकारि।
विश्वानि दुर्गा पिपृतं तिरो नो यूयं पात स्वस्तिभिः सदा नः॥१२॥

12. Excellent *Mitra* and *Varuṇa*, to you this adoration at sacrifices is addressed: remove from us all difficulties, and ever cherish us with blessings.

[सूक्त-६१]

[ऋषि- वसिष्ठ मैत्रावरुणि। देवता- मित्रावरुण। छन्द- त्रिष्टुप्।]

५६४८. उद्वां चक्षुर्वरुण सुप्रतीकं देवयोरेति सूर्यस्ततन्वान्।

अभि यो विश्वा भुवनानि चष्टे स मन्युं मर्त्येष्वा चिकेत।।१।।

1. Spreading around the beautiful light, *Mitra* and *Varuṇa*, of you two divinities, *Sūrya* rises: he who beholds all existing beings apprehends the acts of mortals.

५६४९. प्र वां स मित्रावरुणावृतावा विप्रो मन्मानि दीर्घश्रुदियर्ति।

यस्य ब्रह्माणि सुक्रतू अवाथ आ यत्क्रत्वा न शरदः पृणैथे।।२।।

2. The sage, the solemnizer of sacrifice, the ancient hearer (of holy prayer), earnestly repeats, *Mitra* and *Varuṇa*, your praises: he whose prayers, doers of good deeds, you favour, whose acts (of worship) you recompense not for years.

The Ancient Hearer of Holy Prayer— The text has *dīrghaśrut*, which is explained only by *cirakālam śrotā*, a hearer for a long time, an epithet of *Vasiṣṭha,* but in what sense is somewhat uncertain.

You recompense not for Years— *Ā yatkratvā na śaradaḥ pṛṇaithe* is explained, *yat karma bahūn saṃvatsarān apūrayethe,* whose act you fill or fulfil many years: the Scholiast passes by *na,* which may be the conjunction *and* as well as the negative *not*: in either case the sense is obscure: it may mean that the merit of the worship is so great that it cannot be adequately rewarded except after a long period.

५६५०. प्रोरोर्मित्रावरुणा पृथिव्याः प्र दिव ऋष्वाद्बृहतः सुदानू।

स्पशो दधाथे ओषधीषु विक्ष्वृधग्यतो अनिमिषं रक्षमाणा।।३।।

3. You are vaster, *Mitra* and *Varuṇa*, than the ample earth, vaster, bounteous donors, than the glorious and expansive heaven: you maintain beauty in plants and in people, diligent observers of truth, and vigilantly protecting (us).

You are Vaster— This is said to be implied by the preposition *pra* in the text, put for *prariricāthe,* as in *Sūkta* (xi. *Maṇḍala* i. verse 9) where we have the compound verb *praririce.*

५६५१. शंसा मित्रस्य वरुणस्य धाम शुष्मो रोदसी बद्बधे महित्वा।

अयन्मासा अर्यम्णो जनामवीराः प्र यज्ञमन्मा वृजनं तिराते।।४।।

4. Praise the splendour of *Mitra* and *Varuṇa*, whose strength, by its mightiness, keeps heaven and earth asunder: may the days of

those who differ not worship pass without male descendants: may
he who delights in sacrifice increase in prosperity.

५६५२. अमूरा विश्वा वृषणाविमा वां न यासु चित्रं ददृशे न यक्षम्।

दुहः सचन्ते अनृता जनानां न वां निण्यान्यचिते अभूवन्॥५॥

5. Unperplexed, all-pervading showerers (of benefits), these
(praises) are for you, in which nothing surprising, no adoration
(worthy of you) is beheld: the insincere commendations of men
serve as offences: eulogies of you, although offered in secret, are
not unappreciated.

५६५३. समु वां यज्ञं महयं नमोभिर्हुवे वां मित्रावरुणा सबाधः।

प्र वां मन्मान्यृचसे नवानि कृतानि ब्रह्म जुजुषन्निमानि॥६॥

6. I offer sacrifice to you two with praises, I invoke you, *Mitra*
and *Varuṇa*, when in trouble: may the present hymns be capable of
gratifying you: may these (my) prayers be acceptable to you both.

५६५४. इयं देव पुरोहितिर्युवभ्यां यज्ञेषु मित्रावरुणावकारि।

विश्वानि दुर्गा पिपृतं तिरो नो यूयं पात स्वस्तिभिः सदा नः॥७॥

7. To you, divine *Mitra* and *Varuṇa*, to you this adoration at
sacrifices is addressed: remove from us all difficulties, and ever
cherish us with blessings.

[सूक्त-६२]

[ऋषि– वसिष्ठ मैत्रावरुणि। देवता– मित्रावरुण, १ सूर्य। छन्द– त्रिष्टुप्।]

५६५५. उत्सूर्यो बृहदर्चींष्यश्रेतपुर विश्वा जनिम मानुषाणाम्।

समो दिवा ददृशे रोचमानः क्रत्वा कृतः सुकृतः कर्तृभिर्भूत्॥१॥

1. *Sūrya* spreads his vast and numerous rays over all the
crowds of men: shining bright by day, he is beheld (by all) the
same, the creator, the created, he is glorified by his worshippers.

The Creator, the Created— *Kratvā kṛtaḥ* are explained, *Sarvasya
kartā prajāpatinā saṁpāditaḥ,* the maker of all produced by *Prajāpati.*

५६५६. स सूर्य प्रति पुरो न उद्गा एभिः स्तोमेभिरेतशेभिरेवैः।

प्र नो मित्राय वरुणाय वोचोऽनागसो अर्यम्णे अग्नये च॥२॥

2. Rise up before us, *Sūrya*, with your glorious white horses:
declare us free from sin to *Mitra, Varuṇa, Aryaman,* and *Agni.*

५६५७. वि न: सहस्रं शुरुधो रदन्त्वृतावानो वरुणो मित्रो अग्नि:।
यच्छन्तु चन्द्रा उपमं नो अर्कमा न: कामं पूपुरन्तु स्तवाना:॥३॥

3. May *Varuṇa*, *Mitra*, and *Agni*, the alleviators of pain, the
observers of truth, bestow upon us thousand (of riches): may they,
the givers of delight, grant us excellent (food): glorified by us, may
they fulfil our desires.

५६५८. द्यावाभूमी अदिते त्रासीथां नो ये वां जज्ञु: सुजनिमान ऋष्वे।
मा हेळे भूम वरुणस्य वायोर्मा मित्रस्य प्रियतमस्य नृणाम्॥४॥

4. Indivisible and mighty heaven and earth protect us who, of
fortunate birth, have knowledge of you both: let us not incur the
displeasure of *Varuṇa*, or of *Vāyu*, or of *Mitra*, the best beloved of
men.

५६५९. प्र बाहवा सिसृतं जीवसे न आ नो गव्यूतिमुक्षतं घृतेन।
आ नो जने श्रवयतं युवाना श्रुतं मे मित्रावरुणा हवेमा॥५॥

5. Stretch forth your arms for the prolongation of our
existence, bedew with water the pastures of our cattle, render us
honoured among men: ever youthful *Mitra* and *Varuṇa*, hear these
my invocations.

Yajurveda, 21. 9: Mahīdhara's interpretation is to the same purport as
Sāyaṇa's, with slight variations.

५६६०. नू मित्रो वरुणो अर्यमा नस्त्मने तोकाय वरिवो दधन्तु।
सुगा नो विश्वा सुपथानि सन्तु यूयं पात स्वस्तिभि: सदा न:॥६॥

6. May *Mitra*, *Varuṇa*, Aryaman grant affluence to us and to
our posterity: may all paths be easy of access unto us: and do you
ever cherish us with blessings.

[सूक्त-६३]

[ऋषि– वसिष्ठ मैत्रावरुणि। देवता– १-४ तथा ५ पूर्वार्द्ध– सूर्य, ५ उत्तरार्द्ध
तथा ६ मित्रावरुण। छन्द– त्रिष्टुप्।]

५६६१. उद्वेति सुभगो विश्वचक्षा: साधारण: सूर्यो मानुषाणाम्।
चक्षुर्मित्रस्य वरुणस्य देवश्चर्मेव य: समविव्यक् तमांसि॥१॥

1. The auspicious *Sūrya* rises, the eye of all, the common
(parent) of men: the divine eye of *Mitra* and of *Varuṇa*, who
breaks through the glooms as through (investing) skin.

५६६२. उद्वेति प्रसवीता जनानां महान् केतुरर्णव: सूर्यस्य।

समानं चक्रं पर्याविवृत्सन्यदेतशो वहति धूर्षु युक्त:॥२॥

2. The animator of men arises, the great rain-shedding banner
of *Sūrya* rolling on the universal wheel, which the white steeds
yoked to his car drag along.

The Great Rain-Shedding Banner of Sūrya— *Mahān ketur,
arṇavaḥ sūryasya*, the banner or emblem of *Sūrya* is *Sūrya*, which is
probably all that Sāyaṇa means when he maintains that we have here an
arbitrary change of case, and that for *Sūryasya* we should have *Suryaḥ* in
the nominative.

५६६३. विभ्राजमान उषसामुपस्थाद् रेभैरुदैत्यनुमद्यमान:।

एष मे देव: सविता चच्छन्द य: समानं न प्रमिनाति धाम॥३॥

3. Delighted by the praises (of his worshippers), the radiant
sun rises from the lap of the dawns: that divine sun gratifies my
desires, who limits not the lustre that is common (to all).

५६६४. दिवो रुक्म उरुचक्षा उदैति दूरेअर्थस्तरणिर्भ्राजमान:।

नूनं जना: सूर्येण प्रसूता अयन्नर्थानि कृणवन्नपांसि॥४॥

4. The bright and glorious sun rises from the firmament far-
going, traversing (the heavens), diffusing light: verily all beings
animated by *Sūrya* proceed and execute their assigned labours.

५६६५. यत्रा चक्रुरमृता गातुमस्मै श्येनो न दीयन्नन्वेति पाथ:।

प्रति वां सूर उदिते विधेम नमोभिर्मित्रावरुणोत हव्यै:॥५॥

5. He travels the path which the immortals have prepared for
his course, darting along like a hawk: we worship you, *Mitra* and
Varuṇa, when the sun has risen, with praises and oblations.

५६६६. नू मित्रो वरुणो अर्यमा नस्तमने तोकाय वरिवो दधन्तु।

सुगा नो विश्वा सुपथानि सन्तु यूयं पात स्वस्तिभि: सदा न:॥६॥

6. May *Mitra*, *Varuṇa*, *Aryaman* grant affluence to us and to
our posterity: may all paths be easy of access to us, and do you
ever cherish us with blessings.

[सूक्त-६४]

[**ऋषि**- वसिष्ठ मैत्रावरुणि। **देवता**- मित्रावरुण। **छन्द**- त्रिष्टुप्।]

५६६७. दिवि क्षयन्ता रजस: पृथिव्यां प्र वां घृतस्य निर्णिजो ददीरन्।

हव्यं नो मित्रो अर्यमा सुजातो राजा सुक्षत्रो वरुणो जुषन्त॥१॥

1. Ruling over the water that are in heaven and earth, impelled by you, (the clouds) assume the form of rain may the auspiciously manifested *Mitra*, the royal *Aryaman*, the powerful *Varuṇa*, accept our oblation.

Impelled by You the Clouds Assume the form of Rain— *Pra vām ghṛtasya nirṇijo dadīran* is explained, *yuvābhyām preritā meghā udakasya rūpāṇi prayacchanti,* impelled by you the clouds give the forms of water; or, according to another explanation, *ghṛta* keeps its ordinary sense, the forms of butter, that is, oblations, are given to you.

५६६८. आ राजाना मह ऋतस्य गोपा सिन्धुपती क्षत्रिया यातमर्वाक्।
इळां नो मित्रावरुणोत वृष्टिमव दिव इन्वतं जीरदानू।।२।।

2. Sovereigns, mighty preservers of water, powerful lords of rivers, come to our presence: send down to us munificent *Mitra* and *Varuṇa*, from the firmament, sustenance and rain.

५६६९. मित्रस्तन्नो वरुणो देवो अर्यः प्र साधिष्ठेभिः पथिभिर्नयन्तु।
ब्रवद्यथा न आददिः सुदासं इषा मंदेम सह देवगोपाः।।३।।

3. May *Mitra*, *Varuṇa*, the divine *Aryaman*, conduct us by the most practicable paths, then, (when we desire their guidance), accordingly as *Aryaman* promises to the liberal donor (of oblations), may we, enjoying the protection of the gods, rejoice in abundance, together with posterity.

Rejoice . . . . . Together with Posterity— *Iśa madema saha,* with food rejoice, together with posterity, *putradibhiḥ,* understood.

५६७०. यो वां गर्तं मनसा तक्षदेतमूर्ध्वां धीतिं कृणवद्धारयच्च।
उक्षेथां मित्रावरुणा घृतेन ता राजाना सुक्षितीस्तर्पयेथाम्।।४।।

4. *Mitra* and *Varuṇa*, bedew with water him who fabricates your chariot in his mind, offering high praise, the people well affected towards him.

५६७१. एष स्तोमो वरुण मित्र तुभ्यं सोमः शुक्रो न वायवेऽयामि।
अविष्टं धियो जिगृतं पुरन्धीर्यूयं पात स्वस्तिभिः सदा नः।।५।।

5. *Varuṇa* and *Mitra*, this praise, pure as the *Soma* libation, has been offered to you, and also, *Aryaman*, (to you): protect our rites: be awake to our praises: and do you ever cherish us with blessings.

To *Aryaman*— The text has *vayave*: *Vāyu* is said to be a synonym of *Aryaman*.

[सूक्त-६५]

[ऋषि- वसिष्ठ मैत्रावरुणि। **देवता**- मित्रावरुण। **छन्द**- त्रिष्टुप्।]

५६७२. प्रति वां सूर उदिते सूक्तैर्मित्रं हुवे वरुणं पूतदक्षम्।
     ययोरसुर्यं् मक्षितं् ज्येष्ठं् विश्वस्य् यामन्नाचितां जिगत्नु।।१।।

1. When the sun has risen, I invoke *Mitra* and you, *Varuṇa*, of
pure vigour, whose imperishable and superior might is triumphant
in the crowded conflict over all enemies.

५६७३. ता हि देवानामसुरा तावर्या ता नः क्षिती: करतमूर्जयन्ती:।
     अश्याम मित्रावरुणा वयं् वां द्यावा च यत्र पीपयन्नहां च।।२।।

2. They verily are mighty among the gods: they are rulers: they
below upon us a numerous posterity: may we obtain you, *Mitra*
and *Varuṇa*, whether on earth or in heaven, and wherever the
(passing) days may preserve us.

५६७४. ता भूरिपाशावनृतस्य सेतू दुरत्येतू रिपवे मर्त्याय।
     ऋतस्य मित्रावरुणा पथा वामपो न नावा दुरिता तरेम।।३।।

3. Holders are you of many fetters, barriers against the
irreligious, invincible by hostile mortals: may we cross over all the
danger, *Mitra* and *Varuṇa*, by the path of sacrifice, to you, as (we
cross over) water by a boat.

५६७५. आ नो मित्रावरुणा हव्यजुष्टिं् घृतैर्गव्यूतिमुक्षतमिळाभि:।
     प्रति वामत्र वरमा जनाय पृणीतमुद्नो दिव्यस्य चारौ:।।४।।

4. Come, *Mitra* and *Varuṇa*, to our offered oblation sprinkle
our place of sacrifice with water and with viands (who) in this
world (may present to you such) excellent (donations) that you
may (thereby be induced to) gratify mankind with celestial and
beautiful water.

This passage is very obscurely expressed, although the purpose may
be guessed, with the aid of the Scholiast: it is literally, towards you two
here an excellent to man bestow of water celestial, beautiful (or flowing),
prati vām atra varama janaya pṛṇitam udnaḥ divyasya caroḥ.

५६७६. एष स्तोमो वरुण मित्र तुभ्यं् सोमः शुक्रो न वायवे ऽयामि।
     अविष्टं् धियो जिगृतं् पुरन्धीर्यूयं् पात स्वस्तिभि: सदा नः।।५।।

5. *Varuṇa* and *Mitra*, this praise, pure as the *Soma* libation, has been offered to you, and also, *Aryaman*, (to you): protect our rites: be awake to our praises: and do you ever cherish us with blessings.

[सूक्त-६६]

[ऋषि– वसिष्ठ मैत्रावरुणि। देवता– मित्रावरुण, ४-१३ आदित्यगण, १४-
१६ सूर्य। छन्द– गायत्री, १०-१५ प्रगाथ (समा बृहती, विषमा सतोबृहती),
१६ पुर उष्णिक।]

५६७७. प्र मित्रयोर्वरुणयो: स्तोमों न एतु शूष्य:। नमस्वान्तुविजातयों:॥१॥

1. May this our propitiatory praise, accompanied by oblations, proceed to you, *Mitra* and *Varuṇa*, of reiterated manifestations.

Of Reiterated Manifestations— *Tuvijātayoḥ,* repeatedly born, as presiding over day and night they may be said to be manifest repeatedly in daily succession.

५६७८. या धारयन्त देवा: सुदक्षा दक्षपितरा। असुर्याय प्रमहसा॥२॥

2. You whom the gods uphold for their invigoration, both mighty, masters of strength and of diffusive radiance.

५६७९. ता न: स्तिपा तनूपा वरुण जरितॄणाम्। मित्रं साधर्यतं धिय:॥३॥

3. Protectors of our dwellings, protectors of our persons, *Mitra* and *Varuṇa*, perfect the rites of your adorers.

५६८०. यद्द्य सूर उदितेऽनागा मित्रो अर्यमा। सुवाति सविता भग:॥४॥

4. May *Mitra*, the destroyer of sin, *Aryaman*, *Savitā*, *Bhaga*, bestow (upon us), today at sun-rise what (we pray for).
Sāmaveda. 1351; *Yajurveda,* 33. 20.

५६८१. सुप्रावीरस्तु स क्षय: प्र नु यार्मन्त्सुदानव:। ये नो अंहोऽतिपिप्रति॥५॥

5. May this our dwelling be well protected, liberal deities, on your departure, you who purify us from sin.

५६८२. उत स्वराजो अदितिरदब्धस्य व्रतस्य ये। महो राजान ईशते॥६॥

6. And who are sovereign over all, and, with *Aditi*, preside over this unobstructed and great ceremony.
Uta svarajo aditiradabdhasya vratasya ye, maho rajana iśate, the place of *Aditi,* is rather doubtful, as the text has no copulative: the Scholiast proposes as one reading. *Aditis teṣām mātā,* of them *Aditi* is the mother, or that which follows, *Mitradayo aditiśca, Mitra* and the rest and *Aditi.*

५६८३. प्रति वां सूर उदिते मित्रं गृणीषे वरुणम्। अर्यमणं रिशादसम्॥७॥

7. I glorify you, *Mitra* and *Varuṇa*, and *Aryaman*, the consumer of enemies when the sun has risen.

५६८४. राया हिरण्यया मतिरियमवृकाय शवसे। इयं विप्रा मेधसातये॥८॥

8. May this praise (be effective) for unimpeached strength, alone with golden treasure: may it (be effective), sages, for the fulfilment of (the objects of) the sacrifice.

५६८५. ते स्याम देव वरुण ते मित्र सूरिभिः सह। इषं स्वश्च धीमहि॥९॥

9. May we be thine, divine *Varuṇa*: may we, along with pious worshippers, be, *Mitra*, thine: may we obtain food and water.

May we Obtain Food and Water— *Isham svas ca dhimahi* is explained, *annam udakam ca dharayamahe*, may we retain food and water: this and the two preceding verse form a *Trica*, to be repeated at the morning sacrifice: they occur also *Sāmaveda*. 1067-69.

५६८६. बहवः सूरचक्षसोऽग्निजिह्वा ऋतावृधः।
त्रीणि ये येमुर्विदथानि धीतिभिर्विश्वानि परिभूतिभिः॥१०॥

10. Manifold radiant as the sun, *Agni*-tongued augmenters of sacrifice, you who have limited the three universal sacrifices with comprehensive rites.

Limited the three Universal Sacrifices, Etc.— Trini *ye yemuḥ vidathani dhitibhiḥ viśvani paribhutibhiḥ is explained, ye trini vyaptani kṣityadisthanani paribhavukaiḥ karmahiḥ prayacchanti*, who give the three spread places , earth and the rest, with overcoming acts: it is not very clear what is intended: perhaps merely to say that *Mitra* and the rest are worshipped as the objects of three rites, with definite ceremonies or at definite seasons.

५६८७. वि ये दधुः शरदं मासमादहर्यज्ञमकुं चादृचम्।
अनाप्यं वरुणो मित्रो अर्यमा क्षत्रं राजान आशत॥११॥

11. Who have established the year, and then the month and the day, the sacrifice, the night, and the holy text, they, the royal deities, *Varuṇa*, *Mitra*, *Aryaman*, enjoy unrivalled might.

५६८८. तद्वो अद्य मनामहे सूक्तैः सूर उदिते।
यदोहते वरुणो मित्रो अर्यमा यूयमृतस्य रथ्यः॥१२॥

12. Therefore today at sunrise we solicit you with hymns for (wealth), which *Varuṇa*, *Mitra*, *Aryaman*, bearers of water, you convey.

५६८९. ऋतावान ऋतजाता ऋतावृधो घोरासो अनृतद्विषः।
तेषां वः सुम्ने सुच्छर्दिष्टमे नरः स्याम् ये च सूर्यः॥१३॥

13. Accepters or rites, generated for rites, augmenters of rites, fierce enemies of the neglecter of rites, may we, as well as those men who are your adorers, be in (the enjoyment of) the highest felicity, all confirmed by you.

Those Men who are Etc.— *Teṣām vaḥ sumne succhardiṣṭame,* of those of you in the most blissful opulence, or in happiness, united with a most delightful dwelling, *sukhatame dhane, atyantaramaṇīyagṛhayukte sukhe vā.*

५६९०. उदु त्यद्दर्शतं वपुर्दिव एति प्रतिह्वरे।
यदीमाशुर्वहति देव एतशो विश्वस्मै चक्षसे अरम्॥१४॥

14. That beautiful orb (of the sun) rises on the near margin of the sky as the swift, divine, white-coloured (steed) bears it along for the beholding of all men.

५६९१. शीर्ष्णः शीर्ष्णो जगतस्तस्थुषस्पतिं समया विश्वमा रजः।
सप्त स्वसारः सुविताय सूर्यं वहन्ति हरितो रथे॥१५॥

15. The seven gliding steeds convey the sun, the lord of every individual moving or stationary thing, traversing the whole world in his chariot for the good (of all).

The Lord of Every Individual Moving or Stationary Thing— *Śirṣṇaḥ śirṣṇo jagatas tasthuṣaspatim,* the lord of stationary and moveable head by head: the Scholiast would apparently connect *Śiras* with the horses of the sun, the ablative or genitive being put for the instrumental, *śirasā, svasvaśira sa vahanti sūryam,* they bear the sun by his own head; or the head, says, may be put for the being with a head, *śiraḥ śabdena tad-van padārthaḥ,* that is to say, the whole of such objects, *tasya-kārtsnyam,* or the best of all, *sarvasya śreṣṭham:* he seems rather puzzled: it probably implies only each or individual.

५६९२. तच्चक्षुर्देवहितं शुक्रमुच्चरत्।
पश्येम शरदः शतं जीवेम शरदः शतम्॥१६॥

16. That pure eye (of the universe), beneficial of the gods, rises: may we behold it for a hundred years: may we live a hundred years.

Yajurveda, 36. 24. which adds, śṛṇuyāma śaradaḥ śatam, prabravāma śaradaḥ śatam, adīnaḥ syāma śaradaḥ śatam, bhuyaśca śaradaḥ śatam, may we hear, may we speak, may we be independent, for a hundred years or more.

५६९३. काव्यैभिरदाभ्या यांतं वरुण द्युमत्। मित्रश्च सोमपीतये॥१७॥

17. Unconquerable, resplendent *Varuṇa* and *Mitra*, (induced) by our praises, come to drink the *Soma* juice.

५६९४. दिवो धार्मभिर्वरुण मित्रश्चा यांतमद्रुहा। पिर्बतं सोममातुजी॥१८॥

18. Gentle *Mitra* and *Varuṇa*, destroyers of foes, come from heaven with your glories, and drink the *Soma* juice.

५६९५. आ यांतं मित्रावरुणा जुषाणावाहुतिं नरा। पातं सोममृतावृधा॥१९॥

19. Come, *Mitra* and *Varuṇa*, leaders of rites, propitiated by the oblation, and drink the *Soma,* augmenters of the sacred rite.

[सूक्त-६७]

[**ऋषि**– वसिष्ठ मैत्रावरुणि। **देवता**– अश्विनीकुमार। **छन्द**– त्रिष्टुप्।]

५६९६. प्रति वां रथं नृपती जरध्यै हविष्मता मनसा यज्ञियेन।
यो वां दूतो न धिष्ण्यावजीगरच्छां सूनुर्न पितरा विवक्मि॥१॥

1. Lords of men, (I approach) to adore your chariot with devout praise and oblation, I address it as if it were a messenger to awaken you, adorable deities, as a son (addresses) his parents.

५६९७. अशोच्यग्निः संमिधानो अस्मे उपो अदृश्रन्तमसश्चिदन्ताः।
अचेति केतुरुषसः पुरस्ताच्छ्रिये दिवो दुहितुर्जायमानः॥२॥

2. Kindled by us, *Agni* blazes, the extremities of the darkness are seen nigh at hand, the banner (of the sun) is preceived rising with the glory on the east of the dawn the daughter of heaven.

५६९८. अभि वां नूनमश्विना सुहोता स्तोमैः सिषक्ति नासत्या विवक्सान्।
पूर्वीभिर्यातं पथ्याभिर्वाकस्वर्विदा वसुमता रथेन॥३॥

3. Verily, *Aśvins*, the pious priest repeating (your praises) glorifies you, *Nāsatyās* with hymns: come therefore by formerly-trodden paths to our presence with your chariot, familiar with heaven, laden with treasure.

५६९९. अवोर्वां नूनमश्विना युवाकुर्हुवे यद्वां सुते मांध्वी वसूयुः।
आ वां वहन्तु स्थविरासो अश्वाः पिबाथो अस्मे सुषुता मधूनि॥४॥

4. Relying on you, *Aśvins*, as protectors, desirous of wealth, *Mādhvis*, I invoke you when the *Soma* is effused: may your stout horses bring you (hither): drink the sweet juice poured out by us.

५७००. प्राचींमु देवाश्विना धियं मेऽमृंझां सातयें कृतं वसूयुम्।

विश्वा अविष्टं वाजं आ पुरन्धीस्ता नंः शक्तं शचीपती शचींभिः।।५।।

5. Divine *Aśvins*, render my sincere and undisturbed adoration, offered for the sake of riches, (efficacious) for their acquisition: preserve all my faculties in (the time of) battle: protectors of pious acts (influenced) by our acts, bestow upon us (wealth).

५७०१. अविष्टं धीर्ध्वंश्विना न आसु प्रजावद्रेतो अहं्यं नो अस्तु।

आ वां तोके तनंये तूर्तुजानाः सुरत्नांसो देववींतिं गमेम।।६।।

6. Protect us, *Aśvins*, in these pious acts, may our procreative power fail not: but (through your favour) possessing sons and grandsons, distributing desired riches and enjoying ample wealth, may we accomplish the worship of the gods.

५७०२. एष स्य वां पूर्वगत्वेव सख्यें निधिर्हितो मांध्वी रातो अस्मे।

अहेंळता मनसा यांतमर्वांगश्रन्तां हव्यं मानुषींषु विक्षु।।७।।

7. This treasure given by us has been placed, *Mādhvis*, before you, like (an envoy) who has come to the presence (of a prince) foɪ (acquiring his) friendship: come to our presence with benevolent thoughts, accepting the oblations offered among human beings.

५७०३. एकंस्मिन्योगें भुरणा समाने परि वां सप्त स्नवतो रथौ गात्।

न वांयन्ति सुभ्वों देवयुक्तां ये वां धूर्षु तरणंयो वहंन्ति।।८।।

8. Nourishers of all, the chariot of you two, who are associated in a common purpose, traverses the seven flowing (streams): the excellent horses harnessed by the gods, who bear you rapidly, careering in the car, are never wearied.

५७०४. असश्चतां मघवंद्भ्यो हि भूतं ये राया मंघदेयं जुनन्ति।

प्र ये बन्धुं सुनृतांभिस्तिरन्ते गव्यां पृञ्चन्तो अश्व्यां मघानिं।।९।।

9. Be propitious to those who are affluent (in oblations), who offer the wealth that is to be offered for the sake of riches: they who encourage a kinsman with kind commendations, distributing wealth of cattle and of horses.

Be Propitious— *Asashcata bhutam*, Sāyaṇa says, here means *anuraktau bhavatam*; but he explain it *kutrapi asajyamanʈu;* being anywhere unoccupied, unattached, meaning, be unattached to, or uninterested in, any except the present worshippers. ·

A Kinsman— *Bandhu* may also, it is said, mean the *adhvaryu*, or ministrant priest, *falena badhnati*, whom one binds by a reward.

५७०५. नू मे हवमा शृणुतं युवाना यासिष्टं वर्तिरश्विनाविरावत् ।

धत्तं रत्नानि जरतं च सूरीन् यूयं पात स्वस्तिभिः सदा नः ॥१०॥

10. Ever youthful *Aśvins*, hear today my invocation: came, *Aśvins*, to the dwelling where the oblation is prepared: grant wealth (to the offerer): elevate the worshipper: and do you ever cherish us with blessings.

[सूक्त-६८]

[**ऋषि**– वसिष्ठ मैत्रावरुणि। **देवता**– अश्विनीकुमार।

छन्द– विराट्, ८-९ त्रिष्टुप्।]

५७०६. आ शुभ्रा यातमश्विना स्वश्वा गिरो दस्रा जुजुषाणा युवाकोः ।

हव्यानि च प्रतिभृता वीतं नः ॥१॥

1. Illustrious *Aśvins*, lords of handsome horses, come hither, propitiated; *Dasras*, by the praises of your adorer, and partake of our consecrated oblations.

५७०७. प्र वामन्धांसि मद्यान्यस्थुररं गन्तं हविषो वीतये मे ।

तिरो अर्यो हवनानि श्रुतं नः ॥२॥

2. The exhilarating viands have been prepared for you: come quickly to partake of my oblation: disregarding the invocations of an adversary, listen to ours.

५७०८. प्र वां रथो मनोजवा इयर्ति तिरो रजांस्यश्विना शतोतिः ।

अस्मभ्यं सूर्यावसू इयानः ॥३॥

3. Your chariot, *Aśvins*, in which you ride with *Sūrya*, hastens towards us at our solicitations, traversing the regions as swift as thought, and laden with a hundred blessings.

५७०९. अयं ह यद्वां देवया उ अद्रिरूर्ध्वो विवक्ति सोमसुद्भुवभ्याम् ।

आ वल्गू विप्रो ववृतीत हव्यैः ॥४॥

4. When the stone, seeking to propitiate you two divinities, is raised aloft, and loudly sounds, expressing for you the *Soma* juice, then the pious worshipper brings you back, beautiful divinities, by his oblations.

५७१०. चित्रं ह यद्वां भोजनं न्वस्ति न्यत्रये महिष्वन्तं युयोतम् ।

यो वामोमानं दधते प्रियः सन् ॥५॥

5. Wonderful, verily, is the wealth that is yours: you have liberated from the cave *Atri*, who is dear to you, and enjoys your protection.

You have liberated from the cave Atri— *Nyatraye mahiśvantam yuyotam,* you separated the *mahiśvat* from *Atri*: the Scholiast considers *mahiśvat* as a synonym or *ribisa,* which has occurred before: it is among the 134 words at the end of the *Nighantu* of the *Nirukta,* of which there is no explanation; but in *Mand. I. S.* 116. verse 8, *ribise* is explained, *apagataprakashe pidayantragrhe,* in a dark house of implements of torture. Sāyaṇa elsewhere considers it equivalent to *agni,* or rather *tushagni,* or fire of chaff, as he explains, in the following *Sūkta* 71. v.5, *anhasas* by *ribisad agneh sakashot.* Although the word does not occur, the incident is alluded to more than once in the first *Maṇḍala, Sukta* 112. 7, where the commentary says *Atri* was thrown into a machine-room with a hundred doors, where he was roasted; and again. 118. 7, the same explanation occurs, *śatadvare pidayantragrhe...tushagnim shitenodakena, avarayetham,* you extinguished with cold water the chaff fire by which *Atri* was burnt when thrown into the house of machines of torture with a hundred doors. A reference is made to *Maṇḍala* x. 39. 9.

५७११. उत त्यद्वां जुरते अश्विना भूच्च्यवानाय प्रतीत्यं हविर्दे।
अधि यद्दर्प इतऊति धत्थ:॥६॥

6. Such was your benevolence, *Aśvins*, to *Chyavana,* praising and offering oblations, that you in requital rescued his body from departure.

५७१२. उत त्यं भुज्युमश्विना सखायो मध्ये जहुर्दुरेवास: समुद्रे।
निरीं पर्षदराविा यो युवाकु:॥७॥

7. When faithless friends had abandoned Bhujyu in the midst of the ocean, you brought him to shore, devoted to and relying upon you.

५७१३. वृकाय चिज्जसमानाय शक्तमुत श्रुतं शयवे हूयमाना।
यावघ्न्यामपिन्वतमपो न स्तर्यं चिच्छक्त्यश्विना शचीभि:॥८॥

8. You have granted (his desires) to *Vṛka*, exhausted by his devotions: when called upon you have listened to *Shayu*: you are they who have filled the barren cow (with milk) as (a river) with water: you have (endowed her) with strength, *Aśvins*, by your deeds.

५७१४. एष स्य कारुर्जरते सूक्तैरग्रे बुधान उषसां सुमन्मा।
इषा तं वर्धदघ्न्या पयोभिर्यूयं पात स्वस्तिभि: सदा न:॥९॥

9. This your devoted worshipper, waking before the dawn, praises with hymns: nourish him with food, and let the cow (nourish him) with her milk: and do you ever cherish us with blessings.

[सूक्त-६९]

[**ऋषि**- वसिष्ठ मैत्रावरुणि। **देवता**- अश्विनीकुमार। **छन्द**- त्रिष्टुप्।]

५७१५. आ वां रथो रोदसी बद्धधानो हिरण्ययो वृषभिर्यात्वश्वैः।
घृतवर्तनिः पविभी रुचान इषां वोळ्हा नृपतिर्वाजिनीवान्॥१॥

1. May your golden chariot, drawn by your vigorous horses, blocking up heaven and earth, come to us, following the track of the waters, radiant with (glowing) wheels, laden with viands, the protector of men, the receptacle of food.

५७१६. स पप्रथानो अभि पञ्च भूमा त्रिवन्धुरो मनसा यातु युक्तः।
विशो येन गच्छथो देवयन्तीः कुत्रा चिद्यामश्विना दधाना॥२॥

2. Renowned among the five orders of beings, furnished with three benches, harnessed at will, may it come hither: that (vehicle) wherewith you repair to devout mortals, whatsoever, *Aśvins*, directing your course.

५७१७. स्वश्वा यशसा यातमर्वाग्दस्रा निधिं मधुमन्तं पिबाथः।
वि वां रथो वध्वा३ यादमानोऽन्तान्दिवो बाधते वर्तनिभ्याम्॥३॥

3. Well horsed and celebrated, come, *Aśvins*, to our presence: drink, Dasras, the sweet pledge: your chariot, conveying you, with your spouse, furrows with its two wheels the extremities of the sky.

५७१८. युवोः श्रियं परि योषावृणीत सूरो दुहिता परितक्म्यायाम्।
यद्देवयन्तमवथः शचीभिः परि घ्रंसमोमना वां वयो गात्॥४॥

4. The daughter of *Sūrya* made choice of your chariot at the approach of night: you defend the devout worshipper by your deeds, when the resplendent (sacrificial) food proceeds to you to secure you protection.

५७१९. यो ह स्य वां रथिरा वस्त उस्रा रथो युजानः परियाति वर्तिः।
तेन नः शं योरुषसो व्युष्टौ न्यश्विना वहतं यज्ञे अस्मिन्॥५॥

5. Riders in the chariot, *Aśvins*, come for our purification and welfare to this our sacrifice, at the dawn of day, with that chariot which is clothed in radiance, and which, when harnessed, traverses its (appointed) road.

५७२०. नरा॒ गौरे॑व॒ विद्यु॑तं तृ॒षाणास्माक॒मद्य॒ सव॒नोप॑ यातम्।
पुरु॒त्रा हि वां॒ म॒ति॒भि॒र्हव॑न्ते॒ मा वाम॒न्ये नि य॑म॒न्देव॑य॒न्तः॥६॥

6. Leaders of rites, like (thirsty) cattle, thirsting for the radiant (*Soma*), hasten today to our sacrifice: in many ceremonies to the pious propitiate you with praises: let not other devout worshippers detain you.

५७२१. यु॒वं भु॒ज्युम॑र्ण॒विद्धं॑ स॒मु॒द्र उद्दू॑हथुर॒र्णसो॒ अस्रि॑धानैः।
प॒त॒त्रि॒भि॒रश्र॑मै॒रव्य॑थि॒भि॒र्दंस॑ना॒भि॑र॒श्विना॑ पा॒रय॑न्ता॥७॥

7. You bore up Bhujyu, *Aśvins*, from the waters, when cast into the sea, bearing him to shore by your exertions with your undecaying, unwearied, unharassed horses.

५७२२. नू मे॒ हवमा॒ शृ॑णुतं युवाना॒ यासि॑ष्टं व॒र्तिर॒श्विना॑विरा॒वत्।
ध॒त्तं रत्ना॑नि ज॒रतं॑ च सू॒रीन् यू॒यं पा॑त स्व॒स्तिभिः॒ सदा॑ नः॥८॥

8. Ever youthful *Aśvins*, hear today this my invocation: come, *Aśvins*, to the dwelling where the oblation is prepared, grant wealth (to the offerer), elevate the worshipper, and do you ever cherish us with blessings.

[सूक्त-७०]

[ऋषि- वसिष्ठ मैत्रावरुणि। देवता- अश्विनीकुमार। छन्द- त्रिष्टुप्।]

५७२३. आ वि॒श्ववा॒राश्वि॑ना ग॒तं नः॒ प्र तत्स्थान॒मवा॑चि वां पृथि॒व्याम्।
अ॒श्वो न वा॒जी शुन॑पृ॒ष्ठो अ॒स्था॒द् यत्सेद॑थु॒र्ध्रुव॑से॒ न योनि॑म्॥१॥

1. All-adored Aśvins, come to our (sacrifice), to that place on earth which has been designated yours, which, like a swift, broad-backed horse, awaits you, and on which you are seated as firmly as in a dwelling.

Like a ......broad-backed Horse— *Śuna-priṣṭhaḥ* is, the Scholiast says, *sukhakara*, pleasant, delightful, *vipulactvat*, from its breadth.

As Firmly as in a Dwelling— *A yat sadathur dhruvase na yonim* is not very clear. The comparison is explained, *dhruvaya nivasaya sthanam iva*, like a place for a durable soil.

५७२४. सिषक्ति सा वां सुमतिश्चनिष्ठातापि घर्मो मनुषो दुरोणे।
यो वां समुद्रान्त्सरित: पिपर्त्येतंग्वा चित्र सुयुजां युजान:॥२॥

2. This excellent praise, redolent of food, propitiates you: the
ewer has been heated in the dwelling of the worshipper, which,
reaching you, fills the ocean and the rivers (through the rain it
obtains), associating you (in the rite), like two well-matched horses
in a chariot.

The Ewer has been Heated— *Gharma*: See vol. II. mantra 3869.
The Scholiast connects it with *pravarga,—gharmaḥ pravargaśca.*

५७२५. यानि स्थानान्यश्विना दधाथे दिवो यह्वीष्वोषधीषु विक्षु।
नि पर्वतस्य मूर्धनि सदन्तेषं जनाय दाशुषे वहन्ता॥३॥

3. To whatever places you may descend, *Aśvins*, from heaven,
whether amidst the spreading plants, or among men, or sitting on
the summit of the clouds, be the bearers of food to the man, the
donor (of the oblation).

५७२६. चनिष्टं देवा ओषधीष्वप्सु यद्योग्या अश्नवैथे ऋषीणाम्।
पुरूणि रत्ना दधतौ न्यस्मे अनु पूर्वाणि चख्यथुर्युगानि॥४॥

4. Inasmuch, divine *Aśvins*, as you accept that which is most
acceptable in the plants and in the waters, and those (things) which
are most suitable to you, (the offerings) of the *Ŗsis*, therefore,
bestowing upon us ample riches, (favour us) as you have favoured,
bestowing former couples.

That which is most Acceptable in the Plants and in the Waters—
Meaning, according to the Scholiast, the cakes of meal and the *Soma* juice
offered in sacrifices.

Former Couples— Sacrificers, or institutors of sacrifices,
yajamanas, and their wives.

५७२७. शुश्रुवांसा चिदश्विना पुरूण्यभि ब्रह्माणि चक्षाथे ऋषीणाम्।
प्रति प्र यातं वरमा जनायास्मे वामस्तु सुमतिश्चनिष्ठा॥५॥

5. *Aśvins*, hearing the many prayers of the *Ŗsis*, you look
(favourably) upon (us): come to the sacrifice of this man, and may
your desired devour be (shevn) him.

५७२८. यो वां यज्ञो नासत्या हविष्मान् कृतब्रह्मा समर्योऽ३ भवाति।
उप प्र यातं वरमा वसिष्ठमिमा ब्रह्माण्यृच्यन्ते युवभ्याम्॥६॥

6. Come, *Nasatyas*, to the excellent *Vasiṣṭha*, the worshipper who, accompanied by the priests, is present, offering oblations and repeating praises: these prayers are recited to (bring) you (hither).

५७२९. इयं मनीषा इयमश्विना गीरिमां सुवृक्तिं वृषणा जुषेथाम्।

इमा ब्रह्माणि युवयून्यग्मन्यूयं पात स्वस्तिभिः सदा नः॥७॥

7. This adoration, *Aśvins*, this praise (is for you) be gratified, showerers (of benefits), by this laudation may these eulogies, addressed to you, reach you: and do you ever cherish us with blessing.

ANUVĀKA V

[सूक्त-७१]

[ऋषि– वसिष्ठ मैत्रावरुणि। देवता– अश्विनीकुमार। छन्द– त्रिष्टुप्।]

५७३०. अप स्वसुरुषसो नग्जिहीते रिणक्ति कृष्णीररुषाय पन्थाम्।

अश्वामघा गोमघा वां हुवेम दिवा नक्तं शरुमस्मद्युयोतम्॥१॥

1. Night retires before the dawn, the sister (of the *Aśvins*): the dark night leaves the path clear for the radiant (sun): upon you, who are affluent in horses, affluent in cattle, we call day and night: keep away from us the malevolent.

५७३१. उपायातं दाशुषे मर्त्याय रथेन वाममश्विना वहन्ता।

युयुतमस्मदनिरामममीवां दिवा नक्तं माध्वी त्रासीथां नः॥२॥

2. Come to the mortal, the donor (of oblations) bringing desired wealth in your chariot: keep afar from us famine and sickness: day and night, *Mādhvis*, protect us.

५७३२. आ वां रथमवमस्यां व्युष्टौ सुम्नायवो वृषणो वर्तयन्तु।

स्यूमगभस्तिमृतयुग्भिरश्वैराश्विना वसुमन्तं वहेथाम्॥३॥

3. May your docile and vigorous (horses) bring hither your chariot at the approaching dawn: conduct hither, *Aśvins*, your radiating, wealth-laden chariot, with your rain-bestowing steeds.

५७३३. यो वां रथो नृपती अस्ति वोळ्हा त्रिवन्धुरो वसुमाँ उस्रयामा।

आ न एना नासत्योप यातमभि यद्वां विश्वप्स्यो जिगाति॥४॥

4. With that chariot, lords of men[1], which is your vehicle, which has three benches, is laden with wealth, and is the precursor of day, come, *Nāsatyās*, to us; with that chariot which traverses (the sky) as your all-pervading form.

With that chariot which traverses, Etc.— *Abhi yad vam visvapsnyo jigati* is explained, *yo ratho vam vyaptarūpo abhigacchati.*: or it may mean, since *Vasiṣṭha* praises you,—*visvapsnyaḥ* being a name of *Vasiṣṭha*.

५७३४. युवं च्यवानं जरसोऽमुमुक्तं नि पेदव ऊहथुराशुमश्वम्।
निरंहसस्तमसः स्पर्तमत्रिं नि जाहुषं शिथिरे धातमन्तः ॥५॥

5. You exempted *Chyavana* from decay: you mounted Pedu upon a swift charger: you extricated *Atri* from torture and darkness: you replaced *Jahusha* in his rebellious kingdom.

Exempted Chyavana from decay— See *Ṛg.* i.117.13.

Mounted Pedu, Etc.— *Niranhasa tamasaḥ spartam Atrim;* Sāyaṇa: *anhasaḥ, ribisat tushagneḥ sakaśat, tamasashcha guhantahsthitaccha*: see *Ṛg.* i.118.9.

Replaced Jahusha— See *Ṛg.* i.116.20.

५७३५. इयं मनीषा इयमश्विना गीरिमां सुवृक्तिं वृषणा जुषेथाम्।
इमा ब्रह्माणि युवयून्यग्मन् यूयं पात स्वस्तिभिः सदा नः ॥६॥

6. This adoration, *Aśvins*, this praise (is for you), be gratified, showerer (of benefits), by this laudation: may these eulogies, addressed to you, reach you: and do you ever cherish us with blessings.

[सूक्त-७२]

[ऋषि– वसिष्ठ मैत्रावरुणि। देवता– अश्विनीकुमार। उन्द– त्रिष्टुप्।]

५७३६. आ गोमता नासत्या रथेनाश्वावता पुरुश्चन्द्रेण यातम्।
अभि वां विश्वा नियुतः सचन्ते स्पार्हया श्रिया तन्वा शुभाना ॥१॥

1. Come, *Nāsatyās*, with your cattle-giving, horse-bestowing, wealth-yielding chariot: all praises gather round you, who are resplendent with admirable beauty of person.

All praises— *Viśva niyutaḥ*: *niyut* is here said to mean *stuti*, praise.

─────────────

१. नृपती नृणां यजमानानां पालकौ (सायण)।

५७३७. आ नौ देवेभिरुप यातमर्वाक् सजोषसा नासत्या रथेन।
युवोर्हि नः सख्या पित्र्याणि समानो बन्धुरुत तस्य वित्तम्॥२॥

2. Sharing in satisfaction with the gods, come to our presence, *Nāsatyās*, with your chariot, for the friendship (that prevails) between you and us is from our forefathers: a common ancestor (is ours): acknowledge his affinity.

A Common Ancestor— *Vivasvat* and *Varuṇa* were both sons of *Kaśyapa* and *Aditi*: the *Ādityas* are the sons of the former, *Vasiṣṭha* of the latter, consequently they are first cousins.

५७३८. उदु स्तोमासो अश्विनोरबुध्रञ्जामि ब्रह्माण्युषसश्च देवीः।
आविवासन्रोदसी धिष्ण्येमे अच्छा विप्रो नासत्या विवक्ति॥३॥

3. Praises waken up the *Aśvins*, kindred adorations (arouse them) and the celestial dawns: the sage, addressing these laudations to the adorable heaven and earth glorifies the *Nāsatyās* in their presence.

५७३९. वि चेदुच्छन्त्यश्विना उषासः प्र वां ब्रह्माणि कारवो भरन्ते।
ऊर्ध्वं भानुं सविता देवो अश्रेद्बृहदग्नयः समिधा जरन्ते॥४॥

4. When the dawns arise, your worshippers, *Aśvins*, proffer you praises: the divine *Savitā* casts his splendours on high: the fires, with their (kindled) fuel, greatly glorify you.

५७४०. आ पश्चातान्नासत्या पुरस्तादश्विना यातमधरादुदक्तात्।
आ विश्वतः पाञ्चजन्येन राया यूयं पात स्वस्तिभिः सदा नः॥५॥

5. Come, *Nāsatyās*, from the west, from the east: (come), Aśvins, from the south, from the north, come from every quarter with riches beneficial for the five classes of men: and do you ever cherish us with blessings.

[सूक्त-७३]

[ऋषि- वसिष्ठ मैत्रावरुणि। देवता- अश्विनीकुमार। छन्द- त्रिष्टुप्।]

५७४१. अतारिष्म तमसस्पारमस्य प्रति स्तोमं देवयन्तो दधानाः।
पुरुदंसां पुरुतमा पुराजामर्त्या हवते अश्विना गीः॥१॥

1. Devoted to the gods, and hymning their praise, we have crossed to the opposite shore of this (state of) darkness: the worshipper invokes the *Aśvins*, the doers of many deeds, the most mighty, the first born, the immortal.

५७४२. न्वुं प्रियो मनुष॒: सादि॒ होता॒ नास॒त्या यो यज॑ते व॒न्दते च।

अ॒श्नीतं म॒ध्वो अ॑श्विना उ॒पाक॒ आ वां॑ वोचे वि॒दथे॑षु प्र॒यस्वान्॥२॥

2. The man who is dear to you, *Nāsatyas,* the invoker of the gods, has taken his seat, he who offers worship and repeats praise: be nigh, *Aśvins,* and partake of the libation: supplied with food, I address you at sacrifices.

५७४३. अ॒हेम॑ य॒ज्ञं प॒थामु॒राणा इ॒मां सु॒वृक्तिं॑ वृषणा जुषेथाम्।

श्रु॒ष्टीवे॑व॒ प्रेषि॑तो वा॒मबो॑धि॒ प्रति॒ स्तोमै॑र्जर॑माणो वसि॒ष्ठ:॥३॥

3. Praising (the gods), we prepare the sacrifice for their coming: showerers (of benefits), be propitiated by this pious laudation: despatched like a swift messenger, *Vasiṣṭha* arouses you, glorifying you with hymns.

५७४४. उप॒ त्या व॒ह्नी ग॑म॒तो विशं॑ नो र॒क्षोह॑णा स॒म्भृता॑ वी॒ळुपा॑णी।

सम॒न्धांस्य॑ग्मत म॒त्सरा॑णि॒ मा नो॑ म॒र्धिष्ट॒मा ग॑तं शि॒वेन॑॥४॥

4. May those two, the bearers (of oblations), approach our people, destroyers of *Rakshasas,* well-nourished, strong-handed: accept our exhilarating (sacrificial) viands: injure us not, but come with good fortune.

५७४५. ओ प॒श्चातां॒न्नास॑त्या पु॒रस्ता॑दा॒श्विना॑ यात॒मध॒रादुद॑क्तात्।

आ वि॒श्वत॑: पा॒ञ्चज॑न्येन रा॒या यू॒यं पा॑त स्व॒स्तिभि॒: सदा॑ न:॥५॥

5. Come, *Nāsatyas,* from the west, from the east: come, *Aśvins,* from the south, from the north, come from every quarter with riches beneficial for the five classes of men; and do you ever cherish us with blessings.

[सूक्त-७४]

[**ऋषि**– वसिष्ठ मैत्रावरुणि। **देवता**– अश्विनीकुमार। **छन्द**– प्रगाथ (विषमा बृहती, समासतो बृहती।]

५७४६. इ॒मा ऊं वां॑ दि॒विष्ट॑य उ॒स्रा ह॑वन्ते अश्विना।

अ॒यं वा॑मह्नेऽव॑से श॒चीव॑सू विश्व॑विशं॒ हि गच्छ॒थ:॥१॥

1. These pious praises glorify you, radiant *Aśvins:* I call upon you, who are rich, in acts for preservation, for you repair to every individual.

Sāmaveda, 304; 753: the whole of the *Sūkta* to termed a *Pragatha.*

५७४७. युवं चित्रं दंदथुर्भोजनं नरा चोदेथां सूनृतांवते।
अर्वांग्रथं सर्मनसा नि यंच्छतं पिर्बतं सोम्यं मधुं॥२॥

2. You are possessed, leaders (of rites), of marvellous wealth; bestow it upon him who sincerely praises you: alike favourable-minded, direct your chariot to our presence: drink the sweet *Soma* beverage.

५७४८. आ यांतमुपं भूषतं मध्वः पिबतमश्विना।
दुग्धं पयों वृषणा जेन्यावसू मा नों मर्धिष्टमा गंतम्॥३॥

3. Come, *Aśvins*, tarry near us, drink of the sweet libation: showerers (of benefits), by whom riches are won, milk the rain (from the firmament): harm us not: come hither.

Yajurveda, 33. 88.

५७४९. अश्वांसो ये वामुपं दाशुषो गृहं युवां दीयंन्ति बिभ्रतः।
मधूयुभिर्नरा हयेंभिरश्विना देवा यातमस्मयू॥४॥

4. Yours are the horses that, conveying you, bring you to the dwelling to the donor (of the oblation): divine leader (of rites), favourable inclined towards us, come with your rapid steeds.

५७५०. अधा ह यंतो अश्विना पृक्षः सचन्त सूर्यः।
ता यंसतो मघवंद्भ्यो ध्रुवं यशश्छर्दिरस्मभ्यं नासंत्या॥५॥

5. The pious worshippers now approaching you unite to offer (you sacrificial) food: do you two, *Nāsatyās*, grant to us who are affluent (in offerings) enduring fame and dwelling.

५७५१. प्र ये ययुर्वकासो रथाँ इव नृपातारो जनांनाम्।
उत स्वेन शर्वसा शूशुवुर्नर उत क्षियन्ति सुक्षितिम्॥६॥

6. Those worshippers, the benefactors of men, doing injury to none who repair to you, like waggons (to the farm), either prosper by their own strength, or inhabit an excellent abode.

Like Waggons— The text has only *ratha iva*, like chariots: the Scholiast adds, *vrihyadipurṇa yatha prapnuvanti svamigrham,* loaded with rice and the like, arrive at the house of the owner.

[सूक्त-७५]

[ऋषि- वसिष्ठ मैत्रावरुणि। देवता- उषा। छन्द- त्रिष्टुप्।]

५७५२. व्युर्षा आवो दिविजा ऋतेनाविष्कृण्वाना महिमानमागात्।
अप द्रुहस्तमं आवरजुष्टमंङ्गिरस्तमा पथ्या अजीगः॥१॥

1. The Dawn, the daughter of heaven, has risen: she comes, manifesting her magnificence in light: she scatters our foes as well as the odious darkness, and relumes the paths that are to be trodden (by living beings).

Relumes the Paths that are to be Trodden—*Angirastama pathyaḥ ajigaḥ* is explained, *gantritama padavir udgirati,* she throws up the paths that are to be most traversed, that is, *praninam vyavaharaya prakashayati,* she gives light for the transactions of living beings.

५७५३. महे नों अद्य सुवितायं बोध्युषों महे सौभगाय प्र यंन्धि।

चित्रं रयिं यशसं धेह्यस्मे देवि मर्तेषु मानुषि श्रवस्युम्॥२॥

2. Be unto us today the cause of great felicity: bestow, *Uṣas,* (what is promotive) of great prosperity: give us wonderful riches and reputation: grant, divine benefactress of men, to mortals flourishing male posterity.

Flourishing Male Posterity— The text has *śravasyum,* wishing for food: the comment explains it *annavantam putram,* a son having food.

५७५४. एते त्ये भानवों दर्शतायाश्चित्रा उषसों अमृतास आगुः।

जनयन्तो दैव्यानि व्रतान्यापृणन्तो अन्तरिक्षा व्यस्थुः॥३॥

3. These wonderful, immortal rays of the beautiful Dawn appear, giving birth to the pious rites of divine worship, and filling the firmament, they spread around.

५७५५. एषा स्या युंजाना परांकात्पञ्च क्षिती: परि सद्यो जिंगाति।

अभिपश्यन्ती वयुना जनानां दिवो दुंहिता भुवंनस्य पत्नीं॥४॥

4. Exerting herself, the approaches rapidly from afar (to give light) to the five classes of men, witnessing the thoughts of men, the daughter of heaven, the benefactress of living beings.

५७५६. वाजिनींवती सूर्यस्य योषा चित्रामघा राय ईशे वसूंनाम्।

ऋषिष्टुता जरयन्ती मघोन्युषा उच्छति वह्निभिर्गृणाना॥५॥

5. The bride of *Surya,* the distributress (of food), the possessor of wonderful wealth, she rules over treasures (of every kind) of riches: hymned by the *Ṛṣis,* the waster away of life, the mistress of opulence, he rises glorified by the offerers (of oblations).

५७५७. प्रति द्युतानामरुषासो अश्वाश्चित्रा अदृश्रन्नुषसं वहन्तः।

याति शुभ्रा विश्वपिशा रथेन दधाति रत्नं विधते जनाय॥६॥

6. The bright and wondrous steeds, conveying the resplendent *Uṣas*, are visible: she advances, radiant in her every-way-moving chariot: she bestows wealth upon the man who practises sacred rites.

५७५८. सत्या सत्येभिर्मंहती महद्भिर्देवी देवेभिर्यजता यजत्रैः।

रुजद् दृढ्हानि दर्ददुस्रियाणां प्रति गावं उषसं वावशन्त ।।७।।

7. True with the truthful, great with the great, divine with the deities adorable with the adorable, she disperses the solid (glooms), she displays (the pastures) of the cattle: all creatures, the cattle especially, are longing for the Dawn.

True with the truthful, Great with the Great— *Satya satyebhir, mahati mahadbhir, devi devebhir, yajata yajatraih,* may also be understood, according to the Scholiast, either as applying to *Kiranaih,* rays— the rays of the morning— or to *anyair devaih,* with other deities, associated with whom the Dawn is true, mighty, and adorable.

५७५९. नू नो गोमद्वीरवद्धेहि रत्नमुषो अश्वावत्पुरुभोजो अस्मे।

मा नो बर्हिः पुरुषता निदे कर्यूयं पात स्वस्तिभिः सदा नः ।।८।।

8. Bestow upon us, *Uṣas*, wealth, comprising cattle and horses, abundant food, and male offspring: let not our sacrifice incure reproach among men: and do you (gods), ever cherish us with blessings.

[सूक्त-७६]

[ऋषि– वसिष्ठ मैत्रावरुणि। **देवता–** उषा। छन्द– त्रिष्टुप्।]

५७६०. उदु ज्योतिरमृतं विश्वजन्यं विश्वानरः सविता देवो अश्रेत्।

क्रत्वा देवानामजनिष्ट चक्षुराविरकर्भुवनं विश्वमुषाः ।।१।।

1. The divine *Savitā*, the leader of all, sends upwards the immortal, all-benefiting light: the eye of the gods has been manifested for (the celebration of) religious rites: the Dawn has made all creatures visible.

५७६१. प्र मे पन्थां देवयाना अदृश्रन्नमर्धन्तो वसुभिरिष्कृतासः।

अभूदु केतुरुषसः पुरस्तात्प्रतीच्यागादधि हर्म्येभ्यः ।।२।।

2. The paths that lead to the gods are beheld by me, innocuous and glorious with light: the banner of *Uṣas* is displayed in the east, she comes to the west, rising above high places.

Rising Above High Places— *Unnatapradeshah*— we might else have rendered it above the houses.

५७६२. तानीदहानि बहुलान्यासन्या प्राचीनमुदिता सूर्यस्य।

यतः परि जारइवाचरन्त्युषो ददृक्षे न पुनर्यतीव।।३।।

3. Many are the days that have dawned before the rising of the sun, on which you, *Uṣas*, have been beheld like a wife repairing to an inconstant husband, and not like one deserting him.

Like a Wife Repairing to an Inconstant Husband— *Yatha pari jara ivacaranti.... na punar yantiva* is explained, as in the world a virtuous woman is not seen abandoning a bad and vagrant husband, nor herself going astray.

५७६३. त इद्देवानां सधमाद आसन्नृतावानः कवयः पूर्व्यासः।

गूळ्हं ज्योतिः पितरो अन्वविन्दन्त्सत्यमन्त्रा अजनयन्नुषासम्।।४।।

4. Those ancient sages, our ancestors, observant of truth, rejoicing together with the gods, discovered the hidden light, and, reciters of sincere prayers, they generated the Dawn.

५७६४. समान ऊर्वे अधि सङ्गतासः सं जानते न यतन्ते मिथस्ते।

ते देवानां न मिनन्ति व्रतान्यमर्धन्तो वसुभिर्यादमानाः।।५।।

5. When the common herd (of cattle had been stolen) then, associating, they concurred, nor mutually contended: they obstructed not the sacrifices of the gods, but, unoffending, proceeded with the light (they had recovered).

What this means is not very obvious— it is literally in the common vast assembled they agree, nor do they strive mutually: they injure not the observances of the gods, not harming, going with treasures, or with the *Vasus ; vasubhiḥ* means *ushasam tejobhiḥ,* according to Sāyaṇa.

५७६५. प्रति त्वा स्तोमैरीळते वसिष्ठा उषर्बुधः सुभगे तुष्टुवांसः।

गवां नेत्री वाजपत्नी न उच्छोषः सुजाते प्रथमा जरस्व।।६।।

6. Auspicious *Uṣas*, the *Vasiṣṭhas*, waking at dawn: and praising you, glorify you, glorify you with hymns: *Uṣas*, who are the conductress of the cattle (to pasture), the bestower of food, dawn upon us: shine, well-born *Uṣas*, the first (of the gods).

५७६६. एषा नेत्री राधसः सूनृतानामुषा उच्छन्ती रिभ्यते वसिष्ठैः।

दीर्घश्रुतं रयिमस्मे दधाना यूयं पात स्वस्तिभिः सदा नः।।७।

7. *Uṣas*, the object of the sincere praises of the worshipper, is glorified when dawning, by the *Vasiṣṭhas* bestowing upon us far-famed riches: do you (gods), ever cherish us with blessings.

[सूक्त-७७]

[ऋषि– वसिष्ठ मैत्रावरुणि। देवता– उषा। छन्द– त्रिष्टुप्।]

५७६७. उषो रुरुचे युवतिर्न योषा विश्वं जीवं प्रसुवन्ती चरायै।
अभूदग्निः समिधे मानुषाणामकज्योतिर्बाधमाना तमांसि॥१॥

1. *Uṣas* shines radiant in the proximity (of the sun), like a youthful wife (in the presence of her husband), animating all existence to activity: *Agni* is to be kindled for the good of men: the light disperses the obstructing darkness.

५७६८. विश्वं प्रतीची सप्रथा उदस्थादुश्रद्वासो बिभ्रती शुक्रमश्वैत्।
हिरण्यवर्णा सुदृशीकसन्दृगगवां माता नेत्र्यह्नामरोचि॥२॥

2. Advancing towards all, and spreading widely, the Dawn has risen: clothed in pure and brilliant vesture, she expands: of golden colour and of lovely radiance, she shines the parent of sounds, the leader of days.

The Parent of Sounds— *Gavam mata*: go may here mean speech or articulate sound, which at dawn is uttered by men and birds; or, in its usual sense of "cow", it may refer to the going forth at dawn of cattle to pasture. [Sāyaṇa adds that *gavan mata* may also mean "the productress of sunbeams": *rashminam nirmatri*. Compare the note at the end of this volume to v. 6 of the preceding *Sūkta*.]

५७६९. देवानां चक्षुः सुभगा वहन्ती श्वेतं नयन्ती सुदृशीकमश्वम्।
उषा अदर्शि रश्मिभिर्व्यक्ता चित्रामघा विश्वमनु प्रभूता॥३॥

3. The auspicious *Uṣas*, bearing the eye of the gods (the light), leading her white and beautiful courser (the sun), is beheld, manifested by her rays, distributress of wonderful wealth, mighty over all.

Leading her... Courser the Sun— That is, "making the sun manifest".

Mighty Over all— "Mighty over all," or, perhaps, "risen on account of the whole world (*viz*,. for the good of the transactions of the world);" Sāyaṇa: *viśvan anu, sarvam jagad anulakṣya, prabhuta, pravriddha ; sarvajagadvyavaharayety, arthah.*

५७७०. अन्तिवामा दूरे अमित्रमुच्छोर्वीं गव्यूतिमभयं कृधी नः।

यावय द्वेष आ भरा वसूनि चोदय राधो गृणते मघोनि॥४॥

4. Dawn, *Uṣas*, who are the bearer to us of desirable (wealth), and keep our adversary from us: render the wide earth free from peril: drive away those who hate us: bring to us treasures: bestow, opulent goddess wealth upon him who praises you.

And keep our Adversary from Us— So as to keep our adversary from us: Sāyaṇa: *yathamitro dure bhavati tatha vyucchety arthah.*

५७७१. अस्मे श्रेष्ठेभिर्भानुभिर्वि भाह्युषो देवि प्रतिरन्ती न आयुः।

इषं च नो दधती विश्ववारे गोमदश्वावद्रथवच्च राधः॥५॥

5. Divine *Uṣas*, illume us with your brightest rays, prolonging our existence, bestowing upon us food, (and granting us), you who are adored by all, affluence, comprising cattle, horses, and chariots.

५७७२. यां त्वां दिवो दुहितर्वर्धयन्त्युषः सुजाते मतिभिर्वसिष्ठाः।

सास्मासु धा रयिमृष्वं बृहन्तं यूयं पात स्वस्तिभिः सदा नः॥६॥

6. Well-manifested *Uṣas*, daughter of heaven, do you, whom the *Vasiṣṭhas* magnify with praises, bestow upon us brilliant and infinite wealth; and do you, (gods), ever cherish us with blessings.

[सूक्त-७८]

[ऋषि– वसिष्ठ मैत्रावरुणि। **देवता**– उषा। छन्द– त्रिष्टुप्।]

५७७३. प्रति केतवः प्रथमा अदृश्रन्नूर्ध्वा अस्या अञ्जयो वि श्रयन्ते।

उषो अर्वाचा बृहता रथेन ज्योतिष्मता वाममस्मभ्यं वक्षि॥१॥

1. The first signs of the Dawn are visible, her rays are spreading no high: you bring us, *Uṣas*, desirable (riches) in your vast, descending and resplendent chariot.

५७७४. प्रति षीमग्निर्जरते समिद्धः प्रति विप्रासो मतिभिर्गृणन्तः।

उषा याति ज्योतिषा बाधमाना विश्वा तमांसि दुरितापं देवी॥२॥

2. The kindled fire increases everywhere, (and) the priests, glorifying (the dawn) with hymns: the divine *Uṣas* comes, driving away all the evil glooms by her lustre.

५७७५. एता उ त्या: प्रत्यदृश्रन् पुरस्ताज्ज्योतिर्यच्छन्तीरुषसो विभाती:।
अजीजनन्त्सूर्यं यज्ञमग्निमपाचीनं तमोँ अगादजुष्टम्॥३॥

3. These luminous (beams of the) dawn are beheld in the east
diffusing light: (the dawn) engender sacrifice, fire; the odious
glooms, descending, disappear.

५७७६. अचैति दिवो दुहिता मघोनी विश्वे पश्यन्त्युषसं विभातीम्।
आस्थादृथं स्वधया युज्यमानमा यमश्वास: सुयुजो वहन्ति॥४॥

4. The affluent daughter of heaven is perceived: all creatures
behold the luminous dawn: she ascends her chariot laden with
sustenance, which her easily-yoked horses draw.

५७७७. प्रति त्वाद्य सुमनसो बुधन्तास्माकासो मघवानो वयं च।
तिल्विलयध्वमुषसो विभातीर्यूयं पात स्वस्तिभि: सदा न:॥५॥

5. Affluent (in sacrificial offerings), actuated by one mind, we
and ours awaken you, (Uṣas), today: luminous dawns, soften (the
earth) with unctuous (dews) and do you, (gods) ever cherish us
with blessings.

"**Actuated by one mind**"— The text has sumanasan, i.e., according
to Sāyaṇa, shobhanastutikaḥ, "having (i.e., offering), excellent praises
(or hymns)."

Soften the Earth with Unctuous Dews— The text has only
tilvilayadhvam, a nominal verb from a compound substantive, tila from
sesamum, or its oil and ila, earth:— anoint or make the world possessed
of bland or unctuous soil, jagat snigdhabhumikam kuruta.

[सूक्त-७९]

[ऋषि– वसिष्ठ मैत्रावरुणि। देवता– उषा। छन्द– त्रिष्टुप्।]

५७७८. व्युर्षा आव: पथ्याइ जनानां पञ्च क्षितीर्मानुषीर्बोधयन्ती।
सुसन्दृग्भिरुक्षभिर्भानुमश्रेद्दि सूर्यो रोदसी चक्षसाव:॥१॥

1. Uṣas has dawned upon the paths of men, awaking the five
classes of human beings: She has shed light with her lustrous oxen:
the sun makes heaven and earth manifest with radiance.

"**Upon the paths of men**"— The translation has rendered pathya
jananam, as if the first word represented an acc. pl., probably on account
of the apparently similar expression in verse 1 of hymn lxxv.; but Sāyaṇa,
following the Pada text, takes here pathya for a nom. sing., agreeing with
Uṣaḥ; viz., jananam sarvaprāṇinām pathyā pathi hitā, uṣaḥ, or jananam

hivaya, i.e., "*Uṣas* had dawned beneficial on the path of men, or for the welfare of men.

She has shed Light— *Bhanum aśret*: She has resorted to the sun.

५७७९. व्यंञ्जते दिवो अन्तेष्वक्तून्विशो न युक्ता उषसो यतन्ते।
सं ते गावस्तम आ वर्तयन्ति ज्योतिर्यच्छन्ति सवितेव बाहू।।२।।

2. The dawns send their rays to the ends of the sky. They advance like people arrayed (in martial order): your rays, *Uṣas*, annihilate the darkness; they diffuse light as *Savitā* (spreads out) his arms.

५७८०. अभूदुषा इन्द्रतमा मघोन्यजीजनत् सुविताय श्रवांसि।
वि दिवो देवी दुहिता दधात्यङ्गिरस्तमा सुकृते वसूनि।।३।।

3. The supreme sovereign, the opulent *ushas*, has risen: she has engendered food for our welfare: the divine daughter of heaven, most prompt in movement, bestows treasures upon the pious worshipper.

Most Prompt in Movement— *Angirastama* is explained *gantritama*, most going, as in *Sūkta* lxxv. verse 1; or, according to the Scholiast, it may refer to the *Aṅgirasas*, of whose race the *Bharadvajas*, a branch, are said to be cognate with the night, *angirogotrair bharadvajaih saha ratreṛutpattih*, hence night is elsewhere termed *Bharadvaji*. *ratrirva bharadvaji* Maṇḍala x. 127. The epithet *angirastama*, most *angiras*, is said to be applicable to the dawn because it is the same thing as the end of the night, *ratryarasanasyo-śarūpatvat*: here, however, as well as in the former instance, it is probable that the dawn is said to be per-eminently belonging, to or possessed of, *angiras*, because it is the especial season of fire-worship, of which the *Aṅgirasas* were the institutors.

५७८१. तावदुषो राधो अस्मभ्यं रास्व यावत्स्तोतृभ्यो अरदो गृणाना।
यां त्वां जज्ञुर्वृषभस्या रवेण वि दृळ्हस्य दुरो अद्रेरौर्णोः।।४।।

4. Grant as much wealth as your have bestowed upon thine adorers when (formerly) praised by them: you whom (your worshippers) welcomed with clamour, (loud as the bellowing) of a bull, when you hadst set open the doors of the mountains (where the stolen cattle were confined).

५७८२. देवंदेवं राधसे चोदयन्त्यस्मद्र्यक्सूनृता ईरयन्ती।
व्युच्छन्ती नः सनये धियो धा यूयं पात स्वस्तिभिः सदा नः।।५।।

१. रात्री कुशिक: सौभरो रात्रिर्वा भारद्वाजी (अनु॰ १०.१२७)।

5. Inspiring every individual devout (worshipper) with a desire for wealth, addressing to us the words of truth, diffusing the light of morning, bestow upon us understanding (fit) for the acquirement of riches: and do you, (gods), ever cherish us with blessings.

Addressing to us the Words of Truth— *Asmadryak sunṛta irayanti*, which words Sāyaṇa explains, *asmadryak, asmadabhimukham, sunṛta vacamsi, irayanti prerayanti, i.e.*, "urging speech, (*i.e.*, praises) towards us," *i.e.*, awakening our praises. In other passages *sunṛta* is explained by the Scholiast, *priyasatyavak*, or *priyasatyatmikavak*, kind and truthful speech; and *sunṛtavat*, one who holds kind and truthful speech, or *stutivad*, or *stotri*, one who hymns the gods. Compare note on. v.6, next *Sūkta*.

[सूक्त-८०]

[ऋषि- वसिष्ठ मैत्रावरुणि। देवता- उषा। छन्द- त्रिष्टुप्।]

५७८३. प्रति स्तोमेभिरुषसं वसिष्ठा गीर्भिर्विप्रास: प्रथमा अबुध्रन्।
विवर्तयन्तीं रजसी समन्ते आविष्कृण्वतीं भुवनानि विश्वा॥१॥

1. The pious *Vasiṣṭhas*, first (of all worshippers) awaken with prayers and praises (each succeeding) dawn spreading over the like-bounded earth and heaven making all the regions manifest.

५७८४. एषा स्या नव्यमायुर्दधाना गूढ्वी तमो ज्योतिषोषा अबोधि।
अग्रे एति युवतिरह्रयाणा प्राचिकितत्सूर्यं यज्ञमग्निम्॥२॥

2. Bestowing new existence, dispersing the thick darkness by her radiance, the Dawn is awakened and like an immodest dam. see comes before (the sun), and makes manifest *Sūrya*, sacrifice and *Agni*.

५७८५. अश्वावतीर्गोमतीर्न उषासो वीरवती: सदमुच्छन्तु भद्रा:।
घृतं दुहाना विश्वत: प्रपीता यूयं पात स्वस्तिभि: सदा न:॥३॥

3. May the auspicious dawns ever break upon us redolent of horses, of cattle, of male posterity, shedding moisture, yielding everywhere abundance: and do you, (gods), ever cherish us with blessings.

[सूक्त-८१]

[ऋषि- वसिष्ठ मैत्रावरुणि। देवता- उषा। छन्द- प्रगाथ (विषमा बृहती, समासतो बृहती)।]

५७८६. प्रत्युं अदर्श्यायत्युश्छन्तीं दुहिता दिव:।

अपो महिं व्ययति चक्षसे तमो ज्योतिष्कृणोति सूनरी।।१।।

1. The daughter of heaven is everywhere beheld advancing and shedding light: she drives away the deep darkness that objects may meet the eye: the kind guide of man, she diffuses light.

५७८७. उदुस्रियाः सृजते सूर्यः सचाँ उद्यन्नक्षत्रमर्चिवत्।
तवेदुषो व्युषि सूर्यस्य च सं भक्तेन गमेमहि।।२।।

2. At the same time the sun sends forth his rays, and, rising, renders the planets luminous: so, *Uṣas*, upon your manifestation, and that of *Sūrya*, may we become possessed of sustenance.

Renders the Plants Luminous— For, it is said, the moon and planets shine at night with light derived from the solar ray, *saurena tejasa hi naktam chandraprabhritini nakṣatrani bhasante.*

५७८८. प्रति त्वा दुहितर्दिव उषो जीरा अभुत्स्महि।
या वहसि पुरु स्पार्हं वनन्वति रत्नं न दाशुषे मर्यः।।३।।

3. May we, prompt adorers, awaken you, *Uṣas*, daughter of heaven, bountiful divinity, who bring ample and desirable (wealth) and happiness, like riches, to the donor (of the oblation).

५७८९. उच्छन्ती या कृणोषि मंहना महि प्रख्यै देवि स्वंदृशे।
तस्यास्ते रत्नभाज ईमहे वयं स्याम मातुर्न सूनवः।।४।।

4. Mighty goddess, who, scattering darkness, are endowed with power to arouse the world and make it visible, we pray that we may be dear to you, the distributress of wealth, as sons are to a mother.

५७९०. तच्चित्रं राध आ भरोषो यद्दीर्घश्रुत्तमम्।
यत्ते दिवो दुहितर्मर्तभोजनं तद्रास्व भुनजामहै।।५।।

5. Bring *Uṣas*, such wondrous wealth as may be long renowned: bestow, daughter of heaven, that sustenance which is fit for mortals, such as we may enjoy.

५७९१. श्रवः सूरिभ्यो अमृतं वसुत्वनं वाजाँ अस्मभ्यं गोमतः।
चोदयित्री मघोनः सूनृतावत्युषा उच्छदप स्निधः।।६।।

6. Grant to the pious immortal fame, conjoined with affluence: grant to us food and cattle: and may *Uṣas*, the encourager of the wealthy (sacrificer) the speaker of truth, drive away our foes.

"The speaker of truth:" *sunṛtavatī*, which Sāyaṇa explains, *priyasatyatmika vāk sunṛta, tadvatī; sunṛtavatī* may, therefore, also mean, "possessed of kind and truthful speech", *i.e.,* possessed of hymns, or hymned, sell.. by the pious. Compare note on v. 5 of the preceding *Sūkta*.

[सूक्त-८२]

[ऋषि- वसिष्ठ मैत्रावरुणि। देवता- इन्द्रावरुण। छन्द- जगती।]

५७९२. इद्रावरुणा युवमध्वरायं नो विशे जनायं महि शर्में यच्छतम्।
दीर्घप्रयज्युमति यो वनुष्यति वयं जयेम पृतनासु दूढ्यः ॥१॥

1. *Indra* and *Varuṇa*, bestow upon this man, our employer, a spacious chamber for (the celebration of) the sacrifice; and may we subdue in conflicts such evil-minded persons as may seek to injure him who has been long engaged (in your adoration).

"**A spacious chamber**"— Or it may also mean great happiness: *mahi, mahat, śarma, gṛham sukham va.*

५७९३. सम्राळन्यः स्वराळन्य उच्यते वां महान्ताविन्द्रावरुणा महावसू।
विश्वे देवासः परमे व्योमनि सं वामोजो वृषणा सं बलं दधुः ॥२॥

2. One of you it titled supreme monarch, so is the other: mighty and most opulent are you, *Indra* and all the gods in the highest heaven, showerers (of benefits), have combined your united strength, (your) maid vigour.

"**Supreme Monarch**"— The text says that *Indra* and *Varuṇa* are called *Samraj* and *Svaraj* the former title belonging to *Varuṇa,* as Sāyaṇa infers from ii. 41. 6 and the later to *Indra,* as he infers from i. 61.9 *Samraj* is explained by him, *Samyag rajamanah, i.e.,* thoroughly splendent, and *svaraj, surayam evanyanirapekṣayaive rajamanah, i.e.,* self-splendent, or not dependent for his lustre on any one else.

५७९४. अन्वपां खान्यन्तृन्तमोजसा सूर्यमैरयतं दिवि प्रभुम्।
इन्द्रावरुणा मदे अस्य मायिनोऽपिन्वतमपितः पिन्वतं धियः ॥३॥

3. *Indra* and *Varuṇa*, you have forced open by your strength the barriers of the waters: you have established *Sūrya* as the lord in heaven: in the exhilaration of the inspiring (*Soma*) you have replenished the dry (beds of the rivers): do you also fulfil the objects of our sacred rites.

५७९५. युवामिद्युत्सु पृतनासु वह्नयो युवां क्षेमस्य प्रसवे मितज्ञवः।
ईशाना वस्व उभयस्य कारव इन्द्रावरुणा सुहवां हवामहे ॥४॥

4. The bearers (of offerings) invoke you, *Indra* and *Varuṇa*, in wars, in battles: on banded knees (the *Aṅgirasas* invoke you) for the begetting of prosperity: and we, your worshippers, invoke you, who are entitled to respectful homage, the lords of both celestial and terrestrial treasures.

"**In baules**"— The corresponding word of the text. *priyasat* is rendered by Sāyaṇa, *śatrusenasu* among hostile armies.

"Entitled to respectful homage; *suhava*, Sāyaṇa, *Sakhena hvatavyau,* easily accessible to invocation, easily invoked.

५७९६. इन्द्रावरुणा यदिमानि चक्रथुर्विश्वा जातानि भुवनस्य मज्मना।
क्षेमेण मित्रो वरुणं दुवस्यति मरुद्भिरुग्रः शुभमन्य ईयते ॥५॥

5. *Indra* and *Varuṇa*, inasmuch as you have created by your might all these beings of the world, therefore *Mitra* worships *Varuṇa* for prosperity, while the other, the fierce *Indra*, associated with the *Maruts*, acquires glory.

Therefore *Mitra* Worships *Varuṇa*, Etc.— The sense of the passage is obscure, *kṣemena Mitro Varuṇam duvasyati marudbhir ugraḥ śubham anya iyate*: there is nothing very embarrassing in the words, which are rendered literally in the text. The last clause may also be rendered, according to Sāyaṇa, "along with the *Maruts* the powerful *Indra* sends down rain."

५७९७. महे शुल्काय वरुणस्य नु त्विष ओजो मिमाते ध्रुवमस्य यत्स्वम्।
अजामिमन्यः श्नथर्यन्तमातिरद्भ्रेभिरन्यः प्र वृणोति भूयसः ॥६॥

6. In honour of (*Indra* and *Varuṇa*) the sacrificer and his wife for (the obtaining of) great wealth, confer (by their praises) that strength which is peculiar to each of them, and ever-enduring: one of them, (*Varuṇa*), destroys the unfriendly man neglecting (his worship): the other, (*Indra*), with scanty (means), discomfits numerous (enemies).

Discomfits Numerous Enemies— *Pravṛṇoti bhuyasaḥ*: the expression is equivocal, and may mean, according to the Scholiast, "he exalts many worshippers," *bahun yajamanan utkṛṣṭan karoti*.

५७९८. न तमंहो न दुरितानि मर्त्यमिन्द्रावरुणा न तपः कुतश्चन। यस्य देवा गच्छथो वीथो अध्वरं न तं मर्तस्य नशते परिह्वृतिः ॥७॥

7. Sin contaminates not, difficulties assail not, nor distress at any time afflicts the mortal, *Indra* and *Varuṇa*, to whose sacrifices you, deities, repair, and of which you approve: such a man ruin never destroys.

"Contaminates", "assail", "afflicts", and "destroys" are amplifications— required in the English translation— of the word *naśate,* which, according to Sāyaṇa, means, *vyapnoti,* encompasses, takes hold of.

५७९९. अर्वाङ्नरा॒ दैव्ये॒नाव॒सा ग॒तं शृ॒णु॒तं हवं॒ यदि॑ मे जु॒जोष॑थ:।
युवो॒र्हि स॒ख्यमु॑त वा॒ यदाप्यं॑ मा॒र्डी॒कमि॑न्द्रावरुणा॒ नि य॑च्छतम्॥८॥

8. Leaders of rites, come to our presence with divine protection: if you have any regard for me, hear my invocation: verily your friendship, your affinity, is the source of happiness: grant them, *Indra* and *Varuṇa* (unto us).

५८००. अस्माक॑मिन्द्रावरुणा भरे॒भरे॑ पुरोयो॒धा भ॑व॒तं कृ॒ष्ट्योज॑सा।
यद्वां॒ हव॑न्त उ॒भये॒ अध॑ स्पृ॒धि नर॑स्तो॒कस्य॒ तन॑यस्य॒ साति॑षु॥९॥

9. *Indra* and *Varuṇa*, of irresistible strength, be our preceders in every encounter, for both (past and present) worshippers invoke you to defend them in war, or for the acquirement of sons and grandsons.

५८०१. अ॒स्मे इन्द्रो॒ वरु॑णो मि॒त्रो अ॒र्य॒मा द्यु॒म्नं य॑च्छन्तु॒ महि॒ शर्म॑ स॒प्रथ॑:।
अ॒व॒ध्रं ज्योति॑रदि॒तेर्ऋ॒तावृ॒धो दे॒वस्य॑ श्लो॒कं स॑वि॒तुर्म॑नामहे॥१०॥

10. May *Indra, Varuṇa, Mitra,* and *Aryaman* grant us wealth and a large and spacious habitation; may the lustre of Aditi, the augmentress of sacrifice, be innoxious to us: we recite the praise of the divine *Savitā.*

[सूक्त-८३]

[ऋषि– वसिष्ठ मैत्रावरुणि। देवता– इन्द्रावरुण। छन्द– जगती।]

५८०२. यु॒वां नरा॒ पश्य॑मानास आ॒प्यं प्रा॒चा ग॒व्यन्त॑: पृथु॒पर्श॑वो ययु:।
दासा॑ च वृ॒त्रा ह॒तमार्या॑णि च सु॒दास॑मिन्द्रावरुणा॒व॑सावतम्॥१॥

1. *Indra* and *Varuṇa*, leaders (of rites), contemplating your affinity, and desirous of cattle, the worshippers, armed with large sickles, have proceeded to the east (to cut the sacred grass): destroy, *Indra* and *Varuṇa*, your enemies, whether *Dasas* or *Aryas* and defend *Sudāsa* with your protection.

Armed with Large Sickles— *Prithuparshavaḥ* is explained, *vistirṇaśvaparśuhasta,* holding large rib-bones of horses: the *aśvaparśu* is an implement for cutting the *kuśa* grass[1], either the rib of a horse, or an

---

१. अश्वपर्शूं बर्हिरच्छैति (तै० ब्रा० ३.२.२.१)।

instrument like it: it is frequently alluded to in the *Brahmanas* and *Sutras*:
on the *Taittiriya Samhita, Kanda* 1, *Prapathaka* 1, *Anuvaka* 2; the mantra
ghoshad asi is said, by *Baudhayana*, to be addressed to the *Aśvaparśu*,
"you are the implement, the priest having taken it in his hand. Sāyaṇa,
commenting on the term, understands it literally: *aśvaparśu,
aśvaparśvasthi*, the rib-bone of a horse, the edge of which is as sharp as a
sword, and fit for cutting: *tac ca khadgavat tikṣnadbaratvat lavane
samarthah.*

५८०३. यत्रा नरः॒ समर्य॑न्ते कृ॒तध्व॑जो यस्मिन्ना॒जा भव॑ति॒ किं च॒न प्रि॒यम्।

यत्रा॑ भ॒यन्ते॒ भुव॑ना स्व॒र्दृश॒स्तत्रा॑ न इन्द्रावरुणा॒धि वोचतम्॥२॥

2. Where men assemble with uplifted banners, in what-ever
conflict, there is something unfavourable; where living beings,
looking to heaven, are in fear, there, *Indra* and *Varuṇa*, speak to us
(encouragement).

"There is ....."

Sāyaṇa adds, "every thing is evil". The last part of this verse is
somewhat differently rendered by him: *yatra, ca, yuddhe, bhuvana,
bhuvanani, bhutajatani, svardrishah, śarirapatad urdhvam svargasya
drastaro, vitash ca, bhayante, bibhyati, tatra, tadrishe sangrame, he
indravarunau, no'sman, adhivocatam, asmatpakṣapatavacanau
bhavatam*, i.e., "in whatever (battle) living beings and those seeing
heaven (i.e., gone to heaven, departed) are in fear, there, *Indra* and
Varuṇa, plead our cause."

५८०४. सं भूम्या॒ अन्ता॑ ध्वसि॒रा अद॑ृक्षतेन्द्रावरुणा॒ दि॒वि घोष॒ आ॑रुहत्।

अस्थु॒र्जना॑नामुप॒ मामरा॑तयोऽर्वा॒गव॑सा हवनश्रुता॒ गन्तम्॥३॥

3. The ends of the earth are beheld laid waste: the clamour has
ascended, *Indra* and *Varuṇa*, to heaven: the adversaries of my
people approach me: having heard my invocation, come for my
defence.

५८०५. इन्द्रावरुणा व॒धना॑भिरप्र॒ति भे॒दं व॒न्वन्ता॒ प्र सु॒दास॑मावतम्।

ब्रह्मा॑ण्येषां शृणुतं॒ हवी॒मनि स॒त्या तृत्सू॑नामभवत्पु॒रोहि॑तिः॥४॥

4. *Indra* and *Varuṇa*, you protected *Sudāsa*, over-whelming
the yet unassailed *Bheda* with your fatal weapons: here the prayers
of these *Tṛtsus* in time of battle, so that my ministration may have
borne them fruit.

५८०६. इन्द्रावरुणावभ्या॒ तप॑न्ति मा॒घान्यर्यो॑ व॒नुषा॒मरा॑तयः।

यु॒वं हि वस्व॑ उ॒भयस्य॒ राज॒थोऽध॑ स्मा नोऽवतं पा॒र्ये दि॒वि॥५॥

5. *Indra* and *Varuṇa*, the murderous (weapons) of my enemy distress me: foes among the malignant (assail me): you two are sovereigns over both (celestial and terrestrial) wealth: protect us therefore on the day of battle.

५८०७. युवां हवन्त उभयास आजिष्विन्द्रं च वस्वो वरुणं च सातयै।
यत्र राजभिर्दशभिर्निबाधितं प्र सुदासमावतं तृत्सुभिः सह ॥६॥

6. Both (*Sudāsa* and the *Tṛtsus*) call upon you two (*Indra* and *Varuṇa*), in combats for the acquirement of wealth, when you defend *Sudāsa*, together with the *Tṛtsus*, when attacked by the ten *Rājās*.

५८०८. दश राजानः समिता अयज्यवः सुदासमिन्द्रावरुणा न युयुधुः।
सत्या नृणामद्मसदामुपस्तुतिर्देवा एषामभवन्देवहूतिषु ॥७॥

7. The ten confederated irreligious *Rājās* did not prevail, *Indra* and *Varuṇa*, against *Sudāsa*: the praise of the leaders (of rites), the offerers of sacrificial food, was fruitful: the gods were present at their sacrifices.

५८०९. दाशराज्ञे परियत्ताय विश्वतः सुदास इन्द्रावरुणावशिक्षतम्।
श्वित्यञ्चो यत्र नर्मसा कपर्दिनो धिया धीवन्तो असपन्त तृत्सवः ॥८॥

8. You gave vigour, *Indra* and *Varuṇa*, to *Sudās* when surrounded on all sides by the ten *Rājās* (in the country) where the pious *Tṛtsus*, walking in whiteness, and wearing braided hair, worshipped with oblations and praise.

Walking in Whiteness, Wearing, Etc.— *Śvit yancaḥ kapardinas tṛtsavaḥ*: the epithets are explained, *svaityam nairmālyam gacchantaḥ*, going in, or to, whiteness, or freedom from soil ; and *jaṭilaḥ*, having braided hair. The *Tṛtsus* are styled by Sāyaṇa priests, the pupils of *Vasiṣṭha, Vasiṣṭhaśiṣyāḥ, etatsaṅjñaḥ ṛtvijaḥ*.

५८१०. वृत्राण्यन्यः समिथेषु जिघ्नते व्रतान्यन्यो अभि रक्षते सदा।
हवामहे वां वृषणा सुवृक्तिभिरस्मे इन्द्रावरुणा शर्म यच्छतम् ॥९॥

9. One of you destroys enemies in battle, the other ever protects religious observances: we invoke you, showerers (of benefits), with praises: bestow upon us, *Indra* and *Varuṇa*, felicity.

५८११. अस्मे इन्द्रो वरुणो मित्रो अर्यमा द्युम्नं यच्छन्तु महि शर्म सप्रथः।
अवध्रं ज्योतिरदितेर्ऋतावृधो देवस्य श्लोकं सवितुर्मनामहे ॥१०॥

10. May *Indra, Varuṇa, Mitra, Aryaman*, grant us wealth and a large and spacious mansion: may the lustre of *Aditi*, the augmentress (of sacrifice), be innoxious to us: we recite the praise of the divine *Savitā*.

[सूक्त-८४]

[**ऋषि**– वसिष्ठ मैत्रावरुणि। **देवता**– इन्द्रावरुण। **छन्द**– जगती।]

५८१२. आ वां राजानावध्वरे ववृत्यां हव्येभिरिन्द्रावरुणा नमोभिः।

प्र वां घृताचीं बाह्वोर्दधाना परि त्मना विषुरूपा जिगाति॥१॥

1. Royal *Indra* and *Varuṇa*, I invite you to the sacrifice with oblations and with praise: the butter-dropping (ladle), held in our hands, offers spontaneously (the oblation) to you who are of many forms.

५८१३. युवो राष्ट्रं बृहदिन्वति द्यौयौँ सेतृभिररज्जुभिः सिनीथः।

परि नो हेळो वरुणस्य वृज्या उरुं न इन्द्रः कृणवदु लोकम्॥२॥

2. Your vast kingdom of heaven gratifies (the world with rain), you who bind (the sinner) with bonds not made of rope: may the wrath of *Varuṇa* pass away from us: may *Indra* prepare for us a spacious region.

५८१४. कृतं नो यज्ञं विदथेषु चारुं कृतं ब्रह्माणि सूरिषु प्रशस्ता।

उपो रयिर्देवजूतो न एतु प्र णः स्पार्हाभिरूतिभिस्तिरेतम्॥३॥

3. Render the sacrifice offered in our dwelling fruitful, the prayers uttered by the worshippers successful: may riches come to us sent by the gods: do you two give us increase by you desirable protections.

५८१५. अस्मे इन्द्रावरुणा विश्ववारं रयिं धत्तं वसुमन्तं पुरुक्षुम्।

प्र य आदित्यो अनृता मिनात्यमिता शूरो दयते वसूनि॥४॥

4. Bestow upon us. *Indra* and *Varuṇa*, riches desirable to all, together with a dwelling and abundant food, for the hero, *Āditya*, who punishes beings devoid of truth, gives (to the devout) unbounded treasures.

Āditya— *Āditya*, or the son of *Aditi*, here means *Varuṇa*.

५८१६. इयमिन्द्रं वरुणमष्ट मे गीः प्रावत्तोके तनये तूर्तुजाना।

सुरत्नासो देववीतिं गमेम यूयं पात स्वस्तिभिः सदा नः॥५॥

5. May this my praise reach *Indra* and *Varuṇa*, and, earnestly offered (by me), preserve sons and grandsons: let us, possessed of affluence, present (their) food to the gods: and do you, (duties), ever cherish us with blessings.

[सूक्त-८५]

[ऋषि- वसिष्ठ मैत्रावरुणि। देवता- इन्द्रावरुण। छन्द- जगती।]

५८१७. पुनीषे वामरक्षसं मनीषां सोम्मिन्द्राय वरुणाय जुह्वत्।
घृतप्रतीकामुषसं न देवीं ता नो यामन्नुरुष्यतामभीके।।१।।

1. I offer to you both adoration, uninterrupted by *Rākṣasas,* presenting the *Soma* to *Indra* and to *Varuṇa,*— (adoration), of which the members are radiant as the celestial dawn: may they two protect us at the time of going to battle.

५८१८. स्पर्धन्ते वा उ देवहूये अत्र येषु ध्वजेषु दिद्यवः पतन्ति।
युवं ताँ इन्द्रावरुणावमित्रान्हतं पराचः शर्वा विषूचः।।२।।

2. In the conflict where (combatants) strive against us, in those (contests) in which bright (weapons) fall upon the banners, do you two, *Indra* and *Varuṇa*, slay with your shaft those enemies who have been routed, and are scattered in various directions.

५८१९. आपश्चिद्धि स्वयंशसः सदःसु देवीरिन्द्रं वरुणं देवता धुः।
कृष्टीरन्यो धारयति प्रविक्ता वृत्राण्यन्यो अप्रतीनि हन्ति।।३।।

3. The divine *Soma* (juices), flowing like water, self renowned, (offered) at religious assemblies, support *Indra* and *Varuṇa*: of whom one regulates mankind, distinguished (as good or bad), and the other slays unresisted foes.

Support Indra and Varuṇa— As by the commentary, *somenāpyāyitā hi devatāḥ sve sve sthāne avatiṣṭhante,* "nourished by the *Soma*, the gods abide in their own several stations.

५८२०. स सुक्रतुर्ऋतचिदस्तु होता य आदित्य शवसा वां नमस्वान्।
आववर्तदवसे वां हविष्मानसदित्स सुविताय प्रयस्वान्।।४।।

4. May the devout worshipper derive benefit from sacrifice when offering adoration to you both, sons of *Aditi* (involved) with strength: the who, liberal of oblations invites you for your satisfaction, may he, possessing abundance, be in the enjoyment of happiness.

५८२१. इयमिन्द्रं वरुणमष्ट मे गी: प्रावन्तोके तनये तूतुंजाना।

सुरत्नासो देववीतिं गमेम यूयं पात स्वस्तिभि: सदां न:॥५॥

5. May this my praise reach *Indra* and *Varuṇa*: and earnestly offered (by me), preserve sons and grandsons: let us, possessed of affluence, present (their) food to the gods; and do you, (deities), ever cherish us with blessings.

[सूक्त-८६]

[ऋषि- वसिष्ठ मैत्रावरुणि, **देवता-**वरुण। **छन्द-**त्रिष्टुप्।]

५८२२. धीरा त्वंस्य महिना जनूंषि वि यस्तस्तम्भ रोदंसी चिदुर्वी।

प्र नाकंमृष्वं नुनुदे बृहन्तं द्विता नक्षत्रं पप्रथच्च भूमं॥१॥

1. Permanent in greatness are the births of that *Varuṇa* who propped up the vast heaven and earth, who appointed to (their) two-fold (task) the glorious sun and beautiful constellations, who spread out the earth.

Their Two-fold Task— *Dvita*, of giving light by day and by night.

५८२३. उत स्वया तन्वा३े सं वंदे तत्कदा न्वइन्तर्वर्रुणे भुवानि।

किं मे हव्यमट्टृणानो जुषेत कदा मृळीकं सुमनां अभि ख्यम्॥२॥

2. When may I in my person converse with the deity? When may I (be admitted) to the heart of *Varuṇa*? By what means may he, without displeasure, accept my oblation? When may I, rejoicing in mind, behold that giver of felicity?

५८२४. पृच्छे तदेनो वरुण दिदृक्षूपों एमि चिकितुषो विपृच्छम्।

समानमिन्मे कवयश्चिदाहुरयं ह तुभ्यं वरुणो हृणीते॥३॥

3. Desirous of beholding you, *Varuṇa*, I inquire what is mind offence: I have gone to make inquiry of the wise: the sages verily have said the same thing to me:— this *Varuṇa* is displeased with you.

५८२५. किमागं आस वरुण ज्येष्ठं यत्स्तोतारं जिघांससि सखांयम्।

प्र तन्मे वोचो दूळभ स्वधावोऽवं त्वानेना नमसा तुर ईयाम्॥४॥

4. What has that great wickedness been, *Varuṇa*, that you should seek to destroy the worshipper, your friend? Insuperable, resplendent *Varuṇa*, declare it to me, so that, freed from sin, I may quick approach you with veneration.

५८२६. अर्व दुग्धानि पित्र्या सृज नोऽव या वयं चकृमा तनूभिः।
अर्व राजन्पशुतृपं न तायुं सृजा वत्सं न दाम्नो वसिष्ठम्।।५।।

5. Relax (the bonds) imposed by the ill deeds of our forefathers, and those incurred (by the sins) which we have committed
in our persons: liberate, royal *Varuṇa*, like a calf from its tether,
Vasiṣṭha like a thief nourishing the animal (he has stolen).

"Like a Calf from its Tether.....Like a thief, etc."— Sāyaṇa
supplies "and" to the two comparisons: "liberate *Vasiṣṭha* (*i.e.*, me) like
as a thief (is liberated), who (having performed his penance for the theft
he has committed, at its termination) feeds the animals (with food), and
(*i.e.*, or) like a calf from its tether": *paśutṛpam na tāyum,
stainyaprāyaścittam kṛtvāvasāne ghāsādibhiḥ paśūnām tarpayitāram
stenam iva; damno rajjoḥ, vatsam na, vatsam iva, ca vasiṣṭham, mām
bandhakāt pāpāt, avasṛja vimuñca.*

५८२७. न स स्वो दक्षो वरुण ध्रुतिः सा सुरा मन्युर्विभीदको अचित्तिः।
अस्ति ज्यायान्कनीयस उपारे स्वप्नश्चनेदनृतस्य प्रयोता।।६।।

6. It is not our own choice, *Varuṇa*, out our condition, (that is
the cause of our sinning); it is that which is intoxication, wrath,
gambling, ignorance; there is a senior in the proximity of the
junior: even a dream is a provocative to sin.

Our Condition, that is the cause of our Sinning— The text has
only *na sa svo dakṣo dhrutiḥ*: the latter is explained, the condition
appointed by destiny at the time of birth is the cause of the committal of
sin, not our own power or will, *dhrutiḥ sthirotpattisamaye nirmitā
daivagatiḥ pāpapravṛttau kāraṇam na svabhūtam balam* : this would
make the *Veda* authority for the popular notion of fate and consequent
transmigration.

Intoxication— *Surā*, literally, wine.

Gambling— *Vibhīdaka*, dice, a material of gaming.

There is a senior in the Proximity of the Junior— *Asti jyāyān
kanīyasa upāre*: by the junior, according to the commentator, is to be
understood, man, little and helpless; by the senior, his superior, God,
exercising nigh at hand the restraining faculty, *samīpe niyantṛtvena sthito
jyāyān adhika Iśvaro' sti;* but who, according to Sāyaṇa, somewhat
inconsistently, impels man to wickedness, *sa eva tam pāpe pravartayati:*
to this effect a text is quoted, *eśa hyevāsādhu karma kārayati tam yam
adho ninīṣate*[1], him whom he wishes to lead downwards he causes to do
evil acts.

---

१. कौ० उ० ३.८।

Even a Dream is a Provocative to Sin— *Anṛtasya prayotā,* promoter of the untrue: if so, says Sāyaṇa, how much more likely are we to commit sin when awake.

५८२८. अरं दासो न मीळ्हुषे॑ कराण्यहं देवाय॒ भूर्ण॑येऽना॒गाः।

अचे॑तय॒दचि॑तो दे॒वो अ॒र्यो गृत्सं॑ रा॒ये क॒वित॑रो जुनाति।।७।।

7. Liberated from sin, I may perform diligent service, like a slave, to the divine showerer (of benefits), the sustainer of the world: may he, the divine lord, give intelligence to us who are devoid of understanding: may he who is most wise, guide the worshipper to wealth.

५८२९. अ॒यं सु तुभ्यं॑ वरुण स्वधावो हृ॒दि स्तोम॑ उप॒श्रित॒श्चिद॑स्तु।

शं न॑ः क्षेमे॒ शमु॒ योगे॑ नो अस्तु यू॒यं पा॑त स्व॒स्तिभिः॒ सदा॑ नः।।८।।

8. May this laudation, food-conferring *Varuṇa*, be taken to your heart: may success be ours in retaining what we have, and in acquiring more: and do you, (deities), ever cherish us with blessings.

[सूक्त-८७]

[ऋषि– वसिष्ठ मैत्रावरुणि। देवता– वरुण। छन्द– त्रिष्टुप्।]

५८३०. र॒द॒त्पथो॑ वरुणः॒ सूर्या॑य॒ प्राणाँ॑सि समु॒द्रिया॑ न॒दीनाम्॑।

सर्गो॒ न सृ॒ष्टो अर्व॑तीॠ॒तायञ्च॒कार॑ म॒हीर॑व॒नीरह॑भ्यः।।१।।

1. *Varuṇa* prepared a path for the sun: he set free the waters of the rivers generated in the firmament: hastening (to his task), as a horse let loose rushes to (a flock of) mares, he divided the great nights from the days.

He divided the great nights from the Days— *Varuṇa* is here said to imply the setting sun, by whose departure day ends and night begins.

५८३१. आ॒त्मा ते॒ वातो॒ रज॒ आ न॑वीनो॒त्पशुर्न॑ भूर्णि॒र्यव॑से स॒सवान्॑।

अ॒न्त॒र्म॒ही बृ॒ह॒ती रोद॑सी॒मे विश्वा॑ ते॒ धाम॑ वरुण प्रि॒याणि॑।।२।।

2. Thy spirit is the wind: he sends abroad the waters: he, the cherisher of the world, is the feeder on (sacrificial) food, like an animal upon fodder: all your glories, *Varuṇa*, manifested between the vast and spacious heaven and earth, give delight (to all).

The Spirit is the Wind— *Ātmā te vātaḥ,*— the Scholiast explains,— the wind being sent abroad by you is the support of all living beings, in the form of breath.

५८३२. परि स्पशो वरुणस्य स्मदिष्टा उभे पश्यन्ति रोदसी सुमेके ।
ऋतावान: कवयो यज्ञधीरा: प्रचेतसो य इषयन्त मन्म ॥३॥

3. The excellent spies of *Varuṇa* behold the beautiful heaven and earth, as well as those (men) who, the celebrators of rites, constant in sacrifice, wise and intelligent address (to him their) praise.

The Excellent Spies of *Varuṇa*— Spaśaḥ smadiṣṭāḥ ; the first is rendered *caraḥ*, spies: the epithet is differently explained either *praśastagatayaḥ*, of excellent movement, or *sahapreṣitaḥ*, despatched together: in a former passage. mantra 5065 *spaśaḥ* is explained, *raśmayaḥ* rays, or reins.

५८३३. उवाच मे वरुणो मेधिराय त्रि: सप्त नामाघ्या बिभर्ति ।
विद्वान्पदस्य गुह्या न वोचद्युगाय विप्र उपराय शिक्षन् ॥४॥

4. *Varuṇa* thus spoke to me, possessed of understanding: the cow (speech) has thrice seven appellations: the wise and intelligent *Varuṇa*, giving instruction to me, his worthy disciple, had declared the mysteries of the place (of Brahma).

The Cow— *Aghnyā* is here understood to mean *vāk*, speech; a rather unusual application, although *gauḥ*, the synonym of *aghnyā*, has that meaning: the twenty-one appellations are said to be the seven metres of the *Veda*, as corresponding with the breast, throat, or head; or speech may mean the *Veda*, and as such imply the names of the twenty-one Vedic sacrifices. Some explain here *gauḥ* by *pṛthivi*, earth, having also twenty-one synonyms.

५८३४. तिस्रो द्यावो निहिता अन्तरस्मिन्तिस्रो भूमीरुपरा: षड्विधाना: ।
गृत्सो राजा वरुणश्चक्र एतं दिवि प्रेङ्खं हिरण्ययं शुभे कम् ॥५॥

5. In him are deposited the three heavens, the three earths with their six seasons are shown in him: the most adorable, royal *Varuṇa* has made this golden sun undulating in the sky, he has made it to diffuse light.

The three Earths— Best, middle most, worst see former passage (*Ṛg.* ii.27.8.)[1]

तिस्रो भूमीर्धारयन्

He has made it to Diffuse Light— *Śubhe kam, diptyartham*: see *Ṛg.* v.85.2, [Kam is explained by the Scholiast in his note on v. 3 of the next *Sūkta* as *sukham,* or as an expletive.]

---

१. त्रयो वा इमे त्रिवृतो लोका: (ऐ॰ ब्रा॰ २.१७)।

५८३५. अव॒ सि॒न्धुं व॒रुणो॒ द्यौरि॑व स्थाद् द्र॒प्सो न श्वे॒तो मृ॒गस्तुवि॒ष्मान्।
गम्भी॒रशं॑सो॒ रज॑सो वि॒मानः॑ सु॒पार॑क्ष॒त्रः स॒तो अ॒स्य रा॒जा॥६॥

6. (Radiant) as the sun, *Varuṇa* placed the ocean (in its bed) white as a drop (of water), vigorous as an antelope, objects of profound praise, distributor of water, the powerful transporter beyond sin, the ruler of this existing (world).

White as a Drop of Water— *Drapso na śveto mṛgas tuviṣmān*: the commentator seems to adopt a different construction, and to attach *śveta* to *mṛga: drapso na dravaṇaśīla udabindur iva: śvetaḥ, śubhravarṇo mṛgaḥ, gauramṛga iva; tuviṣmān balavān.*

"Distributor of Water"— According to Sāyaṇa "creator" *nirmata.*

५८३६. यो मृ॒ळया॑ति च॒क्रुषे॒ चिदागो॑ व॒यं स्या॑म॒ वरु॑णे अ॒नाग॑ाः।
अनु॑ व्र॒तान्यदि॑ते॒रृध॑न्तो यू॒यं पा॑त स्व॒स्तिभिः॒ सदा॑ नः॥७॥

7. May we be free from sin against that *Varuṇa*, who has compassion upon him who commits offence, we who are duly observing the rites of the son *Aditi*: and do you, (gods), ever cherish us with blessings.

"Of the son of Aditi"— Sāyaṇa takes *Aditer* as meaning here *adīnasya* "of the mighty (*Varuṇa*) He usually explains it by *akhaṇḍanīya.*

[सूक्त-८८]

[ऋषि- वसिष्ठ मैत्रावरुणि। देवता- वरुण। छन्द- त्रिष्टुप्।]

५८३७. प्र शु॒न्ध्युवं॑ व॒रुणा॑य प्रे॒ष्ठां म॒तिं व॑सिष्ठ मी॒ळ्हुषे॑ भरस्व।
य ईम॑र्वाञ्चं॒ कर॑ते य॒जत्रं॑ स॒हस्रा॑मघं॒ वृष॑णं बृ॒हन्त॑म्॥१॥

1. Offer pure and acceptable praise, *Vasiṣṭha* to the showerer, *Varuṇa*, he who makes the adorable (sun), she donor of thousands, the showerer (of benefits), the vast, manifest before (us).

५८३८. अधा॒ न्व॑स्य सं॒दृशं॑ ज॒गन्वानग्ने॑रनी॒कं वरु॑णस्य मंसि।
स्व॒र्यद॒श्मन्नधि॑पा उ॒ अन्धो॒ऽभि मा॒ वपुर्दृ॒शये॑ निनीयात्॥२॥

2. Hastening into his sight, may I (worthily) glorify the aggregated radiance of *Varuṇa*, when he is the imbiber of the exhilarating beverage (expressed) by the stones: may he render my person of goodly aspect.

The Aggregated Radiance of Varuṇa— *Agner anīkam Varuṇasya* is rendered, *Varuṇasya jvālāsaṅgham.*

५८३९. आ यद्रुहाव वरुणश्च नावं प्र यत्समुद्रमीरयाव मध्यम्।
अधि यदपां स्नुभिश्चराव प्र प्रेङ्ख ईङ्खयावहै शुभे कम्॥३॥

3. When (I, *Vasiṣṭha*) and *Varuṇa* ascend the ship together
when we send it forth into the midst of the ocean, when we
proceed over the waters with swift (sailing vessels), then may we
both undulate happily in the prosperous swing.

With Swift Sailing Vessels— *Snubhiś carāva, gantṛbhir naubhiḥ,*
with going, *viz.,* ships.

Then may we both undulate happily in the Prosperous Swing—
Pra preṅkha īṅkhayāvahai śubhe kam is literally rendered in the text after
the Scholiast who explains it *preṅkhe, naurūpāyām dolāyām eva
preṅkhayāvahai, nimnonnatais tarangair itaś cetaśca pravicalantau
saṅkrīḍāvahai,* let us both sport, being tossed here and there by the up and
down waves, as it were in a swing, in the form of a ship.

५८४०. वसिष्ठं ह वरुणो नाव्याधादृषिं चकार स्वपा महोभिः।
स्तोतारं विप्रः सुदिनत्वे अह्नां यान्नु द्यावस्ततनन्यादुषासः॥४॥

4. So *Varuṇa* placed *Vasiṣṭha* in the ship, and by his mighty
protection made the *Ṛṣi* a doer of good works: the wise *Varuṇa*
placed his worshipper in a fortunate day of days, he extended the
passing days, the passing nights.

In a Fortunate Day of Days— *Sudinatve* is rather the state or
property of a lucky day by its being fruitful, *falatvena.*

He extended the Passing Days, the Passing Nights— *Yān nu
dyāvas tatanan yāduṣāsaḥ. Varuṇa* is here identified with the sun: *uṣasaḥ,*
the Scholiast asserts, here intends *rātriḥ,* nights, *yat* is for *yataḥ,
gacchataḥ.*

५८४१. क्व त्यानि नौ सख्या बभूवुः सचावहे यदवृकं पुरा चित्।
बृहन्तं मानं वरुण स्वधावः सहस्रद्वारं जगमा गृहं ते॥५॥

5. What has become of those our ancient friendships ? Let us
preserve them unimpaired as of old: food-bestowing *Varuṇa,* may
I repair to your vast comprehensive thousand-doored dwelling.

५८४२. य आपिर्नित्यो वरुण प्रियः सन्त्वामागांसि कृणवत्सखा ते। मा त
एनस्वन्तो यक्षिन् भुजेम यन्धि ष्मा विप्रः स्तुवते वरूथम्॥६॥

6. May he your unvarying kin, who was ever dear, though
committing offences against you, still be your friend; adorable
Varuṇa, offending you, let us not enjoy (happiness) ; but do you,
who are wise, bestow on your worshipper a secure abode.

The Unvarying Kin— According to one legend, *Vasiṣṭha* is the son of *Varuṇa*.

Let us not Enjoy Happiness— *Ma ta enasvanto bhujema,* let not us, offending you, enjoy—it is not said what: the Scholiast attaches the prohibitive to the verb, but gives a different turn to the sentence: "being freed from sin through your favour, let us enjoy enjoyments." *tvatprasādāt pāparahitā eva santo bhogān bhuñjāmahai.*

६८४३. ध्रुवासु॒ त्वासु॒ क्षि॒तिषु॒ क्षि॒यन्तो व्य१स्मत् पाशं॑ व॒रुणो मुमोचत्।
अ॒वो व॑न्वा॒ना अदि॑ते॒रुपस्था॒द्यू॒यं पा॑त स्व॒स्तिभिः॒ सदा॑ नः॥७॥

7. While dwelling in these durable worlds, may *Varuṇa* loose our bonds: may we be enjoyers of the protection (which has been given by him) from the lap of *Aditi*, and do you (gods) ever cherish us with blessings.

Aditi— *Aditi* is here explained *Pṛthivī*, earth.

[सूक्त-८९]

[ऋषि— वसिष्ठ मैत्रावरुणि। देवता— वरुण। छन्द— गायत्री, ५ जगती।]

६८४४. मो षु व॑रुण मृ॒न्मयं॑ गृ॒हं रा॑ज॒न्नहं॑ गमम्। मृ॒ळा सु॑क्ष॒त्र मृ॒ळय॑॥१॥

1. May I never go, royal *Varuṇa*, to a house made of clay—grant me happiness, possessor of wealth, grant me happiness.

May I never go to a House made of Clay— *Mo ṣu gṛham mṛnmayam gamam,* the Scholiast adds *tvadīyam*, thine, as if a temple of *Varuṇa* were intended: *su he* interprets *suśobhanam, suvarṇamayam,* very handsome, made of gold ; but its connection in the sentence is not very clear.

Sāyaṇa seems to take *su* as meaning, "but to your beautiful house, *i.e.,* one made of gold."

Grant me Happiness— Sāyaṇa explains *mṛḷaya* as "show mercy".

६८४५. यदेमि॒ प्रस्फु॑रन्नि॒व दृ॒तिर्न ध्मा॒तो अ॑द्रिवः। मृ॒ळा सु॑क्ष॒त्र मृ॒ळय॑॥२॥

2. When, *Varuṇa*, I am throbbing as if (with awe) like an inflated skin, grant me happiness, possessor of wealth, grant me happiness.

"When I am Throbbing— The text adds an epithet, *adrivas,* armed with stones for slinging. After throbbing, Sāyaṇa adds "with cold"; and instead of "I am" he has "I go bound by you". The text seems to allude to the *Varuṇa-pāśa,* a kind of dropsy, (see vol. II, mantra 3057); *cf. Ait. Brahm.* vii. 15, and *Taitt. Saṁh.* ii. 3. 11.

६८४६. क्रत्वः॒ समह॑ दी॒नता॑ प्रती॒पं ज॑गमा शुचे। मृ॒ळा सु॑क्ष॒त्र मृ॒ळय॑॥३॥

3. Opulent and pure (*Varuṇa*), if through infirmity I have done what is contrary (to the law), yet grant me happiness, possessor of wealth, grant me happiness.

५८४७. अपां मध्यै तस्थिवांसं तृष्णाविदज्जरितारम्। मृळा सुक्षत्र मृळय॥४॥

4. Thirst distresses (me) your worshipper in the midst of the waters: grant me happiness, possessor of wealth, grant me happiness.

Thirst Distresses me your Worshipper— Continuing, according to the Scholiast, the allusion to *Vasiṣṭha's* sea voyage: he is thirsty amid the waters because the water of the ocean is saline and unfit for drink. *Lavaṇotkaṭasya samudrajalasya pānānarhatvāt.*

५८४८. यत्किं चेदं वरुण दैव्ये जनेऽभिद्रोहं मनुष्याइश्चरामसि।

अचित्ती यत्तव धर्मा युयोपिम मा नस्तस्मादेनसो देव रीरिषः॥५॥

5. Whatever the offence which we men commit *Varuṇa* against divine beings, whatever law of thine we may through ignorance violate, do not you, divine *Varuṇa*, punish us on account of that iniquity.

ANUVĀKA VI

[सूक्त- ९०]

[ऋषि- वसिष्ठ मैत्रावरुणि। देवता- वायु, ५-७ इन्द्रवायु। छन्द- त्रिष्टुप्।]

५८४९. प्र वीरया शुच्यो ददिरे वामध्वर्युभिर्मधुमन्तः सुतासः।

वह वायो नियुतो याह्यच्छा पिबा सुतस्यान्धसो मदाय॥१॥

1. The sweet and pure *Soma* juices are offered to you, the hero *Vāyu*, by the priests ; therefore harness your *Niyut* steeds, come hither and drink of effused *Soma* for your exhilaration.

Yajus, 33. 70 Mahīdhara explains the first line differently; *pra vīrayā dadrire vām adhvaryubhiḥ*: Sāyaṇa considers *vīrayā* a licence for *vīraya,* and *vām* for *te*. Mahīdhara makes *vīrayā* equivalent to *vīra,* and *vām,* of you two, to the sacrificer and his wife, *he patniyajamānau yuvayoḥ soma dadrire,* your *Soma* libations, wife and sacrificer, are being effused— by the priests.

५८५०. ईशानाय प्रहुतिं यस्त आनट् शुचिं सोमं शुचिपास्तुभ्यं वायो।

कृणोषि तं मर्त्येषु प्रशस्तं जातोजातो जायते वाज्यस्य॥२॥

2. Drinker of the *Soma* juice, *Vāyu*, you elevate him who among mortals offers to you who are the lord an excellent

oblation, the pure *Soma*: repeatedly born, he is born for the acquirement of wealth.

For the Acquirement of Wealth— *Jāyate vājyasya*, the latter is explained *dhanasya prāptaye*.

५८५१. राये नु यं ज॒ज्ञतू॒ रोद॑सी॒मे रा॒ये दे॒वी धि॒षणा॑ धाति दे॒वम्।
अध॑ वा॒युं नि॒युत॑: स॒श्चत॒ स्वा उ॒त श्वे॒तं व॑सु॒धि॒तिं निरे॑के॥३॥

3. His own *Niyut* steeds bear to the place of poverty the white-complexioned dispenser of wealth, *Vāyu*, whom heaven and earth bore for the sake of riches, whom the divine language of praise sustains as a deity for the sake of riches.

Yajuṣ, 27. 24, the explanation is much the same, except in the word *nireke*, which Sāyaṇa renders *dāridryam* from *nitarām riktatā*. Mahīdhara makes it, a place crowded with people, *bahujanākīrṇe sthāne*, deriving it from *nir, nirgata,* and *reka, śunyatā,* emptiness.

५८५२. उ॒च्छन्नु॒षस॑: सु॒दिना॑ अरि॒प्रा उ॒रु ज्योति॒र्विविदु॒र्दीध्या॑ना:।
ग॒व्यं चि॒दूर्व॑मुशि॒जो वि व॑व्रु॒स्तेषा॒मनु॒ प्रदि॑व॒: सस्रु॒रापः॥४॥

4. The blameless dawns (ushering) bright days have broken, and, shining radiantly, (the *Aṅgirasas*) have obtained the vast light (the sun): desirous (to recover it) they have obtained their wealth of cattle, and the ancient waters have subsequently issued for their good.

The *Aṅgirasas*—They are not named in the text, but Sāyaṇa refers the whole to them; by their praise of *Vāyu* the dawn broke, the stolen cattle were rescued, and the obstructed rain set at liberty.

५८५३. ते स॒त्येन॒ मन॑सा दीध्या॑ना: स्वेन॑ यु॒क्तास॒: क्रतु॑ना वहन्ति।
इन्द्र॑वायू वीर॒वाहं रथं॑ वा॒मीशा॑नयो॒रभि॒ पृक्ष॑: सचन्ते॥५॥

5. Those (worshippers) illustrious by sincere adoration, assiduous in the discharge of their own duties, bring to you, *Indra* and *Vāyu*, a hero-bearing chariot, and present to you, two sovereigns, (sacrificial) food.

A Hero-Bearing Chariot— *Vīravāham ratham*, the first is explained either *aśvair vahanīyam*, to be borne by your steeds, or *stotṛbhiḥ prāpaṇīyam*, to be obtained by the worshippers ; *ratham* he renders *yajñam*, the sacrifice.

५८५४. ईशा॑नासो॒ ये द॒धते॒ स्व॑र्णो॒ गोभि॒रश्वे॑भि॒र्वसु॑भि॒र्हिर॑ण्यै:।
इन्द्र॑वायू सू॒रयो॒ विश्व॒मायु॑र॒र्वद्भि॑र्वी॒रै: पृत॑नासु स॒ह्युः॥६॥

6. May those munificent princes who confer upon us prosperity by gifts of cattle, horses, treasure, gold, overcome,

Indra and *Vāyu*, the entire existence (of their enemies) in contests with horses and with heroes.

"**Treasure**"— Sāyaṇa gives a second explanation of *vasubhiḥ*, as an epithet of *hiraṇyaiḥ*, "gold causing us to be settled, *nivāsakaiḥ*.

५८५५. अर्वन्तो न श्रवसो भिक्षमाणा इन्द्रवायू सुष्टुतिभिर्वसिष्ठाः।

वाजयन्तः स्ववसे हुवेम यूयं पात स्वस्तिभिः सदा नः॥७॥

7. We, *Vasiṣṭhas*, (bearing oblation) like horses (bearing burdens), soliciting food, desiring strength, invoke with praises *Indra* and *Vāyu* for (our) sure defence: do you ever cherish us with blessings.

[सूक्त-९१]

[ऋषि– वसिष्ठ मैत्रावरुणि। देवता– वायु, ५-७ इन्द्रवायु। छन्द– त्रिष्टुप्।]

५८५६. कुविदङ्ग नमसा ये वृधासः पुरा देवा अनवद्यास आसन्।

ते वायवे मनवे बाधितायावासयन्नुषसं सूर्येण॥१॥

1. Those venerable worshippers, who by prompted and frequently (adoring *Vāyu*) with reverence were formerly free from reproach, have now illumined *Uṣas* and the sun for sacrificing to *Vāyu* and (the preservation of) embarrassed mankind.

For...The Preservation of Embarrassed Mankind— *Manave bādhitāya* is explained as sons, etc., *manuṣyāṇām bādhitānām putrādinām rakṣaṇārtham* ; or it may be connected with the preceding word *vāyave*, to give oblations to *Vāyu* at the-sacrifice of the hindered *manu, badhitasya manoḥ prajāpater yāge vāyave haviṃṣi dātum.*

५८५७. उशन्ता दूता न दभाय गोपा मासश्च पाथः शरदश्च पूर्वीः।

इन्द्रवायू सुष्टुतिर्वामियाना मार्डीकमीट्टे सुवितं च नव्यम्॥२॥

2. Desiring (adoration), proceeding (in the sky), preservers of mankind, be not disposed, *Indra* and *Vāyu*, to do us harm: protect us through many months and years: our sincere praise, addressed to you both, solicits happiness and excellent wealth.

५८५८. पीवोऽन्नाँ रयिवृधः सुमेधाः श्वेतः सिषक्ति नियुतामभिश्रीः।

ते वायवे समनसो वि तस्थुर्विश्वेन्नरः स्वपत्यानि चक्रुः॥३॥

3. The white-complexioned *Vāyu*, intelligent, glorious with the *Niyut* steeds, favours those men who are well fed, abounding in riches, for they with one mind stand everywhere, ready to (worship) him, and leaders of rites, they perform all the ceremonies, that are productive of excellent offspring.

"Glorious with the Niyut Steeds"— Sāyaṇa seems to explain *niyutam abhiśrīḥ* as the resort or lord of the *Niyut* seeds, *niyutam abhiśrayaṇīyaḥ.*

Those Men who are Well-Fed— *Yajus,* 27. 23. Mahīdhara applies the epithets to the *Niyuts,* Sāyaṇa to *adhyajanān,* wealthy men.

५८५९. यावत्तरस्तन्वो३ यावदोजो यावन्नरश्चक्षसा दीध्यानाः।
शुचिं सोमं शुचिपा पातमस्मे इन्द्रवायू सदतं बर्हिरिदम्॥४॥

4. As much as is your rapidity of body, as much as is your vigour, as much as the leaders (of rites) are illuminated by wisdom, (to such extent), drinkers of the pure (beverage) *Indra* and *Vāyu,* drink this our pure *Soma,* and sit down upon this sacred grass.

५८६०. नियुवाना नियुतः स्पार्हवीरा इन्द्रवायू सरथं यातमर्वाक्।
इदं हि वां प्रभृतं मध्वो अग्रमध प्रीणाना वि मुमुक्तमस्मे॥५॥

5. Harnessing the *Niyuts,* whom the devout (worshippers) desire, to your common car, come, *Indra* and *Vāyu,* hither: this the first (cup) of the sweet beverage is prepared for you ; and then, delighted (by the draught), liberate us (from sin).

"Whom the Devout Worshippers Desire— Rather, "whose worshippers are objects of desire, *spṛhaṇīyastotṛkān.*

५८६१. या वां शतं नियुतो याः सहस्रमिन्द्रवायू विश्ववाराः सचन्ते।
आभिर्यातं सुविदत्राभिरर्वाक्पातं नरा प्रतिभृतस्य मध्वः॥६॥

6. Come to our presence, *Indra* and *Vāyu,* with those munificent *Niyut* steeds, who, the desired of all, wait upon you both by hundreds and thousands: drink, leaders (of rites), of the sweet beverage placed near (the altar).

५८६२. अर्वन्तो न श्रवसो भिक्षमाणा इन्द्रवायू सुष्टुतिभिर्निसिष्ठाः।
वाजयन्तः स्वर्वसे हुवेम यूयं पात स्वस्तिभिः सदा नः॥७॥

7. We, *Vasiṣṭhas,* (bearing oblations) like horses (bearing burdens), soliciting food, desiring strength, invoke with praises *Indra* and *Vāyu* for our sure defence: do you ever cherish us with blessings.

[सूक्त-९२]

[ऋषि- वसिष्ठ मैत्रावरुणि। देवता- वायु, ५-७ इन्द्रवायु। छन्द- त्रिष्टुप्।]

५८६३. आ वायो भूष शुचिपा उप नः सहस्रं ते नियुतो विश्ववार।

उपो॑ ते॒ अन्धो॑ मद्य॑मयामि यस्य॑ देव द॒धिषे॒ पूर्व॑पेय॑म्॥१॥

1. Drinker of the pure (*Soma*), *Vāyu*, come to us as your *Niyuts* are thousands: oh, you who are desired of all, I offer you, the exhilarating (sacrificial) food, of which you, deity, have the prior drinking.

Yajurveda, 7.7.

Offer You— *Upayāmi* has a technical power as especially applicable to the *Soma,* which is brought in a vessel called *upayāma, upayātam pātre gṛhītam.*

५८६४. प्र सोता॑ जीरो अध्व॑रेष्व॑स्थात् सोम॒मिन्द्रा॑य वाय॑वे पिब॒ध्यै।

प्र यद्वां॒ मध्वो॑ अग्रि॒यं भर॑न्त्यध्व॒र्यवो॑ देव॒यन्तः॑ शची॑भिः॥२॥

2. The prompt effuser of the libation offers the *Soma* to *Indra* and to *Vāyu* to drink at the sacrifices, at which devout priests, according to their functions, bring to you two the first (portion) of the *Soma.*

५८६५. प्र याभि॒र्यासि॑ दा॒श्वांस॑मच्छा॑ नियु॒द्भिर्वा॑यविष्ट॒ये दुरो॒णे।

नि नो॒ रयिं॑ सु॒भोज॑सं युवस्व॒ नि वी॒रं ग॒व्यमश्व्यं॑ च॒ राधः॑॥३॥

3. With those *Niyut* seeds, with which you repair, *Vāyu*, to the donor (of the libation), waiting in his hall to offer sacrifice, (come to us), and bestow upon us enjoyable riches, bestow male progeny, and wealth, comprehending cattle, and horses.

५८६६. ये वाय॒व इन्द्र॑मा॒दना॑स आ॒देवा॑सो नितो॒शना॑सो अ॒र्यः।

घ्नन्तो॑ वृ॒त्राणि॑ सू॒रिभिः॑ ष्याम सास॒ह्वांसो॑ यु॒धा नृभि॑र॒मित्रा॑न्॥४॥

4. Overcoming our enemies in war by our warriors, may we be the slayers of foes, through the pious (worshippers) who are the exhilarators of *Indra* and *Vāyu*, the reciters of divine hymns, the destroyers of the adversary.

५८६७. आ नो॑ नियु॒द्भिः श॒तिनी॑भिरध्व॒रं स॑ह॒स्रिणी॑भिरुप याहि य॒ज्ञम्।

वायो॑ अ॒स्मिन्त्स॒वने॑ मादयस्व यू॒यं पा॑त स्व॒स्तिभिः॒ सदा॑ नः॥५॥

5. Come *Vāyu*, to our imperishable sacrifice, with hundreds and thousands of *Niyut* steeds, and be exhilarated at this ceremony: do you (gods) ever cherish us with blessings.

Do you Gods— *Yajus,* 27. 28 Mahīdhara here supplies the ellipse with *Ṛtvijaḥ,* priests.

[सूक्त-९३]

[ऋषि- वसिष्ठ मैत्रावरुणि। **देवता**- इन्द्राग्नी। **छन्द**- त्रिष्टुप्।]

५८६८. शुचिं नु स्तोमं नव॑जातमद्येन्द्रा॒ग्नी वृ॑त्रहणा जुषेथाम्।
उ॒भा हि वां॑ सु॒हवा॒ जोह॑वीमि॒ ता वाजं॑ स॒द्य उ॒शते॒ धेष्ठा॑॥१॥

1. Slayers of enemies, *Indra* and *Agni*, be pleased today by this pious and newly recited praise: repeatedly do we invoke you both, who are worthy of invocation; you are the chief bestowers of food promptly upon him who solicits (it of you).

५८६९. ता सान॑सी॒ शव॑साना॒ हि भू॒तं साकं॒वृधा॒ शव॑सा शूशु॒वांसा॑।
क्ष॒यन्तौ॑ रा॒यो य॑व॒सस्य॒ भूरे॑: पृ॒ङ्क्तं वाज॑स्य स्थवि॑रस्य॒ घृष्वे॑:॥२॥

2. You two are desired of all, the demolishers of (hostile) strength, augmenting together, increasing in vigour, lords of the wealth of corn: do you grant us substantial invigorating food.

"The Demolishers of Hostile Strength"— Sāyaṇa seems to explain *śavasānā hi bhūtam* as, "you acted like an army breaking enemies," (*cf. Pan* iii.1.11. vart.)

Do you Grant us Substantial Invigorating Food— *Prinktam vajasya sthavīrasya ghṛsveḥ* is explained *annasya, sthūlasya, śatruṇām, gharṣakasya, idṛśam annam prayacchatām,* give us such food as is coarse, the destroyer of enemies.

५८७०. उपो॑ ह॒ यद्दि॑दय॒थं वा॒जिनो॑ गु॒र्धीभि॒र्विप्रा॑: प्रम॒तिमिच्छ॑माना॒:।
अर्व॑न्तो॒ न काष्ठां॑ न॒क्षमा॑णा इन्द्रा॒ग्नी जोहु॑वतो॒ नर॑स्ते॥३॥

3. Those sage offerers of oblations, who, desiring your favour, celebrate the sacrifice with holy rites, hasten to worship you, like horse to battle, repeatedly invoking *Indra* and *Agni*.

५८७१. गी॒र्भिर्विप्र॑: प्रम॒तिमिच्छ॑मान॒ ईट्टे॑ र॒यिं य॒शसं॑ पू॒र्वभा॑जम्।
इन्द्रा॒ग्नी वृ॑त्रहणा सु॒वज्रा॒ प्र नो॑ न॒व्येभि॑स्तिरतं दे॒ष्णै:॥४॥

4. The pious sage, desiring your favour, glorifies you with praises for the sake of formerly enjoyed riches, accompanied by celebrity: *Indra* and *Agni*, slayers of *Vṛtra*, bearers of the thunderbolt, exalt us with precious donations.

"Formerly Enjoyed Riches"— Rather, "Riches desirable even in olden time," *pūrvam eva sambhajanīyam.*

५८७२. सं यन्मही मिथती स्पर्धमाने तनूरुचा शूरसाता यतैते।
अदेवयुं विदथे देवयुभिः सत्रा हंतं सोमसुता जनेन।५।।

5. As two large, mutually defiant (armies), emulous in corporal vigour, may contend in war, so do you destroy, by the devout, those who are not devoted to the gods in sacrifice, and, by the man who presents libations, (him who does not offer).

As two large, Mutually Defiant Armies, Emulous in Corporal vigour— *Sām yān mahi mithati spardhamāne tanurucā śūrasātā yataite,* we have here a set of feminine duals without a substantive, literally two large reviling rivalling may strive together: in the best copies there is a blank, which is also left in the printed edition, but in some copies we have *sene,* two armies.

५८७३. इमामु षु सोमसुतिमुप न एन्द्राग्नी सौमनसाय यातम्।
नू चिद्धि परिमम्नाथे अस्माना वां शश्वद्द्विर्ववृतीय वाजैः।।६।।

6. Come with gracious minds, *Indra* and *Agni*, to this our *Soma* libation: you are never regardless of us, therefore I propitiate you with constant (sacrificial) viands.

५८७४. सो अग्न एना नर्मसा समिद्धोऽच्छा मित्रं वरुणमिन्द्रं वोचेः।
यत्सीमागश्चकृमा तत्सु मृळ तदर्यमादितिः शिश्रथन्तु।।७।।

7. Kindled, *Agni*, by this adoration, do you recommend us to *Mitra, Varuṇa*, and *Indra*: whatever sin we may have committed, do you expiate, and may *Aryaman, Aditi* (and *Mitra*) remove it (from us).

५८७५. एता अग्न आशुषाणास इष्टीर्युवोः सचाभ्यश्याम वाजान्।
मेन्द्रो नो विष्णुर्मरुतः परि ख्यन्यूयं पात स्वस्तिभिः सदा नः।।८।।

8. Diligently celebrating these rites, may we, *Agni*, (and *Indra*), at once arrive at your food: let not *Indra. Viṣṇu*, the *Maruts*, abandon us ; and do you (gods) ever cherish us with blessings.

[**सूक्त-९४**]

[**ऋषि**- वसिष्ठ मैत्रावरुणि। **देवता**- इन्द्राग्नी।
छन्द- गायत्री, १२ अनुष्टुप्।]

५८७६. इयं वामस्य मन्मन इन्द्राग्नी पूर्व्यस्तुतिः। अभ्राद्वृष्टिरिवाजनि।।१।।

1. This chief praise, *Indra* and *Agni*, proceeds (copiously) from me your worshipper, like rain from a cloud.

This and the two next stanzas occur in the *Sāmaveda*, 916-18.

५८७७. शृणुतं जरितुर्हवमिन्द्राग्नी वनतं गिरः। ईशाना पिप्यतं धियः॥२॥

2. Hear, *Indra* and *Agni*, the invocation of the worshipper ; accept his adoration. Recompense, lords, his pious acts.

५८७८. मा पापत्वाय नो नरेन्द्राग्नी माभिशंस्तये। मा नो रीरधतं निदे॥३॥

3. Leaders of (rites), *Indra* and *Agni*, subject us not to wickedness, nor to calumny, nor to the reviler.

५८७९. इन्द्रे अग्ना नमो बृहत्सुवृक्तिमेरयामहे। धिया धेना अवस्यवः॥४॥

4. Desiring protection, we offer copious oblations and praise to *Indra* and *Agni*, and prayers with holy rites.

Sāmaveda, 800-802.

५८८०. ता हि शश्वन्त ईळत इत्था विप्रास ऊतये। सबाधो वाजसातये॥५॥

5. Many are the sages who propitiate (*Indra* and *Agni*) in this manner for (their) protection, mutually striving for the acquirement of food.

५८८१. ता वां गीर्भिर्विपन्यवः प्रयस्वन्तो हवामहे। मेधसाता सनिष्यवः॥६॥

6. Eager to offer praise, bearing (sacrificial) food, desirous of wealth, we invoke you, *Indra* and *Agni*, with praises, in the celebration of holy acts.

५८८२. इन्द्राग्नी अवसा गतमस्मभ्यं चर्षणीसहा। मा नो दुःशंस ईशत॥७॥

7. Overcomers of (hostile) men, *Indra* and *Agni*, come with food (to be bestowed) upon us: let not the malevolent have power over us.

५८८३. मा कस्य नो अररुषो धूर्तिः प्रणङ् मर्त्यस्य।

इन्द्राग्नी शर्म यच्छतम्॥८॥

8. Let not the malice of any hostile mortal reach us grant us, *Indra* and *Agni*, felicity.

५८८४. गोमद्धिरण्यवद्वसु यद्वामश्वावदीमहे। इन्द्राग्नी तद्वनेमहि॥९॥

9. We solicit you both for wealth, comprising cattle, gold and horses: may we obtain it of you, *Indra* and *Agni*.

"Gold"— Sāyaṇa explains *hiraṇyavat* as *suvarṇair yuktam, cf.* vol. II. verse 3869.

५८८५. यत्सोम॒ आ सु॒ते नर॒ इन्द्रा॒ग्नी अ॒जोह॑वुः। स॒प्ती॒॑वन्ता स॒पर्य॑वः॥१०॥

10. When adoring leaders (of rites), invoke you two, lords of horses, on the *Soma* being offered, (come hither).

५८८६. उ॒क्थेभि॑र्वृ॒त्रह॒न्तमा॒ या म॒न्दाना॒ चि॒दा गि॒रा।

आङ्गू॒षैरा॑वि॒वा॑सतः॥११॥

11. Utter destroyer of *Vṛtra*, exhilarated (by the *Soma*), you who are worshipped with prayers and hymns and songs, (come hither).

"Utter Destroyers of *Varuṇa*"— Sāyaṇa and Mahīdhara take *vṛtra-hantama* as *āvarakāṇām hantṛtamau*, the latter adds *pāpmānam*.

With Prayers and Hymns and Songs— *Angūṣair, āghoṣair anyais stotraiḥ,* with clamours, with other praises: Mahīdhara, *yajuṣ,* 33. 76, explains it *laukikavākstomaiḥ,* with praises in worldly or vernacular speech, not that of the *Veda*.

५८८७. ताविद्दुःशंसं॒ मर्त्यं॒ दु॒र्विद्वां॑सं र॒क्षस्विन॑म्।

आ॒भोगं॒ हन्म॑ना हतमु॒दधिं॒ हन्म॑ना हतम्॥१२॥

12. Destroy with your fatal (weapons) the mortal who is malignant, ignorant, strong, rapacious: destroy him like a water jar, with your weapons.

Rapacious— *Ābhogam,* the Scholiast says, is he who enjoys good things taken from the worshippers.

[सूक्त-९५]

[**ऋषि**- वसिष्ठ मैत्रावरुणि। **देवता**- सरस्वती, ३ सरस्वान्। **छन्द**- त्रिष्टुप्।]

५८८८. प्र क्षोद॑सा॒ धाय॑सा सस्र॒ एषा॒ सर॑स्वती धरु॒णमायसी॒ पूः।

प्र॒बाब॑धाना र॒थ्ये॑व याति॒ विश्वा॑ अ॒पो म॑हि॒ना सिन्धु॑र॒न्याः॥१॥

1. This *Sarasvatī,* firm as a city made of iron, flows rapidly with all sustaining water, sweeping away in its might all other waters, as a charioteer (clears the road).

Firm as a City made of Iron— *Dharuṇam āyasi pūḥ, ayasa nirmita purīva: dharuṇam* for *dharuṇa, dhārayitrī,* supporter: what is meant by the comparison is not very obvious.

५८८९. एका॑चेत॒त्सर॑स्वती न॒दीनां॒ शुचि॑र्य॒ती गि॒रिभ्य॒ आ स॑मु॒द्रात्।

रा॒यश्चेत॑न्ती॒ भुव॑नस्य॒ भूरे॑र्घृ॒तं पयो॑ दुदुहे॒ नाहु॑षाय॥२॥

2. *Sarasvatī,* chief and pure of rivers, flowing form the mountains to the ocean, understood the request of *Nahuṣa,* and

distributing riches among the many existing beings, milked for him butter and water.

Flowing from the Mountains to the Ocean— *atī giribhya ā samudrāt* is the text.

Milked for him Butter and Water— According to the legend, king *Nahuṣa,* being about to perform sacrifice for a thousand years, prayed to *Sarasvatī,* who thereupon gave him butter and water, or milk, sufficient for that period.

५८९०. स वावृधे नर्यो योष॒णासु॒ वृषा॒ शिशु॒र्वृष॒भो य॒ज्ञिया॑सु।
स॒ वा॒जिनं॑ म॒घव॑द्भ्यो दधाति॒ वि सा॒तये॑ त॒न्वं॑ मामृजीत॥३॥

3. The showerer *Sarasvat,* the friend of man, a showerer (of benefits), even while yet a child, continually increases among his adorable wives (the rains): he bestows upon the affluent worshippers) a vigorous son ; he purifies their persons (to fit them) for the reception (of his bounties).

Sarasvat— Sāyaṇa says *Sarasvat* is the wind *Vāyu* in the firmament, *madhyasthāno Vāyuḥ Sarasvat.*

५८९१. उत॒ स्या न॑: सर॑स्वती जु॒षा॒णोप॑ श्रवत् सु॒भगा॑ य॒ज्ञे अ॒स्मिन्।
मि॒त॒ज्ञुभि॒र्नम॑स्यैरि॒याना॑ रा॒या यु॒जा चि॒दुत्त॑रा॒ सखि॑भ्य:॥४॥

4. May the auspicious and gracious *Sarasvatī* hear (our praises) at this sacrifice, approached as she is with reverence and with banded knees, and most liberal to her friends with the riches she possesses.

५८९२. इ॒मा जु॒ह्वा॑ना यु॒ष्मदा॒ नमो॑भि॒: प्रति॒ स्तोमं॑ सरस्वति जुषस्व।
तव॒ शर्म॑न्प्रि॒यत॑मे॒ दधा॑ना॒ उप॑स्थेयाम शर॒णं न वृ॒क्षम्॥५॥

5. Presenting to you, *Sarasvatī,* these oblations with reverence (may we receive from you affluence): be gratified by our praise and may we, being retained in your dearest felicity, ever recline upon you, as on a sheltering tree.

May we Receive from you Affluence— The text has only *yuṣmad* a, but an inseparable prefix, standing alone implies, in the *Veda,* the verb also: therefore, says the Scholiast, a is for *adadimahi,* may we receive: the rule is *upasargaśruter yogyakriyādhyāhāraḥ,* an *upasarga* in the *Veda* is the indication of the conjenct verb.

५८९३. अ॒यमु॑ ते सरस्वति व॒सि॒ष्ठो द्वा॒रावृ॑त॒स्य॑ सुभगे॒ व्याव॑:।
वर्ध॑ शुभ्रे स्तुव॒ते रा॑सि॒ वाजा॒न् यू॒यं पा॑त स्व॒स्तिभि॒: सदा॑ न:॥६॥

6. Auspicious *Sarasvatī*, for you *Vasiṣṭha* has set open the two doors (the east and west) of sacrifice: white-complexioned (goddess), be magnified ; bestow food on him who glorifies you: and do you (gods) ever cherish us with blessings.

[सूक्त-९६]

[ऋषि– वसिष्ठ मैत्रावरुणि। देवता– सरस्वती, ४-६ सरस्वान्। छन्द– १-२ प्रगाथ (१ विषमा बृहती, २ समासतो बृहती।) ३ प्रस्तार पंक्ति, ४-६ गायत्री।]

५८९४. बृहद्दु गायिषे वचोऽसुर्या नदीनाम्।

सरस्वतीमिन्मंहया सुवृक्तिभिः स्तोमैर्वसिष्ठ रोदसी।।१।।

1. Thou chauntest, *Vasiṣṭha* a powerful hymn to her who is the most mighty of river, worship, *Vasiṣṭha* with well-selected praises, *Sarasvatī*, who is both in heaven and earth.

Who is both in Heaven and Earth— As a goddess, or as eloquence or as a river.

५८९५. उभे यत्ते महिना शुभ्रे अन्धंसी अधिक्षियन्ति पूर्वः।

सा नों बोध्यवित्री मरुत्संखा चोद राधों मघोनाम्।।२।।

2. Beautiful *Sarasvatī*, inasmuch as by your might men obtain both kinds of food, do you, our protectress, regard us: do you, the friend on the *Maruts*, bestow riches upon those who are affluent (in oblations).

Both kinds of Food— *Ubhe andhasī* is said to mean fires celestial and terrestrial, or if food be intended, domestic and wild, *grāmyam āraṇyam vā*.

५८९६. भद्रमिद्द्रद्रा कृणवत्सरस्वत्यकंवारी चेतति वाजिनीवती।

गृणाना जमदग्निवत्स्तुवाना च वसिष्ठवत्।।३।।

3. May the auspicious *Sarasvatī* bestow auspicious fortune upon us: may the faultless-moving food-conferring (goddess) think of us: glorified (as you have been) by *Jamadagni*, (be now) glorified by *Vasiṣṭha*.

५८९७. जनीयन्तो न्वग्रवः पुत्रीयन्तः सुदानवः। सरस्वन्तं हवामहे।।४।।

4. Desiring wives, desiring sons, liberal of donations, approaching him, now worship *Sarsavat*.

५८९८. ये ते सरस्व ऊर्मयो मधुमन्तो घृतश्चुतः। तेर्भिनोंऽविता भव।।५।।

5. With those your waves *Sarasvat*, which are sweet-tasted, the distributors of water, be our protector.

५८९९. पीपिवांसं सरस्वत: स्तनं यो विश्वदर्शत:। भक्षीमहि प्रजामिषम्॥६॥

6. May we recline upon the protuberant breast of *Sarasvat*. Which is visible to all; that we may possess progeny and food.

May we Recline etc.— *Pīpivāṁsam Sarasvatas stanam bhakṣīmahi*, and *stana* here, according to the Scholiast, means of cloud, *megha*.

Sāyaṇa renders this verse "may we obtain the distend and loud-thundering [of breast-like] cloud of *Sarasvat*. Which is visible to all: (may we obtain) progeny and food.

[सूक्त-९७]

[**ऋषि**–वसिष्ठ मैत्रावरुणि। **देवता**– बृहस्पति, १ इन्द्र ३, ९
इन्द्राब्रह्मणस्पती, १० इन्द्राबृहस्पति। **छन्द**– त्रिष्टुप्।]

५९००. यज्ञे दिवो नृषदने पृथिव्या नरो यत्र देवयवो मदन्ति।
इन्द्राय यत्र सवनानि सुन्वे गमन्मदाय प्रथमं वयश्च॥१॥

1. At the sacrifice in the dwellings of man upon earth, where the devout leaders of (rites) rejoice, where the libations to *Indra* are poured out, there may he descend before (other gods) from heaven for his exhilaration: (may his) swift (horses approach).

"In the Dwellings of Men upon Earth"— Sāyaṇa has "at the sacrifice which is the home of the priests upon earth.

५९०१. आ दैव्या वृणीमहेऽवांसि बृहस्पतिर्नो मह आ सखाय:।
यथा भवेम मीळ्हुषे अनागा यो नो दाता परावत: पितेव॥२॥

2. Let us solicit, friends divine protections, for *Bṛhaspati* accepts our (oblations): so may we be without offence towards that showerer (of benefits) who is our benefactor from afar, as a father (of a son).

५९०२. तमु ज्येष्ठं नमसा हविर्भि: सुशेवं ब्रह्मणस्पतिं गृणीषे।
इन्द्रं श्लोको महि दैव्य: सिषक्तु यो ब्रह्मणो देवकृतस्य राजा॥३॥

3. I glorify with homage and with oblations that most excellent and beneficent *Brahmaṇaspati*: may my praise worthy of the deity, attain to the mighty *Indra*, who is the lord of the prayers offered by the devout.

५९०३. स आ नो योनिं सदतु प्रेष्ठो बृहस्पतिर्विश्ववारो यो अस्ति।
कामो राय: सुवीर्यस्य तं दात्पर्षन्नो अति सश्चतो अरिष्टान्।।४।।

4. May that best beloved *Bṛhaspati*, who is the desired of all
sit down in our hall of sacrifice: may he gratify our desire of riches
and of male posterity. Transporting us (at present) embarrassed
uninjured beyond (the assaults of enemies)

५९०४. तमा नो अर्कममृताय जुष्टमिमे धासुरमृतास: पुराजा:।
शुचिक्रन्दं यजतं पस्त्यानां बृहस्पतिमनर्वाणं हुवेम।।५।।

5. May the first-born immortals (by his command) bestow
upon us the food that is necessary for existence let us invoke the
unresisted *Bṛhaspati*, to whom pure praises are addressed, the
adored of householders.

"The First-Born"— Rather, born of vore" *purā jātaḥ, purājā.*

The Adored of Householders— *Pastyānām yajatam* is, literally, the
adorable of houses, *i.e.,* by *metonyney* householders.

५९०५. तं शग्मासो अरुषासो अश्वा बृहस्पतिं सहवाहो वहन्ति।
सहश्चिद्यस्य नीलवत्सधस्थं नभो न रूपमरुषं वसाना:।।६।।

6. May his powerful brilliant horses, wearing a lustrous form
like (that of) the sun, acting together, bring (hither) that *Bṛhaspati*,
in whom strength abides like that of a substantial mansion.

"In whom Strength abides like that of a Substantial Mansion"—
Rather, "to whom belongs strength, and whose friendship bestow a
dwelling." It is interesting to notice, that although Sayama st *milaya,* and
apparently derives it from m+b he yet presentense the correct sense
as=nida. Such facts seem to move that he followed a traditional
interpretation, though he may the thought his own etymonsites.

५९०६. स हि शुचि: शतपत्र: स शुभ्युर्हिरण्यवाशीरिषिर: स्वर्षा:।
बृहस्पति: स स्वावेश ऋष्व: पुरू सखिभ्य आसुतिं करिष्ठ:।।७।।

7. He verily is pure, borne by numerous conveyances, the is he
purifier armed with golden weapons, the object of desire, the
enjoyer of heaven: he *Bṛhaspati* is well domiciled, of goodly
aspect, a most bountiful giver of ample food to his friend.

Armed with Golden Weapons— *Hiraṇyavāśīḥ* may also be
rendered, he whose speech is benevolent, *hitaramaṇīya vāk.*

५९०७. देवी देवस्य रोदसी जनित्री बृहस्पतिं वावृधतुर्महित्वा।
दक्षाय्याय दक्षता सखाय: करद् ब्रह्मणे सुतरा सुगाधा।।८।।

8. The divine heaven and earth, the generatrices of the deity
have by their might, given growth to *Bṛhaspati*: magnify, friends,
the magnifiable, and may he render (the waters) easy to be crossed
and forded for (the attainment of) food.

५९०८. इयं वां ब्रह्मणस्पते सुवृक्तिर्ब्रह्मेन्द्राय वज्रिणे अकारि।

अविष्टं धियो जिगृतं पुरन्धीर्जज्जस्तमर्यो वनुषामराती:॥९॥

9. This praise has been offered as prayer to you both,
Brahmaṇaspati and *Indra*, the wielder of the thunderbolt: protect
our ceremonies: hear our manifold praise: annihilate the assailing
adversaries of your worshippers.

This Prayer has been offered as Prayer— *Iyam suviktir brahma* is
explained *iyam mantrarūpa stutiḥ* this praise in the form of a *mantra,* a
sacred text or prayer.

५९०९. बृहस्पते युवमिन्द्रश्च वस्वो दिव्यस्यैशाथे उत पार्थिवस्य।

धत्तं रयिं स्तुवते कीरये चिद्युयं पात स्वस्तिभि: सदा न:॥१०॥

10. You two, *Bṛhaspati* and *Indra* are lords of both celestial
and terrestrial treasure: grant riches to the worshipper who praises
you: and do you (gods) ever cherish us with blessings.

[सूक्त-९८]

[ऋषि– वसिष्ठ मैत्रावरुणि। देवता– इन्द्र, ७ इन्द्राबृहस्पती।

छन्द– त्रिष्टुप्।]

५९१०. अध्वर्यवोऽरुणं दुग्धमंशुं जुहोतन वृषभाय क्षितीनाम्।

गौराद्वेदीयां अवपानमिन्द्रो विश्वाहेद्याति सुतसोममिच्छन्॥१॥

1. Offer, priests, the shining effused *Soma* to him who is
eminent (among) men: knowing better than the *Gaura* where his
distant drinking-place (is to be found). *Indra* comes daily seeking
for the offerer of the libation.

Knowing better than the Gaura where Etc.— *Gaurād vedīyān
avapānam,* means *avakramya sthitam dūrastham pātavyam somam
gauramṛgād api atiśayena* i.e., knowing the *Soma* that is to be drunk,
through placed afar off, better than an ox or a deer knows the drinking
place or pond which is assessment to go to.

५९११. यद्धिषे प्रदिवि चार्वन्नं दिवेदिवे पीतिमिदस्य वक्षि।

उत हृदोत मनसा जुषाण उशन्निन्द्र प्रस्थितान् पाहि सोमान्॥२॥

2. The pleasant beverage that you, *Indra*, have quaffed in former days, you still desires to drink of daily: gratified in heart and mind, and wishing (our good), drink, *Indra* the *Soma*, that is placed before (you).

५९१२. जज्ञान: सोमं सहसे पपाथ प्र ते माता महिमानमुवाच।

एन्द्र पप्राथोर्व1न्तरिक्षं युधा देवेभ्यो वरिवश्चकर्थ॥३॥

3. As soon as born, *Indra* you have drunk the *Soma* for thine invigoration: your mother (*Aditi*) proclaimed your greatness: hence you have filled the vast firmament. *Indra*. You have gained in battle treasure for the gods.

"**Your Mother Proclaimed your Greatness**"— This refers to *Aditi's* speech *Ṛg*. iv.18.4.

५९१३. यद्योधया महतो मन्यमानान्त्साक्षाम तान् बाहुभि: शाशदानान्।

यद्वा नृभिर्वृतं इन्द्राभियुध्यास्तं त्वयाजिं सौश्रवसं जयेम॥४॥

4. When you enable us to encounter mighty and arrogant (enemies). We are competent to overcome the malignats by our (unarmed) hands alone: and when you. *Indra*, surrounded by your attendant (*Maruts*), fight against them, we shall triumph, aided by you, (in) that glorious war.

५९१४. प्रेन्द्रस्य वोचं प्रथमा कृतानि प्र नूतना मघवा या चकार।

यदेददेवीरसहिष्ट माया अर्थाभवत्केवल: सोमो अस्य॥५॥

5. I proclaim the ancient exploits of *Indra* the recent deeds that *Maghavan* has achieved: when indeed he had overcome the undivine illusion, thenceforth the *Soma* became his exclusive (beverage).

The explanation of the scholiast is rather equivocal, the relation between the *Soma* and *Indra* thenceforth became common or special, peculiar: *tadā prabhṛtyeva Somasya indrasya ca asādhāraṇas sambandho jātaḥ;* but though in the especial degree the drink of *Indra*. It is often presented to *Agni* and other deities.

५९१५. तेवेदं विश्वमभितं: पश्व्यं यत्पश्यसि चक्षसा सूर्यस्य।

गवांमसि गोपतिरेक इन्द्र भक्षीमहि ते प्रयतस्य वस्व:॥६॥

6. Thine is all this animal world around you, which you illume with the light of the sun: you, *Indra*, are the one lord of cattle, thence may we possess wealth bestowed by you.

५९१६. बृहस्पते युवमिन्द्रश्च वस्वो दिव्यस्येशाथे उत पार्थिवस्य।

धत्तं रयिं स्तुवते कीरये चिद्युयं पात स्वस्तिभिः सदा नः ॥७॥

7. You two *Bṛhaspati* and *Indra* are lords of both celestial and terrestrial treasure grant riches to the worshipper who praises you: and do you (gods) ever cherish us with blessings.

[सूक्त-९९]

[**ऋषि**– वसिष्ठ मैत्रावरुणि। **देवता**– विष्णु, ४-६ इन्द्राविष्णु।

छन्द– त्रिष्टुप्।]

५९१७. परो मात्रया तन्वा वृधान न ते महित्वमन्वश्नुवन्ति।

उभे ते विद्म रजसी पृथिव्या विष्णो देव त्वं परमस्य वित्से ॥१॥

1. Expanding with a body beyond all measure, *Viṣṇu* men comprehend not your magnitude: we know these your two worlds (computing) from the earth, but you, divine *Viṣṇu*, are cognisant of the highest.

Your two World Computing from the Earth— That is, the earth and the firmament, which are visible.[1]

५९१८. न ते विष्णो जायमानो न जातो देव महिम्नः परमन्तमाप।

उदस्तभ्ना नाकमृष्वं बृहन्तं दाधर्थ प्राचीं ककुभं पृथिव्याः ॥२॥

2. No being that is or that has been born, divine *Viṣṇu*, has attained the utmost limit of your magnitude by which you have upheld the vast and beautiful heaven, and sustained the eastern horizon of the earth.

Sustained the Eastern Horizon of the Earth— Part put for the whole, the entire earth. Viṣṇu's upholding the three worlds has been mentioned more than once. See *Ṛg.* i. 154. 4

५९१९. इरावती धेनुमती हि भूतं सूयवसिनी मनुषे दशस्या।

व्यस्तभ्ना रोदसी विष्णवेते दाधर्थ पृथिवीमभितो मयूखैः ॥३॥

3. Heaven and earth, abounding with food, abounding with cattle, yielding abundant fodder, you are disposed to be liberal to the man (who praises you): you, *Viṣṇu*, have upheld these two heaven and earth, and have secured the earth around with mountains.

---

१. See *Ṛg.* 10.82.5.

To the Man who Praises You— *Manuṣe stuvate* the *Yajus,* v. 16, reads *manave,* with a similar purport *yajamānāya,* to the institutor of the rite.

Have secured the Earth Around with Mountains— *Dādhartha pṛthivīm mayukhaih;*[1] the last is explained *parvataih,* by mountains: Mahīdhara says by his incarnations displaying his glory, *tejorūpair avatāraih.*

५९२०. उरुं यज्ञाय चक्रथुरु लोकं जनयन्ता सूर्यमुषासमग्निम् ।
दासस्य चिद्वृषशिप्रस्य माया जघ्नथुर्नरा पृतनाज्येषु ॥४॥

4. You two, *Indra* and *Viṣṇu,* have made the spacious world for the sake of sacrifice, generating the sun the dawn, *Agni:* you leaders (of rites) have baffled the devices of the slave *Vṛṣaśipra* in the conflicts of hosts.

५९२१. इन्द्राविष्णू दृंहिताः शम्बरस्य नव पुरो नवतिं च श्नथिष्टम् ।
शतं वर्चिनः सहस्रं च साकं हथो अप्रत्यसुरस्य वीरान् ॥५॥

5. *Indra* and *Viṣṇu,* you have demolished the ninety-nine strong cities of *Śambara:* you have slain at once, without resistance, the hundred thousand heroes of the *Asura Varcin.*

Varcin— See *Ṛg.* ii.14.6.

५९२२. इयं मनीषा बृहती बृहन्तोरुक्रमा तवसा वर्धयन्ती ।
ररे वां स्तोमं विदथेषु विष्णो पिन्वतमिषो वृजनेष्विन्द्र ॥६॥

6. This ample laudation is magnifying you two, who are mighty, wide-striding, endowed with strength: to you two. *Viṣṇu* and *Indra.* I offer praise at sacrifices; grant us food (won) in battles.

५९२३. वषट् ते विष्णवास आ कृणोमि तन्मे जुषस्व शिपिविष्ट हव्यम् ।
वर्धन्तु त्वा सुष्टुतयो गिरो मे यूयं पात स्वस्तिभिः सदा नः ॥७॥

7. I offer, *Viṣṇu,* the oblation placed before you with the exclamation *Vaṣa*—: be pleased, *Śipiviṣṭa,* with my offering: may my laudatory hymns magnify you ; and do you (gods) ever cherish us with blessings.

---

१. See *Tai. S.* 3.4.5.1.

[सूक्त-१००]

[**ऋषि**– वसिष्ठ मैत्रावरुणि, **देवता**–विष्णु। **छन्द**–त्रिष्टुप्।]

५९२४. नू मर्तो दयते सनिष्यन्यो विष्णव उरुगायाय दाशत्।
प्र यः सत्राचा मनसा यजात एतावन्तं नर्यमाविवासात्।।१।।

1. The mortal desirous of wealth quickly obtains it who presents (offerings) to the widely-renowned *Viṣṇu*, who worships him with entirely devoted mind, who adores so great a benefactor of mankind.

"With Entirely Devoted Mind"— Sāyaṇa says, with united praise, *sahāñcatā stotreṇa.*

५९२५. त्वं विष्णो सुमतिं विश्वजन्यामप्रयुतामेवयावो मतिं दाः।
पर्चो यथा नः सुवितस्य भूरेरश्वावतः पुरुश्चन्द्रस्य रायः।।२।।

2. *Viṣṇu*, granter or desires, show to us that favourable disposition which is benevolent to all, unmixed (with exception), so that there may be to us the attainment of easily-acquired, ample, steed-comprising, all-delighting riches .

Granter of Desires— *Evayāvan,* from *eva*, obtainable, desires ; *yāvan,* who enables to obtain.

५९२६. त्रिदेवः पृथिवीमेष एतां वि चक्रमे शतर्चसं महित्वा।
प्र विष्णुरस्तु तवसस्तवीयान्त्वेषं ह्यस्य स्थविरस्य नाम।।३।।

3. This deity, by his great power, traversed with three (steps) the many-lustrous earth ; may *Viṣṇu*, the most powerful of the powerful rule over us, for illustrious is the name of the mighty one.

Earth— Earth *pṛthivī,* according to the comment, is put for *pṛthivyādīn*, or the three worlds.

५९२७. वि चक्रमे पृथिवीमेष एतां क्षेत्राय विष्णुर्मनुषे दशस्यन्।
ध्रुवासो अस्य कीरयो जनास उरुक्षितिं सुजनिमा चकार।।४।।

4. This *Viṣṇu* traversed the earth for a dwelling which he was desirous of giving to his eulogist; firm are the people who are his praisers ; he who is the engenderer of good has made a spacious dwelling (for his worshippers).

Which he was Desirous of giving to his Eulogist— *Manuṣe daśasyan,* according to the Scholiast, we are to understand by the first *stuvate devagaṇāya,* to the company of gods praising him— *Viṣṇu* having taken the three worlds from the *Asuras* to give to them.

"The Engenderer of Good"— Rather, to whom belong fortunate births.

५९२८. प्र तत्ते अद्य शिपिविष्ट नामार्यः शंसामि वयुनानि विद्वान्।
तं त्वा गृणामि तवसमतव्यान्क्षयन्तमस्य रजसः पराके ॥५॥

5. Resplendent *Viṣṇu*, I, the master of the offering, knowing the objects that are to be known, glorify today your name: I who am feeble, praise you who are powerful, dwelling in a remote region of this world.

The *Sāmaveda*, 1626 has a slightly different reading, *pra tat te adya havyam aryaḥ śaṁsāmi*, I, the lord, offer you today an oblation, instead of *nāmaryaḥ śaṁsāmi*, I, the lord, praise your name. The application of *sūrya* is rather equivocal; Sāyaṇa explains it *svāmī stutinām haviṣām vā*, you master of the praises or of the oblation which many mean *Viṣṇu*, or more probably the *yajamāna*.

५९२९. किमित्ते विष्णो परिचक्ष्यं भूत्र यद्ववक्षे शिपिविष्टो अस्मि।
मा वर्पो अस्मदप गूह एतद्यदन्यरूपः समिथे बभूथ ॥६॥

6. What is to be proclaim *Viṣṇu*, of you, when you save. I am *Śipiviṣṭa*? Conceal not from us your real form, although you have engaged under a different form in battle.

You have engaged under a Different form in Battle— *Viṣṇu* is said to have aided *Vasiṣṭha* in battle under an assumed form, and, when questioned, to have said. I am *Śipiviṣṭa*[1], a word to which two senses may be attached one unobjectionable, the other objectionable. In the preceding verse, and in verse 7 of the former *Sūkta*, the word is explained, penetrated, or clothed with rays of light, *raśmibhir ariṣṭa*, the radiant, the splendid: in common use it means a man naturally without prepuce, in which sense it may be here interpreted as implying comparison: in like manner as a man is so denuded, so is *Viṣṇu*, according to his own declaration, uncovered by radiance—*tejasa anācchāditaḥ*; but this is a refinement, and it is probably to be understood as usual: the expression is curious.

५९३०. वषट् ते विष्णवास आ कृणोमि तन्मे जुषस्व शिपिविष्ट हव्यम्।
वर्धन्तु त्वा सुष्टुतयो गिरो मे यूयं पात स्वस्तिभिः सदा नः ॥७॥

7. I offer, *Viṣṇu*, the oblation placed before you with the exclamation *Vaṣaṭ*; be pleased. *Śipiviṣṭa*, with my offering: may my laudatory hymns magnify you and do you (gods) ever cherish us with blessings.

---

१. शिपयोऽत्र रस्मय उच्यते तैराविष्टो भवति। (निरु० ५.७-८)।

[सूक्त-१०१]

[ऋषि– वसिष्ठ मैत्रावरुणि अथवा कुमार आग्नेय।

देवता– पर्जन्य। छन्द– त्रिष्टुप्।]

५९३१. तिस्रो वाच: प्र वद ज्योतिरग्रा या एतद्दुहे मंधुदोघमूर्ध:।

स वत्सं कृण्वन् गर्भमोषधीनां सद्यो जातो वृषभो रौरवीति॥१॥

1. Recite the three sacred texts, preceded by light, which milk the water-yielding udder; for he, the showerer, (thereby) becoming quickly manifest, loudly roars, engendering the (lightning) infant, the embryo of the plants.

The three sacred texts preceded by Light— The texts, it is said, of the three *Vedas,* preceded by *Om.*

The Water-Yielding Udder— The cloud.

The Showerer— *Parjanya,* pleased with the hymns, and in consequence sending rain. [For the "lightning embryo, see Vol. I. mantra 2128, and vol II. 3630.]

५९३२. यो वर्धन ओषधीनां यो अपां यो विश्वस्य जगतो देव ईशे।

स त्रिधातु शरणं शर्म यंसत्त्रिवर्तु ज्योति: स्वभिष्ट्यर्३स्मे॥२॥

2. May he who is the augmenter of plants, the increase of the waters, who rules divine over the whole earth, bestow upon us a three-storied dwelling and felicity: may he grant us the desired light (of the sun) at the three (bright) seasons.

A Three-storied Dwelling— *Tridhātu śaraṇam* is explained *tribhūmikam gṛham,* a house with three earths, either chambers or floors.[1]

The Desired Light at the Three Bright Seasons— The rays of the sun are said to be most powerful at dawn in the spring, at noon is the hot season, and in the afternoon in autumn.

५९३३. स्तरीरुं त्वद्भवति सूत उ त्वद्यथावशं तन्वं चक्र एष:।

पितु: पय: प्रति गृभ्णाति माता तेन पिता वर्धते तेन पुत्र:॥३॥

3. One form of *Parjanyh* is like a barren cow the other produces offspring, he takes whichever form he cleases: the mother receives the milk from the father thence the father, thence the son is nourished.

---

१. त्रीणि वा आदित्यस्य तेजांसि प्रातर्ग्रीष्मे मध्यंदिने शरद्यपराह्ने (तै॰ सं॰ २.१.२.५)।

He takes whichever form he Pleases— The firmament withholds or sends down rain at will.

The Mother receives the milk etc.— The father is the sky, earth the mother, who receives the rain from the former, which, producing the means of offering libations and oblations, returns again to the parent heaven, as well as supports his offspring— all living creatures. [*cf.* Vol. I. verse 814 and note thereon.]

५९३४. यस्मिन् विश्वानि भुवनानि तस्थुस्तिस्रो द्यावंस्त्रेधा सस्रुरापं:।

त्रय: कोशांस उपसेचनासो मध्वं: श्रोतन्त्यभितो विरप्शम्।।४।।

4. In whom all beings exist ; the three worlds abide: from whom the waters flow in three directions (east, west, and south): the three water-shedding masses of clouds (east, west, and north) pour the waters round the mighty (*Parjanya*).

५९३५. इदं वचं: पर्जन्याय स्वराजे हृदो अस्त्वन्तरं तज्जुजोषत्।

मयोभुवो वृष्ट्यं: सन्त्वस्मे सुपिप्पला ओषधीर्देवगोपा:।।५।।

5. This praise is addressed to the self-irradiating Parjanya: may it be placed in his heart; may he be gratified by it; may the joy-diffusing rains be ours: may the plants cherished by the deity be fruitful.

५९३६. स रेतोधा वृषभ: शश्वतीनां तस्मिन्नात्मा जगतस्तस्थुषश्च।

तन्म ऋतं पातु शतशारदाय यूयं पात स्वस्तिभि: सदां न:।।६।।

6. May he, the bull, be the impreginator of the perpetual plans, for in him is the vitality of both the fixed and moveable (world): may the rain sent by him preserve me for a hundred years: and do you (gods) ever cherish its with blessings.

May He— Sāyaṇa makes the sentence indicative. "he is, etc.; and instead of "for" he has "hence, *atas*.

In him is the Vitality— *Tasminn-ātma*: the Scholiast interprets the latter *deha,* body ; probably for bodily existence, the life of the vegetable world depending upon the rain, and that of animals upon corn and the rest.

[सूक्त-१०२]

[ऋषि– वसिष्ठ मैत्रावरुणि अथवा कुमार आग्नेय।

देवता– पर्जन्य। छन्द– गायत्री।]

५९३७. पर्जन्याय प्र गायत दिवस्पुत्राय मीळ्हुषे। स नो यवसमिच्छतु।।१।।

1. Sing aloud to the son of heaven. Parjanya, the sender of rain: may he be pleased (to grant) us food.

५९३८. यो गर्भमोषधीनां गवां कृणोत्यर्वताम्। पर्जन्यः पुरुषीणाम्॥२॥

2. He who is the cause of the impregnation of plants, of cows, of mares, of women.

५९३९. तस्मा इदास्यै हविर्जुहोता मधुमत्तमम्। इळां नः संयतं करत्॥३॥

3. Offer verily to him by the mouth (of the gods *Agni,*) the most savoury oblation, so that he may yield us food unfailingly.

[सूक्त-१०३]

[ऋषि- वसिष्ठ मैत्रावरुणि। देवता- मंडूक। छन्द- त्रिष्टुप्, अनुष्टुप्।]

VII. *Vasiṣṭha,* it is said, having praised *Parjanya,* in order to procure rain, observing the frogs to be delighted by his praises, addressed them in this hymn.

५९४०. संवत्सरं शशयाना ब्राह्मणा व्रतचारिणः।
वाचं पर्जन्यजिन्वितां प्र मण्डूका अवादिषुः॥१॥

1. The frogs, like *Brāhmaṇas,* observant of their vows, practising penance throughout the year, utter aloud praises agreeable to *Parjanya.*[1]

"Practising Penance"— Literally, "lying still", which Sāyaṇa explains as "performing penance for rain".

५९४१. दिव्या आपो अभि यदेनमायन्दृतिं न शुष्कं सरसी शयानम्।
गवामह न मायुर्वत्सिनीनां मण्डूकानां वग्नुरत्रा समेति॥२॥

2. When the waters of the sky fall upon (the troop of frogs) sleeping in the (exhausted) lake like a dry water-skin; then rises together the croaking of the frogs, like the bellowing of cows when joined by their calves.

५९४२. यदीमेनाँ उशतो अभ्यवर्षीत्तृष्यावतः प्रावृष्यागतायाम्।
अख्खलीकृत्या पितरं न पुत्रो अन्यो अन्यमुप वदन्तमेति॥३॥

3. When the rainy season has arrived, and (Parjanya) has sent the rain upon them, thirsty and longing (for its coming), then one frog meets another croaking (his congratulations) as a child (calls to) its father with inarticulate ejaculations.

With Inarticulate Ejaculations— *Akhkhalīkṛtyā* making the imitative sound *akhkhala.*

---

१. This hymn has been translated by Professor Müller, in his *Ancient Sanskrit Lit.,* p. 494.

५९४३. अन्यो अन्यमनु गृभ्णात्येनोरपां प्रंसर्गे यदमन्दिषाताम्।
मण्डूको यदभिवृष्टः कनिष्कन्नृश्रिः सम्पृङ्क्ते हरितेन वाचम्॥४॥

4. One of these two congratulates the other as they are both delighting in the forthcoming of rain; the speckled frog, leaping up repeatedly when moistened by the shower), joins greetings with the green one.

५९४४. यदेषामन्यो अन्यस्य वाचं शाक्तस्येव वदति शिक्षमाणः।
सर्वं तदेषां समृधैवपर्व यत्सुवाचो वदथनाध्यप्सु॥५॥

5. When one of you imitates the croaking of another as a learner (imitates) his teacher, when, loud crying, you converse (leaping) upon the waters, then the entire body is as it were developed.

Then the Entire Body....is Developed— During the dry weather, says the Scholiast, the frogs shrink like a lump of clay; in the rains they expand to their full size.

५९४५. गोमायुरेको अजमायुरेकः पृश्निरेको हरित एकं एषाम्।
समानं नाम बिभ्रतो विरूपाः पुरुत्रा वाचं पिपिशुर्वदन्तः॥६॥

6. One frog has the bellowing of a cow, another the bleating of a goat; one of them is speckled, one is green: designated by a common appellation, they are of various colours and croaking, show themselves in numerous places.

५९४६. ब्राह्मणासो अतिरात्रे न सोमे सरो न पूर्णमभितो वदन्तः।
संवत्सरस्य तदहः परि ष्ठ यन्मण्डूकाः प्रावृषीणं बभूव॥७॥

7. Like *Brāhmaṇas* at the *Soma* libation, at the *Atiratra* sacrifice, you are now croaking around the replenished lake (throughout the night), for on that day of the year you frogs are everywhere about, when it is the day of the serving of the rains.

Croaking Throughout the Night— *Rātrau śabdam kurvāṇaḥ*, is added by the commentator, apparently to make the comparison more appropriate, the *Atirātra* rite being according to him, a nocturnal ceremony, when the priests recite the hymns at night: *rātrim atītya vartate ityatirātraḥ, yathātirātrākhye somayāge Brāhmaṇā rātrau stutaśastrāṇi paryāyeṇa śaṅsanti.* [For the *śastras* used at the *Atirātra,* see Haug's translation of *Aitareya Brāhm.* p. 264.

५९४७. ब्राह्मणासः सोमिनो वाचमक्रत ब्रह्मं कृण्वन्तः परिवत्सरीणम्।
अध्वर्यवो घर्मिणः सिष्विदाना आविर्भवन्ति गुह्या न के चित्॥८॥

8. They utter a loud cry, like *Brāhmaṇas* when bearing the *Soma* libation, and reciting the perennial prayer: like ministrant priests with the *gharma* offering, they hid (in the hot weather) perspiring (in their holes), but now some of them appear.

"**The Perennial Prayer**"— Rather, "the year-long prayer." Sāyaṇa make it refer to *Gavām ayanam*, sacrificial session, which commences and ends with the *atirātra* and lasts a whole year.

Perspiring— *Adhvaryavo gharmiṇaḥ siṣvidānāḥ*: the last may apply to the *adhvaryus* as well the frogs: there is a quibble upon the word *gharmiṇaḥ*, having or bearing the vessel, or performing the rite so termed; or suffering from *gharma*, heat, or the hot season. [For the *pravargya* ceremony and the *gharma*, see Haug's *Ait. Brāhm.* trans. p. 42.]

५९४८. देवहितिं जुगुपुर्द्वादशस्य ऋतुं नरो न प्र मिनन्त्येते।
संवत्सरे प्रावृष्यागतायां तप्ता घर्मा अंश्नुवते विसर्गम्॥९॥

9. These leaders of rites observe the institutes of the gods and disregard not the (appropriate) season of the twelve month; as the year revolves, and the rains return then, scorched and heated, they obtain freedom (from their hiding-places).

५९४९. गोमायुरदाद्जमायुरदात्पृश्रिरदाद्धरितो नो वसूनि।
गवां मण्डूका ददतः शतानि सहस्रसावे प्र तिरन्त आयुः॥१०॥

10. May the cow-toned, the goat-toned, the speckled, the green (frog, severally) grant us riches! May the frogs in the fertilizing (season of the rain), bestowing upon us hundreds of cows, prolong (our) lives!

In the Fertilizing Season of the Rain— *Sahasrasāve* is explained as the generator of thousands of plants, grains, and the like.

[सूक्त- १०४]

[**ऋषि**- वसिष्ठ मैत्रावरुणि। **देवता**- इन्द्रा सोम (रक्षोघ्न), ८, १६, १९-२२, २४ इन्द्र, ९, १२-१३ सोम, १०, १४ अग्नि, ११ देवगण, १७ ग्रावा, १८ मरुद्गण, २३ (पूर्वार्द्ध ऋचा।) वसिष्ठ (उत्तरार्द्ध ऋचा) पृथिवी-अन्तरिक्ष। **छन्द**- त्रिष्टुप्, १-६, १८, २१, २३ जगती, ७ जगती वा त्रिष्टुप्, २५ अनुष्टुप्।]

५९५०. इन्द्रासोमा तपतं रक्ष उब्जतं न्यर्पयतं वृषणा तमोवृधः।
परा शृणीतमचितो न्योषतं हतं नुदेथां नि शिशीतमत्रिणः॥१॥

1. *Indra* and *Soma*, afflict, destroy the *Rākṣasas*; showerers (of benefits) cast down those who delight in darkness: put to flight the

stupid (spirits); consume, slay, drive away, utterly exterminate the cannibals.

५९५१. इन्द्रासोमा समघशंसमभ्यं३घं तपुर्ययस्तु चरुरग्निवाँ इव।

ब्रह्मद्विषे क्रव्यादे घोरचंक्षसे द्वेषो धत्तमनवायं किंमीदिनें।।२।।

2. *Indra* and *Soma*, fall upon the destructive *(Rākṣasa)* and the performer of unprofitable acts, so that, consume (by your wrath), he may perish like the offering cast into the fire: retain implacable hatred to the hater of *Brāhmaṇas*, the cannibal, the hideous, the vile *(Rākṣasa)*.

"**The Performer of Unprofitable Acts**"— Or, as the same word, *aghaśaṃsa,* is rendered in v. 4, "the malignant."

"**To the Hater or Brahmanas**"— *Brahmadviṣe* is explained by Sāyaṇa, *brāhmaṇebhyo, smabhyam dveṣṭre.*

"**The Hideous**"— *Ghoracakṣase* may also mean "rude in speech."

The Vile Rākṣasa— *Kimīdine* is an unusual and rather unintelligible term: the comment explains it *Kimīdānīm iti carate,* to one who goes saying, What now? That is, *Piśunāya,* a spy, an informer; or cruel, vile.

५९५२. इन्द्रासोमा दुष्कृतौ वव्रे अन्तरनारम्भणे तमंसि प्र विध्यतम्।

यथा नातः पुनरेकंश्चनोदयत्तद्वामस्तु सहंसे मन्युमच्छवं:।।३।।

3. *Indra* and *Soma*, chastise the malignant *(Rākṣasas)*, having plunged them in surrounding and inextricable darkness, so that not one of them may again issue from it: so may your wrathful might be triumphant over them.

"**Inextricable**"— Perhaps rather bottomless *ālambana-rahita.* Compare Milton's description of Satan falling in chaos.

५९५३. इन्द्रासोमा वर्तयंतं दिवो वधं सं पृथिव्या अघशंसाय तर्हणम्।

उत्तंक्षतं स्वर्यं३ पर्वतेभ्यो येन रक्षों वावृधानं निजूर्वथ:।।४।।

4. *Indra* and *Soma*, disperse from heaven your fatal (weapon), the extirpator from earth of the malignant *(Rākṣasas)* put forth from the clouds the consuming, (thunderbolt), wherewith you slay the increasing *Rākṣasa* race.

५९५४. इन्द्रासोमा वर्तयंतं दिवस्पर्यंग्नितप्तेभिर्युवमश्महन्मभि:।

तपुर्वधेभिरजरैभिरत्रिणो नि पर्शानि विध्यतं यन्तु निस्वरम्।।५।।

5. *Indra* and *Soma*, scatter around (your weapons) from the sky, pierce their sides with fiery searching adamantine (weapons), so that they depart without a sound.

"Scorching"— The text, after "scorching", adds another epithet, *ajarebhiḥ*, ageless, undecaying.

५९५५. इन्द्रासोमा परि वां भूतु विश्वत इयं मति: कक्ष्याश्वेव वाजिना।
यां वां होत्रां परिह्नोमि मेधयेमा ब्रह्माणि नृपतीव जिन्वतम् ॥६॥

6. May this praise invest you, *Indra* and *Soma*, who are mighty, on every side, as a girth (encompasses) a horse, that praise which I offer to you both with pure devotion: do you, like two kings, accept this my homage.

५९५६. प्रति स्मरेथां तुजयद्भिरेवैर्हतं दुहो रक्षसो भङ्गुरावत:।
इन्द्रासोमा दुष्कृते मा सुगं भूद्यो न: कदा चिदभिदासति दुहा ॥७॥

7. Come with rapid steeds, slay the oppressive mischievous *Rākṣasas* : let there be no happiness, *Indra* and *Soma*, to the malignant, who harasses us with his oppression.

५९५७. यो मा पाकेन मनसा चरन्तमभिचष्टे अनृतेभिर्वचोभि:।
आप इव काशिना सङ्गृभीता असन्त्वस्त्वासत इन्द्र वक्ता ॥८॥

8. May he who with false calumnies maligns me behaving with a pure heart, may such a speaker of falsehood *Indra*, cease to be, like water held in the hand.

५९५८. ये पाकशंसं विहरन्त एवैर्ये वा भद्रं दूषयन्ति स्वधाभि:।
अहये वा तान् प्रददातु सोम आ वा दधातु निर्ऋतेरुपस्थे ॥९॥

9. May *Soma* give to the serpent, or toss upon the lap of *Nirṛti*, those who with designing (accusations) persecute me, a speaker of sincerity, and those who by spiteful (calumnies) vilify all that is good in me.

"Those who by Spiteful Calumnies...in Me"— Rather, "those who with violence vilify me, acting uprightly.

५९५९. यो नो रसं दिप्सति पित्वो अग्ने यो अश्वानां यो गवां यस्तनूनाम्।
रिपु: स्तेन: स्तेयकृद्दभ्रमेतु नि ष हीयतां तन्वा३ तना च ॥१०॥

10. May he, *Agni*, who strives to destroy the essence of our food, of our horse, of our cattle, of our bodies— the adversary, the thief, the robber— go to destruction, and be deprived both of person and of progeny.

५९६०. पर: सो अस्तु तन्वा३े तना च तिस्र: पृथिवीरधो अस्तु विश्वा:।
प्रति शुष्यतु यशो अस्य देवा यो नो दिवा दिप्सति यश्च
नक्तम्।।११।।

11. May he be deprived of bodily (existence) and of posterity; may he be cast down below all the three worlds; may his reputation, Gods, be blighted who seeks our destruction by day or by night.

"May he be Deprived of Bodily Existence"— Literally, "may he exist after his body and progeny," *i.e.,* continue severed from them.

५९६१. सुविज्ञानं चिकितुषे जनाय सच्चासच्च वचसी पस्पृधाते।
तयोर्यत्सत्यं यतरदृजीयस्तदित्सोमोऽवति हन्त्यासत्।।१२।।

12. To the understanding man there is perfect discrimination, the words of truth and falsehood are mutually at variance: of these two, *Soma* verily cherishes that which is true and right: he destroys the false.

The preceding verses are considered to be a malediction upon the *Rākṣasas* by the *Ṛṣi*. To account for the change of tone, Sāyaṇa gives an unusual version of the legend told in the *Mahābhārata* of king *Kalmaṣapāda* being transformed to a *Rākṣasa,* and devouring the 100 sons of *Vasiṣṭha*: here it is said that a *Rākṣasa,* having devoured the *Ṛṣi's* sons, assumed his shape, and said to him, "I am *Vasiṣṭha*, you are the *Rākṣasa*" ; to which *Vasiṣṭha* replied by repeating this verse declaratory of his discriminating between truth and falsehood.

"To the Understanding Man...Variance"— Literally, "to the understanding man truth and falsehood are easily discriminated, their words are mutually at variance."

५९६२. न वा उ सोमो वृजिनं हिनोति न क्षत्रियं मिथुया धारयन्तम्।
हन्ति रक्षो हन्त्यासद्वदन्तमुभाविन्द्रस्य प्रसितौ शयाते।।१३।।

13. *Soma* instigates not the wicked; he instigates not the strong man dealing in falsehood: he destroys the *Rākṣasa,* he destroys the speaker of untruth; and both remain in the bondage of *Indra.*

५९६३. यदि वाहमनृतदेव आस मोघं वा देवाँ अप्यूहे अग्ने।
किमस्मभ्यं जातवेदो तृणीषे द्रोघवाचस्ते निर्ऋथं सचन्ताम्।।१४।।

14. If I am one following false gods, it I approach the gods in vain, then *Agni* (punish me). If (we be not such, then) why, *Jātavedas,* are you angry with us? Let the utterers of falsehood incur your chastisement.

५९६४. अद्या मुरीय यदि यातुधानो अस्मि यदि वायुस्ततप पूरुषस्य।
अधा स वीरैर्दशभिर्वि यूया यो मा मोघं यातुधानेत्याह॑।।१५।।

15. May I this day die if I am a spirit of ill, or if I have ever
injured the life of any man: may you be deprived (*Rākṣasa*) of
your ten sons, who have falsely called me by such an appellation.

५९६५. यो मायातुं यातुधानेत्याह यो वा रक्षाः शुचिरस्मीत्याह॑।
इन्द्रस्तं हन्तु महता वधेन विश्वस्य जन्तोरधमस्पदीष्ट।।१६।।

16. May *Indra* slay with his mighty weapon him who calls me
the *Yātudhāna*, which I am not, the *Rākṣasa*, who says (of
himself), I am pure: may he, the vilest of all beings, perish.

५९६६. प्र या जिगाति खर्गलेव नक्तमप दुहा तन्वं॑ गूह॑माना।
वव्राँ अनन्ताँ अव सा पदीष्ट ग्रावाणो घ्नन्तु रक्षस॑ उपब्दैः।।१७।।

17. May the cruel female fiend who, throwing off the
concealment of her person, wanders about at night like an owl, fall
headlong down into the unbounded caverns: may the stones that
grind the *Soma* destroy the *Rākṣasas* by their noise.

५९६७. वि तिष्ठध्वं मरुतो विक्ष्विच्छत गृभायत रक्षसः सं पिनष्टन।
वयो ये भूत्वी पतयन्ति नक्तभिर्ये वा रिपो दधिरे देवे अध्वरे।।१८।।

18. Stay, *Maruts*, amongst the people, desirous (of protecting
them); seize the *Rākṣasas,* grind them to pieces: whether your fly
about like birds by night, or whether they have offered obstruction
to the sacred sacrifice.

"**Desirous of Protecting them**"— Rather "be pleased (to destroy
the *Rākṣasas*)."

५९६८. प्र वर्तय दिवो अश्मानमिन्द्र सोमशितं मघवन्तं शिशाधि।
प्राक्तादपाक्तादधरादुदक्तादभि जहि रक्षसः पर्वतेन।।१९।।

19. Hurl, *Indra*, your thunderbolt from heaven: sanctify,
Maghavan), (the worshipper) sharpened by the *Soma* beverage:
slay with the thunderbolt the *Rākṣasas,* on the east, on the west, on
the south, on the north.

५९६९. एत उ त्ये पतयन्ति श्र्वयातव इन्द्रं दिप्सन्ति दिप्सवोऽदाभ्यम्।
शिशीते शक्रः पिशुनेभ्यो वधं नूनं सृजदशनिं यातुमद्भ्यः।।२०।।

20. They advance, accompanied by dogs: desirous to destroy
him, they assail the indomitable *Indra*: *Śakra* whets his

thunderbolt for the miscreants; quickly let him hurl the bolt upon the fiends.

५९७०. इन्द्रौ यातूनामभवत् पराशरो हविर्मथीनामभ्याइ३ विवासताम्।

अभीदु ॒शक्रः परशुर्यथा वनं पात्रेव भिन्दन्त्सत एति रक्षसः॥२१॥

21. *Indra* has ever been the discomfiter of the evil spirits coming to obstruct (the rites of) the offerers of oblations: *Sakra* advances, crushing the present *Rākṣasas,* as a hatchet cuts down (the trees of) a forest, as (a mallet smashes) the earthen vessels.

५९७१. उलूकयातुं शुशुलूकयातुं जहि श्वयातुमुत कोकयातुम्।

सुपर्णयातुमुत गृध्रयातुं दृषदैव प्र मृण रक्षं इन्द्र॥२२॥

22. Destroy the evil spirit, whether in the form of an owl, or of an owlet, of a dog, or of a duck, of a hawk or of a vulture; slay the *Rākṣasas, Indra,* (with the thunderbolt) as with a stone.

"A Duck"— Literally, "a ruddy goose, *cakravāka.*

५९७२. मा नो रक्षो अभि नड्यातुमावर्तामपोच्छतु मिथुना या किमीदिनो।

पृथिवी नः पार्थिवात् पात्वंहंसोऽन्तरिक्षं दिव्यात्पात्वस्मान्॥२३॥

23. Let not the *Rākṣasas* do us harm: let the dawn drive away the pairs of evil spirits exclaiming, "What note is this" May the earth protect us from terrestrial, the firmament protect us from celestial, wickedness.

Exclaiming—"What now is This?"—*Kimīdina.* See note on verse 2.

५९७३. इन्द्रे जहि पुमांसं यातुधानमुत स्त्रियं मायया शाशदानाम्।

विग्रीवासो मूरदेवा ऋदन्तु मा ते दृशन्त्सूर्यमुच्चरन्तम्॥२४॥

24. Slay, *Indra,* the *Yātudhāna,* whether in the form of a man, or of a woman doing mischief by her deceptions: may those who sport in murder perish dissipated; let them not behold the rising sun.

"The Yātudhāna"— *i.e., Rākṣasa.*

५९७४. प्रति चक्ष्व वि चक्ष्वेन्द्रश्च सोम जागृतम्।

रक्षोभ्यो वधमस्यतमशनिं यातुमद्भ्यः॥२५॥

25. *Soma,* do you and *Indra* severally watch (the *Rākṣasas),* be vary, be vigilant; hurl the thunderbolt at the malignant *Rākṣasas.*

॥इति सप्तमं मण्डलम्॥

End of the Seventh Maṇḍala

||अथाष्टमं मण्डलम्||

EIGHTH MANDALA

ANUVĀKA 1

[सूक्त- १]

[ऋषि– १.२ प्रगाथ (घौर) काण्व, ३-२९ मेधातिथि-मेध्यातिथि काण्व, ३०-
३३ आसङ्ग प्लायोगि, ३४ शश्वती आङ्गिरसी ऋषिका। देवता– इन्द्र, ३०-
३४ आसङ्ग। छन्द– १-४ प्रगाथ (विषमा बृहती, समासतो बृहती), ४-३२
बृहती, ३३-३४ त्रिष्टुप्।]

५९७५. मा चिदन्यद्वि शंसत सखायो मा रिषण्यत।
इन्द्रमित्स्तोता वृषणं सचा सुते मुहुरुक्था च शंसत॥१॥

1. Repeat, friends, no other praise, be not hurtful (to
yourselves); praise together *Indra*, the showerer (of benefits) when
the *Soma* is effused; repeatedly utter praise (to him).
Sāmaveda, 242, 1660.

५९७६. अवक्रक्षिणं वृषभं यथाजुरं गां न चर्षणीसहम्।
विद्वेषणं संवननोभयङ्करं मंहिष्ठमुभयाविनम्॥२॥

2. A bull rushing (upon his foes), undecaying, like an ox, the
overcomer of (hostile) men, the hater (of adversaries), the
venerable, the displayer of both (enmity and favour), the
munificent, the distributor of both (celestial and terrestrial riches).

The Displayer of both— The text has only *ubhayaṁkaram,* which
the commentator explains *nigrahānugrahayoḥ kartāram.*

The Distributor of both— *Ubhayāvinam.* The Scholiast is rather
puzzled how to interpret the duality here intimated— whether it means as
in the text, or having the faculty of protecting both fixed and moveable
things, or being honoured by both those who recite his praises and those
who offer oblations. The epithets are in the accusative, being governed by
the verb *stota,* "praise," in the first verse. *Cf. Sāmaveda,* 136. Benfey
renders it, *"Den schleundernden, wie einen Büffel stürmendan, wie einen
stier mensch-siegenden, den zornigen, siegenden, zwiefach handelnden,
den hehrsten, zwiebegabeten"*— it seems to me very barbarously, and not
very intelligibly.

५९७७. यच्चिद्धित्वा जना इमे नाना हवन्त ऊतये।
अस्माकं ब्रह्मेदमिन्द्र भूतु तेऽहा विश्वा च वर्धनम्॥३॥

3. Although these people worship you, *Indra*, in many ways to (secure) your protection, (yet) may this our prayer be throughout all days your magnification.

५९७८. वि तर्तूर्यन्ते मघवन् विपश्चितोऽर्यो विपो जनानाम्।

उप क्रमस्व पुरुरूपमा भर वाजं नेदिष्ठमूतये।।४।।

4. The sages (your worshippers), *Maghavan*, the overcomers (of foes), the terrifiers of (hostile) people, pass over various (calamities by your aid): come nigh and bring many sorts of food, and available for our preservation.

५९७९. महे चन त्वामद्रिव: परा शुल्काय देयाम्।

न सहस्राय नायुताय वज्रिवो न शताय शतामघ।।५।।

5. Wielder of the thunderbolt, I would not sell you for a large price, not for a thousand, nor for ten thousand, nor, opulent bearer of the thunderbolt, for a hundred.

For a Large Price— *Śatāya* here signifies infinite, according to the comment. In the *Sāmaveda*, 291 We have *na parādīyase* instead of *na parādeyām*.

५९८०. वस्याँ इन्द्रासि मे पितुरुत भ्रातुरभुञ्जत:।

माता च मे छदयथ: समा वसो वसुत्वनाय राधसे।।६।।

6. You are more precious, *Indra*, than my father, or than my brother, who is not affectionate: you, giver of dwellings, are equal to my mother, for you both render me distinguished on account of celebrity and riches.

५९८१. क्वेयथ क्वेदसि पुरुत्रा चिद्धि ते मन:।

अलर्षि युध्म खजकृत् पुरन्दर प्र गायत्रा अगासिषु:।।७।।

7. Whither has you gone? Where, indeed, are you now? Verily your mind (wanders) amongst many (worshippers): martial, valorous *Purandara*, Come hither; the chaunters are singing (your praise).

Sāmaveda, 271.

५९८२. प्रास्मै गायत्रमर्चत वावातुर्य: पुरन्दर:।

याभि: काण्वस्योप बर्हिरासदं यासद्वज्री भिनत्पुर:।।८।।

8. Raise the sacred chaunt to him who is the destroyer of the cities (of the foes) of his worshipper, (induced) by which may the

thunderer come to sit down at the sacrifice of the sons of *Kaṇva*,
and destroy the cities (of their enemies).

५९८३. ये ते सन्ति दशग्विनः शतिनो ये सहस्रिणः।
अश्वासो ये ते वृषणो रघुद्रुवस्तेभिर्नस्तूयमा गहि॥९॥

9. Come quickly with those your horses which are vigorous
and fleet, and which are traversers of tens, or hundreds, or
thousands (of leagues).

Traversers of Ten, etc.— Or rather, ''Which are traversers of ten
leagues, and are numbered by hundreds and by thousands.''

५९८४. आ त्वंइद्य सबर्दुघां हुवे गायत्रवेपसम्।
इन्द्रं धेनुं सुदुघामन्यामिषमुरुधारामरङ्कृतम्॥१०॥

10. I invoke to-day the all-sufficient *Indra*, as the milch cow
yielding abundant milk, of excellent motion, and easy to be
milked; or, as another (form), the vastdropping, desirable (rain).

Of Excellent Motion— *Gāyatra-vepasam* is explained *praśasya-
vegam*, ''of excellent speed''; or it might have been thought to be a
metaphor, having the form or beauty of the *Gāyatrī*, being the *Gāyatrī*
personified.

The Vast-Dropping, Desirable, etc.— *Anyam isham urudharam* is
rather doubtful; the comment explains it, *uktavilakṣaṇam
bahūdakadharam eśanīyam vṛṣṭim*; this is followed by *Alankṛtam*, which,
being masculine, cane refer only to *Indram*, the doer of enough, all-
sufficient. *Cf. Sāmaveda*, 295. [*Anyam* may mean unparalleled,
adṛṣṭapūrvam, as in hymn 27 of this *Maṇḍala*.]

५९८५. यत्तुदत् सूर एतशं वङ्कू वातस्य पर्णिना।
वहत् कुत्समार्जुनेयं शतक्रतुस्तसरद् गन्धर्वमस्तृतम्॥११॥

11. When *Sūrya* harassed *Etaśa*, *Śatakratu* conveyed (to his
aid) *Kutsa*, the son of *Arjuni*, with his two prancing horses (swift)
as the wind, and stealthily approached the irresistible *Gandharva*.

The Irresistible Gandharva— A name of the sun.
Etaśa— See *Ṛg.* 1.61.15.

५९८६. य ऋते चिदभिश्रिषः पुरा जत्रुभ्यं आतृदः।
सन्धाता सन्धिं मघवा पुरूवसुरिष्कर्ता विह्रुतंपुनः॥१२॥

12. He who without healing materials before the flow of blood
from the necks was the effecter of the re-union, the opulent
Maghavan, again makes whole the dissevered (parts).

To what this alludes is not explained, but possibly it intends to describe the restoration of *Etaśa*, wounded in his conflict with the sun. The verse occurs in *Sāmaveda*, 244. The translation of Langlois. Benfey and Stavenson are very curious.

৫৫৫৬. मा भूम निष्ट्याइवेन्द्र त्वद्रणा इव।

वनानि न प्रजहितान्यद्विवो दुरोषासो अमन्महि।।१३।।

13. May we never be like the abject, *Indra*, through your favour, nor suffer affliction; may we never be like branchless trees; for, thunderer, unconsumable (by foes) we glorify you.

৫৫৫৫. अमन्महीदनाशवोऽनुग्रासंश्च वृत्रहन्।

सकृत्सु तें महता शूर राधसानु स्तोमं मुदीमहि।।१४।।

14. Neither rash nor irate, we verily glorify you, slayer of *Vṛtra*; my we propitiate you, hero, for once (at least) by our praise with great (sacrificial) wealth.

৫৫৫৯. यदि स्तोमं मम श्रवद्स्माकमिन्द्रमिन्दवः।

तिरः पवित्रं ससुवांसं आशवो मन्दन्तु तुग्र्यावृधः।।१५।।

15. If he hear our praise, then may our libations, flowing through the filter, dropping quickly, and diluted with consecrated water, exhilarate *Indra*.

Through the Filter— The text adds an epithet of the filtering-cloth *tiras, i.e.,* placed slantingly. *Āśavaḥ* may mean quickly intoxicating.

Diluted with Consecrated Water— *Tugryāvṛdhaḥ* is explained *vasatīvaryekadhanākhyābhir adbhir vardhamānāḥ,* increasing with the waters termed *vasatīvarī* and *ekadhanā,* water collected and kept apart for the ceremonial (*Cf. Ait. Brāhm.* II.20].

৫৫৫০. आ त्वंद्य सधस्तुतिं वावातुः सख्युरा गहि।

उपस्तुतिर्मघोनां प्र त्वावत्वधा ते वशिम सुष्टुतिम्।।१६।।

16. Come quickly to-day to the collected laudation of your devoted friend: may the subsidiary praise of wealthy (worshippers) reach you, but now I wish (to offer) your complete eulogium.

Laudation— *i.e.,* The laudation made by him together with **many** other priests.

Subsidiary Praise— Sāyaṇa does not recognize this contrast between the two praises, as the explains *upastutiḥ* by *stotram.*

৫৫৫১. सोता हि सोममद्रिभिरेमेनमप्सु धावत।

गव्या वस्त्रैव वासयन्त इन्नरो निर्धुंक्षन्वक्षणाभ्यः।।१७।।

17. Extract the *Soma* juice with the brushing stones, wash it with the consecrated waters; (for by so doing) the leaders (of the rain, the *Maruts*) clothing (the sky with clouds) as with vesture of the hide of the cow, milk, forth (the water) for the rivers.

५९९२. अध ज्मो अर्ध वा दिवो बृह॒तो रोच॒नादधि॑।

अ॒या व॑र्धस्व त॒न्वा॑ गि॒रा ममा॑ जा॒ता सु॑क्र॒तो पृण॑॥१८॥

18. Whether come from the earth or the firmament, or the vast luminous (heaven), be magnified by this may diffusive praise; satisfy, *Śatakratu*, (my) people.

Śatakratu— The text has *Śukratu* as a similar name of *Indra*.

५९९३. इन्द्रा॑य सु म॒दिन्त॑मं॒ सोमं॒ सोता॑ व॒रेण्य॑म्।

शक्र॑ ए॒णं पीप॑यद्विश्व॒या धि॒या हि॒न्वा॒नं न वा॒जय॑म्॥१९॥

19. Pour out to *Indra* the most exhilarating, the most excellent *Soma*, for Śakra cherishes him who is desirous of food, propitiating him by every pious act.

५९९४. मा त्वा॑ सोम॒स्य ग॒ल्दया॒ सदा॒ याच॒न्नहं॑ गि॒रा।

भूर्णिं॑ मृ॒गं न स॒वनेषु॑ चुक्रुधं॒ क ई॑शा॒नं न या॑चिष॒त्॥२०॥

20. May I never, when importuning you in sacrifices with the effusion of the *Soma* and with praise, excite you like a ferocious lion to wrath: who (is there in the world) that does not solicit his lord?

Sāmaveda, 207 but the reading of the first half in Benfey varies, and is apparently faulty; instead of *ma tvā somasya galdayā sadā yācann aham girā*, it is a *tvā somasya galdayā sadā yācanna aham jyā*. It is not easy to make sense of this passage, especially in connection with what follows.

Excite you— *Bhūrṇim* is explained by *bhartāram*, "my lord".

५९९५. मदे॑नेषि॒तं मद॒मुग्रमुग्रेण॒ शव॑सा।

विश्वे॑षां तरु॒तारं॒ मद॑च्युतं॒ मदे॒ हि ष्मा॑ द॒दाति॑ नः॥२१॥

21. (May *Indra* drink) with invigorated strength, the strong exhilarating (*Soma*) offered with animating (laudation): for in his delight he gives us (a son) the overcomer of all (foes), the humbler of their pride.

५९९६. शेवा॑रे॒ वार्या॑ पु॒रु दे॒वो मर्ता॑य दा॒शुषे॑।

स सु॒न्वते॑ च॒ स्तुव॑ते च॒ रासते॑ वि॒श्वगू॒र्तो अरि॑ष्टुः॥२२॥

22. The divine (*Indra*), the accomplisher of all aims, the glorified by his foes, gives vast treasures to the mortal who presents offerings at the sacrifice, to him who pours out the libation, who hymns his praise.

The Glorified by His Foes— *Ari* probably means *prerayitrī*, one who utters a hymn.

५९९७. एन्द्र याहि मत्स्वं चित्रेण देव राधसा।

सरो न प्रास्युदरं सपीतिभिरा सोमेभिरुरु स्फिरम्॥२३॥

23. Come hither, *Indra*, be exhilarated by the wonderful (libatory) affluence and with your fellow-topers (the *Maruts*) fill with the *Soma* juices your vast belly, capacious as a lake.

५९९८. आ त्वा सहस्रमा शतं युक्ता रथे हिरण्ययै।

ब्रह्मयुजो हरय इन्द्र केशिनो वहन्तु सोमपीतये॥२४॥

24. May your thousand, your hundred steeds, *Indra* yokes to your golden chariot, harnessed by prayer, with flowing manes, bring you to drink the *Soma* libation.

Sāmaveda, with the two following verses, 245, 1391.

५९९९. आ त्वा रथे हिरण्ययै हरी मयूरशेप्या।

शितिपृष्ठा वहतां मध्वो अन्धसो विवक्षणस्य पीतये॥२५॥

25. May your two peacock-tailed, white-backed horses, yoked to your golden chariot, bring you to drink of the sweet praiseworthy libation.

६०००. पिबा त्वस्य गिर्वणः सुतस्य पूर्वपा इव।

परिष्कृतस्य रसिन इयमासुतिश्चारुर्मदाय पत्यते॥२६॥

26. Drink you, who are worthy to be glorified, of this consecrated and juicy libation, like the first drinker (*Vāyu*): this excellent effusion issues for your exhilaration.

The First Drinker Vāyu— According to the Scholiast, *pūrvapāḥ* means *Vāyu*, who, having arrived first in the race, drank the *Soma* before the other gods. The allusion is to the principal *graha* libation, called *Aindravāyava*, which *Indra* and *Vāyu* share together. [For the legend, see *Aitareya Brāhm.* II.25.]

६००१. य एको अस्ति दंसना महाँ उग्रो अभि व्रतैः।

गमत्स शिप्री न स यौषदा गमद्ध्वं न परि वर्जति॥२७॥

27. May he who alone overcomes (enemies) through (the power of) religious observances, who by pious acts is rendered mighty and fierce, who is handsome-chinned, approach: may he never be remote; may he come to our invocation; may he never abandon us.

६००२. त्वं पुरं चरिष्ण्वं वधैः शुष्णस्य सं पिणक्।

त्वं भा अनु चरो अध द्विता यदिन्द्र हव्यो भुवः॥२८॥

28. You have broken to pieces the moveable city of *Śuṣṇa* with your weapons; your who are light have followed him; wherefore, *Indra*, you are in two ways to be worshipped.

In Two Ways to be Worshipped— *Dvitā havyaḥ*, by praisers and by sacrificers, *stotṛbhir yaṣṭṛbhiśca*.

६००३. मम त्वा सूर उदिते मम मध्यन्दिने दिवः।

मम प्रपित्वे अपिशर्वरे वसवा स्तोमासो अवृत्सत॥२९॥

29. May my prayers when the sun has risen, those also at noon, those also when evening arrives, bring you back, giver of riches (to my sacrifice).

Also when Evening Arrives— The text, according to Sāyaṇa, adds a fourth time, "also in the night," *śārvare kāle'pi*. For *prapitvā*, see Dr. Goldstücker's Sanskrit Dict. under *abhipitvā* and *apapitvā*.

६००४. स्तुहि स्तुहीदेते घा ते मंहिष्ठासो मघोनाम्।

निन्दिताश्वः प्रपथी परमज्या मघस्य मेध्यातिथे॥३०॥

30. Praise (me), praise (me), *Medhyātithi*, for amongst the wealthy we are the most liberal donors of wealth to you: (praise me as one) who outstrips a horse in speed, follows the right path, and bears the best arms.

६००५. आ यदश्वान्वनन्वतः श्रद्धयाहं रथे रुहम्।

उत वामस्य वसुनश्चिकेतति यो अस्ति याद्वः पशुः॥३१॥

31. When with faith I harness the docile horses in the car, (praise me), for the descendant of *Yādu*, possessed of cattle, know how to distribute desirable riches.

Praise Me— The Scholiast supplies *tadānīm mām evam stuhi*, then verily praise me.

Possessed of Cattle— The text *Yādvaḥ paśuḥ*, literally the *Yādava* animal, but *paśu*, the commentator says, is to be understood as *paśumān*, having animals; or it may be considered as a derivative of *pāś* for *dṛś*, to see, a beholder of subtile objects, *sūkṣmasya draṣṭā*.

६००६. य ऋज्रा मह्यं मामहे सह त्वचा हिरण्यया।
एष विश्वान्यभ्यस्तु सौभंगासङ्ग्स्य स्वन्द्रथः॥३२॥

32. (Praise me, saying,) "He who has presented riches to me with a golden purse: may this rattling chariot of *Asaṅga* carry off all the treasures (of me enemy)."

This Rattling Chariot— Sāyaṇa, to save the accent of *swandrathah*, which, would make it *Bahuvrīhi*, has to resort to a violent ellipsis of *atma*; to avoid this, Wilson has preferred to take it as a *Karmadhāraya*, with an exceptional accent.

६००७. अध प्लायौगिरति दासदन्यानासङ्गो अग्ने दशभिः सहस्रैः।
अधोक्षणो दश मह्यं रुशन्तो नव्गाइव सरसो निरतिष्ठन्॥३३॥

33. (So praise me, saying,) "*Asaṅga*, the son of Plāyoga, has given more than others, *Agni*, by tens of thousands: ten times the (number of) vigorous and brilliant exen (given by him) to me, issue forth like the reeds of a lake."

Ten Times—Sāyaṇa explains daśa as daśa-guṇita-sahasra-saṅkyākāḥ.

६००८. अन्वस्य स्थूरं ददृशे पुरस्तादनस्थ ऊरुर्वरम्बमाणः।
शश्वती नार्यभिचक्ष्याह सुभद्रमर्य भोजनं बिभर्षि॥३४॥

34. *Śaśvatī*, perceiving that the signs of manhood were restored, exclaims, "Joy, husband, you are capable of enjoyment."

[सूक्त- २]

[**ऋषि**– १-४० मेधातिथि काण्व तथा प्रियमेध आङ्गिरस, ४१-४२ मेधातिथि काण्व। **देवता**– इन्द्र, ४१-४२ विभिन्दु। **छन्द**– गायत्री, २८ अनुष्टुप्।]

६००९. इदं वसो सुतमन्धः पिबा सुपूर्णमुदरम्। अनाभयिन्त्ररिमा तें॥१॥

1. Giver of dwellings (*Indra*), drink this effused libation till your belly is full, we offer it, undaunted (*Indra*), to you.

६०१०. नृभिर्धूतः सुतो अश्नैरव्यो वारैः परिपूतः। अश्वो न निक्तो नदीषु॥२॥

2. Washed by the priests, effused by the stones, purified by the woollen filter, like a horse cleansed in a stream.

६०११. तं ते यवं यथा गोभिः स्वादुमकर्म श्रीणन्तः। इन्द्र त्वास्मिन्त्सधमादे॥३॥

3. We have made it sweet for you as the barley-cake mixing it with milk, and therefore, *Indra*, (I invoke) you to this social rite.

६०१२. इन्द्र इत्सोमपा एक इन्द्रः सुतपा विश्वायुः। अन्तर्देवान् मर्त्याँश्च॥४॥

4. *Indra* verily is the chief drinker of the *Soma* among gods and men, the drinker of the effused libation, the acceptor of all kinds of offerings.

The Chief Drinker of the Soma— *Ekaḥ somapāḥ*, he alone is to be presented, it is said, with the entire libation; the other gods are only sharers of a part, *ekadeśa-bhājaḥ*.

६०१३. न यं शुक्रो न दुराशीर्न तृप्रा उरुव्यचंसम्। अपस्पृण्वते सुहार्दम्॥५॥

5. (We praise him) a universal kind-hearted (friend), whom the pure *Soma*, the mixture (of it) made with difficulty, or other satisfying (offerings) do not displease.

६०१४. गोभिर्यदीमन्ये अस्मन्मृगं न व्रा मृगयन्ते। अभित्सरन्ति धेनुभिः॥६॥

6. Whom others pursue with offerings of milk and curds as hunters chase a deer (with nets and snares), and harass with (inappropriate) praises.

६०१५. त्रय इन्द्रस्य सोमाः सुतासः सन्तु देवस्य। स्वे क्षये सुतपाव्नः॥७॥

7. May the three libations be effused for the divine *Indra* in his won dwelling, (for he is) the drinker of the effused juice.

६०१६. त्रयः कोशासः श्रोतन्ति तिस्रश्चम्वः सुपूर्णाः।

समाने अधि भार्मन्॥८॥

8. Three purifying vessels drop (the *Soma*), three ladles are well filled (for the libation), the whole is furnished for the common sacrifice.

The verse alludes to the three daily sacrifices. [The three vessels are the three troughs used in the preparation of the *Soma* libations, the *Droṇakalaśa*, the *Pūtabhṛt*, and the *Āhavanīya*. The three ladles are the three sets of cups *camaṣāḥ*, used in the three libations.]

६०१७. शुचिरसि पुरुनिःष्ठाः क्षीरैर्मध्यत आशीर्तः।

दध्ना मन्दिष्ठः शूरस्य॥९॥

9. You (*Soma*) are pure, distributed in many vessels, mixed at the mid-day sacrifice with milk, and (at the third sacrifice) with curds, the most exhilarating (beverage) of the hero (*Indra*).

६०१८. इमे त इन्द्र सोमास्तीव्रा अस्मे सुतासः।

शुक्रा आशिरं याचन्ते॥१०॥

10. These sharp and pure *Soma* libations effused by us for you solicit you for admixture.

६०१९. तौं आ॒शिरं॑ पुरो॒ळाश॒मिन्द्रे॒मं सोमं॑ श्रीणीहि।

रे॒व॒न्तं हि त्वां॑ शृणोमिं॑ ॥११॥

11. Mix, *Indra*, the milk and *Soma*, (add) the cake the this libation. I hear that you are possessed of riches.

६०२०. हृ॒त्सु पी॒तासों॑ युध्यन्ते दु॒र्मदा॑सो॒ न सु॒रायां॑म्।

ऊ॒ध॒र्न न॒ग्ना ज॑रन्ते॥१२॥

12. The potations (of *Soma*) contend in your interior (for your exhilaration) like the ebriety caused by wine: your worshippers praise you (filled full of *Soma*) like the udder (of a cow with milk).

Like the Ebriety Caused by Wine— *Durmadāso na surāyām,* like bad intoxications, wine, being drunk. The preparation of fermented liquors was therefore familiar to the Hindus, and probably amongst them was wine, the north-west of the Punjab, no doubt their earliest site being the country of the grape; but according to comment on *Manu,* an inferior sort of spirit.

Your Worshippers Praise you, etc.—*Ūdhar na nagnā jarante.*[1] "The praisers praise like an udder," is the literal rendering according to the Scholiast, but *nagna* usually means naked; here it is said to import *stotā,* a praiser, one who does not neglect or abandon the verses of the Veda, *chandāṁsi na jahati.*

६०२१. रे॒वौं इ॒न्द्रे॒व॒तः स्तो॒ता स्या॒त्त्वाव॑तो म॒घोनं॑ः। प्रेदु॑ ह॒रिवः॑ श्रु॒तस्यं॑॥१३॥

13. May the eulogist of you, who are opulent, be opulent; may he even, lord of steeds, surpass one who is wealthy and renowned, like you.

Sāmaveda, 1804.

Surpass one who is Wealthy and Renowned like you— Sāyaṇa renders this last clause "the praiser of any one wealthy and renowned like you would assuredly prosper (much more, then of you)."

६०२२. उ॒क्थं च॒न श॒स्यमां॑न॒मगौ॑र॒रिरा॑ चि॒केत। न गा॒यत्रं॑ गी॒यमां॑नम्॥१४॥

14. (*Indra*), the enemy of the unbeliever, apprehends whatever prayer is being repeated, whatever chaunt is being chaunted.

Sāmaveda, 1805, but the reading of the printed text of Benfey varies. Our text has *agor arir ā ciketa,* the enemy of him who does not praise, *astotuś śatrur Indraḥ*— the *Sāman* has *nago rayir ā ciketa,* translated,

---

१. दुष्टमदा यथा पातारं मादयन्ति तद्वत्त्वां मादयितुं परस्परं युध्यन्त इत्यर्थः।

welch Lied den Bos auch immer spricht, der Schatz beachtet's
nimmermehr.

६०२३. मा न॑ इन्द्र पीयत्न॑वे मा शर्ध॑ते॒ परा॑ दाः।

शिक्षा॒ शचीव॑ः शची॒भिः॥१५॥

15. Consign us not, *Indra*, to the slayer, not to an
overpowering foe; doer of great deeds, enable us by your acts (to
conquer).

Sāmaveda, 1806.

६०२४. व॒यमु॒ त्वा त॒दिद॑र्था॒ इन्द्र॑ त्वा॒यन्त॑ः स॒खा॑यः।

कण्वा॒ उ॒क्थेभि॒र्जर॑न्ते॥१६॥

16. Friends devoted, *Indra*, to you we, the descendants of
Kaṇva, having your praise for our object, glorify you with prayers.

Sāmaveda, 157, 719.

६०२५. न घे॒मन्यदा॒ प॑प॒न् व॒ज्रि॒न्न॒प॒सो॒ न॒वि॒ष्टौ॑। त॒वेदु॒ स्तोमं॑ चिकेत॥१७॥

17. (Engaged), thunderer, in your most recent (worship) I utter
no other praise than that of you, the doer of great deeds, I repeat
only your glorification.

This and the next occur in the *Sāmaveda,* 720-21.

६०२६. इच्छ॒न्ति॑ दे॒वाः सु॒न्व॒न्तं॒ न स्वप्ना॑य स्पृहयन्ति।

यन्ति॑ प्र॒मा॒द॒मत॑न्द्राः॥१८॥

18. The gods love the man who offers libations, they desire not
to (let him) sleep, thence they, unslothful, obtain the inebriating
Soma.

६०२७. ओ षु प्र या॑हि॒ वाजे॑भि॒र्मा॑ हृणीथा अ॒भ्य१॑ स्मान्।

म॒हाँ इ॑व॒ युव॑जानिः॥१९॥

19. Come to us quickly with excellent viands, be not bashful,
like the ardent husband of a new bride.

६०२८. मो षु॑१॑च्च दु॒र्ह॒णा॑वान्त्सा॒यं क॑रद॒रे अस्मत्।

अश्री॒रइ॑व॒ जामा॑ता॥२०॥

20. Let insúperable, delay (coming to us) to-day until the
evening, like an unlucky son-in-law.

Let not Indra Delay, etc.— Who, being repeatedly summoned,
delays his appearance till evening, is the Scholiast's explanation.

६०२९. विद्मा ह्यस्य वीरस्य॑ भूरिदाव॑रीं सुम॒तिम्।
त्रिषु॒ जात॑स्य म॒नांसि॑।।२१।।

21. We know the munificent generosity of the hero (*Indra*): of the purposes of him who is manifest in the three worlds (we are aware).

६०३०. आ तू षि॑ञ्च॒ क॒ण्व॑म॒न्तं न घा॑ वि॒द्म शव॑सा॒नात्।
यश॑स्तरं श॒तमू॑तेः।।२२।।

22. Pour out the libation to him who is associated with the *Kaṇva* (race): we know not any one more celebrated than the very powerful bestower of numerous protections.

In the First Place— Alluding to the *Aindravāyava graha*, see st. 6000.

६०३१. ज्येष्ठे॑न सो॒तरि॒न्द्रा॑य सोम॒ं वी॒राय॒ शक्रा॑य। भरा॑ पि॒बन्न॒र्याय॑।।२३।।

23. Offer, worshipper, the libation in the first place to the hero, the powerful *Indra*, the benefactor of man: may he drink (of it),—

६०३२. यो वेदि॑ष्ठो अव्य॑थिष्व॒श्वा॑व॒न्तं जरि॒तृभ्यः॑।
वाज॑ं स्तो॒तृभ्यो॑ गोम॑न्तम्।।२४।।

24. He who most recognisant of (the merit) of those who give him no annoyance, bestows upon his adorers and praisers food with horses and cattle.

६०३३. पन्यं॑पन्यं॒मित्सो॒तार॑ आ धा॑वत॒ मद॑य। सोम॒ं वी॒राय॒ शूरा॑य।।२५।।

25. Hasten, offerers of the libation, (to present) the glorious *Soma* to the valiant, the hero (*Indra*), for (his) exhilaration.

६०३४. पाता॑ वृ॒त्र॒हा सु॒तमा घा॑ ग॒मन्ना॒रे अस्म॑त्। नि य॑मते श॒तमू॑तिः।।२६।।

26. May the drinker of the *Soma* libation, the slayer of *Vṛtra*, approach, let him not be far from us; let the granter of many protections keep in check (our enemies).

६०३५. एह ह॒री ब्र॒ह्म॒युजा॒ शग्मा॑ व॒क्षतः॑ सखा॑यम्।
गी॒र्भिः श्रु॒तं गिर्व॑णसम्।।२७।।

27. May the delightful steeds who are harnessed by prayer bring hither (ours) friends (*Indra*), magnified by praises, deserving of laudation.

Cf. Sāmaveda, 1658.

६०३६. स्वादव: सोमा आ याहि श्रीता: सोमा आ याहि।

शप्रिनृषीव: शचीवो नायमच्छा सधमादम्।।२८।।

28. Handsome-chinned (*Indra*), the honoured of sages, the doer of great deeds, come, for well-flavoured are the *Soma* juices; come, for the libations are ready mixed: this (your worshipper) now (invites you) to be present at this social exhilarating rite.

Na ayam acchā sadhamādam, "now this (worshipper) in presence (invites) you to be exhilarated with (us)," is the explanation of the Scholiast.

६०३७. स्तुतश्च यास्त्वा वर्धन्ति महे राधसे नृम्णाय।

इन्द्रे कारिणं वृधन्त:।।२९।।

29. They who praising you magnify you, *Indra*, the institutor of rites, and those (hymns which glorify) you have (for their object) great riches and strength.

६०३८. गिरश्च यास्ते गिर्वाह उक्था च तुभ्यं तानि।

सत्रा दधिरे शवांसि।।३०।।

30. Upborne by hymns, those your praises and those prayers which are addressed to you, all combined, sustain your energies.

६०३९. एवेदेष तुविकूर्मिर्वाजाँ एको वज्रहस्त:। सनादमृक्तो दयते।।३१।।

31. Verily this accomplisher of many acts, the chief (among the gods), the wielder of the thunderbolt, he who has ever been unconquered, gives food (to his votaries).

६०४०. हन्ता वृत्रं दक्षिणेनेन्द्र: पुरू पुरुहूत:। महान्महीभि: शचीभि:।।३२।।

32. *Indra*, the slayer of *Vṛtra* with his right hand, the invoked of many in many (places), the mighty by mighty deeds,—

६०४१. यस्मिन् विश्वाश्चर्षणय उत च्यौत्ना जयांसि च।

अनु घेन्मन्दी मघोन:।।३३।।

33. He upon whom all men depend, (in whom) overwhelming energies (abide), he verily is the delighter of the opulent (worshipper).

६०४२. एष एतानि चकारेन्द्रो विश्वा योऽति शुण्वे।

वाजदावा मघोनाम्।।३४।।

34. This *Indra* has made all these (beings), who is thence exceedingly renowned; he is the donor of food to opulent worshippers.

Has made all these beings— *Etāni viśvāni cakāra*, he has made all these, according to comment, either *bhūtajātāni*, all beings, or he has performed all these exploits the death of *Vṛtra*, and the like.

६०४३. प्रभर्ता रथं गव्यन्तमपाकाच्चिद्यमवति। इनो वसु स हि वोल्हा।।३५।

35. He whom, adoring, and desirous of cattle, the protector (*Indra*) defends against an ignorant (foe), becomes a prince, the possessor of wealth.

Desirous of Cattle— *Ratham gavyantam, ratham* is explained *raṁhaṇam*, from *vahi*, to go. It cannot have its usual sense, a car, as it is the epithet of him who becomes the lord, the bearer of riches, *ino vasu sa hi voḷahā*. (इन: ईश्वर:)

६०४४. सनिता विप्रो अर्वद्भिर्हन्ता वृत्रं नृभि: शूर:।
सत्योऽविता विधन्तम्।।३६।।

36. Liberal, wise, (borne by his won) steeds, a hero, the slayer of *Vṛtra*, (aided) by the *Maruts*, truthful, he is the protector of the performer of holy rites.

Wise, Born by his own steeds—Or rather, "wise, attaining his object by his steeds."

६०४५. यजध्वैनं प्रियमेधा इन्द्रं सत्राचा मनसा। यो भूत्सोमै: सत्यमद्वा।।३७।

37. worship, *Priyamedha*, with mind intent upon him, that *Indra*, who is truthful when exhilarated by the *Soma* potations.

Truthful when Exhilarated by the Soma Potations—*Somaiḥ satyamadvā*, in vino veritas conveys a similar notion, but truth, or truthful, as applied to a deity in the Veda, means one who keeps faith with his worshippers, who grants their prayers; so *Indra*, in his cups, is especially bountiful to those who praise him.

६०४६. गाथश्रवसं सत्पतिं श्रवस्कामं पुरुत्मानम्।
कण्वासो गात वाजिनम्।।३८।।

38. Sing, *Kaṇvas*, the mighty (*Indra*), of widelysung renown, the protector of the good, the desirous of (sacrificial) food, present in many places.

६०४७. य ऋते चिद्गास्पदेभ्यो दात् सखा नृभ्य: शचीवान्।
ये अस्मिन्कामममश्रियन्।।३९।।

39. He who, a friend (to his worshippers), the doer of great deeds, tracing the cattle by their foot-marks, being without (other means of detection), restored them to those leaders (of rites) who willingly put their trust in him.

Without other means of Detection— Or rather, "tracing them, though without their footsteps (to guide him)."

६०४८. इत्था धीर्वन्तमद्रिवः काण्वं मेध्यातिथिम्।
मेषो भूतो३ऽभि यन्नयः।।४०।।

40. You, thunderer, approaching in the form of a ram, have come to *Medhyātithi*, of the race of *Kaṇva*, thus propitiating you.

In the form of a ram— *Cf.* Vol. I, *mantra* 600 and *Ṣaḍviṁśā Brāhmaṇa*, 1.1. [The legend is also found in the *Bāṣkala Upaniṣad*, as given in Anquetil du Perron's translation. Dr, Weber compares the Greek legend of Ganymede].

Have come to— Or rather, "did carry off," *ayaḥ, i.e., agamayaḥ.*

६०४९. शिक्षा विभिन्दो अस्मै चत्वार्ययुता ददत्। अष्टा परः सहस्रा।।४१।।

41. Liberal *Vibhindu*, you has given to me four times ten thousand, and afterwards eight thousand.

६०५०. उत सु त्ये पयोवृधा माकी रणस्य नप्त्या। जनित्वनाय मामहे।।४२।

42. I glorify those two (heaven and earth), the augmenters of water, the originators (of beings), the benefactors of the worshipper, on account of their generation (of the wealth so given to me).

Those two Heaven and Earth—The text has *tye payovṛdhā mākī raṇasya naptyā janitvanāya māmahe.* There is no substantive; the Scholiast supplies *dyāvāpṛthivyau*, because, he says, they being pleased such a gift is obtained, *tayoḥ prasannayor evedam dānam labhyate.* The attributives are also in the fem. daul: two of them are unusual; *mākī* is explained by *nirmātryau*, "makers, creators,'] and *naptyā* by *anugrahaśīle, "inclined to be favourable"*; *raṇasya*, of or to the *stotā.*

[सूक्त- ३]

[**ऋषि**– मेध्यातिथि काण्व। **देवता**– इन्द्र, २१-२४ पाकस्थामा कौरयाण।
छन्द– १-२० प्रगाथ (विषमा बृहती, समासतो बृहती), २१ अनुष्टुप्, २२-
२३ गायत्री, २४ बृहती।]

६०५१. पिबा सुतस्य रसिनो मत्स्वा न इन्द्र गोमतः।
आपिर्नो बोधि सधमाद्यो वृधे३ऽस्माँ अवन्तु ते धियः।।१।।

1. Drink, *Indra*, of our sapid libation mixed with milk, and be satisfied: regard thyself as our kinsman, to be exhilarated along with us for our welfare: may your (good) intentions protect us.

Sāmaveda, 239, 1421.

As our Kinsman, etc.—Or rather, "As our kinsman, to be exhilarated along with us, think for our welfare."

This verse is used as a *Pragātha,* as also are 2-20 of this hymn. From the number of *Pragāthas* which this *Maṇḍala* supplies, it is sometimes called the *Maṇḍala* of the *Pragāthas.*

६०५२. भूयाम॑ ते सुम॒तौ वा॒जिनो॑ व॒यं मा न॑: स्तरभि॒मात॑ये।
अ॒स्माञ्चि॒त्राभि॑रवता॒दभि॑ष्टिभिरा न॑: सु॒म्नेषु॑ यामय॥२॥

2. May we be offerers of oblations (to enjoy) your favour; harm us not for the sake of the enemy; protect us with your wondrous solicited (protections), maintain us ever in felicity.

Sāmaveda, 1422

६०५३. इ॒मा उ॑ त्वा पुरूवसो गि॒रो व॑र्धन्तु या मम॑।
पा॒व॒कव॑र्णा: शु॒चय॑ो वि॒पश्चि॑तोऽभि स्तोमै॑रनूषत॥३॥

3. (*Indra*), abounding in wealth, may these my praises magnify you; the brilliant pure sages glorify you with hymns.

Sāmaveda, 250, 1607. *Yajurveda,* 33.81. Mahīdhara considers the *Sūkta* to be addressed to *Āditya*: the epithet *pāvakavarṇa* he renders, with **Sāyaṇa,** *agnisamānatejaska,* radiant as *Agni.*

६०५४. अ॒यं स॒हस्र॒मृषि॑भि: स॒हस्कृ॑त: समु॒द्रइव पप्रथे।
स॒त्य: सो अ॑स्य महि॒मा गृ॒णे शवो॑ य॒ज्ञेषु॑ विप्रराज्ये॥४॥

4. Invigorated by (the praises of) a thousand *Ṛṣis,* this (*Indra*) is as vast as the ocean: the true mightiness and strength of him are glorified at sacrifices, and in the realm of the devout.

Sāmaveda, 1608. *Yajurveda.* 33.83.

६०५५. इन्द्र॒मिद्दे॑वता॒तय॑ इन्द्रं॑ प्रय॒त्य॑ध्वरे।
इन्द्रं॑ स॒मीके॒ वनि॑नो हवामह॒ इन्द्रं॑ धन॑स्य सा॒तये॥५॥

5. We invoke *Indra* for the worship of the gods, and when the sacrifice is proceeding; adoring him, we call upon *Indra* at the close of the rite; we invoke him for the acquirement of wealth.

At the Close of the Rite— *Samīke sampurṇe yāge,* or it may mean *saṅgrāme,* in war. *Sāmaveda,* 249, 1587.

६०५६. इन्द्रो मह्ना रोदसी पप्रथच्छव इन्द्रः सूर्यमरोचयत्।

इन्द्रे ह विश्वा भुवनानि येमिर इन्द्रे सुवानास इन्दवः॥६॥

6. *Indra*, by the might of his strength, has spread out the heaven and earth: *Indra* has lighted up the sun: in *Indra* are all beings aggregated; the distilling drops of the *Soma* flow to *Indra*.

Indra has lighted up the Sun— According to the Scholiast, *Indra* rescues the sun from the grasp of *Svarbhānu*, extricates him from eclipse. *Sāmaveda*, 1588.

६०५७. अभि त्वा पूर्वपीतय इन्द्र स्तोमेभिरायवः।

समीचीनास ऋभवः समस्वरन् रुद्रा गृणन्त पूर्व्यम्॥७॥

7. Men glorify you, *Indra*, with hymns that you may drink the first (of the gods): the associated *Ṛbhus* unite in your praise, the *Rudras* glorify the ancient (*Indra*).

समस्वरन्–तामेद सम्यगस्तुवन्। स्वृ शकापतापमोः।

६०५८. अस्येदिन्द्रो वावृधे वृष्ण्यं शवो मदे सुतस्य विष्णवि।

अद्या तमस्य महिमानमायवोऽनु ष्टुवन्ति पूर्वथा॥८॥

8. *Indra* augments the energy and the strength of this (his worshipper), when the exhilaration of the *Soma* juice is diffused through his body; men celebrate in due order his might to-day as they did of old.

Sāmaveda, 1574. *Yajurveda*, 33.97. Mahīdhara agrees with Sāyaṇa referring the increase of vigour to the *Yajamāna*, *asyaiva yajamānasya vīryam vardhayati*. He is more explicit in applying the incitement to *Indra, Somapānena matta Indro yajamānasya balam vardhayatītyarthaḥ*. The term *viṣṇavi* he agrees in considering an epithet of *made, śarīra-vyāpake*, diffused through the body, or, he says, it may be an equivalent of *yajña*, at sacrifice.

६०५९. तत्त्वा यामि सुवीर्यं तद् ब्रह्म पूर्वचित्तये।

येना यतिभ्यो भृगवे धने हिते येन प्रस्कण्वमाविथ॥९॥

9. I solicit you, *Indra*, for such vigour and for such food as may be hoped for in priority (to others), wherewith you have granted to *Bhṛgu* the wealth taken from those who had desisted from sacrifices, wherewith you have protected *Praskaṇva*.

Taken from those Who had Desisted from Sacrifice— *Yena yatibhyo dhane hite, yatibhyaḥ* is here explained as *karmasu uparatebhyo'yaśtribhyo janebhyo sakāśād dhanam āhṛtya*, having taken the wealth from men not offering sacrifices, or ceasing to perform holy acts (*Cf.* Wilson's edition vol.III. p. 411 st. 5,6]; or *yati* may have its usual sense, and the passage may imply wealth given to *Bhṛgu*, for the benefit of the sages, the *Aṅgirasas*.

६०६०. येना॑ समु॒द्रमसृ॑जो म॒हीरप॒स्तदि॑न्द्र॒ वृष्णि॒ ते॒ शव॑:।
सद्य॒: सो अ॑स्य महि॒मा न स॑न्न॒शे॒ यं क्षो॒णीर॑नुचक्र॒दे॑॥१०॥

10. Wherewith you have sent the great waters to the ocean: such as is your wish-fulfilling strength: that might of *Indra* is not easily to be resisted which the earth obeys.

Such as is Your Wish-Fulfilling Strength—Or, "That Your strength wherewith, etc., is wish-fulfilling."

६०६१. श॒ग्धी न॒ इन्द्र॒ यत्त्वा॑ र॒यिं या॒मि॑ सु॒वीर्य॑म्।
श॒ग्धि वाजा॑य॒ प्रथ॑मं सिषा॒सते॒ श॒ग्धि स्तो॒माय॑ पू॒र्व्य॑॥११॥

11. Grant us, *Indra*, the wealth accompanied by vigour, which I solicit from you; give (wealth) first of all to him desirous of gratifying you, presenting (sacrificial) food; give (wealth), You who are of old, to him who glorifies you.

६०६२. श॒ग्धी नो॑ अस्य॒ यद्ध॒ पौर॒मावि॑थ॒ धियं॑ इन्द्र॒ सिषा॒सत॑:।
श॒ग्धि यथा॑ रु॒शमं॒ श्याव॑कं॒ कृप॑मिन्द्र॒ प्राव॒: स्वर्ण॑रम्॥१२॥

12. Give to this our (worshipper) engaged in celebrating your sacred rites, *Indra*, (the wealth) whereby you have protected the son of *Puru*: grant to the man (asp ring) to heaven (the wealth wherewith) you have preserved, O *Indra*, *Ruśama*, *Śyāvaka*, and *Kṛpa*.

६०६३. कन्न॒व्यो अत॑सीनां तु॒रो गृ॑णीत॒ मर्त्य॑:।
न ही न्व॑स्य महि॒मान॑मि॒न्द्रियं॒ स्वर्गृ॑णन्त॒ आन॒शु॑:॥१३॥

13. What living mortal, the prompter of ever-rising (praises), may now glorify *Indra*? No one of those heretofore praising him have attained the greatness of the properties of *Indra*.

६०६४. क॒दु॑ स्तु॒वन्त॑ ऋतय॒न्त दे॑व॒त ऋषि॒: को विप्र॑ ओहते।
क॒दा हव॑ मघव॒न्निन्द्र॑ सुन्व॒त॒: क॒दु॑ स्तु॒वत॒ आ ग॑म॒:॥१४॥

14. Who, praising you as the deity, (ever) hoped to sacrifice to you? What saint, what sage conveys (his praises to you?) When, opulent *Indra*, have you come to the invocation of one pouring out libations, of one repeating (your) praise?

६०६५. उदु त्ये मधुमत्तमा गिरः स्तोमास ईरते।

सत्राजितो धनसा अक्षितोतयो वाजयन्तो रथाइव॥१५॥

15. These most sweet songs, these hymns of praise ascend (to you), like triumphant chariots laden with wealth, charged with unfailing protections, intended to procure food.

Like Triumphant Chariots, etc.—*Vājayantaḥ annam icchanto rathā iva,* the epithets are somewhat inapplicable to a car, but they are all plur. masec., and can only agree with *rathāḥ. Sāmaveda,* 251, 1362.

६०६६. कण्वाइव भृगवः सूर्याइव विश्वमिद्धीतमानशुः।

इन्द्रं स्तोमेभिर्महयन्त आयवः प्रियमेधासो अस्वरन्॥१६॥

16. The *Bhṛgus,* like the *Kaṇvas,* have verily attained to the all-pervading (*Indra*), on whom they have meditated, as the sun (pervades the universe by his rays): mer of the *Priyamedha* race, worshipping *Indra* with praises glorify him.

Sāmaveda, 1363.

६०६७. युक्ष्वा हि वृत्रहन्तम हरीं इन्द्र परावतः।

अर्वाचीनो मघवन्त्सोमपीतय उग्र ऋष्वेभिरा गहि॥१७॥

17. Utter destroyer of *Vṛtra,* harness your horses come down to us, fierce *Maghavan,* with your attendants from afar to drink the *Soma.*

*Sāmave*da, 301.

With Yours Attendants—Literally, "beautiful ones" (*ṛṣvaiḥ*), *i.e.,* the *Maruts.*

६०६८. इमे हि ते कारवो वावशुर्धिया विप्रासो मेधसातये।

स त्वं नौ मघवन्निन्द्र गिर्वणो वेनो न शृणुधी हवम्॥१८॥

18. These wise celebrators (of holy rites) repeatedly propitiate you with pious praise for the acceptance of the sacrifice: do you, opulent *Indra,* who are entitled to praise, hear our invocation like one who listens to what he desires.

Like one Who listens to What he Desires—*Veno na* (from *vena, kānti-karmā*), *yathā jātābhilāṣaḥ puruṣaḥ kāmayitavyam aikāgryeṇa śṛṇoti,* as a man full of desire listens attentively to that which is agreeable.

६०६९. निरिन्द्र बृहतीभ्यो वृत्रं धनुभ्यो अस्फुरः।

निरर्बुदस्य मृगयस्य मायिनो निः पर्वतस्य गा आजः॥१९॥

19. You have extirpated *Vṛtra* with your mighty weapons; you have been the destroyer of the deceptive *Arbuda* and *Mṛgaya;* you have extricated the cattle from the mountain.

६०७०. निरग्नयो रुरुचुर्निरु सूर्यो नि: सोमं इन्द्रियो रसः।

निरन्तरिक्षादधमो महामहिं कृषे तदिन्द्र पौस्यम्॥२०॥

20. When you had expelled the mighty *Ahi* from the firmament, then the fires blazed, the sun shone forth, the ambrosial *Soma* destined for *Indra* flowed out, and you, *Indra*, did manifest your manhood.

६०७१. यं मे दुरिन्द्रो मरुत: पाकंस्थामा कौरयाणः।

विश्वेषां त्मना शोभिष्ठमुपैव दिवि धावंमानम्॥२१॥

21. Such wealth as *Indra* and the *Maruts* have bestowed upon me, such has *Pākasthāman*, the son of *Kurayāṇa*, bestowed, of itself the most magnificent of all, like the quick-moving (sun) in the sky.

६०७२. रोहिंतं मे पाकंस्थामा सुधुरं कक्ष्यप्राम्। अदाद्रायो विबोधनम्॥२२॥

22. *Pākasthāman* has given me a tawny robust beast of burthen, the means of acquiring riches.

६०७३. यस्मा अन्ये दश प्रति धुरं वहन्ति वह्नयः।

अस्तं वयो न तुग्र्यम्॥२३॥

23. Whose burthen ten other bearers (of loads) (would be required to) convey, such as were the steeds that bore *Bhujyu* home.

See translation, *Ṛg.* i. 116. 4.

६०७४. आत्मा पितुस्तनूर्वासं ओजोदा अभ्यञ्जनम्।

तुरीयमिद्रोहितंस्य पाकंस्थामानं भोजं दातारंमब्रवम्॥२४॥

24. His father's own son, the giver of dwellings, the sustainer of strength like (invigorating) unguents, I celebrate *Pākasthāman*, the destroyer (of foes), the despoiler (of enemies), the donor of the tawny (horse).

[सूक्त-४]

[ऋषि- देवातिथि काण्व। देवता- इन्द्र, १५-१८ इन्द्र तथा पूषा, १९-२१ कुरुङ्ग। छन्द- १-२० प्रगाथ (विषमा बृहती, समासतो बृहती), २१ पुर उष्णिक्।]

६०७५. यदिन्द्र प्रागपागुदङ् न्यग्वा हूयसे नृभिः।

सिमा पुरू नृषूतो अस्यानवेऽसि प्रशर्ध तुर्वशे॥१॥

1. Inasmuch, *Indra*, as you are invoked by the people in the east, in the west, in the north, in the south, so, excellent *Indra*, have you been incited by men on behalf of the son of *Anu*; so, overcomer of foes, (have you been called upon) on behalf of *Turvaśa*.

Sāmaveda, 279, 1231

Inasmuch As—Sāyaṇa, instead of "inasmuch as" and "so," has "although" and "still."

६०७६. यद्वा रुमे रुशमे श्यावके कृप इन्द्र मादयसे सचा ।

कण्वासस्त्वा ब्रह्माभिः स्तोमंवाहस इन्द्रा यंच्छन्त्या गहि ॥२॥

2. Inasmuch, *Indra*, as you have been exhilarated in the society of *Ruma, Ruśama, Śyāvaka,* and *Kṛpa,* so the *Kaṇvas*, bearers of oblations, attract you with their praises, (therefore) come hither.

Sāmaveda, 1232.

६०७७. यथां गौरो अपा कृतं तृष्यन्नेत्यवेरिणम् ।

आपित्वे नं: प्रपित्वे तूयमा गहि कण्वेषु सु सचा पिब ॥३॥

3. As the thirsty *Gaura* hastens to the pool filled with water in the desert, so, (*Indra*,) our affinity being acknowledged, come quickly, and drink freely with the *Kaṇvas*.

Sāma., 252.

६०७८. मन्दन्तु त्वा मघवन्निन्द्रेन्दवो राधोदेयाय सुन्वते ।

आमुष्या सोममपिबश्चमू सुतं ज्येष्ठं तद्दधिषे सहः ॥४॥

4. Opulent *Indra*, may the *Soma* drops exhilarated you, that you may bestow wealth on the donor of the libation; for taking it by stealth (when ungiven), you have drunk the *soma* poured out into the ladle, and have thence sustained pre-eminent strength.

६०७९. प्र चक्रे सहसा सहो बभञ्ज मन्युमोजसा ।

विश्वे त इन्द्र पृतनायवो यहो नि वृक्षाइव येमिरे ॥५॥

5. By his strength he has overpowered the strength (of his foes), he has crushed their wrath by his prowess: all hostile armies have been arrested like trees (immoveable through fear), mighty *Indra*, by you.

All Hostile Armies—Rather, "those wishing to fight," *pṛtanāyavaḥ.*

६०८०. सहस्त्रेणेव सचते यवीयुधा यस्त आनळुपस्तुतिम् ।

पुत्रं प्रावर्गं कृणुते सुवीर्यं दाश्नोति नमउक्तिभिः ॥६॥

6. He who has made his praise attain to you associates himself
with a thousand gallant combatants; he who offers oblations with
reverence begets a valiant son, the scatterer (of enemies).

६०८१. मा भेम मा श्रमिष्मोग्रस्य सख्ये तव।
महत्ते वृष्णो अभिचक्ष्यं कृतं पश्येम तुर्वशं यदुम्॥७॥

7. (Secure) in the friendship of you who are terrible, let us not
fear, let us not be harassed: great and glorious, showerer (of
benefits), are your deeds, as we may behold them in the case of
Turvaśa, of *Yadu*.

६०८२. सव्यामनु स्फिग्यं वावसे वृषा न दानो अस्य रोषति।
मध्वा सम्पृक्ताः सारघेण धेनवस्तूयमेहि द्रवा पिब॥८॥

8. The showerer (of benefits) with his left hip covers (the
world), no tearer (of it) angers him: the delightful (*Soma* juices)
are mixed with the sweet honey of the bee; come quickly hither,
hasten, drink.

No Tearer of it Angers him— *Na dāno asya roṣati, dāno
avakhaṇḍayitā,*[1] or it may mean *dātā,* donor of the oblation.

Delightful—*Dhenavaḥ,* literally, milch cows. *Soma* equally
agreeable is the explanation of the commentator, *dhenuvat prītijanakāḥ
Somāḥ.* This and the preceding occur in *Sāmaveda,* 1606. [Sāyaṇa says,
'mixed with milk sweet as honey.']

With his left hip— *Cf.* translation, *Ṛg.* iii.32.11, where, for "flame,"
we should rather read "hips" as the Scholiast explains *sphigi* in both
places by *kati.*

६०८३. अक्षी रथी सुरूप इद् गोमाँ इदिन्द्र ते सखा।
श्वात्रभाजा वयसा सचते सदा चन्द्रो याति सभामुप॥९॥

9. He who is your friend, *Indra,* is verily possessed of horses,
of cars, of cattle, and is of goodly from: he is ever supplied with
food-comprising riches, and delighting all, he enters an assembly.

Sāmaveda, 277.

With Food-Comprising Riches— Rather, "wealth-associated
food," *śvātrabhājā*[2] *vayasā.*

६०८४. ऋश्यो न तृष्यन्नवपानमा गहि पिबा सोमं वशाँ अनु।
निमेघमानो मघवन्दिवेदिव ओजिष्ठं दधिषे सहः॥१०॥

---

१. दो अवखण्डने।

२. श्वात्रम् इति धननाम।

10. Come like a thirsty deer to the watering place, drink at will of the *Soma*, whence, daily driving down the clouds, you sustainest, *Maghavan*, most vigorous strength.

६०८५. अध्वर्यो द्रावया त्वं सोममिन्द्रः पिपासति।

उप नूनं युयुजे वृषणा हरी आ च॑ जगाम वृत्रहा॥११॥

11. Quickly, priest, pour forth the *Soma*, for *Indra* is thirsty; verily he has harnessed his vigorous steeds, the slayer of *Vṛtra* has arrived.

Sāma., 308.

६०८६. स्वयं चित्स मन्यते दाशुरिर्जिनो यत्रा सोमस्य तृम्पसि।

इदं ते अन्नं युज्यं समुक्षितं तस्येहि प्र द्रवा पिब॥१२॥

12. The man who is the donor (of the oblation), he with (the gift of whose) libation you are satisfied, possesses of himself understanding; this your appropriate food is ready; come, hasten, drink of it.

६०८७. रथेष्ठायाध्वर्यवः सोममिन्द्राय सोतन।

अधि ब्रध्नस्याद्रयो वि च॑क्षते सुन्वन्तो दाश्वध्वरम्॥१३॥

13. Pour out, priests, the *Soma* libation to *Indra* in his chariot: the stones, placed upon their bases, are beheld effusing the *Soma* for the sacrifice of the offerer.

Placed upon their Bases— *Adhi bradhnasya adrayaḥ mūlasya upari,* upon the root or base; this is said to be a broad stone slab placed upon a skin, and called *upara.*

दाशाध्वरम् *dāśa-donar, adhvara* sacrifice.

६०८८. उप ब्रध्नं वावाता वृषणा हरी इन्द्रमपसु वक्षतः।

अर्वाञ्चं त्वा सप्तयोऽध्वरश्रियो वहन्तु सवनेदुप॥१४॥

14. May his vigorous horses, repeatedly traversing the firmament, bring *Indra* to our rites; may your steeds, glorious through sacrifice, bring you indeed to the (daily) ceremonials.

Glorious through Sacrifice— According to Sāyaṇa, *adhvaraśriyaḥ* means sacrifice-haunting, *adhvaram sevamānāḥ.*

६०८९. प्र पूषणं वृणीमहे युज्याय पुरूवसुम्।

स शक्र शिक्ष पुरुहूत नो धिया तुजे राये विमोचन॥१५॥

15. We have recourse to the opulent *Pūṣan* for his alliance: do you, *Śakra*, the adored of many, the liberator (from iniquity), enable us to acquire by our intelligence, wealth and victory.

Pūṣan—*Pūṣan* may be here a name of *Indra*.

६०९०. सं नं: शिशीहि भुरिजोरिव क्षुरं रास्वं रायो विमोचन।
त्वे तन्नं: सुवेदमुस्त्रियं वसु यं त्वं हिनोषि मर्त्यम्॥१६॥

16. Sharpen us like a razor in the hands (of a barber (: grant us riches, liberator (form iniquity), the wealth of cattle easily obtained by us from you, such wealth as you bestow upon the (pious) mortal.

Sam naḥ śiśīhi bhurijor iva kṣuram, that is, *nāpitasya bāhvor iva sthitam kṣuram iva,* like a razor placed as it were in the two arms of a barber.

६०९१. वेमिं त्वा पूषन्तृज्ञसे वेमि स्तोतॅव आघृणे।
न तस्य वेम्यरंणं हि तद्वॅसो स्तुषे पज्राय साम्नै॥१७॥

17. I desire, *Pūṣan*, to propitiate you; I desire, illustrious deity, to glorify you: I desire not (to offer) ungracious praise to any other; (grant riches), bestower of wealth, to him who praises, eulogizes, and glorifies you.

Who Praises, eulogises and Glorifies you— *Stuṣe pajrāya sāmne*[1], the second is explained *prārjakāya stotrāṇām*, to the deliverer (collector?) of praises, or it may be a proper name, that of *Kakṣīvat, Sāman* is rendered *stotram*, the possessive *vat* being understood, *stotravate*, to a praiser: *dhanam dehi* is required to fill up the ellipse.

६०९२. परां गावो यवॅसं कच्चिंदाघृणे नित्यं रेकणॉ अमर्त्य।
अस्माकं पूषन्नविता शिवो भंव महिष्ठो वाजॅसातये॥१८॥

18. Illustrious (*Pūṣan*), my cattle go forth occasionally to pasture, may that wealth (of herds), immortal deity, be permanent; being my protector, *Pūṣan*, be the granter of felicity, be most bountiful in bestowing food.

६०९३. स्थूरं राधं: शताश्वं कुरुङ्गस्य दिविष्टिषु।
राज्ञस्त्वेषस्यं सुभगस्य रातिषु तुर्वॅशेष्वमन्महि॥१९॥

19. We acknowledge the substantial wealth (of the gift) of a hundred horses, the donation made to us amongst men at the holy solemnities of the illustrious and auspicious *Rājā Kuruṅga*.

६०९४. धीभि: सातानिं काण्वस्यं वाजिनः प्रियमेधैरभिद्युभि:।
षष्टिं सहस्रानु निर्मॅजामजे निर्यूथानि गवामृषिं:॥२०॥

---

१. यद्वां पज्रासो अश्विना हवन्ते (ऋ० १.११७.१०)।

20. I, the *Ṛṣi* (*Devatithi*), have received subsequently the complete donation: the sixty thousand herds of pure cattle merited by the devotions of the pious son of *Kaṇva*, and by the illustrious *Priyamedhas*.

६०९५. वृक्षाश्विन्मे अभिपित्वे अररारणुः।
गां भंजन्त मेहनाश्वं भजन्त मेहना॥२१॥

21. Upon the acceptance of this donation to me, the very trees have exclaimed: (See these *Ṛṣis*) have acquired excellent cows excellent horses.

Have Acquired Excellent cows, Excellent horses—*Gām bhajanta mehanā aśvam bhajanta mehanā*, the attributive is explained *manhanīyam, praśasyam*, commendable or excellent; or another sense is given, derived from a fanciful etymology, *me iha na,*[1] of me here not, that is, says the Scholiast, all the people, with the trees at their head, say, a gift such as this that has now been given was never given to me; *ihāsmin rājani tad dānam mama nāsīn mama nāsīd iti vṛkṣa-pramukhāḥ sarve'pi janāḥ procur ityarthaḥ.*

[सूक्त-५]

[**ऋषि**– ब्रह्मातिथि काण्व। **देवता**– अश्विनीकुमार, ३७ उत्तरार्द्ध ३९ चैद्य कशु! **छन्द**– गायत्री, ३७-३८ बृहती, ३९ अनुष्टुप्।]

६०९६. दूरादिहेव॒ यत्सत्य॑रुणप्सुरशिश्वितत्। वि भानुं विश्वधातनत्॥१॥

1. When the shining dawn, advancing hither from afar, whitens (all things), she spreads the light on all sides.

६०९७. नृवद्दस्रा मनोयुजा रथेन पृथुपाजसा। सचेथे अश्विनोषसम्॥२॥

2. And you, *Aśvins*, of goodly aspect, accompany the dawn like leader with your mighty chariot harnessed at a thought.

६०९८. युवाभ्यां वाजिनीवसू प्रति स्तोमा अदृक्षत। वाचं दूतो यथौहिषे॥३॥

3. By you, affluent in sacrifices, may our praises be severally accepted: I bear the words (of the worshipper) like a messenger (to you).

६०९९. पुरुप्रिया ण॑ ऊतये पुरुमन्द्रा पुरूवसू। स्तुषे कण्वासो अश्विना॥४॥

4. We, *Kaṇvas*, praise for our protection the manyloved, the many-delighting *Aśvins*, abounding in wealth,—

---

1. निरु॰ ४.४१

६१००. मंहि॒ष्ठा वा॒ज॒सा॒त॒मेष॑यन्ता शु॒भस्प॒ती। गन्ता॑रा दा॒शुषो॑ गृ॒हम्॥५॥

5. Most adorable bestowers of strength, distributors of food, lords of opulence, repairers to the dwelling of the donor (of the oblation).

६१०१. ता सु॒दे॒वाय॒ दा॒शुषे॑ सु॒मे॒धाम॑वि॒तारि॑णीम्। घृ॒तैर्ग॒व्यूति॑मुक्षतम्॥६॥

6. Sprinkle well with water the pure unfailing pasturage (of his cattle) for the devout donor (of the oblation).

६१०२. आ न॒: स्तोम॒मुप॑ द्र॒वत्तू॒यं श्ये॒नेभि॑रा॒शुभि॑:। यात॒मश्वे॑भिरश्विना॥७॥

7. Come, *Aśvins*, to our adoration, hastening quickly with your rapid falcon-like horses.

६१०३. येभि॒स्तिस्त्र॒: प॑रा॒वतो॒ दि॒वो विश्वा॑नि रोच॒ना। त्रीँर॑क्तू॒न्परि॑दीयथ:॥८॥

8. With which in three days and three nights you traverse from afar all the brilliant (constellations).

६१०४. उ॒त नो॒ गोम॑ती॒रिष॑ उ॒त सा॒तीर॑ह॒र्विद॑। वि प॒थ: सा॒तये॑ सितम्॥९॥

9. Bringers of the day, (bestow) upon us food with cattle, or donations of wealth; and close the path (against aggression) upon our gains.

And close The Path, etc.—*Vi pathaḥ sātaye sitam* is explained *asmākam gavādīnām lābhāya tadupāyarūpān mārgān viśeṣeṇa badhnītam yathānye na praviśanti,* or the *vi* may reverse the sense of *sitam* and imply open, *vimuñcatam pradarśayatam mārgān,* open, or show to us the paths of profit.

६१०५. आ नो॒ गोम॑न्तमश्विना सु॒वीरं॑ सु॒रथं॑ र॒यिम्। वोल्हम॒श्वाव॑ती॒रिष॑:॥१०।

10. Bring to us, *Aśvins*, riches comprising cattle, male offspring, chariots, horses, food.

६१०६. वावृ॒धा॒ना शु॒भस्प॒ती द॒स्त्रा हि॒रण्य॑वर्तनी। पि॒बतं॑ सो॒म्यं मधु॑॥११॥

11. Magnificent lords of good fortune, handsome *Aśvins*, riding in a golden chariot, drink the sweet *Soma* beverage.

Magnificent Lords of Good Fortune— Or lords of bright ornaments,'' or ''of water.''

६१०७. अ॒स्मभ्यं॑ वा॒जिनी॑वसू म॒घव॑द्भ्यश्च स॒प्रथ॑:। छ॒र्दिर्य॑न्त॒मदा॑भ्यम्॥१२॥

12. Affluent in sacrifices, grant to us who are opulent (in oblations) a spacious unassailable dwelling.

६१०८. नि षु ब्रह्म॒ ज॒नानां॒ या॒विष्टं॑ तू॒यमा गतम्। मोष्व॑१॒र्न्याँ उ॒पार॑तम्॥१३॥

13. Do you who ever carefully protect the *Brahman* amongst men, come-quickly: tarry not with other (worshippers).

Who ever Carefully Protect, etc.— *Brahma janānām ya āviṣṭam*: one explanation of the first is *Brāhmaṇa-jātim*, the *Brāhmaṇa* caste; another is given, *parivṛdham stotram havirlakṣaṇam annam vā,* the great praise or sacrificial food.

६१०९. अस्य पिंबतमश्विना युवं मदॅस्य चारुण:।

मध्वोॅ रातस्यॅ धिष्ण्या।।१४।।

14. Adorable *Aśvins*, drink of this exhilarating, delightful, sweet (*Soma* beverage) presented by us.

६११०. अस्मे आ वॅहतं रॅयिं शतवॅन्तं सहॅस्रिणम्। पुरुॅधुं विश्वधॉयसम्।।१५।

15. Bring unto us riches by hundreds and by thousands, desired by many, sustaining all.

Desired by Many— Literally, "to be praised by many," *bahubhiḥ*; or it may mean "giving a home to many," *bahunivāsam*. Benfey explains it "viele speisend."

६१११. पुरुॅत्रा चिद्धि वाॅं नरा विॅह्वयॅन्ते मनीषिण:। वाघॅद्भिरश्विना गॅतम्।।१६।

16. Leaders (of rites), wise men worship you in many places: come to us with your steeds.

६११२. जनाॅसो वृॅक्तबॅर्हिषो हॅविष्मॅन्तो अॅरङ्कृत:।

युवाॅं हॅवन्ते अश्विना।।१७।।

17. Men bearing the clipped sacred grass, presenting oblations, and completely fulfilling (their functions), worship you, *Aśvin*.

६११३. अस्माकॅमद्य वाॅमयं स्तोमो वाॅहिष्ठो अन्तॅम:।

युवाॅभ्याॅं भूत्वश्विना।।१८।।

18. May this our praise to-day be conveyed successfully to you, *Aśvins*, and be most nigh to you.

६११४. यो हॅ वाॅं मध्नुो दॅतिराॅहॅितो रथचॅर्षणे। ततॅ: पिबतमश्विना।।१९।।

19. Drink, *Aśvins*, from the skin (filled) with the sweet (*Soma* juice) which is suspended in view of your car.

६११५. तेनॅ नो वाजिनीवसू पॅश्वैॅ तोकाॅय शं गॅवे। वॅहॅतं पीॅवॅरीॅरिषॅ:।।२०।।

20. Affluent in oblations, bring to us with that (chariot) abundant food, so that there may be prosperity in horses, progeny, and cattle.

६११६. उत नो दिव्या इष उत सिन्धूँरहर्विंदा। अप द्वारेव वर्षथ:॥२१॥

21. Bringers of the day, you rain upon us by the (open) door (of the clouds) the waters of heaven, or (with them fill) the rivers.

६११७. कदा वां तौग्रयो विधत्समुद्रे जहितो नरा।

यद्वां रथो विभिष्पतात्॥२२॥

22. When did the son of *Tugra*, thrown into the ocean, glorify you, leaders (of rites)? then when your chariot and horses descended.

६११८. युवं कण्वाय नासत्यापिरिप्ताय हर्म्ये। शश्वदूतीर्दंशस्यथ:॥२३॥

23. To *Kaṇva* when blinded (by the *Asuras*) in his dwelling, you rendered, *Nāsatyās*, effectual aid.

Kaṇva Blinded—See *Ṛg.* 1.118.7.

Nāsatyās— The Scholiast cites Yāska for an unusual etymology of this title of the *Aśvins*, which is generally explained, those in whom there is no untruth; here one meaning is said to be, born of the nose, *Nāsikāprabhavau*.[1]

६११९. ताभिरा यातमूतिभिर्नव्यसीभि: सुशस्तिभि:। यद्वां वृषण्वसू हुवे॥२४।

24. Rich in showers, come with your newest and most excellent protections when I call upon you.

६१२०. यथा चित्कण्वमावतं प्रियमेधमुपस्तुतम्। अत्रिं शिञ्जारमश्विना॥२५॥

25. In like manner as you protected *Kaṇva*, *Priyamedha*, *Upastuta*, and the praise-repeating *Atri*.

६१२१. यथोत कृत्व्ये धनेंऽशुं गोष्वगस्त्यम्। यथा वाजेषु सोभरिम्॥२६॥

26. And in like manner as (you protected) Anshu when wealth was to be bestowed, and *Agastya* when his cattle (were to be recovered), and Sobhari when food (was to be supplied to him),—

६१२२. एतावद्वां वृषण्वसू अतो वा भूयो अश्विना। गृणन्त: सुम्नमीमहे॥२७।

27. So praising you, *Aśvins*, rich in showers, we solicity of you happiness as great or greater than that (which they obtained).

६१२३. रथं हिरण्यवन्धुरं हिरण्याभीशुमश्विना।

आ हि स्थाथो दिविस्पृशम्॥२८॥

28. Ascend, *Aśvins*, your sky-touching chariot with a golden seat and golden reins.

---

१. निरु० ६.२३।

६१२४. हिरण्ययी वां रभिरीषा अक्षो हिरण्ययः।

उभा चक्रा हिरण्यया।।२९।।

29. Golden is its supporting shaft, golden the axle, golden both the wheels.

६१२५. तेन नो वाजिनीवसू परावतश्चिदा गंतम्। उपेमां सुष्टुतिं मर्म।।३०।।

30. Come to us, affluent in sacrifices, from afar, come to this mine adoration.

६१२६. आ वहेथे पराकात्पूर्वीरश्नंतावश्विना। इषो दासीरमर्त्या।।३१।।

31. Immortal *Aśvins*, destroyers of the cities of the *Dāsas*, you bring to us food from afar.

Pūrvīr aśnantau dāsīḥ, the first word is rendered *purīḥ,* or *bahvīḥ,* many. [In the latter sense, the clause is explained as "taking away much food from the enemy, ye bring it to us".]

६१२७. आ नो द्युम्नैरा श्रवोभिरा राया यातमश्विना। पुरुश्चन्द्रा नासत्या।।३२।।

32. Come to us, *Aśvins*, with food, with fame, with riches, *Nāsatyās*, delighters of many.

६१२८. एह वां प्रुषितप्सवो वयो वहन्तु पर्णिनः। अच्छा स्वध्वरं जनम्।।३३।

33. Let your sleek, winged, rapid (horses) bring you to the presence of the man offering holy sacrifice.

६१२९. रथं वामनुगायसं य इषा वर्तते सह। न चक्रमभि बाधते।।३४।।

34. No hostile force arrests that car of yours which is hymned (by the devout), and which is laden with food.

६१३०. हिरण्ययेन रथेन द्रवत्पाणिभिरश्वैः। धीजवना नासत्या।।३५।।

35. Rapid as thought, *Nāsatyās*, (come) with-your golden chariot drawn by quick-footed steeds.

६१३१. युवं मृगं जागृवांसं स्वदथो वा वृषण्वसू।

ता नः पृङ्क्तमिषा रयिम्।।३६।।

36. Affluent in showers, taste the wakeful desirable *Soma*: combine for us riches with food.

६१३२. ता मे अश्विना सनीनां विद्यातं नवानाम्।

यथा चिच्चैद्यः कशुः शतमुष्ट्रानां ददत्सहस्ना दश गोनाम्।।३७।।

37. Become apprised, *Aśvins*, of my recent gifts, how that *Kaśu*, the son of *Cedi*, has presented me with a hundred camels and ten thousand cows.

६१३३. यो मे हिरण्यसन्दृशो दश राज्ञो अमंहत।
अधस्पदा इच्चैद्यस्य कृष्ट्यश्चर्मम्ना अभितो जनाः ॥३८॥

38. The son of *Cedi*, who has given me for servants ten *Rājās*, bright as gold, for all men are beneath his feet; all those around him wear cuirasses of leather.

Give me for Servitude ten Rājās— Having taken these *Rājās* prisoners in battle, he gives them to me in servitude; *yuddhe parājitān gṛhitvā tān dāsatvenāsmai dattavān.*

Wear Cuirasses of Leather— *Carmamnāḥ* is explained *Carma-mayasya kavacāder dhāraṇe kṛtābhyāsaḥ*, practised in wearing armour of leader; or *carma* may mean *caraṇa sādhanāni aśvādīni vāhanāni*, means of going, vehicles horses, and the like, *i.e.*, exercised in their management in war.

६१३४. माकिरेना पथा गाद्येनेमे यन्तिं चेद्यः।
अन्यो नेत्सूरिरोहते भूरिदावत्तरो जनः ॥३९॥

39. No one proceeds by that path which the *Cedis* follow, no other proud man as a more liberal benefactor confers (favour on those who praise him).

ANUVĀKA II

[सूक्त-६]

[ऋषि– वत्स काण्व। देवता– इन्द्र, ४६-४८ तिरिन्दिर पार्श्वय।
छन्द– गायत्री।]

६१३५. महाँ इन्द्रो य ओजसा पर्जन्यों वृष्टिमाइव। स्तोमैर्वत्सस्य वावृधे ॥१॥

1. *Indra*, who is great in might like *Parjanya* the distributor of rain, is magnified by the praises of *Vatsa*.

Sāmaveda, 1307. *Yajurveda*, 7.40.

६१३६. प्रजामृतस्य पिप्रतः प्र यद्भरन्त वह्नयः। विप्रा ऋतस्य वाहसा ॥२॥

2. When his steeds filling (the heavens) bear onwards the progeny of the sacrifice, then the pious (magnify him) with the hymns of the rite.

Sāmaveda, 1309.

Steeds— The text has *vahnayaḥ* interpreted *vāhakāḥ aśvāḥ*.
The Progeny of the Sacrifice— *i.e.*, *Indra*, [*Cf. infra*, v.28].

६१३७. कण्वा॒ इन्द्रं॒ यद॑क्रत स्तोमै॒र्यज्ञ॑स्य॒ साध॑नम्।

जा॒मि ब्रुव॑त॒ आयु॑धम्॥३॥

3. When the *Kaṇvas* by their praises have made *Indra* the accomplisher of the sacrifice, they declare all weapons needless.

They Declare all Weapons Needless— *Jāmi bruvata āyudham*. The first is explained *prayojanarahitam;* or *āyudham* may imply *Indra*, *ayodhanaśīlam Indram*, when *jāmi*, put for *jāmim*, will have its usual sense, "kinsman."—they call *Indra* bearing weapons, brother, *bhrātaram bruvate*. *Sāmaveda*, 1308.

६१३८. सम॑स्य म॒न्यवे॒ विशो॒ विश्वा॑ नमन्त कृ॒ष्टय॑:। स॒मु॒द्रा॒येव॒ सिन्ध॑व:॥४॥

4. All people, (all) men bow down before his anger, as rivers (decline) towards the sea.
Sāmaveda, 137.

६१३९. ओज॒स्तद॑स्य तित्विष उ॒भे यत्स॒मव॑र्तयत्। इन्द्र॒श्चर्मे॑व॒ रोद॑सी॥५॥

5. His might is manifest, for *Indra* folds and unfolds both heaven and earth, as (one spreads or rolls up) a skin.
Sāmaveda, 182.

६१४०. वि चि॒द्वृ॒त्रस्य॒ दोध॑तो व॒ज्रेण॑ श॒तप॑र्वणा। शिरो॑ बिभेद वृ॒ष्णिना॑॥६॥

6. He has cloven with the powerful hundred-edged thunderbolt the head of the turbulent *Vṛtra*.
Sāmaveva, 1652.

६१४१. इ॒मा अ॒भि प्र णो॑नुमो वि॒पामग्रे॑षु धी॒तय॑:। अ॒ग्ने: शोचि॑र्न दि॒द्युत॑:॥७॥

7. In front of one worshippers we repeatedly utter our praises, radiant as the flame of fire.

६१४२. गु॒हा स॒तीरुप॒ त्मना॒ प्र यच्छोच॑न्त धी॒तय॑:।

कण्वा॑ ऋ॒तस्य॒ धार॑या॥८॥

8. The praises that are offered in secret shine brightly when approaching (*Indra*) of their own will: the *Kaṇvas* (combine them) with the stream of the *Soma*.

६१४३. प्र त॒मिन्द्र॑ नशीमहि र॒यिं गोम॑न्तम॒श्विन॑म्। प्र ब्रह्म॑ पू॒र्वचि॑त्तये॥९॥

9. May we obtain, *Indra*, that wealth which comprises cattle, horses, and food. Before it be known to others.

Before it be known to others— Rather, "so as to know it, *i.e.*, gain it, before other," *anyebhyaḥ pūrvameva jñānāya*.

६१४४. अहमिद्धि पितुष्परि मेधामृतस्य जग्रभ। अहं सूर्य इवाजनि॥१०॥

10. I have verily acquired the favour of the true protector (*Indra*): I have become (bright) as the sun.
Sāmaveda, 152, 1500.

६१४५. अहं प्रत्नेन मन्मना गिरः शुम्भामि कण्ववत्।

येनेन्द्रः शुष्ममिद्धधे॥११॥

11. I grace my words with ancient praise, like *Kaṇva*; whereby *Indra* assuredly enjoys vigour.
Sāmaveda, 1501; reading *janmanā* for *manmanā*].

६१४६. ये त्वामिन्द्र न तुष्टुवुर्ऋषयो ये च तुष्टुवुः। ममेद्वर्धस्व सुष्टुतः॥१२॥

12. Amid those who do not praise you, *Indra*, amid the *Ṛṣis* who do praise you, by my praise being glorified, do you increase.
Sāmaveda, 1502.

६१४७. यदस्य मन्युरध्वनीद्धि वृत्रं पर्वशो रुजन्। अपः समुद्रमैरयत्॥१३॥

13. When his wrath thundered, dividing *Vṛtra* joint by joint, then he drove the waters to the ocean.

६१४८. नि शुष्णं इन्द्र धर्णसिं वज्रं जघन्थ दस्यवि। वृषा ह्युग्र शृण्विषे॥१४॥

14. You have hurled your wielded thunderbolt upon the impious *Śuṣṇa*; you are renowned, fierce *Indra*, as the showerer (of benefits).

६१४९. न द्याव इन्द्रमोजसा नान्तरिक्षाणि वज्रिणम्।

न विव्यचन्त भूमयः॥१५॥

15 Neither the heavens, nor the realms of the firmament, nor the regions of the earth, equal the thunderer *Indra* in strength.
The Realms . . . . . The Regions—The text has only the actual names, but in the plural —the heavens, the firmaments, the earths, *na dyāvo nāntarikṣāṇi na bhūmayaḥ.* See *Ṛg.* ii,27.8.

६१५०. यस्त इन्द्र महीरपः स्तभूयमान आशयत्।

नि तं पद्यासु शिश्रथः॥१६॥

16. You, *Indra*, have cast into the rushing streams him who lay obstructing your copious waters.

६१५१. य इमे रोदसी मही संमीची समजग्रभीत्। तमोभिरिन्द्र तं गुहः॥१७॥

17. You have enveloped with darkness, *Indra*, him who had seized upon these spacious aggregated (realms of) heaven and earth.

६१५२. य इन्द्र यतयस्त्वा भृगवो ये च तुष्टुवुः। ममेदुग्र श्रुधी हवम्॥१८॥

18. Amidst those pious sages, amidst these *Bhṛgus*, who have glorified you, hear also, fierce *Indra*, my invocation.

Those Pious Sages— Sāyaṇa adds, "the *Aṅgirasas*."

६१५३. इमास्त इन्द्र पृश्नयो घृतं दुहत आशिरम्। एनामृतस्य पिप्युषीः॥१९॥

19. These, your spotted cows, the nourishers of the sacrifice, yields, *Indra*, their butter, and this mixture (of milk and curds).

Sāmaveda, 187.

Mixture of Milk and Curds— Or rather, "milk to mix (with the *Soma*)."

६१५४. या इन्द्र प्रस्वस्त्वासा गर्भमचक्रिरन्। परि धर्मेव सूर्यम्॥२०॥

20. These prolific cattle became pregnant, having taken into their mouths, *Indra*, (the products of your vigour) like the all-sustaining sun.

Having taken into their Mouths—The text is *tvā āsā garbham acakriran*, "you with the mouth the embryo they made." According to the Scholiast, the plants that sprang up after the destruction of *Vṛtra* and the consequent fall of rain, were the vigour (*virya*) of *Indra*, and by feeding upon them the cattle multiply. [Sāyaṇa quotes a legend from the *kāṭhaka*, ch. 36, to the effect that after *Indra* killed *Vṛtra*, his virility (*vīrya*) passed into the waters, plants and trees. *Indrasya vai vṛtram jaghnuṣa indriyam vīryam apakrāmat, tad idam sarvam anupraviśad apa oṣadhir vanaspatīn*, etc.] The application of the simile is not very obvious, *pari dharmeva sūryam*, as the rays of the sun generate the sustaining water above the solar orb, as if it was the germ or embryo of all things, *dharma dhārakam poṣakam udakam raśmayo garbharūpeṇa bibhrati tadvat*; or the comparison may be, *yātha dhā sūryaḥ paritaḥ sarvam jagad dhatte tadvat kṛtsnasya jagato dhārakam Indrasya vīryam,* as the sun supports the whole world, so is the vigour of *Indra*, the sustainer of the universe.

६१५५. त्वामिच्छवसस्पते कण्वा उक्थेन वावृधुः। त्वां सुतास इन्दवः॥२१॥

21. Lord of strength, the *Kaṇvas* verily invigorate you by praise: the effused *Soma* juices (invigorate) you.

६१५६. तवेदिन्द्र प्रणीतिषूत प्रशस्तिरद्रिवः। यज्ञो वितन्तसाय्यः॥२२॥

22. *Indra*, wielder of the thunderbolt, excellent praise (is addressed to you) on account of your good guidance, as is a most extended sacrifice.

६१५७. आ न॑ इन्द्र म॒हीमिषं॒ पुरं॒ न द॑र्षि॒ गोम॑तीम्। उ॒त प्र॒जां सु॑वी॒र्य॑म्॥२३॥

23. Be willing to grant us abundant food with cattle: (to grant us) protection, progeny, and vigour.

६१५८. उ॒त त्यदा॒श्वश्व्यं॒ यदि॑न्द्र॒ नाहु॑षीष्व॒ा। अग्रे॒ विक्षु॒ प्रदी॑दयत्॥२४॥

24. May that herd of swift horses, which formerly shone among the people of *Nahuṣa*, (be granted), *Indra*, to us.

६१५९. अ॒भि व्र॒जं न त॑त्निषे॒ सूर॑ उपा॒कच॑क्षसम्। यदि॑न्द्र मृ॒ळया॑सि नः॥२५॥

25. Sage *Indra*, you spread (the cattle) over the adjacent pastures when you are favourably inclined toward us.

६१६०. यद॒ङ्ग त॑वि॒षीय॑स॒ इन्द्र॒ प्ररा॑जसि क्षि॒तीः। म॒हाँ अ॒पार॒ ओज॑सा॥२६॥

26. When you pottest forth your might, you reignest, *Indra*, over mankind: surpassing are you, and unlimited in strength.

६१६१. तं त्वा॑ ह॒विष्म॑तीर्वि॒श उप॑ ब्रुवत ऊ॒तये॑। उ॒रु॒ज्रय॑समि॒न्दु॑भिः॥२७॥

27. The people offering oblations call upon you, the pervader of space, with libations for protection.

६१६२. उ॒प॒ह्वरे॑ गि॒रीणां॑ स॒ङ्गथे॑ च॒ नदी॑नाम्। धि॒या विप्रो॑ अजायत॥२८॥

28. The wise (*Indra*) has been engendered by holy rites on the skirts of the mountains, at the confluence of rivers.

The Wise Indra—The text has only *Vipra*, the sage. Sāyaṇa supplies *Indra*. Mahīdhara (*Yajurveda*, 26.15) understands *medhāvī Somaḥ*. He also interprets *dhiyā* understanding: the *Soma* is produced by the thought that wise men will perform sacrifice by me. Sāyaṇa's conclusion of the purport of the verse is, that men ought to sacrifice in those places where *Indra* is said to be manifested. See also *Sāmaveda*, 143.

६१६३. अतः॑ समु॒द्रमु॒द्वत॑श्चि॒क्त्वाँ अव॑ पश्यति। यतो॑ वि॒पान॒ एज॑ति॥२९॥

29. From the lofty region in which pervading he abides, *Indra* the intelligent looks down upon the offered libation.

The Libation—*Samudram*, the sea: the common explains it here *samundana-śīlam*, the exuding or affluent, the *Soma*. [Another explanation is, that *Indra*, identified with the sun, looks down from the firmament on the ocean (or world), enlightening it by his rays.]

६१६४. आ॒दित्प्र॒त्नस्य॒ रेत॑सो॒ ज्योति॑ष्पश्यन्ति वास॒रम्।
       प॒रो यदि॒ध्यते॑ दि॒वा॥३०॥

30. Then (men) behold the daily light of the ancient shedder of water, when he shines above the heaven.

The daily light— *Indra* is identified with the sun. *Vāsaram,* as an epithet of *jyotiṣ,* is variously explained as *nivāsakam,* clothing, enveloping; or *nivāsahetubhūtam,* the cause of abiding; or [as an adverbial accusative of time "during the day," *atyantasanyoge dvitīyā,*] *kṛtsnamahar udayaprabhṛty āstamanam yāvat,* the light that lasts throughout the day, from sunrise to sunset: *retasaḥ* is also differently explained as *gantuḥ,* the goer, or *udakavataḥ,* water-having. [*Sāmaveda,* 20.

६१६५. कण्वास इन्द्र ते मतिं विश्वे वर्धन्ति पौंस्यम्।

उतो शविष्ठ वृष्ण्यम्॥३१॥

31. All the *Kaṇvas, Indra,* magnify your wisdom, your manhood, and, most mighty one, your strength.

६१६६. इमां म इन्द्र सुष्टुतिं जुषस्व प्र सु मामव। उत प्र वर्धया मतिम्॥३२।

32. Be propitiated, *Indra,* by this my praise; carefully protect me, and give increase to my understanding.

६१६७. उत ब्रह्मण्या वयं तुभ्यं प्रवृद्ध वज्रिवः। विप्रा अतक्ष्म जीवसे॥३३॥

33. Wielder of the thunderbolt, magnified (by our praises), we your worshippers have offered to you these prayers for our existence.

६१६८. अभि कण्वा अनूषतापो न प्रवता यतीः। इन्द्रं वनन्वती मतिः॥३४॥

34. The *Kaṇvas* glorify *Indra;* like waters rushing down a declivity, praise spontaneously seeks *Indra.*

६१६९. इन्द्रमुक्थानि वावृधुः समुद्रमिव सिन्धवः। अनुत्तमन्युमजरम्॥३५॥

35. Holy praises magnify *Indra,* the imperishable, the implacable, as rivers (swell) the ocean.

The Implacable— Literally, "whose wrath is unsubdued by others," *parair anabhibhūto krodho yasya.*

६१७०. आ नो याहि परावतो हरिभ्यां हर्यताभ्याम्। इममिन्द्र सुतं पिब॥३६॥

36. Come to us from afar with your beloved horses; drink, *Indra,* this libation.

६१७१. त्वामिद्वृत्रहन्तम जनासो वृक्तबर्हिषः। हवन्ते वाजसातये॥३७॥

37. Destroyer of *Vṛtra,* men strewing the clipped sacred grass invoke you for the obtaining of food.

६१७२. अनु त्वा रोदसी उभे चक्रं न वर्त्येतशम्।

अनु सुवानास इन्दवः॥३८॥

38. Both heaven and earth follow you as the wheels (of a car follow) the horse; the streams of the *Soma* poured forth (by the priests) follow (you).

६१७३. मन्दस्वा सु स्वर्णर उतेन्द्र शर्यणावति। मत्स्वा विवस्वतो मती॥३९॥

39. Rejoice, *Indra*, at the heaven-guiding sacrifice as *Śaryaṇāvat;* be exhilarated by the praise of the worshipper.

The Heaven-Guiding— or, "to be offered by all the priests," *svarṇare, sarvair ṛtvigbhir netavye.*

Śaryaṇāvat— According to the Scholiast, *Śaryaṇa* is the country of Kurukṣetra, and *Śaryaṇāvat* a lake in the neighbourhood.

६१७४. वावृधान उप द्यवि वृषा वज्रघरोरवीत्। वृत्रहा सोमपातमः॥४०॥

40. The vast wielder of the thunderbolt, the slayer of *Vṛtra*, the deep quaffer of the *Soma*, the showerer, roars near at hand in the sky.

६१७५. ऋषिर्हि पूर्वजा अस्येक ईशान ओजसा। इन्द्र चोष्कूयसे वसु॥४१॥

41. You are a *Ṛṣi*, the first-born (of the gods), the chief, the ruler (over all) by your strength: you give repeatedly, *Indra*, wealth.

६१७६. अस्माकं त्वा सुताँ उप वीतपृष्ठा अभि प्रयः।

शतं वहन्तु हरयः॥४२॥

42. May your hundred sleek-backed horses bring you to our libations, to our (sacrificial) food.

६१७७. इमां सु पूर्व्यां धियं मधोर्घृतस्य पिप्युषीम्।

कण्वा उक्थेन वावृधुः॥४३॥

43. The *Kaṇvas* augment by praise this ancient rite intended (to obtain) an abundance of sweet water.

६१७८. इन्द्रमिद्विमहीनां मेधे वृणीत मर्त्यः। इन्द्रं सनिष्युरूतये॥४४॥

44. The mortal (adorer) selects at the sacrifice *Indra* from among the mighty (gods): he who is desirous of wealth (worships) *Indra* for protection.

६१७९. अर्वाञ्चं त्वा पुरुष्टुत प्रियमेधस्तुता हरी। सोमपेयाय वक्षतः॥४५॥

45. May your horses, praised by the pious priests, bring you, who are the praised of many, down to drink the *Soma*.

६१८०. शतमहं तिरिन्दिरे सहसं पर्शवा ददे। राधाँसि याद्वानाम्॥४६॥

46. I have accepted from *Tirindira*, the son of *Paraśu*, hundreds and thousands of the treasures of men.

Treasures of Man— *Yādvānām*, from *yadu*, a synonym of *manuṣya*, *yadava eva yādvāḥ*, or it may be rendered *yadukulajānām*, of those born of the race of *Yadu*, who have been despoiled by *Tirindira*. [Or it might mean, "I among men have accepted," etc.]

६१८१. त्रीणि शतान्यर्वतां सहस्रा दश गोनाम्। ददुष्पज्राय साम्नैं॥४७॥

47. (These princes) have given to the chaunter *Pajra* three hundred horses, ten thousand cattle.

To the Chaunter Pajra— *Pajrāya Sāmne*, to *Sāman*, the reciter of praises; or to one the race of *Pajra*, as the *Ṛṣi Kakṣīvat*, the repeater of hymns. [*Cf. supra,* verse 6091 and note.]

६१८२. उदानट् ककुहो दिवमुष्ट्राँश्चतुर्युजो ददत्। श्रवंसा याद्वं जनंम्॥४८॥

48. The exalted (prince) has been raised by fame to heaven, for he has given camels laden with four (loads of gold), and *Yādva* people (as slaves.)

[सूक्त-७]

[ऋषि- पुनर्वत्स काण्व। देवता- मरुद्गण। छन्द- गायत्री।]

६१८३. प्र यद्वस्त्रिष्टुभमिषं मरुतो विप्रो अक्षरत्। वि पर्वतेषु राजथ॥१॥

1. When the pious worshipper offers you, *Maruts*, food at the three diurnal rites, then you have sovereignty over the mountains.

Food at the three Diurnal Rites— *Triṣṭubham iṣam*: the epithet is variously explained—chief at the three daily libations, *triṣu savaneṣu praśasyam*; praised by the three deities, *tribhir devaiḥ stutam*; or accompanied by hymns in the *triṣṭubh* metre, *i.e.*, the *Some* offering at the mid-day libation.

६१८४. यदङ्ग तविषीयवो यामं शुभ्रा अचिध्वम्। नि पर्वता अहासत॥२॥

2. When, glorious and powerful (*Maruts*), you fit out your chariot, the mountains depart (from their places).

Mountains depart from their Places— *Nyāhāsata*, from *hā gatau*, they move out of your way through fear.

६१८५. उदीरयन्त वायुभिर्वाश्रासः पृश्निमातरः। धुक्षन्त पिप्युषीमिषम्॥३॥

3. The loud-sounding sons of *Pṛśni* drive with their breezes (the clouds), they milk forth nutritious sustenance.

With Their Breezes— *Vayubhih,* with the winds or the spotted deer, the horses of the *Maruts.*

६१८६. वर्पन्ति मरुतो मिहं प्र वैपयन्ति पर्वतान्। यद्यामं यान्ति वायुभिः॥४॥

4. The *Maruts* scatter the rain, they shake the mountains, when they mount their chariot, with the winds.

६१८७. नि यद्यामाय वो गिरिर्नि सिन्धवो विधर्मणे। महे शुष्माय येमिरे॥५॥

5. He mountains are curbed, the rivers are restrained at your coming, for the upholding of your great strength.

Rather, "when the mountains are curbed at your coming, (and) the rivers are stayed for the sustaining of your great strength,"—the sense running on from v.4.

For the Upholding of your great Strength— *Vidharmaṇe mahe śuṣmāya niyemire, vidharaṇāya mahate yuṣmadīyāya balāya svayam eva niyamyante.* The mountains and rivers are of their own accord restrained for sustaining your great strength; they abide together in one place through fear of our coming and strength, *yuṣmad-yāmād balācca bhītyā ekatraikasthāne niyatā vartante.*

६१८८. युष्माँ उ नक्तमूतये युष्मान्दिवा हवामहे। युष्मान्प्रयत्यध्वरे॥६॥

6. We invoke you for protection by night, (we invoke) you by day, (we invoke) you when the sacrifice is in progress.

६१८९. उदु त्ये अरुणप्सवश्चित्रा यामेभिरीरते। वाश्रा अधि ष्णुना दिवः॥७॥

7. Truly these purple-hued, wonderful, clamorous *Maruts* proceed with their chariots in the height above the sky.

६१९०. सृजन्ति रश्मिमोजसा पन्थां सूर्याय यातवे। ते भानुभिर्वि तस्थिरे॥८॥

8. They, who by their might open a radiant path for the sun to travel, they pervade (the world) with lustre.

६१९१. इमां मे मरुतो गिरमिमं स्तोममृभुक्षणः। इमं मे वनता हवम्॥९॥

9. Accept, *Maruts,* this may praise, (accept), mighty ones, this my adoration, (accept) this my invocation.

६१९२. त्रीणि सरांसि पृश्नयो दुदुहे वज्रिणे मधु। उत्सं कवन्धमुद्रिणम्॥१०॥

10. The milch kine have filled for the thunderer three lakes of the sweet (beverage) from the dripping waterbearing cloud.

The Milch Kine— *Pṛśnayaḥ,* the cows, the mothers of the *Maruts*—*marunmātṛ-bhūtā gāvaḥ,* or it may be put for the sons of *Pṛśni,* the *Maruts.* [Another explanation is *mādhyamikā vācaḥ,* the hymns at the mid-day libation being recited in a middle tone.

Three Lakes— The libations of milk, etc., mixed with the *Soma* at the three diurnal rites; or the libations of *Soma*; filling the three vessels, the *Droṇakalaśa*, the *Adhavanīya*, and the *Pūtabhṛt*.

The Dripping Water-Bearing Cloud— *Utsam kabandham udriṇam* is explained, *utsravaṇaśīlam*, exuding, dropping; *udakam,* water; *udriṇam udakavantam megham,* having water, a cloud. [It probably means, "(they have milked) the dripping water from the cloud."]

६१९३. मरुतो॒ यद्ध॑ वो दि॒वः सु॑म्ना॒यन्तो॑ हवा॑महे ।

आ तू न॒ उप॑ गन्तन ॥११॥

11. When, *Maruts*, desirous of felicity, we invoke you from heaven, come unto us quickly.

६१९४. यू॒यं हि ष्ठा सु॑दान॒वो रु॒द्रा ऋ॑भुक्षणो॒ दमे॑ । उ॒त प्र॒चेत॑सो म॒दे ॥१२॥

12. Munificent, mighty *Rudras*, you in the sacrificial hall are wise (even) in the exhilaration (of the *Soma*).

Mighty Rudras— Explained in the commentary is the sons of *Rudra, rudraputrāḥ*.

६१९५. आ नो॑ र॒यिं म॑द॒च्युतं॑ पुरु॒क्षुं वि॒श्वधा॑यसम् । इ॒यर्ता॑ मरुतो दि॒वः ॥१३॥

13. Send us, *Maruts*, from heaven exhilarating, many lauded, all-sustaining riches.

६१९६. अ॒धीव॒ यद् गि॒रीणां॑ या॒मं शु॒भ्रा अ॑चि॒ध्वम् ।

सु॒वा॒नैर्म॑न्दध्व॒ इन्दु॑भिः ॥१४॥

14. When, bright (*Maruts*), you harness your car over the mountains, then you exhilarate (yourselves) with the effusing *Soma* juice.

६१९७. ए॒ता॒वत॑श्चिदेषां सु॒म्नं भि॑क्षेत॒ मर्त्यः॑ । अदा॑भ्यस्य॒ मन्म॑भिः ॥१५॥

15. A man should solicit happiness of them with praises of such an unconqueable (company).

A Man Should, etc.— Rather, "a man should solicit by his praises the happiness which belongs to them, to such an unconquerable (company)."

६१९८. ये द्र॒प्साइ॑व॒ रोद॑सी॒ धम॑न्त्यनु॒ वृष्टि॑भिः । उ॒त्सं दुह॑न्तो अ॒क्षित॑म् ॥१६॥

16. They who, like dropping showers, inflate heaven and earth with rain, milking the inexhaustible cloud.

६१९९. उद् उ॑ स्वा॒नेभि॑रीरत॒ उद् र॒थैरुद् उ॑ वा॒युभिः॑ । उत्स्तोमैः॑ पृश्निमातरः ॥१७॥

17. The sons of *Pṛśni* rise up with shouts, with chariots, with winds, with praises.

६२००. येनाव तुर्वशं यदुं येन कण्वं धनस्पृतम्। राये सु तस्य धीमहि॥१८॥

18. We meditate on that (generosity) whereby for (the sake of granting them) riches you have protected *Turvaśa* and *Yadu* and the wealth-desiring *Kaṇva*.

६२०१. इमा उ व: सुदानवो घृतं न पिप्युषीरिष:।
वर्धान्काण्वस्य मन्मभि:॥१९॥

19. Munificent (*Maruts*), may these (sacrificial) viands, nutritious as butter, together with the praises of the descendant of *Kaṇva*, afford you augmentation.

६२०२. क्व नूनं सुदानवो मदथा वृक्तबर्हिष:। ब्रह्मा को व: सपर्यति॥२०॥

20. Munificent (*Maruts*), for whom the sacred grass has been trimmed, where now are you being exhilarated? What pious worshipper (detains you as he) adores you?

६२०३. नहि ष्म यद्ध व: पुरा स्तोमेभिर्वृक्तबर्हिष:।
शर्धाँ ऋतस्य जिन्वथ॥२१॥

21. (*Maruts*), for whom the sacred grass is trimmed, it cannot be (that you submit to be detained), for you have derived strength from the sacrifice, formerly (accompanied) by our praises.

For Whom the Sacred Grass is Trimmed *Vṛkta-barhiṣaḥ*[1] may also mean "those by whom the grass has been trimmed"—the priests; when the sense will be, "It cannot be, for, priests, by your praises preceding (those of others) you have propitiated the energies of the *Maruts*, the objects of the sacrifice."

For You have Derived Strength, etc.— Or, "For by the former praises (of others) you have nourished strength connected with the sacrifice."

६२०४. समु त्ये मंहतीरप: सं क्षोणी समु सूर्यम्। सं वज्रं पर्वशो दधु:॥२२॥

22. They have concentrated the abundant waters, they have held together the heaven and earth, they have sustained the sun, they have divided (*Vṛtra*) joint by joint with the thunderbolt.

They have Divided *Vṛtra*, etc.— Sāyaṇa renders it "they have planted the thunderbolt in (*Vṛtra's*) every limb."

---

१. बर्हिरिति यज्ञनाम।

६२०५. वि वृत्रं पर्वशो ययुर्वि पर्वताँ अराजिनः।
चक्राणा वृष्णि पौंस्यम्।।२३।।

23. Independent of a ruler, they have divided *Vṛtra* joint by joint: they have shattered the mountains, manifesting manly vigour.

६२०६. अनु त्रितस्य युध्यतः शुष्ममावत्रुत क्रतुम्। अन्विन्द्रं वृत्रतूर्ये।।२४।।

24. They have come to the aid of the warring *Trita*, invigorating his strength, and (animating) his acts; they have come to the aid of *Indra*, for the destruction of *Vṛtra*.

६२०७. विद्युद्धस्ता अभिद्यव: शिप्राः शीर्षन्हिरण्ययीः।
शुभ्रा व्यंजत श्रिये।।२५।।

25. The brilliant (*Maruts*), bearing the lightning in their hands, radiant above all, gloriously display their golden helmets on their heads.

६२०८. उशना यत्परावत उक्ष्णो रन्ध्रमयातन। द्यौर्न चक्रदद्भिया।।२६।।

26. Glorified, (*Maruts*), by *Uśanas*, when you approach from afar to the opening of the rainy (firmament), then (the dwellers on earth), like those in heaven, are clamorous through fear.

Glorified by Uśanas— *Uśanā, Uśanasā kāvyena ṛṣiṇā stūyamānāḥ*, or it may be for *uśanasaḥ, i.e.*, desiring worshipper, *stotṛṇ kāmayamānāḥ*.

Are Clamorous Through Fear— The text has only *dyaur na cakradad bhiyā*, like heaven, calls out with fear.

६२०९. आ नौ मखस्य दावनेऽश्वैर्हिरण्यपाणिभिः। देवास उप गन्तन।।२७।।

27. Come, gods, to (shew your) liberality at our sacrifice with your golden-footed steeds.

६२१०. यदेषां पृषती रथे प्रष्टिर्वहति रोहितः। यान्ति शुभ्रा रिणन्नप:।।२८।।

28. When the spotted antelope or the swift tawny deer conveys them in their chariot, then the brilliant (*Maruts*) depart, and the rains have gone.

And The Rains have Gone— Sāyaṇa explains *riṇan* as "they flow in every direction," *sarvatra pravahanti*.

६२११. सुषोमे शर्यणावत्याजीके पस्त्यावति। ययुर्निचक्रया नरः।।२९।।

29. The leaders of rites have proceeded with downward chariot-wheels to the *Ṛjīka* country, where lies the *Śaryaṇāvat*, abounding in dwellings, and where *Soma* is plentiful.

६२१२. कदा गच्छाथ मरुत इत्था विप्रं हर्वमानम्।
मार्डीकेभिर्नाधर्मानम्॥३०॥

30. When, *Maruts*, will you repair with joy-bestowing riches to the sage thus adoring you, and soliciting (you for wealth)?

६२१३. कद्ध नूनं कंधप्रियो यदिन्द्रमर्जहातन। को वं: सखित्व ओहते॥३१॥

31. When was it, *Maruts*, who are gratified by praise, that you really deserted *Indra*? Who is there that enjoys your friendship?

The You Really Deserted Indra— That is, they never deserted him, but alone of the gods stood by him in his conflict with *Vṛtra*—an obvious allegory. *Indra* dispersed the clouds with his allies, the winds. In the *Aitareya Brāhmaṇa* 3.20, or *Adhyāya* 12, *Khaṇḍa* 8, *Indra* desired the gods to follow him, which they did; but when *Vṛtra* breathed upon them, they all ran away except the *Maruts*. They remained, encouraging *Indra*, saying, *prahara bhagavo jahi vīrayasva*, Strike, lord, kill, show yourself a hero; as embodied in *Sūkta* 96 of *Maṇḍala* 8.

६२१४. सहो षु णो वज्रहस्तैः कण्वासो अग्निं मरुद्भिः।
स्तुषे हिरण्यवाशीभिः॥३२॥

32. Do you of our race of *Kaṇva* praise *Agni* together with the *Maruts*, bearing the thunderbolt in their hands, and armed with golden lances.

६२१५. ओ षु वृष्णः प्रयज्यूना नव्यसे सुविताय। ववृत्यां चित्रवाजान्॥३३॥

33. I bring to my presence, for the sake of most excellent prosperity, the showerers (of desires), the adorable (*Maruts*), the possessors of wonderful strength.

६२१६. गिरयश्चिन्नि जिहते पर्शानासो मन्यमानाः। पर्वताश्चिन्नि येमिरे॥३४॥

34. The hills, oppressed and agitated by them, move (from their places); the mountains are restrained.

The Mountains are Restrained— *Girayo nijihate parvatāścin niyemire*: the *nijihate* is explained *nitarām gacchanti marudvegena sthānāt pracyavante*, by the violence of the winds they fall from place; for *niyemire*, we have only *niyamyante*. *Parvatāḥ* may be interpreted *meghāḥ*, the clouds, or large hills *mahāntāḥ śiloccayāḥ* in contrast to *girayaḥ*, which are *kṣudrāḥ śiloccayāḥ* small heaps of rock.

६२१७. आक्ष्णयावानो वहन्त्यन्तरिक्षेण पततः। धातारः स्तुवते वयः॥३५॥

35. (Their horses), quickly traversing (space), bear them travelling through the firmament, giving food to the worshipper.

६२१८. अग्निर्हि जानि पूर्व्यश्छन्दो न सूरो अर्चिषा।
ते भानुभिर्वि तस्थिरे॥३६॥

36. *Agni* was born the first among the gods, like the brilliant sun in splendour: then they (the *Maruts*) stood round in their radiance.

The Scholiast intimates that this verse refers to the ceremony called *Āgnimāruta*, when *Agni* is first worshipped, then the *Maruts*.

Brilliant— *Chandas* is explained as *upacchandanīya*, the adorable.

[सूक्त-८]

[**ऋषि**– सध्वंस काण्व। **देवता**– अश्विनीकुमार। **छन्द**– अनुष्टुप्।]

६२१९. आ नो विश्वाभिरूतिभिरश्विना गच्छतं युवम्।
दस्रा हिरण्यवर्तनी पिबतं सोम्यं मधु॥१॥

1. Come to us, *Aśvins*, with all your protections: *Dasras*, riders in a golden chariot, drink the sweet *Soma* beverage.

६२२०. आ नूनं यातमश्विना रथेन सूर्यत्वचा।
भुजी हिरण्यपेशसा कवी गम्भीरचेतसा॥२॥

2. *Aśvin*, partakers of sacrificial food, decorated with golden ornaments, wise, and endowed with profound intellects, come verily in your chariot, invested with solar radiance.

६२२१. आ यातं नहुषस्पर्यान्तरिक्षात् सुवृक्तिभिः।
पिबाथो अश्विना मधु कण्वानां सवने सुतम्॥३॥

3. Come from (the world of) man, come from the firmament, (attracted) by our pious praises; drink, *Aśvins*, the sweet *Soma* offered at the sacrifice of the *Kaṇvas*.

६२२२. आ नौ यातं दिवस्पर्यान्तरिक्षादधप्रिया।
पुत्रः कण्वस्य वामिह सुषाव सोम्यं मधु॥४॥

4. Come to us from above the heaven, you who love the (world) below, (come) from the firmament; the son of *Kaṇva* has here poured forth for you the sweet *Soma* libation.

You Who love The World Below— *Adhapriyā* is explained as "pleased by the *Soma* in the world below, or please by praise."

६२२३. आ नौ यातमुपश्रुत्यश्विना सोमपीतये।
स्वाहा स्तोमस्य वर्धना प्र कवी धीतिभिर्नरा॥५॥

5. Come, *Aśvins*, to drink the *Soma* at our sacrifice, you who are praised (by him) and honoured) by his pious acts, benefactors of the worshipper, sages and leaders of rites.

The second part of the stanza is rendered intelligible by the Scholiast only by taking great liberty with some of the terms; and, after all, the meaning is questionable, *svāhā stomasya vardhanā pra kavī dhītibhir narā*. *Svāhā* he renders as the voc. dual, *svāhākṛtau svāhākāreṇa iṣṭau*, worshipped with the form *svaha*; or *svāhā* may mean *vā* or *stuti, vācā stutau*. *Stomasya* he renders by *stotuḥ*. Or the whole may be in the vocative, and connected with the first part. [Sāyaṇa prefers to connect *dhītibhiḥ* with a supplied imperative, or with *nara, i.e., karmabhir yaṣṭuḥ pravardhakau bhavatam*, or *buddhibhir ātmīyaiḥ karmabhir vā sarveṣām netārau*.]

६२२४. यच्चिद्धि वां पुर ऋषयो जुहूरेऽवंसे नरा।
आ यांतमश्विना गंतमुपेमां सुष्टुतिं ममं॥ ६॥

6. Leaders of rites, when the *Ṛṣis* formerly invoked you for protection, you came; so now, *Aśvins*, come at my devout praises.

६२२५. दिवश्चिद्रोचनादध्या नों गन्तं स्वर्विदा।
धीभिर्वत्सप्रचेतसा स्तोमेभिर्हवनश्रुता॥ ७॥

7. Familiar with heaven, come to us from the sky, or form above the bright (firmament): favourably inclined to the worshipper, (come), induced by his pious acts; hearers of invocations (come, induced) by our praises.

Familiar with Heaven— *Svar-vidā*, explained as *dyulokasya lambhayitārau*, causing to obtain heaven.

Induced by his Pious Acts.— Sāyaṇa connects *dhībhiḥ* with the *Aśvins*, "come with your minds (favourable to us)."

६२२६. किमन्ये पर्यासतेऽस्मत्स्तोमेभिरश्विना।
पुत्रः कण्वस्य वामृषिर्गीभिर्वत्सो अवीवृधत्॥ ८॥

8. What others than ourselves adore the *Aśvins* with praises? The *Ṛṣi Vatsa*, the son of *Kaṇva*, has magnified you with hymns.

६२२७. आ वां विप्र इहावसेऽह्वत्स्तोमेभिरश्विना।
अरिप्रा वृत्रहन्तमा ता नों भूतं मयोभुवा॥ ९॥

9. The wise adorer invokes you hither with praises, *Aśvins*, for protection; sinless, utter destroyers of enemies, be to us the sources of felicity.

६२२८. आ यद्वां योषणा रथमतिष्ठद्वाजिनीवसू।
विश्वान्यश्विना युवं प्र धीतान्यगच्छतम्॥१०॥

10. Affluent in sacrifices, when the maiden (sūrya) mounted your chariot, then, Aśvins, you obtained all your desires.

६२२९. अतः सहस्रनिर्णिजा रथेना यातमश्विना।
वत्सो वां मधुमद्वचोऽशंसीत्काव्यः कविः॥११॥

11. From wheresoever (you may be) come, Aśvins, with your thousandfold diversified chariot: the sage Vatsa, the son of Kavi, has addressed you with sweet words.

The Son of Kavi— Vatsaḥ kāvyaḥ : kāvyaḥ is explained kaveḥ putraḥ, which may mean the son of the sage, that is, of Kaṇva. See v.8.

६२३०. पुरुमन्द्रा पुरूवसू मनोतरा रयीणाम्।
स्तोमं मे अश्विनाविममभि वह्नी अनूषाताम्॥१२॥

12. Delighters of many, abounding in wealth, bestowers of riches, Aśvins, sustainers of all, approve of this mine adoration.

६२३१. आ नो विश्वान्यश्विना धत्तं राधांस्यह्रया।
कृतं नं ऋत्वियावतो मा नौ रीरधतं निदे॥१३॥

13. Grant us, Aśvins, all riches that may not bring us shame, make us the begetters of progeny in due season, subject us not to reproach.

६२३२. यत्रासत्या परावति यद्वा स्थो अध्यम्बरे।
अतः सहस्रनिर्णिजा रथेना यातमश्विना॥१४॥

14. Whether, Nāsatyās, you be far off, or whether you be nigh, come from thence with your thousandfold diversified chariot.

६२३३. यो वां नासत्यावृषिर्गीर्भिर्वत्सो अवीवृधत्।
तस्मै सहस्रनिर्णिजमिषं धत्तं घृतश्चुतम्॥१५॥

15. Give, Nāsatyās, food of many kinds dripping with butter to him, the Ṛṣi Vatsa, who has magnified you both with hymns.

६२३४. प्रास्मा ऊर्जं घृतश्चुतमश्विना यच्छतं युवम्।
यो वां सुम्नाय तुष्टवद्वसूयाद्दानुनस्पती॥१६॥

16. Give, Aśvins, invigorating food, dripping with butter, to him who praises you, the lords of liberality, to obtain happiness; who desires affluence.

६२३५. आ नौ गन्तं रिशादसेमं स्तोमं पुरुभुजा।

कृतं नः सुश्रियो नरेमा दातमभिष्टये॥१७॥

17. Confounders of the malignant, partakers of many (oblations), come to this our adoration; render us prosperous leaders (of rites); give these (good things of earth) to our desires.

६२३६. आ वां विश्वाभिरूतिभिः प्रियमेधा अहूषत।

राजन्तावध्वराणामश्विना यामहूतिषु॥१८॥

18. The *Priyamedhas* at the sacrifices to the gods invoke you, *Aśvins*, who rule over religious rites, together with your protections.

Who Rule Over Religious Rights— A *Brāhmaṇa* quoted for the *Aśvins* being the ministrant priests, the *Adhvaryus*, of the gods, *aśvinau hi devānām adhvaryu.*[1]

६२३७. आ नौ गन्तं मयोभुवाश्विना शम्भुवा युवम्।

यो वां विपन्यू धीतिभिर्गीर्भिर्वत्सो अवीवृधत्॥१९॥

19. Come to us, *Aśvins*, sources of happiness, sources of health; (come), adorable (*Aśvins*), to that *Vatsa*, who has magnified you with sacrifices and with praises.

६२३८. याभिः कण्वं मेधातिथिं याभिर्वशं दशव्रजम्।

याभिर्गोशर्यमावतं ताभिर्नोऽवतं नरा॥२०॥

20. Leaders (of rites), protect us with those protections with which you have protected *Kaṇva* and *Medhātithi*, *Viśa* and *Daśavraja*; with which you have protected *Gośarya*;

Gośarya— Or *Śayu*, whose barren cow the *Aśvins* enabled to give milk. See *Ṛg.* i. 116. 22

६२३९. याभिर्नरा त्रसदस्युमावतं कृत्व्ये धने।

ताभिः ष्वस्माँ अश्विना प्रावतं वाजसातये॥२१॥

21. (And) with which, leaders (of rites), you protected *Trasadasyu* when wealth was to be acquired: do you with the same graciously protect us, *Aśvins*, for the acquirement of food.

६२४०. प्र वां स्तोमाः सुवृक्तयो गिरो वर्धन्त्वश्विना।

पुरुत्रा वृत्रहन्तमा ता नौ भूतं पुरुस्पृहा॥२२॥

१. तै० ब्रा० ३.२.२.१

22. May (perfect) hymns and holy praises magnify you, *Aśvins*: protectors of many, exterminators of foes, greatly are you desired of us.

६२४१. त्रीणि पदान्यश्विनोरावि: सन्ति गुहा पर:।

कवी ऋतस्य पत्मभिर्वाग्जीवेभ्यस्परि।।२३।।

23. The three wheels (of the chariot) of the *Aśvins*, which were invisible, have become manifest: do you two, who are cognizant of the past, (come) by the paths of truth to the presence of living beings.

By The Paths of Truth— *Patmabhir* is explained by *padair,* which meant wheels in the former line; *ṛtasya* is variously explained as truth, water, or the sacrifice, which the paths or wheels are said to cause, *satyasya udakasaya vajñasya vā hetubhūtaiḥ padaiḥ.*

[सूक्त-९]

[**ऋषि**- शशकर्ण काण्व। **देवता**- अश्विनीकुमार। **छन्द**- अनुष्टुप्, १, ४, ६, १४-१५ बृहती, २, ३, ३०, २१ गायत्री, ४ ककुप्, १० त्रिष्टुप्, ११ विराट्, १ जगती।]

६२४२. आ नूनमश्विना युवं वत्सस्य गन्तमवसे।

प्रास्मै यच्छतमवृकं पृथु च्छर्दिर्युयुतं या अरातय:।।१।।

1. Come, *Aśvins*, without fail, for the protection of the worshipper; confer upon him a secure and spacious dwelling; drive away those who make no offerings.

For the Protection of the Worshipper— *Vatsasya avase,* as if it were the name of the *Ṛṣi.* See note on *Sadhvansa* in the preceding *Sūkta.* [Or perhaps Sāyaṇa may mean that *vatsa* is here used for *stotā Cf.* Mahīdhara's note, quoted in s. vi.]

६२४३. यदन्तरिक्षे यद्दिवि यत्पञ्च मानुषाँ अनु। नृम्णं तद्धत्तमश्विना।।२।।

2. Whatever wealth may be in the firmament, in heaven, or among the five (classes) of men, bestow, *Aśvins*, (upon us).

६२४४. ये वां दंसांस्यश्विना विप्रास: परिमामृशु:।

एवेत्काण्वस्य बोधतम्।।३।।

3. Recognize, *Aśvins*, (the devotions) of the son of *Kaṇva*, as (you have recognized) those former sages who have repeatedly addressed pious works to you.

६२४५. अयं वां घर्मो अश्विना स्तोमेन परि षिच्यते।

अयं सोमो मधुमान्वाजिनीवसू येनं वृत्रं चिकेतथः ॥४॥

4. This oblation is poured out, *Aśvin*, to you with praise; this sweet-savoured *Soma* is offered to you, who are affluent with food, (animated) by which you meditate (the destruction of) the foe.

This Oblation— *Gharma* has for one explanation *pravargyam*, a ceremony so called. It is also the name of a sacrificial vessel, as well as of the oblation it contains, *gharmasya haviṣa ādhārabhūto mahāvīro gharmaḥ.* See note on V.2.16.15.

६२४६. यदप्सु यद्वनस्पतौ यदोषधीषु पुरुदंससा कृतम्।

तेनं माविष्टमश्विना ॥५॥

5. Doers of many deeds, *Aśvins*, preserve me with that (healing virtue) deposited (by you) in the waters, in the trees, in the herbs.

Healing Virtue Deposited— The text has only *kritam*, made of done, the Scholiast supplies *bheṣajam*, a medicament. [Sāyaṇa, however, takes *kṛtam* as a Vedic form for the second person dual of the third part, *akārṣṭam*.]

६२४७. यत्रासत्या भुरण्यथो यद्वा देव भिषज्यथः।

अयं वां वत्सो मतिभिर्न विन्धते हविष्मन्तं हि गच्छथः ॥६॥

6. Although, *Nāsatyās*, you cherish (all beings), though, divinities, you heal (all disease), yet this your adorer does not obtain you by praises (only), you repair to him who offers you oblations.

Yet This your Adorer, etc.— The Scholiast explains this to mean that praise, to be efficacious, must be accompanied by offerings.

६२४८. आ नूनमश्विनोर्ऋषिः स्तोमं चिकेत वामया।

आ सोमं मधुमत्तमं घर्मं सिञ्चादथर्वणि ॥७॥

7. When verily you arrive, *Aśvins*, the *Ṛṣi* understands with excellent (comprehension) the praise (to be addressed to you); he will sprinkle the sweet-flavoured *Soma* and the *gharma* (oblation) on *Atharvan* fire.

And the Gharma on the Atharvan Fire— *Gharmam siñcād atharvaṇi*, in the innoxious fire *ahinsake agnau*; or in the fire kindled by the *Ṛṣi* Atharvan, as by a previous text, *tvām atharvo niramanthata. Ṛg.* vi.16.13.

६२४९. आ नूनं रघुवर्तनिं रथं तिष्ठाथो अश्विना।
आ वां स्तोमा इमे मम नभो न चुच्यवीरत॥८॥

8. Abscond at once, *Aśvins*, your light-moving chariot; may these my praises bring you down radiant as the sun.

६२५०. यद्द्य वां नासत्योक्थैराचुच्युवीमहिं।
यद्वा वाणीभिरश्विनेवेत्काण्वस्य बोधतम्॥९॥

9. Acknowledge, *Nāsatyās*, that we may bring you down to-day by the prayers and the praises of the son of *Kaṇva*.

Sāyaṇa explains ti, "Regard (the prayers) of me the son of *kāṇva*, that we may bring you down by these prayers and praises."

६२५१. यद्वां कक्षीवाँ उत यद्व्यश्व ऋषिर्यद्वां दीर्घतमा जुहाव।
पृथी यद्वां वैन्यः सादनेष्वेवेदतो अश्विना चेतयेथाम्॥१०॥

10. Consider (my praises) in the same manner as (you have considered) when *Kakṣīvat* praised you, when the *Ṛṣi Vyaśva*, when *Dīrghatamas*, or *Pṛthin*, the son of *Vena*, glorified you in the chambers of sacrifice.

६२५२. यातं छर्दिष्पा उत नः परस्पा भूतं जगत्पा उत नस्तनूपा।
वर्तिस्तोकाय तनयाय यातम्॥११॥

11. Come (to us as) guardians of our dwelling, become our defenders, be protectors of our dependants, cherishers of our persons: come to the dwelling for (the good of) our sons and grandsons.

Protectors of Our Dependants— *Jagatpā jaṅgamasya prāṇijātasya asmadīyasya pālakau*, protectors of our moveable living beings—either our dependants, or, as M. Langlois renders it, our animals.

For the Good our Sons, Etc.— Or, "come to the dwellings of our sons and grandsons."

६२५३. यदिन्द्रेण सरथं याथो अश्विना यद्वा वायुना भवथः समोकसा।
यदादित्येभिर्ऋभुभिः सजोषसा यद्वा विष्णोर्विक्रमणेषु तिष्ठथः॥१२॥

12. Although, *Aśvins*, you should be riding in the same chariot with *Indra*, although you should be domiciled with *Vāyu*, although you should be enjoying gratification along with the *Ādityas* and *Ṛbhus*, although you be proceeding on the tracks of *Viṣṇu*, (nevertheless come hither).

६२५४. यद्द्याश्विनावहं हुवेय वार्जसातये।
यत्पृत्सु तुर्वणे सहस्तच्छ्रेष्ठमश्विनोरवः ॥१३॥

13. Inasmuch as I invoke you, *Aśvins*, to-day for success in war (therefore grant it), for the triumphant protection of the *Aśvins* is the most excellent for the destruction (of enemies) in battle.

६२५५. आ नूनं यातमश्विनेमा हव्यानि वां हिता।
इमे सोमासो अधि तुर्वशे यदाविमे कण्वेषु वामर्थ ॥१४॥

14. Come, *Aśvins*, these libations are prepared for you: those libation which were presented you by *Turvaśa* and *Yadu*, they are now offered to you by the *Kaṇvas*.

६२५६. यन्नासत्या पराके अर्वाके अस्ति भेषजम्।
तेन नूनं विमदाय प्रचेतसा छर्दिर्वत्साय यच्छतम् ॥१५॥

15. The healing drug, *Nāsatyās*, that is afar off or nigh, wherewith (you repaired) to (his) dwelling for the sake of *Vimada*, do you who are of surpassing wisdom now grant to *Vatsa*.

Sāyaṇa explains it, "together with that (drug) do you, who are of surpassing wisdom, now grant a dwelling to *Vatsa*, as (you did) to *Vimada*."

६२५७. अभुत्स्यु प्र देव्या साकं वाचाहमश्विनोः।
व्यावर्देव्या मतिं वि रातिं मर्त्येभ्यः ॥१६॥

16. I awake with the pious praise of the *Aśvins*; scatter, goddess, (the darkness) at my enlogy: bestow wealth upon (us) mortals.

६२५८. प्र बोधयोषो अश्विना प्र देवि सूनृते महि।
प्र यज्ञहोतरानुषक्प्र मदाय श्रवो बृहत् ॥१७॥

17. *Uṣas*, truth-speaking mighty goddess, awake the *Aśvins*: invoker of the adorable (deities, arouse them) successively; the copious sacrificial food (is prepared) for their exhilaration.

६२५९. यदुषो यासि भानुना सं सूर्येण रोचसे।
आ हायमश्विनो रथो वर्तिर्याति नृपाय्यम् ॥१८॥

18. When, *Uṣas*, you move with your radiance, you shine equally with the sun; and this chariot of the *Aśvins* proceeds to the hall of sacrifice frequented by the leaders (of the rite).

६२६०. यदापीतासो अंशवो गावो न दुह ऊधभिः।

यद्वा वाणीरनूषत प्र देवयन्तो अश्विना ॥१९॥

19. When the yellow *Soma* plants milk forth (their juice) as cows from their udders, when the devout (priests) repeat the words of praise, then, O *Aśvins*, preserve us.

६२६१. प्र द्युम्नाय प्र शवसे प्र नृषाह्याय शर्मणे। प्र दक्षाय प्रचेतसा ॥२०॥

20. Endowed with great wisdom, preserve us for fame, for strength, for victory, for happiness, for prosperity.

For Victory— Sāyaṇa takes *nrishahyaya* as an epithet of *śarmaṇe*, "for happiness to be borne by men," *nṛbhiḥ soḍhavyāya sukhāya*.

६२६२. यन्नूनं धीभिरश्विना पितुर्योना निषीदथः। यद्वा सुम्नेभिरुकथ्या ॥२१॥

21. Although, *Aśvins*, you be seated in the region of the paternal (heaven engaged in) holy rites, or, glorified by us, (abide there) with pleasures, (yet come hither).

In the Region of the Paternal— In the original, *pituḥ,* which is explained as *dyulokasya*, or *yajamānasya*. In the latter sense we must render the clause. "If you abode with your praises in the sacrificial hall of the worshipper, or with the pleasure-conferring (oblations), then come hither."

[सूक्त-१०]

[**ऋषि–** प्रगाथ काण्व। **देवता–** अश्विनीकुमार। **छन्द–** १ बृहती, २ मध्ये
ज्योति (त्रिष्टुप्), ३ अनुष्टुप्, ४ आस्तार पंक्ति, ५-६ प्रगाथ (विषमा बृहती-
समा सतो बृहती)।]

६२६३. यत्स्थो दीर्घप्रसद्मनि यद्वादो रोचने दिवः।

यद्वा समुद्रे अध्याकृते गृहेऽत आ यातमश्विना ॥१॥

1. Whether, *Aśvins*, you are at present where the spacious halls of sacrifice (abound), whether you are in younder bright sphere of heaven, or whether you are in a dwelling constructed above the firmament, come hither.

६२६४. यद्वा यज्ञं मनवे संमिमिक्षथुरेवेत्काण्वस्य बोधतम्।

बृहस्पतिं विश्वान्देवाँ अहं हुव इन्द्राविष्णू अश्विनावाशुहेषसा ॥२॥

2. In like manner, as you have prepared, *Aśvins*, the sacrifice for *Manu*, consent (to prepare it) for the son of *Kaṇva*; for I invoke

Bṛhaspati, the universal gods, *Indra* and *Viṣṇu*, and the *Aśvins*, with rapid steeds.

६२६५. त्या न्व१श्विना हुवे सुद॑ंसंसा गृभे कृता।
    ययोर॑स्ति प्र णः॒ सख्यं॑ दे॒वेष्व॑ध्याप्य॑म्॥३॥

3. I invoke those *Aśvins*, who are famed for great deeds, induced (to come hither) for acceptance (of our oblations), of whom among the gods the friendship is especially to be obtained.

६२६६. ययोरधि॑ प्र य॒ज्ञा अं॒सूरे॒ सन्ति॑ सू॒र्यः॑।
    ता य॒ज्ञस्याध्व॑रस्य प्रचे॒तसा॑ स्व॒धाभि॑र्या पि॒बत॑ः सो॒म्यं मधु॑॥४॥

4. Upon whom (all) sacrifices are dependent, of whom there are worshippers in a place where is no worship, those two familiar with undecaying sacrifices (I invoke) with praises, that you may drink the sweet juice of the *Soma*.

Upon whom all Sacrifices are Dependent— *Yayor adhi pra yajñāḥ, aśvinor upari sarve yāgāḥ prabhavanti,* alluding, the commentator says, to a legend in which it is said that the *Aśvins* replaced the head of the decapitated *yajña*.[1]

There are worshippers in a place where there is no Worship— *Asūre santi sūrayaḥ, stotṛ-rahite deśe yayoḥ stotāraḥ santi* is the explanation of the Scholiast.

६२६७. यद्या॒श्विना॒वप॑गा॒यत्प्रा॒क्स्थो वा॒जिनीवसू।
    यद् दु॒ह्व्यन्व॑वि तु॒र्वशे॒ यदौ॑ हुवे वा॒मथ॑ मा ग॑तम्॥५॥

5. Whether, *Aśvins*, you abide to-day in the west; whether, opulent in food, you abide in the east; whether you sojourn with *Druhyu, Anu, Turvaśu,* or *Yadu,* I invoke you; therefore come to me.

६२६८. यद॒न्तरि॑क्षे प॒तथ॑ः पुरुभुजा॒ यद्वे॒मे रोद॑सी॒ अनु॑।
    यद्वा॒ स्व॒धाभि॑रधि॒तिष्ठ॑थो॒ रथ॒मत॒ आ या॑तमश्विना॥६॥

6. Protectors of many, whether you traverse the firmament, or pass along earth and heaven; whether you ascend your chariot with (all) your splendours; come from thence, *Aśvins*, hither.

---

१. *Taitt. Saṁhitā*, vi. 4.9.5.

[सूक्त-११]

[**ऋषि–** वत्स काण्व। **देवता–** अग्नि। **छन्द–** गायत्री, १ (प्रतिष्ठा) गायत्री, २ वर्धमाना, १० त्रिष्टुप्।]

६२६९. त्वमग्ने व्रतपा असि देव आ मर्त्येष्वा। त्वं यज्ञेष्वीड्यः॥१॥

1. *Agni*, who are a god among mortals, (and among gods), you are the guardian of religious obligations: you are to be hymned at sacrifices.

Among Mortals and Among Gods— The text has only mortals, and the Scholiast asserts that among gods in thereby implied. [Sāyaṇa rather says, "*Agni,* you, the divine, are among mortals (and among gods) the guardian of religious rites."]

६२७०. त्वमसि प्रशस्यो विदथेषु सहन्त्य। अग्ने रथीरध्वराणाम्॥२॥

2. Victor (over enemies), you are to be hymned at solemn rites: you, *Agni*, are the charioteer of sacrifices.

६२७१. स त्वमस्मदप द्विषो युयोधि जातवेदः। अदेवीरग्ने अरातीः॥३॥

3. Do you, *Jātavedas*, drive away from us those who hate us; (drive away), *Agni*, the impious hostile hosts.

६२७२. अन्ति चित्सन्तमह यज्ञं मर्तस्य रिपोः। नोप वेषि जातवेदः॥४॥

4. You desire not, *Jātavedas*, the sacrifice of the man who is our adversary, although placed before you.

६२७३. मर्ता अमर्त्यस्य ते भूरि नाम मनामहे। विप्रासो जातवेदसः॥५॥

5. Prudent mortals, we offer abundant homage to you, who are immortal and all-knowing.

६२७४. विप्रं विप्रासोऽवसे देवं मर्तास ऊतये। अग्निं गीर्भिर्हवामहे॥६॥

6. Prudent mortals, we invoke the sage deity *Agni* with hymns to propitiate him for our protection.

६२७५. आ ते वत्सो मनो यमत्परमाच्चित्सधस्थात्।

अग्ने त्वांकामया गिरा॥७॥

7. *Vatsa*, by the praise that seeks to propitiate you. *Agni*, would draw your thought from the supreme assembly (of the gods).

Atsa— Mahīdhara interprets *Vatsa* by *yajamāna*, the sacrificer dear to *Agni*, as a calf, or child; *vatsa-samaḥ priyaḥ, Yajurveda*, 12.115.

Would Draw their Thought— *Mano yamat, mana āyamayati*, or, as Mahīdhara more explicitly interprets it, *mana ahṛtya gṛhṇāti*, *manonigraham karoti.* For *tvāmkāmayā girā,* Benfey's text, *Sāmaveda,* 8; 1166 reads *tvām kāmaye girā,* I desire you with my hymn.

६२७६. पुरुत्रा हि सदृङ्ङसि विशो विश्वा अनु प्रभुः।

समत्सु त्वा हवामहे॥८॥

8. You look upon many places, you are lord over all people: we call upon you in battles.

You are Lord over all People— This and the next line are found in *Sāmaveda,* 1167-68. In the first stanza the printed *Sāman* reads *diśaḥ* for *viśaḥ*—countries for people.

६२७७. समत्स्वग्निमर्वसे वाजयन्तौ हवामहे। वाजेषु चित्ररांधसम्॥९॥

9. Desiring strength, we call upon *Agni* for protection in battles; upon him who is the granter of wonderful riches (won) in conflicts.

Wonderful Riches won in Conflicts— Benfey renders it "den schatzereichen in dem Kampf."

६२७८. प्रत्नो हि कमीड्यो अध्वरेषु सनाच्च होता नव्यश्च सत्सि।

स्वां चांग्ने तन्वं पिप्रयस्वास्मभ्यं च सौभंगमा यजस्व॥१०॥

10. You, the ancient, are to be hymned at sacrifices: from eternity the invoker of the gods, you sit (at the solemnity) entitled to laudation: cherish, *Agni,* your own person, and grant us prosperity.

[सूक्त-१२]

[ऋषि- पर्वत काण्व। देवता- इन्द्र। छन्द- उष्णिक्।]

६२७९. य इन्द्र सोमपातंमो मदंः शविष्ठ चेततति।

येना हंसि न्यश्त्रिणं तमीमहे॥१॥

1. We solicit, most powerful *Indra,* who are the deep quaffer of the *Soma,* that exhilaration which contemplates (heroic deeds), whereby you slay the devourer (of men).

We Solicit— *tam imahe:* the verb is the burthen of this and the two next verses, and so throughout the *Sūkta* each *tricha* terminates with the same word. [Or it may mean, "We solicit you as possessing that exhilaration," *tādṛṅ-madopetam tvām yācāmahe.*]

That Exhilaration— *Somapātamaḥ madaḥ:* the first by its collocation, should be an epithet, though rather an incompatible one, of the second; but the Scholiast refers to *tvam,* you, understood. *Sāmaveda,* 3૬૧.

६२८०. येना दशग्वमध्रिगुं वेपयन्तं स्वर्णरम्। येना समुद्रमाविथा तमीमहे॥२॥

2. We solicit that (exhilaration) whereby you have defended *Adhrigu,* the accomplisher of the ten (months' rite), and the trembling leader of heaven, (the sun), and the ocean.

Adhrigu— See Vol. I, *mantra* 1235.

The Trembling Leader of Heaven— Sāyaṇa explains it "darkness-dispelling, all-leading," *tamāṁsi varjayantam sarvasya netāram sūryam.*

६२८१. येन सिन्धुं महीरपो रथाँ इव प्रचोदयः।

पन्थामृतस्य यातवे तमीमहे॥३॥

3. We solicit that (exhilaration) whereby you urge on the mighty waters to the sea, in like manner as (charioteers drive) their cars (to the goal), and (whereby) to travel the paths of sacrifice.

६२८२. इमं स्तोममभिष्टये घृतं न पूतमद्रिवः।

येना नु सद्य ओजसा ववक्षिथ॥४॥

4. Accepts, thunderer, this praise (offered) for the attainment of our desires, like consecrated butter; (induced) by which, you, promptly bear us by your might (to our objects).

६२८३. इमं जुषस्व गिर्वणः समुद्रइव पिन्वते।

इन्द्र विश्वाभिरूतिभिर्ववक्षिथ॥५॥

5. Be pleased, you who are gratified by praise, with this our eulogy swelling like the oceans; (induced by which), *Indra*, you bear us with all your protections (to our objects).

६२८४. यो नौ देवः परावतः सखित्वनाय मामहे।

दिवो न वृष्टिं प्रथयन्ववक्षिथ॥६॥

6. (I glorify *Indra*) the deity, who, coming from afar, has given us, through friendship, (riches); heaping (them upon us) like rain from heaven, you have borne us (to our objects).

६२८५. ववक्षुरस्य केतवं उत वज्रो गभस्त्योः।

यत्सूर्यो न रोदसी अवर्धयत्॥७॥

7. The banners of *Indra*, the thunderbolt (he bears) in his hands, have brought (us benefits), when, like the sun, he has expanded heaven and earth.

He has Expanded Heaven and the Earth— When he has refreshed them both with rain, according to the comment.

६२८६. यदि प्रवृद्ध सत्पते सहस्रं महिषाँ अघः।
आदित्त इन्द्रियं महि प्र वावृधे॥८॥

8. Great *Indra*, protector of the good, when you have slain thousands of mighty (foes), then your vast and special energy has been augmented.

६२८७. इन्द्रः सूर्यस्य रश्मिभिर्न्यर्शसानमोषति।
अग्निर्वनेव सासहिः प्र वावृधे॥९॥

9. *Indra*, with the rays of the sun, utterly consumes his adversary: like fire (burning) the forests, he spreads victorious.

६२८८. इयं तं ऋत्वियावती धीतिरेति नवीयसी।
सपर्यन्ती पुरुप्रिया मिमीत इत्॥१०॥

10. This new praise, suited to the season, approaches, (*Indra*), to you; offering adoration and greatly delighting (you), it verily proclaims the measure (of your merits).

Suited to the Season— Or, "connected with sacrifice," *ṛtviyāvatī*.

It Verily Proclaims the Measure— *Mimīta it,* is the burthen of this and the two following verses. It is literally, "verily measures"—it is not said what. Sāyaṇa explains it, *Indra-gatān guṇān paricchinatti*, It, the praise, discriminates the good properties attached to *Indra; māhātmyam prakhyāpayati*, it makes known his greatness.

६२८९. गर्भो यज्ञस्य देवयुः क्रतुं पुनीत आनुषक्।
स्तोमैरिन्द्रस्य वावृधे मिमीत इत्॥११॥

11. The devout praiser of the adorable (*Indra*) purifies in due succession the offering (of the *Soma*); with sacred hymns he magnifies (the might) of *Indra*; he verily proclaims the measure (of his merits).

६२९०. सनिर्मित्रस्य पप्रथ इन्द्रः सोमस्य पीतये।
प्राची वाशीव सुन्वते मिमीत इत्॥१२॥

12. *Indra*, the benefactor of his friend (the worshipper), has enlarged himself to drink the *Soma*, in like manner as the pious praise dilates and proclaims the measure (of his merits).

Proclaims the Measure of his Merits— Literally, like the dilating praise of the worshipper; it proclaims, etc. *Prācī* is explained *prakarṣeṇa stutyam guṇagaṇam prāpnuvatī*.

६२९१. यं विप्रा उक्थवाहसोऽभिप्रमन्दुरायवः।

घृतं न पिप्य आसन्यृतस्य यत्॥१३॥

13. I pour the oblation of the sacrifice, like clarified butter, into the mouth (of that *Indra*), whom wise men, addressing with prayers, delight.

६२९२. उत स्वराजे अदिति: स्तोममिन्द्राय जीजनत्।

पुरुप्रशस्तमूतयं ऋतस्य यत्॥१४॥

14. The excellent praise which *Aditi* brought forth for the imperial *Indra*, for our protection, is that which was (the product) of the sacrifice.

Which was the Product of the Sacrifice— Or rather, "belongs to the sacrifice," *yajñasya sambandhi bhavati.*

६२९३. अभि वह्नय ऊतयेऽनूषत प्रशंस्तये।

न देव विव्रता हरी ऋतस्य यत्॥१५॥

15. The bearers of the oblation glorify (*Indra*) for his excellent protection: now, divinity, let your many actioned horses (bear you to the offering) of the sacrifice.

For his Excellent Protection— Or, "for the sake of his protection and praise."

६२९४. यत्सोममिन्द्र विष्णवि यद्वा घ त्रित आप्त्ये।

यद्वा मरुत्सु मन्दसे समिन्दुभि:॥१६॥

16. Inasmuch as you are exhilarated by the *Soma* shared with *Viṣṇu*, or when (offered) by Trita, the son of the waters, or along with the *Maruts*, so now (be gratified) by (our) libation.

Sāmaveda, 384.

६२९५. यद्वा शक्र परावति समुद्रे अधि मन्दसे।

अस्माकमित्सुते रणा समिन्दुभि:॥१७॥

17. Inasmuch, *Śakra*, as you are exhilarated (by the *Soma*) on the far-distant ocean, so be you gratified now, when the *Soma* is effused by our libations.

On the Far-Distant Ocean— Sāyaṇa takes *samudra* as meaning the *Soma*, i.e., "If you are exhilarated by some distant (offering of) *Soma*."

६२९६. यद्वासि सुन्वतो वृधो यजमानस्य सत्पते।

उक्थे वा यस्य रण्यसि समिन्दुभि:॥१८

18. Inasmuch, protector of the virtuous, as you are the benefactor of the worshipper offering you libations, or by whose prayers you are propitiated, so now (be gratified) by our libations.

६२९७. देवंदेवं वोऽव॑स॒ इन्द्रमि॑न्द्रं॒ गृणीष॒णि॑ ।

अधा॑ य॒ज्ञाय॑ तु॒र्वणे॒ व्या॑नशुः ॥१९॥

19. I glorify the divine *Indra* wherever worshipped for your protection: (my praises) have reached him for the prompt (fulfilment) of the (objects of the) sacrifice.

Divine Indra Wherever Worshipped— *Devam devam Indram Indram.* This, it is said, implies *Indra* as being present at the same time at different ceremonies, or in various forms, as in a former passage, *Ṛg.* vi.47.18. [The verse is addressed to the priests and the *yajamāna*.]

६२९८. य॒ज्ञेभि॒र्यज्ञ॑वाह॒सं॒ सोमे॑भिः॒ सोम॑पा॒तम॑म् ।

होत्रा॑भिरि॒न्द्रं॒ वावृ॑धु॒र्व्या॑नशुः ॥२०॥

20. (His worshippers) have magnified with many sacrifices him to whom the sacrifice is offered, and with many libations the eager quaffer of the *Soma*: (they have magnified) *Indra* with hymns, (their praises) have attained him.

६२९९. म॒हीर॑स्य प्र॒णीत॑यः॒ पू॒र्वीरु॒त प्र॒शस्त॑यः ।

विश्वा॑ व॒सूनि॑ दा॒शुषे॒ व्या॑नशुः ॥२१॥

21. Infinite are his bounties, many are his glories: ample treasures have reached the donor (of oblations).

६३००. इन्द्रं॒ वृ॒त्राय॒ हन्त॑वे दे॒वासो॑ दधिरे पु॒रः ।

इन्द्रं॒ वा॒णीर॑नूषत॒ समो॑जसे ॥२२॥

22. The gods have placed *Indra* (foremost) for the destruction of *Vṛtra*; their praise has been addressed to him to enhance his vigour.

६३०१. म॒हान्तं॑ महि॒ना व॒यं स्तोमे॑भि॒र्हव॑नश्रु॒तम् ।

अ॒र्कैर॒भि प्र णो॑नुमः॒ समो॑जसे ॥२३॥

23. We repeatedly glorify with praises and adorations him who is great with greatness, who hears our invocations, (to enhance) his vigour.

६३०२. न यं वि॒विक्तो॑ रोद॒सी नान्तरि॑क्षाणि व॒ज्रिण॑म् ।

अ॒मादिद॑स्य तित्विषे॒ समो॑जसः ॥२४॥

24. The thunderer, from whom neither the heaven and earth nor the firmament are separated: from the strength of whom, the mighty one, (the world) derives lustre.

६३०३. यदिन्द्र पृतनाज्ये देवास्त्वा दधिरे पुरः।
आदित्ते हर्यता हरी ववक्षतुः॥२५॥

25. When, *Indra*, the gods placed you foremost in the battle, then your beloved horses bore you.

६३०४. यदा वृत्रं नदीवृतं शर्वसा वज्रिन्नवधीः।
आदित्ते हर्यता हरी ववक्षतुः॥२६॥

26. When, thunderer, by your strength you did slay *Vṛtra*, the obstructer of the waters, then your beloved horses bore you.

६३०५. यदा ते विष्णुरोजसा त्रीणि पदा विचक्रमे।
आदित्ते हर्यता हरी ववक्षतुः॥२७॥

27. When your (younger brother) *Viṣṇu* by (his) strength stepped his three paces, then verily your beloved horses bore you.

Viṣṇu by His Strength— *Yadā te Viṣṇur ojasā* might be rendered, "when *Viṣṇu* by your strength"; but the Scholiast renders *te tavānujaḥ.*

Verily your Beloved Horses Bore you— The only reason, apparently, for this phrase—*Ād it te haryatā (kāntau) harī vavakṣatuḥ*—is its having served as the burthen of the two preceding stanzas.

६३०६. यदा ते हर्यता हरी वावृधाते दिवेदिवे।
आदित्ते विश्वा भुर्वनानि येमिरे॥२८॥

28. When your beloved horses had augmented day by day, then all existent beings were subject unto you.

६३०७. यदा ते मारुतीर्विशस्तुभ्यमिन्द्र नियेमिरे।
आदित्ते विश्वा भुर्वनानि येमिरे॥२९॥

29. When, *Indra*, your people, the *Maruts*, were regulated by you, then all existent beings were subject unto you.

Regulated by you— Or, according to Sāyaṇa, subdued the world for you, *tvadartham niyacchanti bhūtajātāni.*

६३०८. यदा सूर्यममुं दिवि शुक्रं ज्योतिरधारयः।
आदित्ते विश्वा भुर्वनानि येमिरे॥३०॥

30. When you had placed younder pure light, the sun, in the sky, then all existing beings were subject unto you.

६३०९. इमां तं इन्द्र सुष्टुतिं विप्र इयर्ति धीतिभिः।
जामिं पदेव पिप्रतीं प्राध्वरे॥३१॥

31. The wise (worshipper), *Indra*, offers you this gratifying sincere praise along with plous rites at the sacrifice, as (a man places) a kinsman in (a prominent) position.

६३१०. यदस्य धार्मनि प्रिये समीचीनासो अस्वरन्।
नाभा यज्ञस्य दोहना प्राध्वरे॥३२॥

32. When the congregated (worshippers) praise him aloud in a place that pleases (him) on the navel (of the earth), in the spot where the libation is effused at the sacrifice, (then).

Then— *Tadānīm dhanam pradehi,* connecting the verse with what follows—*uttaratra sambandha.* The second half of the stanza is very elliptical, *nābhā[1] yajñasya dohanā prādhvare;* the ravel is, as usual, the altar, *yajña* is said to mean here the *Soma,* and *dohana* for *dohane, abhiṣavasthāne.* This is probably an ancient hymn, both by its repetitions and combination of simplicity and obscurity.

६३११. सुवीर्यं स्वश्व्यं सुगव्यमिन्द्र दद्धि नः।
होतेव पूर्वचित्तये प्राध्वरे॥३३॥

33. Bestow upon us, *Indra*, (wealth), comprising worthy male offspring, excellent horses, and good cattle: like the ministrant priest (I worship you) at the sacrifice, (to secure) your prior consideration.

ANUVĀKA III

[सूक्त-१३]

[ऋषि– नारद काण्व। देवता– इन्द्र। छन्द– उष्णिक्।]

६३१२. इन्द्रः सुतेषु सोमेषु क्रतुं पुनीत उक्थ्यम्।
विदे वृधस्य दक्षसो महान्हि षः॥१॥

1. *Indra*, when the *Soma* juices are effused, sanctifies the offerer and the praiser for the attainment of increase giving strength, for he is mighty.

Sanctifies the Offerer and the Praiser— *Kratum punīta ukthyam,* which Sāyaṇa explains *karmaṇām kartāram stōtāram ca;* but he admits,

१. पृथिव्या नाभिस्थानीये।

as an alternative, the sacrifice called *ukthya, ukthyākhyam yāgam.*
Sāmaveda, 381, puts *Indra* in the vocative—*Indra puniṣe*, [So, too, in
Sāmaveda, 746.

६३१३. स प्रॅथमे व्योॅमनि देवानां सदॅने वृॅधः।
सुपारः सुश्रॅवॅस्तमः समॅॅप्सुजित्॥२॥

2. Abiding in the highest heaven, in the dwelling of the gods,
he is the giver of increase, the accomplisher (of works), the
possessor of great renown, the conqueror of (the obstructer of) the
rains.

६३१४. तमॅॅहे वाजॅसातयॅ इन्द्रं भराॅय शुष्मिॅणम्।
भवाॅ नः सुम्ने अन्तॅमः सखाॅ वृॅधे॥३॥

3. I invoke the powerful *Indra* for (aid in) the food-bestowing
combat: be nigh unto us for our happiness; be a friend for our
increase.

This and the preceding occur in *Sāmaveda*, 747-48. [Sāyaṇa remarks
that *bhara* may here mean "sacrifice," most of the words signifying
"combat" having this second meaning also.]

For Our Happiness— Sāyaṇa says, "when wealth or happiness is
sought," *sukhe dhane vā lipsite sati.*

६३१५. इॅयं तं इन्द्र गिर्वणो रातिः क्षॅरति सुन्वतः।
मन्दाॅनो अस्य बर्हिषो वि राॅजसि॥४॥

4. This gift of the offerer of the libation flows to you, *Indra*,
who are gratified by praise, exhilarated by which you reign over
the sacrifice.

Over the Sacrifice— The text has *barhiṣaḥ,* "over the sacred grass
," put for the rite at which it is strewn.

६३१६. नूनं तदिॅन्द्र दद्धि नो यत्त्वाॅ सुन्वन्तॅ ईमहे।
रॅयिं नॅश्चित्रमा भॅराॅ स्वर्विॅदॅम्॥५॥

5. Bestow upon us, *Indra*, that which, when puring out the
libation, we solicit of you; grant us the wondrous wealth that is the
means of obtaining heaven.

Means of Obtaining Heaven— *Svarvidam, svargasya lambhakam*
[the printed text has *sarvasya*]; or it may mean one who possesses or
communicates knowledge of heaven, *svargasya vedītāram, i.e.,* a son.

६३१७. स्तोॅता यत्तॅ विचॅर्षणिरति प्रशॅर्धयद्गिॅरः।
वॅयाइवानुॅ रोहते जुषन्तॅ यत्॥६॥

6. When your discriminating eulogist has addressed to you overpowering praises, then, if they are acceptable to you, they expand like the branches (of a tree).

Overpowering— *I.e.,* Able to overpower enemies, *śatrūṇām prahasanasamarthāḥ.*

६३१८. प्रत्नवज्जनया गिरः शृणुधी जरितुर्हवम्।
मदेमदे ववक्षिथा सुकृत्वने॥७॥

7. Generate your eulogies as of old; hear the invocation of the adorer: you bear in your reiterated exultation (blessings) to the liberal donor (of the oblation).

Generate your Fulogies as of Old— *I.e.,* by granting the expected fruit.

६३१९. क्रीळन्त्यस्य सूनृता आपो न प्रवता यतीः।
अया धिया य उच्यते पतिर्दिवः॥८॥

8. The kind and true words of him who in this hymn is called the lord of heaven sport like waters flowing by a downward (channel).

६३२०. उतो पतिर्य उच्यते कृष्टीनामेक इद्वशी।
नमोवृधैरवस्युभिः सुते रण॥९॥

9. Or he, who is called the one absolute lord of men,—praise him, when the libation is effused, with magnifying songs, imploring his protection.

One Absolute Lord of Men— Sāyaṇa takes it, "who is called the one absolute lord of men by those who magnify him (with songs) and implore his protection."

६३२१. स्तुहि श्रुतं विपश्चितं हरी यस्य प्रसक्षिणा।
गन्तारा दाशुषो गृहं नमस्विनः॥१०॥

10. Praise the renowned, the sapient (*Indra*), whose victorious horses proceed to the dwelling of the devout donor (of the libation).

६३२२. तूतुजानो महेमतेऽश्वेभिः पुषितप्सुभिः।
आ याहि यज्ञमाशुभिः शमिद्धि ते॥११॥

11. Munificently minded, do you, who are quick of movement, come with shining and swift steeds to the sacrifice, for verily there is gratification to you thereby.

६३२३. इन्द्र शविष्ठ सत्पते रयिं गृणत्सु धारय।

श्रवः सूरिभ्यो अमृतं वसुत्वनम्॥१२॥

12. Most powerful *Indra*, protector of the virtuous, secure us who praise you in the possession of riches, (grant) to the pious imperishable all-pervading sustenance.

६३२४. हवे त्वा सूर उदिते हवे मध्यन्दिने दिवः।

जुषाण इन्द्र सप्तिभिर्न आ गहि॥१३॥

13. I invoke you when the sun is risen; I invoke (you) at mid-day: being propitiated, come to us, *Indra*, with your gliding steeds.

६३२५. आ तू गहि प्र तु द्रव मत्स्वा सुतस्य गोमतः।

तन्तुं तनुष्व पूर्व्यं यथा विदे॥१४॥

14. Come quickly; hasten; be exhilarated by the libation mixed with milk; extend the ancient sacrifice, so that I may obtain (its reward).

Extend the Ancient Sacrifice— *Cf.* Haug's *Aitareya Brāhm.*, vol. I, Introduction, p. 74.

६३२६. यच्छक्रासि परावति यदर्वावति वृत्रहन्।

यद्वा समुद्रे अन्धसोऽवितेदसि॥१५॥

15. Whether, *Śakra*, you be afar off, or, slayer of *Vṛtra*, nigh at hand, or whether you be in the firmament, you are the guardian of the (sacrificial) food.

You are the Guardian of the Sacrificial Food— Or, "you are the guardian (by drinking) of the *Soma*," *annasya somalakṣaṇasya pānena rakṣitā bhavasi.*

६३२७. इन्द्रं वर्धन्तु नो गिर इन्द्रं सुतास इन्दवः।

इन्द्रे हविष्मतीर्विशो अराणिषुः॥१६॥

16. May our praises magnify *Indra*! May our effused libations gratify *Indra*! May the people bearing oblations excite pleasure in *Indra*!

Excite Pleasure in Indra— Or, "have rejoiced in *Indra*," *araṁsiṣuḥ.*

६३२८. तमिद्विप्रा अवस्यवः प्रवत्वतीभिरूतिभिः।

इन्द्रं क्षोणीरवर्धयन्वया इव॥१७॥

17. The pious, desiring his protection, magnify him by ample and pleasure-yielding (libations): the earth, (and other worlds, spread out) like the branches of a tree, magnify *Indra*.

६३२९. त्रिकंद्रुकेषु चेतनं देवासो यज्ञमंत्नत।

तमिद्वर्धन्तु नो गिरः सदावृधम्॥१८॥

18. The gods propitiate the superintending adorable (*Indra*) at the *Trikadruka* rites. May our praises magnify him who is ever the magnifier (of his worshippers).

Superintending— *Cetana*, explained *cetayitrī*, causing to be wise. For the *Trikadrukas*, see. *mantra* 2112 and note; for the *abhiplava*, *cf.* Haug's *Aitareya Brāhmaṇa.*, vol. II. p. 285.

६३३०. स्तोता यत्ते अनुव्रत उक्थान्यृंतुथा दधे।

शुचिं: पावक उच्यते सो अद्भुतः॥१९॥

19. Your worshipper is observant of his duty, inasmuch as he offers prayers in due season; for you are he who is called pure, purifying, wonderful.

६३३१. तदिद्रुद्रस्य चेतति यह्वं प्रत्नेषु धामंसु।

मनो यत्रा वि तद्धुर्विचेतसः॥२०॥

20. The progeny of *Rudra* (the *Maruts*) is known in ancient places, and to them the intelligent worshippers offer adoration.

६३३२. यदि मे सख्यामावरं इमस्य पाह्यन्धंसः।

येनं विश्वा अति द्विषो अतारिम॥२१॥

21. If, (*Indra*), you choose my friendship, partake of this (sacrificial) food, by which we may pass beyond (the reach of) all adversaries.

६३३३. कदा तं इन्द्र गिर्वणः स्तोता भवाति शन्तंमः।

कदा नो गव्ये अश्व्ये वसौ दधः॥२२॥

22. When, *Indra*, who delight in praise, may your worshipper be entirely happy? When wilt you establish us in (the affluence of) cattle, of horses, of dwellings?

६३३४. उत ते सुष्टुता हरी वृषणा वहतो रथम्।

अजुर्यस्य मदिन्तमं यमीमहे॥२३॥

23. Or, when will your renowned and vigorous horses bring the chariot of you, who are exempt form decay, that exhilarating (wealth) which we solicit?

That Exhilarating Wealth which we Solicit— We have only *madintamam yam īmahe*, it is not very clear to what the epithet applies; the only substantive is *ratham*, but the Scholiast has *madavantam tvām dhanam*, "You exhilarated, wealth," as if *Indra* was understood, and was the wealth that was solicited. [Sāyaṇa seems to take the verse, "Moreover your renowned and vigorous (or desire-showering) horses bring the chariot of you who are exempt from decay, you, the greatly exhilarated, whom we ask (for wealth)," *atiśayena mādavantam yam tvām dhanam yācāmahe tasya ta ityanvayaḥ*.]

६३३५. तमींमहे पुरुहुतं यहं प्रत्नाभिरूतिभिः।
नि बर्हिषि प्रिये संददर्ध द्विता॥२४॥

24. We solicity with ancient and gratifying (offerings) him who is mighty and the invoked of many: may he sit down on the pleasant sacred grass, and accept the two-fold (offering of cakes and *Soma* juice).

६३३६. वर्धस्वा सु पुरुहुत ऋषिष्टुताभिरूतिभिः।
धुक्षस्वं पिप्युषीमिषमवां च नः॥२५॥

25. Praised of many, prosper (us) with the protections hymned by the *Ṛṣis*, send down upon us nutritious food.

६३३७. इन्द्र त्वमवितेदंसीत्था स्तुवतो अद्रिवः।
ऋतादियर्मि ते धियं मनोयुजं॥२६॥

26. Thunderbolt-bearing *Indra*, you are the protector of him who thus eulogises you: I seek through sacrifice for your favour, which is to be gained by praise.

६३३८. इह त्या संधमाद्या युजानः सोमपीतये।
हरीं इन्द्र प्रतद्वसू अभि स्वर॥२७॥

27. Harnessing your horses, *Indra*, laden with treasure and sharing your exhilaration, come hither to drink of the *Soma*.

६३३९. अभि स्वरन्तु ये तव रुद्रासः सक्षत श्रियम्।
उतो मरुत्वतीर्विशो अभि प्रयः॥२८॥

28. May the sons of *Rudra*, who are your followers, approach and partake of the glory (of the sacrifice); and may (other celestial) people associated with the *Maruts* (partake of the sacrificial) food.

The Glory of the Sacrifice— Sāyaṇa explains *śriyam* by *śrayaṇīyam*, sc. *yajñam*.

६३४०. इमा अस्य प्रतूर्तयः पदं जुषन्त यद्दिवि।
नाभा यज्ञस्य सं दधुर्यथा विदे॥२९॥

29. May those who (are his attendants), victorious (over enemies), be satisfied with the station (which they occupy) in heaven, and may they be assembled at the navel of the sacrifice, that I may thence acquire (wealth).

६३४१. अयं दीर्घाय चक्षसे प्राचिं प्रयत्यध्वरे।
मिमीते यज्ञमानुषग्विचक्ष्य॥३०॥

30. When the ceremony is being prepared in the hall of sacrifice, this (*Indra*), having inspected the rite, regulates (the performance) in due succession for a distant object.

For a Distant Object— For a future rewards, but the phraseology is somewhat obscure; it runs literally, "this (*Indra*) for a long prospect, in the east proceeding sacrifice, measures, having considered in succession the sacrifice," *agam dīrghāya cakṣase prācī prayati adhvare mimīte yajñam anuṣag vicakṣya*.

६३४२. वृषायमिन्द्र ते रथं उतो ते वृषणा हरीं।
वृषा त्वं शतक्रतो वृषा हवः॥३१॥

31. Your chariot, *Indra*, is a showerer (of benefits), showerers (of benefits) are your horses: you also *Śatakratu*, are the showerer (of benefits) the invocation (addressed to you) is the showerer (of benefits).

६३४३. वृषा ग्रावा वृषा मदो वृषा सोमो अयं सुतः।
वृषा यज्ञो यमिन्वसि वृषा हवः॥३२

32. The stone (that bruises the *Soma*) is the showerer (of benefits), so is your exhilaration and this *Soma* Juice that is effused: the sacrifice that you accept is the showerer (of benefits), such also is your invocation.

In this and the two following stanzas we have the usual reiteration of *vṛṣā*,—*Vṛṣā yam Indra te ratha uto te vṛṣaṇa havi,* and so forth, explained, as usual, *kāmānām varṣitā*.

६३४४. वृषा त्वा वृषणं हुवे वज्रिञ्चित्राभिरूतिभिः।
वावन्थ हि प्रतिष्टुतिं वृषा हवः॥३३

33. The showerer (of the oblation) I invoke with manifold and gratifying (praises) you, O thunderer, the showerer (of benefits): inasmuch as you acknowledge the eulogy addressed to you, your invocation is the showerer (of benefits).

[सूक्त-१४]

[**ऋषि**- गोषूक्ति, अश्वसूक्ति काण्वायन। **देवता**- इन्द्र। **छन्द**- गायत्री।]

६३४५. यदिन्द्राहं यथा त्वमीशीय वस्व एक इत्।

स्तोता मे गोषखा स्यात्॥१॥

1. If, *Indra*, I were, as you are, sole, lord over wealth, then should my eulogist be possessed of cattle.
Sāmaveda, 122-1834.

६३४६. शिक्षेयमस्मै दित्सेयं शचीपते मनीषिणे। यदहं गोपतिः स्याम्॥२॥

2. Lord of might, I would give to that intelligent worshipper that which I should wish to give, if I were the possessor of cattle.
Sāmaveda, 1835.

I should wish to Give— "I would wish to give, I would present to that intelligent worshipper," *śikṣeyam asmai ditseyam maniṣiṇe*.

६३४७. धेनुष्ट इन्द्र सूनृता यजमानाय सुन्वते। गामश्वं पिप्युषी दुहे॥३॥

3. Your praise, *Indra*, is a milch cow to the worshipper offering the libations; it milks him in abundance cattle and horses.
Sāmaveda, 1836.

६३४८. न ते वर्तास्ति राधस इन्द्र देवो न मर्त्यः।

यदित्ससि स्तुतो मघम्॥४॥

4. Neither god nor man, *Indra*, is the obstructor of your affluence, (of) the wealth which you, when praised, design to bestow.

६३४९. यज्ञ इन्द्रमवर्धयद्यद्भूमिं व्यवर्तयत्। चक्राण ओपशं दिवि॥५॥

5. Sacrifice has magnified *Indra*, so that he has supported the earth (with rain), making (the cloud) quiescent in the firmament.
Cakrāṇa opaśam divi,—antarikṣe megham opaśam upetya śayānam kurvan, is Sāyaṇa's explanation. Sāmeveda, 121-1639.

६३५०. वावृधानस्य ते वयं विश्वा धनानि जिग्युषः। ऊतिमिन्द्रा वृणीमहे॥६॥

6. We solicity, *Indra*, the protection of you, who are ever being magnified, the conqueror of all the riches (of the enemy).

६३५१. व्यँ१न्तरिक्षमतिरन्मदे सोमस्य रोचना। इन्द्रो यदभिनद्वलम्।।७।।

7. In the exhilaration of the *Soma*, *Indra* has traversed the radiant firmament that he might pierce (the *Asura*) *Vala*.

Sāmaveda, 1640. [Sāyaṇa explains the latter clause, "from which (exhilaration) he pierced *Vala*."]

६३५२. उद्गा आजदङ्गिरोभ्य आविष्कृण्वन्नुहा सती:।

अर्वाञ्चं नुनुदे वलम्।।८।।

8. He liberated the cows for the *Angirasas*, making manifest those that has been hidden in the cave, hurling *Vala* headlong down.

६३५३. इन्द्रेण रोचना दिवो दृल्हानि दृंहितानि च। स्थिराणि न पराणुदे।।९।।

9. By *Indra* the constellations were made stable and firm and stationary, so that they could not be moved by any.

६३५४. अपामूर्मिर्मदन्तिव स्तोम इन्द्राजिरायते। वि ते मदा अराजिषु:।।१०।।

10. Your praise, *Indra*, mounts aloft like the exulting wave of the waters, your exhilarations have been manifested.

६३५५. त्वं हि स्तौमवर्धन इन्द्रास्युक्थवर्धन:। स्तोतॄणामुत भद्रकृत्।।११।।

11. You, *Indra*, are to be magnified by praise, you are to be magnified by prayer; you are the benefactor of those who praise you.

६३५६. इन्द्रमित्केशिना हरी सोमपेयाय वक्षत:। उप यज्ञं सुराधसम्।।१२।।

12. Let the long-maned horses bring the wealth-bestowing *Indra* to the sacrifice to drink the *Soma* juice.

६३५७. अपां फेनेन नमुचे: शिर इन्द्रोदवर्तय:। विश्वा यदजय: स्पृध:।।१३।।

13. You have struck off, *Indra*, the head of *Namuci* with the foam of the waters, when you had subdued all your enemies.

Struck off the Head of Namuci, etc.— This legend, as related in the *Gadā* section of the *Śalya Parvan* of the *Mahābhārata* (printed edition, of Parimal Publications, vol. V) has been previously referred to (vol. II, note on v.2.16.9). Sāyaṇa's version of it slightly varies in the beginning, stating that *Indra*, after defeating the *Asuras*, was unable to capture *Namuci*; on the contrary, he was taken by him. *Namuci*, however, liberated him on the conditions which are enumerated in the *Bharata*—that he would not kill him with any weapon, dry or wet, nor by day or night. In evasion of his oath, *Indra* at twilight, or in a fog, decapitated *Namuci* with the foam of water. [It is also told in the *Taittirīya Saṃhitā*, i.8.7]. *Sāmaveda*, 211. *Yajurveda*, 19.71.

६३५८. मायाभिरुत्सिसृप्सत इन्द्र द्यामारुरुक्षतः। अव दस्यूँरधूनुथाः॥१४॥

14. You have hurled down, *Indra*, the *Dasyus*, gliding upwards
by their devices and ascending to heaven.

६३५९. असुन्वामिन्द्र संसदं विषूचीं व्यनाशयः। सोमपा उत्तरो भवन्॥१५॥

15. You, *Indra*, the most excellent drinker of the *Soma*, destroy
the adverse assembly that offers no libations.

The Most Excellent Drinker of the Soma— Or it may mean "you
who on drinking the *Soma* become pre-eminent." *Viṣūcim* may mean
"discordant," *parasparavirodhena nānā gantrīm.*

[सूक्त-१५]

[**ऋषि**– गोषूक्ति–अश्व सूक्ति काण्वायन। **देवता**– इन्द्र। **छन्द**– उष्णिक्।]

६३६०. तम्वभि प्र गायत पुरुहूतं पुरुष्टुतम्।

   इन्द्रं गीर्भिस्तविषमा विवासत॥१॥

1. Glorify him the invoked of many, the praised of many;
adore the powerful *Indra* with hymns;

   Sāmaveda, 382.

६३६१. यस्य द्विबर्हसो बृहत्सहो दाधार रोदसी।

   गिरीँरज्राँ अपः स्वर्वृषत्वना॥२॥

2. The vast strength of whom, powerful in both (regions), has
sustained the heaven and earth, and by its vigour (upheld) the swift
clouds and flowing waters.

The Swift Clouds— *Girīn ajrān* may mean also the quick
mountains, *i.e.,* before their wings were clipped.

६३६२. स राजसि पुरुष्टुतँ एको वृत्राणि जिघ्नसे।

   इन्द्र जैत्रा श्रवस्या च यन्तवे॥३॥

3. You, the praised of many, reignest: you, single, have slain
many enemies, in order to acquire the spoils of victory and
abundant food.

६३६३. तं ते मदं गृणीमसि वृषणं पृत्सु सासहिम्।

   उ लोककृतुमद्रिवो हरिश्रियम्॥४॥

4. We celebrate, thunderer, your exhilaration, the showerer (of
benefits), the overcomer (of foes) in battle, the maker of the world,
the glorious with your steeds;

Sāmaveda, 383-880. [*Lokakritnu* would see to mean, according to Sāyaṇa, "the provider of a place (for his worshipper)", *sthānasya kartāram*; and *hariśriyam*, "him who is to be served by his steeds," *aśvabhyam sevyam.*]

६३६४. येन ज्योतींष्यायवे मनवे च विवेदिथ।

मन्दानो अस्य बर्हिषो वि राजसि।।५।।

5. Whereby you have made the planets manifest to *Ayu* and to *Manu*, and rule rejoicing over this sacred rite.

Sāmaveda., 881.

६३६५. तद्धा चित्त उक्थिनोऽनु ष्ठुवन्ति पूर्वथा।

वृषपत्नीरपो जया दिवेदिवे।।६।।

6. The reciters of prayer celebrate that your (exhilaration) now as of old: do you daily hold in subjection the waters, the wives of the showerer.

६३६६. तव त्यदिन्द्रियं बृहत्तव शुष्ममुत क्रतुम्।

वज्रं शिशाति धिषणा वरेण्यम्।।७।।

7. Praise sharpens your great energy, your strength, your acts, and your majestic thunderbolt.

Sāmaveda, 1645.

६३६७. तव द्यौरिन्द्र पौंस्यं पृथिवी वर्धति श्रवः।

त्वामापः पर्वतासश्च हिन्विरे।।८।।

8. The heaven invigorates your manhood, *Indra*, the earth (spreads) your renown; the waters, the mountains propitiate you.

Sāmaveda, 1646.

६३६८. त्वां विष्णुर्बृहन् क्षयो मित्रो गृणाति वरुणः।

त्वां शर्धो मदत्यनु मारुतम्।।९।।

9. Viṣṇu, the mighty giver of dwellings, praises you, and *Mitra* and *Varuṇa*; the company of the *Maruts* imitates you in exhilaration.

Sāmaveda, 1647.

६३६९. त्वं वृषा जनानां मंहिष्ठ इन्द्र जज्ञिषे।

सत्रा विश्वा स्वपत्यानि दधिषे।।१०।।

10. You, *Indra*, who are the showerer, have been born the most bountiful of beings; you associate with you all good offspring.

You Associate with you All Good Offspring— That is, you give offspring, and all good things.

६३७०. सत्रा त्वं पुरुष्टुतँ एको वृत्राणि तोशसे।

नान्य इन्द्रात् करणं भूर्य इन्वति॥११॥

11. (*Indra*), the praised of many, you alone destroy many mighty foes: no other *Indra* achieves such great exploits.

६३७१. यदिन्द्र मन्मशस्त्वा नाना हवन्त ऊतये।

अस्माकेभिर्नृभिरत्रा स्वर्जय॥१२॥

12. When (in the combat), *Indra*, they invoke you in many ways with praise for protection, then do you (so invoked) by our leaders overcome all (our enemies).

६३७२. अरं क्षयाय नो महे विश्वा रूपाण्याविशन्।

इन्द्रं जैत्राय हर्षया शचीपतिम्॥१३॥

13. ALL the forms (of *Indra*) have sufficiently entered into our own spacious abode: gratify *Indra* the lord of Shachi, (that he may give us) the spoil of victory.

All the forms of Indra— That is, the various attributes celebrated in our praises.

[सूक्त- १६]

[ऋषि- इरिम्बिठि काण्व। देवता- इन्द्र। छन्द- गायत्री।]

६३७३. प्र सम्राजं चर्षणीनामिन्द्रं स्तोता नव्यं गीर्भिः।

नरं नृषाहं मंहिष्ठम्॥१॥

1. Glorify with hymns the adorable *Indra*, the supreme king of men, the leader (of rites), the overcomer of enemies, the most munificent.

Sāmaveda, 141.

६३७४. यस्मिन्नुक्थानि रण्यन्ति विश्वानि च श्रवस्या। अपामवो न समुद्रे॥२॥

2. In whom all praises, all kinds of sustenance concentrate, like the aggregation of the waters in the ocean.

In Whom All Praises. . . . . Concentrate— Literally, "In whom (as their object) all praises, and all kinds of offspring exultingly meet."

६३७५. तं सुष्टुत्या विवासे ज्येष्ठराजं भरे कृत्नुम्। महो वाजिनं सनिभ्यः॥३॥

3. I worship *Indra* with pious praise, glorious amongst the best (of beings), the achiever of great deeds in war mighty for the acquirement (of wealth).

६३७६. यस्यानूना गभीरा मदा उरवस्तरुत्राः। हर्षुमन्तः शूरसातौ॥४॥

4. Whose unbounded and profound exhilarations are many, protective, and animating in war.

Animating in War— Sāyaṇa explains *harṣamantaḥ* as "exulting in, *i.e.*, eager for, war," *harṣayuktaḥ saṅgrāmotsukaḥ.*

६३७७. तमिद्धनेषु हितेष्वधिवाकाय हवन्ते। येषामिन्द्रस्ते जयन्ति॥५॥

5. (His worshippers) invoke him to take part (in spoiling) the treasures deposited (with the foe): they conquer, of whom *Indra* is (the partisan).

६३७८. तमिच्च्यौत्नैरार्यन्ति तं कृतेभिश्चर्षणयः। एष इन्द्रो वरिवस्कृत्॥६॥

6. They honour him with animating (hymns), men (honour) him with sacred rites, for *Indra* is the giver of wealth.

६३७९. इन्द्रो ब्रह्मेन्द्र ऋषिरिन्द्रः पुरू पुरुहूतः। महान्महीभिः शचीभिः॥७॥

7. *Indra* is Brahmā, *Indra* is the Ṛṣi: *Indra* is the much-invoked of many, mighty with mighty deeds.

Indra is Brahmā— *Indro brahmā, parivṛḍah sarvebhyo'dhikaḥ,* "the augmented or vast, more or greater than all," is the explanation of the commentator. [He explains *ṛṣi* as the beholder of all the *Āryas, sarvasya Āryajātasya draṣṭā.*]

६३८०. स स्तोम्यः स हव्यः सत्यः सत्वा तुविकूर्मिः।

एकश्चित्सन्नभिभूतिः॥८॥

8. He is to be praised, he is to be invoked, he is true, powerful the doer of many deeds; he, being single, is the overcomer (of his foes).

६३८१. तमर्केभिस्तं सामभिस्तं गायत्रैश्चर्षणयः। इन्द्रं वर्धन्ति क्षितयः॥९॥

9. Men who are cognizant (of sacred texts) magnify *Indra* with pious precepts, with sacred songs, and with prayers.

With Pious Precepts, with, etc.— *Tam arkebhis tam sāmabhis tam gāyatrais carṣaṇayaḥ kṣitayaḥ.* The two last equally imply men, but the Scholiast understands the first to be an epithet of the second—the seers or understanders of *Mantras*, or texts, such as those of the *yajus (arka)*, of the Sāyaṇa (*sāman*), and metrical prayers not chanted (*Gāyatra*).

६३८२. प्रणेतारं वस्यो अच्छा कर्तारं ज्योति: समत्सु।

सासह्वांसं युधामित्रान्॥१०॥

10. Him (they magnify) who brings before them the spoil, who gives lustre in combats, who overcomes enemies in battle.

In Battle— Or, "by his weapon," *āyudhena*.

६३८३. स न: पत्रि: पारयाति स्वस्ति नावा पुरुहूत:।

इन्द्रो विश्वा अति द्विष:॥११॥

11. May *Indra*, the fulfiller (of desires), the invoked of many, bear us beyond (the reach of) all our enemies, to welfare, as if by a ship (across the sea).

To Welfare— Sāyaṇa explains *svasti* as "happy," *kṣemeṇa*.

६३८४. स त्वं न इन्द्र वाजेभिर्दशस्या च गातुया च।

अच्छा च न: सुम्नं नेषि॥१२॥

12. Do you, *Indra*, (endow) us with vigour, bestow upon us (wealth, enable us) to go (by the right way), lead us to felicity.

[सूक्त- १७]

[**ऋषि**– इरिम्बिठि काण्व। **देवता**– इन्द्र। **छन्द**– गायत्री, १४, १५ प्रगाथ (विषमा बृहती, समासतो बृहती)।]

६३८५. आ याहि सुषुमा हि त इन्द्र सोमं पिबा इमम्।

एदं बर्हि: सदो मम॥१॥

1. Come: we express, *Indra*, for you, the *Soma* drink: drink it: sit down upon this my sacred grass.

Sāmaveda, 191-666.

६३८६. आ त्वा ब्रह्मयुजा हरी वहतामिन्द्र केशिना। उप ब्रह्माणि न: शृणु॥२

2. Let your long-maned horses, *Indra*, that are yoked by prayers, bring you hither, and do you hear our prayers.

Sāmaveda, 667.

६३८७. ब्रह्माणस्त्वा वयं युजा सोमपामिन्द्र सोमिन:। सुतावन्तो हवामहे॥३॥

3. We *Brāhmaṇas*, offerers of *Soma*, bearing the effused juices, invoke with suitable (prayers) you the drinker of the *Soma*.

Sāmaveda, 668.

We Brāhmaṇas— *I.e.*, *brahmāṇaḥ*, explained in the commentary by *brāhmaṇāḥ*.

६३८८. आ नो॒ याहि॑ सुता॒वतो॒ऽस्माकं॑ सु॒ष्टुती॑रुप॑। पि॒बा सु शि॒प्रिन्न्धस॑:॥४॥

4. Come to us offering the libation, accept our earnest praises; drink, handsome-jawed, of the (sacrificial) beverage.

६३८९. आ ते॑ सिञ्चामि कु॒क्ष्योरनु॑ गा॒त्रा वि धा॑वतु। गृ॒भा॒य जि॒ह्वया॒ मधु॑॥५॥

5. I fill your belly (with the libation): let it spread throughout the limbs: take the honied *Soma* with your tongue.

The Belly— *Kukṣyoḥ,* in the dual, for it is said that *Indra* has two bellies, *Indrasya hi dve udare,* according to another text, fill both the bellies of the slayer of *Vṛtra:* or it may refer only to the right and left sides, or the upper and lower portions of the same belly, *yadvā ekasyaiva udarasya savyadakṣiṇabhedena ūrddhvādhobhāgena vā dvitvam.* [*Cf.* vol.I, mantra 2106 ; vol. II, mantra 2912.]

६३९०. स्वा॒दुष्टे॑ अस्तु सं॒सुदे॒ मधु॑मान्त॒न्वे॒३॒॑तव॑। सोम॒: शर्म॑स्तु ते हृ॒दे॥६॥

6. May the sweet-flavoured *Soma* be grateful to you, who are munificent; (may it be grateful) to your body may it be exhilarating to your heart.

६३९१. अ॒यमु॒ त्वा॑ विचर्षणे॒ जनी॑रि॒वाभि संवृ॑त॑:। प्र सोम॑ इन्द्र सर्पतु॥७॥

7. May this *Soma*, invested (with milk), approach you, observant *Indra*, like a bride (clad in white apparel).

Like a Bride—*Janir iva, jāyā iva,* literally, "like brides". *Śuklair vastraiḥ samvṛtaḥ* is the explanation of the comment. The text has only *samvṛtaḥ,* covered, or invested by, as an epithet of *Soma, payaḥprabhṛtibhiḥ,* by milk and other ingredients.

६३९२. तुवि॑ग्री॒वो व॑पो॒दर॑: सु॒बाहु॑रन्ध॒सो मदे॑। इन्द्रो॑ वृ॒त्राणि॑ जिघ्नते॥८॥

8. Long-necked, large-bellied, strong-armed *Indra*, in the exhilaration of the (sacrificial) food, destroys his enemies.

६३९३. इन्द्र॒ प्रेहि॒ पुर॑स्त्वं वि॒श्वस्ये॒शान॒ ओज॑सा। वृ॒त्राणि॑ वृत्रह॒ञ्जहि॑॥९॥

9. *Indra*, who by your strength are the lord over all, come to us, slayer of *Vṛtra*, subdue our foes.

६३९४. दी॒र्घस्ते॑ अस्त्वङ्कु॒शो येना॒ वसु॒ प्रयच्छ॑सि। यज॑मानाय सु॒न्वते॑॥१०॥

10. Long be your goad, wherewith you bestow wealth upon the sacrificer offering libations.

Goad— Or rather "crook"; *aṅkuśa* is explained by Sāyaṇa as an instrument for drawing towards us things out of reach.

६३९५. अ॒यं त॑ इन्द्र॒ सोमो॑ नि॒पूतो॒ अधि॑ ब॒र्हिषि॑। ए॒हीम॑स्य द्र॒वा पि॑ब॑॥११॥

11. This *Soma* juice, purified (by filtering) through the sacred grass, is for you, *Indra*; come to it; hasten; drink.

Purified through the Sacred Grass— Or rather "purified (by being filtered through the cloth called *daśā pavitra* over the sacred grass (strewed on the *vedi*).
Sāmaveda, 159-725.

६३९६. शाचिगो शाचिपूजनायं रणाय ते सुतः। आख॑ण्डल॒ प्र हू॑यसे॥१२॥

12. Renowned for radiance, renowned for adoration, this libation is for your gratification; destroyer of foes, you are earnestly invoked.

Renowned for Radiance— *Śācigo* is not very satisfactorily explained: *śaktā gāvo yasya*, "he whose cattle are strong." *Śācayaḥ* may also mean, according to Sāyaṇa, *vyaktāḥ*, "manifest," or *prakhyātāḥ*, "famous," and *gāvaḥ* may mean *raśmayaḥ*, rays, *i.e.*, "of renowned or manifest brilliance." So the next epithet, *śācipūjana*, is explained *prakhyātapūjana*, "of renowned adoration," or "whose hymns are renowned." *Sāmaveda*, 726.

६३९७. यस्ते॑ शृङ्ग॒वृषो॑ नपात् प्रणपात्कुण्डपाय्यः।
न्य॑स्मिन्दध्र॒ आ मनः॑॥१३॥

13. (*Indra*), who was the offspring of *Śṛṅgavṛṣa*, of whom the *kuṇḍapāyya* rite was the protector, (the sages) have fixed (of old) their minds upon this ceremony.

Offspring of Śṛṅgavṛṣa— *Yas te Śṛṅgavṛṣo napāt praṇapāt kuṇḍapāyyaḥ* would be more naturally rendered, he who was, *Śṛṅganvṛśa*, your grandson, your great-grandson, *Kuṇḍapāyya*; but Sāyaṇa quotes a legend which describes *Indra* as taking upon himself the character of the son of a *Ṛṣi* named *Śṛṅgavṛṣa* (or *Śṛṅgavṛṣan*), which is therefore here in the genitive case; *napat*, he says, means *apatya*, offspring generally, and is therefore not incompatible with *putra*, "son". *Śṛṅgavṛṣ* may also mean the sun, *i.e.*, *śṛṅgair varṣati*, "he rains with rays"; and *na-pat* may have its etymological sense, not causing to fall, *na pātayitā*, *i.e.*, he who was the establisher of the sun the heaven, *Indra*. Again, *Kuṇḍapāyya*, upon the authority of Pāṇini, 3.1.130, means a particular ceremony, in which the *Soma* is drunk from a vessel called *Kuṇḍa*, and this is said to be *te praṇapāt, tava rakṣitā*, "the protector of you, *Indra*". The construction is loose, and the explanation not very satisfactory. *Sāmaveda*, 727.

६३९८. वास्तोष्पते ध्रुवा स्थूणांसत्रं सोम्यानाम्।
द्रप्सो भेत्ता पुरां शश्वतीनामिन्द्रो॒ मुनीनां सखा॑॥१४॥

14. Lord of dwellings, may the (roof) pillar be strong; may there be vigour of body for the offers of the libation; may *Indra*, the drinker (of the *Soma*), the destroyer of the numerous cities (of the *Asuras*), ever be the friend of the *Munis*.
Sāmaveda, 275.

६३९९. पृदाकुसानुर्यजतो ग॒वेष॒ण॒ एक॒: स॒त्रऽभि भूर्यस॑:।
भूर्णिम॑श्वं॒ नय॑तुजा पु॒रो गृभेन्द्रं॑ सोम॑स्य पी॒तये॑॥१५॥

15. With head uplifted like a serpent, adorable, the recoverer
of the cattle, *Indra* single is superior to multitudes: (the
worshipper) brings *Indra* to drink the *Soma* by a rapid seizure, like
a loaded horse (by a halter).

With head Uplifted Like a Serpent— *Prdākusānu* is explained
prdākuḥ sarpaḥ, a serpent; *sa iva sānuḥ samucchṛtaḥ tadvad
unnataśiraskaḥ,* having the head lifted up in like manner. [Sāyaṇa gives a
second meaning of *sānu,* as *saṁbhajanīya*, to be served or propitiated as
a snake is, with many gems, mantras, medicaments, etc.; *sa yathā
bahubhir maṇimantrauṣadhādibhis saṁsevyo nālpai evam Indro' pi
bahubhis stotrādibhir yatnais sevyaḥ.*]

By a Rapid Seizure— Sāyaṇa explains *gṛbha* as ''means of
seizing,'' *i.e.,* a praise.

[सूक्त-१८]

[**ऋषि**– इरिम्बिठि काण्व। **देवता**– आदित्यगण, ८ अश्विनीकुमार, ९ अग्नि,
सूर्य अनिल। **छन्द**– उष्णिक्।]

६४००. इ॒दं हि नू॒नमे॑षां सु॒म्नं भि॒क्षेत॒ मर्त्य॑:। आ॒दि॒त्याना॑मपू॒र्व्यं स॒वीम॑नि॥१॥

1. Let a mortal now earnestly solicit at the worship of these
Ādityas unprecedented riches.

६४०१. अन॑र्वाणो॒ ह्येषां॒ पन्था॑ आदि॒त्याना॑म्।
अद॑ब्धाः॒ सन्ति॒ पाय॑वः सु॒गेवृध॑:॥२॥

2. The paths of these *Ādityas* are unobstructed and unopposed;
may they yield us security and augment our happiness.

६४०२. तत्सु नः॒ स॒वि॒ता भगो॒ वरु॑णो मि॒त्रो अ॑र्य॒मा।
शर्म॑ यच्छन्तु स॒प्रथो॒ यदी॒महे॑॥३॥

3. May *Savitā, Bhaga, Varuṇa, Mitra,* and *Aryaman* bestow
upon us that ample felicity which we solicit.

६४०३. दे॒वेभि॑र्देव्य॑दिते॒ऽरि॒ष्टभर्मन्त्रा॒ गहि॑। स्म॒त्सू॒रिभि॑: पुरुप्रिये॒ सु॒शर्मभि॑:॥४॥

4. Divine *Aditi,* bringer of safety, beloved of many, come
propitiously with the wise and happy divinities.

Bringer of Safety— Rather, ''whose fostering care is unimpeded.''

६४०४. ते हि पुत्रासो अदितेर्विदुर्द्वेषांसि योतवे।
अंहोश्चिदुरुचक्रयोऽनेहसः ॥५॥

5. These sons of *Aditi* know how to drive away (our) enemies; and, deers of great de ds and donors of security, (they know how to extricate us) from sin.

६४०५. अदितिर्नो दिवा पशुमदितिर्नक्तमद्वयाः।
अदितिः पात्वंहसः सदावृधा ॥६॥

6. May *Aditi* protect our cattle by day, and, free from luplicity, (guard them) by night; may *Aditi*, by her constant favour, preserve us from sin.

Free from Duplicity— *Advayāḥ* is explained as *Kapaṭarahitā*, [*Cf. v.* 14.]

६४०६. उत स्या नो दिवा मतिरदितिरूत्या गमत्।
सा शन्ताति मयस्करदप स्त्रिधः ॥७॥

7. May the monitress *Aditi* come to us for our prosecution by day: may she grant us tranquil felicity, and live away, (our) enemies.

Sāmaveda, 102.

६४०७. उत त्या दैव्या भिषजा शं नः करतो अश्विना।
युयुयातामितो रपो अप स्त्रिधः ॥८॥

8. May the two divine physicians, the *Aśvins*, grant us health: may they drive away from hence iniquity: (may they drive)˙away our foes.

६४०८. शमग्निरग्निभिः करच्छं नस्तपतु सूर्यः।
शं वातो वात्वरपा अप स्त्रिधः ॥९॥

9. May *Agni* with his fires grant us happiness: may the sun beam upon us felicity: may the unoffending wind blow us happiness: (may they all drive) away our foes.

६४०९. अपामीवामप स्त्रिधमर्प सेधत दुर्मतिम्।
आदित्यासो युयोतना नो अंहसः ॥१०॥

10. *Ādityas*, remove (from us) disease, enemies, malignity; keep us afar from sin.

Sāmaveda. 307.

६४१०. युयोता शरुंमस्मदाँ आदित्यास उतामतिम्।

ऋधग् द्वेषः कृणुत विश्ववेदसः॥११॥

11. Keep afar from us, *Ādityas*, malignity, ill-will; do you who are all-wise keep afar those who hate us.

६४११. तत्सु नः शर्म यच्छतादित्या यन्मुमोचति।

एनस्वन्तं चिदेनसः सुदानवः॥१२॥

12. Grant freely to us, generous *Ādityas*, that happiness which liberates even the offending (worshipper) from sin.

६४१२. यो नः कश्चिद्दिरिक्षति रक्षस्त्वेन मर्त्यः।

स्वैः ष एवै रिरिषीष्ट युर्जनः॥१३॥

13. May that man who, from his diabolical nature seeks to do us evil–may he, injuring himself by his own devices, incur that evil.

६४१३. समित्तमघमश्रवद्दुःशंसं मर्त्यं रिपुम्।

यो अस्मत्रा दुर्हणावाँ उप द्वयुः॥१४॥

14. May iniquity pervade that calumniating and hostile mortal who wishes to do us harm, and is treacherous towards us.

Treacherous— *Dvayu,* double—he who professes kindness to our face and maligns us behind our back; *pratyakṣakṛto hitam vadati parokṣakṛtas tu ahitam.*

६४१४. पाकत्रा स्थन देवा हृत्सु जानीथ मर्त्यम्।

उप द्वयुं चाद्वयुं च वसवः॥१५॥

15. Deities, you are (propitious) to sincere (worshippers), you know, *Vasus,* the hearts of men, and distinguish between the single and double minded.

६४१५. आ शर्म पर्वतानामोतापां वृणीमहे।

द्यावाक्षामारे अस्मद्रपस्कृतम्॥१६॥

16. We solicit the happiness of the mountains and of the waters; Heaven and Earth, remove sin far from us.

६४१६. ते नो भद्रेण शर्मणा युष्माकं नावा वसवः।

अति विश्वानि दुरिता पिपर्तन॥१७॥

17. Convey us, *Vasus,* in your vessel, with auspicious felicity, beyond all calamities.

६४१७. तुचे तनाय तत्सु नो द्राघीय आयुर्जीवसे।

आदित्यास: सुमहस: कृणोतन।।१८

18. Radiant *Ādityas* grant to our sons and grandsons to enjoy long life.

Sāmaveda, 395.

६४१८. यज्ञो हीळो वो अन्तर आदित्या अस्ति मृळत।

युष्मे इद्वो अपि ष्मसि सजात्ये।।१९।।

19. The duly-presented sacrifice is ready for you, *Ādityas*; grant us, therefore, happiness: may we ever abide in near relationship with you.

६४१९. बृहद्रूथं मरुतां देवं त्रातारमश्विना। मित्रमीमहे वरुणं स्वस्तये।।२०।।

20. We solicit of the divine protector of the *Maruts*, of the *Aśvins*, of *Mitra*, and of *Varuṇa*, a spacious dwelling for our welfare.

६४२०. अनेहो मित्रार्यमन्नृवद्वरुण शंस्यम्।

त्रिवरूथं मरुतो यन्त नश्छर्दि:।।२१।।

21. *Mitra*, *Aryaman*, *Varuṇa*, and *Maruts*, grant us a secure, excellent, and well-peopled dwelling, a three fold shelter.

A Threefold Shelter— *Trivarūtham*, a guard against heat, cold and wet; or it may mean, according to the Scholiast, *tribhūmikam*, ''three-storied.'' Sāyaṇa, therefore, did not believe that the Hindus of the Vedic period lived in hovels.

६४२१. ये चिद्धि मृत्युबन्धव आदित्या मनव: स्मसि।

प्र सू न आयुर्जीवसे तिरेतन।।२२।।

22. Since, *Ādityas*, we mortals are of kin to death, do you benevolently (exert yourselves to) prolong our lives.

[सूक्त-१९]

[**ऋषि**– सोभरि काण्व। **देवता**– अग्नि, ३४-३५ आदित्यगण, ३६-३७ त्रसदस्यु पौरुकुत्स्य। **छन्द**– १-२६ प्रगाथ (विषमा ककुप्, समासतो बृहती), २७ द्विपदा विराट्, २८-३३ प्रगाथ (समा ककुप्, विषमा सतोबृहती), ३४ उष्णिक्, ३५ सतोबृहती, ३६ ककुप्, ३७ पंक्ति।]

६४२२. तं गूर्धया स्वर्णरं देवासो देवमरतिं दधन्विरे। देवत्रा हव्यमोहिरे।।१।।

1. Glorify (*Agni*), the leader of all (sacred rites): the priests approach the divine lord, (and through him) convey the oblation to the gods.

Sāmaveda, 109-1687.

६४२३. विभूतरातिं विप्र चित्रशोचिषमग्निमीळिष्व यन्तुरम्।

अस्य मेधस्य सोम्यस्य सोभरे प्रेमध्वराय पूर्व्यम्॥२॥

2. Praise, pious *Sobhari*, at the sacrifice this ancient *Agni*, who is the giver of opulence, the wonderfully luminous, the regulator of this rite, at which the *Soma* is presented.

Sāmaveda, 1688.

६४२४. यजिष्ठं त्वा ववृमहे देवं देवत्रा होतारममर्त्यम्।

अस्य यज्ञस्य सुक्रतुम्॥३॥

3. We adore you, the most adorable deity, the invoker of the gods, the immortal, the perfecter of this sacrifice;

Sāmaveda, 112; 1413.

Sāyaṇa explains it "we edore you, the most adorable, the deity among deities, the invoker," etc.]

६४२५. ऊर्जो नपातं सुभगं सुदीदितिमग्निं श्रेष्ठशोचिषम्।

स नौ मित्रस्य वरुणस्य सो अपामा सुम्नं यक्षते दिवि॥४॥

4. *Agni*, the great grandson of (sacrificial) food, the possessor of opulence, the illumer, the shedder of excellent light: may he obtain for us by sacrifice the happiness in heaven (that is the gift) of *Mitra*, of *Varuṇa*, of the waters.

Sāmaveda, 1414. But it reads *apām napātam,* instead of *urjo napātam,* as in our text—from burnt-offerings the rains are generated; from them timber; from timber, fire.

६४२६. यः समिधा य आहुती यो वेदेन ददाश मर्तो अग्नये।

यो नमसा स्वध्वरः॥५॥

5. The man who has presented (worship) to *Agni* with fuel, with burnt offerings, with the *Veda*, with (sacrificial food, and is diligent in pious rites;

With the Veda— Sāyaṇa explains *vedena* by *vedādhyayanena,* "by studying the *Veda.*" Professor Müller, however, says that it means "a bundle of grass." See *Ancient Sanskrit Literature,* p. 28, note, and p. 205.

६४२७. तस्येदर्वन्तो रंहयन्त आशवस्तस्य द्युम्नितमं यशः।

न तमंहो देवकृतं कुतश्चन न मर्त्यकृतं नशत्॥६॥

6. Of him assuredly the rapid horses rush (on the foe): his is most brilliant glory: him no evil, whether the work of gods or of men, ever assails.

६४२८. स्वग्नयो॑ वो अ॒ग्निभिः॑ स्या॒मं सू॑नो सहस ऊ॒र्जां पते।

सु॒वीर॑स्त्व॒मस्म॒यु:।।७।।

7. Son of strength, lord of (sacrificial) food, may we be favoured with your various fires; do you, (Agni), endowed with energy, be well disposed towards us!

Endowed with Energy— Sāyaṇa explains suvīra by "you who are worshipped by noble heroes."

६४२९. प्र॒शंस॑मानो अ॒तिथि॒र्न मि॒त्रियो॒ऽग्नी रथो॒ न वेद्यः॑।

त्वे क्षेमा॑सो अ॒पि स॑न्ति सा॒धव॒स्त्वं राजा॑ रयी॒णाम्।।८।।

8. Agni, when honoured like a guest, is gracious to his praisers; he is to be recognized as a chariot (bringing the fruit of the worship): in you verily the virtuous are confiding; you are the Rājā of riches.

In you the Virtuous are Confiding— Or, perhaps, "in you also are excellent protections," tva kṣemāso api santi sādhavaḥ.

६४३०. सो अ॒द्धा दा॒श्वध्व॒रोऽग्ने॒ मर्तः॑ सु॒भग॒ स प्र॒शंस्यः॑।

स धी॒भिर॑स्तु स॒निता।।९।।

9. Agni, may he who is the offerer of sacrifice obtain his reward: he, auspicious Agni, is worthy of commendation: may he by his pious rites become the giver of wealth.

May .... Reward— This is Sāyaṇa's explanation of the indeclinable word addhā: so addhā, satyaphalaḥ sa bhavatu. [Sāyaṇa takes the second clause also as optative, "may he indeed by worthy of praise."]

The Giver of Wealth— This is in the original the same word (sanitā) as that rendered "effecter of his purposes," in the next verse.

६४३१. यस्य॒ त्वमू॒र्ध्वो अ॑ध्व॒राय॒ तिष्ठ॑सि क्ष॒यद्वी॒रः स सा॑धते।

सो अर्व॑द्भिः स॒निता॒ स विप॑न्युभिः॒ स शूरैः॑ स॒निता॑ कृ॒तम्।।१०।।

10. He over whose sacrifice you preside prospers, having his dwelling filled with male offspring: he is the effecter of his purposes through his horses, through his wise (counsellors), his valiant adherents.

६४३२. यस्याग्निर्वपुर्गृहे स्तोमं चनो दधीत विश्ववार्यः।

हव्या वा वेविषद्विषः॥११॥

11. (So is he) in whose dwelling the all-desired and embodied *Agni* receives praise and food, and conveys oblations to the all-pervading deities.

६४३३. विप्रस्य वा स्तुवतः संहसो यहो मक्षूतमस्य रातिषु।

अवोदेवमुपरिमर्त्यं कृधि वसो विविदुषो वर्चः॥१२॥

12. Son of strength, giver of dwellings, place the prayer of the devout intelligent worshipper, who is most prompt in offerings, below the gods and above mortals.

Below the Gods and above Mortals— ''Spread it throughout the sky'' is the Scholiast's explanation of *avodevam upari-martyam, sarvam nabhaḥ-pradeśam vyāpaya.*

६४३४. यो अग्नि हव्यदातिभिर्नमोभिर्वा सुदक्षमाविवासति।

गिरा वाजिरशोचिषम्॥१३॥

13. He who propitiates the powerful and quick radiating *Agni* with offerings of oblations, with reverential adorations and with praise, (is prosperous).

६४३५. समिधा यो निशिती दाशददितिं धामभिरस्य मर्त्यः।

विश्वेत्स धीभिः सुभगो जनाँ अति द्युम्नैरुद्न इव तारिषत्॥१४॥

14. The mortal who propitiates *Aditi* with his (Agni's) many forms by blazing fuel, prospering through his pious rites, shall surpass all men in renown as (if he had crossed over) the waters.

Aditi— Sāyaṇa takes *Aditim* as an epithet of *Agni, i.e., akhaṇḍanīym,* ''the insuperable.'' His many forms are the *gārhapatya,* etc.

६४३६. तदग्ने द्युम्नमा भर यत्सासहत्सदने कं चिदत्रिणम्।

मन्युं जनस्य दूढ्यः॥१५॥

15. Bestow upon us, *Agni,* that power which may overcome any cannibal (entering) into our abode, the wrath of any malignant (being).

६४३७. येन चष्टे वरुणो मित्रो अर्यमा येन नासत्या भगः।

वयं तत्ते शवसा गातुवित्तमा इन्द्रत्वोता विधेमहि॥१६॥

16. Protected by *Indra,* well knowing the path that through your power, (*Agni*), we should follow, we adore that (radiance) of

your, by which *Varuṇa*, *Mitra*, *Aryaman*, the *Nāsatyās*, and *Bhaga* shine.

६४३८. ते घेदग्ने स्वाध्योऽ३ ये त्वा विप्र निदधिरे नृचक्षसम्।
विप्रासो देव सुक्रतुम्।।१७।।

17. Those verily, *Agni*, are of approved piety who as your worshippers, sagacious deity, have established you as the contemplator of men, the performer of good works.

६४३९. त इद्देदिं सुभग त आहुतिं ते सोतुं चक्रिरे दिवि।
त इद्वाजेभिर्जिग्युर्महद्धनं ये त्वे कार्मं न्येरिरे।।१८।।

18. Auspicious (*Agni*), they have set up the altar, have presented oblations, have expressed the libation on a (fortunate) day; they have won by their efforts infinite wealth who have placed their affection upon you.

६४४०. भद्रो नौ अग्निराहुतो भद्रा राति: सुभग भद्रो अध्वर:।
भद्रा उत प्रशंस्तय:।।१९।

19. May *Agni*, to whom burnt-offerings have been made, be propitious to us: auspicious (*Agni*), may your gifts be blessings, may the sacrifice (we offer) be beneficial, may our praises yield us happiness.

Sāmaveda, 111-1559.

६४४१. भद्रं मन: कृणुष्व वृत्रतूर्ये येना समत्सु सासह:।
अव स्थिरा तनुहि भूरि शर्धतां वनेमा ते अभिष्टिभि:।।२०।।

20. Give us that resolute mind in conflict by which you conquer in combats; humble the many firm (resolves) of our foes: may we propitiate you by our sacrifices.

In Conflict— *Vṛtratūrye,* ''in conflict''; Sāyaṇa says, *saṅgrame.* Mahīdhara, *Yajurveda,* 15.39, explains it *pāpanāśāya,* ''for the extirpation of sin.'' As for *ava sthirā tanuhi,* Mahīdhara takes greater license, and renders the phras, ''make the strong bows without bowstrings,'' *sthirāṇi dhanuṁṣi jyārahitāni kuru.*

६४४२. ईळे गिरा मनुर्हितं यं देवा दूतमरतिं न्येरिरे।
यजिष्ठं हव्यवाहनम्।।२१।।

21. I worship *Agni*, who has been established by Manu with praise, whom the gods have appointed their royal messenger, who is the most adorable, the bearer of oblations.

६४४३. तिग्मजम्भाय तरुणाय राजते प्रयो गायस्यग्नये।
यः पिंशते सूनृताभिः सुवीर्यमग्निर्धृतेभिराहुतः ॥२२॥

22. Offer (sacrificial) food to that bright-shining, everyouthful, royal *Agni*, who, (when gratified) by sincere praises, and worshipped with oblations, bestows excellent male offspring.

६४४४. यदीं घृतेभिराहुतो वाशीमग्निर्भरत उच्चाव च।
असुर इव निर्णिजम् ॥२३॥

23. When *Agni*, worshipped with oblations, sends his voice upwards and downwards, as the sun disperses his rays, (we praise him).

६४४५. यो हव्यान्यैरयता मनुहितो देव आसा सुगन्धिना।
विवासते वार्याणि स्वध्वरो होता देवो अमर्त्यः ॥२४॥

24. The divine (*Agni*), established by *Manu*, the offerer of the sacrifice, the invoker (of the gods), the divine, the immortal, who conveys the oblations in his fragrant mouth, bestows (upon his adorers) desirable (riches).

६४४६. यदग्ने मर्त्यस्त्वं स्यामहं मित्रमहो अमर्त्यः। सहसः सूनवाहुत ॥२५॥

25. *Agni*, son of strength, shining with friendly radiance, and worshipped with oblations, may I, who, although mortal, am as you are, become immortal.

May I . . . . . Become Immortal— Agreeably to the text, *ye yathā yathopāsate te tad eva bhavanti*, "as men worship, such they become." [Or, perhaps, the latter part should be, "May I, although a mortal, become as you, immortal."]

६४४७. न त्वा रासीयाभिशस्तये वसो न पापत्वाय सन्त्य।
न मे स्तोतामतीवा न दुर्हितः स्यादग्ने न पापया ॥२६॥

26. May I not be accused, *Vasu*, of calumniating you, nor, gracious (*Agni*), of sunfulness (against you); let not (the priest) the reciter of my praises be dull of intellect or ill-disposed; (may he not err), *Agni*, through wickedness.

May I not be Accused, Etc.— Rather, "Let me not abuse you by calumny or wickedness," *na tvā rāsīyabhi-śastaye na pāpatvāya*.

६४४८. पितुर्न पुत्रः सुभृतो दुरोण आ देवाँ एतु प्र णो हविः ॥२७॥

27. Cherished by us as a son by a father, let him (*Agni*) in our dwelling convey promptly our oblation to the gods.

६४४९. तवाहमग्न ऊतिभिर्नेदिष्ठाभि: सचेय जोषमा वसो।
सदा देवस्य मर्त्य:॥२८॥

28. *Agni*, granter of dwellings, may I, who am mortal, ever
enjoy pleasure through your proximate protections.

६४५०. तव क्रत्वा सनेयं तव रातिभिरग्ने तव प्रशस्तिभि:।
त्वामिदाहु: प्रमतिं वसो ममाग्ने हर्षस्व दातवे॥२९॥

29. May I propitiate you, *Agni*, by worshipping you, by the
gifts presented to you, by your praises: verily, *Vasu*, they have
called you the benevolent-minded: delight, *Agni*, to give me
wealth.

They have called you, Etc.— Sāyaṇa explains it, "they (the pious
sages) call you my protector," *mama stotur rakṣakam tvām eva
brahmavādinaḥ kathayanti.*

६४५१. प्र सो अग्ने तवोतिभि: सुवीराभिस्तिरते वाजभर्ममभि:।
यस्य त्वं सख्यमोवर:॥३०॥

30. He, *Agni*, whose friendship you acceptest, prospers through
your favours, granting male progeny and ample food.
Sāmaveda, 108, 1822.

६४५२. तव द्रप्सो नील्वान्वाश ऋत्विय इन्धान: सिष्णवा ददे।
त्वं महीनामुषसामसि प्रिय: क्षपो वस्तुषु राजसि॥३१॥

31. Sprinkled, (*Agni*, with the libation), the dripping (juices),
car-borne, agreeable, offered in due season, resplendent, have been
presented to you: you are the beloved of the mighty dawns; you
reign over the things of night.
Sāmaveda, 1823. [Sāyaṇa explains *rājasi*, "you shine amidst," or
"you illuminest."]

६४५३. तमागन्म सोभरय: सहस्रमुष्कं स्वभिष्टिमवसे।
सम्राजं त्रासदस्यवम्॥३२॥

32. We, the Sobharis, have come to the thousand rayed, the
sincerely worshipped, the universal sovereign, the ally of
Trasadasyu, for his protection.

६४५४. यस्य ते अग्ने अन्ये अग्नयं उपक्षितो वयाइव।
विपो न द्युम्ना नि युवे जनानां तव क्षत्राणि वर्धयन्॥३३॥

33. *Agni*, on whom your other fires are dependent, like branches (on the stem of the tree), may I among men, magnifying your powers, become possessed, like (other) votaries, of (abundant) food.

६४५५. यमादित्यासो अद्रुहः पारं नयथ मर्त्यम्।

मघोनां विश्वेषां सुदानवः ॥३४॥

34. Benevolent and generous *Ādityas*, amidst all the offerers of oblations, the man whom you conduct to the limit (of his undertakings obtains his reward).

Whom you conduct to the Limit—The text has only *yam nayatha pāram*, "whom you lead to the opposite bank." The Scholiast supplies the rest.

६४५६. यूयं राजानः कं चिच्चर्षणीसहः क्षयन्तं मानुषाँ अनु।

वयं ते वो वरुण मित्रार्यमन्त्स्यामेदृतस्य रथ्यः ॥३५॥

35. Royal (*Ādityas*), overcomers of (hostile) men, (ye subdue) any one harassing those (who are engaged in sacred rites) and may we, *Varuṇa*, *Mitra*, and *Aryaman*, be the conveyers of the sacrifice (addressed) to you.

६४५७. अदान्मे पौरुकुत्स्यः पञ्चाशतं त्रसदस्युर्वधूनाम्।

मंहिष्ठो अर्यः सत्पतिः ॥३६॥

36. The magnificent lord, the protector of the virtuous, *Trasadasyu*, the son of *Purukutsa*, has given me five hundred brides.

६४५८. उत मे प्रयियोर्वयियोः सुवास्त्वा अधि तुग्वनि।

तिसृणां सप्ततीनां श्यावः प्रणेता भुवद्वसुर्दियानां पतिः ॥३७॥

37. The affluent *Śyāva*, the lord of kine, has given to me upon the banks of the *Suvastu* a present of seventy three (cows).

The printed edition was no comment upon this stanza. The MSS. are imperfect, especially as regards the first half line, *uta me prayiyor vayiyoḥ*. [Durga, in his comment on the *Nirukta*, explains the verse as follows, "Moreover, on the banks of the *Savāstu* (he has given) to me (plenty) of beasts of burden and garments; he, the affluent leader and lord of three seventy noble dark-coloured (cows has given them to me)." He explains *prayiyu* by *dhanam aśvādi*; *vayiyu* by *vastrādi*; *bhuvadvasuḥ* by *bhavayitā vasūnām praśāṣṭāḥ*; *śyāmavarṇānām*, scil. *gavām*.]

[सूक्त-२०]

[**ऋषि**– सोभरि काण्व। **देवता**– मरुद्गण। **छन्द**– प्रगाथ (विषमा ककुप्,
समासतो बृहती।]

६४५९. आ गन्ता मा रिषण्यत प्रस्थावानो माप॑ स्थाता समन्यवः।
स्थिरा॑ चिन्नमयिष्णवः॥१॥

1. Far-travelling (winds), alike wrathful, come hither, harm us
not: benders of the solid (mountains), withdraw not from us.

६४६०. वील्लुपविभिर्मरुत ऋभुक्षण आ रुद्रास॑: सुदीतिभिः।
इषा नो॑ अद्या गता॑ पुरुस्पृहो यज्ञमा सौभरीयवः॥२॥

2. Mighty sons of *Rudra*, *Maruts*, come with brilliant, strong-
wheeled (chariots): desired of many, well disposed to Sobhari,
come to-day to our sacrifice with (abundant) food.

६४६१. विद्मा हि रुद्रियाणां शुष्ममुग्रं मरुतां शिमीवताम्।
विष्णोरेषस्य॑ मील्हुषाम्॥३॥

3. We know the great strength of the active sons of *Rudra*, the
Maruts, the shedders of the diffusive rain.

Shedder of the Diffusive Rain— *Viṣṇor mīḷhuṣām* is explained
vyāptasya eṣaṇīyasya vṛṣṭyudakasya eṣasya sektṛṇām.

६४६२. वि द्वीपानि॑ पाप॑तन्तिष्ठदुच्छुनोभे युञ्जन् रोद॑सी।
प्र धन्वान्यैरत शुभ्रखादयो यदेज॑थ स्वभानवः॥४॥

4. They fall upon the island: the firm-set (trees) are with
difficulty sustained; they agitate both heaven and earth; they urge
on the waters: bright-weaponed, far-shining, whatever (you
approach) you cause to tremble.

Sāyaṇa seems to explain this verse, "The islands fall asunder, the
firmest (trees) experience distress; they (the winds) distress heaven and
earth; the water hurry onward, O bright-weaponed, self-shining ones,
when you agitate them."

६४६३. अच्युता चिद्वो॑ अज्मन्ना नान॑दति पर्वतासो वनस्पतिः।
भूमिर्यामेषु रेजते॥५॥

5. At your coming the unprecipitated mountains and trees
resound; the earth shakes at your passage.

६४६४. अमाय वो मरुतो यातवे द्यौर्जिहीत उत्तरा बृहत्।

यत्रा नरो देदिशते तनूष्वा त्वक्षांसि बाह्वोजसः॥६॥

6. (Alarmed) at your violence, *Maruts*, the heaven seeks to rise higher, abandoning the firmament, where (you) the strong-armed leaders (of rites) display the ornaments of (your) persons.

६४६५. स्वधामनु श्रियं नरो महि त्वेषा अर्मवन्तो वृषप्सवः।

वहन्ते अह्रुतप्सवः॥७॥

7. The radiant, strong, rain-shedding, undisguised leaders of rites display their great glory when accepting the (sacrificial) food.

६४६६. गोभिर्वाणो अज्यते सोभरीणां रथे कोशे हिरण्यये।

गोबन्धवः सुजातास इषे भुजे महान्तो नः स्परसे नु॥८॥

8. The voice (of the *Maruts*) blends with the songs of the Sobharis in the receptacle of their golden chariot: may the mighty well-born *Maruts*, the offspring of the (brindled) cow, (be gracious) to us regard of food, enjoyment, and kindness.

The Voice— Sāyaṇa explains *vāṇa* as "the lute," *vīṇā*.

६४६७. प्रति वो वृषदञ्जयो वृष्णे शर्धाय मारुताय भरध्वम्।

हव्या वृषप्रयाव्णे॥९॥

9. Sprinklers of the libation, present the offerings to the rain-bestowing swift-passing company of the *Maruts*.

६४६८. वृषणश्वेन मरुतो वृषप्सुना रथेन वृषनाभिना।

आ श्येनासो न पक्षिणो वृथा नरो हव्या नो वीतये गत॥१०॥

10. *Maruts* leaders (of rites), come like swift-flying birds in your rain-shedding, strong-horsed chariot, whose wheels bestow showers, to partake of our oblations.

६४६९. समानमञ्ज्यैषां वि भ्राजन्ते रुक्मासो अधि बाहुषु।

दविद्युतत्यृष्टयः॥११॥

11. Their decoration is the same; gold (necklaces) shine (on their breasts), lances gleam upon their shoulders.

६४७०. त उग्रासो वृषण उग्रबाहवो नकिष्टनूषु येतिरे।

स्थिरा धन्वान्यायुधा रथेषु वोऽनीकेष्वधि श्रियः॥१२॥

12. Fierce, givorous, strong-armed, they need not exert (the energy of their) persons: bows and arrows are leady in your chariots; the glory (of conquest) over (hostile) armies is yours.

They need not Exert the Energy, Etc.— Or rather, ''they need not exert themselves to defend their persons,'' *nakistanūsu yetire.*

६४७१. येषामर्णो न सप्रथो नाम त्वेषं शश्वतामेकमिद्धुजे।
वयो न पित्र्यं सहः॥१३॥

13. One illustrious name is given to them all, as widely diffused as water for the gratification (of their worshippers), like invigorating paternal food.

Like invigorating Paternal Food— *Vayo na pitryam sahaḥ.* The latter is explained *prasahanasīlam,* but the exect purport is not very obvious; apparently, it is intended to say that the worshipper may rely upon it.

६४७२. तान्वन्दस्व मरुतस्ताँ उप स्तुहि तेषां हि धुनीनाम्।
अराणां न चरमस्तदेषां दाना मह्रा तदेषाम्॥१४॥

14. Praise them, praise the *Maruts,* for we are (dependent) upon those agitators (of all things) as a menial is upon his lords; therefore are their donations (characterized) by munificence; such are their (gifts).

६४७३. सुभगः स व ऊतिष्वास पूर्वासु मरुतो व्युष्टिषु।
यो वां नूनमुतासति॥१५॥

15. Fortunate was he, *Maruts,* who, in former days, was secure in your protections, as is he who now enjoys them.

६४७४. यस्य वा यूयं प्रति वाजिनो नर आ हव्या वीतये गथ।
अभि ष द्युम्नैरुत वाजसातिभिः सुम्ना वो धूतयो नशत्॥१६॥

16. The sacrificer, to partake of whose oblations you approach, leaders of rites, enjoys, agitators of all things, the felicity you bestow, together with abundant viands, and the gift of strength.

६४७५. यथा रुद्रस्य सूनवो दिवो वशन्त्यसुरस्य वेधसः।
युवानस्तथेदसत्॥१७॥

17. May this (our praise) take effect, so that the ever-youthful sons of *Rudra,* creators of the cloud, (coming) from heaven, may be pleased with us.

६४७६. ये चाहॅन्ति मरुतः सुदानवः स्मन्मीळ्हुषश्चरन्ति ये।

अतॅश्चिदा न उप वस्यॅसा हृदा युवानं आ ववृध्वम्॥१८॥

18. Youthful (*Maruts*), approaching us with benevolent hearts, grant prosperity to those liberal men who worship you, who zealously propitiate you, the showerers of rain, with oblations.

६४७७. यूनं ऊ षु नविष्ठया वृष्णः पावकाँ

अभि सौभरे गिरा। गाय गाइव चर्कृषत्॥१९॥

19. Praise, *Sobhari*, (and attract hither) by a new song the youthful purifying showerers, as (a ploughman) repeatedly drags his oxen.

As a Ploughman, Etc.— Sāyaṇa says, "as a ploughman repeatedly drawing the furrows (praises or addresses) of his oxen."

६४७८. साहा ये सन्ति मुष्टिहेव हव्यो विश्वासु पृत्सु होतृषु।

वृष्णॅश्चन्द्रान् सुश्रवॅस्तमान् गिरा वन्दस्व मरुतो अहं॥२०॥

20. Propitiate with praise the *Maruts*, the senders of rain, the givers of pleasure, the liberal bestowers of food; who are ever victorious in combats, and like a boxer who has been challenged over his challengers.

The Liberal Bestowers of Food— Or, "the most illustrious," *suśravastamān*—Sāyaṇa explains the latter clause, "who are ever victorious in combats and ever challengers, like a challenge-worthy boxer."

६४७९. गावॅश्चिद्घा समन्यवः सजात्येॅन मरुतः सबन्धवः।

रिहते ककुभों मिथः॥२१॥

21. *Maruts*, who are of like wrath, offspring of the maternal cow (*Pṛśni*), related by a common origin, they severally spread through the quarters of the horizon.

Sāmaveda, 404. [Or rather, "Or *Maruts*, alike in energy, your kindred, the cows, severally lick up the quarters of the horizon." Benfey understands by *gavāḥ*, sun's rays.]

६४८०. मतॅश्चिद्धो नृतवो रुक्मवक्षस उपॅ भ्रातृत्वमायॅति।

अधि नो गात मरुतः सदा हि वं आपित्वमस्ति निर्धुवि॥२२॥

22. *Maruts*, dancing (through the air), decorated with golden breast-plates, the mortal (who worships you) attains your brotherhood; speak favourably to us, for your affinity is ever (made known) at the regulated (sacrifice).

६४८१. मरुतो मारुतस्य न॒ आ भैषजस्य॑ वहता सुदानवः।
यू॒यं सं॒खायः॒ सप्तयः॑॥२३॥

23. Generous fiends, *Maruts*, swift gliding (through the air),
bring to us (the boon) of the medicaments that belong to your
company.

६४८२. याभिः॑ सिन्धुम॑व॒थ याभि॒स्तूर्वथ॑ याभि॒र्दश॑स्यथा क्रि॒विम्।
म॒यो॒ नो भू॒तोति॑भि॒र्मयो॑भुवः॒ शि॒वाभि॑रसच॒द्द्विषः॑॥२४॥

24. With those auspicious protections with which you have
guarded the ocean, with which you have destroyed (your enemies),
with which you provided the well (for Gotama), do you who are
the sources of happiness, the unconquerable by your adversaries,
bestow happiness upon us.

The Unconquerable by your Adversaries— *Sāyaṇa* explains
asasacadviṣaḥ as *śatrurahitaḥ,* "destitute of enemies."—For *Gotama,*
see vol. I, *mantra* 945.

६४८३. यत्सिन्धौ॒ यद॒सिक्न्यां॑ यत्स॑मु॒द्रेषु॑ मरुतः॒ सुब॑र्हिषः।
यत्प॒र्वते॑षु॒ भेष॒जम्॥२५॥

25. Whatever medicament there may be in the *Sindhu,* the
Asikni, in the oceans, in the mountains, *Maruts,* who are gratified
by sacrifice,—

६४८४. विश्वं॑ पश्य॑न्तो बिभृथा त॒नूष्वा तेना॑ नो॒ अधि॑ वोचत।
क्ष॒मा र॒पो म॑रुत॒ आतु॑रस्य न॒ इष्क॑र्ता॒ विहु॑तं॒ पुनः॑॥२६॥

26. Do you, beholding every sort, collect them for (the good
of) our bodies, and instruct us in their (uses): let the cure of
sickness (be the portion), *Maruts,* of him amongst us who for his
wickedness is sick; re-establish his enfeebled (frame).

The *Sūktas* of this *Adhyāya* are, for the most part simple. This last has
exceptions.

[सूक्त-२१]

[**ऋषि–** सोभरि काण्व। **देवता–** इन्द्र, १७-१८ चित्र। **छन्द–** प्रगाथ (विषमा
ककुप्, समासतो बृहती।]

६४८५. वयमु॑ त्वाम॑पूर्व्य स्थू॒रं न कच्चि॑द्भर॒न्तोऽव॑स्यवः।
वाजे॑ चि॒त्रं ह॑वामहे॥१॥

1. Unpreceded *Indra*, cherishing you (with sacrificial food), desirous of your protection, we invoke you who are manifold in battle, as (men call upon) some stout (person for help).

As Men Call upon some Stout Person for Help— *Vāje citram, saṅgrāme vividharūpam;* 'he printed *Sāman*, 408 [I.5.1.2.10; II.1.1.22.1.]. (Benfey), reads *vajrin*, "thunderer," for *vāje—Yathā Vrīhyādibhir grham pūrayanto janā annaviṣaye sthūlam guṇādhikam kañcit mānavam āhvayanti,* "as people filling a house with rice and the like call upon some stout, liberal man for food," is the commentator's amplification of the last clause.

Unpreceded—*Apūrvya* is explained "new," *i.e.*, ever new at the three oblations.

६४८६. उप त्वा कर्मन्नूतये स नो युवोग्रश्चक्राम यो धृषत्।
त्वामिद्ध्यवितारं ववृमहे सखाय इन्द्र सानसिम्।।२।।

2. We have recourse, *Indra*, to you for protection at sacred rites: may he who is ever young, fierce, resolute, come to us! We, your friends, *Indra*, rely upon you as our protector and benefactor.
Sāmaveda, 709.

६४८७. आ याहीम इन्द्वोऽश्वपते गोपत उर्वरापते। सोमं सोमपते पिब।।३।।

3. Lord of horses, of cattle, of corn-land, these libations (are for you); come, lord of the *Soma*, drink the effused *Soma* juice.

६४८८. वयं हि त्वा बन्धुमन्तमबन्धवो विप्रास इन्द्र येमिम।
या ते धामानि वृषभ तेभिरा गहि विश्वेभिः सोमपीतये।।४।।

4. Intelligent, but destitute of kin, let us connect ourselves, *Indra*, with you, who abound with kinsmen: come, showerer (of benefits,) with all your glories, to drink the *Soma*.

Intelligent but Destitute of Kin— Or rather, "we your worshippers (*viprāsaḥ*), destitute of kin."

६४८९. सीदन्तस्ते वयो यथा गोश्रीते मधौ मदिरे विवक्षणे।
अभि त्वामिन्द्र नोनुमः।।५।

5. Gathering like (a flock of) birds round your exhilarating heaven-bestowing *Soma* beverage mixed with curds, we repeatedly glorify you, *Indra*.

Sāmaveda, 407. *Vivakṣaṇe* is explained by Sāyaṇa *svargaprāpaṇaśīle*, "causing to obtain *svarga*.

६४९०. अच्छा च त्वैना नमसा वदामसि किं मुहुश्चिद्धि दीधयः।
सन्ति कामासो हरिवो ददिष्ट्वं स्मो वयं सन्ति नो धियः।।६।।

6. We salute you with this adoration: why do you so oft mediate (upon our requests)? Master of bay steeds, let our desires be granted. You are their bestower, we are your (suppliants) and our sacred rites are (addressed to you).

६४९१. नूला इदिन्द्र ते वयमूती अभूम नहि नू तें अद्रिवः।

विद्या पुरा परीणसः ॥७॥

7. We verily are the most recent (objects) of your protection, *Indra*, wielder of the thunderbolt; we have not known of old one greater than you.

We have not Known, Etc.— Sāyaṇa seems to render this latter clause "we knew you not formerly as the mighty one (but now we know you)."

६४९२. विद्या सखित्वमुत शूर भोज्यइमा ते ता वज्रिन्नीमहे।

उतो संमस्मिन्रा शिशीहि नो वसो वाजे सुशिप्र गोमति ॥८॥

8. We acknowledge, hero, your friendship, (the wealth) to be enjoyed through you, and solicit both, thunderer, of you: giver of dwellings, *Indra* of the handsome jaws, sustain us in all abundance and in (store of) cattle.

६४९३. यो न इदमिदं पुरा प्र वस्यं आनिनाय तमु वः स्तुषे।

सखाय इन्द्रमूतये ॥९॥

9. I glorify friends, for your protection, that *Indra* who has brought to us of old this or that excellent (wealth).

Sāmaveda, 400.

६४९४. स वयति गव्यमश्व्यं स्तोतृभ्यो मघवा शतम् ॥१०॥

10. That man glorifies *Indra*, the lord of bay steeds, the protector of the good, the overcomer of enemies, who rejoices (in the fulfilment of his wishes): may *Maghavan* bestow upon us, his worshippers, hundreds of cattle and horses.

६४९५. त्वया ह स्विद्युजा वयं प्रति श्वसन्तं वृषभ ब्रुवीमहि।

संस्थे जनस्य गोमतः ॥११॥

11. With you, showerer (of benefits), for our ally, we bid defiance to one assailing us in a contest (on behalf) of a man possessing herds of cattle.

Sāmaveda, 403.

६४९६. जयेम कारे पुरुहूत कारिणोऽभि तिष्ठेम दूढ्यः।
नृभिर्वृत्रं हन्याम शूशुयाम चावैरिन्द्र प्र णो धियः॥१२॥

12. *Indra*, invoked of many, may we conquer in battle those
contending against us; may we resist the malignant; may we, aided
by the leaders (of rites, the *Maruts*), slay *Vṛtra*; may we be
prosperious, and do you protect our pious works.

The Leaders of Rites—Sāyaṇa explains *nṛbhiḥ* as "wielders of
weapons," *āyudhanetṛbhiḥ*, and *vṛtra* as "the enemy."

६४९७. अभ्रातृव्यो अना त्वमनापिरिन्द्र जनुषा सनादसि।
युधेदापित्वमिच्छसे॥१३॥

13. You, *Indra*, are by your birth brotherless: from ever are
you without a kinsman: the kindred you desire is (that of him) who
engages in war.

Sāmaveda, 399-1389. [Sāyaṇa renders this verse thus, "You, *Indra*,
by your birth are from eternity without a foe, without a controller, without
a kinsman; you desire to show your kinsmanship only by war," *i.e.*, it is
only by fighting that you are the friend of your worshippers.]

६४९८. नकी रेवन्तं सख्याय विन्दसे पीयन्ति ते सुराश्वः।
यदा कृणोषि नदनुं समूहस्यादित्पितेव हूयसे॥१४॥

14. You acknowledge no friendship for the wealthy man (who
makes no offerings); those who are puffed up with wine offened
you: when you institute (the sacrifice), you expelled niggardliness,
and you are invoked as a protector.

Surāśvaḥ, surayā vṛddhāḥ paramattāḥ, intoxicated; or *nāstikāḥ*,
Atheists. For the second line, beginning *Yadā kṛṇoṣi nadanum samūhasi*,
the printed edition gives no commentary. One MS. reads (but no doubt
from some interpolator's hand), Yadā *mānavasya dānādirāhityam
samūhasi nirākaroṣi yastṛītvam karoṣi*, "when you expelled the neglect
of gifts of a man, you make the sacrificing"; but the construction is
questionable. [The verse occurs in *Sāmaveda*, 1390; and Sāyaṇa there
explains the clause, *Yadā kṛṇoṣi nadanum samūhasi*, "when you utter the
inarticulate sound of approbation (to the worshipper, implying, 'He is
mine'), you bring him (wealth)." See Benfey's translation, note.
Professor Müller thus translates the whole verse, *Ancient Sanskrit Lit.*,
p.542, "You never find a rich man to be your friend; wine-swillers
despise you; but when you thunder, when you gather (the clouds), then
you are called like a father."]

As a Protector— Or, "as a father," *pitā iva*.

६४९९. मा ते अमाजुरो यथा मूरास इन्द्र सख्ये त्वावतः।
नि षदाम सचा सुते ॥१५॥

15. Let us not, like foods, *Indra*, be regardless of the friendship of such as you are; let us assemble together when the libation is effused.

Let us not, Like Fools— Sāyaṇa interprets this, "Let not us who are your, *Indra*, be desolate as those who are ignorant of the friendship of such as you are *mā te amājuro yathā mūrāsa indra sakhye tvāvataḥ*. He explains *amājuraḥ* as *gṛhaiḥ putraiḥ dhanādibhiśca saha jīrṇāḥ*.

६५००. मा ते गोदत्र निरराम राधस इन्द्र मा ते गृहामहि।
दृ॒ळ्हा चिदर्यः प्र मृशाभ्या भर न ते दामान आदभे ॥१६॥

16. Let us never, *Indra*, giver of cattle, cease (to benefit) from your wealth; let us not accept it (from another than) you: do you, who are the lord, confirm to us permanent (riches), bestow them upon us; your benefactions cannot be arrested.

Another than you— Sāyaṇa explains *te,* as in the previous verse, *vayam tava svabhūtāḥ*, "we who are thine."

६५०१. इन्द्रो वा घेदियन्मघं सरस्वती वा सुभगा ददिर्वसु।
त्वं वा चित्र दाशुषे ॥१७॥

17. Is it *Indra* who has given to the donor (of the oblation) so much affluence? Is it the auspicious *Sarasvatī* (who has given) the treasure? Or, *Citra*, is it you?

६५०२. चित्र इद्राजा राजका इदन्यके यके सरस्वतीमनु।
पर्जन्यइव ततनद्धि वृष्ट्या सहस्रमयुता ददत् ॥१८॥

18. Verily the *Rājā Citra*, giving his thousands and tens of thousands, has overspread (with his bounty) those other petty princes, who rules along the *Sarasvatī*, as *Parjanya* (overspreads the earth) with rain.

[सूक्त-२२]

[**ऋषि**– सोभरि काण्व। **देवता**– अश्विनीकुमार। **छन्द**– प्रगाथ (विषमा बृहती, समासतो बृहती) ७ बृहती, ८ अनुष्टुप्, ११ ककुप्, १२ मध्येज्योति (त्रिष्टुप्), ९-१०, १३-१८ प्रगाथ (विषमा ककुप्, समासतो बृहती) बृहती।]

६५०३. ओ त्यमह्व आ रथमद्या दंसिष्ठमूतये।
यमश्विना सुहवा रुद्रवर्तनी आ सूर्यायै तस्थथुः ॥१॥

1. I invoke to-day for our protection that splendid chariot, which, adorable *Aśvins*, advancing on the path to battle, you ascended (to go to the wedding) of *Sūrya*.

On the Path to Battle— *Rudravartani,* explained as "having a path which causes weeping in battle," of "whose paths are praised."

६५०४. पूर्वायुषं सुहवं पुरुस्पृहं भुज्युं वाजेषु पूर्व्यम्।
सचनावन्तं सुमतिभिः सोभरे विद्वेषसमनेहसम्॥२॥

2. Celebrate, *Sobhari*, with praises (that chariot), the benefactor of former (encomiasts), the worthily invoked, the desired of many, the preserver, the foremost in battles, the relied upon by all, the scatterer of enemies, the exempt from ill.

६५०५. इह त्या पुरुभूतमा देवा नमोभिरश्विना।
अर्वाचीना स्ववसे करामहे गन्तारा दाशुषो गृहम्॥३॥

3. We incite by our adorations on this occasion the two divine *Aśvins*, the overcomers of foes, that they may come down for our protection and proceed to the dwelling of the donor (of the offering).

६५०६. युवो रथस्य परि चक्रमीयत ईर्मान्यद्वामिषण्यति।
अस्माँ अच्छा सुमतिवाँ शुभस्पती आ धेनुरिव धावतु॥४॥

4. One of the wheels of your car moves in every direction; the other, impellers of actions, remains with you: may your favour, lords of rain, hasten towards us a cow (to her calf)!

Impellers of Actions— *Irmā* is explained *antaryā mitayā prerakau,* "urgers, or impellers, by the property of internal influence or conscience"; or it may mean *udakasya prerayitārau,* "senders of water or rain." [For the two wheels, see vol. I, *mantra* 347].

६५०७. रथो यो वां त्रिवन्धुरो हिरण्याभीशुरश्विना।
परि द्यावापृथिवी भूषति श्रुतस्तेन नासत्या गतम्॥५॥

5. Your celebrated chariot, *Aśvins*, that is three banked, and caparisoned with gold, graces heaven and earth: come with it, *Nāsatyās*.

Three-Banked— Sāyaṇa explains *trivandhura* as "having three seats," or "having two poles, and a bar between them for fastening the harness," *vandhura* being *sārathisthānam* or *dve iṣe tanmadhye rajjusajjanārthako daṇḍaḥ.*

६५०८. दशस्यन्ता मनवे पूर्व्यं दिवि यवं वृकेण कर्षथः।

ता वामद्य सुमतिभिः शुभस्पती अश्विना प्र स्तुवीमहि।।६।।

6. Bestowing upon *Manu* the ancient (rain) from the firmament, you enabled him to cultivate (the soil) with the plough (and reap) the barely: now therefore, *Aśvins*, lords of rain, we glorify you both with praises.

And Reap the Barley— The text has *yavam vṛkena karṣathaḥ*, "you till with the plough barley."

६५०९. उप नो वाजिनीवसू यातमृतस्य पथिभिः।

येभिस्तृक्षिं वृषणा त्रासदस्यवं महे क्षत्राय जिन्वथः।।७।।

7. Rich in food, *Aśvins*, come to us by the paths of sacrifice, those by which showerers (of benefits), you went to gratify *Tṛkṣi*, the son of *Trasadasyu*, with vast wealth.

६५१०. अयं वामद्रिभिः सुतः सोमो नरा वृषण्वसू।

आ यातं सोमपीतये पिबतं दाशुषो गृहे।।८।।

8. Leaders (of rites), affluent in rain, this *Soma* has been expressed by the (grinding) stones for you; come to drink the *Soma*, drink it in the dwelling of the donor.

६५११. आ हि रुहतमश्विना रथे कोशे हिरण्यये वृषण्वसू।

युञ्जाथां पीवरीरिषः।।९।।

9. *Aśvins*, who are rich in rain, ascend your golden chariot, a storehouse (of weapons); bring to us fattening food.

Flattening— *Pīvariḥ*, according to Sāyaṇa, "purifying," or "stout"; *pāvayitṛṇi sthūlāni vā* (*annam*).

६५१२. याभिः पक्थमवथो याभिरध्रिगुं याभिर्बभ्रुं विजोषसम्।

ताभिर्नो मक्षू तूर्यमश्विना गतं भिषज्यतं यदातुरम्।।१०।।

10. With those protections with which you have defended *Paktha*, *Adhrigu*, and *Babhru*, when propitiating you, come to us, *Aśvins*, quickly; administer medicine to the sick.

६५१३. यदध्रिगावो अध्रिगू इदा चिदह्नो अश्विना हवामहे।

वयं गीर्भिर्विपन्यवः।।११।।

11. At the time when hurrying, devout, we invoke you both speedily going to battle, at the dawn of day, with our hymns.

Hurrying, Devout, Etc.— The terms are unusual *yad adhrigāvo adhrigū havāmahe*. The first is explained, *karmasu tvaramāṇāḥ,* "hastening to acts of worship"; the second, *śatruvadhārtham saṅgrāme tvarayā gacchantau; adhrigū* being explained etymoligically *adhṛtagamanau,* "whose going is unwith held."

६५१४. ताभिरा यातं वृषणोप मे हवं विश्वप्सुं विश्ववार्यम्। इषा मंहिष्ठा पुरुभूतमा नरा याभि: क्रिविं वावृधुस्ताभिरा गेतम्॥१२॥

12. Then, showerers, come to my manifold all-propitiating in vocation with those (protections), with which, leaders (of rites), you, who are gratified (by oblations), munificent (in gifts), and the overcomers of numerous (foes), gave augmentation to the well; with such (protections) come hither.

Gave Augmentation to the Well— See i. 112. 5. and note. [The *Aśvins* miraculously filled the well with water, and so rescued *Vandana*.]

६५१५. ताविदा चिदहानां ताविश्विना वन्दमान उप ब्रुवे।

ता ऊ नमोभिरीमहे॥१३॥

13. I address the *Aśvins*, glorifying them at break of day; we solicit them with oblations.

६५१६. ताविद्दोषा ता उषसि शुभस्पती ता यार्मनुद्रवर्तनी।

मा नो मर्ताय रिपवे वाजिनीवसू परो रुद्रावति ख्यतम्॥१४॥

14. We adore those lords of water, leaders on the road of battle, in the evening, at dawn, and at mid-day; therefore, *Rudras* who are rich in food, give us not up hereafter to a mortal adversary.

रुद्रवर्तनी- युद्धे रोदनशीलमार्गौ, स्तूयमानमार्गौ वा।

६५१७. आ सुगम्याय सुग्म्यं प्राता रथेनाश्विना वा सक्षणी।

हुवे पितेव सोभरी॥१५॥

15. Adorable *Aśvins*, bring in your chariot at early dawn happiness to me, soliciting happiness: I, *Sobhari*, invoke you as (did my) father.

६५१८. मनोजवसा वृषणा मदच्युता मक्षुङ्गमाभिरूतिभि:।

आरात्ताच्चिद्भूतमस्मे अर्वसे पूर्वीभि: पुरुभोजसा॥१६॥

16. (*Aśvins*,), who are swift as thought, the showerers (of benefits), prostrators of the arrogant, the givers of enjoyment to many, be ever nigh unto us, for our security, with many and prompt protections.

६५१९. आ नो अश्वावदश्विना वर्तिर्यासिष्टं मधुपातमा नरा।

गोमद्दस्रा हिरण्यवत्।।१७।।

17. *Aśvins*, of goodly aspect, leaders (of rites), deep drinkers of the *Soma* juice, come to our dwelling abounding with horses, with cattle, with gold.

६५२०. सुप्रावर्गं सुवीर्यं सुष्टु वार्यमनाधृष्टं रक्षस्विनां।

अस्मिन्ना वामायानें वाजिनीवसू विश्वां वामानि धीमहि।।१८।।

18. May we obtain from you (wealth) spontaneously bestowed, comprising excellent strength, such as is desired by all, and unassailable by a powerful (foe): may we obtain from you who are rich in food, upon you coming hither, all good things.

[सूक्त- २३]

[ऋषि– विश्वमना वैयश्व। **देवता**– अग्नि। **छन्द**– उष्णिक्।]

६५२१. ईळिष्वा हि प्रतीव्यं१ यजस्व जातवेदसम्।

चरिष्णुधूममगृभीतशोचिषम्।।१।।

1. Adore him who resists (our foes), worship *Jātavedas* the diffuser of smoke, of unobstructed radiance.

Who Resists our Foes— *Prativyam, śatruṣu pratigamana-śīlam agnim; Agni,* who has the property of going against enemies. *Sāmaveda,* 102.

६५२२. दामानं विश्वचर्षणेऽग्निं विश्वमनो गिरा।

उत स्तुषे विष्पर्धसो रथानाम्।।२।।

2. Commend with praise, all-beholding *Viśvamanas,* that *Agni,* who is the giver of chariots to the unenvious (worshipper).

६५२३. येषामाबाध ऋग्मियं इषः पृक्षश्च निग्रभे।

उपविदा वह्निर्विन्दते वसु।।३।।

3. The repeller (of foes), the glorified by hymns, arrests the food and drink, and the bearer of oblations takes away the wealth (of those) of whom he foreknows (the neglect of sacrifice).

Takes away the Wealth of those, Etc.— *Upavidā vindate vasu* is all the text has. The Scholiast explains the first by *upavedanena,* by proximate knowing, that is, *ete havīṁṣi devārtham na prayacchantītyetajñānena teṣām eva dhanam labhate,* "These to not give oblations to the gods"; by this knowledge he takes their wealth. [Sāyaṇa seems to understand the latter part, "those non-sacrificers, whose food and its juices he arrests (sc. as not digesting them?), their wealth, too, he takes away by his divine knowledge (of their guilt)."

६५२४. उद॑स्य शोचि॑रस्थाद्दी॒दियुषो॒ व्यं१श्जर॑म् ।

तपु॑र्जम्भस्य सु॒द्युतो॒ गण॒श्रिय॑:॥४॥

4. The imperishable lustre rises of that *Agni*, who is radiant, bright with blazing teeth, resplendent, and glorious amidst troops (of worshippers).

Troops of Worshippers— *Gaṇaśriyaḥ* is explained by Sāyaṇa "who visits troops of worshippers to take their oblations."

६५२५. उदु॑ तिष्ठ स्व॒ध्व॑र॒ स्तवा॑नो दे॒व्या कृ॒पा ।

अभि॒ख्या भा॒सा बृ॒ह॒ता शु॒शु॒क्वनि॑:॥५॥

5. Rise up with celestial splendour, you who are radiant with great and present lustre, who are worthily worshipped and glorified.

६५२६. अग्ने॑ या॒हि सु॒शस्ति॑भि॒र्हव्या॒ जुह्वा॑न आनु॒षक् ।

यथा॑ दू॒तो ब॒भूथ॑ हव्य॒वाह॑न:॥६॥

6. Proceed, *Agni*, with pious praises, offering in due order the oblations (to the gods), for you are their messenger, the bearer of oblations.

६५२७. अ॒ग्निं व॑: पू॒र्व्यं हु॑वे॒ होता॑रं चर्ष॒णीना॑म् ।

तम॒या वा॒चा गृ॑णे॒ तमु॑ व॒: स्तुषे॑॥७॥

7. I invoke for you, (worshippers), *Agni*, the ancient ministrant priest of man, I praise him with this hymn, I glorify him for you.

६५२८. य॒ज्ञेभि॑रद्भु॒तक्र॑तुं॒ यं कृ॒पा सू॒दय॑न्त॒ इत् ।

मि॒त्रं न॒ जने॑ सु॒धित॒मृता॒वनि॑॥८॥

8. (Worship him who is) of wondrous works, who, gladdened (by offerings), is present like a friend, whom (the priests) by their sacrifices, according to their power, render propitious to the worshipper.

६५२९. ऋ॒ताव॑नम॒मृता॑य॒वो य॒ज्ञस्य॒ साध॑नं गि॒रा । उ॒पो ए॒नं ज॑जुषु॒र्नम॑स॒स्पदे॑॥९॥

9. Pious worshippers, at the place of offerings adore with praise him who is gratified by worship, the completer of the sacrifice.

Adore with Praise— The text has *jujuṣuḥ,* ''they have adored''; but the Scholiast renders it *upāsevadhvam,* expressly stating that the first (the third) person is here put for the second, *madhyamapuruṣasya prathamapuruṣādeśaḥ.*

६५३०. अच्छा नो अङ्गिरस्तमं यज्ञासो यन्तु संयतः।

होता यो अस्ति विक्ष्वा यशस्तमः॥१०॥

10. Let our sacrificers, prepared (with their implements), present themselves before the chief of the *Angirasas,* who is the most renowned offerer of oblations amongst men.

Sacrifices— Or ''sacrifices,'' *yajñaḥ.*

६५३१. अग्ने तव त्ये अजरेन्धानासो बृहद्भाः।

अश्वाइव वृषणस्तविषीयवः॥११॥

11. These your vast blazing flames, undecaying *Agni,* are most powerful, vigorous as horses.

६५३२. स त्वं न ऊर्जां पते रयिं रास्व सुवीर्यम्।

प्रावं नस्तोके तनये समत्स्वा॥१२॥

12. Do you, who are the lord of food, give us riches, with male offspring: defend us, with our sons and grandsons, in battles.

Defend us, Etc.— Or, as Sāyaṇa seems to say, ''defend our wealth, consisting in sons and grandsons, and what has to be guarded in battles.

६५३३. यद्वा उ विश्पतिः शितः सुप्रीतो मनुषो विशि।

विश्वेदग्निः प्रति रक्षांसि सेधति॥१३॥

13. When *Agni,* the lord of man, is sharpened (by sacrifice), and, well pleased, is present in the abode of a man, he verily defends it against all evil spirits.

Sāmaveda, 114.

६५३४. श्रुष्ट्यग्ने नवस्य मे स्तोमस्य वीर विश्पते।

नि मायिनस्तपुषा रक्षसो दह॥१४॥

14. Hero, *Agni,* lord of men, hearing this my present praise, consume the guileful *Rākṣasas* by your flames.

Sāmaveda, 106.

६५३५. न तस्य माययां चन रिपुरीशीत मर्त्यः।

यो अग्नये ददाश हव्यदातिभिः॥१५॥

15. No hostile mortal shall have power by fraud over him who by the (sacred) offerers of the oblation presents (offerings) to *Agni*. *Sāmaveda*, 104.

६५३६. व्यश्वस्त्वा वसुविदमुक्षण्युरप्रीणादृषिः।

महो राये तमु त्वा समिधीमहि।।१६।।

16. The *Ṛṣi Vyaśva*, desirous (of propitiating) the showerer (of rain), has gratified you, the bestower of wealth; so we too kindle you for (the acquirement of) ample riches.

६५३७. उशना काव्यस्त्वा नि होतारमसादयत्।

आयजिं त्वा मनवे जातवेदसम्।।१७।।

17. *Uśanā*, the son of *Kavi*, has established you, *Jātavedas*, as the ministrant priest, you as the offerer of sacrifice, for *Manu*.

६५३८. विश्वे हि त्वा सजोषसो देवासो दूतमक्रत।

श्रुष्टी देव प्रथमो यज्ञियो भुवः।।१८।।

18. All the consentient gods have made you their messenger; may you, divine *Agni*, who are the first (of the deities), quickly become the object of their worship.

Mayest you, Etc.— Sāyaṇa seems to take it, "may you quickly become worthy of the sacrifice, (as bearing our oblations to them)."

६५३९. इमं घा वीरो अमृतं दूतं कृण्वीत मर्त्यः।

पावकं कृष्णवर्तनिं विहायसम्।।१९।।

19. The pious mortal has appointed this immortal, purifying, dark-moving, mighty (*Agni*), his messenger.

६५४०. तं हुवेम यतस्रुचः सुभासं शुक्रशोचिषम्।

विशामग्निमजरं प्रत्नमीड्यम्।।२०।।

20. Let us with uplifted ladles invoke him, the brilliant, bright-shining, undecaying, ancient *Agni*, who is to be adored by men.

६५४१. यो अस्मै हव्यदातिभिराहुतिं मर्तोऽविधत्।

भूरि पोषं स धत्ते वीरवद्यशः।।२१।।

21. The man who by the (holy) presenters of oblations makes offerings to him, receives (from *Agni*) ample nourishment, with male progeny, and fame.

६५४२. प्रथमं जातवेदसमग्निं यज्ञेषु पूर्व्यम्।

प्रति स्रुगेति नर्मसा हविष्मती।।२२।।

22. The ladle charged with the oblation proceeds with reverence at sacrifices to the ancient *Agni*, the first (of the gods), the cognizant of all that exists.

With Reverence— Or, "with the hymn," *stotreņa namaskāreņa vā*.

६५४३. आभिर्विधेमाग्नये ज्येष्ठाभिर्व्यश्वत्।

मंहिष्ठाभिर्मतिभिः शुक्रशोचिषे।।२३।।

23. Let us, like *Vyaśva*, glorify the brilliant *Agni* with these excellent and most pious praises.

६५४४. नूनमर्च विहायसे स्तोमैभिः स्थूरयूपवत्।

ऋषे वैयश्व दम्यायाग्नये।।२४।।

24. *Ŗṣi*, son of *Vyaśva*, adore the far-spreading domestic *Agni*, with praises, like *Sthūrayūpa*.

Sthūrayūpa— Said to be the name of a *Ŗṣi*.

६५४५. अतिथिं मानुषाणां सूनुं वनस्पतीनाम्।

विप्रा अग्निमवसे प्रत्नमीळते।।२५।।

25. Pious men glorify the ancient *Agni*, the guest of men, the son of the trees, for protection.

६५४६. महो विश्वाँ अभि षतो३भि हव्यानि मानुषा।

अग्ने नि षत्सि नमसाधि बर्हिषि।।२६।।

26. Sit down, *Agni*, on the sacred grass, in the presence of all those worshippers diligent (in pious works, induced) by their veneration (to accept) the oblations of men.

६५४७. वंस्वा नो वार्या पुरु वंस्व रायः पुरुस्पृहः।

सुवीर्यस्य प्रजावतो यशस्वतः।।२७।।

27. Grant us (*Agni*) many desirable (things), grant us riches envied by many, (cimprehending) vigour, offspring, fame.

६५४८. त्वं वरो सुषाम्णेऽग्ने जनाय चोदय।

सदा वसो रातिं यविष्ठ शश्वते।।२८।।

28. *Agni*, (who are) the desired of all, the humbler (of foes), the youngest (of the gods), ever bestow riches upon the tranquil and constant man.

Upon the Tranquil and Constant Man— *Suṣāmṇe śaśvate janāya; śobhanasāmavate bahave prādurbhūtaya stotṛṇām,* is all explanation, except that to the first is added *tava prasādāt,* "who enjoys tranquillity from your (*Agni's*) favour." [Sāyaṇa may intent to explain the words as meaning "upon the various reciters of excellent hymns." The *Gaṇaratna-mahodadhi* explains *suṣāman* as *śobhanam sāma priyavacanam yasya* (*cf. Pan.* 8.3.98). In *v.* 28 of the next hymn, *suṣāman* is the name of a king.]

६५४९. त्वं हि सुप्रतूरसि त्वं नो गोमतीरिषः।

महो रायः सातिमग्ने अपां वृधि॥२९॥

29. You verily are a liberal benefactor: bestow upon us, *Agni,* food, with cattle, and the gift of abundant riches.

६५५०. अग्ने त्वं यशा अस्या मित्रावरुणा वह।

ऋतावाना सम्राजा पूतदक्षसा॥३०॥

30. You, *Agni,* are renowned; bring hither the veracious, the purely vigorous, the resplendent deities *Mitra* and *Varuṇa.*

Mitra and *Varuṇa*— This, according to Sāyaṇa, intimates the ordinary association of these two deities with *Agni* at sacrifices.

[सूक्त-२४]

[ऋषि– विश्वमना वैयश्व। देवता– इन्द्र, २८-३० वरु सौषाम्णि।

छन्द– उष्णिक्, ३० अनुष्टुप्।]

६५५१. सखाय आ शिषामहि ब्रह्मेन्द्राय वज्रिणे।

स्तुष ऊ षु वो नृतमाय धृष्णवे॥१॥

1. Let us earnestly, friends, address our prayer to *Indra,* the wielder of the thunderbolt; for you I praise the chief leader (in battles), the resolute (opposer of foes).

Sāmaveda, 390.

६५५२. शवसा ह्यसि श्रुतो वृत्रहत्येन वृत्रहा।

मघैर्मघोनो अति शूर दाशसि॥२॥

2. You are renowned for strength; from the slaying of *Vṛtra,* you are (famed as) *Vṛtrahan:* you surpassest, hero, the opulent in the donation of your riches.

६५५३. स नः स्तवान आ भर रयिं चित्रश्रवस्तमम्।

निरेके चिद्यो हरिवो वसुर्ददिः॥३॥

3. Praised by us, bestow upon us riches of wonderful variety; you, the lord of steeds, who, at the issue (of your weapons) puttest your enemies to flight, are the donor (of treasures).

At the Issue of the Weapons— *Nireke cid vasuḥ* is the text; the Scholiast explains it *tavāyudhanirgamanād eva śatravaḥ palāyante.*

६५५४. आ निरेकमुत प्रियमिन्द्र दर्षि जनानाम्।
धृषता धृष्णो स्तर्वमान आ भर ॥४॥

4. Burst open to your worshippers, *Indra*, the highly prized wealth: glorified by us, do you who are endowed with resolution, bring (us wealth) with a resolute (mind).

६५५५. न ते सव्यं न दक्षिणं हस्तं वरन्त आमुरः।
न परिबाधो हरिवो गविष्टिषु ॥५॥

5. Lord of steeds, in the recovery of the cattle the opponents resist not your left hand nor your right, your enemies (resist you) not.

६५५६. आ त्वा गोभिरिव व्रजं गीर्भिर्ऋणोम्यद्रिवः।
आ स्मा कामं जरितुरा मनः पृण ॥६॥

6. I approach you, thunderer, with praises, as (a cowherd goes) with cattle to the pasture; gratify the desire, satisfy the mind of your adorer.

६५५७. विश्वानि विश्वमनसो धिया नो वृत्रहन्तम।
उग्र प्रणेतरधि षू वसो गहि ॥७॥

7. Fierce destroyer of *Vṛtra*, bringer (of wealth to your worshippers), subduer of enemies, preside over all (the offerings) of us, *Viśvamanas*, with a (favourable) mind.

All the Offerings of Us— Sāyaṇa explains *naḥ* for *mama*, as *pūjāyāṁ bahuvacanam.*

६५५८. वयं ते अस्य वृत्रहन्विद्याम शूर नव्यसः।
वसोः स्पार्हस्य पुरुहूत राधसः ॥८॥

8. May we, hero, slayer of *Vṛtra*, invoked of many become possessed of this your new, desirable, and happiness producing wealth.

६५५९. इन्द्र यथा ह्यस्ति तेऽपरीतं नृतो शवः।
अमृक्ता रातिः पुरुहूत दाशुषे ॥९॥

9. As, *Indra*, inspirer (of men), your strength is irresistible, (so) invoked of many, your munificence to the donor (of oblations) cannot be marred.

Inspirer of Men— The attributive is *Nṛto*, voc, of *Nṛtu*, dancer, or who causes to dance, *i.e.*, agitator, exciter, from *Indra's* faculty of internal impulse in all beings, *sarvasya antaryāmitayā nartayitaḥ: cf. supra*, note on verse 4 in the 2nd *Sukta*.

६५६०. आ वृषस्व महामह महे नृतम राधसे।
दुल्हश्रिद् दूळ्ह मघवन्मघत्तये॥१०॥

10. Most adorable, chief leader (of men), invigorate (yourself with the *Soma*) for (the conquest of) great wealth: consume, *Maghavan*, the strong (cities of the *Asuras*) for the rich spoil.

६५६१. नू अन्यत्रा चिदद्रिवस्त्वन्नो जग्मुराशसं:।
मघवञ्छग्धि तव तन्न ऊतिभि:॥११॥

11. Wielder of the thunderbolt, our solicitations have been formerly addressed to other gods, than you: give us, *Maghavan*, of your (spoil, and guard it) for us with (your) protections.

६५६२. नह्यंङ्ग नृतो त्वदन्यं विन्दामि राधसे।
राये द्युम्नाय शर्वसे च गिर्वण:॥१२॥

12. Verily, impeller (of men), who are to be worshipped by praise, I apply to no other than you for sustenance, riches, reputation, and strength.

६५६३. एन्दुमिन्द्राय सिञ्चत पिबाति सोम्यं मधु।
प्र राधसा चोदयाते महित्वना॥१३॥

13. Effuse the *Soma* juice for *Indra*, let him quaff the *Soma* beverage; he by his might rewards (the donor) with wealth.

Sāmaveda, 36, 1544. The printed edition reads *vadhānsi codayate,* for the *rādhasā codayāte* of the *Ṛgveda* text.

He by his might Rewards, Etc.— Sāyaṇa explains the construction, *svamahattvenaiva annena saha dhanādikam stotṛbhyaḥ prakarṣeṇa codayati*, "he by his might abundantly sends to his worshippers wealth with food."

६५६४. उपो हरीणां पतिं दक्षं पृञ्चन्तमब्रवम्।
नूनं श्रुधि स्तुवतो अश्व्यस्य॥१४॥

14. Let me address the lord of steeds, who associates his strength (with the *Maruts*): now hear the words of the son of *Vyaśva* praising you.

Sāmaveda, 1510, reading *radhaḥ* for *dakṣam*]. *Aśvya* is explained as the son of *Aśva,* or *Vyaśva.*

६५६५. नह्यइन्द्र पुरा चन जज्ञे वीरतरस्त्वत्।
नकीं राया नैवथा न भन्दना।।१५।।

15. No one, *Indra,* has ever been born more mighty than you, no one (surpassing you) in riches; no one (more powerful) in protection; no one (more entitled) to praise.

Sāmaveda, 1411.

६५६६. एदु मध्वो मदिन्तरं सिञ्च वाध्वर्यो अन्धसः।
एवा हि वीरः स्तवते सदावृधः।।१६।।

16. Pour out, priest, the most exhilarating (draught) of the sweet (sacrificial) beverage, for he, the ever-mighty hero, alone is praised.

Sāmaveda, 385, 1684.

Evā hi vīraḥ stavate sadāvṛdhaḥ. The commentator renders in as in the translation, but he does not notice *sadāvṛdha.*

६५६७. इन्द्र स्थातर्हरीणां नकिष्टे पूर्व्यस्तुतिम्।
उदानंश शवसा न भन्दना।।१७।।

17. *Indra,* ruler of horses, no one surpasses your ancient praise, either for force or for fame.

Sāmaveda, 1685, *i.e.,* "None is mightier or more praiseworthy (or richer) than you."

६५६८. तं वो वाजानां पतिमहूमहि श्रवस्यवः।
अप्रायुभिर्यज्ञेभिर्वावृधेन्यम्।।१८।।

18. Desirous of food, we invoke your lord of viands, who is to be magnified by sacrifices (offered) by attentive (worshippers).

Sāmaveda, 1686.

६५६९. एतो न्विन्द्रं स्तवाम सखायः स्तोम्यं नरम्।
कृष्टीया विश्वा अभ्यस्त्येक इत्।।१९।।

19. Come, friends, let us glorify *Indra,* the leader, who is entitled to praise, who, single, overcomes all hostile hosts.

Sāmaveda, 387.

६५७०. अगोरुधाय गविषे द्युक्षाय दस्म्यं वचः।
घृतात्स्वादीयो मधुनश्च वोचत।।२०।।

20. Recite agreeable words, sweeter than clarified butter, or than *Soma,* to the illustious (*Indra*), who is gratified by eulogy, who rejects not praise.

६५७१. यस्यामितानि वीर्या३ न राधः पर्यैतवे।
ज्योतिर्निं विश्वमभ्यस्ति दक्षिणा।।२१।।

21. Whose energies are unbounded; whose wealth cannot be carried away, whose bounty extends like the firmament over all.

६५७२. स्तुहीन्द्रं व्यश्ववदनूर्मिं वाजिनं यममं।
अर्यो गयं मंहमानं वि दाशुषे।।२२।।

22. Glorify *Indra,* the unassailable, the powerful, the regulator (of man), as was done by *Vyaśva;* he, the lord, give a spacious dwelling to the donor (of the oblation).

To the Donor of the Oblation— Sāyaṇa explains *yamam* as *stotṛbhiḥ suniyatam,* "who is conciliated (?) by his praisers"; and *maṅhamānam gayam,* as "honourable wealth," or "a house for the worship of the gods." He gives a passive meaning to *yama,* but *cf.* viii. 103.10.

६५७३. एवा नूनमुपं स्तुहि वैर्यश्च दशमं नवमं।
सुविद्वांसं चर्कृत्यं चरणीनाम्।।२३।।

23. Praise verily at present, son of *Vyaśva,* praise (*Indra*), who is the tenth of the pervading (vital principles), the adorable, the all-wise, to be honoured repeatedly (by sacred rites).

Tenth of the Pervading Vital Principles— The text has simply *daśamam,* the tenth; in explanation of which the Scholiast cites a text which states that there are nine vital airs in the human body, and that *Indra* is the tenth; *nava vai puruṣe prāṇā manuṣyeṣu vartamānā Indras teṣām daśadhā,* etc. [*Cf. Taitt. Brāhm.* i.3.7.4. and *Taitt. Saṁh.* i.7.9]

६५७४. वेत्था हि निर्ऋतीनां वज्रहस्त परिवृजम्।
अहरहः शुन्ध्युः परिपदामिव।।२४।।

24. You are cognizant, wielder of the thunderbolt, of the departure of evil beings, as the purifying sun day by day (is of that) of the Birds) flying in all directions (from their roost).

Sāmaveda, 396.

६५७५. तदिन्द्राव आ भर येना दंसिष्ठ कृत्वने।
द्विता कुत्साय शिश्नथो नि चोदय।।२५।।

25. *Indra*, of goodly aspect, bring to the offerer (of the oblation) that (protection) wherewith to defend him you have twice slain (the foe) for Kutsa; show the same (care of us).

Show the same Care of Us— Sāyaṇa takes it, Bring to us that protection wherewith (you protect your) offerer; send to us (that protection wherewith) you have twice slain (the foe) for *Kutsa*.''

६५७६. तमु॒ त्वा॑ नू॒नमी॑महे॒ नव्यं॑ दंसिष्ठ स॒न्यसे॑।
स त्वं नो॒ विश्वा॑ अभि॒माती॑: सक्षणि॒: ॥२६॥

26. (*Indra*) of goodly aspect, we implore you who are entitled to praise, for (our) preservation; for you are the overcomer of all our adversaries.

६५७७. य ऋ॒क्षादंह॑सो मु॒चद्यो वार्या॒त्सप्त॒ सिन्धु॑षु।
वध॑र्दा॒सस्य॑ तुविनृम्ण नीनम॒: ॥२७॥

27. (He it is) who rescues men from the wickedness of evil beings, who enriches (the dwellers) on the seven rivers: now hurl, you who abound in wealth, your weapon at the *Dāsa*.

Dwellers on the Seven Rivers—*Sapta sindhuṣu, i.e.,* the dwellers on the banks of the seven rivers, the *Ganges,* etc., or on the shores of the seven seas (Sāyaṇa)

६५७८. यथा॑ वरो सु॒षाम्णे॑ स॒निभ्य॒ आव॑हो र॒यिम्।
व्यश्वे॑भ्य: सुभगे वाजिनीवति॒ ॥२८॥

28. As you, *Varu*, have distributed vast wealth to those who have solicited (riches) on behalf of *Susāman*, (so do you now distribute) to the descendants of *Vyaśva*; (and so too you), auspicious food-bestowing (*Uṣas*).

On behalf of Suṣāman— *Varu* is said to have distributed these alms that his father, *Suṣāman,* might go to heaven.

Auspicious Food-Bestowing Uṣas— The text has only *Subhage vājinīvati*. The comment supplies *Uṣas*, on the authority of *Śaunaka*. [Sāyaṇa gives an alternative rendering, which is parallelled by *v.* 2 of the sixth *Sukta* of this *anuvāka*, making *Varu* himself address the stanza to *Uṣas*, and ask her to give him wealth for the sons of *Vyaśva*, as she had given to his father for his suppliants.]

६५७९. आ ना॒र्यस्य॒ दक्षि॑णा॒ व्य॑श्वाँ॒ एतु॒ सोमि॑न:।
स्थू॒रं च॒ राध॑: शत॒वत्स॒हस्र॑वत् ॥२९॥

29. May the gifts of a humane (price), when offering the *Soma* libation, extend to the Vyaśvas, yea, and substantial wealth by hundreds and thousands.

Humane— Sāyaṇa explains *nārya* as *narahitasyāpatyam.*

६५८०. यत्त्वा पृच्छादीजान: कुंहया कुंहयाकृते।
एषो अर्पश्रितो वलो गोंमतीमव तिष्ठति॥३०॥

30. If any ask of you, (*Uṣas*), when anywhere present, where the sacrificer (*Varu* dwells), (reply) the powerful (prince), the refuge of all, a bides on (the banks of) the *Gomatī* river.

In Any ask of you— Sāyaṇa explains *kuhayākṛte* as meaning, ''Oh, you who are honoured by those who ask where *Varu* dwells,'' *sa varuḥ kutra tiṣṭhatītyetadicchayābhilakṣaṇapravṛttair jijñāsubhiḥ puraskṛte* (*Uṣas*). *Valaḥ* he takes as *varaḥ,* sc. *svabalena avārakaḥ śatrūṇām,* ''overwhelmer of enemies.''

[सूक्त-२५]

[ऋषि- विश्वमना वैयश्व। देवता- मित्रावरुण, १-१२ विश्वेदेवा।
छन्द- उष्णिक्, २३ उष्णिग्गर्भा गायत्री।]

६५८१. ता वां विश्वस्य गोपा देवा देवेषु यज्ञियां।
ऋतावांना यजसे पूतदंक्षसा॥१॥

1. You two are the protectors of the universe, divine and to be adored among the gods; therefore, (Vishva manas), you sacrifice to the pair who are observant of truth and endowed with real power.

६५८२. मित्रा तना न रथ्यांई वरुंणो यश्च सुक्रतु:।
सनात्सुंजाता तनंया धृतव्रंता॥२॥

2. *Mitra* and *Varuṇa*, doers of good deeds, (diffusers of) riches, who are the charioteers (of men), well born of old, the sons, (of *Aditi*), observant of vows, (you are worshipped by me).

Charioteers of Man— Or, perhaps, ''bringers, of riches,'' *tanā rathyā.*

You are Worshipped by Me— The text has only the nouns, without any verb, which is supplied by the commentator. [He supplies ''you sacrifice to them'' *tā yajase* from the previous verse.]

६५८३. ता माता विश्ववेंदसासुर्यांय प्रमंहसा। मही जंज्ञानादिंतिर्ऋंतावरी॥३॥

3. The great and veracious *Aditi*, the mother (of the gods), gave birth to those two who are possessed of all affuence, and shining with great splendour, for the (destruction of the) *Asuras.*

६५८४. महान्तां मित्रावरुणा सम्राजां देवावसुरा।
ऋतावांनावृतमा घोषतो बृहत्॥४॥

4. The great *Mitra* and *Varuṇa*, the two sovereign and powerful deities, the observers of truth, illume our solemn rite.

Sovereign— Sāyaṇa, as usual, explains *samraj* as ''perfectly resplendent,'' *samyag dīpyamānau*; and so, too, in *v.* 7.

Powerful— *Asura* is also explained as ''impelling by being the indwelling principle,'' *antaryāmitayā prerakau*.

Illume— The text has *ghoṣataḥ*, which Sāyaṇa renders *svadīptyā prakāśayataḥ*.

६५८५. नपाता शवसो मह: सूनू दक्षस्य सुक्रतू।
सुप्रदानू इषो वास्त्वधि क्षित:॥५॥

5. Grandsons of mighty strength, sons of energy, doers of good deeds, liberal benefactors, they preside over the habitation of food.

६५८६. सं या दानूनि येमथुर्दिव्या: पार्थिवीरिष:।
नभस्वतीरा वां चरन्तु वृष्टय:॥६॥

6. Bestow (upon us) good gifts, viands, whether of heaven or earth: may the water-shedding rains attend upon you.

६५८७. अधि या बृहतो दिवोऽइभि यूथेव पश्यत:।
ऋतावाना सम्राजा नमसे हिता॥७॥

7. (These are they) who look upon the great deities as (a bull contemplates) the herd, sovereigns observant of truth and propitious to adoration.

६५८८. ऋतावाना नि षेदतु: साम्राज्याय सुक्रतू।
धृतव्रता क्षत्रिया क्षत्रमाशतु:॥८॥

8. Observers of truth, doers of good deeds, they sit down for the office of sovereignty; observant of obligations, endowed with strength, they acquire vigour.

Cf. Ṛg I.25.10.

They Acquire Vigour— *Kṣatriyā kṣatram āśatuḥ* is explained *balavantau balam vyāpnutaḥ.*

६५८९. अक्ष्णश्चिद्दातुविर्त्तरानुल्बणेन चक्षसा।
नि चिन्मिषन्तां निचिरा नि चिक्यतु:॥९॥

9. Through knowers of the path, even before the eye (can see), causing (all beings) to open their eyelids, existing from of old, and shining with a mild radiance, verily they have been worshipped.

A rather unintelligible verse, even with the help of the Scholiast. [Sāyaṇa seems to understand it as referring to *Mitra* and *Varuṇa* as respectively presiding over day and night, *ahorātrayor vyāptena tejasā*.]

६५९०. उत नो देव्यदितिरुरुष्यतां नासत्या।

उरुष्यन्तु मरुतो वृद्धशंवस:॥१०॥

10. May the divine *Aditi*, may the *Nāsatyās* also protect us; may the rapid *Maruts* defend us.

६५९१. ते नो नावमुरुष्यत दिवा नक्तं सुदानव:।

अरिष्यन्तो नि पायुभि: सचेमहि॥११॥

11. Munificent and irresistible (*Maruts*), guard our vessel by day and night, so that we may be secure through your protection.

Guard our Vessel— *No nāvam uruṣyata; nāvam yajñiyām* occurs in x.44.6, and seems there to mean the sacrifice.

६५९२. अध्नते विष्णवे वयमरिष्यन्त: सुदानवे।

श्रुधि स्वयावन्तिसन्धो पूर्वचित्तये॥१२॥

12. We, injured (through his protection, offer praise) to the liberal *Viṣṇu*, who harms not (his adorers): do you who goes by thyself alone (to combat), and cause wealth to flow (to the worshipper), hear (our prayer) in behalf of him who has commenced the sacrifice.

Sāyaṇa interprets *Sindho* as *stotṛn prati dhanānām syandanaśīla Viṣṇo,* and *pūrvacittaye* as *prārabdhakarmaṇe yajamānāya.*

६५९३. तद्वार्यं वृणीमहे वरिष्ठं गोपयत्यंम्।

मित्रो यत्पान्ति वरुणो यदर्यमा॥१३॥

13. We solicit that ample, all-desired, all-guarding (wealth) which *Mitra, Varuṇa,* and *Aryaman* hold under their protection.

६५९४. उत न: सिन्धुरपां तन्मरुतस्तदश्विना।

इन्द्रो विष्णुर्मीढ्वांस: सजोषस:॥१४॥

14. Yea, may he who causes the waters to flow (*Parjanya*), the *Maruts*, the *Aśvins*, *Indra*, *Viṣṇu*, may all (these deities) together, the showerers (of benefits, protect) that wealth for us.

६५९५. ते हि ष्मा वनुषो नरोऽभिमातिं कयस्य चित्।

तिग्मं न क्षोद: प्रतिघ्नन्ति भूर्णय:॥१५॥

15. Those desirable leaders (of men), rapid in movement, break down the haughtiness of any (foe) whatever, as an impetuous current (sweeps away all obstacles.)

६५९६. अयमेक॑ इत्था पुरूरु च॒ष्टे वि वि॒श्पति॑:।
तस्य॑ व्र॒तान्यनु॑ व॒श्चरा॑मसि॥१६॥

16. This one, the lord of man (*Mitra*), contemplates many vast things: we follow his rites for you.

६५९७. अनु॑ पूर्वा॒ण्योक॒या॒ सा॒म्रा॒ज्यस्य॑ स॒श्मिम।
मि॒त्रस्य॑ व्र॒ता वरु॑णस्य दी॒र्घश्रु॑त्॥१७॥

17. We observe the ancient rites of the imperial *Varuṇa* and the renowned *Mitra*, (rites) that are good for (our) dwelling.

For our Dwelling— The text has only *Okyā*. The comment renders it *Oko gṛham tasmai hitāni karmāṇi.*

६५९८. परि॒ यो र॒श्मिना॒ दिवोऽन्तान्म॑मे पृ॒थि॒व्या:।
उ॒भे आ प॑प्रौ॒ रोद॑सी महि॒त्वा॥१८॥

18. (*Mitra* is he) who has measured with his rays the limits of both heaven and earth; who has filled both heaven and earth with his greatness.

६५९९. उदु॒ ष्य श॑र॒णे दि॒वो ज्योति॒रयं॑स्त॒ सूर्य॑:।
अ॒ग्निर्न॑ शु॒क्र: समि॑धान आ॒हुत॑:॥१९॥

19. He, *Sūrya*, has uplifted his radiance in the region of the heaven; kindled and invoked with burnt-offerings, he is bright, like *Agni*.

Sūrya— That is, according to the comment, *Mitra* and *Varuṇa. Cf. v.* 21.

६६००. वचो॒ दीर्घप्र॒सद्म॒नीशे॒ वाज॑स्य गो॒मत॑:।
ईशे॒ हि पि॒त्वोऽविष॑स्य॒ दाव॑ने॥२०॥

20. Raise your voice in the spacious hall of sacrifice (to him) who is lord over food derived from cattle, who is able to grant nutritious sustenance.

In the spacious hall of Sacrifice— Sāyaṇa explains *dīrghaprasadmani* as an epithet of *yajñe, vistṛtam sadanam yasmin yajñe.*

६६०१. तत्सूर्यं॑ रोद॑सी उ॒भे दो॒षा वस्तो॑रुप॒ ब्रुवे।
भो॒जेष्व॒स्माँ अ॒भ्युच्च॑रा॒ सदा॑॥२१॥

21. I Glorify by night and day that sun (*Mitra* and *Varuṇa*), and both the heaven and earth; do you (*Varuṇa*) ever bring us to the presence of the bountiful.

That Sun, Mitra and *Varuṇa*— *Tat sūryam* means, according to the Scholiast, the brightness of *Mitra* and *Varuṇa*. [*Sāyaṇa's* words are *sūryam suvīryam, tat Varuṇam Maitram ca tejas.*]

६६०२. ऋज्रमुक्षण्यायने रज्तं हर॑याणे। रथं युक्तम॑संनाम सुषाम॑णि॥२२॥

22. We have received from the son of *Suṣāman*, the descendant of *Ukṣan*, the overcomer (of foes), a well-going chariot of silver, yoked (with a pair of horses.)

६६०३. ता मे॑ अश्व्या॑नां॒ हरी॑णां॒ नितोश॑ना। उ॒तो नु कृ॒त्व्या॑नां॒ नृ॒वाह॑सा॥२३॥

23. Among bay horses these two are pre-eminently the destroyers (of foes), and of those eager in combat; the two strong bearers of men.

६६०४. स्मद॑भीशू कशाव॑न्ता विप्रा॑ नवि॑ष्ठया म॒ती।

म॒हो वा॒जिनाव॒र्व॑न्ता सचा॑सनम्॥२४॥

24. Through this new praise (of *Mitra* and *Varuṇa*) I have obtained at the same moment of the mighty prince, two fast-going sagacious steeds, with whip and reins.

Two Fast-Going Sagacious Steeds—Sāyaṇa explains *viprau* as *medhāvinam ucitau*, "worthy of the praisers of a deity."

[सूक्त-२६]

[**ऋषि**– विश्वमना वैयश्व तथा व्यश्व आङ्गिरस। **देवता**– अश्विनीकुमार, २०-२५ वायु। **छन्द**– उष्णिक्, १६-१७, २१, २५ गायत्री, २० अनुष्टुप्।]

६६०५. युवो॒रु षू रथं॑ हुवे स॒धस्तु॑त्याय सू॒रिषु॑।

अतू॒र्त॑दक्षा वृषणा वृषण्वसू॥१॥

1. (*Aśvins*) of irresistible strength, affluent showerers (of benefits), I invoke your chariot amidst the pious, who are assembled to celebrate your presence.

६६०६. युवं॒ वरो॑ सुषाम्णे॒ महे तने॑ नासत्या।

अवो॑भिर्याथो वृषणा वृषण्वसू॥२॥

2. (Say), *Varu* (Thus), *Nāsatyās*, senders of rain, affluent showerers (of benefits), as you came to *Suṣāman* with your protections to (grant him) great riches, (so come to me).

Say, Varu, Thus— The text has only *Varu*, in the vocative, which the commentator amplifies—*He varunāmaka rājan, evam brūhīti Ṛṣir vadati.*

To Grant him great Riches, so come to Me— *Mahe tane, mahate dhanāya; mahyam āyātam* is supplied by the Scholiast.

६६०७. ता वां॒द्य हं॑वामहे हव्ये॒भिर्वाजिनीवसू।
पूर्वी॑रि॒ष इ॒षय॑न्ता॒वति॒ क्षपः॑॥३॥

3. Affluent in nourishment, we invoke you, who are desirous of (sacrificial) food, on this occasion at dawn with oblations.

At Dawn— *Ati kṣapaḥ kṣapāya atikrame,* "at the passing of night," *uṣaḥ-kāle.*

६६०८. आ वां॒ वाहि॑ष्ठो अश्विना॒ रथो॑ यातु श्रु॒तो नरा।
उप॒ स्तोमा॑न्तुरस्य॑ दर्शथः॒ श्रि॒ये॥४॥

4. Leaders (of rites), let your renowned al-conveying chariot come to us, and (do you) recognize the praises of the zealous (worshipper) for his prosperity.

६६०९. जुहुरा॒णा चि॑दश्विना॒ मन्ये॑थां वृष॒ण्वसू।
यु॒वं हि रु॒द्रा पर्ष॑थो॒ अति॒ द्विषः॑॥५॥

5. *Aśvins*, affluent showerers (of benefits), detect the guileful; verily, *Rudras*, vex your adversaries.

६६१०. द॒स्रा हि विश्व॑मानुष॒ङ्मधू॑भिः॒ परि॑दीय॒थः।
धि॒यञ्जि॒न्वा मधु॑वर्णा॒ शुभ॑स्पतीं॥६॥

6. *Dasras*, who are gratified by sacred rites, of fascinating cimplexion, lords of rain, pass with your fleet (horses) completely round our entire (sacrifice).

Of Fascinating Complexion— *Madhuvarṇā* is explained *ye yuvayo rūpam paśyanti te tatraiva hṛṣṭā bhavanti,* "they who look upon your beauty are delighted."

६६११. उप॑ नो यातमश्विना रा॒या वि॒श्वपु॑षा॒ सह।
म॒घवा॑ना सु॒वीरा॒वन॑प॒च्युता॥७॥

7. Come to us, *Aśvins*, with all-supporting riches, for you are opulent, heroic, overthrown of none.

६६१२. आ मे॑ अस्य प्र॒तीव्य॒ इन्द्र॑नासत्या गतम्।
दे॒वा दे॒वेभि॒रद्य॑ सचन॑स्तमा॥८॥

8. *Indra* and *Nāsatyās*, who are most accessible, come to this may sacrifice: come, gods, to-day, with (other) divinities.

६६१३. वयं हि वां हवांमह उक्षण्यन्तों व्यश्ववत् ।

सुमतिभिरुपं विप्राविहा गंतम् ॥९॥

9. Desirous of you who are bestowers of wealth, we invoke you, as did (your father) *Vyaśva*: come, sagacious *Aśvins*, hither with favourable intentions.

६६१४. अश्विना स्वृषे स्तुहि कुवित्ते श्रवतों हवंम् ।

नेदींयसः कूळयातः पणींरुत ॥१०॥

10. Praise the *Aśvins* devoutly, *Ṛṣi*, that they may repeatedly hear your invocation, and destroy the nearest (approaching enemies) and the Panis.

६६१५. वैयश्वस्यं श्रुतं नरोतो में अस्य वेदथः ।

सजोषंसा वरुणो मित्रा अर्यमा ॥११॥

11. Hear, leaders (of rites), (the invocation) of me the son of *Vyaśva*, and understand its (purport); and may *Varuṇa*, *Mitra*, and *Aryaman* concurrently (grant me wealth).

And Understand Its Purport— Sāyaṇa seems to explain it, "*ye* recognize this my (invocation as devoted to you)."

६६१६. युवादंत्तस्य धिष्ण्या युवानींतस्य सूरिभिः ।

अहंरहर्वृषणा महां शिक्षतम् ॥१२॥

12. Adorable showerers (of benefits), bestow daily upon me (some) of that (wealth) which is given by you, which is brought by you for the worshippers.

६६१७. यो वां यज्ञेभिरावृतोऽधिवस्त्रा वधूरिव ।

सपर्यन्तां शुभे चंक्राते अश्विनां ॥१३॥

13. The man who is enveloped in sacrifices (offered) to you, like a woman with additional raiment, rewarding him, *Aśvins*, you place him in prosperity.

With Additional Raiment— *Adhivastra*, "having another garment over her ordinary clothes."

६६१८. यो वांमुरुव्यचंस्तमं चिकेतति नृपाय्यंम् ।

वर्तिरश्विना परिं यातमस्मयू ॥१४॥

14. Favourably disposed towards me, come, *Aśvins*, to the dwelling of him who knows (how to prepare for you) the most copiously effused (libation) to be drunk by the leaders (of rites).

६६१९. अस्मभ्यं सु वृषण्वसू यातं वर्तिर्नृपाय्र्यम् ।

विषुद्रुहेव यज्ञमूहथुर्गिरा ।।१५ ।।

15. Affluent showerers (of benefits), come to our dwelling for (the libation) to be drunk by the leaders (of rites), for you bring the sacrifice to completion by praise, as the fatal shaft (slays the deer).

As the Fatal Shaft Slays the Deer— The text has only *Viṣudruheva*, which Sāyaṇa explains, *viśvān hinasti śatrūn iti, śaraḥ*. [He explains the allusion as follows: *tena* (*viṣudruha*) *yathā vyādho mṛgam abhilaṣitam deśam prāpayati tadvat stutyā yajñam avaikalyena samāptim prāpayathaḥ*, ''as a hunter by an arrow brings the deer to the desired spot (to its destination?), so ye by praise cause the sacrifice to attain completion.'']

६६२०. वाहिष्ठो वां हवानां स्तोमो दूतो हुवन्नरा । युवाभ्यां भूत्वश्विना ।।१६ ।।

16. *Aśvins*, leaders (of rites), among (all) invocations may my most earnest praise invoke you as a messenger may it be (acceptable) to you.

६६२१. यद्दो दिवो अर्णव इषो वा मदथो गृहे । श्रुतिमिन्मे अमर्त्या ।।१७ ।।

17. Whether, immortal (*Aśvins*), you rejoice in the water of the firmament, or in the dwelling of the worshipper hear this my (invocation).

Or in the Dwelling of the Worshipper— *Iṣo vāgrhe, yuvām icchato yajamānasya* is *Sāyaṇa's* explanation.

६६२२. उत स्या श्वेतयावरी वाहिष्ठा वां नदीनाम् । सिन्धुर्हिरण्यवर्तनिः ।।१८ ।।

18. Verily this *Śvetayāvarī*, the golden-pathed river, is of all rivers the especial bearer of your (praises).

६६२३. स्मदेतया सुकीर्त्याश्विना श्वेतया धिया । वहेथे शुभ्रयावाना ।।१९ ।।

19. *Aśvins*, following a brilliant course, you acquire celebrity by the white river worthily praising you the enricher (of the people on its banks).

The Enricher of the People on its Banks— The river is said to have praised the *Aśvins*, as the *Ṛṣi* lived on its banks. These banks are golden, and consequently enrich those who live near.

६६२४. युक्ष्वा हि त्वं रथासहां युवस्व पोष्या वसो ।

आन्नो वायो मधु पिबास्माकं सवना गहि ।।२० ।।

20. Yoke your chariot-drawing horses, *Vayu*; bring them, *Vasu*, encouraged (to the sacrifice); then drink our *Soma;* come to our daily libations.

६६२५. तवं वायवृतस्पते त्वष्टुर्जामातरद्भुत। अवांस्या वृणीमहे।।२१।।

21. We solicit your protection, *Vayu*, lord of sacrifice wonderful son-in-law of *Tvaṣṭā*.

Wonderful Son-in-Law of Twashtri— Sāyaṇa explains *Tvaṣṭā* here by *Brahmā*, and refers for the connection to the *Itihāsas* and other authorities. Mahīdhara (*Yajurveda*, 27.34) says, *Vāyu*, or the wind, having taken water from *Āditya*, fertilizes it, as rain, and is therefore as it were his son-in-law, identifying *Tvaṣṭā* with *Āditya*.

६६२६. त्वष्टुर्जामातरं वयमीशानं राय ईमहे।

सुतावन्तो वायुं द्युम्ना जनासः।।२२।।

22. We, the offerers of *Soma*, solicit riches from the sovereign, the son-in-law of *Tvaṣṭā*; (may we become) wealthy.

६६२७. वायौ याहि शिवा दिवो वहस्वा स्वश्व्यम्।

वहस्व मह: पृथुपक्षसा रथे।।२३।।

23. Establish, *Vāyu*, happiness in heaven; bear quickly your well-horse (chariot); do you, who are mighty, yoke the broad-flanked (horses) to the car.

Establish, Vāyu, happiness in Heaven— *Vāyu* being considered the supporter of all the celestial luminaries, *sarva-jyotiṣām tvadādhāratvāt*.

६६२८. त्वां हि सुपर्रस्तमं नृषदनेषु हूमहे। ग्रावाणं नाश्वपृष्ठं मंहना।।२४।।

24. We invoke you who are of graceful from, extending through your magnitude your limbs in all directions, to our religious rites, like the stone (for bruising the *Soma*).

Extending . . . . The Limbs in all Directions— *Aśvapṛṣṭham* is literally, ''borne on a horse's back''; but Sāyaṇa here interprets *ashva* by *vyāpta*, and *pṛṣṭha* by *sarvāṅga*.

६६२९. स त्वं नौ देव मनसा वायौ मन्दानो अग्रिय:।

कृधि वाजाँ अपो धिय:।।२५।।

25. Divine *Vayu*, foremost (of the gods), exulting in your won mind, cause our rites to be productive of food and water.

Cause our Rites to be Productive of Food and Water— Sāyaṇa seems to explain the latter clause, ''Give us food and water, and so cause our rites to be duly performed.''

[सूक्त- २७]

[ऋषि– मनु वैवस्वत। **देवता**– विश्वेदेवा। छन्द– प्रगाथ (विषमा बृहती,
समासतो बृहती।]

६६३०. अग्निरुक्थे पुरोहितो ग्रावाणो बर्हिरध्वरे।
ऋचा यामि मरुतो ब्रह्मणस्पतिं देवाँ अवो वरेण्यम्॥१॥

1. *Agni* is the *Purohita* at the sacrifice: the stones, the sacred
grass (are prepared) for the ceremony. I invoke with the holy verse
the *Maruts*, *Brahmaṇaspati*, and all the gods, for their desirable
protection.

Sāmaveda, 48. Sāyaṇa explains *purohita* in its literal meaning, as
"placed in front, (or one the east), on the *uttara vedi*."]

६६३१. आ पशुं गासि पृथिवीं वनस्पतीननुषासा नक्तमोषधीः।
विश्वे च नो वसवो विश्ववेदसो धीनां भूत प्राविताारः॥२॥

2. You come (*Agni*), to the victim, to the dwelling (of the
worshipper), to the touchwood, to the *Soma*, at dawn and at night:
universal deities, givers of wealth, knowing all things, be the
defenders of our pious acts.

To the Dwelling of the Worshipper— *Pṛthivīm*, which is explained
idam devasadanam, "this chamber of the gods." *Oṣadhiḥ* may here also
imply annual plants, according to Sāyaṇa. [Sāyaṇa renders *uṣāsā naktam
oṣadhiḥ*, ("you comest) to dawn and might (these being the times for the
offering), and the *Soma*-grinding stones." He explains *vasavaḥ*, as usual,
by *vāsayitārḥ*, "causers of habitations."]

६६३२. प्र सू न एत्वध्वरो ३ ग्ना देवेषु पूर्व्यः।
आदित्येषु प्र वरुणे धृतव्रते मरुत्सु विश्वभानुषु॥३॥

3. Let the ancient sacrifice proceed first to *Agni*, then to the
gods,—to the *Ādityas*, to *Varuṇa*, observant of obligations, to the
all-resplendent *Maruts*.

६६३३. विश्वे हि ष्मा मनवे विश्ववेदसो भुवन्वृधे रिशादसः।
अरिष्टिभिः पायुभिर्विश्ववेदसो यन्ता नोऽवृकं छर्दिः॥४॥

4. May the universal deities, possessors of all opulence,
destroyers of foes, be (nigh) to *Manu* for his prosperity: do you,
who know all things, secure to us an abode safe from robbers
through your unassailable protections.

An Abode safe from Robbers— *Avṛkam stenarahitam*; or it may imply, "free from any annoyances, *bādhārahitam*."

६६३४. आ नों अद्य समनसो गन्ता विश्वे सजोषसः।
ऋचा गिरा मरुतो देव्यदिते सदने पस्त्ये महि॥५॥

5. Universal deities, united together and of one mind, come this day to us, (attracted) by the sacred praise addressed to you; and do you, *Maruts*, and the might goddess *Aditi*, (come) to the dwelling, (our) abode.

६६३५. अभि प्रिया मरुतो या वो अश्व्या हव्या मित्र प्रयाथन।
आ बर्हिरिन्द्रो वरुणस्तुरा नरं आदित्यासः सदन्तु नः॥६॥

6. Direct, *Maruts*, your beloved horses (to our rite): *Mitra*, (come to our) oblations; and may *Indra*, and *Varuṇa*, and the swift leaders, the *Ādityas*, sit down on our sacred grass.

६६३६. वयं वों वृक्तबर्हिषो हितप्रयस आनुषक्।
सुतसोमासो वरुण हवामहे मनुष्वदिद्धाग्नयः॥७॥

7. Bearing the clipt sacred grass, offering in due order the (sacrificial) food, presenting the effused *Soma*, and having the fires kindled, we invoke you, *Varuṇa*, (and the rest), as did Manus.

Varuṇa— When *Mitra* and *Varuṇa* are named singly, both are intended, and sometimes even more of the *Viśvadevas,* according to the Scholiast. [For *Manu's* sacrifice, *cf.* vol. I, *mantra* 293, and *Śatapatha Brāhmaṇa*, i.8.1.]

६६३७. आ प्र यात मरुतो विष्णो अश्विना पूषन्माकीनया धिया।
इन्द्र आ यातु प्रथमः सनिष्युभिर्वृषा यो वृत्रहा गृणे॥८॥

8. *Maruts*, *Viṣṇu*, *Aśvins*, *Pūṣan*, come hither (induced) by my praise: may *Indra*, the first (of the gods), also come, the showerer (of benefits), he who is praised by (his) worshippers as the slayer of *Vṛtra*.

६६३८. वि नों देवासो अद्रुहोऽच्छिद्रं शर्म यच्छत।
न यद्दूराद्रसवो नू चिदन्ततो वरूथमादधर्षति॥९॥

9. Unoppressive deities, bestow upon us a mansion without defect, so that, subduers (of foes), no one may injure our defences, whether from afar or nigh.

६६३९. अस्ति हि व: सजात्यं रिशादसो देवासो अस्त्याप्यम्।

प्र ण: पूर्वस्मै सुविताय वोचत मक्षू सुम्नाय नव्यसे ।।१०।।

10. There is identity of race among you, deities, destroyers of
foes; there is kindred (with me your worshipper); therefore utter at
once the command for our former prosperity and for new
happiness.

There is kindred with me your Worshipper— The text has
only *asty āpyam,* the Scholiast says, with the *Ṛṣi* of the hymn.

६६४०. इदा हि व उपस्तुतिमिदा वामस्य भक्तये।

उप वो विश्ववेदसो नमस्युराँ असृक्ष्यन्यामिव ।।११।।

11. Deities, possessed of all wealth, I, desirous of offering
worship, address to you verily unprecedented praise, for the sake
of obtaining desired affluence.

६६४१. उदु ष्य व: सविता सुप्रणीतयोऽस्थादूर्ध्वो वरेण्य:।

नि द्विपादश्चतुष्पादो अर्थिनोऽविश्रन्पतयिष्णव: ।।१२।।

12. Devoutly praised (*Maruts*), when the adorable *Savitā* has
risen above you, then bipeds and quadrupeds, and the flying birds,
seeking (their objects), enter (upon their functions).

६६४२. देवन्देवं वोऽवसे देवन्देवमभिष्टये।

देवन्देवं हुवेम वाजसातये गृणन्तौ देव्या धिया ।।१३।।

13. We would invoke each deity among you (gods) for
protection, each deity for the attainment of our desires, each deity
for the acquisition of food, glorifying you with divine praise.

Yajurveda, 33.91.

६६४३. देवासो हि ष्मा मनवे समन्यवो विश्वे साकं सरातय:।

ते नौ अद्य ते अपरं तुचे तु नो भवन्तु वरिवोविद: ।।१४।।

14. May the universal gods with one consent be together the
givers (of riches) to *Manu;* may they, both to-day and hereafter, be
the bestowers of wealth upon us and upon our posterity.

Yajurveda, 33, 94.

६६४४. प्र व: शंसाम्यद्रुह: संस्थ उपस्तुतीनाम्।

न तं धूर्तिर्वरुण मित्र मर्त्यं यो वो धामभ्योऽविधत् ।।१५।।

15. I glorify you, innoxious deities, in the place of praises: no harm befalls the man who, *Mitra* and *Varuṇa*, offers (oblations) to your glories.

६६४५. प्र स क्षयं तिरते वि महीरिषो यो वो वराय दाशति।

प्र प्रजाभिर्जायते धर्मणस्पर्यरिष्टः सर्व एधते।।१६।।

16. He enlarges his dwelling, he has abundant food who offers you (oblations) to obtain a blessing: through his pious acts he is born on every side in his children: all prosper (through your favour) unharmed (by enemies).

६६४६. ऋते स विन्दते युधः सुगेभिर्यात्यध्वनः।

अर्यमा मित्रो वरुणः सरातयो यं त्रायन्ते सजोषसः।।१७।।

17. He gains (wealth) without war, he travels along the roads with quick (horses), whom *Aryaman*, *Mitra* and *Varuṇa*, alike munificent, and acting in concert, protect.

६६४७. अज्रे चिदस्मै कृणुथा न्यञ्चनं दुर्गे चिदा सुसरणम्।

एषा चिदस्मादशनिः परो नु सास्रेधन्ती वि नश्यतु।।१८।।

18. You enable him (*Manu*) to proceed by an unobstructed road; you grant him easy access to difficult passes; May the weapon (of the foe) be far from him, and, inflicting no injury, perish.

६६४८. यदद्य सूर्य उद्यति प्रियक्षत्रा ऋतं दध।

यन्निम्रुचि प्रबुधि विश्ववेदसो यद्वा मध्यन्दिने दिवः।।१९।।

19. Divinities of benevolent vigour, since you preside over the rite to-day, at the rising of the sun, since, possessors of all wealth, (you are present) at his setting, or at his waking, or at the meridian of the day.

Since You Preside over the Rite— Sāyaṇa says, "since ye uphold the house (rendered prosperous)," *grham kalyāṇabhūtam dhārayatha*.

६६४९. यद्वाभिपित्वे अंसुरा ऋतं यते छर्दिर्येम वि दाशुषे।

वयं तद्वो वसवो विश्ववेदस उप स्थेयाम मध्य आ।।२०।।

20. Or since all-wise deities, you accept the sacrifice, bestowing on the zealous donor (of the oblation) a swelling (such as we may worship in) then, possessors of all wealth, distributors of riches, may we worship you in the midst (of that dwelling).

The construction is so loose, that it is impossible to do more than conjecture the meaning *Yadvābhipitve asurā ṛtam yate chardir yema vidāśuṣe* is explained *yadvā asmadyajñam prati yuṣmākam abhiprāptau yajñam gacchate havīṇṣi dattavate yajamānāya gṛham prayacchatha*, "since you give a dwelling to the donor of the oblation proceeding to the rite, which is to bring you to our sacrifice," or, "on your approach to our sacrifice.

६६५०. यद्द्य सूर् उदिते यन्मध्यन्दिन आतुचि᳘ं।

वामं धत्थ मन॑वे विश्ववेद॒सो जुह्वा᳘नाय᳘ प्रचे᳘तसे॥२१॥

21. (Gods), who are possessed of all wealth, bestow the desired (opulence) upon the intelligent *Manu*, offering oblations to you at sunrise, mid-day, and sunset.

Sāyaṇa connects this verse with the next, "since ye give the desired (opulence) to *Manu*," etc., "therefore we solicit of you," etc.

६६५१. वयं त॒द्वः सम्राज आ वृणीमहे पु॒त्रो न ब॑हुपाय्य᳘म्।

अ॒श्याम॒ तदा᳘दित्या᳘ जुह्व॒तो ह॒विर्ये᳘न व॒स्योऽन॑शामहै॥२२॥

22. We solicit of you, resplendent deities, as a son (of a father), that which is to be enjoyed by many; offering oblations, may we obtain that (wealth), *Ādityas*, by which we may possess abundance.

[सूक्त-२८]

[ऋषि- मनु वैवस्वत। देवता- विश्वेदेवा। छन्द- गायत्री, ४ पुर उष्णिक्।]

६६५२. ये त्रि॒ंशति॒ त्रय॑स्परो दे॒वासो॑ ब॒र्हिरास॑दन्। विद॒न्नह॑ द्वि॒तास॑नन्॥१॥

1. May the three-and-thirty divinities sit down upon the sacred grass; may they accept (our offerings), and bestow upon us both (sorts of wealth).

Both Sorts of Wealth— *I.e.,* cattle and money; or, may they give repeatedly, [Sāyaṇa explains *vidan,* "may they acknowledge us as offerers."]

६६५३. वरुणो मित्रो अर्य॑मा स्मद्रा᳘तिषाचो अग्नय॑:।

पत्नीव॑न्तो वष॒ट्कृताः॥२॥

2. May *Varuṇa*, *Mitra*, *Aryaman* and the Agnis, with their wives, honouring the donors (of the oblation), and addressed with the sacrificial exclamation,—

६६५४. ते नौ गोपा अपाच्यास्त उदक्त इत्था न्यक्।

पुरस्तात्सर्वया विशा॥३॥

3. Be our protectors, whether coming with all their attendants from the west, from the north, from the south, from the east.

From the West, Etc.— Sāyaṇa artificially makes out six directions by taking *nyak* as the nadir, and understanding by *itthā* the south and the zenith.

६६५५. यथा वशन्ति देवास्तथेदसत्तदेषां नकिरा मिनत्।

अरावा चन मर्त्यः॥४॥

4. Whatever the gods desire, that assuredly comes to pass: no one can resist their (will), no mortal withholds (their) offerings.

No Mortal withholds their Offerings— Or, perhaps, as Sāyaṇa takes it, "even the non-offering mortal (must give offerings if they will it)."

६६५६. सप्तानां सप्त ऋष्टयः सप्त द्युम्नान्येषाम्।

सप्तो अधि श्रियौ धिरे॥५॥

5. Seven are the lances of the seven (troops of the *Maruts*), seven are their ornaments, they wear seven surpassing glories.

[सूक्त- २९]

[**ऋषि**– मनु वैवस्वत तथा कश्यप-मारीच। **देवता**– विश्वेदेवा।

छन्द– द्विपदा विराट्।]

६६५७. बभ्रुरेको विषुणः सूनरो युवाञ्ज्यङ्क्ते हिरण्ययम्॥१॥

1. One (*Soma*) brown of hue, all-pervading, leader of the nights, ever young, decorates (himself) with golden ornaments.

One Soma Brown of Hue— *Babhru* applies properly to the *Soma* plant, but the other epithets indicate *Soma,* the moon.

Leader of the Nights— *Sunara,* which is explained *suṣṭhu ratrīṇām netā.*

६६५८. योनिमेक आ ससाद द्योतनोऽन्तर्देवेषु मेधिरः॥२॥

2. One (*Agni*) intelligent, resplendent among the gods, is seated in his place (the altar).

६६५९. वाशीमेकौ बिभर्ति हस्त आयसीमन्तर्देवेषु निध्रुविः॥३॥

3. One (*Tvaṣṭā*) immoveably stationed among the gods, holds his iron axe in his hand.

६६६०. वज्रमेको बिभर्ति हस्त आहितं तेन वृत्राणि जिघ्नते।।४।।

4. One (*Indra*) holds his thunderbolt wielded in his hand, by which he slays the *Vṛtras*.

६६६१. तिग्ममेको बिभर्ति हस्त आयुधं शुचिरुग्रो जलाषभेषज:।।५।।

5. One (*Rudra*) brilliant and fierce, (yet) the distributor of healing medicines, holds his sharp weapon in his hand.

६६६२. पथ एक: पीपाय तस्करो यथा एष वेद निधीनाम्।।६।।

6. One (*Pūṣan*) watches the roads like a robber, and is cognizant of hidden treasures.

Pūṣan **Watches the Roads—** *Cf.* Vol. I. *mantra* 499 Sāyaṇa understands the roads to heaven or hell.

६६६३. त्रीण्येक उरुगायो वि चक्रमे यत्र देवासो मदन्ति।।७।।

7. One (*Viṣṇu*) wide-stepping, has traversed the three worlds where the gods rejoice.

६६६४. विभिद्रा चरत एकया सह प्र प्रवासेव वसत:।।८।।

8. Two (the *Aśvins*,) travel with swift (horses) along with one (bride *Sūrya*), like travellers to foreign countries.

६६६५. सदो द्वा चक्राते उपमा दिवि सम्राजा सर्पिरासुती।।९।।

9. Two of like beauty and of royal rank (*Mitra* and *Varuṇa*), worshipped with oblations of clarified butter, have taken their seat in heaven.

६६६६. अर्चन्त एके महि साम मन्वत तेन सूर्यमरोचयन्।।१०।।

10. Some (the *Atris*) when worshipping, call to mind the great *Sāman*, wherewith they light up the sun.

Sāyaṇa explains the *Sāman* as the *trivṛt, pañcadaśa*, etc.

[सूक्त-३०]

[ऋषि- मनु वैवस्वत। देवता- विश्वेदेवा। छन्द- १ गायत्री,
२ पुर उष्णिक्, ३ बृहती, ४ अनुष्टुप्।]

६६६७. नहि वो अस्त्यर्भको देवासो न कुमारक:।
विश्वे सतोमहान्त इत्।।१।।

1. There is no one among you, gods, who is an infant or a youth; you verily are all of mature existence.

All of Mature Existence— *Sato mahāntaḥ*, explained by Sāyaṇa as *sarvasmād vidyamānāt pṛthivyām api ye mahāntas te satomahānta ity ucyante*, literally, "greater than all that is."

६६६८. इति स्तुतासो॑ असथा रिशाद॒सो ये स्थ त्र्यश्च॒ त्रिंशच्च॑।

मनो॑र्देवा यज्ञियास॑ः॥२॥

2. Destroyers of foes, gods, adored by *Manu*, who are three-and-thirty, and are thus hymned.

६६६९. ते न॑स्त्राध्वं॒ ते॑ऽवत त उ॒ नो॒ अधि॑ वोचत।

मा न॑ः प॒थः पित्र्या॒न्मान॒वादधि॒ दूरं॑ नैष्ट परावत॑ः॥३॥

3. Do you preserve us, do you protect us, do you direct us (to our good); lead us not afar from the paternal paths of *Manu*, nor from those still more distant.

From the Paternal Paths of Manu— *Manu* is said to be the universal father, and the paths he enjoins are those of austerity and ceremonial. *Brahmacarya agnihotrādi-karmāṇi yena mārgeṇa bhavanti tam eva asmānnayata*. [Sāyaṇa explains the latter line, "Lead us not away from the far-reaching paternal path of *Manu*, but away from any which is distant therefrom."]

६६७०. ये दे॑वास इ॒ह स्थन॒ विश्वे॑ वैश्वान॒रा उ॒त।

अ॒स्मभ्यं॒ शर्म॑ सप्र॒थो गवेऽश्वा॑य यच्छत॥४॥

4. Gods, who are here present, all to whom this full sacrifice is offered, bestow upon us, upon our cattle and horses, happiness far renowned.

ANUVĀKA V

[सूक्त- ३१]

[ऋषि- मनुर्वैवस्वत। देवता- १-४ यज्ञ स्तुति तथा यजमान प्रशंसा, ५-९ दम्पती, १०-१८ दम्पती-आशीष। छन्द- गायत्री ९-१४ अनुष्टुप् , १० पादनिचृत् , १५-१८ पंक्ति]

६६७१. यो यजा॑ति यजा॑त॒ इत्सुन॒वच्च॑ प॒चाति॑ च। ब्र॒ह्मेदिन्द्र॑स्य चाकनत्॥१॥

1. He who offers oblations (to the gods, again) offers them: he pours forth libations and presents (the sacred cake), he delights in reiterating the praise verily of *Indra*.

The Sacred Cake— The *paśu-puroḍāśa* is explained in the *Nyāya-mala-vistara* as the cake, which is an essential part of the animal sacrifice in the *jyotiṣṭoma, paśu-devatā-sanskāraḥ*.

६६७२. पुरोळाशं यो अस्मै सोमं ररत आशिरम्। पादित्तं शक्रो अंहसः॥२॥

2. *Indra* protects from sin that man who offers him cakes and presents *Soma* mixed with milk.

६६७३. तस्य द्युमाँ असद्रथो देवजूतः स शूशुवत्। विश्वा वन्वन्नमित्रिया॥३॥

3. A brilliant chariot comes to him, sent by the gods, with which, baffling all hostilities, he prospers.

६६७४. अस्य प्रजावती गृहेऽसश्चन्ती दिवेदिवे। इळां धेनुमतीं दुहे॥४॥

4. In his house perpetual abundance, accompanied by progeny, (is present), and milch kine are milked day by day.

Sāyaṇa explains it, "in his house perpetual abundance, accompanied by progeny and cattle, is milked day by day''; or *Ila* may be taken as the goddess of cows, in which case *duhe* is explained, "milks forth, bestows.''

६६७५. या दम्पती समनसा सुनुत आ च धावतः। देवासो नित्ययाशिरा॥५॥

5. Gods, may the husband and wife, who with one mind offer libations and purify them, and (propitiate you) with the *Soma* ever mixed with milk,—

६६७६. प्रति प्राशव्याँ इतः सम्यञ्चा बर्हिराशाते। न ता वाजेषु वायतः॥६॥

6. Constantly associated, may they acquire appropriate (sacrificial) viands; may they be able to offer sacrifice; may they never be wanting in food (given by the gods).

May they never be wanting in food given by the Gods— The phraseology is not very perspicuous, *na ta vājeṣu vayataḥ* is explained *devairdatteṣvanneṣu na gacchataḥ. sarvadā annasahitau tiṣṭhatām.*

६६७७. न देवानामपि ह्नुतः सुमतिं न जुगुक्षतः। श्रवो बृहद्दिवासतः॥७॥

7. They retract not (their promises) to the gods, they withhold not your praise, but offer aboundant (sacrificial) food.

६६७८. पुत्रिणा ता कुमारिणा विश्वमायुर्व्यश्नुतः। उभा हिरण्यपेशसा॥८॥

8. Blessed with youthful and adolescent offspring, and both having their persons richly ornamented, they pass (happily) their whole life.

६६७९. वीतिहोत्रा कृतद्वसू दशस्यन्तामृताय कम्।
समूधो रोशमं हन्तो देवेषु कृणुतो दुवः॥९॥

9. Offering acceptable sacrifices, obtaining the wealth they solicit, presenting gratifying (oblations to the gods), for the sake of

immortality enjoying personal union, they (wife and husband) worship the gods.

Offering Acceptable Sacrifices— Sāyaṇa explains *vītihotra* as "they whose sacrifices procure them happiness," and *kṛtadvasu* as *pātreṣūpayuktadhanau,* "bestowing your wealth on the suppliant."

For the Sake of Immortality— *Amṛtāya;* the comment explains it, for the increase of descendant, *santānābhivṛddhaye.*

६६८०. आ शर्म पर्वतानां वृणीमहे नदीनाम्। आ विष्णोः सचोभुवः॥१०॥

10. We solicit the happiness (afforded) by the mountains, the rivers, and *Viṣṇu,* associated (with the gods).

६६८१. ऐतु पूषा रयिर्भगः स्वस्ति सर्वधातमः। उरुरध्वा स्वस्तये॥११॥

11. May the adorable *Pūṣan,* the possessor of opulence, the most benevolent patron to all, come auspiciously; may a wide path (be open) for our prosperity.

६६८२. अरमतिरनर्वणो विश्वो देवस्य मनसा। आदित्यानामनेह इत्॥१२॥

12. All men with (devout) minds are the unwearied (praisers) of the irresistible deity (*Pūṣan*), verily the (most) sinless of the *Ādityas.*

Unwearied Praisers— Sāyaṇa takes *aramatih* as for *alam-matih,* which he explains as *paryāpta-stutiḥ.*

Verily the most sinless of the *Ādityas—* Sāyaṇa explains this latter clause, "verily (the gifts) of the *Ādityas* are void of evil, (therefore we praise *Pūṣan* for the attainment of food, etc.")

६६८३. यथा नो मित्रो अर्यमा वरुणः सन्ति गोपाः।

सुगा ऋतस्य पन्थाः॥१३॥

13. Since *Mitra, Aryaman* and *Varuṇa* are our protectors, may the paths of the sacrifice be easitly traversed (by them).

६६८४. अग्निं वः पूर्व्यं गिरा देवमीळे वसूनाम्।

सपर्यन्तः पुरुप्रियं मित्रं न क्षेत्रसाधसम्॥१४॥

14. I worship the divine *Agni,* the preceder of you, (gods), with praise, (for the sake) of riches; the worshippers (cherish him), the bountiful perfector of the sacrifice, like a friend.

६६८५. मक्षू देववतो रथः शूरो वा पृत्सु कासु चित्।

देवानां य इन्मनो यजमान इयक्षत्यभिदयर्ज्वनो भुवत्॥१५॥

15. The chariot of the devout worshipper quickly (prevails), as the hero (prevals) in all combats whatever: the celebrator of the

sacrifice, who desires to propitiate the mind of the gods, overcomes those who are no sacrificers.

६६८६. न यजमान रिष्यसि न सुन्वान न देव्यो।

देवानां य इन्मनो यजमान इयक्षत्यभीदयर्ज्वनो भुवत्॥१६॥

16. Devoted to the gods, pouring out to them libations, you, worshipper, shalt not perish: the celebrator of the sacrifice, who desires to propitiate the mind of the gods, overcomes those who are no sacrificers.

६६८७. नकिष्टं कर्मणा नशत्र प्र यौषत्र योषति।

देवानां य इन्मनो यजमान इयक्षत्यभीदयर्ज्वनो भुवत्॥१७॥

17. No one obstructs him by his acts, he is never driven (from his station), he is never separated (from his family): the celebrator of the sacrifice, who desires to propitiate the mind of the gods, overcomes those who are no sacrificers.

६६८८. असदत्रं सुवीर्यमुत त्यदाश्वश्व्यम्।

देवानां य इन्मनो यजमान इयक्षत्यभीदयर्ज्वनो भुवत्॥१८॥

18. To him in this life is a valiant progeny, to him are swift herds of horses; the celebrator of the sacrifice, who desires to propitiate the mind of the gods, overcomes those who are no sacrificers.

[सूक्त-३२]

[ऋषि– मेधातिथि काण्व। देवता– इन्द्र। छन्द– गायत्री।]

६६८९. प्र कृतान्यृजीषिणः कण्वा इन्द्रस्य गाथया। मदे सोमस्य वोचत॥१॥

1. Celebrate with songs the great deeds of *Indra*, the drinker of the stale *Soma*, when in his exhilaration.

Sāyaṇa seems to explain this: ''Proclaim the deeds of the stale *Soma*, in the words of *Indra* when filled with exhilaration.''

६६९०. यः सृबिन्दमनर्शनिं पिप्रुं दासमहीशुवम्। वधीदुग्रो रिणन्नपः॥२॥

2. The fierce (deity) who, liberating the waters, has slain Sṛbinda, Anarśani, Pipru and the slave *Ahiśuva*.

The Slave— Sāyaṇa makes *Dāsa* another proper name. *Dasam ca Ahiśuvam ca.*

६६९१. न्यर्बुदस्य विष्टपं वर्ष्माणं बृहतस्तिर। कृषे तदिन्द्र पौस्यम्॥३॥

3. Pierce the rain-holding domain of the vast *Arbuda*: achieve, *Indra*, this manly exploit.

६६९२. प्रति श्रुतायं वो धृषत्तूर्णाशं न गिरेरधि। हुवे सुशिप्रमूतयें।।४।।

4. I invoke the victorious handsome-jawed *Indra* for your protection, and to hear (your praises), as (a traveller invokes) the water from the cloud.

As a traveller invokes the water from the Cloud— *Turṇāśam na girer adhi.* Sāyaṇa quotes Yāska 5.16. for *turṇāśa*[1] meaning *udaka.* He explains the sense, as a man in hot weather calls for water from the cloud, *yathā gharme 'bhitaptaḥ pumān udakam megham prati hvayati.*

६६९३. स गोर्श्वस्य वि व्रजं मन्दानः सोम्येभ्यं:। पुरं न शूर दर्षसि।।५।।

5. Exhilarated by the *Soma* draughts, you, hero, throw open the pastures of the cattle and horses like a (hostile) city.

Exhilarated by the Soma Draughts— Sāyaṇa explains *somyebhyaḥ* by *somārhebhyaḥ, i.e.,* exhilarated you throw them open to those worthy of the *Soma* or to the worthy offerers of the *Soma.*

६६९४. यदि मे रारणः सुत उक्थे वा दधसे चनं:।
आरादुप स्वधा गहि।।६।।

6. If you are propitiated by my libation and praise, and bestow food (upon me), come with viands from afar.

६६९५. वयं घा ते अपि ष्मसि स्तोतार इन्द्र गिर्वणः:।
त्वं नो जिन्व सोमपाः।।७।।

7. *Indra*, who are pleased by praise, we are your adorers; do you therefore, who are the drinker of the *Soma,* be generous unto us.

Sāmaveda, 230.

६६९६. उत नः पितुमा भर संरराणो अविक्षितम्। मघवन्भूरि ते वसु।।८।।

8. Gratified by us, bring us undiminished food, *Maghavan*, for vast is your wealth.

६६९७. उत नो गोमतस्कृधि हिरण्यवतो अश्विनः:। इळाभिः सं रभेमहि।।९।।

9. Make us (*Indra*) possessed of cattle, of gold, and of horses: may we prosper with abundant viands.

६६९८. बृबदुक्थं हवामहे सुप्रकरस्नमूतयें। साधु कृण्वन्तमर्वसे।।१०।।

<hr>

१. तूर्णाशमुदकं भवति तूर्णमश्नुते (नि० ५.१६)।

10. We invoke *Indra*, who is greatly to be praised, whose arm is stretched out for the protection (of the world), acting nobly for our defence.

Sāmaveda, 217.

६६९९. य: संस्थे चिच्छतक्रतुरादीं कृणोति वृत्रहा।

जरितृभ्य: पुरूवसु:॥११॥

11. The slayer of *Vṛtra*, the accomplisher of a hundred exploits in war, achieves them that he may be the giver of much wealth to his worshippers.

६७००. स न: शक्रश्चिदा शंकदानवाँ अन्तराभर:।

इन्द्रो विश्वाभिरूतिभि:॥१२॥

12. May *Śakra* give us strength, may the liberal *Indra* with all protections be the supplier of our deficiencies.

Supplier of our Deficiencies— *Antarābharaḥ* is explained *chidrāṇām āpūrakaḥ*, or *chidrāpidhāyī*, the filler up or cover of flaws.

६७०१. यो रायोऽ३ वनिर्महान्त्सुपार: सुन्वत: सखा। तमिन्द्रमभि गायत॥१३॥

13. Glorify that *Indra* who is the preserver of riches, the mighty, the converyer beyond (calamity), the friend of the offerer of the libation;

The Conveyer beyond Calamity— Sāyaṇa is more often explained "ready to be brought by praise."

६७०२. आयन्तारं महि स्थिरं पृतनासु श्रवोजितम्। भूरेरीशानमोजसा॥१४॥

14. Him who comes nigh, the mighty, the firm in battles, the acquirer of fame, the lord of vast riches through his prowess.

The Acquirer of Fame— *Śravojitam* might also mean "the winner of wealth or food."

६७०३. नकिरस्य शचीनां नियन्ता सूनृतानाम्। नकिर्वक्ता न दादिति॥१५॥

15. No one puts a limit to his glorious deeds, no one asserts that he is not generous.

६७०४. न नूनं ब्रह्मणामृणं प्राशूनामस्ति सुन्वताम्।

न सोमो अप्रता पपे॥१६॥

16. Verily no debt is due (to the gods) by those *Soma*-partaking *Brāhmaṇas* offering libations; the *Soma* is not drunk without the expenditure of boundless (wealth).

Verily no debt is due, Etc.— A text is quoted to the effect that ''he who has a son, or is chaste, is free from debt,'' that is, to the gods and manes, a *ṛṇo yaḥ putrī yadvā brahmacāri.*[1]

Without the expenditure of Boundless Wealth— *Apratā* is explained *avistīrṇadhanena,* which would rather mean ''by one who has not abundant wealth.''

६७०५. पन्य॒ इदुप॑ गायत॒ पन्य॑ उक्था॒नि॑ शंसत।

ब्रह्मा॑ कृणोत॒ पन्य॒ इत्॥१७॥

17. Sing praises to the adorable (*Indra*), repeat prayers to the adorable (*Indra*), address hymns to the adorable (*Indra*).

६७०६. पन्य॒ आ द॑र्दिरच्छता स॒हस्रा॑ वा॒ज्यव्वृ॑त:।

इन्द्रो॒ यो यज्व॑नो वृध॑:॥१८॥

18. The powerful *Indra,* the discomforter of hundreds and thousands, unchecked (by foes), is adorable; he who is the benefactor of the sacrificer.

६७०७. वि षू चर॑ स्वधा॒ अनु॑ कृष्टी॒नामन्वाहु॑व॒:। इन्द्र॑ पिब॒ सुता॑ना॒म्॥१९॥

19. *Indra,* who are to be invoked of man, come to their offered viands, drink of (their) libations.

६७०८. पिब॒ स्वधैन॑वानामु॒त यस्तुग्र्ये॒ सचा॑। उ॒तायमि॑न्द्र॒ यस्तव॑॥२०॥

20. Drink of the (*Soma*) purchased by the milch cow, that (*Soma*) which is mixed with water, that which, *Indra,* is especially your.

Purchased by the Milch Cow— *Svadhainavānām dhenvā kṛtān somān*: as by the text, *dhenvā kṛṇāti.*[2]

६७०९. अतो॑हि म॒न्युषा॑विणं सुषु॒वांस॑मुपा॒रणे॑। इ॒मं रा॒तं सु॒तं पिब॑॥२१॥

21. *Indra,* pass by the man who offers the libation in anger, him who pours it out upon a spot disapproved of; drink this presented *Soma.*

Sāmaveda, 223, but with some variations].

६७१०. इहि॑ ति॒स्र: परा॑वत इ॒हि पञ्च॑ ज॒नाँ अति॑। धेना॑ इन्द्रावचाक॒शत्॥२२॥

22. *Indra,* who have beheld our praises, proceed in three directions from a distance, pass beyond the five orders of beings.

---

१. एष वा अनृणो य: पुत्री यज्वा ब्रह्मचारिवासी (तै० सं० ६.३.१०.५)।

२. धेन्वा क्रीणाति (तै० सं० ६.१.१०.२)।

In three Directions from a Distance— *I.e.,* Come to us from in front, from behind, and from the side.

६७११. सूर्यो रश्मिं यथा सृजा त्वां यच्छन्तु मे गिरः।
निम्नमापो न सध्र्यक्॥२३॥

23. As the sun disperses his rays, do you disperse (wealth upon me): may my praises rapidly draw you, as waters (reach) the low ground.

६७१२. अध्वर्यवा तु हि षिञ्च सोमं वीराय शिप्रिणे।
भरा सुतस्य पीतये॥२४॥

24. *Adhvaryu,* quickly pour forth the *Soma* to the hero *Indra* with the goodly jaws; bring the *Soma* for his drinking.

६७१३. य उद्नः फलिगं भिनन्न्यईःकिसन्धूँरवासृजत्।
यो गोषु पक्वं धारयत्॥२५॥

25. Who clove the cloud for (the issue of) the rain, who sent down the waters, who placed the mature (milk) in the cattle.

६७१४. अहन्वृत्रमृचीषम और्णवाभमहीशुवम्। हिमेनाविध्यदर्बुदम्॥२६॥

26. The brilliant *Indra* slew *Vṛtra, Aurṇavābha, Ahiśuva*; he smote *Arbuda* with frost.

The Brilliant Indra— For *ṛcīṣama, ṛcā dīptyā sama Indraḥ.* see note on VI, 46.4.

६७१५. प्र वं उग्राय निष्टुरेऽषाळ्हाय प्रसक्षिणे। देवत्तं ब्रह्म गायत॥२७॥

27. Sing aloud (priests) to the fierce, victorious (*Indra*) the overpowerer, the subduer (of foes), the praise inspired by the gods;

६७१६. यो विश्वान्यभि व्रता सोमस्य मदे अन्धसः। इन्द्रो देवेषु चेतति॥२८॥

28. *Indra,* who, in the exhilaration of the quaffed *Soma,* makes known among the gods all pious rites.

६७१७. इह त्या सधमाद्या हरी हिरण्यकेश्या।
वोळ्हामभि प्रयो हितम्॥२९॥

29. May those two golden-maned steeds, together exulting, bring him hither to the salutary (sacrificial) food.

६७१८. अर्वाञ्चं त्वा पुरुष्टुत प्रियमेधस्तुता हरी। सोमपेयाय वक्षतः॥३०॥

30. *Indra,* the glorified of many, let your horses, praised by *Priyamedha,* bring you down to drink the *Soma.*

[सूक्त-३३]

[ऋषि– मेध्यातिथि काण्व। देवता– इन्द्र।
छन्द– बृहती, १६-१८ गायत्री, १९ अनुष्टुप्।]

६७१९. वयं घ त्वा सुतावन्त आपो न वृक्तबर्हिषः।
पवित्रस्य प्रस्रवणेषु वृत्रहन् परि स्तोतार आसते॥१॥

1. We are pouring forth to you the *Soma* juice like water: the praisers, strewing the clipt sacred grass, worship you, slayer of *Vṛtra*, in the streams (falling) from the filter.

Sāmaveda, 864.

६७२०. स्वरन्ति त्वा सुते नरो वसो निरेक उक्थिनः।
कदा सुतं तृषाण ओक आ गमं इन्द्र स्वब्दीव वंसगः॥२॥

2. The leaders (of rites), repeating praises, shout to you, *Vasu*, when the libation issues forth; when, *Indra*, bellowing like a bull, do you come to the dwelling thirsting for the *Soma?*

Sāmaveda, 865, but with *gamat* for *gamaḥ.*]

६७२१. कण्वेभिर्धृष्णवा धृषद्वाजं दर्षि सहस्रिणम्।
पिशङ्गरूपं मघवन् विचर्षणे मक्षू गोमन्तमीमहे॥३॥

3. Resolute (*Indra*), bestow abundantly upon the descendants of *Kaṇva* thousands of viands; wise *Maghavan*, we earnestly solicit you for (wealth) of gold and cattle.

Wealth of Gold and Cattle—*Piśaṅga-rūpam,* "tawny-coloured," is left unexplained by the commentary.

Sāmaveda, 866.

६७२२. पाहि गायान्धसो मद इन्द्राय मेध्यातिथे।
यः संमिश्लो हर्योर्यः सुते सचा वज्री रथो हिरण्ययः॥४॥

4. Drink, *Medhyātithi*, and in the exhilaration of the draught sing to *Indra*, to him who has harnessed his horses, who, when the *Soma* is poured out, is present, the wielder of the thunderbolt, whose chariot is of gold.

Sāmaveda, 289, but the reading differs in some respects, as in the beginning, *pāhi gā andhaso,* instead of *pāhi gāyāndhaso,* and instead of *sute sacā vajrī ratho,* it has *hiraṇyāya indro vajrī.*

६७२३. यः सुष्व्यः सुदक्षिण इनो यः सुक्रतुर्गृणे।
य आकरः सहस्रा यः शतामघ इन्द्रो यः पूर्भिदारितः॥५॥

5. He who is well-handed, both left and right, who is the lord, who is wise, the performer of numerous great acts, the giver of vast wealth, *Indra*, who is the demolisher of cities, who is gratified by praise, is glorified (by us).

६७२४. यो धृषितो योऽवृतो यो अस्ति श्मश्रुषु श्रितः।

विभूतद्युम्नश्च्यवनः पुरुष्टुतः क्रत्वा गौरिव शाकिनः॥६॥

6. He who is the subduer (of foes), the unresisted, practised in combats, possessed of vast wealth, the demander of the libation, the praised of many, who by his acts (of bounty) is like a milch cow to the competent (worshipper).

Practised in Combats— *Śmaśruṣu śritaḥ. Śmaśruṣu* is explained as *yuddha,* a very unusual sense.

The Demander of the Libation— *Cyavana* is literally he who causes to fall or flow, that is, the *Soma*.

६७२५. क ईं वेद सुते सचा पिबन्तं कद्वयो दधे।

अयं यः पुरो विभिनत्त्योजसा मन्दानः शिप्र्यन्धसः॥७॥

7. Who knows him drinking with (the priests) when the *Soma* is effused? What food has he partaken of? He, the handsome-jawed, who, exhilarated by the (sacrificial) beverage, destroys cities by his might.

Sāmaveda, 297, 1696.

६७२६. दाना मृगो न वारणः पुरुत्रा चरथं दधे।

नकिष्ट्वा नि यमदा सुते गमो महाँश्चरस्योजसा॥८॥

8. As a wild elephant emitting the dews of passion, he manifests his exhilaration in many places: no one checks you, (*Indra*), come to the libation; you are mighty, and goes (everywhere) through your strength.

Sāmaveda, 1697.

६७२७. य उग्रः सन्ननिष्टृतः स्थिरो रणाय संस्कृतः।

यदि स्तोतुर्मघवा शृणवद्धवं नेन्द्रो योषत्या गमत्॥९॥

9. He who is fierce, unmoved (by foes) and firm, ready equipped for battle,—if *Maghavan* hear the invocation of his adorer, he will not go apart (from us) but come hither.

Sāmaveda, 1698.

६७२८. सत्यमित्था वृषेदसि वृषजूतिर्नोऽवृतः।

वृषा ह्युग्र शृण्विषे परावति वृषो अर्वावति श्रुतः॥१०॥

10. Verily (*Indra*), in this manner you are the showerer (of benefits), brought by vigorous (steeds) to us, unrested (by foes); fierce (*Indra*), you are celebrated as a showerer (of benefits) when afar; you are celebrated as a showerer (of benefits) when nigh.

Sāmaveda, 263, but with *avita* for *avṛtaḥ*], The usual abuse of *Vṛṣān* occurs in this and the two following verses.

६७२९. वृषंणस्ते अभीशंवो वृषा कशा हिरण्ययी।
वृषा रथो मघवन्वृषणा हरी वृषा त्वं शंतक्रतो।।११।।

11. Showerers (of benefits) are your reins, such also is your golden whip, your chariot, *Maghavan*, is a showerer (of benefits), so are your two horses; and you, too, *Śatakratu*, are the showerer (of benefits).

६७३०. वृषा सोता सुनोतु ते वृषन्नृजीपिन्न भर।
वृषा दधन्वे वृषणं नदीष्वा तुभ्यं स्थातर्हरीणाम्।।१२।।

12. Showerer (of benefits), may the offerer of the libation to you effuse the *Soma* as a showerer; straight-going (*Indra*), bring (us wealth): arrester of your horses, the showerer (of the oblation) has prepared the bountiful *Soma* to be mixed with the waters for you.

६७३१. एन्द्र याहि पीतये मधु शविष्ठ सोम्यम्।
नायमच्छा मघवा शृणवद् गिरो ब्रह्मोक्था च सुक्रतुः।।१३।।

13. Come, most powerful *Indra*, to drink of the *Soma* ambrosia, (for without coming) this *Maghavan*, the achiever of many exploits, hears not our praises, our chaunts, our hymns.

६७३२. वहन्तु त्वा रथेष्ठामा हरयो रथयुजः।
तिरश्चिदर्यं सर्वानानि वृत्रहन्न्येषां या शंतक्रतो।।१४।।

14. *Śatakratu*, slayer of *Vṛtra*, let your horses, yoked to your car, bring you, the lord, riding in your chariot, (to our sacrifices), avoiding those sacrifices (offered) by others.

६७३३. अस्माकमद्यान्तमं स्तोमं धिष्व महामह।
अस्माकं ते सर्वना सन्तु शन्तमा मदाय द्युक्ष सोमपाः।।१५।।

15. Greatest of the great, brilliant drinker of the *Soma*, accept to-day this our present praise; may our sacrifices be most successful in exciting your exhilaration.

६७३४. नहि षस्तव नो मर्म शास्त्रे अन्यस्य रण्यति।
यो अस्मान्वीर आनयत्।।१६।।

16. The hero (*Indra*) who has (ever) guided us delights not in
your punishment, nor in mine; nor in that of any other.

Who has Ever Guided Us— *Śāstra* is explained *śāsana,* governing
or punishing. The Scholiast evidently takes it in the latter sense, as he
adds, *kintu rakṣaṇa eva ramate,* he, *Indra,* delights only in protecting or
preserving.

६७३५. इन्द्रश्चिद्घा तदब्रवीत्त्रिया अंशास्यं मनं:।
उतो अह क्रतुं रघुम्।।१७।।

17. Verily *Indra* said that the mind of a woman is not to be
controlled, he declared also that her intellect was small.

The mind of a Woman, Etc.— According to the comment, this
refers to a legend that *Asaṅga,* the son of *Playoga,* the patron of the *Ṛṣi,*
had been changed to a woman; see the story in the beginning.

६७३६. सप्ती चिद्घा मदच्युता मिथुना वहतो रथम्।
एवेद्धूर्वृष्ण उत्तरा।।१८।।

18. The two horses of *Indra,* hastening to the exhilaration (of
the *Soma*), draw his chariot; the pole of the showerer rests upon
them.

६७३७. अध: पश्यस्व मोपरि सन्तरां पादकौ हर।
मा ते कशप्लकौ दृशन्त्स्त्री हि ब्रह्मा बभूविथ।।१९।।

19. Cast your eyes (son of Playoga) downwards, not upwards:
keep your feet close together; let not (men) behold your ankles, for
from having been a *Brahmā* you have become a female.

You have Become, Female— *Indra* is supposed to say this to
Asaṅga as a female.

[सूक्त- ३४]

[ऋषि- १-१५ नीपातिथि काण्व, १६-१८ सहस्र वसुरोचिष् अङ्गिरस्।।
देवता- इन्द्र। छन्द- अनुष्टुप्, १६-१८ गायत्री।]

६७३८. एन्द्र याहि हरिभिरुप कण्वस्य सुष्टुतिम्।
दिवो अमुष्य शासतो दिवं यय दिवावसो।।१।।

1. Come, *Indra,* with your horses to receive the praise of
Kaṇva; do you, ruling younder heaven, O radiant with oblations,
return thither.

Do you, Ruling Yonder Heaven, Etc.— This line, which constitutes the burden of the hymn, is singularly indistinct, *divo amuṣya śāsato divam yaya divāvaso,* literally, of heaven of that one governing go you to heaven, heaven-affluent. The Scholiast is evidently perplexed; in one interpretation he laters the cases to *divam amuṣmin (Indre) śāsati,* and adds, *tatra vayam sukham āsmahe,* (when *Indra* rules heaven we abide there happily). *Divāvaso* he interprets *dīptahavịṣka.* The gives another explanation (which is followed in the text) *dyunāmakam amum lokam śāsanam kurvanto yuyam svargam gacchata.* In his comment on the passage in the *Sāmaveda,* 348, 1807 he considers *amuṣya* as put for *amuṣmāt pṛthivī-lokāt*—from this world. None are very satisfactory; possibly it is intended to say merely that as *Indra's* presence is necessary in heaven, he is to be allowed to go back as soon as he has partaken of the *Soma* at the sacrifice on earth. [Benefy takes *divam* for the *Soma*-vessel, *dyulokākhya-droṇakalaśa,* and considers the line as addressed to *Indra* and his horses; "von Himmel jenes Herschenden geht ihr zum Himmel, Strahlender."]

६७३९. आ त्वा ग्रावा वदन्निह सोमी घोषेण यच्छतु।

दिवो अमुष्य शासतो दिवं यय दिवावसो।।२।।

2. May the grinding stone, yielding the *Soma* juice as it utters a sound, bring you hither with the noise; do you, ruling younder heaven, O radiant with oblations, return thither.

Sāmaveda, 1809.

६७४०. अत्रा वि नेमिरेषामुरां न धूनुते वृक:।

दिवो अमुष्य शासतो दिवं यय दिवावसो।।३।।

3. The circumference of these (stones) shakes (the *Soma*) at this (rite), as a wolf (terrifies) a sheep do you, ruling younder heaven, O radiant with oblations, return thither.

Sāmaveda, 1808.

६७४१. आ त्वा कण्वा इहावसे हवन्ते वाजसातये।

दिवो अमुष्य शासतो दिवं यय दिवावसो।।४।।

4. The *Kaṇvas* invoke you hither for protection and for food; do you, ruling yonder heaven, O radiant with oblations, return thither.

६७४२. दधामि ते सुतानां वृष्णे न पूर्वपाय्यम्।

दिवो अमुष्य शासतो दिवं यय दिवावसो।।५।।

5. I make offering to you of the libations as the first drink is presented to the showerer; do you, ruling yonder heaven, O radiant with oblations, return thither.

To the Showerer— *Vṛiṣṇe,* which the Scholiast explains as *Vāyu.*
[*Cf. Aitareya Brāhmaṇa,* ii.25.]

६७४३. स्मत्पुरन्धिर्न आ गहि विश्वतोधीर्न ऊतयें।
दिवो अमुष्य शास॑तो दिवं यय दिंवावसो।।६।।

6. (*Indra*) master of the family of heaven, come to us: do you,
who are the sustainer of the universe, (come) for our protection: do
you, ruling yonder heaven, O radiant with oblations, return thither.

Master of the Family of Heaven— *Smatpurandhi* is interpreted
svargakuṭumbin.

६७४४. आ नों याहि महेमते सह॑स्रोते शता॑मघ।
दिवो अमुष्य॒ शास॑तो दिवं यय दिंवावसो।।७।।

7. Sagacious (*Indra*) bestower of numerous protections,
granter of infinite wealth, come unto us: do you, ruling yonder
heaven, O radiant with oblations, return thither.

६७४५. आ त्वा॒ होता॒ मनु॑र्हितो देवत्रा व॑क्षदीड्यः।
दिवो अमुष्य॒ शास॑तो दिवं यय दिंवावसो।।८।।

8. May (*Agni*) the invoker, adorable among the gods, the
benefactor of man, bring you hither: do you, ruling yonder heaven,
O radiant with oblation, return thither.

The Benefactor of Man— Sāyaṇa here explains *manur-hitaḥ* as
"placed by men in their houses," but he allows the meaning in the text in
his Commentary on i.106.5.

६७४६. आ त्वा॒ मदच्युता॒ हरी॑ श्येनं पक्षेंव वक्षतः।
दिवो अमुष्य॒ शास॑तो दिवं यय दिंवावसो।।९।।

9. Let your two steeds, humiliators of the pride (of foes), bring
you as (his) two wings (bear along) the faclcon: do you, ruling
yonder heaven, O radiant with oblations, return thither.

६७४७. आ या॒ह्यर्य आ परि स्वाहा सोम॑स्य पीतयें।
दिवो अमुष्य॒ शास॑तो दिवं यय दिंवावसो।।१०।।

10. Come, lord, from whatever direction, to drink the *Soma*
offered with *svāhā*: do you, ruling yonder heaven, radiant with
oblations, return thither.

६७४८. आ नों याह्युप॑श्रुत्युक्थेषु॑ रणया इह।
दिवो अमुष्य॒ शास॑तो दिवं यय दिंवावसो।।११।।

11. Come to listen to our praises, when they are being recited,—bestow upon us delight: do you, ruling yonder heaven, O radiant with oblations, return thither.

६७४९. सरूपैरा सु नो॑ गहि संभृ॑तै॒: सम्भृ॒ताश्व॑:।
दि॒वो अ॒मुष्य॒ शास॑तो॒ दिवं॒ यय॒ दिंवावसो॥१२॥

12. *Indra*, who are possessed of cherished steeds, come to us with (your) well-fed and like-shaped horses: do you, ruling yonder heaven, O radiant with oblations, return thither.

६७५०. आ या॑हि॒ पर्व॑तेभ्य: समु॒द्रस्याधि॑ वि॒ष्टप॑:।
दि॒वो अ॒मुष्य॒ शास॑तो॒ दिवं॒ यय॒ दिंवावसो॥१३॥

13. Come from the mountains, from above the region of the firmament: do you, ruling yonder heaven, O radiant with oblations, return thither.

६७५१. आ नो॑ गव्या॒न्यश्व्या॑ स॒हस्रा॑ शूर दर्दृहि।
दि॒वो अ॒मुष्य॒ शास॑तो॒ दिवं॒ यय॒ दिंवावसो॥१४॥

14. Bestow upon us, hero, thousands of herds of cattle and horses: do you, ruling yonder heaven, O radiant with oblations, return thither.

६७५२. आ न॑: सहस्र॒शो भ॑रा॒युता॑नि श॒तानि॑ च।
दि॒वो अ॒मुष्य॒ शास॑तो॒ दिवं॒ यय॒ दिंवावसो॥१५॥

15. Bring to us, by thousands, tens of thousands and hundreds (of good things): do you, ruling yonder heaven, O radiant with oblations, return thither.

६७५३. आ यदिन्द्र॑श्च॒ दद्व॑हे स॒हस्रं॒ वसु॑रोचिष:। ओजि॑ष्ठम॒श्व्यं॒ पशु॑म्॥१६॥

16. We, the thousand *Vasurociṣas*, and *Indra* (our leader), when we obtain givorous herds of horses,—

६७५४. य ऋ॒ज्रा वा॒तरं॑हसो॒ऽरुषा॑सो॒ रघु॑ष्यद:। भ्राज॑न्ते॒ सूर्या॑ इव॥१७॥

17. Such as are straight-going, fleet as the wind, bright-coloured, light-footed, and shine like the sun,—

६७५५. पारा॑वतस्य रा॒तिषु॑ द्र॒वच्च॑क्रे॒ष्वाशु॑षु। तिष्ठं॒ वन॑स्य॒ मध्य॑ आ॥१८॥

18. Then (having received) the horses, attached to the rolling-wheeled chariot, given from afar, we depart to the middle of the forest.

Given from Afar— *Pārāvatasya rātiṣu. Pārāvata* is probably the name of a king; "the gifts of *Parāvata*."

[सूक्त-३५]

[**ऋषि**– श्यावाश्व आत्रेय। **देवता**– अश्वनीकुमार। **छन्द**– उपरिष्टात् ज्योति
(त्रिष्टुप्), २२,२४ पंक्ति, २३ महाबृहती।]

६७५६. अग्निनेन्द्रेण वरुणेन विष्णुनादित्यै रुद्रैर्वसुभिः सचाभुवा।
सजोषसा उषसा सूर्येण च सोमं पिबतमश्विना।।१।।

1. Associated with *Agni*, with *Indra*, with *Varuṇa*, with *Viṣṇu*, with the *Ādityas*, the *Rudras*, and the *Vasus*, and united with the dawn and with *Sūrya*, drink, *Aśvins*, the *Soma*.

६७५७. विश्वाभिर्धीभिर्भुवनेन वाजिना दिवा पृथिव्याद्रिभिः सचाभुवा।
सजोषसा उषसा सूर्येण च सोमं पिबतमश्विना।।२।।

2. Powerful (*Aśvins*), associated with all intelligences, with all beings, with heaven, with earth, with the mountains, united with the dawn and with *Sūrya*, drink, *Aśvins*, the *Soma*.

६७५८. विश्वैर्देवैस्त्रिभिरेकादशैरिहाद्भिर्मरुद्भिर्भृगुभिः सचाभुवा।
सजोषसा उषसा सूर्येण च सोमं पिबतमश्विना।।३।।

3. Associated with all the thrice-eleven deities at this ceremony, with the waters, with the *Maruts*, with the *Bhṛgus*, united with the dawn and with *Sūrya*, drink, *Aśvins*, the *Soma*.

६७५९. जुषेथां यज्ञं बोधतं हवस्य मे विश्वेह देवौ सवनाव गच्छतम्।
सजोषसा उषसा सूर्येण चेषं नो वोळ्हमश्विना।।४।।

4. Be gratified by the sacrifice; hear my invocation; recognize, deities, all the offerings in this ceremony; united with the dawn and with *Sūrya*, bring us, *Aśvins*, food.

६७६०. स्तोमं जुषेथां युवशेव कन्यनां विश्वेह देवौ सवनाव गच्छतम्।
सजोषसा उषसा सूर्येण चेषं नो वोळ्हमश्विना।।५।।

5. Be gratified by our praise as youths are delighted (by the voices) of maidens: recognize, deities, all the offerings in this ceremony; united with the dawn and with *Sūrya*, bring us, *Aśvins*, food.

६७६१. गिरो जुषेथामध्वरं जुषेथां विश्वेह देवौ सवनावं गच्छतम्।
सजोषसा उषसा सूर्येण चेषं नो वोळ्हमश्विना॥६॥

6. Be gratified, deities, by our praises, be gratified by the
sacrifice, recognize, deities, all the offerings in this ceremony;
united with the dawn and with *Sūrya*, bring us, *Aśvins*, food.

६७६२. हारिद्रवेव पतथो वनेदुप सोमं सुतं महिषेवावं गच्छथः।
सजोषसा उषसा सूर्येण च त्रिवर्तिर्यातमश्विना॥७॥

7. You alight upon the effused *Soma* as the *Hāridravā* plunges
unto the water: you fall upon it like two buffaloes (plunging into a
pool); united with the dawn and with *Sūrya*, come, *Aśvins*, by the
triple path.

Hāridravā—The Scholiast in a former passage (see Vol. I, *mantra*,
598 and note) makes *hāridravā* a tree; here it is a bird of a yellow colour
probably.

By the Triple Path— *Trir vartir yātam*, "the three daily
ceremonies." [Or "come thrice to our dwelling."]

६७६३. हंसाविव पतथो अध्वगाविव सोमं सुतं महिषेवावं गच्छथः।
सजोषसा उषसा सूर्येण च त्रिवर्तिर्यातमश्विना॥८॥

8. As two geese, as two travellers, as two buffaloes (hasten to
water), ye alight, *Aśvins*, upon the effused *Soma*; united with the
dawn and with *Sūrya*, come, *Aśvins*, by the triple path.

६७६४. श्येनाविव पतथो हव्यदातये सोमं सुतं महिषेवावं गच्छथः।
सजोषसा उषसा सूर्येण च त्रिवर्तिर्यातमश्विना॥९॥

9. Ye hasten like two falcons to the offerer of the libation, ye
alight upon the effused *soma* as two buffaloes (hasten to water);
united with the dawn and with *Sūrya*, come, *Aśvins*, by the triple
path.

६७६५. पिबतं च तृप्णुतं चा च गच्छतं प्रजां च धत्तं द्रविणं च धत्तम्।
सजोषसा उषसा सूर्येण चोर्जं नो धत्तमश्विना॥१०॥

10. Drink, *Aśvins*, the *Soma*, and staiate yourselves; come
hither; give us progeny; give us wealth; united with the dawn and
with *Sūrya*, give us, *Aśvins*, strength.

६७६६. जयतं च प्र स्तुतं च प्र चावतं प्रजां च धत्तं द्रविणं च धत्तम्।
सजोषसा उषसा सूर्येण चोर्जं नो धत्तमश्विना॥११॥

11. Conquer (*Asvins*,) your foes; protect and praise (your worshipper), grant progeny, give wealth, and, united with the dawn and with *Sūrya*, give us, *Asvins*, strength.

६७६७. हतं च शत्रून्यतंतं च मित्रिणं: प्रजां चं धत्तं द्रविणं च धत्तम्।
सजोषंसा उषसा सूर्येण चोर्जं नो धत्तमश्विना॥१२॥

12. Destroy your foes, repair to your friends, grant pogeny, give wealth, and, united with the dawn and with *Sūrya*, give us, *Asvins*, strength.

६७६८. मित्रावरुणवन्ता उत धर्मवन्ता मरुत्वन्ता जरितुर्गच्छथो हवंम्।
सजोषंसा उषसा सूर्येण चादित्यैर्यांतमश्विना॥१३॥

13. Associated with *Mitra* and *Varuṇa*, with Dharma, with the *Maruts*, repair to the invocation of the adorer; repair (to him), *Asvins*, united with the down, with *Sūrya*, and with the *Ādityas*.

६७६९. अङ्गिरस्वन्ता उत विष्णुवन्ता मरुत्वन्ता जरितुर्गच्छथो हवंम्।
सजोषंसा उषसा सूर्येण चादित्यैर्यांतमश्विना॥१४॥

14. Associated with the *Angirasas*, with *Viṣṇu*, with the *Maruts*, repair to the invocation of the adorer; repair (to him), *Asvins*, united with the dawn, with *Sūrya*, and with the *Ādityas*.

६७७०. ऋभुमन्तां वृषणा वाजवन्ता मरुत्वन्ता जरितुर्गच्छथो हवंम्।
सजोषंसा उषसा सूर्येण चादित्यैर्यांतमश्विना॥१५॥

15. Associated with the *Ṛbhus*, and with the *Maruts*, repair, showerers (of benefits), dispensers of food, to the invocation of the adorer; repair (to him), *Asvins*, united with the dawn, with *Sūrya*, and with the *Ādityas*.

६७७१. ब्रह्मं जिन्वतमुत जिन्वतं धियो हतं रक्षांसि सेधंतममीवा:।
सजोषंसा उषसा सूर्येण च सोमं सुन्वतो अश्विना॥१६॥

16. Be propitious to prayer, be propitious to sacred rites, slay the *Rākṣasas*, remedy diseases united with the dawn and with *Sūrya*, (drink), *Asvins*, the *Soma* of the offerer.

Be Propitious to Prayer— *Brahma jinvatam*. The Scholiast renders the substantive by *Brāhmaṇa*.

६७७२. क्षत्रं जिन्वतमुत जिन्वतं नृन्हतं रक्षांसि सेधंतममीवा:।
सजोषंसा उषसा सूर्येण च सोमं सुन्वतो अश्विना॥१७॥

17. Be propitious to the strong, be propitious to men, slay the *Rākṣasas*, remedy diseases; united with the dawn and with *Sūrya*, (drink), *Aśvins*, the *Soma* of the offerer.

Be Propitious to the Strong— *Kṣatram jinvatam uta jivantam nṛn.* The first is explained *kṣatriyam,* the second *yoddhā,* "warriors."

६७७३. धेनूर्जिन्वतमुत जिन्वतं विशो हतं रक्षांसि सेधतममीवा:।

सजोषसा उषसा सूर्येण च सोमं सुन्वतो अश्विना॥१८॥

18. Be propitious to the kine, be propitious to the people, slay the *Rākṣasas*, remedy diseases; united with the dawn and with *Sūrya*, (drink), *Aśvins*, the *Soma* of the offerer.

Be Propitious to the People— *Viśaḥ*, by which Sāyaṇa understands the *Vaiśyas*.

६७७४. अत्रेरिव शृणुतं पूर्व्यस्तुतिं श्यावाश्वस्य सुन्वतो मंदच्युता।

सजोषसा उषसा सूर्येण चाश्विना तिरोअह्न्यम्॥१९॥

19. Humblers of the pride (of your enemies), hear the earnest praise of *Śyāvāśva* offering libations as (you did) that of *Atri*, and, united with the dawn and with *Sūrya*, (drink), *Aśvins*, (the *Soma*) prepared the previous day.

Soma Prepared the Previous Day— *Tiro ahnyam,* according to the Scholiast, is the *Soma* prepared the day before, and drunk at early dawn, at the worship of the *Aśvins*,; *cf.* transl. Vol. I, *mantra* 541.

६७७५. सर्गाँइव सृजतं सुष्टुतीरुप श्यावाश्वस्य सुन्वतो मंदच्युता।

सजोषसा उषसा सूर्येण चाश्विना तिरोअह्न्यम्॥२०॥

20. Humblers of the pride (of your enemies), accept the earnest praises of *Śyāvāśva* offering you libations as if you were accepting oblations; and, united with the dawn and with *Sūrya*, (drink), *Aśvins*, (the *Soma*) prepared the previous day.

६७७६. रश्मीँरिव यच्छतमध्वराँ उप श्यावाश्वस्य सुन्वतो मंदच्युता।

सजोषसा उषसा सूर्येण चाश्विना तिरोअह्न्यम्॥२१॥

21. Humblers of the pride (of your enemies), seize the sacrifices of *Śyāvāśva* offering libations as you seize your reins; and united with the dawn and with *Sūrya*, (drink), *Aśvins*, (the *Soma*) prepared the previous day.

६७७७. अर्वाग्रथं नि यंच्छतं पिबतं सोम्यं मधु।

आ यातमश्विना गंतमवस्युर्वामहं हुवे धत्तं रत्नानि दाशुषे॥२२॥

22. Direct you chariot downwards, drink the *Soma* nectar; come, *Aśvins*, come (hither); desirous of your protection, I invoke you; give precious riches to the donor of the offering.

६७७८. न्खमोवाके प्रस्थिते अध्वरे नरा विवक्षणस्य पीतये।
आ यातमश्विना गंतमवस्युर्वामहं हुवे धत्तं रत्नानि दाशुषे॥२३॥

23. Come, leaders of rites, when the sacrifice, at which your adoration is recited, is commenced, to drink of the *Soma* offered by me; come, *Aśvins*, come (hither); desirous of protection, I invoke you; give precious riches to the donor of the offering.

Offered by Me—Sāyaṇa here takes *vivakṣaṇasya* as an epithet of the speaker, *i.e.*, "at the commenced adoration of me the offerer of libation"; elsewhere, as in viii. 21.5, he takes the word as an epithet of the *Soma*, "heaven-bestowing," *svargaprāpaṇaśīla*.

६७७९. स्वाहाकृतस्य तृम्पतं सुतस्य देवावन्धंस:।
आ यातमश्विना गंतमवस्युर्वामहं हुवे धत्तं रत्नानि दाशुषे॥२४॥

24. Divine (*Aśvins*), partake to satiety of the sacrificial beverage, consecrated with the exclamation *Svāhā*; come, *Aśvins*, come (hither); desirous of protection, I invoke you; give precious riches to the donor of the offering.

[सूक्त-३६]

[**ऋषि**– श्यावाश्व आत्रेय। **देवता**– इन्द्र। **छन्द**– शक्वरी, (७ महापंक्ति।]

६७८०. अवितासि सुन्वतो वृक्तबर्हिष: पिबा सोमं मदाय कं शतक्रतो। यं ते भागमधारयन्विश्वा: सेहान: पृतना उरु ज्रय: समप्सुजिन्मरुत्वाँ इन्द्र सत्पते॥१॥

1. You are the protector of the effuser of the libation, of the strewer of the clipt sacred grass; drink joyfully, *Śatakratu*, the *Soma* for your exhilaration,—that portion which (the gods) assigned you, *Indra*, lord of the virtuous, who are the victor over all (hostile) hosts, the conqueror of many, the subduer of the waters, the leader of the *Maruts*.

The Conqueror of Many— *Uru jrayas*. Sāyaṇa explains *jrayas* here as *vega*, but in viii.6.27 he alternatively explained *urujrayas* as *vistīrṇavyāpin*, "the wide pervader." We might thus render the passage, "the victor over all hostile hosts and over wide space."

६७८१. प्रावं स्तोतारं मघवन्नव त्वां पिबा सोमं मदाय कं शतक्रतो। यं ते
     भागमधारयन् विश्वो: सेहान: पृतना उरु जय: समप्सुजिन्मरुत्वाँ इन्द्र
     सत्पते।।२।।

2. Protect the worshippers, *Maghavan*, protect thyself; drink
joyfully, *Śatakratu*, the *Soma* for your exhilaration,—that portion
which (the gods) assigned you, *Indra*, lord of the virtuous, who are
the victor over all (hostile) hosts, the conqueror of many, the
subduer of the waters, the leader of the *Maruts*.

६७८२. ऊर्जा देवाँ अवस्योर्जसा त्वां पिबा सोमं मदाय कं शतक्रतो। यं ते
     भागमधारयन् विश्वा: सेहान: पृतना उरु जय: समप्सुजिन्मरुत्वाँ इन्द्र
     सत्पते।।३।।

3. You, *Maghavan*, protect the gods with (sacrificial) food, and
yourself by your might; drink joyfully, *Śatakratu*, the *Soma* for
your exhilaration,—that portion which (the gods) assigned you,
Indra, lord of the virtuous, who are the victor over all (hostile)
hosts, the conqueror of many, the subduer of the waters, the leader
of the *Maruts*.

६७८३. जनिता दिवो जनिता पृथिव्य: पिबा सोमं मदाय कं शतक्रतो। यं ते
     भागमधारयन् विश्वा: सेहान: पृतना उरु जय: समप्सुजिन्मरुत्वाँ इन्द्र
     सत्पते।।४।।

4. You, are the generator of heaven, the generator of earth;
drink joyfully, *Śatakratu*, the *Soma* for your exhilaration,—that
portion which (the gods) assigned you, *Indra*, lord of the virtuous,
who are the victor over all (hostile) hosts, the conqueror of many,
the subduer of the waters, the leader of the *Maruts*.

६७८४. जनिताश्वानां जनिता गवांमसि पिबा सोमं मदाय कं शतक्रतो। यं ते
     भागमधारयन् विश्वा: सेहान: पृतना उरु जय: समप्सुजिन्मरुत्वाँ इन्द्र
     सत्पते।।५।।

5. You are the generator of horses, the generator of the cattle;
drink joyfully, *Śatakratu*, the *Soma* for your exhilaration,—that
portion which (the gods) assigned you, *Indra*, lord of the virtuous,
who are the victor over all (hostile) hosts, the conqueror of many,
the subduer of the waters, the leader of the *Maruts*.

६७८५. अत्रीणां स्तोममद्रिवो महस्कृधि पिबा सोमं मदाय कं शतक्रतो। यं
ते भागमधारयन् विश्वाः सेहानः पृतना उरु व्रयः समप्सुजिन्मरुत्वाँ
इन्द्र सत्पते॥६॥

6. Wielder of the thunderbolt, reverence the praise of the *Atris*;
drink joyfully, *Śatakratu*, the *Soma* for your exhilaration,—that
portion which (the gods) assigned you, *Indra*, lord of the virtuous,
who are the victor over all (hostile) hosts, the conqueror of many,
the subduer of the waters, the leader of the *Maruts*.

६७८६. श्यावाश्वस्य सुन्वतस्तथा शृणु यथाशृणोरत्रेः कर्माणि कृण्वतः।
प्र त्रसदस्युमाविथ त्वमेक इन्नृषाह्य इन्द्र ब्रह्माणि वर्धयन्॥७॥

7. Hear (the praises) of *Śyāvāśva* offering the libations, as you
have heard (those) of *Atri* engaged in holy rites: you alone, *Indra*,
have defended *Trasadasyu* in battle, animating his prayers.

[सूक्त-३७]

[**ऋषि**– श्यावाश्व आत्रेय। **देवता**– इन्द्र। **छन्द**– महापंक्ति, १ अतिजगती।]

६७८७. प्रेदं ब्रह्म वृत्रतूर्येष्वाविथ प्र सुन्वतः शचीपत इन्द्र विश्वाभिरूतिभिः।
माध्यंदिनस्य सवनस्य वृत्रहन्नेद्य पिबा सोमस्य वज्रिवः॥१॥

1. You protectest, *Indra*, lord of rites, with all protections in
combats with enemies, this sacrifice of him who offers you the
libations: slayer of *Vṛtra*, irreproachable wielder of the thunderbolt
drink of the *Soma* at the mid-day solemnity.

Who Offers you the Libation— Sāyaṇa explains *Brahma* by
Brāhmaṇan, and takes the whole clause as, "O *Indra*, protect these
Brāhmaṇas with all your protections in combats with enemies, (protect)
those who offer you the libation."

६७८८. सेहान उग्र पृतना अभि द्रुहः शचीपत इन्द्र विश्वाभिरूतिभिः।
माध्यंदिनस्य सवनस्य वृत्रहन्नेद्य पिबा सोमस्य वज्रिवः॥२॥

2. Fierce *Indra*, defeater of hostile armies, lord of rites, (you
protectest) with all your protections; slayer of *Vṛtra*,
irreproachable wielder of the thunderbolt, drink of the *Soma* at the
mid-day solemnity.

६७८९. एकराळस्य भुवनस्य राजसि शचीपत इन्द्र विश्वाभिरूतिभिः।
माध्यंदिनस्य सवनस्य वृत्रहन्नेद्य पिबा सोमस्य वज्रिवः॥३॥

3. You shine the sole sovereign of this world, *Indra*, lord of rites, with all your protections; slayer of *Vṛtra*, irreproachable wielder of the thunderbolt, drink of the *Soma* at the mid-day solemnity.

६७९०. सस्थावाना यवयसि त्वमेक इच्छीपत इन्द्र विश्वाभिरूतिभिः।
माध्यंन्दिनस्य सर्वनस्य वृत्रहन्नेद्व पिबो सोमस्य वज्रिवः॥४॥

4. You alone, *Indra*, lord of rites, separate the combined worlds (heaven and earth) with all your protections; slayer of *Vṛtra*, irreproachable wielder of the thunderbolt, drink of the *Soma* at the mid-day solemnity.

६७९१. क्षेमस्य च प्रयुजश्च त्वमीशिषे शचीपत इन्द्र विश्वाभिरूतिभिः।
माध्यंन्दिनस्य सर्वनस्य वृत्रहन्नेद्व पिबा सोमस्य वज्रिवः॥५॥

5. You, lord of rites, are sovereign over our prosperity and gains, with all your protections; slayer of *Vṛtra*, irreproachable wielder of the thunderbolt, drink of the *Soma* at the mid-day solemnity.

६७९२. क्षत्राय त्वमवसि न त्वंमाविथ शचीपत इन्द्र विश्वाभिरूतिभिः।
माध्यंन्दिनस्य सर्वनस्य वृत्रहन्नेद्व पिबा सोमस्य वज्रिवः॥६॥

6. You are for the strength (of the world); you protect with all your protections, but you need no defender, *Indra*, lord of rites; slayer of *Vṛtra*, irreproachable wielder of the thunderbolt, drink of the *Soma* at the mid-day solemnity.

But you Needest no Defender— So Sāyaṇa takes *na tvamāvitha*. Does it mean, "did you not protect?"

६७९३. श्यावाश्वस्य रेभतस्तथा शृणु यथाशृणोरत्रेः कर्माणि कृण्वतः।
प्र त्रसदस्युमाविथ त्वमेक इन्नृषाह्व इन्द्र क्षत्राणि वर्धयन्॥७॥

7. Hear the praises of *Śyāvāśva* eulogizing you, as you have heard those of *Atri* engaged in pious rites; you alone have protected *Trasadasyu* in battle, augmenting his vigour.

[सूक्त-३८]

[ऋषि– श्यावाश्व आत्रेय। देवता– इन्द्राग्नी। छन्द– गायत्री।]

६७९४. यज्ञस्य हि स्थ ऋत्विजा सस्नी वाजेषु कर्मसु।
इन्द्राग्नी तस्य बोधतम्॥१॥

1. *Indra* and *Agni*, you are the pure ministrants, (encouragers) in offerings and sacred rites,—hear (the praise) of this (your worshipper).

Sāmaveda, 1073.

६७९५. तोशासा रथयावाना वृत्रहणापराजिता। इन्द्राग्नी तस्य बोधतम्॥२॥

2. Destroyers (of foes), riding in one chariot, slayers of *Vṛtra*, invincible; hear, *Indra* and *Agni*, (the praise) of this (your worshipper).

Sāmaveda, 1074.

६७९६. इदं वां मदिरं मध्वधुक्षन्नद्रिभिर्नरः। इन्द्राग्नी तस्य बोधतम्॥३॥

3. The leaders of rites have effused by the stones this sweet exhilarating (beverage) for you; hear, *Indra* and *Agni*, (the praise) of this (your worshipper).

Sāmaveda, 1075.

६७९७. जुषेथां यज्ञमिष्टये सुतं सोमं सधस्तुती। इन्द्राग्नी आ गतं नरा॥४॥

4. Associated in praise, accept the sacrifice; leaders of rites, *Indra* and *Agni*, come hither to the *Soma* effused for this solemnity.

६७९८. इमा जुषेथां सवना येभिर्हव्यान्यूहथुः। इन्द्राग्नी आ गतं नरा॥५॥

5. Accept these sacrifices whereby you have borne away the oblations; leaders of rites, *Indra* and *Agni*, come hither.

६७९९. इमां गायत्रवर्तनिं जुषेथां सुष्टुतिं मम। इन्द्राग्नी आ गतं नरा॥६॥

6. Accept this my earnest praise, following the path of the *gāyatrī*; leaders of rites, *Indra* and *Agni*, come hither.

६८००. प्रातर्यावभिरा गतं देवेभिर्जेन्यावसू। इन्द्राग्नी सोमपीतये॥७॥

7. Rich with the spoils of victory, come, *Indra* and *Agni*, to drink of the *Soma*, with the deities astir in the morning.

६८०१. श्यावाश्वस्य सुन्वतोऽत्रीणां शृणुतं हवम्। इन्द्राग्नी सोमपीतये॥८॥

8. Hear the invocation, *Indra* and *Agni*, of Śyavaśva pouring our the effused juice, (and) the Atris, to drink of the *Soma*.

६८०२. एवा वामह्ऽ ऊतये यथाहुवन्त मेधिराः। इन्द्राग्नी सोमपीतये॥९॥

9. I invoke you both, *Indra* and *Agni*, as the sages have invoked you, for your protection (and) to drink of the *Soma*.

६८०३. आहं सरस्वतीवतोरिन्द्राग्न्योरवो वृणे। याभ्यां गायत्रमृच्यते॥१०॥

10. I solicit the protection of *Indra* and *Agni*, associated with Sarasvati, to whom this *Gāyatrī* hymn is addressed.

Associated with Sarasvati— Sāyaṇa explains *sarasvatīvatoḥ*, "possessors of praise."

[सूक्त-३९]

[ऋषि— नाभाक काण्व। देवता— अग्नि। छन्द— महापंक्ति।]

६८०४. अग्निमस्तोष्यृग्मियमग्निमीळा यजध्यै। अग्निर्देवाँ अनक्तु न उभे हि
विदथे कविरन्तश्चरति दूत्यं१ नभंन्तामन्यके समे॥१॥

1. I glorify the adorable *Agni*, (I invite) *Agni* with praise to the sacrifice, may *Agni* brighten the gods with the oblations at our sacrifice: the sage *Agni* traverses both (worlds discharging his function) as messenger of the gods; may all our adversaries perish.

६८०५. न्यग्ने नव्यसा वचस्तनूषु शंसमेषाम्। न्यराती ररावणां विश्वां अर्यो
अरातीरिरितो युच्छन्त्वामुरो नभंन्तामन्यके समे॥२॥

2. (Propitiated), *Agni*, by our new praise baffle the hostile attempts of these against our persons, consume the enemies of those who are liberal (at sacred rites); may all our foolish assailants depart from hence, may all our adversaries perish.

All our Foolish Assailants— Sāyaṇa here explains *āmuraḥ* by *āmūḍhāḥ*, but in iv.31.9 he explained it by *bādhakaḥ Rākṣasas* etc.

६८०६. अग्ने मन्मानि तुभ्यं कं घृतं न जुह्व आसनि। स देवेषु प्र चिकिद्धि
त्वं ह्यासि पूर्व्यः शिवो दूतो विवस्वतो नभंन्तामन्यके समे॥३॥

3. I pour into your mouth, *Agni*, praises as others (fill it) with delicious butter; do you amidst the gods acknowledge (them), for you are ancient, the giver of happiness, the messenger of *Vivasvat*; may all our enemies perish.

६८०७. तत्तदग्निर्वयो दधे यथायथा कृपण्यति। ऊर्जाहुतिर्वसूनां शं च योश्च
मर्यो दधे विश्वस्यै देवहूत्यै नभंन्तामन्यके समे॥४॥

4. *Agni* grants whatever food is solicited; invoked with offerings, he bestows on the worshippers happiness springing from tranquillity and the enjoyment (of objects of sense); he is requisite for all invocation of the gods: may all our adversaries perish.

Happiness Springing from, Etc.— This is *Sāyaṇa's* interpretation of *śam ca yośca mayaḥ*, which he explains, *śāntinimittam viṣaya-yogajanitam ca sukham*.

६८०८. स चिकेत सहीयसाग्निश्चित्रेण कर्मणा। स होता शश्वतीनां
दक्षिणाभिरभीवृत इनोति च प्रतीव्यंइ नभन्तामन्यके समे ॥५॥

5. *Agni* is known by his most powerful and mainfold deeds: he
is the invoker of the eternals; surrounded by victims, he proceeds
against the foe: may all our adversaries perish.

The Eternails— Sāyaṇa explains *śaśvatīnām* as *bahvīnām
devatānām*.

Against the Foe— This is *Sāyaṇa's* explanation of *pratīvyam*, but in
viii.26.8 he explained it as *yajñam*. Sāyaṇa explains *dakṣiṇābhiḥ* by
paśubhiḥ. B. and R. by "Opferlohn."

६८०९. अग्निर्जाता देवानामग्निर्वेद मर्तानामपीच्यम्। अग्निः स द्रविणोदा
अग्निर्द्वारा व्यूर्णुते स्वाहुतो नवीयसा नभन्तामन्यके समे ॥६॥

6. *Agni* knows the births of the gods; *Agni* knows the secrets of
mankind: *Agni* is the giver of riches; *Agni*, duly worshipped with a
new (oblation), sets open the doors (of opulence): may all our
adversaries perish.

६८१०. अग्निर्देवेषु संवसुः स विक्षु यज्ञियास्वा। स मुदा काव्या पुरु विश्वं
भूमेव पुष्यति देवो देवेषु यज्ञियो नभन्तामन्यके समे ॥७॥

7. *Agni* has his abode among the gods, he (dwells) among
pious people: he cherishes with pleasure many pious acts, as the
earth all (beings); a god adorable among the gods: may all our
adversaries perish.

६८११. यो अग्निः सप्तमानुषः श्रितो विश्वेषु सिन्धुषु। तमागन्म त्रिपस्त्यं
मन्धातुर्दस्युहन्तममग्निं यज्ञेषु पूर्व्यं नभन्तामन्यके समे ॥८॥

8. Let us approach that *Agni* who is ministered to by seven
priests; who takes refuge in all rivers, who has a triple dwelling
place, the slayer of the *Dasyu* for *Mandhātā*, who is foremost in
sacrifices: may all our adversaries perish.

Ministered by Seven Priests— *Yo'gniḥ saptamānuṣaḥ* is left
unexplained by the commentator. The translation is conjectural.
[Professor Müller, *Hist. Sansk. Lit.* p.493, takes it as "acting as seven
priests."]

Mandhatri— Sāyaṇa understands *Mandhātā* is being the same as
Māndhātā, the son of *Yuvanāśva*.

६८१२. अग्निस्त्रीणि त्रिधातून्या क्षेति विदथा कविः। स त्रीँरेकादशाँ इह
यक्षच्च पिप्रयच्च नो विप्रो दूतः परिष्कृतो नभन्तामन्यके समे ॥९॥

9. *Agni*, the sage, inhabits the three elementary regions; may he, intelligent, and richly decorated, the messenger (of the gods), here perform worship to the thrice eleven deities, and satisfy all our desires: may all our enemies perish.

The three Elementary Regions— *Tridhātūni,* - may mean only "threefold," as in v.47.4; but *cf.* I.154.4.

६८१३. त्वं नो अग्न आयुषु त्वं देवेषु पूर्व्य वस्व एक इरज्यसि।

त्वामाप: परिस्रुत: परि यन्ति स्वसेतवो नभन्तामन्यके समे॥१०॥

10. You, ancient *Agni*, among men and gods, are alone to us the lord of wealth; the flowing waters confined within their own banks flow around you: may all our enemies perish.

[सूक्त-४०]

[**ऋषि**– नाभाक काण्व। **देवता**– इन्द्राग्नी।

छन्द– महापंक्ति, २ शक्वरी,१२ त्रिष्टुप्।]

६८१४. इन्द्राग्नी युवं सु न: सहन्ता दासथो रयिम्। येन दृळ्हा समत्स्वा वीळु चित्साहिषीमह्यग्निर्वनेव वात इन्नभन्तामन्यके समे॥१॥

1. Victorious *Indra* and *Agni*, bestow upon us riches whereby we may destroy our powerful enemies in combats as fire fanned by the wind consumes the forests: may all our enemies perish.

६८१५. नहि वां वज्रयामहेऽथेन्द्रमिद्यजामहे शविष्ठं नृणां नरम्। स न: कदा चिदर्वता गमदा वाजसातये गमदा मेधसातये नभन्तामन्यके समे॥२॥

2. Do we not invoke you both? We worship especially *Indra*, who is the strongest leader of men: he comes occasionally with his horses to bestow upon us food; he comes to partake of the sacrifice: may all our enemies perish.

Do We not invoke you Both— Or rather, "we do not invoke you both."

To Bestow upon us Food— Sāyaṇa takes it, "for the receiving of food."

६८१६. ता हि मध्यं भरणामिन्द्राग्नी अधिक्षित:। ता उ कवित्वना कवी पृच्छ्यमाना सखीयते सं धीतमश्नुतं नरा नभन्तामन्यके समे॥३॥

3. They two, *Indra* and *Agni*, are present in the midst of battles: do you two, leaders of rites, who are really sages, when

solicited (by the wise), accept the offering (from him) who seeks
your friendship: may all our enemies perish.

६८१७. अभ्यर्च नभाकवदिन्द्राग्नी यजसा गिरा। ययोर्विश्वमिदं जगदियं द्यौः
पृथिवी महुइंपस्थे बिभृतो वसु नर्भन्तामन्यके सँमे॥४॥

4. Worship, like Nabhāka, *Indra* and *Agni* with sacrifice and
praise, of whom is this universe, upon whose lap this heaven and
the spacious earth deposit their treasure: may all our enemies
perish.

Nabhāka— The *Ṛṣi* of the hymn is *Nābhāka*, perhaps a patronymic:
the text has here *Nabhāka*.

६८१८. प्र ब्रह्माणि नभाकवदिन्द्राग्निभ्यामिरज्यत। या सप्तबुध्नमर्णवं
जिह्वाबारमपोर्णुत इन्द्र ईशान् ओजसा नर्भन्तामन्यके सँमे॥५॥

5. Address like *Nabhāka* your praises to *Indra* and *Agni*, who
overspread (with their lustre) the seven-rooted ocean whose gates
are hidden, and of whom *Indra* by his might is the lord: may all
our enemies perish.

Seven-Rooted ocean whose Gates are Hidden— There is no
explanation of this. *Yā saptabudhnam arṇavam jihmabāram apornutaḥ* is
explained *saptamūlam pihita-dvāram arṇavam tejobhir ācchādayataḥ.*

६८१९. अपि वृश्च पुराणवद् व्रततेरिव गुष्पितमोजो दासस्य दम्भय।
वयं तदस्य सम्भृतं वस्विन्द्रेण वि भजेमहि नर्भन्तामन्यके सँमे॥६॥

6. Cut off (the foe), *Indra*, as an old (pruner) the protruding
(branch) of a creeper; humble the strength of the *Dāsa*; may we
divide his accumulated treasure (despoiled) by *Indra*: may all our
enemies perish.

६८२०. यदिन्द्राग्नी जना इमे विह्वयन्ते तना गिरा। अस्माकेभिर्नृभिर्वयं
सासह्याम पृतन्यतो वनुयाम वनुष्यतो नर्भन्तामन्यके सँमे॥७॥

7. Inasmuch as these people honour *Indra* and *Agni* with gifts
and with praises, so may we, defying hosts, overcome (our foes)
with our warriors; let us praise those seeking praise: may all our
enemies perish.

Let us praise those seeking praise— *Vanuyāma vanuśyataḥ*, the
comment oddly enough explains *stutim icchantaḥ śatrūn vanuyāma.* [The
original rather means, "let us prevail over those desire to conquer."]

६८२१. या नु श्वेताववो दिव उच्चरात उप द्युभिः। इन्द्राग्न्योरनु व्रतमुहाना
यन्ति सिन्धवो यान्तीं बन्धादमुञ्चतां नर्भन्तामन्यके सँम॥८॥

8. Offering oblations, (the worshippers) approach to the worship of *Indra* and *Agni*, who are of a white complexion, and rise from below with bright rays to heaven: they verily have liberated the waters from bondage: may all our enemies perish.

६८२२. पूर्वीष्ट इन्द्रोपमातयः पूर्वीरुत प्रशंस्तयः सूनौं हिन्वस्यं हरिवः।
वस्वों वीरस्यापृचो या नु साधेन्त नो धियो नभेन्तामन्यके समे॥९॥

9. *Indra*, wielder of the thunderbolt, instigator (of acts), may the numerous merits, the many excellences of you, who are the bestower of affluence and of male offspring, perfect our understandings; may all our enemies perish.

The meaning of this verse, even with the help of the Scholiast, is far from intelligible. [Sāyaṇa would seem to take it thus: "*Indra*, wielder of the thunderbolt, instigator (of acts), of you, the gladdener, the brilliant, the hero, the wealth-bestower, numerous (or 'ancient,' *cf.* IV.23.3) are the comparisons, numerous (or 'ancient') are the praises, which exercise our understandings." In his Comm. on IV.23.3 he takes *upamātayaḥ* as *dhanāni*.]

६८२३. तं शिशीता सुवृक्तिभिस्त्वेषं सत्वानमृग्मियम्। उतो नु चिद्य ओजेसा
शुष्णस्याण्डानि भेदति जेषत्स्वर्वतीरपो नभेन्तामन्यके समे ॥१०॥

10. Animate with praises that brilliant adorable *Indra*, the distributor (of riches), who by his might breaks the eggs of *Śuṣṇa*: may he conquer the celestial waters: may all our enemies perish.

The Eggs of Śuṣṇa— *Śuṣṇasya aṇḍāni*, "egg-born offspring": *aṇḍajātānī*, according to the Scholiast.

६८२४. तं शिशीता स्वध्वरं सत्यं सत्वानमृत्वियम्। उतो नु चिद्य ओहेते
आण्डा शुष्णस्य भेदत्यजैः स्वर्वतीरपो नभेन्तामन्यके समे॥११॥

11. Animate that *Indra* to whom sacrifice is due,—sincere, bountiful, adorable;; him who frequents sacrifices, who breaks the eggs of *Śuṣṇa*; you have conquered the celestial waters: may all our enemies perish.

६८२५. एवेन्द्राग्निभ्यां पितृवन्नवीयो मन्धातृवदङ्गिरस्वदवाचि।
त्रिधातुना शर्मणा पातमस्मान् वयं स्याम पतयो रयीणाम्॥१२॥

12. Thus has a new hymn been addressed to *Indra* and *Agni*, as was done by my father, by *Mandhātā*, by *Aṅgiras*; cherish us with a triply defended dwelling: may we be the lords of riches.

Triply Defended Dwelling— *Tridhātunā śarmaṇā, triparvaṇā gṛheṇa*, "with a house of three joints,"—stories? [In i.34.6, *tridhātu* śarma is explained as vātapitta-śleṣma-dhātutrayaśamana viṣayam sukham; in i.85.12, śarma tridhātūni is explained as pṛthivyādiṣu triṣu sthāneṣu avasthitāni sukhāni gṛhāni vā.]

[सूक्त-४१]

[ऋषि– नाभाक काण्व। देवता– वरुण। छन्द– महापंक्ति।]

६८२६. अस्मा ऊ षु प्रभूतये वरुणाय मरुद्भ्योऽर्चा विदुष्टरेभ्यः।
यो धीता मानुषाणां पश्वो गाइव रक्षति नभन्तामन्यके समे॥१॥

1. Offer praise to that opulent Varuṇa, and to the most sage Maruts; (Varuṇa) who protects men by his acts, as (the herdsman guards) the cattle: may all our enemies perish.

By his Acts.— The karmaṇā in the Comm. seems to be a misreading for karmaṇi, "who protects men's religious acts."

६८२७. तमू षु समना गिरा पितृणां च मन्मभिः। नाभाकस्य प्रशस्तिभिर्यः
सिन्धूनामुपोदये सप्तस्वसा स मध्यमो नभन्तामन्यके समे॥२॥

2. (I praise) with a like praise, with the praises of (my) progenitors, with the eulogies of Nabhāka, that Varuṇa who rises up in the vicinity of the rivers, and in the midst (of them) has seven sisters: may all our enemies perish.

Very unintelligible, although Yāska (x.5) is cited in explanation: sindhūnām upodaye saptasvasā sa madhyamaḥ. [Prof. Roth translates it, "der am Ausgang der flüsse ist, deer sieben Schwestern (cf. viii.69.12) Herr ist der mittlere."]

६८२८. स क्षपः परि षस्वजे न्युंस्रो मायया दधे स विश्वं परि दर्शतः।
तस्य वेनीरनु व्रतमुषस्तिस्रो अवर्धयन्नभन्तामन्यके समे॥३॥

3. He embraces the nights: of goodly aspect, and quick of movement, he encompasses the universe by his acts: all who are desirous (of his favour) diligently offer him worship at the three diurnal rites: may all our enemies perish.

Quick of Movement— Sāyaṇa explains usraḥ as utsaraṇaśīlaḥ. Bohtlingk and Roth's Dict. takes it as acc. plur. of usra, "morning."

६८२९. यः ककुभो निधारयः पृथिव्यामधि दर्शतः। स माता पूर्व्यं पदं
तद्वरुणस्य सप्त्यं स हि गोपा वेर्यो नभन्तामन्यके समे॥४॥

4. He, who visible above the earth sustains the points of the horizon, is the measurer (of the universe); that is the ancient abode of Varuṇa, to which we have access; he is our lord, like the keeper of cattle: may all our enemies perish.

The Measurer— Sāyaṇa explains mātā by nirmātā, "the maker."

६८३०. यो धर्ता भुवेनानां य उस्राणामपीच्या३े वेद नामानि गुह्या।
स कविः काव्या पुरु रूपं द्यौरिव पुष्यति नभन्तामन्यके समे॥५॥

5. He who is the sustainer of the worlds, who knows the hidden and secret names of the (solar) rays, he is the sage who cherishes the acts of sages, as the heaven cherishes numerous forms: may all our enemies perish.

६८३१. यस्मिन् विश्वानि काव्या चक्रे नाभिरिव श्रिता। त्रितं जूती संपर्यत
व्रजे गावो न संयुजे युजे अश्वाँ अयुक्षत नभन्तामन्यके समे॥६॥

6. In whom all pious acts are concentrated, like the nave in the (centre of the) wheel, worship him quickly who abides in the three worlds; as men assemble the cattle in their pasture, so do (our foes) collect their horses (to assail us): may all our enemies perish.

६८३२. य आस्वत्क आशये विश्वा जातान्येषाम्। परि धामानि मर्मृशद्वरुणस्य
पुरो गये विश्वे देवा अनु व्रतं नभन्तामन्यके समे॥७॥

7. He who, passing amidst those (regions of the firmament), gives refuge to all their races, and all the deities precede the chariot of *Varuṇa*, when manifesting his glories to perform his worship: may all our enemies perish.

The commentary here is defective, and the passage very obscure; the translation is not entitled to any reliance. [Query, "who going through these regions (of space) rests on all their tribes, surrounding all homes,—all the gods are engaged in worship before *Varuṇa's* dwelling; may all our enemies perish."]

६८३३. स समुद्रो अपीच्यस्तुरो द्यामिव रोहति नि यदासु यजुर्दधे।
स माया अर्किना पदास्तृणान्नाकमारुहन्नभन्तामन्यके समे॥८॥

8. He is the hidden ocean; swift he mounts (the heaven) as (the sun) the sky; when he has placed the sacrifice in those (regions of the firmament), he demolishes with his brilliant radiance the devices (of the *Asuras*); he ascends to heaven: may all our enemies perish.

६८३४. यस्य श्वेता विचक्षणा तिस्रो भूमीरधिक्षितः। त्रिरुत्तराणि पप्रतुर्वरुणस्य
ध्रुवं सदः स सप्तानामिरज्यति नभन्तामन्यके समे॥९॥

9. Of whom, present in the three worlds, the brilliant rays pervade the three realms beyond, the eternal dwelling of *Varuṇa*, he is lord of the seven (rivers): may all our enemies perish.

Sāyaṇa compares ii.27.8, and seems to explain *tri*, ''of whom, the ruler, the brilliant rays pervade the three earths and the three heavens above,—his dwelling-place is immoveable.''

६८३५. यः श्वेताँ अधिनिर्णिजश्चक्रे कृष्णाँ अनु व्रता। स धाम॑ पूर्व्यं॒ ममे॒ यः स्कम्भे॑न॒ वि रोद॑सी अजो॒ न द्यामधा॑रयन्नभ॑न्तामन्य॒के स॑मे॥१०॥

10. He who in his successive functions emits his bright rays or turns them dark, first made his residence (in the firmament), and, as the unborn sun the sky, supports with the pillar (of the firmament) both heaven and earth: may all our enemies perish.

Emits His Bright Rays or Turns them Dark— As presiding over day and night.

[सूक्त-४२]

[**ऋषि**– नाभाक काण्व तथा अर्चनाना आत्रेय। **देवता**– १-३ वरुण, ४-६ अश्विनीकुमार। **छन्द**– १-३ त्रिष्टुप् , ४-६ अनुष्टुप्।]

६८३६. अस्तभ्नाद् द्यामसु॑रो विश्ववेदा॒ अमि॑मीत वरिमाणं॑ पृथिव्याः।
आसी॑दद्विश्वा॒ भुव॑नानि स॒म्राड् विश्वे॒तानि॒ वरु॑णस्य व्र॒तानि॑॥१॥

1. The possessor of all wealth, the powerful *Varuṇa*, has fixed the heaven; he has meted the measure of the earth; he presides as supreme monarch over all worlds; these all are the functions of *Varuṇa*.

६८३७. ए॒वा व॑न्दस्व॒ वरु॑णं बृ॒हन्तं॑ नमस्या धीर॒ममृत॑स्य गो॒पाम्।
स न॑ः शर्म॑ त्रि॒वरू॑थं॒ वि यं॑सत्पा॒तं नो॑ द्या॒वापृथिवी उ॒पस्थे॑॥२॥

2. Glorify then the mighty *Varuṇa*; reverence the wise guardian of ambrosia; may he bestow upon us a thrice sheltering habitation; may heaven and earth preserve us abiding in their proximity.

A Thrice sheltering Habitation— *Trivarūtha* is explained by Sāyaṇa in vi.46.9 as ''sheltering from cold, heat, and rain''; here as *tristhānam*.

६८३८. इ॒मां धियं॑ शिक्ष॑माणस्य देव॒ क्रतुं॒ दक्षं॑ वरुण॒ सं शि॑शाधि।
यया॒ति विश्वा॑ दुरि॒ता तरे॑म सु॒तर्मा॑णम॒धि नावं॑ रुहेम॥३॥

3. Divine *Varuṇa*, animate the sacred acts of me engaging in this your worship: may we ascend the safebearing vessel by which we may cross over all difficulties.

Animate the Sacred Acts.— *Kratum dakṣam,* Sāyaṇa, "sharpen the knowledge and power."

६८३९. आ वां ग्रावाणो अश्विना धीभिर्विप्रा अचुच्यवुः।
नासत्या सोमपीतये नभन्तामन्यके समे॥४॥

4. The acred stones, *Aśvins,* the pious worshippers, *Nāsatyās,* have fallen upon their sacred functions, (to induce you) to drink the *Soma:* may all our enemies perish.

६८४०. यथा वामत्रिरश्विना गीर्भिर्विप्रो अजोहवीत्।
नासत्या सोमपीतये नभन्तामन्यके समे॥५॥

5. In like manner as the pious *Atri, Aśvins,* invoked you with hymns, so (I invoke you), *Nāsatyās,* to drink the *Soma:* may all our enemies perish.

६८४१. एवा वामह्व ऊतये यथाहुवन्त मेधिराः।
नासत्या सोमपीतये नभन्तामन्येके समे॥६॥

6. In like manner as the wise invoke you for protection, so do I invoke you, *Nāsatyās,* to drink the *Soma:* may all our enemies perish.

[सूक्त-४३]

[**ऋषि**– विरूप आङ्गिरस। **देवता**– अग्नि। **छन्द**– गायत्री।]

६८४२. इमे विप्रस्य वेधसोऽग्नेरस्तृतयज्वनः। गिरः स्तोमास ईरते॥१॥

1. These repeaters of laudations recite the praises of the wise creative *Agni,* the uninterrupted sacrificer.

The Uninterrupted Sacrificer— *Astṛta-yajvan* is more literally "the invincible sacrificer."

६८४३. अस्मै ते प्रतिहर्यते जातवेदो विचर्षणे। अग्ने जनामि सुष्टुतिम्॥२॥

2. *Agni, Jātavedas,* to you, the liberal offerer (of the oblation), the all-beholding, I repeat earnest praise.

The Liberal Offerer— Sāyaṇa more frequently explains *pratiharya* as "to accept, desire."

६८४४. आरोकाइव घेदह तिग्मा अग्ने तव त्विषः। दद्भिर्वनानि बप्सति॥३॥

3. Your fierce flames, *Agni,* consume the forest, as wild animals destroy (the plants) with their teeth.

Wild Animals— *Arokāḥ* is an obscure word, Sāyaṇa explains it as *arocamānāḥ paśavaḥ,* but the Comm. to *Śatap. Br.,* iii.1.2.18 explains it as *madhye chidrāṇi*. May it mean here "(your fierce flames) glancing, as it were, through the trees"? *Cf.* Böhtlingk and Roth, *sub voce.*

६८४५. हरयो॑ धूम॒केत॑वो॒ वात॑जूता॒ उप॒ द्यवि॑। यत॑न्ते॒ वृथ॒गग्न॑यः॥४॥

4. The consuming smoke-bannered fires, borne by the wind, spread diversely in the firmament.

६८४६. ए॒ते त्ये वृथ॒गग्न॑य॒ इद्धा॑सः॒ सम॑दृक्षत। उ॒ष॒साम॑िव के॒तवः॑॥५॥

5. These fires separately kindled are beheld like the tokens of the dawn.

६८४७. कृ॒ष्णा रजां॑सि पत्सु॒तः प्र॒याणे॑ जा॒तवे॑दसः। अ॒ग्निर्यद्रोध॑ति क्ष॒मि॑॥६॥

6. Black dust is raised by the feet of Jatavedas when he moves, when *Agni* spreads on the earth.

When Agni spreads the Earth— Sāyaṇa translates *Agnir yad rodhati kṣami*, "when *Agni* heaps (the dry trees) on the ground." Böhtlingk and Roth take *rodhati* as from *rush*, sc. "whatever grows on the earth"; thus connecting these last words of v. 6 with v.7.

६८४८. धा॒सिं कृ॒ण्वा॒न ओष॑धी॒र्बप्स॑दग्नि॒नं वा॑यति। पुन॒र्यन्तरु॒णीर॒पि॑॥७॥

7. Making the plants his food, *Agni* devouring them is never satiated, but falls again upon the young (shrubs).

६८४९. जि॒ह्वाभि॒रह॒ न॒न्नम॑द॒र्चिषा॑ जञ्जणा॒भव॑न्। अ॒ग्निर्वने॑षु रोचते॥८॥

8. Bowing down (the trees) with his tongues (of flame), and blazing with splendour, *Agni* shines in the forests.

६८५०. अप्स्व॑ग्ने॒ सधि॑ष्टव॒ सौष॑धी॒रनु॑ रुध्यसे। गर्भे॒ सञ्जा॑यसे॒ पुनः॑॥९॥

9. Your station, *Agni*, is in the waters: you cling to the plants, and becoming their embryo, are born again.

६८५१. उद॑ग्ने॒ तव॒ तद्घृ॒ताद॒र्ची रो॑चत॒ आहु॑तम्। निसां॑नं जुहो॒इ३॑ मु॒खे॑॥१०॥

10. Your lustre, *Agni*, lambent in the mouth of the ladle, shines when offered from (the oblation of) butter.

६८५२. उ॒क्षान्ना॑य व॒शान्ना॑य॒ सोम॑पृष्ठाय वे॒धसे॑। स्तोमै॑र्विधेमो॒अग्नये॑॥११॥

11. Let us adore with hymns *Agni*, the granter (of desires), the eater of the ox, the eater of the marrow, on whose back the libation is poured.

६८५३. उ॒त त्वा॒ नम॑सा व॒यं होत॑र्वरेण्यक्रतो। अग्ने॑ स॒मिद्धिरी॑महे॥१२॥

12. We solicit you, *Agni*, invoker of the gods, performer of sacred rites, with oblations and with fuel.

Performer of Sacred Rites— Sāyaṇa takes *vareṇyakrato*, "O you who possess desirable knowledge."

६८५४. उत त्वां भृगुवच्छुचे मनुष्वदंग आहुत। अङ्गिरस्वद्धवामहे॥१३॥

13. Holy *Agni*, to whom oblations are offered, we worship you in like manner (as you have been worshipped) by *Bhṛgu*, by Manus, by *Aṅgiras*.

६८५५. त्वं ह्यंग्ने अग्निना विप्रो विप्रेंण सन्त्सता।
सखा सख्यां समिध्यसें॥१४॥

14. You, *Agni*, are kindled by *Agni*; a sage by a sage, saint by a saint, a friend by a friend.

A Saint by a Saint— *San* and *Satā* are explained by Sāyaṇa as respectively *vidyamānaḥ* and *vidyamānena*; and he refers to a passage in the *Aitareya Brāhmaṇa*, i.16, which describes how the fire produced by friction from the two *araṇis* is thrown into the *Āhavanīya* fire, in the *Atithyeṣṭi* ceremony. "In the verse *tvam hyagne*, etc., the one *vipra* (a sage) means one *Agni*, the other *vipra* the other *Agni*; the one *san* (being, existing) means the one, the other *san* (in *satā*) the other *Agni*." (Haug's transl.)

६८५६. स त्वं विप्रांय दाशुषे रयिं देंहि सहस्रिणम्।
अग्नें वीरवतीमिषम्॥१५॥

15. Do you, *Agni*, bestow upon the pious donor (of the oblation) infinite riches and food with male progeny.

६८५७. अग्ने भ्रातः सहस्कृत रोहिदश्व शुचिव्रत।
इमं स्तोमं जुषस्व मे॥१६॥

16. *Agni*, (our) brother, who are elicited by strength, who have red horses, and are (the performer) of pure rites, be propitiated by this my praise.

६८५८. उत त्वांग्ने मम स्तुतौ वाश्रांय प्रतिहर्यते। गोष्ठं गावं इवाशत॥१७॥

17. My praises hasten to you, *Agni*, as cows enter their stalls (to give milk) to the thirsting calves.

६८५९. तुभ्यं ता अंङ्गिरस्तम विश्वाः सुक्षितयः पृथक्।
अग्ने कामांय येमिरे॥१८॥

18. To you, *Agni*, who are the chief of the *Aṅgirasas*, all people have severally recourse for the attainment of their desires.

Have Severally Recourse— *Yemire* seems to be used here as in i.135. 1; iii.59.8. In the latter place Sāyaṇa explains it, ''offer oblations.'' Böhtlingk and Roth render it in all three places, ''sich fügen, gehorchen, true bleiben.''

६८६०. अग्निं धीभिर्मनीषिणो मेधिरासो विपश्चितः। अद्यसद्याय हिन्विरे॥१९॥

19. The wise, the intelligent, the sagacious, propitiate *Agni* with sacrifices for the attainment of food.

६८६१. तं त्वामज्मेषु वाजिनं तन्वाना अग्ने अध्वरम्।

वहिं होतारमीळते॥२०॥

20. Preparing the sacrifice in their mansions, (the worshippers) adore you, *Agni*, the powerful, the bearer (of the oblation), the invoker of the gods.

६८६२. पुरुत्रा हि सदृङ्ङसि विशो विश्वा अनु प्रभुः।

समत्सु त्वा हवामहे॥२१॥

21. You are the lord, you behold all people alike in many places; we therefore invoke you in battles.

This *v.* also occurs in viii.2.8. Sāyaṇa here reads *prabhu* for *prabhuḥ,* but against our MSS.

६८६३. तमीळिष्व य आहुतोऽग्निर्विभ्राजते घृतैः। इमं नः शृणवद्धवम्॥२२॥

22. Adore that *Agni* who shines brightly when fed with offerings of butter, who hears this our invocation.

६८६४. तं त्वां वयं हवामहे शृण्वन्तं जातवेदसम्।

अग्ने घ्नन्तमप द्विषः॥२३॥

23. We invoke you, *Agni*, who are Jatavedas, listening (to our praises), exterminating our foes.

६८६५. विशां राजानमद्भुतमध्यक्षं धर्मणामिमम्।

अग्निमीळे स उ श्रवत्॥२४॥

24. I praise this *Agni*, the sovereign of men, the wonderful, the superintendent of holy acts; may he hear me.

६८६६. अग्निं विश्वायुवेपसं मर्यं न वाजिनं हितम्।

सप्तिं न वाजयामसि॥२५॥

25. We invigorate like a horse that (*Agni*) whose might is everywhere present; who is noble, strong, and benevolent.

Strong— Sāyaṇa takes *maryam na vājinam* a "like a strong man."
Böhtlingk and Roth translate *mari* "Hengst."

६८६७. घ्नन्मृध्राण्यप दि्वषो दह्न रक्षांसि वि्श्वहा।
अग्ने तिग्मेन दीदिहि॥२६॥

26. Slaying the malignant, (driving away) our enemies
everywhere consuming the *Rākṣasas*, do you, *Agni* blaze forth with
bright (radiance).

६८६८. यं त्वा जनास इन्धते मनुष्वदङ्गिरस्तम।
अग्ने स बोधि मे वच॑:॥२७॥

27. Chief of the *Aṅgirasas*, whose men kindle as did *Manus*;
Agni, hear my words.

६८६९. यद॑ग्ने दिवि॒जा अस्य॑प्सुजा वा॑ सहस्कृत। तं त्वा॑ गीर्भिर्ह॑वामहे॥२८॥

28. We worship with praises you, *Agni*, who are born in
heaven or in the waters, elicited by strength.

Born in Heaven, Etc.— Sc. as the sun in heaven, as lightning in the
waters, (*i.e.*, in the firmament), and as generated on earth by friction.

६८७०. तुभ्यं घेत्ते जना इमे विश्वा: सुक्षितय: पृथक्।
धासिं हि॒न्वत्यत्तवे॥२९॥

29. All these people, the inhabitants (of the earth), offer
severally to you (sacrificial) food for your eating and enjoyment.

Prof. Wilson's translation of the eighth *Maṇḍala* ends here; for the
remainder the Editor alone is responsible.—Both trans, and notes.]

६८७१. ते घेद॑ग्ने स्वाध्योऽहा विश्वा॑ नृचक्षस:। तरन्त: स्याम दुर्गहा॑॥३०॥

30. *Agni*, through you, may we, skilled in sacrifices and
beholding men all our days, pass through (all) difficulties.

Beholding men all our Days— Böthlingk and Roth explain *nṛcakṣa-
saḥ* and the Scholiast's *nṛnām draṣṭāraḥ* by "unter Menschen lebend."

६८७२. अग्निं मन्द्रं पुरुप्रियं शीरं पा॑वकशोचिषम्। हृद्बुद्धिर्मन्द्रेभिरीमहे॥३१॥

31. We invoke with cheerful and delightful (hymns) the
gladdening *Agni*, dear to many, who abides in the sacrifice with
purifying brilliance.

६८७३. स त्वम॑ग्ने विभावसु: सृजन्त्सूर्यो॑ न रश्मिभि॑:।
शर्धन्तमांसि जिघ्नसे॥३२॥

32. Shining forth, *Agni*, like the rising sun, displaying your strength by your beams, you destroy the darkness.

६८७४. तत्तें सहस्व ईमहे दात्रं यन्नोपदस्य॑ति। त्वद॑ग्ने वार्यं॒ वसु॑॥३३॥

33. We solicit from you, strong *Agni*, that desirable wealth which is in your gift and which decayeth not.

<h1 style="text-align:center">[सूक्त-४४]</h1>

[ऋषि– विरूप आङ्गिरस। देवता– अग्नि। छन्द– गायत्री।]

६८७५. समिधाग्निं दुवस्यत घृतैबौंधयतातिथिम्। आस्मिन् हव्या जुहोतन॥१॥

1. Honour *Agni* with fuel, awaken him, the guest, with (libations of) butter; offer the oblations in him.

~ This hymn is found in the *Vāj. Saṁh* 3,1,12,30.

६८७६. अग्ने॒ स्तोमं॑ जुषस्व मे व॒र्धस्वानेन॒ मन्म॑ना।

       प्रति॑ सूक्तानि॑ हर्य नः॥२॥

2. *Agni*, accept my praise, be invigorated by this prayer; be favourable to our hymns.

६८७७. अग्निं दू॒तं पुरो॑ द॒धे हव्यवाह॒मुप॑ ब्रुवे। देवाँ॒ आ सा॑दयादि॒ह॥३॥

3. I set *Agni* in the front as the messenger, I adore him as the bearer of the oblations; my he cause the gods to sit down here.

६८७८. उत्ते॑ बृह॒न्तो॑ अर्च॒यः समिधा॒नस्यं॑ दीदिवः। अग्ने॑ शुक्रास॑ ईरते॥४॥

4. Brilliant *Agni*, as you are kindled, your great flames start blazing up.

६८७९. उप॑ त्वा जु॒ह्वो॒३॒॑ मम॑ घृताचीं॑र्यन्तु हर्यत। अग्ने॑ हव्या॒ जुषस्व नः॥५॥

5. Let my ladles, filled with butter, come near you, O propitious one; *Agni*, receive our oblations.

O Propitious One— Sāyaṇa takes *haryata* here as *kāmayamāna*; he more usually explains it as "amiable," "beloved," *spṛhaṇīya*.

६८८०. मन्द्रं॑ होता॑रमृत्विज॑ं चित्रभानुं॑ विभाव॑सुम्।

       अग्निमीळे॑ स उ॑ श्रवत्॥६॥

6. I worship *Agni*, the exhilarating invoker (of the gods), the priest, him who shines forth with various lustre, and is rich in brilliance; may he give ear.

The Priest— Sāyaṇa here explains *ṛtvijam* as *ritau yaṣṭavyam*, "he who is to be worshipped in due season"; in v. 22.2 he explained it as *ṛtu-yaṣṭāram*, "he who offers in due season."

६८८१. प्रत्नं होतॉरमीड्यं जुष्टमग्निं कविक्रेतुम् । अध्वराणामभिश्रियम् ॥७॥

7. (I worship) the beloved *Agni*, the ancient adorable invoker (of the gods), the wise, the frequenter of sacrifices.

The Wise— *Kavikratum* is here explained as *krāntakarmaṇam* (him by whom rites are performed?); in iii.2.4, and iii.14.7, it was explained as *krāntaprajña* and *sarvajña* (*cf.* also i.1.5). It probably means "possessing wise might."

६८८२. जुषाणो अङ्गिरस्तमेमा हव्यान्यानुषक् । अग्ने यज्ञं नय ऋतुथा ॥८॥

8. *Angi*, best of the *Aṅgirasas*, do you, continually accepting these our oblations, conduct the sacrifice at the due seasons.

६८८३. समिधान उ सन्त्य शुक्रशोच इह वॅह । चिकित्वान् दैव्यं जनॅम् ॥९॥

9. Brilliant-flamed giver of good, do you, the knower, when kindled, bring the host of the gods hither.

६८८४. विप्रं होतॉरमद्रुहं धूमकेतुं विभावॅसुम् । यज्ञानां केतुमीमहे ॥१०॥

10. We solicit the wise invoker (of the gods), the beneficent, the smoke-bannered, the resplendent, the banner of the sacrifices.

६८८५. अग्ने नि पॉहि नस्त्वं प्रति ष्म देव रीषतः ।

भिन्धि द्वेषः सहस्कृत ॥११॥

11. Divine *Agni*, produced by strength, do you protect us from the injurer, tear asunder our enemies.

६८८६. अग्निः प्रत्नेन मन्मॅना शुम्भॉनस्तन्वं स्वाम् ।

कविर्विप्रेण वावृधे ॥१२॥

12. The wise *Agni*, beautifying his body with the ancient hymn, has grown in might through the intelligent hymner.

६८८७. ऊर्जो नपॉतमा हुवेऽग्निं पॉवकशोचिषम् । अस्मिन्यज्ञे स्वध्वरे ॥१३॥

13. I invoke *Agni* of purifying lustre, the son of (sacrificial) food, in this inviolable sacrifice.

The Son of Sacrificial Food— For *ūrjo napātam*, see vol.II, mantra 2668 and note.

६८८८. स नों मित्रमहस्त्वमग्ने शुक्रेण शोचिषा । देवैरा सत्सि बर्हिषि ॥१४॥

14. O *Agni*, adorable to your friends, sit down with the gods on our sacred grass with your resplendent radiance.

Adorable to your Friends— In viii.19.25, Sāyaṇa explained *mitramahas* as *anukuladīptimān*. "beneficently shining"; here as *mitrāṇām pūjanīya*.

६८८९. यो अग्निं तन्वो३ दमे देवं मर्तः सपर्यति। तस्मा इद्दीदयद्वसु।।१५।।

15. Whatsoever mortal worships the divine *Agni* in his house (for the attainment of wealth), to him he gives riches.

For the Attainment of Wealth— *Tanvaḥ dhanasya prāptyartham* (*cf. Naigh*. II.10), so Sāyaṇa; but this seems very doubtful; rather, "in his own house."

६८९०. अग्निर्मूर्धा दिवः ककुत्पतिः पृथिव्या अयम्।
       अपां रेतांसि जिन्वति।।१६।।

16. *Agni*, the head (of the gods), the summit of heaven,—he the lord of the earth,—gladdens the seed of the waters.

The Seed— *Retāṁsi*, the movable and immovable productions of the creative waters.

६८९१. उदग्ने शर्चयस्तव शुक्रा भ्राजन्त ईरते। तव ज्योतींष्यर्चयः।।१७।।

17. *Agni*, your pure, bright, shining flames send forth your splendours.

६८९२. ईशिषे वार्यस्य हि दात्रस्याग्ने स्वर्पतिः।
       स्तोता स्यां तव शर्मणि।।१८।।

18. *Agni*, lord of heaven, you preside over (all) that is to be desired or given; may I be your eulogist for happiness.

६८९३. त्वामग्ने मनीषिणस्त्वां हिन्वन्ति चित्तिभिः।
       त्वां वर्धन्तु नो गिरः।।१९।।

19. You, *Agni*, the wise (praise), you they rejoice with (pious) rites; may our praises invigorate you.

६८९४. अदब्धस्य स्वधावतो दूतस्य रेभतः सदा।
       अग्नेः सख्यं वृणीमहे।।२०।।

20. We ever choose the friendship of *Agni*, the unharmed, the strong, the messenger, the praiser (of the gods).

६८९५. अग्निः शुचिव्रततमः शुचिर्विप्रः शुचिः कविः।
       शुची रोचत आहुतः।।२१।।

21. The pure *Agni* shines forth when worshipped the purest offerer, the pure priest, the pure sage.

The Pure Sage— I follow Prof. Wilson in rendering *kavi* as "sage" (*cf*. Say. and *R.V.* i.31.2), but Sāyaṇa here, as more usually, interprets it as *krāntakarman*.

६८९६. उत त्वा॒ धी॒तयो॒ मम॒ गिरो॑ वर्धन्तु वि॒श्वहा॑।
अग्ने॒ स॒ख्य॒स्य॑ बो॒धि न॑:॥२२॥

22. May my rites also and my praises ever invigorate you;
Agni, take thought of our friendship.

६८९७. यद॑ग्ने॒ स्या॒म॒ह॒ं त्वं त्वं वा॑ घा॒ स्या अ॒हम्।
स्युष्टे॒ सत्या॑ इ॒हाशिष॑:॥२३॥

23. *Agni*, if I were you or you wert I, your wishes here should
come true.

If I were you or you wert I— That is, of I were rich like you and
you wert poor like me.

६८९८. वसु॒र्वसु॑पति॒र्हि क॒मस्य॒ग्ने वि॑भाव॒सु:। स्याम॑ ते सु॒मता॒वपि॑॥२४॥

24. *Agni*, you are rich in splendour, the lord of wealth, and the
giver of dwellings; may we too abide in your favour.

६८९९. अग्ने॑ धृ॒तव्र॑ताय ते समु॒द्रायेव॒ सिन्ध॑व:। गिरो॑ वा॒श्रास॑ ईरते॥२५॥

25. *Agni*, my loud praises proceed to you, observant of pious
rites, as rivers to the sea.

६९००. युवा॑नं वि॒श्पतिं॒ क॒विं वि॒श्वाद॑ं पु॒रुवे॑प॒सम्।
अ॒ग्निं शु॒म्भामि॒ मन्म॑भि:॥२६॥

26. I glorify with hymns the ever-young *Agni*, the lord of men,
the wise, the all-devouring, the performer of many acts.

The All-Devouring— *Viśvādam,* the devourer of the entire oblation
(Sāyaṇa).

६९०१. य॒ज्ञानां॒ रथ्ये॑ व॒यं ति॒ग्मज॑म्भाय वी॒ळवे॑। स्तोमै॑रिषेमा॒ग्नये॑॥२७॥

27. Let us seek with our hymns *Agni*, the conductor of the
sacrifices, the mighty, the sharp-jawed.

६९०२. अ॒यम॑ग्ने॒ त्वे अपि॑ जरि॒ता भू॑तु सन्त्य। तस्मै॑ पावक मृळय॥२८॥

28. May this (my family) also be your worshippers, adorable
Agni; O purifier, give them happiness.

Adorable— Sāyaṇa here takes *santya* as *bhajanīya,* elsewhere he
generally explains it as *phalaprada.*

६९०३. धीरो॒ ह्यस्य॒द॒सद् विप्रो॒ न जागृ॑वि: स॒दा। अग्ने॒ दीद॑य॒सि द्यवि॑॥२९॥

29. You verily are wise, seated at the oblation, wakeful as the
seer (for the welfare of living beings); *Agni*, you ever shine in the
sky.

६९०४. पुरा॒ग्ने दु॒रि॒तेभ्यः॑ पु॒रा मृ॒ध्रेभ्यः॑ कवे। प्र ण॒ आयु॒र्वसो॑ तिर॥३०॥

30. Wise *Agni*, giver of dwellings, extend our lives, before sins or assailants (destroy us).

[सूक्त-४५]

[**ऋषि**- त्रिशोक काण्व। **देवता**- इन्द्र, १-इन्द्राग्नी। **छन्द**- गायत्री।]

६९०५. आ घा॒ ये अ॒ग्निमि॒न्धते॑ स्तृ॒णन्ति॑ ब॒र्हिरा॑नु॒षक्।
येषा॒मिन्द्रो॒ युवा॒ सखा॑॥१॥

1. Those (sages) who kindle *Agni*, those of whom the ever-young *Indra* is the friend, continually spread the sacred grass.

Sāmaveda, 133; stanzas 1-3 occur in *Sāmaveda*, 1338. 1-3. *Cf.* also *Vāj. Saṁh.* 7.32.33.24.

६९०६. बृ॒ह॒न्निद्ध्म ए॑षां॒ भूरि॑ श॒स्तं पृ॒थुः स्वरुः॑। येषा॒मिन्द्रो॒ युवा॒ सखा॑॥२॥

2. Ample is their fuel, many their hymns, broad their sacred shaving,—whose friend is the ever-young *Indra*.

Their Sacred Shaving— *Svaru*, which Sāyaṇa leaves unexplained, is the first shaving or splinter from the sacrificial post; see *Indische Stud.* IX, p.222. For its use in the sacrifice, see *Katy*, 6, 4.12; 6, 9,12.

६९०७. अयु॒द्ध इद्यु॒धा वृतं॒ शूर॑ आ॒जति॒ सत्व॑भिः। येषा॒मिन्द्रो॒ युवा॒ सखा॑॥३॥

3. Though before powerless to combat, the hero by his might now subdues one surrounded by allies, (if helped by those) of whom the ever-young *Indra* is the friend.

Powerless to Combat—*Ayuddhaḥ* might mean "unopposed," but Sāyaṇa explains it as *prāg ayoddha eva,* which seems to mean as in the text, though Sāyaṇa explains it differently in i.32.6.

६९०८. आ बु॒न्दं वृ॒त्र॒हा द॑दे जा॒तः पृ॒च्छद्वि मा॒तरम्।
क उ॒ग्राः के ह॑ शृण्विरे॥४॥

4. The slayer of *Vṛtra*, as soon as he was born, seized his arrow, and asked his mother, "who are the terrible, who are renowned?"

Sāmaveda, 216

६९०९. प्रति॑ त्वा श॒वसी॑ वदद्गि॒रावप्सो॒ न यो॑धिषत्।
यस्तै॑ श॒त्रुत्व॑मा॒चके॑॥५॥

5. Your strong mother answered you, "he who wishes your enmity fights as the elephant in the mountain."

As the Elephant— *Apsaḥ* is elsewhere explained by Sāyaṇa as "personal charms," "teeth," etc. (i.124.7), or "beauty" (v.80.6); here he explains it as "a beautiful (elephant)." Dose he take it as=*tantin*? Grassmann explains it as meaning the bosom, or rather that part of the dress which covers it; and hence he takes it here as meaning the cloud which covers the earth and the mountains (*i.e., Vṛtra*).

६९१०. उत त्वं मघवञ्छृणु यस्ते वष्टि ववक्षि तत्।

यद्वीळयासि वीळु तत्।।६॥

6. O *Maghavan*, do you hear (our praise); whosoever desires of you, you bear to him his request; what you fix is sure.

६९११. यदाजि यात्याजिकृदिन्द्रः स्वश्वयुरुप। रथीतमो रथीनाम्।।७॥

7. When *Indra*, the warrior, goes to battle, desirous of gallant steeds, he is the foremost of the lords of chariots.

६९१२. वि षु विश्वा अभियुजो वज्रिन्विष्वग्यथा वृह।

भवा नः सुश्रवस्तमः।।८॥

8. Thunderer, smite all your enemies that they may be scattered,—be to us a most abundant benefactor.

६९१३. अस्माकं सु रथं पुर इन्द्रः कृणोतु सातये। न यं धूर्वन्ति धूर्तयः।।९॥

9. May *Indra*, whom no foes can harm, send before us a beautiful chariot for the acquisition (of our desires).

६९१४. वृज्याम ते परि द्विषोऽरं ते शक्र दावने। गमेमेदिन्द्र गोमतः।।१०॥

10. Strong *Indra*, may we escape your enemies; may we come to you abundantly for your gifts, rich in cattle.

६९१५. शनैश्चिद्यन्तो अद्रिवोऽश्वावन्तः शतग्विनः। विवक्षणा अनेहसः।।११॥

11. (May we come), thunderer, slowly approaching you,—may we be rich in horses, possessed of abundant treasure, ready to offer, and unharmed (by calamity).

६९१६. ऊर्ध्वा हि ते दिवेदिवे सहस्रा सूनृता शता। जरितृभ्यो विमंहते।।१२॥

12. (The sacrificer) gives to your praisers day by day hundreds and thousands of excellent and auspicious gifts.

६९१७. विद्मा हि त्वा धनञ्जयमिन्द्र दूळ्हा चिदारुजम्।

आदारिणं यथा गर्यम्।।१३॥

13. We know you, *Indra*, as the conqueror of wealth, the breaker of firm obstacles, the opener, and (guarding from harm) as a house.

The Opener— Sāyaṇa explains *ādāriṇam* as *ādartāram* (*cf.* viii.24.4), and seems to connect it with *dṛḷhā arujam*. It is explained in the St. Petersb. Dict. as "anziehend, reizend," and by Grassmann as "erschliessend, machend."

६९१८. कुकुहं चित्त्वा कवे मन्दन्तु धृष्णविन्दवः।
आ त्वां पणिं यदीमहे॥१४॥

14. Wise (*Indra*), overcomer of enemies, when we solicit you the barterer, may the drops of the *Soma* exhilarate you the exalted one.

The Barterer— *Paṇi* seems used here as in i.33.3, where it is said, "Mighty *Indra*, bestowing upon us abundant wealth, take not advantage of us, like a dealer," *mā paṇir bhūr asmād adhi, i.e.,* do not demand from us the strict price of your gifts. Here *Indra* is represented as selling them for the offered *Soma*-libations.

६९१९. यस्तै रेवाँ अदाशुरिः प्रममर्षं मघत्तये। तस्यं नो वेद आ भर॥१५॥

15. Grant to us the possessions of that rich man who, through his niggardliness, reviles you as to your bestowal of wealth.

६९२०. इम उ त्वा वि चक्षते सखाय इन्द्र सोमिनः।
पुष्टावन्तो यथा पशुम्॥१६॥

16. These friends, effusing the *Soma*, look on you, *Indra*, as men with their fodder ready (look) on their cattle.

Sāmaveda, 136

६९२१. उत त्वाबधिरं वयं श्रुत्कर्णं सन्तमूतये। दूरादिह हवामहे॥१७॥

17. We invoke you here from afar for our protection, who are never deaf. and whose ears are always open to hear.

६९२२. यच्छुश्रूया इमं हवं दुर्मर्षं चक्रिया उत। भवेरापिर्नो अन्तमः॥१८॥

18. If you hear this our prayer, then display your invincible power and be our nearest kinsman.

६९२३. यच्चिद्धि ते अपि व्यथिर्जगन्वांसो अमन्महि।
गोदा इदिन्द्र बोधि नः॥१९॥

19. Whenever, repairing to you in our distress, we offer our praises, attend to us, *Indra*, as a giver of cattle.

६९२४. आ त्वां रम्भं न जिव्रयो ररभ्मा शवसस्पते।
उशमसि त्वा सधस्थ आ॥२०॥

20. Lord of might, we lean on you as the aged on a staff; we long for you in the sacrifice.

६९२५. स्तोत्रमिन्द्राय गायत पुरुनृम्णाय सत्वने। नकिर्यं वृण्वते युधि॥२१॥

21. Sing the praise to *Indra*, who is rich in wealth and bountiful, whom nine can stay in battle.

६९२६. अभि त्वा वृषभा सुते सुतं सृजामि पीतये।
तृम्पा व्यश्नुही मदम्॥२२॥

22. When the *Soma* is effused, I pour out the libation to you, showerer (of blessings), for your drinking; satiate yourself, enjoy the exhilarating draught.

Sāmaveda, 161, 731

६९२७. मा त्वा मूरा अविष्यवो मोपहस्वान आ दभन्।
माकीं ब्रह्मद्विषो वन:॥२३॥

23. Let not fools, seeking protection, nor mockers trouble you; favour not the enemies of the *Brāhmaṇas.*

Enemies of the Brāhmaṇas— *Brahmadviṣaḥ,* which Sāyaṇa explains *brāhmaṇānām dveṣṭṛn.* Benfey (Sama V. Lex.) Translates it, "Fiend der Frommen." This and the next verse occur in *Sāmaveda,*732

६९२८. इह त्वा गोपरीणसा महे मन्दन्तु राधसे। सरौ गौरो यथा पिब॥२४॥

24. Let (the worships) gladden you here with the *Soma* mixed with milk, for the attainment of great wealth; drink it as the buffalo a lake.

६९२९. या वृत्रहा परावति सना नवा च चुच्युवे।
ता संसत्सु प्र वोचत॥२५॥

25. Proclaim in our assemblies those perpetual and ever new riches which the slayer of *Vṛtra* sends from afar.

६९३०. अपिबत् कद्रुव: सुतमिन्द्र: सहस्रबाह्वे। अत्रादेदिष्ट पौंस्यम्॥२६॥

26. *Indra* drank the *Soma* offering of Kadru, (he smote the enemies) of the thousand-armed; there did his might shine forth.

Sāmaveda, 131—Sāyaṇa takes *Kadravaḥ* as "belonging to a *Ṛṣi* named *Kadru*"; but it must be the gen, or abl. of *Kadru,* the well-known mother of the *nāgas.* Benfey takes the isolated *sahasrabahve* as a Vedic dative without guna in the sense of "battle." He translates the verse, "Der Kadru Trank hat eingeschlürft, *Indra* zur tausendarmgen Scholacht!" The *Sāmveda* reads *ādadiṣta* for *ādediṣta.*

६९३१. स॒त्यं त॒नुर्वशे॒ यदौ॑ वि॒दानो॑ अह्नवा॒य्यम्। व्यान॑ट् तु॒र्वणे॒ शमि॑॥२७॥

27. Well knowing those (sacrificial) deeds of Turvasa and Yadu, he overcame Anhavāyya in battle.

Turvasha, Yadu— These names are associated in i.36.18; 54.6; 174. 9; and elsewhere. Nothing is known of *Ahnavayya*. The St. Petersburg Dict. takes it as an adj. (a+*hnu*), "nicht zu leugnen, nicht zu beseitigen." Perhaps the sentence may mean, "he prevailed indisputably in battle."

६९३२. त॒र॒णिं वो॒ जना॑नां त्र॒दं वाज॑स्य गो॒मतः॑। स॒मानमु॒ प्र शं॑सिषम्॥२८॥

28. I praise our common (*Indra*), the deliverer of your families, the slayer (of your enemies, the bestower) of riches in cattle.

Sāmaveda, 204.

६९३३. ऋ॒भु॒क्ष॒णं न वर्त॑व उ॒क्थेषु॑ तुग्र्या॒वृध॑म्। इन्द्रं॒ सोमे॒ सचा॑ सु॒ते॥२९॥

29. (I praise) in hymns the mighty *Indra*, the augmenter of waters, for the attainment of wealth, when the *Soma* is effused with (song);

६९३४. यः कृ॒न्तदि॑द्धि॒ योन्यं॑ त्रि॒शोका॑य गि॒रिं पृ॒थुम्।

गोभ्यो॑ गा॒तुं निरे॑तवे॥३०॥

30. Who clove for Trishoka the broad womb-like cloud, (and made) a path for the cows to issue forth.

The Cows— *Go* here means "water, rain."

६९३५. यद्दधि॑षे॒ मन॑स्य॒सि म॒न्दानः॑ प्रे॒दिय॑क्षसि। मा तत्क॑रिन्द्र मृ॒ळय॑॥३१॥

31. Whatever you undertake in your exhilaration, whatever you purpose in your mind or are thinking to bestow,—O *Indra*, do it not, but bless us.

Do it not but bless Us— Sāyaṇa understands this, "do it not, for you have done it for us,—only make us happy." Could it be that the worshipper had a feeling of nemesis? Or would he monopolize all?

६९३६. द॒भ्रं चि॒द्धि त्वाव॑तः कृ॒तं शृ॒ण्वे अधि॒ क्षमि॑।

जि॒गात्वि॑न्द्र ते॒ मनः॑॥३२॥

32. *Indra*, the least deeds of one like you are renowned in the earth; may your care visit me.

The least deeds of one, Etc.— This seems to be *Sāyaṇa's* interpretation; but Dr. Muir gives a more natural version (*Sansk. Texts*, vol. v, p.III), "little has been heard of as done upon earth by one such as you are."

६९३७. तवेदु ताः सुकीर्तयोऽसन्वृत प्रशंस्तयः। यदिन्द्र मृळयासि नः॥३३॥

33. Yours be those ascriptions of praise, your those hymns, through which, *Indra*, you bless us.

६९३८. मा न एकस्मिन्नागसि मा द्वयोरुत त्रिषु। वधीर्मा शूर भूरिषु॥३४॥

34. Slay us not for one sin, not for two, not for three; O hero, slay us not for many.

६९३९. बिभया हि त्वावत उग्रादभिप्रभङ्गिणः। दस्मादहमृतीषहः॥३५॥

35. I am afraid of one like you, terrible, the smiter of enemies, the destroyer, who endures hostile attacks.

६९४०. मा सख्युः शूनमा विदे मा पुत्रस्य प्रभूवसो।

आवृत्वद्भूतु ते मनः॥३६॥

36. Wealthy (*Indra*), may I never have to tell you of the destitution of my friend or my son; may your mind be favourable towards me.

Sāyaṇa's interpretation of this verse is very obscure, as he explains *śūnam* by *vṛddham*; but the verse is cleared up by his comment on ii.27.17, where he explains *śūnam* as *śunyam, dāridryam*, "may I never have to tell a kinsman's destitution to an opulent, kind, and munificent patron."

६९४१. को नु मर्या अमिथितः सखा सखायमब्रवीत्।

जहा को अस्मदीषते॥३७॥

37. "Who, O mortals," said (*Indra*), "unprovoked, has ever, as a friend, slain his friend? Who fleeth from me?"

This is said by *Indra* in answer to *vv.* 34,35.

६९४२. एवारे वृषभा सुतेऽसिन्वन्भूर्यावयः। श्वघ्नीव निवता चरन्॥३८॥

38. Showerer (of benefits), when the ready *Soma* was effused, you did devour much, without stint, rushing down like a gamester.

Sāyaṇa's Comm. is lost to much of this verse. He explains *asinvan* as *na badhnan*; in vii.39.6 he explained it is *apratibadhnān*, "not hindering the desires of mortals." The St. Petersburg Dict. renders it "unersättlich."

६९४३. आ त एता वचोयुजा हरी गृभ्णे सुमद्रथा।

यदीं ब्रह्मभ्य इद्ददः॥३९॥

39. I draw hither your two steeds, harnessed to a beautiful chariot and yoked by hymns, since you give wealth to the *Brāhmaṇas*.

६९४४. भिन्धि विश्वा अप द्विषः परि बाधो जही मृधः।
वसु स्याहं तदा भर॥४०॥

40. Cleave asunder all the hostile hosts, frustrate their destructive attacks, and bestow on us their desirable wealth.

Sāmaveda, 134, 1074.

६९४५. यद्वीळाविन्द्र यत्स्थिरे यत्पर्शाने परांभृतम्। वसु स्याहं तदा भर॥४१॥

41. Bestow on us, *Indra,* that desirable wealth, which is deposited in strongholds, in fastnesses, and in places which can stand an attack.

Sāmaveda, 207, 1072. Sāyaṇa explains *parśāne* as *vimarṣaṇkṣame,* *cf.* Müller, *var. lect.* p.32. Benfey take it as "a well" (so Schol. S.V. *kupadi*), and quotes a note from Stevenson, "when the English took Poonah ten lakhs of rupees belonging to the Peshva were found built into the side of a well." B. and R. take it as "Abgrund, Kluft."

६९४६. यस्य ते विश्वमानुषो भूरेर्दत्तस्य वेदति। वसु स्याहं तदा भेर॥४२॥

42. Bestow on us, *Indra,* that desirable wealth which all men recognize as given abundantly by you.

Sāmaveda, 1071, with *var. lect.*

[सूक्त-४६]

[ऋषि– वश अश्व्य। देवता– २१-२४ पृथुश्रवा कानीत, २५-२८, ३२ वायु। छन्द– गायत्री, १ पादनिचृत् , ५ ककुप् , ७ बृहती, ८ अनुष्टुप् , ९ सतो-बृहती, ११-१२ प्रगाथ (बृहती, विपरीता पंक्ति), १३ द्विपदा (जगती) , १४ बृहती पिपीलिकामध्या, १५ ककुमन्यंकुशिरा, १६ विराट्, १७ जगती, १८ उपरिष्टाद् बृहती, १९ बृहती, २० विषमपदा बृहती, २१-२४ पंक्ति, २२ संस्तार पंक्ति, २५-२८ प्रगाथ (विषमा बृहती, समा सतोबृहती) ३० द्विपदा विराट्, ३१ उष्णिक्, ३२ पंक्ति।]

VIII. 6.4. The Deity Vāyu— The Schol. on v. 33. remarks that *vāyu* may be considered the deity of v. 21.24, since even where the gift is the direct subject, it must be regarded as the result of *Vāyu's* favour.

६९४७. त्वावतः पुरूवसो वयमिन्द्र प्रणेतः। स्मसि स्थातर्हरीणाम्॥१॥

1. O wealthy *Indra,* the leader (of rites), we belong to one like you, ruler of horses.

Sāmaveda, 193.

We Belong to one like you— Sāyaṇa adds, "since none other is like You, we are Yours."

६९४८. त्वां हि सत्यमद्रिवो विद्य दातारमिषाम्। विद्य दातारं रयीणाम्॥२॥

2. You, thunderer, we verily know to be the giver of food, you we know to be the giver of riches.

६९४९. आ यस्य ते महिमानं शतमूते शतक्रतो। गीर्भिर्गृणन्ति कारवः॥३॥

3. O *Śatakratu*, wielding a hundred protections, whose greatness the worshippers praise with their hymns.

६९५०. सुनीथो घा स मर्त्यो यं मरुतो यमर्यमा। मित्रः पान्त्यदुहः॥४॥

4. Fortunate in sacrifice is that mortal whom the guileless *Maruts*, whom *Aryaman* and *Mitra*, protect.

६९५१. दधानो गोमदश्ववत्सुवीर्यमादित्यजूत एधते। सदा राया पुरुस्पृहा॥५॥

5. He who is directed by *Āditya* ever increases, possessing abundance of kine and horses and vigorous children; he increases in wealth longed for by many.

६९५२. तमिन्द्रं दानमीमहे शवसानमभीर्वम्। ईशानं राय ईमहे॥६॥

6. We solicit a gift from this *Indra*, the displayer of might, the fearless; we solicit wealth from the lord.

६९५३. तस्मिन्हि सन्त्यूतयो विश्वा अभीरवः सचा।

तमा वहन्तु सप्तयः पुरूवसुं मदाय हरयः सुतम्॥७॥

7. In him abide united all secure protections; lord of vast wealth, may his gliding steeds bear him to the expressed *Soma* juice for his exhilaration.

All secure Protections— Sāyaṇa says that this may also refer to the troops of the *Maruts* who accompany *Indra*.

६९५४. यस्ते मदो वरेण्यो य इन्द्र वृत्रहन्तमः।

य आददिः स्वर्नृभिर्यः पृतनासु दुष्टरः॥८॥

8. That exhilaration of your, *Indra*, which is preeminent, which utterly destroys your enemies, which wins wealth from men, and is invincible in battles;

From Men— Sāyaṇa explains *nṛbhiḥ* by *śatrubhyaḥ*, "from your foes."

६९५५. यो दुष्टरो विश्ववार श्रवाय्यो वाजेष्वस्ति तरुता।

स नः शविष्ठ सवना वंसो गहि गमेम गोमति व्रजे॥९॥

9. Which is invincible in contests,—O you desired by all,—well worthy of praise and the deliverer (from enemies); come

to our oblations, most mighty one, giver of dwellings; may we obtain a stall full of kine.

The Deliverer from Enemies— Sāyaṇa explains *'tarutṛ'* in viii.1.28 by *jetṛ*.

६९५६. गव्यो षु णो यथा पुराश्वयोत रंथया। वरिवस्य मंहामह॥१०॥

10. Lord of wealth; visit us as of old, to give us cows, horses and chariots.

Sāmaveda, 186.

६९५७. नहि तें शूर राधसोऽन्तं विन्दामि सत्रा।

दशस्या नौ मघवन्निंदद्रिवो धियो वाजेभिराविथ॥११॥

11. Verily, hero, I find no limit to your wealth; O *Maghavan*, the thunderer, bestow (your gifts) quickly upon us, and bless our offerings with (abundant) food.

६९५८. य ऋष्वः श्रावयत्सखा विश्वेत् सं वेद जनिमा पुरुष्टुतः।

तं विश्वे मानुषा युगेन्द्रं हवन्ते तविषं यतस्रुचः॥१२॥

12. The graceful *Indra*, whose friends extol him, knows, praised of many, all births; him, the mighty, all men invoke at all times, seizing the ladles (for oblation).

All Men—Sāyaṇa takes *viśve mānuṣā* as 'all the priests, *adhvaryus*, etc., associated with men,' *sarve'py adhvaryvādayo manuṣyasambandhinaḥ.*

६९५९. स नो वाजेष्वविता पुरूवसुः पुरः स्थाता। मघवा वृत्रहा भुवत्॥१३॥

13. May *Maghavan*, the wealthy, the slayer of *Vṛtra*, stand before us as our defender in battles.

६९६०. अभि वो वीरमन्धसो मदेषु गाय गिरा महा विचेतसम्।

इन्द्रं नाम श्रुत्यं शाकिनं वचो यथा॥१४॥

14. At the time of the exhilaration of the *Soma*, sing, according to your hymns, with a loud voice, you wise hero *Indra*, the humbler of enemies, the strong, the ever worthy to be praised.

Sāmaveda, 265.

Your Wise Hero— Sāyaṇa takes *vaḥ* as=*yuyānr*, or as *yuṣmākam hitayā*. *vaco yathā* he explains as "in the *gāyatrī* or *triṣṭubh* metre." Benfey translates it, "im wahren Sinne des Worts." *Nāma* Sāyaṇa explains, but apparently without any necessity, *śatrūṇām nāmakam, cf.* Benfey's Gloss, *vṛṣaṇamān*. The St. Petersburg Dict. takes it as simply "freilich, gerade."

६९६१. ददी रेक्णस्तन्वे॒ दिदिर्वसु॒ ददिर्वजे॑षु पुरुहूत॒ वाजि॑न॑म्। नू॒नम॑थ॑॥१५॥

15. (*Indra*), invoked by many, speedily give me wealth; give riches, give abundance of food in battle.

Speedilty— It is curious that Sāyaṇa seems to have misread the *atha* of the text for *adya*.

६९६२. विश्वे॑षामिरज्य॒न्तं॒ वसू॑नां सास॒ह्वांस॑ चि॒दस्य॒ वर्प॑सः।

कृ॒पय॑तो नू॒नम॒त्यथ॑॥१६॥

16. (We praise you), the lord of all riches, the subduer of this obstructor waging (attacks),—speedily give us abundant (wealth).

Abundant— Here again Sāyaṇa seems to read *adyāpi* or *apyādya* for *atyatha. Ati* Should however be connected with the obscure word *kṛpyataḥ.*

६९६३. म॒हः सु वो॒ अर॑मिष॒े स्तवा॑महे मी॒ळ्हुष॑े अरङ्ग॒माय॒ जग्म॑ये।

यज्ञे॑भि॒र्गी॒र्भिर्वि॒श्वम॑नुषां मरु॒तामि॑यक्षसि॒ गाय॑े॒ त्वा॒ नर्म॑सा गि॒रा॥१७॥

17. I desire the coming of you, the mighty one; we give praise with oblations and hymns to the showerer who hastens readily (to the sacrifice); associated with the *Maruts*, you are worshipped of all men; I glorify you with adoration and praise.

You are worshipped of all Men— Sāyaṇa explains *viśvamanuṣām marutām iyakṣasi* as *etair ijyase marutām sambandhī tvam.* But it would be better to render it, "you show favour to all men and the *Maruts*" (*cf.* vi.49.4), or "to the *Maruts* who are known to all men."

६९६४. ये पा॑तय॒न्ते अ॒ज्म॑भि॒र्गिरीणां॒ स्नु॒भिरे॑षाम्।

यज्ञं॑ म॒हि॒ष्व॒र्णीनां॒ सुम्नं॒ तु॒विष्व॑णीनां॒ प्राध्व॑रे॥१८॥

18. (We present) the oblation to those loud-sounding (*Maruts*) who rush along with the streaming trains of the clouds; may we obtain in the sacrifice the happiness which those deep-roarers bestow.

Streaming Trains— Sāyaṇa generally explains *ajman* by *gamanam* (as in i.166.5) or *saṅgrāma* (as in i.112.17); here he explains it *balair balakarair udakaiḥ.* Here it seems impossible to resist comparing Virgil's "immensum coelo venit agmen aquarum."

६९६५. प्र॒भ॒ङ्गं॒ दुर्म॑तीनामिन्द्र॒ शविष्ठ॑ भर।

र॒यिम॒स्मभ्यं॑ यु॒ज्यं॒ चोदयन्मते॒ ज्येष्ठं॑ चोदयन्मते॥१९॥

19. (We worship) the crusher of the malevolent; most powerful *Indra*, bring to us suitable wealth, O inspirer,— (bring) most excellent (wealth), O inspirer.

O Inspirer— *Codayanmate* is explained by Sāyaṇa as *dhanam prerayanti matir yasya*, "you whose mind sends wealth to his worshipper." In v.8.6 it is applies to the eye." and he there explains it, "having the mind as its instigator", Böhtligk and Roth compare v.43.9, and translate it, "die Andachtlietend, fördernd."

६९६६. सनित: सुसनितरुग्र चित्र चेतिष्ठ सूनृत।
प्रासहा सम्राट् सहुरिं सहन्तं भुज्युं वाजेषु पूर्व्यम्॥२०॥

20. O bountiful, most bountiful, mighty, wonderful, best giver of knowledge and supremely truthful, by your prowess, universal ruler, (bring to us) inconflicts ample wealth, overpowering those who attack us, and causing enjoyment.

Two of the epithets in this verse, *bhujyum* and *pūrvyam,* are applies in viii.22.2 to the chariot of the *Aśvins;* and *pūrvya* is there explained by Sāyaṇa as "going before (in battle)," and *bhujyu* as "the preserver of all."

६९६७. आ स एतु य ईवदाँ अदेव: पूर्तमाददे।
यथा चिद्रशों अश्य: पृथुश्रवसि कानीतेऽस्या व्युष्याददे॥२१॥

21. "Let him draw near, who, though not a god, would receive this complete living gift,—since *Vaśa*, the son of *Aśva*, receives it at the dawn of this (morning) at the hands of *Pṛthuśravas*, the son of *Kanīta*.

This verse is supposed to be spoken by *aśva* or his friends, Sāyaṇa explains *ivat* as usual by *gamanavad, gavādilakṣaṇam*, and *pūrtam* as *pūrṇam*; but Böthlingk and Roth take *ivat* as=*iyat*, "such, so great", and *pūrtam* in its sense of "pious works."

Kānīta— *Kānīta* is also explained by Sāyaṇa as "the son of a maiden," *kanyāyāḥ putraḥ.*

६९६८. षष्टिं सहस्त्राश्व्यस्यायुतासनमुष्ट्राणां विंशतिं शता।
दश श्यावीनां शता दश त्र्यरुषीणां दश गवां सेहस्त्रा॥२२॥

22. "I have received sixty thousand horses, and tens of thousands;—a score of hundreds of camels— a thousand brown mares— and ten times ten thousand cows with three red patches.

Sāyaṇa says, "having the head, back, and sides white (or bright)"; he also omits one *dasa* in his explanation.

This and the two following stanzas are spoken by *Vaśa.*

६९६९. दश श्यावा ऋधद्रयो वीतवारास आशव:।
मह्या नेमिं नि वावृतु:॥२३॥

23. "Ten brown horses bear along the wheel (of my chariot), of mature vigour, of complete power, and trampling down obstacles.

Of Complete Power— Sāyaṇa explains *vītavārāsaḥ* as *krāntabalaḥ prāptabala vā*; but it rather means "having sleek tails."

६९७०. दानासः पृथुश्रवसः कानीतस्य सुराधसः।
रथं हिरण्ययं ददन् मंहिष्ठः सूरिर्भूद्वर्षिष्ठमकृत श्रवः॥२४॥

24. "These are the gifts of the wealthy *Pṛthuśravas*, the son of *Kanīta*; he, bestowing a golden chariot, has proved himself most liberal and wise, he has won most abundant fame."

६९७१. आ नो वायो महे तने याहि मखाय पाजसे।
वयं हि ते चकृमा भूरि दावने सद्यश्चिन्महि दावने॥२५॥

25. Come to us, *Vāyu*, to bestow great wealth and glorious strength; we have offered (libations) to you the giver of abundant (wealth), we have offered immediately to you the giver of great (gifts).

६९७२. यो अश्वेभिर्वहते वस्त उस्राश्चिः सप्त सप्ततीनाम्।
एभिः सोमेभिः सोमसुद्भिः सोमपा दानाय शुक्रपूतपाः॥२६॥

26. He who is borne on horses and surrounds himself with thrice seven times seventy cows,—he comes to you with these *Soma*-libations and *Soma*-priests, to offer to you, drinker of the *Soma*, drinker of the bright pure *Soma*.

He— Sc. Pṛthuśravas.

६९७३. यो म इमं चिदु त्मनामंदच्चित्रं दावने।
अरट्वे अक्षे नहुषे सुकृत्वनि सुकृत्तराय सुक्रतुः॥२७॥

27. He who of his own will has been pleased to give me this honoured gift, he, performer of good works, (has determined) on a pre-eminently good action, amidst *Aratva*, *Akṣa*, *Nahuṣa* and *Sukṛtvan*.

Aratva, Akṣa, Nahuṣa, Sukṛtvan— These are either the officers of *Pṛthuśravas* or other kings.

६९७४. उचथ्ये वपुषि यः स्वराळुत वायो घृतस्नाः।
अश्वेषितं रजेषितं शुनेषितं प्राज्म तदिदं नु तत्॥२८॥

28. He who is self-resplendent in his glorious body, who is bright, O *Vāyu*, like *ghī*, has given me this food, brought by horses, brought by camels, brought by dogs.

Self-Resplendent in his Glorious Body— Sāyaṇa gives an alternative, "he who is lord over (the kings) *Ucathya* and *Vapus*."

Brought by Camels— The Schol, says that *rajas* means a camel or an ass.

६९७५. अर्ध प्रियमिषिराय षष्टिं सहस्रासनम्। अश्वानामित्र वृष्णाम्॥२९॥

29. I have now received (a gift) dear to the beneficent king, sixty thousand bulls vigorous like horses.

६९७६. गावो न यूथमुप यन्ति वध्रय उप मा यन्ति वध्रयः॥३०॥

30. As the cows to the herd, so repair the oxen; so the oxen repair to me.

६९७७. अध यच्चारथे गणे शतमुष्ट्राँ अचिक्रदत्।
अध श्वित्नेषु विंशतिं शता॥३१॥

31. Since, when the herd were wandering (to the wood), he called a hundred camels (to give them to me), and two thousand from among the white herds (of cows).

६९७८. शतं दासे बल्बूथे विप्रस्तरुक्ष आ ददे।
ते तं वायविमे जना मदन्तीन्द्रगोपा मदन्ति देवगोपाः॥३२॥

32. I, the sage, accept the hundred from the slave *Balbūtha*, the cowherd; we here are your, O *Vāyu*,—those who have *Indra* and the gods for protectors rejoice (though your favour).

The Cowherd— Sāyaṇa seems to take *tarukṣa* as *gavāśvādīnām tārakaḥ*, but it is given as a proper name in the guṇa to *Pan*. IV. 1.105. He says that "a hundred" means here an indefinite number.

६९७९. अध स्या योषणा मही प्रतीची वशमश्व्यम्।
अधिरुक्मा वि नीयते॥३३॥

33. This tall maiden, adorned with gold, is led towards me, *Vaśa*, the son of *Aśva*.

[सूक्त-४७]

[ऋषि– त्रित आप्त्य। **देवता**– आदित्यगण, १४-१८ आदित्यगण तथा उषा।
छन्द– महापंक्ति।]

६९८०. महि वो महतामवो वरुण मित्र दाशुषे। यमादित्या अभि द्रुहो रक्षथा
नेमघं नंशदनेहसौ व ऊतयः सुऊतयो व ऊतयः॥१॥

1. *Mitra* and *Varuṇa*, you are great, and great is your protection to the offerer; no evil, *Ādityas*, harms him whom you guard from the injurer; your aids are void of harm, your aids are true aids.

६९८१. विदा देवा अघानामादित्यासो अपाकृतिम्। पक्षा वयो यथोपरि
व्यइस्मे शर्म यच्छतानेहसो व ऊतयः सुऊतयो व ऊतयः॥२॥

2. Divine *Ādityas*, you know the averting of evils; as birds (spread) their wings over (their) young, grant us happiness; your aids are void of harm, your aids are true aids.

६९८२. व्यइस्मे अधि शर्म तत्पक्षा वयो न यन्तन। विश्वानि विश्ववेदसो
वरूथ्या मनामहेऽनेहसो व ऊतयः सुऊतयो व ऊतयः॥३॥

3. Grant us that happiness of yours, as birds (spread) their wings; O you possessed of all wealth, we solicit all riches suitable for our dwelling; your aids are void of harm, your aids are true aids.

६९८३. यस्मा अरासत क्षयं जीवातुं च प्रचेतसः। मनोर्विश्वस्य घेदिम
आदित्या राय ईशतेऽनेहसो व ऊतयः सुऊतयो व ऊतयः॥४॥

4. To whomsoever these wise *Ādityas* grant a dwelling and the means of life, (for him) they master the wealth of every man; your aids are void of harm, your aids are true aids.

Of Every Man— The Schol, adds, "who does not offer sacrifice."

६९८४. परि णो वृणजन्नघा दुर्गाणि रथ्यो यथा। स्यामेदिन्द्रस्य
शर्मण्यादित्यानामुतावस्यनेहसो व ऊतयः सुऊतयो व ऊतयः॥५॥

5. May our sins avoid us as charioteers inaccessible place; may we abide in *Indra*'s happiness and in the protection of the *Ādityas*; your aids are void of harm, your aids are true aids.

६९८५. परिह्वृतेदना जनो युष्मादत्तस्य वायति। देवा अदभ्रमाश वा
यमादित्या अहेतनानेहसो व ऊतयः सुऊतयो व ऊतयः॥६॥

6. Only by painful means does a living man obtain the wealth which you bestow; but he whom you, divine *Ādityas*, visit, wins great (riches); your aids are void of harm, your aids are true aids.

By Painful Means—Sc. by penance, religious observances, etc.

A living Man— Sāyaṇa explains *ana* as *prāṇa-yuktaḥ*, "endowed with life," just as in IV.30.3 he explained it *prāṇarūpeṇa balena*; but it seems better to take it in both places as the particle "certainly." Might we translate the line, "verily men succumb through the loss of the wealth given by you?" In the second line Sāyaṇa unites *āśa vaḥ* into one word, *āśavaḥ,* "swiftly moving."

६९८६. न तं तिग्मं चन त्यजो न द्रासदभि तं गुरु। यस्मा उ शर्म सप्रथ
आदित्यासो अराध्वमनेहसों व ऊतयः सुऊतयों व ऊतयं:॥७॥

7. Him fierce wrath touches not, nor heavy (calamity), to whom, *Ādityas,* you have given great happiness; your aids are void of harm, your aids are true aids.

Fierce Wrath— I have taken *tigmam* as agreeing with the neuter *tyājas.* Sāyaṇa makes it agree with *tam,* and translates the sentence, "him though fierce (or harsh) wrath touches not."

You have given great Happiness— Sāyaṇa here takes *saprathas* as a masculine nom. plural; but elsewhere (as i.22.15; 94.13) he had explained it properly as a neuter nom, sing, agreeing, as here, with *śarma.*

६९८७. युष्मे देवा अपि ष्मसि युध्यन्तइव वर्मसु। यूयं महो न एनसो
यूयमभांदुरुष्यतानेहसों व ऊतयः सुऊतयों व ऊतयं:॥८॥

8. Deities, may we abide in you as warriors in their armour; do you defend us from great evil, do you defend us from little; your aids are void of harm, your aids are true aids.

६९८८. अदितिर्न उरुष्यत्वदिति: शर्म यच्छतु। माता मित्रस्य रेवतोंऽर्यम्णो
वरुणस्य चानेहसों व ऊतयः सुऊतयों व ऊतयं:॥९॥

9. May *Aditi* defend us, may *Aditi* grant us happiness, the mother of the wealthy *Mitra, Aryaman* and *Varuṇa;* your aids are void of harm, your aids are true aids.

६९८९. यद्देवा: शर्म शरणं यद्भद्रं यदनातुरम्। त्रिधातु यद्वरूथ्यं तदस्मासु
वि यन्तनानेहसों व ऊतयः सुऊतयों व ऊतयं:॥१०॥

10. Grant to us, deities, that happiness which is a refuge, auspicious, and free from sickness, which is threefold and fit for a (secure) shelter; your aids are void of harm, your aids are true aids.

Threefold— This phrase *tridhātu* is explained by Sāyaṇa's note on *varūthya* in vi. 67.2, and *trivarūtha* in viii.18.21, as protecting against cold, heat, and wind or wet.

६९९०. आदित्या अव हि ख्यताधि कूलादिव स्पश:। सुतीर्थमर्वतो यथानु
नो नेषथा सुगमनेहसों व ऊतयः सुऊतयों व ऊतयं:॥११॥

11. *Ādityas,* look down upon us as those who look from the shore; as (men lead) their horses to a secure *Ghāṭa,* so conduct us

along a good path; your aids are void of harm, your aids are true aids.

Who look from the Shore— Sāyaṇa takes *spaśah* as for *spaṣṭah*, "visible." It is derived from the lost root spas, "to see," preserved in common Sanskrit in the words *spaśa*, "a spy," and *spaṣṭa*, and the mutilated *paśya, cf.,* spicio. Sāyaṇa explains the image "as a man standing on the shore looks down on the water below or on some one in it."

६९९१. नेह भद्रं रक्षस्विने नावयै नोपया उत। गर्वे च भद्रं धेनवे वीराय च
श्रवस्यतेऽनेहसो व ऊतयः सुऊतयो व ऊतयः॥१२॥

12. Let there not be prosperity here to our powerful (foe), nor to him who threaten or assails us; but let there be prosperity to our cattle, our milch kine, and our male offspring desirous of food; your aids are void of harm, your aids are true aids.

Nor to him who threatens or assails Us— Rather, "neither to threaten nor to assail us."

६९९२. यदाविर्यदपीच्यं देवासो अस्ति दुष्कृतम्। त्रिते तद्विश्वमाप्त्य आरे
अस्मद्दधातनानेहसो व ऊतयः सुऊतयो व ऊतयः॥१३॥

13. Deities, whatever evil is manifest, whatever is concealed, (let it be not found) in *Trita Āptya*, keep it far from us; your aids are void of harm, your aids are true aids.

Sāyaṇa necessarily interprets the line in this way, as he holds that *Trita Āptya* is the *Ṛṣi* of the hymn. Prof. Roth no doubt gives the true meaning when he says that *Trita Āptya* was a deity dwelling in remote distance, and consequently evil was sought to be transferred to him, *cf. Atharva V.* XIX.56.4. He would render it, "keep it far from us in *Trita Aptya.*" See Dr. Muir's *Sanskrit Texts,* vol. v. p.336.

६९९३. यच्च गोषु दुष्वप्न्यं यच्चास्मे दुहितर्दिवः। त्रिताय तद्विभावर्याप्त्याय
परा वहानेहसो व ऊतयः सुऊतयो व ऊतयः॥१४॥

14. Daughter of heaven, (*Uṣas*), whatever ill-omened dream threatens our cattle our ourselves, keep it, O brilliant one, far from *Trita Āptya*; your aids are void of harm, your aids, are true aids.

Far from *Trita Āptya*— Here the dative *Tritāya Āptyāya* might suggest the more appropriate rendering, "keep it far away for *Trita Āptya.*" Verses 14-15 are prescribed in Āśvalāyana's *Gṛhya Sūtras* to be recited after an unpleasant dream.

६९९४. निष्कं वा घा कृणवते स्रजं वा दुहितर्दिवः। त्रिते दुष्वप्न्यं
सर्वमाप्त्ये परि ददास्यनेहसो व ऊतयः सुऊतयो व ऊतयः॥१५॥

15. Daughter of heaven, whatever ill-omened dream threatens *Trita Āptya*, we transfer it to the worker of gold ornaments or to the maker of garlands: your aids are void of harm, your aids are true aids.

It is singular that here Sāyaṇa gives an alternative interpretation, agreeing with Prof. Roth's explanation of stt.13,14, "whatever evil dream threatens the worker of gold ornaments or the maker of garlands, that evil, abiding in *Trita Āptya* (or the son of the waters), we *Tṛtas* throw off from ourselves." This seems to mean, "we throw it off on *Trita Āptya*."

६९९५. तदंन्नाय तदंपसे तं भागमुंपसेदुषैं। त्रितायं च द्विताय चोषें दुष्वप्न्यं
वहानेहसौं व ऊतयं: सुऊतयौं व ऊतयं:॥१६॥

16. *Uṣas*, bear (elsewhere) the ill-omened dream for *Trita* and *Dvita*, who eat and do)in dreams) that (which is eaten and done amiss when awake) and who obtain that (inauspicious) portion; your aids are void of harm, your aids are true aids.

Bear Elsewhere— *I.e.,* let the eating of honey etc., perceived in a dream, produce happiness as in a waking state.

Trita and Dvita— Here Sāyaṇa has only the proper interpretation. For *Dvita cf. Śat. Brāhmaṇa,* i.2.3.1.

६९९६. यथा कलां यथा शफं यथ ऋणं सन्नयांमसि। एवा दुष्वप्न्यं
सर्वमाप्त्ये सं नंयामस्यनेहसौं व ऊतयं: सुऊतयौं व ऊतयं:॥१७॥

17. As (in the sacrifice) we put severally together the proper parts and the hoofs, and as we discharge a debt, so we transfer all the ill-omened dream that rests on *Āptya*; your aids are void of harm, your aids are true aids.

Sāyaṇa's explanation is, "as in the sacrifice they place together the *kalā*, sc. the heart, etc., as fit to be cut to pieces, and the *śapha*, sc. the hoof, bones, etc., as unfit." He also proposes another explanation, in which the *kalā* is the *śapha* or "hoof." But the words *śapha* and *kalā* occur together in the *Taitt. Saṁhitā*, vi.1.10, where the process of buying the *Soma* is described; and Sāyaṇa there takes *śapha* as the eighth part of a cow, and *kalā* as a very small portion.

That rests of Āptya— Or we may take it, "we transfer all the ill-omened dream to *Āptya*."

६९९७. अजैष्माद्यासनाम चाभूमानांगसो वयम्। उषो यस्मांदुष्वप्न्यादभैष्माप
तदुच्छत्वनेहसौं व ऊतयं: सुऊतयौं व ऊतयं:॥१८॥

18. May we be to-day victorious, and obtain (happiness); may we be free from evil; *Uṣas*, may that ill dream depart, of which we were afraid; your aids are void of harm, your aids are true aids.

[सूक्त-४८]

[ऋषि- प्रगाथ काण्व। देवता- सोम। छन्द- त्रिष्टुप्, ५ जगती।]

६९९८. स्वादोरभक्षि वयसः सुमेधाः स्वाध्यो वरिवोवित्तरस्य।
विश्वे यं देवा उत मर्त्यासो मधु ब्रुवन्तो अभि सञ्चरन्ति॥१॥

1. May I, the wise and devout, enjoy the delicious, abundantly honoured *Soma* food, which all gods and mortals, pronouncing sweet, seek to obtain.

६९९९. अन्तश्च प्रागा अदितिर्भवास्यवयाता हरसो दैव्यस्य।
इन्दविन्द्रस्य सख्यं जुषाणः श्रौष्टीव धुरमनु राय ऋध्याः॥२॥

2. You enter within, and unimpaired, you avert the anger of the gods; *Soma*, enjoying the friendship of *Indra*, may you bring us to wealth as a swift (horse) its burden.

You enter within— Sāyaṇa adds, "the heart or the sacrificial chamber."

७०००. अपाम सोमममृता अभूमागन्म ज्योतिरविंदाम देवान्।
किं नूनमस्मान्कृणवदरातिः किमु धूर्तिरमृत मर्त्यस्य॥३॥

3. We drink the *Soma*, may we become immortal; we have attained the light of (heaven), we have known the gods; what now could the enemy do to us, or what, O immortal, should the aggriever do to the mortal?

Sāyaṇa in his comment on this verse (*Taitt, Samhitā*, iii.2.5) says that "the past tense is used in the sense of wish," *asaṁsadyotanāya bhūtārthanir desah.*

७००१. ख्यं उरुशंस धीरः प्र ण आयुर्जीवसे सोम तारीः॥४॥

4. O *Soma*, drunk by us, be bliss to our hearts, as a father is indulgent to a son or a friend to a friend; O *Soma*, worthy of wide praise, do you, wise one, extend our years that we may live.

७००२. इमे मा पीता यशस उरुष्यवो रथं न गावः समनाह पर्वसु।
ते मा रक्षन्तु विस्रसश्चरित्रादुत मा स्रामाद्यवयन्त्विन्दवः॥५॥

5. May these glory-conferring protecting *Soma*-streams knit together my joints as cows draw together a chariot falling in pieces; may they keep us from a loosely-knit worship; may they deliver me from sickness.

Cows— *Gavaḥ* may equally apply to the *Soma* streams, as the *Soma* is mixed with milk, and may be thus considered the product of the cows.

A Loosely-Knity Worship— When the *Soma* is drunk, the ceremony becomes consolidated.

७००३. अग्निं न मा मथितं सं दिदीपः प्र चक्षय कृणुहि वस्यसो नः।
अथा हि ते मद आ सोम मन्ये रेवाँइव प्र चरा पुष्टिमच्छ॥६॥

6. *Soma*, kindle me like the fire ignited by attrition, brighten (our eyes) and make us rich; I praise you now for exhilaration; come now, full of wealth, to nourish us.

७००४. इषिरेण ते मनसा सुतस्य भक्षीमहि पित्र्यस्येव रायः।
सोम राजन् प्र ण आयूंषि तारीरहानीव सूर्यो वासराणि॥७॥

7. May we partake of you, effused, with a longing mind as (men enjoy) paternal wealth; King *Soma*, prolong our lives, as the sun the world-establishing day.

७००५. सोम राजन् मृळया नः स्वस्ति तव स्मसि व्रत्या इ स्तस्य विद्धि।
अलर्ति दक्ष उत मन्युरिन्दो मा नो अर्यो अनुकामं परा दाः॥८॥

8. King *Soma,* bless us for our welfare; we worshippers are your, do you recognize it; the enemy goes strong and fierce, O *Soma*; give us not over to him as he desires.

७००६. त्वं हि नस्तन्वः सोम गोपा गात्रेगात्रे निषसत्था नृचक्षाः।
यत्ते वयं प्रमिनाम व्रतानि स नो मृळ सुषखा देव वस्यः॥९॥

9. O *Soma*, you are the guardian of our bodies, you dwell in each limb as the beholder of man; though we impair your rites, yet, divine one, bless us, you who are possessed of most excellent food and good friends.

७००७. ऋदूदरेण सख्या सचेय यो मा न रिष्येद्धर्यश्व पीतः।
अयं यः सोमो न्यधाय्यस्मे तस्मा इन्द्रं प्रतिरमेम्यायुः॥१०॥

10. May I obtain a wholesome friend who, when quaffed, will not harm me, O lord of bay horses; I ask of *Indra* a long permanence for this *Soma* which has been placed within us.

७००८. अप त्या अस्थुरनिरा अमीवा निरत्रसन्तमिषीचीरभैषुः।
आ सोमो अस्माँ अरुहद्विहाया अगन्म यत्र प्रतिरन्त आयुः॥११॥

11. May those irremovable sicknesses depart; let those strong (pains) which have made us tremble, be afraid; the mighty *Soma* has climbed into us, we have attained that (draught) by which men prolong life.

७००९. यो न॒ इन्दुः॑ पितरो हृत्सु पीतोऽम॒र्त्यो॑ मर्त्याँ॑ आ॒विवेश॑।
तस्मै॒ सोमा॑य ह॒विषा॑ विधेम मृ॒ळी॒के अ॑स्य सुम॒तौ स्या॑म॥१२॥

12. That *Soma* which, drunk into our hearts, has entered, immortal, into us mortals,—to h im, fathers, let us do worship with oblations; may we abide in his bliss and favour.

७०१०. त्वं सोम॑ पितृ॒भिः॑ सं॒विदा॑नोऽनु॒ द्यावा॑पृथि॒वी आ त॑तन्थ।
तस्मै॒ त इ॑न्दो ह॒विषा॑ विधेम व॒यं स्या॑म॒ पत॑यो रयी॒णाम्॥१३॥

13. *Soma*, you in conjunction with the fathers do stretch our successively heaven and earth,—to you let us do worship with oblations, may we be lords of wealth.

७०११. त्रा॒तारो॑ दे॒वा अधि॑ वोचता नो॒ मा नो॒ नि॒द्रा ई॑श॒त मोत ज॒ल्पिः॑।
व॒यं सोम॑स्य वि॒श्वह॑ प्रि॒यासः॑ सु॒वीरा॑सो वि॒दथ॑मा वदेम॥१४॥

14. Guardian gods, speak favourably to us; let no dreams nor the censurer overpower us; may we be ever dear to *Soma*; possessed of brave offspring, may we utter our hymn.

७०१२. त्वं नः॑ सोम वि॒श्वतो॑ वयोधा॒स्त्वं स्व॑र्विदा वि॒शा नृ॒चक्षाः॑।
त्वं न॑ इन्द ऊ॒तिभिः॑ स॒जोषाः॑ पा॒हि प॒श्चाता॒दुत वा॑ पुरस्ता॑त्॥१५॥

15. You, *Soma*, give us food from every side; you are the bestower of heaven; enter us, beholder of men; O *Soma*, rejoicing with your protecting powers, guard us from behind and before.

With your Protecting Powers— Sāyaṇa, as often elsewhere (*cf.* i.84.20), understands by *ūtyaḥ* the *Maruts* as *gantāraḥ* (*ava gatau*).

[As Sāyaṇa gives no commentary here, the St. Petersburg Dict., Grassmann's Lexicon and translation and ludwig's translation and notes have been consulted for this translation.

These eleven apparently spurious hymns are called the *Vālakhilya*, containing *Vargas* XIV-XXXI. They are not reckoned in the division by *Maṇḍalas* and *Anuvakas*. Sāyaṇa takes no notice of them in his commentary. Professor Wilson omitted these *Khila mantras* in his translation.]

[VĀLAKHILYAS]

[सूक्त-४९]

[ऋषि- प्रस्कण्व काण्व। **देवता-** इन्द्र।
छन्द- प्रगाथ (विषमाबृहती, समा सतोबृहती।)]

७०१३. अभि प्र व: सुराधसमिन्द्रमर्च यथा विदे।
यो जरितृभ्यो मघवा पुरूवसु: सहस्रेणेव शिक्षति॥१॥

1. I would praise to you the bounteous *Indra* as is fit, the wealth-abounding *Maghavan*, who loves to help with thousandfold treasure those who praise him.

७०१४. शतानीकेव प्र जिगाति धृष्णुया हन्ति वृत्राणि दाशुषे।
गिरेरिव प्र रसा अस्य पिन्विरे दत्राणि पुरुभोजस:॥२॥

2. He rushes on boldly like a weapon with a hundred edges, he smites the enemies of his worshipper; the gifts of him who feeds many, swell like the streams of a mountain.

७०१५. आ त्वा सुतास इन्दवो मदा य इंद्र गिर्वण:।
आपो न वज्रिन्नवोक्यं सर: पृणन्ति शूर राधसे॥३॥

3. The expressed exhilarate *Soma*-juices, O *Indra*, lover of hymns, fill you for bounty, O hero, O thunderer, as the waters flow to their accustomed lake.

७०१६. अनेहसं प्रतरणं विवक्षणं मध्व: स्वादिष्ठमीं पिब।
आ यथा मन्दसान: किरासि न: प्र क्षुद्रेव त्मना धृषत्॥४॥

4. Drink the incomparable, helpful, swelling beverage, the sweet of the *Soma*, that in your exultation you may pour out treasure for us, just as the mill-stone pours out meal.
The St. Petersb. Dict. takes *dhṛṣad* as =*dṛṣad*.

७०१७. आ न: स्तोममुप द्रवद्धियानो अश्वो न सोतृभि:।
यं ते स्वधावन्त्स्वदयन्ति धेनव इन्द्र कण्वेषु रातय:॥५॥

5. Come quickly to our praise—urged on by the *Soma*-pressers like a horse—which the milch-kine make sweet, for you, O *Indra*, of independent mighty; there are gifts [for you] among the *Kaṇva's*.

Grassmann proposes to read *somam*.

७०१८. उग्रं न वीरं नमसोप॑ सेदिम विभू॑तिमक्षि॒तावसुम्।
उद्री॑व॒ वज्रि॑न्नवतो न सि॒ञ्चते॑ क्ष॒रन्तीन्द्र॑ धी॒तय॑:॥६॥

6. We have approached you with homage like a mighty hero,
the pre-eminent one, of imperishable wealth; O *Indra*, thunderer,
our prayers flow forth as an abundant fountain pours out its
streams.

Read *siñcate* unaccented.

७०१९. यद्ध॑ नू॒नं यद्वा॑ य॒ज्ञे यद्वा॑ पृथि॒व्यामधि॑।
अतो॑ नो य॒ज्ञमाशुभि॑र्महेमत उग्र उ॒ग्रेभि॒रा ग॑हि॥७॥

7. Whether you are now present at a sacrifice, or whether you
are abroad on the earth, come from thence with your swift steeds
to our sacrifice, O you of lofty counsel; come, strong one, with the
strong [steeds].

७०२०. अ॒जि॒रासो॒ हर॑यो॒ ये त॒ आशवो॒ वाता॑इव प्रस॒क्षिण॑:।
येभि॒रप॑त्यं॒ मनु॑ष: परी॒यसे॒ येभि॒र्विश्वं॒ स्व॑र्दृ॒शे॥८॥

8. Agile and swift are your steeds, overpowering like the
winds; with which you encircle the race of *Manus*, with which the
whole heaven becomes visible.

Or perhaps 'with which you encircle all, a very sun to (*cf*. IX.61.18).

७०२१. ए॒ता॒वत॑स्त ईमह॒ इन्द्र॑ सु॒म्नस्य॒ गोम॑त:।
यथा॒ प्रावो॒ मघ॑वन् मे॒ध्यातिथिं॒ यथा॒ नीपा॑तिथिं॒ धने॑॥९॥

9. O *Indra*, we long for such a bounty of yours, rich in kine;
(help us), *Maghavan*, as you did help *Medhyātithi* with wealth, as
you did help *Nīpātithi*;

७०२२. यथा॒ कण्वे॒ मघ॑वन्त्र॒सद॑स्य॒वि यथा॒ पक्थे॒ दश॑व्रजे।
यथा॒ गोश॑र्ये॒ अस॑नो॒रृजि॒श्वनीन्द्र॒ गोम॒द्धिर॑ण्यवत्॥१०॥

10. As you, *Maghavan*, did give abundant kine and gold to
Kaṇva and *Trasadasyu*, to *Paktha* and *Daśavraja*; as you did give
them to *Gośarya* and *Ṛjiśvan*.

[सूक्त-५०]

[ऋषि- पुष्टिगु काण्व। **देवता-** इन्द्र।
छन्द- प्रगाथ (विषमा बृहती, समासतो बृहती।]

७०२३. प्र सु श्रुतं सुराधसमर्चा शक्रमभिष्टये।
य: सुन्वते स्तुवते काम्यं वसु सहस्रेणेव मंहते॥१॥

1. I would praise the far-famed, the bounteous *Śakra*, for the sake of his protection, who gives desirable wealth by thousands to the presser of the *Soma* and the offerer of hymns.

७०२४. शतानीका हेतयो अस्य दुष्टरा इन्द्रस्य समिषो मही:।
गिरिर्न भुज्मा मघवत्सु पिन्वते यदीं सुता अमन्दिषु:॥२॥

2. Invincible are his hundred-edged weapons, the mighty arrows of *Indra*; he pours forth blessings on his liberal worshippers like a mountain rich in springs, when the effused *Soma* has exhilarated him.

७०२५. यदीं सुतास इन्दवोऽभि प्रियममन्दिषु:।
आपो न धायि सवनं म आ वसो दुघाइवोप दाशुषे॥३॥

3. When the effused *Soma*-drops have exhilarated the beloved one, my oblation is offered abundantly like the waters, O gracious *Indra*—it is like the milch kine to the worshipper.

७०२६. अनेहसं वो हवमानमूतये मध्व: क्षरन्ति धीतय:।
आ त्वा वसो हवमानास इन्दव उप स्तोत्रेषु दधिरे॥४॥

4. The prayers which consecrate the *Soma* flow froth to the incomparable one who calls you for his favour, the *Soma*-drops which invoke you, O gracious one, have set you in the midst of the hymns.

This line is very obscure.

७०२७. आ न: सोमे स्वध्वर ईयानो अत्यो न तोशते।
यं ते स्वदावन्त्स्वदन्ति गूर्तय: पौरे छन्दयसे हवम्॥५॥

5. H rushes hurrying like a horse to the *Soma* offered in our festival, which the hymns make sweet to you, O you that love sweet viands, you approve the summons to the satisfying beverage.

Paura may be a proper name (*cf.* Vol., III verse 4268), 'You approve the summons to (the house of) *Paura*.'

७०२८. प्र वीरमुग्रं विविचिं धनस्पृतं विभूतिं राधसो मह:।
उद्रीवं वज्रिन्नवतो वसुत्वना सदा पीपेथ दाशुषे ॥६॥

6. Praise the mighty hero, wide-grasping, spoil-harrying, who has control over vast treasure; you, O thunder eve pour forth wealth to the worshipper like an abundant fountain.

७०२९. यद्ध नूनं परावति यद्वा पृथिव्यां दिवि।
युजान इन्द्र हरिभिर्महेमत ऋष्व ऋष्वेभिरा गहि ॥७॥

7. Whether you are in the far distance or in the earth or in heaven, O *Indra*, god of lofty counsel, yoke your steeds, come hither, lofty one, with the lofty.

७०३०. रथिरासो हरयो ये ते अस्त्रिध ओजो वातस्य पिप्रति।
येभिर्नि दस्युं मनुषो निघोषयो येभि: स्व: परीयसे ॥८॥

8. Your harmless steeds which draw you chariot, which surpass the strength of the wind, with which you silence the enemy of man and with which you goes round the sky.

Or 'of Manus,' *dasyum manuṣaḥ.*

७०३१. एतावतस्ते वसो विद्याम शूर नव्यस:।
यथा प्राव एतशं कृत्व्ये धने यथा वशं दशव्रजे ॥९॥

9. May we once more know you as such, O gracious hero, as when you did aid *Etaśa* in the decisive battle, or *Vaśa* against *Daśavraja*.

७०३२. यथा कण्वे मघवन् मेधे अध्वरे दीर्घनीथे दमूनसि।
यथा गोशर्ये असिषासो अद्रिवो मयि गोत्रं हरिश्रियम् ॥१०॥

10. As you was willing to give, O *Maghavan*, to *Kaṇva* in the sacrificial feast, or to *Dīrghanītha* the friend of the house, as you was willing to give, O slinger, to *Gośarya*, so give to me a herd of kine shining like gold.

[सूक्त-५१]

[ऋषि– श्रुष्टिगु काण्व। **देवता**– इन्द्र।
छन्द– प्रगाथ (विषमा बृहती, समासतो बृहती)।]

७०३३. यथा मनौ सांवरणौ सोममिन्द्रापिब: सुतम्।

नीपातिथौ मघवन् मेध्यातिथौ पुष्टिगौ श्रुष्टिगौ सचा॥१॥

1. As you did drink, O *Indra*, the effused *Soma* beside *Manu*, the descendant of *Saṁvaraṇa*, by *Nīpātithi* and *Medhyātithi*, by *Puṣṭigu* and *Śruṣṭigu*, O *Maghavan* [so do you drink it here].

७०३४. पार्षद्वाण: प्रस्कण्वं समसादयच्छयानं जिव्रिमुद्धितम्।
सहस्राण्यसिषासद् गवामृषिस्त्वोतो दस्यवे वृक:॥२॥

2. The descendant of *Pṛṣadvana* entertained the aged *Praskaṇva* who lay rejected (by his kindred); aided by you the seer *Dasyave-vṛka* desired to obtain thousands of cows.

७०३५. य उक्थेभिर्न विन्धते चिकिद्य ऋषिचोदन:।
इन्द्रं तमच्छा वद नव्यस्या मत्यरिष्यन्तं न भोजसे॥३॥

3. Sing that *Indra* with the new hymn who has no lack of praises, who is wise and the inspirer of seers, who is as it were eager to enjoy.

७०३६. यस्मा अर्कं सप्तशीर्षाणमानृचुस्त्रिधातुमुत्तमे पदे।
स त्विंमा विश्वा भुवनानि चिक्रददादिज्जनिष्ट पौंस्यम्॥४॥

4. He to whom they sang the seven-headed hymn with its three parts in the highest region, he has made all these worlds tremble, and has thus brought forth his power.

I.e., sung by seven divine singers in heaven.

७०३७. यो नौ दाता वसूनामिन्द्रं तं हूमहे वयम्।
विद्या ह्यस्य सुमतिं नवीयसीं गमेम गोमति व्रजे॥५॥

5. We invoke that *indra* who gives us wealth; for we know his new favour; may we obtain a stall rich in cows.

७०३८. यस्मै त्वं वसो दानाय शिक्षसि स रायस्पोषमश्नुते।
तं त्वा वयं मघवन्निन्द्र गिर्वण: सुतावन्तो हवामहे॥६॥

6. He whom you help, O gracious one, to give, obtains abundance of wealth; bringing the *Soma* we invoke you, *Indra*, *Maghavan*, you that love hymns.

७०३९. कदा चन स्तरीरसि नेन्द्र सश्चसि दाशुषे।
उपोपेन्नु मघवन् भूय इन्नु ते दानं देवस्य पृच्यते॥७॥

7. Never are you niggardly, *Indra*, and give not to the worshipper; but your godlike gifts, O *Maghavan*, are poured forth more and more.

७०४०. प्र यो नंनक्षे अभ्योजंसा क्रिविं वधै: शुष्णं निघोषयन्।
यदेदस्तंभीत्प्रथयंत्रमूं दिवुमादिज्जनिष्ट पार्थिव:॥८॥

8. He who overpowered *Krivi* by his might and silenced *Suṣṇa* with his weapons, when he spread abroad yonder sky and propped it up, then first the dweller on earth was born.

७०४१. यस्यायं विश्व आर्यो दासं: शेवधिपा अरिं:।
तिरश्चिंदर्ये रुशमे पवीरवि तुभ्येत् सो अंज्यते रयिं:॥९॥

9. That wealth, which every *Ārya* here covets and every miserly *Dāsa*, is sent direct to you, the pious *Ruśama Paviru*.

७०४२. तुरण्यवो मधुंमन्तं घृतंश्चुतं विप्रांसो अर्कमांनृचु:।
अस्मे रयि: पंप्रथे वृष्ण्यं शवोऽस्मे सुंवानास इन्दवं:॥१०॥

10. The zealous seers have sung a hymn, sweet with *Soma* and dropping *ghī*; wealth and manly strength have spread themselves among us, and so too the expressed *Soma* drops.

[सूक्त-५२]

[ऋषि– आयु काण्व। देवता– इन्द्र।
छन्द– प्रगाथ (विषमा बृहती, समासतो बृहती)।]

७०४३. यथा मनौ विवंस्वति सोमं शक्रांपिब: सुतम्।
यथां त्रिते छन्दं इन्द्र जुजोषस्यायौ मांदयसे सचां॥१॥

1. As you, *Śakra*, did drink the effused *Soma* from *Manu Vivasvat*, as you did accept the hymn from *Trita*, so do you gladden yourself with *Āyu*.

७०४४. पृषंध्रे मेध्यें मातरिश्वनीन्द्र सुवाने अमन्दथा:।
यथां सोमं दशंशिप्रे दशोंण्ये स्यूमंरश्मावृज्जूनसि॥२॥

2. You did enjoy, *Indra*, the effused drink with *Pṛṣadhra*, *Medhya* and *Mātariśvan*, just as you did drink the *Soma* with *Daśaśipra*, *Daśoṇya*, *Syumaraśmi*, and *Rjunas*.

७०४५. य उक्था केवंला दधे य: सोमं धृषितापिबत्।

यस्मै विष्णुस्त्रीणि पदा विचक्रम उप मित्रस्य धर्मभिः॥३॥

3. [It is *Indra*] who has appropriated the hymns for himself, who has bravely drunk the *Soma*, for whom *Viṣṇu* strode the three steps according to the ordinances of *Mitra*.

७०४६. यस्य त्वमिन्द्र स्तोमेषु चाकनो वाजे वाजिञ्छतक्रतो।
तं त्वा वयं सुदुघामिव गोदुहो जुहूमसि श्रवस्यवः॥४॥

4. O *Śatakratu*, you who are bountiful to him whose praises and oblations you delight in, we, desiring wealth, invoke you, as the milkers call a cow which bears abundant milk.

७०४७. यो नो दाता स नः पिता महाँ उ ईशानकृत्।
अर्यामनुग्रो मघवा पुरूवसुर्गोरश्वस्य प्र दातु नः॥५॥

5. He who gives to us is our father, the mighty, the strong, he who acts as the sovereign, may he, the strong rich *Maghavan*, give us kine and horses, even without our asking for it.

७०४८. यस्मै त्वं वसो दानाय मंहसे स रायस्पोषमिन्वति।
वसूयवो वसुपतिं शतक्रतुं स्तोमैरिन्द्रं हवामहे॥६॥

6. He to whom you give a present that he may give obtains abundance of wealth; we, desiring wealth, invoke with our praises *Indra Śatakratu*, the lord of wealth.

Cf. supra, III.6.

७०४९. कदा चन प्र युच्छस्युभे नि पासि जन्मनी।
तुरीयादित्य हवनं त इन्द्रियमा तस्थावमृतं दिवि॥७॥

7. Never are you heedless, you guard both races, (gods and men); O fourth *Āditya*, to you belongs the *Indra* invocation, the ambrosia has risen to heaven.

I.e., with *Varuṇa, Mitra* and *Aryaman.*

७०५०. यस्मै त्वं मघवन्निन्द्र गिर्वणः शिक्षो शिक्षसि दाशुषे।
अस्माकं गिर उत सुष्टुतिं वसो कण्ववच्छृणुधी हवम्॥८॥

8. (As you hear) the worshipper who you favour, O *Indra*, *Maghavan*, liberal one, you that love hymns, so, gracious one, hear our hymns and our invocation of praise, like *Kaṇva's*.

७०५१. अस्तावि मन्म पूर्व्यं ब्रह्मेन्द्राय वोचत।
पूर्वीर्ऋतस्य बृहतीरनूषत स्तोतुर्मेधा असृक्षत॥९॥

9. The old hymn has been sung, you have utter the prayer to *Indra*; they have shouted many *bṛhatī*-verses of the rite, many hymns of the worshipper have they poured forth.

७०५२. समिन्द्रो रायौ बृहतीरधूनुत सं क्षोणी समु सूर्यम्।

सं शुक्रास: शुच॑य: सं गवा॑शिर: सोमा॒ इन्द्र॑ममन्दिषु:॥१०॥

10. *Indra* has heaped together vast stores of wealth, the two worlds and the sun; the bright pure *Soma*-drink mixed with milk, has exhilarated *Indra*.

[सूक्त-५३]

[ऋषि- मेध्य काण्व। देवता- इन्द्र।

छन्द- प्रगाथ (विषमा बृहती, समासतो बृहती)।]

७०५३. उपमं त्वा॑ मघोनां ज्येष्ठञ्च वृषभाणाम्।

पूर्भित्तमं मघवन्निन्द्र॒ गोविद॑मीशानं रा॒य ईमहे॥१॥

1. We come to you, O *Maghavan Indra*, the highest of *Maghavans*, the strong of bulls, the mightiest breaker of forts, the provider of kine, the lord of wealth.

७०५४. य आयुं॑ कुत्स॑मतिथि॒ग्वमर्द॑यो वावृधानो दिवेदि॑वे।

तं त्वा॒ वयं॒ हर्य॑श्वं शत॒क्रतुं॒ वाजयन्तौ॑ हवामहे॥२॥

2. You who, waxing in might day by day, did destroy *Āyu*, *Kutsa*, and *Atithigva*, we invoke you, *Śatakratu*, with your bay horses, rousing you by our offerings.

७०५५. आ नो॑ विश्वे॑षां रसं॒ मध्व॑: सिञ्चन्त्वद्रय:।

ये परा॑वति॒ सुन्विरे॒ जनेष्वा॒ ये अ॑र्वा॑वतीन्द॑व:॥३॥

3. Let the stones pour forth the honey-juice for us all, the *Soma*-drops which have been pressed by men afar or near.

७०५६. विश्वा॑ द्वेषां॑सि जहि चाव॑ चा॒ कृधि विश्वं॑ सन्वन्त्वा॒ वसु॑।

शीर्ष्टे॑षु चित्ते म॒दिरासो॑ अं॒शवो॒ यत्रा॒ सोम॑स्य तृ॒म्पसि॑॥४॥

4. Smite all our enemies and drive them away, may we all obtain their wealth; even among the *Śiṣṭas* are you exhilarating *Soma*-plants, where you fill yourself with the *Soma*.

७०५७. इन्द्र॒ नेदी॑य॒ एदि॑हि मि॒तमे॑धाभिरूतिभि॑:।

आ शंन्त॑म॒ शन्त॑माभिर॒भिष्टिभिरा॒ स्वापे॑ स्वा॒पिभि॑:॥५॥

5. *Indra*, come very near with your firmly-wise protections; come, O most healthfull, with your most healthfull aid, come, good kinsman, with you good kinsmen.

७०५८. आजितुं सत्पतिं विश्वचर्षणिं कृधि प्रजास्वाभगम्।
प्र सू तिरा शचीभिर्ये तं उक्थिनः क्रतुं पुनत आनुषक्॥६॥

6. Make rich in children that chief of all men, who is victorious in battle and a strong protector; proper thoroughly with your powers your singers who continually purify their minds.

७०५९. यस्ते साधिष्ठोऽवसे ते स्याम भरेषु ते।
वयं होत्राभिरुत देवहूतिभिः ससवांसो मनामहे॥७॥

7. May we be in battle as one who is the sure to gain your protection; we worship you with invocations and prayers when we obtain our desire.

७०६०. अहं हि ते हरिवो ब्रह्म वाज्ययुराजिं यामि सदोतिभिः।
त्वामिदेव तममे समश्वयुर्गव्युरग्रे मथीनाम्॥८॥

8. With your help, O lord of bay steeds, I always go into prayer and into battle, seeking spoil; it is your whom I insist upon, when I go, longing for horses and kine, at the head of plunders.

The St. Petersb. Dict. would read *matīnām* for *mathīnām*, 'in the beginning of my prayers.'

[सूक्त-५४]

[ऋषि– मातरिश्वा काण्व। देवता– इन्द्र, ३-४ विश्वेदेवा।
छन्द– प्रगाथ (विषमा बृहती, समासतो बृहती)।]

७०६१. एतत्त इन्द्र वीर्यं गीर्भिर्गृणन्ति कारवः।
ते स्तोभन्त ऊर्जमावन् घृतश्रुतं पौरासो नक्षन्धीतिभिः॥१॥

1. The singers with their hymns, O *Indra*, this might of yours; singing loudly, they have brought you sacred viands dropping with ; the offerers have drawn near with their prayers.

Or perhaps 'the *Pauras*', *cf. sup.* II.5.

७०६२. नक्षन्त इन्द्रमवसे सुकृत्यया येषां सुतेषु मन्दसे।
यथा संवर्ते अमदो यथा कृश एवास्मे इन्द्र मत्स्व॥२॥

2. They have drawn near *Indra* with holy rites for his protection, they in whose libations you rejoice: as you did rejoice in *Samvarta* and *Kṛśa*, so now, *Indra*, do you rejoice in us.

७०६३. आ नो विश्वे सजोषसो देवासो गन्तनोप न:।
वसवो रुद्रा अवसे न आ गमञ्छृण्वन्तु मरुतो हवम्॥३॥

3. You gods, come all with one accord to us; let the *Vasus* and *Rudras* come for our protection, let the *Maruts* hear our call.

७०६४. पूषा विष्णुर्हवनं मे सरस्वत्यवन्तु सप्त सिन्धव:।
आपो वात: पर्वतासो वनस्पति: शृणोतु पृथिवी हवम्॥४॥

4. May *Pūṣan*, *Viṣṇu*, *Sarasvatī*, and the seven rivers, favour my call; may the waters, the wind, the mountains, the trees, the earth, hear my call.

७०६५. यदिन्द्र राधो अस्ति ते माघोनं मघवत्तम।
तेन नो बोधि सधमाद्यो वृधे भगो दानाय वृत्रहन्॥५॥

5. With yours own special gift, O *Indra*, best of *Maghavans*, be you our boon-companion for good, our liberal benefactor, O slayer of *Vṛtra*.

७०६६. आजिपते नृपते त्वमिद्धि नो वाज आ वक्षि सुक्रतो।
वीती होत्राभिरुत देववीतिभि: ससवांसो वि शृण्विरे॥६॥

6. O lord of battle, lord of men, mighty in action, do you guide us in the conflict; far-famed are those who obtain their desires by sacrificial feasts, by invocations, and by entertaining the gods.

७०६७. सन्ति ह्याश्र्य आशिष इन्द्र आयुर्जनानाम्।
अस्मान्रक्षस्व मघवन्नुपावसे धुक्षस्व पिप्युषीमिषम्॥७॥

7. Our prayers abide in the true one, in *Indra* is the life of men; draw near to us, *Maghavan*, for our protection; milk forth the streaming drink.

७०६८. वयं त इन्द्र स्तोमेभिर्विधेम त्वमस्माकं शतक्रतो।
महि स्थूरं शश्वयं राधो अह्रयं प्रस्कण्वाय नि तोशय॥८॥

8. O *Indra*, we would worship you with hymns; O *Śatakratu*, you are ours; pour down upon *Praskaṇva* great, solid, inexhaustible, exuberant abundance.

[सूक्त-५५]

[ऋषि- कृशकाण्व। देवता- प्रस्कण्व। छन्द- गायत्री, ३,५ अनुष्टुप्।]

७०६९. भूरीदिन्द्रस्य वीर्यं व्यख्यमभ्यायति। राधस्ते दस्यवे वृक।।१।।

1. Great indeed is *Indra's* might; I have beheld it; your gift approaches, O *Dasyave-vṛka*.

Sc. 'O foe to the *Dasyu*.'

७०७०. शतं श्वेतास उक्षणो दिवि तारो न रोचन्ते। महा दिवं न तस्तभुः।।२।।

2. A hundred white oxen shine like stars in the heaven, by their size they have almost held up the heavens.

७०७१. शतं वेणूच्छतं शुनः शतं चर्माणि म्लातानि।

शतं मे बल्बजस्तुका अरुषीणां चतुःशतम्।।३।।

3. A hundred bamboos, a hundred dogs, a hundred dressed hides, a hundred bunches of *balbaja* grass, and four hundred red mares are mine.

७०७२. सुदेवाः स्थ काण्वायना वयोवयो विचरन्तः।

अश्वासो न चङ्क्रमत।।४।।

4. May you have the gods propitious to you, O descendants of *Kaṇva*, living through youth on youth; step out vigorously like steed.

७०७३. आदित्साप्तस्य चर्किरन्नानूनस्य महि श्रवः।

श्यावीरतिध्वसन्पथश्चक्षुषा चन सन्नशे।।५।।

5. Let them praise the seven-yoked team, great is the strength of that which is not yet full-grown; the dark-brown mares haves rushed along the paths so that no eye can follow them.

[सूक्त-५६]

[ऋषि- पृषध काण्व। देवता- प्रस्कण्व, ५- अग्नि, सूर्य।
छन्द- गायत्री, ५- पंक्ति।]

७०७४. प्रति ते दस्यवे वृक राधो अदर्श्यह्ह्रियम्। द्यौर्न प्रथिना शवः।।१।।

i. Your inexhaustible gift has appeared, O *Dasyave-vṛka*, its fullness is in extent like the sky.

७०७५. दश॒ मह्यं॑ पौत॒क्रत॒: सह॒स्रा दस्य॑वे॒ वृक॑:। नित्या॒द्राये॒ अम॑ंहत॥२॥

2. *Dasyave-vṛka*, the son of *Putakrata*, has given to me ten thousand from his own store;

७०७६. श॒तं मे॒ गर्द॑भानां श॒तमूर्णा॑वतीनाम्। श॒तं दा॒साँ अति॒ स्रज॑:॥३॥

3. A hundred asses a hundred woolly sheep, a hundred slaves, beside garlands.

७०७७. तत्रो॒ अपि॒ प्राणी॑यत पूत॒क्रताये॒ व्यक्ता। अश्वा॑नामि॒न्न यूथ्या॑म्॥४॥

4. There too has been brought for *Putakrata* a well adorned mare, which is not one of the common horses of the herd.

७०७८. अचे॒त्यग्निश्चि॑कितु॒र्हव्य॑वाट् स सु॒मद्र॑थ:। अ॒ग्नि: शु॒क्रेण॑ शो॒चिषा॑ बृ॒हत् सूरो॑ अरोचत दि॒वि सूर्यो॑ अरोचत॥५॥

5. The shining *Agni* has appeared, the bearer of the oblation, with his chariot; *Agni* has gleamed forth brilliantly with his bright flame as Sura, he has gleamed forth in heaven as *Sūrya*.

[सूक्त-५७]

[ऋषि– मेध्य काण्व। देवता– अश्विनीकुमार। छन्द– त्रिष्टुप्।]

७०७९. यु॒वं दे॑वा॒ क्रतु॑ना॒ पूर्व्ये॑ण यु॒क्ता रथे॑न त॒विषं॑ य॒जत्रा।
आ ग॑च्छतं नासत्या॒ शची॑भिरि॒दं तृ॒तीयं॒ सव॑नं पिबाथ:॥१॥

1. You have come quickly, you two gods, with your car, endued with ancient might, O sacred *Aśvins*; truthful ones, with your powers, drink this third libation.

७०८०. यु॒वां दे॒वास्त्रय॑ एकाद॒शास॑: स॒त्या: स॒त्यस्य॑ दॅदृशे पुर॒स्तात्।
अ॒स्माकं॑ य॒ज्ञं सव॑नं जुषा॒णा पा॒तं सोम॑मश्विना दीद्य॒ग्नी॥२॥

2. The three-and-thirty truthful gods saw you before the truthful one; O *Aśvins*, gleaming with fire, drink the *Soma*, enjoying our offering, our libation.

I.e., before the Sun; the dawns are compared to 'truthful active women' in *Ṛgveda*, I.79.1.

७०८१. प॒ना॒य्यं तद॑श्विना कृ॒तं वां॑ वृ॒षभो॑ दि॒वो रज॑स॒: पृ॒थि॒व्या:।
स॒हस्रं॒ शंसा॑ उ॒त ये ग॒विष्ठौ॒ सर्वाँ॒ इत्ताँ उप॑ याता पिब॒ध्यै॥३॥

3. That work of yours, O *Aśvins*, is worthy of wonder, the bull of the heavens, the firmament and the earth; and your thousand blessings in battle, for all these come hither to drink.

I.e., the Sun, which they may be said to reveal, as they come with the earliest dawn.

७०८२. अयं वां भागो निहितो यज्ञेमा गिरो नासत्योप यातम्।

पिब॑तं सोमं॑ मधु॑मन्तमस्मे प्र दा॒श्वांस॑मवतं श॒चीभि॑:।।४।।

4. O sacred ones, this your portion has been placed for you; O truthful ones, come to these your praises; drink among us the sweet *Soma*; succour your worshipper with your powers.

[सूक्त-५८]

[ऋषि– मेध्य काण्व। देवता– विश्वेदेवा, १ विश्वेदेवा अथवा ऋत्विज्।

छन्द– त्रिष्टुप्।]

७०८३. यमृत्विजो॑ बहुधा॒ कल्पय॑न्त: सचेत॑सो यज्ञमिमं॑ वह॑न्ति। यो अ॒नूचा॒नो ब्रा॒ह्मणो॒ युक्त॑ आसी॒त्का स्वित्तत्र॒ यज॑मानस्य॒ संवित्।।१।।

1. He whom the wise priests bring, when they arrange the offering in many ways, who was employed as a learned *Brāhmaṇa*, what is the offerer's knowledge regarding him?

७०८४. एक॑ एवा॒ग्निर्ब॑हुधा॒ समि॑द्ध एक॑: सूर्यो॑ विश्व॒मनु॒ प्रभू॑त:।

एकै॒वोषा॒: सर्व॑मिदं॒ वि भा॒त्येक॑ वा॒ इदं॒ वि ब॑भूव॒ सर्व॑म्।।२।।

2. *Agni* is one, though kindled in various ways: one is the Sun, pre-eminent over all; one Dawn illumines this all; one is that which has become this all.

७०८५. ज्योति॑ष्मन्तं केतु॑मन्तं त्रि॒चक्रं॒ सुखं॒ रथं॑ सुष॒दं भूरि॑वारम्।

चित्रा॒मघा॒ यस्य॒ योगे॒ऽधिज॑ज्ञे॒ तं वां॑ हुवे॒ अति॑ रि॒क्तं पि॑ब॒ध्यै।।३।।

3. The brilliant chariot, diffusing splendour, rolling lightly on its three wheels, offering an easy seat, and full of many gifts, at whose yoking the Dawn was born, rich in marvellous treasures, I invoke that your chariot (O *Aśvins*), come you hither to drink.

[सूक्त-५९]

[ऋषि– सुपर्ण काण्व। देवता– इन्द्रावरुण। छन्द–जगती।]

७०८६. इमानि॑ वां भा॒गधेया॑नि सिस्रत॒ इन्द्रा॑वरुणा॒ प्र म॒हे सु॒तेषु॑ वाम्।

यज्ञेय॑ज्ञे ह॒ सर्व॑ना भुरण्य॒थो यत्सु॒न्वते॒ यज॑मानाय॒ शिक्ष॑थ:।।१।।

1. These your offered portions stream forth, O *Indra* and *Varuṇa*, to your honour in the oblations; at every sacrifice you hasten to the oblations, when you help the offerer who presses out the *Soma*.

७०८७. निषिध्वरीरीरोषधीरापं आस्तामिन्द्रावरुणा महिमानमाशत।

या सिस्रतू रजंस: पारे अध्वनो ययो: शत्रुनकिरादेव ओहते॥२॥

2. The plants and the waters were efficacious; they have attained their power, O *Indra* and *Varuṇa*; you who have gone beyond the path of the firmament, no godless man is worth being called your enemy.

७०८८. सत्यं तदिन्द्रावरुणा कृशस्यं वां मध्वं ऊर्मिं दुहते सप्त वाणीं:।

ताभिर्दाश्वांसमवतं शुभस्पती यो वामदंब्धो अभि पाति
चित्तिभि:॥३॥

3. True, O *Indra* and *Varuṇa*, is that saying of *Kṛśa's*, 'the seven sacred voices distil a stream of honey;' for their sake help the worshipper, O you lords of splendour, who reverences you devoutly in his thoughts.

Cf. *Ṛgveda*, IX.103,3, 'the *Soma* streams through the sheep's wool round the honey-dropping vessel, the seven voices of the sacred bards shout to it.'

७०८९. घृतप्रुष: सौम्यां जीरदानव: सप्त स्वसार: सदने ऋतस्यं।

या हं वामिन्द्रावरुणा घृतश्चुतस्ताभिर्धत्तं यजमानाय शिक्षतम्॥४॥

4. The seven sister-streams of the *Soma*, in the hot the offering, pour forth *ghi*-dripping streams of yours, O *Indra Varuṇa*, provide for and help the offerer.

७०९०. अवोचाम महते सौभगाय सत्यं त्वेषाभ्यां महिमानमिन्द्रियम्।

अस्मान्त्स्विन्द्रावरुणा घृतश्चुतस्त्रिभि: साप्तेभिरवतं शुभस्पती॥५॥

5. To our great happiness we have declared to these two brilliant ones the true might of *Indra*; O *Indra* and *Varuṇa*, lords of splendour, help us, the offerers of *ghī*, with the company of thrice seven.

This obscure phrase occurs in a hymn to *Indra* (*Ṛgveda*, i.133,6), 'O irresistible one, you destroy not men with the warriors, with the thrice seven warriors.'

७०९१. इन्द्रावरुणा यदृषिभ्यो मनीषां वाचो मतिं श्रुतमदत्तमग्रे।

यानि स्थानान्यसृजन्त धीरा यज्ञं तन्वानास्तपसाभ्यपश्यम्।।६।।

6. O *Indra* and *Varuṇa*, I have seen what you formerly gave to
the seers, wisdom, power of song, and fame, and the places which
the wise have prepared for themselves, as they spread the web of
the sacrifice with holy austerities.

७०९२. इन्द्रावरुणा सौमनसमदृप्तं रायस्पोषं यजमानेषु धत्तम्।

प्रजां पुष्टिं भूतिमस्मासु धत्तं दीर्घायुत्वाय प्र तिरतं न आयुः।।७।।

7. O *Indra* and *Varuṇa*, give to the offerers cheerfulness
without levity, and abundance of wealth; give to us offspring,
food, prosperity; prolong our lives to length of days.

ANUVĀKA VII

[सूक्त-६०]

[ऋषि– भर्ग प्रागाथ। देवता–अग्नि।

छन्द– प्रगाथ (विषमा बृहती, समासतो बृहती)।]

७०९३. अग्न आ याह्यग्निभिर्होतारं त्वा वृणीमहे।

आ त्वामनक्तु प्रयता हविष्मती यजिष्ठं बर्हिरासदे।।१।।

1. *Agni*, come hither with the fires, we choose you as our
invoking priest; let the presented offering anoint you, the chief
sacrificer, to sit down on the sacred grass.
   Sāmaveda, 1552.

७०९४. अच्छा हि त्वा सहसः सूनो अङ्गिरः स्रुचश्चरन्त्यध्वरे।

ऊर्जो नपातं घृतकेशमीमहेऽग्निं यज्ञेषु पूर्व्यम्।।२।।

2. Angiras, son of strength, the ladles go to find you in the
sacrifice; we praise the ancient *Agni* in our offerings, the grandson
of food, butter-haired.
   Butter-Haired— Similarly *Agni* is called *ghṛtapṛṣṭhā*, "butter-
backed," in v.4.3. The *pradīpta-kalaśa-sthānīya-jvālāḥ* of Sāyaṇa seems
to be a mislection for *pradīptakeśa, cf.* v.37.1.

७०९५. अग्ने कविर्वेधा असि होता पावक यक्ष्यः।

मन्द्रो यजिष्ठो अध्वरेष्वीड्यो विप्रेभिः शुक्र मन्मभिः।।३।।

3. *Agni*, you, wise, are the creator (of consequences); O purifier, you are the involving priest, worthy of worship; bright one, you are to be praised in our sacrifices by the priests with hymns, yourself the chief ministrant worthy to be rejoiced in.

७०९६. अद्रोघमा वंहोशतो यविष्ठ्य देवाँ अजस्र वीतये।
अभि प्रयांसि सुधिता वसो गहि मन्दस्व धीतिभिर्हित:॥४॥

4. Most youthful, eternal one, bring the longing gods to me guileless, to eat (the oblation); giver of dwellings, approach the well-placed food; rejoice, being set in your place with praises.

७०९७. त्वमित्सप्रथा अस्यग्ने त्रातर्ऋतस्कवि:।
त्वां विप्रास: समिधान दीदिव आ विवासन्ति वेधस:॥५॥

5. Deliverer *Agni*, you, the truthful and the seer, are widely spread; O kindled blazing one, the wise praisers wait on you.
Sāmaveda, 41.

७०९८. शोचा शोचिष्ठ दीदिहि विशे मयो रास्व स्तोत्रे महाँ असि।
देवानां शर्मन् मम सन्तु सूरय: शत्रूषाह: स्वग्नय:॥६॥

6. Most resplendent (*Agni*), shine forth and illuminate (us); give happiness to your people, to your worshipper, for you are great; may my priests abide in the bliss of the gods, subduing their enemies, possessing bright fires.

My Priests— Sāyaṇa explains *sūrayaḥ* by *stotaro medhāvinaḥ, asmākam putrādayo vā.*

७०९९. यथा चिद्वृद्धमंतसमग्ने सञ्जूर्वसि क्षमि।
एवा दह मित्रमहो यो अस्मधुग् दुर्मन्मा कश्च वेनति॥७॥

7. As, *Agni*, you consumest old timber on the earth, so, cherisher of friends, do you burn our injurer, whosoever evil-mided wishes (our ill).

७१००. मा नो मर्ताय रिपवे रक्षस्विने माघशंसाय रीरध:।
अस्त्रेधद्भिस्तरणिभिर्यविष्ठ्य शिवेभि: पाहि पायुभि:॥८॥

8. Subject us not to a strong mortal enemy, nor to the malevolent; O most youthful, guard us with your unharming delivering auspicious protections.

७१०१. पाहि नो अग्न एकया पाह्युत द्वितीयया।
पाहि गीर्भिस्तिसृभिरूर्जाम्पते पाहि चतसृभिर्वसो॥९॥

9. *Agni*, protect us by one (*rich*), or protect us by a second; lord of strength, protect us by three songs; protect us, giver of dwellings, by four.

This *v.* occurs in *Sāmaveda*, 36, 1544; and in *Yajurveda*, 27.43. In the latter, *Mahidhara* explains the four as the *Ṛk, Yajuṣ, Sāman,* and *Nigada.*

७१०२. पा॒हि वि॒श्व॒स्माद्र॒क्षसो॑ अ॒राव्णः॒ प्र स्म॒ वा॒जेषु॑ नोऽव।
त्वामि॑द्धि॒ नेदि॑ष्ठं॒ दे॒व॒ता॑तय आपिं॑ न॒क्षा॑महे वृ॒धे॥१०॥

10. Protect us from every impious *Rākṣasa*, shield us in battles; we approach you, our nearest neighbour, our kinsman, for sacrifice and for increase.

Impious— Literally, "not giving (sacrificial) gifts." *Sāmaveda*, 1545.

७१०३. आ नो॑ अग्ने व॒यो॒वृ॒धं र॒यिं पा॑वक॒ शंस्य॑म्।
रास्वा॑ च न उप॒माते पुरु॒स्पृहं॑ सु॒नी॒ती स्व॒यश॑स्तरम्॥११॥

11. Purifying *Agni*, bestow upon us food-augmenting excellent wealth; and (bring) us, O meter-our of good, by auspicious guidance, (a treasure) desired by many and bringing its own fame. *Sāmaveda*, 43.

७१०४. येन॒ वंसा॑म पृत॒नासु॒ शर्धं॑तस्तरन्तो अ॒र्य आ॒दिशः॑।
स त्वं नो॑ वर्ध॒ प्रय॑सा श॒चीवसो॒ जिन्वा॒ धियो॑ वसु॒विदः॑॥१२॥

12. By which we may escape and destroy in battles our impetuous weapon-aiming enemies; O you who by wisdom establish our rites, bless us with food, prosper our wealth-obtaining offerings.

७१०५. शि॒शा॒नो वृ॒षभो॑ य॒थाग्निः॒ शृङ्गे॒ दवि॑ध्वत्।
ति॒ग्मा अ॒स्य हन॑वो॒ न प्र॒तिधृ॑षे सु॒जम्भः॒ सह॑सो य॒हुः॥१३॥

13. *Agni* tosses his horns, sharpening them as a bull; his sharp jaws are not to be resisted; he is mighty toothed, this son of strength.

Sharpening them as a Bull— *Cf.* Virgil, *Georg.* III.232.

Not to be Resisted— Sāyaṇa in his Comm. curiously takes *na* twice, once as=*iva* (*hanava iva*), and then again with *pratidhṛṣe*.

७१०६. नहि ते॑ अग्ने वृषभ प्र॒तिधृ॑षे॒ जम्भा॑सो॒ यद्वि॒तिष्ठ॑से।
स त्वं नो॑ होतः सु॒हुतं॑ ह॒विष्कृ॑धि॒ वंस्वा॑ नो॒ वार्या॑ पुरु॥१४॥

14. Since you spread out on all sides, your teeth, bull *Agni*, are not to be resisted; O offerer, do you make our oblation rightly presented; give us many precious (gifts).

७१०७. शेषे॒ वने॑षु मा॒त्रो॒: सं त्वा॒ मर्ता॑स इन्धते।
अत॑न्द्रो ह॒व्या व॑हसि हविष्कृत॒ आदि॑द्दे॒वेषु॑ राजसि॥१५॥

15. You sleep within your mothers in the woods, mortals kindle you; unwearied you bear the offerings of the sacrificer, then you shine among the gods.

Sāmaveda, 46.

Your Mothers— This refers to the two *aranis* or pieces of wood from which the sacrificial fire is produced by attrition. *Cf.* III.29.2.

७१०८. स॒प्त होता॑रस्तमि॒दीळ॑ते त्वा॒ग्ने सु॒त्यज॑मह॒यम्।
भि॒न॒त्स्य॒द्रिं तप॑सा॒ वि शो॒चिषा॒ प्राग्ने॑ तिष्ठ॒ जना॒ँ अति॑॥१६॥

16. The seven priests praise you, *Agni*, giver of good things and unfailing; you cleave the cloud with your fierce splendour; go forth, having overcome our enemies.

Having Overcome our Enemies— Sāyaṇa gives another interpretation, taking *janan* not as *asmādvirodhi-janān* but *asmān*, "proceed to the gods with the oblation, having left us behind."

७१०९. अ॒ग्निर॑ग्निं वो॒ अ॒ध्रिगुं॑ हु॒वेम॑ वृ॒क्तब॑र्हिष:।
अ॒ग्निं हि॒तप्र॑यस: शश्व॒ती॒ष्वा॒ होता॑रं चर्ष॒णीनाम्॥१७॥

17. Now that we have cut the sacred grass, let us invoke for you *Agni*, *Agni* the irresistible; having placed the oblations, let us invoke *Agni*, abiding in many (places), the offerer of sacrifices for men.

Addressed to the sacrificers or to the gods— *Agni* the offerer of Sacrifices—When *Agni* is satisfied, living beings obtain their desires by the rain which he causes. *Cf. Manu,* III.76.

७११०. के॒तेन॒ शर्म॑न्त्सचते सु॒षाम॒ण्यग्ने॑ तु॒भ्यं चिकि॑त्वना।
इ॒ष॒ण्य॒या न॑: पुरु॒रूप॑मा॒ भर॒ वाजं॑ ने॒दिष्ठ॑मू॒तये॑॥१८॥

18. (The sacrificer) worships you by praises, *Agni*, with the experienced (priests) in the rite celebrated with beautiful *Sāman* hymns; bring us of your own accord for our protection food of various kinds which may be always in our reach.

७१११. अग्ने॑ जरि॒तर्वि॒श्पति॑स्तेपा॒नो दे॑व रक्ष॒स:।
अप्रो॑षिवा॒नृग्ह॑प॒तिर्म॑हाँ अ॑सि॒ दिव॒स्पायुर्दुरो॑णयु:॥१९॥

19. Divine *Agni*, worthy of praise, you are the guardian of men, the consumer of the *Rākṣasas*; you are great, you the never-absent guardian of the (worshipper's) house, the protector of heaven, ever present in the dwelling.

Worthy of Praise— *Jaritṛ* usually means "the singer of praises,"—here, as applied to *Agni* it is explained by Sāyaṇa as-*stutya*. *Sāmaveda*, 39.

७३१२. मा नो॒ रक्ष॒ आ वे॑शीदाघृणीवसो॒ मा यातु॒र्यातु॑माव॒ताम् ।
परोग॒व्यूत्य॒निरा॑मप॒ क्षुध॒मग्ने॒ सेध॑ रक्षे॒स्विन॑: ॥२०॥

20. O you of brilliant wealth, let not the *Rākṣasa* enter us, nor the torment of the evil spirits; *Agni*, drive away further than a *gavyuti* from us poverty, hunger, and the strong demons.

Gavyuti— This is a measure=two *krośas*, Sāyaṇa adds that it implies an unlimited distance.

Hunger— Sāyaṇa explains *kṣudham* unnecessarily as *kṣapayitāram*, "the destroyer."

[सूक्त-६१]

[ऋषि– भर्ग प्रागाथ। देवता– इन्द्र। छन्द– प्रगाथ (विषमा बृहती,
समासतो बृहती)।]

७३१३. उ॒भयं॑ शृणव॒च्च न॒ इन्द्रो॑ अ॒र्वागि॒दं वचः॑ ।
स॒त्रा॒च्या म॑घवा॒ सोम॑पीतये धि॒या शवि॑ष्ठ॒ आ ग॑मत् ॥१॥

1. May *Indra* listen to both these our hymns; may the mightiest *Maghavan* come to us, (pleased) with our devoted offering, to drink the *Soma*.

Sāmaveda, 290, 1233. (*Satrācyā dhiyā* should rather mean, "come to us with your whole mind," *cf.* VIII.2.37).

Both our Hymns— *I.e.,* whether recited (*śāstra*) or sung praises (*stotra*).

७३१४. तं हि स्व॒राजं॒ वृष॑भं॒ तमोज॑से धि॒षणे॑ निष्टत॒क्षतुः॑ ।
उ॒तोप॒मानां॑ प्रथ॒मो नि षी॑द॒सि सोम॑कामं॒ हि ते॒ मनः॑ ॥२॥

2. Him, self-resplendent, have heaven and earth formed as the showerer, him (they have formed) for strength; therefore you sit down first of your peers; your mind loved the *Soma*.

Sāmaveda, 1234.

७११५. आ वृषस्व पुरूवसो सुतस्येन्द्रान्धसः।
विद्मा हि त्वा हरिवः पृत्सु सासहिमधृष्टं चिद्धृष्वणिम् ॥३॥

3. *Indra*, possessor of much wealth, pour the effused *Soma* within you; possessor of (bright) coursers, we know you, the overpowerer in battles, the unconquerable, the conqueror.

७११६. अप्रामिसत्य मघवन्तथेदसदिन्द्र क्रत्वा यथा वशः।
सनेम वाजं तव शिप्रिन्नवसा मधू चिद्धन्तो अद्रिवः ॥४॥

4. *Indra, Maghavan* of unbroken truth, it ever comes to pass as you in your knowledge may'st desire; by your protection, O handsome-jawed, may we obtain food, speedily, O thunderer, subduing our enemies.

७११७. शग्ध्यूइ षु शचीपत इन्द्र विश्वेभिरूतिभिः।
भगं न हि त्वा यशसं वसुविदमनु शूर चरामसि ॥५॥

5. *Indra*, lord of rites, give us (our desire) with all your helping powers; hero, we worship you as happiness, the glorious, the obtainer of wealth.

Sāmaveda, 253, 1579.

All your helping Powers— Sc. The *Maruts*.

७११८. पौरो अर्श्वस्य पुरुकृद् गवामस्युत्सो देव हिरण्ययः।
नकिर्हि दानं परिमर्धिषत्त्वे यद्द्याामि तदा भर ॥६॥

6. You are the increaser of horses, the multiplier of cows; you, deity, with your golden body are a very function; none can harm the gifts laid up for me in you; bring me whatever I ask.

Sāmaveda, 1580.

७११९. त्वं ह्योहि चेरवे विदा भगं वसुत्तये।
उद्वावृषस्व मघवन् गविष्टय उदिन्द्राश्वमिष्टये ॥७॥

7. You are (bounteous), come; may you obtain wealth to distribute to the worshipper; shower your bounty, *Maghavan*, on me desiring cows, shower it, *Indra*, on me desiring horses.

Sāyaṇa's text leaves *cerave* in the first line unexplained. In the *Sāmaveda* Comm. it is explained *cetayitre*, which (like *medhāvin*) probably only means "the worshipper." The St. Petersburg Dictionary gives it as "begehend (einheiliges Work)."—*Sāmavede*, 240, 1581.

७१२०. त्वं पुरू सहस्राणि शतानि च यूथा दानाय मंहसे।
आ पुरन्दरं चकृम विप्रवचस इन्द्रं गायन्तोऽवसे॥८॥

8. You grant many hundreds and thousands of herds as a gift (to the offerer). Uttering long praises, we, hymning *Indra*, the destroyer of cities, bring him before us for our protection.
Sāmaveda, 1582.

Uttering Long Praises— Benfey takes *vipravacas* as "Lieder der Lobsänger habend."

७१२१. अविप्रो वा यदविविधद् विप्रो वेन्द्र ते वचः।
स प्र ममन्दत्त्वाया शतक्रतो प्राचामन्यो अहंसन॥९॥

9. *Indra*, whether it be the unskilled or the skilled who celebrated your praise, each rejoices in his desire for you, O *Śatakratu*, whose wrath presses ever forwards, who meet the foe, proclaiming "it is I."

७१२२. उग्रबाहुर्मेक्षकृत्वां पुरन्दरो यदि मे शृणवद्ध्ववम्।
वसूयवो वसुपतिं शतक्रतुं स्तोमैरिन्द्रं हवामहे॥१०॥

10. If the strong-armed slayer of enemies, the destroyer of cities, will but hear my invocation, we, desiring wealth, will with our praises call one *Indra Śatakratu*, the lord of wealth.

७१२३. न पापासो मनामहे नारायासो न जल्हवः।
यदिन्द्रं वृषणं सचा सुते सखायं कृणवामहै॥११॥

11. We are not evil who worship him, nor too poor to offer gifts, nor destitute of sacred fires,—since assembled together, when the *Soma* is effused, we make *Indra*, the showerer, our friend.

We are not Evil— Sāyaṇa takes *manamahe* as a transitive verb, *cf.* v.6.1; more probably it means "to appear,"—"we do not appear evil," etc.

७१२४. उग्रं युयुज्म पृतनासु सासहिमृणकातिमदांभ्यम्।
वेदा भृमं चित्सनिता रथीतमो वाजिनं यमिदु नशत्॥१२॥

12. We join (to our rite) the mighty *Indra*, the subduer of enemies in battles, the inviolate, him to whom praise is due as a debt; he, the best of charioteers, knows (among steeds) the strong racer, and (among men(he, the bounteous (knows) the offerer whom he is to reach.

Sāyaṇa's explanation of this verse is obscure; he seems to take
vājinam twice over, with a difference in meaning in each clause. I have
supposed that *veda* is to be repeated in the second clause; but this is
doubtful.

७१२५. यत॑ इन्द्र॒ भया॑महे॒ ततो॑ नो॒ अभ॑यं कृधि।

मघ॑वञ्छग्धि॒ तव॒ तन्न॒ ऊति॑भि॒र्वि द्विषो॒ वि मृधो॑ जहि।।१३।।

13. *Indra*, give us security from him of whom we are afraid;
Maghavan, be strong for us with your protections; destroy our
enemies, destroy those who harm us.

Sāmaveda, 274, 1321 (with *ūtaye* for *ūtibhih*).

७१२६. त्वं हि रा॑धस्पते॒ राध॑सो॒ मह॑: क्षय॒स्यासि॑ विध॒त:।

तं त्वा॑ व॒यं म॑घवन्निन्द्र गिर्वण॒: सुता॑वन्तो हवामहे।।१४।।

14. Lord of wealth, you are (the bestower) of great wealth and
a dwelling-place upon your worshipper; as such, we invoke you,
bearing the *Soma*, O *Maghavan*, *Indra*, who are to be honoured
with hymns.

Sāmaveda, 1322 (with *vidharta* for *vidhataḥ*).

७१२७. इन्द्र॒: स्पळु॑त वृत्र॒हा प॑र॒स्पा नो॒ वरे॑ण्य:।

स नो॑ रक्षिष॒च्चर॑मं॒ स म॑ध्य॒मं स प॒श्चात्पा॑तु न॒: पुर॑:।।१५।।

15. *Indra*, the all-knower, the slayer of *Vṛtra*, the protector, is
to be chosen by us; may he guard our (son), our last (son), our
middle (son), may he protect us from behind and before.

७१२८. त्वं न॑: प॒श्चाद॑ध॒रादु॑त्तरा॒त्पुर॒ इन्द्र॒ नि पा॑हि वि॒श्वत॑:।

आ॒रे अ॒स्मत्कृ॑णुहि॒ दैव्यं॒ भय॑मा॒रे हे॒तीरदे॑वी:।।१६।।

16. *Indra*, protect us from the west, from the south, from the
north, from the east, protect us from every side; keep far from us
supernatural alarm, keep far the weapons of the demons.

Sāyaṇa in vi.19.9 explained the four terms in the text as referring to
the four quarters; here his Comm. makes them refer to the six directions
in space, "protect is from the west, from the east, from below (this
includes the upper direction), from the north (this includes the south)."

७१२९. अ॒द्या॒द्या श्व॒: श्व॒ इन्द्र॒ त्रास्व॑ प॒रे च॑ न:।

विश्वा॑ च नो जरितॄन्त्सत्पते॒ अहा॒ दिवा॒ नक्तं॑ च रक्षिष॒:।।१७।।

17. Save us, *Indra*, every to-day, every tomorrow, and every succeeding day; lord of the good, protect us, your praisers, in all days, by day and by night.

७१३०. प्रभङ्गी शूरो मघवा तुवीमघः सम्मिश्लो वीर्याय कम्।
उभा ते बाहू वृष्णा शतक्रतो नि या वज्रं मिमिक्षतुः॥१८॥

18. *Maghavan* is the shatterer, the hero, great in wealth, and the conductor to victory (over our enemies). *Śatakratu*, both your arms, which grasp the thunderbolt, are the showerers (of blessings).

This and the previous verse occur in *Sāmaveda*, 1459.

The Conductor to Victory— Sāyaṇa's interpretation of *sammiślo vīryāya* (*samyak miśrayitā śatrūṇām vīryakaraṇāya*) may, perhaps, mean, "bringing us into successful collision with our enemies," *cf.* his Comm. on *Sāmaeda., 289*. The text more probably means, "mingling, or associated, with us to display his might."

[सूक्त-६२]

[**ऋषि**– प्रगाथ काण्व। **देवता**– इन्द्र। **छन्द**– पंक्ति, ७, ९, बृहती।]

७१३१. प्रो अस्मा उपस्तुतिं भरता यज्जुजोषति। उक्थैरिन्द्रस्य माहिनं वयो
वर्धन्ति सोमिनो भद्रा इन्द्रस्य रातयः॥१॥

1. Present the offering of praise to *Indra*, since he enjoys it; (the priests) augment the ample food of the *Soma*-loving *Indra* with their recited hymns; *Indra's* gifts are worthy of praise.

७१३२. अयुजो असमो नृभिरेकः कृष्टीरयास्यः।
पूर्वीरति प्र वावृधे विश्वा जातान्योजसा भद्रा इन्द्रस्य रातयः॥२॥

2. Without a fellow and unlike the other gods, he alone, unconquerable, surpasses the men of former times, he surpasses in might all beings; *Indra's* gifts are worthy of praise.

Unlike the other Gods— Sāyaṇa explains *nṛbhiḥ* By *devaiḥ*. Another interpretation takes "he" as the *ṛṣi* of the hymn, in which case *nṛbhiḥ* will mean its ordinary sense, "men," not "gods."

७१३३. अहितेन चिदर्वता जीरदानुः सिषासति।
प्रवाच्यमिन्द्र तत्तव वीर्याणि करिष्यतो भद्रा इन्द्रस्य रातयः॥३॥

3. He, the swift giver, wishes to bestow blessings (upon us) with his unurged courser; your greatness, *Indra*, as you are about

to display your powers, should be proclaimed; *Indra*'s gifts are
worthy of praise.

७१३४. आ याहि कृणवाम त इन्द्र ब्रह्माणि वर्धना।

येभि: शविष्ठ चाकनो भद्रमिह श्रवस्यते भद्रा इन्द्रस्य रातयः॥४॥

4. *Indra*, come hither; let us perform for you our sacred rites
augmenting your vigour; by which (rites), most mighty one, you
desire to bless him who wishes for food; *Indra*'s gifts are worthy
of praise.

७१३५. धृषतश्चिद्धृषन्मनः कृणोषीन्द्र यत्त्वम्।

तीव्रैः सोमैः सपर्यतो नमोभिः प्रतिभूषतो भद्रा इन्द्रस्य रातयः॥५॥

5. You have made your mind, *Indra*, more resolute than the
resolute, since you (wish to give the desires) of him who worships
you with the intoxicating *Soma* juices and adorns you with
adorations; *Indra*'s gifts are worthy of praise.

७१३६. अव चष्ट ऋचीषमोऽवताँ इव मानुषः। जुष्ट्वी दक्षस्य सोमिनः

सख्यायं कृणुते युजं भद्रा इन्द्रस्य रातयः॥६॥

6. *Indra*, who is well-deserving of the hymn, looks down (with
favour) upon us as a (thirsty) man (looks down) on wells; and
being well-pleased he makes the energetic *Soma*-offerer his friend;
Indra's gifts are worthy of praise.

His Friend— Sāyaṇa takes *yujam* as *ātmānam*; but the line rather
means "he makes the skilled *Soma*-offerer's friend his friend."—Another
interpretation is that he makes the *Soma* the friend of the worshipper.

७१३७. विश्वे त इन्द्र वीर्यं देवा अनु क्रतुं ददुः।

भुवो विश्वस्य गोपतिः पुरुष्टुत भद्रा इन्द्रस्य रातयः॥७॥

7. *Indra*, by the example of your power and knowledge the
gods attain the same; O hymned by many, you are the herdsman of
the universe; *Indra*'s gifts are worthy of praise.

The Heardsman— Sāyaṇa takes *gopati* as "lord of waters" or "of
hymns"; but in VIII.69.4 he seems to adopt the common meaning. He
would explain the construction of *viśvasya* as if it characterized the *go of
gopatiḥ*.

७१३८. गृणे तदिन्द्र ते शव उपमं देवतातये।

यद्धंसि वृत्रमोजसा शचीपते भद्रा इन्द्रस्य रातयः॥८॥

8. *Indra*, I laud that might of your which is near at hand to the worshipper,—(I laud you) that you slewest *Vṛtra*, O lord of rites, by your strength; *Indra*'s gifts are worthy of praise.

Sāmaveda, 391 (with *upamam*).

To the Worshipper— Or, "for the sake of the offering."

७१३९. समनेव वपुष्यतः कृणवन्मानुषा युगा।
विदे तदिन्द्रश्चेतनमध श्रुतो भद्रा इन्द्रस्य रातयः॥९॥

9. As a woman who shows no partiality wins her lovers to her, so *Indra* confers periods of time on mankind; it is *Indra* who has performed that knowledge-giving achievement, therefore he is renowned; *Indra*'s gifts are worthy of praise.

Who shows no Partiality— Sāyaṇa takes *samanā* as *samānamanaska yoṣit*, and explains *yuga* as "years, half-years, seasons, months," etc.; but the explanation utterly breaks down. Prof. Roth explains the first line, "er macht die Menschen zue einem bewundernden Zuschauerkries, *d. h.* zieht aller Augen auf sich."

७१४०. उज्जातमिन्द्र ते शव उत्त्वामुतव क्रतुम्।
भूरिंगो भूरि वावृधुर्मघवन्तव शर्मणि भद्रा इन्द्रस्य रातयः॥१०॥

10. *Maghavan*, rich in cattle, (those who abide) in your happiness have greatly augmented your might when it was born, (they have greatly augmented) you, *Indra*, and your knowledge; *Indra*'s gifts are worthy of praise.

Greatly Augmented— By their *Soma*-offerings and hymns.

७१४१. अहं च त्वं च वृत्रहन्त्सं युञ्याव सनिभ्य आ।
अरातीवा चिंदद्रिवोऽनु नौ शूर मंसते भद्रा इन्द्रस्य रातयः॥११॥

11. May I and you, slayer of *Vṛtra*, be close you united until wealth is obtained; hero, wielding the thunderbolt, even the niggard concedes (that our union gives wealth); *Indra*'s gifts are worthy of praise.

७१४२. सत्यमिद्वा उ तं वयमिन्द्रं स्तवाम नानृतम्। महाँ असुन्वतो वधो भूरि
ज्योतींषि सुन्वतो भद्रा इन्द्रस्य रातयः॥१२॥

12. Let us praise that *Indra* with truth, not with untruth, great is the destruction of him who offers not but to him who offers abundant *Soma*-oblations, *Indra*'s gifts are worthy of praise.

Indra's Gifts are worthy of Praise— Sāyaṇa merely says, "to him who offers abundant *Soma*-oblations (*bhūri jyotiṁṣi*) great is the favour conferred by *Indra*." I have ventured to connect it with the last clause, as Sāyaṇa does not explain this recurring burden. A more natural explanation would be, "to him who offers the *Soma* great are the blessings (*bhūri jyotiṁṣi*)."

[सूक्त-६३]

[ऋषि- प्रगाथ काण्व। देवता- इन्द्र, १२ देवगण।
छन्द- गायत्री, १, ४, ५, ७ अनुष्टुप्, १२ त्रिष्टुप्।]

७१४३. स पूर्व्यो महानां वेन: क्रतुभिरानजे।
यस्य द्वारा मनुष्पिता देवेषु धियं आनजे॥१॥

1. He, (*Indra*), the chief of those to be honoured, desirous of our offerings, approaches; he, the doors of whose favour, the sacred rites. *Manu*, the (universal) father, attained among the gods.
Sāmaveda, 355. The Comm. there gives a different interpretation, as it explains the first *ānaje* by, *ātmānam vyaktikaroti* and the second by *āgamayati*; and *Manuḥ*, which is here left unexplained, is there=*jñātā sarvasya Indraḥ*.

७१४४. दिवो मानं नोत्सदन्त्सोमपृष्ठासो अद्रय:। उक्था ब्रह्म च शंस्या॥२॥

2. May the stones which press out the *Soma* never forsake *Indra*, the maker of heaven, nor the praises and hymns which are to be uttered.

७१४५. स विद्वाँ अङ्गिरोभ्य इन्द्रो गा अवृणोदपं। स्तुषे तदस्य पौंस्यम्॥३॥

3. He, the wise *Indra*, discovered the cows to the *Aṅgirasas*; I glorify that his might.
Discovered the Cows— When carried off by the *Paṇis*, see I.6.5; I.11.5.

७१४६. स प्रत्नथा कविवृध इन्द्रो वाकस्य वक्षणि:।
शिवो अर्कस्य होमन्यस्मत्रा गन्त्ववर्वसे॥४॥

4. As in former times, so now too is *Indra* the blesser of the worshipper and the bearer of him who praises him may he come among us auspicious for our protection at the oblation of the *Soma*.

७१४७. आदू नु ते अनु क्रतुं स्वाहा वरस्य यज्यव:।
श्वात्रमर्का अनूषतेन्द्र गोत्रस्य दावने॥५॥

5. Forthwith, *Indra*, as they offer to *Agni* the lord of *Svāhā*, the singers successively praise your deeds, for your attainment of wealth.

As they Offer to Agni— *I.e.,* as they make the oblation to you in the fire.

७१४८. इन्द्रे विश्वानि वीर्या कृतानि कर्त्वानि च। यमर्का अध्वरं विदुः॥६॥

6. In that *Indra*, whom the singers know as the unharming, all past and future powers abide.

७१४९. यत्पाञ्जन्यया विशेन्द्रे घोषा असृक्षत।
अस्तृणाद् बर्हणा विपो३ ऽर्यो मानस्य स क्षयः॥७॥

7. When praises are addressed to *Indra* by the men of the five classes, he destroys their enemies by his might; he, the lord, is the abode of the worshipper's homage.

७१५०. इयमु ते अनुष्टुतिश्चकृषे तानि पौंस्या। प्रावश्चक्रस्य वर्तनिम्॥८॥

8. This praise is your, for you have achieved those exploits; you have guarded the road of our chariot-wheel (to the sacrificial rite).

७१५१. अस्य वृष्णो व्योदन उरु क्रमिष्ट जीवसें। यवं न पश्व आ ददे॥९॥

9. When the various sustenance, given by *Indra*, the showerer, is obtained, all men step our with wide strides for (dear) life; they receive it as cattle barley.

७१५२. तद्दधाना अवस्यवो युष्माभिर्दक्षपितरः। स्याम मरुत्वतो वृधे॥१०॥

10. Presenting our praise, and desiring protection, may we with you (O priests) be lords of food, to offer sacrifice to (*Indra*) attended by the *Maruts*.

७१५३. बळृत्वियाय धाम्न ऋक्वभिः शूर नोनुमः। जेषामेन्द्र त्वया युजा॥११॥

11. Hero, by our hymns we offer praise to you, who appear at the time of sacrifice, and wear auspicious splendour; with you as our ally may we conquer (our enemies).

७१५४. अस्मे रुद्रा मेहना पर्वतासो वृत्रहत्ये भरहूतौ सजोषाः।
यः शंसते स्तुवते धायि पज्र इन्द्रज्येष्ठा अस्माँ अवन्तु देवाः॥१२॥

12. The *Rudras*, the showering clouds, and (*Indra*) who rejoices with us in the battle-challenge which brings *Vṛtra's* destruction, and who comes in his might to the reciter and singer of his praises—may these gods, with *Indra* at their head, protect us.

Sāyaṇa gives an alternative explanation of the first part of this verse, "May the showering mountain-like (or 'filling,' 'gratifying') *Maruts,* the sons of *Rudra,* allies in the battle-challenge which brings *Vṛtra's* destruction." This verse also occurs in *Yajurveda,* XXXIII.50, but Mahīdhara's Commentary differs widely from Sāyaṇa's. "May the gods who shower wealth upon us, the *Rudras,* and those who have stated festivals (*parvataḥ*), who are unanimous in the battle-challenge for the destruction of *Vṛtra,*—may these gods with *Indra* at their head protect us and him who recites or mutters the praises, or having accumulated wealth, offers oblations." The St. Petersburg Dict. translates the clause *yaḥ saṁsate stuvate dhāyi pajra Indrajyeṣṭhā asmān avantu devāḥ,* in pretty close agreement with *Sāyaṇa's* interpretations as followed in the text. "Die Götter mit *Indra* an der Spitze, der zu Gunsten des Anrufenden and Lobenden sich fiest macht (oder 'feist' *d.h.* 'kräfgig ist,') mögen uns gnädig sein."

[सूक्त-६४]

[ऋषि– प्रगाथ काण्व। देवता– इन्द्र। छन्द– गायत्री।]

७१५५. उत्त्वा मन्दन्तु स्तोमाः कृणुष्व राधो अद्रिवः।
अर्व ब्रह्मद्विषो जहि॥१॥

1. May our praises exhilarate you; thunderer, make food for us, destroy the haters of the *Brahmans.*
Sāmaveda, 194, 1354

७१५६. पदा पणीँररा॑धसो नि बाधस्व महाँ असि। नहि त्वा कश्चन प्रति॥२॥

2. Crush with your foot the *Paṇis* who offer no oblations; you are mighty; there is none so ever like unto you.
Sāmaveda, 1355

७१५७. त्वमीशिषे सुतानामिन्द्र त्वमसुतानाम्। त्वं राजा जनानाम्॥३॥

3. You, *Indra,* are the lord of the *Soma* effused or not effused, you are the king of all men.
Sāmaveda, 1356

७१५८. एहि प्रेहि क्षयो दिव्याइ घोषत्र्रर्षणीनाम्। ओभे पृणासि रोदसी॥४॥

4. Come hither, come forth from heaven to our dwelling, shouting for the sake of men; you fill both heaven and earth.

Come Hither . . . . of Men— Another interpretation is, "Come hither, and (having accepted the oblation) proceed gladly, praising the sacrificer (sc. *divi* for *divam*).

You Fillest both heaven and Earth— Sāyaṇa adds, "with splendour or with rain."

७१५९. त्यं चित्पर्वतं गिरिं शतवन्तं सहस्रिणम्। वि स्तोतृभ्यो रुरोजिथ॥५॥

5. Do you hurst, for your worshippers, the gnarled cloud with its hundreds and thousands of showers.

The Gnarled Cloud— *Parvata* and *giri* both mean "cloud" as well as "mountain"; but as the former is a *yogarūḍha pada* (*i.e.,* a compound term whose parts, when it is analyzed, have the same meaning as the whole), it is here taken in its analyzed sense as *parvavat*, "having knots," "gnarled."

७१६०. वयमुं त्वा दिवा सुते वयं नक्तं हवामहे। अस्माकं काममा पृण॥६॥

6. We invoke you when the *Soma* is effused by day, we invoke you by night; fulfil our desire.

७१६१. क्व १ स्य वृषभो युवा तुविग्रीवो अनानतः। ब्रह्मा कस्तं संपर्यति॥७॥

7. Where is that ever-youthful showerer, strong-necked and bowing to none? What hymner worships you?
Sāmaveda, 142.

Showerer— So Sāyaṇa, but usually *vṛṣabha* means "a bull." For *tuvigrīva, cf.* i.187.5.

७१६२. कस्य स्वित्सवनं वृषा जुजुष्वाँ अव गच्छति।

इन्द्रं क उ स्विदा चके॥८॥

8. To whose offering does the showerer come down pleased? Who can praise *Indra*?

७१६३. कं ते दाना असक्षत वृत्रहन्कं सुवीर्या।

उक्थे क उ स्विदन्तमः॥९॥

9. In what character, O slayer of *Vṛtra*, do the sacrificial offerings honour you, or the brave praises in the hymn? Who is nearest (in time of battle)?

Who is nearest in time of Battle— Sāyaṇa takes it thus, adding *yuddhe* to *ka u svid antamaḥ*. But it would have seemed more natural to connect these words with the preceding *śastre*.

७१६४. अयं ते मानुषे जने सोमः पूरुषु सूयते। तस्येहि प्र द्रवा पिब॥१०॥

10. For you is this *Soma* effused among men by me of mortal race; draw near, hasten, drink it.

Among men by me, Etc.— Sāyaṇa explains *mānuṣe jane* by *mayi* (but *cf.* I.48.11), and *puruṣu* by *manuṣyeṣu madhye* or *Purunāmasu rājasu*.

७१६५. अयं तै शर्यणावति सुषोमांयामधि प्रियः।
आर्जीकीयें मदिन्तमः॥११॥

11. This is your beloved most exhilarating *Soma* which grows in the *Śaryaṇāvat* take by the *Suṣomā* river in the *Ārjīkīya* country.

Śaryaṇāvat Lake— *Cf.* VIII.7.29— Sāyaṇa seems to have read *adhi śritaḥ* for *adhi priyaḥ*; he places this lake in the back part of *Kurukṣetra*.

In the Arjikiya Country— Sāyaṇa adds that the *Soma* thus grows in a very distant country (*scil.* to one in the South of India). According to Yāska, *Nirukta*, IX.26 *Ārjīkīya* is a name of the *Vipāś*; see Professor Roth's *Lit and Hist. of the Veda*, pp.137-140.

७१६६. तमद्य राधंसे महे चारुं मदांय घृष्वये। एहीमिन्द्रं द्रवां पिबं॥१२॥

12. Come to-day, *Indra*, hasten, drink this grateful *Soma* for our great wealth, and for your own foe-crushing exultation.

Grateful— Sāyaṇa explains *cāru* as *cāraṇaśīla*, "quickly moving"; but in IX.61.9 he explains it as *kalyāṇa-svarūpa*.

Foe-Rushing Exultations— Sāyaṇa takes *ghṛṣvi* as *śutrūṇām gharṣaṇaśīla*; it more probably means "lively," "vehement."

[सूक्त-६५]

[ऋषि- प्रगाथ काण्व। देवता- इन्द्र। छन्द- गायत्री।]

७१६७. यदिन्द्रं प्रागपागुदङ्न्यग्वा हूयसे नृभिंः। आ यांहि तूर्यमाशुभिंः॥१॥

1. Whether you are invoked by us, the leaders of rites, from the east, the west, the north, or the south, come hither quickly with your rapid steeds.

The first part of this verse occurs in *Sāmaveda*, 279, 1231.

७१६८. यद्वां प्रस्रवणे दिवो मादयांसे स्वर्णरि। यद्वां समुद्रे अन्धंसः॥२॥

2. Whether you rejoice in the ambrosia-fountain of heaven, or in some other heavenward-leading sacrifice (on earth), or in the ocean-like firmament of the waters;

Ocean-like firmament of the Waters— *Andhas* properly means "food"; according to Sāyaṇa it here implies water as the cause of food. *Yadvā samudre andhasas* might mean, "or in the *Soma-vat*."

७१६९. आ त्वां गीर्भिर्महामुरुं हुवे गांमिव भोजंसे। इन्द्र सोमंस्य पीतयें॥३॥

3. *Indra*, by my praises I invoke you, great and strong one, to drink the *Soma*, as a bull to eat (his fodder).

७१७०. आ तं इन्द्र महिमानं हरयो देव ते महः। रथे वहन्तु बिभ्रतः॥४॥

4. Let your steeds, *Indra*, bearning you in your chariot, bring hither your might, (may they bring hither) your splendour, O divine one.

७१७१. इन्द्रं गृणीष उ स्तुषे महाँ उग्र ईशानकृत्। एहि नः सुतं पिब॥५॥

5. *Indra*, you are invoked, you are praised, the great, the strong, the wielder of sovereignty; come hither and drink our libation.

७१७२. सुतावन्तस्त्वा वयं प्रयस्वन्तो हवामहे। इदं नो बर्हिरासदे॥६॥

6. Bearing the effused *Soma* and the sacrificial food, we invoke you, *Indra*, to sit on our sacred grass.

७१७३. यच्चिद्धि शश्वतामसीन्द्र साधारणस्त्वम्। तं त्वा वयं हवामहे॥७॥

7. Because you are common to many worshippers, therefore, *Indra*, we invoke you.

Therefore we Invoke you— Sc. we invoke you before the others.

७१७४. इदं ते सोम्यं मध्वधुक्षन्नद्रिभिर्नरः। जुषाण इन्द्र तत्पिब॥८॥

8. The priests have milked for you with their stones this nectar of the *Soma*; drink it, *Indra*, well pleased.

७१७५. विश्राँ अर्यो विपश्चितोऽति ख्यस्तूयमा गहि।

अस्मे धेहि श्रवो बृहत्॥९॥

9. Do you, the lord, pass by all other worshippers and come quickly to us, and bestow on us abundant food.

Food. *Śravas* may also mean "glery."

७१७६. दाता मे पृषतीनां राजा हिरण्यवीनाम्। मा देवा मघवाँ रिषत्॥१०॥

10. May (*Indra*) the king give me cows adorned with gold; O gods, let not *Maghavan* be harmed.

७१७७. सहस्रे पृषतीनामधि श्रन्दं बृहत्पृथु। शुक्रं हिरण्यमा ददे॥११॥

11. Upon a thousand cows I obtain gold, abundant, delightful, wide-spread, and pure.

Upon a thousand Cows I obtain Gold— The Scholiast seems to explain this as if the cows came as it were laden with gold from *Indra*.

৩১৭৮. नपातो दुर्गहस्य मे सहस्त्रैण सुराधसः। श्रवो देवेष्वंक्रत॥१२॥

12. Plunged as I am in sorrow, my children, by the favour of
the gods, obtain food, and are blessed with abundance in a
thousand cattle.

Sāyaṇa takes *napātaḥ* as a genitive singular=*arakṣitasya*, and would
understand the verse, "destitute of a protector as I am and plunged in
sorrow, (my dependants) by the favour of the gods," etc. But it is better
to take *napātaḥ* as a nominative plural.

[सूक्त-६६]

[ऋषि– कलि प्रागाथ। देवता– इन्द्र। छन्द– प्रागाथ (विषमा बृहती,
समासतो बृहती), १५ अनुष्टुप्।]

৩১৭৯. तरोभिर्वो विदद्वसुमिन्द्रं सबाधं ऊतयें।

बृहद् गायन्तः सुतसोमे अध्वरे हुवे भरं न कारिणम्॥१॥

1. Thronging together, (worship) for your protection *Indra* full
of might and the revealer of wealth; (worship him), chanting the
Bṛhat-Sāman at his sacrifice where the *Soma* is effused; I invoke
him as (men invoke) a beneficent master of a household.

Sāmaveda, 237, 687.

৩১৮০. न यं दुध्रा वरन्ते न स्थिरा मुरो मदे सुशिप्रमन्धसः।

य आदृत्या शशमानाय सुन्वते दाता जरित्र उक्थ्यम्॥२॥

2. He, the handsome-jawed, whom, in the intoxication of the
Soma, the fierce (demons) withstand not, nor the firm gods, nor
mortal (men),—who confers glorious wealth on him who
reverently praises him, offers the *Soma*, and sings hymns;

Sāmaveda, 688, but reading *madeṣu śipram* for *made suśipram*.—
Sāyaṇa does not explain *ādṛtya*; but the St. Petersburg Dict. derives it
from *dṛi*, 'to tear,' in the sense of "aufthuend d.h. mit offener Hand"; but
Benfey prefers the usual meaning, and renders it "ehrfurchtsvill." The
yaḥ in the printed commentary should probably by placed before *data, cf.*
var. Lect. *Ādṛtya* can hardly be taken with *madāya*, as it is always
construed with the accusative; but it may apply to *Indra, i.e.,* "who with
favouring regard confers," etc., (*cf.* I.103.6). *Made* also can hardly be
other than a locative, though Sāyaṇa takes it as a dative, and seems to
connect it with *ādṛtya.*

७१८१. य: शक्रो मृक्षो अश्व्यो यो वा॒ कीजो॑ हिरण्यय॑:।
स ऊर्वस्य॑ रेजयत्यपा॑वृतिमिन्द्रो॑ गव्य॑स्य वृत्रहा॑॥३॥

3. He *Śakra*, who is the purifier (of his worshippers), and well-skilled in horses, who is wonderful and goldenbodied,—He, *Indra*, the slayer of *Vṛtra*, shakes the hiding-place of the numerous herd of kine.

This is a very obscure stanza. Sāyaṇa explains *mṛkṣaḥ* by *stotṛṇāṁ śodhakaḥ* or *paricaraṇīyaḥ*, and *aśvyaḥ* as *aśvakuśalaḥ;* but he adds another explanation, which takes the two words together, as *aśvaḥ prakṣ ālitaḥ*, "a well-washed horse." Again, he explains *kījaḥ* as *adbhutaḥ*, "wonderful," but this seems only based on an etymological guess, *kim asya katham jāta iti vacanāt*. The St. Petersburg Dict. takes *mṛkṣa* as a currycomb or some such instrument, "Striegel, Kamm oder ähnlich," ("*Indra* wird mit einem kratzenden Werkzeuge verglichen, das den Verschluss der Heerde aufreisst"), and *kīja* as some similar instrument.

Numerous herd of Kine— Here, again, we have an obscure word in *apāvṛti*. Sāyaṇa explains it as *apavaraṇīyam*, "to be opened," referring apparently to the cave of the *paṇis* (I.6.5).

७१८२. निखा॑तं चि॒द्य: पुरुसम्भृ॑तं वसू॒दिद्दप॑ति दा॒शुषे॑।
वज्री॑ सु॒शिप्रो॑ हर्य॑श्व इत् क॑र॒दिन्द्र॑: क्रत्वा॒ यथा॑ वश॑त्॥४॥

4. He who verily pours forth to the offerer the buried wealth accumulated by many, he, *Indra*, the thunderer, handsome-jawed, borne on bay steeds, does as he pleases, (when propitiated) with sacrifice.

Accumulated by Many— The *Saṁhitā* text reads *puru-sambhṛtam* as a compound; Sāyaṇa in his Comm. divides the two words, "the buried wealth, plentious and accumulated." He takes the wealth as the accumulated stores from former sacrifices.

When propitiated with Sacrifice— Sāyaṇa says that sacrifice is here the *upādhi* or necessary preliminary condition.

७१८३. यद्वा॑वन्थ॒ पुरुष्टुत॒ पुरा॑ चि॒च्छूर॑ नृणाम्।
वयं॒ तत्त॑ इन्द्र॒ सं भ॑रामसि य॒ज्ञमुक्थं तुरं॒ वच॑:॥५॥

5. Hero, praised of many, what of old time you did desire from your votaries, that, *Indra*, we hasten to bring to you,—oblation and recited praise.

Sāyaṇa makes the construction rather complicated by taking *chid* "as
(*upamārthe, Nirukta,* I.4), "as of old time (you received'st) from your
votaries, so now we hasten to bring you what you did desire."

७१८४. सचा सोमेषु पुरुहूत वज्रिवो मदाय द्युक्ष सोमपाः।
त्वमिद्धि ब्रह्मकृते काम्यं वसु देष्ठः सुन्वते भुवः॥६॥

6. Bearer of the thunderbolt, invoked of many, radiant, drinker
of the *Soma,* be present at our libations for your exhilaration; for
you are an abundant giver of desirable wealth to him who utters
your praises and effuses the *Soma.*

७१८५. वयमेनमिदा ह्योऽपीपमेह वज्रिणम्।
तस्मा उ अद्य समना सुतं भरा नूनं भूषत श्रुते॥७॥

7. To-day and yesterday we have here refreshed him, the
thunderer; bring to him to-day our libation effused for (success in)
battle; let him now hasten hither on hearing our praise.

For success in Battle— *Sāmaveda,* 272, 1691; but reading *savane*
for *samanā*. Sāyaṇa takes the latter word as meaning "for battle," but it
is properly an adverb. The St. Petersb. Dict. translates it here, "in gleicher
Weise."

७१८६. वृकश्चिदस्य वारण उरामथिरा वयुनेषु भूषति।
सेमं नः स्तोमं जुजुषाण आ गहीन्द्र प्र चित्रया धिया॥८॥

8. The obstructing robber, the destroyer of travelling enemies,
is obedient to him in his ways; hasten, *Indra,* (drawn) by our
gorgeous rite, welcoming this our hymn.

Sāmaveda, 1692.

The destroyer of Tavelling Enemies— This is Sāyaṇa's
interpretation of *vṛkaś cid vāraṇa urāmathiḥ* (thus connecting the last
word with the etymological root *ur,* "to go"); but Yāska (*Nirukta,* v.21)
takes the words literally, "the obstructing wolf, destroying the sheep,"
which is far preferable.

In his ways— *Vayuneṣu* may also mean *prajñāneṣu,* "in his
counsels."

७१८७. कदू न्वस्याकृतमिन्द्रस्यास्ति पौंस्यम्।
केनो नु कं श्रोमतेन न शुश्रुवे जनुषः परि वृत्रहा॥९॥

9. What act of might is there, unperformed by *Indra*? Who has
not heard of his famous (heroism)? He, the slayer of *Vṛtra,* (is
renowned) from his birth.

७१८८. कदू॒ महीरधृ॑ष्टा अस्य॒ तवि॑षी: क॒दु वृ॒त्र॒घ्नो अस्तृ॑तम्।
इन्द्रो॒ विश्वा॑न्॒ बेक॒नाटाँ अह॒र्दृश॑ उ॒त क्रत्वा॑ प॒णीँरभि॑॥१०॥

10. When were his mighty forces ever languid? When was
aught undestroyed before the slayer of *Vṛtra*? *Indra* by his energy
overpowers all the huckstering usurers who see only this world's
days.

Huckstering Usurers— *Cf. Nirukta*, VI.26. The text may also be
interpreted "usurers and hucksters". *Ahardṛśaḥ*, lit. "seeing the day," is
explained as seeing only the light of this world and dwelling in deep
darkness after death. The Schol refers to *Manu*, VIII.102, for a censure on
usurers and traders.

७१८९. व॒यं घा॑ ते॒ अपू॒र्व्येन्द्र॒ ब्रह्मा॑णि वृत्रहन्।
पु॒रू॒तमा॑स: पुरुहूत व॒ज्रिवो॒ भृ॒तिं न प्र भ॑रामसि॥११॥

11. *Indra*, slayer of *Vṛtra*, invoked of many, we, your many
worshippers, offer new hymns to you, thunderer, as your wages.

As your Wages— Sāyaṇa remarks that the use of wages as an
illustration is not inappropriate, as both the hymns and the wages are
given by a definite rule (*niyamena*).

७१९०. पू॒र्वीश्चि॒द्धि त्वे॑ तु॒विकूर्मिन्ना॒शसो॑ हवन्त इन्द्रो॒तय॑:।
तिर॒श्चिद॑र्य: सव॑ना व॒सो गहि॒ शवि॑ष्ठ श्रु॒धी मे॒ हव॑म्॥१२॥

12. *Indra*, doer of many great deeds, (other worshippers invoke
the manifold hopes and protections which abide in you; but
rejecting the enemy's oblations, come to us bestower of dwellings;
O mightiest, hear my appeal.

७१९१. व॒यं घा॑ ते॒ त्वे इद्विन्द्र॒ विप्रा॒ अपि॑ ष्मसि।
न॒हि त्वद॒न्य: पु॑रुहूत॒ कश्च॒न मघ॑वन्न॒स्ति म॒र्डि॒ता॥१३॥

13. *Indra*, we are your, therefore we, your worshippers, depend
on you; other than you, *Maghavan*, invoked of many, there is no
giver of happiness.

७१९२. त्वं नो॑ अ॒स्या अम॑तेरु॒त क्षु॒धो॒३ऽभिश॑स्तेर॒व स्पृ॑धि।
त्वं न॑ ऊ॒ती तव॑ चि॒त्रया॑ धि॒या शिक्षा॑ शचिष्ठ गातु॒वित्॥१४॥

14. Deliver us from this poverty, hunger, and calumny; give us
(our desire) by your protection and wondrous working; O
mightiest, you know the right way.

O **Mightiest**— Sāyaṇa explains *saciṣṭha* in IV.20.9, as *atiśayena prājña*, and in IV.43.3, *śaktimattara*.

७१९३. सोम॒ इद्धः॒ सुतो॑ अस्तु॒ कल॑यो मा बि॑भीतन।
अपेदे॒ष ध्व॒स्मायति॑ स्व॒यं घैषो॑ अपा॑यति॥१५॥

15. Let your effused *Soma* juice be only (for *Indra*); O sons of *Kali*, fear not; that malignant (spirit) departs, of his own accord he departs.

[सूक्त-६७]

[ऋषि— मत्स्य साम्मद अथवा मैत्रावरुणि मान्य अथवा अनेक मत्स्य
जालनद्ध। देवता— आदित्यगण। छन्द— गायत्री।]

VII 7.8 **Sammada**— See Prof. Aufrecht in his edition of the *Ṛgveda*, p.477, (but *cf.* Prof. Müller's transl., Pref. p. IXIV).

७१९४. त्यान्नु॒ क्ष॒त्रियाँ॒ अव॑ आदि॒त्यान्या॑चिषामहे। सुमृ॒ळीकाँ॑ अभि॒ष्टये॑॥१॥

1. We solicit for protection those *Kṣatriyas*, the *Ādityas* who bless (their votaries) abundantly to the attainment of their desires.

७१९५. मि॒त्रो नो॒ अत्यँह॑तिं॒ वरु॑णः प॒र्षद॒र्यमा॑। आ॒दि॒त्यासो॒ यथा॑ वि॒दुः॥२॥

2. May the *Ādityas*, *Mitra*, *Varuṇa*, and *Aryaman*, bear us across our distress, as they know it well.

७१९६. तेषां॒ हि चि॒त्रमु॒क्थ्यं१॒ वरू॑थम॒स्ति दा॒शुषे॑। आ॒दि॒त्याना॒मरङ्कृ॒ते॑॥३॥

3. To those *Ādityas* belongs wonderful wealth, worthy of all praise, (laid up) for the offerer of oblations and the sacrificer.

७१९७. म॒हि वो॑ मह॒तामवो॒ वरु॑ण मित्रा॒र्यमन्। अवाँ॑स्या वृ॒णीमहे॑॥४॥

4. You are great, *Varuṇa*, *Mitra*, and *Aryaman*, and great is your protection; your protections we implore.

७१९८. जी॒वान्नो॒ अभि॒ धेत॑नादि॒त्यासः॑ पु॒रा ह॒थात्। कद्ध॒ स्थ हवनश्रु॑तः॥५॥

5. *Ādityas*, hasten to us are our death, while we are yet alive; where are you, hearers of prayer?

Where are You— Sāyaṇa takes *kat* and *ke*, ''who?'' but the *Nirukta* (VI.27) explains it as *kva*.

७१९९. यद्वः॑ श्रा॒न्ताय॑ सु॒न्वते॒ वरू॑थम॒स्ति य॒च्छर्दि॑ः।
तेना॑ नो॒ अधि॑ वोचत॥६॥

6. Whatever wealth, whatever dwelling is yours (to give) to the wearied offerer of libations,—with these speak to us a kindly answer.

७२००. अस्ति देवा अंहोरुर्वस्ति रत्नमनांगसः। आदित्या अद्भुतैनसः॥७॥

7. Great, O deities, is (the guilt) of the sinner, but to the sinless is happiness; *Ādityas*, you are void of sin.

७२०१. मा नः सेतुः सिषेदयं महे वृणक्तु नस्परिं। इन्द्र इद्धि श्रुतो वशी॥८॥

8. Let not the snare bind us; may *Indra*, the renowned, the subduer of all, deliver us for a glorious act.

७२०२. मा नौ मृचा रिपूणां वृजिनानांमविष्यवः। देवां अभि प्र मृक्षत॥९॥

9. O deities, ready to protect, mole us not with the destructive net of our wicked enemies.

Sāyaṇa gives another interpretation of this verse, taking *abhipramrkṣ ata* from *mṛj* instead of *mṛṣ*. "Let us not (be tormented) by the destructive net of our enemies, deliver us from it."

७२०३. उत त्वामंदिते मह्यहं देव्युपं ब्रुवे। सुमृळीकामभिष्टये॥१०॥

10. I address you, who give abundant delight, the great goddess *Aditi*, for the attainment of my desire.

७२०४. पर्षि दीने गंभीर आँ उग्रंपुत्रे जिघांसतः।
मार्किस्तोकस्यं नो रिषत्॥११॥

11. You protect on every side; let not (the net) of the destroyer hurt our children, in this shallow water full of mighty offspring.

Full of mighty Offspring— Sāyaṇa takes *ugraputre* as a loc. agreeing with "water"; the St. Petersburg Dict. as a voc. agreeing with *Aditi*, "O mother of mighty children."

७२०५. अनेहो नं उरुव्रज उरूचि वि प्रसर्तवे। कृधि तोकायं जीवसे॥१२॥

12. Wide-traversing, far-reaching goddess, put forth your power to come to us, innocent ones, that our children my live.

७२०६. ये मूर्धानं क्षितीनांमदब्धासः स्वयंशसः। व्रता रक्षन्ते अद्रुहं॥१३॥

13. You who are the heads of men, unharming, and of self-sustained glory, who, benevolent ones, protect our rites.

७२०७. ते नं आस्नो वृकाणांमादित्यासो मुमोचंत। स्तेनं बद्धमिंवादिते॥१४॥

14. *Ādityas*, deliver us from the jaws of the destroyers like a bound thief; O *Aditi*, (deliver us).

७२०८. अपो षु णं इयं शरुरादित्या अप॑ दुर्मतिः । अ॒स्मदेत्व॒जघ्नुषी ।।१५।।

15. *Ādityas*, let this net, let the malevolent design turn away from us innocuous.

७२०९. शश्वद्धि व॑: सुदानव॒ आदि॑त्या ऊ॒तिभि॒र्वयम्।
पुरा॒ नूनं॑ बु॒भुज्म॒हे॑ ।।१६।।

16. Bounteous *Ādityas*, by your protections we have continually possessed enjoyments from of old.

७२१०. शश्व॑न्तं हि प्र॒चेतस॑: प्रति॒यन्तं॑ चि॒देन॑सः। दे॒वाः॑ कृणु॒थ जी॒वसे॑।।१७।।

17. Wise deities, keep away from us, that we may live, the many doers of sin who come against us.

This verse might be better rendered, "O wise deities, you help to life many a one who turns from sin."

७२११. तत्सु नो॒ नव्यं॑ स॒न्य॑स आदि॑त्या॒ यन्मुमोच॑ति।
बन्धाद् ब॒द्धमि॑वादिते ।।१८।।

18. *Ādityas* and *Aditi*, let that which releases us as a prisoner from his bond, be ever the object of our praise and worship.

That which releases Us— According to Sāyaṇa this may be either the net or your favour. In the form case the net itself is supposed by the favour of the gods to become as it were the instrument of deliverance.

७२१२. नास्माक॑मस्ति तत्तर॑ आदि॑त्यासो अति॒ष्कदे॑।
यू॒यमस्म॒भ्यं मृ॑ळत ।।१९।।

19. Not to us is there strength enough to burst from this (net); O *Ādityas*, do you grant us your favour.

७२१३. मा नो॒ हेति॒र्विव॑स्वत॒ आदि॑त्याः कृत्रि॒मा शरुः॑।
पुरा॒ नु ज॒रसो॑ वधीत् ।।२०।।

20. Let not this weapon of *Vivasvat*, this net made with hands, *Ādityas*, destroy us before old age.

Vivasvat— *I.e., Yama*, properly the son of *Vivasvat*.

Before old Age— Sāyaṇa says 'purā' pūrve 'nu' idānīm, sarvadetyarthaḥ, 'jarasaḥ' idānīm jīrṇān, "let it not destroy us, now and of old infirm"; but this seems needlessly artificial.

७२१४. वि षु द्वेषो॒ व्यं॑हति॒मादि॑त्यासो॒ वि सं॑हितम्।
विष्व॒ग्विव॒ वृ॑हता॒ रपः॑ ।।२१।।

21. *Ādityas*, utterly destroy our enemies, destroy wickedness, destroy the closely drawn net, destroy evil everywhere.

[सूक्त-६८]

ऋषि– प्रियमेध आङ्गिरस। देवता– इन्द्र , १४-१९ ऋक्ष अश्वमेध।
छन्द– गायत्री, १,४,७,१०।]

७२१५. आ त्वा रथं यथोतयें सुम्नाय वर्तयामसि।
तुविकूर्मिमृतीषहमिन्द्र शविष्ठ सत्पते॥१॥

1 Most powerful *Indra*, protector of the good, we bring you here, rich in achievements and subduer of enemies, as a car for our protection and weal.

Sāmaveda, 354, 1771 (with a slight variation).

७२१६. तुविशुष्म तुविक्रतो शचीवो विश्वया मते। आ पप्राथ महित्वना॥२॥

2 Great in power, rich in deeds, mighty one, adorable, you have filled (all things) with your universal majesty.

Sāmaveda, 1772.

Adorable— *Mate* is left unexplained by Sāyaṇa, unless *pūjanīya*, 'adorable,' is its interpretation; he explains it as *stotavya* in VIII.18.7. The St. Petersburg Dict. reads *viśvayamati* as an epithet of *Indra*, '[der überall seine Gedanken hat.''

७२१७. यस्य ते महिना मह: परि ज्मायन्तमीयतु:।
हस्ता वज्रं हिरण्ययम्॥३॥

3. You mighty one, whose hands in your might grasp the all-pervading golden thunderbolt.

Sāmaveda, 1773.

The All-Pervading— *Jmāyantam* Sāyaṇa explains as *pṛthivyām sarvato vyāpnuvantam*, the St. Petersburg Dict. as "bahnbrechend.''

७२१८. विश्वानरस्य वस्पतिमनानतस्य शवस:।
एवैश्च चर्षणीनामूती हुवे रथानाम्॥४॥

4. I invoke (*Indra*) the lord of that might which subdues all enemies and bows to none,—(I invoke him) followed by your onsets as his soldiers and (surrounded) by the protection of your chariots (O *Maruts*).

Sāmaveda, 364. The construction of the latter part is obscure. Sāyaṇa gives another interpretation, which takes *vah* as applying to the sacrificers instead of the *Maruts*, "I invoke him to come with his protections in the onsets of your soldiers and chariots." This partly agrees with Benfey, "Euren Gebieter allherrschender and unbeugsamer Gewalt ruf ich durch Lieder, dass or schützt die Manschen und die Wagen."

७२१९. अभिष्टये सदावृधं स्वर्मीळ्हेषु यं नरः। नाना हवन्त ऊतये।।५।।

5. (I invoke him) to come to our help, whose might ever waxes more and more,—to whom men appeal for aid in various ways in battles.

७२२०. परोमात्रमृचीषममिन्द्रमुग्रं सुराधसम्। ईशानं चिद्रसूनाम्।।६।।

6. (I invoke) *Indra*, the unlimited, worthy of praise, the mighty, possessing excellent wealth, the lord of treasures (for his votaries).

७२२१. तंतमिद्राधसे मह इन्द्रं चोदामि पीतये।
यः पूर्व्यामनुष्टुतिमीशे कृष्टीनां नृतुः।।७।।

7. To him, to him, *Indra*, do I direct my praise, that he may quaff the *Soma* to may great gain,—to him, the bringer of success, who rules over the praises of the offerers at the opening of the sacrifice.

At the opening of the sacrifice— Sāyaṇa explains *pūrvyām* as *yajña-mukhasthām,* but it might be taken in its usual meaning "ancient".

७२२२. न यस्य ते शवसान सख्यमानंश मर्त्यः।
नकिः शर्वांसि ते नशत्।।८।।

8. You mighty one, whose friendship no mortal reaches, whose might no one attains.

७२२३. त्वोतासस्त्वा युजाप्सु सूर्ये महद्धनम्। जयेम पृत्सु वज्रिवः।।९।।

9. Protected by you, O thunderer, with you as our ally, may we win great wealth in battles, that we may bathe in the water and behold the sun.

Bathe in the water and behold the Sun— These words *apsu sūrye* are explained by Sāyaṇa, "that we may perform our accustomed bathings in the water, and, when the sun is risen, may set about our accustomed tasks."

७२२४. तं त्वा यज्ञेभिरीमहे तं गीर्भिर्गिर्वणस्तम।
इन्द्र यथा चिदाविथ वाजेषु पुरुमाय्यम्।।१०।।

10. We address you with sacrificial gifts, (we address you with songs, O *Indra* most worthy of song, as you have protected me, the offerer of many praises, in battles.

The Offerer of Many Praises— *Purumāyyam*, lit. "possessing much wisdom." The St. Petersburg Dict. takes it as a proper name.

७२२५. यस्य ते स्वादु सख्यं स्वाद्वी प्रणीतिरद्रिवः। यज्ञो विंतन्तसाय्यः।।११।

11. You, the thunderer, whose friendship is sweet, sweet too is your liberality, and your sacrifice pre-eminently to be performed.

७२२६. उरु णस्तन्वे३ तनं उरु क्षयाय नस्कृधि।
उरु णो यन्धि जीवसे।।१२।।

12. Give ample (wealth) to our own selves, give ample (wealth) to our children, give ample (wealth) to our dwelling, grant us (our desire) that we may live.

To our own Selves— Sāyaṇa here explains *tanve tane* as *ātmajāya tat-putrāya*; but in VI.46.12 and VII.104.10 he explains it as given in the translation.

७२२७. उरुं नृभ्यं उरुं गवं उरुं रथाय पन्थाम्। देववीतिं मनामहे।।१३।।

13. We solicit a spacious (road) for our servants, a spacious (road) for our cattle, a spacious road for our chariot, and (an abundant) sacrifice.

७२२८. उप मा षड् द्वाद्वा नरः सोमस्य हर्या। तिष्ठन्ति स्वादुरातयः।।१४।।

14. Six princes come to me in pairs, bearing pleasant gifts, in the exhilaration of the *Soma*.

७२२९. ऋज्राविन्द्रोत आ ददे हरी ऋक्षस्य सूनवि। आश्वमेधस्य रोहिता।।१५।

15. I receive two straight-going steeds from *Indrota*, two day from the son of *Ṛkṣa*, two roan from the son of *Aśvamedha*.

Indrota, Etc.— These prices with their respective fathers are the six of V.14. The sons of *Ṛkṣa* and *Aśvamedha* had originally commenced the sacrifice, but *Indrota* and his father *Atithigva* came to see it and added their gifts. The sons alone are mentioned; the son is the father's second self, *pitṛ-putrayor abhedāt*.

७२३०. सुरथाँ आतिथिग्वे स्वभीषूँराक्षे। आश्वमेधे सुपेशसः।।१६।।

16. (I receive) two steeds with excellent chariots from the son of *Atithigva*, two with excellent reins from the son of *Ṛkṣa*, two with excellent ornaments from the son of *Aśvamedha*.

७२३१. षळश्वाँ आतिथिग्व इन्द्रोते वधूमतः। सचा पूतक्रतौ सनम्।।१७।।

17. I have received together (with my other gifts) six horses with their mares from the pious Indrota, the son of *Atithigva*. Together— *Scaha*, *i.e.*, together with the gifts of *Ṛkṣa* and *Aśvamedha*. The Schol. remarks that the use of this word implies that *Indrota's* gift is incidental and no part of the original sacrifice.

७२३२. ऐषु चेतद्वृषण्वत्यन्तर्क्ष्ज्रेष्व॑रुषी। स्व॒भीशुः कशावती॥१८॥

18. Among these straight-going steeds is numbered a mature roan mare with excellent reins and whip.

With excellent reins and whip— Sāyaṇa takes *kaśāvatī* as *dṛptā*, "proud," "spirited."

७२३३. न युष्मे वा॑जबन्धवो निनित्सुश्चन मर्त्यः। अव॒द्यमधि॑ दीधरत्॥१९॥

19. O princes, givers of food, even the lover of calumny has thrown no censure on you.

[सूक्त-६९]

[ऋषि– प्रियमेध आङ्गिरस। देवता– इन्द्र, ११ पूर्वार्द्ध– विश्वेदेवा, ११ उत्तरार्द्ध एवं १२ – वरुण। छन्द– अनुष्टुप्, २ उष्णिक्, ४-६ गायत्री, ११, १६ पंक्ति, १७, १८ बृहती।]

७२३४. प्रप्र वस्त्रिष्टुभमिषं मन्दद्वीरायेन्दवे।
धिया वो॑ मेधसा॒तये॑ पुर॒न्ध्या विवासति॥१॥

1. Present your sacrificial food with a three-fold song of praise to *Indu*, gladdener of heroes; he will bless you in your religious rites to the accomplishment of your sacrifice.

Sāmaveda, 360 (with vandad-vīrāya for mandadvīrāya). Sāyaṇa here takes puraṅdhyā as bahuprajñayā, but in VII. 97.9 he took puraṅdhiḥ as bahvīr stutiḥ.

Indu— The Schol. explains this as *Indra*, "he who rules (*ind*) or besprinkles (*und*) with rain." *Triṣṭubham* rather means here a song of praise generally.

७२३५. नदं व॒ ओद॑तीनां नदं योयु॑वतीनाम्।
पतिं वो॑ अघ्न्यानां धेनूनामिषुध्यसि॥२॥

2. (Invoke) for yourselves the author of the dawns, (I invoke) for you the roarer of the rivers; (I invoke) for you the lord of the inviolable ones; (O sacrificer), you desire kine.

Sāmaveda, 1512. Benfey translates it "der Morgenröthen Sänger, Sänger der immer nahenden, den Herrn der unverletzbaren, der Küh', begehrest du für euch."

The Author of the Dawns—*Nada* is here explained *utpādaka; Indra* is called the author of the dawns as being identified with the sun, as one of the twelve *Ādityas.*

The Inviolable ones— *Aghnyānām,* sc. cows.

౭౨౩౬. ता अस्य सूददोहसः सोमं श्रीणन्ति पृश्नयः।
जन्मन्देवानां विशस्त्रिष्वा रोचने दिवः॥३॥

3. These white kine, giving milk wells, mix the *Soma* for him at the three oblations, rising (in consequence to the brilliant home of the sun, the birthplace of the gods).

This verse occurs in the White *Yajurveda,* XII.55, and is there thus explained by Mahīdhara, ''These various in the text) which makes both these words equally mean *pravṛddha,* ''when the bright fertilizing rivers (or the white milch cows) flow with full waters (or with distended udders), then take, etc.'' In VI.48.11 he explains *dhenum sṛjadhvam anapasphurām* as ''release the cow unobstructed,'' *anapabādhanīyām* as ''release the cow unobstructed,'' *anapabādhanīyām*; and in IV.42.10, *tam dhenum dhattam anapasphurantīm*; as ''grant us that cow (riches) uninjured,'' *anavahiṁsitām.* But Mahīdhara in his comm. on this last verse in the White *Yajurveda,* VII.10, explains *anapasphurantīm* as ''not going to another,'' *i.e.,* ''not running away,'' which will give a good sense in all the passages (*cf.* Prof. Goldstücker's *Dict.*). Similarly, the St. Petersburg Dict. translates *anapauraḥ* as ''not struggling against being milked,'' and *apasphurām* as ''bursting forth,'' *i.e.,* ''when the white milch cows come without starting away, then take the gushing *Soma* for *Indra* to drink.''

౭౨౩౭. अभि प्र गोपतिं गिरेन्द्रमर्च यथा विदे। सूनुं सत्यस्य सत्पतिम्॥४॥

4. Worship with your praise, as he himself knows,—that lord of kine, *Indra,* the son of *Satya,* the protector of the good.

Satya=truth, *Yajña.*

౭౨౩౮. आ हरयः ससृज्रिऽरुषीरधि बर्हिषि। यत्राभि सन्नवामहे॥५॥

5. Let the brilliant bay (horses) drop him down on the cut grass, where we will hymn his praise.

౭౨౩౯. इन्द्राय गाव आशिरं दुदुह्रे वज्रिणे मधु। यत्सीमुपह्वरे विदत्॥६॥

6. The cows have milked the intoxicating draught for *Indra,* the thunderer, when he finds it near him.

౭౨౪౦. उद्यद् ब्रध्नस्य विष्टपं गृहमिन्द्रश्च गन्वहि।
मध्वः पीत्वा सचेवहि त्रिः सप्त सख्युः पदे॥७॥

7. When *Indra*, and I ascend to our home, the world of the sun, then, having drunk the sweet (*Soma*), let us be united in the twenty-first sphere of the (universal) friend.

৩২৪१. अर्चंत प्रार्चंत प्रियमेधासो अर्चंत।
अर्चन्तु पुत्रका उत पुरं न धृष्ण्वर्चत॥८॥

8. Worship *Indra*, worship him pre-eminently, worship him, you of the family of *Priyamedha*; let your sons also worship him; worship him as a strong city.

৩২৪२. अव॑ स्वराति गर्गरो गोधा परि॑ सनिष्वणत्।
पिङ्गा परि॑ चनिष्कददिन्द्राय ब्रह्मोद्यतम्॥९॥

9. The drum utters its sound, the leathern guard twangs, the tawny bowstring leaps to and fro; let the hymn be raised to *Indra*.

৩২৪३. आ यत्पतन्त्येन्य॑: सुदुघा अनपस्फुर॑:।
अपस्फुरं गृभायत सोममिन्द्राय पातवे॥१०॥

10. When the bright fertilizing rivers flow with diminished waters, then take the overflowing *Soma* for *Indra* to drink.

৩২৪४. अपादिन्द्रो अपादग्निर्विश्वे॑ देवा अमत्सत।
वरुण इदिह क्षयत्तमापो॑ अभ्यनूषत वत्सं संशिश्वरीरिव॥११॥

11. *Indra* drank (the *Soma*), *Agni* drank it, the *Viśve Devās* were gladdened; let *Varuṇa* fix his dwelling here, the waters have praised him as cows (low) meeting their calves.

The Waters— Another interpretation of *apaḥ* is "hymns," from a forced derivation, *āpana-śīlaḥ*.

৩২৪५. सुदेवो अ॑सि वरुण यस्य॑ ते सप्त सिन्धव॑:।
अनुक्षरन्ति काकुदं सूर्म्यं॑ सुषिरामिव॥१२॥

12. You are a glorious god, *Varuṇa*, across whose palate the seven rivers keep pouring as a fair-flowing (stream) into an abyss.

Across whose palate the seven Rivers, Etc.— The last words *sūrmyam suṣiram iva* are left unexplained in the Comm; I have followed Yāska's interpretation, *Nirukta*, v.27. Sāyaṇa has given a current metaphorical explanation of them in his Introd. vol. I, p.38, where they are quoted as applied by the grammarians to enforce the need of studying grammar, the seven rivers being taken to mean the seven declensional affixes (*cf.* Ballantyne's *Mahābhāṣya*, p.34, where another explanation is offered, "across whose palate the seven rivers keep flowing a (fire penetrates and purifies) a beautiful perforated iron image''). Sāyaṇa, however, here takes the seven rivers as the Ganges, etc., and *Varuṇa's* palate as the ocean. Prof. Roth takes *sūrmyam suṣiram* as fem. acc. agreeing with *kakudam*, ''welchem die seiben Flüsse zustromen, wie in einen schaumendan hohlen Schlund.''

७२४६. यो व्यतीँरफाणयत् सुयुक्ताँ उप दाशुषे।
तक्वो नेता तदिद्वपुरुपमा यो अमुच्यत॥१३॥

13. He who directs towards the worshipper his well-yoked prancing steeds,—he, (*Indra*), the swift bearer of blessing, (produces) rain,—he, who being comparable only to himself is delivered (from all his enemies).

Comparable only to Himself— Sāyaṇa obscurely interprets *upamā* as *upamāna-bhūta*. The St. Petersburg Dict. takes it as an adverb, ''in close proximity.''

७२४७. अतीदु शक्र औहत इन्द्रो विश्वा अति द्विषः।
भिनत्कनीनं ओदनं पच्यमानं परो गिरा॥१४॥

14. *Śakra* verily overpowers; *Indra* overpowers all his enemies; he, worthy of love, abiding beyond, cleaves the cloud smitten by his thunder-voice.

The Cloud Smitten— The words *odanam pacyamānam* would usually mean ''rice when cooked''; but Sāyaṇa takes *odana* as ''a cloud'' on Yāska's authority (*Naigh.*, I.10), and *pacyamāna* as *tāḍyamāna*, but *cf.* the next verse.

७२४८. अर्भको न कुमारकोऽधि तिष्ठन्नवं रथम्।
स पक्षन्महिषं मृगं पित्रे मात्रे विभुक्रतुम्॥१५॥

15. (*Indra*), like a young boy, has mounted his splendid chariot; he makes ready for his father and mother the great deer-like many-functioned cloud.

He makes Ready— Here Sāyaṇa seems to take *pac* in its usual signification, ''to cook, to mature''; he explains it as *vṛṣṭyabhimukham karoti*, ''*Indra* makes the cloud ready for raining.'' *Mṛga*, ''deer-like,'' he explains as ''wandering hither and thither like a deer,'' or ''to be sought by all.'' Perhaps we might translate the line as a ude metaphor of primeval times, ''he roasts (with his thunderbolt) the wild mighty buffalo (the cloud) for his father and mother.''

७२४९. आ तू सुशिप्र दम्पते रथं तिष्ठा हिरण्ययम्।
अध घुक्षं सचेवहि सहस्रपादमरुषं स्वस्तिगामनेहसम्॥१६॥

16. Handsome-jawed (*Indra*), householder, mount your golden chariot; then let us meet mounted together on that bright thousand-footed brilliant auspiciously moving sinless (car).

७२५०. तं घेमित्था नमस्विन उप स्वराजमासते।
अर्थं चिदस्य सुधितं यदेतव आवर्तयन्ति दावने ॥१७॥

17. (The priests), presenting praise, thus worship that self-resplendent (*Indra*); they obtain his well-stored wealth, when (his horses) bring him on his way for the offering.

His horses— Or "their praises."

७२५१. अनु प्रत्नस्यौकस: प्रियमेधास एषाम्।
पूर्वामनु प्रयतिं वृक्तबर्हिषो हितप्रयस आशत ॥१८॥

18. The *Priyamedhas* have reached the ancient dwelling place of these deities, having strewed the sacred grass and placed their oblations after the manner of a pre-eminent offering.

After the Manner of a Pre-Eminent Offering— *Pūrvām anu prayatim;* Sāyaṇa explains *pūrva* by *mukhya*, "principal," and *anu* by *lakṣīkṛtya*. But it might mean, "after the manner of former offerings," *cf.* I.126.5.

[सूक्त-७०]

[ऋषि– पुरुहन्मा आङ्गिरस। देवता– इन्द्र। छन्द– बृहती, १-६ प्रगाथ (विषमा बृहती, समासतो बृहती), १३ उष्णिक्, १४ अनुष्टुप्, १५ पुर उष्णिक्।]

७२५२. यो राजा चर्षणीनां याता रथेभिरध्रिगु:।
विश्वासां तरुता पृतनानां ज्येष्ठो यो वृत्रहा गृणे ॥१॥

1. I praise that *Indra* who is the lord of men, who proceeds irresistible in his chariots, the breaker-through of all armies, the pre-eminent one, the slayer of *Vṛtra*.

Sāmaveda, 273, 933. Sāyaṇa explains *tarutā* by *tārakaḥ*, which may mean "deliverer"; in VIII.1.21 he explained it by *geta*, "conwueror."

७२५३. इन्द्रं तं शुम्भ पुरुहन्मन्नवसे यस्य द्विता विधर्तरि।
हस्ताय वज्र: प्रति धायि दर्शतो महो दिवे न सूर्य: ॥२॥

2. *Puruhanman*, honour that *Indra* for your protection, for in your upholder there is a two-fold might; he holds in his hand (to smite his enemies) the glorious thunderbolt great as the sun in heaven.

Sāmaveda, 934, but with *mahān devaḥ* for *maho dive*.

A two-fold might— To smite your enemies and to favour your friends.

७२५४. नकिष्टं कर्मणा नशद्यश्चकारं सदावृधम्।

इन्द्रं न यज्ञैर्विश्वगूर्तमृभ्वसमधृष्टं धृष्ण्वोजसम्॥३॥

3. None can touch him by his deeds, who has made *Indra* his friend by sacrifices,— (*Indra*) ever giving fresh strength, to be hymned by all, great, unconquered, of ever-daring might.

Sāmaveda, 243,1155, with a slight variation.

७२५५. अषाळ्हमुग्रं पृतनासु सासहिं यस्मिन्महीरुरुज्रयः।

सं धेनवो जायमाने अनोनवुर्द्यावः क्षामो अनोनवुः॥४॥

4. (I laud) him who is not to be withstood, the mighty, the conqueror in hostile hosts; whom, when he was born, the strong rushing cows welcomed and the heavens and the earths praised.

Sāmaveda, 1156, with *kṣamiḥ* for *kṣāmaḥ*.

The Strong Rushing Cows— Benfey conjectures that these cows are the *Maruts*, the sons of *Pṛśni;* Sāyaṇa allows another interpretation, "mankind offering oblations of clarified butter, etc."

The Earths— The plural is used, because, according to a text, "the worlds are threefold," *trivṛto lokaḥ*.

७२५६. यद् द्यावं इन्द्र ते शतं शतं भूमीरुत स्युः।

न त्वां वज्रिन्त्सहस्रं सूर्या अनु न जातमष्ट रोदसी॥५॥

5. *Indra*, were there an hundred heavens to compare with-you, or were there an hundred earths,—O thunderer, not even a thousand suns would reveal you,—yea, no created thing would fill you, nor heaven and earth.

Sāmaveda, 278, 862.

Not even a thousand Suns— Sāyaṇa compares *Kaṭha Upan.*, V.15, "there (in *Brāhmaṇa*) the sun shines not."

No created thing would fill you— Sāyaṇa compares *Chāndogya Up.*, III.14, "the soul within my heart is greater than the earth, greater than the sky, greater than the heaven, greater than all these worlds."

७२५७. आ पप्राथ महिना वृष्ण्या वृषन्विश्वा शविष्ठ शवसा।

अस्मां अव मघवन्गोमति व्रजे वज्रिञ्चित्राभिरूतिभिः॥६॥

6. Mightiest showerer (of blessings), you have filled all (our hosts) with your vast bountiful power; O *Maghavan*, thunderer,

guard us with your manifold protections, (when we march) against
the well-stocked cowpen of our enemies.

Sāmaveda, 863.

৩২৫৫. न सीमदेव आपदिषं दीर्घायो मर्त्य:।
एतंग्वा चिद्व एतंशा युयोज॑ते हरी॒ इन्द्रो॑ युयोज॑ते॥৩॥

7. O long-lived *Indra*, the mortal who has not you as his deity
obtains no food; (he who praises not) that steed-borne *Indra*, who
yokes to his car the two variegated, who yokes the two bay steeds.

Sāmaveda, 268, with *apa tad* for *āpad*, *etaśaḥ* for *etaśa* and *indro
hari* for *harī indraḥ*. Sāyaṇa's comm. on this verse seems to be corrupt.

৩২৫৯. तं वो॑ म॒हो महाय्य॑मिन्द्रं॑ दाना॒य॑ सक्ष॒णिम्।
यो गा॒धेषु॒ य आर॑णेषु॒ हव्यो॒ वाजे॒ष्वस्ति॒ हव्य॑:॥৫॥

8. Great (priests), worship that *Indra* who is propitiated by
gifts; who is to be invoked in the shallows and in the depths, and
who is to be invoked in battles.

Is propitiated by Gifts— *Dānāya sakṣaṇim*, lit. "who follows for a
gift.'

৩২৬০. उद्दू॒ षु णो॒ वसो॑ महे मृ॒शस्व॑ शूर॒ राध॑से।
उद्दू॒ षु म॒ह्यै म॑घवन्म॒घत्त॑य उ॒दिन्द्र॑ श्रव॑से महे॥৯॥

9. O hero, giver of dwellings, raise us up to enjoy abundant
food; raise us up, *Maghavan*, for abundant wealth; raise us up,
Indra, for abundant fame.

৩২৬৭. त्वं न॑ इन्द्र ऋ॒तयु॒स्त्वानि॑दो॒ नि तृ॑म्पसि।
मध्ये॒ वसिष्व॑ तुविनृम्णो॒र्वोर्नि॑ दा॒सं शिश्न॑थो ह॒थै॑:॥৭०॥

10. *Indra*, who delight in offerings, you satisfy us abundantly
with (the possessions of him) who despises you; O you possessed
of vast wealth, shelter us between your thighs; you smite down the
Dāsa with your blows.

৩২৬২. अ॒न्यव्र॑तम॒मानु॑षम॒यज्व॑नम॒देव॑युम्।
अव॒ स्व: सखा॑ दुधुवीत॒ पर्व॑त: सु॒घ्नाय॒ दस्युं॒ पर्व॑त:॥৭৭॥

11. May your friend, *Parvata*, hurl down from heaven him
who follows other rites, the enemy of men, him who offers not
sacrifice and who worships not the gods; may *Parvata* hurl the
Dasyu down to the stern smiter (death).

Parvata— In I.122.3, Sāyaṇa identifies *Parvata* with *Parjanya*; in VII.37.8 he calls him a god, the friend of *Indra*; here he describes him as a *ṛṣi*, the friend of *Indra, tava sakhi-bhūtaḥ Parvata ṛṣiḥ*.

The Enemy of Men— *Amānuṣam*, Sāyaṇa explains it as "the enemy of the men who sacrifice to *Indra*."

७२६३. त्वं नं इन्द्रासां हस्तेँ शविष्ठ दावनेँ।
धानानां न सं गृभायास्मयुद्धिः सं गृभायास्मयुः॥१२॥

12. Most powerful *Indra*, in your favour towards us, take these cows in your hand, as fried grain, to give to us; yea, take them twice in your favour towards us.

७२६४. सखायः क्रतुमिच्छत कथा राधाम शरस्यं।
उपस्तुतिं भोज: सूरियों अह्रयः॥१३॥

13. Associated priests, give good head to the sacrifice, for how can we (worthily) perform the praise of (*Indra*) the destroyer, who is the recompenser of enemies, the sender of reward, the unvanquished?

The recompenser of Enemies— *Bhojaḥ*, which Sāyaṇa explains as *śatrūṇām bhojayitā;* Prof. Wilson translated it in VIII. 3.24 "the despoiler of enemies." In II.14.10, Sāyaṇa explained it *phalasya dātāram rakṣitāram ca*.

७२६५. भूरिभिः समह ऋषिभिर्बर्हिष्मद्धिः स्तविष्यसे।
यदित्थमेकमेकमिच्छरं वत्सान्परादद:॥१४॥

14. *Indra*, the common object of our worship, you are praised by many sacrificing *Ṛṣis*; for it is you, destroyer of foes, who thus give calves in succession to your worshippers.

In Succession— *Ekam ekam*, "one by one," *i.e.,* according to Sāyaṇa "many." He adds that "calves" here includes "cow."

७२६६. कर्णगृह्या मघवा शौर देव्यो वत्सं नस्त्रिभ्य आनयत्।
अजां सूरिं धातवे॥१५॥

15. May Maghavan, taking them by the ears, lead the cows with their calves from our three (destructive enemies), as the owner leads a goat to drink.

Sāyaṇa in this interpretation reads *vatsam na* for *vatsam naḥ,* and explains it as *vatsa-sahitaḥ.* *Śauradevyaḥ* he explains as "cow," *i.e.,* connected with, or won in, battle (*sauradevam*).

[सूक्त-७१]

[ऋषि- सुदीति तथा पुरुमीळ्ह आङ्गिरस यद्वा द्वयोरेकः। देवता- अग्नि।
छन्द- गायत्री, १०-१५ प्रगाथ (समासतो बृहती, विषमा बृहती]

७२६७. त्वं नौ अग्ने महोभिः पाहि विश्वस्या अरातेः।
उत द्विषो मर्त्यस्य॥१॥

1. *Agni*, do you protect us by great wealth from every niggard
and mortal foe.

Sāmaveda, 6. Sāyaṇa explains *mahobhiḥ* by *mahadbhir dhanaiḥ*, or
by *pūjābhiḥ*, "by our worship." In his comm. on the *Sāmaveda*, he takes
it as *mahadbhiḥ pālanaiḥ*, "by your great protections.' *Arāteḥ* also may
either mean "from the non-giver," or "from the non-giving (*i.e.*,
niggardliness) of every one."

७२६८. नहि मन्युः पौरुषेय ईशे हि वः प्रियजात। त्वमिदसि क्षपावान्॥२॥

2. O you who was born loved, no human anger can harm
you,—you only are the lord of night.

Sāyaṇa explains this, that we will protect you from men by day, and
you wilt protect thyself by night from evil spirits, as fire then burns
brightest.

७२६९. स नो विश्वेभिर्देवेभिरूर्जो नपाद्भद्रशोचे। रयिं देहि विश्ववारम्॥३॥

3. Son of strength, auspicious in brilliance, associated with all
the gods, give us all desirable wealth.

With all the Gods— Sāyaṇa reads *sa no vasva upamāsi* from V.9 for
sa no viśvebhir devebhiḥ.

७२७०. न तमग्ने अरातयो मर्तं युवन्त रायः। यं त्रायसे दाश्वांसम्॥४॥

4. That sacrificing mortal whom you, *Agni*, protect the
niggardly cannot separate from wealth.

७२७१. यं त्वं विप्र मेधसातावग्ने हिनोषि धनाय। स तवोती गोषु गन्ता॥५॥

5. Wise (*Agni*), he whom in his performance of the sacrifice
you incite to attain wealth, by your protection walks (lord) among
crowds of cattle.

Cf. I.86.3.

७२७२. त्वं रयिं पुरुवीरमग्ने दाशुषे मर्ताय। प्र णो नय वस्यो अच्छ॥६॥

6. You, *Agni* give to the offerer wealth comprehending many
male descendants; conduct us to affluence.

७२७३. उरुष्या णो मा परा दा अघायते जातवेदः। दुराध्ये३ मर्ताय॥७॥

7. Defend us, Jatavedas; deliver us not over to the malevolent, to the man whose thoughts are evil.

७२७४. अग्ने मार्किष्टे देवस्य रातिमदेवो युयोत। त्वमीशिषे वसूनाम्॥८॥

8. *Agni*, let not the godless take away the wealth which you, the divine, have given, for you are the lord of treasures.

७२७५. स नो वस्व उप मास्यूर्जो नपान्माहिनस्य। सखे वसो जरितृभ्यः॥९॥

9. Son of strength, the friend, the giver of dwellings, you met our abundant treasure to us your praisers.

७२७६. अच्छा नः शीरशोचिषं गिरो यन्तु दर्शतम्।
अच्छा यज्ञासो नमसा पुरूवसुं पुरुप्रशस्तमूतये॥१०॥

10. Let our voices come near the beautiful (*Agni*) him who bears devouring flames; let our sacrifices with our oblations come near him, for our protection, who is rich in wealth and rich in praise;

Sāmaveda, 1554.

७२७७. अग्निं सूनुं सहसो जातवेदसं दानाय वार्याणाम्।
द्विता यो भूदमृतो मर्त्येष्वा होता मन्द्रतमो विशि॥११॥

11. (Let them come near) *Agni*, *Jātavedas*, son of strength, for the giving of all desirable good things; who is doubly immortal as (perpetually burning) amongst priest amongst the sacrificers.

Sāmaveda, 1555. Sāyaṇa gives another interpretation, "who is doubly immortal (amongst gods) and amongst men," a being equivalent to *ca*. *Viśi*, which he explains as put for the plural *vikṣu yajamāna-rūpasu*, more probably means "in the house," or "in the family."

७२७८. अग्निं वो देवयज्ज्ययाग्निं प्रयत्यध्वरे।
अग्निं धीषु प्रथममग्निमर्वत्यग्निं क्षैत्राय साधसे॥१२॥

12. I praise *Agni*, (O sacrificers), for the inauguration of you divine offering; (I praise him) when the sacrifice is proceeding; (I praise) *Agni* first of the gods, at our rites; (I praise) *Agni* when the enemy approaches; (I praise) *Agni* for the attainment of land.

For the attainment of land— Sc. as the fruit of the sacrifice. The St. Petersburg Dict. says "Zur Regelung der Feldmark."

७२७९. अग्निरिषां सख्ये ददातु न ईशे यो वार्याणाम्।
अग्निं तोके तनये शश्वदीमहे वसुं सन्तं तनूपाम्॥१३॥

13. May *Agni* in his friendship give us food for he is the lord of all desirable things; we solicit abundance for our sons and grandsons from *Agni*, who is the giver of dwellings and the protector of our bodies.

May Agni give us— Or taking *naḥ* for *mahyam* and *sakhye* as a dative (against the accent), "may *Agni* give food to me his friend."

७२८०. अग्निमीळिष्वावंसे गाथाभिः शीरशोचिषम्।
अग्निं रायें पुरुमीळ्ह श्रुतं नरोऽग्निं सुदीतयें छर्दिः॥१४॥

14. Laud with your hymns for our protection *Agni*, whose splendour lie outspread; laud *Agni* for wealth, O *Purumīḷha*, for other offerers are lauding that far famed one on their own behalf; solicit of *Agni* a house for (me) *Suditi*.

Whose splendours lie outspread— This is here Sāyaṇa's explanation of *śīraśociṣam* (*śayanasvabhāva-rociṣkam*), but he gave a different explanation iv v.10 (*aśana-śīla-jvalam*).

Sāmaveda, 49. This verse is supposed to be addressed by *Suditi* to *Purumīḷha*.

७२८१. अग्नि द्वेषो योतवै नौ गृणीमस्यग्निं शं योश्च दातवे।
विश्वासु विश्ववितेव हव्यो भुवद्वस्तुर्ऋषूणाम्॥१५॥

15. We praise *Agni* that he may keep off our enemies; we praise *Agni* that he may give us joy and security; he may we be worshipped as the giver of dwellings to the *Ṛṣis*, he who is as it were the protector of all men.

[सूक्त-७२]

[ऋषि– हर्यत प्रागाथ। देवता– अग्नि अथवा हवि स्तुति। छन्द– गायत्री।]

७२८२. हविष्कृणुध्वमा गमदध्वर्युर्वनते पुनः। विद्वाँ अस्य प्रशासनम्॥१॥

1. (Priests), present the oblation, for (*Agni*) has come; the *Adhvaryu* again offers (the sacrifice), well-skilled in its offering.

७२८३. नि तिग्ममभ्यंशुं शुं सीदद्धोता मनावधि। जुषाणो अस्य सख्यम्॥२॥

2. The *Hotā* sits down by (*Agni*'s) hot flame, rejoicing in his friendship towards the offerer.

Hot Flame— Sāyaṇa takes *aṁśu* as here equivalent to *Agni*; the St. Petersburg Dict. translates it "the stalks of the *Soma*-plant."

७२८४. अन्तरिच्छन्ति तं जनै रुद्रं परो मनीषयां। गृभ्णन्ति जिह्वया ससम्॥३॥

3. For the sake of the offerer, they seek by their skill to place *Rudra* in the fore front; they seize him, as he sleeps, with their tongues.

With their Tongues— Sc. "with their hymns," the cause being used for the effect.

७२८५. जाम्यंतीतपे धनुर्वयोधा अरुहद्वनम्। दृषदं जिह्वयावधीत्।।४।।

4. (*Agni*), the giver of food, scorches the vast bow (of the sky); he mounts the water; he smites the cloud with his tongue.

With his Tongue— Sāyaṇa here takes *jāmi* as *pravṛddham, sarvam atiricya vartamānam*, but the true meaning is probably "him own." He gives another interpretation of the later part of the verse as referring to a forest-conflagration, in which case *vanam* and *dṛṣadam* are taken in their usual acceptation, "he mounts the forest, he smites the rock with his tongue."

७२८६. चरन्वत्सो रुशन्निह निदातारं न विन्दते। वेति स्तोतव अम्ब्यम्।।५।।

5. Roaming like a calf and bright-shining, he finds here no hinderer; he seeks a chanter to praise him.

Here— *Iha* "here" may either mean "in this world," *asmin loke*, or "in the sky," *antarikṣe*; in the latter case *Agni* will mean the lightning, and the praiser (*ambya*) will be the thunder.

७२८७. उतो न्वस्य यन्महदश्वावद्योजनं बृहत्। दामा रथस्य ददृशे।।६।।

6. As soon as the great stout harness of his horses in seen (in the sky), the traces of his chariot.

७२८८. दुहन्ति सप्तैकामुप द्वा पञ्च सृजतः। तीर्थे सिन्धोरधि स्वरे।।७।।

7. Seven milk one (cow), the two direct the five, on the resounding shore of the river.

Ekam, "the one (cow)," is explained as the *gharma*, or earthen vessel so called, which is used to boil milk, etc., in the *Pravargya* ceremony. The "seven" are the seven officiating priests or assistants, two of whom, the *pratiprasthātā* and the *adhvaryu*, are said to direct in the performance the other five, *viz.*, the *yajamāna* or institutor, the *brāhmaṇa* (or *brahman*), the *hotā*, the *agnīdhra*, and the *prastotā*. The "resounding shore" refers to the exclamations used in the sacrifice performed by the *ṛṣi* of the hymn.

७२८९. आ दशभिर्विवस्वत इन्द्रः कोशमचुच्यवीत्।
खेदया त्रिवृता दिवः।।८।।

8. Invoked by the ten (fingers) of the worshipper, *Indra* has caused the cloud to fall from heaven by his threefold ray.

The Ten— The fingers are called "the ten sisters" in III.29.13.

Indra— Sāyaṇa says that *Indra* may also here stand for *Agni* or *Āditya*.

His threefold Ray— *Khedayā trivṛtā;* Sāyaṇa explains *khedayā* by *raśminā,* and *trivṛtā* by *tri-prakāravartanavatā,* "revolving in three ways." *Khedayā* occurs again in 77.3, and is there explained *rajjvā.* The St. Petersburg Dict. explains it as "vielleicht Hamme, Schlägel oderein ähnliches Werkzeug dem *Indra* zukommend."

७२९०. परि त्रिधातुरध्वरं जूर्णिरिति नवीयसी। मध्वा होतारो अञ्जते॥९॥

9. The three-hued fresh impetuous (blaze) goes swiftly round the sacrifice; the priests anoint it with butter.

Three-Hued— Sc. red, white, and black.

७२९१. सिञ्चन्ति नमसावतमुच्चाचक्रं परिज्मानम्। नीचीनबारमक्षितम्॥१०॥

10. They pour out with reverence the inexhaustible cauldron, as it goes round circular above and with an opening below.

Sāmaveda, 1604.

The inexhaustible Cauldron— Sc. the *gharma* or *mahāvīra,* the contents of which are thrown into the *Āhavanīya* fire. The St. Petersburg Dict. takes *avata* (which properly means "a cistern") as a metaphor for a cloud (see under *parijman*).

७२९२. अभ्यारमिद्द्वयो निषिक्तं पुष्करे मधु। अवतस्य विसर्जने॥११॥

11. The reverent priests drawing near pour the superfluous butter into the large (spoon), when they set the cauldron down.

Sāmaveda, 1603.

The Large Spoon— Sc. the *upayamanī* spoon from which the sacrificer drinks the milk.

Down— Sc. on the stool, *āsandyām.*

७२९३. गाव उपावतावतं मही यज्ञस्य रप्सुदा। उभा कर्णा हिरण्यया॥१२॥

12. Draw nigh, ye cows, to the cauldron; (the two kinds of milk) in the sacrifice are plentiful and fruit giving; both ears (of the vessel) are golden.

White Yajurveda, 33.19. *Sāmaveda,* 117, 1602, reading *upa vadāvate* for *upāvatāvatam.*

The two kinds of Milk— The milk of a cow and a goat is poured into the *Gharma* or *Mahavīra. Rapsudā* is a very hard word (see Benfey's glossary). Sāyaṇa gives several attempts to explain it; thus it may be *āripsoḥ phalaprade,* "giving fruit to one who is about to begin," or *lipsvor aśvinor dātavye,* "to be presented to those who desire to receive it (sc. the Aśvins)," or (since *rap* is "to praise"), *mantreṇa dātavye* or *dohanīye,* "to be rightly offered or milked (*sud*) with hymns." Mahīdhara gives a totally different explanation, which is adopted by Benfey; he takes *rapsu* as *rūpa* (but *Naigh.,* III.7 gives only *psu*), and renders the line "O cows, approach the altar-trench (*catvala*), for heaven and earth (*mahi*) give beauty to the sacrifice; both your ears are golden."

७२९४. आ सुते सिंञ्चत श्रियं रोद॑स्योरभिश्रियम्। रसा द॑धीत वृष॑भम्॥१३॥

13. Drop into the milked (stream) the admixture, which reaches, (as it boils), heaven and earth; set the bull in the liquor.

Sāmaveda, 1480. *White Yajurveda,* 33.21.

The Admixture— This is the goat's milk which is poured into the cow's milk in the *Gharma.*

Heaven and Earth— Or the *Aśvins. Cf. Nirukta,* XII.1.

The Bull in the Liquor— The 'bull,' *vṛṣabha,* is explained as *Agni,* and the liquor (*rasa=rase*) is the goat's milk. Sāyaṇa adds, "The goat is dedicated to *Agni,* hence the contact of its milk with fire is proper."

७२९५. ते जा॑नत स्वमोक्यं॒ सं वत्सासो न मातृभिं॑:।
मिथो न॑सन्त जामिभिं॑:॥१४॥

14. They know their own abode; as calves with their mothers, so they severally assemble with their kin.

Sāmaveda, 1481.

Know their own Abode— I.e.a the cows come to the *Gharma* to be milked, as to their stall.

७२९६. उप॒ स्रक्वे॑षु बप्स॑त: कृण्वते धरुणं दिवि।
इन्द्रे॑ अग्ना नम॒: स्व॑:॥१५॥

15. (The priests) minister in the sky the supporting (milk) to (*Agni*) who devours with his jaws; they minister all the food to *Indra* and *Agni.*

Sāmaveda, 1482.

All the Food— Or *swar* may be taken, like *divi,* as "in the sky."

७२९७. अधुक्षत्पिप्युषीमिषमूर्जं॑ सप्तप॑दीमरि:। सूर्य॑स्य सप्त र॒श्मिभिं॑:॥१६॥

16. The wind by means of the sun's seven rays milks the nourishing food and drink from the seven-stepped one.

This is the literal meaning of *saptapadīm,* but Sāyaṇa explains it as "the middle tone with gliding foot, which is personified in the cow that is milked into the *gharma,*" *sarpaṇa-svabhāva-pādām mādhyamikām vācam gharmadhugrūpeṇāvasthitām.* (The thunder is often called the *mādhyamikā vāk,* and we have in I.164.28,29 a similar comparison of the lowing cow, while being milked, to the cloud as it thunders while raining.) The cow (*soma-krayani*) which is given as the price of the *Soma*, has to take seven steps, and it is considered to be *vāk* personified, see *Taitt. Saṁhitā*, VI.1.7.8. The St. Petersb, Dict. takes *saptapadīm* as an epithet of *iṣam ūrjam*, "für alle Bedürfnisse genügend."

७२९८. सोमस्य मित्रावरुणोदिता सूर आ ददे। तदातुरस्य भेषजम्॥१७॥

17. *Mitra* and *Varuṇa*, I take the *Soma* when the sun is risen; it is medicine to the sick.

I Take— Sāyaṇa explains *adade* as *svīkaroti*, "he takes," unless we should read *svīkaromi*.

७२९९. उतो न्वस्य यत्पदं हर्यतस्य निधान्यम्। परि द्यां जिह्वयातनत्॥१८॥

18. *Agni*,—standing in the place which I, the eager offerer, choose as the spot for presenting the oblations,—fills the sky on every side with his blaze.

In the place— Sc. the *uttara-vedi* or altar outside the enclosure.

[सूक्त-७३]

[**ऋषि–** गोपवन आत्रेय अथवा सप्तवधि । **देवता–** अश्विनीकुमारौ।
छन्द– गायत्री]

७३००. उदीराथामृतायते युञ्जाथामश्विना रथम्। अन्ति षद्भूतु वामवः॥१॥

1. Rise, *Aśvins*, on my behalf, as I prepare to sacrifice; yoke your ear; let your protection abide near me.

७३०१. निमिषश्चिज्जवीयसा रथेना यातमश्विना। अन्ति षद्भूतु वामवः॥२॥

2. Come, *Aśvins*, in your chariot which moves quicker than the twinkling of an eye; let your protection abide near me.

७३०२. उप स्तृणीतमत्रये हिमेन घर्ममश्विना। अन्ति षद्भूतु वामवः॥३॥

3. *Aśvins*, you covered the hot (fire) with cold (water) for *Atri*; let your protection abide near me.

Water for *Atri*— *Cf. Rgveda*, I.116.8.

७३०३. कुह स्थः कुह जगमथुः कुह श्येनेव पेतथुः।
अन्ति षद्भूतु वामवः॥४॥

4. Where are you? Whither are you gone? Whither have you flown like hawks? Let your protection abide near me.

७३०४. यद्द्य कर्हि कर्हि चिच्छ्रूयातमिमं हवम्।
अन्ति षद्भूतु वामवं:॥५॥

5. If to-day, at some time, in some place, you would but hear my invocation,—let your protection abide near me.

७३०५. अश्विना यामहूतेमा नेदिष्ठं याम्याप्यम्। अन्ति षद्भूतु वामवं:॥६॥

6. The *Aśvins* are earnestly to be invoked in emergency; I enter into close friendship with them; let your protection abide near me.

I Enter into close Friendship—*Cf.* var. lect., and the commentary on I.36.12.

७३०६. अवंन्तमत्रये गृहं कृणुतं युवमश्विना। अन्ति षद्भूतु वामवं:॥७॥

7. *Aśvins*, you made a sheltering house for *Atri*; let your protection abide near me.

A sheltering house for Atri— Sāyaṇa adds, "When being burned in the cell of the consecrated fire."

७३०७. वरेथे अग्निमातपो वदते वल्वत्रये। अन्ति षद्भूतु वामवं:॥८॥

8. You stayed the fire from its fierceness for *Atri*, while he praised you acceptably; let your protection abide near me.

७३०८. प्र सप्तवध्रिराशसा धारामग्नेरंशायत। अन्ति षद्भूतु वामवं:॥९॥

9. Through his praise of you *Saptavadhri* set the fire's flame-point (to his basket); let your protection abide near me.

Cf. Ṛgveda, V.78.5.

७३०९. इहा गंतं वृषण्वसू शृणुतं मं इमं हवम्।
अन्ति षद्भूतु वामवं:॥१०॥

10. Come hither, lords of abundant wealth, hear this my invocation; let your protection abide near me.

७३१०. किमिदं वां पुराणवज्जरंतोरिव शस्यते। अन्ति षद्भूतु वामवं:॥११॥

11. Why is this (repeated invocation) addressed to you as if you were decrepit like old men? Let your protection abide near me.

As if you were Decrepit—Sāyaṇa explains it, "as we see in the world that an old man does not come, though often called, so too is it with you."

७३११. समानं वां सजात्यं समानो बन्धुरश्विना। अन्ति षद्भूतु वामवं:॥१२॥

12. *Aśvins*, your relationship is common and you have a common kinsman; let your protection abide near me.

Sāyaṇa's Comm. is here obscure, but he explains the text as meaning
that the two *Aśvins* were both born from the wife of the sun (sc. *Vicasvat*),
who had assumed the form of a mare. (*Cf.* VII.72.2 and the passage from
the *Bṛhaddevatā* quoted in the Comm.) He seems to explain the common
kinsman as meaning either the sacrificial ladle or the *ṛṣi* himself (*cf.*
VIII.27.10).

७३१२. यो वां रजांस्यश्विना रथो वियाति रोदसी।

अन्ति षद्भूतु वामवः॥१३॥

13. Your chariot, *Aśvins*, moves swiftly through the worlds,
through heaven and earth; let your protection abide near me.

७३१३. आ नो गव्येभिरश्वैः सहस्त्रैरुप गच्छतम्।

अन्ति षद्भूतु वामवः॥१४॥

14. Come to us with thousands of herds of cattle and horses;
let your protection abide near me.

७३१४. मा नो गव्येभिरश्वैः सहस्त्रेभिरति ख्यतम्।

अन्ति षद्भूतु वामवः॥१५॥

15. Pass us not by with your thousands of herds of cattle and
horses; let your protection abide near us.

Pass us not By— I have adopted this explanation of *mā ati khyatam*
from Sāyaṇa's Comm. on I.4.3. He here takes *atikhyaḥ* as for
pratikhyaḥ(*pratyākhyaḥ*), "do not reject (or neglect) us,"etc.

७३१५. अरुणप्सुरुषा अभूदकर्ज्योतिर्ऋतावरी। अन्ति षद्भूतु वामवः॥१६॥

16. The purple-tinted Dawn has appeared, the mistress of the
sacrifice spreads her light; let your protection abide near me.

Mistress of the Sacrifice— *Ṛtāvarī* is sometimes explained as
yajñavatī, sometimes as *satyavatī*, "truthful".

७३१६. अश्विना सु विचाकशद्वृक्षं परशुमाँ इव।

अन्ति षद्भूतु वामवः॥१७॥

17. *Aśvins*, the splendidly-brilliant (sun cleaves the darkness)
as the woodman with his axe a tree; let your protection abide near
me.

७३१७. पुरं न धृष्णवा रुज कृष्णया बाधितो विशा।

अन्ति षद्भूतु वामवः॥१८॥

18. O bold *Saptavadhri*, distressed by the entangling and detaining (basket), break through it as through a city; let your protection (*Aśvins*) abide near me.

This is supposed to be addressed by Saptavadhri to himself, or by Gopavana to Saptavadhri.

Distressed by . . . . Basket— So Sāyaṇa; but kṛṣṇayā ye bādhito viśā probably means "distressed by the black people."

[सूक्त-७४]

[**ऋषि**– गोपवन आत्रेय। **देवता**– अग्नि, १३-१५ श्रुतर्वा आर्क्ष्य।
छन्द– गायत्री, १, ४, ७, १०, १३-१५ अनुष्टुप्।]

७३१८. विशोविशो वो अतिथिं वाजयन्तः पुरुप्रियम्।
अग्निं वो दुर्यं वचः स्तुषे शूषस्य मन्मभिः॥१॥

1. Food-desiring (priests, worship) *Agni*, who is the guest of all mankind, beloved of many; I address to him in your behalf a domestic homage with hymns, for the attainment of happiness;
Sāmaveda, 87, 1564.

Domestic— *Duryam* is explained by Sāyaṇa (II.38.5) as gṛhyam gṛhe bhavam. Should not the *guhā hitam* of the Comm. here be gṛhe or gṛhāya hitam "placed in, or suitable for, the house," cf. VIII. 1.11, gṛhebhyo hitā.

७३१९. यं जनासो हविष्मन्तो मित्रं न सर्पिरासुतिम्। प्रशंसन्ति प्रशस्तिभिः॥२॥

2. (That *Agni*), to whom clarified butter is offered, whom man, bearing oblations, worship with praises as a friend;
Sāmaveda, 1565.

As a Friend— *Mitram na* is also explained "like the sun."

७३२०. पन्यांसं जातवेदसं यो देवतात्युद्यता। हव्यान्यैरयद्दिवि॥३॥

3. *Jātavedas*, the earnest praiser of his worshipper, who sends to heaven the oblations presented in the sacrifice.
Sāmaveda, 1566.

७३२१. आगन्म वृत्रहन्तमं ज्येष्ठमग्निमानवम्।
यस्य श्रुतर्वा बृहन्नार्क्षो अनीक एधते॥४॥

4. We have come to that most excellent *Agni*, mightiest destroyer of the wicked, the benefactor of men, in whose army (of rays) *Śrutarvān*, the mighty son of *Ṛkṣa*, waxes great.

Sāmaveda, 89, but with *aganma* for *āganma*, and reading the second line as *ya sma śrutarvānnārkṣye bṛhadānīka idhyate*, "who with his host of rays is kindled in *Śrutarvān*, the son of *Ṛkṣa*."

७३२२. अमृतं जातवेदसं तिरस्तमांसि दर्शतम्। घृताहवनमीड्यम्॥५॥

5. (We have come) to the immortal *Jātavedas*, who shows light across the darkness, well worthy of praise, and receiving the offerings of *ghī*;

७३२३. सबाधो यं जना इमेऽग्निं हव्येभिरीळते। जुह्वानासो यतस्रुच:॥६॥

6. That *Agni*, whom these crowding worshippers honour with oblations, offering to him with up-lifted ladled.

७३२४. इयं ते नव्यसी मतिरग्ने अधाय्यस्मदा।
मन्द्र सुजात सुक्रतोऽमूर दस्मातिथे॥७॥

7. This new hymn has been made by us for you, O joyful, well-born *Agni*, glorious in deeds, unbewildered, beautiful, the guest (of man);

Has been made by us for you— Sāyaṇa explains *adhāyy asmadā* as "has been borne (or conceived) in us for you," *asmāsu dhṛtam abhūt*.

७३२५. सा ते अग्ने शन्तमा चनिष्ठा भवतु प्रिया। तया वर्धस्व सुष्टुत:॥८॥

8. *Agni*, may it be dear to you, most pleasant and most agreeable— well praised by it, to you wax great.

Most pleasant and most Agreeable— Sāyaṇa explains *caniṣṭhā* as *atiśayenānnavatī*, "most richly endowed with food," but in vii.70.2 he allowed in a similar phrase the alternative rendering *kamanīyatamā*.

७३२६. सा द्युम्नैर्द्युम्निनी बृहदुपोप श्रवसि श्रव:। दधीत वृत्रतूर्ये॥९॥

9. May this (hymn) the rich source of wealth, heap abundance on our abundance (with stores won from our enemies) in battle.

७३२७. अश्वमिद्गां रथप्रां त्वेषमिन्द्रं न सत्पतिम्।
यस्य श्रवांसि तूर्वथ पन्यंपन्यं च कृष्टय:॥१०॥

10. (Worship), you men, the bright (*Agni*), who goes like a horse and fills our chariots (with spoil), who protects the good like *Indra*, and by whose might ye ravage the stores (of your enemies) and all their wonderful (wealth).

Who goes like a Horse— Sāyaṇa explains *gām* by *gantāram*, as in i.121.9, and iv.22.8.

Wonderful— Lit. "worthy to be piaised," *paṇyam*.

७३२८. यं त्वा॑ गोपव॑नो गि॒रा चनि॑ष्ठदग्ने अङ्गिरः।
स पा॑वक श्रुधी॒ हव॑म्॥११॥

11. *Agni, Angiras,* whom *Gopavana* by his praise has made the
especial giver of food,—O purifier, hear his prayer.

But with *tam* and *janiṣṭhad* or *yam* and *caniṣṭhad;* on the latter hard
word *cf.* Benfey's *Sāma-V.* Gloss. It would seem to mean "has
gladdened"

७३२९. यं त्वा॑ जना॒स ई॑ळ॒ते स॒बाधो॑ वाज॑सातये। स बो॑धि वृत्रतू॒र्ये॑॥१२॥

12. O you whom the crowding worshippers praise for the
obtainment of food, attend to them for the destruction of their
enemies.

For the Destruction of their Enemies— Or as in *v.*9) "in battle,"
*vṛtraturye. Sāma V.,*1565,

७३३०. अ॒हं हु॑वान आर्क्षे॒ श्रुत॑र्वणि मद॒च्युति॑।
श॒र्धा॑सीव स्तु॒का॒विनां॑ मृक्षा॒ शीर्षा॑ च॒तुर्णा॑म्॥१३॥

13. Summoned before *Śrutarvān,* the son of *Ṛkṣa,* the humbler
of the pride of his enemies, (I stroke) with my hand the heads of
the four horses (which he has given me), as (men stroke) the long
wool of rams.

With my Hand— Sāyaṇa reads *vṛkṣā,* which he explains *keśavantī,*
but he also gives another explanation, *hastena,* which might apply to the
true reading *mṛkṣā.* In fact this word seems to suggest his supplied verb
unmṛjāmi. The St. Petersb. Dict. takes *mṛkṣā),* has the Ist person Sing.
Imperative of *mrakṣ* (for *mṛkṣāni),* "let me stroke."

७३३१. मां च॒त्वार॑ आश॒वः श॒विष्ठ॑स्य द्रवि॒त्नवः॑।
सु॒रथा॑सो अ॒भि प्रयो॑ वक्ष॒न्वयो॒ न तुग्र्य॑म्॥१४॥

14. Four swift horses of that most mighty king, yoked to a
splendid car, bear me forth to seize the substance (of my enemies),
as the ships bore home the son of *Tugra.*

The Son of Tugra— For *Bhujyu's* legend *cf.* Vol. I, verse 1216
Vayaḥ "birds" seems a poetical metaphor for "ships."

७३३२. स॒त्यमि॒त्त्वा॑ महेनदि प॒रुष्ण्यव॑ देदिशम्।
नेमा॑पो अ॒श्वदा॑तरः श॒विष्ठा॑दस्ति॒ मर्त्यः॑॥१५॥

15. Verily I address you, O great river *Parushni;* O waters,
there is no mortal who gives horses more liberally than this most
mighty (monarch).

[सूक्त-७५]

[ऋषि– विरूप आङ्गिरस। देवता– अग्नि। छन्द– गायत्री।]

७३३३. युक्ष्वा हि देवहूतमाँ अश्वाँ अग्ने रथीरिव। नि होता पूर्व्यः सदः॥१॥

1. *Agni*, like a charioteer yoke your god-invoking steeds; eat thyself first, the invoker.

White Yajurveda. 13.37.

७३३४. उत नो देव देवाँ अच्छा वोचो विदुष्टरः। श्रद्विश्वा वार्या कृधि॥२॥

2. Divine (*Agni*), proclaim us to the gods as profoundly killed; assure to us all desirable things;—

Profoundly skilled— Sāyaṇa explains *viduṣṭaras* as *vidvattamān*; but it is really an epithet of *Agni*, "you most wise."

७३३५. त्वं ह यद्यविष्ठ्य सहसः सूनवाहुत। ऋतावा यज्ञियो भुवः॥३॥

3. Since you are truthful and worthy of sacrifice, O most youthful, son of strength and everywhere honoured with offerings.

७३३६. अयमग्निः सहस्त्रिणो वाजस्य शतिनस्पतिं। मूर्धा कवी रयीणाम्॥४॥

4. This *Agni* is the lord of hundredfold and thousandfold food; he is the head, the seer, (the lord) of wealth.

Yajurv-V., 15.21 Mahīdhara takes *Murdha* with *rayīṇām*, "you who are the head (or best) of wealth."

७३३७. तं नेमिमृभवो यथा नमस्व सहूतिभिः। नेदीयो यज्ञमङ्गिरः॥५॥

5. O *Angiras*, with the deities associated in the invocate on, draw this offering near you as the *Ṛbhus* (bend the circumference of a wheel.

Cf. vii. 32.20.

७३३८. तस्मै नूनमभिद्यवे वाचा विरूप नित्यया। वृष्णे चोदस्व सुष्टुतिम्॥६॥

6. *Virūpa*, with constant voice address your praise to this well-pleased showerer (of blessings).

With Constant Voice— Sāyaṇa naturally takes *nityayā vācā* as alluding to the eternal nature of the hymns, *utpatti-rahitayā vācā mantrarūpayā*.

Well-pleased— Sāyaṇa explains *abhidyave* here as *abhigatatṛptaye*; his more usual explanation is *abhigatadīptaye*.

७३३९. कमु ष्विदस्य सेनयाग्नेरपाकचक्षसः। पणिं गोषु स्तरामहे॥७॥

7. What strong enemy shall we overthrow, to win kine, by the help of the host of this *Agni* of unmeasured radiance?

The Host— Sāyaṇa explains ''the host'' as the rays.

७३४०. मा नो॑ देवानां॒ विश॒: प्रस्नाती॑रिवोष्ना॑:। कृशं॒ न हा॑सुरघ्न्या॑:॥८॥

8. May he not (forsake) us, the liegemen of the gods, as the milk-streaming cows (forsake not); the kine abandon not a little (calf).

७३४१. मा न॒: समस्य दूढ्ये॑: परि॑द्वेषसो अं॒हति॑:।

ऊर्मि॒र्न नाव॒मा व॑धीत्॥९॥

9. Let not the onset of any evil-minded adversary harm us as the wave (overwhelms) a ship.

७३४२. नम॑स्ते अग्न॒ ओज॑से गृ॒णन्ति॑ देव कृ॒ष्टय॑:। अमै॑रमित्र॒मर्दय॥१०॥

10. Divine *Agni*, men utter your praises for the attainment of strength; by strength destroy the enemy.
Sāmaveda, 11, 1648.

७३४३. कुवित्सु नो॒ गवि॒ष्टये॒ऽग्ने॑ संवे॒षिषो॑ र॒यिम्। उ॒रु॒कृ॒दुरुणस्कृधि॥११॥

11. *Agni*, send us abundance of wealth to satisfy our desires; giver of free space, grant us abundant room.
Sāmaveda, 1649. Sāyaṇa takes *gaviṣṭi* in its etymological sense as *gavām eṣaṇāya*. I have given it a general meaning.

७३४४. मा नो॒ अस्मि॒न्महा॑धने॒ परा॑ व॒र्गभा॑रभृद्य॒था। संव॒र्गं सं र॒यिं ज॑य॥१२॥

12. Leave us not in this conflict as a bearer his burden win for us the plundered wealth of our foes.
Sāmaveda, 1650, with *agne* for *asmin.*

७३४५. अन्य॒मस्म॒द्द्रिया इय॑मग्ने॒ सिष॑क्तु दुच्छुना॑।

वर्धा॑ नो॒ अमव॑च्छव॑:॥१३॥

13. *Agni*, may your plagues pursue some other to terrify him; increase our vigorous strength in battle.

७३४६. यस्याजु॑ष॒न्नम॑स्विन॒: शमी॑मदु॒र्मख॑स्य वा। तं घे॑दग्निर्वृधाव॑ति॥१४॥

14. *Agni* especially protects (in battle) that praiser or zealous sacrificer whose offerings he has attended.
Especially Protects— Sāyaṇa explains *vṛdhā avati* as *viśeṣeṇa gacchati.* It rather means ''*Agni* protects him with blessing.''

७३४७. परस्या॒ अधि॑ संव॒तोऽव॑राँ अ॒भ्या त॑र। यत्राह॒मस्मि॒ ताँ अ॑व॥१५॥

15. Deliver us wholly from the hostile army, shield those among whom I am (lord).
Yajurveda, II.71.

७३४८. विद्या हि ते पुरा वयमग्ने पितुर्यथावसः। अधा ते सुम्नमीमहे॥१६॥

16. We know your protection, *Agni*, as of a father in former times, therefore we (again) desire of you that happiness.

[सूक्त -७६]

[ऋषि- कुरुसुति काण्व। देवता- इन्द्र। छन्द- गायत्री।]

७३४९. इमं नु मायिनं हुव इन्द्रमीशानमोजसा। मरुत्वन्तं न वृञ्जसे॥१॥

1. I invoke now for the destruction of my enemies the wise *Indra* attended by the *Maruts*, ruling all by his power.

७३५०. अयमिन्द्रो मरुत्सखा वि वृत्रस्याभिनच्छिरः। वज्रेण शतपर्वणा॥२॥

2. *Indra*, attended by the *Maruts*, has cleft the head of *Vṛtra* with his hundred-jointed thunderbolt.

७३५१. वावृधानो मरुत्सखेन्द्रो वि वृत्रमैरयत्। सृजन्त्समुद्रिया अपः॥३॥

3. *Indra* increasing in might, attended by the *Maruts*, has torn *Vṛtra* asunder, letting loose the waters of the firmament.

७३५२. अयं ह येन वा इदं स्वर्मरुत्वता जितम्। इन्द्रेण सोमपीतये॥४॥

4. This is that *Indra*, by whom assisted by the *Maruts*, yonder heaven was conquered, to quaff the *Soma*.

Yonder Heaven— Sāyaṇa gives as alternative renderings of *svaḥ* "all (sacrificial) actions," and this world," *sarvam karma yadvedam sarvam jagat.*

७३५३. मरुत्वन्तमृजीषिणमोजस्वन्तं विरप्शिनम्। इन्द्रं गीर्भिर्हवामहे॥५॥

5. We invoke with our praises the mighty *Indra*, accompanied by the *Maruts*, the vigorous accepter of the residue of the oblation.

The Residue of the Oblation— *Rjiṣiṇam*, the residue of the *Soma* (*ṛjiṣa*) being offered at the *tṛtīya* evening oblation.

७३५४. इन्द्रं प्रत्नेन मन्मना मरुत्वन्तं हवामहे। अस्य सोमस्य पीतये॥६॥

6. With an ancient hymn we invoke *Indra* with the *Maruts*, to drink this *Soma*.

७३५५. मरुत्वाँ इन्द्र मीढ्वः पिबा सोमं शतक्रतो। अस्मिन्यज्ञे पुरुष्टुत॥७॥

7. *Indra*, *Śatakratu*, showerer (of blessings), drink the *Soma* at this offering, accompanied by the *Maruts*, O invoked of many.

७३५६. तुभ्येदिन्द्र मरुत्वते सुताः सोमासो अद्रिवः।
हृदा हूयन्त उक्थिनः॥८॥

8. Thunderer *Indra*, to you with the *Maruts* are these *Soma*-libations effused,— they are offered to you in faith, with recited hymns.

In Faith— Sāyaṇa explains *manasā* as *bhaktyā*.

७३५७. पिबेदिन्द्र मरुत्संखा सुतं सोमं दिविष्टिषु। वज्रं शिशान ओजसा॥९॥

9. Drink, *Indra*, with your friends the *Maruts*, this *Soma* effused on the recurring sacred days, and sharpen your thunderbolt with (renewed) vigour.

Cf. i.86.4. *Diviṣṭiṣu* may also mean "in these solemnities which are means to obtain heaven," *cf.* viii.4.19.

७३५८. उत्तिष्ठन्नोर्जसा सह पीत्वी शिप्रे अवेपयः। सोममिन्द्र चमू सुतम्॥१०॥

10. Rising up in your strength, *Indra*, you did shake your jaws, when you had quaffed the *Soma* Pressed between the two boards.

Sāmaveda, 988. (Benfey, "schüttelst die Lippen du,") *Yajur-V.*, 8.39.

७३५९. अनु त्वा रोदसी उभे क्रक्षमाणमकृपेताम्। इन्द्र यद्दस्युहाभवः॥११॥

11. Let heaven and earth follow you, *Indra*, as you smitest, when you beat down the *Dasyu*.

Sāmaveda, 989, with *spardhamānam adadetam* for *krakṣamāṇam akṛpetām*. Sāyaṇa takes *anu akṛpetām* as *anukalpayetām*. Grassmann derives it from *krap*, "heaven and earth longed after you, as you smotest, etc."

७३६०. वाचमष्टापदीमहं नवस्रक्तिमृतस्पृशम्। इन्द्रात् परि तन्वं ममे॥१२॥

12. I make this sacrificial hymn, reaching to the eight points (of the sky) and rising to a ninth (the sun in the zenith), though it is less than (the dimensions of) *Indra*.

Sāma-V., 990, with *ṛtāvṛdham* for *ṛtaspṛśam*. Benfey takes *aṣṭ apadīm navasraktim* as referring to the metre of the hymn, "einen achtfüssigen Gesang, aus neun Gliedern bestechenden lieblichen web' um *Indra* ich." Sc too Grassmann.

[सूक्त -७७]

[ऋषि– कुरुसुति काण्व। देवता– इन्द्र। छन्द– गायत्री, १०-११ प्रगाथ
(समा बृहती, विषमा सतोबृहती)।]

७३६१. जज्ञानो नु शतक्रतुर्वि पृच्छदिति मातरम्।
क उग्राः के ह शृण्विरे॥१॥

1. As soon as he was born *Śatakratu* asked his mother, who are the mighty, who are renowned?

Cf. viii.45.4.

७३६२. आर्दौ शवस्यब्रवीदौर्णवाभमहीशुवम्। ते पुत्र सन्तु निष्ठुर:॥२॥

2. His strong mother answered,—*Aurṇavābha* and *Ahiṣuva*, be these, my son the foes whom you shalt overcome.

Cf. viii.32,26.

Whom you shalt overcome— Sāyaṇa explains *niṣṭuraḥ* as *tava nistāraṇīyāḥ;* the St. Petersb. Dict. gives "die keinen Ueberwinder haben."

७३६३. समित्तान्वृत्रहाखिदत्खे अराँइव खेदया। प्रवृद्धो दस्युहाभवत्॥३॥

3. The slayer of *Vṛtra* dragged them along as spokes (are tied fast) with a rope in the nave of a chariot wheel; he swelled in vigour, the slayer of enemies.

With a Rope— *Cf.* note on viii.72.8.

७३६४. एकंया प्रतिधापिबत्साकं सरांसि त्रिंशतम् इन्द्र: सोमस्य काणुका॥४।

4. At one draught *Indra* drank at once thirty lakes filled with *Soma*.

Yāska comments on this verse in *Nirukta*, v. 11. He gives the explanation in the text as that of the ceremonialists (*yājñikaḥ*) which applies the verse to the thirty *uktha* vessels presented at the mid-day offering; the *nairuktāḥ* take the verse as referring to the fifteen days and nights in which the collected light of the moon is gradually absorbed. Yāska is evidently uncertain as to the meaning of the word *kāṇukā*, which he explains in several ways, either as a neuter plural agreeing with *sarāṁsi*, or as a nom, sing, agreeing with *Indra*.

७३६५. अभि गन्धर्वमतृणदबुध्नेषु रज: स्वा। इन्द्रो ब्रह्मभ्य इद्वृधे॥५॥

5. In the realms (of the sky) where the foot finds-no resting-place, *Indra* shattered the cloud to bring increase to the *Brāhmaṇas*.

The Cloud— The *gandharva*, *Gandharvam*.

To the Brāhmaṇas— *Brahmebhyah*.

७३६६. निरांविध्यद् गिरिभ्य आ धारयत्पक्कमोदनम्। इन्द्रो बुन्दं स्वाततम्॥६॥

6. *Indra* smote (rain) from the clouds with his farstretched arrow, he secured boiled rice (for men).

७३६७. शतब्रध्न इषुस्तव सहस्रपर्ण एक इत्। यमिन्द्र चकृषे युजम्॥७॥

7. That single shaft of your, *Indra*, which you make your ally, is hundred-pointed, thousand-feathered.

७३६८. तेन॒ स्तोतृ॑भ्य आ भ॑र नृभ्यो॒ नारि॑भ्यो॒ अत्त॑वे।
　　　स॒द्यो जा॒त ऋ॑भुष्ठिर॒॥८॥

8. Forthwith increased (by our offerings), do you, mighty and firm, by that (weapon) bring (wealth) for sustenance to us your praisers, our children, and our wives.

७३६९. ए॒ता च्यौत्ना॑नि॒ ते कृ॒ता वर्षि॑ष्ठानि॒ परी॑णसा। हृ॒दा वी॒ड्व॑धारयः॒॥९॥

9. These gigantic far-reaching efforts were put forth by you; you did fix them firm in your thought.

These Gigantic Far-Reaching Efforts— *Cyautnāni* is generally explained as *balāni*, "powers," "energies"; here Sāyaṇa takes it as referring to "the mountains," as the supporters or stays of the earth, *bhūmeḥ kīla badhadhāraṇāni* (see *var. lect. cf.* VII.99.3.

७३७०. विश्वे॑त्ता॒ विष्णु॒राभ॑रदुरुक्र॒मस्त्वे॑षि॒तः।
　　　श॒तं म॑हि॒षान्क्षीर॑पा॒कमो॑द॒नं व॒राह॑मिन्द्र॒ एमु॑षम्॒॥१०॥

10. The wide-traversing Sun, despatched by you, brings (to the world) all these (waters which you createst); he brings hundreds of cattle and rice boiled in milk; it is *Indra* who slays the water-stealing boar.

The Scholiast offers two interpretations of this verse. The first, that of the grammatical school (*nairukta*), is given in the text. The sun (here called *Viṣṇu*), as the bringer of rain, is said to bring the cattle and food which the rain produces; the "boar" *varāha* is one of the personifications of the cloud as smitten by *Indra's* thunderbolt (*cf. Nirukta*, v.4). The mythological school (*aitīhasikā*) take the verse more literally, and their explanation is given in the *Caraka Brāhmaṇa*. The legend is, however, told more distinctly in the *Taitt. Saṁh.*, VI.2.4. It is there related that "the personified sacrifice concealed itself from the gods, and assuming the form of *Viṣṇu*, entered the earth. The gods, stretching our their hands, sought in vain to lay hold of it; but wherever it turned, *Indra*, outstripping it, stood in front of it. It said to him, 'Who is this that, outstripping me, always stands in front of me?' He answered, 'I slay in inaccessible places, but who are you?' 'I can bring out from inaccessible places.' Then it said to him, 'You say that you can slay in inaccessible places,—if this be so, the boar *vāmamoṣa* (*Vāmamuṣa* in *Ch. Br.*) guards for the asuras, behind the seven mountains, the wealth which the gods must obtain; prove your title by slaying that boar.' *Indra*, seizing up a tuft of *darbha*-grass, pierced those mountains and slew him. Then he said to the sacrifice, 'You said that you could bring out from inaccessible places; bring him out from thence.' It brought out all the instruments of the sacrifice (according to

the Comm. the altar, *Soma*-jars, cups, etc.), and gave them to the gods.''
The legend of the *Caraka* only differs in making the boar hide behind
twenty-one stone cities. The seven mountains, according to the Schol., are
the four *dīkṣās* or initiatory rites and the three *upasads*; the boar
vāmamoṣa (''stealer of precious things'') is the personified ceremony of
pressing the *Soma*-juice. The whole legend appears to have arisen from
the present passage and that in I.61.7.

७३७१. तुविक्षं ते सुकृतं सूमयं धनुः साधुबुन्दो हिरण्ययः।
उ_भा ते॑ बाहू॒ रण्या॒ सुसंस्कृत ऋदूपे चिंदूदुवृधा॑।।११।।

11. Far-darting is your well-made auspicious bow, unfailing is
your golden arrow; your two warlike arms are ready equipped,
destructively overthrowing, destructively piercing.

This difficult verse is explained in Yāska's *Nirukta*, VI.33; but his
explanation of *ṛdūpe cid ṛdūvṛdhā* is very doubtful and confused, *cf.* Prof.
Roth's Comm. The St. Petersburg Dict. explains the words ''like two bees
delighting in sweetness,'' taking *ṛdu* as for *mṛdu*, sc. the *madhu* or *Soma*-
juice.

[सूक्त-७८]

[ऋषि– कुरुसुति काण्व। देवता– इन्द्र। छन्द– गायत्री, १० बृहती)।]

७३७२. पुरोळाशं नो॑ अन्ध॒स इन्द्र॒ सहस्रमा भर। शता च॑ शूर गोनाम्॑।।१।।

1. (Accepting) our offering of sacrificial viands, O hero *Indra*,
bring us thousands and hundreds of cows.

७३७३. आ नो॑ भर॒ व्यञ्जनं॑ गामश्वमभ्यञ्जनम्। सचा॑ मना हिरण्यया॑।।२।।

2. Bring us condiments, cows, horses, and oil, (bring us) with
them precious golden (vessels).

Precious Golden Vessels— Sāyaṇa explains *mana* by *mananīyāni*,
the St. Petersb, Dict. takes it as ''a vessel'' or ''a weight,'' *i.e.*, ''with a
weight of gold.''

७३७४. उत नः॑ कर्णशोभना पुरूणि॑ धृष्ण॒वा भर। त्वं हि श्रृण्विषे व॑सो।।३।।

3. O resolute one, bring us many ear-ornaments; giver of
dwellings, you are renowned.

७३७५. नकीं॑ वृधीक इन्द्र॒ ते॒ न सुषा न सुदा उत॑।
नान्यस्त्वच्छूर वाघतः॑।।४।।

4. There is no prosperer other than you, no divider of the spoil,
no giver of boons; O hero, there is no (leader) of the sacrificer
other than you.

७३७६. नकीमिन्द्रो निर्कर्तवे न शक्र: परिशक्तवे। विश्वं शृणोति पश्यति।।५।।

5. *Indra* cannot be brought low, he cannot be over-powered,—he hears, he sees all.

७३७७. स मन्युं मर्त्यानामदब्धो नि चिकीषते। पुरा निदश्चिकीषते।।६।।

6. Unharmed he brings low the wrath of mortals; ere any on can reproach him, he brings him low.

७३७८. क्रत्व इत्पूर्णमुदरं तुरस्यास्ति विधत:। वृत्रघ्न: सोमपाव्न:।।७।।

7. The belly of the *Soma*-drinker, the eager slayer of *Vṛtra*, is filled by the sacrificer's offering.

७३७९. त्वे वसूनि सङ्गता विश्वा च सोम सौभगा। सुदात्वपरिह्वृता।।८।।

8. In you, O drinker of the *Soma*, are treasures stored, and all precious things and unblemished gifts.

Drinker of the Soma— *I.e.,* Soma, here applied to *Indra,* as possessing it (*somavān*) or as identified with it after drinking it.

७३८०. त्वामिद्यवयुर्मम कामो गव्युहिरण्ययु:। त्वामश्वयुरेषते।।९।।

9. To you my desire hastens, seeking barley, cows and gold,—to you it hastens seeking horses.

Barley— *Yava* properly means barley, but may be here used generally. The St. Petersburg Dict. remarks *sub-v.,* that in the *Atharvaveda,* and still more in the *Brāhmaṇas, yava* and *vrīhi* (rice) are the principal kinds of corn, while rice is not mentioned by name in the *Ṛgveda.*

७३८१. तवेदिन्द्राहमाशसा हस्ते दात्रं चना ददे।

दिनस्य वा मघवन्त्सम्भृतस्य वा पूर्धि यवस्य काशिना।।१०।।

10. I take my sickle also in hand, *Indra*, with a prayer to you; fill it, *Maghavan*, with a handful of barley already cut or piled.

It would appear as if the field were a barren one and the poet sought from *Indra* a harvest which he had not sown.

[सूक्त-७९]

[ऋषि- कृत्नु भार्गव। **देवता-** सोम। **छन्द-** गायत्री, ९ अनुष्टुप्।]

७३८२. अयं कृत्नुरगृभीतो विश्वजिदुद्भिदितिसोम:। ऋषिर्विप्र: काव्येन।।१।।

1. This all-creating *soma*, obstructed by none, the conqueror of all, the producer of fruit, the seer, the wise, (is to be praised) with a hymn.

The Conqueror of All, Etc.— *Viśvajit* and *udbhid* are also the
names of two special *Soma* ceremonies, and the *Soma* may be addressed
under these names as the principal means of their accomplishment.

७३८३. अभ्यूर्णोति यन्नग्नं भिषक्ति विश्वं यतुरम्।
प्रेमन्धः ख्यन्निः श्रोणो भूत्॥२॥

2. He covers what is naked, he heals all that is sick, the blind
sees, the lame walks.

७३८४. त्वं सोम तनूकृद्भ्यो द्वेषोभ्योऽन्यकृतेभ्यः।
उरु यन्तासि वरूथम्॥३॥

3. *Soma*, you offer us a wide shelter from the wasting enmities
wrought by our foes.

Yajurveda, 5.35. Sāyaṇa seems to take *yantāsi* as *bhavasi*; Mahīdhara
explains it, "you the restrain (*yanta*) from enmities, etc., you are a wide
shelter."

७३८५. त्वं चित्ती तव दक्षैर्दिव आ पृथिव्या ऋजीषिन्।
यावीरघस्य चिद् द्वेषः॥४॥

4. O *Rjiṣin*, by your wisdom and might drive away the enmity
of our oppressor from the heaven and the earth.

O Rjiṣin— *I.e.,* you who possess the remains of the *Soma*, offered in
the third *savana, cf. Taitt. Samhitā* VI.1.6. *Rjīṣin* is translated in the St.
Petersburg Dict "vorstürzend, ereilend."

७३८६. अर्थिनो यन्ति चेदर्थं गच्छानिद्दुषो रातिम्।
ववृज्युस्तृष्यतः कामम्॥५॥

5. The petitioners seek for wealth, they attend the bounty of
the liberal; (by you) men pour out the desire of the thirsty.

७३८७. विदद्यत्पूर्व्यं नष्टमुदीमृतायुमीरयत्। प्रेमायुस्तारीदतीर्णम्॥६॥

6. (*Soma*) urges him on when the sacrificer obtains (by
offerings) him old lost wealth, he lengthens out his unending life.

He Lengthens out his unending life— There, is no Comm. for this
last clause.

७३८८. सुशेवो नो मृळयाकुरद्दृप्तक्रतुरवातः। भवा नः सोम शं हृदे॥७॥

7. Most gracious and conferring joy, void of pride in your acts,
and never failing, dwell, *Soma*, auspiciously in our hearts.

७३८९. मा न: सोम सं वीविजो मा वि बीभिषथा राजन्।
मा नो हार्दि त्विषा वधी:॥८॥

8. O *Soma*, cause us not to tremble, frighten us not, O king; smite not our hearts with your brightness.

७३९०. अव यत्स्वे सधस्थे देवानां दुर्मतीरीक्षे।
राजन्नप द्विष: सेध मीढ्वो अप स्निध: सेध॥९॥

9. When in my house I watch against the enemies of the gods, then, O king, drive away those who hate us,—O showerer of blessings, drive away those who would harm us.

Showerer of Blessings— Sāyaṇa explains *mīḍhvaḥ* "effuser of the Soma," *somarasasya sektā*, but it seems more natural to take it here as elsewhere (as II.8.1. of *Agni*) *phalasya sektā*, or (as VII.89.7. of *Varuṇa*) *kāmānāṁ sektā*.

[सूक्त-८०]

[ऋषि– एकद्यू नौधस। देवता– इन्द्र, १० देवगण।
छन्द– गायत्री, १० त्रिष्टुप् ।]

७३९१. नह्यं१न्यं बळाकरं मर्डितारं शतक्रतो। त्वं न इन्द्र मृळय॥१॥

1. Other than you, *Śatakratu*, I know no bestower of happiness; *Indra*, do you make us happy.

७३९२. यो न: शश्वत्पुराविथामृध्रो वाजसातये। स त्वं न इन्द्र मृळय॥२॥

2. O you, the invulnerable, who have always in former times protected us for the battle, do you, *Indra*, make us happy.

७३९३. किमङ्ग रध्रचोदन: सुन्वानस्याविदेदसि। कुवित्स्विन्द्र ण: शक:॥३॥

3. Director of the worshipper, you are the guardian of the offerer; help us mightily.

७३९४. इन्द्र प्र णो रथमव पश्चाच्चित्सन्तमद्रिव:। पुरस्तादेनं मे कृधि॥४॥

4. *Indra*, protect our chariot; though now left behind, set it in the front, O thunderer.

७३९५. हन्तो नु किमाससे प्रथमं नो रथं कृधि। उपमं वाजयु श्रव:॥५॥

5. Up, why sit you still? Make our chariot the first; our food-seeking offering is near you.

Food-Seeking— Here, as elsewhere, Sāyaṇa explains *vājayu* by *annam icchat;* the St. Petersburg Dict. takes it as "wettlaufend, eilig"; Grassmann renders it "güterreich." Sāyaṇa explains *Śravas* by *annam* as usual, *i.e., havirlakṣaṇam*. The clause may perhaps mean "the race is glorious and swift."

७३९६. अर्वां नो वाज़्युं रथं सुकरं ते किमित्परिं।
अस्मान्त्सु जिग्युर्ष्वस्कृधि ॥६॥

6. Protect our food-seeking chariot; everything is easy for you to do; make us completely victorious.

७३९७. इन्द्र दृह्स्व पूरसि भद्रा तं एति निष्कृतम्। इयं धीर्ह्नत्वियांवती ॥७॥

7. *Indra*, be firm (in battle), you are (strong as) a city; to you, the repeller (of enemies), comes this auspicious sacrifice, offered in due season.

You are Strong as a City— Or, according to another interpretation, "be firmly settled (in our sacrifice), you are the fulfiller of desires," *pūrakaḥ kāmānām asi*.

The Repeller of Enemies— *Niṣkṛitam* is here taken a actively, *i.e., Niṣkartāram*. It may be also taken passively, "this auspicious sacrifice comes to your appointed (place)."

७३९८. मा सीमंवद्य आ भांगुर्वी काष्ठां हितं धनम्। अपावृक्ता अरत्नयः ॥८॥

8. Let not reproach reach us; far off is the goal; there is the wealth stored; may our enemies be excluded.

७३९९. तुरीयं नामं यज्ञियं यदा करस्तदुंश्मसि। आदित्पतिर्न ओहसे ॥९॥

9. When you assume your sacrificial fourth name, we long for it; then you forthwith carry us as a protector.

Sacrificial Fourth Name— The four names are explained to be the *nakṣatra* or constellation-name, (*i.e., Arjuna*, as connected with the constellation *Arjunekṣu* or *Phalgunyau*? see *Śatap Brāhm.*, II.1.2.11, where it is, however, called the hidden name *guhyam nāma*), the hidden name, the revealed name, and the sacrificial name *somayājin*.

७४००. अवीवृधद्यो अमृता अमन्दीदेकद्यूर्दैवा उत यांश्च देवीः।
तस्मां उ राधः कृणुत प्रशस्तं प्रातर्मक्षू धियावंसुर्जगम्यात् ॥१०॥

10. O immortal gods and all you goddesses, *Ekadyū* has honoured you (with his praise) and rejoiced you (with his *Soma*-offerings); make his substance abundant; and may (*Indra*), who rewards pious acts with wealth, come speedily in the morning.

[सूक्त-८१]

[ऋषि- कुसीदी काण्व। देवता- इन्द्र। छन्द- गायत्री।]

७४०१. आ तू न॑ इन्द्र क्षुमन्तं चि॒त्रं ग्रा॒भं सं गृ॑भाय। म॒हाह॒स्ती दक्षि॑णेन॥१॥

1. *Indra*, lord of the mighty hand, do you seize for us with your right hand marvellous praise-exciting (riches), worthy to be seized.

Sāmaveda,167, 728, Sāyaṇa supplies *dhanam* "wealth," and takes *kṣumantam* as *śabdamantam stutyam*. Benfey takes *grābham* (*grahaṇārham*) as referring to the thunderbolt, "ergreife nun für uns den donnernden, den Flammengriff."

७४०२. विद्मा हि त्वा॑ तुविकू॒र्मिं तु॒विदे॒ष्णं तु॒वीम॑घम्। तु॒विमा॒त्रमवो॑भिः॥२॥

2. We know you the achiever of many great deeds, the bestower of many gifts, the lord of much wealth, vast in size, and full of protection (for your worshippers).

Sāmaveda, 729.

७४०३. न॒हि त्वा॑ शूर॒ देवा॒ न मर्ता॑सो दि॒त्सन्त॑म्। भी॒मं न गां वा॑र॒यन्ते॥३॥

3. Hero, when you desire to give, neither gods nor men can stay you, as (they cannot stay) a terrible bull.

७४०४. एतो न्विन्द्रं॒ स्तवा॑मे॒शानं॒ वस्वः॑ स्व॒राज॑म्। न राध॑सा म॒र्धिष॒न्नः॥४॥

4. Hasten hither, let us glorify *Indra* the lord of wealth, the self-resplendent, let none vex, us by his wealth.

७४०५. प्र स्तो॒षदु॒प गा॑सिष॒च्छ्रव॑त्सा॒मं गी॒यमा॑नम्। अ॒भि राध॑सा जुगुरत्॥५॥

5. May (*Indra*) sing the prelude, may he sing the accompaniment, may he listen to our hymn as it is chanted; may he, endowed with wealth, accept us favourably.

May he sing the Accompaniment— *I.e.,* let him act as *prastotā* and the *upagātā*; for the functions of these assistants at a *Sāman*. see Prof. Haug's notes, *Ait. Brāhm.*, III.23; VII.1.

७४०६. आ नो॑ भर॒ दक्षि॑णे॒नाभि स॒व्येन॒ प्र मृ॑श। इन्द्र॒ मा नो॒ वसो॒र्निर्भा॑क्॥६॥

6. Bring us (gifts) with your right hand, and with your left bestow them on us; exclude us not, *Indra*, from wealth.

७४०७. उप॑ क्रमस्व॒ भर॑ धृष॒ता धृ॑ष्णो॒ जना॑नाम्। अ॒दा॒शूष्ट॑रस्य॒ वेदः॑॥७॥

7. Come hither, and bring us, daring one, with your resolute (mind), the wealth of him who is pre-eminently a niggard amongst men.

७४०८. इन्द्र य उ नु ते अस्ति वाजो विप्रेभि: सनित्व:।
अस्माभि: सु तं सनुहि।।८।।

8. O *Indra*, give us a abundantly that wealth which is your, and which is to be obtained by the wise (worshippers).

७४०९. सद्योजुर्वस्ते वाजा अस्मभ्यं विश्वश्चन्द्रा:। वशैश्च मधू जरन्ते।।९।।

9. May your all-rejoicing riches speedily come to us; full of desires, men immediately offer their praises.

[सूक्त -८२]

[ऋषि- कुसीदी काण्व। देवता- इन्द्र। छन्द- गायत्री।]

७४१०. आ प्र द्रव परावतोऽर्वावतंश्च वृत्रहन्। मध्व: प्रति प्रभर्मणि।।१।।

1. Hasten, slayer of *Vṛtra*, from afar or from nigh to the exhilarating (*Soma*-libations) in the sacrifice.

७४११. तीव्रा: सोमास आ गहि सुतासो मादयिष्णव:।
पिबा दधृग्यथोचिषे।।२।।

2. Come hither, the strong intoxicating *Soma* is effused: drink, since you are boldly devoted to it.

७४१२. इषा मन्दस्वादु तेरं वराय मन्यवे। भुवत्त इन्द्र शं हृदे।।३।।

3. Rejoice yourself with this food,—may it forthwith avail to (quench) your foe-restraining anger, may it produce happiness, *Indra*, in your heart.

७४१३. आ त्वशत्रवा गहि न्युखकथानि च हूयसे। उपमे रोचने दिव:।।४।।

4. O you who have no enemies, come hither; you are summoned from the resplendent heaven to the hymns at this our rite near at hand in this world illumined (by the sacred fires).

It would be more obvious to take *upame rochane livaḥ*, with the St. Petersb. Dict., as "in the highest splendour of heaven". Sāyaṇa, however, takes *divaḥ* as *svatejasā dīpyamānād dyulokāt*, "from the world of heaven illumined by its won splendour," *i.e.*, by the deities residing there; *rocane* as *agnibhir dīpyamāne loke*, and *upame* as *samīpe, asmadīye yajñe ca*.

७४१४. तुभ्यायमद्रिभि: सुतो गोभि: श्रीतो मदाय कम्।
प्र सोम इन्द्र हूयते।।५।।

5. *Indra*, this *Soma*, effused for you by the stones and mixed with milk, is offered auspiciously (in the fire) for your exhilaration.

७४१५. इन्द्र श्रुधि सु मे हवंमस्मे सुतस्य गोमंतः।
वि पीतिं तृप्तिमंश्नुहि॥६॥

6. *Indra*, hear with favour may call; be present at the drinking of this our libation mixed with milk, and be satisfied.

७४१६. य इंन्द्र चमसेष्वा सोमंश्चमूषु ते सुतः। पिबेदंस्य त्वमीशिषे॥७॥

7. Whatever *Soma* has been poured into the cups and the bowls for you, drink it, *Indra*—you are the sovereign.

Sāmaveda, 162.

The Bowls— The *Soma* libations are poured from two kinds of vessels, the *camasas, i.e.,* cups, and the *grahās*, or saucers (here called *camu*), *cf.* Haug, *Ait. Br.* trans., p.118.

७४१७. यो अप्सु चन्द्रमांइव सोमंश्चमूषु ददृशे। पिबेदंस्य त्वमीशिषे॥८॥

8. Whatever *Soma* is seen in the vessels like the moon (reflected) in the waters, drink it,—you are the sovereign.

In the Vessels— *i.e.,* it is thus seen in the eight *grahās*. Sāyaṇa gives another interpretation of *apsu* "in the waters" as *antarikṣe* "in the sky," *nirmalatayā*, the *Soma* being likened to the moon for its purity.

७४१८. यं ते श्येनः पदांभरत्तिरो रजांस्यस्पृतम्। पिबेदंस्य त्वमीशिषे॥९॥

9. Whatever *Soma* the hawk bore for you with its feet, having won it, till then inviolate, from the (guardians of the) upper worlds, drink it,—you are the sovereign.

Whatever the Hawk Bore— This alludes to the legend given in the *Taitt. Saṁhita,* VI.I. (*Cf.* also *Ait. Brahm.*, III.25-27), which tells how the *Gāyatri* as a hawk brought the *Soma* from heaven. The portions which she seized with her feet became the morning and the midday libation, that which she seized with her bill became the evening libation.

[सूक्त-८३]

[**ऋषि**– कुसीदी काण्व। **देवता**– विश्वेदेवा। **छन्द**– गायत्री।]

७४१९. देवानामिदवो महत्तदा वृणीमहे वयम्। वृष्णांमस्मभ्यंमूतये॥१॥

1. We solicit that might protection of the desire-raining deities in our own behalf, for our own help.

Sāmaveda, 138.

७४२०. ते नं: सन्तु युज: सदा वरुणो मित्रो अर्यमा। वृधासंश्च प्रचेतस:॥२॥

2. May those (deities) *Varuṇa, Mitra,* and *Aryaman,* be ever our allies and supremely wise helpers.

७४२१. अर्ति नो विष्पिता पुरु नौभिरपो न पर्षथ। यूयमृतस्य रथ्य:॥३॥

3. Charioteers of the sacrifice, do you conduct us through the many wide-spread (forces of our enemies) as in ships across the waters.

Sāyana's comm. is not quite clear, but I have taken it as in II.27.7. If we omit the words *no'smān* (found only in B.) and take *nah* for *asmākam,* his interpretation will run, "conduct our (sacrifices) to completion through the many widespread (forces of our enemies)."

७४२२. वामं नो अस्त्वर्यमन्वामं वरुण शंस्यम्। वामं ह्यावृणीमहे॥४॥

4. Be wealth ours, *Aryaman,*— wealth worthy to be praised. *Varuṇa;* it is wealth which we ask.

७४२३. वामस्य हि प्रचेतस ईशानासो रिशादस:। नेमादित्या अघस्य यत्॥५॥

5. Mighty in wisdom, repellers of enemies, you are the lords of wealth; be not mine the wealth, *Ādityas,* which belongs to sin.

Be not Mine— I think that *na* is omitted in the Comm. before *prāpnotu.*

७४२४. वयमिद्व: सुदानव: क्षियन्तो यान्तो अध्वन्ना। देवा वृधाय हूमहे॥६॥

6. Bounteous deities, whether we dwell at home or go abroad on the road, we invoke you only to be nourished by our oblations.

Whether we dwell at home or go abroad on the Road— The Schol. explains this, "whether we remain at home to perform the *agnihotra,* etc., or go forth in the roads to collect fuel, etc."

To be nourished by our Oblations— Or "to enrich us with wealth."

७४२५. अधि न इन्द्रैषां विष्णो सजात्यानाम्। इता मरुतो अश्विना॥७॥

7. Come to us, *Indra, Viṣṇu, Maruts,* and *Ādityas,* from the midst of these your brethren.

Yajurveda, 33,47.

Your Brethren— Sc. *Mitra,* etc.

७४२६. प्र भ्रातृत्वं सुदानवोऽधं द्विता समान्या। मातुर्गर्भे भरामहे॥८॥

8. Bounteous (deities), we forthwith proclaim aloud that brotherhood of yours in mother's womb, (first) in common union, then as born in diverse manner.

This alludes to a legend partly given in *Taitt. Saṁhitā*, VI.5.6. There *Aditi* is represented as offering a certain offering to the gods, and as conceiving four of the *Ādityas* on eating the remainder which they gave to her. Thinking to conceive a still nobler offspring, she next eats the whole of the second offering herself, but she only conceives a barren egg. She then offers the third offering to the *Ādityas* and conceives *Vivasvat*. But this legend says nothing of the birth of *Pūṣan* and *Aryaman* as alluded to by the Scholiast.

७४२७. यूयं हि ष्ठा सुदानव इन्द्रज्येष्ठा अभिद्यव:। अधा चिद्व उत ब्रुवे।।९।।

9. Bounteous (deities) with *Indra* as your chief, be present here in your radiance; again and again I praise you.

[सूक्त -८४]

[ऋषि– उशना काण्व। देवता– अग्नि। छन्द– गायत्री।]

७४२८. प्रेष्ठं वो अतिथिं स्तुषे मित्रमिव प्रियम्। अग्निं रथं न वेद्यम्।।१।।

1. I praise *Agni* your most beloved guest, dear as a friend, who brings wealth as a chariot;
Sāmaveda, 5, 1544.

७४२९. कविमिव प्रचेतसं यं देवासो अधं द्विता। नि मर्त्येष्वादधु:।।२।।

2. Whom the gods have set like a wise seer in a twofold function among mortals.
Sāmaveda, 1245, reading prashamsyam and iti for pracetasam and adha.

A two-fold function among Mortals— *Agni's* two functions are the *Gārhapatya* and *Āhavanīya* fires, or it may refer to his offices connected with the sacrifice in heaven and earth.

७४३०. त्वं यविष्ठ दाशुषो नृँ: पाहि शृणुधी गिर:। रक्षा तोकमुत त्मना।।३।।

3. Ever-youthful (*Agni*), protect your offerers, hear our praises, and thyself guard our offspring.
Sāmaveda, 1246; *Yajurveda*, 13.52. Benfey takes the last clause ''bewahre uns und unsern Spross,'' which Mahīdhara also gives as an alternative rendering.

७४३१. कया ते अग्ने अङ्गिर ऊर्जो नपादुपस्तुतिम्। वराय देव मन्यवे।।४।।

4. Divine *Agni Aṅgiras*, son of food, with what voice (shall I utter) my praise to you, most excellent scorner of enemies?
Sāmaveda, 1549. For a different explanation of *varāya manyave. see* VIII.82.3.

Son of Food— Sāyaṇa here as elsewhere gives the alternative rendering "grandson of the sacrificial offering."

७४३२. दाशेम॒ कस्य॒ म॒न॑सा य॒ज्ञस्य॑ सहसो यहो। क॒दु॒ वोच॒ इदं नर्मः॥५॥

5. Son of strength, what worshipper's (offerings) shall we present to you with devoted mind, and when shall I utter to you this praise?

Sāmaveda, 1550. Benfey translates kasya manasā yajñasya "mit welcher Feien Ersinnung?"

७४३३. अधा॒ त्वं हि न॒स्करो॒ विश्वा॑ अ॒स्मभ्यं सु॒क्षिती॑:।
वार्ज॒द्रविणसो॒ गिरः॑॥६॥

6. Cause all our praises to bring to us excellent dwellings and abundance of wealth in food.

Sāmaveda, 1551.

७४३४. कस्य॑ नू॒नं प॒रीणसो॒ धियो॑ जिन्वसि दम्पते।
गोषाता॒ यस्य॑ ते॒ गिरः॑॥७॥

7. Whose many offerings do you gladden, Agni, you who are the lord of the house, and whose praises bring wealth of kine?

Sāmaveda, 34, with pariṇasi and satpate for pariṇasaḥ and dampate.

The lord of the House— Sāyaṇa takes dampate as jāyāpatisvarūpa, since abides in the Gārhapatya fire, but cf.VIII.69.16. The last clause may mean "whose praises are heard in the rite which brings wealth of kine."

७४३५. तं मर्जयन्त सु॒क्रतुं पुरो॒यावा॑नमाजिषु। स्वेषु क्ष॒येषु॑ वा॒जिन॑म्॥८॥

8. They keep him bright in their houses, (Agni) famed for glorious deeds, the mighty one who presses forward in battles.

७४३६. क्षेति॒ क्षेमे॑भिः सा॒धुभि॒र्नकि॒र्यं घ्नन्ति॒ हन्ति॒ यः।
अग्ने॑ सु॒वीरं॑ एधते॥९॥

9. He who dwells at home with all-efficient protections, whom none can harm, but who himself harms (his enemies),—he, Agni, (your worshipper), waxes strong with heroic offspring.

[सूक्त-८५]

[ऋषि- कृष्ण आङ्गिरस। देवता- अश्विनीकुमार। छन्द- गायत्री।]

७४३७. आ मे॒ हवं॑ नासत्या॒श्विना॑ गच्छतं यु॒वम्। मध्व॑: सोम॒स्य पीतये॑॥१॥

1. Nāsatyās, Aśvins, come you to may invocation that ye may drink the exhilaration Soma.

७४३८. इमं मे स्तोमर्मश्विनेमं मे शृणुतं हर्वम्। मध्वः सोमस्य पीतये॥२॥

2. *Aśvins*, hear this my hymn, this my invocation that you may drink the exhilarating *Soma*.

७४३९. अयं वां कृष्णो अश्विना हवते वाजिनीवसू।
मध्वः सोमस्य पीतये॥३॥

3. *Kṛṣṇa* invokes you, *Aśvins* rich in sacrifices, that you may drink the exhilarating *Soma*.

७४४०. शृणुतं जरितुर्हवं कृष्णस्य स्तुवतो नरा। मध्वः सोमस्य पीतये॥४॥

4. Leaders (of all), hear the invocation of *Kṛṣṇa*, the hymner, who praises you,—that ye may drink the exhilarating *Soma*.

७४४१. छर्दिर्यन्तमदाभ्यं विप्राय स्तुवते नरा। मध्वः सोमस्य पीतये॥५॥

5. Leaders, give to the sage who praises you an unassailable dwelling that you may drink the exhilarating *Soma*.

७४४२. गच्छतं दाशुषो गृहमित्था स्तुवतो अश्विना।
मध्वः सोमस्य पीतये॥६॥

6. *Aśvins*, come to the house of the offerer who thus praises you, that you may drink the exhilarating *Soma*.

७४४३. युञ्जाथां रासभं रथे वीड्वङ्गे वृषण्वसू। मध्वः सोमस्य पीतये॥७॥

7. You who possess showering wealth, yoke the ass to your firmly built chariot, that ye may drink the exhilarating *Soma*.

Yajurveda, II.13, has part of this verse, but much of it is quite different. Sāyaṇa takes the verse as addressed to the *Aśvins*, Mahīdhara as addressed to the *adhvaryu* priest and the sacrificer, or to the sacrificer and his wife.

७४४४. त्रिवन्धुरेण त्रिवृता रथेना यातमश्विना। मध्वः सोमस्य पीतये॥८॥

8. *Aśvins*, come hither with your three-seated triangular car, that you may drink the exhilarating *Soma*.

Three-Seated triangular Car— For *trivandhureṇa* cf. I.34.9; I.47.2; VIII.22.5, etc., Sāyaṇa continually vacillates in his interpretation; here he takes it as *triphalakasaṁghaṭitena*, "compacted of three pieces." He also gives as a second interpretation of *trivṛta* "defended by three sets of plates."

७४४५. नू मे गिरो नासत्याश्विना प्रावतं युवम्। मध्वः सोमस्य पीतये॥९॥

9. *Nāsatyās*, *Aśvins*, hasten quickly to my praises, that you many drink the exhilarating *Soma*.

[सूक्त-८६]

[ऋषि- कृष्ण आङ्गिरस अथवा विश्वक काष्णि।
देवता- अश्विनीकुमार। छन्द- जगती।]

७४४६. उभा हि दस्रा भिषजां मयोभुवोभा दक्षस्य वर्चसो बभूवथुः। ता वां
विश्वको हवते तनूकृथे मा नो वि यौष्टं सख्या मुमोचंतम्॥१॥

1. *Dasras*, physicians, sources of happiness, you both were (the objects) of *Dakṣa*'s praise; *Viśvaka* now invokes you for the sake of his son; sever not our friendships, but fling loose (your reins and gallop hither).

Objects of Dakṣa's Praise— This seems to allude to the thousand *Ṛks* uttered by *Dakṣa* or *Prajāpati*, *i.e.*, the *Aśvinā Śastra*, which was won by the *Aśvins* in a race, see I.116.2 (Comm.) and *Ait. Brahm., iv.7.

Sever not our Friendships— Sc. as worshipper and the object of worship.

७४४७. कथा नूनं वां विर्मना उप स्तवद्ध्वं धियं ददथुर्वस्यं इष्टये। ता वां
विश्वको हवते तनूकृथे मा नो वि यौष्टं सख्या मुमोचंतम्॥२॥

2. How *Vimanas* once praised you, and you gave him understanding for the attainment of excellent wealth! *Viśvaka* now invokes you for the sake of his son; sever not our friendships, but fling loose (your reins and gallop hither).

७४४८. युवं हि ष्मा पुरुभुजेममेधतुं विष्णाप्वे ददथुर्वस्यंइष्टये। ता वां
विश्वको हवते तनूकृथे मा नो वि यौष्टं सख्या मुमोचंतम्॥३॥

3. Gladdeners of many, you have given to *Viṣṇāpu* this prosperity for the attainment of excellent wealth; *Viśvaka* now invokes you for the sake of his son; sever not our friendships, but fling loose (your reins and gallop hither).

Viśnapu— This is the name of the *Ṛṣi*'s son or grandson.

७४४९. उत त्यं वीरं धनसामृजीषिणं दूरे चित्सन्तमर्वसे हवामहे। यस्य
स्वादिष्ठा सुमतिः पितुर्यथा मा नो वि यौष्टं सख्या मुमोचंतम्॥४॥

4. We summon that hero to our protection, (the enjoyer) of wealth, the possessor of the *Soma*, who now dwells afar off and whose hymn is most pleasing (to the gods) like his father's, sever not our friendships, but fling loose (your reins and gallop hither).

We Summon that Hero— The *Ṛṣi* here prays for the presence of his absent son *Viṣṇāpu*. The Schol. only adds in explanation that "it is for the son to protect the father."

The Possessor of the Soma— *Ṛjīṣin* is generally an epithet of *Indra* and is always explained by Sāyaṇa as here, "possessor of the stale *Soma*" *ṛjīṣa* (*cf.* III.32.1; 36.10, etc.); but there is a word *ṛjīṣa* in I.32.6, applied to *Indra*, which Sāyaṇa there explains as "enemy-repelling," and *ṛjīṣin* must have some such meaning here. The St. Petersburg Dict. always explains it in the *Ṛgveda* as "vorsturzend, ereilend."

७४५०. ऋतेन देव: सविता शमायत ऋतस्य शृङ्गमुर्विया वि पप्रथे। ऋतं
सासाह महि चित्पृतन्यतो मा नो वि यौष्टं सख्या मुमोचतम्।।५।।

5. The sun-god by truth extinguishes his beams (in the evening): he spreads abroad (in the morning) the horn of truth; truth verily overcomes the might of the eager assailant; therefore sever not our friendships, but fling loose (your reins and gallop hither).

Sāyaṇa takes the stanza as a praise of truth, *satyapraśaṁsā*. He seems to explain the verse as implying that as the sun swerves not from his appointed course, and as truth or adherence to right conquers earthly foes, so the *Aśvins* must fulfil the duties of ancient friendship and hear the *Ṛṣi's* prayer.

[सूक्त-८७]

[**ऋषि**– कृष्ण आङ्गिरस अथवा घुम्नीक वासिष्ठ अथवा प्रियमेध आङ्गिरस।
देवता– अश्विनीकुमार। **छन्द**– प्रगाथ (विषमा बृहती, समासतो बृहती)।]

७४५१. घुम्नी वां स्तोमों अश्विना क्रिविर्न सेक आ गंतम्।
मध्व: सुतस्य स दिवि प्रियो नेरा पातं गौराविवेरिणे।।१।।

1. *Aśvins*, your praise is filled with plenty as a well (with water) in time of rain; hasten hither; it is especially dear to the *Soma* when it is effused in the brilliant (offering); drink, leaders (of rites), as two *Gauras* (drink), at a pool.

Cf. VIII.4.3

Your Praise is filled with Plenty—*I.e.*, it brings abundance to the worshipper. (In 89.2, *dyumnī* is explained "glorious".) Another interpretation takes *Dyumnī* as for *Dyumnīko*. "*Aśvins, Dyumnīka* is your praiser."

७४५२. पिबतं घर्मं मधुमन्तमश्विना बर्हि: सीदतं नरा।
ता मन्दसाना मनुषो दुरोण आ नि पातं वेदसा वय:।।२।।

2. Drink, *Aśvins*, the exhilarating (*Soma*) as it drops (into the vessels),—seat yourselves, leaders, on the sacrificial grass; rejoicing in the house of the worshipper, drink the sacred beverage with the oblation.

As it Drops— *Gharma* may also be taken for the earthen pot called *mahāvīra*, and signify the milk boiled in it, "Drink, *Aśvins, the exhilarating* (*Soma*) and the milk."

In the house of the Worshipper— Literally "in the house of the man" *manuṣo duroṇe, i.e.,* the sacrifice which is as a home to the deities, *cf.* v.76.4.

Drink the Sacred Beverage with the Oblation— Or this clause may mean "protect our lives together with our wealth."

७४५३. आ वां विश्वाभिरूतिभिः प्रियमेधा अहूषत।
ता वर्तिर्यातमुप वृक्तबर्हिषो जुष्टं यज्ञं दिविष्टिषु॥३॥

3. The worshippers have invoked you with an protections; come in the early mornings to the dwelling of him who has clipped the sacred grass, to the offering loved (by all the gods).

The Worshippers— *Priyamedhaḥ,* literally "those whose sacrifice are acceptable." The commentator also suggests that it may refer to the *Ṛṣi Priyamedha* (VIII.68, 69), the plural being used as honorific.

With all your Protections— Or *viśvābhir ūtibhiḥ* may mean "with prayers for all desirable blessings."

७४५४. पिबतं सोमं मधुमन्तमश्विना बर्हिः सीदतं सुमत्।
ता वावृधाना उप सुष्टुतिं दिवो गन्तं गौराविवेरिणम्॥४॥

4. *Aśvins*, drink the exhilarating *Soma*, sit down in your radiance on the sacrificial grass; waxing strong (through the libation), come from heaven to our praises as two *Gadras* to a pool.

७४५५. आ नूनं यातमश्विनाश्वेभिः प्रुषितप्सुभिः।
दस्रा हिरण्यवर्तनी शुभस्पती पातं सोममृतावृधा॥५॥

5. Come, *Aśvins*, with your glossy steeds; *Dasras*, riding in golden chariots, lords of good fortune, upholders of truth, drink the *Soma*.

७४५६. वयं हि वां हवामहे विपन्यवो विप्रासो वाजसातये।
ता वल्गू दस्रा पुरुदंससा धियाश्विना श्रुष्ट्या गंतम्॥६॥

6. We, your wise praisers, invoke you to the enjoyment of the sacrificial viands; come quickly, *Dasras*, at the sound of our

praise, *Aśvins*, graceful in your movements, abounding in mighty deeds.

[सूक्त-८८]

[ऋषि– नोधा गौतम। **देवता–** इन्द्र।
छन्द– प्रगाथ (विषमा बृहती, समा सतोबृहती)।]

७४५७. तं वो॒ दस्ममृती॒षहं॒ वसो॑र्मन्दा॒नम॑न्ध॑सः।
अ॒भि व॒त्सं न स्व॒सरे॑षु धे॒नव॒ इन्द्रं॑ गी॒र्भिर्न॑वामहे॥१॥

1. We offer praise with our hymns, as cows (low) to their calf in the stalls, to that handsome *Indra* of yours. (O priests), the overcomer of enemies, who rejoices in the excellent beverage.

Yajurveda, 26.11; *Sāmaveda*, 236, 685.

In the Stalls— Sāyaṇa takes *svasareṣu* in this sense, but he quotes Yāska (*Nir.*, V.4) to show the word may also mean "days." (*Cf*. Prof. Roth's note in his edition, p.56.) Sāyaṇa takes it as 'days' in the first clause, "we praise you in the days," and 'stalls' in the second.

In the Excellent Beverage— I take *vasoḥ*, or rather the gloss *vasayituḥ*, as Sāyaṇa explains it in vi.16.25.

७४५८. द्यु॒क्षं सु॒दानुं॒ तवि॑षीभि॒रावृ॑तं गि॒रिं न पुरु॑भो॒जस॑म्।
क्षु॒मन्तं॒ वाजं॑ श॒तिनं॑ स॒हस्रि॑णं म॒क्षू गोम॑न्तमीमहे॥२॥

2. We solicit the radiant bounteous (*Indra*), surrounded by powers as a mountain (by clouds), the supporter of many,—(we solicit him) speedily for renowned food, rich in cattle, and multiplied an hundred and a thousand fold.

Sāmaveda, 686.

The Supporter of Many— Or "to be fed by the offerings of many," *purubhojasam*.

Renowned— Sayaṇa's explanation of *kṣumantam* is not clear, but he seems to take it as "causing praises by means of the children which it will produce," *śabdavantam, anena putrādikam lakṣyate, stotrādīni kurvāṇam. Kṣumantam vājam* occurs in II.1.10; 4.8, and is there explained *śabdavantam kīrtimantam*. (Grassmann explains it as *nahrungsreich'*.) Sāyaṇa adds that another interpretation of the verse takes all the adjectives as agreeing with *vājam*.

७४५९. न त्वा॑ बृह॒न्तो अ॒द्रयो॒ वर॑न्त इन्द्र वी॒ळव॑ः।
यद्दि॒त्ससि॑ स्तुव॒ते माव॑ते॒ वसु॑ न॒किष्ट॒दा मि॑नाति ते॥३॥

3. The vast firm mountains cannot stop you, *Indra*, whatever wealth you would give to a worshipper such as I none can hinder you therein.

Sāmaveda, 296.

७४६०. योद्धासि क्रत्वा शर्वसोत दंसना विश्वा जाताभि मज्मना।
आ त्वायमर्क ऊतये ववर्तति यं गोर्तमा अजीजनन्।।४।।

4. By your exploits and might you are a warrior you overpower all beings by your deeds and prowess, this hymn which the *Gotamas* have made, causes you to turn hither for their protection.

This Hymn which the Gotamas, Etc.— This seems the obvious meaning of the words a *tvāyam arka ūtaye vavartati yam Gotamā ajījanan.* But Sāyaṇa, hilding the eternity of the Veda, explains the line, "this hymn (or this praiser) brings you hither for their protection, whom they have made manifest (in their sacrifice)."

७४६१. प्र हि रिरिक्ष ओजसा दिवो अन्तेभ्यस्परि।
न त्वा विव्याच रजं इन्द्र पार्थिवमनु स्वधां ववक्षिथ।।५।।

5. *Indra*, by your might you extend beyond the limits of heaven, the region of the earth cannot contain you: deign to bring us food.

Sāmaveda, 312, but with *yo, sadobhyas,* and *ati viśvam* for *hi, antebhyas,* and *anu svadhām;* agreeing in the last clause with i.81.5.

७४६२. नकिः परिष्टिर्मघवन्मघस्य ते यद्दाशुषे दशस्यसि।
अस्माकं बोध्युचथस्य चोदिता मंहिष्ठो वाजसातये।।६।।

6. None can hinder your bounty, *Maghavan*, when you give wealth to your votary; most liberal sender (of wealth), listen to our praise for the attainment of food.

[सूक्त-८९]

[ऋषि– नृमेध आङ्गिरस तथा पुरुमेध आङ्गिरस। देवता– इन्द्र। छन्द– १-४ प्रगाथ (विषमा बृहती, समा सतोबृहती) , ५-६ अनुष्टुप्, ७ बृहती।]

७४६३. बृहदिन्द्राय गायत मरुतो वृत्रहन्तमम्।
येन ज्योतिरजनयन्नृतावृधौ देवं देवाय जागृवि।।१।।

1. Priests sing to *Indra* the most sin-destroying *Bṛhat-Sāman*, by which the upholders of truth produced the divine all-waking luminary for the god.

Yajurveda, 20.30; *Sāmaveda*, 258.

Brhat Sāman— This is a certain *Sāman*, but here it means a mighty hymn.

By which the Upholders, Etc.— That is, the *Visve devāh* produced the sun for *Indra* by means of the *Brhat Sāman*. Mahīdhara takes it as meaning that they produced *Indra's* own wakeful radiance thereby.

७४६४. अपाधमदभिशंस्तीरशस्तिहाथेन्द्रौं द्युम्न्याभवत्।
देवास्तं इन्द्र सख्यायं येमिरे बृहद्द्वानो मरुद्गण।।२।।

2. *Indra*, the destroyer of those who offer not praise, has driven away the malevolent and has become glorious; I *Indra* of mighty splendour, lord of the troops of *Maruts*, the gods press you for your friendship.

Yajurveda, 3.3.95.

The Malevolent— Sāyana takes *abhiśastīh* as 'injuries' or 'the injuries,' sc. enemies. Mahidhara, as usual, takes it as 'calumnies,' *abhiśapan*.

The Gods Press You— Sāyana explains *yemire* by *tvām niyacchanti*, but Mahīdhara more correctly preserves the middle meaning (*cf.* v. 32.10), "the gods anxiously devote themselves to win your friendship." *Cf.* Sāyana's own explanation in VIII.98.3.

७४६५. प्र व इन्द्राय बृहते मरुतो ब्रह्मार्चत।
वृत्रं हनति वृत्रहा शतक्रतुर्वज्रेण शतपर्वणा।।३।।

3. Priests, utter forth the hymn to your great *Indra*: let *Satakratu*, the slayer of *Vrtra*, smite *Vrtra* with his hundred-edged thunderbolt.

Yajurveda, 33.96; *Sāmaveda*, 257.

७४६६. अभि प्र भर धृषता धृषन्मनः श्रवंश्चिते असद् बृहत्।
अर्षन्त्वापो जवंसा वि मातरो हनों वृत्रं जया स्वः।।४।।

4. Daring-souled (*Indra*), there is abundance of food with you,—boldly bring it to us; let our mothers (the waters) impetuously spread over the earth; smite *Vrtra*, and conquer all.

Our Mothers— The waters are called mothers from the passage in the *Taitt. Up.*, II.1, "from the waters comes the earth, from the earth the plants, from the plants food, from food semen, from semen man."

७४६७. यज्जायंथा अपूर्व्यं मर्घवन्वृत्रहत्यांय।
तत्पृथिवीमंप्रथयस्तदस्तभ्ना उत द्याम्।।५।।

5. *Maghavan*, who had none before you, when you was born for the slaying of *Vṛtra*, then you did spread abroad the earth, then you did prop up the heavens.
Sāmaveda, 601, 1429.

७४६८. तत्तें यज्ञो अंजायत तद्कं उत हस्कृति:।
तद्दिश्वंमभिभूरसि यज्जातं यच्च जन्त्वम्।।६।।

6. Then was the sacrifice produced for you, then too the joyous hymn; then did you surpass all, whatever has been or will be born.
Sāmaveda, 1430.

७४६९. आमासु पक्कमैरंय आ सूर्यं रोहयो दिवि।
घर्मं न सामन्तपता सुवृक्तिभिर्जुष्टं गिर्वणसे बृहत्।।७।।

7. In the immature (cows) you produced the mature (milk), you caused the sun to arise in heaven, (Priests), excite (*Indra*) with your praises as men heat the *Gharma* with *Sāman*-hymns; (sing) the acceptable *Bṛhat sāman* to him who is to be honoured by song.
Sāmaveda, 1431.

The Mature Milk— *Cf.* I.62.9.

You caused the Sun to arise in Heaven— Sāyaṇa here repeats the legend of the *Paṇis* and the stolen cows of the *Aṅgirasas*. The *Ṛṣis* implored *Indra* for help, who, seeing that the stronghold of the *Asuras* was enveloped in thick darkness, set the sun in the sky to dispel it.

As men heat the Gharma with Sāman Hymns— For the ceremony of heating the *Mahavīra* or *Gharma* pot, used in the *Pravargya* ceremony, see Prof. Haug's *Ait. Brāhm.*, Vol. II. p. 42. The *Sāman* hymns repeated during the heating are given in *Ait. Brāhm.*, I.21

[सूक्त-९०]

[ऋषि– नृमेध आङ्गिरस तथा पुरुमेध आङ्गिरस। देवता– इन्द्र।
छन्द– प्रगाथ (विषमा बृहती, समा सतोबृहती)।]

७४७०. आ नो विश्वासु हव्य इन्द्रं: समत्सु भूषतु।
उप ब्रह्माणि सर्वनानि वृत्रहा परमज्या ऋचीषम:।।१।।

1. May *Indra*, who is to be invoked in all battles regard our hymns and our libations, he the slayer of *Vṛtra*, who crushes the mightiest (foes), who is worthy of his praise.
Sāmaveda, I.3.2.3.7; II.7.1.2.1, but with *Indra* and its adjectives in the accusative for the nominative, and *bhuṣata* for bhuṣatu, *i.e.,* "(priests) honour *Indra*, etc."

Who crushes the Mightiest Foes— *Paramajyāḥ* also occurs in VIII.1.30. *Sayana's* first explanation is inadmissible, "he whose bowstring (*Jya*) is most excellent (*parama*)" (*cf.* Wilson's transl., vol. v, p.428); but he adds another, taken in the text, rightly connecting it with the root *jyā*, to which he gives the sense of *hiṁsā*. (Benfey in his Dict. connects this root in the sense of 'overpowering' with. The St. Pertersburg Dict. explains it "die höchste Obergewalt hebend."

७४७१. त्वं दाता प्रथमो राधसामस्यसि सत्य ईशानकृत्।
तुविद्युम्नस्य युज्या वृणीमहे पुत्रस्य शर्वसो महः॥२॥

2. You are the chief giver of wealth, you are truthful and make your worshippers rulers; we solicit (blessings) worthy of you, lord of vast riches, mighty son of strength.

Sāmaveda, 1493.

Mighty Son of Strength— Sāyaṇa obscurely explains this phrase, "son of strength, because produced as the cause of strength in order to destroy enemies" (*cf.* VIII.92.14). This strength, or victory through strength, is the final cause of his production or manifestation by the rite; and the final cause being then taken for the efficient, 'strength' may thus be called the father.

७४७२. ब्रह्मा त इन्द्र गिर्वणः क्रियन्ते अनतिद्भुता।
इमा जुषस्व हर्यश्व योजनेन्द्र या ते अमन्महि॥३॥

3. *Indra*, who are the object of hymns, unexaggerated praises are offered by us; lord of bay steeds, accept these fitting hymns, which we have meditated for you.

Unexaggerated— *Anatidbhuta* is an obscure word; Sāyaṇa explains it *sarvān atikramya na bhavanti, indraguṇavyāpakāni yathārthabhūtāni.* The St. Petersb. Dict. explain it "unübertroffen," and derives it from *atibhūta* with an alliterative reference to *adbhuta*.

Hymns— *Yojana* is also explained by Sāyaṇa as *stotra* in i.88.5.

७४७३. त्वं हि सत्यो मघवन्ननानतो वृत्रा भूरि न्यृञ्जसे।
स त्वं शविष्ठ वज्रहस्त दाशुषेऽर्वाङ्रयिमा कृधि॥४॥

4. You are truthful, *Maghavan*; unhumbled yourself, you humble many enemies; most mighty thunderer, cause wealth to meet your worshipper.

७४७४. त्वमिन्द्र यशा अस्यृजीषी शवसस्पते।
त्वं वृत्राणि हंस्यप्रतीन्येक इदनुत्ता चर्षणीधृता॥५॥

5. You, *Indra*, lord of strength, are the glorious possessor of the offered *Soma*; alone with (your thunderbolt), that protector of

men, you smite the enemies that none else cloud oppose or drive
away.

Sāmaveda, 248, 1411, but with *śavasas patiḥ* for *pate, purvanuttās*
for *anuttā,* and *carṣaṇīdhṛtiī* for *dhṛtā.*

७४७५. तमु॒ त्वा नू॒नम॑सुर॒ प्रचेत॑सं रा॒धो भा॒गमि॑वेमहे।
महीव॒ कृत्तिं॑: शर॒णा तं इन्द्र॒ प्र तं॒ सुम्ना॒ नो अश्रवन्।।६।।

6. Living one, who possess supreme knowledge, we verily ask
you for wealth as though it were an inheritance your abode (in
heaven), *Indra,* is vast like your glory; may your blessings fill us.

Sāmaveda, 1412.

Living One— *Asura* is explained *balavān Prāṇvān.*

The Abode in heaven is vast like your Glory— This is Sāyaṇa's
interpretation, following Yāska, *Nir.,* v.2 More probably it means "your
protection is as a vast cloak or "hide," see Prof. Roth's note in his
edition.

[सूक्त-९१]

[ऋषि– अपाला आत्रेयी। देवता– इन्द्र। छन्द– अनुष्टुप्, १-२ पंक्ति।]

VIII.9.11. Sāyaṇa quotes a legend from the *Sātyāyaṇa Brāhmaṇa* to
illustrate this hymn. *Apālā,* the daughter of Atri, being afflicted with a
disease of the skin, was repudiated by her husband; she returned to her
father's hermitage, and there practised penance. One day she went our to
bathe, intending to make a *Soma* offering to *Indra,* and as she was
returning, she found some *Soma* plants in the road. She gathered them and
ate them as she walked. *Indra,* hearing the sound of her jaws, thought it
was the sound of the *Soma* stones, and appeared to her, asking whether
there were any *Soma* stones bruising there. She explained the reason of
the sound, and *Indra* turned away. She called after him, "why do you turn
away? You go from house to house to drink the *Soma,* now then drink the
Soma ground by my teeth and eat fried grains of barley." She then added,
without paying him respect, "I know not whether you are *Indra*, but if
you come to my house I will pay you die honour." Feeling however sure
that it was really *Indra,* she addressed the latter half of the third verse to
the *Soma* in her mouth. *Indra* then, falling in love with here drank the
Soma as she wished. She then triumphantly exclaimed (v.4): "I have been
repudiated by my husband and yet *Indra* comes to me." *Indra* then
granted her a boon and she thus chose, "my father's head is bald, his field
is barren, and my body is destitute of hair; make these things grow."
Indra granted the three boons. For this hymn and legend, *cf.* Prof. Kuhn
in *Indische Stud.* I.pp.118,119, and Prof. Aufrecht, *ib,* IV.1-8; Grimm, in
his *Deutsche Myth.*, p.118-21, and *Norddeutsche Sagen*, p.443.

७४७६. कन्याइ३ वार्॑वायती सोममपि॑ स्रुताविन्दत्।

अस्तं॒ भर॑न्त्यब्रवीदिन्द्रा॑य सुनवै त्वा शक्रा॒य सुनवै त्वा॥१॥

1. A young woman going to the water found *Soma* in the path; as she carried it home she said, I will press you for *Indra*, I will press you for *Śakra*.

This verse is said by *Apālā*, as *Indra* comes up and questions her.

७४७७. असौ य ए॑षि॒ वीर॑को गृहंगृ॑हं विचा॒क॑शत्।

इमं ज॒म्भ॑सुतं पिब धा॒नाव॑न्तं कर॒म्भिण॑मपू॒पव॑न्तमुक्थिन॑म्॥२॥

2. You who go from house to house a hero bright in your splendour, drink this *Soma* pressed by my teeth together with fried grains of barley, the *karambha*, cakes and hymns.

Apālā says this as *Indra* turns to depart.

The Karambha— A mixture of fried barley meal and batter er eurds.

७४७८. आ च॒न त्वा॑ चिकित्सामो॒ऽधि॑ च॒न त्वा॒ नेम॑सि।

शनै॒रिव॑ शनकै॒रिवेन्द्रा॑येन्दो॒ परि॑ स्रव॥३॥

3. We wish to know you, but here we know you not, O *soma*, flow forth for *Indra* first slowly, then quickly.

First Slowly, then Quickly— This is *Sāyaṇa's* explanation of the words *śanair iva śanakair iva*; but it is better to translate them, with Prof. Aufrecht, "allämhlig und allmähliger tropfe."

७४७९. कु॒विच्छक॑त्कु॒वित्कर॑त्कु॒विन्नो॒ वस्य॑सस्करत्।

कु॒वित्प॑तिद्वि॒षो यती॑रिन्द्रे॒ण सङ्गमा॑महै॥४॥

4. May (*Indra*) repeatedly make us powerful, may he do abundantly for us, may he repeatedly make us very rich; often hated by our husband and forced to leave him, may we be united to *Indra*.

७४८०. इ॒मानि॑ त्री॒णि वि॒ष्टपा॒ तानी॑न्द्र॒ वि रो॑हय।

शिर॒स्तत॒स्योर्वरा॒मादि॑दं म॒ उपो॒दरे॑॥५॥

5. These three places,—do you cause them all to grow,—my father's (bald) head, his (barren) field, and my body.

७४८१. असौ च॒ या न॒ उर्व॒रादि॒मां त॒न्वं॑ मम॑।

अथो॑ त॒तस्य॒ यच्छिर॒: सर्वा॒ ता रो॑मशा कृधि॥६॥

6. This field which is our (father's), and this my body and the head of my father,—do you make all these bear a crop.

Do you make all these bear a Crop— Lit. make them all hairy" *romaśani, Cf. Propertius.* IV.2.14, et coma lactenti spicea fruge tumet."

७४८२. खे र॒थ॒स्य खेऽन॑स॒: खे यु॒ग॒स्य॑ शतक्रतो।
अपा॒लामि॑न्द्र॒ त्रिष्पूत्व्यकृ॑णो॒: सूर्य॑त्वचम्॥७॥

7. Thrice, *Śatakratu*, did you purify *Apālā*, in the hole of the chariot, in the hole of the cart, and in the hole of the yoke, and you did make here with a skin resplendent like the sun.

Thrice did you Purify Apālā, etc.— Sāyaṇa says that *Indra* dragged her through the wide hole of his chariot, the narrower hole of the cart, and the small hole of the yoke, and she east off three skins. The first skin became a hedge-hog, the second an alligator, the third a chameleon. I suppose, with Prof. Aufrecht, that the hole or space of the chariot and cart represents the opening between the four wheels; the hole of the yoke seems to me to mean the opening through which the animal's head passed, corresponding to Homer's II.19.406.

[सूक्त-९२]

[ऋषि– श्रुतकक्ष आङ्गिरस अथवा सुकक्ष आङ्गिरस। देवता– इन्द्र।
छन्द– गायत्री, १- अनुष्टुप्।]

७४८३. पान्तमा वो॒ अन्ध॑स॒ इन्द्र॑मभि॒ प्र गा॑यत।
विश्वासाहं॒ शतक्र॑तुं॒ मंहि॑ष्ठं चर्षणीनाम्॥१॥

1. Sing priests, that *Indra*, who drinks your offered beverage,—the foe-subduing *Śatakratu*, most liberal of men.

Sāmaveda, 155, 713.

Most Liberal of Men— Or "to be most honoured of men," *Maṁhiṣṭ hacarṣaṇīnām.*

७४८४. पुरु॒हू॒तं पुरु॑ष्टुतं॒ गाथा॑न्यं॒ सन॑श्रुतम्। इन्द्र॒ इति॑ ब्रवीतन॥२॥

2. Proclaim that deity as *Indra*, who is invoked by many, who is praised by many, who is worthy of songs and renowned as eternal.

Sāmaveda, 714.

७४८५. इन्द्र॒ इन्नो॑ म॒हानां॒ दाता॑ वा॒जानां॑ नृ॒तु:। म॒हाँ अ॒भिज्ञा य॑मत्॥३॥

3. May *Indra* who causes all to rejoice, be the given of plenteous food to us; may he, the mighty, bring us (riches) up to our knees.

Sāmaveda, 715, with *mahonām* for *mahānām*.

Who causes all to Rejoice— *Nṛtuḥ=nartayitā*, "he who causes all to dance," *cf.* II.22.4. Sāyaṇa gives another explanations as "bringer *(neta)* of kine to your votaries." The St. Petersh. Dict. renders it "lebhaft, beweglich."

७४८६. अपादु शिप्रयन्धसः सुदक्षस्य प्रहोषिणः। इन्दोरिन्द्रो यवाशिरः॥४॥

4. *Indra*, the handsome-jawed, has drunk of the dropping *Soma*-beverage cooked with barley, (the offering) of *Sudakṣa* assiduous in sacrifice.

Sāmaveda, 145.

Sudakṣa— This is explained as the name of a *Ṛṣi*. Benfey takes *sudakṣasya prahoṣiṇaḥ* as epithets of the *Soma*, "des kraftigen, aufregenden."

७४८७. तम्वभि प्राचतेन्द्रं सोमस्य पीतये। तदिद्ध्यस्य वर्धनम्॥५॥

5. Loudly praise that *Indra* that he may drink the *Soma*,—it is this which gives gim strength.

७४८८. अस्य पीत्वा मदानां देवो देवस्यौजसा। विश्वाभि भुवना भुवत्॥६॥

6. The god, having quaffed its exhilarations, by the strength of the divine *(Soma)* has conquered all worlds.

७४८९. त्यमु वः सत्रासाहं विश्वासु गीर्ष्वायतम्। आ च्यावयस्यूतये॥७॥

7. Bring hither for our protection *Indra* the conqueror of many, who pervades all your praises;

Sāmaveda, I.2.2.3.6; II.8.1.10.1. This verse is addressed by the sacrificer to the praising priest.

७४९०. युध्मं सन्तमनर्वाणं सोमपामनपच्युतम्। नरमवार्यक्रतुम्॥८॥

8. The warrior, whom none oppose and none can harm, the quaffer of the *Soma*, the leader whose deeds cannot be hindered.

Sāmaveda, 1643.

७४९१. शिक्षा ण इन्द्र राय आ पुरु विद्वाँ ऋचीषम। अवा नः पार्ये धने॥९॥

9. O you worthy of our praise, you who know all things, repeatedly give us riches, protect us by the wealth our enemies.

Sāmaveda, 1644.

७४९२. अतश्चिदिन्द्र ण उपा याहि शतवाजया। इषा सहस्रवाजया॥१०॥

10. Come to us, *Indra*, from thence with food of an hundred-fold strength, of a thousand-fold strength.

Sāmaveda, 215.

From Thence— *I.e.,* from heaven or from our enemies' abode.

७४९३. अयां धीवतो धियोऽवेद्धि: शक्र गोदरे। जयेम पृत्सु वेज्रिव:॥११॥

11. *Śakra*, let us go, proved in deeds, to deeds; thunderer, cleaver of mountains, let us conquer in battles by your steeds.

By your steeds— Sāyaṇa says "by steeds given by you."

७४९४. वयमुं त्वा शतक्रतो गावो न यवसेष्वा। उक्थेषु रणयामसि॥१२॥

12. We refresh you, *Śatakratu*, with our praises, as (the herdsman) the cattle with (different kinds of) pasture.

७४९५. विश्वा हि मर्त्यत्वनानुकामा शंतक्रतो। अगन्म वज्रिन्नाशसं:॥१३॥

13. All mortal natures, *Śatakratu*, are moved by desire; we feel wishes. O thunderer.

७४९६. त्वे सु पुत्र शवसोऽवृत्रन् कामंकातय:। न त्वामिन्द्रातिं रिच्यते॥१४॥

14. O son of strength, men, uttering their desires, abide happily in you; none, *Indra*, surpasses you.

७४९७. स नौ वृषन्त्सनिष्ठया सं घोरया द्रविंत्वा। धियाविड्ढि पुरन्ध्या॥१५॥

15. Showerer (of blessings), protect us by your action, which is most bounteous yet awful, foe-terrifying yet many-cherishing.

So Sāyaṇa, who explains *purandhyā* by *bahūnām dhārayitryā*: but he himself explains the word in V.35.8 (*no ratham ava purandhyā*) by *śobhanabuddhyā*. I should therefore prefer to translate the verse, "Showerer, protect us by your care, by your good providence, which is bounteous and yet awful and foe-terrifying."

७४९८. यस्तें नूनं शंतक्रतविन्द्र द्युम्नितंमो मद:। तेनं नूनं मदें मदे:॥१६॥

16. Rejoice us, *Indra*, *Śatakratu*, as you rejoice in that most glorious exhilaration of the *Soma*;

Sāmaveda, 116.

Rejoice Us— Benfey takes it "des rauschs berausche rich."

७४९९. यस्तें चित्रश्रवस्तमो य इन्द्र वृत्रहन्तंम:। य ओजोदातंमो मद:॥१७॥

17. That *Soma* of your, *Indra*, which is most widely renowned, most destructive of your enemies, and most renovating to your strength.

७५००. विद्मा हि यस्ते॑ अद्रिव॒स्त्वादत्त॑: सत्य॒ सोमपा॑:।
विश्वा॑सु॒ दस्म॑ कृ॒ष्टिषु॑॥१८॥

18. Thunderer, smiter of enemies, truthful drinker of the *Soma*, we know (the wealth) which is given by you to all your votaries.

७५०१. इन्द्रा॑य॒ मद्व॑ने सु॒तं परि॒ शोभ॑न्तु नो॒ गिर॑:। अ॒र्कम॑र्चन्तु का॒रव॑:॥१९॥

19. Let our voices praise on every side the (*Soma*) effused to the exhilarated *Indra*; let the priests do honour to the (*soma*) honoured of all.

Sāmaveda, 158, 722.

७५०२. यस्मि॒न् विश्वा॒ अधि॒ श्रियो॒ रण॑न्ति स॒प्त सं॒सद॑:।
इन्द्रं॑ सु॒ते ह॑वामहे॥२०॥

20. We invoke, now that the *Soma* is effused, that *Indra* in whom all graces are at their height, and in whom the seven associated priests rejoice.

Sāmaveda, 723.

७५०३. त्रि॒कद्रु॑केषु॒ चेत॑नं दे॒वासो॑ य॒ज्ञम॑त्नत। तमिद्व॑र्धन्तु नो॒ गिर॑:॥२१॥

21. The gods extended the heaven-revealing sacrifice in the *Trikadruka* days,—may our praise prosper it.

Sāmaveda, 724. The verse has already occurred in VIII.13.18, and Sāyaṇa there took *yajñam Indra*, sc. *yaṣṭavyam*.

Trikadruka Days— These are the first three days of the *ābhiplava*, a religious ceremony which lasts six days and is a part of the *Gavamayana* sacrifice. The first three days are severally called *jyotis*, *go* and *āyus*, the last three *go*, *āyus* and *jyotis*.

७५०४. आ त्वा॑ विशन्त्विन्द॑व: समु॒द्रमि॑व॒ सिन्ध॑व:।
न त्वामि॒न्द्राति॑ रिच्यते॥२२॥

22. Let the *Soma*-drops enter you as the rivers the sea: none, *Indra* surpasses you.

Sāmaveda, 197, 1660.

७५०५. विव्य॒क्थ महि॑ना वृष॑न्भ॒क्षं सोम॑स्य जागृवे। य इ॑न्द्र॒ ज॒ठरे॑षु ते॥२३॥

23. *Indra*, showerer (of blessings), wakeful one, you have attained by your might the drinking of the *Soma* which enters into your belly.

Sāmaveda, 1661.

७५०६. अरं॒ त इ॑न्द्र॒ कुक्ष॑ये॒ सोमो॑ भवतु वृत्रहन्। अरं॒ धाम॑भ्य॒ इन्द॑व:॥२४॥

24. *Indra*, slayer of *Vṛtra*, may the *Soma* be enough for your belly, may the drops be enough for your (various) bodies.

Sāmaveda, 1662. Sāyaṇa explains *dhāmabhyaḥ* for your various bodies or splendours, *nānāvidhebhyaḥ śarīrebhyas tava tajobhyo vā.*

७५०७. अरमश्वाय गायति श्रुतकक्षो अरं गवे। अरमिन्द्रस्य धाम्ने॥२५॥

25. *Śrutakakṣa* sings enough for a horse, enough for a cow, enough for a house of *Indra*.

Sāmaveda, 118, with *gāyata śrutakakṣa* or *gāyati śrutakakṣaḥ*.

Sings for a horse, cow, Etc.— It is not clear whether these gifts are past or future ones,—Sāyaṇa allows both interpretations. He explains *Indrasya dhāmne* as "for a house given by *Indra*." Benfey takes it as *Indra's* heaven.

७५०८. अरं हि ष्मा सुतेषु णः सोमेष्विन्द्र भूषसि। अरं ते शक्र दावने॥२६॥

26. When our *Soma*-libations are effused, you are abundantly able (to drink them),—may they be enough for you, the bounteous.

Abundantly Able— Sāyaṇa takes *bhūṣasi* as for *bhavasi*, or as=*prāpaya*, "bring us abundant wealth." The St. Petersb. Dict. derives it from *bhūṣ* "sich ernstlich bemühen um."

७५०९. पराकात्ताच्चिदद्रिवस्त्वां नक्षन्त नो गिरः। अरं गमाम ते वयम्॥२७॥

27. May our praises reach you, thunderer, even from afar; may we obtain your (wealth) abundantly.

७५१०. एवा ह्यसि वीरयुरेवा शूर उत स्थिरः। एवा ते राध्यं मनः॥२८॥

28. You verily love to smite the mighty, you are a hero and firm (in battle), your mind is to be propitiated (by praise).

Sāmaveda, 232, 824.

The Mighty— Benfey takes *Virayu* as "helden-liebend."

७५११. एवा रातिस्तुवीमघ विश्वेभिर्धायि धातृभिः।

अर्धा चिदिन्द्र मे सचा॥२९॥

29. Lord of great wealth, your bounty is possessed by all your worshippers; therefore, *Indra*, be also my ally.

Sāmaveda, 825.

७५१२. मो षु ब्रह्मेव तन्द्रयुर्भुवो वाजानां पते। मत्स्वा सुतस्य गोमतः॥३०॥

30. Be not like a laze *Brāhmaṇa*, O lord of food; rejoice thyself by drinking the effused *Soma* mixed with milk.

Sāmaveda, 826. *Brāhmaṇa* is explained here by Sāyaṇa as a *Brāhmaṇa*, but *cf.* Haug's *Ait. Brāhm.* pref., p.20, and his transl., p. 376.

७५१३. मा न॑ इन्द्रा॒भ्या॑इ॒दिश॑: सू॒रो अ॑क्तु॒ष्वा य॑मन्।
त्वा यु॒जा व॑नेम॒ तत्॥३१॥

31. *Indra*, let not the threatening prowling (demons) obstruct us at night; let us smite them with you as our helper.

Sāmaveda, 128, with *yamata* for *yaman*.

७५१४. त्वये॒दिन्द्र॑ यु॒जा व॒यं प्रति॑ ब्रुवीमहि॒ स्पृध॑:।
त्वम॒स्माकं॒ तव॑ स्मसि॥३२॥

32. With you, *Indra*, as our helper, let us answer our enemies; you are ours, we are your.

७५१५. त्वामि॒द्धि त्वा॒यवो॒ऽनुनो॑नु॒वत॑श्चरा॑न्। सखा॑य इन्द्र का॒रव॑:॥३३॥

33. *Indra*, may your friends, the chanters, worship you, devoted to your service and again and again reciting your praise.

[सूक्त-९३]

[**ऋषि**– सुकक्ष आङ्गिरस। **देवता**– इन्द्र, ३४ इन्द्र तथा ऋभुगण।
छन्द– गायत्री।

७५१६. उद्घे॒दभि॑ श्रु॒ताम॑घं॒ वृष॒भं नर्या॑पसम्। अस्ता॑रमेषि॒ सूर्य॑॥१॥

1. You risest, O sun, on (the sacrifice of *Indra*) the showerer (of blessings), the bountiful giver, famed for his wealth, the benefactor of men;

Sāmaveda, 125, 1450. *Indra* is himself one of the twelve *Ādityas*.

७५१७. नव॒ यो न॑व॒तिं पुरो॑ बि॒भेद॑ बा॒ह्वोज॑सा। अहिं॑ च वृत्र॒हाव॑धीत्॥२॥

2. Who cleft the ninety-nine cities by the strength of his arm, and, slayer of *Vṛtra*, smote *Ahi*.

Sāmaveda, 1451.

The Ninety-nine Cities—*Cf.* II.19.6.

Ahi— Sc. the cloud.

७५१८. स न॒ इन्द्र॑: शि॒व: सखा॑श्वा॒वद्गोम॒द्यव॑मत्। उ॒रुधा॑रेव दोहते॥३॥

3. May *Indra*, our auspicious friend, milk for us, like a richly-streaming (cow), wealth of horses, kine, and barley.

Sāmaveda, 1452.

७५१९. यद॒द्य कच्च॑ वृत्रहन्नु॒दगा॑ अ॒भि सूर्य॑। सर्वं॒ तदि॑न्द्र ते॒ वशे॑॥४॥

4. Whatsoever, O Sun, slayer of *Vṛtra*, you have risen upon to-day,—it is all, *Indra*, under your power.

Yajurveda, 33.35. Sāmaveda, 126.

७५२०. यद्वा प्रवृद्ध सत्पते न मरा इति मन्यसे। उतो तत्सत्यमित्तव।५॥

5. When, swelling in your might, lord of the good, you think "I shall not die," that thought of yours is indeed true.

Lord of the Good— According to Sāyaṇa "lord of the *nakṣatras.*"

७५२१. ये सोमास: परावति ये अर्वावति सुन्विरे।
सर्वांस्ताँ इन्द्र गच्छसि।६॥

6. You go at once, *Indra*, to all those *Soma*-libations which are effused afar or effused near.

७५२२. तमिन्द्रं वाजयामसि महे वृत्राय हन्तवे। स वृषा वृषभो भुवत्।७॥

7. We invigorate that (great) *Indra* for the slaying of mighty *Vṛtra*; may he be a bounteous showerer (of wealth).

Sāmaveda, 119, 1222.

७५२३. इन्द्र: स दामने कृत ओजिष्ठ: स मदे हित:।
द्युम्नी श्लोकी स सोम्य:॥८॥

8. *Indra* was created for giving he, the most mighty was set over the exhilarating *Soma*; he, the glorious one the lord of praise, is worthy of the *Soma.*

Sāmaveda, 1223, with *bale* for *made.*

Indra was Created— Sāyaṇa adds "by *Prajāpati* all the time of creation."

७५२४. गिरा वज्रो न सम्भृत: सबले अनपच्युत:।
ववक्ष ऋष्वो अस्तृत:॥९॥

9. The mighty (*Indra*), unassailed by his foes, hastens to confer wealth on his worshippers,—rendered keen by their praises as a weapon, full of strength and invincible.

Sāmaveda, 1224, with *ugro* for *ṛṣvaḥ.*

७५२५. दुर्गे चित्र: सुगं कृधि गृणान इन्द्र गिर्वण:। त्वं च मघवन् वश:॥१०

10. *Indra*, worthy of our praise, do you, hymned by us, make our path plain even in the midst of difficulties, (hear us), *Maghavan*, if you love us;

७५२६. यस्य ते नू चिदादिशं न मिनन्ति स्वराज्यम्।
न देवो नाधिगुर्जनं:॥११॥

11. You whose command and rightful empire neither god nor irresistible hero can harm.

Rightful empire— Sāyaṇa gives another explanation of *svarājya* as *svargasvāmitva*.

७५२७. अधा॑ ते॑ अप्र॑तिष्कुतं दे॒वी शुष्मं॑ सप॒र्यत॒: । उ॒भे सुशि॒प्र रोद॑सी ॥१२॥

12. Yea, deity of the handsome jaw, the two goddesses, heaven and earth, both worship your resistless consuming might.

७५२८. त्वमे॑तद॑धारय: कृ॒ष्णासु॒ रोहि॑णीषु च । प॒रु॒ष्णीषु॒ रुश॒त् पय॑: ॥१३॥

13. It is you that keep this bright milk in the black, red, and spotted cows.

७५२९. वि यद॑हेर॒ध त्विषो॒ विश्वे॑ दे॒वासो॒ अक्र॑मु: ।

विद॒न्मृग॑स्य॒ ता अम॑: ॥१४॥

14. When all the gods fled in various directions from the splendour of the demon *Ahi*, and when fear of the deer seized them.

Fear of the Deer— *Cf.* I.80.7; v. 32.3;; 43.2.

७५३०. आदु॑ मे॒ निव॑रो भु॒वद् वृ॒त्रह॒दिष्ट॒ पौस्य॑म् । अ॒जा॑तशत्रुरस्तृत॒: ॥१५॥

15. Then was my *Indra* the repeller; then did the smiter of *Vṛtra* put forth his might, he who has no existent enemies, the invincible.

७५३१. श्रु॒तं वो॑ वृ॒त्रह॑न्त॒मं प्र शर्ध॑ चर्षणी॒नाम् । आ शुषे॒ राध॑से म॒हे ॥१६॥

16. (Priests), I bring to you men, for great wealth, that renowned and mighty one who utterly destroyed *Vṛtra*.

Sāmaveda, 208, with *āśiṣe* for *āśuṣe*. I should prefer to take *carṣaṇīnām* as governed by the epithets of *Indra*, "renowned and mighty amongst men."

७५३२. अ॒या धि॒या च॑ ग॒व्यया॑ पु॒रुणा॑मन्नुरुष्टुत । यत्सोमे॑सोम॒ आभ॑व: ॥१७॥

17. O you bearing many names and praised by many, when you are present at our various *Soma*-libations, may we be endowed with a kine-desiring mind.

Sāmaveda, 188.

May We be endowed with a kine-desiring Mind— Sāyaṇa explains this to mean "may we obtain kine." *Gavyayā* should mean "with a desire for milk." Might it be rendered "Come with this mind, with this desire for milk, when you are present at our *Soma* offerings?"

७५३३. बोधिन्मना इदस्तु नो वृत्रहा भूर्यासुतिः।
शृणोतु शक्र आशिषम्।।१८।।

18. May the slayer of *Vṛtra*, to whom many libations are offered, know our desires,—may *Śakra* hear our praises.

Sāmaveda, 140, reading *bodhanmanāḥ*.

७५३४. कया त्वं न ऊत्याभि प्र मन्दसे वृषन्।
कया स्तोतृभ्य आ भर।।१९।।

19. Showerer (of blessings), with what coming of your do you gladden us, with what coming bring you (wealth) to your worshippers?

Yajurveda, 36.7; *Sāmaveda*, 1586.

७५३५. कस्य वृषा सुते सचा नियुत्वान्वृषभो रणत्। वृत्रहा सोमपीतये।।२०।।

20. At whose hymn-accompanied libations does the showerer, the lord of the *Niyuts,* the slayer of *Vṛtra*, rejoice to drink the *Soma*?

७५३६. अभी षु णस्त्वं रयिं मन्दसानः सहस्रिणम्।
प्रयन्ता बोधि दाशुषे।।२१।।

21. Rejoicing (in our oblations), bring us wealth a thousandfold; remember that you are the giver to your votary.

७५३७. पत्नीवन्तः सुता इम उशन्तो यन्ति वीतये।
अपां जग्मिर्निचुम्पुणः।।२२।।

22. These *Soma*-libations with their wives proceed (to *Indra*) longing to be drunk; the stale *Soma*, pleasing to the taste, goes to the waters.

This a very obscure verse; Sāyaṇa follows the explanation given by Yāska, *Nir.*, V.18. The epithet *patnīvantaḥ* ''with their wives or protectresses'' is said to allude to the two kinds of water, the *Vasatīvaryaḥ* and the *Ekadhanāḥ*, used in the *Soma* offerings. (*Cf. Ait. Brāhm.*, II.20.) At the time of the *Avabhṛtha*, or concluding ceremonies of purification, the *ṛjīṣa* or stale *Soma* is thrown into the waters. The epithet *nicuṁpuṇaḥ*, which Yāska *explains nīcamānena pṛṇāti*, is derived by Mahīdhara (*Yajurveda*, 3.48) from the root *cup* 'lente incedere,' and similarly the St. Petersb. Dict. explains it 'senlöpfrig.'

७५३८. इष्टा होत्रा असृक्षतेन्द्रं वृधासो अध्वरे। अच्छावभृथमोजसा।।२३।।

23. The sacrificing priests, invigorating (*Indra*) by their offerings at the sacrifice, have by their might dismissed him to the *Avabhṛtha*.

Sāmaveda, 151, with *vridhantah*.

७५३९. इह त्या सधमाद्या हरी हिरण्यकेश्या। वोळ्हामभि प्रयो हितम्॥२४॥

24. May those two golden-maned steeds together exulting bring him to our wholesome offering.

See viii.32.29.

७५४०. तुभ्यं सोमाः सुता इमे स्तीर्णं बर्हिर्विभावसो।
स्तोतृभ्य इन्द्रमा वह॥२५॥

25. Resplendent (*Agni*), these *Soma*-libations are effused for you, and the clipt grass is spread; bring *Indra* hither for his worshippers.

Sāmaveda, 213, but with some variations.

७५४१. आ ते दक्षं वि रोचना दधद्रत्ना वि दाशुषे।
स्तोतृभ्य इन्द्रमर्चत॥२६॥

26. May he give strength and his brilliant heaven and precious things to you his worshipper, and to his praising priests; worship *Indra*.

७५४२. आ तें दधामीन्द्रियमुक्था विश्वा शतक्रतो।
स्तोतृभ्य इन्द्र मृळय॥२७॥

27. I prepare, *Śatakratu*, your strong (*Soma*) and all your praises; be gracious, *Indra*, to your hymners.

७५४३. भद्रम्भद्रं न आ भरेषमूर्जं शतक्रतो। यदिन्द्र मृळयासि नः॥२८॥

28. Bring us what is most auspicious, *Śatakratu*, (bring us) food and strength, if you have favour to us, *Indra*.

Sāmaveda, 173.

७५४४. स नो विश्वान्या भर सुवितानि शतक्रतो। यदिन्द्र मृळयासि नः॥२९॥

29. Bring us all blessings, *Śatakratu*, if you have favour to us, *Indra*.

७५४५. त्वामिद्वृत्रहन्तम सुतावन्तो हवामहे। यदिन्द्र मृळयासि नः॥३०॥

30. Bearing the effused libation, we invoke you, mightiest slayer of *Vṛtra*, if you have favour to us, *Indra*.

७५४६. उप नो हरिभिः सुतं याहि मंदानां पते। उप नो हरिभिः सुतम्॥३१

31. Come with your steeds to our effused libation, lord of the Soma,—come with your steeds to our effused libation.

Sāmaveda, 150, 1790.

७५४७. द्विता यो वृत्रहन्तमो विद इन्द्रः शतक्रतुः।
उप नो हरिभिः सुतम्॥३२॥

32. *Indra*, *Śatakratu*, mightiest slayer of *Vṛtra*, you whose power is known in a two-fold way, come with your steeds to our effused libation.

Sāmaveda, 1791.

Whose power is known in a two-fold Way— *I.e.,* You are known in your terrible from as the slayer of *Vṛtra*, etc., and in your merciful from as the protector of the world. *Cf. sup*.70.2. The St. Petersb. Dict. explains *dvita* as 'besonders.'

७५४८. त्वं हि वृत्रहन्नेषां पाता सोमानामसि। उप नो हरिभिः सुतम्॥३३॥

33. Slayer of *Vṛtra*, you are the drinker of these *Soma* juices, come with your steeds to our effused libation.

Sāmaveda, 1792.

७५४९. इन्द्र इषे ददातु न ऋभुक्षणमृभुं रयिम्। वाजी ददातु वाजिनम्॥३४॥

34. May *Indra* bring to us the bounteous *Ribhu Ṛbhukṣaṇa* to partake of our sacrificial viands; may he, the mighty, bring the mighty (*Vāja*).

Sāmaveda, 199.

Ṛbhukṣaṇa— *Ṛbhukṣaṇa* was the eldest and *Vāja* the youngest of the three brothers. The *Ṛbhus* have a share in the evening libation between *Prajāpati* and *Savitā*, see *Ait. Brāhm.*, III.30. This verse is addressed to the *Ṛbhus* in the evening libation on the ninth day of the *Dvādaśaha* ceremony (*ib.*, V.21).

[सूक्त-९४]

[ऋषि- बिन्दु अथवा पूतदक्ष आङ्गिरस। देवता- मरुद्गण। छन्द- गायत्री।

७५५०. गौर्धयति मरुतां श्रवस्युर्माता मघोनाम्। युक्ता वह्नी रथानाम्॥१॥

1. The cow (*Pṛśni*), the food-desiring mother of the wealthy *Maruts*, drinks (the *Soma*),—she is worthy of all honour, who yokes (the mares) to their chariots,

Sāmaveda, 149.

The Cow— *Cf.* I.23.10; II.34.2, etc.

७५५१. यस्या देवा उपस्थे व्रता विश्वे धारयन्ते। सूर्यामासा दृशे कम्॥२॥

2. She, in whose presence all the gods observe their functions, and the sun and moon move in peace to enlighten the world.

७५५२. तत्सु नो विश्वे अर्य आ सदा गृणन्ति कारवः। मरुतः सोमपीतये॥३

3. Therefore all our priests in their worship always sing the *Maruts* that they may drink the *Soma*.

Sāyaṇa explains this verse, "all our priests in their worship always sing that (might of the *Maruts*) that they may drink the *Soma*; the *Maruts* (are to be invoked by us)."

७५५३. अस्ति सोमो अयं सुतः पिबन्त्यस्य मरुतः।
          उप स्वराजो अश्विना॥४॥

4. This *Soma* is effused (by us); the self-resplendent *Maruts* drink of it, and the *Aśvins*.

Sāmaveda, 174, 1785. The construction would rather indicate that *svarājaḥ* is an epithet of *asya* (*somasya*) not of *marutaḥ*.

७५५४. पिबन्ति मित्रो अर्यमा तना पूतस्य वरुणः। त्रिषधस्थस्य जावतः॥५॥

5. *Mitra*, *Aryaman*, and *Varuṇa* drink (the *Soma*), purified by the straining cloth, abiding in three places, and granting posterity.

Sāmaveda, 1786.

Abiding in three Places— "The *Soma* juice, when it is extracted, is poured into the *Ādhavanīya*, a kind of trough. Thence it is poured into a cloth, in order to strain it. This cloth is called *Pavitra* or *Daśāpavitra*. Below the cloth is another trough called *Pūtabhṛt*" (Haug). These are the "three places" of the text.

Granting Posterity—*Jāvataḥ* is a hard word. Sāyaṇa explains it *stutyajanavantam* "having reference to praise-worthy persons"; I have adopted the rendering of the St. Petersburg Dict. "an Nachkommenschaft reich, der Nachkommenschaft geben kann."

७५५५. उतो न्वस्य जोषमाँ इन्द्रः सुतस्य गोमतः। प्रातर्होतेव मत्सति॥६॥

6. *Indra* also is eager in the morning to drink this effused (*Soma*) mixed with milk, as a priest (to praise the gods).

Sāmaveda, 1787.

७५५६. कदत्विषन्त सूर्यस्तिर आपैव स्निधः। अर्षन्ति पूतदक्षसः॥७॥

7. When do the sages flash like waters across (to sky)? When do the *Maruts*, pure in vigour, destroyers of enemies, come to our offering?

७५५७. कद्वो॒ अ॒द्य म॒हानां॑ देवाना॒मवो॑ वृणे। त्मना॑ च द॒स्मव॑र्चसाम्॥८॥

8. O shall I to-day possess your protection, mighty deities, beautifully bright in yourselves (though unadorned)?

७५५८. आ ये विश्वा॑ पार्थि॑वानि प॒प्रथ॒न्नीचना॑ दि॒वः। म॒रुतः॑ सोम॑पीतये॥९॥

9. (We invoke) those *Maruts* to drink our *Soma*, who have spread our all the things of earth and the luminaries of heaven.

७५५९. त्यान्नु॑ पू॒तद॑क्षसो दि॒वो वो॑ मरुतो हुवे। अ॒स्य सोम॑स्य पी॒तये॑॥१०॥

10. O *Maruts*, I invoke you, resplendent, of pure vigour, to drink this *Soma*.

७५६०. त्यान्नु॑ ये वि रोद॑सी त॒स्तभुर्म॒रुतो॑ हुवे। अ॒स्य सोम॑स्य पी॒तये॑॥११॥

11. I invoke those *Maruts* to drink this *Soma*, who have established heaven and earth.

७५६१. त्वं नु मारु॑तं ग॒णं गि॑रि॒ष्ठां वृ॒ष॒णं हुवे। अ॒स्य सोम॑स्य पी॒तये॑॥१२॥

12. I invoke that band of the *Maruts*, abiding in the clouds, the showerers, to drink this *Soma*.

[सूक्त-९५]

[ऋषि– तिरश्ची आङ्गिरस। देवता– इन्द्र। छन्द– अनुष्टुप्]

७५६२. आ त्वा॒ गिरो॑ र॒थीरि॒वास्थुः॑ सु॒तेषु॑ गिर्वणः।
अ॒भि त्वा॒ सम॑नूषते॒न्द्रं वत्सं॒ न मा॒तरः॑॥१॥

1. O *Indra*, worthy of praise when the *Soma* is effused our songs hasten to you as charioteer (to his go, they low towards you as cows towards their calves.
Sāmaveda, 349.

७५६३. आ त्वा॑ शु॒क्रा अ॑चुच्यवुः सु॒तास॑ इन्द्र गिर्वणः।
पिबा॒ त्व१ँ स्या॒न्ध॑स इन्द्र वि॒श्वासु॑ ते हि॒तम्॥२॥

2. *Indra* worthy of praise, let the bright *Soma*-libations come to you; drink your portion of the beverage; *Indra*, in all places it is fit for you.

७५६४. पिबा॒ सोमं॒ म॒दाय॒ कमि॑न्द्र श्ये॒नाभृ॑तं सु॒तम्।
त्वं हि श॒श्व॑तीनां॒ पती॒ राजा॑ वि॒शाम॑सि॥३॥

3. Drink to your fill, *Indra*, the effused *Soma* brought, by the hawk, you are the lord of all the divine hosts, you are the self-resplendent.

Brought by the Hawk— *Cf.* I.80.2.

The Lord of all the divine Hosts— Sāyaṇa taken *śaśvatīnām* with *viśām*, as *bahunām marudgaṇān sarveṣām devagaṇānām ca.*

७५६५. श्रुधी हवं तिरश्च्या इन्द्र यस्त्वा सपर्यति ।
सुवीर्यस्य गोमंतो रायस्पूर्धि महाँ असि ॥४॥

4. Hear, *Indra*, the prayer of *Tiraści* who worships you, and satisfy him with wealth bringing gallant offspring and cattle,—for you are mighty.

Sāmaveda, 346, 882.

७५६६. इन्द्र यस्ते नवीयसीं गिरं मन्द्रामजीजनत् ।
चिकित्विन्मनसं धियं प्रत्नामृतस्य पिप्युषीम् ॥५॥

5. To him who has made for you this newest joy-giving hymn, do you, *Indra*, (extend) your ancient truthful providence to which all hearts are known.

Sāmaveda, 884, with *yas to Indra* for *Indra yas te.*

७५६७. तमु ष्टवाम यं गिर इन्द्रमुक्थानि वावृधुः ।
पुरूण्यस्य पौंस्या सिषासन्तो वनामहे ॥६॥

6. Let us praise that *Indra* whom our chants and hymns have magnified; we worship him, desirous to honour his many deeds of might.

Sāmaveda, 885.

७५६८. एतो न्विन्द्रं स्तवाम शुद्धं शुद्धेन साम्ना ।
शुद्धैरुक्थैर्वावृध्वांसं शुद्ध आशीर्वान्ममत्तु ॥७॥

7. Come let us praise the purified *Indra* with a pure *Sāman* and with pure recited hymns; let the pure (*Soma*) mixed with milk gladden him waxing strong.

Sāmaveda, 350, 1402, with *śuddhaiḥ* in the second line for *śuddha.*

Sāyaṇa illustrates this and the following verses by a egend from the *Sātyāyana Brāhmaṇa. Indra*, after the slaughter of *Vṛtra*, being polluted by the guilt of *Brahmanicide*, begged the *Ṛṣis* to purify him by their *Sāman* hymns. They accordingly said these verses and he became purified; and they then offered him the *Soma*, etc.

७५६९. इन्द्र शुद्धो न आ गहि शुद्धः शुद्धाभिरूतिभिः।
शुद्धो रयिं नि धारय शुद्धो ममद्धि सोम्यः॥८॥

8. Come to us, *Indra*, purified; purified with your pure protecting hosts; purified establish wealth in us; purified and now worthy of the *Soma*, rejoice.

Sāmaveda, 1403.

The Pure Protecting Hosts— The *Maruts*.

७५७०. इन्द्र शुद्धो हि नो रयिं शुद्धो रत्नानि दाशुषे।
शुद्धो वृत्राणि जिघ्नसे शुद्धो वाजं सिषाससि॥९॥

9. Purified, *Indra*, give us wealth; purified give to your worshipper precious things; purified you smite your enemies; purified you desire to give us food.

Sāmaveda, 1404.

[सूक्त-९६]

[**ऋषि**– तिरश्ची आङ्गिरस अथवा द्युतान मारुत। **देवता**– इन्द्र, १४ चतुर्थ चरण– मरुद्गण, १५ इन्द्राबृहस्पती। **छन्द**– त्रिष्टुप्, ४ विराट्]

७५७१. अस्मा उषास आतिरन्त याममिन्द्राय नक्तमूर्म्याः सुवार्चः।
अस्मा आपो मातरः सप्त तस्थुर्नृभ्यस्तराय सिन्धवः सुपाराः॥१॥

1. For him the dawns prolonged their rising; for *Indra* the nights uttered auspicious voices by night; for him the waters, the mothers, the seven rivers, stood, offering an easy passage for men to cross over.

The nights uttered auspicious Voices by night— Sāyaṇa's explanation is, "All men read the *Veda*, etc., in the latter half of the night; therefore the voices of the night were auspicious; they studied the *Veda* under *Indra's* direction."

७५७२. अतिविद्धा विथुरेण चिदस्त्रा त्रिः सप्त सानु संहिता गिरीणाम्।
न तद्देवो न मर्त्यस्तुर्याद्यानि प्रवृद्धो वृषभश्चकार॥२॥

2. By him the thrower, unaided, were pierced asunder the thrice seven table-lands of the mountains heaped together; neither god nor mortal could do what he, the showerer, in his full-grown strength has done.

Pierced Asunder the thrice seven tablelands—For this legend compare *surpra*, note on VIII.8.8.10.

७५७३. इन्द्रस्य॒ वज्र॒ आय॑सो॒ निमि॑श्ल॒ इन्द्र॑स्य बा॒ह्वोर्भूयि॑ष्ठमो॒जः।
शीर्ष॒न्निन्द्र॑स्य॒ क्रत॑वो निरे॒क आ॒सन्ने॑षन्त॒ श्रुत्या॑ उ॒पा॒के॥३॥

3. *Indra's* iron thunderbolt is grasped firmly in his hand; enormous strength resides in his arms: when he goes forth (to battle), there is ample employment for his head and his mouth, and (his followers) rush near him to hear his commands.

Ample Employment for his head and his Mouth— *I.e.,* his head is employed in fitting the helmet, etc., and his eyes in seeing the enemy; and the mouth issues its various orders.

७५७४. मन्ये॑ त्वा य॒ज्ञिय॑ यज्ञि॒याना॒ मन्ये॑ त्वा च्य॒वन॑मच्युता॒नाम्।
मन्ये॑ त्वा॒ सत्व॑नामिन्द्र के॒तुं मन्ये॑ त्वा वृ॒षभं॑ चर्ष॒णीनाम्॥४॥

4. I think you the most worthy among those worthy of sacrifice: I think you the overthrower of the imperishable (mountains); I think you, *Indra,* the banner of warriors; I think you the showerer (of blessings) to men.

Of the imperishable Mountains— Sāyaṇa adds another interpretation "of the heroes not to be overthrown."

The Banner of Warriors— Another but less likely interpretation is "the manifester of thyself to your worshippers."

७५७५. आ यद्व॒ज्रं बा॒ह्वोरि॑न्द्र॒ धत्से॑ मद॒च्युत॒मह॑ये॒ हन्त॒वा उ॑।
प्र पर्व॑ता॒ अन॑वन्त॒ प्र गाव॒ः प्र ब्र॒ह्माणो॑ अभि॒नक्ष॑न्त॒ इन्द्र॑म्॥५॥

5. When, *Indra,* you grasp in your arms your pride humbling thunderbolt to smite *Ahi,* when the mountain clouds loudly roar and the cows loudly bellow, then the *Brāhmaṇas* offer their worship to *Indra.*

The Cows— The cows are the waters pent within the clouds.

The Brāhmaṇas— Sāyaṇa explains *brahmāṇaḥ* as "the Brāhmaṇas," or as "the mountains, etc."

७५७६. तमु॑ ष्ट्वां॒ य इ॒मा ज॒जान॒ विश्वा॑ जा॒तान्य॒वरा॑ण्य॒स्मात्।
इन्द्रे॑ण मि॒त्रं दि॑धिषेम गी॒र्भिरु॒पो नमो॑भिर्वृष॒भं वि॑शेम॥६॥

6. Let us praise that *Indra* who produced all the things, to him all beings are subsequent; may we maintain friendship with *Indra* by our hymns, let us bring the showerer (of blessings) near us by our praises.

May We maintain friendship with Indra— Sāyaṇa takes *mitram* as for *maitrīm;* but he offers another interpretation, "let us say by our hymns 'may we be friends with *Indra.*'"

७५७७. वृत्रस्य त्वा श्वसथादीर्षमाणा विश्वे देवा अजहुर्ये सखायः।
मरुद्भिरिन्द्र सख्यं ते अस्त्वथेमा विश्वाः पृतना जयासि ॥७॥

7. All the gods who were your friends forsook you, flying
away at the snorting of *Vṛtra*; O *Indra*, let there be friendship to
you with the *Maruts*: then do you conquer all these hostile armies.
Sāmaveda, 324.
Friendship with the *Maruts—* Cf. *Ait. Brāhm.*, III.20. The *Maruts*
alone did not leave him.

७५७८. त्रिः षष्टिस्त्वा मरुतो वावृधाना उस्राइव राशयो यज्ञियासः।
उप त्वेमः कृधि नो भागधेयं शुष्मं त एना हविषा विधेम ॥८॥

8. These sixty-three *Maruts* were worthy of sacrifice
nourishing your vigour like cows gathered together: we come to
you, do you grant us our portion; so will we produce strength in
you by this offering.
These sixty-three *Maruts—* *Triḥ Śaṣṭiḥ* would properly mean
"thrice sixty,' but Sāyaṇa takes it expressly as sixty-three, and explains it
by adding that there were nine companies of the *Maruts*, each composed
of seven. The *White Yajurveda*, 17.81-86 (*cf.* 39.7), gives six companies
of seven each; and Sāyaṇa in his Comm. on *Taitt. Saṁh.*, I.5.11, where he
quotes II.2.5, (*saptagaṇa vai Marutāḥ*) similarly gives the same number
(42), but with apparently differing names; he adds however, "the other
gāna is to be sought in another *śākhā*." Here he quotes five *gānas* from
the *Samhitā*, Iv. 6.5; a sixth, he says, is found in a *Khila* or supplementary
portion, and the three *ganas* remaining to make up the total of 63 he takes
from the *Taitt Āraṇyaka*. IV.24,25.

७५७९. तिग्ममायुधं मरुतामनीकं कस्त इन्द्र प्रति वज्रं दधर्ष।
अनायुधासो असुरा अदेवाश्चक्रेण ताँ अपं वप ऋजीषिन् ॥९॥

9. Your sharp bow, the host of *Maruts*, and your thunderbolt
who, *Indra*, has ever withstood? The *Asuras* are weaponless and
abandoned by the gods, drive them away by your discus, O *Ṛjīṣin*.
Cf. VIII.86.4.

७५८०. मह उग्राय तवसे सुवृक्तिं प्रेरय शिवतमाय पश्वः।
गिर्वाहसे गिर इन्द्राय पूर्वीर्धेहि तन्वे कुविदङ्ग वेदत् ॥१०॥

10. Send forth an excellent hymn to great (*Indra*), the strong,
might, and most fortunate, (that he may prosper) my cattle; utter
many praises to *Indra* who is borne by praise, may he speedily
give much wealth to me.

Who is Borne by Praise— *Cf.* I.30.5; 61.4.

७५८१. उक्थवाहसे विभ्वे मनीषां दुणा न पारमीरय नदीनाम्।
नि स्मृश धिया तन्वं श्रुतस्य जुष्टतरस्य कुविदङ्ग वेदत्॥११॥

11. Send forth your praise to mighty *Indra* who is borne by
hymns, as (a sailor sends a traveller) in a ship across the rivers;
bring to me by your rites that wealth which belongs to him
renowned and beneficent; may he speedily give much wealth.

Sāyaṇa illustrates this and the following verses by a legend that
Indra, aided by *Bṛhaspati* and the *Maruts*, slew the *asure Kṛṣṇa*, who
with 10,000 other *asuras* had occupied the river *Aṁśumatī*, which is said
to be the Yamunā. He adds a different legend from the *Bṛhaddevatā*,
which, however, not being declared by a *ṛṣi*, is not to be implicitly
received. (On this *cf.* Müller's remarks in Var. Lectt.) This other account
is to the effect that the *Soma*, being afraid of *Vṛtra*, took refuge with the
Kurus by the river *Aṁśumatī*. *Indra* followed it with *Bṛhaspati* and the
Maruts, and begged it to return. It however refused, and attempted to
resist; but it was ultimately conquered and carried back to the gods, who
drank it and in consequence vanquished the demons. *Drapsa* is a common
word for *Soma*, 'the dropping,' and can hardly mean 'swift-moving' as
Sāyaṇa takes it. Benfey refers the line to the cloud, taking *Aṁśumatī* as
the sunlight, "In die Aneumati sinkt niedereilend, herschreiten' mit
zehntausenden der schwarze."

७५८२. तद्दिविड्ढि यत् इन्द्रो जुजोषत्स्तुहि सुष्टुतिं नमसा विवास।
उप भूष जरितर्मा रुवण्यः श्रावया वाचं कुविदङ्ग वेदत्॥१२॥

12. Perform those rites of your that *Indra* may accept them;
praise him to whom praise belongs, worship him with your
service; O priest, adorn thyself, grieve not (for poverty); let *Indra*
hear your praise, may he speedily give much wealth.

७५८३. अव द्रप्सो अंशुमतीमतिष्ठदियानः कृष्णो दशभिः सहस्रैः।
आवत्तमिन्द्रः शच्या धमन्तमप स्नेहितीनृमणां अधत्त॥१३॥

13. The swift-moving *Kṛṣṇa* with ten thousand (demons) stood
on the *Aṁśumatī*; by his might *Indra* caught him snorting (in the
water); he, benevolent to man, smote his malicious (bands).

७५८४. द्रप्समपश्यं विषुणे चरन्तमुपह्वरे नद्यो अंशुमत्याः।
नभो न कृष्णमवतस्थिवांसमिष्याामि वो वृषणो युध्यताजौ॥१४॥

14. "I have seen the swift-moving (demon) lurking in an inaccessible place, in the depths of the river *Aṁśumatī*, (I have seen) *Kṛṣṇa* standing there as (the sun) in a cloud; I appeal to you, showerers; conquer him in battle."

This is *Indra's* speech to the *Maruts*. I suppose the simile means that, though the demon thinks to conceal himself, he is seen as clearly by *Indra* as the sun is behind a cloud.

७५८५. अर्धं द्रप्सो अँशुमत्या उपस्थेऽधारयत्तन्वं तित्विषाण:।
विशो अदेवीरभ्याइ चरन्तीर्बृहस्पतिना युजेन्द्र: ससाहे॥१५॥

15. Then the swift-moving one shining forth assumed his own body by the *Aṁśumatī*, and *Indra* with *Bṛhaspati* as his ally smote the godless hosts as they drew near.

The Godless House— Sāyaṇa explains *adevīḥ* as "not shining, dark," or "not to be praised" (Virgil's "illaudati").

७५८६. त्वं ह त्यत्सप्तभ्यो जार्यमानोऽशत्रुभ्यो अभव: शत्रुरिन्द्र। गूळ्हे
द्यावापृथिवी अन्वविन्दो विभुमद्भ्यो भुवनेभ्यो रणं धा:॥१६॥

16. As soon as you was born, *Indra*, you was an enemy to those seven who had no enemy; you recovered the heavens and earth when concealed (in darkness); you cause joy to the mighty worlds.

Sāmaveda, 326.

Those Seven who had no Enemy— Sc. *Kṛṣṇa, Vṛtra, Namuci, Śambara,* etc. Another interpretation is "you was an enemy to those who had no enemy, on behalf of the seven sages (the *Aṅgirasas*), *i.e.,* in order to recover their cows."

७५८७. त्वं ह त्यदप्रतिमानमोजो वज्रेण वज्रिन्धृषितो जघन्थ।
त्वं शुष्णस्यावातिरो वधत्रैस्त्वं गा इन्द्र शच्येदविन्द:॥१७॥

17. Thunderer, you, the resolute one, did smite that unrivalled might with your bolt; you destroyed *Śuṣṇa* with your weapons, you recovered the cows, *Indra*, by your wisdom.

७५८८. त्वं ह त्यद्वृषभ चर्षणीनां घनो वृत्राणां तविषो बंभूथ।
त्वं सिन्धूँरसृजस्तस्तभानान् त्वमपो अजयो दासपत्नी:॥१८॥

18. You, showerer, was the mighty destroyer of the hindrances of your worshippers; you did set free the obstructed rivers, you did win the waters which the *Dāsas* had mastered.

७५८९. स सुक्रतू रणिता यः सुतेष्वनुतमन्युर्यो अहेव रेवान्।
य एक इन्नर्यपांसि कर्ता स वृत्रहा प्रतीदन्यमाहुः॥१९॥

19. He who noble in his exploits rejoices in the *Soma*-libations, he whose wrath cannot be repelled and who is wealthy as the days, he who alone performs the rites for his worshipper,—he, the slayer of *Vṛtra*, men say, is a match for all others.

Who is wealthy as the Days— Sāyaṇa adds "wealth is produced in the days, not in the nights."

७५९०. स वृत्रहेन्द्रश्चर्षणीधृतं सुष्टुत्या हव्यं हुवेम।
स प्राविता मघवा नोऽधिवक्ता स वाजस्य श्रवस्यस्य दाता॥२०॥

20. *Indra* is the slayer of *Vṛtra*, the cherisher of men; let us invoke him worthy of invocation, with an excellent hymn; he is *Maghavan*, our protector, our encourager, he is the bestower of food that brings fame.

७५९१. स वृत्रहेन्द्र ऋभुक्षाः सद्यो जज्ञानो हव्यो बभूव।
कृण्वन्नपांसि नर्या पुरूणि सोमो न पीतो हव्यः सखिभ्यः॥२१॥

21. As soon as he was born, he, *Indra*, the slayer of *Vṛtra*, the chief of the *Ṛbhus*, was worthy to be invoked; he, performing many sacred acts for men, is worthy to be invoked for his friends like the quaffed *Soma* juice.

[सूक्त-९७]

[ऋषि- रेभ काश्यप। देवता- इन्द्र। छन्द- बृहती ; १०, १३ अतिजगती;
९१-९२ उपरिष्टाद्बृहती; १४ त्रिष्टुप; १५ जगती।]

७५९२. या इन्द्र भुज आभरः स्वर्वाँ असुरेभ्यः।
स्तोतारमिन्मघवन्नस्य वर्धय ये च त्वे वृक्तबर्हिषः॥१॥

1. *Indra*, lord of heaven, with those good things which you have carried off from the *Asuras* do you prosper, O *Maghavan*, your praiser and those who have spread for you the clipped grass.

Sāmaveda, 254.

७५९३. यमिन्द्र दधिषे त्वमश्वं गां भागमव्ययम्।
यजमाने सुन्वति दक्षिणावति तस्मिन् तं धेहि मा पणौ॥२॥

2. Those horses, those cows, that imperishable wealth which you have seized (from your cnemies),—bestow them on the

sacrificer who offers the *Soma* and is liberal to the priests,—not on the niggard.

७५९४. य इन्द्र सस्त्यव्रतोऽनुष्वापमदेवयुः।
स्वैः ष एवैर्मुरत्पोष्यं रयिं संनुतर्धैहि तं ततः॥३॥

3. Let him, *Indra*, who sleeps away careless of the gods and offering no sacrifices,—let him lose his precious wealth by his own evil courses, and then do you stow him away in some hidden place.

By his own Evil Courses— Sāyaṇa adds "by gambling, etc."

७५९५. यच्छक्रासि परावति यदर्वावति वृत्रहन्।
अतस्त्वा गीर्भिर्द्युगदिन्द्र केशिभिः सुतावाँ आ विवासति॥४॥

4. Whether, *Śakra*, you are in the far-distant region, or whether, slayer of *Vṛtra*, you are in the lower,—the sacrificer longs to being you, *Indra*, from thence by his hymns as by heaven-going steeds;

Sāmaveda, 264.

Whether you . . . . Lower— Whether you are in the heaven or in the firmament.

Heaven-Going— Sāyaṇa takes *dyugat* as an instrumental plural with its case-termination dropped. The St. Petersb. Dict. takes it as an adverb "durch den Himmel her."

७५९६. यद्वासि रोचने दिवः समुद्रस्याधि विष्टपि।
यत्पार्थिवे सदने वृत्रहन्तम यदन्तरिक्ष आ गहि॥५॥

5. Or whether you are in the brightness of heaven, or whether in some region in the midst of the sea, or whether, mightiest slayer of *Vṛtra*, in some abode in the earth, or whether in the firmament,—come to us.

७५९७. स नः सोमेषु सोमपाः सुतेषु शवसस्पते।
मादयस्व राधसा सूनृतावतेन्द्र राया परीणसा॥६॥

6. *Indra*, drinker of the *Soma,* lord of strength, now that our *Soma*-libations have been effused, do you gladden us with wholesome food and ample wealth.

With wholesome Food— *Sunṛitāvata* "truthful, is also explained "accompanied by truthful words"; Sāyaṇa adds that it really means "accompanied by children." It should rather be "gladden us with generous gifts."

७५९८. मा न॑ इन्द्र प॒रा वृ॑ण॒ग्भवा॑ न॒: सध॑मा॒द्य॑: ।

त्वं न॑ ऊ॒ती त्व॒मिन्न॑ आ॒प्यं मा न॑ इन्द्र प॒रा वृ॑णक् ॥७॥

7. Leave us not, *Indra*, but share our joy; you are our protection, you are our kindred; *Indra*, leave us not.

Sāmaveda, 260, with *sadhamādye*. *Cf.* also VIII.3.1.

७५९९. अ॒स्मे इ॑न्द्र स॒चा सु॒ते नि ष॑दा पी॒तये॒ मधु॑ ।

कृ॒धी ज॑रि॒त्रे म॑घव॒न्नवो॑ म॒हद॒स्मे इ॑न्द्र स॒चा सु॒ते ॥८॥

8. Sit with us, *Indra*, at the oblation to drink the *Soma;* *Maghavan*, perform a mighty protection for your worshipper, (seated) with us at the oblation.

७६००. न त्वा॑ दे॒वास॑ आशत॒ न मर्त्या॑सो अद्रिव: ।

विश्वा॑ जा॒तानि॒ शव॑सा॒भिभूर॑सि॒ न त्वा॑ दे॒वास॑ आशत ॥९॥

9. Thunderer, neither gods nor mortals equal you by their acts; you surpass all beings by your might, the gods equal you not.

७६०१. विश्वा॑: पृत॒ना अ॑भि॒भूतरं॒ नरं॑ स॒जूस्त॑तक्षु॒रिन्द्रं॑ ज॒जनु॒श्च राज॑से ।

क्रत्वा॒ वरि॑ष्ठं॒ वर॒ आमु॑रि॒मुतो॒ग्रमोजि॑ष्ठं॒ तव॑सं तर॒स्विन॑म् ॥१०॥

10. The assembled (priests) have roused *Indra*, the leader, the conqueror in all battles; they have created him (by their hymns) to shine,—him the mightiest in his acts, the smiter of enemies for spoil, the terrible, the most powerful, the stalwart the furious.

Sāmaveda, 370, 930, with several variations in the second line.

७६०२. सम॑ीं रे॒भासो॑ अस्वरन्निन्द्रं॒ सोम॑स्य पी॒तये॑ ।

स्व॑र्प॒तिं यदीं॑ वृ॒धे धृ॒तव्र॑तो॒ ह्योज॑सा स॒मूति॑भि: ॥११॥

11. The *Rebhas* have together praised *Indra* that he may drink the *Soma*; when (they praise) the lord of heaven that he may wax strong (by the oblations), then he, observant of pious rites, is united to his strength and his protecting guards.

Sāmaveda, 932, with *samu* and *svaḥ patiḥ* for *sam īm* and *svarpatim*.

Is United to his strength and his Protecting Guards—Sc. by the praises of the worshippers he acquires strength, and the *Maruts* are his guards.

७६०३. नेमिं॑ नमन्ति च॒क्षसा॒ मेषं॒ विप्रा॑ अ॒भिस्व॑रा ।

सु॒दी॒तयो॑ वो अ॒द्रुहोऽपि॒ कर्णे॑ तर॒स्विन॑: स॒मृक्व॑भि: ॥१२॥

12. At the first sight (the *Rebhas*) bow to him who is the circumference of the wheel, the priests (worship) with their praise (*Indra*) the ram; radiant and unharming, do you also, full of earnestness, sing in his ear with your hymns.

Sāmaveda, 931, with *abhsvare*.

The Ram— Alluding to the legend of *Indra's* carrying off *Medhātithi* in the form of a ram. *Cf.* I.51.1; VIII.2.40.

७६०४. तमिन्द्रं जोहवीमि मघवानमुग्रं सत्रा दधानमप्रतिष्कुतं शवांसि। मंहिष्ठो गीर्भिरा च यज्ञियो ववर्तद्राये नो विश्वा सुपथा कृणोतु वज्री॥१३॥

13. Again and again I invoke the strong *Indra*, *Maghavan*, who alone really possesses might, the irresistible; may he draw nigh through our songs, most bounteous and worthy of sacrifice; may he, the thunderer, make all things prosperous for our wealth.

Sāmaveda, 460, with some variations.

७६०५. त्वं पुर इन्द्र चिकिदेना व्योजसा शविष्ठ शक्र नाशयध्यै। त्वद्द्विश्वानि भुर्वनानि वज्रिन् द्यावा रेजेते पृथिवी च भीषा॥१४॥

14. *Indra*, mightiest *Śakra*, you know how to destroy those cities (of *Sambara*) by your strength at you all worlds tremble, thunderer,—heaven and earth (tremble) with fear.

७६०६. तन्म ऋतमिन्द्र शूर चित्र पात्वपो न वज्रिन्दुरिताति पर्षि भूरि। कदा न इन्द्र राय आ दशस्येर्विश्वप्स्न्यस्य स्पृहयाय्यस्य राजन्॥१५॥

15. *Indra*, hero assuming many forms, may that truthfulness of your protect me; bear us, thunderer, over our many sins as over waters; when, radiant *Indra*, wilt you give us some wealth, desirable to all, manifold in its kinds?

[सूक्त-९८]

[ऋषि– नृमेध आङ्गिरस। देवता– इन्द्र।
छन्द– उष्णिक्, ७,१०-११ ककुप्, ९,१२ पुर उष्णिक्।]

७६०७. इन्द्राय साम गायत विप्राय बृहते बृहत्। धर्मकृते विपश्चिते पनस्यवे॥१॥

1. Sing a *Sāman* to *Indra*, a *Bṛhat* to the mighty sage, to the performer, of religious rites, the all-knowing one who longs for praise.

Sāmaveda, 388, 1025, with *brahmakṛte* for *dharmakṛte*.

७६०८. त्वमिन्द्राभिभूरसि त्वं सूर्यमरोचयः।

विश्वकर्मा विश्वदेवो महाँ असि॥२॥

2. You are the conqueror, *Indra*; you has lighted in the sun; you are the maker of all, the lord of all the gods, the mighty

Sāmaveda, 1026, For *viśvadeva* compare *supra* v.82.7.

७६०९. विभ्राजञ्ज्योतिषा स्वरगच्छो रोचनं दिवः।

देवास्त इन्द्र सख्यायं येमिरे॥३॥

3. You have pervaded the light of the sky, illumining heaven by your splendour; the gods, *Indra*, submissively solicit your friendship.

Sāmaveda, 1027.

The Light of the Sky— I have here taken *rocanam divaḥ* in its usual meaning. Sāyaṇa explains the line "you have pervaded and illumined by your light heaven which manifests the sun (as being its receptacle)."

७६१०. एन्द्र नो गधि प्रियः सत्राजिदगोह्यः।

गिरिर्न विश्वतस्पृथुः पतिर्दिवः॥४॥

4. Come to us, *Indra*, beloved one, triumphant, and whom none can conceal—lord of heaven, vast on all sides as a mountain.

Sāmaveda, 313, 1247.

७६११. अभि हि सत्य सोमपा उभे बभूथ रोदसी।

इन्द्रासि सुन्वतो वृधः पतिर्दिवः॥५॥

5. Truthful drinker of the *Soma*, you surpass heaven and earth; O *Indra*, you are the fosterer of him who prepares the libation, you are the lord of heaven.

Sāmaveda, 1248.

७६१२. त्वं हि शश्वतीनामिन्द्र दर्ता पुरामसि।

हन्ता दस्योर्मनोर्वृधः पतिर्दिवः॥६॥

6. You, *Indra*, are the stormer of many hostile cities, the slayer of the *Dasyu*, the fosterer of man, the lord of heaven.

Sāmaveda, 1249, with *dhartā* for *dartā*.

The Fosterer of Man— Sāyaṇa explains *manoḥ* as "the man who offers sacrifice."

७६१३. अधा हीन्द्र गिर्वण उप त्वा कामान्महः संसृज्महे।

उदेव यन्त उदभिः॥७॥

7. *Indra* worthy of hymns, we send our earnest praises to you as men going by water (splash their friends) with handfuls.

Sāmaveda, 406, 710, with some variations.

Praises— Or "desires," "prayers," *cf.* I.81.8.

Splash their friends with Handfuls— The Scholiast adds "in sport." Sāyaṇa, in his Comm. on the corresponding phrase in the *Sāmaveda,* (not found in the Bibl. Ind. ed.), *udeva gmanta udabhiḥ,* explains it "as men going by the water, *i.e.,* a river, or the waters, *i.e.,* the sea (I read in Benfey's quotation *samudralokṣaṇaḥ*), desire an eightfold gain." Benfey translates it "wir sprengten dir, wie Wellen übe Wellen gehn."

७६१४. वार्ण त्वा॑ यव्याभि॒र्व॑र्ध॑न्ति॒ शूर॒ ब्रह्मा॑णि ।

वा॒वृ॒ध्वांसं॑ चि॒दद्रि॑वो दि॒वेदि॑वे ॥ ८ ॥

8. As the lake (swells) with the rivers, so our praises, O hero, O thunderer, augment you as you grow more and more day by day.

Sāmaveda, 711.

Grow More and More— Sāyaṇa takes *brahmāṇi vavṛdhvāṁsam* "swelling with our praises even more than the lake."

७६१५. यु॒ञ्जन्ति॒ हरी॑ इ॒षिर॒स्य गा॒र्थ्यो॑रौ॒ रथं॑ उ॒रुयु॑गे । इन्द्र॑वाह॒ वचो॑युजा ॥ ९ ॥

9. (The priests) by their hymn yoke in the swift deity's yoked at a word.

Sāmaveda, 712, adding *svar-vida.*

७६१६. त्वं नं॒ इन्द्रा॒ भरँ॒ ओजो॒ नृ॒म्णं॒ शत॑क्रतो विच॒र्षणे ।

आ वी॒रं पृ॑तना॒षहं॑ ॥ १० ॥

10. *Indra,* all-beholding *Maghavan,* bring us strength and wealth; (we solicit you) the host-overpowering champion.

Sāmaveda, 405, 1169.

The host-overpowering Champion— So Sāyaṇa, supplying *tvām āyācāmahe.* The true construction is undoubtedly "bring us a host-overpowering champion," sc. a son.

७६१७. त्वं हि नः॒ पि॒ता व॑सो॒ त्वं मा॒ता श॑त॑क्रतो ब॒भूवि॑थ ।

अ॒था ते॑ सु॒म्नमी॑महे ॥ ११ ॥

11. You have been our father, O giver of dwellings, you our mother O *Śatakratu;* we pray for that happiness which is your.

Sāmaveda, 1170.

७६१८. त्वां शुष्मिन् पुरुहूत वाज॒यन्त॒मुप॑ ब्रुवे शतक्रतो।

स नो॑ रास्व सु॒वीर्य॑म्।।१२।।

12. Mighty *Śatakratu*, invoked by many, I praise you desirous
of offerings; do you give us wealth.

Sāmaveda, 1171, with *sahaskṛta for śatakrato*.

[सूक्त-९९]

[**ऋषि–** नृमेध आङ्गिरस। **देवता–** इन्द्र।

छन्द– प्रगाथ (विषमा बृहती, समासतो बृहती)।]

७६१९. त्वा॒मिदा ह्यो॒ नरो॑ऽपीप्य॒न्वज्रि॑न्भूर्ण॑यः।

स इ॑न्द्र स्तोम॑वाहसा॒मि॒ह श्रु॒ध्युप॒ स्व॒स॒र॒मा ग॑हि।।१।।

1. Thunderer, your worshippers, ready with their oblations,
have to-day and yesterday made you drink (the *Soma*); listen,
Indra, here to us who offer you praise and come you to our
dwelling.

Sāmaveda, 302, 813, with *stomavāhasaḥ* for-*sām*.

७६२०. मत्स्वा॒ सुशिप्र हरि॑व॒स्तदी॑महे॒ त्वे आ भू॒षन्ति॑ वे॒धसः॑।

तव॒ श्रवां॑स्युप॒मान्यु॒क्थ्या॒ सु॒तेष्विन्द्र॑ गिर्वणः।।२।।

2. Handsome-jawed lord of steeds, rejoice (in the libation); we
pray to you, your votaries come to you *Indra*, worthy of praise,
may your food be a pattern and excellent.

Sāmaveda, 814, with *ukthya* for *ukthyā* Sāyaṇa takes *upamāni* as
upamāna-bhūtāni; it means rather 'magnificent.'

७६२१. श्राय॒न्तइव॒ सूर्यं॒ विश्वेदिन्द्र॑स्य भक्षत।

वसू॑नि जा॒ते जन॑मान॒ ओज॑सा॒ प्रति॑ भा॒गं न दीधिम।।३।।

3. As the gathering (rays) proceed to the son, so (the *Maruts*)
proceed) to *Indra*, and by their power divide all his treasures
among those who have been or will be born; may we meditate on
our share.

Sāmaveda, 267, 1319, reading *jāto janimani* and *dīdhimaḥ*.
Yajurveda, 33,41.

This is an obscure verse and Yāska's interpretation (*Nir.*, VI.8)
throws but little light. Sāyaṇa gives another explanation, in which he
takes *bhakṣata* as=*bhajata*, and not as=*vibhajante*, "(O worshippers), as
the gathering (rays) proceed to the sun, so do you enjoy all the wealth of

Indra; and let us possess like an inheritance the treasures which by his power (he distributes) to him that has been or will be born.'' Mahīdhara's explanation seems much simpler and better, ''the gathering (rays) proceeding to the sun distribute all *Indra's* treasures (to living beings, sc. as rain, corn, etc.) may we too by our power leave those treasures as an inheritance to him who has been or will be born.''

७६२२. अनर्शरातिं वसुदामुप॑ स्तुहि भद्रा इन्द्रस्य रात॑यः।
सो अ॑स्य॒ काम॑ विध॒तो न रोष॑ति मनो॑ दाना॒य॑ चोद॒यन्॥४॥

4. Praise him the bestower of wealth, whose gifts are never evil; *Indra's* gifts are fortunate; he directs his mind to the gift and mars not the desire of his worshipper.

Sāmaveda, 1320, with *alarśirātim* for *anarśarātim.*

७६२३. त्वमि॑न्द्र प्रतू॒र्तिष्व॒भि विश्वा॑ अ॒सि स्पृध॑ः।
अश॒स्तिहा ज॑निता वि॒श्वतू॒रसि त्वं तूर्य॑ तरुष्य॒तः॥५॥

5. *Indra,* you conquer in battles all opposing hosts O opposer who beat down those who would oppose you are the smiter of the wicked, the bringer (of evil to your enemies), and the destroyer of all.

Sāmaveda, 311, 1637, with *vṛtratuḥ* for *viśvatuḥ. Yajurveda,* 33,66. Mahīdhara takes *tūrya* as an imperative=*māraya,* not as a vocative.

७६२४. अनु॑ ते शुष्मं॑ तु॒रय॑न्तमीयतुः क्षो॒णी शि॒शुं न मा॒तरा॑।
विश्वा॑स्ते॒ स्पृध॑ः श्नथयन्त म॒न्यवे॑ वृ॒त्रं यदि॑न्द्र तू॒र्वसि॑॥६॥

6. Heaven and earth follow your destructive energy as mothers their child; since you smite *Vṛtra,* all the hostile hosts, *Indra,* faint at your wrath.

Sāmaveda, 1638. *Yajurveda,* 33,67.

Faint— The texts of *R.V., S.V.,* and *Y.V.* read *śnathayanta,* which properly means ''to kill,'' but must here have a passive meaning. Sāyaṇa and Mahīdhara read *sratha yanta,* which they explain *khinnā bhavanti,* ''they are wearied affected.'' Benfey translates it ''sinkt kraftlos,'' and add in Gloss. ''*cnath (snath)* hat heir wehl unzweifelhaft die Bed. voi *crath* 'laxari' 'erschlaffen,'' *Śrathayanta* is probably the right reading.

७६२५. इ॒त ऊ॒ती वो॒ अ॒जरं॑ प्रहे॒तार॒मप्र॑हितम्।
आ॒शुं जे॒तारं॑ हे॒तारं॑ र॒थीत॑ममतू॒र्तं तु॒ग्र्यावृध॑म्॥७॥

7. (Worshippers), summon hither for protection him who never grows old, the repeller (of enemies), himself never repelled, the

swift conqueror, the driver, the best of charioteers, unharmed of any, the augmenter of water.

Sāmaveda, 283.

७६२६. इष्कर्तारमनिष्कृतं सहस्कृतं शतमूर्तिं शतक्रतुम्।
समानमिन्द्रमवंसे हवामहे वसंवानं वसूजुवंम्॥८॥

8. We solicit for our protection *Indra*, the consecrator of others but himself consecrated by none, produced by strength, possessing an hundredfold protection, possessing hundredfold knowledge, a common deity to many, hiding treasures in his store-house and sending wealth (to his votaries).

The Consecrator of others— Mahīdhara (*Yajurveda*, 12.110) explains *iṣkartāram* as *yajñaniṣpādakam*, but Sāyaṇa takes it as *śatrūṇām* (?) *saṁskartāram*. As one of the meanings of *saṁskāra* is the investiture with the sacred thread, and *vrātya* is the name for one in whose youth the customary observances have been omitted and who has not received his investiture with the sacred thread, the epithet *aniṣkṛtam* may perhaps illustrate the application of the term *vrātya* to the Supreme Being in *Praśna Upan.*, II.11, *cf.* Śaṅkara's comm. *"prathamajātatvād anyasya saṁskartur abhāvād asaṁskṛto vrātyas tvām svabhāvata eva śuddhaḥ."* Grassmann explains *iṣkartāram aniṣkṛtam* as 'director, yourself undirected.'

[सूक्त-१००]

[ऋषि- १-३, ६-१२ नेम भार्गव; ४-५ इन्द्र। देवता- इन्द्र, १०-११ वाक्।
छन्द- त्रिष्टुप्, ६ जगती, ७-९ अनुष्टुप्।]

७६२७. अयं तं एमि तन्वा पुरस्ताद्दिश्वे देवा अभि मां यन्ति पश्चात्।
यदा महं दीधरो भागमिन्द्रादिन्मया कृणवो वीर्याणि॥१॥

1. I here go before you with my son, the *Viśve devās* follow after me; if, *Indra*, you keep wealth for me, then put forth your strength on my side.

I here go strength on my Side— *I.e.*, if you wish to give me the wealth of my enemies, come and help me to overcome them.

७६२८. दधामि ते मधुनो भक्षमग्रे हितस्तें भागः सुतो अस्तु सोमं:।
असंश्च त्वं दक्षिणतः सखा मेऽधा वृत्राणि जङ्घनाव भूरि॥२॥

2. I offer the beverage of the exhilarating drink first to you, let the effused enjoyable *Soma* be placed within you; be you a friend on my right hand, then will we two smite our many enemies.

७६२९. प्र सु स्तोमं भरत वाज॒यन्त इन्द्रा॑य सत्यं यदि॑ सत्यम॒स्ति।
नेन्द्रो॑ अस्तीति॒ नेम॑ उ त्व आह॒ क ई॑ ददर्श॒ कम॒भि ष्टवाम।।३।।

3. Offer fervently, may war-loving companions, true praise to
Indra, if he truly exists; *Nema* says "verily there is no *Indra*,"
who has ever seen him? whom shall we praise?

७६३०. अयम॒स्मि जरित॒: पश्य॑ मेह॒ विश्वा॑ जातान्यभ्य॑स्मि म॒ह्ना।
ऋ॒तस्य॑ मा प्र॒दिशो॑ वर्धयन्त्यादर्दि॒रो भुव॑ना दर्दरीमि।।४।।

4. (*Indra* speaks) "Here I am, worshipper, behold me here; I
overpower all beings by my might; the offerers of sacrifice
magnify me by their praises; I, the shatterer, shatter the worlds.

७६३१. आ यन्मा॑ वेना॑ अरु॑हन्नृतस्य॑ एक॑मासी॒नं हर्यतस्य॑ पृष्ठे।
मन॑श्चिन्मे हृद॒ आ प्रत्य॑वोचद॒चिक्र॑दञ्छिशु॒मन्त॑: सखा॑य:।।५।।

5. "When the lovers of sacrifice ascended to me sitting alone
on the back of my well-loved (firmament), then my mind verily
proclaimed to my heart, 'my friends with their children are crying
to me."

On the back of my well-loved Firmament— *Haryatasya pṛṣṭhe* is
explained by the Schol. as *kāntasya antarikṣasya pṛṣṭhe*.

७६३२. विश्वेत्ता॑ ते॒ सर्व॑नेषु॒ प्रवाच्या॑ या च॒कर्थ॑ मघवन्निन्द्र सुन्व॒ते।
पारा॑वतं॒ यत्पुरुसम्भृ॑तं व॒स्व॒पावृ॑णो॒: शरभाय॑ ऋषि॒बन्धवे।।६।।

6. Verily all those deeds of your, *Maghavan*, are to be
proclaimed, which you have achieved for him who offers libations
in the sacrifices; that wealth of *Pārāvat*, collected by many; you
have opened to *Śarabha*, the kinsman of the *Ṛṣi*.

Pārāvat— Sāyaṇa only adds "a certain enemy so called." *Pārāvata*
probably means "brought from afar."

Collected my Many— Sāyaṇa takes *puru-sambhṛtam* adverbially
(but perhaps only as an alternative rendering, see var. lect.); "that wealth
of *Pārāvat* you have opened to *Śarabha*, so that it now is collected by
many." He only adds that *Śarabha* was a *Ṛṣi*.

७६३३. प्र नू॒नं धा॑वता पृथङ्नेह॒ यो वो॑ अवा॑वरीत्।
नि षीं॑ वृत्रस्य॒ मर्म॑णि व॒ज्रमिन्द्रो॑ अपीपतत्।।७।।

7. Haste now severally forward; he is not here who stopped
you way,—has not *Indra* let fall his thunderbolt in the very vitals
of that enemy?

I have ventured to give an independent version of this verse, as I do
quite understand *Sāyaṇa's* Comment. He apparently reads *ni* for *na* of the
second line; and seems to explain the verse; "that enemy who was
running forward and stayed not apart and did not hinder you,—*Indra* has
thrown (*nyapīpatat*) his bolt in the vitals of that enemy."

७६३४. मनोजवा अर्यमान आयसीमंतरत्पुरंम्।
दिवं सुपर्णो गत्वाय् सोमं वज्रिण आभरत्॥८॥

8. *Suparṇa*, rushing swift as thought, passed through the iron
city; then having gone to heaven he brought the *Soma* to the
thunderer.

He brought the Soma to the Thunderer— This alludes to the
legend of the *Gāyatrī* as a bird fetching the *Soma* from heaven. Sāyaṇa
explains *āyasīm* "iron" as *hiraṇmayīm* "golden," in allusion no doubt to
the other legend which represents the cities of the demons as made of iron
on the earth, silver in the firmament, and gold in heaven (*Ait. Brāhm.*,
I.23).

७६३५. समुद्रे अन्तः शयत उद्ना वज्रो अभीवृतः।
भरन्त्यस्मै संयतं पुरःस्रवणा बलिम्॥९॥

9. The thunderbolt lies in the midst of the sea, covered with the
waters; (the foes) flying in front of the battle bring offerings of
submission to it.

७६३६. यद्वाग् वदन्त्यविचेतनानि राष्ट्री देवानां निषसाद मन्द्रा।
चतस्र ऊर्जं दुदुहे पर्यांसि कं स्विदस्याः परमं जगाम॥१०॥

10. When *Vāk*, the queen, the gladdner of the gods, sits down
(in the sacrifice) uttering things not to be understood, she milks
water and food for the four quarters (of the earth); whither now is
her best portion gone?

Sāyaṇa quotes the *Nirukta*, XI.28, and explains *Vāk* here as the
thunder (*cf.* VIII.69.14); by the "best portion" he understands the rain,
"which sinks in the earth or is taken up by the sun's rays." The verse
appears to mean the same as Tennyson's lines in the "Talking Oak"

"Low thunders bring the mellow rain
Which makes me broad and deep."

The sacrifice brings rain ushered in by thunder; and then it is asked
"whither is the thunder gone now that it has passed?"

७६३७. देवीं वाचमजनयन्त देवास्तां विश्वरूपाः पशवो वदन्ति।
सा नो मन्द्रेषमूर्जं दुहाना धेनुर्वागस्मानुप सुष्टुतैतु॥११॥

11. The gods produced the goddess *Vāk*; her do animals of every kind utter; may she, *Vāk*, the all gladdening cow, yielding meat and drink, come to us, worthily praised.

Sāyaṇa adds to explain this verse, "the thunder entering into all beings, becomes the speaker of moral truth," *eṣā mādhyamikā vāk sarvaprāṇyantargatā dharmābhivādinī bhavati.*

Animals of every Kind— Sāyaṇa adds "whether their utterance be articulate or inarticulate."

७६३८. सखें विष्णो वितरं वि क्रमस्व द्यौर्देहि लोकं वज्राय विष्कभें।

हनांव वृत्रं रिणचांव सिन्धूनिन्द्रस्य यन्तु प्रसवे विसृष्टाः।।१२।।

12. O *Viṣṇu* my friends, stride forth lustily; O heaven, give room to contain the thunderbolt; let us smite *Vṛtra*, let us open the rivers; let them flow, set free, at the command of *Indra*.

Give Room to contain the Thunderbolt— Sāyaṇa here quotes the following passage from the *Bṛhaddevatā*. "*Vṛtra* had enveloped the three worlds and stood there in his fierce energy; *Indra* could not conquer him, and he went to *Viṣṇu* and said, 'I will smite *Vṛtra*, do you stride forth and stand by my side, and let the heavens give room for my uplifted thunderbolt.' *Viṣṇu* consented and did so, and the heavens gave an open space. All this is related in this verse."

[सूक्त-१०१]

[**ऋषि**– जमदग्नि भार्गव। **देवता**– १ से ५ तृतीय चरण तक मित्रावरुण, ५ चतुर्थ चरण ६ आदित्यगण, ७-८ अश्विनीकुमार, ९-१० वायु, ११-१२ सूर्य, १३ उषा अथवा सूर्यप्रभा, १४ पवमान, १५-१६ गौ। **छन्द**– १-२, ५-१२ प्रगाथ (विषमा बृहती, समासतो बृहती), ३ गायत्री, ४ सतोबृहती, १३ बृहती, १४-१६ त्रिष्टुप्।

७६३९. ऋधगित्था स मर्त्यः शशमे देवतांतये।

यो नूनं मित्रावरुणावभिष्टयें आचक्रे हव्यदांतये।।१।।

1. That man verily consecrates the oblation for the sacrifice, who brings quickly *Mitra* and *Varuṇa* to the offerer for the attainment of his desires.

Yajurveda, 33,87. Mahīdhara differs from Sāyaṇa in his explanation, and gives it thus: "Verily that man who worships *Mitra* and *Varuṇa* for the attainment of his desires and the giving of oblations, becomes thereby perfectly tranquil and able to perform the sacrifice" (*rdhag devatātaye*).

७६४०. वर्षिष्ठक्षत्रा उरुचक्षसा नरा राजांना दीर्घश्रुत्तमा।

ता बा॒हुता॒ न दंस॑ना रथर्यतः सा॒कं सूर्य॑स्य र॒श्मिभिः॑॥२॥

2. Those two leaders of rites, great in might, far-seeing, resplendent, and most far-hearing, perform their deeds like two arms, by the help of the rays of the sun.

Like two Arms— Sāyaṇa adds, as an explanation, "that is, they obtain the sacrifice as the arms accomplish an object."

७६४१. प्र यो वां मित्रावरुणाजिरो दू॒तो अद्र॑वत्। अ॒यः॒शीर्षा॒ मदे॑रघुः॥३॥

3. *Mitra* and *Varuṇa*, he who hastens to appear before you, becomes the messenger of the gods; he wears an iron helmet, he exults in his wealth.

An Iron Helmet— Sāyaṇa says "golden," as often elsewhere (*ayas-śīṣā*).

७६४२. न यः॒ संपृ॑च्छे न पुन॒र्हवी॑तवे न सं॒वादा॑य र॒मते॑।

तस्मा॒न्नो॒ अ॒द्य स॒मृते॑रुरुष्य॒तं बा॒हुभ्यां॒ न उ॑रुष्यतम्॥४॥

4. He who has no pleasure in questioning, nor in repeated calling nor in dialogue,—defend us to-day from him and from his encounter, defend us from his arms.

७६४३. प्र मि॒त्राय॒ प्रार्य॒म्णे स॒चथ्य॑मृ॒तावसो॑।

वरू॒थ्यं१॒॑ वरु॑णे छ॒न्द्यं॒ वचः॒ स्तोत्रं॒ राज॑सु गायत॥५॥

5. O you rich in offerings, sing to *Mitra*, sing to *Aryaman*, a reverential hymn produced in the sacrificial chamber; sing a propitiating address to *Varuṇa*; sing a hymn of praise to the kings.

Sāmaveda, 255, with *varūthye* for *varūthyam*.

Produced in the sacrificial Chamber— Sāyaṇa explains *varūthyam* as *yajñagṛhe bhavam*; the St. Petersb. Dict. gives it as "Schutz gewahrend."

To the Kings— Sc. *Mitra, Aryaman* and *Varuṇa*.

७६४४. ते हि॒न्विरे॑ अ॒रुणं॒ जेन्यं॒ वस्वेकं॑ पु॒त्रं ति॒सृणा॑म्।

ते धामा॒न्यमृ॑ता॒ मर्त्या॑नाम॒दब्धा॒ अभि च॑क्षते॥६॥

6. It was these who sent the red victory-giving *Vasu*, the one son of the three (worlds); they the invincible, the immortal, overlook the abodes of men.

Victory-Giving— Elsewhere Sāyaṇa explains *jenya* when connected with *vasu* as *jetavya*, "what is to be conquered or won," *cf.* II.5.1,

VII.74.3; here he takes it actively as *jayasādhanam*. The St. Petersh. Dict. explains it as "edel von Abkunft, ächt, wahr."

Vasu— Sāyaṇa by his explanation *vāsakam* seems here to take *Vasu* as for *Vasum*, sc. the Sun, as one of the *Vasus*, as he adds "they send him for the dispelling of the darkness of the three worlds." But it would be more natural to take it in its ordinary meaning 'wealth,' *i.e.*, gold. "It was these who sent the red gold victory-giving," or "the reward of victory."

७६४५. आ मे वन्नांस्युद्यता द्युमत्तमानि कर्त्वा।
उभा यातं नासत्या सजोषसा प्रति हव्यानि वीतयें ॥७॥

7. O associated *Nāsatyas*, come both of you to my uplifted glorious praises and my rites, come to partake of my offerings.

७६४६. रातिं यद्वामरक्षसं हवामहे युवाभ्यां वाजिनीवसू।
प्राचीं होत्रां प्रतिरन्तावितं नरा गृणाना जमदग्निना ॥८॥

8. Deities rich in food, when we solicit your bounty, that (wealth) which demons cannot thwart,—then, helping our praise directed to the east, come, leaders of rites, worshipped by *Jamadagni*.

Helping— Perhaps rather "inspiring," *cf.* IV.6.1.

७६४७. आ नौ यज्ञं दिविस्पृशं वायो याहि सुमन्मभिः।
अन्तः पवित्र उपरि श्रीणानोऽयं शुक्रो अयामि ते ॥९॥

9. Come, *Vāyu*, to our heaven-reaching sacrifice with its beautiful hymns of praise; this bright *Soma* has been kept for you, poured out upon the middle of the straining cloth.

Yajurveda, 33,85.

७६४८. वेत्यध्वर्युः पथिभी रजिष्ठैः प्रति हव्यानि वीतयें।
अधा नियुत्व उभयस्य नः पिब शुचिं सोमं गवाशिरम् ॥१०॥

10. The ministrant priest comes by the straightest paths, he beings the oblations for your enjoyment; then lord of the *Niyut* steeds, drink of both kinds, the *Soma* pure and that mixed with milk.

The Priest Comes— *i.e.*, from the *havirdhāna*, a cart for the *Soma*.

७६४९. बण्महाँ असि सूर्य बळादित्य महाँ असि।
महस्तै सतो महिमा पनस्यतेऽद्धा देव महाँ असि ॥११॥

11. Verily you are great, O Sun; verily, *Āditya*, you are great;
the greatness of you, the great one, is praised; verily you are great,
O god.

Sāmaveda, 276, 1788, with *paniṣṭama mahnnā* for *panasyate addhā*.
Yajurveda, 33.39.

७६५०. बट् सूर्य॑ श्रव॑सा म॒हाँ अ॑सि स॒त्रा दे॑व म॒हाँ अ॑सि।
      म॒ह्ना दे॒वाना॑म॒सुर्यः॑ पु॒रोहि॑तो वि॒भु ज्योति॒रदा॑भ्यम्॥१२॥

12. Verily, O sun, you are great in fame; O god, you are indeed
might among the gods in might; you are the slayer of the *Asuras*,
and the preceptor (of the gods); your glory is widespread and to be
marred by none.

Sāmaveda, 1789. *Yajurveda*, 33.40.

The Slayer of the Asuras— Sāyaṇa explains *asuryaḥ* by *asurāṇām
hantā*; Mahīdhara takes it "beneficent to living beings." The true
meaning is no doubt that given in the St. Petersb. Dict. "unkörperlich,
geistlich, göttlich."

७६५१. इ॒यं या नीच्य॑र्किणी॑ रू॒पा रोहि॑ण्या कृ॒ता।
      चि॒त्रेव॒ प्रत्य॑दर्श्याय॒त्य॒इ॒न्तर्द॒शसु॒ बा॒हुषु॑॥१३॥

13. She who was created beautiful and bright, bending
downwards and receiving all praise, has been seen within (the
world), like a brindled cow, advancing to the ten regions (spread
our) like arms.

She— This is explained to be *Uṣas*, the dawn, or the light of the Sun.

७६५२. प्र॒जा ह॑ ति॒स्रो अ॒त्याय॑मीयु॒र्न्य॑इ॒न्या अ॒र्क॒म॒भितो॑ विविश्रे।
      बृ॒ह॒द्ध तस्थौ॒ भुव॑नेष्व॒न्तः पव॑मानो हरि॒त आ वि॑वेश॥१४॥

14. Three kinds of creatures went to destruction; the others
came before *Agni*; the mighty one (the Sun) stood within the
worlds; (*Vāyu*), the purifier, entered the quarters of the sky.

This very obscure verse is explained in the *Śatapatha Brāhmaṇa*,
II.5.1, which gives as legend to the effect that *Prajāpati* desired to create,
and after intense meditation produced in succession three kinds of
creatures—birds, small snakes (*sarisṛpa*), and serpents; but they all died.
He then reflected on the cause of the failure; and, perceiving it to be the
want of nourishment, he caused milk to be produced in his own breasts.
After this he created a fourth kind which were thus fed and lived. The
'others' are those which thus survived.

The Mighty One— The mighty one' is explained as the Sun. Sāyaṇa, however, adds that others (as, *e.g. Śatapatha Brāhmaṇa*) take it as *Prajāpati*.

७६५३. माता रुद्राणां दुहिता वसूनां स्वसादित्यानाममृतस्य नाभिः।

प्र नु वोचं चिकितुषे जनाय मा गामनागामदितिं वधिष्ट ॥१५॥

15. (She who is) the mother of the *Rudras*, the daughter of the *Vasus*, the sister of the *Ādityas*, the home of ambrosia,—I have spoken to men of understanding,—kill not her, the sinless inviolate cow.

७६५४. वचोविदं वाचमुदीरयन्तीं विश्वाभिर्धीभिरुपतिष्ठमानाम्।

देवीं देवेभ्यः पर्येयुषीं गामा मावृक्त मर्त्यो दभ्रचेताः ॥१६॥

16. The divine cow, who herself utters speech and gives speech to others, who comes attended by every kind of utterance, who helps me for my worship of the gods,—it is only the fool who abandons her.

Gives speech to others— Sāyaṇa adds that men are silent while they are hungry, but begin to speak when they have eaten food.

[सूक्त-१०२]

[ऋषि— प्रयोग भार्गव अथवा अग्नि बार्हस्पत्य अथवा अग्नि-पावक अथवा
सहसः पुत्र-गृहपति, यविष्ठश्च यद्वा एकः ।

देवता— अग्नि। छन्द— गायत्री।]

७६५५. त्वमग्ने बृहद्वयो दधासि देव दाशुषे। कविर्गृहपतिर्युवा ॥१॥

1. Divine *Agni*, the ever young, the wise, the protector of the household, it is you who give abundant food to the worshipper.

७६५६. स न ईळानया सह देवाँ अग्ने दुवस्युवा। चिकिद्विभानवा वह ॥२॥

2. Resplendent one, do you, the all-knower, bring the gods hither with this our reverential hymn of praise.

७६५७. त्वया ह स्विद्युजा वयं चोदिष्ठेन यविष्ठ्य। अभि ष्मो वार्जसातये ॥३॥

3. O ever youthful one, with you as our ally, the sender of wealth, we overcome (our enemies) for the attainment of food.

Sāmaveda, 403.

७६५८. और्वभृगुवच्छुचिमप्नवानवदा हुवे। अग्निं समुद्रवाससम् ॥४॥

4. Like *Aurva Bhṛgu* and like *Apanvān*, I invoke the pure *Agni*, dwelling in the midst of the sea.

Aurva Bhṛgu— For the legend of *Aurva*, the descendant of *Bhṛgu* (he is sometimes called the son, sometimes the grandson, and sometimes only the descendant), see Muir's *Sanskrit Texts*, I.447,476. He became the submarine fire. Benfey takes *Aurvabhṛgu* as a *dvandva* compound, "like *Aurva* and *Bhṛgu*."

Apnavāna— We have *Apnavān* mentioned as one of the *Bhṛgus* in IV.7.1.

Dwelling in the Midst of the Sea— Sāyaṇa explains *samudravāsasam* by *samudramadhyavartinām*. It should properly mean "clothed or hidden by the sea."

७६५९. हुवे वातस्वनं कविं पर्जन्यक्रन्दं सहः। अग्निं समुद्रवाससम्॥५॥

5. I invoke *Agni* dwelling in the midst of the sea, the wise one, roaring like the wind, might, with a voice like *Parjanya*'s.

७६६०. आ सवं सवितुर्यथा भगस्येव भुजिं हुवे। अग्निं समुद्रवाससम्॥६॥

6. I invoke *Agni* dwelling in the midst of the sea, like the energy of *Savitā*, like the enjoyments granted by *Bhaga*.

Like the Energy of Savitā— Sāyaṇa only explains *savam savituḥ* by *prerakasya devasya prasavam*, but *cf.* viii.100.12.

Like the Enjoyments Granted by Bhaga— *Sāyaṇa only explains Bhagasyeva bhujim by Bhagākhyasya devasya bhogam iva.* The St. Petersburg Dict. explains *bhuji* "Gewährung von Genuss, Gunst,"—*i.e.,* "like the favour of *Bhaga*."

७६६१. अग्निं वो वृधन्तमध्वराणां पुरूतमम्। अच्छा नप्त्रे सहस्वते॥७॥

7. (Draw) near to *Agni* the strong, the mightiest, him who expands (with his flames), the grandson of the invincible ones.
Sāmaveda, 21, 946.

The Grandson of the invincible ones— Sāyaṇa takes *adhvarāṇām* as *ahiṃsyānām balinām*. Benfey's transl. is far better, "Eurem *Agni*, dem Segnenden, ihm dem Opferverschendsten, dem stärkereichen Enkel zu" (rufen wir an.)

७६६२. अयं यथा न आभुवत्त्वष्टा रूपेव तक्ष्या। अस्य क्रत्वा यशस्वतः॥८॥

8. (Draw near) that he may deal with us as a carpenter deals with the timber he has to cut; may we become renowned by his skill.
Sāmaveda, 947.

७६६३. अयं विश्वा अभि श्रियोऽग्निर्देवेषु पत्यते। आ वाजैरुप नो गमत्॥९॥

9. Among the gods *Agni* has to do with all the successes (of men); may he come to us with abundance of food.

Sāmaveda, 948.

७६६४. विश्वेषामिह स्तुहि होतृणां यशस्तमम्। अग्निं यज्ञेषु पूर्व्यम्॥१०॥

10. Praise at our rite *Agni*, the most glorious of all ministrant priests, the foremost in the sacrifices.

७६६५. शीरं पावकशोचिषं ज्येष्ठो यो दमेष्वा। दीदाय दीर्घश्रुत्तमः॥११॥

11. (Praise him) the dweller in the sacrifice, of purifying radiance, who shines, the chief of the gods and omniscient, in the house (of the sacrificers).

७६६६. तमर्वन्तं न सानसिं गृणीहि विप्र शुष्मिणम्।
    मित्रं न यातयज्जनम्॥१२॥

12. O priest, glorify him, who is welcome and strong as a horse, and who like a friend conquers all our foes.

Who Conquers all our Foes— The St. Petersburg Dict. explains *yātayajjanam* "die Leute vereinigend."

७६६७. उप त्वा जामयो गिरो देदिशतीर्हविष्कृतः।
    वायोरनीके अस्थिरन्॥१३॥

13. The sister praises of the worshipper rise to you, proclaiming your glories; they stand kindling you in the presence of *Vāyu*.

Sāmaveda, 13, 1570.

In the Presence of Vāyu— Sāyaṇa explains *anīke* as *samīpe tvām samedhayantyas*. Benfey takes *vayor anīke* "im Windesstrom."

७६६८. यस्य त्रिधात्ववृतं बर्हिस्तस्थावसन्दिनम्। आपश्चिन्नि दधा पदम्॥१४॥

14. The waters find their place in him, for whom the triple-jointed grass is spread unlimited and untied (in the sacrifice).

Sāmaveda, 1571.

The waters find their Place in Him— The waters rest in *Agni*, who abides as lightning in the firmament.

The triple-jointed Grass . . . . United— Sāyaṇa does not explain *tridhātu*, but in the *Sāmaveda*, he explains it by *triparvan*. He adds that the sacred grass is not tied in bundles in the sacrifice.

७६६९. पदं देवस्य मीळ्हुषोऽनाधृष्टाभिरूतिभिः। भद्रा सूर्य इवोपदृक्॥१५॥

15. Auspicious is the place of the god who pours forth all desires with his inviolable protections; auspicious is his appearance like the Sun's.

Sāmaveda, 1572.

७६७०. अग्ने घृतस्य धीतिभिस्तेपानो देव शोचिषा।
सा देवान्वक्षि यक्षि च॥१६॥

16. Divine *Agni*, blazing with radiance, through our oblations of *ghī*, bear (our sacrifice) to the gods and offer it.

७६७१. तं त्वाजनन्त मातरः कविं देवासो अङ्गिरः। हव्यवाहममर्त्यम्॥१७॥

17. The gods, as mothers, have borne you *Aṅgiras*, the seer, the immortal, the bearer of the oblation.

७६७२. प्रचेतसं त्वा कवेऽग्ने दूतं वरेण्यम्। हव्यवाहं नि षेदिरे॥१८॥

18. The gods seat you in your place, O wise *Agni*, the seer, the messenger, the most excellent, the bearer of the oblation.

Seat you in your Place— For *ni ṣedire cf.* iv.7.5.

७६७३. नहि मे अस्त्यघ्न्या न स्वधितिर्वनन्वति। अथैतादुग्भरामि ते॥१९॥

19. No cow is mine, and no axe is at hand to cleave wood, but yet I being both these to you.

७६७४. यदग्ने कानि कानि चिदा ते दारूणि दध्मसि। ता जुषस्व गविछ्य॥२०॥

20. Most youthful (*Agni*), when we offer any kinds of timber to you, do you accept them all.

This is partly found in *Yajurveda*, II.73.

Any kinds of Timber— Sāyaṇa here quotes a passage from the *Taittirīya Saṁhitā.*, v.1.10, to the effect that in ancient times they only offered to *Agni* wood cut with the axe, until the ṛṣi *Prayoga* by this verse caused him to accept wood blown down by the wind or by other accidents.

७६७५. यदत्युपजिह्विका यद्रुमो अतिसर्पति। सर्वं तदस्तु ते घृतम्॥२१॥

21. Whatever timber the ant has gnawed, whatever the emmet has infested,—may it all be welcome to you as *ghī*.

Yajurveda, 11.74.

७६७६. अग्निमिन्धानो मनसा धियं सचेत मर्त्यः।
अग्निमीधे विवस्वभिः॥२२॥

22. Let a man, when he kindles *Agni*, perform the ceremony with a (devout) mind; he kindles him with the priests.

Sāmaveda, 19, with *indhe* for *idhe*.

[सूक्त-१०३]

[ऋषि— सोभरि काण्व। देवता— अग्नि, १४ अग्नि तथा मरुद्गण। छन्द—
बृहती, ५ विराड्रूपा; ७, ९, ११, १३ सतोबृहती; ८, १२ ककुप्, १०
हंसीयसी (गायत्री), १४ अनुष्टुप्।]

७६७७. अदर्शि गातुवित्तमो यस्मिन्न्व्रतान्यादधुः।
उपो षु जातमार्यस्य वर्धनमग्निं नक्षन्त नो गिरः॥१॥

1. He, in whom they offer the sacrifices, has appeared,—he who knows all ways; our praises rise to *Agni*, auspiciously born, the helper of the *Ārya*.

Sāmaveda, 47, 1515, with *nakṣantu* for *nakṣanta*.

Arya— *Arya* here seems to mean the member of the *Āryan* race as opposed to the non-*Āryan*. Sāyaṇa explains it by *uttamavarṇa*, a man of the highest caste.

७६७८. प्र दैवोदासो अग्निर्देवाँ अच्छा न मज्मना।
अनु मातरं पृथिवीं वि वावृते तस्थौ नाकस्य सानवि॥२॥

2. *Agni*, when invoked by *Divodāsa*, ran along the mother Earth as with might, towards the gods; he took his place in the height of heaven.

Sāmaveda, 51, 1517 with *deva Indraḥ* for *devān acchā*, and *śarmaṇi* for *sānavi*.

This is an obscure verse, and Sāyaṇa does not explain it at all clearly. The *Sāmaveda*, text takes *na* not as a negative, but as 'like,' *deva Indro na*. Sāyaṇa here leaves *pravivavṛte* unexplained; the Comm. on the *Sāmaveda*, explains it *anyarūpam karoti*. I have followed the translation suggested by the St. Petersb. Dict.

७६७९. यस्मादेजन्त कृष्टयश्चर्कृत्यानि कृण्वतः।
सहस्रसां मेधसाताविव त्मनाग्निं धीभिः संपर्यत॥३॥

3. Since men tremble before those who perform the sacred sacrifices, therefore do ye devoutly worship in the solemn rite *Agni* the bestower of thousands of kine.

७६८०. प्र यं राये निनीषसि मर्तो यस्ते वसो दाशत्।
स वीरं धत्ते अग्न उक्थशंसिनं त्मना सहस्रपोषिणम्॥४॥

4. *Agni*, bestower of dwellings, that mortal whom you wish to lead to wealth, and who gives offerings to you possesses of himself a strong son, a reciter of hymns and a lord of great wealth.

Sāmaveda, 58, with *yah* for *yam*.

A Lord of great Wealth— *Sahasraposiṇa* explained as *bahudhanam*, but literally meaning 'nourisher of thousands.'

७६८१. स दृळ्हे चिद्भि तृणत्ति वाजमर्वता स धत्ते अक्षिति श्रवः।
त्वे देवत्रा सदा पुरूवसो विश्वा वामानि धीमहि॥५॥

5. Lord of vast wealth, he (your worshipper) spoils with his steed food laid up even in strongholds, he possesses imperishable wealth; in you divine we ever possess all desirable treasures.

७६८२. यो विश्वा दयते वसु होता मन्द्रो जनानाम्।
मधोर्न पात्रा प्रथमान्यस्मै प्र स्तोमा यन्त्यग्नये॥६॥

6. To him the invoker of the gods, who ever rejoicing distributes all wealth to men,—to *Agni* proceed our praises like the principal cups of the exhilarating *Soma*.

Sāmaveda, 44, 1583.

७६८३. अश्वं न गीर्भी रथ्यं सुदानवो मर्मृज्यन्ते देवयवः।
उभे तोके तनये दस्म विश्पते पर्षि राधो मघोनाम्॥७॥

7. The liberal worshippers with their hymns honour you harnessed to the ear like a horse; graceful lord of men, grant wealth to us rich in children and grandchildren.

Sāmaveda, 1584.

With their Hymns Honour you— This alludes to the common idea that the chariots of the gods are yoked by the praises of their worshippers.

Rich in Children and Grandchildren— So Sāyaṇa; but the Pada text takes *ubhe* and *toke* as dual, see Benfey's note.

७६८४. प्र मंहिष्ठाय गायत ऋताव्ने बृहते शुक्रशोचिषे।
उपस्तुतासो अग्नये॥८॥

8. Singers of hymns, sing aloud to the mighty *Agni*, most bounteous, observant of truth and radiant with brightness.

Sāmaveda, 107, 878.

७६८५. आ वंसते मघवा वीरवद्यशः समिद्धो द्युम्न्याहुतः।
कुविन्नो अस्य सुमतिर्नवीयस्यच्छा वाजेभिरागमत्॥९॥

9. The wealthy and glorious (*Agni*), when invoked and kindled, pours forth on his votaries abundance of food with children; may his ever fresh favour continually come to us with all kinds of food.

Sāmaveda, 879, with *bhavīyasi* for *navīyasi*.

७६८६. प्रेष्ठमु प्रियाणां स्तुह्यासावातिथिम्। अग्निं रथानां यमम्॥१०॥

10. Praise, singer of hymns, the guest, *Agni*, the dearest of the dear, the driver of chariots.

Singer of Hymns— Sāyaṇa explains *āsāva* a *stotā*; the St. Petersb. Dict. takes it as 'Somatrankbereiter.'

७६८७. उदिता यो निदिता वेदिता वस्वा यज्ञियो ववर्तति।
दुष्टरा यस्य प्रवणे नोर्मयो धिया वाजं सिषासतः॥११॥

11. (Praise him) the knower, worthy of the sacrifice, who brings to us treasures which have come up (from the depths) and are far-renowned,—whose (flames), as he hastens to wage the battle by means of our sacred rite and hard to be passed through as waves rushing down a declivity.

Far-Renowned— Sāyaṇa explains *niditā* by *śrutāni*. The St. Petersb. Dict. gives it as "verwahrt, versteckt."

By Means of our Sacred Rite— *Dhiyā* is explained by *karmaṇā*. The offering is supposed to give the god strength for the battle.

७६८८. मा नो हृणीतामतिथिर्वसुरग्निः पुरुप्रशस्त एषः।
यः सुहोता स्वध्वरः॥१२॥

12. May none hinder *Agni* from coming to us, our guest, the giver of dwellings, praised by many,—(*Agni*) who is the excellent invoker of the gods, who offers an excellent sacrifice.

Sāmaveda, 110, reading *hṛṇītha atithim* for *hṛṇītam atithiḥ*.

७६८९. मो ते रिषन्ये अच्छोक्तिभिर्वसोऽग्ने केभिश्चिदेवैः।
कीरिश्चिद्धि त्वामिट्टे दूत्याय रातहव्यः स्वध्वरः॥१३॥

13. *Agni*, giver of dwellings, let not those come to harm, who approach you in whatsoever manner with hymns of praise; the worshipper who offers his libation and duly performs the rite praises you that you may be the bearer of the sacrifice.

७६९०.   आग्ने याहि मरुत्सखा रुद्रेभिः सोमपीतये।

सोभर्या उप सुष्टुतिं मादयस्व स्वर्णरि।।१४।।

14. *Agni*, who have the *Maruts* as your friends, come with the *Rudras* to drink the *Soma*; come to the praises of *Sobhari*; delight yourself at our solemn rite.

।।इति अष्टमं मण्डलम्।।

End of the Eighth Maṇḍala

तृतीयभागस्य मन्त्रानुक्रमसूची

अधा मही न आयस्यना ७,१५,१४

अधा ह यन्तो अश्विना ७,७४,५

अधा हि विश्ववीड्योऽसि ६,२,७

अधा हीन्द्र गिर्वण: ८,९८,७

अधा होता न्यसीदो ६,१,२

अधि न इन्द्रैषां ८,८३,७

अधि बृबु: पणीनां ६,४५,३१

अधि या बृहतो दिव: ८,२५,७

अधि श्रिये दुहिता ६,६३,५

अधीव यद्गिरीणां ८,७,१४

अधुक्षत् पिप्युषीमिषम् ८,७२,१६

अध्वर्यवा तु हि षिञ्च ८,३२,२४

अध्वर्यवोऽरुणं दुग्धमंशुम् ७,९८,१

अध्वर्यो द्रावया त्वं ८,४,११

अध्वर्यो वीर प्र महे ६,४४,१३

अनर्वाणो ह्येषां पन्था ८,१८,२

अनर्शरातिं वसुदामुप स्तुहि ८,९९,४

अनु तदुर्वी रोदसी ७,३४,२४

अनु तन्नो जास्पति: ७,३८,६

अनु ते दायि मह इन्द्रियाय ६,२५,८

अनु ते शुष्मं तुरयन्तमीयतु: ८,९९,६

अनु त्रितस्य युध्यत: ८,७,२४

अनु त्वा रोदसी उभे ८,७६,११

अनु त्वा रोदसी उभे चक्रं ८,६,३८

अनु त्वाहिघ्ने अध देव ६,१८,१४

अनु द्यावापृथिवी ६,१८,१५

अनु पूर्वाण्योक्या ८ २५,१७

अनु प्रलस्यौकस: ८,६९,१८

अनु प्र येजे जन ओजो ६,३६,२

अनेनो वो मरुत: ६,६६,७

अनेहसं वो हवमानमूतये ८,५०,४

अनेहसं प्रतरणं विवक्षणं ८,४९,४

अनेहो न उरुव्रजे ८,६७,१२

अनेहो मित्रार्यमन् ८,१८,२१

अन्तरिच्छन्ति तं जने ८,७२,३

अन्तरैश्चक्रैस्तनयाय ६,६२,१०

अन्तश्च प्रागा अदितिर्भवा ८,४८,२

अन्ति चित् सन्तमह ८,११,४

अन्तिवामा दूरे अमित्रमुच्छ ७,७७,४

अन्यदद्य कर्वरमन्यदु ६,२४,५

अन्यमस्मद्भिया इयम् ८,७५,१३

अन्यव्रतममानुषं ८,७०,११

अन्यो अन्यमनु गृभ्णाति ७,१०३,४

अन्वपां खान्यतृन्तमोजसा ७,८२,३

अन्वस्य स्थूरं ददृशे पुरस्तात् ८,१,३४

अप त्या अस्थुरनिरा ८,४८,११

अप त्वं वृजिनं रिपुं ६,५१,१३

अप स्वसुरुषसो नग्जिहीते ७,७१,१

अपादित उदु नश्चित्रतम: ६,३८,१

अपादिन्द्रो अपादग्नि: ८,६९,११

अपादु शिप्र्यन्धस: ८,९२,४

अपाधमदभिशस्ती: ८,८९,२

अपाम सोमममृता अभूम ८,४८,३

अपामीवामप स्रिधं ८,१८,१०

अपामुपस्थे महिषा ६,८,४

अपामूर्मिर्मदन्त्रिव ८,१४,१०

अपां फेनेन नमुचे: ८,१४,१३

अपां मध्ये तस्थि वां सं ७,८९,४

अपि पन्थामगन्महि ६,५१,१६

अपिबत् कद्रुव: सुतम् ८,४५,२६

अपि वृश्च पुराणवत् ८,४०,६

अपि हु सविता ७,३८,३

अपूर्व्या पुरुतमानि ६,३२,१

अपो षु ण इयं शरु:८,६७,१५

अप्रामिसत्य मघवन् ८,६१,४

अप्स्वग्ने सधिष्टव ८,४३,९

अबोधि जार उषसां ७,९,१

अब्जामुक्थैरहिं ७,३४,१६

अभि कण्वा अनूषत ८,६,३४

अभि क्रत्वेन्द्र भूरध ७,२१,६

अभि गन्धर्वमतृणात् ८,७७,५

अभि त्वं वीरं गिर्वणसम् ६,५०,६

अभि त्वा पाजो रक्षस: ६,२१,७

आ तू न इन्द्र क्षुमन्तं ८,८१,१

आ तू पिश्व कण्वमन्तं ८,२,२२

आ तू सुशिप्र दंपते ८,६९,१६

आ ते दक्षं वि रोचना ८,९३,२६

आ ते दधामीन्द्रियं ८,९३,२७

आ ते मह इन्द्रोत्युग्र ७,२५,१

आ ते वत्सो मनो यमत् ८,११,७

आ ते सिञ्चामि कुक्ष्यो: ८,१७,५

आत्मा ते वातो रज ७,८७,२

आत्मा पितुस्तनूर्वासः ८,३,२४

आ त्व१ग्घ सधस्तुतिं ८,१,१६

आ त्व१ग्घ सबर्दुघां ८,१,१०

आ त्वशत्रवा गहि ८,८२,४

आ त्वा कण्वा इहावसे ८,३४,४

आ त्वा गिरो रथीरिवास्थु: ८,९५,१

आ त्वा गीर्भिर्महामुरुं ८,६५,३

आ त्वा गोभिरिव व्रजं ८,२४,६

आ त्वा ग्रावा वदन्निह ८,३४,२

आ त्वा ब्रह्मयुजा हरी ८,१७,२

आ त्वा मदच्युता हरी ८,३४,९

आ त्वा रथं यथोतये ८,६८,१

आ त्वा रथे हिरण्यये ८,१,२५

आ त्वा रम्भं न जिव्रयो ८,४५,२०

आ त्वा विशन्त्विन्दव: ८,९२,२२

आ त्वा शुक्रा अचुच्यवु: ८,९५,२

आ त्वा सहस्रमा शतं ८,१,२४

आ त्वा सुतास इन्दवो ८,४९,३

आ त्वा हरयो वृषणो ६,४४,१९

आ त्वा होता मनुर्हितो ८,३४,८

आ दशभिर्विवस्वत ८,७२,८

आदित्रल:स्य रेतसो ८,६,३०

आदित्या अव हि ख्यता ८,४७,११

आदित्यानामवस ७,५१,१

आदित्या रुद्रा वसवो ७,३५,१४

आदित्या विश्वे मरुतश्च ७,५१,३

आदित्यासो अदितयः ७,५२,१

आदित्यासो अदिति: ७,५१,२

आदित्सापत्स्य चर्किरन् ८,५५,५

आदीं शवस्यब्रवीद् ८,७७,२

आदु मे निवरो भुवत् ८,९३,१५

आदू नु ते अनु क्रतुं ८,६३,५

आ देवो ददे बुध्न्या ७,६,७

आ देवो यातु सविता ७,४५,१

आ दैव्या वृणीमहे ७,९७,२

आ धृर्षस्मै दधाता ७,३४,४

आधेण चित् तद्वेकं ७,१८,१७

आ न इन्द्र महीमिषं ८,६,२३

आ नः सहस्रशो ८,३४,१५

आ नः सोमे स्वध्वर ८,५०,५

आ नः स्तोममुप द्रवत ८,५,७

आ नः स्तोममुप द्रवद्धियानो ८,४९,५

आ नार्यस्य दक्षिणा ८,२४,२९

आ निरेकमुत प्रियं ८,२४,४

आ नूनं यातमश्विना रथेन ८,८,२

आ नूनं यातमश्विनाश्वेभि: ८,८७,५

आ नूनं यातमश्विनेमा ८,९,१४

आ नूनं रघुवर्तनिं ८,९,८

आ नूनमश्विना युवं ८,९,१

आ नूनमश्विनोर्ऋषि ८,९,७

आ नो अग्ने वयोवृधं ८,६०,११

आ नो अद्य समनसो ८,२७,५

आ नो अश्वावदश्विना ८,२२,१७

आ नो गन्तं रिशादसेमां ८,८,१७

आ नो गन्तं मयोभुवा ८,८,१९

आ नो गव्यान्यक्ष्या ८,३४,१४

आ नो गव्येभिरश्व्यै: ८,७३,१४

आ नो गव्येभिरश्व्यैर्वसव्यै: ६,६०,१४

आ नो गोमन्तमश्विना ८,५,१०

आ नो दधिक्रा पथ्यां ७,४४,५

आ नो दिव आ पृथिव्या ७,२४,३

आ नो देव: सविता त्रायमाणो ६,५०,८

आ नो देव शवसा ७,३०,१

आ नो देवेभिरुप देवहूतिम् ७,१४,३

आ नो देवेभिरुप यातं ७,७२,२

आ नो द्युम्नैरा श्रवोभि: ८,५,३२

आ नो नियुद्भि: शतिनीभि: ७,९२,५

उत स्या नः सरस्वती घोरा ६,६१,७
उत स्या नः सरस्वती जुषाणोप ७,९५,४
उत स्या नो दिवा ८,१८,७
उत स्या श्वेतयावरी ८,२६,१८
उत स्वया तन्वा३ सं वदे ७,८६,२
उत स्वराजे अदितिः ८,१२,१४
उत स्वराजो अदितिः ७,६६,६
उताद परुषे गवि ६,५६,३
उतासि मैत्रावरुणो ७,३३,११
उतेदानीं भगवन्तः ७,४१,४
उतो घा ते पुरुष्या ७,२९,४
उतो न्वस्य जोषमाँ ८,९४,६
उतो न्वस्य यत्पदं ८,७२,१८
उतो न्वस्य यन्महत् ८,७२,६
उतो पतिर्य उच्यते ८,१३,९
उतो हि वां रत्नधेयानि ७,५३,३
उत्तिष्ठन्नोजसा सह ८,७६,१०
उत्ते बृहन्तो अर्चयः ८,४४,४
उत्ते वयश्चिद्वसतेरपप्तन् ६,६४,६
उत्त्वा मन्दन्तु स्तोमाः ८,६४,१
उत्पूषणं युवामहे ६,५७,६
उत्सूर्यो बृहदर्चींष्यश्रेत् ७,६२,१
उदग्ने तव तद् घृतात् ८,४३,१०
उदग्ने भारत द्युमत् ६,१६,४५
उदग्ने शुचयस्तव ८,४४,१७
उदभ्राणीव स्तनयन् ६,४४,१२
उदस्य बाहू शिथिरा ७,४५,२
उदस्य शुष्माद्भानुः ७,३४,७
उदस्य शोचिरस्थादाजुह्वा ७,१६,३
उदस्य शोचिरस्थाद् दीदियुषो ८,२३,४
उदानट् ककुहो दिवं ८,६,४८
उदावता त्वक्षसा ६,१८,९
उदिता यो निदिता वेदिता ८,१०३,११
उदिन्वस्य रिच्यते ७,३२,१२
उदीरयन्त वायुभिः ८,७,३
उदीराथामृतायते ८,७३,१
उदु ज्योतिरमृतं ७,७६,१
उदु तिष्ठ सवितः ७,३८,२

उदु तिष्ठ स्वध्वर ८,२३,५
उदु त्यच्चक्षुर्महि ६,५१,१
उदु त्यद्दर्शतं वपुः ७,६६,१४
उदु त्ये अरुणप्सव ८,७,७
उदु त्ये मधुमत्तमा ८,३,१५
उदु ब्रह्माण्यैरत ७,२३,१
उदु श्रिय उषसो ६,६४,१
उदु ष्य देवः सविता दमूना ६,७१,४
उदु ष्य देवः सविता ययाम ७,३८,१
उदु ष्य देवः सविता हिरण्यया ६,७१,१
उदु ष्य वः सविता ८,२७,१२
उदु ष्य शरणे दिवो ८,२५,१९
उदु स्तोमासो अश्विनोः ७,७२,३
उदु त्रियाः सृजते सूर्याः ७,८१,२
उदु स्वानेभिरीरत ८,७,१७
उदू अयाँ उपवक्तेव ६,७१,५
उदू षु णो वसो महे ८,७०,९
उद्गा आजदङ्गिरोभ्य ८,१४,८
उदेदभि श्रुतामघ ८,९३,१
उद् घ्याममिवेत् तृष्णजो ७,३३,५
उद्घद् ब्रध्नस्य विष्टपं ८,६९,७
उद्यस्य ते नवजातस्य ७,३,३
उद्व्रां चक्षुर्वरुण ७,६१,१
उद्व्रां पृक्षासो मधुमन्तो अस्थुः ७,६०,४
उद्वेति प्रसवीता जनानां ७,६३,२
उद्वेति सुभगो विश्वचक्षाः ७,६३,१
उप क्रमस्वा भर ८,८१,७
उप च्छायामिव ६,१६,३८
उप त्वा वह्नी गमतो विशं ७,७३,४
उप त्वा कर्मन्नूतये ८,२१,२
उप त्वा जामयो गिरो ८,१०२,१३
उप त्वा जुह्वो३ मम ८,४४,५
उप त्वा रण्वसंदृशं ६,१६,३७
उप त्वा सातये नरो ७,१५,९
उप नः सुनवो गिरः ६,५२,९
उप नो यातमश्विना ८,२६,७
उप नो वाजिनीवसू ८,२२,७
उप नो हरिभिः सुतं ८,९३,३१

कण्वा इन्द्रं यदक्रत ८,६,३
कण्वा इव भृगवः ८,३,१६
कण्वास इन्द्र ते मतिं ८,६,३१
कण्वेभिर्धृष्णवा धृषत् ८,३३,३
कथा नूनं वां विमना ८,८६,२
कदत्विषन्त सूरयः ८,९४,७
कदा गच्छाथ मरुतः ८,७,३०
कदा चन प्र युच्छस्युभे ८,५२,७
कदा चन स्तरीरसि ८,५१,७
कदा त इन्द्र गिर्वणः ८,१३,२२
कदा भुवन रथक्षयाणि ६,३५,१
कदा वां तौग्र्यो विधत् ८,५,२२
कदू स्तुवन्त ऋतयन्त ८,३,१४
कदू न्व१स्याकृतं ८,६६,९
कदू महीरधृष्टा अस्य ८,६६,१०
कद्ध नूनं कधप्रियो यद् ८,७,३१
कद्रो अद्य महानां ८,९४,८
कं ते दाना असक्षत ८,६४,९
कन्नव्यो अतसीनां ८,३,१३
कन्या वारवायती ८,९१,१
कमु ष्विदस्य सेनयाग्नेः ८,७५,७
कया ते अग्ने अङ्गिरः ८,८४,४
कया त्वं न ऊत्याभि ८,९३,१९
कया नो अग्ने वि वसः ७,८,३
कर्णगृह्या मघवा शौरदेव्यः ८,७०,१५
कर्हि स्वित्तदिन्द्र यज्जरित्रे ६,३५,३
कर्हि स्वित्तदिन्द्र यत्नृभिर्नॄन् ६,३५,२
कविं केतुं धासिं ७,६,२
कविमिव प्रचेतसं ८,८४,२
कस्तमिन्द्र त्वावसुं ७,३२,१४
कस्य नूनं परीणसो ८,८४,७
कस्य वृषा सुते सचा ८,९३,२०
कस्य स्वित्सवनं वृषा ८,६४,८
का ते अस्त्यरंकृतिः ७,२९,३
काव्येभिरदाभ्या ७,६६,१७
किमङ्ग त्वा ब्रह्मणः सोम ६,५२,३
किमङ्ग रध्रचोदनः ८,८०,३

किमन्ये पर्यासते ८,८,८
किमस्य मदे किम्वस्य ६,२७,१
किमाग आस वरुण ज्येष्ठं ७,८६,४
किमित्ते विष्णो ७,१००,६
किमिदं वां पुराणवत् ८,७३,११
कीरिश्चिद्धि त्वामवसे ७,२१,८
कुत्सा एते हर्यश्वाय ७,२५,५
कुविच्छकत्कुवित्करत् ८,९१,४कुवित्सु
कुवित्सस्य प्र हि व्रजं ६,४५,२४
कुविदङ्ग नमसा ये ७,९१,१
कुह स्थः कुह जग्मथुः ८,७३,४
कृतं नो यज्ञं विदथेषु ७,८४,३
कृते चिदत्र मरुतो रणन्त ७,५७,५
कृधि रत्नं यजमानाय ७,१६,६
कृष्णा रजांसि पत्सुतः ८,४३,६
केतेन शर्मन्त्सचते ८,६०,१८
को नु मर्या अमिथितः ८,४५,३७
क्रत्व इत्पूर्णमुदरं ८,७८,७
क्रत्वः समह दीनता ७,८९,३
क्रत्वा दा अस्तु श्रेष्ठोऽद्य ६,१६,२६
क्रत्वा हि द्रोणे अज्यसे ६,२८
क्रीळन्त्यस्य सूनृता ८,१३,८
क्व१त्यानि नौ सख्या ७,८८,५
क्व१त्या वल्गू पुरुहूताद्य ६,६३,१
क्व नूनं सुदानवो ८,७,२०
क्व१स्य वृषभो युवा ८,६४,७
क्वेयथ क्वेदसि ८,१,७
क्षत्रं जिन्वतमुत ८,३५,१७
क्षत्राय त्वमवसि ८,३७,६
क्षप उस्रश्च दीदिहि ७,१५,८
क्षेति क्षेमेभिः साधुभिर्निकिर्यं ८,८४,९
क्षेमस्य च प्रयुजश्च ८,३७,५
खे रथस्य खेऽनसः ८,९१,७
गच्छतं दाशुषो गृहं ८,८५,६
गन्तेयान्ति सवना ६,२३,४
गमद्वाजं वाजयन्निन्द्र ७,३२,११
गम्भीरेण न उरुणा ६,२४,९

गर्भे नु सन्नन्वेषामवेद ४,२७,१
गर्भे मातुः पितुष्षिता ६,१६,३५
गर्भो यज्ञस्य देवयुः ८,१२,११
गव्यो षु णो यथा ८,४६,१०
गाथश्रवसं सत्पतिं ८,२,३८
गाव उपावतावतं ८,७२,१२
गावश्चिद् घा समन्यवः ८,२०,२१
गावो न यूथमुप यन्ति ८,४६,३०
गावो भगो गाव इन्द्रो ६,२८५
गिरयश्चिन्नि जिहते ८,७,३४
गिरिश्च यास्ते गिर्वाहः ८,२,३०
गिरा य एता युनज्द्धरी ७,३६,४
गिरा वज्रो न संभृतः ८,९३,९
गिरो जुषेथामध्वरं ८,३५,६
गीर्भिर्विप्रः प्रमतिमिच्छमान ७,९३,४
गुहा सतीरुप त्मना ८,६,८
गृणे तदिन्द्र ते शव ८,६२,८
गृभीतं ते मन इन्द्र ७,२४,२
गृहमेधास आ गत ७,५९,१०
गोभिर्यदीमन्ये अस्मत् ८,२,६
गोभिर्वाणो अज्यते ८,२०,८
गोमद्धिरण्यवद्वसु ७,९४,९
गोमायुरदादजमायुरदाद् ७,१०३,१०
गोमायुरेको अजमायुरेकः ७,१०३,६
गौर्धयति मरुतां ८,९४,१
ग्नाश्च यन्नरश्च ६,६८४
ग्रावाणः सोम नो ६,५१,१४
घृतप्रुषः सौम्या ८,५९,४
घृतवती भुवनानामभि ६,७०,१
घृतेन द्यावापृथिवी ६,७०,४
घ्नन्मृध्राण्यप द्विषो ८,४३,२६
चकार ता कृणवन्नु ७,२६,३
चत्वारो मा पैजवनस्य ७,१८,२३
चनिष्ठं देवा ओषधीषु ७,७०,४
चरन् वत्सो रुशन्निह ८,७२,५
चित्र इन्द्राजा राजका ८,२१,१८
चित्रं ह यद्वां भोजनं ७,६८,५

छर्दिर्यन्तमदाभ्यं ८,८५,५
जज्ञानः सोम सहसे पपाथ ७,९८,३
जज्ञानो नु शतक्रतुः ८,७७,१
जनं वज्रिन्महि चिन्मन्य ६,१९,१२
जनाय चिद्य ईवत ६,७३,२
जनासो वृक्तबर्हिषो ८,५,१७
जनिता दिवो जनिता ८,३६,४
जनिताक्षाणां जनिता ८,३६,५
जनिष्वा देववीतये ६,१५,१८
जनीयन्तो न्वग्रवः ७,९६,४
जनूश्चिद् वो मरुतस्त्वेष्येण ७,५८,२
जयतं च प्र स्तुतं ८,३५,११
जयेम कारे पुरुहूत ८,२१,१२
जातो यदग्ने भुवना ७,१३,३
जाम्यतीतपे धनुः ८,७२,४
जिह्वाभिरह नन्नम ८,४३,८
जीमूतस्येव भवति प्रतीकं ६,७५,१
जीवात्रो अभि धेतना ८,६७,५
जुषस्व नः समिधमग्ने ७,२,१
जुषाणो अङ्गिरस्तमेमा ८,४४,८
जुषेथां यज्ञमिष्टये ८,३८,४
जुषेथां यज्ञं ___ मे विश्वेह ८,३५,४
जुष्टी नरो ब्रह्मणा वः ७,३३,४
जुहुराणा चिदश्चिना ८,२६,५
ज्मया अत्र वसवो ७,३९,३
ज्येष्ठेन सोतरिन्द्राय ८,२,२३
ज्योतिष्मन्तं केतुमन्तं ८,५८,३
त इद्देवानां सधमाद ७,७६,४
त इद्देदिं सुभग ८,१९,१८
त इत्रिण्यं हृदयस्य ७,३३,९
त उग्रासो वृषण ८,२०,१२
तं त्वा वयं सुध्यो ६,१७
तं त्वा समिद्धिरङ्गिरो ६,१६,११
तं पृच्छन्ती वज्रहस्तं ६,२२,५
तं पृच्छन्तोऽवरासः ६,२१,६
तं वः सखायः सं ६,२३,९
तं व इन्द्रं चतिनमस्य ६,१९,४

मा नो मृचा रिपूणां ८,६७,९

मा नो रक्ष आ ८,६०,२०

मा नो रक्षो आ अभि ७,१०४,२३

मा नो वधी रुद्र ७ए ४६,४

मानो वृकाय वृक्ये ६,५१,६

मा नोऽहिर्बुध्यो ७,३४,१७

मा नो हृणीतामतिथिर्वसु ८,१०३,१२

मा नो हेतिर्विवस्वत ८,६७,२०

मा पापत्वाय नो ७,९४,३

मा भूम निष्ट्या इवेन्द्र ८,१,१३

मा भेम मा श्रमिष्मो ८,४,७

मायाभिरुत्सिससृप्सत ८,१४,१४

मा व एनो अन्यकृतं ६,५१,७

मा वो दात्रान्मरुतो ७,५६,२१

मा शूने अग्ने ७,१,११

मा सख्युः शूनमा ८,४५,३६

मा सीमव आ ८,८०,८

मा स्वेधत सोमिनो ७,३२,९

मित्रं न यं सुधितं ६,१५,२

मित्रस्तन्नो वरुणो देवो अर्यः ७,६४,३

मित्रस्तन्नो वरुणो मामहन्त ७,५२,२

मित्रस्तन्नो वरुणो रोदसी ७,४०,२

मित्रा तना न रथ्या ८,२५,२

मित्रावरुणवन्ता उत ८,३५,१३

मित्रो नो अत्यंहतिं ८,६७,२

मिम्यक्ष येषु रोदसी ६,५०,५

मूर्धानं दिवो अरतिं ६,७,१

मो ते रिषन्ये अच्छोक्तिभि ८,१०३,१३

मो षु त्वा वाघतश्चनारे ७,३२,१

मो षु ब्रह्मेव ८,९२,३०

मो षु वरुण मृन्मयं ७,८९,१

मो ष्व्द्य दुर्हणावान् ८,२,२०

यं युवं दाश्वध्वराय ६,६८,६

यं वर्धयन्तीद्गिरः ६,४५,५

यः शग्मस्तुविशग्म ६,४४,२

यः सत्राहा विचर्षणि ६,४६,३

य आपिर्नित्यो वरुण ७,८८,६

य आयुं कुत्समतिथिग्व ८,५३,२

य आनयत्परावतः ६,४५,१

य आस्ते यश्च चरति ७,५५,६

य आस्वत्क आशये ८,४१,७

य इद्ध आविवासति ६,६०,११

य इन्द्र चमसेष्वा ८,८२,७

य इन्द्र यतयस्त्वा ८,६,१८

य इन्द्र शुष्मो मघवन् ७,२७,२

य इन्द्र सस्त्यव्रतो ८,९७,३

य इन्द्र सोमपातमो ८,१२,१

य इन्द्राग्नी सुतेषु ६,५९,४

य इमे रोदसी मही ८,६,१७

य ईं राजानावृतुथा ६,६२,१

य उग्रइव शर्यहा ६,१६,३९

य उक्था केवला ८,५२,३

य उक्थेभिर्न विन्धते ८,५१,३

य उग्रः सत्रनिष्ट्टतः ८,३३,९

य उद्नः फलिगं भिनन्त्यक् ८,३२,२५

य ऋक्षादंहसो मुचद् ८,२४,२७

य ऋज्वा महां ८,१,३२

य ऋजा वातरंहसो ८,३४,१७

य ऋते चिदभिश्रिषः ८,१,१२

य ऋते चिद्गास्पदेभ्यो ८,२,३९

य ऋष्वः श्रावयत्सखा ८,४६,१२

य एक इत्तमु ष्टुहि ६,४५,१६

यह एक इद्धव्यश्चर्षणीनाम् ६,२२,१

य एको अस्ति दंसना ८,१,२७

य एनमादिदेशति ६,५६,१

य ओजिष्ठ इन्द्र तं ६,३३,१

यं विप्रा उक्थवाहसो ८,१२,१३

यः ककुभो निधारयः ८,४१,४

यः कृन्तदिद्दि योन्यं ८,४५,३०

यः पञ्च चर्षणीरभि ७,१५,२

यः शक्रो मृक्षो अश्व्यो ८,६६,३

यः श्वेताँ अधिनिर्णिज ८,४१,१०

यः संस्थे चिच्छत्क्रतु ८,३२,११

यः समिधा य आहुती ८,१९,५

यः सुषव्यः सुदक्षिण ८,३३,२

यः सृविन्दमनर्शनिं ८,३२,२

येन सिन्धुं महीरपो ८,१२,३
येना दशग्वमधिगुं ८,१२,२
येनाव तुर्वशं यदुं ८,७,१८
येना समुद्रमसृजो ८,३,१०
ये पाकशंसं विहरन्त ७,१०४,९
ये पातयन्ते अज्मभि ८,४६,१८
येभिः सूर्यमुषसं ६,१७५
येभिस्तिस्रः परावतो ८,५,८
ये मूर्धानः क्षितीनाम् ८,६७,१३
ये राधांसि ददत्यश्या ७,१६,१०
ये वां दंसांस्यश्विना ८,९,३
ये वायव इन्द्रमादनास ७,९२,४
येषामर्णो न सप्रथो ८,२०,१३
येषामाबाध ऋग्मिय ८,२३,३
येषामिळा घृतहस्ता ७,१६,८
ये सोमासः परावति...सर्वस्ताँ ८,९३,६
यो अग्निं हव्यदातिभिॅ ८,१९,१३
यो अग्निं तन्वो दमे ८,४४,१५
यो अग्निः सप्तमानुषः ८,३९,८
यो अद्रिभित्प्रथमजा ६,७३,१
यो अपाचीने तमसि ७,६,४
यो अप्सु चन्द्रमा इव ८,८२,८
यो अश्वेभिर्वहते ८,४६,२६
यो अस्मै हविषाविधत्र ६,५४,४
यो अस्मै हव्यदातिभि ८,२३,२१
यो गर्भमोषधीनां ७,१०२,२
यो गृणताभिदासिथापि ६,४५,१७
यो दुष्टरो विश्ववार ८,४६,९
यो देह्यो३ अनमयद्वधस्नै ७,६,५
योद्धासि कृत्वा शवसोत ८,८८,४
यो धर्ता भुवनानां ८,४१,५
यो धृषितो योऽवृतो ८,३३,६
यो न इदमिदं पुरा ८,२१,९
यो न इन्दुः पितरो ८,४८,१२
यो नः कश्चिद्रिरिक्षति ८,१८,१३
यो नः शश्वत्पुराविथा ८,८०,२
ये नः सनुत्यो अभिदासद् ६,५,४
यो नः स्वो अरणो यश्च ६,७५,१९

योनिमेक आ ससाद ८,२९,२
योनिमेक इन्द्र सदने ७,२४,१
यो नो अग्ने दुरेव ६,१६,३१
यो नो दाता वसूनाम् ८,५१,५
यो नो दाता स नः पिता ८,५२,५
यो नो देवः परावतः ८,१२,६
यो नो मरुतो अभि दुर्हणायु ७,५९,८
यो नो रसं दिप्सति ७,१०४,१०
यो ब्रह्मणे सुमतिमायजाते ७,६०,११
यो म इमं चिदु त्मना ८,४६,२७
यो मा पाकेन मनसा ७,१०४,८
यो मायातुं यातुधानेत्याह ७,१०४,१६
यो मूळयाति चक्रुषे ७,८७,७
यो मे हिरण्यसंदृशो ८,५,३८
यो यजाति याजत इत् ८,३१,१
यो रजांसि विममे पार्थिवानि ६,४९,१३
यो रयिवो रयिन्तमो ६,४४,१
यो राजा चर्षणीनां ८,७०,१
यो रायो अवनिर्महान् ८,३२,१३
यो वर्धन ओषधीनां ७,१०१,२
यो वां यज्ञेभिरावृतो ८,२६,१३
यो वां यज्ञो नासत्या ७,७०,६
यो वां रजांस्यश्विना ८,७३,१३
यो वां रथो नृपती ७,७१,४
यो वां गर्तं मनसा ७,६४,४
यो वां नासत्यावृषि ८,८,१५
यो वामुरुव्यचस्तमं ८,२६,१४
यो वामृजवे क्रमणाय ६,७०,३
यो विश्व दयते वसु ८,१०३,६
यो विश्वान्यभि व्रता ८,३२,२८
यो वेदिष्ठो अव्यथिष्व ८,२,२४
यो वो देवा घृतस्नुना ६,५२,८
यो व्यतीर्फाणयत् ८,६९,१३
यो ह वां मधुनो दृति ८,५,१९
यो हव्यान्येरयता मनुर्हितो ८,१९,२४
यो ह स्य वां रथिरा ७,६९,५
रथं वामनुगायसं ८,५,३४
रथं हिरण्यवन्धुरं ८,५,२८

स इतन्नुं स वि ६,९,३
स इत्तमोऽवयुनं ६,२१,३
स इत्सुदानुः स्ववाँ ६,६८,५
स इदस्तेव प्रति धाद् ६,३,५
स ई रेभो न प्रति ६,३,६
स ई स्पृधो वनते ६,२०,९
स ई पाहि य ऋजीषी ६,१७,२
सकृद्ध घौरजाबत ६,४८,२२
सकृद्ध घौरजायत ६,४८,२२
स क्षपः परि षस्वजे ८,४१,३
सखाय आ शिषामहि ८,२४,१
सखायः क्रतुमिच्छत ८,७०,१३
सखायस्त इन्द्र विश्वह ७,२१,९
सखायो ब्रह्मवाहसे ६,४५,४
सर्खे विष्णो वितरं ८,१००,१२
स गृत्सो अग्निस्तरुणश्चिद् ७,४,२
स गोमधा जरित्रे ६,३५,४
स गोरश्वस्य वि व्रजं ८,३२,५
स घा नो देवः ७,४५,३
सचस्व नायमवसे ६,२४,१०
सचा सोमेषु पुरुहूत ८,६६,६
स चिकेत सहीयसा ८,३९,५
स चित्रश्चित्रं चितयन्तमस्मे ६,६,७
स जायमानः परमे व्योमनि व्रता ६,८,२
स जायमानः व्योमन् वायुर्न ७,५,७
सजूर्देवेभिरपां ७,३४,१५
सजोषस्त्वा दिवो नरो ६,२,३
स तत्कृद्धीगितस्तूयमग्ने ६,५,६
स तु श्रुधि श्रुत्या यो ६,३६,५
स तु श्रुधीन्द्र नूतनस्य ६,२१,८
सत्यं तत्तुर्वशे यदौ ८,४५,२७
सत्यं तदिन्द्रावरुणा ८,५९,३
सत्यमित्तन्न त्वावाँ ६,३०,४
सत्यमित्त्वा महेनदि ८,७४,१५
सत्यमित्था वृषेदसि ८,३३,१०
सत्यमिद्वा उ तं वयम् ८,६२,१२
सत्या सत्येभिर्महती ७,७५,७
सत्रा मदासस्तव ६,३६,१

सत्रा त्वं पुरुष्टुतँ ८,१५,११
सत्रे ह जाताविषिता ७,३३,१३
स त्वं दक्षस्य वृको ६,१५,३
स त्वं न इन्द्राकवाभिः ६,३३,४
स त्वं न इन्द्र वाजेभि ८,१६,१२
स त्वं न ऊर्जा पते ८,१३,१२
स त्वं नश्चित्र ६,४६,२
स त्वं नो अर्वत्रिदाया ६,१२६,
स त्वं नो देव मनसा ८,२६,२५
स त्वं विप्राय दाशुषे ८,४३,१५
स त्वमग्ने विभावसुः ८,४३,३२
स त्वमस्मदप द्विषो ८,१०,३
सदस्य मदे सद्धस्य ६,२७,२
सदिद्धि ते तुविजातस्य ६,१८,४
स दृळ्हे चिदभि तृणत्ति ८,१०३,५
सदो द्वा चक्राते उप ८,२९,९
सद्यश्चिद्यस्य चर्कृतिः ६,४८,२१
सद्यश्चिन्नु ते मघवत्रभिष्टौ ७,१९,९
सद्यो अध्वरे रथिरं जनन्त ७,७,४
सद्योजुवस्तो वाजा ८,८१,९
स न इन्द्र त्वयताया ७,२०,१०;२१,१०
स न इन्द्रः शिवः ८,९३,३
स न ईळानया सह ८,१०२,२
स नः पप्रिः पारयाति ८,१६,११
स नः पृथु श्रवाय्यम् ६,१६,१२
स नः शक्रश्चिदा शकद् ८,३२,१२
स नः सोमेषु सोमपाः ८,९७,६
स नः स्तवान रयिः ८,२४,३
सना ता त इन्द्र भोजनानि ७,१९,६
सनितः सुसनितरुग्र ८,४६,२०
सनिता विप्रा अर्वद्भि ८,२,३६
सनितासि प्रवतो दाशुषे ७,३७,५
सनिर्मित्रस्य पप्रथ ८,१२,१२
स नीव्याभिर्जरितारम् ६,३२,४
सनेम्यस्मद्द्युोत ७,५६,५
सनेम तेऽवसा नव्य ६,२०,१०
स नो नियुद्भिः पुरुहूत ६,२२,११
स नो नियुद्भिरा पृण ६,४५,२१

स वीरो अप्रतिष्कुत ७,३२,६
स वृत्रहेन्द्र ऋभुक्षाः ८,९६,२१
स वृत्रहेन्द्रश्चर्षणीधृत् ८,९६,२०
स वेतसुं दशमायं ६,२० ८
सव्यामनु स्फिग्यं ८,४,८
स श्चितानस्तन्यतू ६,६,२
ससंदृक्ते स्वनीक ७,३,६
स सत्पतिः शवसा ६,१३,३
स सत्यसत्वन्महते ६,३१५
स समुद्रो अपीच्य ८,४१,८
स सर्गेण शवसा ६,३२५
स सुक्रतुर्ऋत्तचिदस्तु ७,८५,४
स सुक्रतुर्यो वि दुरः पणीनां ७,९,२
स सुक्रतू रणिता यः सुतेषु ८,९६,१९
स सूर्यं प्रति पुरो ७,६२,२
स सोम आमिश्लतमः ६,२९,४
सस्तु माता सस्तु पिता ७,५५,५
स स्तोम्यः स हव्यः ८,१६,८
सस्वश्चिद्धि तन्वः ७,५९,७
सस्वश्चिद्धि समृतिस्त्वेष्ये ७,६०,१०
सहस्रशृङ्गो वृषभो ७,५५,७
सहस्रेणेव सचते यवीयुधा ८,४,६
सहस्रे पृष्टीनाम् ८,६५,११
स हि क्षयेण क्षम्यस्य ७,४६,२
स हि धीभिर्हव्यो ६,१८,६
स हि यो मानुषा युगा ६,१६,२३
स हि विश्चाति पार्थिवा ६,१६,२०
स हि विश्चानि पार्थिवाँ ६,४५,२०
स हि शुचिः शतपत्रः ७,९७,७
सहो षु णो वज्रहस्तैः ८,७,३२
सा ते अग्ने शंतमा ८,७४,८
सा द्युम्नैर्द्युम्निनी ८,७४,९
सा नो विश्चा अति द्विषः ६,६१९
सांतपना इदं हवि ७,५९,९
सा वह योक्षभि ६,६४५
सा विट् सुवीरा मरुद्भिरस्तु ७,५६,५
सास्माकेभिरेतरी ६,१२४
साहा ये सन्ति मुष्टिहेव ८,२०,२०

सिञ्चन्ति नमसावतम् ८,७२,१०
सिन्धूँरिव प्रवण आशुया ६,४६,१४
सिषक्ति सा वां सुमति ७,७०,२
सीदन्तस्ते वयो यथा ८,२१,५
सुगस्ते सुगस्ते अग्ने सनविन्तो ७,४२,२
सुगोत ते सुपथा ६,६४,४
सुज्योतिषः सूर्य दक्षपितृन् ६,५०,२
सुतः सोमो असुतादिन्द्र ६,४१,४
सुत इत्त्वं निमिश्ल ६,२३,१
सुतावन्तस्त्वा वयम् ८,६५,६
सुदेवाः स्थ काण्वायना ८,५५,४
सुदेवो असि वरुण ८,६९,१२
सुनीथो घा स मर्त्यो ८,४६,४
सुनोता सोमपाव्ने ७,३२,८
सुपर्ण वस्ते मृगो ६,७५,११
सुप्रावर्ग सुवीर्यं ८,२२,१८
सुप्रावीरस्तु स क्षयः ७,६६,५
सुभगः स व ऊतिषु ८,२०,१५
सुरथाँ आतिथिग्वे ८,६८,१६
सुविज्ञानं चिकितुषे ७,१०४,१२
सुवीरं रयिमा भर ६,१६,२९
सुवीर्यं स्वश्च्यं ८,१२,३३
सुशेवो नो मृळयाकु ८,७९,७
सुषोमे शर्यणावति ८,७,२९
सूरो न यस्य दृशतिरेपा ६,३,३
सूर्यस्येव वक्षथो ७,३३,८
सूर्यो रश्मिं यथा सृजा ८,३२,२३
सृजन्ति रश्मिमोजसा ८,७,८
सेदग्निरग्नींत्यस्त्वन्या ७,१,१४
सेदग्निर्यो वनुष्यतो ७,१,१५
सेदुगो अस्तु मरुतः ७,४०,३
सेमां वेतु वषट्कृतिम् ७,१५,६
सेहान उग्र पृतना ८,३७,२
सो अग्न ईजे शशमे ६,१,९
सो अग्न एना नमसा ७,९३,७
सो अद्धा दाश्वध्वरो ८,१९,९
सोता हि सोममद्रिभि ८,१,१७
सोम इद्धः सुतो अस्तु ८,६६,१५